Dictionary of Literary Biography

1   *The American Renaissance in New England*, edited by Joel Myerson (1978)

2   *American Novelists Since World War II*, edited by Jeffrey Helterman and Richard Layman (1978)

3   *Antebellum Writers in New York and the South*, edited by Joel Myerson (1979)

4   *American Writers in Paris, 1920-1939*, edited by Karen Lane Rood (1980)

5   *American Poets Since World War II*, 2 parts, edited by Donald J. Greiner (1980)

6   *American Novelists Since World War II, Second Series*, edited by James E. Kibler Jr. (1980)

7   *Twentieth-Century American Dramatists*, 2 parts, edited by John MacNicholas (1981)

8   *Twentieth-Century American Science-Fiction Writers*, 2 parts, edited by David Cowart and Thomas L. Wymer (1981)

9   *American Novelists, 1910-1945*, 3 parts, edited by James J. Martine (1981)

10   *Modern British Dramatists, 1900-1945*, 2 parts, edited by Stanley Weintraub (1982)

11   *American Humorists, 1800-1950*, 2 parts, edited by Stanley Trachtenberg (1982)

12   *American Realists and Naturalists*, edited by Donald Pizer and Earl N. Harbert (1982)

13   *British Dramatists Since World War II*, 2 parts, edited by Stanley Weintraub (1982)

14   *British Novelists Since 1960*, 2 parts, edited by Jay L. Halio (1983)

15   *British Novelists, 1930-1959*, 2 parts, edited by Bernard Oldsey (1983)

16   *The Beats: Literary Bohemians in Postwar America*, 2 parts, edited by Ann Charters (1983)

17   *Twentieth-Century American Historians*, edited by Clyde N. Wilson (1983)

18   *Victorian Novelists After 1885*, edited by Ira B. Nadel and William E. Fredeman (1983)

19   *British Poets, 1880-1914*, edited by Donald E. Stanford (1983)

20   *British Poets, 1914-1945*, edited by Donald E. Stanford (1983)

21   *Victorian Novelists Before 1885*, edited by Ira B. Nadel and William E. Fredeman (1983)

22   *American Writers for Children, 1900-1960*, edited by John Cech (1983)

23   *American Newspaper Journalists, 1873-1900*, edited by Perry J. Ashley (1983)

24   *American Colonial Writers, 1606-1734*, edited by Emory Elliott (1984)

25   *American Newspaper Journalists, 1901-1925*, edited by Perry J. Ashley (1984)

26   *American Screenwriters*, edited by Robert E. Morsberger, Stephen O. Lesser, and Randall Clark (1984)

27   *Poets of Great Britain and Ireland, 1945-1960*, edited by Vincent B. Sherry Jr. (1984)

28   *Twentieth-Century American-Jewish Fiction Writers*, edited by Daniel Walden (1984)

29   *American Newspaper Journalists, 1926-1950*, edited by Perry J. Ashley (1984)

30   *American Historians, 1607-1865*, edited by Clyde N. Wilson (1984)

31   *American Colonial Writers, 1735-1781*, edited by Emory Elliott (1984)

32   *Victorian Poets Before 1850*, edited by William E. Fredeman and Ira B. Nadel (1984)

33   *Afro-American Fiction Writers After 1955*, edited by Thadious M. Davis and Trudier Harris (1984)

34   *British Novelists, 1890-1929: Traditionalists*, edited by Thomas F. Staley (1985)

35   *Victorian Poets After 1850*, edited by William E. Fredeman and Ira B. Nadel (1985)

36   *British Novelists, 1890-1929: Modernists*, edited by Thomas F. Staley (1985)

37   *American Writers of the Early Republic*, edited by Emory Elliott (1985)

38   *Afro-American Writers After 1955: Dramatists and Prose Writers*, edited by Thadious M. Davis and Trudier Harris (1985)

39   *British Novelists, 1660-1800*, 2 parts, edited by Martin C. Battestin (1985)

40   *Poets of Great Britain and Ireland Since 1960*, 2 parts, edited by Vincent B. Sherry Jr. (1985)

41   *Afro-American Poets Since 1955*, edited by Trudier Harris and Thadious M. Davis (1985)

42   *American Writers for Children Before 1900*, edited by Glenn E. Estes (1985)

43   *American Newspaper Journalists, 1690-1872*, edited by Perry J. Ashley (1986)

44   *American Screenwriters, Second Series*, edited by Randall Clark, Robert E. Morsberger, and Stephen O. Lesser (1986)

45   *American Poets, 1880-1945, First Series*, edited by Peter Quartermain (1986)

46   *American Literary Publishing Houses, 1900-1980: Trade and Paperback*, edited by Peter Dzwonkoski (1986)

47   *American Historians, 1866-1912*, edited by Clyde N. Wilson (1986)

48   *American Poets, 1880-1945, Second Series*, edited by Peter Quartermain (1986)

49   *American Literary Publishing Houses, 1638-1899*, 2 parts, edited by Peter Dzwonkoski (1986)

50   *Afro-American Writers Before the Harlem Renaissance*, edited by Trudier Harris (1986)

51   *Afro-American Writers from the Harlem Renaissance to 1940*, edited by Trudier Harris (1987)

52   *American Writers for Children Since 1960: Fiction*, edited by Glenn E. Estes (1986)

53   *Canadian Writers Since 1960, First Series*, edited by W. H. New (1986)

54   *American Poets, 1880-1945, Third Series*, 2 parts, edited by Peter Quartermain (1987)

55   *Victorian Prose Writers Before 1867*, edited by William B. Thesing (1987)

56   *German Fiction Writers, 1914-1945*, edited by James Hardin (1987)

57   *Victorian Prose Writers After 1867*, edited by William B. Thesing (1987)

58   *Jacobean and Caroline Dramatists*, edited by Fredson Bowers (1987)

59   *American Literary Critics and Scholars, 1800-1850*, edited by John W. Rathbun and Monica M. Grecu (1987)

60   *Canadian Writers Since 1960, Second Series*, edited by W. H. New (1987)

61   *American Writers for Children Since 1960: Poets, Illustrators, and Nonfiction Authors*, edited by Glenn E. Estes (1987)

62   *Elizabethan Dramatists*, edited by Fredson Bowers (1987)

63   *Modern American Critics, 1920-1955*, edited by Gregory S. Jay (1988)

64   *American Literary Critics and Scholars, 1850-1880*, edited by John W. Rathbun and Monica M. Grecu (1988)

65   *French Novelists, 1900-1930*, edited by Catharine Savage Brosman (1988)

66   *German Fiction Writers, 1885-1913*, 2 parts, edited by James Hardin (1988)

67   *Modern American Critics Since 1955*, edited by Gregory S. Jay (1988)

68   *Canadian Writers, 1920-1959, First Series*, edited by W. H. New (1988)

69   *Contemporary German Fiction Writers, First Series*, edited by Wolfgang D. Elfe and James Hardin (1988)

70 *British Mystery Writers, 1860-1919,* edited by Bernard Benstock and Thomas F. Staley (1988)

71 *American Literary Critics and Scholars, 1880-1900,* edited by John W. Rathbun and Monica M. Grecu (1988)

72 *French Novelists, 1930-1960,* edited by Catharine Savage Brosman (1988)

73 *American Magazine Journalists, 1741-1850,* edited by Sam G. Riley (1988)

74 *American Short-Story Writers Before 1880,* edited by Bobby Ellen Kimbel, with the assistance of William E. Grant (1988)

75 *Contemporary German Fiction Writers, Second Series,* edited by Wolfgang D. Elfe and James Hardin (1988)

76 *Afro-American Writers, 1940-1955,* edited by Trudier Harris (1988)

77 *British Mystery Writers, 1920-1939,* edited by Bernard Benstock and Thomas F. Staley (1988)

78 *American Short-Story Writers, 1880-1910,* edited by Bobby Ellen Kimbel, with the assistance of William E. Grant (1988)

79 *American Magazine Journalists, 1850-1900,* edited by Sam G. Riley (1988)

80 *Restoration and Eighteenth-Century Dramatists, First Series,* edited by Paula R. Backscheider (1989)

81 *Austrian Fiction Writers, 1875-1913,* edited by James Hardin and Donald G. Daviau (1989)

82 *Chicano Writers, First Series,* edited by Francisco A. Lomelí and Carl R. Shirley (1989)

83 *French Novelists Since 1960,* edited by Catharine Savage Brosman (1989)

84 *Restoration and Eighteenth-Century Dramatists, Second Series,* edited by Paula R. Backscheider (1989)

85 *Austrian Fiction Writers After 1914,* edited by James Hardin and Donald G. Daviau (1989)

86 *American Short-Story Writers, 1910-1945, First Series,* edited by Bobby Ellen Kimbel (1989)

87 *British Mystery and Thriller Writers Since 1940, First Series,* edited by Bernard Benstock and Thomas F. Staley (1989)

88 *Canadian Writers, 1920-1959, Second Series,* edited by W. H. New (1989)

89 *Restoration and Eighteenth-Century Dramatists, Third Series,* edited by Paula R. Backscheider (1989)

90 *German Writers in the Age of Goethe, 1789-1832,* edited by James Hardin and Christoph E. Schweitzer (1989)

91 *American Magazine Journalists, 1900-1960, First Series,* edited by Sam G. Riley (1990)

92 *Canadian Writers, 1890-1920,* edited by W. H. New (1990)

93 *British Romantic Poets, 1789-1832, First Series,* edited by John R. Greenfield (1990)

94 *German Writers in the Age of Goethe: Sturm und Drang to Classicism,* edited by James Hardin and Christoph E. Schweitzer (1990)

95 *Eighteenth-Century British Poets, First Series,* edited by John Sitter (1990)

96 *British Romantic Poets, 1789-1832, Second Series,* edited by John R. Greenfield (1990)

97 *German Writers from the Enlightenment to Sturm und Drang, 1720-1764,* edited by James Hardin and Christoph E. Schweitzer (1990)

98 *Modern British Essayists, First Series,* edited by Robert Beum (1990)

99 *Canadian Writers Before 1890,* edited by W. H. New (1990)

100 *Modern British Essayists, Second Series,* edited by Robert Beum (1990)

101 *British Prose Writers, 1660-1800, First Series,* edited by Donald T. Siebert (1991)

102 *American Short-Story Writers, 1910-1945, Second Series,* edited by Bobby Ellen Kimbel (1991)

103 *American Literary Biographers, First Series,* edited by Steven Serafin (1991)

104 *British Prose Writers, 1660-1800, Second Series,* edited by Donald T. Siebert (1991)

105 *American Poets Since World War II, Second Series,* edited by R. S. Gwynn (1991)

106 *British Literary Publishing Houses, 1820-1880,* edited by Patricia J. Anderson and Jonathan Rose (1991)

107 *British Romantic Prose Writers, 1789-1832, First Series,* edited by John R. Greenfield (1991)

108 *Twentieth-Century Spanish Poets, First Series,* edited by Michael L. Perna (1991)

109 *Eighteenth-Century British Poets, Second Series,* edited by John Sitter (1991)

110 *British Romantic Prose Writers, 1789-1832, Second Series,* edited by John R. Greenfield (1991)

111 *American Literary Biographers, Second Series,* edited by Steven Serafin (1991)

112 *British Literary Publishing Houses, 1881-1965,* edited by Jonathan Rose and Patricia J. Anderson (1991)

113 *Modern Latin-American Fiction Writers, First Series,* edited by William Luis (1992)

114 *Twentieth-Century Italian Poets, First Series,* edited by Giovanna Wedel De Stasio, Glauco Cambon, and Antonio Illiano (1992)

115 *Medieval Philosophers,* edited by Jeremiah Hackett (1992)

116 *British Romantic Novelists, 1789-1832,* edited by Bradford K. Mudge (1992)

117 *Twentieth-Century Caribbean and Black African Writers, First Series,* edited by Bernth Lindfors and Reinhard Sander (1992)

118 *Twentieth-Century German Dramatists, 1889-1918,* edited by Wolfgang D. Elfe and James Hardin (1992)

119 *Nineteenth-Century French Fiction Writers: Romanticism and Realism, 1800-1860,* edited by Catharine Savage Brosman (1992)

120 *American Poets Since World War II, Third Series,* edited by R. S. Gwynn (1992)

121 *Seventeenth-Century British Nondramatic Poets, First Series,* edited by M. Thomas Hester (1992)

122 *Chicano Writers, Second Series,* edited by Francisco A. Lomelí and Carl R. Shirley (1992)

123 *Nineteenth-Century French Fiction Writers: Naturalism and Beyond, 1860-1900,* edited by Catharine Savage Brosman (1992)

124 *Twentieth-Century German Dramatists, 1919-1992,* edited by Wolfgang D. Elfe and James Hardin (1992)

125 *Twentieth-Century Caribbean and Black African Writers, Second Series,* edited by Bernth Lindfors and Reinhard Sander (1993)

126 *Seventeenth-Century British Nondramatic Poets, Second Series,* edited by M. Thomas Hester (1993)

127 *American Newspaper Publishers, 1950-1990,* edited by Perry J. Ashley (1993)

128 *Twentieth-Century Italian Poets, Second Series,* edited by Giovanna Wedel De Stasio, Glauco Cambon, and Antonio Illiano (1993)

129 *Nineteenth-Century German Writers, 1841-1900,* edited by James Hardin and Siegfried Mews (1993)

130 *American Short-Story Writers Since World War II,* edited by Patrick Meanor (1993)

131 *Seventeenth-Century British Nondramatic Poets, Third Series,* edited by M. Thomas Hester (1993)

132 *Sixteenth-Century British Nondramatic Writers, First Series,* edited by David A. Richardson (1993)

133 *Nineteenth-Century German Writers to 1840,* edited by James Hardin and Siegfried Mews (1993)

134 *Twentieth-Century Spanish Poets, Second Series,* edited by Jerry Phillips Winfield (1994)

135 *British Short-Fiction Writers, 1880-1914: The Realist Tradition,* edited by William B. Thesing (1994)

136 *Sixteenth-Century British Nondramatic Writers, Second Series,* edited by David A. Richardson (1994)

137 *American Magazine Journalists, 1900-1960, Second Series*, edited by Sam G. Riley (1994)

138 *German Writers and Works of the High Middle Ages: 1170-1280*, edited by James Hardin and Will Hasty (1994)

139 *British Short-Fiction Writers, 1945-1980*, edited by Dean Baldwin (1994)

140 *American Book-Collectors and Bibliographers, First Series*, edited by Joseph Rosenblum (1994)

141 *British Children's Writers, 1880-1914*, edited by Laura M. Zaidman (1994)

142 *Eighteenth-Century British Literary Biographers*, edited by Steven Serafin (1994)

143 *American Novelists Since World War II, Third Series*, edited by James R. Giles and Wanda H. Giles (1994)

144 *Nineteenth-Century British Literary Biographers*, edited by Steven Serafin (1994)

145 *Modern Latin-American Fiction Writers, Second Series*, edited by William Luis and Ann González (1994)

146 *Old and Middle English Literature*, edited by Jeffrey Helterman and Jerome Mitchell (1994)

147 *South Slavic Writers Before World War II*, edited by Vasa D. Mihailovich (1994)

148 *German Writers and Works of the Early Middle Ages: 800-1170*, edited by Will Hasty and James Hardin (1994)

149 *Late Nineteenth- and Early Twentieth-Century British Literary Biographers*, edited by Steven Serafin (1995)

150 *Early Modern Russian Writers, Late Seventeenth and Eighteenth Centuries*, edited by Marcus C. Levitt (1995)

151 *British Prose Writers of the Early Seventeenth Century*, edited by Clayton D. Lein (1995)

152 *American Novelists Since World War II, Fourth Series*, edited by James and Wanda Giles (1995)

153 *Late-Victorian and Edwardian British Novelists, First Series*, edited by George M. Johnson (1995)

154 *The British Literary Book Trade, 1700-1820*, edited by James K. Bracken and Joel Silver (1995)

155 *Twentieth-Century British Literary Biographers*, edited by Steven Serafin (1995)

156 *British Short-Fiction Writers, 1880-1914: The Romantic Tradition*, edited by William F. Naufftus (1995)

157 *Twentieth-Century Caribbean and Black African Writers, Third Series*, edited by Bernth Lindfors and Reinhard Sander (1995)

158 *British Reform Writers, 1789-1832*, edited by Gary Kelly and Edd Applegate (1995)

159 *British Short-Fiction Writers, 1800-1880*, edited by John R. Greenfield (1996)

160 *British Children's Writers, 1914-1960*, edited by Donald R. Hettinga and Gary D. Schmidt (1996)

161 *British Children's Writers Since 1960, First Series*, edited by Caroline Hunt (1996)

162 *British Short-Fiction Writers, 1915-1945*, edited by John H. Rogers (1996)

163 *British Children's Writers, 1800-1880*, edited by Meena Khorana (1996)

164 *German Baroque Writers, 1580-1660*, edited by James Hardin (1996)

165 *American Poets Since World War II, Fourth Series*, edited by Joseph Conte (1996)

166 *British Travel Writers, 1837-1875*, edited by Barbara Brothers and Julia Gergits (1996)

167 *Sixteenth-Century British Nondramatic Writers, Third Series*, edited by David A. Richardson (1996)

168 *German Baroque Writers, 1661-1730*, edited by James Hardin (1996)

169 *American Poets Since World War II, Fifth Series*, edited by Joseph Conte (1996)

170 *The British Literary Book Trade, 1475-1700*, edited by James K. Bracken and Joel Silver (1996)

171 *Twentieth-Century American Sportswriters*, edited by Richard Orodenker (1996)

172 *Sixteenth-Century British Nondramatic Writers, Fourth Series*, edited by David A. Richardson (1996)

173 *American Novelists Since World War II, Fifth Series*, edited by James R. Giles and Wanda H. Giles (1996)

174 *British Travel Writers, 1876-1909*, edited by Barbara Brothers and Julia Gergits (1997)

175 *Native American Writers of the United States*, edited by Kenneth M. Roemer (1997)

176 *Ancient Greek Authors*, edited by Ward W. Briggs (1997)

177 *Italian Novelists Since World War II, 1945-1965* edited by Augustus Pallotta (1997)

178 *British Fantasy and Science-Fiction Writers Before World War I*, edited by Darren Harris-Fain (1997)

179 *German Writers of the Renaissance and Reformation, 1280-1580*, edited by James Hardin and Max Reinhart (1997)

180 *Japanese Fiction Writers, 1868-1945*, edited by Van C. Gessel (1997)

181 *South Slavic Writers Since World War II*, edited by Vasa D. Mihailovich (1997)

182 *Japanese Fiction Writers Since World War II*, edited by Van C. Gessel (1997)

183 *American Travel Writers, 1776-1864*, edited by James J. Schramer and Donald Ross (1997)

184 *Nineteenth-Century British Book-Collectors and Bibliographers*, edited by William Baker and Kenneth Womack (1997)

185 *American Literary Journalists, 1945-1995, First Series*, edited by Arthur J. Kaul (1998)

186 *Nineteenth-Century American Western Writers*, edited by Robert L. Gale (1998)

187 *American Book Collectors and Bibliographers, Second Series*, edited by Joseph Rosenblum (1998)

188 *American Book and Magazine Illustrators to 1920*, edited by Steven E. Smith, Catherine A. Hastedt, and Donald H. Dyal (1998)

189 *American Travel Writers, 1850-1915*, edited by Donald Ross and James J. Schramer (1998)

190 *British Reform Writers, 1832-1914*, edited by Gary Kelly and Edd Applegate (1998)

191 *British Novelists Between the Wars*, edited by George M. Johnson (1998)

192 *French Dramatists, 1789-1914*, edited by Barbara T. Cooper (1998)

193 *American Poets Since World War II, Sixth Series*, edited by Joseph Conte (1998)

194 *British Novelists Since 1960, Second Series*, edited by Merritt Moseley (1998)

195 *British Travel Writers, 1910-1939*, edited by Barbara Brothers and Julia Gergits (1998)

196 *Italian Novelists Since World War II, 1965-1995*, edited by Augustus Pallotta (1998)

197 *Late Victorian and Edwardian British Novelists, Second Series*, edited by George M. Johnson (1998)

198 *Russian Literature in the Age of Pushkin and Gogol: Prose*, edited by Christine A. Rydel (1998)

Documentary Series

1 Sherwood Anderson, Willa Cather, John Dos Passos, Theodore Dreiser, F. Scott Fitzgerald, Ernest Hemingway, Sinclair Lewis, edited by Margaret A. Van Antwerp (1982)

2 James Gould Cozzens, James T. Farrell, William Faulkner, John O'Hara, John Steinbeck, Thomas Wolfe, Richard Wright, edited by Margaret A. Van Antwerp (1982)

3 Saul Bellow, Jack Kerouac, Norman Mailer, Vladimir Nabokov, John Updike, Kurt Vonnegut, edited by Mary Bruccoli (1983)

4 Tennessee Williams, edited by Margaret A. Van Antwerp and Sally Johns (1984)

5 American Transcendentalists, edited by Joel Myerson (1988)

6 Hardboiled Mystery Writers: Raymond Chandler, Dashiell Hammett, Ross Macdonald, edited by Matthew J. Bruccoli and Richard Layman (1989)

7 Modern American Poets: James Dickey, Robert Frost, Marianne Moore, edited by Karen L. Rood (1989)

8 The Black Aesthetic Movement, edited by Jeffrey Louis Decker (1991)

9 American Writers of the Vietnam War: W. D. Ehrhart, Larry Heinemann, Tim O'Brien, Walter McDonald, John M. Del Vecchio, edited by Ronald Baughman (1991)

10 The Bloomsbury Group, edited by Edward L. Bishop (1992)

11 American Proletarian Culture: The Twenties and The Thirties, edited by Jon Christian Suggs (1993)

12 Southern Women Writers: Flannery O'Connor, Katherine Anne Porter, Eudora Welty, edited by Mary Ann Wimsatt and Karen L. Rood (1994)

13 The House of Scribner, 1846-1904, edited by John Delaney (1996)

14 Four Women Writers for Children, 1868-1918, edited by Caroline C. Hunt (1996)

15 American Expatriate Writers: Paris in the Twenties, edited by Matthew J. Bruccoli and Robert W. Trogdon (1997)

16 The House of Scribner, 1905-1930, edited by John Delaney (1997)

17 The House of Scribner, 1931-1984, edited by John Delaney (1998)

Yearbooks

1980 edited by Karen L. Rood, Jean W. Ross, and Richard Ziegfeld (1981)

1981 edited by Karen L. Rood, Jean W. Ross, and Richard Ziegfeld (1982)

1982 edited by Richard Ziegfeld; associate editors: Jean W. Ross and Lynne C. Zeigler (1983)

1983 edited by Mary Bruccoli and Jean W. Ross; associate editor: Richard Ziegfeld (1984)

1984 edited by Jean W. Ross (1985)

1985 edited by Jean W. Ross (1986)

1986 edited by J. M. Brook (1987)

1987 edited by J. M. Brook (1988)

1988 edited by J. M. Brook (1989)

1989 edited by J. M. Brook (1990)

1990 edited by James W. Hipp (1991)

1991 edited by James W. Hipp (1992)

1992 edited by James W. Hipp (1993)

1993 edited by James W. Hipp, contributing editor George Garrett (1994)

1994 edited by James W. Hipp, contributing editor George Garrett (1995)

1995 edited by James W. Hipp, contributing editor George Garrett (1996)

1996 edited by Samuel W. Bruce and L. Kay Webster, contributing editor George Garrett (1997)

1997 edited by Matthew J. Bruccoli and George Garrett, with the assistance of L. Kay Webster (1998)

Concise Series

Concise Dictionary of American Literary Biography, 6 volumes (1988-1989): *The New Consciousness, 1941-1968; Colonization to the American Renaissance, 1640-1865; Realism, Naturalism, and Local Color, 1865-1917; The Twenties, 1917-1929; The Age of Maturity, 1929-1941; Broadening Views, 1968-1988.*

Concise Dictionary of British Literary Biography, 8 volumes (1991-1992): *Writers of the Middle Ages and Renaissance Before 1660; Writers of the Restoration and Eighteenth Century, 1660-1789; Writers of the Romantic Period, 1789-1832; Victorian Writers, 1832-1890; Late Victorian and Edwardian Writers, 1890-1914; Modern Writers, 1914-1945; Writers After World War II, 1945-1960; Contemporary Writers, 1960 to Present.*

Russian Literature in the Age of Pushkin and Gogol: Prose

Russian Literature in the Age of Pushkin and Gogol: Prose

Edited by
Christine A. Rydel
Grand Valley State University

A Bruccoli Clark Layman Book
Gale Research
Detroit, Washington, D.C., London

Library of Congress Cataloging-in-Publication Data

Russian literature in the age of Pushkin and Gogol. Prose / edited by Christine A. Rydel.
    p. cm.–(Dictionary of literary biography; v. 198)
"A Bruccoli Clark Layman book."
Includes bibliographical references and index.
ISBN 0-7876-1853-5 (alk. paper)
1. Russian prose literature–19th century–Bio-bibliography–Dictionaries. 2. Authors, Russian–Biography–Dictionaries. I. Rydel, Christine. II. Series.
PG3093.R79 1998
016.89173'3–dc21   98-35579
                                                                                    CIP

10 9 8 7 6 5 4 3 2 1

This book is dedicated to the memory of my mentors,
Carl R. Proffer and Edward J. Brown,
who helped at the beginning
and to
Edward Alan Cole,
who helps me now.

Contents

Plan of the Series xiii

Introduction xv

Sergei Timofeevich Aksakov (1791–1859) 3
Irina Makarova

Vissarion Grigor'evich Belinsky (1811–1848) 24
Derek Offord

Aleksandr Aleksandrovich Bestuzhev (Marlinsky)
(1797–1837)...54
Lew Bagby

Nikolai Aleksandrovich Bestuzhev
(1791–1855) 80
Lew Bagby

Faddei Venediktovich Bulgarin (1789–1859) 87
Ronald D. LeBlanc

Petr Iakovlevich Chaadaev (1794–1856).............101
George L. Kline

Vladimir Ivanovich Dal' (Kazak Vladimir
Lugansky) (1801–1872) 110
Joachim T. Baer

Nadezhda Andreevna Durova (Aleksandr Andreevich Aleksandrov) (1783–1866) 119
Jehanne M Gheith

Ivan Sergeevich Gagarin (1814–1882) 126
Richard Tempest

Elena Andreevna Gan (Zeneida R-va)
(1814–1842) 132
Veronica Shapovalov

Nikolai Vasil'evich Gogol (1809–1852) 137
Amy Singleton Adams

Timofei Nikolaevich Granovsky
(1813–1855) 167
Edward Alan Cole

Nikolai Ivanovich Grech (1787–1867) 177
Ruth Sobel

Ivan Vasil'evich Kireevsky (1806–1856) 183
Rosina Neginsky

Ivan Ivanovich Lazhechnikov
(1790 or 1792–1869) 194
Veronica Shapovalov

Nikolai Ivanovich Nadezhdin (1804–1856) 206
Leonard A. Polakiewicz

Vasilii Trofimovich Narezhny (1780–1825) 215
Ronald D. LeBlanc

Vladimir Fedorovich Odoevsky
(1804 or 1803–1869) 221
Neil Cornwell

Ivan Ivanovich Panaev (1812–1862) 244
Carolyn Jursa Ayers

Nikolai Filippovich Pavlov (1803–1864) 249
Carolyn Jursa Ayers

Aleksei Alekseevich Perovsky (Antonii
Pogorel'sky) (1787–1836)...............................256
Thomas Berry

Mikhail Petrovich Pogodin (1800–1875) 264
Dan I. Ungurianu

Nikolai Alekseevich Polevoi (1796–1846)...........272
Mary Jo White

Osip Ivanovich Senkovsky (Józef-Julian Sekowski,
Baron Brambeus) (1800–1858) 281
Louis Pedrotti

Vladimir Aleksandrovich Sollogub
(1813–1882) 292
Maxim D. Shrayer

Orest Mikhailovich Somov (1793–1833).............305
John Mersereau Jr.

Nikolai Vladimirovich Stankevich
(1813–1840) 317
Edward Alan Cole

Aleksandr Ivanovich Turgenev (1784–1845) 325
Vladimir Shatskov

Aleksander Fomich Vel'tman (1800–1870)........331
Brian J. Horowitz

Mikhail Nikolaevich Zagoskin (1789–1852) 344
Dan I. Ungurianu

Checklist of Further Readings............................357

Contributors 361

Cumulative Index..365

Plan of the Series

. . . Almost the most prodigious asset of a country, and perhaps its most precious possession, is its native literary product — when that product is fine and noble and enduring.

Mark Twain*

The advisory board, the editors, and the publisher of the *Dictionary of Literary Biography* are joined in endorsing Mark Twain's declaration. The literature of a nation provides an inexhaustible resource of permanent worth. We intend to make literature and its creators better understood and more accessible to students and the reading public, while satisfying the standards of teachers and scholars.

To meet these requirements, *literary biography* has been construed in terms of the author's achievement. The most important thing about a writer is his writing. Accordingly, the entries in *DLB* are career biographies, tracing the development of the author's canon and the evolution of his reputation.

The purpose of *DLB* is not only to provide reliable information in a convenient format but also to place the figures in the larger perspective of literary history and to offer appraisals of their accomplishments by qualified scholars.

The publication plan for *DLB* resulted from two years of preparation. The project was proposed to Bruccoli Clark by Frederick C. Ruffner, president of the Gale Research Company, in November 1975. After specimen entries were prepared and typeset, an advisory board was formed to refine the entry format and develop the series rationale. In meetings held during 1976, the publisher, series editors, and advisory board approved the scheme for a comprehensive biographical dictionary of persons who contributed to North American literature. Editorial work on the first volume began in January 1977, and it was published in 1978. In order to make *DLB* more than a reference tool and to compile volumes that individually have claim to status as literary history, it was decided to organize volumes by

*From an unpublished section of Mark Twain's autobiography, copyright by the Mark Twain Company

topic, period, or genre. Each of these freestanding volumes provides a biographical-bibliographical guide and overview for a particular area of literature. We are convinced that this organization—as opposed to a single alphabet method—constitutes a valuable innovation in the presentation of reference material. The volume plan necessarily requires many decisions for the placement and treatment of authors who might properly be included in two or three volumes. In some instances a major figure will be included in separate volumes, but with different entries emphasizing the aspect of his career appropriate to each volume. Ernest Hemingway, for example, is represented in *American Writers in Paris, 1920–1939* by an entry focusing on his expatriate apprenticeship; he is also in *American Novelists, 1910–1945* with an entry surveying his entire career, as well as in *American Short-Story Writers, 1910–1945, Second Series* with an entry concentrating on his short stories. Each volume includes a cumulative index of the subject authors and articles. Comprehensive indexes to the entire series are planned.

Since 1981 the series has been further augmented by the *DLB Yearbooks,* which update published entries and add new entries to keep the *DLB* current with contemporary activity. There have also been *DLB Documentary Series* volumes which provide biographical and critical source materials for figures whose work is judged to have particular interest for students. One of these companion volumes is entirely devoted to Tennessee Williams.

We define literature as the *intellectual commerce of a nation:* not merely as belles lettres but as that ample and complex process by which ideas are generated, shaped, and transmitted. *DLB* entries are not limited to "creative writers" but extend to other figures who in their time and in their way influenced the mind of a people. Thus the series encompasses historians, journalists, publishers, book collectors, and screenwriters. By this means readers of *DLB* may be aided to perceive literature not as cult scripture in the keeping of intellectual high priests but firmly positioned at the center of a nation's life.

DLB includes the major writers appropriate to each volume and those standing in the ranks behind them. Scholarly and critical counsel has been sought in deciding which minor figures to include and how full their entries should be. Wherever possible, useful references are made to figures who do not warrant separate entries.

Each *DLB* volume has an expert volume editor responsible for planning the volume, selecting the figures for inclusion, and assigning the entries. Volume editors are also responsible for preparing, where appropriate, appendices surveying the major periodicals and literary and intellectual movements for their volumes, as well as lists of further readings. Work on the series as a whole is coordinated at the Bruccoli Clark Layman editorial center in Columbia, South Carolina, where the editorial staff is responsible for accuracy and utility of the published volumes.

One feature that distinguishes *DLB* is the illustration policy—its concern with the iconography of literature. Just as an author is influenced by his sur-roundings, so is the reader's understanding of the author enhanced by a knowledge of his environment. Therefore *DLB* volumes include not only drawings, paintings, and photographs of authors, often depicting them at various stages in their careers, but also illustrations of their families and places where they lived. Title pages are regularly reproduced in facsimile along with dust jackets for modern authors. The dust jackets are a special feature of *DLB* because they often document better than anything else the way in which an author's work was perceived in its own time. Specimens of the writers' manuscripts and letters are included when feasible.

Samuel Johnson rightly decreed that "The chief glory of every people arises from its authors." The purpose of the *Dictionary of Literary Biography* is to compile literary history in the surest way available to us—by accurate and comprehensive treatment of the lives and work of those who contributed to it.

The *DLB* Advisory Board

Introduction

During the years this volume covers, roughly from the Napoleonic to the Crimean Wars, or the reigns of Alexander I (reigned 1801–1825) and his younger brother Nicholas I (reigned 1825–1855), modern Russian culture—including its prose literature—emerged as an autonomous phenomenon, no longer dependent on the patronage of the state. These years also saw Russian literature begin to play a role in European culture, especially with the work of Russia's national poet, Aleksandr Pushkin. However, Pushkin was certainly not the first to encounter the West. Although some examples of Westernization predate Peter the Great (reigned 1682–1725), his reign marks Russia's decisive adoption of European civilization in preference to its traditional ways. From that time onward, the state functioned as the sole source of patronage with either the inclination or the resources to effect sweeping Westernization.

Although Peter's revolution had some cultural aspects to it, the tsar was primarily interested in acquiring modern military technology and the infrastructure to support it. For most of the eighteenth century, as Russia's court and gentry strove to Europeanize themselves, literary culture remained an imitative enterprise, awkward and undistinguished: a kind of hothouse plant, as it were. Consequently, Russian culture could not be considered truly European throughout most of the period commonly called the Enlightenment, although the situation began to change during its later, sentimental phase. Under Catherine the Great (reigned 1763–1796), some writers—notably Nikolai Ivanovich Novikov, Aleksandr Nikolaevich Radishchev, and Nikolai Mikhailovich Karamzin—sought escape from the cloying embrace of the state, only to be silenced in the period of reaction brought on by the French Revolution. After the assassination of Catherine's son and heir, Paul I (reigned 1796–1801), the movement toward cultural autonomy surfaced anew, possessed of undiminished vigor in a new atmosphere symbolized by a young, presumably enlightened and liberal, Alexander I.

In comparison with the Western countries whose culture it sought to emulate, agricultural Russia was distinguished by its lack of a bourgeois public life; nevertheless, in the age of Pushkin and Nikolai Gogol, a true reading public developed. The vast majority of the Russian people were peasants who followed the traditional ways of old Russia, as did the merchant class. The relatively small percentage who were gentry relied on state service to augment income from their estates, for they could barely afford to maintain the Western lifestyle Peter I inaugurated. The wealthier gentry favored the French language, engaged tutors for their children, and sought to place their sons in the elite guards regiments. The range of civil society was not large, and many of these sons flocked together in Masonic lodges and other secret societies devoted to such activities as discussing literature and, even more dangerous, politics.

Typically hosted by a wealthy family, the salon provided another setting for cultural growth. Nevertheless, this elite, which looked mainly to St. Petersburg and Moscow, eventually formed the core of a genuine public, once the possibility of reasonably unfettered journalism and literature emerged along with a fully developed modern Russian language. These developments distinguish the reign of Alexander I as much as Russia's victory over Napoleon and its subsequent involvement as one of the leading powers of Europe. Added to these factors were the growing number and prestige of universities and a burgeoning population of literate civil servants, the latter a particularly important aspect of the reign of Nicholas I. In this milieu, Russian writers found a public that could and would support their efforts.

Thus Russian literature emerged as a freestanding province of European culture in the years following Napoleon's invasion; in consequence, Russian culture made its debut, so to speak, in the age of European Romanticism. In essence, Russia ceased to imitate and began to participate. Russian writers no longer had to be described by reference to Western models (such as "the Russian Voltaire" or "the Russian Sterne") because they participated fully in the general European culture of their times. (However, European writers still provided inspiration for this new generation of Russian authors.) In fact, considering subsequent periods of Russian cultural history, one is tempted to think that only during the Romantic age were Russian thought and writing completely synchronized with the rest of Europe, in part because of the nature of Romanticism: not a unified movement, Romanticism could incorporate Russia's version because the movement bore the impress of the national differences it often celebrated. Of course, while the characteristic art of the time was poetry, the Romantic style marked Russian prose, too, although less vividly. Particularly in the works of its early practitioners, Russian Romantic prose carries with it some traces of the earlier age. Nevertheless, one would hesitate to categorize the prose of the great ones—Pushkin, Gogol, and Mikhail Iur'evich Lermontov—as neoclassical or even sentimental. Compared to the best writers of the preceding age, they spoke a completely different language.

This language, however, was unintelligible to Russia's rulers and may have done as much as the Decembrist Revolt of 14 December 1825 to open the ever-widening abyss between the government and the literate public, or "the split between the state and society." For its part, the Russian state remained static while the modern culture to which it had given birth continued to develop. In a sense, the state, to the bitter end, remained locked into the model of "enlightened despotism" that had suited it so well in the eighteenth century. To be sure, the period of the French Revolution and the Napoleonic Wars constituted a kind of Time of Troubles for enlightened despotism; but just as in the case of the original Time of Troubles in the early seventeenth century, the Russian state emerged amazingly unscathed by the revolutionary experience through which it had passed. Indeed, the reactionary policies of Alexander I after 1815 seemed to many to have betrayed the promises he at least symbolized in 1801. But the nascent Russian public had in fact been profoundly affected by its collision with the storm-center of modern life; and when idealistic Guards officers attempted to use some regiments to effect a constitutional revolution during a brief and confused interregnum, many thoughtful Russians, most of whom could not approve of the uprising, were able to understand it in a way that the state could not. Whatever the political ideas of the Decembrists, their new patriotism and dedication to a concept of Russia as something more than the dynasty resonated with the new age. But the new ruler, while sadly acknowledging that much was wrong, nevertheless set his face resolutely against all change.

Nicholas I was called "the gendarme of Europe" for his foreign policy, but he was even more the gendarme in his own land. His model for the entire empire was the ordered parade ground of his professional army. He also sought to freeze Russian culture in place through censorship, the Third Section (a special political police force), and punishment. Nicholas's ideological and educational program found its voice in his Minister of Education, Count Sergei Semenovich Uvarov, who formed the repressive policy of "Official Nationality," which sought to counterattack an onslaught of European ideas by espousing "the truly Russian conservative principles of Orthodoxy, Autocracy, and Nationality, our last anchor of salvation and the best guarantees of Russian strength and greatness." However, this policy was not unique to Russia but was typical of "restoration ideologies" common in Europe after the Napoleonic age. Although the levels of repression in Russia were not even comparable to those the later Soviets employed, the relatively small scale of the writing population made Russian culture extremely vulnerable to authoritarian methods, and the biographies of writers during the period from 1825 to 1855 are full of arrests, imprisonments, exiles, and brutal service in the ranks for trivial and even imaginary offenses. The situation was worsened twice by French revolutions. The first was in 1830 and the second, which spread throughout central Europe in 1848, resulted in a severe and effective crackdown on all intellectual activity in Russia. It is therefore somewhat surprising to discover that this was an age of great intellectual vitality and literary creativity, including the birth of a vigorous critical tradition. The "men of the forties" were distinguished by a great breadth of learning and high ideals for their country; but the state regarded them with a suspicion born of incomprehension, and until the regime brought ruin down upon itself and Russia in the Crimean War, Russian writers were treated as though they were dangerous revolutionaries. In this historical context, Russia's great literary tradition emerged. The hothouse flower of eighteenth-century Russian literature now found itself transplanted in the open air, where it flourished in spite of the harsh political, social, and ideological climate of the Russian State.

Against this historical background developed what was arguably Russia's richest period of cultural growth, not accidentally called the Golden Age. The years between 1815 and 1855 witnessed four decades of debate in a search for a national identity. For probably the first time in its history, Russian culture tried to acquire a kind of legitimacy by building on ideological underpinnings that set the stage for the main arenas of the debate: politics, philosophy, language, and literature. Two tendencies, conveniently labeled liberal and conservative, divided the intellectuals, though not always neatly and efficiently, into opposing camps. Politically the conservatives remained on the side of a strong autocratic state, while the liberals, symbolized most notably by the Decembrists, fought for either a constitutional monarchy or a republican form of government. In temperament the Decembrists fell into a European tradition as children of the Enlightenment and the French revolutions.

The same divisions characterized the debates about language and literature. The conservatives, who followed the teachings of Admiral Aleksandr Semenovich Shishkov, advocated retention of old Slavonic forms and semantic roots; the liberals, on the other hand, followed the reforms of Karamzin, who sought to simplify the language by modernizing and "civilizing" it, thus making it into a language "suitable for the salon," in effect, a native substitute for French. The arguments about language expanded into polemics over whether Russian literature should remain entrenched in its own form of neoclassicism or plunge headlong into the heady waters of Romanticism. Not unexpectedly, the Shishkovites stood firmly on the side of neoclassicism, while the Karamzinists, for the most part, opted for the Romantic experiment. At first, though, the polemics over language and literary movements focused mainly on the dominant genres of the day: lyrics, ballads, and verse narratives. Prose really came into its own in the 1830s, when poetry began to recede into the literary background. And while many of the formal questions of the debates—for example, language and style—played a prominent role in the development of poetry, most of the philosophical and ideological concerns of the day found a forum in prose, whether fiction, criticism, essays, memoirs, sketches, reminiscences, notebooks, or diaries.

One of the most defining events in Russian history and cultural life dominates a fair portion of both the poetry and prose of the era, either openly or in code: the Decembrist Revolt, the terrible event that ushered in the reign of Nicholas I on a tragic note. On that day young liberal Guards officers brought some regiments onto the Senate Square in St. Petersburg to demonstrate for a constitutional monarchy. The day ended with cannon fire clearing the square and with the arrest of the idealistic conspirators. A similar uprising in the south of Russia also ended in defeat for the conspirators. In the end five Decembrists were hanged and scores exiled to Siberia. The gentry was shocked as never before, both at the actions of its sons and at the ruthless punishment meted out to them by the regime. Nicholas I, who kept on his desk a record of the in-terrogations as a guide to the ills of Russia, lived in perpetual fear of another revolution. Nicholas's "villains," on the other hand, became the most celebrated heroes in all of Russian literature, especially in the civic strain of Romanticism, which, it may be argued, grew directly out of the revolt. Over the years this civic branch of Russian Romanticism has acquired various epithets: Literary Decembrism, Decembrist Romanticism, Civicism, Decembrist Civicism, and Decembrist Romantic Civicism—all the inventions of Soviet literary critics.

Perhaps another source of the civic strain of Russian literature was the resurgence of freemasonry, which, like the Decembrist Revolt, was a by-product of the European Enlightenment, though its origins are clouded in more ancient times. Viewed with suspicion by both church and state, freemasonry heralded the beginnings of true civil society in Russia. Even more than the aristocratic salon, the Masonic lodge offered a venue where men could meet free of the restraints of class and rank. Much of Russian political discourse had to be carried on in Masonic code, underscoring the backward state of Russian political life compared to that of Europe. Ultimately neither the Decembrist Revolt nor freemasonry posed any threat to either the church or the state. Nevertheless, the tsar found it necessary to force Russians to conform to the doctrine of Official Nationality, of which two main components were orthodoxy and autocracy. The third element, nationality (more precisely, national spirit, a loose rendering of the Russian term *narodnost'*), became not only the major issue under discussion but also perhaps the defining principle of Russian Romanticism. The debate about the exact meaning of *narodnost'* continues into the present.

On a philosophical level, investigations into Russia's national identity, its national spirit, its *narodnost'*, essentially its "Russianness," commenced well before the tsar made it an issue. Two writers and critics, Prince Petr Andreevich Viazemsky and Orest Mikhailovich Somov, initially used the term in the early 1820s simply to define an "author's faithfulness to distinctive traits of his national culture." One of the first groups to probe the true meaning of *narodnost'* was the *Obshchestvo liubomudriia* (Society of Wisdom Lovers), which met between 1823 and the end of 1825. It began as a circle of Moscow University graduates and young men who worked in the Moscow Archives of the Ministry of Foreign Affairs and thus received the affectionate nickname *arkhivnye iunoshi* (archive youth). Desiring a philosophical tradition in Russia, the *Liubomudry* (a direct rendering into the Slavic form of the word "philosophers") gathered secretly to discuss the

German metaphysics of thinkers such as Immanuel Kant, Johann Gottlieb Fichte, Benedict de Spinoza, Georg Wilhelm Hegel, and especially Friedrich Wilhelm von Schelling. However, the group–principally the writer Vladimir Fedorovich Odoevsky, the poet Dmitrii Vladimirovich Venevitinov, the future Slavophile Ivan Vasil'evich Kireevsky, the historian Mikhail Petrovich Pogodin, the literary historian and critic Stepan Petrovich Shevyrev, and various members of the circle of Semen Egorovich Raich–concerned themselves most with literary questions. They wanted to create a new Russian literature based on Romantic aesthetics and philosophy and grounded in German idealist Romantic historicism. They prudently disbanded in December 1825 after having destroyed all of their protocols. Some of them later went on to participate as Slavophiles in the great debate with the Westernizers that initially grew out of Russia's eternally complex relations with the West and ultimately lasted for many decades.

This great debate developed within the context of Romanticism, which further removed the question from a state that, permanently wedded to the style and mentality of enlightened despotism, never understood the terms of the new dialogue. The figure of Petr Iakovlevich Chaadaev illustrates this situation. A young officer in the service of Alexander I, he became personally alienated from the autocracy and almost simultaneously shifted from interest in the French Enlightenment to the new European Romanticism and German philosophy. When he published an essay stating that Russia had no past, present, or future, the tsar, thinking him simply mad, sentenced him to medical treatment. The tsar did not understand what Chaadaev meant when he said that having chosen Orthodoxy instead of Roman Catholicism, Russia had placed itself on a path to nowhere. Chaadaev redeemed himself with another essay, titled *Apologie d'un fou* (An Apology of a Madman, written in 1837 but not published until 1862). The question Chaadaev posed was answered in two different ways, by the Westernizers and the Slavophiles. Of course, the state never understood either of these camps, for they both spoke the language of idealism.

The Westernizers–chief among whom were Vissarion Grigor'evich Belinsky, Aleksandr Ivanovich Herzen, and Timofei Nikolaevich Granovsky–saw Russia's destiny as permanently merged with the civilization of Europe. Their view of *narodnost'* in this period was that Russia was behind the West but on the same path. The movement, though, was not homogeneous. Belinsky and Herzen became increasingly radical, for example, whereas Granovsky

represented a moderate approach akin to Western liberalism. Although their ideas differed markedly from one another, their answer to Chaadaev basically disregarded the question of religion, which he saw as fundamental. The Slavophiles–made up of Ivan and Petr Vasil'evich Kireevsky, Konstantin and Ivan Sergeevich Aksakov, Aleksei Stepanovich Khomiakov and Iurii Fedorovich Samarin–on the other hand, took exception to this issue, for they saw Orthodoxy as being essential to *narodnost'*. The Slavophile concept of seeing religion as a basic element of nationalism was typical of European Romantics. Their concept of Orthodoxy was essentially different from that entertained by the regime. To the Slavophile the core idea of Orthodoxy was *sobornost'* (communal spirit or harmony). For example, one of their number described the Russian peasant land commune, the *mir,* as a "moral choir," primarily because it lacked the concept of private property. Slavophiles saw Western culture as dangerously individualistic, competitive, mechanistic, and soulless. The attitudes of the Slavophiles and the Westernizers toward Peter the Great reflect their basic differences: Westernizers revered him as a hero who set Russia on the path of progress, while Slavophiles abhorred him as the tsar who broke the organic continuity of Russian development. It may not be too extreme to say that some of them saw Peter the Great as the Antichrist.

At the same time that this philosophical division was taking place, the old literary polemics that had divided the conservatives from the liberals broke down into vicious quarrels between the literary aristocrats and the plebeians whose main audience were the *chinovniki* (bureaucrats). Their numbers increased dramatically in the reign of Nicholas I, reflecting the growth of the administrative bodies, particularly in St. Petersburg but also in Moscow and the provincial cities. They came to dominate the reading public. The increasing demand for literate servitors outstripped the growth of the gentry and compelled the state to draw on a class of people described in the documents as the *raznochintsy*. The term means "people of diverse rank" or "people of no particular estate." This new class did not fit into the traditional social categories of Russia or of the West. Lacking a true bourgeois ethos, its members made their way upward from squalor by means of a rudimentary training in literacy. In the succeeding, post-Nicolaevan age, the *raznochintsy* became the breeding ground for the radical intelligentsia. A *raznochinets* usually was an individual with a basic education suitable for working in a large chancery, copying and filing the vast amount of paperwork a bureaucracy produces. With the appearance of the *raznochintsy* and the rise of the *chinovniki,* a decidedly plebeian element entered the literary scene of Russia and ultimately shifted the public's taste for poetry to a hunger for prose.

The rise of the plebeian element also parallels the gradual change of venue for the arbiters of taste. With the literary aristocrats dominating the early years of the century, most of the trend-setting took place in literary salons and in societies, both formal and frivolous, dedicated to discussions of language, literature, and culture. Among the most formal of the societies are those connected, not surprisingly, with the conservative tendency; the preeminent example of these was the *Beseda liubitelei russkogo slova* (Colloquy of Lovers of the Russian Word), which took Shishkov's side in the language controversy. Based in St. Petersburg, this society espoused a patriotic, nationalistic bias, though later some Decembrists and their sympathizers also joined their ranks; among them were Pavel Aleksandrovich Katenin, Vil'gel'm Karlovich Kiukhel'beker, Aleksandr Sergeevich Griboedov, and Vladimir Fedoseevich Raevsky. Others of the more formal societies also shifted orientation with the change of political climate. For example, the *Vol'noe obshchestvo liubitelei slovesnosti, nauk i khudozhestv* (Free Society of Lovers of Letters, Sciences, and the Arts, 1801–1825) originally focused on libertarian thought but came to be more conservative after 1807. On the other hand, the *Vol'noe obshchestvo liubitelei rossiiskoi slovesnosti* (Free Society of Lovers of Russian Literature, 1816–1825) was initially conservative but turned more republican in 1819 after the election of a new president, Fedor Nikolaevich Glinka. At their gatherings, young men would read aloud and discuss their own works as well as many popular intellectual topics, chief among which was the meaning of history. The membership at one time included Kiukhel'beker, Somov, Griboedov, Kondratii Fedorovich Ryleev, Aleksandr Aleksandrovich Bestuzhev (Marlinsky), Nikolai Ivanovich Gnedich, and Baron Anton Antonovich Del'vig. They published a monthly journal, *Sorevnovatel' prosveshcheniia i blagotvoreniia* (The Champion of Enlightenment and Beneficence, 1818–1825) that advocated pre-Romanticism–highlighting such ideas as *narodnost',* the importance of Russian history and culture, and the creative, individualistic spirit of the artist. Perhaps the most scholarly of the groups was the *Obshchestvo liubitelei rossiiskoi slovesnosti* (Society of Lovers of Russian Literature, 1811–1930); connected with Moscow University, it published a series of its proceedings as well as major works such as the dictionary of Vladimir Ivanovich Dal'.

Nothing could be farther from these "serious" societies than the St. Petersburg literary group Arzamas (1815–1818), whose meetings parodied those of the Freemasons and the *Beseda liubitelei russkogo slova.* Made up mainly of former students of the lyceum for the gentry at Tsarskoe Selo, noblemen related by marriage and family ties, and advocates of the Karamzin reforms, this group exerted the longest-lasting influence on Russian letters. Its membership, which included the young Pushkin, shared in Enlightenment ideals but also liked to enjoy themselves. Their meetings reflected their fun-loving spirit, and their familiar correspondence celebrated the cult of friendship so important to the Romantic sensibility. The most brilliant representatives of the age belonged to this society: Bestuzhev, Viazemsky, Pushkin, his uncle Vasilii L'vovich Pushkin, Aleksandr Ivanovich Turgenev; the poets Vasilii Andreevich Zhukovsky, Ivan Ivanovich Dmitriev, and Denis Vasil'evich Davydov; and Karamzin. Another group, *Zelenaia lampa* (Green Lamp, 1819–1820), was made up of poets, theater enthusiasts, and political conspirators who gathered after theatrical performances to discuss poetry, theater affairs, ancient Russian history, and politics. The group also enjoyed ties to the proto-Decembrist society, *Soiuz Blagodenstviia* (Union of Welfare). Before most of these groups understandably ceased to meet after December 1825, more than four hundred various societies and groups existed during their heyday. Not all of the meetings took place in formal gatherings; the intellectuals also met at the soirees and salons that dominated the St. Petersburg social scene.

Moscow, on the other hand, became the training ground for the future Russian radical intelligentsia, whose precursors met in the famous circle (1830–1831) that formed around the young, popular philosopher and poet, Nikolai Vladimirovich Stankevich. Its eclectic membership included the Westernizers Belinsky and A. I. Turgenev, the Slavophile K. S. Aksakov, the anarchist Mikhail Aleksandrovich Bakunin, the future conservative publisher and literary theorist Mikhail Nikiforovich Katkov, and the liberal historian Granovsky. They ultimately followed different theoretical paths; nevertheless, they acquired their early philosophical inclinations from their reading of Schelling, Kant, Fichte, Schiller, Johann Wolfgang von Goethe, and later in the 1840s, Hegel. In many ways Belinsky emerged as the most influential member of the group in forming the nature and character of the Russian intelligentsia, whose ideas and political platforms persisted well into the twentieth century. Belinsky was another source of the civic trend in Russian literature that evolved and spread in the later decades of the century. Though a critic not without taste and aesthetic acumen, Belinsky placed greater value on the social aspects and reforming potential of literature than on its artistic merit. His literary criticism and annual surveys of literature generally formed the taste of the Russian readership and both made and broke the careers of his contemporary writers.

Belinsky's influence spread with the rise of professional journalism, a phenomenon that resulted from the growth of a true reading public. Herein lie the origins of the final split in the first half of the nineteenth century, what the noted historian Nicholas V. Riasanovsky calls "the parting of ways," or the end of harmony between government and society. The social base of the reading public was rapidly broadening at the expense of the aristocracy. Though journalistic enterprises had sprung up in the eighteenth century, they lay principally in the hands of the aristocrats. Limited in scope and readership, these enterprises were not particularly profitable. The nineteenth century saw a gradual evolution of journalism; whereas the earlier almanacs and journals on the whole were published to broadcast the views and philosophies of various circles and societies, later journals and newspapers (albeit not without political and theoretical biases) were published not only to satisfy the reading public but also to realize a profit for their publishers. The most important and influential among them was Aleksandr Filippovich Smirdin, a bookseller, publisher, and owner of a lending library. He advanced the cause of Russian literature by publishing affordable editions of eighteenth- and nineteenth-century poetry and prose. His commitment to publishing cheap editions of literature also broadened the base of Russian readership. So far-reaching was his influence on Russian literature that Belinsky called the decade of the 1830s the "Smirdin period in Russian literature."

The complex history of the rise of journalism in Russia clearly demands attention, especially since the authors whose biographies make up this present volume published mainly in periodicals, that is, almanacs, journals, and newspapers. Almanacs surfaced in the 1820s and early 1830s in limited runs; some appeared only once. Especially important was *Poliarnaia zvezda* (Polar Star, 1823–1825; three annuals), which espoused a Romantic Civic Decembrist orientation. This St. Petersburg almanac, edited by the Decembrists Bestuzhev and Ryleev, followed a set format that included both belles lettres and critical articles, such as Bestuzhev's "Glances (*vzgliady*) at Russian Literature," annual surveys of Russian literature that also were "sociopolitical manifestoes"

encouraging writers to rely on national models and to eschew mindless imitation of French neoclassicism. A manuscript for a fourth annual, *Zvezdochka* (Little Star for 1826) was confiscated after the Decembrist Revolt. The *Liubomudry* also published an almanac, *Mnemozina* (Mnemosyne, Moscow, 1824–1825; four volumes) under the editors Kiukhel'beker and V. F. Odoevsky. This almanac favored Russian literature over translations or articles about contemporary literary polemics and German idealist philosophy. Baron Del'vig's *Severnye tsvety* (Northern Flowers, 1825–1832; eight volumes) best portrays the state of Russian literature in this period. At least eighty authors, chiefly sympathetic to European Romanticism and Karamzin's reforms, published their works in this elegant, beautifully illustrated, pocket-sized tome. The champion and theoretician of Russian Romanticism, Somov, coedited the final five volumes, the last of which was a memorial to Del'vig. Not unlike Del'vig's popular and profitable almanac, Egor' Vasil'evich Alad'in's *Nevskii al'manakh* (Nevsky Almanac, 1825–1833, 1846–1847) provided another forum for the major writers of the day. Patterned after *Poliarnaia zvezda*, the almanac published poetry and prose in the Romantic and sentimental modes. In 1827 the almanac ran into censorship problems when it printed the Somov and Bestuzhev stories that were to have appeared in *Zvezdochka*, which had been suppressed after December 1825. This popular illustrated almanac enjoyed commercial success but never achieved critical renown. At a much later time two almanacs, *Fiziologia Peterburga* (Physiology of Petersburg, 1844) and *Peterburgskii sbornik* (Petersburg Collection, 1845) published representative works of the Natural School.

The journals that came out in both St. Petersburg and Moscow also expressed the political and literary positions of their editorial boards. Partisan politics and literary loyalties made the journals a natural forum for polemical debate. Karamzin's *Vestnik Evropy* (Herald of Europe, 1802–1830) was the most distinguished journal of the early nineteenth century in Russia. The twentieth-century critic Iurii Mikhailovich Lotman credits Karamzin and this journal with creating the modern Russian reading public. After Karamzin left as main editor in 1803, five different editors steered it from its early Romantic/sentimental proclivities to its later anti-Romantic stance. Its influence ebbed after 1825. Nikolai Alekseevich Polevoi's *Moskovskii telegraf* (Moscow Telegraph, 1825–1834) took up the liberal, Western banner, publishing translations of writers as diverse as Honoré de Balzac, Victor Hugo, Benjamin Constant, Sir Walter Scott, James

Fenimore Cooper, Washington Irving, Charles Robert Maturin, and E. T. A. Hoffmann. Polevoi was a *raznochinets* critic, playwright, publisher, and historian who tried to refute Karamzin's *Istoriia gosudarstva Rossiikogo* (History of the Russian State, 1816–1818; revised, 1818–1829) with his own *Istoriia russkogo naroda* (History of the Russian People, 1829–1833), an act that put him squarely in the middle of controversy. Polevoi at first tried to use his "encyclopedic" journal (with sections on literature, the arts, philosophy, history, archaeology, agriculture, economics, and the natural sciences) to propagate Romanticism, with help from such literary aristocrats as Prince Viazemsky, from whom he broke away as a result of his critical review of Karamzin's history. The government closed the journal after Polevoi's scathing review of a patriotic play, *Ruka Vsevyshnego otechestvo spasla* (The Hand of the Almighty Saved the Fatherland, 1834), by the popular and well-protected author Nestor Vasil'evich Kukol'nik.

Two professors at Moscow University, Pogodin and Nikolai Ivanovich Nadezhdin, also entered the journalistic arena with short-lived periodicals. Founded by the *Liubomudry,* Pogodin's *Moskovskii vestnik* (Moscow Herald, 1827–1830) displayed a marked bias toward German Romanticism and at first was strong in literature. However, after the departure of most of the major contributors in 1829, Pogodin indulged his taste for history in the pages of the journal. This narrow focus lost readership, and the publication soon closed. Nadezhdin's *Teleskop* (Telescope, 1831–1836) met a more dramatic end. Billing itself as a "journal of contemporary enlightenment," the encyclopedic *Teleskop* was rather progressive, and both future Slavophiles and Westernizers contributed to its pages. Belinsky published his well-known "Literaturnye mechtaniia" (Literary Reveries) in the journal's supplement, *Molva* (Rumor). The journal was closed after it published the first of Chaadaev's "Philosophical Letters." In the wake of the controversy Nadezhdin was exiled and the censor who passed the essay lost his job. Pogodin returned to journalism and a career as an editor when he, along with Shevyrev—a literary historian, critic and minor poet—headed the literary criticism section of *Moskvitianin* (Muscovite, 1841–1856). A predominantly Slavophile literary and historical journal, it stood behind the doctrine of Official Nationality, emphasizing the religious and moral nature of Russia. Belinsky became one of the most vociferous critics of the stance of this journal. However conservative *Moskvitianin* may have been, it never reached the "patriotic" heights—or depths—of some of the St. Petersburg publications, such as those edited by Osip Ivanovich Senkovsky, Faddei

Venediktovich Bulgarin, and Nikolai Ivanovich Grech.

As its title implies, *Syn otechestva* (Son of the Fatherland, 1812–1852) was a strongly patriotic journal published by Smirdin under the editorial guidance of the men sometimes referred to as the "Unholy Triumvirate": Senkovsky, Bulgarin, and Grech. This historical-political journal, which added literature in 1818 (though the literary section declined in the 1830s and 1840s), entered into polemics with almost every other journal of the day. Financed by Smirdin, Senkovsky and Grech became editors of one of the most commercially successful journals, *Biblioteka dlia chteniia* (Library for Reading, 1834–1865). One of the first encyclopedic journals, *Biblioteka dlia chteniia* was able to attract the best talent in Russia and thus did much to popularize Russian literature. Despite its patriotic orientation, it also published foreign authors such as Balzac, Scott, George Sand, and William Makepeace Thackeray. The variety it offered certainly contributed to a wide readership. Senkovsky, however, was quite imperious with his authors; he reserved the right to edit and rewrite texts without authorial permission. This policy, together with a cavalier attitude toward payment of fees, made him quite unpopular with writers. After Senkovsky's departure from the journal because of illness in 1848, *Biblioteka dlia chteniia* continued to decline, for it was no longer able to compete with the journals that had earlier challenged its authority as the preeminent arbiter of taste.

One of the first journals that challenged *Biblioteka dlia chteniia* was *Sovremennik* (The Contemporary, 1836–1866), founded by Pushkin as a purely literary endeavor that championed good literature above all. Though it was nonpolitical, it took a stance for Enlightenment ideals and against Official Nationality. After Pushkin's death in 1837, his friends Viazemsky, Zhukovsky, Odoevsky, Andrei Aleksandrovich Kraevsky, and Petr Aleksandrovich Pletnev (who took complete control from 1838 to 1846) edited the journal. When Ivan Ivanovich Panaev and Nikolai Alekseevich Nekrasov purchased it in 1846, with Nekrasov as editor, *Sovremennik* became the voice of the progressives and the leading literary journal in Russia until it closed in 1866. After Kraevsky left *Sovremennik,* he published what became the chief rival of *Biblioteka dlia chteniia*: *Otechestvennye zapiski* (Notes of the Fatherland, 1839–1884), a scholarly literary journal, encyclopedic in scope and Western in orientation. Its chief weapon against the conservatives was Belinsky, who in his critical articles advocated the Natural School and realism and opposed "outmoded" Romanticism, the Slavophiles, and the duo of Bulgarin and Grech. However, articles and poems by Lermontov, Nekrasov, Herzen, and Ivan Sergeevich Turgenev also enhanced the reputation of the journal. After working as a book reviewer and contributor, Nekrasov left in 1846 for *Sovremennik;* Belinsky followed, thus depriving Kraevsky of his chief writers. As a result *Otechestvennye zapiski* fell into decline until Nekrasov returned in 1867 after the demise of *Sovremennik.* He, along with the prose writer Mikhail Evgrafovich Saltykov (Shchedrin), turned it into the leading populist journal of the 1870s. It fell into decline after Nekrasov's death and was closed for political reasons in 1884.

Newspapers did not enjoy the same success as did the journals. Moscow had a few papers that lasted only about a year, while St. Petersburg had more. Only four newspapers in the capital lasted ten years or longer. One of the best papers did not survive—mainly because of low readership: Del'vig and Somov's *Literaturnaia gazeta* (Literary Gazette, 1830–1831). Inspired by Pushkin and Viazemsky, it published excellent examples of contemporary prose, poetry, and criticism. Various factors—chief among them the inexperience of the editors, Bulgarin's steady stream of public denunciations and attacks, the opposition of the government, prohibition against publishing any political news, and a high price—guaranteed this newspaper a short life. *Severnaia pchela* (The Northern Bee, 1825–1862), on the other hand, survived for many years. This four-page newspaper, "whose notoriety in Russian literary history exceeds its size and quality," according to one critic, received the patronage of the government, especially the gendarmes of the Third Section, the special police of the tsar's personal chancery. The only newspaper allowed to publish political news (which the gendarmes supplied to the editors, Bulgarin and Grech, in exchange for their informing on perceived enemies of the state), it was the only St. Petersburg daily paper and the only one read at court. *Severnaia pchela* wielded its greatest influence for about fifteen years, from the late 1820s to the middle of the 1840s. It published some of the best writers, including Pushkin, whom the editors denounced publicly after the great poet had begun to publish in the rival *Literaturnaia gazeta.* Pushkin was in good company; Bulgarin also attacked Gogol, Nekrasov, and Fyodor Dostoyevsky, among others. Not above duplicity, Bulgarin even took bribes in return for good reviews. In the last two years of its existence—without Bulgarin at its helm—the paper started to become more liberal.

Russian belletristic prose truly developed in the 1830s, simultaneously with the rise in popularity of literary journals. However, Karamzin, the leading prose writer of the end of the eighteenth century, in a way embodies the entire history of Russian culture in the first half of the nineteenth century. In his youth he was a liberal republican child of the Enlightenment; in the 1790s he wrote fictionalized travel notes and short stories according to the sentimental paradigm, not unlike Western models. Karamzin became less liberal after the French Revolution and ultimately evolved into the classic representative of Russian conservatism. Appointed as official historiographer by the tsar, he became the chief apologist for the Russian state and the chronicler of its legitimacy. His *Istoriia gosudarstva Rossiiskogo* was the first account of the national past genuinely accessible to the public, and it was enormously successful. Along with the 1812 war against Napoleon, *Istoriia gosudarstva Rossiiskogo* served to awaken *narodnost'* on the eve of the Romantic age, and it remained an important influence throughout that period and beyond. It was essential to the doctrine of Official Nationality and a cultural treasure house for the entire Romantic period in Russian literature. As a long prose work, it stands at the source of a tradition that culminated in Leo Tolstoy's *Voina i mir* (War and Peace, 1865–1869). In matters of style Karamzin's name stood for a French-inspired modernization of the language into writing understandable to the ladies of the salons. Karamzin remained above the fray during the controversies over the old and the new language, but when his *Istoriia* appeared, even his opponents were mollified by its elegant and suitably elevated diction.

Karamzin's sentimental fiction also set the standard for subsequent Russian prose. After his fictionalized travel account, *Pis'ma russkogo puteshestvennika* (Letters of a Russian Traveler, 1791–1801) began to appear in his *Moskovskii zhurnal* (Moscow Journal), Karamzin became known as the "Russian Sterne." Growing out of the tradition of freemasonry, the Enlightenment, and Western models, this work nevertheless exemplifies a moderate approach to the excess of tender feeling and copious outpouring of tears that characterized Western sentimentalism. But the humanitarian ideals of freemasonry persisted in Karamzin's works and helped put Russia on the path to the later civic strain of the Natural School and realism in literature. His own stories, models of the "small" genre, deal with topics that were later carried over to become Romantic motifs as well: Russian history, the cult of friendship, Gothic Romance, adventure, doomed love, and silence. However, an underlying tone of playful irony prevents his stories from becoming mawkish. Karamzin inspired entire generations of Russian prose writers, most notably the early practitioners of short-story writing that dominated the Russian literary scene from the middle of the 1820s until the great age of the Russian novel that characterized the second half of the nineteenth century. Karamzin is a transitional figure whose development as a writer parallels the age in which he lived. His place in literary history shows him evolving from the last of the Western models (the Russian Sterne) to the first of a long line of great Russian prose writers.

Though it is much easier to classify poetry as Romantic or neoclassical, John Mersereau Jr. offers some unifying characteristics of Romantic prose. Chief among them are the Romantic narrator's tendency to rely on metaphor rather than on metonymy, to tell rather than show, to emphasize plot and setting over psychological analysis, to intrude into the tale, to provide rather than reveal motivation for characters, to subordinate psychology to intrigue, to dwell on the exotic and bizarre rather than the mundane, and to allow the supernatural to dominate where deemed appropriate. Favorite genres also unify the period and include historical novels, society tales, utopias, travel notes, anecdotes, hussar tales, novels of manners, confessions, adventure stories, supernatural tales, and the *künstlernovelle* and *künstleroman*—stories and novels in which the heroes are artists, musicians, or writers. Another genre that gained popularity later was the family chronicle, the best example of which is a fictionalized autobiographical trilogy of Sergei Timofeevich Aksakov. Within these genres Russian writers explored various themes of Romanticism: nostalgia for the past, world-weariness, boredom, the cult of the ego, the torture of genius, the poet against the crowd, the poet as the link between God and mere mortals, *sehnsucht* (yearning) for the supernatural and/or the infinite, Romantic love and friendship, the lure of madness, pantheism, mysticism, and perhaps the most defining characteristic for Russia—a search for national identity, *narodnost'*.

In the 1830s Russian literature began to develop in another direction, arguably as a result of a persistent civic strain in Russian letters that became more pronounced with the rise in popularity of Belinsky and his critical articles. Writers descended from the ether to land in the dirt and grime of commonplace, quotidian life among the Russian lower classes. The transition from Romanticism to realism that took place in narrative prose (circa 1842–1855) evolved into the Natural School (not to be confused with French naturalism). Bulgarin first used the term in a derogatory way to describe what he thought Gogol's works represented; Belinsky later used the term simply to mean "realism." Though its practitioners did not follow strict guidelines, they share some common features that the critic Viktor Vladimirovich Vinogradov elucidates in his work *Gogol and the Natural School* (1925). Members of the Natural School concentrate on the "voice of nature"—that is, on the details of face and clothing, usually insulting and dirty. They rely on downward similes and metaphors, in the main comparing humans to animals; they also emphasize unattractive details of human behavior, such as nose-blowing and spitting. Characters speak an ugly, inarticulate language, relying on particles and prepositions more than nouns, verbs, and adjectives in stupid, illogical conversations not devoid of swearing and scatology. Events generally take place in dark, gray, muddy, snowy locales, most frequently the streets, marketplaces, taverns, and attics of St. Petersburg. The characters are, on the whole, average or below-average people, rarely villainous; they often appear in schematic pairs. The favorite character type was the petty clerk, the most famous of which is Gogol's Akakii Akakievich, the protagonist of his "Shinel'" (The Greatcoat, 1842). These writers also seem to favor poor students, artists, writers, and prostitutes. The chief genre of this informal school was the *ocherk,* or physiological sketch, which was really a collection of observations on St. Petersburg life. *Ocherki* are literary equivalents of art sketches from nature; they also resemble the French feuilleton and *physiologie,* favored devices of the *école frénétique,* which espoused a strong social and philanthropic program for literature. The Natural School obviously wandered far from the tender sensibilities of an earlier age as Russian prose resolutely forged on to realism.

Though novels became the favored genre of realism, they also appeared in Russia as early as the second decade of the nineteenth century. Meant simply to entertain the public, they copied Western picaresques and adventure novels. The first "novelists" were Vasilii Trofimovich Narezhny with his picaresque *Rossiiskii Zhil'blaz* (A Russian Gil Blas, 1814) and Bulgarin with his moralizing adventure novel *Ivan Vyzhigin* (1829) and his less successful historical novels, *Dimitrii Samozvanets* (Dimitrii the Pretender, 1830) and *Mazepa* (1833–1834). Historical novels were the rage among the reading public, perhaps because the Russians were still feeling patriotic after the defeat of Napoleon. Also, Karamzin's history awakened in the Russians a true interest in their past. The favorite Western model for Russian historical novels was the work of Sir Walter Scott, which authors as diverse as Mikhail Nikolaevich Zagoskin, Ivan Ivanovich Lazhechnikov, and Pushkin followed; but where Zagoskin and Lazhechnikov followed the mold, Pushkin broke it with the best historical novel of the period, *Kapitanskaia dochka* (The Captain's Daughter, 1833–1836).

The first real novel of import, however, was Pushkin's *Evgeny Onegin* (Eugene Onegin, written 1823–1831, published 1833), an unclassifiable novel in verse that created true Russian types that became the models for future Russian literary characters. Mikhail Iur'evich Lermontov's *Geroi nashego vremeni* (A Hero of Our Time, 1840) also gave Russia a true Romantic hero, Pechorin, in this ironically titled novel made up of five tales that unite the principal Romantic genres (travel notes, adventure tale, doomed love story set in an exotic locale, society tale, and supernatural story). The hero becomes the uniting principle as the chronology of events is wrenched to provide a deep psychological portrait of Pechorin. (For discussion of the prose works of these two poets, see the companion to this volume, *Russian Literature in the Age of Pushkin and Gogol: Poetry and Drama*.) Like his predecessors, Gogol mixes genres in his novel *Mertvye dushi* (Dead Souls, 1842), subtitled a *poema*—that is, a narrative in verse; however, he wrote his novel in highly poetic prose. Ostensibly a picaresque, *Mertvye dushi* goes beyond conventional genre lines. Usually classified as Romantics, Pushkin, Lermontov, and Gogol transcend any attempt at categorization. While their works may embody some of the characteristics of the age in which they were written, these three authors stand out as literary giants among their contemporaries. These three writers, once and for all, gave Russian literature the legitimacy it had begun to seek decades before. The eighteenth-century hothouse flower was now blossoming freely in the public garden of classical world literature.

—Christine A. Rydel

Note on Bibliography

The authors of the essays have provided the fullest bibliographical data available to them at the time of writing. For more detailed bibliographical information, please refer to Kseniia Dmitrievna Muratova, ed., *Istoriia russkoi literatury XIX veka: Bibliograficheskii ukazatel'* (Moscow and Leningrad: Akademiia Nauk SSSR, 1962). This work has been the main source for the bibliographies of individual authors. Other more modern sources provided information for some of the incomplete citations in Muratova's bibliography.

Note on Dates, Names, and Transliterations

All dates in this volume appear in Old Style, that is, according to the Julian calendar, which the Russians used until 1918. To convert to the Gregorian calendar (New Style), add twelve days.

Russian names appear in the text as they do in the Library of Congress transliteration system, with the following exceptions: Moscow appears in the bibliography instead of Moskva, and names that would end in "skii" generally appear as "sky" (for example, Viazemsky instead of Viazemskii). For a few well-known authors, such as Leo Tolstoy, the commonly accepted English spellings have been used. Also, the diacritical marks have been omitted over the letter *e* in names like Fedor, Shevyrev, and Kishinev. Using *e* instead of *yo* in names gives the reader a more accurate means of conducting further research in library catalogues.

Acknowledgments

This book was produced by Bruccoli Clark Layman, Inc. Karen L. Rood is senior editor for the *Dictionary of Literary Biography* series. In-house editors are Penelope M. Hope and Tracy Simmons Bitonti.

Administrative support was provided by Ann M. Cheschi, Beverly Dill, Renita Hickman, and Tenesha S. Lee.

Bookkeeper is Neil Senol.

Copyediting supervisors are Phyllis A. Avant and Samuel W. Bruce. The copyediting staff includes Christine Copeland, Margo Dowling, Thom Harman, Melissa D. Hinton, Jannette L. Giles, Nicole M. Nichols, and Raegan E. Quinn. Freelance copyeditors are Rebecca Mayo and Jennie Williamson.

Editorial associate is Jeff Miller.

Layout and graphics staff includes Janet E. Hill, Mark J. McEwan, and Alison Smith.

Office manager is Kathy Lawler Merlette.

Photography editors are Margo Dowling, Melissa D. Hinton, Margaret Meriwether, and Paul Talbot. Photographic copy work was performed by Joseph M. Bruccoli.

Production manager is Marie L. Parker.

SGML supervisor is Cory McNair. The SGML staff includes Linda Drake, Frank Graham, Jennifer Harwell, and Alex Snead.

Systems manager is Marie L. Parker. Software support was provided by Stephen Rahe.

Database manager is Javed Nurani. Kim Kelly performed data entry.

Typesetting supervisor is Kathleen M. Flanagan. The typesetting staff includes Pamela D. Norton, Karla Corley Price, and Patricia Flanagan Salisbury. Freelance typesetters include Deidre Murphy and Delores Plastow.

Walter W. Ross and Steven Gross did library research. They were assisted by the following librarians at the Thomas Cooper Library of the University of South Carolina: Linda Holderfield and the interlibrary-loan staff; reference-department head Virginia Weathers; reference librarians Marilee Birchfield, Stefanie Buck, Stefanie DuBose, Rebecca Feind, Karen Joseph, Donna Lehman, Charlene Loope, Anthony McKissick, Jean Rhyne, and Kwamine Simpson; circulation-department head Caroline Taylor; and acquisitions-searching supervisor David Haggard.

Assistance with Russian translation was provided by Alexander A. Prokopenko and Valery A. Ganiev.

The editor owes special thanks to Harold Segel for inviting her to edit this volume, and to Professor James West of the University of Washington and Professor Richard Tempest of the University of Illinois, Urbana-Champaign, who provided aid on more than one occasion. The editor is also grateful to Professor Dan Ungurianu of the University of Missouri–Columbia and Professor Amy Singleton Adams of the College of the Holy Cross, both of whom displayed extraordinary professionalism and thoughtful consideration. As always, the editor

thanks Lydia C. Thriersen. Sincere gratitude is due to Associate Vice President for Academic Affairs at Grand Valley State University, John Gracki, who generously provided funding necessary for the completion of this project. Ursula K. Franklin has helped with questions relating to French language and literature; the editor is grateful for her professional advice and her supportive friendship. Theresa Tickle of the Slavic library at the University of Illinois, Urbana-Champaign, went out of her way at especially busy times to provide assistance in tracking down obscure references; the editor appreciates her successful efforts. Thanks also go to Paul Talbot, photography editor at Bruccoli Clark Layman. Very special thanks are due to the in-house editors, Penelope M. Hope and Tracy Simmons Bitonti; every author should be blessed with editors such as these. Deepest appreciation, however, goes to the editor's own "unholy triumvirate": James Norris Class and Wayne Louis Robart, whose technical skills and dedication to help finish this volume went far beyond the call of duty, deserve much more than mere thanks; and Edward Alan Cole, colleague and friend, who did much more to help than can be enumerated, knows to what extent the editor values everything he has done for her.

Russian Literature in the Age of Pushkin and Gogol: Prose

Sergei Timofeevich Aksakov
(20 September 1791 – 30 April 1859)

Irina Makarova
Russian State (Herzen) Pedagogical University

and

Christine A. Rydel
Grand Valley State University

BOOKS: *Zapiski ob uzhen' eryby* (Moscow, 1847);
Zapiski ruzheinego okhotnika Orensburgskoi gubernii (Moscow, 1852; corrected and enlarged edition, Moscow, 1853);
Rasskazy i vospominaniia okhotnike o raznykh okhotakh (Moscow: L. Stepanova, 1855);
Semeinaia khronika (Moscow: L. Stepanova, 1856);
Vospominaniia prezhnei zhizni (Moscow, 1856);
Literaturnye i teatral'nye vospominaniia (Moscow, 1856); first published in *Russkoe bogatstvo*, 4 (1856);
Detskie gody Bagrova-vnuka (Moscow: Katkov, 1858);
Istoriia moego znakomstva s Gogolem (Moscow: M. G. Volochaninov, 1890);
Alenkii tsvetochek (St. Petersburg: N. G. Martynov, 1886);
Raznye sochineniia (Moscow: L. Stepanova, n.d.).
Editions and Collections: *Polnoe sobranie sochinenii*, 4 volumes (St. Petersburg: Martynov, 1886);
Sobranie sochinenii, 6 volumes (St. Petersburg: Prosveshchenie, 1909–1910);
Polnoe sobranie sochinenii, 4 volumes (St. Petersburg: Deiatel', [1912–1913]);
Izbrannye sochineniia (Moscow-Leningrad, 1949);
Sobranie sochinenii, 4 volumes (Moscow: Goslitizdat, 1955–1956);
Semeinaia khronika. Detskie gody Bagrova-vnuka (Moscow: Goslitizdat, 1958);
Sobranie sochinenii, 5 volumes (Moscow: Pravda, 1966);
Semeinaia khronika (Moscow: Khudozhestvennaia literatura, 1991);

Sergei Timofeevich Aksakov, 1830

Okhota pushche nevoli: Sbornik proizvedenii (Kiev: Dnipro, 1991);
Detskie gody Bagrova-vnuka; Semeinaia khronika (Ufa: Bashkirskoe knizhnoe izdatel'stvo, 1991);
Rasskazy o rodnoi prirode (N. p.: Prapor, 1992);

Alen'kii tsvetochek (Moscow: Molodaia gvardiia, 1992);

Alen'kii tsvetochek (Moscow: Sovetskaia Rossiia, 1993).

Editions in English: *Memoirs of the Aksakov Family* [*A Family Chronicle*, part I], translated by "a Russian lady" (Calcutta: "Englishman" Press, 1871);

Years of Childhood, translated by J. D. Duff (London: Arnold, 1916; New York: Longmans, Green, 1916);

A Russian Gentleman (*Semeinaia khronika*), translated by Duff (London: Arnold, 1917; New York: Longmans, Green, 1917);

A Russian Schoolboy, translated by Duff (London: Arnold, 1917; New York: Longmans, Green, 1917)–comprises *Recollections* and *Butterfly Collecting*;

Chronicles of a Russian Family, translated by M. C. Beverly (London: Routledge, 1924; New York: Dutton, 1924)–comprises *Family Chronicle, Years of Childhood, Recollections*;

"Notes on Angling," in *Rod and Line*, edited by Arthur M. Ransome (London: Cape, 1929);

Years of Childhood, translated by Alex Brown (New York: Vintage, 1961);

The Little Scarlet Flower, translated by James Riordan (Moscow: Progress, 1976).

Though early in life he looked backward for inspiration, Sergei Aksakov laid the groundwork for the great Russian realist novels of Ivan Turgenev, Ivan Aleksandrovich Goncharov, and Leo Tolstoy. An early advocate of the neoclassical tradition of the late eighteenth century, he largely ignored the Romantic movement in the early decades of the nineteenth century and became one of the first writers of realistic prose in Russia. The clear, precise, and almost laconic style of his autobiographical novels, reminiscences, literary sketches, and works on hunting and fishing set the standard for Russian literary language for many decades. Enormously popular in the 1840s and 1850s, Aksakov became known as the "patriarch" of Russian literature in spite of writing his major works during the last fifteen years of his life. Perhaps the most Russian of the writers of his era, his works still retain their freshness and appeal, especially for the Russian reader, though he unfortunately remains largely unknown in the West.

Sergei Timofeevich Aksakov was born in Ufa on 20 September 1791 of a not particularly wealthy but distinguished family that descended from noble Varangians, one of whom constructed the Church of the Dormition of the Mother of God at the Kievo-Pecherskaia Lavra (Kiev-Cave Monastery),

where he is buried. One of his descendants, a certain Ivan Fedorovich, was nicknamed Oksak (Turkic/Tatar for "lame"), hence the family name Oksakov that later became Aksakov. In the pre-Petrine era Sergei Timofeevich's ancestors served the state as boyars, provincial governors, scriveners, attorneys, and courtiers not only in Moscow but also in other areas of the realm. Aksakov's own father, Timofei Stepanovich, served as a zemstvo court official in Ufa, the capital city of the region. Aksakov's autobiographical works provide a fairly detailed description of the personality of his father, "a nature lover, weak-willed, quiet, bashful, poorly educated man." However, the most memorable portrait to emerge in Aksakov's 1856 autobiographical novel *Semeinaia khronika* is that of his paternal grandfather under the fictional name of Stepan Mikhailovich Bagrov.

Aksakov's grandfather was a pioneer of the Bashkirian steppes at the easternmost edge of European Russia, the area known as Zavolzh'e, (the lands on the left bank of the Volga that encompass the Saratov and Simbirsk regions, among others). Feeling that life in Ufa was closing in on him, Stepan Aksakov moved his family and serfs to these virgin lands. By all accounts the elder Aksakov dealt equitably with the Bashkirians, paying them a low but not unfair price for the fifty thousand acres that made up his estate, Novo-Aksakovo, situated on the Buguruslan River about 160 miles from Ufa. Here grandfather Aksakov, like his alter ego Stepan Mikhailovich Bagrov in his grandson's 1858 book *Detskie gody Bagrova-vnuka* (Childhood Years of Bagrov the Grandson), managed his estate in a "medieval, or rather, even patriarchal" manner. At Novo-Aksakovo, where as a young boy he spent much of his childhood, Sergei Timofeevich first became acquainted with the wonders of nature and acquired early his passion for hunting and fishing in all forms, which he learned from his father.

Aksakov's mother, on the other hand, exerted an altogether different influence on her son. Maria Nikolaevna, née Zubova, came from the urban service "aristocracy." Reputed to be a local beauty, she was the daughter of the deputy lord-lieutenant of Ufa. An imperious, intelligent, and well-educated woman, Maria Nikolaevna took responsibility for educating her most beloved son. Much more sophisticated than her husband, she kept abreast of literary trends both in Russia and abroad. Under her tutelage young Sergei learned to read and write by age four. Sergei was a sickly lad who spent his earliest years recuperating from various illnesses and reading book after book. Mother and son grew close, a situation that worked to the detriment of both parties. Aksakov documents in his 1856 *Vospomminaniia prezhnei zhizni* (Reminiscences of a Life Gone By) how his first separation from his mother almost cost them their lives.

Aksakov first entered the Kazan gymnasium in January 1801. During this first stay the nervous and coddled youngster suffered pangs of loneliness and separation from his mother. As a result he fell ill with a serious nervous ailment, which he characterized later as "falling sickness." According to one account, when Maria Nikolaevna learned of her son's affliction, she went to take care of him, traveling in bad weather in spite of her own health, which was delicate since she had just given birth to another child. She supposedly never fully recuperated from this episode. Sergei spent the next year convalescing and regaining his health.

In the spring of 1802 (1801 according to Aksakov's own, probably mistaken, account) Sergei Timofeevich entered the gymnasium in earnest. There he received a less than adequate education, even though he singled out a few gifted teachers, among them Ivan Ipat'evich Zapolsky (physics) and especially Grigory Ivanovich Kartashevsky (mathematics), who married Aksakov's sister Natalia Timofeevna in 1817. While at the gymnasium, Sergei boarded with Zapolsky and Kartashevsky. In 1804 the gymnasium was reorganized into the University of Kazan by transferring the best of the students from the gymnasium into the new institution and promoting the teachers to professors. Aksakov took classes simultaneously in the gymnasium and the university. Although there were no defined departments, students took courses in higher mathematics, logic, science, classical literature, anatomy, and history. Though he never finished the entire course of study, Aksakov received an *attestat* (certificate of attendance) in 1807 with subjects listed that he had only heard of and which were still not taught at the university.

Aksakov's school days nevertheless contributed much to the formation of his character and personality, especially the extracurricular activities in which he participated. During the years in Kazan he developed interests that grew into passions that stayed with him until his death: hunting, fishing, literature, and especially the theater. His 1858 essay "Sobiranie babochek" (Butterfly Collecting) describes what he called a "story from student life"—his foray into the world of lepidoptery, a pursuit that occupied his last year at the university. His initial attempt at writing began even earlier.

Aksakov published his first short pieces, mainly poetry, in a handwritten high-school journal, *Arkadskie pastushki* (Arcadian Shepherds). These

Maria Nikolaevna Aksakov, the writer's mother

early poems attest to Aksakov's brief flirtation with Nikolai Mikhailovich Karamzin's sentimentalism; he even used "mythological" pseudonyms such as Adonisov, Irisov, Daphnisov, and Amintov. His poems "K solov'iu" (To a Nightingale) and "K nevernoi" (To An Unfaithful One), melancholy love lyrics, were successful in their limited sphere. Buoyed by the positive reaction to his fledgling efforts, Aksakov founded, along with his friend Ivan Ivanovich Panaev and the future mathematician Dmitry Matreevich Perevoshchikov, the "more serious" *Zhurnal nashikh zaniatii* (Journal of Our Activities). By this time (1806–1807) Aksakov had already emerged as one of Karamzin's adversaries and a follower of the conservative Adm. Aleksandr Semenovich Shishkov, author of a famous dictionary and of *Rassuzhdeniia o starom i novom sloge rossiiskogo iazyka* (Discussion of the Old and New Style of the Russian Language, 1803), a source of Aksakov's own brand of moderate, nonideological Slavophilism.

While at the university Aksakov developed his passion for the theater. Reputed to be quite talented, he refined his skills of elocution, which later opened doors to the cultural circles of St. Petersburg. Aksakov could also boast of an incredible memory; he was able to memorize entire plays, acting out all of the roles with insight and naturalness. He enthusiastically engaged in acting in and staging productions of such playwrights as Aleksandr Petrovich Sumarokov and August Friedrich Ferdinand von Kotzebue in the gymnasium/university student amateur group. Aksakov also enjoyed attending the excellent public theater in Kazan, where famous actors from the capital toured. Aksakov himself acknowledges that one of them, the eminent Petr Alekseevich Plavil'shchikov, opened his eyes to the "new world of theatrical art." Later Aksakov would establish himself as an able theater critic.

In 1807 Aksakov left the university. At that time his family received an inheritance from Aunt Kuroedova (the model for Kurolesova in *Semeinaia khronika*) that enabled them to move first to Moscow and in the following year to St. Petersburg, where Aksakov's sister could receive the best education in the finest schools of the capital. At the advice of his former mathematics teacher Kartashevsky, Aksakov entered service in 1808 as a translator for the Commission for the Codification of Laws, which the reform-minded Mikhail Speransky later headed. Aksakov worked in this position until the end of September 1810, when he became a member of the "Expedition" on Government Revenues, where he seems to have worked little. Aksakov remained in civil service until he received a full discharge on 19 October 1819.

During the St. Petersburg years Aksakov took full advantage of the cultural life of the capital. When he arrived there still in his late teens, he quickly developed a new group of friends, the most important of whom were the famous tragic actor Iakov Emel'ianovich Shusherin and Admiral Shishkov. With Shusherin, Aksakov practiced and perfected his declamatory skills, and he considered his friendship with the actor, who introduced him to a wide circle of theatrical personalities, a major event in his life. Aksakov later portrayed the actor in an 1854 sketch "Iakov Emel'ianovich Shusherin i sovremennye emu teatral'nye znamenitosti" (Iakov Emel'anovich Shusherin and Theatrical Celebrities of His Times). Aksakov remained active in the theatrical life of both capitals from 1812 to 1830, a period he describes in theatrical reminiscences that provide valuable portraits of celebrities and include many facts that contribute greatly to the history of Russian theater in the first third of the nineteenth century.

Aksakov became involved with other leading figures of St. Petersburg society as well, including an old family friend, Vasily Vasil'evich Romanovsky, a leading Martinist; Aleksandr Fedorovich Labzin; and the conservative Shishkov. These three individuals were prominent in the esoteric movements of the day, especially Freemasonry, which appealed little to Aksakov. His 1852 reminiscence "Vstrecha s Martinistami" (A Meeting with Martinists) discusses the mystical program of this fashionable group that made up part of St. Petersburg society in the early nineteenth century and characterized some of the spiritual tendencies of the times.

On the other hand, early support of Admiral Shishkov's linguistic views prepared Aksakov for a long and fruitful association with the chief proponent of the "old style" of Russian literary language. One of Aksakov's colleagues at the Commission for the Codification of Laws, Aleksandr Ivanovich Kaznacheev, introduced his famous uncle Shishkov and Aksakov. Aksakov frequented the admiral's salon, where he met some of the most distinguished writers of the late eighteenth and early nineteenth centuries: the poet Gavrila Derzhavin, the fabulist Ivan Ivanovich Dmitriev, and the comic dramatist Count Aleksandr Aleksandrovich Shakhovskoy, who at that time was the director of the Imperial Theater. In this salon Aksakov was able to pursue two of his passions: literature and the theater. In Admiral Shishkov's home Aksadov staged many theatrical performances; attended meetings of Shishkov's circle, Beseda liubitelei russkogo slova (Colloquy of Lovers of the Russian Word), as a "silent observer"; and practiced his declamatory skills, which especially captured the attention of Derzhavin, whose home Aksakov frequently visited. Aksakov makes both Shishkov and Derzhavin come alive in two essays: "Vospominanie ob Aleksandre Semenoviche Shishkove" (Reminiscence of Aleksandr Semenovich Shishkov, 1856) and "Znakomstvo s Derzhavinym" (My Acquaintance with Derzhavin, 1852–1856).

Life in civil service held little appeal for Aksakov, who was much more interested in the theater. Because of his noble birth he was not allowed to appear on the professional stage, but he did act in many amateur theatricals. So in 1811 he quit government work and left for Moscow, where he lived until Napoleon's 1812 invasion, when he returned to the Orenburg estate. He spent the next several years traveling in the country as well as in Moscow and St. Petersburg. During his final sojourn in Moscow, through Shusherin's introductions Aksakov befriended many literary figures.

Aksakov's works have no story or recollection of the major historical event of this time: Napoleon's invasion. Though one chapter of his *Literaturnye i teatral'nye vospominaniia* (Literary and Theatrical Reminiscences, 1856) is titled "1812," he merely mentions "Moscow events" of that year and does not dwell on their significance or their repercussions except to note in passing Moscow's "rebirth from the ashes." Aksakov consistently describes only that part of Moscow that touched on his own life–literary and theatrical circles. However, an 1814 poem, "A. I. Kazhacheevu" (To A. I. Kaznacheev), expresses righteous anger that even after Napoleon's assault Russian society still indulges in Gallomania. Aksakov cannot imagine how the citizens of Moscow, their city in ruins, their holy churches reduced to ashes, can curry favor of the very people who desecrated maidens and killed their wives and children. He expected a return to Russian customs and language; rather, he finds the enemy in the homes of his friends. The lyrical narrator exclaims: "I v samon torzhestve ia vizhu nash pozor!" (And in our very celebrations I see our disgrace!) The poem stands on the side of Aksakov's friend, Admiral Shishkov. As Andrew Durkin notes, it "is his most thoroughly Shishkovian effort, not only in its rather archaic diction but also in its ascription of the lapses in public morality to thoughtless imitation of French customs and uncritical use of the French language." Shishkov's influence persists in another of Aksakov's "public epistles" in which he rejects certain Romantic principles in favor of a "classical," rationalistic, analytic approach to poetry, "Poslanie k kn. Viazemskomu" (Epistle to Prince Viazemsky, 1821).

Aksakov continued to write verses in the 1820s that treat themes that remained a part of his artistic work until his death: the glories of the Russian countryside around his ancestral home, the joys of hunting and fishing, nostalgia for the past, the importance of family, and the superiority of rural life over urban existence. Some of the best poems of this period include: "Vot rodina moia" (Behold My Homeland), "Ob okhote" (About Hunting), "Osen'. Bratu Arkadiiu Timofeevichu v Peterburg" (Autumn. To my brother Arkadii Timofeevich in St. Petersburg), and "Rybach'e gore. Russkaia idilliia" (A Fisherman's Misfortune. A Russian Idyll). After 1830 Aksakov wrote verses of a purely personal nature, usually in celebration of events in his family. In spite of being a dedicated prose writer, Aksakov was a poet at heart and never ceased reading poetry. He may have published his own lyrics and translations of poems and drama in verse, but he never took his own poetry seriously. When he was older, he wrote to Turgenev that his own poetry included "all of the shortcomings of its time" and added that he "never created any original poetry."

Though not particularly interesting in respect to mechanics or content, Aksakov's poetry nevertheless attracts one with its simplicity and sincerity of expression. Often his poetry exhibits a joking tone when he describes incidents from family life or tales of hunting and fishing. The autobiographical

The Aksakov family home in Znamenskoe, Orenburg Province

nature of the poetry is probably the feature most important for the contemporary reader. However, a few pieces are poetically rather strong–for example, "Plach dukha berezy" (Lament of a Birch Tree's Spirit, 1853) and "17 oktiabra (A. N. Maikovu)" (October 17 [For Apollon Nikolaevich Maikov], 1857). The former is a birch tree's lyrical monologue after some unknown hand has ruthlessly felled it, thereby terminating thirty years of enjoying the other wonders of nature. The tree addresses its destroyer: "And so, tireless old man, / You will go mushroom hunting, / But you will no longer find in its accustomed place / The birch tree you love so much. / For now across your path / Lies its fresh corpse, / And quietly it moves its branches / As it conducts its own wake." Here man destroys the harmony of nature. Yet in "17 oktiabria (A. N. Maikovu)" the lyrical narrator once again finds communion in nature despite bad weather: "Again the rains, again the fogs, / And falling leaves and naked woods, / And darkened fields, / And the low, grey firmament. / Again autumn weather! / But full of gentle moistness, / it fills my heart with joy: / I love this time of year."

Aksakov's lyrical hero is a man who has a keen understanding of nature and constantly tries to unlock its mysteries. He hunts and fishes but also is capable of simply looking at the landscape, seemingly without any purpose. Although the poetry is technically undistinguished, it does possess a certain degree of lyricism that testifies to its author's rich poetic understanding of life and the abundance of feeling he has for it. Even though Aksakov's poetry is full of shortcomings, it suggests the lyrical vein from which sprang forth many of his works, especially those devoted to hunting and fishing.

In 1816 Aksakov married the daughter of one of Aleksandr Vasil'evich Suvorov's generals, Ol'ga Semenovna Zaplatina. Her mother was a Turk, Igel'-Siuma, who had been captured during the siege of Ochakov in 1788 when she was twelve years old and then taken to be baptized and raised as a Russian in Kursk in the family of General Voinov. She gave birth to Ol'ga Semenovna in 1792 and died when she was only thirty years old. By family accounts Ol'ga Semenovna was a strict but loving mother, not as indulgent with her offspring as her husband, who shared with her the duties of raising and educating their children. Rarely separated from each other, the Aksakovs seem to have enjoyed a happy marriage and fulfilling family life. Of the two, Ol'ga Semenovna appears to have been the more practical, and it was she who managed the family affairs. She also "participated in the intellectual discussions taking place in her drawing room on an equal footing with the men."

Directly after their marriage the Aksakovs moved to his father's estate, Novo-Aksakovo (Novoe Bagrovo in *Semeinaia khronika*), where they lived for five years. The first of their fourteen children (nine of whom survived), Konstantin Sergeevich, was born in 1817. Their family grew rapidly; by 1821 the Aksakovs had four children. At this time the elder Aksakov, Timofei Stepanovich, agreed to give his son his own estate, Nadezhino (Parashino in *Semeinaia khronika*), in the Belebeev region of Orenburg province. But before Sergei Timofeevich moved his family there, he took them to spend the winter of 1821 in Moscow, where he renewed his acquaintance with old friends from the literary and theatrical spheres: the novelist and dramatist Mikhail Nikolaevich Zagoskin, the vaudeville writer Dmitry Ivanovich Pisarev, dramatist and theater director Fedor Fedotovich Kokoshkin, and the playwright Count Shakhovskoy, among others. In the 1820s he also published a translation of Nicolas Boileau-Despréaux's tenth satire, for which the Obshchestvo liubitelei rossiiskoi slovesnosti (Society of Lovers of Russian Literature) rewarded him with full membership. From 1812 until 1830 Aksakov translated many works of classical and neoclassical texts, including, according to Andrew R. Durkin, "Sophocles's *Philoctetes* (409 B.C., from a

French version by La Harpe), Molière's *L'École des maris* (1661) and *L'Avare* (1669), Nicholas Boileau's eighth and tenth *Satires* (1666) and Sir Walter Scott's *Peveril of the Peak* (1823). Aksakov undertook the latter only to complete a translation (from a French version) undertaken by his friend Aleksandr Ivanovich Pisarev, who died in 1828."

After this brief Moscow sojourn the Aksakovs moved to their estate, where Aksakov led the life of a country squire; besides fulfilling the duties of a loving husband and paterfamilias, he enjoyed the sports of hunting and fishing. Though a proponent of peaceful, Russian rural life, in 1826 Aksakov moved his family back to Moscow; he spent the rest of his life either in that city or in its environs. Several reasons may account for his decision to leave Orenburg province, chief among them his lack of success in farming and managing the estates. In addition he needed a steady job to support his growing family and to make arrangements for their formal education. Recalling his own unhappy experiences in boarding school, Aksakov did not want to subject his children to the terrible conditions in Russian schools, both public and private. (One son, Mikhail, did attend a boarding school in St. Petersburg and died in 1841, when he was fourteen years old.) And by all accounts Ol'ga Semenovna was not overly fond of life in Orenburg Province, an area she saw as primitive compared to her native Kursk. Ol'ga Semenovna's discontent and Aksakov's own desire to participate in the cultural life of the "second" capital most likely precipitated their move to Moscow.

In the city Aksakov renewed his ties with his former circle of friends and engaged in literary and journalistic activity that included his translations as well as theatrical reviews and commentaries. In a more practical vein, through the patronage of Admiral Shishkov, who was then the minister of education, Aksakov gained a post on the newly reorganized and more powerful Moscow censorship committee. He began his duties in late 1827 and served until January 1829. For some of that time he even acted as chief censor. Following the retirement of Admiral Shishkov, a committee reorganization led to Aksakov's dismissal, for the new minister of education, Karl Andreevich Lieven, did not require his services. In spite of this situation Aksakov returned in June 1830 to his work as a censor, a post he held until early 1832, when he was relieved of his duties, supposedly for allowing unacceptable material to appear in print. These years in civil service were a difficult period in his life, for any wrong decision could have led to consequences even more serious than mere discharge.

Though Aksakov was happy to quit the civil service, he nevertheless felt that his dismissal was an act of cruel injustice. In this mood he wrote the 1832 "Stansy" (Stanzas), a dignified poem that describes his position with uncharacteristic sharpness. "Believe me, I have enough strength / to endure the tsar's injustice / . . . No earthly power will tarnish / the rightness of my actions, / And my honor, my holy banner, / Shines with the brightness of purity!"

During the time that Aksakov worked as a censor he also was active in journalism, mainly as a critic. He began his critical activities with an analysis of a translation of Jean-Baptist Racine's *Phèdre* (1677) his review appeared in the first issue of *Vestnik Evropy* (Herald of Europe) in 1824 in the form of a letter to the editor. In the 1820s he regularly submitted his essays and reviews to Mikhail Petrovich Pogodin's *Moskovskii vestnik* (Moscow Herald), Nikolai Filippovich Pavlov's *Ateneia* (Athenei), and Semeon Egorovich Raich's *Galateia* (Galatea). In the late 1820s Aksakov convinced Pogodin to run a special drama supplement to *Moskovskii vestnik,* which Aksakov wrote singlehandedly. His theatrical critiques and reviews appeared in that journal under the pen name "Liubitel' russkogo teatra" (A Lover [amateur] of the Russian Theater).

Young Aksakov is usually portrayed as a man who had little to do with the social currents of his time. He supposedly lived easily and happily, enjoyed declamation, went to the theater, met his friends, and never paid much attention to social disturbances. However, several episodes in Aksakov's life suggest that he concerned himself with the social issues of his time. Aksakov's famous feuilleton "Rekomendatsia ministra" (Recommendation of a Minister), which was anonymously published on the pages of *Moskovskii vestnik,* belies this position. The feuilleton's satirical aim was perhaps too good and provoked a powerful negative reaction in the official circles of Moscow and St. Petersburg. In it a minister must receive a petitioner who is unknown to him but comes bearing a letter from a well-connected individual who "cannot be refused." And though the petitioner is a complete fool, the minister must recommend him for a position for which others are much more qualified. Over the course of years the erstwhile petitioner becomes an "important person" in his own right and even acquires a reputation for his intelligence–much to the dismay of the minister.

The feuilleton's intent was quite clear: to poke fun at representatives of the highest governmental power in Nicolaevan Russia. This barb could not go unnoticed and immediately caught the attention of Nicholas I himself, who reacted with great anger. The events surrounding "Recommendations of a

Aksakov in 1835

Minister" troubled Aksakov for a long time. Eventually Count Shakhovskoy defended Aksakov and sent a special letter to Count Benkendorf, the chief of the Third Section, in which he stated that Aksakov was a man "of good intent, a friend of peace and order" who wrote the ill-fated feuilleton "not out of malicious rebelliousness." Shakhovskoy's intercession on Aksakov's behalf was successful. Aside from "Rekomendatsiia ministra" Aksakov published two satirical miniatures in the same first issue of *Moskovskii vestnik* in the section titled "Nravy" (Morals). One of them, "Edinodushie" (Total Agreement), was signed with only the initial *A,* and the other one, "Sovremennyi vopros" (Contemporary Question), was printed without a signature. Aksakov, it seems, intended to produce a whole cycle of "morality-conscious" satirical miniatures. In a letter to the editor of *Moskovskii vestnik* he asks whether or not he would be allowed "to publish some essays about wrongdoings, for the most part like the ones that can be found on the pages of police papers." In the next, the second issue of *Moskovskii vestnik,* several humorous miniatures appeared again in the "Morals" section, most likely written by Aksakov. However, publication of such materials in *Moskovskii vestnik* soon ended.

In 1829 Pogodin, the publisher of *Moskovskii vestnik,* decided to make some major revisions in the journal, and for this task he enlisted Aksakov's help. Unfortunately Pogodin's plan never materialized. Conflicts within the staff, Aleksandr Sergeevich Pushkin's departure from the journal, an insufficient number of subscribers: all of these greatly undermined the publication, forcing it to become a special historical paper and later to close for good. By the end of 1830 *Moskovskii vestnik* had ceased to exist.

After this unfortunate attempt Pogodin and his friends decided to create a new journal. Their plan was to begin to publish, together with Nikolai Ivanovich Nadezhdin, a biweekly publication called *Fonar'* (Lantern), with three supplements: "Rusalka" (Water Sprite), or "Nympha" (Nymph), to be published two times a week with pictures of the latest fashions; "Literaturnaia rasprava" (Literary Combat), or "Mech i shchit" (Sword and Shield), which was to publish polemics once a week; and "Moskovskaia vesternitsa" (Moscow Heraldess), or "Nravy i teatr" (Morals and the Theater), which was to come out weekly. Aksakov was supposed to be the editor of the latter two supplements. The original plans did not materialize. Instead *Fonar'* became *Teleskop,* and instead of three supplements, only one came out: *Molva* (Rumor).

In the 1830s Aksakov became Nadezhdin's unofficial associate in the journal *Teleskop* (Telescope) and its supplement *Molva.* In the 1840s and 1850s much of Aksakov's writing appeared in Pogodin's *Moskvitianin* (the Muscovite) because Pogodin's journal paid substantial fees to the debt-burdened Aksakov. Durkin writes that he "set Pogodin a number of strict conditions, including the right to withhold pieces the censors might mutilate, and insisted on complete autonomy: 'In order to receive four thousand rubles, it's necessary to write about forty printer's signatures a year, but in a given year I may not even manage to write ten. So I am not accepting any obligation and I will give you whatever comes, when it comes. Of course, upon your receipt of the articles I will receive my money without delay.'" In the 1850s Aksakov also became associated with journals such as the Slavophile *Russkaia beseda* (Russian Conversation) and Mikhail Nikiforovich Katkov's conservative *Russkii vestnik* (Russian Herald).

Aksakov's first artistic prose piece, a short sketch called "Buran" (The Blizzard), appeared in 1833 in the almanac *Dennitsa* (Day Star), published by a well-known ethnographer, historian, and friend, Mikhail Aleksandrovich Maksimovich. Because Aksakov did not want to bring down on the publisher of *Dennitsa* the wrath of his literary enemy, Boris Nikolaevich Polevoy, the sketch appeared anonymously. When the piece was republished in

1858, Aksakov provided an introduction describing the writing of the sketch as well as Polevoy's embarrassment at having praised the literary merits of his "opponent's" work. In the short introduction Aksakov also stresses that the incident actually occurred and emphasizes the role memory plays in his art. A verse fragment in Aksakov's notebook, *Kniga dlia vsiakoi vsiachiny* (A Book of Odds and Ends, 1815–1820s), is the source for the sketch. Though D. S. Mirsky in *A History of Russian Literature from Its Beginnings to 1900* labels "Buran" as experimental and immature, it is not without merit and includes stylistic and thematic elements of Aksakov's later prose. Almost a prose poem, it relates how a group of five peasant drovers are trapped on the open steppes of the Orenburg region by an unexpected blizzard. In contrast to the practical language of the peasants, full of regionalisms and colloquialisms, the lyrical style of the nature passages underlines the theme of man pitted against nature. In this as in all of Aksakov's works the force of nature dominates man, who must seek and find his place in it and adjust to it. The peasants are divided: the young and inexperienced versus an old man who has learned some of the secrets of nature and can interpret its code.

Aksakov wrote this story at Maksimovich's request while working as an inspector at the Konstantinov School. He took up this post in 1833 and two years later became director of the school in its restructured form as the Konstantinov Surveying Institute. He appears to have been instrumental in the reorganization of the institute and performed his duties as director responsibly and well. Nevertheless, he resigned in 1839, ostensibly because the work upset him and had a bad effect on his health. Actually he resigned because an inheritance he received after his father's death in 1837 (his mother had died in 1833) allowed him to retire and live a comfortable life as a private citizen.

In the 1830s Aksakov's circle of acquaintances changed; Pisarev died, and Kokoshkin and Shakhovskoy faded into the background, though Zagoskin remained a personal friend. Aksakov also became much more involved with the young university circle founded by Pavlov, Nadezhdin, Pogodin, and his own son Konstantin. At the same time he fell under the influence of Nikolai Vasil'evich Gogol, with whom in 1832 he began a friendship that lasted until Gogol died. From their earliest days in Moscow the Aksakovs entertained a variety of friends at their Saturday "open house." These gatherings brought together people from various levels of society: gentry, journalists, dramatists, actors, and representatives of university life. There was always much to eat and drink as people conversed, listened to musical recitals, played cards, heard authors' works in progress, and in the later 1830s and 1840s engaged in the philosophical and political discussions led by Aksakov's sons and their Slavophile associates. Aksakov's wife and their daughter, Vera, also took part in the lively debates, and the Aksakov home exemplified Russian hospitality at its best.

Aksakov numbered Vissarion Grigorievich Belinsky among his new acquaintances, though their relations were not always felicitous. Aksakov met Belinsky in 1833, and their relationship during the 1830s was quite friendly. The young critic, always welcome in Aksakov's home, met Gogol for the first time there. Aksakov helped Belinsky when he had money problems and in 1837 facilitated the publication of his *Osnovaniia russkoi grammatiki* (Essentials of Russian Grammar). In 1838 Aksakov, in his capacity as director of the Konstantinov Surveying Institute, offered Belinsky the position of instructor of Russian language. After brief service in the school Belinsky decided to leave and devote himself fully to work at the journal *Moskovskii nabliudatel'* (Moscow Observer).

Through his son Konstantin, Aksakov became increasingly aware of the spiritual interests of the younger generation and was attracted to Belinsky's "practical" activities. Although considering Belinsky's ideas questionable and sometimes even wrong, Aksakov admired his intellect, talent, fervor, and belief in those ideas. Nevertheless, something went awry between the two. In October 1839 Aksakov, accompanied by his houseguest Gogol and his daughter Vera, made a trip to St. Petersburg to enlist his youngest son, Mikhail, in the Corps of Pages. In his *Istoriia moego znakomstva s Gogolem* (History of My Acquaintance with Gogol, 1890) Aksakov, with his usual conscientiousness, describes every detail of this six-week journey to the capital. His prodigious memory touches on many events, yet he neglects to mention the name of a person with whom he met on several occasions—Belinsky. This omission foreshadows Aksakov's later rather unfriendly, and in some ways hostile, relationship with the critic. The rise of social unrest, already a major issue in the 1840s, sped up the process of division and dissent among various intellectual circles and social strata. Spurred on by these social changes, Aksakov and Belinsky found themselves on opposite sides of the barricade, thus becoming political enemies.

Aksakov's friendship with Gogol was much more lasting and complex. In the summer of 1832 when Pogodin brought Gogol to meet Aksakov, Gogol's two-volume *Vechera na khutore bliz Dikanki* (Evenings on a Farm Near Dikanka, 1831–1832), had al-

Olga Semenovna, Aksakov's wife

ready made him well known in Russia. This meeting grew into a friendship that lasted twenty years and played an important role in Aksakov's literary life. It was Gogol who first encouraged Aksakov to write. Aksakov read his prose to Gogol even before anyone else realized that Aksakov possessed any belletristic talent.

Gogol's early works overwhelmed Aksakov, who perceived them as forging a new direction in art. Yet Aksakov was not fond of the Romanticism in young Gogol's work; he considered it a limiting factor and a trait unworthy of such a talented writer. Aksakov's dislike of Romanticism had a long history. Even in the theater he opposed the Romantics, especially those who were keen on German mysticism. But every visit of Gogol to the Aksakov home and every page from Gogol's new works became causes for celebration. As one critic wrote, "Aksakov was the high priest in the cult of Gogol." Nevertheless, small quarrels erupted between the two, though they seldom developed into anything serious. In *Istoriia moego znakomstva s Gogolem* there are negative remarks about Gogol's insincerity, aloofness, and constant unwillingness to bare his soul to those supposedly close to him. Two weeks after Gogol's death, in an open letter to friends of the deceased writer, Aksakov remarked, "Even with his friends he sometimes, or actually always, was not candid."

Aksakov noticed a dangerous turn in Gogol's spiritual development long before his final emotional breakdown. Though Aksakov himself was a religious man, he disapproved of any form of mysticism or fanaticism and viewed them as destroyers of the creative process. Gogol's increasingly mystical attitudes in fact began to frighten Aksakov. In 1844 Gogol wrote from Nice that he was sending his friends in Moscow a New Year's gift, "a remedy against spiritual unease." Aksakov was overjoyed at the prospect of what he expected to be the second volume of *Mertvye dushi* (Dead Souls, 1842); he was dismayed to receive instead the work of a medieval mystical philosopher: Thomas à Kempis's fifteenth-century *Imitation of Christ*. According to Durkin, "Always a foe of religious hypocrisy and doubtless stung by Gogol's lack of ordinary sympathy [in telling a man who was going blind to read a chapter of the book at a time], Aksakov heatedly replied that he had read Thomas à Kempis before Gogol had even been born and had no use for mysticism." But after Gogol's return to Russia their relationship once again became calm and peaceful in spite of Gogol's continuing spiritual drama.

Ralph Matlaw calls Aksakov's *Istoriia moego znakomstva s Gogolem* "as much a spiritual autobiography of Aksakov as a biography of Gogol." Based on Aksakov's correspondence with Gogol as well as on a long friendship, *Istoriia moego znakomstva s Gogolem* remained unpublished until thirty-one years after Aksakov's death. In discussing Aksakov's work on Gogol, Mirsky states that the writer "was not as a rule a student of other people's minds. He took people as they came, as parts of his world, and gave them a sensual rather than a mental reality. But in the case of Gogol the elusive and evasive personality of the great writer caused him such bitter disappointment and disillusionment that he was forced to make an exceptional effort to understand the workings of the strange man's mind, where genius and baseness were so strangely mingled. The effort was painful but extraordinarily successful, and Aksakov's memoir is to this day our principal approach to the problem of Gogol."

By the beginning of the 1840s Aksakov was already a well-known literary figure who possessed a reputation as a man of exquisite taste. Celebrated writers and actors of the time began to seek his acquaintance. A kind, soft, and considerate person, Aksakov often attracted the sympathies of people of many different political beliefs. He was a definite moral authority on questions relating to literature and household life. A good father, he was especially close to his son Konstantin, the renowned Slavophile. This affection helps explain Aksakov's "general sympathy" for the Slavophile doctrines; as Durkin says, the Slavophiles "were, after all, the younger generation of his own set and included his own sons. On a practical level too their doctrines were congenial, tending to approve the status quo as far as the gentry's economic position was concerned and to enhance the gentry's significance in the political sphere." However, Aksakov remained indifferent "to specific Slavophile issues and tenets, and indeed to public affairs and philosophical issues generally." Nevertheless, his home in Moscow became a center of the Slavophiles with his sons Konstantin and Ivan as leaders of the movement. There they and their friends took part in constant discussions, and the family patriarch often found himself among the discussants.

Aksakov believed in the Slavophiles' sincere love for the people and was convinced that the Slavophiles were the ones who could best defend the people's interests. He also felt that only the Slavophiles could preserve and protect indigenous Russian culture from harmful foreign influence. In addition, he shared their negative opinion of Peter the Great and held him responsible for many of the hardships that had fallen upon contemporary Russia—a result of the tsar's misguided attempts to turn Russia into a western country. He admired the Slavophiles' respect for national traditions, heritage, and folk customs. Indifferent to theories, Aksakov was mostly interested in various aspects of national identity.

In 1843 Aksakov had the good fortune to purchase a summer home in the country—Abramtsevo. Located about thirty-five miles from Moscow on the river Bor' near the Khot'kov monastery and about eight miles from the St. Sergius-Trinity monastery in Sergiev Posad (Zagorsk), the estate was made up of three parts, consisting in all of about 185 acres. A large manorial home with a mezzanine stood in the middle of an extensive park. The estate provided Aksakov with richly diverse nature, widespread forests, a huge pond, and unlimited possibilities for fishing and mushroom hunting. According to Durkin, by the late 1840s Abramtsevo "became Aksakov's principal residence and at least part of the family often spent the entire year there, despite the old house's unsuitability as a year-round residence." This home became the center of hospitality and cultural life for the Aksakovs. Abramtsevo was ideally located; the estate allowed Aksakov to live in the ru-

A 1969 photograph of Aksakov's summer home, Abramtsevo

ral setting he loved while being close enough to Moscow to permit him access to the intellectual circles of the "second capital." In later years the rich merchant and patron of the arts Savva Mamontov bought the estate, which in the late nineteenth century became a center of folk and Russian revival art, visited by such painters as Valentin Aleksandrovich Serov, Il'ia Efimovich Repin, and Mikhail Aleksandrovich Vrubel'. According to Matlaw, one of the reasons Aksakov bought the estate was to escape "unpleasant experiences he had undergone for publishing two satires that dealt sharply with corruption and malpractice in government." Another reason for the move was his health problems.

Two years later, in 1845, Aksakov went blind in his left eye. Durkin quotes a letter in which Aksakov describes his malaise to his old friend Panaev. "In 1845 I became blind in my left eye; I underwent a great deal of treatment in order to save the right one; I caught cold in the bad eye (while fishing, of course) and suffered an inflammation in it and such rheumatic pains in my head that I was on the verge of going mad. In 1847 I was unexpectedly cured by the doctors and since then, although I am often ailing, I see, thank God, the light of day with my right eye, I can read a bit, write a bit (especially with a

pencil), I can fish and I can hunt for mushrooms, of which I am a great fancier." Unfortunately, the disease that originally afflicted his left eye gradually infected the right one, causing a progressive deterioration of his vision that eventually led to total blindness. It became increasingly hard to write on his own, and he often relied on family members, dictating his work usually to his daughters. On 10 March 1845 Aksakov wrote a letter to Gogol telling him that it probably would be the last handwritten one he would ever receive: "Let these words help you remember the last efforts of my vision." The worse his illness became, the more Aksakov wrote. In fact, Aksakov's reputation as a writer rests on the prose narratives he wrote during the last fifteen years of his life.

The quiet, well-paced, peaceful life in Abramtsevo brought back many memories of childhood to Aksakov: he remembered the joys of communing with nature, his first catch, his first hunt. Even before he moved to the country, Aksakov had begun work in 1840 on his memoirs, the first excerpts of which were published anonymously in 1846 in *Moskovskii literaturnyi i uchebnyi sbornik* (Moscow Literary and Educational Collection). This excerpt eventually grew into what most critics consider his masterpiece, *Semeinaia khronika*. But during his years at Abramtsevo, Aksakov turned more and more to nature; his written works reflect his passion for its delights.

Even as a child Aksakov had displayed a keen interest in fishing, which he later described in his fictional memoir, *Detskie gody Bagrova-vnuka*. Yet as an adult he abandoned the fishing pole for the gun, and hunting became another passion in his life. In his later years Aksakov again became quite interested in fishing. Even when he was old and blind, he regularly went out to the lake to fish. He could sit for hours on the shores of the river Bor' in Abramtsevo, where, while enjoying one of the greatest pleasures of his life, he accumulated a vast amount of material for his book. In 1845 Aksakov began work on *Zapiski ob uzhen'e ryby* (Notes on Fishing, 1847). On 8 October of the same year he wrote to his son Ivan, "I have a compilation of a book about fishing and dictation of my memoirs ahead of me." In 1846 he finished the book, which came out the following year.

Zapiski ob uzhen'e ryby is saturated with Aksakov's passion for the sport as well as a profound feeling for nature, the essence of which lies not in aesthetic admiration of the beauties of nature but in man's search to understand the secrets of the world around him. In Aksakov's opinion mere admiration of the splendors of nature is nothing more than superficial attraction to the landscape or to decoration for its own sake for those trite, dry people who are caught up in the "muddy maelstrom" of their own vulgar little affairs. Aksakov's poem "Poslanie k M. A. Dmitrievu" (Epistle to Mikhail Aleksandrovich Dmitriev, 1851) provides a clue to his attitude toward nature: "There is, though / an equalizer / Eternally young and alive, / A miracle worker and healer,– / To whom I sometimes go. / I go to the world of nature, / A world of tranquility, freedom, / to the kingdom of fish and sandpipers, / To my native waters, / To the wide expanse of steppe meadows, / To the cool shade of forests / And–to my youthful years." Aksakov believed that all of man's base passions fall silent before the grandeur of nature.

Aksakov wanted to write a book on fishing that was practical but one whose author was clearly literate and "intimately knowledgeable in his subject." He wanted to convey the observant narrator's own disposition toward nature. Durkin quotes an excerpt from one of Aksakov's letters to Gogol about his aim in writing this book. "I have undertaken to write a book about angling, not only in its technical aspect, but in relation to nature in general; my passionate angler likewise passionately loves the beauties of nature as well; in a word, I have fallen in love with my work and I hope that this book will be pleasant not only for the lover of fishing, but also for everyone whose heart is open to the impressions of early morning, late evening, luxuriant midday, etc." Another aspect of the "passionate angler," according to Matlaw, lies in his method of dwelling not on the pleasures of the sport and not on its idyllic qualities but on the "loving detail and expert analyses of angling and of fishes."

Aksakov kept meticulous notes and records on the fish he caught. The book systematically discusses every aspect of fishing, such as all manner of gear and all types of bait. The second section includes essays on different types of fish. These data as well as his own observations of piscine behavior provide his readers with entertaining and enlightening pictures of fish life. His description of the "training" of carp even anticipates Ivan Petrovich Pavlov's experiments with conditioned responses. "Carp that are being bred in ponds can easily be trained to come to be fed at a designated time and at a designated place; if you continuously ring a little bell during their feeding time, they will get so used to it, that they will start gathering at the sound of the bell even at other times. One could probably train other fish to do the same." Such observations helped to establish the "authenticity (as distinct from the accuracy)" of his notes, a characteristic important to the author. Aksakov hoped that his book would appeal to more than just fishermen; in this regard *Zapiski ob uzhen'e ryby* was quite successful. Its popularity surprised even Aksakov, who took the opportunity of the publication of a second edition to expand the existing chapters and add a new one. The sincere, personal tone of the text, with its reliance on memory to recall the narrator's past, most assuredly contributed to the book's extraordinary reception.

Soon afterward (in 1851) Aksakov finished his *Zapista ruzheinego okhotnika Orensburgskoi gubernii* (Notes of a Rifle Hunter of the Orenburg Province). In May of the same year a small excerpt from this work, "Prolet i prilet ptits" (Migration of Birds), was published in *Moskovskie vedomosti* (Moscow News), and in March 1852 the entire book came out in a separate edition with a dedication to his "brothers and friends"–Nikolai and Arkadii. The popularity of the book led to a demand for a second edition six months later. Unfortunately Aksakov faced problems with the censorship committee: for some reason a censor thought that the hunting jargon in the book was meant to be satirical of the army and the government. By the end of January 1853 Aksakov was successful in his battle with the committee, and the second edition appeared two weeks later. This edition won even more critical acclaim than the first and thus became established as a major work of Russian literature.

Like its companion volume on fishing, the book on hunting conveys an aura of authenticity. Aksakov kept the same records on the number of birds he had caught as he had on his fishing tally. He was also conscious of the style of his narration and, according to Durkin, wanted it to be "in harmony with its subject." Yet again he does not dwell on the intrinsic beauty of nature but tries to convey its rich variety, focusing on intricate detail in his description of various game fowl and also managing at the same time to impart the essence of his subject. Vivid pictures of the animals emerge. As Gogol said to Aksakov, "In your birds there is more life than in my people." Naturalists, scientists, and nature writers also lauded Aksakov for his works on fishing and hunting. Here is a sample of Aksakov's style:

Kak krasivy ee pestrye, temnye, krasno-zheltye, korichnevye i svetlo-serye per'ia! Kak ona stroino, kruglo i krepko slozhena! Kak ona zhiva, provorna, lovka i milovidna vo vsekh svoikh dvizheniiakh! . . . Ona otlichaetsia provorstvom svoego bega i neobyknovennoiu siloiu i bystrotoiu svoego priamogo, kak strela, poleta. Vzlet ili pod"em ee bystr, shumen i mozhet ispugat', esli chelovek ego ne ozhidaet.

How beautiful [its] motley, dark, reddish-yellow, brown and light [grey] feathers are! How symmetrically, roundly and firmly [it] is built! How alive, quick, dexterous and handsome all [its] motions are! . . . [It] is distinguished by the speed with which [it] runs and by his swift, straight [as an arrow] line of flight. He takes off quickly and noisily and can startle a person who is taken unawares. (translation by Richard Noel Porter)

Matlaw says that the style of *Zapiski* is free of literariness but is conversational, spontaneous, and real. Though it retains an air of oral composition, it is also "consciously wrought." He goes on to note that "it is the expression of something grounded in the native tradition, of a purity of vocabulary unequaled in Russian." Aksakov rarely uses foreign words and then only for effect.

Aksakov's aesthetic principles forbade him to depict nature without its connection to man. He believed that without a human presence in the works the reader would remain indifferent to descriptions of nature. Nevertheless, Matlaw says, Aksakov showed that nature existed "independent of man, sufficient unto itself, with life and movement and grandeur that endow it with a kind of active existence. To be sure, man moves and acts within it through ordinary necessity . . . [but] only as one of

Aksakov in 1856

its lesser dependents." Most readers and critics of Aksakov, according to Matlaw, agree that nature plays the starring role in his prose. What man learns from nature and how he reacts to it tell exactly who and what he is. For Aksakov nature teaches his characters "the richness and complexity of life, the limits of man's activity."

In the beginning of the 1850s Aksakov intended to publish an annual miscellany, an "Okhotnichii sbornik" (Collection of Works on Hunting), which would include not only nature stories by various belletrists but also articles by natural scientists. When he showed the plan of the journal to the Moscow censorship committee, it denied his request for publication. Reputedly the committee considered some of the materials in the journal to be of "poor taste." In 1853 the main censorship committee allowed Aksakov to publish a separate volume with only his works in it. The book appeared in 1855 under the title *Rasskazy i vospominaniia okhotnike o raznykh okhotakh* (Tales and Reminiscences of a Hunter on Various Types of Hunting) and included short discourses on snaring, falconry, spear fishing, fox hunts, and wolf hunts as well as a collection of five *Melkie okhotnich'i rasskazy* (Little Hunting Stories). *Rasskazy i vospominaniia* brought together two elements that run through most of Aksakov's works: hunting tales and memoirs. The last of Aksakov's works that combine these traits is his 1858 "Sobiranie babochek" (Butterfly Collecting), a memoir of his days at Kazan University and a treatise on butterfly collecting. These works are minor yet helpful, for they define, Durkin says, "Aksakov's notion of the hunt and elucidat[e] the significance of hunting as a human activity, the major theme of *Notes on Fishing* and *Notes of a Hunter*.

Aksakov tried many times to write a story of his own life. His efforts finally culminated in a trilogy, *Vospominaniia prezhnei zhizni,* consisting of *Semeinaia khronika, Detskie gody Bagrova-vnuka,* and *Vospominaniia*. Work on these volumes became the main focus of the last ten years of his life. The trilogy, though fiction, is largely autobiographical and is the culmination of the elements of memoir writing that are present in Aksakov's works from "Buran" to "Ocherk zimnego dnia" (Sketch of a Winter Day), written just before his death in 1859. Even his *Zapiski ob uzhen'i ryby,* on hunting and fishing, include quite a bit of autobiographical material.

In the beginning of 1856 the first three *otryvki* (fragments) from *Semeinaia khronika,* "Stepan Mikhailovich Bagrov," "Mikhailo Maksimovich Kurolesov," and "Zhenitba molodogo Bagrova" (The Marriage of Young Bagrov), along with *Vospominaniia,* were published in a separate edition. The extraordinary success of the book prompted Aksakov to add two more fragments that had already appeared in journals to the second edition for the complete work. Long before he finished *Semeinaia khronika,* Aksakov foresaw troubles with the censorship committee regarding its publication. In the summer of 1854 he informed Panaev that the censors would probably mutilate *Semeinaia khronika*. When Aksakov sent a part of the book to Pogodin for publication in *Moskvitianin,* he added the following note: "I could only wish that the censors would not mutilate it; I have already thrown out much that is interesting and have replaced it with ellipses. If the censor leaves out too much—it would be better not to publish it." The source of all Aksakov's troubles with the censors were the segments of the book that dealt with the complex and often contradictory life on a Russian manor that depended so heavily on the Russian serf system. Nevertheless, at the end of September 1855 *Semeinaia khronika* passed the review and was soon published—mainly through the influence of the minister of education, who saw a great need for such literature.

While preparing the book for publication, Aksakov faced not only difficulties with the censors but also protests from his family. Some of the Aksakovs opposed parts of the work that they thought presented the family in a negative light. This discord within Aksakov's inner circle at times made his life quite miserable. He decided to avoid such conflicts by fictionalizing both characters and geographical locations. In a special epilogue to the reader in the first edition Aksakov wrote that he regretted he could not present his reading public with a complete book, for about half of *Semeinaia khronika* was censored. He also had to leave out much in *Vospominaniia*. In the second edition he added another address to the reader. "In publishing the second edition of my book with the addition of two new excerpts, I find it necessary to forewarn my benevolent readers, that I wrote parts of *Family Chronicle* based on stories from Bagrov family members, my close neighbors, and that these parts have nothing in common with my own personal recollections, other than some places and some names which I assigned arbitrarily." Aksakov persisted with this ruse until the end of his life. It was officially over when in 1870, in an introduction to the fourth edition of *Semeinaia khronika,* his son Ivan wrote about the close ties among the parts of the trilogy and explained the reasons behind his father's "forewarnings" to his readers.

In the "epilogue" to *Semeinaia khronika* Aksakov states quite clearly his ideas and thoughts about the book, in a way providing a thesis for the narrative.

Farewell, my dark and light images, my good and bad people, or would it be better to say, images, in which there are light and dark sides and people in which there are both good and evil qualities. You are neither great heroes nor famous personalities; in quiet and in obscurity you walked along your chosen earthly path in life and long ago, very long ago you left it behind; but you were people, and your internal and external life was full of poetry, and as interesting and instructive to us as we and our life will in turn be interesting and instructive to our descendants. You were also characters in a great and mighty pageant . . . and you will also become a memory.

Part of the originality of *Semeinaia khronika* lies in its relationship between fact and fiction in an atmosphere of historical accuracy counteracted by fictional bias. Reality remains within the constricting borders of the book. The narrator presents events and characters' personal lives as subordinate to history. Nevertheless, Aksakov follows his own impulses to provide an aesthetic representation of real life. In 1857 he said, "I am not able to substitute a fabrication for reality. I tried several times to write fictitious events and fictional people. All that came out was total junk, and it sounded funny even to me." To make the structure of this fictional memoir even more complex, he merges real history with literary models to produce a rich narrative.

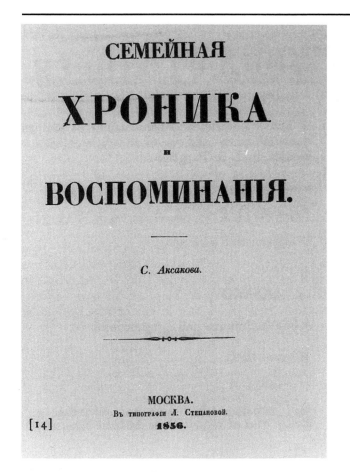

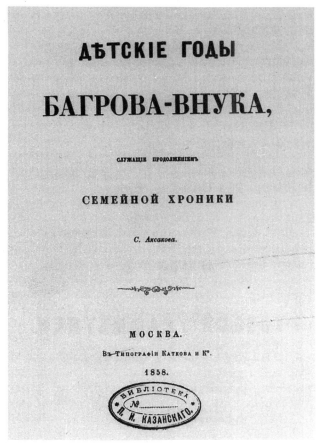

Title pages for two of Aksakov's most important works–A Family Chronicle and Recollections *(1856) and* The Childhood Years of Bargrov-Grandson *(1858)*

Within the form of an "historical memoir" Aksakov introduces echoes of earlier literary sources in a variety of genres: historical chronicles, historical documents, Gothic novels, *plutovaia* (rogue) literature (for example, Russian tales of Savva Grudtsyn and Frol Skobeev), sentimental romances, sentimental adventure novels, the *ocherk* (sketch), fairy tales, and even folktales (with grandfather Stepan Mikhailovich Bagrov akin to a *bogatyr',* a folk hero of great physical and moral strength). Stepan Mikhailovich also resembles Homeric and biblical archetypes, especially an Old Testament patriarch.

Dealing with the last third of the eighteenth century, *Semeinaia khronika* sees Russia from a positive point of view. Matlaw writes that Aksakov created a book that describes "the immensity of Russia and the implications of its sense of space." It also "conveys the special qualities of frontier life." Stepan Mikhailovich Bagrov, the narrator/author's grandfather, left a good estate because he felt cramped and settled his family in Bashkir territory across the Volga near Ufa. The first chapter of the book, Matlaw says, describes the new estate as well

as the troubles of moving the whole family and their serfs to a new homestead. The narrator describes all features of life–meals, farming, milling, and recreation–to produce an idyllic, though not ideal, depiction of Russian life on the steppe. The first chapter, or fragment, introduces the majestic figure of Stepan Mikhailovich, an "elemental creature in spontaneous communion with life and nature." He emerges as a character of great integrity, exhibiting qualities of "simplicity, strong moral sense, wisdom, understanding, fundamental nobility of character, deep religious sense." However, Stepan Mikhailovich also acts arbitrarily at times and indulges in terrible rages from which no one remains immune.

Mikhailo Maksimovich Kurolesov, whose name derives from the verb *kurolesit'*–(to play tricks), acts as an antithesis to Stepan Mikhailovich. The second fragment tells the tale of his treachery and ghastly demise. Kurolesov, a poor fortune hunter, secretly marries Stepan Mikhailovich's extremely young, rich cousin Praskovia, an act that angers old Bagrov, who eventually makes peace with the couple. On the surface Kurolesov seems to be a good manager and husband but secretly indulges in debauches, sadistic behavior, and wild acts; he whips people and even terrorizes the police. Kurolesov manages to lead a double life for fourteen years until someone sends Praskovia a letter that exposes her husband's depravity. She goes to her estate, Parashino, and witnesses his debauchery. With newfound courage she confronts him after having prayed through the night. Kurolesov beats her and locks her up until Stepan Mikhailovich comes to rescue her with an "army" of serfs. Ultimately, a vengeful retainer poisons Kurolesov.

The next three fragments deal with the courtship and marriage of old Bagrov's son, Alexei Stepanich. Unlike the villain who married his cousin for her riches, Alexei marries for love. He meets Sofia Nikolavna Zubina, an educated woman who enjoys respect and admiration in the social circles of Ufa. After the death of her stepmother, who had treated her harshly, Sofia cares for her invalid father. Extremely popular in society for her beauty, intelligence, and practicality, she feels sorry for the shy, immature, blushing Alexei and agrees to marry him. Alexei has trouble receiving permission from his father to marry Sofia; his sisters stand in the way of his happiness by slandering Sofia, charging that she is poor and of low lineage. In the course of a correspondence between father and son, Alexei threatens to commit suicide if his father does not grant him permission to marry. The wedding takes place with old Bagrov's blessing, but he and his wife do not attend the ceremony. Though the story is sentimental, the description of the wedding strangely enough seems rather objective. The fragment ends with the couple's arrival at Novoe Bagrovo and a description of the customs and amenities surrounding the introduction of the new couple to family, friends, and serfs.

The fourth fragment describes the couple's first days with the Bagrovs. Sofia initially does not like country life. Gradually Stepan wins her over, and the two grow to love and respect each other. Sofia and Alexei set off on a round of visits to all of the neighboring relatives, mainly because Stepan Mikhailovich demands that they follow the protocol that custom demands. Some of the places the couple visits are simply wretched: one of Alexei's sisters is still upset at the marriage and treats Sofia badly, even to the extent of giving the couple a room infested with rats. Sofia becomes angry at the weak Alexei, who does not defend her. The final episode of the fragment—a ceremonial dinner back at Novoe Bagrovo—reveals how old Stepan has greatly changed his original opin-

ion of his daughter-in-law, whom he now genuinely likes and even treats as his own daughter.

In the final fragment the newlyweds have returned to Ufa, where Sofia struggles to win back the affections of her own weak, dying father, whose servant, a Kalmuk, has gained absolute power over him. The couple move to their own home, and Alexei begins his work at the law courts. Sofia becomes pregnant, much to the joy of her father-in-law, who eagerly awaits the birth of a grandson. Stepan Mikhailovich becomes extremely angry when Sofia delivers a daughter. Unfortunately the little girl soon dies, and Sofia nearly perishes. Her grief at the loss of her child is compounded when her father also dies. But life does go on, and Sofia once again becomes pregnant. The book ends with a famous passage in which, after first crossing himself in thanksgiving after learning of the birth of the long-awaited child, old Stepan Mikhailovich gleefully inscribes his grandson's name in the family tree.

Pervym dvizheniem Stepana Mikhailycha bylo perekrestit'sia. Potom on provorno vskochil s posteli, bosikom podoshel k shkafu, toroplivo vytashchil izvestnuiu nam rodoslovnuiu, vzial iz chernilitsy pero, provel chertu ot kruzhka s imenem "Aleksei," sdelal kruzhok na kontse svoei cherty i v seredine ego napisal: "Sergei."

Stepan Mikhailovich's first movement was to cross himself. Then he nimbly jumped from his bed, went barefoot to the cupboard, hastily pulled out the familiar family tree, took the pen from the inkstand, drew a straight line from the circle that contained the name, Alexei, made a circle at the end of the line, and in its center wrote: "Sergei."

Thus the author announces his own birth at the end of his own "prehistory." Nevertheless, Aksakov always insisted that *Semeinaia khronika* was a *khudozhestvennoe proizvedenie* (work of art) in spite of its memoiristic nature. The narrator, who reveals much about himself as he relates the story of his ancestors, is conscious of his role in the chronicle. He tries to be objective and impartial but does not always succeed; for the most part he creates no positive or negative types but shows at least two sides of the people he describes.

The narrator introduces the main characters with a physical portrait that he follows with a psychological profile. As an omniscient narrator he tells his readers immediately about the character of each person he describes. His methods of characterization are calm and orderly; he does not rely on tricks of repetition of one physical characteristic (as do Gogol, Goncharov, and Tolstoy). He also does not dwell on psychological analysis "from the inside."

In the chronicle he rarely uses interior monologue or psychological eavesdropping; he simply informs his readers of what they need to know. The reader must then deduce the characters' thoughts by observing their actions. And though he employs the device of many contrasting pairs (old Bagrov and his wife, Sophia and Aleksei, Kurolesov and Praskovia, Aleksei and Kurolesov, and the two daughters—Aleksandra the Sly and Tatiana the Simple), he never resorts to the schematic dualism of Gogol or the more sophisticated and extensive juxtapositions of Tolstoy. Characters rarely change; only spectacularly dramatic events can provide external motivation for change. As a result the characters are generally one-sided, though at times they reveal conflicting traits. More than any of the characters, Stepan Mikhailovich exhibits this tension of opposing elements: his furious rages and arbitrary decisions lend an aura of realistic "humanness" to his depiction as a heroic/patriarchal archetype.

The structure of *Semeinaia khronika* also reinforces one of the basic themes of the book: contrasts. While the first chapter introduces a good man, albeit one who flies into terrible rages, the second one describes a man almost totally evil. The second chapter also paints a picture of a terrible marriage based on venal motives and contracted between a man of the world and an immature girl. But then the focus switches in the next fragment to the courtship between an immature, shy young man who genuinely falls in love with a sophisticated, seemingly mature, socially adept young woman. Their marriage, though not without problems, is a good one—especially in contrast to Praskovia and Kurolesov's. The third fragment also shows Alexei as alienated in the city, a situation that is reversed in the next chapter when the couple goes to the country, and Sofia finds herself in strange territory.

Chapters two and three act out one of the basic themes in Aksakov's works—country life versus city life. In his works a person's reaction to the countryside provides a clue to his character. The more estranged an individual is from nature, the more negative he is. The fourth fragment recounts the gradual transformation of Sofia from being merely a daughter-in-law to being Stepan Bagrov's genuine daughter. Perhaps the regard and affection Sofia receives from Stepan Mikhailovich strengthens her in her attempt to regain the love of her own estranged father in the last chapter of the book. And when *Semeinaia khronika* ends with Stepan Bagrov's inscribing his new grandson's name in the family tree, Aksakov completes the final contrast: a book that begins by looking back ends by looking forward, a device not uncommon in Aksakov's works.

Konstantin Sergeevich Aksakov, Aksakov's son, who was an important Slavophile

Published along with *Semeinaia khronika, Vospominaniia* is a real memoir that relates Aksakov's experiences upon leaving home to study at the gymnasium in Kazan where he spent his school days. Based on his own experiences, this work is the closest of all his "autobiographical" works to historical fact. Besides documenting and portraying the daily lives of students and teachers, his early interest in theater and literary work, and various events from his young life, *Vospominaniia* also firmly places Aksakov's experiences in their historical context. The opening of the Kazan university coincided with the beginning of Russia's war against Napoleon. Aksakov writes of how "electrifying" the events of the war seemed to him and his classmates. "The famous Bagration was our favorite; when we heard that he, together with a small dispatch, was left to cover the retreat of the army, a mission that was nothing short of suicidal, but still managed to fight his way through a whole army of Frenchmen, a 'hurrah' of such proportions thundered through the air that I cannot even describe it."

But ultimately the main foci of the work are memory "of the golden age of childhood happiness . . . and the fiery, mistaken, unreasonable, yet pure and honorable" time of youth as well as Aksakov's youthful search for something "higher, even if it does seem like madness." These gymnasium days were clearly important to the young (and old) Aksakov. Nostalgic and sentimental in tone, *Vospominaniia* treat Aksakov's personal past as a gradual integration of a young boy into the social world of adults. The source of most of the information today about Aksakov's school days, the work also dwells on the process of education on both a general and a particular scale. This memoir reveals Aksakov's first forays into two worlds that became lifelong passions: theater and literature.

Aksakov endows this genuine memoir with artistic touches, especially its structure, which Durkin describes as a "cyclical journey, with change and development in the self rendered tangible by the hero's recurrent visits to places that remain constant." The young boy's response to life in the city and the country change with time and provide glimpses of the internal, emotional, and psychological evolution taking place as Sergei moves toward manhood. Aksakov describes the events that contribute to this process against the backdrop of the seasons almost schematically, with negative occurrences in the winter and positive ones in the spring.

The complex process of the creation of a child's personality told mainly from the child's point of view comprises the main theme of the last part of the "autobiographical" trilogy, *Detskie gody Bagrova-vnuka,* which Aksakov initially conceived as a book for children and dedicated to his granddaughter Ol'ga Grigor'evna. It continues the saga of the Bagrovs by concentrating on the earliest, preschool years in the life of Serezha, whose birth ended *Semeinaia khronika.* Serezha, along with a narrator, tells his own story; the two narratives complement each other to form a single voice that creates "a single coherent universe." The narrator must rely on his memory to relate the remembered events in the voice of the child, who tells his tale in the present tense. In the introduction to the book Aksakov even discusses the reliability of his memory. Within the text Serezha says of himself, "My mind is quite older than my years."

Serezha's travels from one place to another to form the basic structure of the memoir with the act of traveling, an important element of the work. Serezha's perceptions of people and places change during the course of travel. These changes, according to Durkin, act as milestones in the young boy's perceptual, social, and ethical development. In an address to the reader Aksakov states that his book describes a world of childhood influenced by the events of everyday life.

The larger world around Serezha constantly invades his own small universe. New and different sides of life constantly present themselves to the youngster. He makes the great discovery that not everything is perfect in this world. He observes the shortcomings that are part of his environment yet never tries to confront or rise above them. Even this early in life, Durkin says, the young Aksakov establishes himself as an "impartial observer of the reality around him."

Life, though, always presents new and complex problems to a child. Nature and the people around him force him to make moral decisions and demand his active participation. They make him ask questions such as What is good? What is evil? Who is right? and Who is wrong? Aksakov manages to sustain in the narrative the feelings a child would have as he confronts moral questions. Yurii Samarin, the Slavophile philosopher, describes how Aksakov achieves this effect: " . . . in his inner world he was able to preserve the simplicity of childhood and the warmth of youth while acquiring the sober wisdom of old age. Namely because of this rare combination of apparently incompatible attributes, the individual who was Sergei Timofeevich commanded irrefutably universal respect and sympathy."

After hearing Aksakov read from the book, Leo Tolstoy wrote in his diary, "'Childhood' is delightful." Later, in a letter to the critic Vasily Petrovich Botkin, Tolstoy wrote the following about *Detskie gody Bogrova-vnuka:* "It does not possess the concentrated, youthful force of poetry, but uniformly sweet poetry of nature spills out over everything; as a result at times it may seem boring, but on the other hand, it is unusually calming and striking in its clarity, fidelity and proportionality of reflection." Aksakov's own views of the book were complex and often contradictory. He was unsure that his friends were correct when many of them told him that *Detskie gody Bagrova-vnuka* was his best work; yet in an 1857 letter to Panaev he wrote that this book was the most important of his works in respect to its ideas about education. Mirsky deems this work Aksakov's most characteristic and seems to support the author's own appraisal of its value when he calls it a "story of a peaceful and uneventful childhood, exceptional only for the exceptional sensibility of a child encouraged by an exceptionally sympathetic education." Mirsky also considers it "a masterpiece of realistic narrative."

A self-contained piece of children's literature, *Alenkii tsvetochek* (The Little Crimson Flower) provides an added dimension to the narrative. The housekeeper, Pelageia, relates this fairy tale whose plot is borrowed from the Russian translation of "Beauty and the Beast." It is the most folklore-oriented of Aksakov's works. A writer who tries to create a literary fairy tale based on folklore encounters many difficulties, not the least of which is stylization. However, Aksakov successfully uses elements of folk language and specific fairy-tale traits to compose a piece that has strong ties to the Russian-folklore tradition.

The 1850s were some of the most intense years in Aksakov's literary life. In the first half of the decade he wrote various sketches and memoirs of leading personalities in the worlds of theater and literature: "Znakomstvo s Derzhavinym" (My Acquaintance with Derzhavin), "Biografiia M. N. Zagoskina" (Biography of M. N. Zagoskin, 1853), "Iakov Emel'ianovich Shusherin i sovremennye emu teatral'nye znamenitosti" (Iakov Emel'ianovich Shusherin and His Contemporary Theatrical Celebrities), "Neskol'ko slov o M. S. Shchepkine"(A Few Words About Mikhail Semenovich Shchepkin), and "Vospomineniia ob Aleksandre Semenoviche Shishkove" (Reminiscences of Aleksandr Semenovich Shishkov). Not meant to be comprehensive biographies, these works concentrate on peculiar characteristics of their subjects, showing them caught up in their obsessions and passions. Critics single out Aksakov's sketch of Shishkov for special praise; Mirsky even calls it delightful. Aksakov wrote about Shishkov from the perspective of old age. Three decades after wholeheartedly embracing both the man and his ideas, Aksakov realized that his excessive enthusiasm was misplaced. In his youth Aksakov exaggerated Shishkov's importance and mistook his pedantry for brilliance. Nevertheless, his portrait of his former mentor emerges, according to Matlaw, on the whole as "a sympathetic and appreciative depiction of a kindly man and a somewhat distraught scholar."

Aksakov's ability to make people come alive contributed greatly to his success as a memoirist. Dmitrij Čiževskij notes that it "is especially interesting that Aksakov was able to describe his early literary enthusiasm for works such as the epics and didactic novels of Mikhail Matveevich Kheraskov, works considered unbearably dull since the 1830s, in such a way that readers of a later day feel close to them." This ability accounts for the importance of Aksakov's *Literaturnye i teatrol'nye vospominaniia* which grew into a long series of sketches. Though its sections that deal with the 1820s received little attention when they appeared in the periodical press, they are still a valuable source for the historians of both theater and literature. Mirsky characterizes them as delightful and at times amusing; however, they provide "no profound intuitions into other people's souls." This work formed the basis for Aksakov's collection called *Raznye sochineniia* (Various Works, n.d.), which also includes many short pieces.

Aksakov in 1892

In the last months before his death Aksakov also wrote his "Sobiranie babochek" (Butterfly Collecting), which describes his brief foray into lepidoptery while he was still at the university in Kazan. It is also fitting perhaps that his last work, "Ocherk zimnego dnia" (Sketch of a Winter Day), echoes his first prose piece, "Buran." Aksakov's last work describes the weather on the day of a hunt in winter when he was only twenty-one. Relying on his memory, he relates the details that give the sketch its quiet, poetic power. It returns to Aksakov's basic theme of the fusion of man and nature.

During the last years of his life Aksakov tried to experiment in other genres, not merely autobiographical and biographical ones. Fairly recently a fragment of a novel, "Kopyt'ev," was discovered. Dated 1857, it most likely never was finished. Aksakov also managed to keep up an active correspondence that reflects his concerns for the state of Russia and the problems of art and literature. He also received Moscow's intelligentsia at Abramtsevo, where Turgenev and Tolstoy were frequent visitors. Panaev's *Literaturnye vospominaniia* (Literary Reminiscences, 1928) and Mikhail Nikolaevich Longinov's *Vospominaniia o S. T. Aksakove* (Reminiscences of S. T. Aksakov, 1859) in *Russkii vestnik* (no. 8, 1859) provide much information about Aksakov's final days. Longinov describes Aksakov's physical decline after the onset of eye disease in 1845. This affliction forced him to spend time in darkened rooms. Unused to such a sedentary life, he "ruined his organism." In the spring of 1858 his illness became critical and caused him great pain and suffering, which he bore bravely and patiently. He spent the summer of 1858 at Abramtsevo, where, in moments of respite from severe pain, he dictated his final works. He continued in this vein in

Moscow: he engaged in literary activities in spite of his constant pain. Aksakov died 30 April 1859 of kidney failure and is buried in the Simonov monastery in Moscow.

Aksakov was not a man of "progressive" ideas; he was always quite apprehensive about the wave of revolutionary-democratic literature that exemplified his time. Yet his views were broad enough not to reduce his understanding of the literature to political sympathy or antipathy. He showed how the new realism was related to classical models. And his opinions on theater and education were enlightened. He saw the theater as an important way to influence society, and he tried to rid the stage of its artificiality. As a pedagogue he hated meaningless memorization and lobbied for classroom activities that would foster the creative abilities of youth.

During most of his professional life, beginning with his theater essays and critiques of the 1820s, Aksakov fought for art that reflected the depth of the multifaceted nature of life. His belief that the source of all art is reality and that every artist has the sacred responsibility to express it truthfully without idealizing it was unwavering. Aksakov reaffirmed this belief many times in his letters, discussions with friends, essays, and especially in his memoirs and autobiographical works. About *Semeinaia khronika,* Mirsky asserts that Aksakov "came nearer than any other Russian writer, even than Tolstoy in *War and Peace,* to a modern, evolutionary, continuous presentation of human life, as distinct from the dramatic and incidental presentation customary to the older novelists."

That Aksakov practiced in his works what he believed becomes irrefutably evident in the universal assessment of his work as "objective." He never tries to influence the reader by judging characters; instead he allows the reader to judge the characters by their actions and their behavior. As one critic says, Aksakov treats people the same way he does fish and birds: "Although the pike is not very likable, it is described with the same poetic love as other animals." Aksakov's objective narrative also shows the good and bad of Russia under serfdom. Though the Bagrovs and even the evil Kurolesov wield great power, they use it so wisely that their peasants and serfs rarely complain. Aksakov's talents are so great that his works remain classics even when their "issues" have long since lost their relevance. He also had the ability to make a man as ordinary as Aleksei Stepanovich in *Semeinaia khronika* interesting. The measured balance of his narration parallels his language, the "middle style" that became the standard of realistic writing in Russia. Critics have described his style as limpid, easy,

spontaneous, transparent, pure, graceful, and natural.

Aksakov's high moral principles, honesty, and spiritual well-being won him the respect of his contemporaries and the adulation of generations of critics. What all seem to admire the most in the man is his Russianness: "In his person Aksakov incarnated the best in traditions and customs that may be truly deemed Russian." For the Western reader Aksakov more than any other author reveals what it meant to be a Russian in the late eighteenth and early nineteenth centuries. But for the Russian readers, especially through his remarkable autobiographical trilogy, Aksakov helped to preserve an important part of the collective memory.

Letters:

L. N. Maikov, ed., "Pis'ma S. T., K. S., I I. S. Aksakovy k I. S. Turgenevu," *Russkoe obozrenie,* no. 8 (1894): 460–484; no. 9: 5–38; no. 10: 478–501; no. 11: 7–30; no. 12: 591–601.

References:

P. V. Annenkov, "S. T. Aksakov i ego *Semeinaia khronika,*" in *Vospominaniia i kriticheskie ocherki: Sobranie statei i zametok 1849–1868 godov,* 2 volumes (St. Petersburg, 1879), volume 2, pp. 109–132;

Annenkov, *Zamechatel'noe desiatiletie,* in *Literaturnye vospominaniia,* edited by B. M. Eikhenbaum (Leningrad: Academia, 1928);

A. S. Arkhangel'skii, "S. T. Aksakov: Detstvo i studenchestvo," *Russkoe obozrenie,* 34 (July 1895): 37–56; 34 (August 1895): 498–513; 35 (September 1895): 63–69;

Nonna Hordowsky Carr, "S. T. Aksakov in Russian Literary Criticism Before 1917," dissertation, University of Colorado, 1976;

V. V. Danilov, "S. T. Aksakov, S. N. Glinka i V. V. Izmailov v Moskovskom tsenzurnom komitete," *Izvestiia po russkomu iazyku i slovesnosti,* volume 1, book 2 (Akademiia Nank USSR, 1928), pp. 507–524;

N. A. Dobroliubov, "Derevenskaia zhizn' pomeshchika v starye gody," in *Sobranie sochinenii,* 9 volumes (Moscow: Gosudarstvennoe izdatel'stvo khudozhestvennoi literatury, 1962), volume 2, pp. 290–293;

Andrew R. Durkin, "Pastoral in Aksakov: The Transformation of Poetry," *Ulbandus Review,* 2 (1979): 62–75;

Durkin, *Sergei Aksakov and Russian Pastoral* (New Brunswick, N.J.: Rutgers University Press, 1983);

Durkin, "Two Instances of Prose Pastoral: Nemcova and Aksakov," in *American Contributions to the Ninth International Congress of Slavists, Kiev, September, 1983,* edited by Paul Debreczny, volume 2: *Literature, Poetics, History* (Columbus, Ohio: Slavica, 1983), pp. 125–133;

S. Durylin, "Gogol' i Aksakovy (s tremia neizdannymi zapiskami Gogolia)," in *Zven'ia,* 3–4 (Moscow & Leningrad: Academia, 1934), pp. 325–364;

Pamela Evans, "The Portrayal of Childhood." dissertation, University of Toronto, 1980;

Kathryn B. Feuer, "*Family Chronicle:* The Indoor Art of Sergei Aksakov," *Ulbandus Review,* 2 (1979): 86–102;

Marsha Gayle Gauntt, "S. T. Aksakov's *The Family Chronicle:* An Exceptional Novel," dissertation, University of California, Los Angeles, 1975;

Xenia Glowacki-Prus, "The Biographical Sketches of S. T. Aksakov," *New Zealand Slavonic Journal,* 2 (1977): 1–12;

Glowacki-Prus, "Sergey Aksakov as a Biographer of Childhood," *New Zealand Slavonic Journal,* 2 (1974): 19–37;

Richard Gregg, "The Decline of a Dynasty: From Power to Love in Aksakov's *Family Chronicle,*" *Russian Review,* 50 (January 1991): 35–47;

A. S. Khomiakov, "Sergei Timofeevich Aksakov," in *Polnoe sobranie sochinenii,* volume 3 (Moscow: Russkii arkhiv, 1900–1907), pp. 369–375;

V. P. Kriazheva, "Iz istorii ideino-tvorcheskikh sviazei S. T. Aksakova s Gogolem," *Uchenye zapiski Leningradskogo gosudarstvennogo pedagogicheskogo instituta im. Gertsena,* 245 (1963): 217–235;

Kriazheva, "K voprosu ob esteticheskikh vzgliadakh S. T. Aksakova," *Uchenye zapiski Leningradskogo gosudarstvennogo pedagogicheskogo instituta im Gertsena,* 273 (1965): 32–49;

I. Kruti, "S. T. Aksakov v istorii russkoi teatral'noi kritiki," in *Teatr: Sbornik statei i materialov* (Moscow: VTO, 1945), pp. 183–199;

Zenon Kuk, "*Detskie gody Bagrova-vnuka* by Sergei T. Aksakov: A Marvel of 'Pure' Russian," *Proceedings of the Kentucky Foreign Language Conference: Slavic Section,* 3, no. 1 (1985): 35–43;

Marcus C. Levitt, "Aksakov's *Family Chronicle* and the Oral Tradition," *Slavic and East European Journal,* 32 (Summer 1988): 198–212;

Valerian Maikov, *N. V. Gogol' i S. T. Aksakov. K istorii literaturnykh vlianii* in *Russkoe obozrem'e,* no. 5 (1891): 438–455;

S. I. Mashinskii, "Iz istorii tsenzorskoi deiatel'nosti S. T. Aksakova [po novym materialam]," *Izvestiia Akademii nauk SSSR,* 18 (May/June 1959): 238–252;

Mashinskii, "Novye materialy o S. T. Aksakove," *Izvestiia Akademii nauk SSSR,* 14 (May/June 1955): 239–254;

Mashinskii, *S. T. Aksakov: Zhizn' i tvorchestvo* (Moscow: Khudozhestvennaia literatura, 1973; second expanded edition);

Ralph Matlaw, "Sergey Aksakov: The Genius of Ingenuousness," in S. T. Aksakov, *The Family Chronicle,* translated by M. C. Beverley (New York: Dutton, 1961), pp. vii-xxiv;

D. S. Mirsky, *A History of Russian Literature from Its Beginnings to 1900,* edited by Francis J. Whitfield (New York: Vintage, 1958);

Viktor Ostrogorskii, *Sergei Timofeevich Aksakov: Kritiko-biograficheskii ocherk* (St. Petersburg: Martynov, 1901);

Jerome Joseph Rinkus, "The World View of Sergei Aksakov," dissertation, Brown University, 1971;

V. I. Shenrok, "S. T. Aksakov i ego sem'ia," *Zhurnal Ministerstva narodnogo prosveshcheniia,* no. 10 (1904): 355–418; no. 11: 245–271; no. 12: 229–290;

V. D. Smirnov, *Aksakovy, ikh zhizn' i literaturnaia deiatel'nost': Biograficheskii ocherk,* in *Zhizn' zamechatel'nykh liudei. Biograficheskaia biblioteka F. Pavlenkova* (St. Petersburg, 1895);

Andrew Baruch Wachtel, *The Battle for Childhood: Creation of a Russian Myth* (Stanford: Stanford University Press, 1990);

Patrick Joseph Wreath, "A Critical Study of S. T. Aksakov," dissertation, Cornell University, 1969.

Papers:

Letters, manuscripts, and other materials are in Aksakov *fondy* (files) in the following archives: Rossiiskii gosudarstvennyi arkhiv literatury i iskusstva (RGALI), Moscow; Institut russkoi literatury i iskusstva. Pushkinskii dom (PD), St. Petersburg; Rossiiskaia gosudarstvennaia biblioteka, rukopisnyi otdel, Moscow.

Vissarion Grigor'evich Belinsky

(30 May 1811 – 26 May 1848)

Derek Offord
University of Bristol

BOOKS: *Osnovaniya russkoi grammatiki dlia per-vonachal'nogo obucheniya* (Moscow, 1837);

Nikolai Alekseevich Polevoi (St. Petersburg: E. Prats, 1846).

Editions and Collections: *Sochineniia,* 12 parts (Moscow: K. T. Soldatenkov and N. M. Shchepkin, 1859–1862);

Sochineniia, 4 volumes (St. Petersburg: F. Pavlenkov, 1900);

Polnoe sobranie sochinenii, volumes 1–11, edited by S. A. Vengerov (St. Petersburg, 1900); volumes 12–13, edited by V. S. Spiridonov (Moscow-Leningrad: Goslitizdat, 1926, 1948);

Sobranie sochinenii, 3 volumes, edited by F. M. Golovenchenko (Moscow: Goslitizdat, 1948);

Polnoe sobranie sochinenii, 13 volumes (Moscow: AN SSSR, 1953–1959); the definitive edition compiled by the Institute of Russian Literature of the Academy of Sciences of the USSR.

Editions in English: *Belinsky, Chernyshevsky, and Dobrolyubov: Selected Criticism,* edited by Ralph E. Matlaw (New York: Dutton, 1962);

Russian Philosophy, volume 1, edited by James M. Edie, James P. Scanlan, and Mary-Barbara Zeldin (Chicago: Quadrangle Books, 1965), pp. 280–320;

Selected Philosophical Works (Moscow: Goslitizdat, 1948; Westport, Conn.: Hyperion Press, 1981);

A Documentary History of Russian Thought: From the Enlightenment to Marxism, edited by W. J. Leatherbarrow and D. C. Offord (Ann Arbor, Mich.: Ardis, 1987), pp. 117–135.

Vissarion Grigor'evich Belinsky

Vissarion Grigor'evich Belinsky is by general agreement the greatest Russian literary critic and the father of the radical intelligentsia. His career spans the years 1834 to 1848 and coincides with the middle period of the repressive reign of Nicholas I, with the flowering of Russian literature in the early part of its golden age and with the intense debate about the relationship of Russia to the West. Criticism is molded by Belinsky into a tool not merely for the discussion of literature and aesthetics but also for the expression of opinions on many other subjects, notably morality, history, and society. His essays are not so much appraisals of works of art, although they do include that element, as free-ranging enquiries apropos of those works. Belinsky's career is commonly divided into three broad phases: an early infatuation with the thought of Friedrich Wilhelm Joseph von Schelling, which lasted from 1834 to 1836 and which was associated with the search for a national character reflected in culture; an equally unrestrained enthusiasm for Georg Wilhelm Friedrich Hegel, which was associated in the period from 1838 to 1840 with exaltation of art for its own sake and with a notorious political conservatism and glorification of the status quo; and a final period beginning in 1840 and eventually associated more with radical French influences than with German philosophical ones, in which Belinsky stresses the need for art to mirror society and expresses sympathy for the downtrodden. This schema represents a more or less crude simplification, although a necessary one.

Since Belinsky was a restless spirit incessantly searching for meanings and values that would satisfy him and was intensely receptive to art and ideas, his views were in a state of constant flux, and there are more gradations in their development than the schema suggests. At the same time there is, for all his volte-faces, a unity to his work that flows both from certain beliefs that remain constant (in the greatness of such artists as Homer, William Shakespeare, Johann Wolfgang von Goethe, Aleksandr Sergeevich Pushkin, and Nikolai Vasil'evich Gogol; in the supreme importance of art for a people and of artistry in the work of art; and in the integrity of the true artist) and from the general characteristics of his thought (its thirst for ultimate values and truths, its striving for classification within grand patterns, and its fierce passion). The character of his work, particularly its remorselessness and ardor, earned him among contemporaries the sobriquet "furious Vissarion."

Belinsky was born on 30 May 1811 in Viapori (Swedish name Sveaborg) in Finland, then part of the Russian Empire. His paternal grandfather, Nikifor, was a priest in Penza Province. His father, Grigorii, qualified as a doctor in the St. Petersburg Medical Academy and at the time of the birth of Vissarion, his first son, was serving with the Baltic fleet. In 1816 Grigorii took up an appointment as district doctor in Chembar, Penza Province, and it was there that Vissarion spent his most unhappy childhood. He was educated for a while in the local school and from 1825 at the *gimnaziia* in Penza. He did not complete the course at the *gimnaziia,* however, leaving in 1828 to prepare himself at home for the entrance examinations for Moscow University, at which he registered with a state bursary in 1829. In 1832, however, he was expelled from the university for missing lectures, for friction with the authorities, and for writing a juvenile play, *Dmitrii Kalinin,* that included tirades against serfdom. There followed a period of great hardship that doubtless exacerbated the serious lung disease that had already begun to manifest itself during Belinsky's university years.

It is essential when approaching Belinsky's work to bear in mind its historical context. Although Russia had been thrown into closer contact with the West as a result of the Napoleonic Wars and was subsequently subject to increasing Western cultural influence, the autocratic regime allowed no practical application of the new ideas that came from the West. Indeed, Nicholas I (ruler from 1825 to 1855), who came to power in the wake of the Decembrist Revolt (1825), tightened state supervision of his subjects through a new secret police force (the Third Section, established in 1826), imposed stricter censorship, and through Minister of Education S. S. Uvarov introduced the theory of Official Nationality (promotion of orthodoxy, autocracy, and nationality as the guiding principles of the Russian Empire). Idealistic men, civilizing and humanizing forces, could express themselves only in the most abstract way, not through any practical activity, let alone through any overt political grouping. Therefore, throughout the period in which Belinsky was active, particularly in the 1830s, intellectual life had a rather abstruse character. It tended to seek oblique answers to the great questions that troubled Russians, such as the meaning of the national life and their destiny as a people, in art, a field that seemed relatively innocuous from the political point of view. There is much in Belinsky's early essays that is typical of the atmosphere of this repressive post-Decembrist age in Russia, notably the tendency to take refuge in vague abstractions, the cultivation of a noble idealism, and intoxication with German Romantic philosophy, particularly the philosophy of Schelling, which was avidly discussed in the Stankevich circle (named for poet and philosopher Nikolai Vladimirovich Stankevich) frequented by Belinsky in the early 1830s.

Belinsky's first major essay, "Literaturnye mechtaniia" (Literary Reveries), was published in ten installments in Nikolai Ivanovich Nadezhdin's journal *Molva* (Rumor) in 1834. This debut, which immediately attracted attention, was notable for its pioneering attempt to apply a philosophical system to the history of Russian literature and for the warmth of feeling with which it discussed literature. Belinsky begins by lamenting the current poverty of Russian literature and provocatively asserting that in a sense Russia has no literature, if by literature one means a coherent corpus of works expressing the spirit of a people—its inner life and pulse.

Each people, according to Belinsky, plays its particular role, decreed by Providence in the great family of mankind, and makes a contribution to the general repository of achievement in the universal quest for self-perfection. Thus the Germans have excelled in the field of speculation and analysis; they have given ideas. The English with their practical activity have given inventions. The French have given laws of fashion and set tone; their life is social: it belongs to the drawing room. The Italians are distinguished by their artistic tendency and lead a life of love and creativity. Literature is the expression of such distinctive characteristics, an expression or symbol of a people's inner life. The Russians, on the other hand, he felt did not as yet have a clear physiognomy or distinctive national character (*samobytnost'*, originality, and *narodnost'*, national distinctiveness, are the terms Belinsky uses) because the Westernization of Russia precipitated by Peter the Great (ruler from 1696 to 1725) had created a divorce in Russian life between people (*narod*) and society (*obshchestvo*). Russian literature reflected this rift between the superficially Westernized nobility and the masses, who remained in a state of pre-Petrine backwardness.

The first attempts, by Antiokh Dmitrievich Kantemir and Vasily Kirillovich Trediakovsky in the eighteenth century, to produce literary works of a Western sort were not inspired by poetic feeling, and the first literary genius, Mikhail Vasil'evich Lomonosov, the Peter the Great of Russian literature, unable to express himself in a Russian way, was forced into imitativeness. *Narodnost'* did begin to find expression from the age of Catherine II (ruler from 1762 to 1796), especially in the verse of Gavriil Romanovich Derzhavin and the fables of Ivan Andreevich Krylov, but even in the Alexandrine age (1801–1825) Russian literature remained imitative despite its growing importance. Pushkin, an unselfconscious artist and son of his age, found in Romanticism a distinctive form for the expression of his feelings and a means of overthrowing the foreign influence of neoclassicism. The Pushkin period (1820s) was a time when the Russians refelt, rethought, and relived the entire intellectual life of the West and when Russia began to glimpse if not a literature then at least the specter of it, for there was life and momentum in it. And yet in general the history of Russian literature to 1834 is the history of unsuccessful attempts by Russians to create by blind imitation of foreign models a literature of their own. Russia did not yet have true *narodnost'* in its literature, nor could it have, because its society was too young and had yet to liberate itself from Western tutelage.

In the second half of 1835 Belinsky became de facto editor of *Teleskop* (The Telescope) and *Molva* in Nadezhdin's absence from Moscow and gave the publications a distinctive direction, especially through his own critical articles, chief among them an essay, "O russkoi povesti i povestiakh g. Gogol'ia" (About the Russian Novella and the Novellas of Mr. Gogol). Belinsky sets out in this work to explain why the novel and the *povest'* have become the dominant literary forms of the age; draws a distinction between different types of art (or "poetry" as he prefers to say); accounts for the current ascendancy of the *povest'*, surveying the development of the Russian *povest'* in particular; discusses the nature of the creative process; and gives a highly enthusiastic review of Gogol's early stories in the collections *Vechera na khutore bliz Dikan'ki* (Evenings on a Farm near Dikanka), published in 1831–1832; *Mirgorod,* published in 1835; and *Arabeski* (Arabesques), published in 1835.

The question as to the modern ascendancy of the novel and the *povest'* is interconnected for Belinsky with a division of "poetry" into two types, "ideal" (*ideal'naia*) and "real" (*real'naia*), and with the emergence of the individual as a subject of interest to the artist. In poetry of the first type the poet re-creates life according to his own ideal (*peresozdaet*), which is determined by his view of things and by his attitude toward the world, his age, and his people. In real poetry, on the other hand, the poet reproduces life in all its nakedness and truth (*vosproizvodit*) and is faithful to all the details and nuances of reality (*deistvitel'nost'*). For peoples in the early stages of their history, of whom Belinsky takes as an example the ancient Greeks, man with free will, passions, feelings and thoughts, wishes and privations, does not exist because his individuality is not yet acknowledged and his ego is fused with the identity of his people. As the European peoples matured, though, according to Belinsky the idea of man as an individual distinct from his people and of interest by himself was born. The songs of the troubadours—expressing the sorrow of love, or the lament of an imprisoned princess, or a desire for vengeance or exploit—reflected this change. At last the epic poem was supplanted by the novel. Miguel de Cervantes destroyed the ideal tendency of poetry, which by the late sixteenth century was false, and Shakespeare for once and for all reconciled and combined poetry and life. In recent times, Belinsky says, Goethe, Friedrich von Schiller, and Sir Walter Scott have emulated Shakespeare. Thus is born real poetry, the poetry of life and reality, the true poetry of Belinsky's time. Its hallmark is faithfulness to reality; it does not re-create so much as reproduce reality. Its hero is man as an individual, an autonomous being and free agent, a riddle whose solution can be achieved only through full consciousness.

For the portrayal of man in relation to social life the novel seemed to Belinsky to be the most suitable form, but in fact the *povest'* prevails, perhaps because contemporary life is too varied, complex, and fragmented, and readers want it to be reflected in all its forms. The *povest'* will accommodate whatever one wishes: a sketch of mores, a mordant gibe at an individual or society, some deep mystery of the soul, or the play of passions. Concise and swift, light and deep, it can tear individual pages out of the great book of life. Belinsky proceeds to survey the development of the Russian *povest'*, which really only dates from the 1820s. He discusses such writers as Aleksandr Ivanovich Odoevsky, Mikhail Petrovich Pogodin, Nikolai Alekseevich Polevoy, and Nikolai Filippovich Pavlov before turning to Gogol, whose *povesti* are distinguished by the simplicity of their invention, *narodnost'*, complete truthfulness to life, originality, and comic animation always overshadowed by a deep sense of sadness and dejection. The root of all these virtues lies in Gogol's being a poet of real life.

Belinsky then advances his view of the nature of the creative process: first an idea is conceived by the artist; then it comes to be embodied in certain images and to take on life. Artistic creation for Belinsky is a "mysterious clairvoyance, poetic somnambulism." The artist has nowhere actually seen the characters he creates and does not copy them from reality; rather he has perceived everything in a prophetic dream, in radiant moments of poetic revelation. The work of art is not a contrivance but the apprehension of some higher, mysterious power located in the artist and outside him. The answer to the question of whether or not the poet is a free creator is therefore ambiguous. On the one hand, he is a slave to his subject in that he is not sovereign in its choice and development and in that he does not create to order or of his own volition. On the other hand, his age, people, individuality, life, opinions, and level of culture are all reflected in his work.

Applying these considerations to Gogol, Belinsky without hesitation confidently identifies him as a writer of talent whose work includes poetry of reality. Gogol transcends the depiction that might be achieved through ratiocination, labor, and careful and faithful copying (*kopirovka*) of reality and rises to true creativity (*tvorchestvo*). He takes the mundane, the prosaic, and the vulgar (*poshloe*), such as the quarrel between the two Ivans or the life of the Old World landowners who simply ate and drank and died, and he amuses his readers with it; but then in addition he makes his readers part from this world with a sense of sadness. Gogol's works therefore embody poetry, philosophy, and truth, and what he depicts is not so much copied from reality as divined by feeling in a moment of poetic revelation. They are also imbued with *narodnost'*, which is a prerequisite for a truly artistic work inasmuch as *narodnost'* is to be understood as a faithful depiction of the mores, customs, and character of a people.

As well as his major article on Gogol, Belinsky published in 1835 pieces on the poets Evgeny Abramovich Baratynsky and Aleksei Vasil'evich Kol'tsov and a celebrated damaging review of Vladimir Grigor'evich Benediktov, whose Romantic verse was at that time held in high regard. Alongside skill and descriptive flair Belinsky finds in Benediktov's poetry a predilection for the flowery phrase, imprecise and strained diction, looseness of thought, and deficiency of feeling and fantasy.

The most important articles Belinsky produced in 1836 are a survey of Russian literature for the second half of 1835 and a critical piece about the literary critical stance of the journal *Moskovskii nabliudatel'* (The Moscow Observer). The first of these works, the initial example of a genre to which Belinsky was later to attach much importance, reiterates his view of the barrenness of the Russian literary landscape as yet and again discusses the nature of *narodnost'* in literature, a reflection of the individual character of a people. He emphasizes the obligation of a journal to develop and extend the taste for reading among the public and to cultivate through the literary works it publishes and through its literary criticism a sense of the beautiful. For aesthetic sense, he argues—and the point is perhaps the most important one in the essay—is the basis of the good and moral. Prosperity may flourish in North America; civilization may have reached its height; and the prisons may be empty. But if, as people say, there is no art there, no love of the beautiful, then Belinsky despises that prosperity and has neither respect for the civilization nor confidence in its morality.

In the second of his major articles in 1836 he takes *Moskovskii nabliudatel'* to task for being more concerned with literary decency than with artistry and beauty. The proper function of criticism, Belinsky argues, is to explain the laws of artistic creation in theory and to confirm their truth in practice. As for the critic himself, his gift is a rare one and therefore highly prized, for there are few people naturally endowed to the highest degree with aesthetic sense. The critic needs profound feeling, ardent love of art,

The Chembarsk College, which Belinsky attended from 1822 to 1825 (drawing by B. I. Lebedev, from Belinsky v zhizni, *1948)*

erudition, and an objective mind. In Russia, where taste is uneducated and literature largely imitative, the influence of good criticism may be especially beneficent and of bad criticism correspondingly destructive. The article is also notable for its reiteration of Belinsky's other shibboleths during this period. Discussing the question of the artist's relationship to reality, Belinsky takes the example of the historical dramatist or novelist such as Schiller or Scott: he cannot be and should not be a slave of history any more than of actual life because in either event he would become a copyist rather than a creator; he is therefore faithful to history in a spiritual rather than a factual way. Belinsky also contrasts the application of "taste" and "feeling" to the judgment of works of art and exalts the latter: taste, the property of the eighteenth century when the word *art* was equivalent to *savoir-faire,* implies a cold judgment of the sort appropriate to a paté or a Burgundy whereas feeling, which Belinsky associates with the nineteenth century, implies for him a reverential, self-abnegating, and ecstatic contemplation.

Characteristic of Belinsky's early Schellingian period as a whole are a view of the world as the breath of an eternal idea; a misty vision of harmonious union achieved through altruistic love between man and his fellows and between man and the world; the belief that runs counter to the eighteenth-century cosmopolitanism that peoples have distinctive characteristics and fulfill through their collective lives one aspect of the development of the eternal idea; a view of art as the expression of the distinctive spirit of a people; the belief that art is an end in itself; and a view of the creative process of the true poet as an unconscious, intuitive apprehension of reality. Already apparent too in the early articles of the period from 1834 to 1836 in general are Belinsky's exaltation of the role of the poet, his equation of that role with altruism and service, and his insistence upon the integrity and freedom of the artist.

He also broaches the subject of the role of the critic, which he sees as manifold: thoroughly to appraise a writer, as is done in the West; to determine his influence on contemporaries and posterity; to examine the spirit of his work in general rather than its isolated merits and defects; to analyze the circumstances of his life to see if he might have done more and why he did what he did; and to plot his place in his literature. The aim of the Russian critic should be not so much to broaden man's understanding of the beautiful as to disseminate in his own land ideas on this subject that are already well known elsewhere. The first and main question that criticism must resolve is whether or not a work is beautiful and whether or not an author is a "poet." Already clear too are his literary preferences: among the artists he most admires are Homer, Shakespeare, Goethe, Schiller, Lord Byron, and Scott. German thought and literature are in general admired, while French culture is seen as artificial and sterile. Some of Belinsky's faults are already apparent too, though one should bear in mind of course his immaturity: the style is often rambling and wordy, though there are purple passages with a poetry of their own. The argumentation is not always easy to follow, nor are ideas elegantly expressed. There are many flattering generalizations on the nature of the Russian people. Most important for Belinsky's disciples, perhaps, is the moral fervor that informs his work and manifests itself in contempt for the empty society dandy and in tirades contrasting selfless service of an ideal with pursuit of place or wealth.

Belinsky wrote one other major work in 1836, a review of a book on moral philosophy by theologian Vasilii Mikhailovich, who took the name Filaret when he became Metropolitan (bishop) of Moscow. This review is important as the only surviving article that reflects the influence of Johann Gottlieb Fichte, with whose ideas Belinsky had become acquainted under the tutelage of Mikhail Aleksandrovich Bakunin, with whom Belinsky was staying at Premukhino in the late summer when the article was written. Much of Belinsky's original draft of this article, which was capable of being construed as critical of the reality of Nicholas's Russia, albeit in quite abstract terms, was omitted by Nadezhdin, fearing the consequences of its publication for his journal. (Belinsky at the time saw revolutionary implications in Fichte's doctrine of the freedom of the personality and scented in it the smell of blood, as he later wrote.) What remains of the article nevertheless ranges over many subjects. First, Belinsky outlines opposing theories of cognition, the a priori and a posteriori theories. He inclines to the a priori view, contending that facts and phenomena do not exist in themselves but reside in the individual, that external objects only stimulate in the ego the concepts that the ego attributes to them. Second, Belinsky erodes the boundaries among goodness, truth, and beauty. Each good act, he asserts, is also a true and beautiful act. Moreover, these three values are endowed with a religious sense. Third, Belinsky de-

fines good in absolute terms and lays down a demanding ethic. The model of human perfection, as he sees it, is Christ, and all should try to raise themselves to the ideal Christ represents. Even the good man who fails to improve as much as he might is seen as ignoble. Fourth, Belinsky offers a definition of man's place in the cosmos and of his relationship to others. Man is an organ of the consciousness of nature, a vessel of the spirit of God, a member of the great family called mankind. No individual can attain full and perfect development of his consciousness; that is possible only for mankind as a whole. Therefore, each man must love mankind as the idea of the complete development of consciousness, which constitutes his own goal too. Finally, in a lyrical concluding passage Belinsky asserts the existence of pattern in the universe and of meaning in life. There is much in life that is bad: sins, doubt, despair, inner disharmony, and revulsion at life. Yet there is much more that is beautiful: tears of repentance before the cross and moments of comfort and faith. The soul may find reconciliation and glimpse a new land and heaven.

Late in 1836 Nadezhdin's *Teleskop* was closed following the publication in it of Petr Iakovlevich Chaadaev's first "Philosophical Letter," and Belinsky found himself without a means of livelihood. In 1837 he published a grammar of the Russian language on which he had been working since 1834, but the book was unsuitable for teaching purposes in schools and did not sell. He also became quite ill and from June to September was forced to recuperate in the Caucasian spa town of Piatigorsk. At the same time he increasingly turned his back on the concerns of everyday life and sank deeper into a mood of abstract contemplation, in which he was encouraged by acquaintance with Bakunin, who became his principal philosophical mentor during this period. Philosophy and art, for Belinsky and his friends, seemed to hold the key to all questions from the sublime to the most trivial and mundane. Those who did not share this predilection for immersion in philosophical speculation to the exclusion of all other activity were viewed with contempt in Belinsky's circle. To have the reputation of a solid or respectable man in society was considered disgraceful, and descriptions such as "good fellow" or "bon vivant" were terms of abuse. In particular Belinsky and friends such as Bakunin, Vasily Petrovich Botkin, and Konstantin Sergeevich Aksakov avidly read and endlessly debated the works of Hegel who, as Belinsky understood him, enabled one to reconcile oneself with reality and all its defects. Recognition of reality as rational and of might as right gave Belinsky a sense of liberation.

Belinsky believed in his Hegelian phase that truth may only be perceived through higher reason (*razum,* or the Hegelian *Vernunft*), not by means of ordinary reason or understanding (*rassudok,* or the Hegelian *Verstand*) and empiricism. Mechanistic explanations of phenomena represent only that fragmentary view of reality of which the understanding is capable. Reason, on the other hand, makes possible a deeper explanation of the inner essence and development of things. Phenomena that develop out of themselves have rationality (*razumnost'*) and are endowed with a certain sanctity. Furthermore, life consists in movement, which is dialectical, proceeding through a struggle of opposites that finds resolution in a higher synthesis, whereas death consists in stasis, a condition exemplified by oriental societies. The individual is part of a living whole, a social organism. Societies and states, like people, are flesh and blood animated by spirit, not artificial inventions that move mechanically. Art is an instrument of the truth that reason seeks to illuminate. The artist must not moralize or represent ephemeral, local, or factional interests. As for the creative process, the artist continues to be seen as not entirely in control of his work; inspiration does not come when he wishes and as he wills it.

In 1838 Belinsky found a new outlet for his views as editor of *Moskovskii nabliudatel',* from which Shevyrev had recently departed. The journal became a vehicle for the propagation of German culture: works by Goethe, E. T. A. Hoffmann, and other German writers were published there together with philosophical discourses, especially on aesthetics; articles in a Hegelian spirit; and excerpts from the works of Hegel himself. It was here that Belinsky published the earliest expression of his own Hegelian mode, an article that was conceived as a theoretical preamble to a series that was to deal with Denis Ivanovich Fonvizin and Mikhail Nikolaevich Zagoskin, the eighteenth-century dramatist and nineteenth-century historical novelist respectively. (Only the preamble was actually written.) The article covers many subjects. First, Belinsky presents a naive and boastful discussion of the supposedly many-sided character of the Russians and their destiny to inherit the distinctive qualities of all other peoples. Second, he compares the character and culture of the Germans and the French. Whereas the German regards any individual phenomenon as a mysterious hieroglyph or sacred symbol whose inner life and spirit and whose relation to the general he may penetrate through his capacity for contemplation, the Frenchman is able to see only the external form of an object and fails to perceive the object as the expression of an idea or to grasp its relation-

ship to the world as a whole. For the German, life is a sacred mystery that may be apprehended by the grace of God and through revelation, while for the Frenchman everything in life is as clear, sharply defined, and accessible to the understanding as $2 \times 2 = 4$.

Most importantly, Belinsky dwells in this article on the views of Heinrich Theodor Rotscher, a disciple of Hegel in the field of aesthetics. Any phenomenon is thought in form. The forms that thought assumes, according to the Hegelian view, are elusive and innumerable in their infinite variety, but in all of them is one moving, developing idea of being, an idea that passes through various stages and moments in its development. It is in this movement and development of the unified eternal idea that the life of the world consists, and discovery of this movement and development is the task of philosophy.

Belinsky proceeds to argue that for a higher understanding of life both reason and feeling need to be engaged. Feeling is immediate contemplation of truth, unconscious reason; without it a man has only a finite understanding (*rassudok*), not reason (*razum*). The potential conflict between mind and feeling is obviated by the development of a conscious reason or a unification of feeling and reason in an organic and concrete whole. There is a struggle between feeling and thought in man, but this struggle, which has the end of synthesizing these apparently incompatible faculties, is a necessary part of man's process of development, without which there is no life. The struggle proceeds in all spheres of knowledge, including the understanding of a work of art: it is impossible, according to Rotscher, to understand a work of art without understanding it in its totality and without seeing in it a particular, finite manifestation of the general infinite idea. To understand the general, it is necessary to detach the idea from the form and find the absolute significance and place of this idea in the dialectical movement of the general idea, like a link in a chain. But it is also necessary to trace through the images of the work of art the idea that has been torn away from it, to lose it again in the form, to see it, and to show it to others in its organic unity with the form. Belinsky repeats a mythological allusion deployed by Rotscher to illustrate the idea: the critic as thinker who tears the idea away from the work of art and thus destroys it is like Pallas, who tore the beating heart out of the body of Dionysus, who had been tortured by the Titans, while the critic as creator, which is what the critic becomes in the second act of the critical process, is like Zeus who kindled new life from Dionysus's heart.

Rotscher does not engage in psychological criticism, the function of which is to explain the characters in a work of art, still less in the criticism of "spontaneous feeling" that simply praises the good passages and criticizes the bad ones in a work. Nor, again, is his criticism the sort of contextual commentary favored by the French, which may be quite valuable when applied to works of primarily historical significance, such as those of Voltaire, but is unilluminating when applied to timeless works of art such as the plays of Aeschylus, Sophocles, or Shakespeare. Instead, Rotscher engages in philosophical criticism, whose aim is to identify the general and the absolute in a particular, finite manifestation.

The indigestibility of the work being published in *Moskovskii nabliudatel'*, particularly, the liberal helpings of Rotscher, were not to the taste of all readers of the journal. Complaints came in, subscriptions fell, and in 1839 the journal ceased to appear. Belinsky again found himself with no means of livelihood. He plunged into a new spiritual crisis, feeling at odds with himself and his environment. Salvation came quickly, however, in the form of an invitation in June 1839 to take up the position of critic on Andrei Aleksandrovich Kraevsky's St. Petersburg journal *Otechestvennye zapiski* (Notes of the Fatherland). Belinsky accepted the invitation with alacrity and began writing for *Otechestvennye zapiski* almost at once. In October 1839 he moved to St. Petersburg.

The move to St. Petersburg and employment with a new journal, however, did not immediately bring a change of orientation. On the contrary, during the first months of his St. Petersburg period Belinsky produced his clearest statements of belief in art as an end in itself and the most notorious expressions of his Hegelian reconciliation with the reality of life in Russia under Nicholas I.

The first of the articles shortly to become infamous was written apropos of a work by Fedor Nikolaevich Glinka, published in 1839, on the battle of Borodino. Just as Belinsky opposes mechanistic theories such as the eighteenth-century materialists' explanation of the universe as the coupling of atoms, so too he in this article criticizes theories that seek to explain the origin of political societies in terms of a social contract. Such cosmological and political theories seem to Belinsky to fall into the error of trying to make clear to the understanding things which are not accessible to it. In fact, civil society arranges itself without the consciousness or the willingness of the people of whom it is composed. The state is the highest moment of social life and its highest and only rational form. Only when he becomes a member of a state does a man stop being a slave to nature and become instead its master, and only as a member of a state is he a truly rational being.

Belinsky goes on to defend the divine right of kings, whose word is law, supporting his argument with quotations from *Richard II* (3.3.72ff), Shakespeare's play probably written and acted in 1595 and published in 1598, and from the gospel according to St. Matthew (7:29). Only dumb animals, he contends, live without authority. Man, even in his natural condition before he became corrupted, acknowledged authority and lived in rational forms of subjugation. Feeling told him that the father was higher than the son and that the son must obey, and the idea of the father developed into the idea of the king. The king is God's deputy on earth, Belinsky says. The king's power and sanctity are thrown into relief by comparison with the essential lack of substance attached to the office of the president of the United States. The president is merely society's highest official, a man with a real title but a spectral personality, the head of a state that is a symbol without essence. The monarch, on the other hand, is linked to his subjects by bonds of spirit and moral law; he embodies the personality of the state, and his subjects in serving him serve the state. The magic force of the idea included in his name endows the whole people with one identity, and the infinite number of individuals merges into a single body, or living soul.

Belinsky says that the individual's inner subjective world, his ego, is in conflict with the outer objective world, his nonego. However, in order to be a real person and not an apparition one must be a particular expression of the general, a finite manifestation of the infinite. The individual must therefore renounce his subjective personality and submit to the universal and general, acknowledging it alone as true and real. Admittedly a moment of rejection is necessary in a man's spiritual development. Yet the quarrel with reality cannot be an end in itself; it must finish with reconciliation. Society is the highest reality, and reality either demands complete acknowledgment of itself on the part of its individual members, or it crushes them under the leaden weight of its giant palm. Anyone who has torn himself away from society without reconciliation perishes like Pushkin's Aleko, who mistakenly thought he could forever escape from society by attaching himself to a wandering crowd of gypsies. Peter the Great, by subordinating natural parental feeling to the interests of the state in persecuting his son and heir, seems to Belinsky a heroic example of the triumph of moral law, striving to realize a general good over the selfish will of man. Peoples as a whole achieve this triumph when a sense of private interests is lost and when everybody thinks above all about the fatherland, merging into a common mass at the head of which stands the king. Russia was thus at the time of the Battle of Kulikovo (1380), in the Time of Troubles (1598–1613), and in 1812.

Belinsky's article on Wolfgang Menzel, a minor German literary critic and historian who had criticized Goethe for standing above topical issues, includes a further glorification of the state and justification of the subordination of the individual to it. It also links this political stance to the realm of aesthetics inasmuch as Belinsky argues here for an uncommitted art.

Belinsky repeatedly denigrates Menzel, who had rejected Hegel's philosophy of monarchy as the highest rational form of the state. He sees Menzel as one of those "little great men" who see the state as a machine that can be operated at will by mediocrities rather than as the realization of a divine idea, a living organism with interdependent parts and a will of its own that is higher than the will of any individual. The little great men hear only dissonances and discord in the world, not the music of the spheres. They argue as if man were able to change the world, as if there were no Providence. The French in particular are the object of Belinsky's scorn: standing by a machine called "la sainte guillotine," they thought to remake everyone in the image of the Romans.

Belinsky's central contention in this article is that the poet falls into error when he ceases to be a poet, allows his personality to interfere in the free process of creation, and starts to moralize. Belinsky rejects the basic idea of Menzel's criticism that art must serve society. In fact, Belinsky believes art does in a sense serve society by expressing society's consciousness and inspiring society's members with elevated thoughts about what is good and true. But it serves society not as a means to an end but as an end in itself. If mankind demands that art make a contribution to society and treat the poet as a contractor, then literature will be flooded with dissertations, allegories, moralizing, and factional polemic. This outcome, according to Belinsky, is seen in French literature with its declamatory moralizing and sententiousness (Belinsky cites Pierre Corneille, Jean Racine, Nicolas Boileau, Molière, and Fénelon as examples), its impudent blasphemy (as in Voltaire), its deification of animal passion (as in the works of Victor Hugo, Alexandre Dumas, and Eugène Sue), and its advocacy of Saint-Simonism and social and sexual equality (as in what Belinsky considers to be the absurd and scandalous novels of George Sand, which threaten the institutions of marriage and the family).

True poetry, Belinsky believes, has as its content eternal and universal questions. By the same token the true artist through his marvelous images realizes the divine idea for its own sake, not for some end external and alien to it. His inspiration is so free that he cannot command it himself or choose precisely what and when he will create. Menzel is wrong, Belinsky thinks, to rebuke Goethe for having nothing to say about the French Revolution, which he lived through, and because he did not demand the consolidation of a fragmented Germany into a political whole, an objective that could not be achieved at that time. A genius always has an instinctive grasp of truth and reality. For him whatever is is rational, necessary, and real, and only that which is rational, necessary, and real is. Goethe therefore did not demand or desire the impossible but loved to enjoy that which necessarily existed.

Belinsky then draws a Hegelian distinction between the ethical (*nravstvennoe*) and the moral (*moral'-noe*). The former stands in the same relation to the latter as reason (*razum*) to understanding (*rassudok*), the lofty to the mundane, the tragic to the everyday, wisdom to cunning, art to craft. The concept of ethical knowledge (*nravstvennost'*, or Hegelian *Sittlichkeit*) is a law of the reason that lies in the mysterious depth of the spirit, while morality (*moral'nost'*, or Hegelian *moralität*) is an intellectual conception of ethical knowledge on the part of superficial people who sense a need for such a law but do not bear such a law within themselves. Belinsky sees ethical knowledge as an absolute, universal, and eternal concept, whereas morality is often a relative, transient, and mutable concept that relates to the lower, practical side of life, just as the concept of honor that flows from it. Infringement of the inner ethical law gives rise to spiritual suffering (*kara*) in a person, while the breaking of the moral code entails a less fearsome social sanction (*nakazanie*). But the inner ethical law does not exist for everybody, because it is within man, not outside him, and is only to be found in a deep and powerful spirit.

Returning to the contention that everything that exists is rational, necessary, and real, Belinsky wonders at the perfection in the Creator's design and at the folly of those who, judging the infinite kingdom of the spirit by their own moral premises, see history as a madhouse or a dungeon full of criminals rather than as a pantheon full of glorious, immortal representatives of mankind who have carried out the destinies of God. Such error arises, Belinsky believes, out of a limited and purely intellectual understanding of reality that is capable of looking only at one side of an object. The man endowed with reason perceives the inner necessity in the rise and fall of peoples and even in the terrible crimes of history.

Art, finally, Belinsky says, is a reproduction (*vosproizvedenie*) of reality. Consequently, he says, its task is not to correct or embellish reality, like the work of recent French writers, literary sansculottes, but to show reality as it is. The truly artistic work elevates and broadens the spirit of man to contemplation of the infinite, reconciles him with reality rather than turning him against it, and strengthens him for struggle with adversity. Art achieves these ends only when it succeeds in revealing what is general and rationally necessary in particular phenomena and when it presents those phenomena in objective fullness, wholeness, and completeness. The sufferings of the subjective spirit may be the object of art, but when they are the laments of the poet, they cannot be artistic, because one who cries from suffering does not stand above it and therefore cannot see its rational necessity.

In 1840 Belinsky also produced a wide-ranging critical article on, or rather apropos of, Aleksandr Sergeevich Griboedov's masterpiece *Gore ot uma* (Woe from Wit), published in a cut version in 1833. Belinsky begins by offering a view of the history of art as divisible into two great phases, the classical and the romantic. The former found expression, properly speaking, only among the ancient Greeks, whose world was an external, objective one in which society meant everything and man meant nothing. The latter phase, which Belinsky identifies with the Middle Ages, is characterized by a youthful, idealistic striving informed by Christianity and reflected in the institution of knight-errantry. From the time of Shakespeare and Cervantes comes an art that is neither Classical (not created by Greeks or Romans) nor Romantic (not created by knights-errant or troubadours). This new art, modern art, consists in the reconciliation of the Classical, with its plasticity of form, and the Romantic, with its wealth of content.

Belinsky proceeds again to deploy many Hegelian concepts or arguments. First, he applies to art a dialectical schema describing the relationship of the general to the particular. The ideal is a general absolute idea that renounces its generality to become a specific phenomenon, and having become specific, returns to its generality. In Shakespeare's *Othello* (first performed in 1604), for example, the idea of jealousy has taken on a concrete form, but since Othello, thanks to the general idea embodied in him, is a typical character rather than a specific individual, a second renunciation of the

idea (or a return of the general idea to itself) takes place. Second, Belinsky offers a definition of reality as the wholeness of the visible and spiritual worlds, the worlds of facts and ideas. He sees reality as spirit revealing itself to itself. Man inhabits the world of reality and is a real person or true being when he feels or thinks or is aware of himself as a vessel of the spirit, a finite part of the general and infinite, or when he serves king and country on account of an elevated view of his duties toward them, or of a desire to be a tool of truth and goodness, or of an awareness of himself as part of society. Everything particular, coincidental, or irrational, on the other hand, is illusoriness, the antithesis of reality, its negation, something seeming but not being. Man eats, drinks, gets dressed; this is the world of illusions, because man's spirit in no way participates in these processes.

Belinsky returns by means of this juxtaposition of rational reality as affirmation of life and illusory reality as negation of life to a distinction that he has made between two types of poetry, the poetry of affirmation and the poetry of negation, and between tragedy (which he associates with poetry of affirmation) and comedy (which is to be found in the poetry of negation). He proceeds to illustrate the distinction by reference to the work of Gogol, which embodies both types. "Taras Bul'ba," for instance, depicts a hero representing a society bound together by daring while the tale of the two Ivans depicts a world of contingency and irrationality.

Only in the last quarter of his article does Belinsky turn to examination of Griboedov's play, though his examination of it is informed by the more-general themes that he has developed earlier in the article. On one level he is enthusiastic about *Gore ot uma*: it is written not in hexameters but in free verse, which hitherto had been used only for fables. It is couched not in bookish language but in living Russian. Every word breathes originality. It is full of turns of phrase so felicitous that they at once became proverbial; it dispenses with artificial love, *raisonneurs,* and the devices of conventional drama; and it reveals fresh, vigorous talent. Yet most things in the play exist only in themselves and have no relation to the whole. The point is thrown into relief by a lengthy analysis of Gogol's *Revizor* (The Inspector General), published in 1836, with which Belinsky has prefaced his discussion of *Gore ot uma* and which had the purpose of showing the wholeness (*totalität*) of Gogol's play, the coherence of its self-contained world. There is in *Gore ot uma,* Belinsky contends, no idea that is realized in the play's action. To those who hold that the play illustrates disharmony between an intelligent, deep per-

Belinsky in 1838

son and the society in which he lives, Belinsky objects that society is always more correct and higher than the individual and that individuality is only real to the extent that it expresses society through itself. In spite of its several masterly scenes and characters, Belinsky sees *Gore ot uma* as marred by the inconsistency and falsity of its basic idea and by the existence of an ulterior purpose on Griboedov's part: namely to ridicule contemporary society through satire.

In 1840 Belinsky also wrote a famous review of the work of the Romantic prose writer Marlinsky (the nom de plume of Aleksandr Aleksandrovich Bestuzhev) that struck a severe blow against Romanticism and undermined Marlinsky's reputation. In Marlinsky's novellas Belinsky finds platitudes, flat characters, contrivances, unrealistic dialogue, a tendency to dazzle with effects, and implausible plots. In the heroes and heroines he detects moralizing and sensuality but not feeling. Marlinsky speaks for his novella; the novella does not speak for itself. A talent such as Marlinsky's, Belinsky says, does not mature but becomes more and more strained.

By this time Belinsky was beginning to curse his infamous reconciliation with reality. His change of heart and sense of self-revulsion is fully reflected in his personal correspondence, particularly in his voluminous letters to Botkin, but it also finds expression in his published work. For example, in his two famous articles on Mikhail Tur'evich Lermontov, published in 1840 and 1841, Belinsky begins for the first time to extol the hero in conflict with his society and therefore to move away somewhat from the position he had occupied in his articles on Glinka, Menzel, and Griboedov, although he does remain in many respects under Hegel's sway.

In the first of the articles on Lermontov, which is devoted to *Geroi nashego vremeni* (A Hero of Our Time, 1840), Belinsky praises Lermontov for the naturalness of his plot, which develops without strain; for the excellence of his characterization; and for allowing events to flow logically from the nature of the characters. As for Pechorin, Belinsky thinks he should not be condemned too severely, for his vices are to be found in readers, too, and to a greater degree. Pechorin shows a strength of spirit and power of will that Belinsky finds admirable. In his vices something great glints like lightning in dark storm clouds. He is full of poetry. His nature is deep, and his instinct for truth is strong. His passions are storms that cleanse the sphere of the spirit. In order to arrive at the truth a person may have to make many detours. (Belinsky seems here to foreshadow a Dostoevskian theme and hints at the possibility of the emergence of harmony out of discord, the resolution of spiritual crisis through religious faith.) Lermontov is implicitly congratulated for confronting reality in the spirit of the modern age and modern art.

Belinsky reads Lermontov's novel not as a "wicked irony" but as a portrait of a hero of the time, and he rejects the charge of egoism leveled against Pechorin. He analyzes Pechorin as a divided self, one half of which carries out actions and the other half of which judges himself for those actions. Pechorin's is a transitional condition of the spirit in which all the old things are being destroyed but in which there is as yet nothing new. In this state man is only a potentiality of something real in the future and but an apparition in the present. (Belinsky seems to be speaking of himself here, and indeed it is tempting to see his literary criticism in general as on one level a tortured externalization of his own spiritual crises.) Thus arises the condition bedeviling the "superfluous man" (as such characters later came to be known), the state of spleen or reflection (*refleksiia*), an unaccountable ennui in which feelings and ideas are dissected and fragmented and lack fullness and freshness. Action is paralyzed as it is for Shakespeare's Hamlet, the apotheosis of reflection. Terrible though this state of reflection is, Belinsky also sees it as necessary. It is one of the great moments of the spirit. Through it the transition from the immediacy of feeling to the higher plane of rational consciousness may be effected.

In the second of his articles on Lermontov, in which Belinsky discusses among other subjects Lermontov's verse, he still retains a Hegelian framework, emphasizing the participation of particular phenomena in the whole and taking an elitist view of the poet as a chosen one who may despise the crowd. Belinsky begins by contrasting poetry (and science in the broad sense denoted by *nauka* and the German *Wissenschaft*), which may be fully appreciated only through reason, with the so-called exact sciences, which engage only understanding. An intelligent person is bound to understand that parallel lines never meet in infinity, but more than intelligence is required to grasp what is of value in Homer's *Iliad* or Shakespeare's *Macbeth* (probably written and performed in 1606 but not published until 1623). Art belongs to the superexperiential and supersensual sphere in which reason operates, and receptivity to it is therefore an innate gift rather than a skill that can be acquired through education or exercise. Together with the view of poetry as a form of spiritual revelation goes an elitist attitude toward the poet. Like Mozart in Pushkin's "little tragedy," Belinsky exalts the few chosen ones, priests of beauty, and despises the criterion of utility and the masses who demand its application.

Belinsky proceeds in his prescriptive vein to discuss how a man may live a rewarding life. The fullness of an individual's life, he says, depends on the degree to which he participates in the general life of mankind and banishes mundane personal considerations. To live, then, does not mean simply to eat and drink for a certain span, to struggle for rank and money, and to swat flies and play cards in one's spare time. Such an existence is worse than death and lower than animal life, for an animal at least uses all its resources. To live means to feel and to think, to suffer and to experience bliss. The importance of suffering in this conception of a full life is striking and perhaps indicative of the spiritual crisis Belinsky himself was undergoing at this time: the capacity to suffer, Belinsky argues, determines the capacity for bliss. Those who have not cried shall not delight. Thus suffering fulfills, in terms of personal experience, the function of a Hegelian antithesis without which a felicitous synthesis is not possible.

A further important element in the second article on Lermontov is Belinsky's discussion of the relationship between art and reality and his speculation on which is superior. He believes, for example, that a picture of a landscape executed by a talented painter is more beautiful than a comparable real landscape because the picture forms a beautiful entity in which all parts are subordinated to the whole and directed toward a single end and in which nothing is contingent or superfluous. The great artist distills from the untidiness of the familiar world the essence of reality. He discards fragmented or coincidental phenomena and entertains only ideals or typical images, so that such names as Othello, Ophelia, Onegin, and Molchalin, a character in Griboedov's *Gore ot uma,* may be seen not as proper nouns but as common nouns. In art, therefore, reality is more like reality than reality itself. Art, borrowing material from reality, raises it to generic, typical significance and creates an elegant whole from it. However, the artist stands to reality in the relation not of a slave but of a creator: his hand is not guided by reality; rather he introduces his ideals into reality and through them transforms it. Thus poetry is the essence of reality, the finest ether, the triple extract, the quintessence of life. The poet then is the noblest vessel of the universal spirit, the one chosen by the heavens.

Belinsky turns to the crucial question of the purpose of art. He still affirms that beauty, like truth and goodness, is an end in itself. So too is poetry, in which beauty is expressed and worshiped. Poetry may indeed have the effect of elevating a man's soul and inspiring him to good deeds, but this effect is achieved without any utilitarian intention on the part of the artist. The poet may inject his own ideals into his creation, but he cannot be required to subjugate his free inspiration to various current demands. Free as the wind, he obeys only his own inner calling, the mysterious voice of the God who moves him; and like Pushkin he dismisses the clamor of the rabble for support in topical controversy.

Turning almost halfway through the essay to Lermontov, Belinsky praises the poet's freshness, charm, and energy; the simplicity of his images; the power and sonority of his verse; the fullness of his feeling; and the depth and variety of his ideas. Belinsky maintains that there is a correlation between the greatness of a poet and the degree to which the development of his talent and the historical development of his society are linked. The point is clarified by a comparison between Pushkin and Lermontov in which Belinsky deplores the bleakness of Russia under Nicholas I. Whereas from the beginning of his career Pushkin wrote poetry that is joyful, playful, colorful, and full of hope, Lermontov's poetry from the first is joyless, hopeless, gloomy, severe, and lacking faith in human life and feeling (though at the same time thirsting for life and having an abundance of feeling). Thus, Lermontov is a national poet in whom the historical moment of Russia has found expression. The age is in general an age of reflection, and reflection is therefore a legitimate subject for poetry and one which all the great modern poets, such as Byron, Goethe, and Schiller, have acknowledged.

Belinsky also returns in 1841 to a genre at which he had tried his hand once before and which a decade earlier had been in vogue in Russian journals: the annual survey of the state of Russian letters. As in his literary debut, Belinsky is concerned in his "Russkaia literatura v 1841 godu" (Russian Literature in 1841) with the definition of *literature*. A literature is the consciousness of a people. Like a mirror it reflects a people's spirit and the intuitive view of the world with which a people's members are born. It reveals the purpose of a people, the place a people occupies in the great family of nations, and the moment expressed by a people in the universal historical development of the spirit of mankind. Belinsky makes some generalizations on the cultures of the Germans, the French, and the English. Finally, he explains the current dearth of literature in Russia as a result of the lack of inner life or coherent outlook in Russia's immature society. The past of Russian literature is far from brilliant and its present dull, Belinsky concludes, parodying a famous utterance of Count Aleksandr Khristofovovich Benkendorf (Head of the Third Section) on the destiny of Russia; but for the future, Belinsky says, one should by no means despair.

Belinsky also wrote in 1841 a lengthy review of two works on Peter the Great and of a new edition of a seventeenth-century work by Grigory Karpovich Kotoshikhin, in which Belinsky made his first extended excursion into the field of history. Belinsky's view of Peter the Great is set in the framework of a Hegelian conception of history and of the role of certain peoples in it. Belinsky sees history as the actual development of the general or absolute idea in the form of political societies. The essence of history is that which is rational and necessary. This essence is linked to the past and in the present includes its future. The content of history is general, that is to say, the fate of mankind. Just as the history of a people is not the history of the millions of individuals who constitute it but rather the history of a certain number of those individuals in whom the spirit and destinies of the people have been expressed, so humanity as a whole is not the sum of all the peoples of the globe but only of those several peoples who express the idea of humanity. Some peoples, such as the Chinese, may have seemed to form impressive civilizations but belong to humanity, Belinsky contends, only to the same degree as their teeming herds of cattle.

Belinsky offers an extended contrast of Asia and Europe that illustrates his distinction between historical and nonhistorical peoples. Asia was the cradle of the human race, but he thinks it has remained a cradle. The life of the Asiatic is a static life of primeval natural immediacy (*neposredstvennost'*). Europe, unlike Asia, has been characterized since pagan times by moral mobility and mutability. Belinsky finds in European history enormous variety, diversity, and movement. Using feeling and inspiration, the European gave free rein to his capacity for thought, judgment, and analysis. He brought into play his reason, which breaks down immediacy. He constantly introduced his ideals into life and realized them. Noble relations between the sexes; the refinement of morals, art, and science; the subjugation of the unconscious forces of nature, over matter. The triumph of the spirit, respect for the human personality, the sanctity of human law—everything of which mankind is proud—is the result of the development of European life. Everything European is human, and everything human is European.

Against this background Belinsky develops a Westernist and etatist conception of Russian history, according to which Russia only began to participate in the life of mankind when Peter the Great had initiated Westernization through his authoritarian state. Belinsky is uninterested in the academic debate over the beginnings of Russian history and is dismissive of the significance of the pre-Muscovite period. For him Russian history begins with the rise of Muscovy and the attendant growth of a strong centralized state. Even the history of the Muscovite state, though, is only an introduction to the history of the Russian state. This state began with Peter the Great, a demigod who breathed life into the colossal but slumbering body of ancient Russia. Peter the Great made Russia part of Europe not just in a geographical sense but also by eradicating the Asiatic quality introduced into the life of the Russians, a Christian people, by the Tatars. However, that a great man, Peter the Great, was needed to bring Russia into the mainstream of humanity did not mean, Belinsky argues, that the Russian people were not already potentially a people of historical significance. No genius can make anything out of a people who lack substance. The best one can make of a sugar beet is sugar; only from granite, marble, or bronze can one create a lasting monument. The vices of the Russian people—for example, the immurement of women, bribery and corruption, intellectual laziness, ignorance, contempt for oneself, and intolerance of foreigners—are not inherent. Rather they are external and coincidental—the consequences of unfortunate historical conditions; therefore, they may be dispersed by the light of knowledge and education. The difference, then, between pre-Petrine and post-Petrine Russia is the difference between a country in an immediate, natural, and patriarchal state, on the one hand, and a country participating in the rational movement of historical development on the other. The Russian people were the same people in both ages. Peter the Great did not re-create that people; rather he led them out of crooked paths onto the highway of universal historical life.

Belinsky also published in 1841 an article on a Russian translation of Goethe's Roman elegies in which he argues that the poet, above all people, feels kinship with human life in all of its forms. No one finds it so easy as the poet to recapture the life and spirit of other peoples: like the zoologist Georges Cuvier, who from one bone dug up out of the earth could define the genus, species, size, and appearance of an animal, so the poet on the basis of a few facts—Shakespeare using Plutarch, for example—can re-create a whole tribe of beings who were once young and vigorous. He is able to put himself in any position, any country, any age in a man's life and to share any experience outside his own. Belinsky also considers in this article the route by which humanity develops (it moves ceaselessly forward in a spiral), the nature of poetry (it is a lofty, inspired art rather than a craft), the relationship of poetry to life (it is not copying but free reproduction), the nature of beauty (it is the sister of truth and morality), the moral utility of great art, and the current state of Russian literature (it is characterized by petty and insignificant works and marred by commercial considerations).

The article "Razdelenie poezii na rody i vidy" (The Division of Poetry into Genuses and Species), also published in 1841, is an exhaustive attempt to classify what Belinsky defines as the genuses of literature (epic, lyric, and dramatic) and their respective species (epics, historical novels, idylls, songs, odes, elegies, epistles, and satires; tragedies and comedies), and to exemplify his classification by reference to the writers whom he most admires, especially Homer, Shakespeare, Goethe, Schiller, Scott, James Fenimore Cooper, Pushkin, and Gogol. Of particular interest, given the movement in Russia toward prose, is Belinsky's examination of the novel, which he sees as the epic of the modern age. All the generic and essential signs of the epic are to be found, he believes, in the novel, with the difference that the novel has other elements and a different coloring. Its task is to draw together everything that is contingent from everyday life and from historical events and to penetrate into their spirit. The sphere of the novel, however, he sees as much broader than the sphere of the epic. It arises out of the most recent civilization of the Christian peoples—in the age of humanity, when all civil, social, familial, and general human relations had become highly complex and dramatic.

Belinsky also wrote in 1841 many pieces that were conceived as parts of a theoretical and critical course on Russian literature. (They were not published in his lifetime, and the plan for such a course was never realized.) One such piece was an unfinished essay on the "idea of art." In another piece Belinsky examined Russian folk poetry and its significance. Perhaps the most interesting of these pieces, as an expression of the socialist content that Belinsky's messianism had by this date taken on, is an essay to which Nikolai Khristoforovich Ketcher subsequently gave the title "Obshchee znachenie slova literatura" (The General Meaning of the Word Literature). In this piece Belinsky dwells on the free participation of the citizens of ancient Greece in state and social affairs and glimpses the outlines of a new Hellas, a socialist heaven on earth in which art will be permeated with social interests.

In the course of 1842 Belinsky's more radical mood, consonant with the spirit of the age as he now understood it, found expression in many ways. In his survey of the state of Russian literature in 1841, for example, he commends contemporary literature on account of its preoccupation with life and reality, by which he understands society. Moreover, he takes a progressive view on the role of women in society. Rejecting the notion that woman is suitable only to procreate, act as nursemaid, cook for her husband, dance, and gossip, he defends her right to equality and argues that if she stands lower than man in terms of moral development then the reason lies not in her nature but in man's abuse of his strength and in the semibarbaric, oriental character of Russian society. However, he believes times are changing: woman is becoming aware of her human rights and is proving her abilities, as the work of such women as George Sand attests.

In the same article Belinsky renews the attack on Romanticism that he had waged in his articles on Benediktov and Marlinsky, though now, as the movement is in retreat, he acknowledges its positive aspect. Romanticism represents the inner world of man, the world of the spirit and the heart. This fantastic sealed world, in which the Middle Ages dwelt exclusively, has appeal, but it is separate from the external world in which real life, nature, and history unfold. Therefore, the modern age, while not entirely relinquishing it, has added new elements to it and has reconciled it with history and with practical activity. One may no longer succumb to the charm of this inner world and take refuge in it, disregarding the external world. That way lie self-indulgence and self-destruction. Nor, on the other hand, may one live entirely in the external world. The man who does so is likely to lack deep moral principles and a sure view of reality and to prove cold, dry, tough, and unloving. Such a man is a citizen, warrior, merchant, or anything else, but never a human being; one may never trust him or be his friend.

Belinsky's increasing insistence on the need for contemporary relevance in art finds expression in two essays of 1842 on minor poets Apollon Nikolaevich Maikov and Aleksandr Ivanovich Polezhaev. Great demands are now made of the poet, Belinsky argues at the beginning of his essay on Maikov. The poet has to be excellent, not merely talented, if he is to be known at all. The time when rhymed trinkets or a modicum of sensation and feeling in poetry would satisfy the reading public is gone. The modern poet must express deep feelings and ideas in artistic form and must show development in the spirit of the time. Society wishes to see in him not an entertainer but a representative of its spiritual life, an oracle capable of answering the most abstruse questions, a doctor who discovers within himself the general pains and sorrows. Maikov, in Belinsky's view, writes poetry of two types: anthological verse, in the spirit of the ancients, and verse in which he sets out to be a contemporary poet. Maikov's anthological poetry gave grounds, Belinsky believed, for hoping that the poet had a bright future, but it lacked the tragic element that was such an important part of the Hellenic world. As for the second type of verse Belinsky finds not a poet of modernity in ideas, form and feelings, sympathy and antipathy, hopes and wishes, but only a practitioner, for the most part, of empty rhetoric.

In the essay on Polezhaev, Belinsky again emphasizes the importance of historical context for the artist and of content as a criterion in the judgment of art. The conditions for greatness in a poet, he contends, are both internal (within the poet's own nature) and external (in the history of his people, for poetry springs from the national soil, and in the historical moment at which the poet catches humanity). A Chinese poet, Belinsky believes, might possess the gifts of a Schiller but would always remain limited by the supposed poverty of Chinese life. Where there is vital life, on the other hand, there is

material for poetry, and it is on living reality and contemporary interests that the poet must concentrate. Content and the thought that the poet brings to bear on it, rather than the quality of his verse or even the richness of his feeling, will be the yardsticks by which his talent is judged. Thought makes itself felt in poetry as a certain view of a certain side of life, as a principle (*principe*) by which the poet's creations are inspired and live. Thought for poetry is like oil for a lamp: when the lamp has oil, it burns with an even and pure flame, but without oil it flares up at times, gives off sparks, smokes, and gradually goes out. Polezhaev was not a great poet, but given his unusual strength of feeling, the power of his verse, and the concision and acuity of his expression, he might have become one had he lived at another time and been provided with an historical worldview. As it was, Belinsky believes Polezhaev became caught up in his own feelings and failed to develop or mature. He presents the sad spectacle of a strong nature ruined by wild, unbridled passions—a fate for which no one but Polezhaev himself, Belinsky believes, was to blame. (It is a view of Polezhaev with which Nikolai Aleksandrovich Dobroliubov, stressing the effect on the poet of conditions in Russia under Nicholas I, was to disagree.)

Perhaps the most important statement of Belinsky's views in 1842 is his long article in three installments, "Rech' o kritike" (Speech about Criticism), in which he responds to a recent lecture delivered by Aleksandr Vasil'evich Nikitenko at St. Petersburg University. This article, or rather its first installment, amounts to a manifesto of Belinsky's views on the roles of art and criticism in the post-Hegelian period of his career.

Criticism and art are both forms of consciousness of reality and of the age, Belinsky thinks, but criticism is philosophical consciousness whereas art is spontaneous or immediate consciousness. He believes criticism is particularly important for the present time, chiefly a thinking and judging time. The thinking element has now merged with the artistic; a work of art is dead if it portrays life only to portray life and lacks any powerful subjective impulse originating in the prevailing thought of the age. Art, then, should be a wail of suffering or a dithyramb of delight, a question or an answer to a question.

This new formulation of the relationship between art and society entails a change in Belinsky's view of the importance of beauty in a work. It remains axiomatic for Belinsky that beauty is a necessary condition of art and that without beauty there is not and cannot be art. Beauty, he asserts, is not everything in art, although he himself, he admits, was once an ardent advocate of the opposing view.

The process of apprehending art always begins with the search for beauty, and the quality of art as an end in itself is always the first moment of this process. To pass by this moment means never to understand art. However, to remain at this moment, Belinsky contends, means to understand art in a one-sided way. Everything living moves and develops, including art, for art is not a dead and motionless algebraic formula.

In the modern age, then, art requires a rational content that has historical sense as an expression of contemporary consciousness. The age emphatically rejects art for art's sake. Even the most powerful talent may now captivate the public only for a limited time if it confines itself to "birdsong," that is, creates a personal world that has nothing in common with historical and philosophical actuality and tries to shut out worldly sufferings. Belinsky therefore takes a fresh view of George Sand, as a writer whose work is infused with humanity and love of truth. It now makes Belinsky indignant to think that there are those who consider themselves higher than their suffering brethren who vainly turn to them, their eyes full of supplication and expectation.

Turning to the subject of criticism, Belinsky lists Nikitenko's categories of criticism—personal, analytical or philosophical, and artistic. Personal criticism, Belinsky argues, is the province of those critics who rely on their own views, feelings, and tastes. As far as analytical criticism is concerned, or historical criticism as this type of criticism is called in France and Germany, Belinsky concedes that it meets a need. Each work of art should indeed be examined in relation to its age and society and to the life and character of its author. At the same time, though, definition of the degree of aesthetic merit in a work must be the first business of the critic. For if a work does not have the seal of creativity and free inspiration, then it can have no value, and its content, however topical, will be rendered senseless and absurd through being expressed in a forced way. Criticism for Belinsky should therefore embody elements of both aesthetic and historical criticism, as Nikitenko has defined them. Historical criticism without aesthetic, and aesthetic without historical, will be equally one-sided and false.

Poets do not inevitably write, Belinsky continues, in the spirit of their age. On the contrary, there are societies in which the most gifted individuals sometimes feel themselves isolated and at odds with their surroundings. In such societies—and here Belinsky's familiar moral engagement merges with an implicit condemnation of Russian life—prevailing concepts may be diametrically opposed to reality. Those societies are characterized by lack of religion,

decay, fragmentation, individualism, and egoism. They live by old traditions in which people no longer believe and which are contrary to new truths discovered by science and applied in historical movements. It is easy for their members to accept their vices as inevitable and to flee from reality or take a rosy view of it and sing like little birds. People may be abetted in this flight from reality by the German view of art, in which, alongside profundity and truth, there are also philistinism and an antisocial dimension.

In the second installment of the article on Nikitenko's speech, Belinsky engages in battle with the Slavophiles, whom he sees as shortsighted people, Old Believers, champions of ignorance and *narodnost'* misunderstood. This battle is conducted through reexamination of the reforms of Peter the Great, the progenitor of Russian civilization. Belinsky also traces what he sees as the striving of Russian literature away from artificiality and imitativeness toward naturalness and originality, from the bookish to the living and social. This installment of the article—whose structure has by this point become ragged—ends with a long discussion of eighteenth-century writers, in particular the satirist Kantemir and the dramatist Aleksandr Petrovich Sumarokov, whom Belinsky assesses much more sympathetically than in his earlier phases, since his preoccupation with the relationship of literature and society makes him now see greater importance and usefulness in the didactic element of their work.

Belinsky's increasingly radical mood in 1842 finds further expression in a reassessment of the work of the poet Baratynsky. While Belinsky continues to state views formulated during his Hegelian phase on developing and static societies and on the reconciliation of opposites, he also invokes the new scientific spirit and acknowledges the achievements of the industrial age. Baratynsky's poetry, Belinsky believes, is no longer so valuable as it once had been, because its content now has a false note, particularly inasmuch as Baratynsky supposes poetry to be incompatible with the modern scientific age and art to be incompatible with thought. Railways, steamers, industrial development—these achievements of the age are triumphs over matter, space, and time, and humanity as a whole will in the future benefit from them. True, Belinsky believes the mercantile spirit is now too dominant. But that means only that humanity in the nineteenth century has entered a transitional phase in its development. Transitional phases are phases of rotting and decay, to be sure, but not for humanity as a whole, which will arise again young and strong. In any case Belinsky believes the advancement of human knowledge is not confined to mathematics and technology or reflected only in the development of railways and machines.

Most importantly Belinsky is determined to reconcile thought, reason, and analysis in the spirit of the age with feeling, which at an earlier stage he had seen as the paramount quality in poetic creation. He now disputes that reason and feeling are at odds with one another. Nor is thought inimical to art; rather it is the prevalence of one over the other that is damaging. A predominance of feeling over mind may make a man fanatical or superstitious and weak-minded, while a predominance of mind may make a man immoral, egoistic, or pedantic—a dry dialectician who sees only logical formalities but no soul or content in things. Thus, reason and feeling are like the land and the sun: the former has nutritional power and holds the germ of its fruits; the latter arouses that power.

In his survey of the state of Russian literature in 1842 Belinsky is again concerned with the demise of Romanticism, which he hopes to see supplanted by a new spirit of realism; the article again reflects a strong awareness of Russia's being in a transitional period. The old Romanticism, which in its time had seemed so frightening to supporters of Classicism, he gently mocks for its alleged emptiness and for its mistaken evaluations of such writers as Schiller, Byron, and Hoffmann. Romanticism did, it is true, have a positive effect in Russia: it cleared the way for an independent literature by breaking down neoclassical prejudices and taboos. But now he thinks Romanticism too has had its day, having been killed off in the 1830s by prose, in which Belinsky sees a virile, mature literature that has grown closer to reality. That is not to say, though, that the artist, having abandoned the exaggeration, falsehood, or childish fantasy associated with the "ideal" in the Romantic period, should now slavishly copy facts from reality. Rather he should filter them through his fantasy and illuminate them with a general significance. Indeed a portrait of a man by a great painter, Belinsky argues, produces a better likeness of its subject than a daguerreotype, for the painting draws out of the subject everything that is concealed from others and even from the subject himself.

From 1843 Belinsky's principal preoccupations may be seen as the creation of a realistic literature and polemic with the Slavophiles. The first task was reflected in an emphasis in his work on the importance of the depiction of contemporary society in art; in a search in literature for what was of general, typical significance; in acceptance of the role of reason, as well as poetic fantasy and inspiration, in the artistic process; in an interest in satire (reflected in an essay of 1845 on the work of the eighteenth-century satirist Kantemir); in a demand that humanistic values and sympathy for the poor be injected into art; and in encouragement of, and contributions to, the formation of a Natural School that upheld the rights of the weak and of women and censured apathy, ignorance, and routine. The second task became necessary with the gathering of the Slavophiles beginning with the early 1840s into a distinct group expressing their views through Pogodin's journal *Moskvitianin* (The Muscovite). The war with the Slavophiles was waged both by means of scathing criticism of their values and by the promotion of a counteracting Westernism. Belinsky's crowning achievement during this period may be seen as his huge series of articles on Pushkin. He also continued to the last to produce annual surveys of the state of Russian literature. Meanwhile his personal circumstances changed: on 12 November 1843 he married Mariia Vasil'evna Orlova, the daughter of a priest, whom Belinsky had known since 1835 and to whom he had become close during a visit to Moscow in June through August 1843. Mariia bore him a daughter, Ol'ga, on 13 June 1845 and a son, Vladimir, on 24 November 1846.

In his survey of Russian literature for 1843 Belinsky discusses the directions Russian literature might take in its current state of crisis. In fact, he does not find the present poverty of Russian literature dispiriting, for in essence contemporary Russian literature is superior to the literature of earlier times. Whereas in the 1820s and 1830s works by writers other than Pushkin, Griboedov, and Gogol might have had value as experiments in various manners, by the 1840s it was not enough, Belinsky maintained, for a writer to show novelty. In order to set literature on a new path, genius, or at least great talent, was now required in a writer.

Belinsky's principal purposes in this survey are to discuss the relationship between literature and reality as he sees it and to assert the high purpose of literature as both a faithful echo and inspector (*revizor*) of public opinion. He begins his examination of these questions with a comparison of classical satire and modern prose genres, which themselves may include a satirical element but which must treat contemporary society in a more realistic way. The vices that the satirist of earlier times used to censure, Belinsky believes, were not really vices at all but abstract ideas about vices, rhetorical tropes, sheep and windmills with which a Don Quixote could do battle. Nowadays, on the other hand, he thinks the reading public requires the portrayal of real people, not imaginary ones. This demand for realism compels modern writers to depict society and its essence, which lies in its mores, customs, concepts, attitudes, and so forth, as well as in its external forms such as costumes and hairstyles, for it is in society that real people live. Moreover, in seeking to explain why the individual is as he is, Belinsky thinks, the modern writer must examine the general factors that have shaped him rather than what is untypical in him, his idiosyncrasies; and these factors too are to be found in society. In this literature of the modern world the classical satirist's heroes of virtue and monsters of wrongdoing have gone out of fashion, for the mass of society is made up of ordinary people, who are neither good nor evil and who, while not idiots, are mostly uneducated and ignorant. Belinsky believes Russian literature is not alone in finding comic material in contemporary reality; other European literatures currently have an even more humorous tendency than the Russian. Belinsky cites Dickens, for instance *Oliver Twist* (1837–1838) and *Barnaby Rudge* (1841), to show that even in England with its thousand-year-old civilization there are just as many cranks, eccentrics, ignoramuses, fools, rogues, swindlers, and thieves as anywhere else.

Belinsky does not argue that people themselves have changed. On the contrary, he thinks people in the present age are intrinsically no better or worse than people of another time, nor are people of one nationality any better or worse than people of another. At all times and in all places there are abuses, vices, oddities, and disparities between words and deeds and between moral concepts and true morality. It is social forms and relationships, not people, that change from one time and place to another. Society improves, and the law of the development of mankind as a whole is predicated on this improvement. However, Belinsky believes progress is possible only when literature is not an idle amusement but a faithful mirror of society and an expression of its consciousness.

This discussion of the demand for realism and the need to treat society in modern literature leads Belinsky to a further attempt at definition of the relationship between art and reality and an acceptance of the role of consciousness in the creative process. Taking his material from reality, the artist must not embellish it, reconstruct it, or view it in the light of an outdated moral code but must depict it as it is and from a contemporary viewpoint. Moreover, Belinsky incorporates a role for the mind as well as for the poetic fantasy in the creative process: fantasy is only one of the faculties that shape the poet's work; in addition to fantasy the poet needs a profound mind that discerns the idea in the fact and the

general significance in the particular phenomenon. Poets who rely on fantasy alone always seek the content for their works in the land of fairy tales or in distant antiquity, whereas poets who have profound minds as well as a creative fantasy find their ideals around them.

Belinsky ends his discussion of these questions with renewed praise of Gogol, who he believes combines creative fantasy and a profound mind to an extraordinary degree. Unfortunately, though, Gogol was not yet widely appreciated. For the crowd generally considers comedy, humor, and irony, which arouse laughter, as inferior to what arouses more elevated feelings and does not understand that there are points at which the comic coalesces with the tragic and provokes a form of laughter that is not light and joyful but sickly and bitter. The crowd does not realize that a poet who depicts what is base and squalid may also be a priest of that same beauty that is served by poets who depict what is elevated; they do not see the radiant models behind the grim facade.

Belinsky's conversion to a radical position on contemporary issues is completed in his article of 1844 on the work *Les mystères de Paris* (1842–1843) by the French writer Eugène Sue. This article may be seen as a model for the Russian radical conception of the bourgeoisie; it also raises the question of the role of environment in determining behavior and as a possible cause of crime.

Belinsky begins by deploring the use of money as the main yardstick by which success appears to be measured in the modern age. He therefore considers the basic idea of Sue's novel as true and noble, inasmuch as the author had wanted to confront a debauched, egoistic society that worshiped the golden calf with the spectacle of the sufferings of the unfortunate who are condemned, as a result of society's materialism, to ignorance and poverty and therefore to vice and punishment. Sue takes the reader through the taverns where criminals and loose women congregate, through the prisons crowded with suspects and convicts, the hospitals and asylums, and the attics and cellars where the poor huddle. The bourgeois is depicted as a bloated, self-satisfied gentleman with the head of an ass and the body of a bull who has grown rich at the expense of the poor and the orphaned. Having whipped up the Russian working class against the monarchy in the revolution of 1830, the bourgeoisie emerged from their dens after the battle and clambered over the corpses to positions of power from which they then excluded everyone else by means of an electoral property qualification. The proprietor looks at any worker in the same way that the planter looks at the

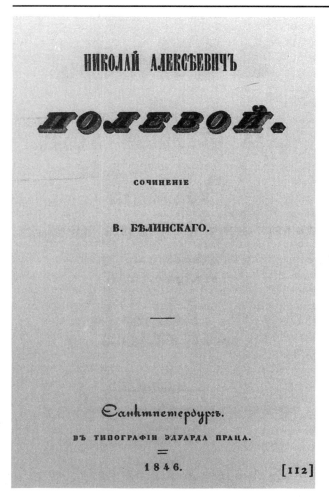

НИКОЛАЙ АЛЕКСѢЕВИЧЪ

ПОЛЕВОЙ.

СОЧИНЕНІЕ

В. БѢЛИНСКАГО.

Санктпетербургъ.

ВЪ ТИПОГРАФІИ ЭДУАРДА ПРАЦА.

1846.

[112]

Title page for a biography of Nikolai Aleksandr Polevoi, one of the few works by Belinsky published in book form

Negro. True, the proprietor cannot make a man work for him by force, but he can withhold work from the worker and make him die of hunger. The favorite rule of the bourgeois is everyone for himself. He observes the civil law but does not want to hear of the laws of humanity and morality.

Belinsky does, however, find encouraging features in French life and in particular puts forth an optimistic view of the French masses that was shortly to be echoed by radical Russian thinkers describing the Russian *narod*. Sue himself, as man and artist, Belinsky holds in low esteem. He seems to Belinsky to share bourgeois values and to be ignorant of the true vices and virtues of the people. Sue does not suspect that it is the whole system of French legislation and the structure of French society rather than any particular law that lie at the root of society's ills. As for the artistic status of Sue's *Les mystères de Paris*, the work is, in Belinsky's opinion, false and absurd in terms of plot and characterization. Nevertheless,

as a Frenchman, Sue was not without sympathy for the fallen and the weak, for humanity and love of mankind are, Belinsky supposes, the most pronounced traits of the French national character. Sue's work raises questions that are of importance to Belinsky in the Russian context. What right does one have to consider oneself better than the poor and to judge them? Can one be sure that any person brought up in such conditions from childhood would be any more honest and moral? When the criminal is executed, does his family have any means of livelihood other than crime?

Throughout the last five years of his life—in particular in his annual surveys of Russian literature in 1844, 1845, and 1846—Belinsky fiercely attacks the Slavophiles, often presenting their thought as a vestigial manifestation of Romanticism. Thus the survey of Russian literature for 1844 takes the form of a critical appraisal of the poetry of Nikolai Mikhailovich Iazykov and the leading Slavophile thinker Aleksei Stepanovich Khomiakov, both of whom had had volumes of poetry published in 1844. Belinsky sees Iazykov as a poet who poses as a Russian daredevil (*udalets*) but who at heart is a Russian barin. His dashing and reckless escapades, his drunkenness and youthful unruliness are for show. Poetry for Iazykov, Belinsky says, is a masquerade: he tries to hide his tailcoat with a homespun one; he strokes his false beard; and he flaunts coarseness of feeling and expression. He mistakenly equates *narodnost'* with vulgarity. To these faults in Iazykov's poetry Belinsky adds a long and damaging list of examples of loose, florid, or strained expressions and of fine-sounding lines with vague meaning.

In Khomiakov's poetry Belinsky finds even greater artificiality and sham than in Iazykov's. Khomiakov sings hymns to pre-Petrine Russia, in which he likes to see similarities with modern Russia; but there is no truth in them. Belinsky dislikes Khomiakov's paternalistic instructions to his compatriots about the need for humility. Most of all he takes issue with the prediction apparently included in Khomiakov's poem "Mechta" (A Dream) of the impending ruin of the West and the assignment of Russia to the East. Russia, Belinsky believes, belongs to Europe by virtue of its geographical position and its being a Christian power. It also belongs to Europe because its new civil society is European, and its history has already been merged inextricably with the destiny of Europe. Khomiakov seems to Belinsky to invite such forces of darkness as the Turks and the Tatars to exult over the supposed death of civilization.

It was also early in 1845 that the two-part anthology *Fiziologiia Peterburga* (Physiology of St. Petersburg) was published, which marked the formation of a Natural School of writers producing short prose sketches of a supposedly realistic and authentic nature on contemporary subjects and particularly the poor strata of the population. As well as influencing the general tone and orientation of the anthology, Belinsky contributed two pieces of his own to each part. In an introduction to the anthology as a whole he placed the genre of the physiological sketch in the mainstream of Russian realistic literature. In the long article "Peterburg i Moskva" (St. Petersburg and Moscow), which also appeared in the first part of the anthology, he compared the character of the two capitals and argued, against the Slavophile view, that St. Petersburg, far from being an artificial creation, reflected historical necessity, while Moscow, a patriarchal city, provided fertile ground for Romantic, idealistic theories of all kinds. In the second part of the anthology he published two more pieces. Belinsky also wrote reviews of both volumes in which he countered attacks against the humanistic tendency of the collection and defended in particular the sketches by Nikolai Alekseevich Nekrasov, Vladimir Ivanovich Dal', and Ivan Ivanovich Panaev that were published in the volumes.

In a review, also published in 1845, of Count Vladimir Aleksandrovich Sollogub's novella *Tarantas* (The Carriage, 1845) Belinsky again reiterates his view that the present age is inimical to pure art. As in all critical epochs, when an old way of life is being challenged and is breaking up but there is as yet no more than a presentiment of the new, art is not a master but a slave and serves ends that are peripheral to itself. At the same time his attack on Slavophilism (in particular Ivan Vasil'evich Kireevsky (the hero of Sollogub's work was called Ivan Vasil'evich) comes to a crescendo in this piece.

In his survey of Russian literature for 1845 Belinsky continues his twofold task of attacking the Slavophiles and defending a committed, even satirical, form of art. He begins by attempting to characterize the "Romantics of life," people who may be quite intelligent but are fruitlessly so because they are quite impractical. In their youth, a time of strength and vitality when one should live, these Romantics merely speculate about life. They even dress themselves up in such attire as a Tatar hat, Tatar robe, and little morocco-leather boots. (Belinsky is mocking the Slavophile fondness for native costume.) The illness from which these Romantics suffer, he says, is disharmony with reality. They seem to wish to live apart from life. They first compose a program for life and then live in conformity to it. There is, however, a formidable weapon that can be

deployed against everything that is false and comic in reality, namely humor. Only a writer armed with this weapon—and Belinsky has Gogol in mind—may lend a new direction to literature and kill off Romanticism. The principal service of the new literary school, which has constituted the most important development in Russian literature since 1836 when Gogol's *Mirgorod* cycle and *Revizor* appeared, is that it has turned from the higher ideals of human nature and life to the so-called crowd. This school has singled the crowd out as its hero, studies it carefully, and introduces it to itself. In the process the new school has fulfilled the desire of Russian literature to become fully national, original, and independent and has made literature an expression and mirror of Russian society.

The year 1845 was richer in literary works than the preceding one, but its main significance for Belinsky lay in the fact that the tendency he described had become more sharply defined. Belinsky praises Iakov Petrovich Butkov's "Peterburgskie vershiny" (St. Petersburg Heights), Aleksandr Ivanovich Herzen's *Kto vinovat?* (Who Is to Blame?), pieces in the anthology *Fiziologiia Peterburga,* including the sketches by Kazak Lugansky (the nom de plume of Dal') and Nekrasov, and especially Sollogub's *Tarantas.* Above all modern writers, though, stands George Sand, three of whose novels had appeared in translation in *Otechestvennye zapiski* in 1845.

Between 1843 and 1846 Belinsky also wrote eleven articles on—or in the case of the first three articles, apropos of—Pushkin. The series was prompted by the appearance in the period 1838–1841 of a collection of Pushkin's works, which Belinsky found wanting in many respects.

The first article in Belinsky's series offers a general view of the significance of Pushkin's work and begins to explore the literary-historical background against which Pushkin should be seen. Only six years after Pushkin's death the character of Russian society had changed to such an extent that Pushkin seemed to Belinsky already to belong to a different age. Consequently, Pushkin appears before posterity in a twofold light. He is no longer a poet as unconditionally great for the present and future as he was for the past. His work has unqualified merits and temporary merits, artistic significance and historical significance. However, in order to achieve this aim Belinsky finds it necessary to examine the relationship between Pushkin and the past of Russian literature; indeed he believes that to write about Pushkin means to write about the whole of Russian literature before him, for his predecessors explain him and he them. Belinsky draws encouragement from this thought, for it indicates that Russian literature, for all its poverty, has vitality, is developing organically, and has a history.

Belinsky reiterates his idea that Russian literature is not an indigenous but a transplanted growth and that the main feature in its history up until Pushkin is therefore a constant striving to rid itself of the results of the artificial transplantation and to establish roots in its new soil. An innovation sent to Russia from Europe, the idea of poetry as practiced by the likes of Trediakovsky and Lomonosov was understood as the art of celebrating solemn occasions. There consequently arose a rhetorical tradition, characterized by falsehood and platitudes and removed from reality. And yet parallel to this tendency there also developed from the beginning a satirical tendency that found expression in Kantemir's depiction of the conflict between the moribund Muscovite and new post-Petrine worlds and that remained a distinctive feature of Russian literature. An important step in the transition of Russian poetry from rhetoric to life was taken by Derzhavin, about whom Belinsky had just written a separate article, which he asked his readers to read in conjunction with the introductory articles in the series on Pushkin.

The second of Belinsky's articles in the series on Pushkin is a prolix survey of Krylov, Nikolai Mikhailovich Karamzin, Ivan Ivanovich Dmitriev, Vladislav Aleksandrovich Ozerov, Vasily Andreevich Zhukovsky, and Konstantin Nikolaevich Batiushkov, the principal purpose of which is to define and trace the development of Romanticism, which Belinsky believes found expression in Russia chiefly in the poetry of Zhukovsky. Romanticism lies in man's inner world, Belinsky says, the life of his soul and heart. It therefore manifests itself in feeling and love. Belinsky tries to trace the historical development of Romanticism by showing how love, chiefly romantic love, has been manifested in various times and places.

In the Orient where man, as Belinsky persists in seeing him, is the son of nature and lives a life close to animality, love still expresses, as it always has, no more than the sensual desire of one sex for the other and has failed to move on to its higher, more spiritual and moral moments. In ancient Greece, on the other hand, love manifested itself only in the highest moment of its development; here sensual striving was irradiated and inspired by the idea of beauty, which the Greeks, a moral-aesthetic people, worshiped. At the same time Romanticism, as the mystical essence of the life of the heart, had a gloomy side for the Greeks and was always held in check by other sides of the Hellenic spirit. In the Middle Ages, which Belinsky sees as an ultraroman-

tic epoch, Romanticism was a boundless force that, being limited by nothing, went to extremes of contradiction and senselessness. The medieval world was governed not by reason but by heart and fantasy. Woman was queen of this Romantic world, and veneration of her was expressed through the rituals of courtly love. The world of the Middle Ages worshiped beauty as ancient Greece had done but introduced a spiritual element into the concept. Whereas the Greeks had understood beauty in terms of elegant form animated by grace, medieval man conceived beauty as a sensual expression of moral qualities, a concept more spiritual than corporeal. To capture beauty of this sort in art, sculpture was an inadequate medium; only painting was equal to the task.

Romanticism, Belinsky says, lives on in the modern world as an organic synthesis of the Romanticism of all previous ages. The modern age he sees as an age of equilibrium between the inner, spiritual side of man–romance (*romantika*)–on the one hand and conscious reason on the other. Romanticism remains a requirement of the spiritual nature of man: the heart is the basis, the root soil, of his existence, and without love and hatred, sympathy and antipathy man is but an apparition. At the same time Belinsky thinks that no one in the modern age may find full satisfaction in the life of the heart alone. To attempt to build happiness only on love would be to renounce one's human dignity. The real world, in which man is above all a son and citizen of his country, has an equal if not greater claim on modern man. Knowledge, art, civil activity–all constitute for modern man a side of life that should be organically linked with his inner spiritual world but must not be replaced by it. Only through the harmonious interaction of both sides of his being may modern man build happiness on the solid foundation of consciousness rather than on the sandy bank of contingency.

The modern world, according to Belinsky, attributes to woman the same needs and capacities as to man. He believes that the mutual respect that is the only foundation for true human love has given rise to equality between the sexes during the modern age. Man can no longer be a lord or woman a slave. Both sides have established similar rights and obligations. Belinsky thinks that love in the modern age, as well as being simpler and more natural than love in other ages, is also more spiritual and moral. Man in the modern age will not worship woman simply because she is beautiful, as the Greeks did, nor will he discard her like a toy that has bored him as soon as he is sated with her possession. He will not perceive her, as medieval man did, as some incorporeal being of a higher nature but will fully recognize her as a human being. The ideal of the modern age is not an ethereal maiden proud of her innocence or inhabiting a world of dreams but a woman who realizes the life of her heart in actuality.

Russia did not experience the Middle Ages in the same way as Western Europe and therefore could not have a native Romanticism. Yet poetry without Romanticism, Belinsky says, is like a body without a soul. It was the great service of Zhukovsky to Russian literature to acquaint and animate it with the Romanticism of the Middle Ages through his translations of German and English poets, particularly Schiller, who at the beginning of the nineteenth century had resurrected that Romanticism. And yet Zhukovsky's poetry, with its sorrow at the transience and treacherousness of earthly happiness and his conviction that something more constant than the here and now lay only in the world beyond the grave, could no longer be accepted without demurral. To sustain oneself with noble thoughts and feelings; to equate personal happiness with love for a woman and to lament that when she is snatched away by death, the chance of happiness in this world has vanished; and to succumb to resignation and passive contemplation of the beauty of the universe—that is moral asceticism, the one-sidedness in which the error of ultra-Romanticism lies. Man's demand for personal happiness is legitimate and just, Belinsky says, but happiness cannot lie in the heart and love of a woman alone. It lies too, Belinsky argues in an elevated passage with huge periods and biblical resonance, in the world of social activity where thought and feeling are translated into exploit (*podvig*). This is the world of perpetual struggle between the past and future and of historical progress. Belinsky exalts those who in the midst of this chaos and suffering do not lose sight of the lodestar that guides them toward their goal. These individuals bear within them the ideal of a better existence, a new kingdom of God on earth, and they do everything in their power to bring it into being.

In the third article in his series Belinsky concentrates on the poetry of Batiushkov, whom Belinsky sees as a distinguished poet but one who lacks profundity and independence and whose verse is more graceful than energetic, and on the work of Nikolai Ivanovich Gnedich, whose translation of the *Iliad* conveys the Hellenic spirit, which Belinsky believes must be understood if art in general is to be appreciated fully and deeply.

In the fourth article, which serves at last as an introduction to the work of Pushkin, Belinsky emphasizes Pushkin's debt to Derzhavin, Zhukovsky, and Batiushkov. Without these predecessors Belinsky thinks Russia would have had no Pushkin, though one could not define what precisely he derived from each. Belinsky sees Pushkin as, unlike previous Russian poets, gradually developing both as a poet and as a man. That Pushkin's works differ markedly from one another in both form and content as the years go by indicates to Belinsky an organic vitality that derives both from Pushkin's own genius and from the fact that his poetry grows out of a living, and therefore mutable, reality. The article also examines the poetry from Pushkin's years at the lycée when he was a gifted poet who promised Pushkin but was not yet Pushkin.

In the fifth article Belinsky's main purpose is to identify the pathos that he believes provides the key to understanding any poet. A poet's works, however varied they may be, according to Belinsky have a common physiognomy, emanating as they do from one personality, a single and indivisible ego. The critic must first of all seek the poet's personality. Each person is born to realize through his personality, to a greater or lesser extent, one of the infinitely diverse facets of the human spirit, and the worth and importance of a personality lies in this mission of realization (*realizatsiia*) of spirit. The great poet has a strong personality that is worth studying; indeed the deeper and stronger his personality, the more he is a poet. The key to the poet's originality lies not in any abstract philosophical or rational idea, some syllogism, dogma, or rule, but in what Belinsky calls pathos, a powerful force that moves the poet to undertake the toil and exploit, comparable in a sense to the labor of childbirth, that are required to bring his embryonic creation into the world. Pathos drives a poet to love an idea as a beautiful living object and to contemplate it not merely with his reason, understanding, feeling, or any other single faculty but also with his whole moral being. Belinsky chooses the word *pathos* in preference to *passion* to describe this love that gives rise to the poetic idea because its connotations for him are moral, spiritual, and heavenly rather than sensual, corporeal, and earthly. Pathos transforms simple intellectual comprehension of an idea into a love of it that is full of energy and passionate striving.

In the case of Pushkin, Belinsky says, the poet's pathos lies in the charm, grace, and artistry of his verse. This pathos accounts for all the merits of Pushkin's poetry. It has plasticity and simplicity, and acoustic wealth and the power of the Russian language. It is tender, malleable, dense, bright, transparent, pure, fragrant, and strong. It has proportionality: everything is present to the right extent, occurs in its rightful place, and is in harmony with the other parts; nothing is either superfluous or

Belinsky in 1881 (Portrait by I. Astafev)

lacking. In contrast to a poet such as Schiller, who is a champion of what is noble and humane, Pushkin is first and foremost an artist filled with love for what is aesthetically beautiful. Pushkin's pathos enabled him to draw comprehensively on contemporary reality, with all its prose as well as its poetry, for his subject matter and to present it unadorned. Belinsky believes all subjects are for the true artist equally filled with poetry. Pushkin's *Evgeny Onegin* (1823–1831), for example, is a poem of contemporary reality which ranges over the four seasons, town and country, and the lives of the urban dandy and of rural landowners who discuss haymaking, wine, relatives, and kennels. At the same time the pathos of artistry breeds tolerance. Thus, in his small pieces Pushkin never curses or rejects. The general coloring of his poetry, and of his lyric poetry in particular, suggests an inner beauty in man. Even his sadness, profound as it may be, has a pacific and healing quality. His poetry therefore exhibits a tender and noble quality, a refinement of feeling, and a power to nurture humaneness that endow it with great morally educative value.

However, the pathos Belinsky has detected in Pushkin also accounts for what Belinsky sees as defects in his work. His humaneness and tolerance of the discords in life breed resignation. It is as if he accepts their inevitability and conceives no ideal of a better reality or has no faith in the possibility of its attainment. In this respect Pushkin belongs to a school of poetry that is already passé in Europe. Belinsky sees poetry as now engaged and imbued with a spirit of analysis. Much of Pushkin's work lacks the topical interest that comes only when an artist addresses the disquieting questions of his day. The artistic *profession de foi* (profession of faith) of Pushkin as an uncommitted poet is included in his poem "Chern'" (The Mob), in which the poet proudly scorns the rabble's plea that he use his lyre to improve its lot and asserts that the poet was born for inspiration, sweet sounds, and prayers, not for cupidity, conflict, or worldly agitation. Poetry should not be regarded, Belinsky still believes, as didactic thoughts in rhyme; the poet should not be required to sing hymns to virtue or castigate vice with satire. And yet the crowd, Belinsky now contends, cannot be ignored, for it is a repository of the popular spirit, an immediate source of the mysterious psyche of popular life. The work of a poet worthy of the description national (*narodnyi,* or *natsional'nyi*) must reflect the spiritual substance of his people; one is therefore entitled to demand that a poet's work either furnish answers to contemporary questions or at least be filled with regret that these serious intractable questions exist.

It is only in the sixth article of his series on Pushkin that Belinsky begins to examine Pushkin's first major works, his early narrative poems. "Ruslan i Liudmila" (Ruslan and Ludmila), for all its immaturity, did represent significant novelty and technical progress in Russian poetry. The poem "Brat'ia razboiniki" (The Robber Brothers) Belinsky finds false, strained, and melodramatic. Of much more interest to him, though, are the poems "Kavkazskii plennik" (The Captive of the Caucasus) and "Bakhchisaraiskii fontan" (The Fountain of Bakhchisarai). In "Kavkazskii plennik" Pushkin appeared as both fully himself and fully a representative of his age. Belinsky found in this poem a dual pathos. First, Pushkin was captivated in it by the poetic life of the wild mountain dwellers of the Caucasus, in which the poem was set, and by the magnificent beauty of the landscapes he described. Second, through his elegiac characterization of the captive, which delighted contemporaries, Pushkin portrayed a disillusioned soul typical of his time. This yearning of the young for lost youth, disenchantment without prior enchantments, spiritual torpor at the time when the soul should be most active, hot-blooded passion in conjunction with spiritual frigidity, a thirst for activity manifesting itself in absolute inactivity and apathetic indolence, senility before youth—these are salient features of the Russian hero from Pushkin on. It was not Pushkin, however, who invented these "superfluous men," as they were later to be known; he was merely the first to point them out. They were a sad but necessary phenomenon that sprang from a society in a stage of transition from adolescence to youth.

Turning to "Bakhchisaraiskii fontan," Belinsky finds at the core of this poem the profound idea of the regeneration of a savage soul through love. In Pushkin's "Tatar Girei," Girei, sated with sensual love in the harem, suddenly realizes a more human and higher feeling toward a woman who is foreign to his world. His captive Mariia embodies everything European: she is a maiden of the Middle Ages—a meek, modest being, devout in a childlike way. The feeling aroused by her in Girei is a Romantic, chivalrous feeling that causes upheaval in the Tatar's despotic, marauding nature. Girei is reborn through his encounter with her, and if he has not fully become a human being as a result, at least he is no longer an animal.

The seventh article in Belinsky's Pushkin series is devoted to the narrative poems *Tsygany* (The Gypsies) and *Poltava*. In *Tsygany*, Belinsky believes, Pushkin was no longer giving voice to the moral mood of contemporary society; rather he had become a tutor of future generations. It was Pushkin's intention in *Tsygany*, Belinsky thinks, to show in his hero, Aleko, a man so offended at the degradation of human dignity in civilized society, with its prejudices, decencies, and love of gold, that he turns his back on that society and seeks freedom in the company of gypsies. However, the whole course of the poem, its dénouement, and particularly the character of the old gypsy, who plays an important role in it, show that in fact the poet has created in Aleko not a champion of human dignity but a scathingly satirical portrait of him and people like him. Aleko is one of those "liberals" whose words and deeds are at odds with one another. He cannot personally live up to the standards invoked in his diatribe against civilization, for he is ruined by egoism, which finds expression in his jealousy of Zemfira, the gypsy woman who is unfaithful to him.

Belinsky proceeds to deliver an impassioned tirade against jealousy and vengefulness. He sees jealousy as a manifestation of petty tyranny that breeds a thirst for vengeance, an animal passion that arises in a man who confuses love with sensuality and seeks to exercise his rights over a woman who no longer loves him. Such possessive love may exist in marriage, for matrimony entails obligation, but it is a profanation of true love, which may be experienced only by a morally developed person. This ti-rade leads Belinsky into consideration of the nature of morality. The morally developed being is guided by the impulses of the heart illuminated by reason. His morality cannot be confined to a theoretical level; rather its true measure is practical activity. The evidence that indicates whether a man is moral or immoral should therefore be sought not in his statements about intellectual systems or in his preference for one moral doctrine over another but in the conduct of his human relationships.

Belinsky's thoughts lead him to a defense of free love. Fundamental to true morality as he sees it is a religious respect for the human worth of any individual. If a man in the position of Aleko, who has prompted these observations of Belinsky's, is a truly moral being, then he respects in the woman he loves the rights of a free personality and consequently the natural leanings of her heart. He will not construe her sudden cooling toward him as a crime or infidelity. The only course of action open to the morally developed man when he no longer is loved is to give his blessing to his former partner's new love and to bury his suffering deep in his heart. Many people brought up on fiction replete with jealousy, betrayals, daggers, and poisons, Belinsky says, will find such conduct prosaic. They may even scorn a man capable of it on the grounds that he lacks the concept of honor, for according to notions that have come down in distorted form from the Middle Ages a man must wash away dishonor with blood as Aleko wishes to do. Belinsky thinks there is no place, though, for such barbarous practices in the enlightened modern age.

Belinsky returns with relish to the subject of the despotic egoism of which he thinks Aleko's jealousy and medieval vengefulness are symptomatic. Aleko considers himself ahead of the whole of Europe on the path toward civilized respect for the rights of the personality, and yet through his refusal to renounce a selfish claim on Zemfira, as on a slave or chattel, he proves himself a Turk at heart. Proud and wicked, Aleko was not born for a life among the wild but meek children of nature who have no laws. He wanted freedom (*volia*) only for himself, as the simplehearted old gypsy, who knows no theories of morality, tells Aleko. The old gypsy then banishes Aleko from the gypsy encampment (and in the old gypsy's statement, Belinsky believes, the whole sense of the poem lies).

Aleko, as Belinsky sees him, is perhaps not entirely without hope. For as he sits on a stone, covered in blood and with a knife in his hands after taking his vengeance, he seems to acknowledge through his silence the punishment (*kara*) that has overtaken him; from this moment the beast in him might have died, and the resurrection of the man might have begun. Such, Belinsky believes, is the nature of this man that he could rise to humanization only at the price of a terrible crime and a terrible punishment for it. Belinsky's idea is suggestive of a major Dostoevskian theme, and indeed it is tempting to see Belinsky's excited tract on *Tsygany* with its diatribe on egoism (treated in Ivan Sergeevich Turgenev's *Rudin,* 1856) and its defense of free love (developed in Aleksandr Vasil'evich Druzhinin's novella *Polin'ka Saks,* 1847) as itself a seminal influence on the Russian novel.

Turning to *Poltava,* Belinsky holds that in this poem Pushkin wanted to attempt an epic in a new spirit. In seeking subject matter for his epic, Pushkin had come to rest on the greatest epoch of Russian history, the reign of Peter the Great, and in particular on the Battle of Poltava, which was the greatest event in that reign, for the success of all of Peter the Great's labors hinged on the outcome of that battle. In *Poltava* the battle, and Peter the Great too, appeared only in the last of the poem's three songs; the other two songs were taken up with the love of Mazeppa and Mariia and with Mazeppa's relations with Mariia's parents. Consequently, the battle becomes an episode in the love story of Mazeppa and its dénouement. The subject matter is accordingly lowered and its epic quality undermined. Thus *Poltava,* despite the magnificence of its verse, is flawed: it is a poem without a hero and fails to make on the reader a unified and altogether satisfying impression.

Finally, in *Graf Nulin* (Count Nulin) Belinsky finds a set of tableaux in the style of the painters of the Flemish school, who excel in presentation of the prose of reality. In truth, though, Belinsky has little to say about this poem, no doubt because its frivolity holds no appeal for a man of such high moral seriousness.

The eighth article in Belinsky's series on Pushkin is the first of two on *Evgenii Onegin,* Pushkin's favorite creation, which Belinsky sees as having great artistic merit as well as historical and social significance. In it, he believes, the poet's personality found exceptionally full and clear expression. Belinsky's essay is a prolix piece, which has a threefold purpose. First, Belinsky engages in polemic with the Slavophiles on the question of national character. Second, he argues that *Evgenii Onegin* is a faithful poetic depiction of Russian reality at a particularly interesting moment in its development, when Russian society was beginning to take shape. In this sense the work is an historical poem, a "poem of Russian life," an "encyclopedia of Russian life," and a work that was "national" in the highest degree. Third,

Belinsky seeks to convince his readers that Onegin is not the cold egoist he is usually believed to be.

Belinsky takes issue at the beginning of the article with those who do not realize that *Evgenii Onegin* is a highly national work because they believe that a Russian in a tailcoat or corset has ceased to be a Russian and that the Russian spirit makes itself felt only where there are homespun coats, bast shoes, raw vodka, and sour cabbage. True nationality in a poet, says Gogol in a passage that Belinsky is fond of quoting, lies not in a description of a *sarafan* (a Russian peasant woman's dress) but in an ability to look at even an alien world through the eyes of his national element and to feel and speak in such a way that it seems to his compatriots that they themselves are feeling and speaking. The poet capable of divining the national psyche is equally faithful to reality in descriptions of any social stratum and able to make characters from all strata speak with the same authenticity.

Understanding that the novel was the genre required for the portrayal of contemporary society and taking that society as he found it with all its coldness, prose, and banality (*poshlost'*), Belinsky saw Pushkin as concentrating on the landowning gentry, the stratum in which almost all progress to date had occurred and to which he himself belonged. In the process he revealed the inner life of this segment of Russian society and Russian society in general in the 1820s. Pushkin was not to blame for this society's developing so fast that by the time Belinsky was writing in the 1840s the society of the 1820s seemed remote.

Turning to Pushkin's characterization in *Evgenii Onegin,* Belinsky embarks on a protracted, strained, and at times somewhat banal defense of Onegin against the charge of immorality leveled at him by those who believed that he was an egoist and even that Pushkin intended to portray him as such. In fact, Belinsky argues, life in St. Petersburg society did not kill feeling in Onegin but merely bred in him indifference to fruitless passions and trivial entertainments. Belinsky quotes among others three stanzas from the first chapter of the work, which he believes demonstrate that Onegin, far from being cold, dry, and stale, was a sensitive, poetic soul. (Belinsky's reading of the stanzas in question seems suspect, however; he does not dwell on Pushkin's hint that Onegin's ennui may be a pose.) An embittered mind, Belinsky maintains, may be a sign of a higher nature dissatisfied with itself as well as with other people. In any case, such faults as Onegin does possess are the product not of his nature, passions, or personal mistakes but of the age in which he lives.

Belinsky returns from this preliminary discussion of Onegin's character to fresh consideration of the subject of egoism, which, as in his appraisal of "Tsygany," Belinsky here treats as the cardinal sin. If Onegin is an egoist at all, as his detractors claim, then he is an egoist who suffers. Belinsky believes he finds evidence for this view in the passages, omitted by Pushkin from his final version, that describe Onegin's visit to the Caucasus. Here is a character who feels alien to everything that goes on around him. To the dull-witted rabble, to whom youth, health, wealth, intelligence, and feeling are sufficient preconditions for happiness, such suffering seems modish eccentricity, but to Belinsky it is authentic and untheatrical. To experience so much by the age of twenty-six without having tasted life, to be so exhausted and weary without having done anything, to reach a point of such unconditional rejection without having held any convictions—this fate amounts to death.

Belinsky continues his apologia with some rather sterile observations on why in chapter three Onegin failed to fall in love with Tat'iana, the inexperienced girl who sent him her letter, and yet in chapter eight did fall in love with Tat'iana, the composed wife of a general in St. Petersburg society. In both events, Belinsky argues, Onegin acted neither morally nor immorally. Finally, Belinsky defends Onegin by taking issue with Pushkin. At one point in *Evgeny Onegin* Pushkin likens all people to the primogenitrix Eve: unsatisfied by what is given to them, they are lured to the forbidden tree by the serpent. Belinsky claims to hold a more optimistic view of human nature. Man, he believes, is born not for evil and crime but for good and for what he calls "rationally-legitimate" enjoyments of life's blessings. Evil lurks not in man but in society, and since societies, if they are seen as forms of human development, are still far from perfection, it is unsurprising that one sees many crimes in them.

The ninth article in Belinsky's series on Pushkin, and his second on *Evgeny Onegin,* is devoted almost exclusively to discussion of the heroine of Pushkin's novel in verse, Tat'iana. His article deals with the position of women in Russian society and with the effect of Russian society on the way in which Russian women express their natures. His view of Tat'iana the woman, as well as Tat'iana the character, is an admiring one.

In all strata of Russian society, Belinsky begins, man plays the first role; but one could not say that woman plays the second role because in truth she does not play any role at all. Only in the upper stratum could an exception be found to this rule, and even there the exception is true only up to a point. In spite of their copying of European customs, the Russians remain unchivalrous, and such attentiveness to women as they do show, smacks of theatricality and falsity. Whereas in Europe woman really is the queen of society, in Russia she is not even a human being. In fact, she is nothing but a prospective bride. To get married is her only wish, the object of her existence.

Russian reality, being squalid, breeds in many young women, if in their childhood their parents leave them to their own devices, a belief that only that is good which is diametrically opposed to this reality. These "ideal maidens," as Belinsky calls them, despise the crowd and earthly things. They are voracious readers, especially of Romantic fiction, and they live in a state of nervous exaltation. And yet in this world of moral cripples one occasionally finds exceptions who have genius in their natures. Such is Pushkin's Tat'iana, whose nature is unified, constant, thoughtful, deep, passionate, and loving. There is a sharp contrast between Tat'iana and her environment: she is like a rare and beautiful flower that has grown in the crevice of a wild cliff. And yet even Tat'iana, while retaining her natural simplicity, is at the same time inevitably deformed by her environment, Belinsky argues, and exhibits that bookishness of feeling that characterizes the Russian educated class. Consequently, although it was not a book that kindled her passion, her passion was bound to take a somewhat bookish form.

Tat'iana's true nature and the influence of society are both evident in her explanation to Onegin in chapter eight. Here she represents everything typical of a Russian woman with a deep nature who is at the same time mindful of convention: ardent passion, sincere, simple feeling, and purity on the one hand and wounded self-esteem, vain pride in virtue, and servile fear of public opinion on the other. Tat'iana does not love society and would happily leave it forever for the country; yet while she remains in society, public opinion will always be her idol. Pride in her virtue is expressed in her vow of eternal faithfulness to the one to whom she has been given (not the one, Belinsky notes, to whom she has given herself); that is to say, faithfulness to a relationship not sanctified by love is a profanation of feeling. Thus although Nature created Tat'iana for the role of a woman whose life was predominantly the life of the heart and for whom to love was to live, society re-created her as a woman locked in marriage to a man she did not love but determined to fulfill strictly her external obligations.

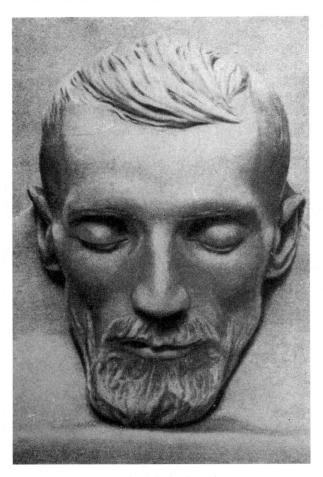

Belinsky's death mask

The tenth article in Belinsky's series on Pushkin is devoted entirely to *Boris Godunov* (written in 1825, published in 1831). Belinsky sees this historical drama as Pushkin's Waterloo, for the poet deployed his full genius in it yet still suffered a decisive defeat. There are two main reasons for this failure. One, Belinsky believes, is that the play lacks drama because of the nature of Russian history: pre-Petrine Russia differs from the Western European states in that its history is predominantly quietist rather than dramatic. (It lacks conflicts that result in the triumph of new ideas or principles.) Another, Belinsky says, is that instead of divining the secret of Godunov's personality and his historical significance by means of his own poetic instinct, Pushkin slavishly followed Karamzin's conception of the character in his history of the Russian state. Pushkin portrayed Godunov as a melodramatic rogue tormented by his conscience. In fact, the key to Godunov's personality lay in his having no hereditary right to power but rising to it from a position of equality with other nobles. A ruler taking supreme power in these circumstances, if he is to have legitimacy, must be endowed with genius of the sort possessed by Peter the Great, whereas Godunov was only an able minister. Lacking these insights into the character of Godunov, Belinsky thinks, Pushkin created a character without wholeness or fullness.

The eleventh and final article of his series on Pushkin Belinsky uses to examine, or at least mention in passing, the large number of works produced by the poet from 1830 until his death. In general the works produced after Pushkin's famous Boldino autumn of 1830 are less highly regarded by Belinsky than the narrative poems and *Evgenii Onegin,* and for the most part they therefore merit only cursory treatment. Among the works Belinsky now surveys are the narrative poem *Domik v Kolomne* (The Little House in Kolomna), a work too light for Belinsky's taste; "Andzhelo," which Belinsky finds unworthy of Pushkin's talent; the little tragedies, which Belinsky prizes highly, particularly *Kamennyi gost'* (The Stone Guest) and the *skazki* (fairy tales), most of which Belinsky dismisses as the product of a false striving for *narodnost'*. Central to Belinsky's assessment of *Mednyi vsadnik* (The Bronze Horseman) in this article is his veneration of Peter the Great. Confronted with the clash of Pushkin's poor Evgeny, the unfortunate ordinary man, with the "giant on the bronze horse," symbol of the mighty state, the reader's reaction, Belinsky believes, is ambivalent: while not rejecting sympathy for personal grief, he recognizes the triumph of the general over the individual. The sight of the Giant steadfastly rising above universal destruction and thus symbolizing the indomitable nature of his creation makes readers aware that he could not protect the lot of individuals while promoting the interests of the people and the state and that historical necessity is on his side. Perhaps the most notable feature of the eleventh article on Pushkin, though, is Belinsky's relatively low opinion of Pushkin's prose works, which Belinsky clearly thinks have little substance. His sketchy treatment of them—he devotes only about two pages to them in his whole series of more than four hundred pages—reflects this evaluation.

Pushkin was above all a poet-artist, Belinsky argues in his concluding assessment of the place of Pushkin in Russian literature, and his nature prevented him from being anything more than that. He gave Russia poetry as art and would consequently remain for Russians an exemplary master of poetry, a teacher of art. Among the qualities of his poetry is an ability to develop in people a sense of the beautiful and of humanity. The time would come when he would be regarded in Russia as a classical poet

Belinsky's grave (left) in St. Petersburg (photograph by Christine Rydel)

whose works could help to form moral as well as aesthetic sense.

By the beginning of 1846 when the series of articles on Pushkin was complete, Belinsky was again in extremely bad health. The poorly paid work for *Otechestennyue zapiski* was exhausting him both mentally and physically. He resolved to leave the journal and to publish a large almanac. He did contribute an article to the collection *Peterburgskii sbornik* (St. Petersburg Collection), published by Nekrasov early in 1846, but his own almanac was not produced. In spring 1846 Belinsky went to the Crimea, at the expense of his literary friends, in an attempt to recuperate. After his return he started to write for the journal *Sovremennik* (The Contemporary), which had been acquired by Nekrasov and Panaev while Belinsky was in the Crimea, and it was in this journal that his survey of Russian literature for 1846 was published. By the spring of 1847, though, his doctor was advising him to take the waters in Silesia, and in May, overwhelmed now by grief at the

death of his infant son in March, he set out, again at friends' expense, for Salzbrunn. It was here that he wrote his famous letter to Gogol, a furious attack on that writer prompted by Gogol's apparent defense of the existing order in his *Izbrannye mesta iz perepiski s druz'iami* (Selected Passages from a Correspondence with Friends, 1847). In this letter, which was not published in Belinsky's lifetime but was widely known throughout Russia and which has been seen as his testament, Belinsky defended the sacred vocation of the writer in Russia, where autocracy and censorship made imaginative literature a beacon of free conscience.

From Silesia, Belinsky, in the company of Pavel Vasil'evich Annenkov, traveled in Germany, Switzerland, and France, returning to Russia in November 1847. He wrote a final survey of Russian literature, for 1847, in which he again advocated judicious Westernization, defended the Natural School, and welcomed the appearance of such works as the earliest sketches in Turgenev's cycle *Zapiski okhot-*

nika (Sportsman's Sketches, 1847–1851) titled "Khor and Kalinych." However, the survey was Belinsky's last substantial essay. During the St. Petersburg winter his health again deteriorated, and he died at the age of thirty-six on 26 May 1848.

The importance of Belinsky in Russian literary history and also in Russian intellectual history can hardly be overestimated. He emerged as the dominant Russian critic at a time when Russian literature was entering its golden age. He presided over its development, helped to mold the taste of an inexperienced reading public, cultivated its awareness of concepts such as beauty, poetry, and artistry, and compelled it to think about such questions as the purpose of art, the relationship of the artist to his society, and the function of literary criticism. He established a canon of works—especially those of Pushkin, Gogol, and Lermontov—that he believed were landmarks and undermined the claims of other writers—such as Benediktov, Marlinsky, and Iazykov—who enjoyed much popularity for a while, to inclusion in this canon (though he did not deny their importance from the point of view of literary history). A few of his evaluations, such as those of Dal' and James Fenimore Cooper, may be seen as eccentric, but most have stood the test of time. He gave coherence to the literature that was emerging and related it to the awakening society from which it sprang, thereby contributing significantly to the nourishment of his people's self-awareness. He helped to nurture in Russians a passionate love of literature and persuaded them that literature was to be treated with the utmost seriousness both as a manifestation of the state of their nation and society and as a vehicle for the pursuit of the ultimate aesthetic and moral values of beauty, goodness, and truth.

As a literary critic Belinsky may be seen in retrospect, if his whole corpus of work is considered, as a protean figure in whose writings the kernel of both the mainstreams of Russian criticism in the decades after his death may be found. His insistence during his early period, particularly in its Hegelian phase, that art was an end in itself and that the true artist is receptive to the whole of reality and serenely pursues truth and beauty without partisanship, continued to find expression in the 1850s and beyond in a school of criticism whose leading representative was Druzhinin and to which Turgenev was sympathetic. This school, and the writers whom they championed, came to be known as the Pushkin School of Russian literature on account of their celebration of Pushkin's Olympian detachment and their rejection of any intended social or political role for literature. On the other hand, the

distinctive characteristics of Belinsky as a critic in his final years—a view of literature as a mirror of society, sympathy for the oppressed, enthusiasm for the Natural School, which supposedly recorded the plight of the little man, the demand that the Russian writer use his gift with a sense of civic responsibility to expose injustice in his repressive society—were enthusiastically taken up by the militant radical thinkers who emerged after the Crimean War (1853–1856). These thinkers—notably Dobroliubov, Nikolai Gavrilovich Chernyshevsky, the nihilist Dmitry Ivanovich Pisarev, and their epigones of more or less revolutionary complexion—championed Gogol, whom they supposed to be a negative talent and a vehement critic of Russian reality; constructed an aesthetic that identified beauty not as a transcendent value but as an attribute of the actual world; and encouraged writers to concentrate on such politically fruitful material as the nature and plight of the masses. This stream of Russian literary criticism emerged finally in the Soviet view of art and the doctrine of Socialist Realism.

Imaginative literature in the age of Nicholas I was the main sphere of cultural life, the yardstick by which the development of the nation was judged, and the principal means of expression of the free conscience. It is therefore difficult and misleading to attempt to separate this literature and the criticism of Belinsky that contributed so much to its promotion from the more general debate about ethical and social matters and the nature and destiny of the Russian people. (Political matters, though perhaps implicit in the discussions, were not overtly examined in the 1830s and 1840s.) The significance of Belinsky on this broader level, although it was almost exclusively as a literary critic that he wrote, is no less great. He served as one of the major channels through which Western European ideas—in particular German philosophy and later radical French ideas—flowed into Russia. As a Westernizer close to Herzen and Timofei Nikolaevich Granovsky, Belinsky denounced Slavophilism and argued for a judicious acceptance of those elements of Western civilization that would enable Russia to progress. In the field of history he endorsed the view of Peter the Great as a providential ruler who had laid foundations for the modernization and civilization of Russia and depicted Ivan IV (in his second essay on Lermontov) as a tragic figure who had appeared before circumstances were propitious for this great mission. Above all he stamped his personality with its restless quest for truth and its furious sense of moral engagement on the nascent Russian intelligentsia.

The distinctive character of Belinsky's work, as much as the work of any other Russian thinker, imparted to Russian thought in this its major formative phase enduring virtues and defects. Among the defects are a proclivity to schematic generalization, intolerance and scorn for moderation, a tendency to stretch material on a Procrustean bed of theoretical abstraction, and a willingness to follow ideas to conclusions from which might flow injustices no more tolerable than those to whose eradication Belinsky's short life was dedicated. Chief among his virtues are idealism, integrity, sincerity, selfless energy, courage, and thirst for truth.

Letters:

Pis'ma, 3 volumes, edited by E. A. Liatsky (St. Petersburg: M. M. Stasiulevich, 1914).

References:

Pavel V. Annenkov, *The Extraordinary Decade. Literary Memoirs,* translated by Irwin Titunik, edited by Arthur Mendel (Ann Arbor: University of Michigan Press, 1968);

Isaiah Berlin, in *Russian Thinkers,* edited by Henry Hardy and Aileen Kelly (London: Hogarth Press, 1978), pp. 150–185;

Herbert E. Bowman, *Vissarion Belinski, 1811–1848: A Study in the Origins of Social Criticism in Russia* (New York: Russell & Russell, 1969);

Edward J. Brown, in *Stankevich and His Moscow Circle 1830–1840* (Stanford, Cal.: Stanford University Press, 1966), pp. 120–132 and passim;

Richard Hare, in *Pioneers of Russian Social Thought* (London & New York: Oxford University Press, 1951), pp. 32–68;

Evgeny Lampert, in *Studies in Rebellion* (London: Routledge & Kegan Paul, 1957), pp. 46–107;

Pavel Ivanovich Lebedev-Poliansky, *V. G. Belinskii: literaturno-kriticheskaia deiatel'nost'* (Moscow-Leningrad, 1945);

Literaturnoe nasledstvo, nos. 55–57 (Moscow: AN SSSR, 1948–1951);

Thomas Garrigue Masaryk, *The Spirit of Russia,* volume 1 (London: G. Allen & Unwin, 1919), pp. 350–378;

Rufus W. Mathewson, in "Belinsky. 'My Heroes Are the Destroyers,'" *The Positive Hero in Russian Literature* (Stanford, Cal.: Stanford University Press, 1975), pp. 25–45 and passim;

Vera Stepanovna Nechaeva, *V. G. Belinskii: nachalo zhiznennogo puti i literaturnoi deiatel'nosti, 1811–1830* (Moscow: Stepanovnev, 1949);

Nechaeva, *V. G. Belinskii: uchenie v universitete i rabota v "Teleskope" i "Molve," 1829–1836* (Moscow: AN SSSR, 1954);

Nechaeva, *V. G. Belinskii: zhizn' i tvorchestvo, 1836–1841* (Moscow: AN SSSR, 1961);

Nechaeva, *V. G. Belinskii: zhizn' i tvorchestvo, 1842–1848* (Moscow: AN SSSR, 1967);

Iu. Oksman, *Letopis' zhizni i tvorchestva V. G. Belinskogo* (Moscow: Gosuder stvennoe i zdatel'stvo Khudozhestvennoi literatury, 1958);

Victor Terras, *Belinskij and Russian Literary Criticism: The Heritage of Organic Aesthetics* (Madison: University of Wisconsin Press, 1974);

Andrzej Walicki, in *A History of Russian Thought from the Enlightenment to Marxism* (Stanford, Cal.: Stanford University Press, 1979), pp. 120–128, 134–149, 417–421, and passim;

René Wellek, "Social and Aesthetic Values in Russian Nineteenth-Century Literary Criticism (Belinskii, Chernyshevskii, Dobroliubov, Pisarev)," in *Continuity and Change in Russian and Soviet Thought,* edited by Ernest J. Simmons (New York: Russell & Russell, 1967), pp. 381–397.

Aleksandr Aleksandrovich Bestuzhev
(Marlinsky)
(23 October 1797 – 7 June 1837)

Lew Bagby
University of Wyoming

BOOKS: *Poezdka v Revel'* (St. Petersburg: A. Pliushar, 1821);

Andrei, kniaz' Pereiaslavskii, published anonymously (Moscow: S. Selivanovskii, 1828);

Russkie povesti i rasskazy Aleksandra Marlinskogo, volumes 1–2 (parts 1–8) (St. Petersburg & Moscow: III otdelenie, 1832–1834); *Polnoe sobranie sochinenii,* volume 3 (parts 9–12) (St. Petersburg: III otdelenie, 1838–1839);

Editions and Collections: *Sochineniia* (Moscow: Goskhudlitizdat, 1935);

Izbrannye povesti, edited by G. V. Prokhorov (Leningrad: Khudozhestvennaia literatura, 1937);

Sobranie stikhotvorenii (Leningrad: Sovetskii pisatel', 1948);

Sochineniia v dvukh tomakh, 2 volumes, edited by N. N. Maslin (Moscow: Khudozhestvennaia literatura, 1958);

Poliarnaia zvezda izdannaia A. Bestuzhevvym i K. Ryleevvym, edited by V. A. Arkhipov, V. G. Bazanov, and Ia. L. Levkovich (Leningrad: AN SSSR, 1960);

Polnoe sobranie stikhotvorenii, edited by M. A. Briskman (Leningrad: Sovetskii pisatel', 1961);

Povesti i rasskazy, edited by A. L. Ospovat (Moscow, 1976);

Sochineniia v dvukh tomakh, 2 volumes, edited by V. I. Kuleshov (Moscow: Khudozhestvennaia literatura, 1981);

Fregat "Nadezhda": Povesti, edited by V. I. Sakharov (Odessa, 1983);

Revel'skii turnir: Istoricheskie povesti, edited by V. I. Sakharov (Odessa, 1984);

Romanticheskie povesti, edited by V. V. Dement'iev and others (Sverdlovsk: Sredne-Uralskoe knizhnoe izdatel'stvo, 1984);

Noch' na Korable: povesti i rasskazy (Moscow: Khudozhestvennaia literatura, 1988).

Edition in English: *The Tatar Chief; or, A Russian Colonel's Head for a Dowry,* translated by G. C. Hebbe (New York: W. H. Colyer, 1846).

OTHER: "An Evening on Bivouac," translated by Lauren G. Leighton, in *Russian Romantic Prose: An Anthology,* edited by Carl R. Proffer (Ann Arbor, Mich.: Translation Press, 1979), pp. 138–144;

"The Test," translated by Lewis Bagby, in *Russian Romantic Prose: An Anthology,* pp. 145–195;

Ammalat-bek: A Caucasian Tale, excerpts, translated by Bagby, in *The Ardis Anthology of Russian Ro-*

manticism, edited by Christine Rydel (Ann Arbor: Ardis, 1984), pp. 212–241;

"A Glance at Russian Literature in the Course of 1824 and the Beginning of 1825," translated by Leighton, in *Russian Romantic Criticism,* edited by Leighton (New York: Greenwood Press, 1987), pp. 69–84;

"On Romanticism and the Novel," translated by Leighton, in *Russian Romantic Criticism,* pp. 137–160.

In his daily behavior, in his beliefs, in his fiction and criticism, and in his political code, Aleksandr Bestuzhev was an extreme representative of the Romantic generation. His stories feature dashing young men quick with wit, short on patience, practiced with a sword and pistol, and ready for dramatic and violent action, preferably of their own design. His literary criticism espoused European models of the Romantic aesthetic code and in no uncertain terms belabored the older generation's classical orientation. He was a renowned literary critic in the debates of the early nineteenth century, a passable poet in the Golden Age of Russian verse, and the most popular writer of prose fiction in the 1830s. His renown lasted well into the 1840s and 1850s, although he was ignored by later generations.

Aleksandr Aleksandrovich Bestuzhev was born in St. Petersburg to Aleksandr Fedoseevich Bestuzhev and Praskovya Mikhailovna Bestuzheva on 23 October 1797. The fifth of eight children, he was the most Dionysian in temperament and the most prolific as a writer, having established his reputation as a literary critic, poet, and translator by 1820. He was also a rising star in the military and at court. At the same time, Bestuzhev was a leading member of the Northern Society, a conspiratorial group of (for the most part) military officers who plotted the overthrow of the sovereign and organized, however ineptly, the "first Russian revolution": on 14 December 1825 Bestuzhev was the first to bring rebel troops to the Senate Square, where the Decembrist Revolt was staged as though in live theater. The one-day disaster ended with the consolidation of Nicholas I's power and the deaths of many participants, spectators, and Decembrists (as the instigators came to be called). In its aftermath Bestuzhev dressed the part of a dandy and turned himself over to the police. He prostrated himself before the tsar and sought his forgiveness. The remainder of Bestuzhev's life was spent in exile, first in Finland and Siberia, then in the Caucasus, where he fought as a common soldier in the war for hegemony in the region.

Bestuzhev was a cause célèbre in exile. Young officers flocked to his side in order to model themselves after him. He was a living example of the romantic-heroic code taken from the pages of literature and performed on the stage of life. This public attention, and the fame he won publishing in the 1830s under the pen name Marlinsky (though few readers knew that Marlinsky was Bestuzhev), spurred him on toward greater aspirations, which found their object in self-mythologization and self-glorification. He fell in battle on 7 June 1837; his body was never recovered and his end (or whereabouts) never conclusively ascertained. Wild rumors spread that he had not been killed but whisked away into mountain retreats where he lived the remainder of his life among the Caucasian peoples whose heroic and literary romantic qualities he had extolled in his tales and letters.

Bestuzhev's self-made myth did not last long. His extreme form of Romanticism was roundly attacked for its excesses and uniformity. His social type was later discredited by Leo Tolstoy and Ivan Turgenev, though both had admired him greatly in their youth: "Do you know," Turgenev once confessed to Tolstoy, "that I used to kiss Marlinsky's name on journal covers?" As a new, Realist page turned in Russian history, Bestuzhev was all but forgotten by the intelligentsia. Among a broad readership, however, his popularity remained intact well into the Soviet era.

Bestuzhev was a profoundly conflicted person. His quest for a heroic persona was predicated upon a realization of romantic ideals that precluded admission of less romantic aspects of the self. A study of his many works, fiction and otherwise—his diary and letters; the government documents pertaining to the Decembrist Revolt, to Bestuzhev's part in it, and to his interrogation; and memoirs that give some indication of the man behind the mask—delivers up a sense of Bestuzhev's human traits, those which the romantic, heroic persona would not admit.

A psychological understanding of Bestuzhev must in some way accommodate the distinction between the man and his persona. Since critics, like Bestuzhev's contemporaries, have read his fiction as a coded diary and have viewed his behavior and speech in life as a guide to his literature, the question is not whether he resembled his fictional heroes but how he created this effect. It is quite an accomplishment that Bestuzhev managed to convince his readership that his art represents his person.

It is possible to view Bestuzhev's equation of self to art as a form of communication in which his personality and his idea of himself stand out in re-

Portrait of Bestuzhev by his brother Nikolai, 1823–1824
(Institute of Russian Literature [Pushkin House],
St. Petersburg)

lief. For purposes of description, "Bestuzhev" is used here to indicate the man, "Marlinsky" his heroic persona. For Bestuzhev, the pen name Marlinsky at first operated as a disguise, then functioned as a secret code, and finally came to represent his whole identity. Originally he had taken the name Marlinsky in 1817 when he was stationed near Peterhof, the tsar's summer palace, at Marli. By 1819 the name became a mask by which he sequestered his well-known identity and literary biases from his opponents in the polemics of the day. He rarely used it at this time, but it attests early in his career to a recourse to disguise. Later, in exile, Bestuzhev was allowed to publish only under this pseudonym, thus rendering it into a code meant to disclose rather than hide his identity from a public that, for all intents and purposes, considered him dead. At this period in his life (1830–1837) Marlinsky became the repository of the identity Bestuzhev conceived for himself and propagated in daily life and in his fiction, letters, and criticism.

This persona, acquired from the confluence of life and art during this period à la George Gordon, Lord Byron, seemed to be an adequate means for fully expressing his personality. The dynamic changes wrought in the years following the Napoleonic Wars forged new ideas of personality that influenced Bestuzhev directly. The concern with the search for identity that was characteristic during this epoch appealed to young minds seeking a unique sense of self (oblivious though they may have been to the uniformity in their quest for uniqueness). The heroic persona supplied an aestheticized form of personality as fluid and as vital as the times in which Bestuzhev lived.

However, the Decembrist Revolt, its aftermath (interrogation, humiliation, isolation, physical punishment, deprivation), and exile challenged the integrity of Bestuzhev's idea of himself. Introspection and analytic skill were required to render the persona new, yet Bestuzhev (unlike his older brothers and oldest sister) lacked these qualities. Consequently, the next stage in the development of Bestuzhev's persona represented an imaginative continuation of the basic heroic outline of the past, but with new Byronic characteristics attached to it: weariness of life; impatience with man's imperfections; a keen sense of one's superiority and consequent isolation from the herd; a consciousness of the transitory nature of life; a combative, self-confident, and assertive grasp of the heroic individual's right to define reality and self; the glorification of the ego and its authority in all matters; and the idea of death as the consummate act of a titanic will. Bestuzhev wove these features into his view of himself and the world and encoded them onto the pages of his fiction and letters. It is therefore not surprising that readers were willing to mythologize him after his disappearance.

In his earliest years Bestuzhev's life had moved forward with the illusion of regularity and even predictability. Surrounded by a loving family and parents dedicated to their children, Bestuzhev was nurtured to believe in his potential as a participant on the broad social, literary, and political stages. His dream of becoming a naval officer was dashed early when he found he had little capacity for mathematics, so he turned to a career as a guard officer. He excelled, perhaps more for his good looks and dashing character than for his skills as a surveyor of roadways. In fact, Bestuzhev became an exemplar of the extreme code of behavior that distinguished guard officers from others—at the gaming tables, on the dueling grounds, and in the boudoirs of the *belles dames* of society. Bestuzhev was known for his quick wit, satiric sketches, intemperate acts of daring, and flair with the pen. By the time he turned twenty, he had already established himself as a bearer of the new, Romantic word against those who either espoused the cloying and sweet manners of the sentimental age or against those who advanced a narrow, nationalistic program of purifying Russia from the pernicious influences of the West.

In the name of an indigenous Russian element (*narodnost'*), Bestuzhev advanced his cause both against French influences and feudal Russian practices. But he could not mask that he had gone to school on Sir Walter Scott, Byron, Washington Irving, and Ann Radcliffe. In effect, he argued Anglophilia from a Francophobic base. Aleksandr Pushkin could not help noticing, and in a letter of 12 January 1824 he addressed Bestuzhev as "my dear Walter [Scott]."

Bestuzhev was supported in his literary interests by his father, a member of the ancient nobility whose family name had fallen on hard times in the eighteenth century. The family's problems were compounded by the fact that Bestuzhev's father had married a woman from the merchant class, a dramatic political gesture representative of his liberal leanings (and surely the urging of his heart) that had an impact on him and his family. All the children were subsequently rendered sensitive to class issues and, when pressed, stood for the liberal cause against the exclusive and elitist tendencies of their father's class. Those who suffered most, it can be argued, were the daughters, Elena, Olga, and Mariya, who never married.

Bestuzhev was consumed by fiction, not only of the literary variety but also of those kinds that infect daily life. From the Cadet Corps of Engineers, where he enrolled at age nine, to the Guard Officer Corps, where in 1822 he became adjutant to General Augustine Betancourt, Bestuzhev created a lively self-image both in the literary debates and in his personal escapades. His older brother Nikolai reproached him for his behavior, finding it lacking in rationality and devoid of that quest for the Golden Mean taught them by their father, who died when Bestuzhev was thirteen years old. With Nikolai at the family helm, Bestuzhev pursued his own course, something he might not have done under the stern eye of his father. Upon finishing school Bestuzhev entered the Light Dragoon Regiment, a military corps known for its flamboyant and hedonistic style. Perfecting the egocentric code of the small but powerful world in which he moved, Bestuzhev rose to a position of prominence. His name was heard in association with higher positions, not only in the military but also at court; his career looked bright, and his future seemed assured.

Signs of this promise were to be seen not only in his stature in the guard and among members of the court but also in his publication venture: together with the poet Kondratii Fedorovich Ryleev, and with the assistance of the writer Orest Mikhailovich Somov and many of their lettered friends, Bestuzhev published one of the first literary journals to experience popular commercial success in Russia. It was called *Poliarnaia zvezda* (The Polar Star) and appeared annually from 1823 to 1825. Bestuzhev and Ryleev received from the Dowager rare gifts for its original issue. The journal caused a sensation for its stylistic brilliance, its polemical nature, and the quality of its content. The 1823 edition included pieces by all the leading figures of the literary scene: Pushkin, Ryleev, Somov, Faddei Venediktovich Bulgarin, Evgenii Abramovich Baratynsky, Petr Aleksandrovich Pletnev, Prince Petr Andreevich Viazemsky, Nikolai Ivanovich Gnedich, Fedor Nikolaevich Glinka, Vasilii Andreevich Zhukovsky, Denis Vasilievich Davydov, Anton Antonovich Del'vig, Ivan Andreevich Krylov, Nikolai Ivanovich Grech, and Osip Ivanovich Senkovsky. Bestuzhev's work was confined to literary criticism and prose fiction; his hand at poetry was weak, and he knew better than to print anything that might be compared with the verse of the Pushkin Pleiad.

Bestuzhev's political leanings are indicative of the manner in which he operated in society; he attempted to be accepted by several quite disparate groups of people. He once claimed, "I am more a Democritus in image than at heart," a comment that suggests something of his ambivalence in matters that were of great import for him and Russian society. The liberal tendencies which were nurtured in his family found a new home in 1820, when he joined the *Vol'noe obshchestvo liubitelei rossiiskoi slovesnosti* (Free Society of Lovers of Russian Literature), an organization that discussed Enlightenment ideals, but many key members of which gradually emerged as leading figures in an underground political movement. Bestuzhev joined their revolutionary secret society in 1823. That society had grown out of another, *Soiuz blagodentstviia* (the Union of Welfare). Rebellions in Spain, Italy, Portugal, Piedmont, and Greece inspired the military officers belonging to the Union of Welfare to form the so-called Northern Society in St. Petersburg. (There was another branch, the Southern Society, in Tulchin.) They supported civil liberties and the end of autocracy in Russia.

Bestuzhev's colleague and friend Ryleev was inducted into the Northern Society in 1823, and he quickly brought Bestuzhev into the organization after him. That same year, Bestuzhev visited Moscow to spread the cause of the society and to gather support from Moscow liberals. He was successful in this endeavor: he recruited many members, including his brothers Nikolai and Mikhail, and he introduced two of the most daring and rash members—Aleksandr Ivanovich Yakubovich and Petr Grigor'evich Kakhovsky.

If Bestuzhev believed wholeheartedly in the cause he served, he could not represent its voice, which was something of a surprise to his comrades, for they saw him as a man of letters who enjoyed a rather brilliant career in the literary arena. Bestuzhev, however, was short on substantive political rhetoric and the modes of discourse it required. He cast himself as a man of action and left the details of political reform to others. Although he was privy to the workings, tactics, and internal debates of the Northern Society and rose to a position of prominence in its ruling central committee, the *Duma,* he could not distinguish himself as one of its thinkers. Even Ryleev counted more on Nikolai Bestuzhev's mind than Aleksandr's, considering the latter entirely too rash to warrant serious attention on theoretical and political matters. Bestuzhev's skills were more successfully used to inspire others, particularly in consort with Ryleev. The two, in fact, represented the improvisational wing of the Northern Society. Bestuzhev and Ryleev's style was declamatory, not analytic. Neither was prepared to see the insurgency in tactical or military terms, only as a grand historical gesture. To effect their ends they composed underground songs meant to instill revolutionary fervor in the masses, particularly among common soldiers. The songs were designed to elicit hostility toward the government and a desire to bring about change at the top.

In the fall of 1825 Bestuzhev and Ryleev occupied adjacent quarters. Their rooms were the center for discussions about revolt. The plan, from the perspective of the right flank, was to assassinate the tsar, Alexander I. But on 27 November 1825 Alexander I died, leaving a vacuum at the top that neither of his brothers, Constantine or Nicholas, was eager to fill. Several weeks of indecision, ridiculed in the Western press, ensued. Constantine's desire to bypass the throne led to Nicholas's ascent and precipitated the Decembrist Revolt. Utilizing the confusion surrounding succession and fearing the rise of the hated Nicholas to power, the members of the Northern Society elected to force the senate to adopt a constitutional form of government and thus forestall Nicholas. They planned to take Senate Square on the first day of Nicholas's reign, to arrest the tsar and his family (regicide was still considered by the most extreme members of the group), and to gain control of the government. Prince Sergei Petrovich Trubetskoi was to assume temporary power during the transition to a constitutional form of government.

Beginning with Trubetskoi's absence on the day of the revolt (he went into hiding), the Decembrist affair was an abject failure. No sooner did Bestuzhev bring out the first troops to occupy Senate Square than it became obvious that the insurgents could not rally sufficient numbers to be successful. They were surrounded by an army loyal to the new tsar and were scattered when Nicholas I ordered his troops to fire on the rebels and the masses that had gathered in support of them.

The day of the rebellion marked a seminal moment in Bestuzhev's life and in his attempt to make his literary self-perception into reality, to write his romantic, literary persona onto Russian cultural history. But his ambivalence was given more range than he surely had planned. If Bestuzhev was the first to lead insurgents out into formation on Senate Square, he was also the first to reveal to the new tsar that the plans of the Northern Society had included regicide. After six months of interrogations Bestuzhev was sentenced to beheading, but Nicholas I commuted the sentence to loss of noble rank, hard labor for twenty years in Siberia, and permanent exile. For more than six months of imprisonment in the Peter and Paul Fortress, Bestuzhev suffered with the personal knowledge that he had failed his heroic ideal, not during the revolt but in its aftermath—his testimony may have influenced the punishment inflicted upon the leaders of the society. For their participation Ryleev and four others were hanged.

The tsar's first interview with Bestuzhev occurred shortly after the latter's arrest. From Nicholas I's memoirs and notes it is clear that Bestuzhev sought his forgiveness immediately. This is also clear in a long letter of self-justification (published in *Iz pisem i pokazanii dekabristov,* 1906) that Bestuzhev wrote the tsar within the first month of his incarceration and interrogation. Seeking to flatter the tsar while simultaneously fending off accusations from his comrades that he, Bestuzhev, had maligned Nicholas I in public, Bestuzhev wrote:

> You, Emperor, already know how, inflamed by this sorrowful state of Russia and seeing all elements prepared for a change, [we] came to the decision to revolt. Now let me dare to elaborate before Your Highness that we, in doing this, thought our actions founded on the laws of the people. . . . In addition, Batenkov and I said that we had at this time (that is, close to December 14), a political right [to revolt] based on the fact of the interregnum. For Your Highness had refused the crown, and we know that the Grand Duke's abdication was already here. (Our error consisted in the fact that we did not know that Your Highness had been named the Heir to the throne [in Alexander I's will]). . . . Your Imperial Highness, let the following confession of how we viewed Your personal character before [December 14] serve as proof of the respect which I have for Your magnanimity. We were quite familiar with the gifts which nature bestowed upon You; we knew that You, Em-

peror, were engaged in the study of governance and that you read a great deal. . . . The anecdotes which bespeak the harshness of Your Highness frightened many of us. But I must confess that never once did I ever say that the Emperor Nicholas with his mind and strictness would ever become a despot all the more dangerous because his perspicacity threatens all intelligent and well-intentioned people with exile; or that He, being enlightened Himself, would deliver death blows to enlightenment [in Russia]; or that our fate would be decided from the moment He would take the throne; or that consequently we may as well die today [December 14] as tomorrow.

Bestuzhev prostrates himself before the sovereign who proceeded over the next two decades to exercise the despot's will Bestuzhev and his comrades foresaw over so-called Enlightenment ideals in Russia. Yet Bestuzhev carefully cloaks his complicity through allusions and stylistic feints that are technically true, but in spirit disingenuous: he does not respect the tsar himself, but the tsar's "magnanimity"; Bestuzhev acknowledges that he and his comrades knew Nicholas was a student of governance, but he hardly mentions that not one of them believed he was an apt student; Bestuzhev alludes to Nicholas's "harshness," but only as a delusion, it would appear, shared by the insurgents. So as to leave no doubt about his allegiance to the tsar, Bestuzhev concludes his letter most abjectly:

> Experience has revealed to me my errors, repentance has washed clean my soul, and I am pleased now to be disposed to whatever Providence delivers. . . . From the few signs which have penetrated my dark cell, I doubt not that Your Royal Highness will heal all the ills of Russia, will quiet and correct for the better the wandering of misguided minds and thus exalt the Fatherland. I am convinced that the Heavens themselves have bestowed on us through You another Peter the Great, even greater than he, for in our time and with Your gifts, Emperor, to be such as Peter is but a small task. This thought for the time being lessens my sufferings for myself and for my brothers. Prayers dedicated to the happiness of a Fatherland which is not separated from Your Highness's true glory now fly [from my cell] to the throne of You, the Most High.

Even though their crimes, relatively speaking, were not of the magnitude of Aleksandr's, Bestuzhev's brothers, Nikolai and Mikhail, received more harsh sentences than Aleksandr. A comparison of the brothers' testimonies underscores why—Aleksandr was more cooperative and forthcoming with evidence than either Nikolai or Mikhail. In his testimony Bestuzhev revealed a deep-seated conflict between core personality characteristics and his persona ideal, between

Bestuzhev's mother, Praskovya Mikhailovna Bestuzheva (portrait by V. Pogonkin, Pushkin Museum of Fine Arts, Moscow)

Bestuzhev the man and Marlinsky his mask. Once confronted by the futility of his actions, Bestuzhev's bravado deflated. He confessed the error of his ways, condemned his rash behavior, and quietly accepted his fate.

Bestuzhev paid a high price for depicting himself as a patriot among conspirators. He revealed the inner workings of the Northern Society and exposed all but his brothers' involvement in plans of regicide. This confessing was done in a manner that defeated his heroic self image, for in selecting techniques by which to diminish his complicity he opted to present himself as something of a buffoon engaged in nothing more than empty speech:

> Obolensky and Ryleev said . . . that it was necessary to eliminate the whole [royal] family. I don't know what their reason was, but it seemed [they reasoned that the destruction of the tsar's family] would eliminate the possibility of a royalist counterinsurgency. I adhered to this plan for I knew that you might find one assassin, but not enough [to murder the entire royal family]. . . . I was convinced that it would be impossible to find such people. Yakubovich and I insisted that no less than ten [assassins] would be required [for the job], and thus by this colossal figure the blow to the Sacred Head was avoided. In a word, I made a loud noise (*Ia byl krikun*), but I was not a villain.

Bestuzhev presents himself as rebel in word but not in deed. His behavior worked against the radicals' linkage of words and deeds; this nullification redoubled the crisis of identity and forced Bestuzhev to confront the vacuousness of a persona he had generated in the press and in society. During the investigation Bestuzhev was held accountable for frivolous speech, for his propensity to be clever and to play the wit on any occasion, even the most serious. Through the conditions of his imprisonment and interrogation he was asked to question the nature of his heroic self-idea and to examine the consequences of his prior discourse. Bestuzhev's response was both clever and psychologically ominous—he utilized the marlinism (a term created to describe his flamboyant style) in his responses to the investigatory commission to repress personal guilt and to obscure his part in the conspiracy. In this fashion the marlinism took on new functions, expressing in symbolic form the content of a reality he wished to hide: for example, "Up until that time only a dress blade did I carry, and such a delicate little one, *like a gesture,* and by which it would have been impossible to either *cut or gut* a man." Bestuzhev's discourse could never be the same either in fiction or in other forms; the marlinism now became a marker of the chasm separating his voice from his self-concept.

In the guise of a faithful citizen and dutiful soldier willing to serve the government, Bestuzhev was the only Decembrist allowed in exile to resume a literary career. However, for the remainder of his life Bestuzhev was viewed with great suspicion by Nicholas I. The tsar monitored his every official move and insisted that Bestuzhev use his pen name, Marlinsky, when appearing in print. Nicholas I also selected Bestuzhev's place of exile in Siberia and later agreed to his removal from there to the Caucasus to fight against the indigenous peoples.

Bestuzhev began his exile in October 1827. He traveled from Fort Slava in Finland, where he had been temporarily imprisoned, to Siberia. He left Finland a few days after his brothers Nikolai and Mikhail. He traveled with a fellow Decembrist through Yaroslavl, Vyatka, Perm, and then to Ekaterinburg, where he was given a warm and hospitable greeting by provincial officials. From there the two prisoners moved on through Tobolsk and Krasnoyarsk to Irkutsk. There Bestuzhev was reunited for three weeks with his brothers. From Irkutsk he was taken along the distant reaches of the Lena River to Yakutsk, where he arrived on Christmas Eve 1827. Yakutsk was the antithesis of life in the capital city. There were twenty-five hundred inhabitants—Buriats, Tungus, Great Russians in government service, and Siberians of Russian extraction. Most were illiterate, and by Bestuzhev's reckoning only one family subscribed to a journal. The town consisted of yurts, huts, and log cabins, all surrounded by the vast emptiness of the northeastern Siberian expanses. Vegetation was sparse, and due to the short growing season, vegetables were nearly impossible to cultivate. Winter at sixty-two degrees latitude was severe, and the temperature often remained at forty degrees below zero or lower. Mail was received twice a month. Bestuzhev spent his time indoors reading and writing letters to his family and friends, entertaining himself with plans for the future, and indulging memories.

This period was a time of stasis for Bestuzhev. He wrote little except personal letters, and he could hardly indulge his persona's social manners where society was lacking. Nevertheless, it was a period of nascent creativity, of the potential for a rebirth. Bestuzhev read with renewed vigor the works of Homer, Dante, Johann Wolfgang von Goethe, Friedrich Schiller, William Shakespeare, Thomas More, and Byron. He studied the indigenous peoples of northeastern Siberia and engaged in a scientific expedition (led by the German natural scientist Georg Adolph Erman) to gather astronomical data. He became an amateur ethnographer, linguist, folklorist, and natural scientist.

Within six months Bestuzhev was joined by a fellow Decembrist, Zakhar Grigor'evich Chernyshev, who brought with him a portrait of Bestuzhev done in Chita by his brother Nikolai. Bestuzhev requested by post that another be done "mustache down and without sideburns." Even in Siberia he did not cease in his efforts to create an image of himself. He wrote to his mother and sisters for money, clothes, amenities, books, dictionaries, a fur coat, a neckerchief, colored gloves, summer undergarments, a single-breasted evening jacket in black, and material from which he might fashion other items of clothing. A lack of society in Yakutsk notwithstanding, Bestuzhev seems to have engaged in two affairs and to have arranged good relations with the regional governor, who gave balls and organized dinners to which he invited "the rebels." But after the transfer of Chernyshev to another community, Bestuzhev slipped into a brief despair relieved only by a plan for escape from his solitude—he requested transfer to the Caucasus to join his youngest brothers, Pavel and Petr, who were distinguishing themselves in battle à la Marlinsky.

On 10 February 1829 Bestuzhev wrote to the official indirectly responsible for overseeing the Decembrists in Siberian exile, Count Ivan Ivanovich Dibich:

Your highness' generous mercy, which I have had the pleasure of experiencing before, emboldens me to make a request of you which is both humble and impassioned: I ask that Your Highness intercede for me before the most generous Monarch that I might be assigned the post of common soldier to serve you in pursuit of victory. A great soul reared in battle can well understand the suffering of a soldier who has been sentenced to wither away in frivolity while the glory of Russian weapons thunders above the cradle of the ancient world, above the grave of Mohammed. But in beseeching your mercy, I seek neither reward nor distinction. I seek only the opportunity to spill my blood for the glory of the Emperor, that I might honorably end my life, a life given by him, so that over my dust the name of a criminal shall not hang. Forgiven by the most highly generous of Monarchs, I feel all the more the magnitude of my crime and am more completely consumed by repentance. But together with these feelings my consciousness opens before me the limitlessness of His mercy, and therefore I beseech you to inform His Imperial Highness of my humble request. If he, who decides the fate of battles and of empires, might have a free moment to take from civic and military duties, please turn his attention to his unfortunate servant. Only in the Emperor's mercy lie my hopes, only in your intercession can I find anyone to take my part. Other than your highness I have no other protector, no other means by which to serve in word and in deed the Most High Emperor, whose throne you, by unalterable right, may approach. Awaiting with great trepidation a word on my fate, and suffused with great respect for you and a zealous devotion to you, I have the honor of abiding, your highness and most kind sir, as your most devoted servant Alexander Bestuzhev.

Bestuzhev's rhetoric was effective, at least within certain limits. Count Dibich delivered the plea to Nicholas I, who responded in clever conformity to Bestuzhev's description of his motives ("I seek neither reward nor distinction"): "Alexander Bestuzhev shall be transferred as a common soldier to the active regiments of the Caucasus Corps with the proviso that in the event of distinction in battle he will not be promoted, but that word of his accomplishments will be reported to me." Bestuzhev was not aware of this proviso and went to the Caucasus to distinguish himself specifically in order to receive recognition and promotion to officer status. High rank could potentially restore his noble station and eventually lead to his freedom. He was mistaken in this calculation, and he paid the consequences by assuming that the warrior-hero's identity, to be restored in leaving the stasis of Yakutsk for the front lines of the Caucasus, could surpass any limitations. His heroic self now acquired new characteristics: a mysterious, criminal past; a sense of the tragic proportions of life and of fate; an indelible feeling of isolation; and heroic proximity to death. He assumed, in other words, that this image of self, derived from his reading, was not only substantive but also adequate to reality.

Upon his arrival in the Caucasus, Bestuzhev visited his brothers Pavel and Petr, but then was almost immediately swept into engagement against the Turks. He was removed from Tiflis, the cultural center. The influence he exercised over young officers (who saw the more grandiose Decembrists such as Bestuzhev as models for their behavior) was deemed dangerous. He was transferred, consequently, to Derbent on the Caspian Sea, where he remained for four years. Here, thanks to his sister Elena's tireless efforts and skill at dealing with publishers and the censor, he began to write for publication again. Within three years his work and the name Marlinsky became household items. His success allowed him to secure the economic well-being of his family—his mother and sisters on the family estate, Pavel and Petr in the Caucasus, and Nikolai and Mikhail in Siberia. He began to make unprecedented sums for his work—ten thousand rubles for the first two volumes of a three-volume collection of his work to date (1832–1834).

During the initial years of exile in the Caucasus, Bestuzhev created more than fiction under the pen name Marlinsky. He also reinvented his self-image, the one built out of a combination of literary archetypes (which his fiction propagated), his code of behavior in daily life as written in the annals of Russian military history, memoirs of those who visited him in the Caucasus, and his letters to family and friends (particularly his publishers, Nikolai and Ksenofont Alekseevich Polevoi). Of the many letters that have survived from the time, there are few that do not advertise the persona Marlinsky in archetypal heroic terms. He dressed like the local natives, spoke with them in their sundry tongues, rode like the Cherkes across the valleys and mountains of the land between the Black and Caspian Seas, and confessed in a rather self-congratulatory tone: "all the natives of the mountains are crazy about me." Bestuzhev was experiencing a complete coincidence between his lived experience and his persona.

In a letter written just months before his disappearance, Bestuzhev addressed his mother, to whom he was wont to confess almost everything sincerely, "I so completely rely on that Providence which has so far saved me from ill, that without the least anxiety, not to mention fear, I approach all dangers [with equanimity]. Fear is a feeling unknown to me. Whatever will be, will be; whatever will not, will not. This is my faith." There is no dissembling here. Bestuzhev's words present with utter conviction an inner consciousness so complemented

Elena Aleksandrovna Bestuzheva, who worked with publishers on behalf of her brothers Aleksandr and Nikolai (1828 portrait by V. Pogonkin, Pushkin Museum of Fine Arts, Moscow)

by literariness that his idea of himself appears thoroughly united with his authentic self. Yet the Byronic proportions of this idea cannot be overlooked. Bestuzhev saw himself as an outcast, a loner, an isolated and doomed man, a martyr. He wrote to his brother Pavel:

> My God, my God, when shall I end this impoverished nomadic existence on foreign soil, far from every means toward gainful occupation?! I pray but for one thing—that I be given a tiny corner where I might lay down my staff and, serving the Emperor in some state service, I might also serve Russian letters with the pen. Clearly this is not desired. Let it be so.

Bestuzhev cast himself as a prophet in the wilderness, forsaken in his own country:

> Not in vain is my fate like that of Byron. What calumny did they not cast at him? What did they not accuse him of doing? So it is with me. My greatest misfortunes appear to others to be crimes. My conscience is clean, but my head is bespattered by disgrace and slander. . . . I am not an inhabitant of the earth; but what can be done when, it seems, everything has conspired to hinder the outpouring of my unspoken truths!

Bestuzhev refers here to his growing awareness that he is not destined to fulfill his secret wish—to be promoted and win his freedom. He refers, too, to scandals and trauma associated with his name. In 1832 his brother Petr began to suffer paranoia. He stopped eating for fear of poisoning, kept to his bed, and ranted even at those, including Bestuzhev, who attempted to care for him. Bestuzhev sought Petr's removal from the Caucasus and won his return home, where, within a few years, he died insane. Then, in 1833, Bestuzhev underwent a scandalous round of inquiries connected with the death of his landlady's young daughter. It was the stuff of fiction. Olga Nestertsova, the victim, would visit Bestuzhev's room to do his laundry, sew for him, and, according to rumor, service other needs. One evening she pranced across the room and threw herself onto Bestuzhev's bed. Under a pillow lay a pistol Bestuzhev kept loaded to forestall thieves, because crime was rampant at that time in Derbent. As the girl alighted on the bed, the pistol fired and the bullet punctured her lung. Two days later she drowned in her blood, but not without having confessed Bestuzhev's innocence in the matter to her mother, a local priest, several officers summoned to the scene, and the physician attending her. Given the sensationalism of the case, its prurient interest, melodrama, and romantic literariness, the case did not end with Bestuzhev's official exoneration. For most of the following year he was subjected to social humiliation by people he had alienated in Derbent.

These events neatly fit the archetypal image of the martyr and loner, the misfit and outsider, that Bestuzhev cultivated in his fiction and personal letters. Bestuzhev's tragic implication in Nestertsova's death inclined toward narrative form, but not in the sense of building a fantasy in which imagination takes the dominant role in structuring discourse. The impulse was in the opposite direction—Bestuzhev's life became fictionalized, renderable in the narrative shape he had educated his readers to expect of him. In being calumniated "like Byron" in society, Bestuzhev found evidence to sustain the belief that a heroic identity fit life and letters both in triumph and, better yet, adversity. The self took on mythic proportions. In fact, Bestuzhev's letters during the Caucasus years become more explicitly religious or spiritual, not in the sense of church tradition and dogma but in relation to his idea of himself and the capacity of that idea to regenerate itself successfully. For him the Marlinsky persona became a capacious idea into which life and death cycles could be absorbed. He began to throw himself into battle with a fearlessness that became more and more detached from mortal considerations:

> I have stopped believing that a bullet can touch me, and the whistle of the shot has become for me nothing but the whistle of the wind, even less remarkable, for the wind at least makes me turn my head, whereas bullets make no impression on me. . . . And so it is, we lose all our pleasures through habit, and the dangers of battle finally bore us when they cease to boil our blood. I, however, am not entirely asleep, and the shouts of a skirmish beckon me like the voice of a beloved lady; they fling me into the fire and into the frenzy of oblivion.

In 1835 Bestuzhev bid farewell to Derbent and began to travel the central mountains and the western and northern slopes of the Caucasus. He saw continuous battle, suffered many diseases that began to waste him, and gradually lost his physical strength. Malaria, intestinal parasites, tapeworm, hemorrhoids, scurvy, and other diseases took their toll not only on his body but also on his spirit. He was sent infrequently to the local watering holes of the Russian aristocracy to take the cure for his ill health, but he was not allowed to remain there long because of the sympathy he elicited from the civilian population. He was kept under constant surveillance; his apartments were searched; and his letters were intercepted and read. Bestuzhev could no longer avoid the realization that his suffering was connected to the tsar and that he could not expect release through distinguishing himself in battle. He began to lose heart and became more serious, brooding, and quick-tempered. Bestuzhev saw little before him but interminable marches and battles in futile military service for the remaining years of his sentence. There was only one thing for him to do, and that was to make a good show of himself. He had within his control the ability to display the integrity of his romantic heroic ideal.

Bestuzhev arrived on Adler Promontory on the Black Sea in June 1837. He made out his last will and testament, apparently for the first time in his life. He wrote his brother Pavel, "I embrace you my dear brother. If God does not grant that we meet again, be happy. You know that I have loved you greatly. This, however, is not an epitaph. I don't think about dying, nor do I long for it to come soon. However, in any event it is best to bid you farewell. When you show this letter to mother, do not reveal this part. Why worry her needlessly?" The next day Bestuzhev again displayed great bravery in battle: he carried the front lines far into the woods, but they were cut off and surrounded. The following day, in the aftermath of the battle, Bestuzhev's remains were sought in the woods, but none could be located. Bestuzhev simply disappeared. Although some witnesses among his troops believed he had been hacked to pieces by the Cherkes natives, there was no conclusive proof that he had died nor any evidence that he was abducted or carried away into the mountains by the natives with whom he shared a mutual attraction. The mystery of his fate created legends as his readers supplied a variety of "endings" that conformed to their favorite Marlinsky plots: he had plotted and faked his death only to be taken into the mountains to live among the natives; he had been killed by a jealous lover in a duel; he had drowned in one of the mighty rivers of the Caucasus; he had gone down a hero in battle.

Each of the "readings" of Bestuzhev's end underscores the linkage of life to literature, which was a belief characteristic of a generation of readers and writers in Russia. This shared belief conditioned the personal, subjective responses the public made to Bestuzhev's life and demise. The image of the romantic hero he projected was received as biographical fact. The rumors carried Bestuzhev's Marlinsky existence forward in time, conferring on him the honor he had sought in society—immortality.

Bestuzhev's readers included private citizens and literati, but they also included government officials and even the tsar. It was as difficult for Nicholas I to accept the death of the hero as it was for the general public. A Cherkes native was conscripted to find Bestuzhev (or his grave) so that rumors could be put to rest. The agent discovered no concrete evidence to support any hypothesis about Bestuzhev's disappearance, and Nicholas I called off further investigations.

As in fiction, Bestuzhev's life was now demarcated by a beginning, middle, and end. But to lift the hero's literary plot out of fiction and place it into life, an entire career was required that could encompass life and letters in such a manner as to prove their coincidence both to the writer himself and to his public. Byron supplied the model for Bestuzhev's belief in the possibility of realizing this desire. Byron had achieved immortality through the identification of fiction with reality, at once sacrificing himself to the romantic ideal of freedom and self-will and bestowing upon the world a body of work that has withstood the test of time. In this last respect, however, Bestuzhev failed in his quest for immortality; the quality of his texts was not sufficient. Later generations dismissed Bestuzhev's art, and in time his name lost the heroic ring that had so moved young Turgenev and Tolstoy.

Bestuzhev's contribution to the literary debates of the second and third decades of the nineteenth century represent his most substantial contribution to letters in that period. He was considered a primary voice for the radical wing of Romantic aesthetics, the one labeled "Decembrist" or "Civic" by Soviet scholars. He entered the literary arena as a critic, not as a poet or writer of prose fiction. He began his assaults on classicist aesthetics, Francophile sentimentalism, and resistance to language innovations from the West in a dramatic, even self-serving, fashion. He wished to make a name for himself and consequently developed his marlinist techniques both to draw attention to himself as critic and to take the high ground in the debates raging at the time over the Russian literary language.

Bestuzhev's contributions to the debates clearly aligned him with the reformers and proto-Westernizers, but this assessment must be tempered by his resistance to French influences in the verbal arts. In his early career Bestuzhev was more interested in English literature than either French or German, and thus his railings against borrowings from France ring a false note. He could be as slavish as the next writer, yet he saw his turn toward British models as innovative. Nonetheless, Bestuzhev managed to distinguish himself in a variety of debates, particularly against Pavel Aleksandrovich Katenin, whom he virtually drove from the literary arena for several years after a vitriolic disagreement concerning lexical and stylistic matters.

In the period from 1818 to the Decembrist Revolt in 1825, Bestuzhev translated approximately twenty works from English, German, and French sources (particularly English) on literary and political topics, and he published more than thirty articles of criticism, essays, critiques, feuilletons, reviews, and letters to the editors of a variety of journals. He also translated a host of theoretical works from Europe, including Francis Bacon, William Wordsworth, and Schiller, and involved himself in anything that caused a row in literary society. He occasionally attacked some of his political compatriots (Somov, Viazemsky, and Vil'gel'm Karlovich Kiukhel'beker). But it was with the publication of his and Ryleev's *Poliarnaia zvezda* that Bestuzhev established himself as a major figure in Russian literary criticism. In each of the three issues of *Poliarnaia zvezda* Bestuzhev contributed a major assessment of Russian literary tradition, from its beginnings to the Romantic period. Interestingly, against his desire that Russian literature exemplify its own national characteristics (*narodnost'*), in order to develop his argument Bestuzhev borrows heavily from Western European literary commentaries. He utilized particularly Jean-Charles-Léonard Simonde de Sismondi's *De la littérature du midi de l'Europe* (1813) as well as the work of August and Friedrich Schlegel. De-

rivativeness aside, Bestuzhev argued for an organic and evolutionary development in Russia of a modern school, one that characterized the radical wing of his generation. His claims were widely refuted by his detractors, upheld vehemently by his supporters, and debated with passion by all sides.

The substance of the squabbles ultimately had more to do with the status of the verbal arts in Russia than with any specific detail. Bestuzhev, his friends, and his opponents advanced the cause of literature in society. By delivering a sometimes melodramatic forum for crystallizing public attention on the arts, they effectively elevated the central issues with which they were uniformly involved and consequently propelled Russian literary discourse to a new level. *Poliarnaia zvezda* played an important role in creating a larger audience, a larger reading public, and a commercially viable literary industry. It was the most popular, widely read, and influential literary almanac in Russia at the time. It innovated what later became known as the "thick" journal of the second half of the nineteenth century. Bestuzhev contributed greatly to the development of a larger intellectual community in two ways, both as a publisher of this powerful journal and as a literary critic who lent theoretical substance to the Romantic cause. He not only gave it a local definition and described its continuity with Russia's literary past but also developed a language through which to analyze specific works from a theoretical and linguistically informed base. Through his extensive practice in a variety of professional guises, from publisher to translator and from critic to literary theoretician, Bestuzhev guaranteed his place in Russian letters. But there was an additional area in which he practiced, one integrally related to his project of fixing a literary identity for himself, not as a professional but as a figure of heroic proportions.

Each issue of *Poliarnaia zvezda* also carried at least one piece of historical fiction by Bestuzhev. It can be claimed, of course, that he used to his advantage a publisher's prerogative to include his own works in the journal. Ryleev did the same and published many of his most famous poems, including the politically oriented collection *Dumy* (Meditations, 1825); in fact it had been a common practice in Russia and Europe for a long time. Nevertheless, Bestuzhev managed to establish his credibility as a premier writer of fiction despite the obvious advantage that accrued to him as editor and publisher. Bestuzhev, in addition to his annual piece of literary criticism, published works of Russian and Livonian history: "Roman i Ol'ga. Starinnaia povest'" (Roman and Olga: A Tale of Old) and "Vecher na bivuake" (An Evening on Bivouac) in 1823; "Zamok

Neigauzen. Rytsarskaia povest'" (Castle Neihausen: A Knight's Tale) and "Roman v semi pis'makh" (A Novel in Seven Letters) in 1824; and "Revel'skii turnir" (The Revel Tournament) and "Izmennik" (The Traitor) in 1825. Another tale, "Krov' za krov'" (Blood for Blood), was to be included in a small issue of *Poliarnaia zvezda* for 1826 (the terminal issue); the story was suppressed in the aftermath of the Decembrist Revolt and was not published until later in 1826, in *Nevskii al'manakh* (Neva Almanac), and only then under another title, "Zamok Eizen" (Castle Eisen).

Bestuzhev's fiction in the pre-Decembrist period was dedicated exclusively to historical topics gleaned from Nikolai Mikhailovich Karamzin's *Istoriia Gosudarstva Rossiiskogo* (History of the Russian State, 1816–1818; revised, 1818–1829) and from chronicles, specifically the fourteenth-century *Sofiisky vremennik* (The Sofian Chronicle) and the Livonian *Heinrich's Chronik* of the sixteenth century. In addition to the tales published in *Poliarnaia zvezda* Bestuzhev also wrote "Poezdka v Revel'" (Journey to Revel, 1820–1821), "Gedeon" (1821), "Listok iz dnevnika gvardeiskogo ofitsera" (A Leaf from a Guard Officer's Diary, 1821), "Eshche listok iz dnevnika gvardeiskogo ofitsera" (Another Leaf from a Guard Officer's Diary, 1821), "Zamok Venden (otryvok iz dnevnika gvardeiskogo ofitsera)" (Castle Wenden [A Fragment from a Guard Officer's Diary], 1821), and "Noch' na korable (iz zapisok gvardeiskogo ofitsera na vozvratom puti v Rossiiu posle kampanii 1814 goda)" (Night on a Ship [From the Notes of a Guard Officer on the Return Trip to Russia after the Campaign of 1814], 1822), all published in various journals and collected in *Russkie povesti i rasskazy Aleksandra Marlinskogo* (1832–1834). It is apparent from the titles that the texts form something of a complete cycle of work focusing on the borderlands between Russia and Livonia, or, at a more comprehensive level, between Western and Russian societies. An examination of four of the works of this period delivers a reasonable idea of Bestuzhev's thematic interests, character archetypes, and stylistic techniques.

"Poezdka v Revel'" is presented in the form of travel notes. This genre permitted Bestuzhev to develop his narrator's identity in complete conformity with the persona of Marlinsky. At the same time the free and open range allowed by the genre supplied the author with ample opportunity to display his gifts as a writer. The shifts from prose to poetry, from historical investigation to critiques of contemporary society, and from minute observation of Livonian customs to the Russian past, display the narrator's erudition, worldliness, and style. Bestu-

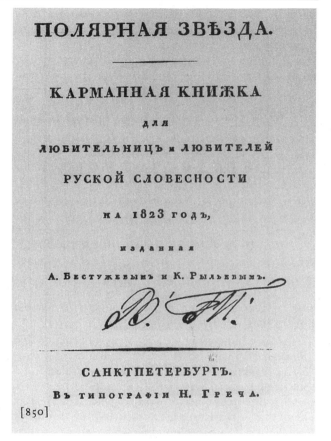

Title page for the first volume of Poliarnaia zvezda *(The Polar Star), the literary almanac edited and published by Bestuzhev and Kondratii Fedorovich Ryleev*

zhev's experiments in the travel genre allowed him to work on character development, setting scenes, and describing local color, all of which were of great importance to him as he moved to the historical genre. In addition Bestuzhev experimented with a new style of writing, one that involved experimentation with the Russian language in a manner of great interest to the Romantic generation. His innovations were of real importance to several of his contemporaries, including Pushkin and Viazemsky, who utilized Bestuzhev's contributions to Romantic, poetic language in their work of the early 1820s.

Freedom of expression was a crucial part of the Romantic canon to which Bestuzhev subscribed, and consequently his narrators play a dominant role in his tales, particularly the historical tales that soon followed "Poezdka v Revel'." The least intrusive is the narrator in Bestuzhev's first published historical tale, "Roman i Ol'ga," a story involving the love of a relatively impoverished noble youth, Roman, for Ol'ga, the daughter of a wealthy nobleman who will not allow the couple to wed. When Roman saves Ol'ga's father from certain death, he receives Ol'ga's hand in marriage. This story represents an anomalous form, interesting for its contribution to a budding historical tradition in the Romantic era but of limited value as a model of the Bestuzhevan form of romance. Its contributions, however, are not insignificant: in "Roman i Ol'ga" Bestuzhev saturates his prose with daring metaphors and striking similes; extensively utilizes aphorisms that play on words in a manner that came to be known as marlinism; stylizes his prose through an assertive use of rhythms, assonance, and alliteration (poetic devices borrowed as much from the poetry of the day as from the Karamzinian prose tradition); introduces interior speech to delineate character; develops historical detail for local coloration; creates a suspenseful plot with Byronic digressions (utilized to "brake" the action for suspense); delivers up a strong female dramatis persona to match the qualities of the hero; and elaborates in clever detail a political subplot that represents a running commentary on contemporary Russian life.

More in keeping with his general practice than "Roman i Ol'ga," however, is "Izmennik," a story set in the Time of Troubles (1598–1613), a period of extremes toward which the romantic and revolutionary Bestuzhev was drawn. Its excesses are typical of his ultra-Romantic style (which combines Radcliffian Gothic elements with self-conscious, modernist Byronic overtones). The story concerns a young man who is betrayed in love, loses in sibling rivalry, and remains misunderstood in society. These experiences cause him to become ferocious, vengeful, and hateful, qualities that lead him to call upon the devil to do his work. Following the adage "call upon the Devil and he appears," a pre-Dostoyevskian demon appears in the guise of a friend and helper to lead the protagonist, Vladimir Sitsky, to his end. It takes five chapters to get there, and getting there is the least of Bestuzhev's interests. Thus, the first four chapters comprise only half of the entire work; the second half consists of the fifth and final chapter. In it Vladimir delivers a romantic confession (a typical feature of the romantic tale, fully expected by the reader familiar with Western archetypes) and commits his heinous act of revenge.

In the first chapter the protagonist's character is established—he once led the city of Pereiaslavl but was ousted for what he calls a misunderstanding. In the second chapter, two carpenters are introduced to develop Vladimir's character further; he is as much a mystery to them as his brother, Mikhail, is a shining example of virtue. The carpenters also reveal that Mikhail and Vladimir had competed for the hand of the fair Elena, a contest Mikhail had won. The third chapter takes place in a dark forest,

as in folklore and Gothic tales, where Vladimir tries to conjure the devil. He fails even when he cajoles, taunts, and challenges the evil force to appear. Yet an old friend of his arrives upon the scene and offers his services. The implication, of course, is that this "friend" has been Vladimir's nemesis all along and will lead him further down the road to perdition. This friend, Khvorostinin, convinces Vladimir to defect to the Polish side so that he might avenge himself simultaneously on Mikhail, Elena, and Pereiaslavl. In the final chapter, where Bestuzhev concentrates all his descriptive powers, the Poles with Vladimir attack Pereiaslavl; the brothers meet in mortal combat. Mikhail refuses to fight his own kin, so Vladimir, who feels no such compunction, slays him. Elena dies too, from grief. This information is reported rather than depicted—Vladimir, in the aftermath of the battle, overhears two Poles discussing the events of the day and the death of Elena. The soldiers, who do not know Vladimir is at hand, abuse him and call him a traitor to his own people. Vladimir, suffering from wounds inflicted during the battle, dies with the image of his brother before him and carries his guilt with him into the next world.

The heroine of the story, as in "Roman i Ol'ga," is represented as a strong and independent individual. Her strength of character is depicted in a dramatic scene prior to the Polish army's assault on the city. Elena steals out of Pereiaslavl into the enemy camp and confronts Vladimir. She tells him that she will go with him wherever he wishes as long as he does not take Mikhail's life. This courageous and selfless act on Elena's part establishes her as one of an extended series of long-suffering heroines in nineteenth-century Russian literature. Yet in a typical Bestuzhevan twist on the Gothic tradition, the episode is revealed to be Vladimir's dream. Although this turn might suggest that Elena's role as a powerful female figure is nothing but illusion, the contrary can be asserted on psychological grounds. The dream sequence is of interest in regard to Vladimir's delineation. In his dream he responds to Elena's act with a correspondingly large gesture—he will not take Elena away from Mikhail, nor will he attempt to avenge himself on his brother and their city. He promises to return to Pereiaslavl to fight for their cause. The dream, in other words, represents his conscience. He does not obey it, however, which complicates his depiction in two ways: first, it underscores the Gothic motif (his actions are controlled by an evil force); second, the dream indicates Bestuzhev's awareness of complexity in human character, something which infrequently occurs in his stories.

"Izmennik" develops a binary opposition of characters, a typical characteristic of Bestuzhev's prose. Vladimir represents a Gothic/Byronic hybrid character (that is, a Western literary phenomenon, symbolized by his going over to the Polish side); Mikhail represents Vladimir's opposite, someone positive and genuinely Russian. The nationalistic element is clearly displayed here. To the conventional traits of the Byronic hero there is added the machinations of the devil. This feature intensifies the Byronic type's curse in general—he is doomed even before the narrative commences. Mikhail, on the other hand, is not fully developed in this work, even less in fact than the shadowy Elena. This deficiency in Mikhail's delineation suggests a political, social, and literary problem that extends well into the second half of the nineteenth century (as evident particularly in Turgenev's novels). The dichotomy, too, is so persistent that it informs socialist realist character delineation in the Soviet era.

As much as Bestuzhev's heroes are defined along a series of binary oppositions (the most inclusive set represented by the categories "good" versus "evil"), so too are Bestuzhev's narrative forms. He wrote Gothic tales with tragic overtones at the same time as he produced tales of comedic romance. The comedic stories, such as "Roman i Ol'ga" and sundry other folklore-based narratives, are structured along the following line: the departure of the hero on a quest, his descent into a netherworld of evil and corruption, his confrontation with the forces of death, his emergence through victory on a prenarrative plane of life-affirming values, and his marriage to a heroine. "Roman i Ol'ga" and "Revel'skii turnir" represent this pole in the Bestuzhev scheme of genres.

"Revel'skii turnir" is a thoroughly political tale, a fact Bestuzhev attempted to hide from the censor through utilizing a narrative tone at odds with the serious Decembrist import of the tale. There is a decided conflict, consequently, between the content of the story and the narrator's persona. The tale is as follows: Edvin loves Minna. He is a wealthy merchant, she the daughter of a knight, Burtnek. For reasons of class, they cannot marry. Minna will preside as queen of a tournament and will be presented in marriage to the knight who can defeat Burtnek's enemy, Ungern. Donnerbats, a bully and drunkard, is encouraged by the girl's father, who in his prejudice prefers an uncouth and slovenly knight to a rich and educated merchant. At the tournament an unfamiliar knight appears, defeats Ungern, and thus wins Minna. The mysterious masked man is Edvin. But class delineation, social etiquette, and law are threatened by the prospect of a marriage between the two. The crowd engages in debate; fighting breaks out between knights and merchants in the crowd; and Burtnek then recognizes the inevitable and, desiring peace in the kingdom, agrees to the marriage.

The theme develops out of the material presented in "Roman i Ol'ga," where Roman was originally kept from marrying Olga by her father (Roman was less wealthy than Olga). In "Revel'skii turnir," however, the complication is not based on monetary deficiency (Edvin may even be more wealthy than Burtnek), but difference in class. This theme carries an autobiographical element: Bestuzhev's mother was from the merchant class. Thus, this "tale of old" in fact represents a commentary on radical politics of the late eighteenth and early nineteenth century that is both personal and broadly social.

The motifs organized around this theme are similar to those found in "Roman i Ol'ga": an unwilling father, a worthy suitor, threat of marriage to a third party, military prowess proven in the face of death, and other accoutrements of plot. These invariant features of comedic narrative are of interest to the reader's appreciation of Bestuzhev's story types, but of greater interest is the way in which Bestuzhev executes his tale. This is his second-longest work of the pre-Decembrist period. The story is divided into seven chapters, most of which are entirely static (as in "Izmennik"), that is, they do not advance the plot or develop character. In the place of plot movement is a figure who becomes more dominant with each passing year—the narrator, who exercises willful control over the story line much in the manner of "Poezdka v Revel'." The narrator frequently addresses his readers, inserts superfluous detail, and indulges character dialogue that brakes the action and impedes progress toward the conclusion of the plot. These techniques serve to depict the narrator himself and to raise the persona of the author, with whom he is rhetorically related, to the highest of hierarchical values in Bestuzhev's texts.

In the first chapter this propensity is immediately displayed. Readers are introduced to Burtnek and Ungern and given the outlines of a plot complication. The remainder of the chapter, which represents more than one-fifth of the entire narrative, is dedicated to the development of a variety of speech types: anecdotes, jokes, witticisms, word play, and marlinist devices. In this way Bestuzhev indicates that the primary event in the narrative is voice, not action; speech, not plot; and discourse, not character development. Inessential conversations, apostrophes to the reader and to the dramatis personae,

Kondratii Fedorovich Ryleev, Bestuzhev's friend and fellow Decembrist

and digressions by the narrator dominate. Dialogue unrelated to plot or character foregrounds the author's persona, permitting Bestuzhev to diminish the political theme while developing his Marlinsky persona extensively.

If Bestuzhev's contribution to Russian prose was of limited value in the 1820s, it must be understood that Russia had yet to develop a substantial tradition in prose; it was the Golden Age of Russian verse. But it is certain that Bestuzhev's contributions went a long way toward developing the style, character types, and themes that riveted his readership in the 1830s when he picked up the pen again in exile and created cultural documents that have not been unraveled from his personal identity for more than 150 years.

During the 1830s Bestuzhev wrote approximately thirty stories and tales under the pen name Marlinsky. Half of them treat the Caucasus, where he lived and fought in exile, and the other half a variety of genres: the sea stories "Leitenant Belozor" (Lieutenant Belozor, 1831), "Fregat 'Nadezhda'" (The Frigate 'Hope,' 1832), and "Morekhod Nikitin"

(The Sailor Nikitin, 1834); the tales of horror "Vecher na kavkazskikh vodakh na 1824 godu" (An Evening at a Caucasian Spa in 1824, 1830), "Sledstvie vechera kavkazskikh vodakh v 1824 godu" (A Sequel to an Evening at a Caucasian Spa in 1824, 1830), "Strashnoe gadanie. Rasskaz" (A Terrible Divination: A Story, 1830), and "Latnik. Rasskaz partizanskogo ofitsera" (The Cuirassier: A Partisan Officer's Story, 1831); one historical tale, "Naezda: povest' 1613-go goda" (The Raid: A Tale of the Year 1613, 1831); and the society tale "Ispytanie" (The Test, 1830). These stories appeared in various journals and were collected in *Polnoe sobranie sochinenii* (1838–1839). The Caucasian narratives, however, represent Bestuzhev's major achievement in fiction during his exile. What is noteworthy about the history piece, society tale, sea stories, and Gothic tales is the speed with which Bestuzhev wrote and published them. All appeared between 1830 and 1832 (with the exception of "Morekhod Nikitin"). The dramatic effect these tales had on the audience may be due in some measure to the rapidity with which Marlinsky's name appeared in print. Although he was virtually unknown in 1830, by 1833 he had become a household name. A consequence of his quick delivery, however, was a uniformity that Vissarion Grigor'evich Belinsky, the leading critic of the day, scorned in his famous essay "Literaturnye mechtaniia" (Literary Reveries), published in the journal *Molva* (Rumor) in 1834. He said that Bestuzhev's talent was one-dimensional and that his stories and characters lacked depth. Belinsky found Bestuzhev's style pretentious, more interested in sound play than in substance, and he found it implausible that all Bestuzhev's characters, independent of class and race distinctions, expressed themselves in the same manner, which is to say, like the narrator: "There is more phrase-making in [Bestuzhev] than real ideas, more rhetorical bombastics than the expression of [authentic] feeling." Nevertheless, Belinsky had to acknowledge that Marlinsky was the rage and that his audience would have labeled him the "Russian Balzac" had it not been more appropriate, from their perspective, to call Balzac the "French Marlinsky."

Belinsky's biases represent a turn in Russian culture, one that would leave Bestuzhev permanently behind. Nevertheless, an objective appreciation of Bestuzhev's contribution to Russian prose in the 1830s must accommodate not only Belinsky's point of view but also Bestuzhev's aesthetics. In fact, Bestuzhev's prose represented popular culture, the art of a growing mass readership, the aesthetics of entertainment, and the belief that life and literature are inextricably linked in a self-mirroring relationship. For Bestuzhev, the uniformity of his prose constituted evidence in support of the fundamental idea governing his every move in life and letters. Wit, flashy figures of speech, impassioned declamations, and emotional tirades represented the language of art and of life for him. Bestuzhev experienced the effectiveness of these forms of speech each day; his audience responded to them in his fiction; and his family and friends harkened to his style in his letters. The orientation toward artificial plots, implausible circumstances, and unnatural relationships that Belinsky denigrated was no more nor less abnormal for Bestuzhev than the conditions in which he found himself in exile—caught between vastly different cultures, languages, religious beliefs, and value systems; constrained to fight an enemy he more frequently admired than hated; and more sympathetic to their behavioral (heroic) code than that of the next generation of Russians. For Bestuzhev, his experiences in exile validated his fiction. His narratives did not distort the reality he attempted to depict; they represented an opportunity to inscribe his idea of life and authentic, heroic selfhood onto Russian culture. Two works of the period indicate the extent to which Bestuzhev questioned his beliefs and then reaffirmed them—the society tale "Ispytanie" and *Ammalat-bek: Kavkazskaia byl'* (Ammalat-bek: A Caucasian Legend, 1832), first published in *Moskovskii telegraf.*

In 1830 the journal *Syn otechestva* (Son of the Fatherland) published in four installments Bestuzhev's first work of prose in exile, "Ispytanie." It was an immediate success and marked the emergence of a "new" author, Marlinsky, whose popularity immediately surpassed that of Bestuzhev in the 1820s. It is a fast-paced society tale that condenses the values of Bestuzhev's generation. It may represent both a polemical response to Pushkin's *Evgeny Onegin* (written 1823–1831) and a Decembrist tract that takes a critical stance in relation to the military officer's and society gentleman's code of behavior.

The hussars Gremin and Strelinsky are stationed near Kiev. Gremin, upon learning that Strelinsky will travel to Petersburg, asks his friend to make contact with a certain Alina, a recently widowed society belle with whom he was once enamored. Gremin wants Strelinsky, a Don Juan, to test Alina's love for him. Strelinsky warns Gremin that he cannot be responsible for his actions with Alina, but Gremin convinces him that their friendship is sufficient to restrain Strelinsky from falling in love with Alina as he tests her faithfulness to Gremin.

Strelinsky arrives in Petersburg and falls in love with Alina; she returns his feelings, and they begin a courtship. Gremin arrives, learns of Strelin-

sky's betrayal, and considers a duel. Enter Olga, Strelinsky's sister, who immediately attracts Gremin's attention. Despite the luring of his heart toward Olga, Gremin's pride overtakes him, and he challenges Strelinsky. As the two meet in the morning light to fulfill the duties of their code, Olga arrives, shames the two for their misguided behavior, confesses her love to Gremin, and begs them to end the affair amicably. They do so; the artificial love triangle is dissolved; and marriages are planned along predictable lines.

"Ispytanie" addresses Decembrist themes from the perspective of the failed revolt. It asks indirectly what possibilities there are for political, social, and economic reform in the aftermath of 14 December 1825 and the execution of five Decembrist leaders. Bestuzhev's society tale answers forthrightly that the course of action available to characters of the Gremin variety are extremely limited. For Strelinsky and Alina, a pre-Tolstoyan flight from vacuous urban society to the countryside, where they plan on making agrarian reforms and alleviating the plight of the serfs, represents a possibility of some hazy, theoretical promise.

Bestuzhev also addressed heroic behavior patterns, questioned their value, and then reasserted them in a feminine guise. At the end of the story Gremin's rash adherence to the gentleman officer's code reveal that it endangers lives in a senseless way. Olga's behavior, archetypically feminine in its impulse toward life, nurturing, and relationships, becomes a heroic counterpoint. The death wish of the men's military code is superseded by Olga's life-affirming and dramatic efforts. Here, in a rare moment, Bestuzhev suggests a more balanced notion of the heroic in life and letters.

From a rhetorical point of view Bestuzhev successfully integrates the theme linking literature and life within his story through the figure of his alter ego, the narrator. The narrator is cast in the third person; he is dramatized and intrusive, self-conscious at times, most often reliable, and authoritative when delivering interpretive comments. There are moments, however, when his perspective is limited. As in the first period of Bestuzhev's creativity, the dramatized narrator performs several services. He reminds the reader he is always dealing with fiction and with the consciousness that creates it: he states at one digressive moment, "Each person has his own fantasies, and each author his own way of telling a story."

The narrator establishes criteria for judging the narrative in all its disparate elements. As a self-conscious narrator he is willful (as in the digressive second chapter on the Haymarket) and ironic (for example, when he satirizes his protagonists and their callow understanding of the world). Readers are asked to adopt the formal distance these traits develop rhetorically, participating in the reception of the text in the spirit of its generation. When the narrator ironically describes Alina, who nonetheless represents the ideological (Decembrist) center of the tale, readers are asked to view the passage from the narrator's perspective:

> Rays of the cold morning sun had already begun to play on the diamond colors of the large window panes of the grafinya Zvezdich's bedroom, but within, behind the triple canopy, a mysterious darkness lay and the goddess of sleep flew to and fro on gentle wings. Nothing is more sweet than morning dreams. As we sleep initial duty is fulfilled toward fatigue, but as one's soul gradually overcomes the body's demands, dreams become more and more delicate. The eyes, turned inward, see more sharply, visions become illuminated clearly and the sequence of ideas, images and dream occurrences become more orderly and even real. One's memory may retain these creations intact. But this is a matter for the heart alone. . . . It beats, yet it is enthralled by the dream's sweet presence. It alone is the witness to their momentary existence. Such dreams guarded Alina's sleep, and although there was nothing quite definite in them, nothing of the stuff out of which romantic poems or historical novels are fashioned, they yet contained everything essential to enchant a youthful imagination. Her initial dreams were, however, less colorful than entertaining.

The narrator makes fun of the romance of the unconscious and the idea that Alina's dreams are literary. The narrator suggests readers are to take the literary material here described with a grain of salt, effectively debunking the assumed linkage of literature and life. While criticizing the belief in literary plots that encompass his characters' psyches, he simultaneously preserves the validity of the theme at another level—the one that links narrator and reader.

Elsewhere, too, the narrator assaults his characters' idea that literature equals life: "In the book of love most charming of all is the page on faux pas: and to each his own. Alina was now no longer the seventeen year old, attracted to every kind of social model or to the seductive logic of anxious seducers, who was swept away by her first dalliance, as by a new toy, and, imagining herself the heroine of some novel, wrote three passionate letters to Prince Gremin." The narrator suggests that the reader familiar with Romantic literary archetypes join him in his critique. He encourages the reader to engage in the task of generating the tale he refuses to narrate, at

least once it has proven to conform completely to literary expectation:

> no matter how sure [Strelinsky] was that he loved and was loved in return, the wondrous words, "I love you," had died upon his lips twenty times without being uttered as if he were required for some reason to conceal them. The Countess [Alina] also, like all women it seems, was as afraid of the words, "I love you," as of a pistol shot, as if each of its letters were made of blazing silver! And no matter how prepared she was for that word from Strelinsky, no matter how sure she was that it had to happen one day, all the blood in her heart rushed to her head when Strelinsky, having seized the right moment, with trepidation began to express, but then concealed his love. . . . I leave it to the reader to complete such scenes for himself. I think that each with either a sigh or a smile may recall and then draw the details of similar moments in his youth. And, surely, each will err only slightly.

Bestuzhev's narrator alternates between facetious and reliable discourse, between a judgment of man's hypocrisy and a castigation of myopic obeisance to a literary model. In each instance the narrator represents the point of view of the author. The limitations the narrator feigns are subverted by the reliability of his judgments. For instance, in describing the ball at which Strelinsky and Alina meet, the narrator exposes the duplicity of high society by summarizing its actions and by peering into what might be considered its collective mind:

> Skimming along the mirror-finished parquet floor, like aerial apparitions, behind their mothers and aunts who were all dolled up for the occasion, the young girls enchantingly, how enchantingly, responded with a slight nod to the courteous bows of the cavaliers whom they knew, and with smiles in response to the knowing glances of their girl friends. And the entire time lorgnettes were directed at them, and every lip was busy analyzing them. Yet, not a single heart beat with true affection for any of them . . . perhaps.

The narrator shifts his perspective from person to person, from couple to couple, stepping into their minds and discovering therein mean pettiness and egocentricity, self-righteousness and false pride: "And so our admirer, having first sat with her mother, an old, successful manipulator, listens with rapt attention to her nonsense, then showers greetings upon the daughter herself, and while dancing, makes goo-goo eyes at her and licks his lips, for he is adding up her riches in his mind."

The complexity in narrator roles that derives from Bestuzhev's play with voices in the text is best revealed in the final chapter of the story, where, because of the narrator's many guises, Bestuzhev places reliable commentary in the personage of another character introduced specifically for this task—the unnamed physician who attends the duel between Strelinsky and Gremin. (Early in Bestuzhev's career a Doctor Loncius played a similar role in "Revel'skii turnir.") After observing the happy resolution of the conflict, this physician states that he must return to his office to make notes for a study he is composing: "'A dissertation, I am sure, on the passions of oysters!' Gremin said smiling. 'On the contrary,' the doctor replied, 'it's on the felicitous foolishness of man.'" Perhaps the most important element of the exchange between the doctor and Gremin is its covert representation of the author's point of view. In that exchange Gremin and Strelinsky are compared to oysters in which the precious pearl of individuality has not yet been developed. By implication, the narrator possesses the prized object.

The linkage of art and life is tenuous. Bestuzhev's narrator takes pains to show the reader that this story is not meant to encapsulate the real world. Furthermore, its characters are not meant to be fully delineated. Through the faults of character, and through the corrective perspectives of the narrator, Bestuzhev's message is made clear—the relationship between fiction and reality must be reconstituted; not dismissed altogether, but reformulated.

This new conception of fiction, of course, was not at all similar to Belinsky's. Bestuzhev's notion of art now incorporated the model "art equals life" from a dialogic perspective. His experiences during and after the revolt, and then in exile, suggested that a new arrangement was more appropriate for the propagation of literature as a molding force in the lives of his readers. Strelinsky's and Gremin's behavioral models are shown to be inadequate to reality, life-threatening, and consequently in desperate need of change. Through satire Bestuzhev underscores the necessity of transformation in the callow heroes' code. As a consequence, the narrator takes a superior position to his characters, effectively distancing himself from them intellectually, morally, and emotionally. The narrator's sundry guises reaffirm a standard of behavior that links social reality and literature—the notion of the self as a series of masks proscribed by social convention. But the performances of selfhood in daily life do not represent the only level on which the modeling takes place. The narrator is developed by Bestuzhev in such a way as to suggest the author's presence. As Alina states to Strelinsky at the masked ball, "The more you conceal your identity, the more surely I know it."

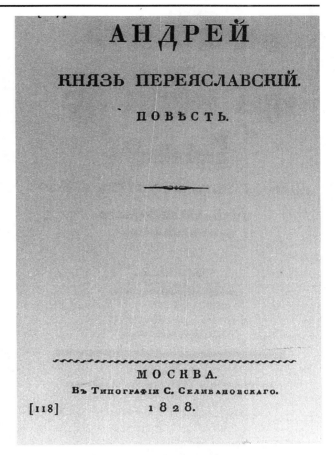

Title page for Bestuzhev's tale Andrei, kniaz' Pereiaslavskii (Andrei, Prince of Pereiaslavl), published anonymously because the author was in exile

Poetry and prose were read at this historical moment with the belief that depth was secured in the identification of author and text. Bestuzhev exploited this belief in "Ispytanie," teasing the reader to fuse author and narrator together:

There are moments in life, hours even, of heavy ineffable sadness. . . . The mind, as though paralyzed, suddenly gets lost. But one's feelings, poisoned by a full understanding of a great disaster, like an avalanche, rushes down one's heart and smothers it in the frigid cold of despair, a mute, but deep, senseless and torturous despair! At such times the eyes have no tears, the lips no words, and even worse, a sadness takes form in the heart, more acrid than bitter tears. And the heart itself, like some subterranean being overflowing with blazing sulphur, strains to throw from itself the heavy burden which is crushing it, but it cannot.

Through the narrator, then, direct association could be made with the persona that Bestuzhev, not without justification, propagated in reality. It is a peculiarity of Bestuzhev's prose of the 1830s that it asserted the linkage of letters and life through the agency not of fictional plots and characters but of the rhetorical apparatus from which fiction is built. The reality to be gleaned from Bestuzhev's new prose was the reality of his life not as it was in fact (Bestuzhev's) but as he perceived it (Marlinsky's).

The didactic intent of "Ispytanie" represents one of its more radical features, suggesting again Bestuzhev's belief that fiction can indeed influence life. The society tales, sea stories, and historical tale that Bestuzhev wrote in rapid succession advanced the same set of values elaborated in "Ispytanie." Although many of these narratives represent, at a superficial glance, the same type of fiction Bestuzhev wrote in the 1820s, there are marked differences. Bestuzhev's protagonists possess those heroic qualities that also endanger their lives. Where this was an implicit, perhaps unconscious, element in the prose of the 1820s, Bestuzhev made it an explicit theme in the 1830s. In many instances the hero is killed, a new event in the Bestuzhev canon. As the protagonist loses his ability to make the world conform to his will, the narrator takes on more of his heroic qualities. The link between protagonist and author is broken in favor of a new bond between the author and his narrator. From 1830 through 1834 Bestuzhev's readers thought they were apprehending the authentic voice of Marlinsky (and for those few in the know, of Aleksandr Bestuzhev). In either case there were the beliefs, shared by reader and writer alike, that fiction embodied the writer himself and that the man represented a sensitive warrior-poet-hero straight out of fiction.

Through his experiences in the Caucasus, Bestuzhev became reconvinced of the value of the heroic ethic. His apprehension of the Caucasian mountain peoples permitted a deepening of the Romantic to such an extent that the code, which he had questioned roundly in "Ispytanie," became an adequate representation of what the real world required of him (and his heroes). Rather than continuing to debunk the hero of the Gremin and Strelinsky variety, Bestuzhev now elaborated the image through projecting it upon the Caucasian natives, the warriors whom he saw as titanic, even mythological, beings. This turn is apparent in what may be the most popular tale of his career, *Ammalat-bek.*

Bestuzhev's fiction about the Caucasus represents the most substantial artistic contribution he made to Russian letters. It generated all manner of response: from the departure of his young readers to fight in the Caucasian wars he described, to the creation of a host of literary clones; from the generation of political debate about the wisdom of the government campaign against the mountain peoples, to

Mikhail Iur'evich Lermontov's paintings of selected scenes from *Ammalat-bek;* and from the production of stage plays based on this work, to outright negation of their aesthetic value. *Mulla Nur,* his second most influential work of the period, appeared in 1836. Between these two dates several minor tales appeared: "Krasnoe pokryvalo" (The Red Veil, 1832), "Rasskaz ofitsera byvshego v plenu u gortsev" (The Story of an Officer Who was a Captive of the Mountain Tribes, 1834), and "On byl ubit" (He Was Killed, 1836). All these works bore the stamp of marlinism.

Tolstoy was fond of these tales as a boy, although later in his life he attempted to debunk the Romantic illusions of the Marlinsky text in order to establish his authority over them. In Tolstoy's *Kazaki* (The Cossacks, 1863) the protagonist arrives in the Caucasus under the spell of Marlinsky's work only to have his expectations frustrated at every step. Alexandre Dumas was impressed by *Ammalat-bek* and translated it into French, later publishing the same translation as his own work under a new title, *Sultanetta.* In the preface to his translation Dumas (perhaps unaware of the previous publication of the story in Russian) wrote, "Among the papers left in [Marlinsky's] room when he died was a manuscript. This manuscript had been read subsequently by several persons, and, among their number, by the daughter of the officer in command in my time, who spoke of it to me as a story full of interest. At her recommendation I had it translated, and finding the little romance, as she had done, not only very interesting, but also remarkably strong in local coloring, I resolved to publish it." The story was also translated into German, Danish, Czech, Polish, and English. Virtually all commentators have noted the interest these Caucasian stories hold for the ethnographer, anthropologist, folklorist, historian, and literary critic. *Ammalat-bek* is a veritable encyclopedia of Dagestan legends, sayings, beliefs, and lexicon. From the epigraph, "Slow to Offend–Quick to Avenge," to the thirty-five footnotes Bestuzhev appends to explain the language of the natives, *Ammalat-bek* is replete with the local color that struck Dumas.

Obvious in all the Caucasian tales is the interdependence of life and literature. In his two most significant works in this genre Bestuzhev took characters and plots from local legends and from authentic historical personages. Explaining *Ammalat-bek* to his publishers, the Polevoi brothers, Bestuzhev wrote on 13 August 1831:

all the events written [in this story] are not made up. . . . As concerns the conclusion of the tale, it has been taken by [me] from local legends. . . . Many witnesses have told me that they had more than once heard Verkhovsky [Ammalat-bek's Russian guardian and friend] describe Ammalat's heady passion for the Seltaneta, who was praised abroad for her beauty. . . . Legend indicates, too, that the Avar khan himself demanded Verkhovsky's head if Ammalat was to win the khan's daughter in marriage. . . . As concerns Ammalat's bestial robbery of Verkhovsky's grave, I have not departed from the original story one iota; soldiers recall the event to this day with indignation. . . . All the anecdotes about [Ammalat's] daring in riding and shooting described in chapter one circulate even now in Dagestan.

Claims of this type have obscured the most cardinal feature of *Ammalat-bek*—it is fictionalized. Ammalat-bek is the head of a village near Dagestan. He protects his people from the Russians who occupy his village while they wage war with mountain tribes. One day the Sultan Akhmet khan of the Avar mountain tribe comes to Ammalat's village, confronts the Russian captain in charge, incites the villagers to resist, and kills the captain. Since Ammalat is responsible for what transpires in his village, he must either face imprisonment or flee with the ruthless sultan into the mountains. He chooses the latter.

Once in the sultan's village, Ammalat falls in love with Akhmet Khan's daughter, the Sultaneta. Before their love can bloom fully, they are separated. Ammalat leaves to raid a Russian camp. The raid fails; many of the Avars are killed; and Ammalat is taken captive. Ermolov, the general in command of the Caucasian campaign, sentences Ammalat to death. A Colonel Verkhovsky pleads for Ammalat's life, stating that he will take responsibility for him. Ermolov agrees, and Ammalat becomes Verkhovsky's ward. The young, idealistic, and compassionate officer educates Ammalat, teaching him to read and write. Ammalat is impressed but not convinced that his way of life is any less valuable. He longs for his sultana and, upon hearing that she is dying (pining away for him), receives permission from Verkhovsky to visit her.

Ammalat visits the sultana and she recovers. Against her wishes, Ammalat returns to the Russians and Verkhovsky. Tormented by the sense of duty that draws him back to the Russian side, by his love for the Sultaneta, and by his captivity, Ammalat begins to resent his benefactor. Hearing of this, the Sultan calls Ammalat to a secret meeting in a cave. There he tells Ammalat that Verkhovsky has been ordered by Ermolov to exile Ammalat to Siberia. Were Ammalat to kill Verkhovsky, the sultan would give his daughter to him in marriage. Ammalat vows to avenge himself. He slays Verkhovsky

along the shore of the Caspian within view of the Russian army.

To prove to the Sultan that he has indeed killed Verkhovsky, Ammalat steals into the graveyard where the officer's body is buried, digs into the grave and decapitates the corpse. He carries the grim proof of his revenge to the Sultan, whom he finds on his deathbed. Half-crazed, Ammalat presents the severed head to the Sultan. Horrified by this blood offering at the very moment he attempts to make peace with eternity, the Sultan curses Ammalat and promptly dies. His wife and daughter, who do not know of the Sultan's deceit, are provoked by Ammalat's insensitivity toward the dying man and blame him for the death. Ammalat is cast out of the community.

During a Russian attack on the village of Anapa, a stronghold of the tribal counterinsurgency, a Caucasian native defies Russian forces with utter daring. He rides within rifle range and challenges their skill. A young Russian officer, Verkhovsky's brother, mortally wounds the brave man. The Russians bring the rider, revealed to be Ammalat, to their lines, where he dies horrified at the specter of his mentor's face.

The theme of death runs throughout the story, from the murder at the outset in Ammalat's house and his death sentence for permitting the crime under his roof to Verkhovsky's murder; from the removal of Verkhovsky's head in a scene of Gothic grotesquery to the sudden death of Ammalat's nemesis, Sultan Akhmet; and from the death of a faithful old steed at Ammalat's hands to Ammalat's wish-fulfilling demise in battle at the conclusion of the story. This is the stuff of Bestuzhev's persona as it directly touches the central fascination of his life both at conscious and unconscious levels. In his youth Bestuzhev had found solace from mortal fear in the flamboyant, fearless persona of the folkloric hero. Undaunted bravado and heroic action supplanted fear. It did not, however, eliminate death anxiety; heroism merely responded to the stimulus. If death was remanded to the unconscious, fear had been assuaged through a choice of behavioral modes.

In exile Bestuzhev discovered death at another level: it could act as a palliative. Once a frightening specter, death became a balm with mythic powers attached to it. Death turned into a conscious construct, again related to the hero (but not to a callow, folkloric one). The mythic hero's confrontation with mortality constituted a transformational ground of lasting value. The hero might in fact die, but unlike the young prince (or fool) Ivan of Russian folklore, brought back from mutilation and dis-

Drawings by Mikhail Iur'evich Lermontov of scenes from Bestuzhev's 1832 Caucasian tale Ammalat-bek: *at top, Ammalat-bek delivers Verkhovsky's head to the dying khan; below, Ammalat-bek in his final battle (from* Literaturnoe nasledstvo, *volumes 43–44, book I, 1941)*

memberment through the Waters of Life and the Waters of Death, the mythic hero is reconstituted by his audience. Immortality is bestowed on authentic historical figures who die gloriously enough to warrant their resurrection by the community in its lore; Ammalat was a case in point. At this level of apprehension, death becomes an aesthetic phenomenon subject to personal control as a theme both in fiction and life.

In *Ammalat-bek* Bestuzhev purposefully informed his final draft with the mythic powers of death. Where, for example, the conclusion of the draft reads: "[Ammalat] fell, the icy hand of death choked out the final breath of his chest, and the imprint of a final ennui fixed upon his brow. It was frightful to see his eyes rolled back," the canonical version is much more extended, focusing clearly on the process of dying and heroic suffering. Death is a solution to the problems of life, and disfiguration holds the potential for a wholeness that eludes the body not yet exposed to its mortality. In the following passage (cited in F. Z. Kanunova, *Estetika russkoi romanticheskoi povesti*, 1973) the italicized portions represent Bestuzhev's additions to the original draft:

> *The shot had gone straight into [Ammalat's] heart. The ligature attached to the main artery broke apart from the sudden rush of blood which gushed through the bindings!* . . . With just a few twitches of the body and several wheezes from his breast, the icy hand of death choked out the final breath of *the mortally wounded man's* chest, and the imprint of a final ennui fixed upon his brow, *an ennui which had slowly gathered whole years of repentance in one sudden moment in which the soul strains to be released from the body, feels equally the tortures of life and of insignificance, feels suddenly all the pangs of the past and all the fears of the future.* It was frightful to see *the dead man's disfigured face.*

Bestuzhev consigns mythic, death-dealing forces to an imagistic space lying between public and private spheres. Whereas death is associated with enclosures, the ongoing life of the community is related to open spaces. At the meeting point of the two, dramatic tension of a carnivalesque nature is created. *Ammalat-bek*, in fact, begins on a festive day that Bestuzhev describes in a manner suggesting the life-death celebration of carnival:

> It was *juma* [a day of rest]. . . . The sea, eternally lapping the beach, rolls in like mankind itself come to play upon the firmament. The spring day was drawing toward evening and all the town's inhabitants, called out surely more by the freshness of the evening air than by idle curiosity, left their dwellings and gathered in crowds along both sides of the road. Women without veils, in colored scarves rolled into turbans upon their heads, in long silk gowns drawn up to the length of short *arkhaluki* (tunics), and in wide-cut pants, sat in rows as lines of children formed in front of them. The men congregated in circles. They stood, sat on their haunches, or sauntered around in groups of two or three. Elder men smoked tobacco from small wooden pipes. Happy chatter was heard all around, and at times the clang of horseshoes and the cry *"Kach, kach!"* (Watch out!) from riders preparing for their races rose above the throng.

The phrase "women without veils" reinforces the break both with normal routine and with the sacred code lying at the heart of carnival. Mankind "come to play" reinforces this idea, as do Bestuzhev's appeals to all the senses: shouts and cries, the taste of tobacco, the scent of roses ("Millions of glowing roses just like sunsets spill in red from the cliffs"). Figurative embraces, where man and plant life are equated, perform the same function ("Almond trees, resembling cupolas, stand ablaze in silver bloom; about them tall vines entwine their leaves in spirals"). An atypical mixture of discrete categories is apparent throughout the text as well, reinforcing the carnival idea. Public celebrations ("You might imagine that on this *juma* the outskirts of Buynaki are even more animated [than usual] with a picturesque mixture of folk") are accompanied by rude speech ("a large crowd of soldiers . . . gathered to heap abuse on the [Russian] train").

Within Ammalat's house a scene unfolds spatially distinct from the *juma* scene but related to it thematically. In public, in the open air, Sultan Akhmet incites Ammalat's village to revolt against the Russian forces occupying it, and while the fight is in progress, he visits Ammalat's house. Within this enclosure a Russian captain enters to arrest the Sultan, whom Ammalat defends out of obeisance to custom—the Sultan is a guest in his domicile. The Sultan murders the captain and initiates Ammalat's life as a fugitive.

Bestuzhev continues the pattern of alternating scenes from the public domain (war, battles, arrests, sentencings, and a variety of confrontations) with the private world of enclosures (associated with death in almost every instance). When the Sultan tricks Ammalat into killing Verkhovsky, their meeting takes place in a cave: "They inched along the steep ledge in continual danger of falling, grabbing onto sweetbriar roots for safety, and finally, after much difficulty, they landed at a narrow opening into a small cave at water level. . . . Therein, Sultan-Akhmet-Khan lay upon a carpet and seemed to be waiting patiently while Ammalat gazed about in the thick smoke which swirled around him."

Ammalat murders Verkhovsky in the open air, that is, in the public eye: "An alarm went along

Bestuzhev's brother Mikhail Aleksandrovich Bestuzhev (1838 portrait by Nikolai Bestuzhev, Institute of Russian Literature [Pushkin House], St. Petersburg)

the front lines, soldiers and Don Cossacks responded quickly to the shot. But they arrived too late. They could neither prevent the vicious crime nor catch the fleeing murderer. Within five minutes the bloody body of the treacherously killed colonel was surrounded by a crowd of soldiers and officers." Then Ammalat beheads Verkhovsky in a deep grave: "It seemed to him that the flame of his torch enveloped him, that hell's own spirit world, dancing and howling in laughter, wound about him . . . With a labored groan he tore himself upward, crawled out unconsciously from the narrow grave and began to run, fearing even to look back." This scene reinforces, too, the notion of sleep as it is linked with the unconscious: "Neither revenge, nor pride, nor even love—in other words, no single passion of his which had moved him to kill the man earlier—could now bestow on him the courage to perform this nameless, godless act of mutilation. Turning the head back to reveal the neck, in a dark forgetfulness reminiscent of sleep, Ammalat began to chop Verkhovsky about the neck." These gruesome physiological details, belonging to ancient sacrificial rites in which the king is dismembered, complete the carnival grotesque.

The drama unfolds between two spheres, the public and private, between life and death. Bestuzhev underscores this intermediate ground, this threshold, as central to the tragic moral of the tale. In the graveyard scene, the distinction is made quite clear: "No stars in the sky; clouds upon the mountains; a wind from the high ridges, like a nocturnal fowl, was striking the forest with its wings; an involuntary shudder coursed through Ammalat at the very threshold of the dead, whom he was daring to disturb." Later, when Ammalat delivers Verkhovsky's head to the sultan, the threshold is underlined: "Surkhay silently pointed to the door, and in utter confusion Ammalat crossed a decisive threshold."

At the conclusion of the tale there is a suggestion that fear of death has not been entirely assuaged. The conscious thematization of death, in other words, may not deliver release from mortal dread. As the sultan dies, Ammalat reads the following on the warrior's face: "The khan lay upon a mattress in the middle of the room, disfigured by a ravaging disease. Invisibly, but unmistakably, death hovered over him. The slowly extinguishing gaze of the dying man showed clearly that he was facing death in utter terror." The hero is not exempt; heroism is no cure. Ammalat's death monologue reflects the same ultimate anxiety even when death has been sought consciously as a solution to the problems of life. But as Verkhovsky's brother observes, there is something to be read in the dead man's face that transcends mortal fear: "A reptilian trace of anguish, well-marked grooves upon the cheeks, deep wrinkles on the forehead, earned not by time but by exhausted passion, and bloody scars disfigured a handsome face whereon some unknowable, torturous pain, something surely more horrible than death, had etched itself." Ammalat gives voice in his last moment to the content of that something "more horrible than death": "'It was so stifling on this earth . . . and so cold in that grave! . . . How horrible to be a corpse! . . . I am a fool. I have sought death. . . Oh, let me return to the good earth! . . . Let me live, even if only one more day, if only one more short hour! . . . Find out for yourself how it is to die!'" Worse than death, it appears, is the longing for life in the face of certain demise.

If only momentarily, Bestuzhev arrests this anguish in a public space that stands on the threshold of art and life. Ammalat was an historical personage who became a legendary figure for his people. Bestuzhev's story extends the legend to a larger audience (widened yet again by Dumas). Immortality may indeed be accessible to the one who dies dramatically enough to stimulate an audience to generate the myth. Bestuzhev's fiction of the 1830s is of lasting value not only as an expression of ultra-Romanticism on Russian soil but also because it gives testimony to a persistent belief in the validity of Romantic art to depict life adequately, which is to say the life of the archetypal romantic hero, artist, and warrior.

Closure of the Ammalat type is what occurred, in fact, with Bestuzhev himself. Whether or not he sought death on 7 June 1837 (masking his intent in heroism), doubts about his demise raised the Marlinsky persona to the level of social text. Somewhere within this cultural narrative it did not matter whether he was actually alive or dead. Although he was now lost to Russian culture as a productive member from whom letters, stories, travel notes, heroic behavior in battle, and a prominent pose in society could be expected, the Marlinsky idea was firmly attached to Bestuzhev's name and has remained, albeit often with prejudice, in the collective mind of the public through the twentieth century.

Letters:

"Pis'ma Aleksandra Aleksandrovicha Bestuzheva k N. A. i K. A. Polevym, pisannye v 1831–1837 godakh," *Russkii vestnik,* 32 (1861): 285–335; 33 (1861): 425–487;

"Pis'mo Bestuzheva (Marlinskogo) k A. M. Andreevu," *Russkii arkhiv* (1869): 606–608;

"Aleksandr Bestuzhev na Kavkaze, 1829–1837: neizdannye pis'ma ego k materi, sestram i brat'iam," *Russkii vestnik,* 87 (1870): 458–524; 88 (1870): 46–85;

"Aleksandr Bestuzhev v Iakutske; neizdannye pis'ma ego k rodnym, 1827–1829," *Russkii vestnik,* 87 (1870); 213–264;

"Pis'mo A. A. Bestuzheva (Marlinskogo) k A.S. Pushkinu," *Russkii arkhiv,* 1 (1881); 425–427;

"Pis'mo Aleksandra Bestuzheva–grafu Dibichu," *Russkaia starina,* 11 (1881): 886–887;

"Neizdannye pis'ma A. A. Bestuzheva k Polevym," *Russkoe obozrenie,* 10 (1894): 819–834;

"Pis'ma A. Bestuzheva–F. V. Bulgarinu," *Russkaia starina,* 2 (1901): 392–404;

"Zapiski A. A. Bestuzheva predstavlennaia Nikolaiu I," in *Iz pisem i pokazanii dekabristov,* edited by A. K. Borozdin (St. Petersburg: M. V. Pirozhkov, 1906), pp. 35–44;

"Pis'ma A.A. Bestuzheva iz ssylki," *Byloe,* 5 (1925): 116–120;

M. K. Azadovskii, ed., *Vospominaniia Bestuzhevykh* (Moscow-Leningrad: AN SSSR, 1951);

"Pis'mo Aleksandra Bestuzheva k P. A. Viazemskomu (1823–1825)," *Literaturnoe nasledstvo,* volumes 59–60, edited by K. Bogachevskaia (Moscow: AN SSSR, 1956), pp. 191–230.

References:

Mikhail P. Alekseev, *Etiudy o Marlinskom* (Irkutsk: Izdatel'stvo Irkutskogo universiteta, 1928);

Lewis Bagby, *Alexander Bestuzhev-Marlinsky and Russian Byronism* (University Park: Pennsylvania State University Press, 1995);

Bagby, "Alexandr Bestuzev-Marlinskij's 'Roman i Ol'ga': Generation and Degeneration," *East European Journal,* 25, no. 4 (1981): 1–15;

Bagby, "Bestuzev-Marlinskij's 'Morechod Nikitin': Polemics in Ambiguity," *Russian Literature,* 22 (1988): 311–342;

Bagby, "Bestuzev-Marlinskij's 'Mulla Nur': A Muddled Myth to Rekindle Romance," *Russian Literature,* 11 (1982): 117–128;

Bagby, "Bestuzev-Marlinskij: Personality-Persona," *Russian Literature,* 22 (1987): 247–310;

Bagby, "Notes on Sentimental and Romantic Prose (and Literary Evolution)," *Russian Literature,* 14 (1983): 103–148;

Dominique Barlesi, "Fonction et Langue de Personnages dans les Nouvelles Historiques de Bestuzev-Marlinskij," *Revue des Etudes Slaves,* 49 (1973): 7–23;

Glynn Barratt, *The Rebel on the Bridge: A Life of the Decembrist Baron Andrey Rozen, 1800–84* (Athens: Ohio University Press, 1975);

V. Bazanov, *Ocherki dekabristskoi literatury: publitsistika, proza, kritika* (Moscow: Khudozhestvennaia literatura, 1953);

Bazanov, *Ocherki dekabristskoi literatury: poeziia* (Moscow: Khudozhestvennaia literatura, 1957);

A. K. Borozdin, ed., *Iz pisem i pokazanii dekabristov* (St. Petersburg: M. V. Pirozhkov, 1906);

E. A. Chamokova, *Proza A. A. Bestuzheva-Marlinskogo 30-kh godov XIX veka* (Leningrad, 1968);

Horst von Chmielewski, *Aleksandr Bestuzev-Marlinskii* (Munich: Sagner, 1966);

Dmitrij Cizevskij, *History of Nineteenth-Century Russian Literature, Volume I: The Romantic Period,* translated by Richard Noel Porter, edited by Serge A. Zenkovsky (Nashville: Vanderbilt University Press, 1974), pp. 100–104;

L. G. Frizman, *Literaturno-Kriticheskie raboty dekabristov* (Moscow: Khudozhestvennaia literatura, 1978), pp. 29–137;

Sergei Golubov, *Bestuzhev-Marlinskii* (Moscow: Molodaia gvardiia, 1960);

Ia. Gordin, *Sobytie i liudi 14 dekabria* (Moscow: Sovetskaia rossiia, 1985);

Janusz Henzel, *Proza Aleksandra Biestuzewa-Marlinskogo w okresie Petersburgskim* (Wrocław: Zakład Narodwy im. Ossolińskich, 1964);

S. G. Isakov, "O 'livonskikh' povestiakh dekabristov," *Uchenye zapiski Tartuskogo Gosudarstvennogo*

Universiteta: Trudy po russkoi i slavianskoi filologii: literaturovedenie, 8 (1965): 33–80;

Isakov, "O livonskoi teme v russkoi literature 1820–1830-kh godov," *Uchenye zapiski Tartuskogo Gosudarstvennogo Universiteta: Trudy po russkoi i slavianskoi filologii III,* 98 (1960): 144–193;

R. Iu. Iusufov, "Dagestanskaya tema v tvorchestve A. A. Bestuzeva-Marlinskogo," *Dagestan i russkaia literatura kontsa XVIII i pervoi poloviny XIX vv.* (Moscow: Nauka, 1964), pp. 83–143;

Faina Zinovev'na Kanunova, *Estetika russkoi romanticheskoi povesti: A. A. Bestuzhev-Marlinskii i romantiki belletristy. 20-30-kh godov XIX v* (Tomsk: Izdatel'stvo Tomskogo universiteta, 1973);

Kanunova, *Iz istorii russkoi povesti kontsa XVIII-pervoi treti XIX v.* (Tomsk: Izdatel'stvo Tomskogo universiteta, 1969);

Simon Karlinsky, "Bestuzev-Marlinskij's 'Journey to Revel' and Pushkin," in *Pushkin Today,* edited by David M. Bethea (Bloomington: Indiana University Press, 1993), pp. 59–72;

N. Kotliarevskii, *Dekabristy kn. A. I. Odoevskii i A. A. Bestuzhev-Marlinskii: ikh zhizn' i literaturnaia deiatel'nost'* (St. Petersburg: M. M. Stasiulevich, 1907);

N. Kovarsky, "The Early Bestuzhev-Marlinsky," in *Russian Prose,* edited by Boris Eikhenbaum and Iu. Tynyanov, translated and edited by Ray Parrott (Ann Arbor: Ardis, 1985), pp. 109–126;

Neil B. Landsman, "Decembrist Romanticism: A. A. Bestuzhev-Marlinsky," in *Problems of Russian Romanticism,* edited by Robert Reid (Aldershot, Hants, England / Brookfield, Vt.: Gower, 1986), pp. 64–95;

Kh. D. Leemets, "K voprosu o semanticheskoi strukture metaforicheskogo epiteta v russkoi proze nachala XIX v. (na materiale proizvedenii A. Marlinskogo)," *Uchenye zapiski Tartuskogo Gosudarstvennogo Universiteta: Trudy po russkoi i slavianskoi filolgii,* 17 (1971): 190–199;

Lauren G. Leighton, *Alexander Bestuzhev-Marlinsky* (New York: Twayne, 1976);

Leighton, "Bestuzhev-Marlinskii's 'The Frigate Hope': A Decembrist Puzzle," *Canadian Slavonic Papers* (1980): 171–186;

Leighton, "Bestuzhev-Marlinsky as a Lyric Poet," *Slavonic and East European Review,* 47 (January 1969): 308–322;

Leighton, "The Great Soviet Debate Over Romanticism: 1957–1964," *Studies in Romanticism,* 22 (1983): 41–64;

Leighton, "Marlinism: istoriia odnoi stilistiki," *Russian Literature,* no. 12 (1975): 29–60;

Leighton, "Marlinskij's 'Ispytanie': A Romantic Rejoinder to *Evgenij Onegin,*" *Slavic and East European Journal,* 13 (Summer 1969): 200–216;

Leighton, "Marlinsky," *Russian Literature Triquarterly,* 3 (May 1972): 249–268;

Leighton, "Pushkin and Marlinskij: Decembrist Allusions," *Russian Literature,* 14 (1983): 351–382;

Leighton, "Romanticism, Marxism-Leninism, Literary Movement," *Russian Literature,* 14 (1983): 183–200;

Leighton, *Russian Romanticism: Two Essays* (The Hague: Mouton, 1975);

Iu. Levin, "Ob obstoiatel'stvakh smerti A. A. Bestuzheva-Marlinskogo," *Russkaia literatura,* 2 (1962): 219–222;

Iu. M. Lotman, "The Decembrist in Everyday Life," in *The Semiotics of Russian Culture,* by Lotman and B. Uspenskii, edited by Ann Shukman (Ann Arbor: Department of Slavic Languages and Literatures, University of Michigan, 1984), pp. 71–124;

Lotman, "Dekabrist v povsednevnoi zhizni (Bytovoe povedenie kak istoriko-psikhologicheskaia kategoriia)," in *Literaturnoe nasledie dekabristov,* edited by V. G. Bazanov and V. E. Vatsuro (Leningrad: Nauka, 1975);

Lotman, "Puti razvitiia russkoi prozy 1800-kh-1810-kh godov." *Uchenye zapiski Tartuskogo Gosudarstvennogo Universiteta: Trudy po russkoi i slavianskoi filologii IV,* 104 (1961): 3–57;

Lotman, "The Theater and Theatricality as Components of Early Nineteenth-Century Culture," in *The Semiotics of Russian Culture,* pp. 125–142;

Lotman and B. Uspenskii, "Spory o iazyke v nachale XIX v. kak fakt russkoi kul'tury ('Proisshestvie v tsarstve tenei, ili sud'bina rossiiskogo iazyka'–neizvestnoe sochinenie Semena Bobrova)," *Uchenye zapiski Tartuskogo Gosudarstvennogo Universiteta: Trudy po russkoi i slavianskoi filologii XXIV–literaturovedenie,* 358 (1975): 168–322;

Iu. V. Mann, *Poetika russkogo romantizma* (Moscow: Nauka, 1976), pp. 235–240, 284–325;

N. Maslin, "O romantizme A. Marlinskogo," *Voprosy literatury,* 78 (1958): 141–169;

Anatole G. Mazour, *The First Russian Revolution, 1825: The Decembrist Movement, Its Origins, Development, and Significance* (Stanford, Cal.: Stanford University Press, 1961);

B. Meilakh, "Literaturno-esteticheskaia programma dekabristov," *Voprosy literatury i estetiki* (Leningrad: Sovetskii pisatel', 1958), pp. 252–301;

John Mersereau, Jr., *Baron Delvig's 'Northern Flowers', 1825–1832: Literary Almanac of the Pushkin Pleiad*

(Carbondale: Southern Illinois University Press, 1967) pp. 8–16;

Mersereau, *Russian Romantic Fiction* (Ann Arbor: Ardis, 1983), pp. 45–47, 53–63, 67–68;

N. I. Mordovchenko, *Russkaia kritika pervoi chertverti XIX veka* (Moscow-Leningrad: Akademia Nauk, 1959);

V. D. Morozov, *Ocherki po istorii russkoi kritiki vtoroi poloviny 20-30-kh godov XIX veka* (Tomsk: Izdatel'stvo Tomskogo universiteta, 1979);

M. V. Nechkina, *Dvizhenie dekabristov,* 2 volumes (Moscow: AN SSSR, 1955);

Nechkina, *Vosstanie 14 dekabria 1825* (Moscow: AN SSSR, 1951);

M. G. Nersisian, *Dekabristy v Armenii* (Erevan: Izdatel'stvo Erevanskogo universiteta, 1975);

R. Neuhauser, *Towards the Romantic Age: Essays on Sentimental and Preromantic Literatures* (The Hague: Martinus Nijhoff, 1974);

S. A. Ovsiannikova, "A. A. Bestuzhev-Marlinskii i ego rol' v dvizhenii dekabristov," *Ocherki iz istorii dvizheniia dekabristov* (Moscow: AN SSSR, 1954), pp. 404–450;

N. N. Petrunina, "Dekabristskaia proza i puti razvitiia povestvovatel'nykh zhanrov," *Russkaia literatura,* 1 (1978): 26–47;

Petrunina, "Proza dekabristov (romanticheskaia povest' pervoi poloviny 1820-kh gg)," *Istoriia russkoi literatury,* volume 2, edited by E. N. Kupreianova (Leningrad: Nauka, 1981), pp. 179–188;

A. A. Pokrovskii, ed., *Vosstanie dekabristov: Materialy,* volume 1 (Moscow-Leningrad: Gosudarstvennoe izdatel'stvo, 1925), pp. 425–473;

A. K. Popov, *Russkie pisateli na Kavkaze* (Baku: Azerba idzhanskoe gosudarstvennoe izdatel'stvo, 1949);

A. V. Popov, *Dekabristy-literatory na Kavkaze* (Stavropol': Knizhnoe izdatel'stvo, 1963);

"Popytka brat'ev A. A. i M. A. Bestuzhevykh izdavat' zhurnal, 1818–1823," *Russkaia starina,* 8 (1900): 391–395;

Carl Proffer, "Washington Irving in Russia: Pushkin, Gogol, Marlinsky," *Comparative Literature,* 20 (1967): 329–342;

E. M. Pul'khritudova, "Literaturnaia teoriia dekabristskogo romantizma v 30-e gody XIX veka," *Problemy romantizma* (Moscow: Iskusstvo, 1967), pp. 232–291;

Pul'khritudova, *Razvitie dekabristskogo romantizma v 30-kh gody XIX veka* (Moscow, 1966);

A. N. Pypin, "Sverstnik Pushkina: A. Bestuzhev-Marlinskii," *Istoriia Russkoi literatury,* volume 4 (St. Petersburg: M. M. Stasiulevich, 1907), pp. 419–479;

A. I. Reviakin and I. A. Reviakina, "Aleksandr Aleksandrovich Bestuzhev-Marlinskii: 1797–1837," *Istoriia russkoi literatury XIX veka* (Moscow, 1977), pp. 154–173;

M. Sadykhov, *Pisateli-dekabristy i Azerbaidzhan* (Baku: Azerbaidzhanskoe gosudarstvennoe izdatel'stvo, 1967);

Van Shaduri, *Dekabristskaia literatura i gruzinskaia obshchestvennost'* (Tbilisi: Zaria vostoka, 1958);

Aleksandr P. Sharupich, *Dekabrist Aleksandr Bestuzhev: Voprosy mirovozzreniia i tvorchestva* (Minsk: Izdatel'stvo Ministerstva vysshego, srednego spetsial'nogo i professional'nogo obrazovaniia BSSR, 1962);

Sharupich, *Romantizm Aleksandra Bestuzheva* (Minsk: Izdatel'stvo Ministerstva vysshego, srednego spetsial'nogo i professional'nogo obrazovaniia BSSR, 1964);

Mark S. Simpson, *The Russian Gothic Novel and its British Antecedents* (Columbus, Ohio: Slavica Publishers, 1986);

N. L. Stepanov, "Pisatel'-dekabrist (A. Bestuzhev-Marlinskii)," in his *Poety i prozaiki* (Moscow: Khudozhestvennaia literatura, 1966), pp. 180–217;

E. Tarasov, "Iakutskaia ssylka Bestuzheva-Marlinskogo," *Dekabristy na katorge i v ssylke,* volumes 8–9 (Moscow, 1925), pp. 249–264;

A. Titov, "Aleksandr Bestuzhev–geroi zabytogo romana," *Russkaia literatura,* 1 (1959): 133–138;

V. Vasil'ev, *Bestuzhev-Marlinskii na Kavkaze* (Krasnodar: Krasnodarskoe knigoizdatel'stvo, 1939);

Vasil'ev, "Dekabrist A. A. Bestuzhev-Marlinski kak pisatel'-etnograf," *Nauchno-pedagogicheskii sbornik Vostochnogo Pedagogicheskogo Instituta v Kazani* (Kazan', 1926), pp. 56–76;

V. Vatsuro, "Lermontov i Marlinskii," *Tvorchestvo M. Iu. Lermontova* (Moscow: Nauka, 1964), pp. 341–362;

Vatsuro and others, eds., "A. A. Bestuzhev." *Pisateli-dekabristy v vospominaniiakh sovremennikov,* volume 2 (Moscow: Khudozhestvennaia literatura, 1980), pp. 119–173.

Papers:
The Bestuzhev family archives are located at the Institute of Russian Literature (Pushkin House) and the Russian National Library in St. Petersburg.

Nikolai Aleksandrovich Bestuzhev

(13 April 1791 – 15 May 1855)

Lew Bagby

University of Wyoming

BOOKS: *Zapiski o Gollandii 1815 goda* (St. Petersburg: Imperatorskogo vospitatel'nogo doma, 1821);

Plavanie Fregata Provornogo v 1824 godu (St. Petersburg: Morskaia tipografiia, 1825).

Editions and Collections: *Rasskazy i povesti starogo moriaka N. Bestuzheva* (Moscow: Grachev, 1860);

Stat'i i pis'ma (Moscow-Leningrad: Obshchestvo politikatorzhan, 1933);

Opyt istorii rossiiskogo flota (Leningrad: Izdatel'stvo sudostroitel' noi promyshlennosti, 1961);

Izbrannaia proza, edited by Ia. Levkovich (Moscow: Sovetskaia Rossiia, 1983).

Nikolai Bestuzhev, a Renaissance man of his time, was an artist, historian, economist, political thinker, writer of fiction, dramatist, natural scientist, agronomist, astronomer, ethnographer, mechanic, and inventor. He was also a revolutionary; thus from 14 December 1825 until his death in 1855 Bestuzhev lived in permanent exile in Siberia, first in Chita and then, upon his release from prison, in Selenginsk. Through his ordeal he lived with his brother Mikhail and, after the deaths of his mother and brother Pavel in 1846, with his sisters, Elena, Olga, and Maria, who moved to Siberia to be with him.

Nikolai Aleksandrovich Bestuzhev was the first child born to Aleksandr Fedoseevich Bestuzhev, a member of the Russian nobility, and Praskovya Mikhailovna Bestuzheva of the merchant class. In this marriage the Bestuzhev family symbolically embodied part of the liberal agenda of Russian Enlightenment thinking in the waning years of the eighteenth century. The union conferred on the family a mark of democratic distinction while simultaneously consigning it to secondary status among the ranks of the nobility, for whom such political dramatics had their place in European fiction, but not in everyday Russian life. Nikolai Bestuzhev carried on the traditions of his parents' union, bestowing on the nineteenth century a legacy of great dis-

Nikolai Aleksandrovich Bestuzhev (watercolor self-portrait; Collection of I. S. Zil'bershtein, Moscow)

tinction and, from the perspective of the government and its supporting cast of nobles and gentry, infamy.

Prior to the Decembrist Revolt, Bestuzhev graduated from the Naval Academy, where his distinguished record permitted him to serve as instructor and mentor to new cadets. He wrote his impressions of his naval voyages of 1815, 1817, and 1824 to Holland, France, and Spain publishing them serially as short pieces, such as *Zapiski o Gollandii 1815 goda* (Notes on Holland for the Year 1815), first published in *Sorevnovatel' prosveshcheniia i blagotvorennia* (The Champion of Enlightenment and Beneficence) in 1821. In 1819 he served as assistant director of the Baltic lighthouses in Russia. By 1823 he had been promoted to the illustrious position of director of the Naval Museum in St. Petersburg. There he began a history of the Russian navy; it remained incomplete because of his exile and was not published until 1961 under the title *Opyt istorii rossiiskogo flota* (An Experimental History of the Russian Navy). After the Decembrist Revolt he wrote a major tract on free trade and industrialization in Russia (though this work has been attested to only in the memoirs of Bestuzhev's fellow exiles), published his observations on Siberian natives (described in M. K. Azadovskii's 1924 study), studied natural science, worked on developing a modern chronometer, designed a simplified bolt for rifles, produced a special conveyance for travel in Siberia, built an observatory for meteorological studies, made gold jewelry, and worked at the lathe to produce furniture and other items necessary for creating a semblance of normal life in Siberia. He, like so many of the Decembrist insurgents of officer rank and their families, helped develop a Siberian intelligentsia. Collectively they opened schools, built libraries, and developed hospitals.

In all his creative work Bestuzhev proved to be engaged and dispassionate simultaneously. In his many paintings of exile he preserved the portraits of his fellow revolutionaries as well as images of their prisons, cells, natural environment, daily lives, and the factories where they were forced to work. These were potentially emotional subjects for Bestuzhev to represent figuratively, but the objectivity with which they are depicted indicate the exercise of a great intellect and the breadth of his capacities to study, examine, analyze, and synthesize information from all sources. In this way he was the complete opposite of his brother Aleksandr Aleksandrovich Bestuzhev (Marlinsky), who represented the Dionysian romantic personality par excellence. Nikolai was Apollonian.

This distinctive quality of mind is also to be found in Bestuzhev's writing—letters, memoirs, essays, reports, and fiction. Prior to the Decembrist Revolt, Bestuzhev participated actively in the literary life of the capital city. He wrote quasi-romantic tales; travel notes; fables; poetry; translations of Thomas More, Lord Byron, Sir Walter Scott, and Washington Irving; and essays on a variety of topics. In 1821 he participated actively in the life of the *Vol'noe obshchestvo liubitelei rossiiskoi slovesnosti* (Free Society of Lovers of Russian Literature). Within a year he was serving on its editorial board, and by 1825 he was the chief editor of all prose submissions to the journal of the society. His own contributions were in genres popular at the time—travel notes and histories in which the emphasis was on the peculiarities of a people, their land, habits, and daily life. But unlike the sentimentalist notes codified earlier by

Nikolai Mikhailovich Karamzin, Bestuzhev's work did not milk the reader's affections. He attempted merely to present objective information in a readable, reliable, and thus authoritative, form. Rather than coaxing the reader to follow the narrator's argument or sentiments, Bestuzhev maneuvered his reader into the dispassionate zone where facts speak for themselves. In many respects, in his travel literature and reports on foreign lands Bestuzhev permits the reader greater latitude than the usual sentimentalist tract and calls upon the reader to produce comparisons and conclusions (often to the disadvantage of Russia) on his or her own terms. His *Zapiski o Gollandii 1815 goda* is a case in point. As Bestuzhev attested during interrogation after the revolt, his experience in Holland represented his entrance into liberal politics (1815 was the year in which Holland ratified a democratic form of government). In *Zapiski o Gollandii 1815 goda,* however, the political theme is understated—essential historical facts are presented, but the reader is left to do the work and is not urged along a direct ideological path by the narrator.

Bestuzhev's trust in the mental capacities of his audience is greater than that of many writers of his generation. This trust is apparent, too, in his paintings and ethnographic treatises. Nevertheless, he was not a dispassionate personality—he was deeply committed to Enlightenment ideals in education, politics, history, economics, and law. But where others, such as his brother Aleksandr or their friend and colleague Kondratii Fedorovich Ryleev, engaged in more bombastic forms of representation (the rhetoric of emotion) and manipulated the reader's feelings more directly, Bestuzhev had faith that reason performs the function of persuasion and that it does so with greater clarity, honesty, and integrity than emotional appeal.

This belief does not mean that Bestuzhev was incapable of traditional sentimental or Romantic modes of discourse. His "Ob udovol'stviiakh na more" (On the Pleasures of the Sea, published in Aleksandr Bestuzhev and Ryleev's *Poliarnaia zvezda,* 1824), indicates how much in control of that type of rhetoric he was. Since the narrative is about the senses, it is justifiable generically (in his mind) to represent the object world from the perspective of the subject and his emotions. Viewed from the isolated perspective it affords (and without reference to Bestuzhev's other work), the text gives the impression that Bestuzhev was a run-of-the-mill secondary literary figure bent on reproducing the dominant literary style. Nothing

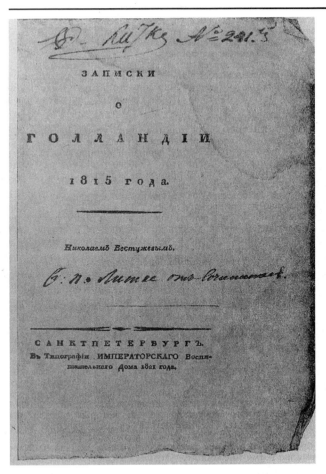

Title page for Bestuzhev's Zapiski o Gollandii 1815 goda
*(Notes on Holland for the Year 1815), inscribed "To P. Litke,
from Author" (from M. Iu. Baranovskaia,* Dekabrist
Nikolai Bestuzhev, *1954)*

tail. The meager attempt at psychological understanding remains flat, the vocabulary formulaic, and the metaphors devoid of interest. Clearly, Bestuzhev's reason could not give over to the flamboyant tastes of the Romantic. He remained throughout his life an Enlightenment figure.

What Bestuzhev's fiction lacked, however, his objective reportage possessed—drama, tension, and inherent interest. His "14 dekabria 1825 goda" (published in Aleksandr Ivanovich Herzen's *Poliarnaia zvezda,* 1861), which gives a brief account of the day of the revolt from a personal perspective, is a testimony to concise language and compact description. This precision is not so much a function of the relation of the memoir to direct experience but of Bestuzhev's belief in the value of representational, historical discourse. The same cannot be said with any assurance about his fictional works. Romantic ardor had no place in his fictional vocabulary—he could not produce it. But vivid life—where the thing has the capacity to represent itself without the necessity of metaphoric adornment or rhetorical embellishment, without recourse to fantasy or detachment from reality—arrested Bestuzhev's attention and commanded his allegiance:

> With the fifth and sixth round the column trembled, and when I looked around I saw between me and all others in flight at the other end of Senate Square hundreds of sacrifices to freedom raked by grapeshot. I had to follow the general movement and, with a dead feeling in my soul, picked my way among those who had been killed. There was no motion among them, no cries, no moans, not a groan, only in the intervals between shots could the hot blood streaming along the pavement, melting the snow, turning crimson, freezing, be heard.

Bestuzhev's fiction published in the aftermath of the Decembrist Revolt, although accomplished sufficiently to be counted as a serious contribution to a growing Russian prose tradition, harkens back to the Sentimentalist era. "Traktirnaia lestnitsa" (The Inn Stairs, published in *Severnye tsvety,* 1825) is typical of the frame tales of the early part of the century in general and of Washington Irving's example in particular. It recounts the pathetic tale of an old man, whom the narrator meets in Copenhagen at an inn, and his clandestine relations with a married woman. It is a morality tale about the fruits of illicit love (an illegitimate child) and the tragedy thereby produced. "Pokhorony" (The Funeral, 1829), although of psychological interest in the aftermath of the revolt, is also a throwback to earlier models. Its belaboring of a set of binary oppositions (rich/poor, high society/lower-class life, external appearance/internal reality) is too automatic, and its sentimental

could be farther from the truth. His capacity to elicit the discourse mode required by any genre in which he practiced is in keeping with his intellectual abilities, his belief in the control of emotion by reason, his trust in order, and his faith in rationality. In this way he was diametrically opposed to many of his contemporaries.

Bestuzhev's tendencies toward reportage, object-orientation, and dispassionateness did him a disservice when he was writing fiction. For example, his "Gugo Fon-Brakht: Proizshestvie XIV stoletiia" (Hugo von Bracht: An Episode from the Fourteenth Century, published in *Sorevnovatel' prosveshcheniia i blagotvoreniia,* 1823) is as wild and romantic a tale (in terms of content) as any of his brother Aleksandr's famous Livonian tales; yet even though the story is full of violence, upheaval, daring, and dastardly deeds (seduction, sea battles, murders, live burial), the narrative remains undramatic. No tension is built, no suspense maintained, no dialogue re-created, and no critical confrontation developed in dereference to a dog's proverbial faithfulness to its master (as in Byron's "Darkness," a popular poem at the time) helps consign the work to tertiary status.

"Shlissel'burgskaia stantsiia: istinnoe proisshest-vie" (Schlisselburg Station: A True Event, written in 1830–1832) stands on the border of fiction and auto-biography. Typical of Bestuzhev, because this piece has an objective correlative, its narrator bears an authoritative voice that carries the story forward with complete commitment to its purposes—to enter-tain and edify. The "fiction" is merely a mask for the memoir it is. Although presented in the guise of fiction, with descriptions of character, setting, and local color, with a plot, dialogue, narrator's digres-sions, asides, and other such accoutrements, the work was really occasioned by the prodding of fam-ily and friends as to the reasons Bestuzhev never married.

The original title of the work in fact was "Otchego ia ne zhenat" (Why I Am Not Married). Its plot is simple. The narrator is traveling in foul weather to the Lake Ladoga region. He stops to change horses, is delayed in receiving them, and subsequently meets a young, beautiful widow who is likewise delayed. They draw close together dur-ing their time at the post station, but nothing comes of the relationship later. The story was first pre-sented by Bestuzhev's sister Elena to *Semeinyi krug* (The Family Circle) for publication in 1858, but she withdrew it from consideration because the censor declared that the story would have had to appear without the author's name. This condition was be-cause Bestuzhev lived in exile, along with many fel-low Decembrists, and in 1826 Tsar Nicholas I had declared that their work was not allowed to appear in print under their real names. His ruling lasted in some publishing quarters well after his death. When the Bestuzhev family archivist, M. I. Semevsky, at-tempted to extract the heroine's true identity from Bestuzhev's brother Mikhail, the latter refused to di-vulge the secret. Mikhail merely attested that the fig-ure of the heroine had been altered in the story in order to protect the object of Bestuzhev's interest from exposure (she was already married, and he de-cided never to marry because he would give his heart to no other).

"Shlissel'burgskaia stantsiia" is one of the more interesting of Bestuzhev's works. Clearly the fusion of the formal characteristics of fiction with the objective and personal facts from his biography engendered the very discourse the author was in-clined to avoid when writing romantic fiction (which is detached, in his opinion, from the every-day world). The failure of his experiments in fiction is here countered by an aesthetic success that can

Portrait by Bestuzhev of fellow Decembrist Sergei Krivtsov, 1828 (from V. V. Afanas'ev, ed., I Love My Native Land: In Lermontov's Footsteps, 1989)

only be explained by the relationship of the subject matter to reality. It was when Bestuzhev engaged what he viewed as the real world that his talents were summoned with conviction. His prose style be-came adequate to the reality he wished to depict, and his rhetoric was filled with the voice of author-ity that derives from the Enlightenment writer's confidence in his knowledge of the matter at hand.

The fiction Bestuzhev created that made the greatest aesthetic impact is actually not fiction, but the appearance of it. In this contradiction the image of the man emerges. An Enlightenment figure of the late eighteenth century, Bestuzhev could never make the transition to the Romantic age. His is a literature of fact that neither engages the excesses of fantasy nor allows the willfulness of the Romantic code, as embodied in its art, to affect his perception of world, self, or other. In this respect he was the polar oppo-site of his younger brother, Aleksandr, who gave over wholly to the proposition that art informs life and that meaningfulness in the formation of a world-view, of a self, and of relations with others was manifest at the moment when lived experience coin-cided either with plots represented on the pages of European and Russian works or with stage produc-tions in St. Petersburg and Moscow.

Watercolor self-portrait of Bestuzhev painting in Chita, circa 1828–1830 (The Institute of Russian Literature [Pushkin House], St. Petersburg)

Bestuzhev was an empiricist and rationalist and thus prefigured many of the beliefs (without the excesses) of the post-Romantic generation (which included Nikolai Gavrilovich Chernyshevsky and Nikolai Aleksandrovich Dobroliubov). Thus, his work printed under the pretext of artfulness is highly referential. It was not uncommon in this period, even for ultra-Romantics such as his brother Aleksandr, to read fictional pieces as texts encoded with personal information about the author. Those readers privileged with personal or biographical information, which would permit them to ascertain the direct relationship of the text to fact, experienced the coincidence of the two domains as the moment of discovery, the epiphany toward which the reading was directed. Bestuzhev dispensed with the conceit and displayed himself in an unmediated fashion. For example, since he had already published works such as "Ob udovol'stviiakh na more," reference to his naval career or maritime propensities, registered across the boundaries of fiction and fact (in works such as "Shlissel'burgskaia stantsiia"), render his fiction mere biography: "I was already approaching Schlisselburg, but as a man who had served at sea and only rarely had enjoyed the opportunity of travel on land, particularly in a Russian post coach, felt quite distinctly the difference between land and sea transportation, although in this instance I certainly had the right to claim that I was traveling on a sea of muck accompanied by bounces, knocks and bumps." The biographical reference gives the passage its "moment of insight," but only for those readers initiated in the code through which biography and this semifictive account converged. Other readers remained in the dark about the secret heart of the text, which, given the deficiencies of the work, comprises one of its greater pleasures.

The impulse to direct fictional narrative toward a reality coefficient, which interested Bestuzhev most, makes his literature of fact polemical. He assaults the conceits of writers, such as his brother, who in daily life and in fiction generate public personas from a Byronic cloth: "Don't believe people, madam: their wealth often consists of no more than ornate phrases," says the narrator of "Shlissel'burgskaia stantsiia" to his traveling companion—that is, to the woman with whom Bestuzhev fell in love. Bestuzhev's narrator presents himself as the counterpoint to the phrasemongers of his generation, to the mindless and empty forms of personality that debased the authenticity Bestuzhev represented in his person.

Bestuzhev warned his younger brother Aleksandr that he should be wary of the Romantic's code of ethics. Because the ego was valued beyond the needs of the community and the self was deemed a

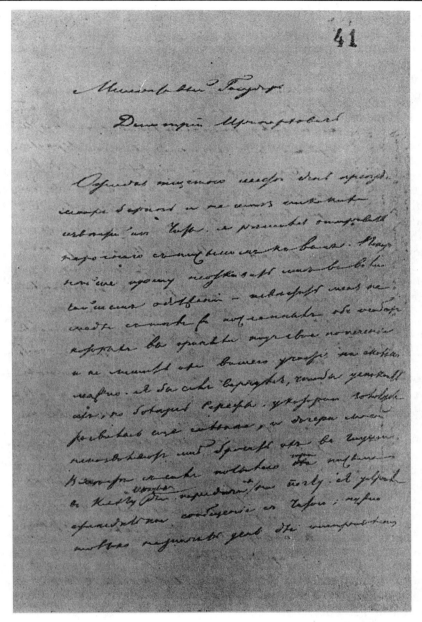

Letter from Bestuzhev to Dmitrii Irinarkhovich Zavalishin, 10 May 1853 (from M. Iu. Baranovskaia, Dekabrist Nikolai Bestuzhev, *1954)*

demigod, Bestuzhev found that code morally bankrupt. Seeing that Aleksandr was inclined to follow the behavioral model of his contemporaries, he challenged the values posited by them in order to wrest his brother from the clutches of a flashy, egocentric lifestyle. Bestuzhev lambasted the "militaire's" propensity for dueling—it advanced a superficial value (dominance) over any substantive principle. Bestuzhev believed first and foremost that one must maintain a consistent set of rules that apply in all circumstances in life. He was opposed to the frivolous use of language by aristocratic youths for whom the word signified the opportunity for wit rather than the occasion for referencing "the thing in itself." He railed against the devaluation of proportion and measure in conducting one's daily affairs both in the public and private sphere, and he loathed the sundry masks worn in his brother's guard officer world for the sole purpose of manipulating others' perceptions. He could not abide the relativity of values in the Romantic generation. Neither could he accept the mutability of the sign such relativity asserted.

For Bestuzhev, there is an objective and verifiable exterior world, not only of things but also of principles and personalities. In all he endeavored to accomplish in his life, he founded his activities on the notion that the "thing in itself" existed and on the belief that its essence is immutable.

This belief lay at the heart of all Bestuzhev's creativity—from the special conveyance he built to manage the difficulties of travel in Siberia to the paintings he made of his surroundings and friends in exile. Bestuzhev's greatest legacy, perhaps, lies in these paintings. They preserve an historical moment in Russian cultural history that would otherwise be lost. The significance of these works, however, lies beyond their mere historical value. It is Bestuzhev's technique which arrests attention, and that is because it is another part of his understanding that the world of appearances has substance which can be made concrete through representational art.

Bestuzhev's portraits of the Decembrists do not attempt to capture some hidden, subsurface "truth" emanating from the individual's face; consequently the portraits do not indulge the subjectivist mannerisms of Romantic art. Rather, Bestuzhev delivers an unembellished representation of the figure as presented to his eyes during the process of painting, during the process of rendering the subject in as objective a manner as possible. The clothes on the figures are those worn on the occasion; they are not symbolic of anything deep, mysterious, or profound. They are signs of the "thing in itself." The variety in the portraits is due to human difference—not ideologically or theoretically, but in fact.

Much the same can be said of Bestuzhev's landscapes. His representations of the fortresses in which they were incarcerated, factories where they worked, and domiciles in which they lived, are rendered in a fashion that suggests objectivity before any subjective principle or hidden purpose (political or otherwise). The three-dimensional images are drawn with a kind of mathematical exactitude, not necessarily pleasing to the eye but certainly suggestive of Bestuzhev's desire to deliver the object without bias. He endeavored to eliminate the problem of point of view through a dry and scientific capturing of objective space—the intersection of lines, the meeting place of man-made structures against the background of nature, the crossing point of order and what might first appear to be disorder (but which is for Bestuzhev another level of order).

Bestuzhev was at heart an Enlightenment man, and he shared little with the next generation other than, in broad outline, its political beliefs. He was at his best with his tools, implements and intellect, and least inspired when using the mode of fiction. His contribution to Russian intellectual and cultural history cannot be denied. He was a unique force in Russian politics, a consistent and active source of energy in the development of a more modern Siberia, and a powerful witness to the compelling nature of materialist and empirical philosophy.

Letters:

M. K. Azadovskii, ed., *Vospominaniia Bestuzhevykh* (Moscow-Leningrad: AN SSSR, 1951);

Dekabristy, edited by L. M. Ivanova (Moscow, 1955), pp. 233–254.

Biographies:

M. Iu. Baranovskaia, *Dekabrist Nikolai Bestuzhev* (Moscow: Goskul'tprosvetizdat, 1954);

Il'ia Samoilovich Zil'bershtein, "Nikolai Bestuzhev i ego zhivopisnoe nasledie," in *Literaturnoe nasledstvo,* volume 60, part 2 (Moscow-Leningrad: AN SSSR, 1956), pp. 7–429;

Zil'bershtein, *Khudozhnik, dekabrist Nikolai Bestuzhev* (Moscow: Izobrazitel'noe iskusstvo, 1988).

References:

M. K. Azadovskii, *Nikolai Bestuzhev—etnograf'* (Irkutsk, 1924);

Lidia K. Chukovskaia, *Dekabrist Nikolai Bestuzhev, issledovatel' Buriatii* (Moscow-Leningrad: Gosudarstvennoe izdatel'stvo geograficheskoi literatury, 1950);

Ia. Gordin, *Sobytie i liudi 14 dekabria* (Moscow: Sovetskaia Rossiia, 1985);

S. I. Mashinskii, ed., *Pisateli-dekabristy v vospominaniiakh sovremennikov,* volume 2 (Moscow: Khudozhestvennaia literatura, 1980);

Anatole G. Mazour, *The First Russian Revolution, 1825: The Decembrist Movement, Its Origins, Development, and Significance* (Stanford, Cal.: Stanford University Press, 1961);

John Mersereau Jr., *Russian Romantic Fiction* (Ann Arbor: Ardis, 1983), pp. 49–51, 63–64, 80–81;

Vladimir Orlov, ed., *Dekabristy: antologiia,* volume 2 (Leningrad: Khudozhestvennaia literatura, 1975);

Galina E. Pavlova, *Dekabrist Nikolai Bestuzhev—istorik russkogo flota* (Moscow: Voenizdat, 1953);

Pavel E. Shchegolev, ed., *Vospominaniia brat'ev Bestuzhevykh* (Petrograd: Izdatel'stvo Ogni, 1917).

Papers:

The Institute of Russian Literature (Pushkin House) and the Russian National Library in St. Petersburg house the Bestuzhev family archives.

Faddei Venediktovich Bulgarin

(24 June 1789 – 1 September 1859)

Ronald D. LeBlanc
University of New Hampshire

BOOKS: *Sochineniia*, 5 volumes (St. Petersburg: N. Grech, 1827–1828);

Kartina voiny Rossii s Turtsiei (St. Petersburg, 1829);

Ivan Vyzhigin, nravstvenno-satiricheskii roman, 4 volumes (St. Petersburg: Pliushar, 1829);

Vospominaniia o nezabvennom Aleksandre Sergeeviche Griboedove (St. Petersburg: N. Grech, 1830);

Dimitrii Samozvanets, istoricheskii roman, 4 volumes (St. Petersburg: A. Smirdin, 1830);

Sochineniia, 12 volumes (St. Petersburg: A. Smirdin, 1830);

Kartina voiny Rossii s Turtsiei v tsarstvovanie Imperatora Nikolaia I (St. Petersburg: N. Grech, 1830);

Petr Ivanovich Vyzhigin, nravoopisatel'nyi-istoricheskii roman XIX veka, 4 volumes (St. Petersburg: I. Zaikin, 1831);

Mazepa, 2 volumes (St. Petersburg: A. Smirdin, 1833–1834);

Pamiatnye zapiski tituliarnogo sovetnika Chukhina, ili Prostaia istoriia obyknovennoi zhizni, 2 volumes (St. Petersburg: A. Smirdin, 1835);

Sochineniia, 3 volumes (St. Petersburg: Guttenbergov, 1836);

Rossiia v istoricheskom, statisticheskom, geograficheskom i literaturnom otnosheniiakh: ruchnaya kniga dlia russkikh vsekh soslovii, 2 volumes (St. Petersburg: Pliushar, 1837–1838);

K portretu Nikolaia Ivanovicha Grecha (St. Petersburg: N. Grech, 1838);

Letniaia progulka po Finliandii i Shvetsii v 1838 godu (St. Petersburg: Ekspeditsii zagotovlennia gosudarstvennykh bumag, 1839);

Polnoe sobranie sochinenii, 7 volumes (St. Petersburg: N. Grech, 1839–1844);

Komary. Vsiakaia vsiachina, roj pervyi (St. Petersburg: Journal de S. Petersbourg, 1842);

Ocherki russkikh nravov; ili, Litsevaia storona i iznanka roda chelovecheskogo (St. Petersburg: M. D. Ol'khin, 1843);

Suvorov (St. Petersburg: M. D. Ol'khin, 1843);

Vospominaniia; otryvki iz vidennago, slyshannago i ispytannago v zhizni, 6 volumes (St. Petersburg: M. D. Ol'khin, 1846–1849);

Sochineniia (Moscow: Sovremennik, 1990);

Vsiakaia vsiachina: literaturno-kriticheskie stat'i (Kharkov: Osnova, 1991).

Edition in English: *Ivan Vejeeghen; or, Life in Russia*, 2 volumes, translated by George Ross (London: Whittaker, Treacher, 1831; Philadelphia: Carey & Lea, 1832).

OTHER: *Severnyi arkhiv*, edited by Bulgarin and Nikolai Ivanovich Grech (1822–1828);

Literaturnye listki, edited by Bulgarin (1823–1824);

Syn otechestva, edited by Bulgarin and Grech (1825–1840);

Russkaia Taliia, edited by Bulgarin (St. Petersburg: N. Grech, 1825);

Severnaia pchela, edited by Bulgarin and Grech (1825–1859);

Detskii sobesednik, edited by Bulgarin (1826–1827);

Ekonom, edited by Bulgarin and V. P. Burnashev (1841–1853);

Kartinki russkikh nravov, 6 volumes, edited by Bulgarin (St. Petersburg: Iu. Iungmeister, 1842).

Few figures in Russian literary history have been as universally reviled and categorically condemned as Faddei Bulgarin (Tadeusz Bułharyn). This nineteenth-century Polish expatriate is seldom remembered in his adopted country for any of his literary accomplishments. Instead he is known mainly for his unscrupulous practices as a journalist, his alleged service as a spy for the tsar's secret police, his espousal of archreactionary political views as a newspaper editor, and his merciless hounding, as a literary critic, of the great national poet Aleksandr Pushkin. Bulgarin's name, in fact, has become virtually synonymous in Russia with viciousness, opportunism, and avarice of the most amoral kind. Such widespread disdain for Bulgarin's disagreeable personality traits and unethical conduct has unfairly colored critical judgment of his considerable achievements as a writer, as well as his important contributions to Russian literature as a critic, journalist, and publisher. Probably few peo-

Faddei Venediktovich Bulgarin (portrait by Vasilii Fedorovich Timm; from Russkii khudozhestvennyi listok *[Russian Art Sheet])*

ple today realize that Bulgarin was a literary pioneer who introduced several important prose genres into Russian literature, a popular and prolific novelist who wrote the first Russian best-seller, as well as a successful editor and publisher who helped give shape to nineteenth-century Russian journalism.

The story of Bulgarin's life is so muddied by rumors, accusations, and justifications that it is difficult to reconstruct a truly accurate biography of this writer. The three main sources upon which subsequent biographical accounts of his life have been based are all, in one way or another, patently unreliable. Bulgarin's own *Vospominaniia* (Memoirs, 1846–1849), for example, cannot be trusted, since the author obviously attempts to cover up some of the more embarrassing episodes from his past. Nikolai Ivanovich Grech likewise provides a less-than-reliable biographical sketch of Bulgarin in his *Zapiski o moei zhizni* (Notes about My Life, 1886), since those memoirs were written after the two longtime friends had quarreled irreconcilably in 1853. Finally, Mikhail Lemke's *Nikolaevskie zhandarmy i literatura 1826–1855 gg.* (The Gendarmes of Nicholas I and Russian Literature, 1826–1855, 1909) is a strongly biased and polemical work that relies more on un-

substantiated hearsay than on factual evidence. What is known for certain is that Tadeusz Bułharyn was born in Pieryszew, an estate in the Minsk province of Belorussia, on 24 June 1789. Both of his parents hailed from a long line of Polish nobility, and the family held estates in the western part of Russia. His father, Benedykt Bułharyn, was a civil-military commissar who took an active part in the revolutionary uprising led by Tadeusz Kościuszko in 1794 in reaction to the Second Partition of Poland. A staunch republican, the elder Bułharyn was exiled to Siberia in 1796, reportedly for killing a Russian general, Voronov, during the Polish insurrection; but he was pardoned by Paul I a year later, and he apparently died soon thereafter, around 1799. Shortly after her husband's arrest, Bulgarin's mother (née Aniela Buczyńska) took her family to live in St. Petersburg, where in 1798 young Faddei was accepted into the school of the Corps of Cadets. Immersed in an academic atmosphere that introduced him to contemporary works of European and Russian literature, Bulgarin soon began writing fables, satires, poems, and play fragments. Although he attended Orthodox church services in St. Petersburg during the years of his schooling in the Russian capital, Bulgarin claimed that in order to please his mother he remained a Roman Catholic throughout his life. Indeed, all five of his children (four sons and a daughter) would later be brought up Catholic as well.

Upon his graduation from the Corps of Cadets in 1806, Bulgarin was commissioned as a cornet in the Russian army and assigned to an Uhlan regiment stationed in the capital. In 1807 his regiment was sent to Prussia, where Bulgarin saw his first military action in the Battle of Friedland against the French army. Bulgarin was decorated with the Order of St. Anna, Third Class, for his valor in that battle, reportedly suffering a serious stomach wound from which he had to spend several weeks recuperating at the hospital in Königsberg. During the next few years, while Russia was at war with Sweden, Bulgarin was stationed mainly in Finland and was later transferred to the garrison at Kronstadt as a result of satiric verses he allegedly composed about the regimental commander, the Grand Duke Konstantin. In 1811, while living in Revel, where he seems to have fallen upon particularly hard times both financially and emotionally, Bulgarin was discharged from the army for poor conduct. He spent time next in Warsaw and Paris, where, seemingly motivated by a latent patriotism that had awakened in his soul, Bulgarin enlisted in the Polish Legion of Napoleon's army. He saw action in the French campaigns in Spain and Italy and then served in Marshall Oudinot's corps that fought against Russian forces under the command of Prince Wittgenstein in Lithuania and Belorussia in 1813. Bulgarin, who had long been an admirer of Napoleon, claims that during this time he actually met the French emperor personally, an event he would later describe in his military sketch, "Znakomstvo s Napoleonom na avanpostakh pod Bautsenom v 1813 g." (Becoming Acquainted with Napoleon at the Outpost near Bautzen in 1813), included in the 1830 edition of his collected works. Captured by Prussian forces in France and turned over to the Russians as a prisoner of war, Bulgarin made his way back to Warsaw, where he was released as a result of the tsar's manifesto of August 1814, which granted full amnesty to those Poles who had served on the enemy side during the war.

In his memoirs Bulgarin tried to conceal the fact that he had once fought against the Russians during the Napoleonic invasion. His literary opponents during the late 1820s and early 1830s, however, would take advantage of every opportunity to embarrass Bulgarin publicly about his service in the French army. Indeed, his enemies repeatedly exploited Bulgarin's war record to make their point that this Polish renegade had long been an unscrupulous opportunist who lacked any firm moral code or personal loyalties. In fairness to Bulgarin, however, it should be pointed out that this alleged coward and turncoat was in fact decorated for bravery in combat and that he enlisted in the Polish Legion at a time when Russia and France were officially at peace with one another. Moreover, his family's freedom-loving heritage (his father named him Tadeusz in honor of Kościuszko) no doubt inclined him toward wishing to see his Polish homeland become an independent country liberated by Napoleon rather than remain a Russian colonial possession ruled by tsarist monarchs. Indeed, the peculiar circumstances of his birth, upbringing, and education placed him in the unfortunate position of feeling himself forever an "alien," split in his loyalties to both his native country, Poland, and his adopted country, Russia. While Bulgarin's legendary opportunism is indisputable, it must nonetheless be granted that this young soldier found himself in a highly confusing and unenviable situation during the Napoleonic Wars, one that merely exacerbated his already deeply ambivalent emotions and conflicting loyalties.

During the years 1816 to 1820 Bulgarin seems to have divided his time equally between St. Petersburg, where he worked for a while in the legal profession, and Wilno (now Vilnius), the university city in Lithuania that was at that time a center of intellectual and literary activity. Although Bulgarin never officially enrolled as a student at Wilno University, he did attend lectures there and became closely acquainted with some of the professors (such as Joachim Lelewel) and students (such as Adam Mickiewicz). More important, Bulgarin became associated in Wilno with a literary group known as the *Towarzystwo Szubrawców* (Society of Scamps), many of whose members contributed to the satirical periodical *Wiadomości Brukowe* (Pavement News), edited by Kazimierz Kontrym. As supporters of the values of the Polish Enlightenment, the members of the *Towarzystwo Szubrawców* directed their satire primarily against the obscurantism, conservatism, and provincialism of feudal Polish landowners and village clergy. Gallomania, an obsession with Parisian fashions, resistance to Enlightenment, intellectual and social backwardness, and moral vice—these were some of the favorite targets of these Polish satirists. Along with Józef-Julian Sekowski (who later would likewise become a Russified Pole, Osip Ivanovich Senkovsky), Bulgarin was granted honorary membership in the *Towarzystwo Szubrawców*. Under the pseudonym Derfintos, Bulgarin even contributed satiric pieces to the *Wiadomości Brukowe,* which thus provided the fledgling author with much of his literary and journalistic apprenticeship, influencing the stylistic as well as thematic direction of his later prose fiction. According to Zofia Mejszutowicz, Bulgarin's activities in Wilno between 1816 and 1820, and especially his close association there with the *Towarzystwo Szubrawców,* left a lasting imprint not only on his literary method but also on his ideological orientation: this early exposure to the rich literary traditions and cultural values of his homeland resulted in a "Polishness" that never fully disappeared in Bulgarin's works.

Bulgarin's career as a journalist began in earnest in 1820, when he settled in St. Petersburg. During that year he met Grech, who would become his close friend, ideological ally, and business partner for the next thirty years; their close relationship lasted until they quarreled over money in 1853. In his new, self-appointed role as spokesman for Polish literature and culture in Russia, Bulgarin wrote an essay, "Kratkoe obozrenie polskoi slovesnosti" (A Short Survey of Polish Literature, 1820), that Grech agreed to publish in his journal, *Syn otechestva* (The Son of the Fatherland). In 1825 Grech invited Bulgarin to help him edit *Syn otechestva,* while Bulgarin had founded two new journals of his own, which he would later invite Grech to edit with him: *Severnyi arkhiv* (The Northern Archive) in 1822 and *Literaturnye listki* (Literary Pages) in 1823. Whereas *Severnyi arkhiv* was oriented toward historical, geo-

Title page for the only volume of Russkaia Taliia (Russian Thalia), Bulgarin's theater almanac

graphical, and scientific issues, *Literaturnye listki* was devoted exclusively to literature and literary criticism. In 1825 Bulgarin was granted official permission to publish *Severnaia pchela* (The Northern Bee), which would remain for many years the only private newspaper in Russia that was allowed to print political news. Bulgarin's journalistic accomplishments during the 1820s also include *Detskii sobesednik* (A Child's Conversationalist, 1826–1827), a magazine published for the moral edification of Russian youth, and *Russkaia Taliia* (Russian Thalia, 1825), an annual theater almanac designed to include both original plays and drama criticism. Although only one volume of *Russkaia Taliia* was ever published, it included excerpts from the text of Aleksandr Sergeevich Griboedov's controversial stage comedy, *Gore ot uma* (Woe from Wit), completed by May 1824 but not published in full until 1861.

The first half of the 1820s constitutes what many consider to be the "liberal" years of Bulgarin's life and career. It was during this period that he was accepted as a member of the progressive *Vol'noe*

obshchestvo liubitelei rossiiskoi slovesnosti (Free Society of Lovers of Russian Literature, 1816–1825); became acquainted with Kondratii Fedorovich Ryleev, Vil'gel'm Karlovich Kiukhel'beker, and several other Russian Decembrists; married Elena Ivanovna Von Ide, a first cousin of Aleksandr Aleksandrovich Bestuzhev (Marlinsky); contributed to the three volumes of *Poliarnaia zvezda* (The Polar Star, 1823–1825), published by Ryleev and Bestuzhev; and became a close friend of Griboedov, the gifted playwright about whom he later wrote *Vospominaniia o nezabvennom Aleksandr Sergeevich Griboedove* (Reminiscences about the Unforgettable Aleksandr Sergeevich Griboedov, 1830). His *Severnaia pchela* was initially a liberal newspaper that included among its contributors such progressive writers as Ivan Andreevich Krylov, Fedor Nikolaevich Glinka, Nikolai Mikhailovich Iazykov, and even Pushkin. Bulgarin's close links with both the Russian Decembrists and the Polish Szubrawcy eventually led to his falling under suspicion by government officials who were investigating possible subversive activities at Wilno University. All this early liberalism disappeared suddenly, however, after the ill-fated uprising of 14 December 1825. Following this failed revolt, Bulgarin sought to dissociate himself completely from any potentially suspicious elements—be they Polish, Catholic, liberal, or Decembrist—and to prove his patriotism by zealously supporting the Russian government in whatever way possible. Thus he reportedly provided tsarist officials with a verbal portrait of Kiukhel'beker, who at the time was evading arrest for complicity in the Decembrist revolt.

To demonstrate further his strong loyalty to the Russian throne, Bulgarin also cooperated quite extensively with the Third Section, the tsar's secret police, writing reports for them concerning various literary and theatrical matters in Russia. In an 1826 report titled "O tsenzure v Rossii i o knigopechatanii voobshche" (About Censorship in Russia and Bookprinting in General), for example, Bulgarin suggested ways that the tsarist regime could guide public opinion in the direction it wanted (without having to resort to force) and could also eliminate dangerous freethinking among the citizenry. In addition, *Severnaia pchela,* which in 1826 published Count Aleksandr Khristoforovich Benckendorff's official version of the Decembrist revolt, now began to receive government patronage. It quickly became a conservative organ that was staunchly committed to advancing the tsar's doctrine of "Official Nationality" and condemned any form of European liberalism. It was during the second half of the 1820s that Bulgarin began to acquire the odious reputation of a soulless opportunist and shameless toady that would follow him throughout the remainder of his career and that would persist even after his death. By 1829 it had become widely known that Bulgarin was enjoying official protection as a journalist in exchange for working as an informant for the Third Section. Many satiric epigrams were written about Bulgarin, attacking him for being a chameleon, an opportunist, and a mercenary. One contemporary, Prince Petr Andreevich Viazemsky, noted that Bulgarin resembled the legendary hare in Russian folklore, running back and forth between two opposing camps. When he saw in 1826 that his relationship with men of letters who were liberal Decembrists could only jeopardize his personal and professional well-being, the ever-pragmatic Bulgarin simply intensified his efforts to curry favor with archconservatives and reactionaries (such as Benckendorff, Leontii Vasil'evich Dubel't, Maksim Iakovlevich Fon-Fok, Aleksandr Semenovich Shishkov, and Count Aleksei Andreevich Arakcheev) who held positions of power within the tsarist government.

During the first half of the 1820s, prior to the Decembrist revolt, Bulgarin had managed to establish a reputation for himself not only as an enterprising journalist, editor, and publisher but also as a popular and prolific writer of prose fiction. Initially, Bulgarin capitalized upon his personal experiences during the Napoleonic campaigns, as is evident in such first-person narratives as "Voennaia shutka'" (A Military Joke, 1823), "Voennaia zhizn'" (Military Life, 1824), and "Eshche voennaia shutka" (Yet Another Military Joke, 1825), all of which merely relate humorous wartime anecdotes. Likewise, his early writings on historical themes, such as "Osvobozhdenie Trembovli, istoricheskoe proisshestvie XVII veka" (The Liberation of Trembowla, a Historical Event of the Seventeenth Century, 1823) and "Marina Mnishekh, supruga Dimitriia Samozvantsa" (Marina Mniszech, the Spouse of Dimitrii the Impostor, 1824), are not exactly sophisticated or original works. Soon, however, Bulgarin was making significant contributions to the development of Russian prose fiction in two genres: the satirical sketch on contemporary mores and manners (nravy) and the utopian tale.

A seminal model for Bulgarin's nravy was provided by French journalist Victor-Joseph Etienne Jouy, who wrote satiric sketches of contemporary life in the weekly feuilleton section of the Paris newspaper Gazette de France. Using an authorial alter ego named L'Hermite de la Chaussée d'Antin, Jouy would observe the colorful inhabitants of Paris and vividly describe life in the city streets, ca-

fés, shops, and offices. Bulgarin in effect "Russified" this genre by depicting the manners and customs of the various social classes in the Russian capital. In his attempt to paint the city of St. Petersburg verbally, by means of short sketches such as "Progulka za gorod" (A Stroll beyond the City, 1823), "Progulka po trotuaru Nevskogo Prospekta" (A Stroll along the Sidewalk of Nevskii Prospekt, 1824), and "Progulka v Ekateringof" (A Stroll to Ekaterinhof, 1824), Bulgarin merely followed the pattern Jouy had established in his tableaux of Parisian mores and manners. Like Jouy's promenades, Bulgarin's progulki are constructed in compliance with the eighteenth-century aesthetic requirement that literature bring not only pleasure but also benefit: that satire instruct readers through edifying examples of moral virtue and amuse them through comic scenes of social life. In a highly laudatory review that appeared in Poliarnaia zvezda in 1824, Bestuzhev praised Bulgarin for bringing the Paris Hermit to life on the shores of the Neva. Bulgarin's colleague Grech likewise commented favorably on the way his friend's satiric sketches of contemporary mores and manners were pleasing the reading public in Russia.

Bulgarin also achieved success as a writer during the 1820s in the genre of the utopian tale. Whereas the nravy revealed Bulgarin to be an accurate, perceptive, and humorous observer of contemporary Russian social mores, his utopian tales showed that the author also possessed the necessary powers of imagination to be able to put in fictional form his critique of current social problems. In "Pravdopodobnye nebylitsy, ili Stranstvovanie po svetu v dvadtsat' deviatom veke" (Plausible Fables, or a Journey around the World in the Twenty-ninth Century, 1824) published in Literaturnye listki, the action takes place in a mythical kingdom in Siberia during the year 2824. In the tradition of Louis Sébastien Mercier's L'An deux mille quatre cent quarante, rêve s'il en fut jamais (1770; translated as Memoirs of the Year Two Thousand Five Hundred, 1772) and Julius Von Voss's Ini: Roman aus dem ein und zwanzigsten Jahrhundert (Ini: Novel from the Twenty-first Century, 1810), Bulgarin's utopian tale borders on science fiction, for it shows readers what fantastic technical inventions will be achieved by their descendants a thousand years in the future. The author is quick to point out, however, that all these scientific wonders—ranging from fast food, prefabricated housing, and air travel to x-ray apparatuses, duplicating machines, and computers—have been reached through the proper development of education, science, and morality.

A similar didacticism is present in Bulgarin's "Neveroiatnye nebylitsy, ili Puteshestvie k sredotochiiu Zemli" (Implausible Fables, or A Journey to the Center of the Earth, 1825) published in *Severnyi arkhiv*. This tale is set in the present rather than the future and focuses not on the material benefits that science can bring to humankind but on the moral strengths and weaknesses of members of contemporary Russian society. Using the narrative device of the allegorical journey, suggested perhaps by Ludvig Holberg's *Nicolai Klimii iter subterraneum novam* (1741), Bulgarin's story takes the reader on a trip under the surface of the earth, where the narrator visits three different underground civilizations that are designed to represent stages of human enlightenment and moral development: Ignorantsiia (Land of Ignorance), where spider-like creatures with tiny heads and huge bellies live in constant darkness and find their happiness entirely in the satisfaction of the physical appetite for food and drink; Skotiniia (Land of Beasts), whose ape-like inhabitants, in addition to eating, sleeping, and heaping unwarranted praise upon themselves, are concerned only with the latest fashions, their physical appearance, and frivolous social amusements; and finally Svetoniia (Land of Light), which is inhabited by human-like creatures who have attained true enlightenment and as a result have become kind, considerate, peace loving, modest, and honest.

Bulgarin later published a third utopian tale, "Stsena iz chastnoi zhizni v 2028 godu ot Rozhdestva Khristova" (A Scene from Private Life in 2028 A.D., 1830), that again portrays a Golden Age in Russia's future. Focusing upon achievements in science, morality, and education, this story shows what Russians could become if only they would eliminate some of the vices in contemporary social life that Bulgarin crusaded against: bribery among government officials, corruption in the legal profession, gentry Gallomania, miseducation of the young, and sloth and ignorance.

Although neither Bulgarin's *nravy* nor his utopian tales could be called great literature, they did satisfy the ever-growing demand for prose fiction from a burgeoning reading audience in Russia, providing the public with entertaining, amusing, yet informative reading material about contemporary life in their country. As his fame, ability, and confidence as a writer grew, Bulgarin sought recognition not merely as a feuilletonist but also as a novelist. During the second half of the 1820s, therefore, he shifted his attention away from short satirical sketches written after the manner of Jouy and turned to the long, quasi-picaresque novel of mores and manners made famous by Alain René Lesage in

Histoire de Gil Blas de Santillane (1715–1735). When Bulgarin wrote his first and most successful novel, *Ivan Vyzhigin,* in 1829, the artistic method he had used in his short works of fiction did not change much, however, for he continued in this longer narrative form to capitalize on his talent for relating, in a lively and amusing manner, his keen observations about the society in which he lived. Excerpts from *Ivan Vyzhigin* had begun to appear in the "*Nravy*" section of *Severnyi arkhiv* as early as 1825, at which time the subtitle for the forthcoming novel was "Russkii Zhilblaz" (The Russian Gil Blas). But when the novel finally appeared in book form in 1829, it was subtitled *nravstvenno-satiricheskii roman* (A Moral-Satirical Novel), a change that illustrates quite explicitly how *Ivan Vyzhigin* can be seen as merely a novel-length evolution of Bulgarin's earlier satirical *nravy*. The change in subtitle also signals Bulgarin's desire to underscore the originality of his novel and to mask its indebtedness to such obvious precursors as Lesage's *Gil Blas* and Vasilii Trofimovich Narezhny's more recent *Rossiiskii Zhilblaz, ili Pokhozhdeniia kniazia Gavrily Simonovicha Chistiakova* (The Russian Gil Blas, or The Adventures of Prince Gavrilo Simonovich Chistiakov, 1814).

In Bulgarin's *Ivan Vyzhigin* the reader follows the picaresque adventures of the eponymous hero, who begins his life as a poor, nameless orphan but is actually the natural son of the wealthy Prince Miloslavsky. Adopted by a negligent landowner in provincial Belorussia and abused by an unscrupulous Jew, young Ivan makes his way to Moscow, where through a birthmark he is recognized by a rich society lady (his mother), who initially claims that she is his aunt. A drastic change takes place in the hero's way of life as the former village urchin is transformed almost overnight into an urbane gentleman who learns how to dance, sing, play the piano, and speak French. While in Moscow he also falls madly in love with a beautiful young woman whose sudden departure for Orenburg prompts Ivan to follow in hot pursuit and thus launches him upon a long series of adventures that take him from the Kirgiz steppe back to Moscow again, as well as from the war with Turkey to high society life in St. Petersburg. These extensive travels across the physical and moral geography of his country, peregrinations that bring Ivan Vyzhigin into contact with a wide range of social and professional types, serve mainly to inculcate in Bulgarin's protagonist essentially the same eighteenth-century Enlightenment morals and bourgeois values that Lesage's Gil Blas had learned from his travels and experiences: namely, that perseverance, adaptability, and prudence will ultimately be rewarded in life with worldly success and personal happiness. By the end of the novel Ivan Vyzhigin manages to discover his true noble lineage, inherit Prince Miloslavsky's fortune of a million rubles, marry the virtuous woman he loves, and then retire with her to his gentry estate in the countryside.

Few readers today would seriously maintain that *Ivan Vyzhigin* is a well-written novel; most would agree instead that its characters are flat, its storyline contrived, its satire heavy-handed, and its style feuilletonistic. The American Slavist John Mersereau Jr. has aptly summarized the artistic merits of *Ivan Vyzhigin* by calling it "a penitential chore to read." What makes Bulgarin's novel such penitential reading is, among other things, its transparent and oppressive didacticism. The author's depiction of contemporary social manners and his portrayal of the hero's character are both subordinated to his intention to teach the rather trite moral lesson that, as he himself puts it in the preface, "all evil results from shortcomings in moral upbringing, while for all goodness people are indebted to Faith and enlightenment." It is with ample justification, therefore, that Bulgarin's literary opponents complained of the tiresome moral sententiousness that permeates his novel. Despite its obvious artistic mediocrity, however, *Ivan Vyzhigin* received an overwhelmingly favorable response from the reading public in Russia, where it enjoyed an unprecedented commercial success and became an instant best-seller. The first edition of two thousand copies sold out so quickly (reportedly in just seven days) that a second edition had to be printed right away and a third one a year later. By 1832 an estimated seven thousand copies of the novel had been sold in Russia, and *Ivan Vyzhigin* had already been translated into French, German, Swedish, English, Italian, Dutch, and Spanish. Readers in Russia seem to have been especially pleased that *Ivan Vyzhigin* provided them at last with a domestic rather than foreign novel, one that dealt with contemporary life in their own country rather than abroad in Europe.

The tremendous popularity enjoyed by Bulgarin's first novel of mores and manners encouraged the author in 1831 to write a sequel, *Petr Ivanovich Vyzhigin, nravoopisatel'nyi-istoricheskii roman XIX veka,* a "moral-historical novel of the nineteenth century" that followed the adventures of Ivan Vyzhigin's son Petr during the period of the Napoleonic Wars. Unlike *Ivan Vyzhigin,* however, whose commercial success netted the publisher of the third edition, Aleksandr Filippovich Smirdin, nearly one hundred thousand rubles in profit, *Petr Ivanovich Vyzhigin* turned out to be a total failure. A rival publisher, Ivan Ivanovich Zaikin, who hurried to offer Bulga-

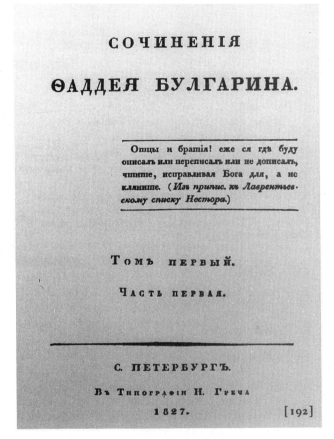

Title page for the first volume of Bulgarin's Sochineniia *(Works), published by Nikolai Ivanovich Grech*

rin the unheard-of sum of thirty thousand rubles for the rights to the manuscript of this sequel, eventually suffered a huge financial loss over the book. Nevertheless the initial commercial success of *Ivan Vyzhigin* encouraged other mediocre Russian authors during the 1830s to attempt to duplicate Bulgarin's achievement by exploiting the novel of mores and manners rather for its commercial than its artistic possibilities. In 1831, for example, Ivan Gurianov wrote *Novyi Vyzhigin na makar'evskoi iarmarke* (A New Vyzhigin at the Makar'ev Fair), while in 1832 Gennadii Simonovsky published a novel titled *Russkii Zhilblaz, pokhozhdenie Aleksandra Sibiriakova, ili shkola zhizni* (A Russian Gil Blas: The Adventures of Aleksandr Sibiriakov, or The School of Life). Bulgarin's best-seller prompted not only imitations such as these two epigones but also several parodies. The little-known writer Aleksandr Anfimovich Orlov wrote a whole series of short satiric chapbooks that poked fun at the characters in, as well as the style of, Bulgarin's *Vyzhigin* novels. In these pamphlets Orlov provided humorous, if apocryphal, accounts of the further adventures of Ivan Vyzhigin, of his son Petr, and of other, newly discovered Vyzhigin progeny. In his *Rodoslovnaia Ivana Vyzhigina, syna Vanki Kaina* (The Genealogy of Ivan Vyzhigin, Son of Vanka Kain, 1831), for example, Orlov reconstructed the history of Ivan Vyzhigin's forebears and linked Bulgarin's picaresque hero genealogically with such notorious eighteenth-century robbers as Vanka Kain and Cartouche.

In the aftermath of *Ivan Vyzhigin* a bitter polemic quickly arose among Russian literary critics over the relative artistic merits of Bulgarin's best-selling novel. It is difficult to assess accurately how Russian writers, readers, and critics at the time truly felt about *Ivan Vyzhigin,* since the contemporary debate that surrounded it was fueled by personal animosities and feuds as well as by professional jealousies and rivalries. Bulgarin's friends and allies praised his novel as a work of high literary merit, while his personal and professional enemies denigrated it as a piece of insipid, pedestrian prose. Russian critical opinion during this time was divided into two main camps: the literary aristocrats, including upper-class writers such as Pushkin, Viazemsky, and Vladimir Fedorovich Odoevsky, who continued to regard literature as a noble and refined pursuit undertaken by poets inspired by the Muse; and the literary democrats, made up of plebeian writers such as Bulgarin, Grech, and Nikolai Alekseevich Polevoi, who sought to shatter the elitist exclusivity of the institution of literature in Russia and to widen the ranks of its readers and writers by opening it up to members of the middle and lower classes. During this period (called the "Age of Smirdin" because of that bookseller and publisher's extensive enterprises) the traditional system of literary patronage was being replaced more and more by a new system of literary commerce; as a result increased prominence was accorded to the middlemen of the literary marketplace: editors, publishers, booksellers, and others engaged in the printing and selling of books or journals. Many contemporary men of letters witnessed with profound misgivings the passing of the Golden Age of poetry in Russia and the subsequent turn to prose fiction during the 1830s. The rise of the novel in early nineteenth-century Russia provoked grave concern among many literary aristocrats, who feared that as a result of the democratization, professionalization, and commercialization of Russian letters, the aesthetic quality of literature would decline. In their opinion Bulgarin's novel provided a salient example of how a successful literary commodity in Russia no longer necessarily had to be a true work of art. For journalists such as Grech, Polevoi, and Bulgarin, on the other hand, the success of *Ivan Vyzhigin* was important for advancing their goal of popularizing prose fiction in

Russia. They hoped to create and control a growing readership, an audience that not only would pay to read Russian novels such as *Ivan Vyzhigin* but also would subscribe to their periodicals.

The critical polemic that surrounded *Ivan Vyzhigin* was thus a dispute over the future direction of Russian literature as well as a battle to win the allegiance of Russian readers. The bitter controversy that arose in 1830 between the plebe Bulgarin and the mandarin Pushkin, which was characterized by an exchange of vicious personal attacks against each other in the pages of contemporary journals, was driven in part by the rivalry between the great national poet and the best-selling novelist as they competed over a Russian reading public that Pushkin had once dismissed as a mere "rabble" (*chern'*). Indeed, some scholars have argued that Pushkin's decision during the 1830s to turn away from poetry and condescend to write in such a lowly genre as prose was prompted by the need he felt to counter the popular successes being enjoyed by Bulgarin, a hack writer with vulgar bourgeois values, who threatened to corrupt the Russian reading public both morally and intellectually. The polemic started when Bulgarin, reacting angrily to an unfavorable review in Anton Antonovich Del'vig's *Literaturnaia gazeta* (Literary Gazette) of his 1830 historical novel, *Dimitrii Samozvanets,* believed that Pushkin had written the review, and he made some highly derogatory remarks about the poet's literary talent as well as his family's genealogy in an article titled "Anekdot" (Anecdote, 1830), published in *Severnaia pchela.* Bulgarin also wrote a scathing review of chapter 7 of Pushkin's *Evgeny Onegin* (written 1823–1831, published in full in 1833), which he described as "une chute complète." Pushkin responded by publishing an article, "Torzhestvo druzhby, ili Opravdannyi Aleksandr Anfimovich Orlov" (The Triumph of Friendship, or Aleksandr Anfimovich Orlov Justified, 1831), that appeared under the pseudonym Feofilakt Kosichkin in *Teleskop* (The Telescope). As the title clearly suggested to contemporaries, this article was written as a rejoinder to Grech's impassioned defense of Bulgarin in a recent volume of *Syn otechestva,* where he had lashed out virulently against Orlov's parodies of *Ivan Vyzhigin,* dismissing them as "stupid little books" that could not be compared with Bulgarin's novels. Pushkin uses a mock defense of his purported "friend" Orlov not merely to discredit the aesthetic quality of Bulgarin's popular novels by placing them on a par with Orlov's parodic chapbooks; he also seeks to invalidate Grech's overly favorable reviews of the works written by his close friend and business partner. Pushkin wished to expose the unscrupulous tactics of Bulgarin and

Grech, who were unfairly using their considerable power as journalists, editors, and critics to influence public opinion concerning new works of Russian literature.

In a second article, titled "Neskol'ko slov o mizintse g. Bulgarina i o prochem" (A Few Words about Mr. Bulgarin's Little Finger and Other Matters, 1831), Pushkin's pseudonym Feofilakt Kosichkin once again takes offense at a remark made by Grech (that Bulgarin had more intelligence and talent in his little finger than many critics had in their heads) and uses it to launch a counterattack against the author of *Ivan Vyzhigin*. In the article, Kosichkin provides the outline for a pamphlet novel to be titled "Nastoiashchii Vyzhigin. Istoriko-nravstvenno-satiricheskii roman XIX veka" (The Real Vyzhigin: A Historical-Moral-Satirical Novel of the Nineteenth Century), that he threatens to publish unless Grech and Bulgarin cease their polemical attacks in *Severnaia pchela*. This outline of *Nastoiashchii Vyzhigin* reveals that Pushkin planned to include some embarrassing incidents from Bulgarin's adventuresome biography (mainly from his military service record and his rumored spying for the secret police) within the narrative structure of the novel of mores and manners that Bulgarin had helped to popularize in Russia. In this way Pushkin would be able to ridicule his personal and professional nemesis at the same time as he mocked the type of moral-satirical novel that had become Bulgarin's literary trademark. As a more properly artistic rather than journalistic response to Bulgarin's debasement of Lesage's picaresque model, Pushkin also planned to write a "Gil Blas-type" novel of his own, titled "Russkii Pelam" (A Russian Pelham). Patterned after Edward Bulwer-Lytton's *Pelham, or The Adventures of a Gentleman* (1828), Pushkin's novel would relate the adventures of a gentleman rather than a rogue, and it would appeal to a cultured, refined, and aesthetically developed reader rather than the relatively unsophisticated audience targeted by Bulgarin's popular moral-satirical novels. "Nastoiashchii Vyzhigin" was something Pushkin merely proposed in his article; "Russkii Pelam," on the other hand, was a project that he seriously worked on but did not finish.

Bulgarin's attempt at the end of the 1820s to gain recognition for himself as the "Russian Lesage" by producing novels of contemporary mores and manners was followed by efforts at the beginning of the 1830s to establish himself as the "Russian Walter Scott" by writing novels on Russian history. Bulgarin's interest in history extended back to the beginning of the 1820s, as evidenced by the themes of

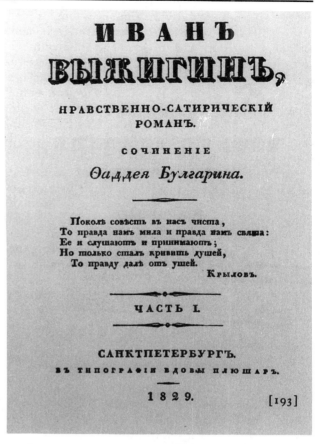

Title page for Ivan Vyzhigin, *Bulgarin's "moral-satirical novel," which became the first best-selling novel in Russia*

some of his earliest literary works (such as "Osvobozhdenie Trembovli" and "Marina Mnishekh"). As was the case with many of his contemporaries, Bulgarin's interest in the historical past of Russia was sparked not only by the upsurge of nationalist sentiment that swept across Europe during the Romantic period but also by the appearance of the first eight volumes of Nikolai Mikhailovich Karamzin's monumental *Istoriia gosudarstva Rossiiskogo* (History of the Russian State, 1816–1818; revised, 1818–1829). As a student of the liberal Polish historian Joachim Lelewel and a supporter of the constitutionalist views of the Decembrists, Bulgarin had taken issue with the conservative ideology espoused by Karamzin, whose monarchist views on Russia represented the class interests of the traditional, serf-owning nobility. Indeed, Bulgarin was instrumental in popularizing within Russian intellectual circles Lelewel's strong critique of Karamzin, "Razsmotrenie *Istorii gosudarstva Rossiiskogo* g. Karamzina" (An Examination of Mr. Karamzin's *History of the Russian State*), which Bulgarin translated and then published in issues of *Severnyi arkhiv* between 1822 and 1824. By the time he wrote his first historical novel in 1830, however, Bulgarin had long abandoned his liberal views and adopted more conservative ones. He had also established a pattern in his literary works of strongly emphasizing his support of autocratic rule in Russia as well as his loyalty to the tsar. The historical novels he wrote during the 1830s, as a result, read largely as "official" histories filled with loyalist sentiments, fervid expressions of patriotism, and monarchist values.

The title "father of the Russian historical novel" (or the "Russian Walter Scott") belongs by rights not to Bulgarin, however, but to Mikhail Nikolaevich Zagoskin, who early in 1829 published *Iurii Miloslavskii, ili Russkie v 1612 g.* (Iurii Miloslavsky, or The Russians in 1612). Set during the Time of Troubles (1598–1613), when Russia underwent a period of widespread social upheaval and political turmoil following the death of the last ruler in the line of Riurik, Zagoskin's novel enjoyed a spectacular success among Russian readers. The tsar liked *Iurii Miloslavskii* so much that he ordered Bulgarin imprisoned briefly for having written an unfavorable review of it in *Severnaia pchela*. Bulgarin published his first historical novel, *Dimitrii Samozvanets,* in 1830, and it too was a popular success among Russian readers hungry for novels about their national past. Bulgarin set his novel during the same historical period, the Time of Troubles; unlike Zagoskin, however, Bulgarin chose not to follow Scott's formula of making average fictional characters—rather than famous real-life personages—serve as the central figures in the drama. The main heroes in *Dimitrii Samozvanets* are Dimitrii, Boris Godunov, Marina Mniszech, and other well-known historical personages. And whereas in Scott's novels the love intrigue, suspense, and adventure are all subordinated to major events of history, in *Dimitrii Samozvanets* the melodramatic effects dominate the narrative. The protagonist in Bulgarin's novel, as a result, bears closer affinities with a romantic adventurer out of popular fiction than with the actual impostor who for a short while became the ruler of Russia. Pushkin was not far off the mark when he sarcastically referred to the eponymous hero of *Dimitrii Samozvanets* as a "Vyzhigin of the eighteenth century," since Bulgarin's protagonist is portrayed in a manner that makes him indeed resemble a literary picaro.

As a rule the characterizations in *Dimitrii Samozvanets* are rather weak; Bulgarin's characters all seem to act in a manner that is highly implausible, exaggerated, and inconsistent. This artistic shortcoming no doubt reflects the lingering influence that Gothic romances and sentimental fiction continued to exert upon the author's style. Even Bulgarin's ostensible strength as a writer—his skill in vividly describing social mores and manners—is not satisfactorily exploited in his historical novel, where the local color (descriptions of clothing, weapons, and food) is not successfully integrated into the narrative story line. In his recreation of the historical Russian past, Bulgarin seems unable to escape the mind set of his own century and thus fails to establish any psychological verisimilitude in his novel, which remains essentially a period piece that lacks a true historical perspective.

The publication of *Dimitrii Samozvanets* only fueled the author's conflict with Pushkin, who suspected that Bulgarin, through his connections with the Third Section, had been instrumental in delaying official approval of Pushkin's *Boris Godunov* (1831), which dealt with the same theme as Bulgarin's historical novel. Pushkin had written his play in 1825, but he had been forced to submit it for inspection to Tsar Nicholas I, who had taken it upon himself beginning in 1826 to act as the poet's personal censor. It is likely that Bulgarin was called upon to read Pushkin's manuscript for the tsar, since he frequently served as the government expert on literary matters. Bulgarin, in any case, is widely believed to have been the author of the anonymous report, "Zamechaniia na komediiu o tsare Borise i Grishke Otrep'eve" (Remarks on the Comedy about Tsar Boris and Grishka Otrep'ev, 1826), which led the tsar to prohibit the publication of *Boris Godunov* and to recommend that Pushkin transform his play into an historical novel à la Scott. Whether or not Bulgarin was in fact the author of the "Zamechaniia" and thus served as the censor of *Boris Godunov,* the serious charges (including plagiarism of the play) leveled against him by Pushkin and his friends only further damaged his already seriously tarnished reputation as a man of letters in Russia.

Although Bulgarin continued to write works of fiction throughout most of the 1830s, he was again never able to match the early commercial and artistic successes he enjoyed as a novelist with *Ivan Vyzhigin* and *Dimitrii Samozvanets*. In *Petr Ivanovich Vyzhigin,* for example, Bulgarin failed miserably in his attempt to synthesize the genre of the satiric novel of mores and manners (such as *Ivan Vyzhigin*) with the genre of the historical novel (such as *Dimitrii Samozvanets*). *Mazepa* (1833–1834), meanwhile, is perhaps Bulgarin's most unsuccessful historical novel, as the author proved unable to match, let alone surpass, the artistic achievements of George Gordon, Lord Byron (*Mazeppa, A Poem,* 1819), Ryleev (*Voinarovsky,* 1824), and Pushkin (*Pol-*

tava, 1829), all of whom had earlier treated the subject of the famous Cossack leader from the time of Peter the Great. Although Bulgarin apparently sought to provide an in-depth character study, focusing narrative attention primarily on the rise and fall of this colorful historical figure from Ukraine, his *Mazepa* emerges as a one-dimensional villain who, like Satan or Judas, abstractly personifies evil.

In 1835 Bulgarin published his final novel, *Pamiatnye zapiski tituliarnogo sovetnika Chukhina, ili Prostaia istoriia obyknovennoi zhizni* (The Memoirs of the Titular Councilor Chukhin, or The Simple History of an Ordinary Life). Borrowing a device that Pushkin had applied with consummate skill and great success in his *Povesti pokoinogo Ivana Petrovicha Belkina* (Tales of the Late Ivan Petrovich Belkin, 1830), Bulgarin claimed to be a mere editor who was publishing "notes" on contemporary Russian mores and manners that were written by a simple government clerk named Veniamin Chukhin. Just as Bulgarin's earlier *Mazepa* paled miserably in comparison with other Russian historical novels, such as Pushkin's *Kapitanskaia dochka* (The Captain's Daughter, 1833–1836) and Gogol's "Taras Bul'ba" (1835), so too did his *Zapiski Chukhina* fail to match the level of artistry attained in the prose fiction then being written by Russian authors—not only by major figures such as Pushkin, Gogol, and Mikhail Iur'evich Lermontov, but also by minor writers such as Odoevsky, Aleksei Alekseevich Perovsky (Antonii Pogorel'sky), and Aleksandr Fomich Vel'tman. Bulgarin himself seems to have recognized his serious limitations as a novelist and to have realized that his early successes were due largely to the fact that his novels had filled a literary vacuum that no longer existed. After 1835 Bulgarin all but abandoned literature and concerned himself chiefly with his journalistic duties. He apparently understood that Russian literature had developed to a point where a lesser writer such as himself could no longer reasonably expect to compete against truly creative literary talents. Although he did publish a biography of General Aleksandr Vasil'evich Suvorov (1843), two collections of satiric sketches (1842 and 1843), and his memoirs, Bulgarin during the 1840s devoted nearly all his time to literary criticism rather than literature.

As a critic Bulgarin sought mainly to fight against what he perceived to be the baneful influence of the new realistic tendency in Russian prose. Whereas Bulgarin the novelist had polemicized during the 1830s with Pushkin and the literary aristocrats as they competed against each other for the burgeoning Russian readership, Bulgarin the critic polemicized during the 1840s mainly with Vissarion Grigor'evich Belinsky, who championed the socially progressive literature being written by a younger generation of Russian prose artists. Unlike "official" democrats such as Bulgarin, Grech, and Senkovsky, who loyally supported the tsar and his autocratic form of government, these young writers were social and political progressives who challenged the status quo in Nicolaevan Russia. Indeed, Bulgarin accused the liberal journal to which Belinsky contributed his essays, *Otechestvennye zapiski* (Notes of the Fatherland), of working to undermine the foundations of tsarist autocracy in Russia. In an 1846 issue of his *Severnaia pchela,* Bulgarin bestowed the pejorative title of "Natural School" (*natural'naia shkola*) upon the group of young writers who were responsible for developing this realistic tendency in Russian prose fiction. In their physiological sketches of native life, whether of life among the lower classes in St. Petersburg or of the peasants in the Russian countryside, writers such as Nikolai Alekseevich Nekrasov, Evgenii Grebenka, Iakov Petrovich Butkov, Panteleimon Aleksandrovich Kulish, Ivan Ivanovich Panaev, and Dmitrii Vasil'evich Grigorovich treated the theme of social injustice and inequality with a sentimental humanitarianism that sought to evoke sympathy, pity, and compassion for the plight of the poor and the downtrodden. According to Belinsky these Natural School writers were following the fine example set by Gogol, whose prose works succeeded magnificently in stripping the veil from contemporary life and capturing what Belinsky called the "poetry of reality." To Belinsky's mind, Gogol had stepped forward upon the death of Pushkin in 1837 to become the leading light on the national literary scene. The Age of Pushkin had now been superseded by the Gogolian period of Russian literature with its aesthetic emphasis upon critical realism.

Bulgarin, however, saw in the prose works by Gogol and the writers of the Natural School the threat of a serious moral decline in society. In his scathing reviews of such works as the play *Revizor* (The Inspector General, 1836) and the novel *Mertvye dushi* (Dead Souls, 1842), Bulgarin took Gogol strongly to task for describing only the unseemly aspects of contemporary social reality (*byt*) and for focusing exclusively on the dark and dirty side of native life: the drunkenness, banality, and backwardness of everyday existence in Russia. Gogol's characters, according to Bulgarin, were grotesque caricatures whose trivial thoughts and base physical urges merely exaggerated the negative features of people living in contemporary society. Like the seventeenth-century Flemish genre paintings by David Teniers, Gogol's prose fiction provided

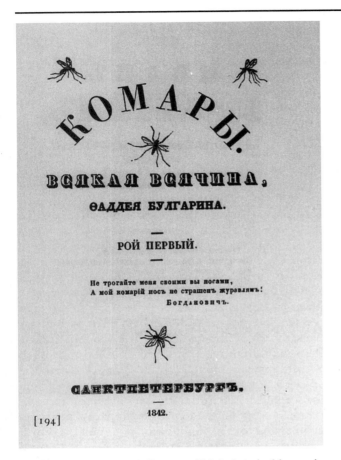

Title page for Bulgarin's Komary. Vsiakaia vsiachina, roj
pervyi *(Mosquitoes: Miscellany, First Swarm)*

crude and dirty pictures of common life in Russia. In response to this "filthy tendency" that he observed in the prose works written by Gogol and the members of the Natural School, Bulgarin published two collections of satiric sketches in which he sought to provide edifying models for depicting everyday life in Russia. *Kartinki russkikh nravov* (Pictures of Russian Manners, 1842) was a six-volume series edited by Bulgarin, with the first two volumes comprising of his own sketches and the other four collecting works by Ivan Petrovich Miatlev, Grech, Dal', and Nestor Vasil'evich Kukol'nik. *Ocherki russkikh nravov* (Sketches of Russian Manners, 1843) also collects pieces by Bulgarin. Although Bulgarin's *nravy* treated themes similar to the physiological sketches drawn by the Natural School writers, his brand of "word painting" (*bytopisanie*) continued to be guided by an archaic eighteenth-century aesthetic that prescribed instructing readers morally as well as amusing them satirically. There is, accordingly, a highly abstract, generalized, and rationalistic quality to Bulgarin's depiction of social virtues and vices. Unlike most Russian writers during the Romantic period, who viewed themselves as adver-

saries of the existing order and thus assumed a posture of hostility toward the government, Bulgarin remained a staunch defender of the status quo. His inclination as a writer, therefore, was to idealize contemporary life in tsarist Russia rather than to criticize it or to call for radical change.

During the 1830s Bulgarin had managed to become one of the most powerful figures on the literary and journalistic scene in Russia. As a novelist he had attained sufficient popularity and commercial success to be considered a serious literary rival to Pushkin. In fact, when he and Pushkin were inducted together into the prestigious *Obshchestvo liubitelei rossiiskoi slovesnosti* (Society of Lovers of Russian Literature, 1811–1930) in 1834, they were referred to as the two leading lights in Russian letters. As a journalist and critic Bulgarin joined forces during the late 1830s and early 1840s with Grech and Senkovsky, the editor of the enormously successful journal *Biblioteka dlia chteniia* (Library for Reading, 1834), to form what one critic would later call the " journal triumvirate" (*zhurnalnyi triumvirat*), an alliance that for many years enjoyed an unfair monopoly over the periodical press in Russia and collectively maintained a virtual stranglehold upon the free and open expression of liberal opinion. By the late 1840s, however, Bulgarin was fast losing his authority as a publicist, just as earlier he had suddenly lost his popularity as a writer. In both instances Bulgarin simply failed to keep pace with the rapid changes taking place in Russia and lost touch with actual social conditions. During the last ten years of his life Bulgarin withdrew more and more from public life. He did manage to land a civil-service appointment, becoming a member of the State Commission for Horse Breeding in 1844 and receiving regular promotions thereafter, so that by 1857 he had attained the rank of Actual State Councilor. He now spent the majority of his time, however, not in the capital but on his country estate, Karlovo, located near Dorpat in Estonia. Having succeeded in alienating countless people over the years with all his personal and professional feuding, Bulgarin lived the last years of his life in nearly total isolation from the public spotlight. According to Grech, Bulgarin displayed an increasingly hostile disposition during his declining years, manifesting many of the symptoms of what might today be diagnosed as a psychoneurotic personality: sudden and violent mood swings; extreme nervousness, suspiciousness, and irritability; feelings of deep depression and paranoia; and a persecution complex. Two years after suffering a debilitating stroke that left his right side partially paralyzed, Bulgarin died of apoplexy at his Karlovo estate on 1 September 1859. This influential man of letters had acquired such widespread ill repute by then and had become so intensely hated in Russia that his death was met with almost complete public silence.

Bulgarin remains a highly enigmatic and controversial figure in the history of Russian literature. Despised during his lifetime as an unprincipled opportunist and intriguer, he has been unfairly treated after his death in criticism and scholarship. As several scholars have observed, Bulgarin is remembered today not as an actual literary personage but as a moral reptile of mythic proportions: a larger-than-life symbol of absolute evil, amorality, and mediocrity, with a reputation that has obscured his significant contributions to Russian literary culture. As a pioneering writer of prose fiction, Bulgarin helped to introduce and popularize on Russian soil several new literary genres: the satiric sketch, the feuilleton, the travel account, the military anecdote, and the utopian tale. Although his novels lack intrinsic artistic worth, the commercial success of *Ivan Vyzhigin* and *Dimitrii Samozvanets* did stimulate a widespread demand among contemporary Russian readers for original domestic novels. Moreover, when Bulgarin's popularity as a writer waned, he was succeeded by more talented Russian novelists who were able to capitalize on the interest he had awakened in the genre. As one of the first professional men of letters in Russia, Bulgarin helped to make a career in literature a financially profitable activity in his adopted country; as a journalist, editor, and publisher (antiliberal political ideology aside), he was also instrumental in democratizing the institution of literature in Russia by helping to broaden the ranks of its readers and writers.

Although Bulgarin officially remained a bête noir throughout the long years of Communist rule in Russia, during which time his works were not republished and his name was seldom mentioned, several scholars nonetheless undertook to reexamine Bulgarin's legacy fairly and objectively. As early as the 1920s some of the Russian Formalists argued that notorious literary figures such as Bulgarin, Grech, and Senkovsky ought to be recognized for their sociological rather than moral significance: that is, as middle-class writers who were among the first to produce mass literature in Russia and to appeal to new nonaristocratic readers. The Soviet writer Veniamin Aleksandrovich Kaverin, meanwhile, challenged the notion that the so-called journal triumvirate enjoyed a monopoly over the contemporary periodical press. In their studies on Bulgarin, critics such as Aleksandr L. Pogodin and Zofia Mejszutowicz sought to emphasize that this influential writer had a positive impact upon the development of Russian literature, preparing the soil for the success of Gogol, the Natural School, and literary realism. Rehabilitative efforts such as these gained added impetus during the final years of Soviet rule, when Bulgarin's works were once again allowed to be published and his role in Russian literary history was discussed with greater openness. Bulgarin's rehabilitation is likely to continue in the post-glasnost' and post-Soviet period as critics in Russia persist in exploding the myths that surround this much-despised writer and in unearthing the "other" Bulgarin who has long remained buried beneath official versions of him as a colossal symbol of evil.

References:

N. N. Akimova, "Bulgarin i Gogol' (literaturnaia biografiia i literaturnaia reputatsiia)," *Russkaia literatura,* 3 (1996): 3–18;

Akimova, "Bulgarin i Gogol' (massovoe i elitarnoe v russkoi literature: problema avtora i chitatelia)," *Russkaia literatura,* 2 (1996): 3–22;

Gilman H. Alkire, "Gogol' and Bulgarin's *Ivan Vyzhigin,*" *Slavic Review,* 28, no. 2 (1969): 289–296;

Alkire, "The Historical Novels of Faddej Bulgarin," dissertation, University of California at Berkeley, 1966;

A. Altunian, "Vlast' i obshchestvo. Spor literatora i ministra (Opyt analiza politicheskogo teksta)," *Voprosy literatury,* 1 (1993): 173–214;

Nikolai A. Engel'gardt, "Gogol' i Bulgarin," *Istoricheskii vestnik,* 97, no. 1 (1904): 154–173;

Engel'gardt, "Gogol' i romany dvadtsatykh godov," *Istoricheskii vestnik,* 87, no. 2 (1902): 561–580;

Iurii Fokt, "*Ivan Vyzhigin* i *Mertvyia dushi,*" *Russkii arkhiv,* no. 8 (1902): 596–603;

V. V. Gippius, "Pushkin v bor'be s Bulgarinym v 1830–1831 gg.," *Vremennik pushkinskoi komissii,* volume 6 (Moscow-Leningrad: Akademiia nauk, 1941), pp. 235–255;

Nikolai Ivanovich Grech, "Izvestie N. I. Grecha o zhizni i sochineniiakh F. V. Bulgarina," *Russkaia starina,* 4 (1871): 514–520;

Grech, *Zapiski o moei zhizni* (St. Petersburg: Suvorin, 1886);

A. Ianov, "Zagadka Faddeia Bulgarina," *Voprosy literatury,* 9–10 (1991): 98–125;

Veniamin Aleksandrovich Kaverin, *Baron Brambeus: Istoriia Osipa Senkovskogo, zhurnalista, redaktora "Biblioteka dlia chteniia"* (Moscow: Nauka, 1966);

Ronald D. LeBlanc, "Faddei Bulgarin's *Russkii Zhilblaz*," in his *The Russianization of Gil Blas: A Study in Literary Appropriation* (Columbus, Ohio: Slavica, 1986), pp. 145–200;

LeBlanc, "Gogol's Chichikov: Russian Picaro or Real Vyzhigin?" *Canadian-American Slavic Studies*, 23, no. 4 (1989): 409–428;

LeBlanc, "Making *Gil Blas* Russian," *Slavic and East European Journal*, 30, no. 3 (1986): 340–354;

Mikhail Lemke, *Nikolaevskie zhandarmy i literatura 1826–1855 gg.* (St. Petersburg: S. V. Bunin, 1909);

Sophia Lubensky, "The First Russian Novel in English: Bulgarin's *Ivan Vyžigin*," *Russian Language Journal*, 126–127 (1983): 61–68;

Nataliia N. L'vova, "Kapriz mnemoziny," in *Sochineniia*, by Bulgarin (Moscow: Sovremennik, 1990), pp. 5–22;

Zofia Mejszutowicz, *Powieść obyczajowa Tadeusza Bułharyna* (Kraków: Polska Akademia Nauk, 1978);

Mejszutowicz-Bocheńska, "Tadeusz Bułharyn w zyciu literackim Rosji pierwszej połowy w. XIX," in *Polacy w zyciu kulturalnym Rosji*, edited by Ryszard Łużnyj (Kraków: Polska Akademia Nauk, 1986), pp. 41–50;

John Mersereau Jr., *Russian Romantic Fiction* (Ann Arbor: Ardis, 1983);

Frank Mocha, *Tadeusz Bułharyn (Faddej V. Bulgarin) 1789–1859: A Study in Literary Maneuver* (Rome: Institutum Historicum Polonicum Romae, 1974);

V. F. Pereverzev, "Pushkin v bor'be s russkim plutovskim romanom," in his *U istokov russkogo real'nogo romana* (Moscow: Khudozhestvennaia literatura, 1937), pp. 44–77;

Aleksandr L. Pogodin, "*Ivan Vyzhigin,* roman Faddeia Bulgarina," *Zapiski russkogo nauchnogo instituta v Belgrade*, 9 (1933): 141–181;

Pogodin, "Russkie pisateli-poliaki," in *Z zagadnień kulturalno-literackich wschodu i zachodu*, edited by Marjan Zdziechowski (Kraków: Gebethner i Wolff, 1933–1934), pp. 107–121;

Pogodin, "Tadeusz Bułharyn," *Przeglad współczesny*, 11, no. 122 (1932): 496–507;

V. A. Pokrovskii, *Problema vozniknoveniia russkogo "nravstvenno-satiricheskogo" romana (O genezise "Ivana Vyzhigina")* (Leningrad: Akademiia Nauk, 1933);

Abram Reitblat, "Vidok Figliarin (Istoriia odnoi literaturnoi reputatsii)," *Voprosy literatury*, 3 (1990): 73–101;

Reitblat, "Bulgarin i ego chitateli," in *Chtenie v dorevoliutsionnoi Rossi,* (Moscow: Rossiiskaia gosudarstvennaia biblioteka, 1992), pp. 55–66;

Reitblat, "Bulgarin i III otdelenie v 1826–1831 gg.," *Novoe literaturnoe obozrenie*, no. 2 (1993): 113–129;

M. Samupere, "Neizvestnyi Faddei," *Raduga*, no. 4 (1991): 30–41;

Walter Schamschula, *Der russische historische Roman vom Klassizismus bis zur Romantik* (Meisenheim am Glan: Verlag Anton Hain, 1961);

Zdzisław Skwarczyski, "*Wiadomości Brukowe* a pierwszy rosyjski romans moralno-satyryczny *Iwan Wyżigin*," in *Z polskich studiów slawistycznych*, edited by Jo'sef Magnuszewski (Warsaw: Państwowe Wydawnictwo Naukowe, 1963), pp. 77–104;

Dzhakoma Strano, "Povest' Gogolia *Ivan Shpon'ka* kak parodiia romana Bulgarina *Ivan Vyzhigin*," *Russica Romana*, 3 (1996): 51–76;

Jurij Striedter, *Der Schelmenroman in Russland: Ein Beitrag zur Geschichte des russischen Romans vor Gogol'* (Berlin: Erich Blaschker, 1961);

Nicholas P. Vaslef, "Bulgarin and the Development of the Russian Utopian Genre," *Slavic and East European Journal*, 12, no. 1 (1968): 35–43;

Vaslef, "Faddej V. Bulgarin: His Contribution to Nineteenth-Century Russian Prose," dissertation, Harvard University, 1966;

N. I. Vorob'eva, "O kruge chteniia F. V. Bulgarina (po materialam ego biblioteki)," in *Chtenie v dorevoliutsionnoi Rossii*, edited by Abram I. Reitblat (Moscow: Rossiiskaia gosudarstvennaia biblioteka, 1995), pp. 79–90;

S. D. Zubkov, "Iz sposterezhen' nad dvoma romanami (Pustoliubov-Stolbikov–proti Vyzhigina)," *Radians'ke literaturoznavstvo*, no. 5 (1975): 31–43.

Petr Iakovlevich Chaadaev
(27 May 1794 – 14 April 1856)

George L. Kline
Bryn Mawr College

BOOKS: *Oeuvres choisies de Pierre Tchadaief publiées pour la première fois par le P[ère] Gagarin,* edited by Ivan Sergeevich Gagarin, S.J. (Paris & Leipzig: A. Franck, 1862);

Sochineniia i pis'ma P. Ia. Chaadaeva, 2 volumes, edited by Mikhail Osipovich Gershenzon (Moscow: A. I. Mamontov, 1913–1914);

Lettres philosophiques adressées à une Dame, edited by François Rouleau (Paris: Librairie des Cinq continents, 1970);

Stat'i i pis'ma, edited by Boris Nikolaevich Tarasov (Moscow: Sovremennik, 1987; enlarged edition, 1989);

Sochineniia, edited by V. Iu. Proskurina (Moscow: Izd-vo Pravda, 1989);

Oeuvres inédites ou rares, edited by Raymond T. McNally, Rouleau, and Richard Tempest (Meudon, France: Bibliothèque slave, Centre d'études russes, 1990);

Polnoe sobranie sochinenii i izbrannye pis'ma, 2 volumes, edited by S. G. Blinov, Z. A. Kamensky, and others (Moscow: Izd-vo Nauka, 1991).

Editions in English: *Philosophical Letters and Apology of a Madman,* translated by Mary-Barbara Zeldin (Knoxville: University of Tennessee Press, 1969);

The Major Works of Peter Chaadaev: A Translation and Commentary, translated by McNally (Notre Dame, Ind.: University of Notre Dame Press, 1969);

Philosophical Works of Peter Chaadaev, in *Sovietica,* edited by McNally and Richard Tempest, volume 56 (Dordrecht & Boston: Kluwer Academic Publishers, 1991).

Petr Iakovlevich Chaadaev

Petr Chaadaev was one of the most brilliant, cultivated, and perceptive Russians of his time. Despite having been declared officially insane and publicly silenced by Tsar Nicholas I in 1836 after the publication of his "First Philosophical Letter," Chaadaev maintained friendly contacts and lively intellectual interchanges with some of his most distinguished contemporaries, including Aleksandr Pushkin and Aleksei Stepanovich Khomiakov. In Germany in 1826 he had met Friedrich Wilhelm Joseph von Schelling, who expressed a high opinion of the qualities of Chaadaev's mind and spirit. Most of the Western European celebrities who visited Moscow in the two decades after 1836 managed to meet Chaadaev—among them Hector Berlioz, the Marquis de Custine, Franz Liszt, and Prosper Mérimée.

Petr Iakovlevich Chaadaev was born on 27 May 1794 in Moscow to a family of prosperous landed gentry of Lithuanian origin on his father's side. His mother's father was the noted Prince Mikhail Mikhailovich Shcherbatov, author of *A Discourse on the Corruption of Morals in Russia,* written in the late 1780s but first published abroad, by Aleksandr Ivanovich Herzen, in 1858. Chaadaev was raised by his aunts and uncles after the early deaths of his parents. Like other children of the Russian gentry during this period, he was attended by French and German governesses and taught by French and German tutors. He became entirely fluent in French at an early age and acquired a good reading knowledge of German. (He told Schelling in 1833 that he had read all of Schelling's works in the original.)

Chaadaev studied for three years at Moscow University (1808–1811) but left to join the Russian army as a cadet officer of the famous Semenovsky Guard Regiment. He saw action in such major battles of the war against Napoleon as Borodino, Kulm, and Leipzig, and was decorated with the Iron Cross and the Order of Anna, Fourth Class. On 1 April 1814 he entered Paris with the Russian army of occupation under Tsar Alexander I. Chaadaev returned to Russia in 1816 and was given important assignments involving direct contact with the tsar and his court, especially in 1820 in connection with a revolt in the Semenovsky Regiment. Chaadaev had been selected to serve in the Imperial Court, but he abruptly resigned his commission in March 1821 for reasons that have never been fully clarified. One of the reasons appears to have been his proud independence and his unwillingness, despite the high honor involved, to become what he called (in a 2 January 1821 letter to Princess Anna Mikhailovna Shcherbatova) a kind of elegant "plaything."

During the 1820s Chaadaev enjoyed the reputation of a brilliant wit but was also considered a dandy and something of a snob. He mellowed somewhat in later years but always retained a concern for his appearance and his public image. As reported by P. Bartenev in his 1884 commentary on Pushkin's correspondence, Chaadaev's friend Pushkin referred to him once as "heureux à force de vanité" (roughly, "self-satisfied in his vanity").

Chaadaev and Pushkin had met at Tsarskoe Selo (near St. Petersburg) in 1816. Chaadaev's unit was stationed there, and Pushkin was just finishing his education at the celebrated Lycée. Their ages were, respectively, twenty-two and seventeen. They remained close friends for the next twenty-one years until Pushkin's death in 1837. Only a handful of Chaadaev's letters to Pushkin, and even fewer of Pushkin's letters to Chaadaev, have survived. It appears that during a period of emotional distress Chaadaev regrettably destroyed many of Pushkin's letters to him. However, the letters that remain, especially Pushkin's unsent letter of October 1836 (which Chaadaev did not see until some years after Pushkin's death) in response to the publication of

Chaadaev's "First Philosophical Letter," are intellectual, cultural, and literary documents of the highest order.

Pushkin the schoolboy admired Chaadaev the war hero—someone who, though only a few years older, had taken part in the battles about which Pushkin had only dreamed. The adolescent Pushkin was also aware, precociously, of the gaps in his education and turned eagerly to the brilliant and prematurely bookish Chaadaev for help in filling them. With the passage of time the relationship between the two gifted friends became more nearly equal. Although, as his contemporaries P. V. Annenkov and Ia. I. Saburov attest, it was Chaadaev who "forced Pushkin to think," it was Pushkin who persuaded Chaadaev to study Nikolai Mikhailovich Karamzin's monumental *Istoriia gosudarstva Rossiiskogo* (History of the Russian State, 1816–1818; revised, 1818–1829) and ultimately to revise his earlier harshly negative judgments of the role of Peter the Great in Russian history. As Chaadaev later put it (in a 1 November 1843 letter to Aleksandr Turgenev), Russia might well have become just another "Swedish province" without Peter.

Although Pushkin's warm affection for and loyalty to Chaadaev continued to the end, his intellectual respect for Chaadaev's views appears to have slackened somewhat. He was cool to Chaadaev's favored utopian dream of establishing "the Kingdom of God on earth," and this coolness—a result of Pushkin's realism and skepticism—caused Chaadaev at times to be both puzzled and distressed.

Chaadaev, who in the "First Philosophical Letter" had complained that Russia had produced no William Shakespeares or Johann Wolfgang von Goethes, suggested in the early 1830s that Pushkin might indeed be Russia's "new Dante," a truly national poet of supreme gifts. Pushkin wrote several splendid, warm, and appreciative poems to Chaadaev. The following lines—from the nineteen-year-old poet to the twenty-four-year-old thinker—are among the most celebrated:

My zhdem s tomlen'em upovan'ia
Minuty vol'nosti sviatoi.

(We await in languishing hope
The moment of sacred freedom.)
....
Moi drug, otchizne posviatim
Dushi prekrasnye poryvy!
Tovarishch, ver': vzoidet ona,
Zvezda plenitel'nogo schast'ia,
Rossiia vsprianet oto sna,
I na oblomkakh samovlast'ia

Napishut nashi imena!

(My friend, let us devote the splendid
Impulses of our souls to our fatherland!
Comrade, believe in this: a star of captivating
Happiness will rise,
Russia will awaken from its slumber,
And our names will be written
On the ruins of the autocracy!)

Pushkin spoke more specifically about Chaadaev's talent, his character, and his fate in another well-known four-line poem, circa 1820: "On vyshnei voleiu nebes / Rozhden v okovakh sluzhby tsarskoi; / On v Rime byl by Brut, v Afinakh Perikles, / A zdes' on—ofitser gusarskii (By Heaven's High Will he was born / To the shackles of the Tsar's service; / In Rome he would have been a Brutus, in Athens a Pericles, / But here [in Russia] he is [only] a Hussar officer.)"

In 1821 Pushkin in Caucasian exile wrote a poem to Chaadaev telling him how much he missed and needed him, eloquently expressing his gratitude for the help that Chaadaev had given him in earlier years:

V minuty gibeli nad bezdnoi potaennoi
Ty podderzhal menia nedremliushchei rukoi;

(At the moment when I was about to plunge into a hidden
    abyss,
You held me back with a vigilant hand.)
. . . .
Kogda uslyshu ia serdechnyi tvoi privet?
Kak obnimu tebia! Uvizhu kabinet,
Gde ty vsegda mudrets, a inogda mechtatel'
I vetrenoi tolpy besstrastnyi nabliudatel'.

(When will I hear your heartfelt greeting?
How I shall embrace you! I picture the study
Where you sit—always the wise man, sometimes a dreamer,
And an unimpassioned observer of the changeable crowd.)

The two men in fact met again in Moscow in 1826 following a six-year separation, after Chaadaev returned from Western Europe and Pushkin from his internal exile.

Following his resignation from military service, Chaadaev attempted to find a position with the Russian diplomatic corps, but was rebuffed. He was offered instead a civil service position in the Ministry of Finance, but turned it down, pleading insufficient knowledge and experience in financial matters.

As for Chaadaev's personal finances, although he had independent means, he did not have savings sufficient to support him for what turned out to be a three-year sojourn in Western Europe (1823–1826).

His trip had a threefold motivation: to improve his health (on doctor's orders); to become acquainted firsthand with the thought and culture of Western Europe and with some of its leading representatives as well as to purchase books for his growing personal library; and to be away from a country which at that time he felt to be culturally and socially deficient. In later years he experienced serious and continuing financial problems. His voluminous correspondence with his brother Mikhail (much of it published for the first time in 1990) deals almost exclusively with money matters and reveals a quite different Chaadaev, apparently obsessed with debts, loans, mortgages, and property rights, and sometimes embarrassingly nagging and importunate in his dealings with his often difficult, unresponsive, and uncooperative brother.

The way Chaadaev raised the money for his European trip was by selling some of his serfs in 1823. Although this practice was common enough at the time among members of the Russian landed gentry, scholar Raymond T. McNally sees in this action a contradiction, or at least a severe tension, with Chaadaev's own sharp and sustained critique of the institution of serfdom in Russia. In any case, Chaadaev himself makes no reference to this tension in any of his essays, notes, or letters and appears not to have considered it a moral problem.

Chaadaev's impressions of individuals, cultures, politics, and the social orders in the half-dozen European countries which he visited were, on this trip, overwhelmingly positive. But events of later decades, including the July Revolution of 1830 in France, the Polish uprising of the same year, and the revolutions of 1848, changed his views sharply. He had never approved of violent revolution as a means of social and political change, and he had called the failed Decembrist revolt (1825) an "immense calamity" for Russia. In the 1840s he came to see Western Europe as increasingly secularized and revolutionary in spirit. In a 26 September 1849 letter to Khomiakov he even expressed the quasi-Slavophile view that it was the world-historical mission of Russia to "save" Western Europe from its own secularizing and revolutionizing tendencies. Some commentators take this claim at face value, but others treat it as ironic. In any case, his earlier enthusiasm for West European politics had by the late 1840s and early 1850s mostly been dissipated. He sensed a decline in the greatness of European affairs, symbolized by the contrast between the uncharismatic adventurer, Louis Napoleon, and the charismatic Napoleon Bonaparte.

Chaadaev completed his most significant work, eight "Philosophical Letters," between 1829

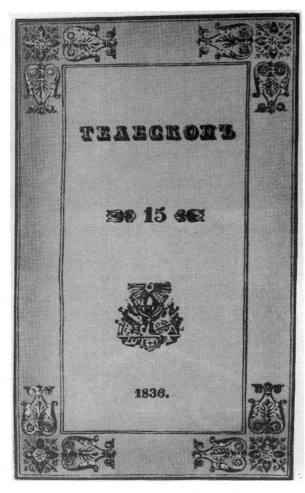

Cover of the issue of Teleskop *(Telescope) in which Chaadaev's "First Philosphical Letter" was published*

and 1831, composing them in a forceful, concise, and elegant, if faintly old-fashioned French. Why French? Because it was, as he and Pushkin agreed, *la langue de l'Europe* (the language of Europe), and he was addressing a Europe-wide audience. The first two letters were especially critical of the thought and culture, the social institutions and the national psychology of Russia. Although not yet published, some of the letters had been copied and circulated in manuscript among certain of Chaadaev's friends and acquaintances.

By 1836, when he was forty-two, Chaadaev had written a good deal—not only the "Philosophical Letters" but also several long and philosophically significant letters to such correspondents as Pushkin, Khomiakov, Count Adolphe de Circourt, Aleksandr Ivanovich Turgenev, and Princess Sophia Sergeevna Meshcherskaia—but he had published almost nothing. In January of that year a Russian

translation of the "First Philosophical Letter," the text which was harshest and most uncompromising in its critical assault on Russia's historical past, present, and future, appeared in the Moscow journal *Teleskop* (Telescope). Chaadaev's attitude toward this event was ambivalent. On the one hand, he was delighted to have a larger audience, at long last, for his unconventional views. On the other hand, he had significantly tempered certain of his more extreme views in the seven years since composing the "First Philosophical Letter." His position was now less stark, more balanced, with greater nuance. Chaadaev sometimes suggested, after the dismal fact and against the weight of the evidence, that Nikolai Ivanovich Nadezhdin, the editor of *Teleskop,* had published the "First Letter" without the author's knowledge or consent.

In any case, the impact of this publication was accurately described by Herzen in his memoirs, *Byloe i dumy* (My Past and Thoughts, 1852–1868), as like that of a "pistol shot in a dark night." Publication of *Teleskop* was permanently suspended; Nadezhdin was exiled; the censor who had passed the "First Philosophical Letter" (apparently in a fit of distraction, while playing cards) was dismissed. Chaadaev was officially declared insane in the report of Count Aleksandr Khristoforovich Benckendorff, head of the Third Section (secret police) to the governor-general of Moscow, for "only a madman" could write such nasty and unflattering things about his own country. He was placed under house arrest with daily medical and police surveillance. The title of Chaadaev's *Apologie d'un fou* (Apology of a Madman, written in 1837 but not published until 1862) is an ironic reference to his officially proclaimed "instant insanity."

As it happened, Prince Dmitrii Vladimirovich Golitsyn, the military governor-general of Moscow, Chaadaev's powerful friend and protector, was away from Moscow when the storm broke. Shortly after returning to the city a month later, Golitsyn put a stop to the medical surveillance and granted Chaadaev permission to leave his home on condition that he not leave the city limits and that he return home each night. By February 1837 some of Chaadaev's confiscated papers had been returned. Tsar Nicholas I gave the order to call off both police and medical surveillance as of October of that year. But the ban on Chaadaev's works remained in full and damaging effect to the end of his life. He could neither be published nor mentioned by name (whether praised or blamed) in any publication issued within the borders of the vast Russian empire.

The other seven "Philosophical Letters" had all been completed by 1831. But none of them, or the *Apologie d'un fou,* was to be published during Chaadaev's lifetime. This barrier was especially frustrating to the author, who had, in effect, completed a full-scale philosophical treatise which, in François Rouleau's complete 1970 edition, comes to nearly two hundred pages. The first publication of three of the "Philosophical Letters" and the *Apologie* (in Paris, in French, edited by Ivan Sergeevich Gagarin, S.J.) did not appear until 1862, half a dozen years after Chaadaev's death. The remaining five "Philosophical Letters"–Numbers 2, 3, 4, 5, and 8–were published in Russian translation by Dmitrii Shakhovskoi in *Literaturnoe nasledstvo,* volumes twenty-two through twenty-four (Moscow, 1935). The original French texts of these letters were published by McNally in *Forschungen zur osteuropäischen Geschichte,* volume eleven (Berlin, 1966).

The impression which Chaadaev's "First Philosophical Letter," left on the consciousness of Russian society was, as Osip Mandel'shtam described it, as sharp and indelible as the mark that a diamond cuts in glass. It is now abundantly clear to serious students of Chaadaev's work–and Chaadaev said as much in a letter to an unidentified correspondent, written between October and December 1854–that his strong critique of the Russia of his time was motivated by love of his country and the desire to reform rather than hatred or the rage to repudiate. In Chaadaev's words, he had come to love his country as Peter the Great had taught him to do: loving the truth first of all and keeping his eyes open to the flaws and gaps in Russia's historical past and present. In another formulation, Chaadaev was always a Russian patriot, but his patriotism was negative rather than positive. However, the cultivated Russian public as well as the political and ecclesiastical authorities in Russia regarded him as flatly unpatriotic, as a renegade, almost a traitor.

Surveying the historical scene, Chaadaev found unity, universality, and organic religious or spiritual togetherness (*sobornost',* in the term that Khomiakov was to make famous) in Western Europe with its powerful tradition of Roman Catholic Christianity. In contrast, he found exclusiveness, divisiveness, and even self-centeredness in Russia, with its unworldly and antisocial tradition of Russian Orthodox asceticism and spirituality.

Chaadaev had met and corresponded with Schelling and was especially impressed by the latter's mature "philosophy of revelation." He had closely studied such French "Christian traditionalists" as François Guizot, Joseph de Maistre, Louis Bonald, and Félicité Lamennais. Aleksandr Turgenev, Chaadaev's friend and correspondent, even referred to him, only partly in jest, as "our Moscow Bonald" and "our Moscow Lamennais." But, as McNally has made clear, Chaadaev was influenced only by Lamennais's early work, in particular, the four-volume *Essai sur l'indifférence en matière de religion* (Essay on Indifference Toward Religion, 1817–1823), which he had been studying closely while he was completing the "First Philosophical Letter." He found the later Lamennais, the author of the "democratic" and even "radical" *Paroles d'un croyant* (Words of a Believer, 1834), highly uncongenial.

In any case, Chaadaev meditated deeply on the role that religion and the churches in general, and Christianity and the Roman Catholic Church in particular, had played and continued to play in the history of the West. He was the first Russian philosopher of history in at least two senses: first, he ascribed a special ontological status to the realm of the historical–the general historical process and particular historical events–and was sensitive to the "sacred flow" of history. He was profoundly moved by what Vasilii Vasil'evich Zenkovsky aptly calls the "theurgical restlessness" of those who are called upon to do "God's work in history." Second, he turned a searching critical and analytical gaze on Russian history in the light of world history, raising for the first time the fateful and much-to-be-discussed question of the relationship between Russia and the West.

For Chaadaev, separateness, fragmentation, and self-centeredness are all forms of "falling away" from the ideal dynamic and universal unity in which Divine Providence sustains people, societies, and nature. For him, Christ represents not just the spirit of sacrifice but also and especially a "horror of division, a passionate love of unity." Chaadaev sharply criticized the Protestant Reformation. But he made certain distinctions, condemning John Calvin more harshly than Martin Luther, at least in part because of Calvin's role in causing Michael Servetus to be burned at the stake as a heretic. And he expressed a great admiration for Anglicanism, in part because of the impressive Anglican Charles Cook, whom he had met in Florence, and in part because of Khomiakov's ecumenical relations with certain Anglican churchmen. Yet his general assessment of Protestantism was strongly negative. For him it did not represent, as it did later for Vladimir Sergeevich Solovev, the principle of free religious searching; rather, it represented disunity, fragmentation, the denial of Christian unity. (These were standard arguments of Counter-Reformation Roman Catholic critics.) When Pushkin responded to Chaadaev's blanket rejection of Protestantism (in the "First Philosophical Letter") by making the sensible and valid point that, after all, the principle of Christian unity is embodied in Christ himself, and that Christ is central for Protestants too, Chaadaev (at least based on the existing record) was reduced to silence.

Chaadaev was no less critical of the Renaissance than of the Reformation. But here his reasons were of a different order; namely, that the Renaissance had brought back into Christian Europe such pagan and explicitly anti-Christian values and attitudes as pride, competitiveness, self-centeredness, and sensuality.

Taking an encompassing view, Chaadaev discerns in the great cosmic "totality of [all] beings" a unity that is absolute and objective, transcending the world of sense experience. In the realm of history and culture it is the nations of western Europe that exemplify such unity. In Chaadaev's unforgettable image, these nations have walked "hand in hand" down the broad path of the centuries. On any given day—for example, at Christmas or Easter—Christians throughout Europe, whatever their vernacular language or their local customs, take part in the same liturgy, using the same language (Latin), reciting the same texts, hearing the same music, taking part in the same gestures.

All of this unity, as Chaadaev realized, was truer of medieval Europe than it was of the Europe of his own time. Chaadaev clearly had a special sympathy for the European Middle Ages. But McNally may be going too far when he claims that Chaadaev tended to view Western Europe as a whole through the "rose-colored glasses of romantic medievalism." Chaadaev was arguably no more a Romantic than was Georg Wilhelm Friedrich Hegel.

Chaadaev was firmly convinced that Russia had violated the unity of Christendom, withdrawing into a self-isolation that was started by Photius, Patriarch of Constantinople, when he excommunicated Pope Nicholas I. More generally, the source of Russian Orthodox Christianity, according to Chaadaev, was "wretched and despised" Byzantium. Only some years after 1829 did he come to recognize his error and admit that, in the tenth century, Byzantine culture was in fact powerful and flourishing, and that the schism between the Eastern and Western churches did not begin with Photius. At that point, Chaadaev turned to the much-invoked "Tatar yoke," something about which he had had nothing to say in the "First Philosophical Letter," for the explanation of the cultural and social backwardness of Russia.

Chaadaev saw the Russians of his time as locked into their cultural and spiritual separateness, ignorant of what had been happening in Western Europe: "We [Russians] live only in the narrowest of presents, without past and without future, in the midst of a flat calm." A chief symptom of willful Russian self-isolation, for Chaadaev, is the fact that in Russia serfdom was introduced several centuries after the coming of Christianity to Russia in 988. In contrast, in Western Europe Christian pressures had brought about the eventual abolition of slavery and serfdom. This point, as Chaadaev in 1829 had yet to discover, had been forcefully and convincingly made by Hegel. More telling, according to Chaadaev, was the fact that for several generations the Russian Orthodox Church and its hierarchy had been thunderously silent about this great moral and social evil.

For Chaadaev, who in a 27 May 1839 letter to Princess Sophia Meshcherskaia called himself "quite simply . . . a Christian philosopher,"—but could perhaps be more accurately described in Zenkovsky's expression as a "theologian of culture"—the history and culture of Western Europe had been unified and made fruitful by Western, that is, Roman Catholic, Christianity. "It is Christianity," he declared, "which has accomplished everything in Europe." However, as Boris Niklolaevich Tarasov (among others) has noted, Chaadaev's "Christian philosophy" is somewhat untraditional. He omits several topics of central significance to other Christian philosophers, for example, the question of (original) sin, the question of the salvation of the individual soul, the sacraments of the church. Chaadaev was mainly interested in religion, and Christianity in particular, as an historical force, one that creates and sustains both social order and the values of high culture.

Chaadaev was even more outspokenly Eurocentric than Hegel—with whose works he became familiar only after he had written the eight "Philosophical Letters." He was scornful of the culture and religion of China and India. He dismissed the civilization of Japan and the Christianity of Abyssinia (that is, the Coptic Christianity of what is now Ethiopia) as "absurd aberrations" from "divine and human truths." But by "divine and human truths" he appears to mean something like "the norms of nineteenth-century Western Europe."

In the "First Philosophical Letter" Chaadaev insisted that Russia must eventually retrace the path of Western European historical development, including all of its steps or stages. But in later writings he admitted that he had been too hasty in making this claim, that such a step-by-step retracing would not be possible. The harsh view expressed in the "First Letter"—that Divine Providence guides and has guided the historical development of Western Europe but has somehow neglected backward and self-isolated Russia—is somewhat softened in the *Apologie* and other late writings. Chaadaev admitted

First page of a manuscript for Chaadaev's "Third Philosophical Letter" (Dashkov Collection, Institute of Russian Literature [Pushkin House], St. Petersburg)

that there had been "some exaggeration" in his earlier "quasi-indictment of a great people" (*espèce de réquisitoire contre un grand peuple*) and that he had failed to give due credit to the Russian Orthodox Church, "so humble, at times so heroic, which alone attenuates the emptiness of our chronicles."

Anticipating certain themes developed more than a decade later by such Slavophiles as Khomiakov and Ivan Vasil'ievich Kireevsky, Chaadaev went so far as to suggest that Russia has a special mission on the stage of world history: it is destined to solve many of the social problems and to "perfect the greater part of the ideas" that have had their origin in older (presumably Western European) societies. Chaadaev remained wary of the extreme religious nationalism of the emerging Slavophile movement (he called them *nos slavons fanatiques*), seeing it as fundamentally incompatible with that Christian universalism for which "there is neither Greek nor Jew" (Colossians 3:10–11) and by extension neither Russian nor Frenchman, neither German nor Englishman. He rejected what he called the Slavophiles' "retrospective utopia" as involving an "arrogant apotheosis of the Russian people." This movement, Chaadaev declared in a 20 May 1842 letter to Schelling, threatened to turn Russia away from that "religious humility, . . . that modesty of spirit which has always been the distinctive trait of our national character."

One of the many paradoxes of Chaadaev's life and thought is the plain biographical fact that this first Russian Westernizer remained to the end of his life a close and faithful friend of the senior Moscow Slavophile, Khomiakov, whereas his contacts with the senior Westernizers–Herzen, Vissarion Grigor'evich Belinsky, Timofei Nikolaevich Granovsky–were for the most part casual and episodic.

Another paradox is that after a lifetime of criticizing serfdom in Russia, when Alexander II ascended the Russian throne in 1855 the ill and aging Chaadaev declared (according to eyewitnesses) that he was going to lock himself up in his study in order to write a treatise defending the continuation of serfdom. There appear to have been two reasons for this surprising development–one frivolous, the other serious. The frivolous reason was Chaadaev's personal disappointment when he saw Alexander II up close at an official function in Moscow. He had always had a special regard for charismatic leaders (such as Alexander I). But it was not merely that he found Alexander II uncharismatic. Rather, as he is reported to have said: "J'ai regardé avec beaucoup d'attention le nouvel Empereur et je suis bien affligé; voyez ses yeux qui n'expriment rien, mais rien de tout" (I have scrutinized the new Emperor very closely and I am terribly distressed; look at his eyes, which are absolutely expressionless). Presumably Chaadaev drew the hasty conclusion that a tsar with expressionless eyes could not be trusted to emancipate the Russian serfs. His more serious reason may have been that he feared the violence and bloodshed that might well accompany a too-precipitate emancipation and felt that the process of freeing the serfs would have to be slow, deliberate, and extended over a considerable period of time.

Chaadaev never married. He was loved by a noblewoman, Avdot'ia Sergeevna Norova, but her frail health prevented her from marrying; she died in 1835. Chaadaev died from a heart attack on 14 April 1856 and was buried near Norova in Moscow.

Almost all of Chaadaev's texts were composed in French, a language with which Chaadaev, like his friend Pushkin, was entirely at home. Yet he never lost his native fluency in Russian, in contrast to the Francophone noblemen described in the opening chapters of Leo Tolstoy's *Voina i mir* (War and Peace, 1865–1869), who had let their conversational

Chaadaev's grave at Donskoi Monastery in Moscow

Russian wither from neglect so that when it became temporarily unfashionable (in 1812) for a Russian to speak, read, or write the language of Napoleon's invading armies, they had to turn to their own semiliterate or illiterate servants for lessons in colloquial Russian. It sometimes seems as though Chaadaev is unaware of which language he is using, so frequent are his shifts from French to Russian and back again, often within a single letter, sometimes within a single paragraph or sentence.

It is particularly charming to find Chaadaev writing in French to Pushkin (French was the usual language of their correspondence) to urge him to write his own letters in Russian, the language of Pushkin's métier as Russia's national poet. One peculiar result of this pervasive bilingualism is the dichotomy between the formality of French–in which language Chaadaev addresses such close friends as Pushkin with the decorous *vous*–and the intimacy of Russian–in which the same friends are addressed with the informal *ty*. This difference of course makes Russian translations of Chaadaev's (and Pushkin's) French letters systematically misleading, since they invariably use the decorous and formal Russian *vy* to render the French *vous*.

Chaadaev sometimes opened himself to misinterpretations of a more serious kind involving the substance of his thought as well as his style and tone. His addiction to hyperbolic statement, to irony, and even to mimicry sometimes obscured his own position. Thus, when he said in the "First Philosophical Letter" that Russia had borrowed from Western Europe only "useless luxuries" (*luxe inutile*), he probably did not mean to be taken literally. He was well aware that Russian borrowing from the West included such necessary, nonluxury items as the steel plow, the printing press, and the loom. Presumably, what he meant to say was that there had been altogether too much borrowing of frivolous and luxurious items—of furniture, clothing, items for comfort and convenience.

Chaadaev's mimicry is perhaps most clearly in evidence in a brief essay with the misleading title "*L'Univers* 15 janvier 1854." The essay was not published in that French journal or anywhere else during Chaadaev's lifetime. In that work he deliberately assumes the persona of a Frenchman, or at least a Western European. The article begins: "Les Russes ne cessent de reprocher notre ignorance dans tout ce qui touche à leur pays" (The Russians continue to reproach us [Western Europeans] for being ignorant of everything that concerns their country). It continues: "il n'existe pas de peuple au monde qui nous soit moins connu que le peuple russe" (there is no people [or 'nation'] in the world that is less well known [to West Europeans] than the Russian people [or 'nation']). Clearly, Chaadaev is enjoying this switching of roles as he mimics the stance of a Frenchman or a German and pretends to view Russia from abroad, in ignorance. Then, of course, he goes on to explain Russia to the West, as though from the viewpoint of a fellow Western European. The reader who emerges from this text in some confusion as to Chaadaev's intentions is surely to be forgiven.

A final tension deserves to be noted briefly. Chaadaev repeatedly praised the submissiveness of human reason, celebrating the Christian virtues of meekness, modesty, the long-suffering and self-abnegating love of one's neighbor, and organic religious togetherness. He was critical of Immanuel Kant's stress on the autonomy of reason and called Kant's *Critique of Pure Reason* (1781) an "Apology for Adamite Reason." He was critical of the Renaissance in Western Europe for reintroducing such pagan, anti-Christian "virtues" as pride and self-assertiveness. Yet the texture and tone of much of his writing in fact displays those same characteristics. In this sense Chaadaev's rhetoric sometimes tends to veil or even undermine the central moral and social message of this profound and serious Christian philosopher.

Biographies:

Mikhail Osipovich Gershenzon, *P. Ia. Chaadaev: Zhizn' i myshlenie* (St. Petersburg: M. M. Stasiulevich, 1908);

Pavel Semenovich Shkurinov, *P. Ia. Chaadaev: Zhizn', deiatel'nost', mirovozzrenie* (Moscow: Izdatel'stvo Moskovskogo universiteta, 1960);

Aleksandr Aleksandrovich Lebedev, *Chaadaev,* Zhizn' zamechatel'nykh liudei, no. 19 (Moscow: Molodaia gvardiia, 1965);

Boris Nikolaevich Tarosov, *Chaadaev,* Zhizn' zamechatel'nykh liudei, Selected Series, volume 1, second enlarged edition (Moscow: Molodaia gvardiia, 1990).

References:

Heinrich Falk, S. J., *Das Weltbild Peter J. Tschaadajews nach seinen acht "Philosophischen Briefen": Ein Beitrag zur russischen Geistesgeschichte des 19. Jahrhunderts* (Munich: Isar Verlag, 1954);

Osip Mandel'shtam, "Petr Chaadaev," in his *Sobranie sochinenii,* volume 2, edited by Gleb Struve and Boris Filippov (Washington, D.C.: Inter-Language Literary Associates, 1966), pp. 326–334;

Raymond T. McNally, *Chaadayev and His Friends: An Intellectual History of Peter Chaadayev and His Russian Contemporaries* (Tallahassee: Diplomatic Press, 1971);

Charles Quénet, *Tchaadaev et les Lettres Philosophiques: Contribution à l'étude du mouvement des idées en Russie* (Paris: Lib. ancienne Honoré Champion, 1931);

Studies in Soviet Thought, special Chaadaev issue, edited by McNally, 32, no. 4 (1986);

Boris Nikolaevich Tarasov, "P. Ia. Chaadaev i russkaia literatura pervoi poloviny XIX veka," in Chaadaev, *Stat'i i pis'ma* (Moscow: Sovremennik, 1989), pp. 5–37;

Andrzej Walicki, *A History of Russian Thought: From the Enlightenment to Marxism,* translated by Hilda Andrews-Rusiecka (Stanford, Cal.: Stanford University Press, 1979), pp. 81–91;

Vasilii Vasil'evich Zenkovsky, *A History of Russian Philosophy,* volume 1, translated by George L. Kline (London: Routledge & Kegan Paul, 1953), pp. 148–170.

Papers:

The primary collections of Chaadaev materials are the Pypin Archive, the Shakhovskoi Archive, and the Dashkov Collection, all at the Institute of Russian Literature (Pushkin House), St. Petersburg; and the Obleukhov Collection and the Chaadaev and Zhikarev Collection, both at the State Library (formerly the Lenin Library), Moscow.

Vladimir Ivanovich Dal'
(Kazak Vladimir Lugansky)
(10 November 1801 – 11 September 1872)

Joachim T. Baer
University of North Carolina at Greensboro

BOOKS: *Russkiia skazki iz predaniia narodnago izustnago na gramotu grazhdanskuiu perelozhennyia . . . Piatok pervyi,* as Kazak Vladimir Lugansky (St. Petersburg: Pliushar, 1832);

Opisanie mosta navedennago na reke Visle dlia perekhoda otriada General-Leitenanta Ridigera (St. Petersburg, 1833);

Byli i nebylitsy Kazaka Vladimira Luganskogo, as Lugansky, 2 volumes (St. Petersburg: N. Grech, 1833–1835);

Nakhodchivoe pokolenie, volume 5 of *Kartinki russkikh nravov,* edited by Faddei Venediktovich Bulgarin (St. Petersburg: Iu. Iungmeister, 1842);

Soldatskie dosugi Kazaka V. Luganskogo, as Lugansky (St. Petersburg, 1843);

Pokhozhdeniia Khristiana Khristianovicha Viol'damura i ego Arsheta . . . S al'bomom kartin, as Lugansky (St. Petersburg: M. D. Ol'khin, 1844);

Rozyskanie o ubienii Evreiami khristianskikh mladentsev i upotreblenii krovi ikh (St. Petersburg: po prikazaniiu g. ministra vnutrennikh del, 1844); republished as *Zapiska o ritual'nykh ubiistvakh* (St. Petersburg, 1913; St. Petersburg: A. S. Suvorin, 1914);

Povesti, skazki i rasskazy Kazaka Luganskogo, as Lugansky, 4 volumes (St. Petersburg: Gutenberg, 1846);

Sochineniia, Kazaka Luganskogo, as Lugansky, 4 volumes (St. Petersburg: A. Smirdin, 1846);

O narechiiakh russkogo iazyka. Po povodu opyta oblastnago Velikorusskago slovaria izdannago Vtorym Otdeleniem Imperatorskoi Akademii Nauk. Iz V. knizhki "Vestnik Imperatorskago Russkago Geograficheskago Obshchestva za 1852 god" (St. Petersburg, 1852);

Matrosskie dosugi (St. Petersburg: Morskoi Uchenyi Komitet, 1853);

Michman Potseluev, ili zhivuchi ogliadyvaisia, as Lugansky (St. Petersburg, 1855);

Sochineniia. Novoe polnoe izd., 8 volumes (Moscow: M. O. Vol'f, 1861);

Poslovitsy russkago naroda. Sbornik poslovits, pogovorok, rechenii, prislovii, chistogovorok, pribautok, zagadok, poverii i proch (Moscow: Imp. obshchestva istorii i

drevnostei rossiiskikh universitetskoi tipografii, 1862);

Tolkovyi slovar' zhivago velikorusskago iazyka, 4 volumes (Moscow: Ob-vo liubitelei ross. slovesnosti, A. Semen, 1863–1866); second edition, corrected and enlarged from the author's manuscript, 4 volumes (St. Petersburg & Moscow, 1880–

1882); third edition, enlarged and edited by I. A. Boduena-DeKurtena, 4 volumes (St. Petersburg & Moscow, 1903–1909);

Dva-soroka byval'shchchinok (St. Petersburg: M. O. Vol'f, 1880);

O pover'iakh, suever'iakh i predrassudkakh russkago naroda (St. Petersburg: M. O. Vol'f, 1880).

Editions and Collections: *Sochineniia . . . Povesti i razskazy,* third edition, 8 volumes (St. Petersburg & Moscow: M. O. Vol'f, 1883–1884);

Polnoe sobranie sochinenii Vladimira Dalia, 10 volumes (St. Petersburg & Moscow: M. O. Vol'f, 1897–1898);

Sobranie izbrannykh sochinenii dlia detei shkol'nogo vozrasta (Petrograd & Moscow: M. O. Vol'f, 1915);

Izbrannye proizvedeniia, compiled by N. N. Akopova (Moscow: Pravda, 1983);

Povesti i rasskazy, compiled by Iu. M. Akutin and A. A. Il'in-Tomich (Moscow: Sovetskaia Rossiia, 1983);

Polnoe sobranie sochinenii v vos'mi tomakh, 8 volumes projected (Moscow: Stolitsa, 1995–).

OTHER: "Khmel', son i iav'" in *Russkie povesti XIX veka 40-50-x godov,* volume 1 (Moscow: Goslitizdat, 1952).

Most educated Russians know Vladimir Ivanovich Dal' as the author of the four-volume *Tolkovyi slovar' zhivago velikorusskago iazyka* (Reasoned Dictionary of the Living Great-Russian Language, 1863–1866) on which Dal' worked for approximately fifty years of his life. They also know him as the author of *Poslovitsy russkago naroda* (Proverbs of the Russian People, 1862). Thus, Dal's main achievement in the estimate of most educated Russians is as a collector of words, proverbs, songs, and fairy tales. Few know his contribution to Russian dialectology, *O narechiiakh russkogo iazyka* (On the Dialects of the Russian Language, 1852), and fewer still are familiar with his artistic writing: his artfully transformed fairy tales, *Russkiia skazki . . . Piatok pervyi* (Russian Fairy Tales . . . First Group of Five, 1832); his collection of stories *Byli i nebylitsy* (True Stories and Inventions, 1833–1835); his stories with an ethnographic bent, such as "Bolgarka" (A Bulgarian Woman, 1837) and "Podolianka" (A Podolyan Woman, 1839); and his contribution in Russian literature to the tradition of the so-called physiological sketch, realistic depictions of the lower classes: "Peterburgskii dvornik" (A Petersburg Caretaker), published in *Literaturnaia gazeta* (Literary Gazette) in 1844; "Denshchik" (An Orderly), published in *Finskii vestnik* (Finland Herald) in 1845; "Chukhontsky v Pitere" (Finns in St. Petersburg), published in *Finskii vestnik* in 1846; and "Ural'skii Kazak" (A Cossack from the

Urals), published in Aleksandr Pavlovich Bashutsky's almanac *Nashi, spisannye s natury* (Ours, Copied from Life) in 1843. Yet Dal's artistic contribution, while not as enduring in importance as his activity as a collector, was important at the time and was recognized by his far-greater contemporary, Aleksandr Pushkin. Only two years older than Dal', Pushkin was favorably disposed toward Dal's first collection of artistically transformed fairy tales and soon sent him one of his own, "Skazka o rybake i rybke" (Fairy Tale of the Fisherman and the Fish, 1833), with an autographed dedication on a copy of the manuscript that read "Here is One From Thy Own. To the Fairy Tale Writer, the Cossack from Lugansk, from the Fairy Tale Writer Aleksandr Pushkin."

When the two writers met in Orenburg in 1833, Pushkin encouraged Dal' to write more prose: "If I were in your place I would write a novel immediately, right now." Dal' continued writing prose but never wrote a novel. The importance of Dal's contribution to artistic literature was rediscovered in the twentieth century by the great literary scholar Boris Eikhenbaum. In essays discussing Nikolai Semenovich Leskov and Mikhail Alekseevich Kuzmin he also found a place for Dal' as a representative of that early tradition in Russian literature in which the focus was not ideological but philological, and he assigned Dal' a place in Russian literature as forerunner of the later "philological school" or "younger line": Leskov, Kuzmin, Evgenii Ivanovich Zamiatin, Boris Andreevich Vogau (better known as Boris Pilniak), Aleksei Mikhailovich Remizov, and others. On the one hand, Eikhenbaum saw literary phenomena in terms of cycles; on the other, in terms of the simultaneous coexistence of varying traditions, for example, Dal' and Aleksandr Aleksandrovich Bestuzhev (Marlinsky) in the 1830s. The presence of a writer such as Dal' was an interesting theoretical problem for a representative of the Formalist School such as Eikhenbaum. He prefaces his 1924 essay "V poiskakh zhanra" (In Search of Genre) with an epigraph from Dal': "There is a certain kind of alternating cycle in all things, but there is also variety."

Vladimir Ivanovich Dal's background was Danish-German. His Danish father came to Russia originally as a Protestant theologian, but after receiving additional training in Germany, worked as a medical doctor in the Imperial service; his German mother, Maria Ivanovna Freitag, was a daughter of a cultured woman who had translated works of the German writers Salomon Gessner and August Wilhelm Iffland into Russian. Dal' was born on 10 November 1801 in Lugansk (Ukraine) and later signed his works Kazak Vladimir Lugansky (Cossack Vladimir of Lugansk). Dal's father, even though Danish-born, became a fer-

The house in Lugansk where Vladimir Ivanovich Dal' was born

vent Russian patriot who experienced the 1812 Napoleonic invasion of Russia, regretting that his sons were still too young to do battle with the invaders. Dal's early education was narrow (mathematics and drawing); after he turned fourteen, he entered the Naval Cadet School in St. Petersburg. He finished his training and served for five years as a naval officer, feeling even more Russian than he had when he was younger. He recognized this allegiance clearly after a brief visit to Denmark, the country of his forebears, a visit to which he had looked forward with great anticipation but from which he came away knowing that he had "nothing in common with the Danes, the homeland of my ancestors." Neither did he feel any attraction to the Germans, his forebears on his mother's side. What interested him with ever-greater passion were Russian things—the Russian language spoken by the humble people and their customs and beliefs. He left the naval service in 1824 and entered the medical school of the University of Derpt (Tartu, Estonia) from which he graduated with honors three years later. Dal' participated as a physician in Russian campaigns against Turkey (1828–1829) and Poland (1831). He did not leave Russian territory after that.

As a physician in the Imperial service, Dal' did not wish to submit to the standard method of practicing medicine but chose homeopathy as a manner of treatment. This decision caused difficulties with his superiors. Furthermore, in 1832 he published his first artistic work, *Russkiia skazki . . . Piatok pervyi,* which also aroused suspicion for its unorthodox use of the Russian language and its focus on the lives of humble peo-

ple and their irreverent attitude toward authority. Dal' had to leave St. Petersburg for an assigned post as administrator in the Orenburg province. The years that followed (first in Orenburg, later in Nizhny-Novgorod) turned Dal's life in the direction he had secretly desired all along: collecting and recording Russian lexical material and folklore. High moments during Dal's eight years of service in Orenburg were visits by Pushkin in September 1833 in search of material for his *Istoriia Pugachevskogo bunta* (History of the Pugachev Uprising, 1834) and by Vasilii Andreevich Zhukovsky in the suite of the Tsarevich Alexander in 1837. Pushkin looked upon Dal's artistic style, so strong in philological experiments, more kindly than did Zhukovsky. Dal' was present when Pushkin died in January 1837. Pushkin, the story goes, gave Dal' his ring with an emerald stone; until he died, Dal' wore the ring on his right hand. This biographical detail perhaps makes Dal' Pushkin's heir in a sense, but only remotely. Beyond some minor details, the two had little in common. Dal' was married twice: first to Iuliia Andre in 1833, and after Andre's death to Ekaterina L'vovna Sokolova in 1841. He had a son and daughter from his first marriage and three daughters from his second. Dal' was reticent about personal matters and once replied (to the great linguist Iakov Karlovich Grot): "Judge the work and leave the person out. What do you need it for?"

In 1839 Dal' took part in a disastrous expedition against the Sultan of Khiva and afterward was transferred to the Ministry of the Interior in St. Petersburg. As an administrator Dal' conducted studies of the Old Believers and other sects; as an artist he wrote several physiological sketches, a popular form at that time in France and Russia. His productivity encompassed textbooks for children on botany (1849) and zoology (1849) and the popular anthology *Soldatskie dosugi* (A Soldier's Leisure, 1843). With this latter work Dal' became an active contributor to the production of second-rate, popular reading material. The demands of administrative duties and artistic interests could not be reconciled in the capital, and Dal' consequently once more took a post in the provinces.

In Nizhny-Novgorod, starting in 1849, he served as head of the Office for Administration of the Crown Properties. He became friends with Pavel Ivanovich Melnikov (Andrei Pechersky), who had interests similar to Dal's and who became his helper and disciple. Dal's *Poslovitsy russkago naroda* was completed in 1852 but was not allowed to appear in print until 1862, because it was considered too simple and unsophisticated to be worthy of the print medium. After its publication Dal' commented that "my collection was destined to pass through many tortures long before it came out in print." When it did appear, one critic called it "a monument to people's stupidities." Dal' continued collecting words for his *Tolkovyi slovar' zhivago velikorusskago iazyka* and published its first edition in 1863–1866. The second edition was published posthumously in 1880–1882.

After working in government service for many years, Dal' retired in 1859 and settled in Moscow. In the last decade of his life he became a spiritualist and began reading the works of Swedish scientist and philosopher Emmanuel Swedenborg. He decided to transcribe the Holy Scriptures into popular language, finishing the "Five Books of Moses" (Pentateuch) and titling the work "Bytopisanie" (Writ of Life); apparently this project was never published. It is not difficult to see that Dal's enthusiasm and passion for the spoken Russian word ("which we treat with such condescension in our society") had turned into a kind of fanaticism. A common interest in folklore and spiritualism led to a friendship between Dal' and I. O. Lapshin, a state official in Moscow. Lapshin arranged spiritualist seances in his Moscow apartment that were attended by other writers such as Vladimir Sergeevich Solovev.

Dal's mystic inclination grew until he died in September 1872; one of his last wishes was to be baptized in the Russian Orthodox faith before his death. Because of his extraordinary love of things Russian (not refined, but simple things), it bothered Dal' that he not only had a non-Russian name (perhaps part of the reason he signed his work Kazak Vladimir Lugansky) but also was a Lutheran by baptism. When friends would ask him occasionally whether he was Russian or German, Dal' answered that it was the "spirit, the soul, which determined a person's adherence to one or the other nationality." And if one looked further at "the manifestation of the spirit, at a person's thought and at the language in which that thought was expressed, then there could be no doubt that he was Russian." Dal's insistence on his Russianness must not be taken lightly. It is a feature of his character and mind; with its accompanying fanaticism and intellectual limitations, it puts him somewhat in the company of such characters as the assistant procurator in Leo Tolstoy's novel *Voskresenie* (Resurrection, 1899): "Vrede, however, was a conservative, and furthermore, like all Germans serving in Russia he was especially devoted to orthodoxy."

Dal' made his reputation early in life with his collection of artistically reworked fairy tales, *Russkiia skazki . . . Piatok pervyi.* They were a manifestation of what came to be seen as *narodnost'* (native spirit) in art. Zhukovsky, Pushkin, Petr Pavlovich Ershov, and Dal' became enthusiastic about the richness of native life in popular fairy tales and legends, reworking them according to their own artistic methods. For Dal',

however, what mattered most was not the material itself, which could be expressed in a variety of forms, but the choice of words and phrases in the artistic transformation of the material, as he explained in the first volume of his *Polnoe sobranie sochinenii* (Complete Collected Works, 1897–1898): "Not the fairy tales themselves were important to me but the Russian word which with us has lived in such neglect that it could not show itself among people without a special pretext or cause. The fairy tale was such a pretext."

Dal' wanted his group of five fairy tales to be reproduced in *na gramotu grazhdanskuiu perelozhennye* (native speech), "adapted to the popular manner of life" and "embellished with current proverbs." Narrated by a simple peasant (Dem'ian), Dal's fairy tales became a model of philological play, a "fireworks" of linguistic "excesses," as Eikhenbaum once said of Leskov (*chrezmernyi pisatel'*), who followed Dal' as a representative of the "younger school." Entertainment and joy was all that mattered, and the inherent humor in Dal's fairy tales delighted Pushkin. Zhukovsky, on the other hand, recognized the "peasant" language at its foundation and dismissed Dal's style as *muzhitskii* (a mouzhik's). More fairy tales followed, not all of them as brilliant and successful as the "First Group of Five." Fundamentally, Dal' was interested only in the possibilities of word play, ornamentation through proverbs, rhythmic prose, and details of *byt* (everyday life), for which the fairy tales gave him ample opportunity. It was an artfully developed style with focus on the idiosyncrasies of a humble narrator; the unabashed linguistic excess and exaggeration found imitators in Dal's time, a tradition that has been humorously called *lapotnaia shkola* (the "bast shoe" school).

Dal's prose tales, which followed the fairy tales, were not so brilliant stylistically. The critic V. Gofman commented: "It is curious that V. Dal' apparently did not succeed with a *skaz* on a basis which was not folkloristic, i.e., outside of the stylization of the fairy tales." Dal's prose tales can be divided into groups, such as stories in a non-Russian setting, stories of poor officials, biographical stories, and stories with emphasis on *byt*. Dal' essentially lacked the storyteller's gift of developing a plot with suspense and eventual denouement. On the other hand, he observed well and was always sympathetic to his subject. The stories in the first group, published in *Moskovskii telegraf* (The Moscow Telegraph), include "Tsyganka" (A Gypsy Woman, 1830), "Bolgarka," and "Podolianka," followed by stories of Kazakh life: "Bikei i Mauliana" (1833) and "Maina." Attention to the details of the life of these non-Russian people makes these stories noteworthy. Critic M. I. Fetisov called them "a small encyclopedia of Kazakh life."

Dal' in the 1830s

the way on various herbal preparations with their folk names and uses:

> Maliny li, businy li, shalfeiu, lipovogo tsveta, kipreiu, ivana-da-mar'i, romashki s landyshami, ili uzh zavarit' nastoiashchego chaiu? I Van'ka rassudil, chto buznya p'etsia na noch' dlia ispariny, malina posle bani, shalfei durnuiu pogodu, lipovyi tsvet so svezhimi sotami, ivan-da-mar'ia i romashka, kogda ne mozhetsia, kiprei, to-est' koporskii ili ivan-chai, po nuzhde, za nedostatkom luchshego, i potomu polagal zavarit' segodnia nastoiashchego, kitaiskogo chaiu, chto y bylo ispolneno.

Dal's prose tales of everyday life, "Kolbasniki i borodachi" (Sausage Makers and Bearded Fellows), published in *Otechestvennye zapiski* in 1844, and "Otets s synom" (Father and Son), published in the same journal in 1848, are at the borderline of the next group of his work, the physiological sketches. Dal' always paid special attention to details in the speech of his characters. The merchant Grebnev in "Otets s synom" speaks as a merchant of his time would speak, with a Dalian twist toward exaggeration. This speech is characterized by a wealth of folk sayings, presented in a concentrated and unbroken series, deliberately exaggerated and impossible to translate precisely. In this passage, for example, the speaker is discussing how need gives rise to labor; he says that bread does not need a stomach but that a stomach needs bread, and he concludes that one cannot make fish soup without fish:

> Stalo byt', brattsy moi, trud, rabota, remeslo—rozhdaiutsia iz potreby, potomu chto na vsiakuiu potrebu est' pomekha, zapiataia. Khleb za briukhom ne khodit, a briukho za khlebom. Vsiakuiu potrebu, protianuv ruku s mesta, ne dobudesh'; podle izby gribki ne rastut, a podi narezh' lozy, spleti vershu, postav' ee umeiuchi na sterzhne, znaia, chto ryba protiv vody idet, da opiat' podi dostan' iz nee rybu—da togda i poesh' ushitsy.

Gogol's genius inevitably left traces in Dal's style as it did elsewhere. The use of metonymy in Dal' is reminiscent of Gogol's strength in the use of this device, particularly in reference to certain characters and the suggestive associations of their names: in Gogol, Korobochka (Little Box), Sobakevich (Doggy), Nozdrev (Nostril), Bashmachkin (Shoe); in Dal', Shilokhvostov (Pintail), Igrivyi (Playful or Naughty), Viol'damur (from the Italian *viola d'amore* or French *viole d'amur,* tenor violin or viola of love).

Dal's efforts in the tradition of the physiological sketch have long been considered some of his most successful accomplishments. First developed in France, the physiological sketch achieved great popularity in Russia as an element of the Natural School. In 1845 Nikolai Alekseevich Nekrasov edited an anthol-

Another group of stories develops the theme of the poor official, a tradition to which all major and minor writers paid their due. They represent a mixture of sentimentalism and naturalism: "Bedovik" (Poor Fellow), published in *Otechestvennye zapiski* (Notes of the Fatherland) in 1839; "Zhizn' cheloveka ili progulka po Nevskomu prospektu" (A Man's Life, or a Walk Along the Nevsky Boulevard), published in *Moskvitianin* (The Muscovite) in 1843; and *Pokhozhdeniia Khristiana Khristianovicha Viol'damura i ego Arsheta* (Adventures of Christian Christianovich Viol'damur and his Arshet, 1844). Dal' intersperses his narrative style, wherever appropriate, with folk sayings and metaphoric expressions, often lending it a humorous twist.

Dal's biographical tales continue his method of combining feeling with naturalism. They reveal at times a certain imitativeness of Nikolai Gogol, but they lack his hyperbole, tendency for the grotesque, and extraordinary wealth of comparisons. Dal's talent rests in the interplay of life and language without the serious subcurrent of Gogol's absurd world. Gogol's linguistic escapades lose much in translation; Dal's folklife details simply cannot be exactly translated. For example, in this passage one person is asking another what kind of tea they should brew, commenting along

ogy titled *Fiziologiia Peterburga* (A Physiology of Petersburg), preceded by an introductory essay by Vissarion Grigori'evich Belinsky and including Dal's "Peterburgskii dvornik," which had already been published a year earlier in *Literaturnaia gazeta*. Here, Dal' succeeds in combining several aspects of his talent: excellent observation, an eye for detail, and a sensitive ear for the mannerisms of speech of his simple hero, Grigorii. He presents a day in the lives of a St. Petersburg custodian and his tenants in a succinct sequence of typical situations. The narrative language is vivid, and the dialogues are representative of the speech of the hero and the tenants:

> —Prinesi! Tut vot liuboe; libo po vodu idi, libo ulitsu meti; a kak nadziratel' poidet, tak vot i budem my s toboi u prazdnika.
> —U prazdnika? Da mne chto za prasdniki! Tam vy sebe, pozhalui, prazdnuite, a ty vody prinesi!

Belinsky saw Dal's physiological sketches as "exemplary creations of their kind whose secret V. I. Lugansky has so profoundly grasped." He went on to say that next to Gogol, Dal' is "until now the most gifted writer in Russian literature." Other physiological sketches followed: "Denshchik," "Ural'skii kazak," and *Nakhodchivoe pokolenie* (An Inventive Tribe), the last one finding a place as the fifth booklet of Faddei Venediktovich Bulgarin's *Kartinki russkikh nravov* (Pictures of Russian Manners, 1842). Dal's success with this genre rests in his talent for succinctness and his lack of sentimentality. The genre does not require the development of a story line but a sharp eye and a well-tuned ear, both of which he possessed. It should be added that Gogol valued this trait of Dal's and spoke highly of him, as in this excerpt from an 1846 letter to his friend, the critic Petr Aleksandrovich Pletnev:

> In my opinion he is more important than all other story tellers and creators of fantasies. I may perhaps not be impartial in this situation, the reason being that this writer more than any other appeals to my own personal taste and to the idiosyncrasy of my own requirements. Every line of his teaches me something and makes me think, bringing me closer to an appreciation of Russian ways and our national life. Furthermore, everyone will agree with me that this writer is useful and beneficial to all of us at the present time. His works are a living and truthful account of Russia.

Dal' continued to write sketches. Andrei Aleksandrovich Kraevsky, editor of *Otechestvennye zapiski,* aptly titled a set of Dal's stories, which began to appear in 1848 and came out for many years in various periodicals, "Kartiny iz russkogo byta" (Scenes from Russian Daily Life). A second group of such short prose works, "Novye kartiny iz russkoi zhizni" (New Scenes from Russian Life), followed in *Russkii vestnik* (The Russian Herald) in 1867 and 1868.

In addition to its folklore character, Dal's late work shows clear moral tendencies. The stories in the second series encourage readers to live and die in harmony with God's design ("Obmiran'e" [Dying]), to respect the skill in their craftsmanship and the high moral standards of the Old Believer Schismatics ("Dedushka Bugrov" [Grandfather Bugrov]), and to be merciful to the needy ("Kruzhevnitsa" [The Lace Maker]). The times, however, demanded other material, and Dal' seemed no longer in tune with what the critics were seeking. In 1861 Nikolai Aleksandrovich Dobroliubov, writing for the journal *Sovremennik* (The Contemporary), gave Dal's work a scathingly negative review:

> After the noise which Mr. Dal' made with his unfortunate fantasy about the fact that a knowledge of reading and writing was ruinous for national morals, after the justified reproaches and the subjection to public disgrace, which were poured on him at that time from all sides—and especially after his unfortunate attempts to defend himself, which spoiled his cause completely—after all these disgraceful stories which he created, one is sorely at a loss to say anything in praise of something written by Mr. Dal'. You may expect that this remark will be followed by a "but," or a "however." Don't look for it, or you will be disappointed: we don't even want to say anything in praise of Mr. Dal'.
>
> Truthfully speaking, from his stories you don't even learn a penny's worth about the Russian people, and in the stories themselves you don't find a drop of indigenousness. On a single page of sketches by Uspensky, or in the stories of the life of simple folk by Shchedrin, you find more national elements and more about the people than in all the works of Dal' combined.
>
> Mr. Dal' does not have, nor did he ever have, any clear idea in his concepts (for what sort of concept can there be without any idea), except what he found in the heap of trifles which he has remembered from national life.

Dal' was not concerned with the social aspects of the situations he presented. If the question of an ideology were to be raised with regard to Dal', then the only appropriate response would be "native Russianness" (*narodnost'*), which is closely linked to the Slavophile worldview. But ideas were not Dal's major concern. In his fairy tales, stories, and sketches—even in the least artistically embellished works, his *Soldatskie dosugi* and *Matrosskie dosugi* (A Sailor's Leisure, 1853)—he chose unsophisticated material and wrote for unsophisticated people. But in his best work he was an experimenter with style. He found imitators who carried his artistic philological experiments further in the nineteenth century and in the twen-

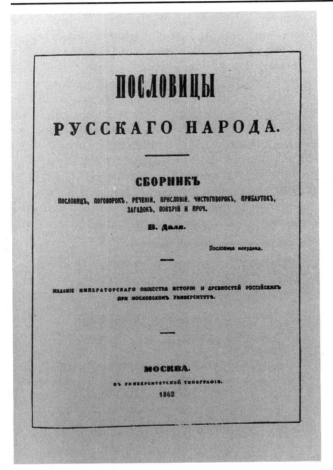

Title page for Dal's Poslovitsy russkago naroda *(Proverbs of the Russian People), a collection of sayings, riddles, catch phrases, and popular beliefs*

tieth. Devices from Dal' can be found in Leskov's "Administrativnaia gratsiia (Zahme Dressur v zhandarmskoi aranzhirovke)" (Administrative Grace [Zahme Dressur in a Gendarme Arrangement]), written in 1893; in Remizov's "Emaliol'" (included in a 1910–1912 collection) and Pilniak's "Mat'machekha" (Colt's Foot, included in a 1924 collection); and in works by Melnikov (Pechersky) and Zamiatin. Dal's achievement as an artist was not understood until a Formalist such as Eikhenbaum grasped the law of the cyclical nature and the variety of artistic movements operating side by side in literary history: "There is some kind of sequential circuit in everything, but there also is a difference." He gave Dal' a place in the literary history of the nineteenth century; since that time readers have learned to appreciate him as an artist: "The rise of this younger line (Dal', Mel'nikov-Pechersky, Leskov), suppressed and lost in the Russian prose of the period of Dostoevsky and Tolstoy, is profoundly significant."

Native Russians and students of the Russian language have long recognized the importance of Dal's *Tolkovyi slovar'.* It is the result of one man's dedication to a single task spanning more than five decades. Dal's interest in such a project was apparently ignited when, while traveling in 1819, he heard a coachman use the word *zamolazhivaet* (it is clouding over), a dialectal expression of the Tula region. He recorded it, and from then on he never stopped recording until he died in 1872. Dal' was not a trained linguist such as Grot, Aleksandr Khristoforovich Vostokov, Izmail Ivanovich Sreznevsky, Aleksei Aleksandrovich Shakhmatov, and Jan Niecislaw Baudouin de Courtenay; nevertheless he set his mind with a sort of missionary zeal to restore the Russian language to its "unperverted" state, cleansed of all foreign words. This singleminded effort has retained its value more than one hundred years after it first appeared. And while scholars such as V. I. Chernyshev have assessed it critically and discussed its shortcomings, the final conclusion is entirely on the positive side: "that's why the *Tolkovyi Slovar'* of Dal' until now is and must be a reference work for any Russian linguist and writer, a book which clarifies many mysteries of understanding and usage of words in the Russian language in the area of its lexicology and phraseology on the basis of the language of the entire Russian people, a language which has been preserved since ancient times and has developed in its dialects and literary usage." The Russian poet Osip Mandel'shtam compared the *Tolkovyi slovar'* indirectly to the Greek Acropolis, "a minor Kremlin, a winged fortress of nominalism, endowed with the Hellenic spirit for a tireless battle with the formless chaos, nonexistence, which is threatening our history from all sides." Vladimir Nabokov speaks of the *Tolkovyi slovar'* with admiration in his autobiography, *Speak, Memory* (1966), and Aleksandr Solzhenitsyn's first wife, Natal'ia Reshetovskaia, mentions in her recollections of her life with her husband how "he considered it absolutely imperative to study Dal' regularly, ideally every day. He used to say that he needed to create within himself an internal ambience of the Russian language, to become suffused with its spirit."

Tolkovyi slovar' is organized in terms of *gnezda* (word "nests"). *Poslovitsy russkago naroda,* too, had been grouped in semantic units, and Dal' found it productive to apply this method to his dictionary as well. The proverbs were published in 1862 under 179 topics (*Bog-vera*—God-Faith; *Vera-grekh*—Faith-Sin; *Izuverstvo-raskol*—Fanaticism-Schism; *Izuverstvo-khanzhestvo*—Fanaticism-Bigotry). In *Tolkovyi slovar'* words are grouped according to "affinities" of word meanings such as *TRI, troit', troit'-troenie, troinoi, troika.* This system was a compromise between the alphabetical arrangement, which Dal' considered too "fatiguing," and the arrangement by word roots. It has been called an "alphabet-nest" system. A full discussion of Dal's method may be found in a 1958 study by Mikhail Varfolomeevich Kankava. Dal' not only wanted to record all Russian words in circulation but also suggested some of his own inventions to replace foreign influences in the Russian language: *lovkosilie* instead of *gimnastika*, *sebiatnik* instead of *egoist*, *iarostivost'* instead of *energiia*, *nebozem* instead of *gorizont*. Dal's suggested replacements were not adopted by Russian native speakers. Scholars in the twentieth century have come to value Dal's dictionary as a collection of "the store of knowledge of the Russian people, its entire way of life, all its concepts and beliefs, of everything that finds expression in the Russian word."

Samples of Dal's own collecting activity find their way into the tale "Savelii Grab, ili Dvoinik" (Savelii Grab, or The Double), published in volume two of the anthology *Sbornik Kukol'nika, Skaza za skazkoi* (Kukol'nik's Collection of Tales and More Tales) in 1842; the hero is himself a collector. Dal' handed over some of his collections to others: his songs to Petr Vasil'evich Kireevsky, his fairy tales to Aleksandr Nikolaevich Afanas'ev, and the birch bark drawings to the Imperial Library in St. Petersburg. His collection *O pover'iakh, suever'iakh i predrassudkakh russkago naroda* (On the Beliefs, Superstitions and Prejudices of the Russian People) was published both during his lifetime as a series in Nestor Vasil'evich Kukol'nik's journal *Illiustratsiia* (Illustration) in 1845 and 1846 and posthumously as a book in 1880. The entries on such topics as the *domovoi* (house spirit), *vodianoi* (water sprite) and *oboroten'* (werewolf) vary in length. They are in fact short essays that may possibly have been useful to such writers as Maksim Gorky (*Detstvo* [Childhood], 1913) and Fedr Kuzmich Sologub (*Melkii bes* [The Petty Demon], 1907). The essays on *zagovory* (charms) and *primety* (signs) are particularly detailed. This collection closes with a short piece on *klady* (treasures).

Dal' also wrote historical narratives, one dealing with the ill-fated Khiva expedition with Count Vasilii Alekseevich Perovsky in 1839–1840 ("Pis'ma o Khivinskom pokhode" [Letters on the Khiva Expedition]), published in *Russkii arkhiv* in 1867; another with the adventures of a Russian captured by the Turkomans of the Khiva Sultanate ("Rasskaz Grushina" [Grushin's Tale]); and a third with the Russian invasion of Afghanistan and the siege of the Herat Fortress ("Rasskaz ob osade kreposti Gerata" [A Tale of the Siege of the Herat Fortress]). This last tale is of great interest, for it depicts the collision of imperialist interests between Russia and Great Britain in that part of the world in the 1830s. The fortress, with defenses directed by an English officer, was under siege for nine

Title page for the second, revised edition of Tolkovyi slovar' zhivago velikorusskago iazyka (Reasoned Dictionary of the Living Great-Russian Language), a project on which Dal' spent nearly fifty years

and one-half months. Dal's description, slanted in favor of the Russians, with the Persians depicted as being cowardly and the English as being duplicitous, illustrates the tendencies toward bias during a period of hegemonic power rivalries. Equally biased in favor of Russian political designs are "Pis'ma o Khivinskom pokhode" and "Rasskaz Grushina."

Dal' was a model of the Russian chauvinist in the nineteenth century, highly focused on all things Russian and uninterested in the broad interconnections among various cultures. This characteristic can be seen as a limiting factor in his life, but it can also be viewed as a source of strength. To Dal', the recording of native Russian culture equaled the search for truth by a philosopher. Through his diligence and commitment to the collecting, compiling, and recording of Russia's native language and beliefs, he has preserved an essential part of Russian culture. He has also created for himself a monument, attractive in its diversity and richness, that will continue to be important. Dal's work delights and inspires readers and writers wherever the Russian word in all of its manifestations commands interest and respect.

Biographies:

Maia Iakovlevna Bessarab, *Vladimir Dal'* (Moscow: Moskovskii Rabochii, 1968); revised and augmented as *Vladimir Dal', Kniga o doblestnom grazhdanine Rossii i velikom bortse za russkii iazyk* (Moscow: Sovremennik, 1972);

Vladimir I. Porudominskii, *Dal', Zhizn' zamechatel'nykh liudei*, series 17, no. 505 (Moscow: Molodaia gvardiia, 1971).

References:

Joachim T. Baer, "Dal' and Leskov als Vertreter des künstlerischen Philologismus," *Zeitschrift für slavische Philologie*, 37, no. 1 (1973): 179–190;

Baer, "Philologism and Conservatism in Nineteenth-Century Russian Literature," *Slavic Studies*, 16: 125–144;

Baer, "Remizov, Zamiatin and Pil'niak: Drei Meister des 'künstlerischen Philologismus' in der Russischen Literatur," in *Korrespondenzen, Festschrift für Dietrich Gerhardt aus Anlass des 65. Geburtstages*, edited by Engle-Braunschmidt u. Schmücker (Giessen: Schmitz Verlag, 1977), pp. 16–27;

Baer, *Vladimir Ivanovich Dal' as a Belletrist* (The Hague: Mouton, 1972);

Baer, "Vladimir Ivanovich Dal'–Collector and Recorder of Native Russian Culture," *Die Welt der Slaven*, 22, no. 2 (1977): 225–241;

A. V. Blyum, "Dal's Dictionary and the Censorship: New Material on Baudouin de Courtenay," *Oxford Slavonic Papers*, 23 (1990): 61–66;

N. Bogoslovsky, ed., *N. V. Gogol o literature* (Moscow, 1952), pp. 211–212;

Dagmar Burkhart, "Die semiotischen Dimensionen des russischen Sprichworts," in *Beitrage zur russischen Volksdichtung*, edited by Klaus-Dieter Seemann (Wiesbaden: Harrassowitz, 1987), pp. 13–37;

V. I. Chernyshev, "Tolkovyi slovar' russkogo iazyka (Kriticheskii otzyv)" and "Vladimir Ivanovich Dal' i ego trudy v oblasti izucheniia russkogo iazyka i russkogo naroda," in *Izbrannye trudy*, volume 1 (Moscow, 1970), pp. 351–439;

V. Chicherov, "Sbornik Vladimira Dalia 'Poslovitsy russkogo naroda,'" introduction to Dal's *Poslovitsy russkogo naroda* (Moscow: Goslitizdat, 1957), pp. v–xxviii;

Boris Eikhenbaum, *Skvoz' literaturu: sbornik statei* (Leningrad: Academia, 1924);

Iu. P. Fesenko, ed., "Dva rukopisnykh nabroska V. I. Dalia 'Silistriia' i 'Kulevich,'" *Russkaia Literatura: Istoriko-Literaturnyi-Zhurnal*, 3 (1990): 146–150;

M. I. Fetisov, *Pervye russkie povesti na Kazakhskie temy* (Alma-Ata: AN KazSSR, 1950), pp. 80–152;

V. Gofman, "Fol'klornyi skaz Dalia" in *Russkaia proza*, edited by Boris Eikhenbaum (Leningrad: Akademia, 1926), pp. 232–261;

Mikhail Varfolomeevich Kankava, *V. I. Dal' kak leksikograf* (Tbilisi: Tsodna, 1958);

Fryderyk Listwan, "Nowelistyka Włodzimierza Dala, Wybrane zagadnienia," *Slavia-Orientalis*, 31, nos. 1–2 (1982): 15–26;

Listwan, "'Polskie momenty' w życiu i twórczości Władzimierza Dala," *Slavia-Orientalis*, 35, no. 4 (1986): 523–527;

Listwan, "Włodzimierz Dal a tradycja folklorystyczna: Bajki," *Slavia-Orientalis*, 31, nos. 3–4 (1982): 129–140;

Osip Mandel'shtam, *O prirode slova* (Khar'kov: Istoki, 1922);

R. Pletnev, "K stodesiatiletiiu smerti V. I. Dalia," *Novyi Zhurnal*, 153 (December 1983): 262–266;

N. V. Popova, "Avtorskie otstupleniia v Slovare V. I. Dalia," *Russkaia rech'* (November–December 1988): 81–83;

Vladimir I. Porudominskii, "Dal' i Pushkin," *Russkaia rech'* (September–October 1987): 31–39; (January–February 1988): 13–18;

Porudominskii, "Gogol' i Dal': Iz tvorcheskikh obshchenii," *Russkaia rech'* (September–October 1988): 10–16; (November–December 1988): 9–17;

Porudominskii, "Lev Tolstoi i Vladimir Dal'," *Russkaia rech'* (March–April 1987): 36–45;

Reshetovskaia, Natal'ia, *V spore so vremenem* (Moscow: Izdatel'stvo Agentstva pechati Novosti, 1975);

L. G. Samotnik, "V. I. Dal' i problemy sibirskogo narechiia," in *Russkoe narodnoe slovo v istoricheskom aspekte*, edited by V. N. Rogova and others (Krasnoiarsk: Krasnoiarskii gosudarstvennyi universitet, 1984);

G. P. Smolitskaia, "K 130-letiiu so dnia rozhdeniia: Vladimir Ivanovich Dal' 1801–1872," *Russkaia rech'* (November–December 1991): 3–11;

A. A. Zrazhevskii, "O literaturnykh psevdonimakh V. I. Dalia," *Russkaia rech'* (November–December 1991): 18–23.

Nadezhda Andreevna Durova
(Aleksandr Andreevich Aleksandrov)
(September 1783 – 21 or 23 March 1866)

Jehanne M Gheith
Duke University

BOOKS: *Kavalerist-devitsa. Proisshestvie v Rossii* (St. Petersburg: I. Butovsky, 1836);

God zhizni v Peterburge, ili Nevygody tret'ego poseshcheniia (St. Petersburg: A. Voeikov, 1838);

Povesti i rasskazy, 4 parts (St. Petersburg: V. Poliakov, 1838);

Zapiski Aleksandrova (Durovoi). Dobavlenie k "Devitse-kavalerist" (Moscow: Nikolai Stepanov, 1839);

Gudishki (St. Petersburg: Shtab otdel'nogo korpusa vnutrennei strazhi, 1839);

Klad (St. Petersburg: Shtab otdel'nogo korpusa vnutrennei strazhi, 1840);

Ugol (St. Petersburg: Shtab otdel'nogo korpusa vnutrennei strazhi, 1840);

Yarchuk: Sobaka-dukhovidets (St. Petersburg: Rossiiskaia akademiia, 1840).

Editions and Collections: *Zapiski kavalerist-devitsy;* (Kazan', 1960; incomplete edition, Moscow, 1962);

Izbrannye sochineniia kavalerist-devitsy N. A. Durovoi (Moscow: Moskovskii rabocii, 1983);

Izbrannoe (Moscow, 1984);

Editions in English: *The Cavalry Maiden,* translated by John Mersereau and David Lapeza (Ann Arbor, Mich.: Ardis, 1988);

The Cavalry Maiden, edited and translated by Mary F. Zirin (Bloomington: Indiana University Press, 1988).

Nadezhda Andreevna Durova in the uniform of the Mariupol' Hussars, circa 1810 (portrait by an unknown artist)

Nadezhda Andreevna Durova's literary and military careers are closely linked, for the latter gave rise to her most successful literary persona, that of the female officer. Although she published for only four years (1836–1840) before retiring to relative obscurity, Durova made a significant mark on Russian literature. Her military memoirs are an unusual achievement in any literature, for while many women have fought in wars, few have recounted their experiences. These journals are among the first published autobiographies in Russia; Durova was also one of the first Russian women to publish a substantial body of prose fiction.

Disguised as a man, using the name Aleksandr Vasil'evich Sokolov (according to her service records), Durova joined the military on 17 September 1806. She served in the cavalry throughout the Napoleonic Wars (including the Battle of Borodino) and saw combat in 1807 and 1812–1814. Durova was the only Russian woman until the twentieth century to win the St. George Cross, a high military honor, awarded her for saving an officer's life in her first battle in 1807. Two of the three regiments in which Durova served were Polish-Lithuanian, and she was stationed for long periods in the western borders of what was then the Russian empire; she also briefly served as orderly to Field Marshal Kutuzov in 1812. Durova was steadily (but slowly) promoted throughout her time in the military, and when she retired in 1816, she left with the rank of *shtabs-rotmistr* (captain).

Nadezhda Andreevna Durova was born and grew up in the Kama-Volga region and also spent four or five years of her youth with her maternal grandmother in Ukraine. Durova's father, Andrei Vasil'evich Durov, born in Ufa province, was a cavalry captain of Polish ancestry. Her mother, born Nadezhda Ivanovna Aleksandrovicha, eloped with Durov in the early 1780s and thus alienated her father, who forgave her only after the birth of her first child (Nadezhda) in 1783. A. V. Durov left the military for financial reasons and in 1789 became the *gorodnichii* (mayor) of Sarapul. His daughter Nadezhda was raised from an early age by Astakhov, a hussar orderly (a common practice in this period). With Astakhov she learned to be comfortable in the martial world of horses, sabers, and pistols. At the age of four Nadezhda was given back into her mother's care, and the relationship between mother and daughter became increasingly strained. At eighteen she married Vasilii Stepanovich Chernov, a jurist, but left him after the birth of their son, Ivan. In 1804 she returned home to her parents. Durova decided to escape the female realm, claiming this as one main reason for joining the army in 1806.

Her imposture was discovered by officials in 1807 (largely through the efforts of her father). Durova's case merited a personal interview with Tsar Aleksandr I, who at first wanted to send her back to her father. When Durova insisted that serving in the military was vitally important to her, the tsar relented; he promoted her to the rank of officer, transferred her to the Mariupol' hussars (a more prestigious regiment), and rechristened her with a name based on his own: Aleksandrov. Aleksandr I also insisted that she keep her new name "above reproach," a command Durova took seriously: such a relationship with a ruler is perhaps unique in Russian history, and Durova's frequent admiring references to Aleksandr I not only reflect classical rhetorical traditions and her own desire to participate in autocratic and patriarchal structures but also indicate that she was aware of the unusual nature of their relationship. After this interview Durova was under the personal protec-

tion of the tsar and no longer needed to worry about discovery; her financial situation was also alleviated, for she could apply to him for funds, as she did on occasion. She retired in 1816 partly because she had not received the promotions she felt were commensurate with her service and partly at her father's request. It was difficult for Durova to leave the military. In 1860, nearly forty-five years after the fact, she writes: "I nearly despaired when the first sentry I passed did not come to attention . . . as he was supposed to at the sight of an officer. . . . I could not bear this complete alienation from the main element of my life."

Little is known about Durova from her retirement to Elabuga and Sarapul in 1816 until she embarked on a literary career in 1836 at the age of fifty-three. Aleksandr Pushkin facilitated Durova's entrée into the literary world; Durova's brother Vasilii, slightly acquainted with Pushkin, mediated the initial correspondence between the two. Durova wrote to the poet in 1835, offering her memoirs for his revision and publication: "Your wonderful pen can make them engrossing for our female readers." Pushkin responded that the memoir needed no revision and published a fragment of it (the first to reach him) in his journal *Sovremennik* (The Contemporary). This selection, "Zapiski N. A. Durovoi, izdavaemye A. S. Pushkinym" (Notes of N. A. Durova, published by A. S. Pushkin), included Pushkin's preface. Durova's cousin, Ivan Butovsky, published the full text of *Kavalerist-devitsa. Proisshestvie v Rossii* (The Cavalry Maiden: It Happened in Russia) later in 1836; convinced by Petr Aleksandrovich Pletnev that Pushkin was too busy to publish and edit the full text, Durova had, much to her later regret, relieved Pushkin of these duties.

The correspondence between Pushkin and Durova reveals a great deal about Durova as author, Pushkin as editor-publisher, and the literary mores of the 1830s. As Durova, a woman from the provinces and a literary outsider, impatiently confronted Russia's nascent literary institutions, she expressed her frustration in no uncertain terms; Pushkin responded elegantly, in amused and amusing detail.

Unlike most Russian authors, Durova had no formal education. For this reason, perhaps, critics (sometimes admiringly, sometimes disparagingly) frequently note the *nebrezhnyi* (careless) quality of her work. Nevertheless, Durova had read widely, and her fiction refers to various Western European authors (for example, Pierre Corneille, Voltaire, and Sir Walter Scott).

Durova published in the major journals of the period: *Biblioteka dlia chteniia* (Library for Reading), *Otechestvennye zapiski* (Notes of the Fatherland) and *Sovremennik,* and her works were highly regarded by prominent critics, including Vissarion Grigor'evich Belinsky and Nikolai Alekseevich Polevoi. In many ways her fiction is typical of the late Romantic period in Russia. She is usually adept in her use of suspense and the gruesome or shocking (à la Ann Radcliffe, whose works Durova had read). Durova's subjects are rarely Russian, and much of her fiction utilizes unusual narrative perspectives, covering a wide range of gender, class, and ethnic or religious positions and possibilities. Durova's unconventional angle of vision as a military officer and a woman is reflected in many of her works.

Durova-Aleksandrov's posture as a man is not exactly an imposture or masquerade, for these two identities seem to have merged for her; she moves lightly from one to the other throughout her autobiographical and semiautobiographical works—*Zapiski* (Notes), *Zapiski Aleksandrova (Durovoi). Dobavlenie k "Devitse-Kavalerist"* (Notes of Aleksandrov [Durova]. Addendum to the Cavalry Maiden, 1839), *God zhizni v Peterburge, ili Nevygody tret'ego poseshcheniia* (A Year of Life in Petersburg, or The Disadvantages of the Third Visit, 1838), and "Elena, T-skaia krasavitsa" (Elena, the Belle of T, 1837)—in which Durova alternates use of masculine and feminine forms, in narrative passages referring to herself in feminine forms and switching to masculine in conversation with others. This systematic alternation causes a kind of disjuncture that cannot be reproduced in English and causes narrative tension, as Durova constantly reminds the reader of her double-gender identity. Her own usage of the double identity clearly confused the reviewers of her day, who, when referring to Durova, randomly alternated feminine and masculine forms, sometimes calling her both Durova and Aleksandrov in a single paragraph.

Durova's figure called into question traditional definitions of gender boundaries. She was well aware of this fact as her description of her first meeting with Pushkin indicates (in *God zhizni*). She notes that he became visibly confused when she referred to herself using masculine forms, but she continued to do so because this usage had become part of her nature. On bidding Durova farewell, Pushkin kissed her hand, to which she responded: "O my God! I got out of that habit [masculine ending] so long ago!," and she snatched her hand away. She continues the account: "Not even the shadow of an ironic smile appeared on Aleksandr Sergeevich's face, but I dare say that at home he did not restrain himself, and . . . undoubtedly laughed wholeheart-

Durova, age fourteen

edly over this exclamation." Dual awareness and self-irony are typical of Durova; she was comfortable in her masculine role, unwilling to give it up even for Pushkin, whom she admired greatly; yet she was quite conscious of the enigma her double-gender identity posed for others.

Kavalerist-devitsa, is generally acknowledged as Durova's masterpiece. This text moves from her childhood years to descriptions of her life in the military, and its language is direct and lively. *Kavalerist-devitsa* is hybrid in genre, a cross between diary and memoir; according to Durova it was written as a diary and edited some twenty years later. Because Durova's original manuscripts have not survived, the history of the writing and editing process remains unclear; but her claim would account for two striking features of the narrative: a fairly coherent self-presentation and a sense of immediacy.

Kavalerist-devitsa differs from the usual military memoir in several ways. First, as a female officer Durova's perspective necessarily diverged from that of male memoirists, many of whom had been trained for a military career. Durova notes that "everything they (her fellow officers) find ordinary is quite extraordinary to me," and her memoir focuses on "ordinary," mainly peacetime, events, the

The Battle of Borodino (1812), in which Durova was injured (painting by an unknown artist)

daily round of military life that most male memoirists did not deem worthy of description. Although Durova includes her own feats of bravery in her account, unlike most military memoirists she focuses neither on them nor on the movements of battle. Rather, she concentrates on the joy of unrestricted movement and the chance to explore various locations and cultures.

The passionate desire for freedom Durova frequently expresses in *Kavalerist-devitsa* indicates that she sought in military life the freedom of movement traditionally open to the male sex rather than freedom from all forms of external discipline. On entering the military, she exclaims: "You, young women of my own age, . . . only you can value my happiness! You, who must account for every step, who cannot go fifteen feet without supervision and protection, who from the cradle to the grave are eternally dependent and eternally guarded, God knows from whom and from what— . . . only you can comprehend the joyous sensations that fill my heart at the sight of vast forests, immense fields, . . . and at the thought that I can roam them all with no one to answer to and no fear of anyone's prohibition."

Throughout her autobiographical writings Durova both rejects traditional female roles and shows sympathy for members of her sex. This tension is reflected in her not mentioning her marriage or motherhood. Throughout *Kavalerist-devitsa* she carefully changes dates so as to erase these years, claiming to have joined the army at the age of sixteen, when in fact she was twenty-three in 1806. As late as 1860 she continued to mystify her birthdate, saying, "I was born in 1788, in September. I don't know exactly what date." Several cogent reasons have been advanced for Durova's reticence: perhaps the marriage was so painful that she did not want to remember it, as A. Saks intimates; perhaps, as Mary Fleming Zirin suggests, factors of censorship or self-censorship were responsible.

Although Durova in many ways left the conventionally feminine realm, she continued to be deeply interested in the role and position of women in Russia. While she did not focus on "women's issues" to the same extent as did other female authors of the 1830s (for example, Elena Gan and Mariia Zhukova), she frequently included women's perspectives in her works or showed particular concern for female readers. Her military journals discuss women much more than the usual military memoir, and in different ways, showing how women lived rather than making them objects of sexual interest or exploit. Durova's other fiction, too, sometimes made women's concerns central (for example, "Elena" and "Nurmeka"), and in an untitled, unpublished article written in 1858, she encouraged women to take up socially useful roles. In choosing to enter the military and to publish her memoirs, Durova herself provided an alternative model for a woman's life.

Of Durova's other autobiographical works "Nekotorye chertyiz detskikh let" (A Few Traits from Childhood Years, 1838) and *God zhizni,* like *Kavalerist-devitsa,* provide a coherent self-presentation. In "Nekotorye cherty detskikh let" Durova, even more than in *Zapiski kavalerist-devitsa,* portrays her mother as continually restricting her daughter's freedom. *God zhizni* tells of Durova's unhappy encounters with Petersburg society. With sometimes fierce irony Durova describes how provincial values and habits clash with those of the capital: in Petersburg she is briefly lionized, only to find that society's "friendship" cannot survive more than two visits.

Zapiski Aleksandrova (Durovoi). Dobavlenie k "Devitse-kavalerist" is a series of apparently unconnected tales of Durova's life in the military. Many of the stories are absorbing and occasionally provide background for unexplained events in *Kavalerist-devitsa. Dobavlenie* is a kind of literary workshop; Durova includes several tales that appear in different form elsewhere.

In light of modern theories of autobiography (the self or selves that recount are necessarily different from the self in the moment of telling) Durova's autobiographical works provide a fascinating study in self-presentation; the fragmentary *Dobavlenie* seems to represent an earlier stage of the other two narratives and thus illustrates the ways she reworked material to create a cohesive picture of her "self."

Durova's stories tend to interweave; works not only join and separate, as in the examples above, but also implicitly comment on one another. In "Literaturnye zatei" (Literary Ventures), part of *Dobavlenie,* she describes a storytelling fest in which each officer must narrate an interesting event from his life. For her turn Durova tells "Elena," a story first published in 1837 and later included as "Igra sud'by" (The Play of Fate) in her *Povesti i rasskazy* (Novellas and Stories, 1839). "Elena" is about a beautiful and (initially) innocent girl, married at thirteen to a debauched army officer and literally destroyed (through syphilis) by men's mistreatment and a society in which her mother's main goal is to see her daughter "settled." Portraying the (secretly) female officer telling this story to male officers, Durova again indicates her concern for women in Russia. She does not polemicize, nor does she retell Elena's story in "Literaturnye zatei"; rather she leaves it up to the reader to connect the two works.

Besides the military journals, "Pavil'on" (The Pavilion, 1839) is Durova's most renowned work. The influential Belinsky was one of the critics who praised it highly. The story has two narrative centers: the relationship between the priest Venedikt and his son, Valerian (born before Venedikt became a priest) and the secret hidden in the pavilion of the title. This story, rich in Gothic motifs, ends in a bloody scene in that same pavilion.

Durova's portrayal of the strained relations between father and son is noteworthy as an early example of a theme that later took on great significance in Russian literature (for example, in the works of Fedor Dostoyevsky and Ivan Turgenev):

the relationship between generations. Durova powerfully depicts the strong bond between Venedikt and Valerian and Venedikt's sense of guilt for forcing his son to become a priest, a career for which he was not suited by nature. Grief and guilt drive Venedikt mad after witnessing Valerian's murderous passion.

In addition to *Dobavlenie* and "Pavil'on" Durova published several other works in 1839, *Gudishki* (Hooters), "Dva slova iz zhiteiskogo slovaria" (Two Words from the Dictionary of Everyday Life), "Sernyi kliuch" (The Sulphur Spring) and *Povesti i rasskazy.* "Dva slova" is a witty and poignant explication of the word *vospominaniia* (ball or recollection) in the lives of three society women of different ages (seventeen, forty, and sixty); "Sernyi kliuch" is a fairy tale–like tragic love story among the Cheremys (or Mariitsy), a tribal people of the Ural region. *Gudishki,* Durova's longest work (two hundred thousand words), is based on a Lithuanian legend and attempts to explain the existence of twelve villages named Gudishki encountered by the female officer-narrator in Durova's earlier story, "Gudishki" (in *Dobavlenie*). The novel, narrated by a Jewish tavern keeper, is a lurid tale of Lithuanian gods, a demon-child, near-incestuous desire, and human greed.

Povesti i rasskazy includes one new work, "Nurmeka," in addition to three that had been published earlier under different titles: "Igra sud'by" (previously "Elena"), "Liudgarda, kniazhna Gota" (previously "Pavil'on"), and "Cheremiska" (previously "Sernyi kliuch"). "Nurmeka," an historical novella set in the time of Ivan IV, depicts nationality, gender, and familial relationships in intriguing ways. This novella, an unusually sympathetic portrayal of Muslim life, treats Islamic customs with respect, though superficially. Durova here encourages readers to sympathize with the Tatars in their (ultimately unsuccessful) attempt to retake the city of Kazan' from Russian domination; she even reverses the image of the "Mongol yoke," as characters complain, instead of the "Russian yoke."

The story, "a transvestite masquerade," as Zirin aptly puts it, centers on secrets, substitution, and mystery, particularly the uncertain identity of the main character, Nurmeka, whose mother, Kizbek, keeps "her" veiled, allowing no one to see her face. Rumors of the girl's beauty spread, and the bravest, wealthiest Tatar men vie for her hand in marriage. In a reworking of a fairy-tale motif Kizbek exacts an unusual *kalym* (bride-price): the successful suitor must bring back the key to Kazan', a task that ultimately proves impossible.

Durova's fantastic tales (for example, *Gudishki,* the 1839 novel; *Klad* [Buried Treasure, 1840], *Yar-*

Durova in the 1860s

chuk: *Sobaka-dukhovidets,* [Yarchuk: The Dog Who Saw Spirits, 1840]) were generally less well received than those works based on her own experience. *Klad* is an unlikely tale of robbery and undiscovered treasure; the main protagonists are the children of a Tatar father and a Jewish mother. *Yarchuk,* set in seventeenth-century Bohemia, depicts the power of evil embodied in a demonic beauty and a dog that exposes spirits. Unlike these works *Ugol* (The Nook, 1840) at first appears to be a typical society tale, but here again Durova departs from literary conventions both by giving two serving women important roles and by closing with a nearly happy ending. *Ugol* also treats class in ways unusual for the period, describing the efforts of Fedulova, a merchant's wife and daughter of a freed serf, to enter high society.

It is unclear why Durova stopped publishing in 1840. Her own answer in later years was that she wanted to maintain a high artistic standard and no longer felt that she could: "I couldn't write now the way I did before, and I don't want to appear in the world with just anything."

Even after Durova retired she continued to wear men's clothes, to refer to herself using masculine forms, and to use the name Aleksandrov. For the last twenty-five years of her life she lived mainly in Elabuga on a meager annual pension of one thou-

sand rubles for her years of military service; when she died, she left only one ruble. She was known in Elabuga for her charity to people and animals and for her lively, sometimes eccentric behavior.

Durova died on 21 March 1866 (possibly 23 March) and was buried with military honors. The site was nearly forgotten, but in 1901 the Lithuanian dragoons erected a monument on her tomb, and a marble bust of Durova was placed in Elabuga in 1962. Until recently her literary works had fared less well.

Durova's life and personality—inferred from her literary works—have been the basis of many fictional depictions: this elision of life and fiction is, on one level, a tribute to her creative and compelling use of autobiographical materials. She is important in Russian literature not only because of her own works but also as the subject of fictionalized treatments, as Russians struggled to comprehend this anomalous figure. Durova has been variously mythologized in works ranging from A. Bogatyrev's 1957 opera *Nadezhda Durova* and L. A. Churilova's (Charskaia's) relatively sympathetic portrayal in *Smelaia zhizn'* (A Bold Life, 1908) to Konstantin A. Lipskerov and A. Kochetkov's play, *Nadezhda Durova* (1942), in which Durova's biography is exploited to encourage women's patriotism during World War II. These works not only reveal Durova's continued influence on Russian culture but also disclose attitudes about women's and men's roles in various eras.

Letters:

Leonid Grossman, ed. *Pis'ma zhenshchin k Pushkinu* (Moscow: Sovremennye problemy, 1928), pp. 118–128, 242–248;

Zapiski kavalerist-devitsy (Kazan', 1960), pp. 183–198;

"Vse,chto ia mog pripomit': Avtobiografiia N. A. Durovoi," *Nedelia,* no. 26 (1962);

Bibliographies:

N. N. Golitsyn, *Biograficheskii slovar' russkikh pisatel'nits* (St. Petersburg: V. S. Balashev, 1889), pp. 88–89;

Russkii biograficheskii slovar', volume 6 (St. Petersburg: Glavnoe upravlenie udelov, 1906), pp. 722–726;

Voennaia entsiklopediia, volume 9 (St. Petersburg: I. D. Sytin, 1912), pp. 243–244.

Biographies:

E. S. Nekrasova, "Nadezhda Andreevna Durova," *Istoricheskii vestnik,* no. 9 (September 1890): 585–612;

A. Saks, *Kavalerist-devitsa* (St. Petersburg: Vestnik russkoi konnitsy, 1912).

References:

V. V. Afanas'ev, "Divnyi fenomen nravstvennogo mira," introduction to Durova's *Izbrannoe* (Moscow: Sovetskaia Rossiia, 1984), pp. 5–28;

Vissarion Grigor'evich Belinsky, *Polnoe sobranie sochinenii,* volume 3 (Moscow: Akademia Nauk SSSR, 1953), pp. 148–157; volume 4 (Moscow: Akademia Nauk SSSR, 1954), pp. 308–309, 315–318, 382–383;

M. Sh. Fainshtein, "Sotrudnitsa pushkinskogo *Sovremennika*," *Pisatel'nitsy pushkinskoi pory: Istoriko-literaturnye ocherki* (Leningrad: Nauka, 1989), pp. 155–160;

Barbara Heldt, "Mothers and Daughters," *Terrible Perfection* (Bloomington: Indiana University Press, 1987), pp. 77–86;

Heldt, "Nadezhda Durova: Russia's Cavalry Maid," *History Today,* 33 (February 1983): 24–28;

Irina Mikhailovna Iudina, "Zhenshchina–voin i pisatel'nitsa Neizvestnye avtografy 'Kavalerist-devitsy' N. A. Durovoi," *Russian Literature,* no. 2 (1963): 130–135;

Vladimir Murav'ev, "Kavalerist-devitsa Nadezhda Durova," introduction to *Izbrannye sochineniia kavalerist-devitsy N. A. Durovoi* (Moscow: Moskovskii rabochii, 1988), pp. 5–24;

Petr Aleksandrovich Pletnev, *Sochineniia i perepiska,* volume 2 (St. Petersburg, 1885), pp. 267–268;

Aleksandr Pushkin, *Perepiska,* volume 2 (Moscow: Khudozhestvennaia literatura, 1982), pp. 482–483, 486, 490–505;

Pushkin, "Zapiski N. A. Durovoi," *Izbrannye* (Moscow: Moskovskii rabochii, 1988), pp. 553–559;

B. V. Smirensky, "Nadezhda Durova," in *Zapiski Kavalerist-devitsy* (Kazan', 1960), pp. iii–xxiv;

Mary Fleming Zirin, article about and translation of N. A. Durova's "My Childhood Years," in *The Female Autograph,* edited by Domna C. Stanton and Jeanine Parisier Plottel, volumes 12–13 (New York: New York Literary Forum, 1984), pp. 119–142;

Zirin, "*A Woman in the 'Man's World'*: The Journals of Nadezhda Durova (1783–1866)," in *Revealing Lives: Autobiography, Biography and Gender,* edited by Marilyn Yalom and Susan Groag Bell (Buffalo, N.Y.: State University of New York Press, 1990), pp. 43–51.

Papers:

The manuscript of an untitled, unpublished article by Durova from 1858 is in the Manuscript Division of the Russian National Library, archive of Mikhail Petrovich Pogodin.

Ivan Sergeevich Gagarin

(20 July 1814 – 20 July 1882)

Richard Tempest

University of Illinois at Urbana–Champaign

BOOKS: *La Russie sera-t-elle catholique?* (Paris: C. Douniol, 1856);

Les starovères, l'église russe et le pape (Paris: C. Douniol, 1857);

Tendances catholiques dans la société russe (Paris: C. Douniol, 1860);

La réforme du clergé russe (Paris: Joseph Albanel, 1867);

Les hymnes de l'église grecque (Paris, 1868);

L'église russe et l'immaculée conception (Paris: E. Plon, 1876);

Vie du P. Maro Folloppe de la Compagnie de Jésus: les jesuites de Russie, 1805–1816 (Paris: E. Plon, 1877);

Les archives russes et la conversion d'Alexandre I (Lyon, 1877);

Dnevnik; Zapiski o moei zhizni; Perepiska, edited by Richard Tempest and François Rouleau (Moscow: Iazyki russkoi kul'tury, 1996).

Editions in English: *The Russian Clergy,* translated by Ch. Du Gard Makepeace (London: Burns & Oates, 1872).

TRANSLATION: *O primirenii Russkoi Tserkvi s Rimskoiu* (Paris, 1858).

OTHER: *Études de théologie, de philosophie et d'histoire,* nos. 1–6 (1857–1858);

Petr Iakovlevich Chaadaev, *Oeuvres choisies de Pierre Tchadaïef publiées pour la première fois par le P[ère] Gagarin de la Compagnie de Jésus* (Paris & Leipzig: A. Franck, 1862).

Ivan Sergeevich Gagarin

In his youth Gagarin was a Russian diplomat and served in Munich, London, and Paris. His wide circle of friends and contacts included Fedor Ivanovich Tiutchev, Mikhail Iurievich Lermontov, Petr Iakovlevich Chaadaev, Aleksandr Ivanovich Turgenev, Prince Petr Andreevich Viazemsky, Friedrich Wilhelm Joseph von Schelling, and Félicité de Lamennais. As a friend of Prince Petr Vladimirovich Dolgorukov, with whom he shared lodgings in St. Petersburg, he was suspected by some of complicity in Aleksandr Pushkin's fateful duel, though the scholarly consensus now is that he was guiltless in the affair. In 1842 Gagarin converted to Catholicism and subsequently took Holy Orders in the Society of Jesus. From the 1850s through the 1880s he lived, with some interruptions, in Paris, where he published polemical tracts on the history of the Russian Church and worked for a union between the Russian and the Roman churches in Catholicism. During this period he corresponded with Ivan Turgenev and Nikolai Semenovich Leskov, and conducted a public debate

126

with his Slavophile opponents in Russia. On two occasions Gagarin played a notable role as a literary intermediary. In 1836 he was instrumental in arranging the publication of Tiutchev's poems in Pushkin's journal *Sovremennik* (The Contemporary), and in 1862 he performed a similar, albeit posthumous, service for Chaadaev by bringing out *Oeuvres choisies de Pierre Tchadaïef publiées pour la première fois par le P[ère] Gagarin de la Compagnie de Jésus,* the first book publication of three of Chaadaev's eight "Philosophical Letters" and his "Apology of a Madman."

Ivan Sergeevich Gagarin was born in Moscow into a rich and noble family. His father, Prince Ivan Sergeevich Gagarin (1777–1862), was a member of the Senate. His mother, Varvara Mikhailovna, née Pushkina (1779–1854), a devout and kindly woman, exercised considerable influence on the formation of his character. Gagarin was educated at home under the supervision of a French tutor. In 1831 Gagarin entered government service as a student at the Moscow Archive of the Ministry of Foreign Affairs. Early on he conceived a revulsion toward "tyranny and oppression" and, inspired by his readings in the classics, drew up constitutions for an imaginary republic "as fantastical as Plato's." According to Gagarin's "Notes sur mon histoire," he was a shy and bookish adolescent who spent much of his time daydreaming: " . . . My favourite diversion during this period was the long hours I spent pacing the vastness of a sepulchral hall, my head filled with fantasies of this nonexistent world, which so enchanted me." But the young Gagarin's political views were foreign to his parents, who covered him with reproaches every time he mentioned his utopia.

On 4 May 1833 Gagarin was appointed to the position of attaché at the Russian mission in Munich. Here he renewed his studies and attended lectures at the university. In Gagarin's archive at Meudon is a note, dating from September 1833, in which Friedrich Schelling invited him to tea at his house where he was expecting "several scholars and young French professors." This metaphysical tea party was just one of the many occasions when Schelling and the young Russian met. The famous philosopher, a correspondent of the thinker Chaadaev, commended him to Gagarin as "one of the most remarkable men not only in Russia, but in Europe." In Munich Gagarin lost his utopian convictions. He remained passionately opposed to serfdom and political injustice but concluded that "all revolutionary doctrines put might before right." He also became an agnostic.

Gagarin drew close to Tiutchev, his diplomatic colleague at the embassy, and was one of the select few who were aware that Tiutchev wrote poetry. The two spent hours in conversation, drinking tea and smoking cigars. In the summer of 1835 Gagarin visited Holland, the Rhineland, and Prague, where he was introduced to the exiled French king Charles X and members of his family. Gagarin was particularly taken by the pretty Duchess de Berry (Marie-Caroline de Bourbon-Sicile), the mother of Count Chambord Ferdinand-Marie-Dieudonné d' Artois, the youthful Bourbon pretender. The future Jesuit had an eye for beautiful women, especially highborn ones, according to Gagarin's own diary, which he began keeping during this journey and in which he continued to make intermittent entries throughout his diplomatic career.

In November 1835 Gagarin met the poet and critic Viazemsky, whose personality briefly tempted him to embrace "a literary existence." Gagarin's aesthetic sensibilities were conventional: he admired Napoleon I; George Gordon, Lord Byron; and Johann Wolfgang von Goethe, whom he called "the great triad of the age"; indeed, in his diary entries for the summer of 1834 he consciously strove to imitate the style of Goethe's *Aus Einer Reise am Rhein.* Elsewhere he quotes the poet Dmitrii Vladimirovich Venevitinov and expresses his admiration for George Sand's novel *Jacques* (1834).

Like the young Leo Tolstoy, the painfully self-conscious Gagarin would draw up elaborate and rigid rules of personal conduct which, again like Tolstoy, he consistently failed to obey. He was a frequent visitor to the palaces of the Bavarian royal family and in his diary chronicled the minutiae of court and society life in Munich. The last months of 1834 were a difficult time for Gagarin. He was worried by his lack of religious faith, longed to fall passionately in love, and dreamed of finding an exalted cause to which he could devote himself body and soul. He agonized over certain temptations of the flesh, wondering whether he should "purchase experience through weakness"—that is, lose his virginity to a woman of easy virtue. In December 1834 he went on a gambling spree (the only such incident in his life) and after losing all his winnings, railed against those "depraved modern writers" who "extolled" games of chance. (This may be a reference to Pushkin's tale "The Queen of Spades," 1833.)

Late in 1835 Gagarin arrived in St. Petersburg to take up new duties at the foreign ministry. With him he brought a selection of Tiutchev's poems, which he showed to the poet Vasilii Andreevich Zhukovsky, Viazemsky, and Pushkin. In

THE RUSSIAN CLERGY.

Translated from the French of

FATHER GAGARIN, S.J.

BY

CH. DU GARD MAKEPEACE, M.A.

LONDON: BURNS AND OATES,
17, 18 Portman Street and 63 Paternoster Row.
1872.

Title page for the English translation of Gagarin's ecclesiastical history

1836 the latter published several of them in the journal *Sovremennik,* thus launching Tiutchev's literary reputation. Gagarin moved in the same circles as Pushkin and Baron George Charles d'Anthès-Heeckeren, both of whom he saw almost daily, and while in Moscow he made Chaadaev's acquaintance. His conversations with Chaadaev were an important factor in Gagarin's eventual decision to become a Catholic. After the publication of Chaadaev's "First Philosophical Letter," for which the thinker was declared insane by the government, Gagarin carried an offprint of the famous article to Pushkin in St. Petersburg.

In July 1837 Gagarin traveled to England as a diplomatic courier and the following February arrived in Paris to take up a new appointment as attaché at the Russian embassy there. In Paris he frequented the salon of Sophie Swetchine, a Russian-born Catholic, and saw much of Alek-sandr Turgenev, the diarist and epistolerian, whom he had already met in Munich. Toward the end of his stay in France, Gagarin grew friendly with the poet Viktor Grigor'evich Tepliakov. In a diary entry for 4 June 1841, A. Turgenev refers to a walk he took in the park with Gagarin and Tepliakov, during which the three men recited Lermontov's verses on Napoleon I. A letter Tepliakov sent to Gagarin in December 1841 from Rome testifies to their common affection for the recently killed Lermontov. Gagarin's Paris diary, which in its discursiveness and profusion of detail resembles A. Turgenev's journals, describes Gagarin's encounters with Count Louis-Mathieu Molé (Louis-Philippe's prime minister in 1836–1839), Antoine Pierre Berryer (the parliamentary leader of the legitimists), Charles Morny (Louis-Napoleon's half brother), the religious writers de Lamennais and Ferdinand, baron d'Eckstein, and literary figures such as Delphine Gay, Charles Nodier and Eugène Sue. He collected accounts of the doings and sayings of famous men: Napoleon I, Charles X, Louis-Philippe, Charles-Maurice de Talleyrand-Périgord (prince de Bénévent), Klemens Wenzel Nepomuk Lothar Metternich, the Marquis de Lafayette, and the Grand Duke Constantine. His friend Berryer was a particularly valuable informant, on one occasion reporting to him secret details of Napoleon's betrothal to the Archduchess Marie-Louise, details that Berryer had heard from Metternich himself.

The personality of the future Jesuit was a strange mixture of the sensual and the austere: finding French cuisine dangerously tempting, he resolved to eat just one meal a day, which consisted of a dish of meat and vegetables. Like that other diaristic quidnunc, A. Turgenev, Gagarin was an inveterate gossip. His journal abounds in colorful and even scandalous stories of Parisian society life:

> There is much talk at my club of the unusual bet won yesterday at the Jockey Club by one Seidwitz, a young Saxon formerly in the service of Austria who had taken part in the apprehension of the famous Hungarian brigand Szubri: he wagered that in the space of three hours he would make three rides on horseback, each one of three leagues, drink three bottles of wine, and f— three women. Which he accomplished, to his great glory, at the Jockey Club and in the foyer of the Opéra (entry for 16 April 1842).

But the equestrian, alcoholic, and sexual exploits of this Saxon Dolokhov did not impress Gagarin, whose account concludes with a curt pun: "It goes without saying that he is a strapping fool!"

Gagarin attended recitals by Franz Liszt, which he enjoyed, and by Hector Berlioz, which he did not: "Perhaps there is much science here, but what a cacophony. . . . There is something elaborate and yet bizarre in all this." His musical interests afforded him the opportunity to witness the following scene:

> Today I heard what are, I believe, two of the foremost talents in Paris: Rachel in the role of Roxanne and Chopin on the pianoforte. . . . Next to me sat Georges (sic!) Sand, a woman of about forty, with beautiful black eyes and a dark complexion, whose expression seemed rather ordinary; she was much looked at, which displeased her; Mme d'Hauponville, the daughter of the Duke de Broglie, approached her to within three paces and pointed a lorgnette at her; Georges Sand calmly lifted her own, very large lorgnette and stared at Mme d'Hauponville until the latter desisted (entry for 26 April 1842).

Gagarin's Paris post lasted four years, although in 1839 to 1840 he spent several months in Russia, where he joined the "Les Seize" circle and came into close contact with Lermontov. The two often met in the salon of Ekaterina Andreevna Karamzina, the widow of the celebrated historian, and at the St. Petersburg homes of A. Turgenev and Baron Petr Aleksandrovich Valuev, another member of the circle.

Gagarin had a high opinion of Lermontov's poetry, which in an 1840 letter to the Slavophile Iurii Samarin he termed "sublime." The young diplomat was the most erudite and cosmopolitan member of Les Seize. His experiences among the *literati* of Munich, London, and Paris put him in a position to act as the group's informant about the West European cultural scene. Some of Lermontov's poetry of the period—for example, "Duma" (Meditation, 1838), arguably displays the indirect influence of Chaadaev's ideas, for which Gagarin may have acted as a conduit. Together with his cousin, the artist Grigorii Gagarin, he helped Vladimir Aleksandrovich Sollogub in his work on the novel *Tarantas* (The Traveling Cart, 1845). Indeed, Sollogub's protagonist, Ivan Vasil'evich, was partly modeled on Ivan Gagarin.

On 7 May 1840 Gagarin was promoted to junior secretary at the Paris embassy. He secretly converted to Catholicism on 19 April 1842 and two months later traveled to Russia in order to settle his affairs and resign from the diplomatic service. His diary offers only hints of the spiritual process that led to his decision to become a Catholic. The only person in Russia whom he told about his conversion was Samarin, his cousin and closest friend. With him Gagarin attended the meetings of the Moscow Slavophiles. He also saw Chaadaev and Aleksandr Ivanovich Herzen, the writer and future political exile. Gagarin may have served as the model for the character of Anatolii Stolygin in Herzen's 1847 novel *Dolg prezhde vsego* (Duty Comes First). In 1843 Gagarin returned to France where on 12 August he became a Jesuit novice and spent two years at the monastery of St. Acheul near Amiens. There he was visited by A. Turgenev and by Father Vladimir Sergeevich Pecherin, another Catholic convert, who describes the probationary Jesuit as "a fresh and pious novice" with "a kind of sacred revulsion" toward money.

Meanwhile Gagarin had become a cause célèbre. Wild rumors about him circulated in Russia. Both A. Turgenev and Herzen for a while believed that Gagarin would return to his native country to spread the faith; Herzen in particular wondered at Gagarin's wish to seek "martyrdom." Pecherin reports a conversation he had in 1846 with two Jesuit missionaries, according to whom Gagarin was slated to become the head of the Russian branch of the Jesuit order if and when it was legalized in Russia. Upon joining the priesthood Gagarin studied theology for four years. In 1853 a Russian court tried him in absentia as a defector and an apostate. In 1857 he petitioned Alexander II for permission to return home to see his father, who, however, asked that Gagarin's request be denied. In 1859–1860 Gagarin traveled to Jerusalem and French Syria and in 1862–1864 taught church history at Gazir in modern Lebanon. In his most famous book, *La Russie sera-t-elle catholique?* (Will Russia Be Catholic?, 1856), and in his other writings Gagarin argued that a union of the Catholic and the Russian churches would guarantee the latter's religious and administrative independence, ensure freedom of conscience, and make revolution in Russia impossible. These works created a considerable stir in his native country, particularly among his old Slavophile friends and contacts such as Tiutchev, Samarin, and Aleksei Stepanovich Khomiakov, who harshly criticized them.

In Paris, Gagarin headed a circle of Russian Catholics who shared his views and wished to acquaint the West with their country's history and culture. To this end he started a journal, *Études de théologie, de philosophie et d'histoire,* six issues of which appeared between 1857 and 1858. He also founded the Musée Slave, now known as the Bibliothèque Slave. He became a close friend of the exiled Decembrist Nikolai Ivanovich Turgenev, A. Turgenev's younger brother, and corresponded with him on a variety of historical and political topics. When the rumors that N. Turgenev was involved in Pushkin's death resurfaced, Gagarin refuted them in an article that appeared in 1865 in the newspaper *Birzhevye vedomosti* (News of the Stock Market). The article was reprinted that same year in the journal *Russkii Arkhiv* (Russian Archive). In June 1875 at the request of the Slavophile Ivan Sergeevich Aksakov, the writer Leskov visited Gagarin in Paris and had conversations with him on religious and ecclesiological topics. Leskov describes Father Gagarin as "a kindly country gentleman" who still carried with him "the atmosphere of Pushkin's circle." In his memoirs the acerbic Pecherin also refers to the former Russian aristocrat's old-world airs, although in less flattering terms: " . . . He receives 12,000 francs a year from Russia. O, sainte pauvreté!! pauvre homme!"

In 1879 Aksakov brought out some of Tiutchev's unpublished poems, which he had received from Gagarin, who had jealously guarded them for forty years. The daughter of the memoirist Aleksandra Smirnova-Rosset reports that Gagarin "preserved into his old age ardent feelings of love for his country." Indeed, shortly before his death Gagarin asked the imperial authorities to issue him a restricted Russian passport (that is, one that would not give him the right of abode in Russia). He died without ever seeing his homeland again—one more in a long line of Russian idealists who tasted what William Shakespeare in *King Richard II* called "the bitter bread of banishment."

Letters:

V. A. Bil'basov, *Istoricheskie monografii,* volume 2 (St. Petersburg, 1901)—Samarin's letters to Gagarin concerning Lermontov; *Russkaia Starina,* no. 1 (1911)—Gagarin's correspondence with Pecherin; *Indiana Slavic Studies,* 4 (1967)—Leskov's letters to Gagarin; *Simvol,* nos. 1–7 (1979–1982)—Gagarin's correspondence with Samarin and Ivan Kireevsky, Leskov's letter to Gagarin of 18 June 1875; *Revue des études slaves,* fasc. 3 (1982): 478–479—Tepliakov's letter to Gagarin of 14 December 1841; *Simvol,* nos. 9–11 (1983–1984)—Gagarin's correspondence with Mikhail Zhikharev concerning Chaadaev, his letter to Nikolai Trubetskoi and correspondence with Mikhail Semevsky concerning Pushkin's death, Tiutchev's letters to Gagarin, Gagarin's correspondence with I. Aksakov concerning Tiutchev; *Sim-*

vol, no. 13 (1985)—Gagarin's correspondence with Dolgorukov; *Simvol,* no. 17 (1987)—Gagarin's correspondence with Leskov; *Literaturnoe nasledstvo,* no. 97, volumes 1–2 (1988–1989)—Gagarin's correspondence with Tiutchev, I. Aksakov, and Aleksandra Bakhmeteva (see also index); *Simvol,* no. 22 (1989)—Gagarin's letters to A. Turgenev; *Simvol,* no. 27 (1992)—Schelling's letter to Gagarin.

References:

Stella Lazarevna Abramovich, *Pushkin v 1836 godu* (Leningrad: Nauka,1989);

M. P. Alekseev, "Po sledam rukopisei I. S. Turgeneva vo Frantsii," *Russkaia literatura,* no. 2 (1963): 53–85;

Adrien Boudou, *Le Saint-Siège et la Russie—leurs relations diplomatiques au XIX siècle, 1814–1847* (Paris, 1922);

Boudou, *Le Saint-Siège et la Russie—leurs relations diplomatiques au XIX siècle, 1848–1883* (Paris, 1925);

A. S. Buturlin, "Imel li I. S. Gagarin otnoshenie k paskviliu na A. S. Pushkina?," *Izvestiia AN SSSR. Otdelenie literatury i iazyka,* 28, issue 3 (1969): 277–285;

Petr Iakovlevich Chaadaev, *Polnoe sobranie sochinenii i izbrannye pis'ma,* volumes 1–2 (Moscow, 1991);

Peter K. Christoff, *A. S. Khomjakov* (The Hague: Mouton, 1961);

Christoff, *I. V. Kireevsky* (The Hague, 1972);

Christoff, *Iu. F. Samarin* (Boulder: University of Colorado Press, 1991);

Christoff, *K. S. Aksakov* (Princeton, N.J.: Princeton University Press, 1982);

Charles Clair, "Premières années et conversion du prince Jean Gagarin," *Revue du monde catholique,* 19, nos. 6–9 (1883);

N. Ia. Eidel'man, *Gertsen protiv samoderzhaviia: sekretnaia politicheskaia istoriia Rossii XVIII–XIX vekov i vol'naia russkaia pechat',* (Moscow, 1984);

Gregory L. Freeze, *The Parish Clergy in Nineteenth-Century Russia: Crisis, Reform, Counter-Reform* (Princeton, N.J.: Princeton University Press, 1983);

Emma Gershtein, *Sud'ba Lermontova* (Moscow: Khudozhestvennaia literatura, 1986);

A. Gratieux, *A. S. Khomiakov et le mouvement slavophile,* 2 volumes (Paris, 1939);

Dennis Linehan, "Jean-Xavier Gagarin and the Foundation of *Études,*" *Diakonia,* 21, no. 2 (1987): 89–98;

David M. Matual, "Ivan Gagarin: Russian Jesuit and Defender of the Faith," *Diakonia,* 24 (1991): 5–18;

V. I. Mil'don and A. L. Ospovat, "Gagarin," *Russkie pisateli 1800–1917. Biograficheskii slovar',* volume 1 (Moscow, 1989), pp. 509–510;

T. L. Nikol'skaia, "Gagarin," *Lermontovskaia entsiklopediia* (Moscow: Sovetskaia èntsiklopediia, 1981), pp. 98–99;

The Philosophical Letters of Peter Chaadaev, translated and edited by Raymond T. McNally and Richard Tempest (Dordrecht & Boston: Kluwer Academic Publishers, 1991);

P. O. Pirling, "Gagarin," *Russkii Biograficheskii Slovar',* volume 4 (Moscow, 1914), pp. 69–74;

J. G. A. M. Remmers, *De Herenigingsgedachte van I. S. Gagarin, S. J. (1814–1882)* (Tilburg, 1951);

M. J. Rouèt de Journel, "L'Oeuvre des Saints Cyrille et Méthode et la Bibliothèque Slave," *Revue des études slaves,* no. 3 (1923), pp. 90–104;

Journel, *Une russe catholique* (Paris, 1953);

Russkoe obshchestvo 30-kh godov XIX veka, ed. I. A. Fedosov (Moscow, 1989);

L. Shur, "Iz istorii Slavianskoi Biblioteki," *Simvol,* no. 14 (1985): 247–253;

Shur, "K biografii I. S. Gagarina," *Simvol,* no. 12 (1984): 200–203;

Pierre Tchaadaev, *Oeuvres inédites ou rares* (Meudon, 1990);

Richard Tempest, "Mezhdu Reinom i Senoi: molodye gody Ivana Gagarina," *Simvol,* no. 32 (1994): 200–240; includes Russian translation of the "Notes sur mon histoire";

Fedor Ivanovich Tiutchev, *Sobranie sochinenii v dvukh tomakh* (Moscow, 1984).

Papers:

Gagarin's books, diaries, autobiography, correspondence, and other personal papers are in the Bibliothèque Slave, Meudon, France; Gagarin's letter to Viazemsky of 30 September 1839 is in the Rossiiskii Gosudarstvennyi Arkhiv Literatury i Iskusstva (formerly TsGALI), f. 197. Other Gagarin materials are in TsGILA, f. 892 and Gosudarstvennyi Arkhiv Rossiiskoi Federatsii (formerly TsGAOR) and Rossiiskaia Natsional'naia Biblioteka (formerly GPB), f. 109 and f. 728. Gagarin's letters to Samarin are in the Rossiiskaia Gosudarstvennaia Biblioteka (formerly VGBIL), f. 265.

Elena Andreevna Gan
(Zeneida R-va)
(11 January 1814 – 24 June 1842)

Veronica Shapovalov
San Diego State University

BOOKS: *Sochineniia,* as Zeneida R-va, 4 volumes (St. Petersburg, 1843);
Polnoe sobranie sochinenii, as Elena Gan, 6 volumes (St. Petersburg: N. F. Mertts, 1905).

Elena Gan entered the history of Russian literature as a talented author of society tales. In the 1830s and 1840s her novellas enjoyed great popularity, but by the end of the nineteenth century they began to be forgotten. After 1905 her works were no longer republished, and not until the 1970s and 1980s was there a resurgence of interest in the work of early nineteenth-century authors, including the stories by Gan.

Elena Andreevna Fadeeva was born to an old noble family in Rzhishchev, not far from Kiev, on 11 January 1814. Her mother, Elena Pavlovna Fadeeva, née Dolgorukaia, came from a famous family of princes and was raised in Rzhishchev by her maternal grandmother, Elena Bandre-du-Plessy, who, together with her friend and neighbor Countess Dzialynskaia, instilled in Elena Pavlovna an interest in archaeology, botany, and history along with a desire to attain knowledge independently. Elena Pavlovna had an extensive education, which was quite unusual for a woman in that era, and was known for her sharp intelligence. She corresponded with leading European scientists and helped them in their research on the South of Russia and the Caucasus.

Gan's father, Andrei Mikhailovich Fadeev, had no wealth, title, or career at the time of his marriage. Consequently, the Dolgoruky family objected to the union, and Gan's parents eloped. The marriage took place in a small chapel not far from Rzhishchev. Gan was one year old when her father finally obtained a permanent job as a member of the Office of Foreign Settlers in Ekaterinoslavl'. He served there for fifteen years, carrying out duties that included constant travel around the colonies to inspect the needs of the settlers. Gan had a brother, Rostislav Andreevich Fadeev, a military writer and publicist, and two sisters, Ekaterina and Nadezhda.

Gan's mother sought to educate her daughters at home in the same way that she had been educated, while Rostislav studied at the Artillery School in St. Petersburg. When Gan was eight years old, her father visited Bessarabia on business and had occasion to share accommodations with Aleksandr Pushkin in the house of Gen. Ivan Nikitich Inzov. In his memoirs Fadeev wrote that he could not sleep at night because Pushkin kept late hours, writing and reciting his new works to his roommate. Later, to make up for the inconvenience, Pushkin gave Fadeev a present of two manuscripts: "Kavkazskii plennik" (The Prisoner of the Caucasus, 1820–1821) and "Bakhchisaraiskii fontan" (The Fountain of Bakhchisarai, 1822). Fadeev presented the manuscripts to his wife, who was enthralled with them. These manuscripts were treasured and read over and over again—thus began Pushkin's influence on Gan, who shared her mother's admiration of the poet.

When Gan was thirteen, her mother became ill and was paralyzed on her right side. Although this did not incapacitate her (she learned to draw with her left hand in order to continue illustrating records of the plant specimens that she collected), Gan had to take on many more responsibilities and hence became more independent. This year marked the beginning of her adult life; in her works her heroines also undergo the same change at the age of thirteen because they either lose their mothers or face some other great modification in their upbringing. Because her mother was no longer able to provide for her education, and Ekaterinoslavl' lacked qualified teachers, Gan decided to continue her schooling by herself. By that time she knew French and was familiar with history, botany, and other subjects. On her own she learned German, Italian, and English and became seriously interested in Russian and Western European literature.

Her mother's illness necessitated a voyage to the Crimea for Gan's entire family. They stayed at an old estate belonging to a wealthy local family; on the premises was a library of several hundred books comprising not only modern European literature but also the classics. The Greek settlements in the Crimea inspired Gan to read Homer, Sophocles, and Plutarch. She knew about Pushkin's travels in the Crimea and read all his works with great zest, interrupting her reading only to fantasize about the romantic landscape of cliffs, sea, and ruins surrounding her. Even as a child Gan was set apart from her peers by her highly developed taste for all beautiful things and by her independent mind, fiery imagination, and artistic creativity. At night, after reading the works of her favorite poets, she would be inspired to write her own poetry or short stories, though she usually burned these the next day.

E. S. Nekrasova has noted that Gan was compelled to write almost despite herself. The heroine of Gan's *Naprasnyi dar* (A Futile Gift, 1842), published in the journal *Otechestvennye zapiski* (Notes of the Fatherland), wrote with the same motivation: "She took the pencil almost unknowingly, without any participation of her will in this act: something inside of her was constricted, something in her heart was begging her to let it free; emotion welled up in her chest, thoughts swarmed in her head—yet language seemed to her poor and weak."

In 1830, at the age of sixteen, Gan met her future husband, the captain of an equestrian artillery, Petr Alekseevich Gan, who was twice as old as Elena. He became her husband the same year, and soon after the wedding was sent away to the Polish campaign while Elena Gan stayed with her parents. In 1831 her first child was born in the absence of her husband—a daughter, also named Elena, who would become the famous theosophist Elena Blavatskaia.

The following years Gan spent constantly moving from place to place, following her husband wherever his military command sent him. She had a son, Aleksandr, who died while still an infant. Exhausted by the unsettled life, she moved to Odessa to be with her parents. In 1835 Gan gave birth to her second daughter, who would become a writer known as Vera Petrovna Zhelikhovskaia. Soon Gan became disillusioned, not so much with the transient life of a military wife, but with her husband. He shared none of her interests in poetry and literature and did not understand her esoteric thoughts. He was more preoccupied with worldly pleasures of food and drink and the shallow social life of the military. More precisely, he seemed set on living his life in the company of men and banished Gan to the world of wifely duties: housekeeping and raising children. Gan, who had moved beyond that world from the moment her mother began her education, could not accept such a mental exile.

In 1836 Gan's husband was transferred to St. Petersburg. The city had a great influence on Gan. Her brother-in-law acted as her guide as she went sightseeing and exploring in both the capital and its suburbs. In an undated letter to her relatives (quoted by Zhelikhovskaia) she wrote that she was fascinated with the Kazan' Cathedral and the Peter and Paul Fortress. She began going to the theater, where she saw many plays and operas; she also visited art galleries and became familiar with paintings by such artists as Karl Briullov and Orest Kiprensky. In a private gallery she had a chance to see Pushkin. Describing this meeting in an undated letter to her relatives (quoted by E. S. Nekrasova), she wrote that when she recognized Pushkin, she completely forgot about the paintings. She remembered that Pushkin smiled, noticing her attention. In spite of her many activities, she still found time for self-education: she studied history, foreign languages, and literature. Following her mother's example, she continued to educate her own daughters.

Gan made many acquaintances in St. Petersburg and attended literary readings and musical soirees in the homes of her relatives—the Sushkovs and Beklemishevs. There she heard excerpts from the first Russian national opera, *Zhizn' za tsarya* (A Life for the Tsar, 1836; renamed *Ivan Susanin*) by Mikhail Ivanovich Glinka. However, even in the capital among her friends and acquaintances, she felt lonely. She wrote to her sister on 25 June 1836, "In the whole of Petersburg there is not a soul I consider to be close to mine."

In St. Petersburg she met Osip Ivanovich Senkovsky, a writer and the editor of the journal *Teleskop* (Telescope), and developed a friendship with him that affected her life greatly. Some scholars speculate that her involvement with Senkovsky was romantic, but Gan's family strongly denied any such allegations. It was Senkovsky who noticed Gan's talent and encouraged her to write. According to Nekrasova, Gan started her literary career as a translator: she did an abridged translation of Edward Bulwer-Lytton's novel *Godolphin* (1833) that was published under the title of *Liubov' i chestoliubie* (Love and Ambition) in the monthly journal *Biblioteka dlia chteniia* (The Library for Reading). In 1837 Gan's novella *Ideal* (The Ideal) appeared in the same journal.

The plot of *Ideal* concerns an unhappy marriage. The heroine, Ol'ga Gol'tsberg, is disappointed and disillusioned with her husband. Her dissatisfaction with her marriage leads her to idealize her favorite poet, Anatoii. She reads his works over and over, but has never met him. Finally coincidence brings them together; Ol'ga is in a position to grab happiness, but to do so would mean causing the unhappiness of her husband. However, her fascination with the poet does not last. She discovers that Anatolii is a shallow and immoral man; she subsequently realizes that life can satisfy only those who make few demands. Conse-

Gan's daughter, theosophist Elena Blavatskaia (widely known as Madame Blavatsky)

quently, she is faced with the question of what to do, given her unfathomable capacity for feeling and her endless ability to love. Ol'ga comes to realize that love must be what she feels for the Savior and that her goal must be the heavens. The plot, however, is but a small part of *Ideal*. Reviewing her work, critic Vissarion Grigor'evich Belinsky noted that to Gan plot has little significance; it functions as a libretto for an opera, and every digression that Gan's work includes is like the music in the opera. It is in these digressions that Gan expounds on the value of life and humanity and expresses despair at the position of any woman who is superior to her milieu.

Although Gan was still young, she was amazingly perceptive about her experience as a woman. As a well-educated person, she understood that the blandness and emptiness of women's lives were caused by lack of education and a solid basis of knowledge. With this insight Gan was ahead of her contemporaries. She was solving the "issue of women" in the manner that it was understood in Russian society only in the 1860s and 1870s. Gan stands at the beginning of the history of feminism in Russian literature.

In many ways Gan is often compared to George Sand. Like the French writer, Gan believed in the significance of the life of the heart for a woman. How-

ever, Gan considered the only valid form for such a life to be marriage. Yet she confesses in *Ideal* that the odds are one thousand to one that a woman with an unusual soul ends up joining her fate to that of the most ordinary and prosaic man. In *Ideal* she expresses for the first time her dilemma—she is a creative intellectual, a woman with a strong spirit and ambition who at the same time wants to love and to devote herself completely to her beloved. Gan wrote *Ideal* and her other works under the pen name Zeneida R-va; A. V. Starchevskii suggests that the first name was inspired by a character in Senkovsky's 1834 novella *Liubov' i smert'* (Love and Death). She used the pseudonym not so much out of modesty, but for fear of provoking anger in her provincial society. Significantly, she was one of only a few women of her era to use a female pen name consistently.

In 1835 Gan's father received a post in Astrakhan' as "the head guardian of the Kalmyk people." Gan joined her family there in 1837, taking her children and separating from her husband. She spent the summer of 1837 in the Caucasus, where she became friends with the exiled Decembrist Sergei Ivanovich Krivtsov, with whom she later corresponded. Inspired by the success of *Ideal,* Gan wrote *Vospominanie Zheleznovodska* (A Recollection of Zheleznovodsk). This work demonstrates the author's slightly ironic attitude towards the popular genre of the adventure story in the Caucasus. In *Vospominanie Zheleznovodska* the heroine is about to embark on a trip to the mountains. The story recounts her wild adventures, including a kidnapping, imprisonment in a small village in the mountains, and desperate plans to escape. In the final scene, however, the author's irony comes through as the heroine awakens from her sleep and discovers that all her adventures have been but a dream. However, Gan did not deem *Vospominanie Zheleznovodska* worth publishing, and it appeared in print only after her death, in the 1843 edition of her works.

Her next work, *Utballa* (published in *Biblioteka dlia chteniia* in 1838), was inspired by her journey to the Caucasus; it centers on the profound love of a woman who is ready to give up her entire life for one minute of happiness with the man she loves and to endure the most atrocious suffering for this love. For the man, however, the woman is merely an episode in his life, an accident that is quickly forgotten. In the course of the story Gan raises the question of the social position of the illegitimate child. The heroine of the story, Utballa, is the illegitimate daughter of a Kalmyk woman and a wealthy Russian merchant. Society, intent on upholding a superficial moral code, contemptuously punishes Utballa for her illegitimacy. Gan defends the blameless child and condemns society for its prejudice.

The plot of *Utballa* generates more interest than *Ideal*. Though it includes elements of both an adventure story and a romance, Gan's main theme of the loneliness an educated woman feels in society recurs. An educated intellectual who has to live among the nomads, Utballa finds herself in a position similar to Gan's other intelligent, talented women characters who cannot escape the judgments and customs of society. Death and destruction await all of them, be it Utballa, who is mercilessly murdered by a crowd, or the poet Aniuta in *Naprasnyi dar,* who dies as a result of being ostracized and banished from society. In *Utballa* Gan acquaints the reader with the customs and life of the Kalmyks. She describes their dwellings, games, entertainment, customs, and social order. However, the abundance of ethnographical details never interferes with the narration. The story includes breathtakingly beautiful descriptions, especially of the steppes and the horseback rides the heroine takes to dull her sorrow.

At the end of 1837 Gan returned to her husband and lived in poor conditions in a small provincial town. She did not have a room of her own and could work only at night, when her family did not bother her. In the first months of 1838 Gan toiled over her new tale, *Dzhellaledin,* published in *Biblioteka dlia chteniia* in 1838. Like *Utballa,* it combines elements of romance, adventure, and society tales. The story was inspired by Pushkin's Southern poems "Bakhchisaraiskii fontan" and "Tsygany" (The Gypsies, 1824). The main character, Dzhellaledin, the son of the Crimean Khan Sagib-Girei, resembles both of Pushkin's heroes Khan Girei and Aleko. The love triangle in *Dzhellaledin*–Liudmila, Emina, and Dzhellaledin–also reminds one of the love triangle in "Bakhchisaraiskii fontan." Dzhellaledin, like Aleko, despises Western people and does not recognize any other will but his own. *Dzhellaledin* stands apart from many Oriental tales of the 1830s because of the sincerity of feeling and passion with which the story is written.

In 1838 Gan went to the Caucasus with her mother. There she worked on the novella *Medal'on* (The Locket, published in *Biblioteka dlia chteniia* in 1839), which she completed in only two weeks. Unlike *Utballa* and *Dzhellaledin, Medal'on* is a society tale with a strong element of suspense and even mystery. In its description of spa society, Gan's *Medal'on* is the predecessor of Mikhail Iur'evich Lermontov's "Kniazhna Meri" (Princess Mary), a section of his novel *Geroi nashego vremeni* (A Hero of Our Time, 1837–1840). Like Gan's other heroines, the main character in *Medal'on,* Sophia, is a talented, beautiful, and educated woman; however, unlike the others, she is not lonely. Sophia and her sister represent a small community of women who become quite strong in the defense of

their honor. *Medal'on* was greeted by the public with great enthusiasm; however, Gan was little inspired by this success. Her health had begun to fail her (she developed tuberculosis), and her doctor forbade her to work. She also had to abandon the nomadic lifestyle she had earlier led with her husband. Soon after *Medal'on* was published, her bad health forced her to move to Odessa. There she met the poets Vladimir Grigor'evich Benediktov and Andrei Ivanovich Podolinsky. Gan spent long hours talking to Benediktov who, in turn, read his poems to her; he even dedicated one of them to her. In 1839 she gave birth to her fourth child, Leonid. In Odessa, Gan worked on two novellas: *Sud sveta* (Society's Judgment), published in *Biblioteka dlia chteniia* in 1840, and *Teofaniia Abbiadzhio,* published in *Biblioteka dlia chteniia* in 1841.

Sud sveta, like *Ideal,* incorporates many elements of Gan's personal life. In the work she depicts the boredom of her own existence as well as the gossip the provincials spread about a young woman writer. For the first time in Gan's fiction a heroine realizes unequivocally that an intellectual life will not satisfy all of the needs of a woman, who must have an emotional life as well. As in her previous stories, Gan's heroine, Zeneida, is much stronger and wiser than Vlodinsky, who thinks that he loves her. She possesses the strength of mind to realize the emptiness of society, the injustice of its judgment, and the inequality of standards for men and women.

In 1841 Gan returned once again to her husband as a response to his persistent requests. She avoided social encounters and concentrated on her work. That same year, she published *Teofaniia Abbiadzhio,* one of her best-loved and most successful tales. In this story Gan returns to one of her favorite themes—the impossibility of happiness for a woman, since she sacrifices all for the sake of her family. Teofaniia sacrifices her possible happiness for the sake of her fiancé, Dolin'i, and her friend, Ol'ga; however, Dolin'i and Ol'ga are not happy in their marriage. To save her family from poverty, Teofaniia marries Ertino, an old friend of her father. Everybody sees her marriage as a happy one; Teofaniia, however, is profoundly unhappy.

In creating the image of woman's selfless love, Gan displays not only her talent but also her high ideals. This story exemplifies the theory that poets create their lives in their work—a theme especially relevant to female authors who seem to incorporate themselves into their characters, perhaps because a patriarchal society tends to repress women's thoughts and emotions in intellectual spheres. Though male authors also speak through the words of their characters, they are not limited to this mode of expression. This difference was true especially in the nineteenth century, when men had broader freedom of expression in society than women. *Teofaniia Abbiadzhio* reveals much about its author, especially her moral character.

Gan continued to work in spite of her weak health. In 1841 she moved to Saratov, where her father was appointed director of the Chamber of State Property and later became the governor. There she worked on some new long stories. In January 1842 Belinsky published a review in *Otechestvennye zapiski* in which he praised Gan's works. After its publication two prestigious journals, *Otechestvennye zapiski* and *Moskvitianin* (The Muscovite), invited Gan to join them. She accepted the invitations and published *Naprasnyi dar* and another tale, *Liubon'ka,* in *Otechestvennye zapiski* in 1842. *Naprasnyi dar,* like so many others, has a strong autobiographical element. Aniuta, the main character of the tale, is set apart from the multitude by her talent. If Aniuta decides to pursue her vocation, she, as a creative woman in a repressive society, suffers agony and pain. The provincial society considers Aniuta to be insane. She faces an impossible choice—in order to get a job as a governess to support her mother and herself, she has to quit creative writing. The moral conflict results in serious illness. When Aniuta meets people who care and who understand her talent, it is too late to save her life. Until the end of her career Gan investigated the ramifications of this theme of the alienation of the gifted woman. While Gan was working on *Naprasnyi dar,* her health completely deteriorated. In the early spring of 1842 she moved to Odessa, where she died on 24 June 1842.

Gan's works go beyond the boundaries of the classic definition of "society tale" and differ greatly from the works of her contemporaries in this genre. Gan introduced several elements of adventure and romance into her society tales. In many of them she pays equal attention to the spiritual life of her characters and to the narration. She moved outside the genre of the society tale because as a woman she both shared and challenged the assumptions of her era about gender and the writer's source of inspiration.

Letters:

"Avtografy izvestnykh i zamechatel'nykh liudei," *Starina i novizna,* 9 (1905): 333–336;

Mikhail Osipovich Gershenzon, "Materialy po istorii russkoi literatury i kul'tury. Russkaia zhenshchina 30kh godov," *Russkaia mysl',* 12 (1911): 54–73.

References:

Joe Andrew, "Elena Gan and 'A Futile Gift,'" in his *Narrative and Desire in Russian Literature, 1822-49:* *The Feminine and the Masculine* (New York: St. Martin's Press, 1993), pp. 85–138;

Bik. A-ov, "Elena Andreevna Gan (Zeneida R-va)," introduction to Gan's *Polnoe sobranie sochinenii* (St. Petersburg, 1905), pp. iii-xviii;

Hugh Anthony Aplin. "M. S. Zhukova and E. A. Gan: Women Writers and Female Protagonists. 1837-1843," dissertation, University of East Anglia, 1988;

Nina Awsienko, "The Burdens of 'Superfluous' Talent," *Journal of Russian Studies,* 29 (1975): 13–14;

A. I. Beletskii, "Turgenev i russkie pisatel'nitsy 30kh–60kh godov," in *Tvorcheskii put' Turgeneva* (Petrograd, 1923), pp. 157–160;

Vissarion Grigor'evich Belinsky, "Sochineniia Zeneidy R-voi," in his *Polnoe sobranie sochinenii,* volume 7 (Moscow: Akademia Nauk, 1955), pp. 648–678;

Nadezhda Andreevna Fadeeva, "Elena Andreevna Gan i Osip Iv. Senkovsky (v 1836–38)," *Russkaia starina,* 66 (1890): 1–68;

Fadeeva, "Vospominaniia o Rostislave Fadeeve," in *Sobranie sochnenii,* by Rostislav Andreevich Fadeev (St. Petersburg, 1890), volume 1, pp. 1–68;

N. N. Fatov, "Bibliograficheskie materialy dlia izucheniia zhizni i tvorchestva E. A. Gan," *Izvestiia otdeleniia russkogo iazyka i slovesnosti imperatorskoi Akademii nauk,* 19, no. 2 (1914): 211–263;

L. Kuzmich, "Elena Gan—zabytaia pisatel'nitsa," *Novyi zhurnal,* no. 71 (1963): 294–302;

Marion Meade, *Madame Blavatsky: The Woman Behind the Myth* (New York: Putnam, 1980);

E. S. Nekrasova, "Elena Andreevna Gan (Zeneida R-va) 1814–1842: Biograficheskii ocherk," *Russkaia starina,* 8 (1886): 335–354; 9 (1886): 553–574;

Marit Bjerkung Nielsen, "The Concept of Love and Conflict of the Individual vs. Society in Elena Gan's *Sud sveta,*" *Scando-Slavica,* 24 (1978): 125–138;

Nielsen, *Elena Andreevna Gan (Zeneida R-va) 1814-1842* (Oslo: Universitetet i Oslo, Slavisk-baltisk institutt, 1979);

A. V. Starchevskii, "Roman odnoi zabytoi romanistki," *Istoricheskii vestnik,* 8 (1886): 203–234; 9 (1886): 509–531;

Vera Petrovna Zhelikhovskaia, "Elena Andreevna Gan: Pisatel'nitsa-romanistka v 1835-1842 gg.," *Russkaia starina,* 3 (1887): 733–766.

Nikolai Vasil'evich Gogol

(20 March 1809 – 21 February 1852)

Amy Singleton Adams
College of the Holy Cross

BOOKS: *Gants Kiukhel'garten. Idilliia v kartinakh,* as V. Alov (St. Petersburg, 1829);

Vechera na khutore bliz Dikan'ki, 2 volumes (St. Petersburg: Departament narodnogo prosvescheniia, 1831–1832);

Arabeski. Raznye sochineniia, 2 volumes (St. Petersburg: vdova Pliushar s synom, 1835);

Mirgorod, 2 volumes (St. Petersburg: Departament vneshnei torgovli, 1835);

Revizor (St. Petersburg: A. Pliushar, 1836);

Pokhozhdeniia Chichikova, ili Mertvye dushi. Poema, part 1 (Moscow: Universitetskaia tipografiia, 1842); part 2 (Moscow: Universitetskaia tipografiia, 1855);

Sochineniia, 4 volumes (St. Petersburg: A. Borodina, 1842);

Vybrannye mesta iz perepiska s druz'iami (St. Petersburg: Departamenta vneshnei torgovli, 1847);

Razmyshleniia o bozhestvennoi liturgii (St. Petersburg: P. A. Kulish, 1857).

Editions and Collections: *Sochineniia i pis'ma,* 6 volumes (St. Petersburg: P. A. Kulish, 1857);

Polnoe sobranie sochinenii N. V. Gogolia (Moscow: A. I. Mamontov, 1867);

Sochineniia, 7 volumes, edited by Nikolai S. Tikhonravov and Vladimir Ivanovich Shenrok, tenth edition (St. Petersburg: A. F. Marks, 1889–1896);

Polnoe sobranie sochinenii N. V. Gogolia, edited by P. V. Bykov (St. Petersburg: M. O. Vol'f, 1900);

Sochineniia (Berlin: Petropolis, 1900);

Sochineniia: polnoe sobranie, edited by V. I. Iakovenko (St. Petersburg: F. Pavlenkov, 1902);

Polnoe sobranie sochinenii N. V. Gogolia: s ego biografiei i primechaniiami v 3-kh tomakh, 3 volumes, edited by A. I. Kirpichnikov (Moscow: I. D. Sytin, 1902);

Vse dramaticheskie proizvedeniia N. V. Gogolia (St. Petersburg: Obshchestvennaia pol'za, 1902);

Polnoe sobranie khudozhestvennykh proizvedenii N. V. Gogolia, edited by Kirpichnikov (Moscow: I. D. Sytin, 1909);

Nikolai Vasil'evich Gogol

Sochineniia: polnoe sobranie v odnom tome, fourth edition (Petrograd: F. Pavlenkov, 1916);

Polnoe sobranie sochinenii, 10 volumes (Berlin: Slovo, 1921);

Sobranie sochinenii, 6 volumes, edited by N. S. Ashukin (Moscow: Khudozhestvennaia literatura, 1937);

Polnoe sobranie sochinenii, 14 volumes, edited by N. L. Meshcheriakov and Vasilii V. Gippius (Moscow: Akademiia nauk SSSR, 1937–1952);

Sobranie khudozhestvennykh proizvedenii, 5 volumes (Moscow: Akademiia nauk SSSR, 1951–1952);

Sochineniia, 2 volumes (Moscow: Khudozhestvennaia literatura, 1959);

Sobranie sochinenii v semi tomakh, 7 volumes (Moscow:
Sovremennik, 1983);

Sobranie sochinenii v vos'mi tomakh, 8 volumes, edited
by V. R. Shcherbin (Moscow: Pravda, 1984).

Editions in English: *The Collected Works,* 6 volumes,
translated by Constance Garnett (New York:
Knopf, 1922–1927; London: Chatto & Windus, 1922–1928);

Chichikov's Journeys; or, Home Life in Russia, translated
by Bernard Guilbert Guerney (New York: The
Readers Club, 1942); republished as *Dead
Souls* (New York: Rinehart, 1948); revised edi-
tion (New Haven & London: Yale University
Press, 1996);

Selected Passages from Correspondence with Friends, translated, with an introduction, by Jesse Zeldin
(Nashville: Vanderbilt University Press,
1969);

The Theater of Nikolai Gogol: Plays and Selected Writings,
translated by Milton Ehre and Fruma Gott-
schalk, edited by Ehre (Chicago: University of
Chicago Press, 1980);

Arabesques, translated by Alexander R. Tulloch (Ann
Arbor, Mich.: Ardis, 1982);

The Complete Tales of Nikolai Gogol, 2 volumes, edited
by Leonard J. Kent (Chicago: University of
Chicago Press, 1985);

*Hanz Kuechelgarten, Leaving the Theater, and Other
Works,* edited by Ronald Meyer (Ann Arbor,
Mich.: Ardis, 1990).

PLAY PRODUCTIONS: *Revizor,* St. Petersburg,
Aleksandriiskii Teatr, 19 April 1836; Moscow,
Bolshoi Teatr, 24 May 1836;

Zhenit'ba, St. Petersburg, 9 December 1842;

Igroki, Moscow, 5 February 1843.

Nikolai Vasil'evich Gogol is the father of Russia's Golden Age of prose realism. Later nineteenth-
century Russian authors wrote in the shadow of Gogol's thematics and sweeping aesthetic vision;
twentieth-century modernists acknowledge Gogol
as an inspiration. Gogol defined the contours of the
Russian literary landscape with his early collections,
Vechera na khutore bliz Dikan'ki (Evenings on a Farm
near Dikanka, 1831–1832) and *Mirgorod* (1835).
Playful and horrific, these folk-inspired tales of
good and evil evolve into the elusive morality and
fantastic realism of Gogol's Petersburg stories.
Characters and themes from the latter provide the
basis for some of Fyodor Dostoyevsky's great novels. Gogol's plays are social satires that revolutionized the very idea of the stage in Russian theater.

Pokhozhdeniia Chichikova, ili Mertvye dushi (The Adventures of Chichikov, or Dead Souls, 1842), Gogol's
epic poem in prose, is the point where discussions of
Russian national identity often begin. With *Mertvye
dushi* Gogol provided Russia with its first world-
class novel, which, although sui generis, is strongly
reminiscent of the picaresque.

Many readers compare Gogol's genius with
that of Miguel de Cervantes, Laurence Sterne, and
James Joyce. Gogol's work shows extraordinary manipulation of language, confusion of the ridiculous
and sublime, and a blossoming desire to capture in
verbal images the cultural essence and national mission of Russia. Despite such recognition from his
critics and readers, Gogol has been one of the most
misunderstood writers of the modern age. The
swarm of seemingly irrelevant details, inconsisten-
cies, and contradictions that characterize Gogol's
life and work have misled readers who look for
monolithic purpose or truth. In his critical biography of Gogol, Victor Erlich says that "we are still far
from agreement as to the nature of his genius, the
meaning of his bizarre art, and his still weirder life."
Vladimir Nabokov calls Gogol "the strangest prose-
poet Russia has ever produced." Despite the oddities of Gogol's personality, the explosive complexity
of his work captures the fragmentation of the
nineteenth-century consciousness. Gogol's effort to
overcome the social, cultural, and ultimately spiritual disunity he perceived in Russia motivates his
work. Gogol's attempt to reconcile the contradictions inherent in his vision of true social and spiritual cohesiveness contributed to his death. Yet the
works that his aesthetic pilgrimage produced are
unequaled in world literature.

Nikolai Vasil'evich Gogol was born on 20
March 1809 in the small Ukrainian town of Velikie
Sorochintsy in the Mirgorod district, Poltava
province. He was the first surviving child of Maria
Ivanovna and Vasilii Afanas'evich Gogol-Ianovsky,
landowners of modest means. Gogol's parents were
alarmed by their son's tiny size and fragile health.
To bolster his chances of survival, they named him
for St. Nikolai, whose icon the neighboring town of
Dikanka revered. They also built a small church in
the name of their infant son on his home estate of
Vasil'evka. The circumstances of his parents' marriage underscores the seemingly spiritual nature of
Gogol's birth; he was the product of what the family
considered a divinely ordained union. At thirteen,
Gogol's father, Vasilii Afanas'evich, saw the Virgin
Mary in a dream; pointing to a baby girl, she told
him that the child would someday be his wife. Vasilii Afanas'evich recognized his neighbors' seven-

The house in Sorochinsk where Gogol was born

month-old daughter, Maria Ivanovna Kosiarovskaia, whom he later married.

Young Nikolai was the darling of the Gogol-Ianovsky family, even after the birth of his siblings: Maria in 1811, Ivan in 1812, Anna in 1821, Elizaveta in 1823, and Ol'ga in 1825. The conditions of Gogol's childhood resound in his writing. His mother instilled in him colorful beliefs about heaven and hell; his father, who wrote Ukrainian folk comedies, showed Gogol the beauty of the surrounding countryside and the humor of its inhabitants; Gogol's paternal grandmother filled his mind with Cossack legends, ancient songs, and terrifying folktales.

The Gogol-Ianovsky home was a lively place, filled with visitors who enjoyed the family's hospitality and the abundance of their table. However, despite the richness of the land, Gogol's father was a dreamy man who managed his estate and affairs poorly. When Gogol left for school at age ten, a distant relative and family benefactor, Dmitrii Prokof'evich Troshchinsky, financed the boy's education.

In the spring of 1821 Gogol arrived at the High School for Advanced Study in Nezhin. Students and teachers at Nezhin did not warm quickly to Gogol, whose physical repulsiveness exacerbated his social ineptitude. The other boys thought the mottled skin of Gogol's pointed face and his unusually long, thin nose gave him a birdlike appearance. This epithet would be repeated throughout Gogol's life. The Nezhin school offered a nine-year course of study in religious education, Russian language and literature, Latin, Greek, German, French, physics, mathematics, political science, geography, history, military science, drawing, and dancing. However, Gogol took little interest in his schoolwork. He preferred instead to invent elaborate fabrications, assign nicknames to students, and write satirical verses about the teachers. Held at a distance by Gogol's insightful mockery, the community at the Nezhin school called him the "mysterious dwarf."

In 1825, during Gogol's fourth year at school, Vasilii Afanas'evich Gogol-Ianovsky died, leaving his sixteen-year-old son the male authority in the family (Gogol's brother, Ivan, drowned in 1819 at the age of seven). Bolstered by his new place in the family, Gogol returned to school that August with renewed vigor. He finally made friends among the boys who shared his growing interest in literature. The family benefactor, Troshchinsky, lent the students books from his personal library; French authors predominated in this collection, but there were also works of British, Spanish, and Russian literature. The students eventually decided to establish their own library of books and periodicals—of which Gogol was the librarian—by pooling their meager resources. Among the new talents of the day, Aleksandr Pushkin especially impressed Gogol. Pushkin's work, notably his novel in verse *Evgeny Onegin* (Eugene Onegin, 1823–1831, published in full in 1833), inspired Gogol and his fellow students to try their own hands at poetry.

Gogol's first literary endeavors were long, youthful poems that are no longer extant. On Sundays the students met to critique each others' work. When Gogol offered the group the story "Brat'ia Tverdoslavichi" (The Brothers Tverdoslavich) in 1826, all agreed that prose did not suit him, and Gogol destroyed the work. Ironically it was not until Gogol published his first collection of stories that Russian readers and writers alike would challenge the supremacy of the poetic genre.

Readings of student poetry gave way to theatrical performances. In a converted gym Gogol and his boyhood friends performed works of Denis Ivanovich Fonvizin, Ivan Andreevich Krylov, and Iakov Borisovich Kniazhnin along with the Ukrainian comedies of Gogol's father. Gogol was in his element on stage. Dressed as a crotchety old man or a female gossip, he displayed such dramatic talent and confidence that many thought Gogol would become an actor. Any aspirations he had for the stage remained unrealized, but those who were moved to tears and laughter when Gogol read his work in progress in Russian drawing rooms testify to the writer's great talent for losing himself in his characters.

During his final year at school, Gogol's thoughts turned increasingly to St. Petersburg. From his provincial distance Gogol perceived the Russian capital as a wondrous city of wealth and opportunity. There, he wrote friends and family, he would make a name for himself and serve Russia in government service or law. In his letters blind enthusiasm, conventional Christian piety, and a fascination with the latest fashions color Gogol's depiction of the civil servant. He arrived in St. Petersburg in December 1828 armed with letters of introduction that proved rather ineffectual. Gogol was insulted by the humble positions offered to him, disillusioned by the mindless workings of the civil bureaucracy, and irritated by the constraints of his own poverty. He finally accepted a post that paid poorly but demanded little of his time, and encouraged by the March 1829 publication of his short lyric "Italiia" (Italy) in *Syn otechestva* (Son of the Fatherland), he devoted himself to writing.

Gogol's first attempt to establish a literary identity and sympathetic readership in St. Petersburg ended in humiliating failure. In May 1829 Gogol published *Gants Kiukhel'garten* (Hanz Kuechelgarten) under the name V. Alov at his own expense. Initially ignored by the reading public and the critics, the idyll received two scornful reviews in June 1829 in *Severnaia pchela* (The Northern Bee) and *Moskovskii telegraf* (The Moscow Telegraph). Gogol was so disgraced by this reception that he bought and burned all remaining copies of *Gants Kiukhel'garten*.

Gants Kiukhel'garten is a menagerie of borrowings from Johann Heinrich Voss's *Luise: Ein laendliches Gedicht in drei Idyllen* (1795) and also from George Gordon, Lord Byron; Thomas Moore; Vicomte François-Auguste-René de Chateaubriand; Vasilii Andreevich Zhukovsky; Vil'gel'm Karlovich Kiukhel'beker; and Pushkin. Donald Fanger says in *The Creation of Nikolai Gogol* (1979) that, despite its unremarkable poetics, *Gants Kiukhel'garten* shows the first stirrings of Gogol's understanding of the artist's vocation. In addition many motifs and images that later become important to Gogol's work are already present in the poem. Nabokov detects the spirit of Gogol's Ukrainian stories in a graveyard scene; the quiet home life and overladen tables depicted in *Gants Kiukhel'garten* are seen again in the well-fed domesticity of "Starosvetskie pomeshchiki" (Old World Landowners, 1835).

In *Gants Kiukhel'garten* the title character forsakes the comforts of his idyllic German country home and his love, Luisa, for the wonders of Greece. Unable to find meaning in the ancient ruins, he returns to sing the praises of his homeland. The poem opens with a description of the village Luenensdorf as it is reflected in water, an inverted perspective that foreshadows Gogol's tendency to view the nature of his subject through a skewed lens: "Plenitel'no oborotilos' vse / Vniz golovoi v serebrianoi vode: / Zabor, i dom, i sadik v nei takie zh" (All things are turned enchantingly around, / Reversed, head first, within the silver water: / The fence and house and garden—all repeated).

The confusion of the village and its lifelike reflection is echoed immediately in Gogol's introduction of an elderly pastor, the heroine's grandfather. Dozing in a garden chair, the old man cannot distinguish dream from reality, a major theme in Gogol's later work. The pastor is awakened by a beautiful woman, whose lily whiteness is shared by almost every woman in Gogol's work. Like the artist Piskarev in Gogol's "Portret" (The Portrait, 1835), the pastor must wake up once again before he realizes

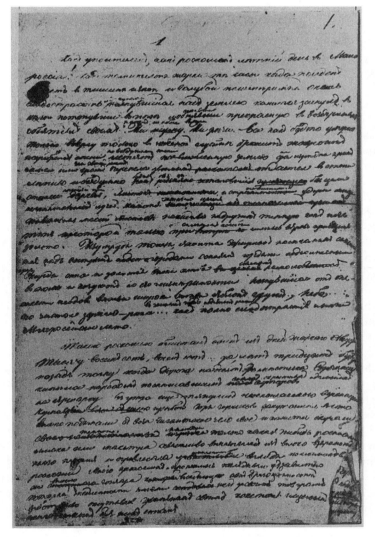

Page from the manuscript for "Sorochinskaia iarmarka" *(The Fair at Sorochinsk), one of the stories in Gogol's* Vechera na khutore bliz Dikan'ki *(Evenings on a Farm near Dikanka, 1831–1832)* *(from David Magarshack,* Gogol: A Life, *1957)*

that his granddaughter, Luisa—and not the heavenly creature of his dream—is standing before him.

With a sigh Luisa tells her grandfather about the mysterious agonies of young Gants. Oblivious to the present, Gants is engrossed with thoughts of a distant and glorious past, which comes to life for him in the ancient volumes he pores over at night. For Gogol the spatial and temporal estrangement of Gants from his object of intrigue is fundamental to the artist's unique ability to perceive beauty in a world of banalities. Gants longs to transcend the comfortable materialism of his provincial home, arriving in the dreamlike world of classical antiquity. "O, kak chudesno vy svoi mir / Mechtoiu, greki, naselili! / Kak vy ego obvorozhili! / A nash—i beden

on, i sir, / I raskvadrachen ves' na mili" (How marvelous was the world wherein / You dwelt, O Greeks, as in a dream! / How you charmed it, made it gleam! / And ours: it's pallid, bare and thin, / And squared off by a mileage scheme).

In Athens, however, Gants discovers that he cannot resurrect the past among the ruins and that for such empty dreams he abandoned his home: "Zachem on put' siuda napravil, / Ne dlia istlev-shikh li mogil / Krov bezmiatezhnyi svoi ostavil, / Pokoi svoi tikhii pozabyl?" (Why did he direct his path here? / Not, surely, for these graves of dust / Did he abandon his peaceful home, / Forget his quiet room?). He returns home a bent and weary pilgrim and pledges to celebrate only the pleasures of this world ("Ia svoiu Germaniiu poiu" [Of my own Germany I'll sing]).

Yet even as Gants vows to remain a disciple of earthly beauty, he grieves for the loss of his unrealizable dreams: "Proshchaias's nimi on navek, / Kak by po starom druge vernom, / Grustit v zabvenii userdnom" (On parting with those dreams for good, / It seems old faithful friends he's leaving, / And for them, lost in thought, is grieving). *Gants Kiukhel'garten* offers an early glimpse of the problematics of Gogol's own artistic aspirations. The artist needs "dusha zheleznoi voli" (a soul of iron will) to avoid worldly vanities or, lacking such resistance, should withdraw into the modest pleasures of family life. Yet as Gogol's earliest work intimates, the quiet solitude of home can be detrimental to the dreams essential to the artistic soul.

To recover from the devastating June 1829 critique of *Gants Kiukhel'garten,* Gogol left for Lübeck, Germany, in July of that year; he financed his travel with the money his mother had sent for him to pay the interest on the estate mortgage. Gogol's sudden departure reveals several tendencies that would soon establish a pattern in his life: a love-hate relationship with a perceived readership; the idea of travel as a remedy for personal and artistic crises; and a cunning willingness to deceive those closest to him, especially when in need of money.

Recalling his hero Gants, Gogol was disillusioned by the ordinariness of Lübeck and returned to St. Petersburg six weeks later. He took a position in the department of public buildings in the ministry of interior, where he worked until he transferred to the ministry of the court in April 1830. The publication of several of his early pieces proved to be the curative Germany was intended to be. "Bisavriuk" (Bisavriuk), later revised as "Vecher nakanune Ivana Kupala" (St. John's Eve), appeared anonymously in the February 1830 issue of *Otechestvennye zapiski* (Notes of the Fatherland); "Glava iz istoricheckogo romana," a chapter from the incomplete historical novel "Get'man" (The Hetman), was published under the signature "OOOO" by *Severnye tsvety* (Northern Flowers) in December of the same year.

The following January *Literaturnaia gazeta* (The Literary Gazette) published a chapter from "Strashnyi kaban" (The Terrible Boar, another chapter of which appeared in March), signed "P. Glechik," along with "Mysli o geografii [dlia detskogo vosrasta]" (Some Thoughts on Teaching Geography to Children), signed "G. Ianov," and "Zhenshchina" (Woman), the first essay to use Gogol's name. The latter is a short, unrestrained meditation reworked from Gogol's school days and displaying the influence of the eternal feminine in German romanticism on the author. Woman balances man's contemptible corporeality; she is "poèziia" (poetry), the "iazyk bozh'ii" (language of the gods), the intangible Idea. All aesthetic inspiration stems from woman, who is the divine model from which the artist derives the material. Woman's ethereal purity defines the limits of her gender in Gogol's later characterizations; when a female character displays too forceful a bodily presence in his work, Gogol invariably emphasizes her often-grotesque manliness.

The director of *Literaturnaia gazeta,* Anton Antonovich Del'vig–a close friend of Pushkin and the poet Zhukovsky–took note of Gogol. Both Del'vig and Zhukovsky considered Gogol's civil position inappropriate for the new author. Through another friend of Pushkin, Petr Aleksandrovich Pletnev, Zhukovsky arranged for Gogol to teach history at the Patriotic Institute for the daughters of the nobility. Gogol took up his post on 10 March 1831. With waning enthusiasm Gogol relied on his weak knowledge to teach natural science, history, and geography. Most of all, students enjoyed listening to Gogol's hilarious Ukrainian anecdotes that he had collected from his family. These tales of Little Russia (as Ukraine was known prior to 1917) make up the first volume of his Dikanka stories.

In May, Pletnev invited Gogol to a reception in honor of Pushkin. Gogol was entranced by Pushkin, who greeted the younger writer amicably. This meeting between the two great writers was the first of many.

By the time Gogol's various preliminary work appeared in print, he had completed the stories that make up the first volume of *Vechera na khutore bliz Dikan'ki.* Although this collection established Gogol as a writer, several reviewers treated the originality of the work as a shortcoming. In his journal *Severnaia pchela* Faddei Venediktovich Bulgarin described the generally low qualities of *Vechera* as a lack of imagination, impoverished descriptions, and a shallowness of characterization. He wrote that Gogol's work was interesting only as a folkloric representation of the Russian or Slavic national spirit as preserved by the Ukrainian people. Others argued that the merit of the work–and the claim that the author was himself Ukrainian–suffered from ethnographical inaccuracies and an unlikely mingling of the Ukrainian and Russian languages. Combining cultural prejudice with a misunderstanding of innovative literary forms, Nikolai Alekseevich Polevoi flippantly noted in 1832 in the *Moskovskii telegraf* that the two volumes of *Vechera* must indeed be the work of a Ukrainian, who could not distinguish between significant and insignificant detail. Surprisingly the usually oversensitive Gogol was unfazed by this criticism. In addition to growing self-confidence and the prospect of financial success, Gogol had Pushkin's support and approval. Pushkin regarded Gogol's tales as fresh and lively; where others pointed out weakness, Pushkin saw strength.

Four stories comprise the first volume of *Vechera*. Gogol borrowed these tales from traditional folklore, but his use of authenticating detail–specifically Ukrainian customs, dress, and beliefs–to launch flights into the fantastic resulted in works of original literary prose. The deceptively simple beekeeper Rudyi Panko narrates the tales, directly addressing the readers and coaxing them into realms of the irrational that border the everyday world. The first part of *Vechera* is both playful and horrible; at times good and evil are no more than merriment and bedevilment while at other times they produce nightmarish tales and images. In these stories the boundaries between real and unreal blur as reality gives way to magical dream worlds and the laws of time and space are rendered mutable.

In "Sorochinskaia iarmarka" (The Fair at Sorochinsk) the hopes of the handsome young Grits'ko are dashed when the mean-spirited and domineering stepmother of the lovely Paraska will not allow the two to marry. At the Sorochintsy fair Grits'ko wagers that a gypsy cannot convince Paraska's father to permit the marriage. A rumor is circulating at the fair that scraps of the devil's red jacket have been seen, a sign of bad luck. Gripped by the fear of this jacket, Paraska's father is easy prey for the gypsy who, in the melee the devil story creates at the fair, beguiles him into accepting Grits'ko as a son-in-law.

The structure of "Sorochinskaia iarmarka" frames the interplay between the real and the fantastic in the devilish folktale. With his opening paean to a hot summer day in Little Russia, Gogol paints a detailed portrait that encompasses the fathomless sky, golden haystacks, and flittering insects. The artist's eye captures the beauty of the natural surroundings. "Nagnuvshiesia ot tiazhesti plodov, shirokie vetvi chereshen, sliv, iablon', grush; nebo, ego chistoe zerkalo–reka v zelenykh, gordo podniatykh ramakh kak polno sladostrastiia i negi malorossiiskoe leto!" (The broad branches of cherries, of plums, apples, and pears bent under their load of fruit, the sky with its pure mirror, the river in its green, proudly erect frame–how full of delight is the Little Russian summer!). The description of the colorful procession of wagons to the fair lacks the lofty tone of Gogol's verbal landscape, yet its naturalistic

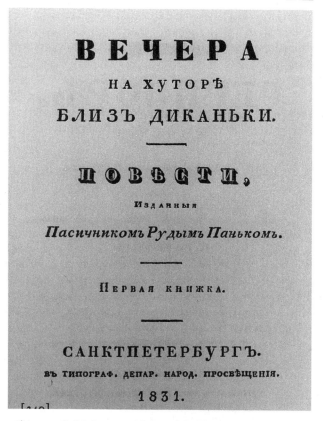

Title page for Vechera na khutore bliz Dikan'ki, *a collection of Gogol's folktales narrated by the character Rudyi Panko, who is credited as the author*

detail grounds the scene with the same sense of reality.

By the end of "Sorochinskaia iarmarka," however, the laws of the material world no longer motivate human action. The dancing crowd at Paraska and Grits'ko's wedding seems overcome by an all-encompassing force that grotesquely transforms even the oldest of guests into puppetlike automatons: "Starushki, na vetkhikh litsakh kotorykh veialo ravnodushie mogily, [tolkali] mezhdu novym, smeiushchimsia, zhivym chlovekom" (Old women, whose ancient faces breathed the indifference of the tomb, [shoved] their way between the young, laughing, living human beings). A mysterious power animates the soulless and the lifeless, blurring the boundary between living and dead. It is as if the mere telling of the story of the devil's jacket and its use in the gypsy's hoax introduces the irrational into the material world, confounding its laws of cause and effect.

Again, in "Maiskaia noch', ili Utoplennitsa" (A May Night, or The Drowned Maiden) an inner narrative affects the outcome of the love story that frames it. In this tale Levko's desire to wed Ganna is frustrated by his own father, the lecherous, one-eyed mayor of the town. Interjected into this love triangle is the legend that surrounds a deserted lakeside house on the outskirts of the village. Levko tells Ganna how the daughter of the Cossack officer who lived in the house was tormented by her stepmother, a witch. In her sorrow the girl drowned herself and, according to Russian folk belief, became a mermaid. One night the girl dragged her stepmother into the pond. The witch transformed herself into a mermaid to escape punishment, and any living man who can distinguish the stepmother among the other mermaids will be rewarded.

Attempting to curtail his father's interest in Ganna, Levko gathers the young men of the village together to create general confusion and to expose the mayor's lechery with satirical ditties. In the midst of this foolishness Levko wanders off and falls asleep by the deserted house of local legend. He dreams that the spurned daughter of the Cossack officer and her fellow mermaids surround him, compelling him to pick out the evil stepmother. He succeeds; the Cossack's drowned daughter gives him a note; and he awakes. The division between dream and reality blurs when, still groggy from sleep, Levko opens his clenched hand to find a note from the local commissar instructing the mayor to marry Levko to Ganna. As in "Sorochinskaia iarmarka" authentic details and realistic descriptions provide the base from which the fantastic arises. But whereas the strange phenomena in "Sorochinskaia iarmarka" have plausible explanations—rumor, the gypsy's intrigue—the appearance of the commissar's letter in "Maiskaia noch'" does not.

"Vecher nakanune Ivana Kupala" shares with "Maiskaia noch'" the confusion of the magic and the real, but with disastrous results. A wealthy Cossack forbids his beautiful daughter Pidorka to marry the poor, kinless Petro. As in "Sorochinskaia iarmarka," devilry casts its shadow on Petro's attempts to overcome the father's obstinacy. However, the nature of the demonic in "Vecher nakanune Ivana Kupala" is more clearly sinister.

In exchange for a trunk full of treasure, Petro enters into a murderous pact with Bisavriuk, a mysterious drifter thought to be the devil incarnate. Petro accompanies Bisavriuk into the forest on St. John's Eve to pick the red flower of a fern that blossoms once a year on that day. If Petro can pick the flower at midnight, it will show him where the treasure is buried. He succeeds, but when he tries to grasp the trunk of gold and jewels, it recedes from him further into the earth. The forest witch appears to him and demands that he cut off the head of a six-year-old child. That child is Ivas', Pidorka's

younger brother. Overcome by the sight of the wealth that awaits him, Petro kills the boy after only a moment's hesitation.

Waking the next day, Petro remembers nothing. Pidorka reports that her brother has disappeared in the forest, presumably carried off by gypsies. Now a rich man, Petro realizes his dream and marries Pidorka. But the couple never knows happiness; Petro's soul troubles him to the point of madness. A year later, again on St. John's Eve, Petro suddenly remembers the gruesome details of his night in the woods with Bisavriuk. In his horror he is reduced to a smoking pile of ashes and his remaining treasure turned into pottery shards. Pidorka enters a convent.

"Vecher nakanune Ivana Kupala" intensifies the theme, introduced in "Sorochinskaia iarmarka," of desire that provides an opportunity for evil to infiltrate the material world. The ghastly tale also establishes a system of crime and punishment wherein the innocent (Ivas') and the beautiful (Pidorka) suffer horribly from others' misdeeds. Gogol's stunning use of language counterbalances the eerie pessimism of "Vecher nakanune Ivana Kupala." Pidorka's message of love to Petro, conveyed by Ivas', for example, displays rich images and the cadence of folk parallelism and repetition. In 1831 in the journal *Teleskop* (Telescope), Nikolai Ivanovich Nadezhdin remarked on the linguistic beauty of both this tale and "Maiskaia noch'." Such instances, he wrote, provide examples of successfully combining Ukrainian folk language with Russian literary language.

"Propavshaia gramota" (The Lost Letter), narrated by the local sexton, humorously treats themes found in the other Dikanka stories. In it the sexton's grandfather must retrieve from a den of witches a letter he was entrusted to deliver to Empress Catherine. Like Petro in "Vecher nakanune Ivana Kupala," he finds himself deep in the forest at night. However, to recover the letter he need not commit murder but must beat the witches at the card game *durak* (fool). He finally outwits them by secretly making the sign of the cross over the cards. Outraged, the witches fling his letter back and send him flying through the woods on a devilishly spirited steed. The grandfather wakes up the next morning on the roof of his own house.

Because he rushes off to deliver the letter without blessing his house, the sexton's grandfather is revisited every year at that same time by a strange force that compels his wife to dance. Recalling "Sorochinskaia iarmarka," the sexton concludes: "Za chto ni primetsia, nogi zatevaiut svoe, i vot tak i dergaet pustit'sia vprisiadku" (No matter what anyone did, her legs would go their own way, and something forced her to dance). Readers of Gogol have noted the influence of the Ukrainian *vertep* (folk puppet theater) in the plot and characterization in these early tales; indeed, at times human characters spontaneously transform into puppetlike beings.

The second volume of *Vechera* appeared in 1832. Like its predecessor, this collection creates a world where dreams and devilish magic coexist with the rational world. Again it is often desire—erotic or material—that initiates the interaction between these two realms. In "Noch' pered Rozhdestvom" (Christmas Eve) Gogol introduces for the first time the struggle between the artist and the devil, a theme that frequently appears in his later work and looms large in his ideas about the nature of art and the artist.

Like "Maiskaia noch'" and "Vecher nakanune Ivana Kupala," "Noch' pered Rozhdestvom" is set on a magical night when the natural and supernatural converge. Carolers roam the town while above them a witch gathers stars in her sleeve and the devil steals the moon. Using the mundane to describe these fantastic events, Gogol underscores their playful proximity: "[Chert] vdrug skhvatil . . . obeimi rukami mesiats, krivliaias' i duia, perekidyval ego iz odnoi ruki v druguiu, kak muzhik, dostavshii golymi rukami ogon' dlia svoei liul'ki" ([The devil] suddenly seized the moon with both hands; grimacing and blowing, he kept flinging it from one hand to the other, like a peasant who has picked up an ember for his pipe with bare fingers).

On this night the blacksmith Vakula has gone to visit the lovely but conceited Oksana in defiance of the wishes of her father, the rich Cossack Chub. The design of the love plot is typical of Gogol with one important addition: Vakula is an artist. His greatest achievement—a picture of St. Peter driving a defeated devil out of hell on Judgment Day—so infuriated the devil that he swore to avenge himself on Vakula. Disregarding the blacksmith's talents, Oksana taunts him, making ludicrous stipulations for their marriage—she demands from him the slippers of the Empress Catherine—and asking Vakula if his mother is a witch.

The blacksmith's mother, Solokha, is indeed the very witch who was earlier gathering stars. When she slides back down the chimney into her house, a smitten devil follows her. However, Solokha's many suitors begin to visit. At the first knock she hides the devil in one of the many empty sacks lying on her floor. She fills the other sacks with each successive visitor: the mayor, the sexton, and her favorite—the Cossack Chub. Arriving home after Oksana's snub, the blacksmith is irritated to see

Gogol in 1834 (portrait by Aleksei Gavrilovich Venetzianov; from David Magarshack, Gogol: A Life)

that his mother has left *drian'* (trash) lying around, and he hauls the sacks outside for disposal. The devil is in the sack slung over Vakula's shoulder when the blacksmith meets a crowd of carolers and Oksana, who again teases him about the empress's slippers. The humiliated blacksmith runs away, leaving his mother's remaining suitors to be discovered by the carolers in a delightfully slapstick scene.

Meanwhile, Vakula approaches the wizard Puzatyi Patsiuk (whose Turkish pose and violation of the Christmas fast suggest his alliance with the devil) to exchange his soul for the slippers. Ready to oblige, the devil crawls out of the sack on Vakula's back. But the blacksmith outsmarts him and forces the devil to take him to meet the empress in St. Petersburg. The fanciful treatment of the spirit world in the representation of Vakula's flight echoes the fantastic opening of the tale. The magical brightness of St. Petersburg will never appear so innocent in Gogol's later stories as it does in "Noch' pered Rozhdestvom." Likewise the brief portrait of the Cossack regiment with which Vakula is presented to the empress will lose its vibrancy when it becomes Gogol's primary focus in "Taras Bul'ba" (one of the stories in *Mirgorod,* 1835). Vakula returns from St. Petersburg with the empress's slippers and marries Oksana with her father's blessing. In a final declaration of victory Vakula paints on the church wall an even more contemptuous picture of the devil, which causes passersby to spit in disgust.

The historical context for "Strashnaia mest'" (A Terrible Vengeance) is the struggle of the Ukraine for independence presented in Gogol's unfinished novel "Get'man" and later in "Taras Bul'ba." However, the bloody and ambiguous contest between good and evil eclipses the historical theme. The relentless lack of the comic in "Strashnaia mest'" reflects the predestined demise of a Cossack family; the tale is classically tragic as it opens with a wedding and ends with the death of an entire family. Gogol divides the story into two parts. First he presents the tale of the Cossack Danilo and his wife Katerina, who are killed by Katerina's sorcerer-father. In the second part of "Strashnaia mest'" an ancient curse provides an explanation for the bloodshed, infanticide, and incest in the first half of the story. By redirecting the horror of Danilo and Katerina's suffering back through the centuries, Gogol not only lessens its effect but also blurs the distinction between good and evil. In the end the sorcerer is as much a victim of fate as those he murders.

The story of Danilo and Katerina paints a richly symbolic picture of evil. It is noteworthy that in 1833 Gogol wrote a letter to his mother admitting that as a child he had not been inspired by any feeling until she described to him the horror of the Last Judgment. Although in many tales Gogol's artists pit themselves against images of evil, he himself acknowledges that these same images can awaken the artist's sensibilities. In addition to an increasingly complex representation of evil, Gogol introduces the notion of a second self, or double, in "Strashnaia mest'" and also utilizes the themes of changelings and deceptive identities.

"Strashnaia mest'" opens with the alarming appearance of a hideous sorcerer at a wedding attended by Danilo, his wife, Katerina, and their infant son. Boating home along the Dnieper River, the family witnesses a strange sight that recalls in a noncomic way the graveyard scene in *Gants Kiukhel'garten*. In a riverside burial ground corpses rise wailing from their graves and, as quickly as they appeared, fade away. Danilo bravely dismisses this frightening sight but immediately voices his concern about the strange behavior of Katerina's father, who has recently returned from living twenty years in Turkic lands. Like the Cossack sorcerer Puzatyi Patsiuk in "Noch' pered Rozhdestvom," the non-Christian traits of Katerina's father underscore his wicked-

ness; he will not drink, eat pork, or toast the success of the Cossacks, the traditional defenders of Orthodox Christianity. His red jacket recalls the devil's coat that wreaks so much havoc in "Sorochinskaia iarmarka" although the devilry in the latter tale is playful rather than destructive. In "Strashnaia mest'" the diabolic is protean and powerful. The sorcerer can transform his shape and summon his daughter's soul, her spirit double. But Katerina's father cannot change his destiny. As fated, he kills every member of his family. He attempts to repent, but when the Bible of the monk to whom he has turned for redemption drips with blood, the sorcerer kills the holy man as well. "Strashnaia mest'" is an oppressive tale of unmitigated grief. Here innocent victims of evil cannot seek refuge in convents and monasteries, as did Pidorka in "Vecher nakanune Ivana Kupala," and the devil cannot be outsmarted; there is no escape from the "terrible vengeance."

In contrast to the inevitability of "Strashnaia mest'," the dynamics of evasion motivate "Ivan Fedorovich Shpon'ka i ego tetushka" (Ivan Fedorovich Shpon'ka and His Auntie). As Ivan Shpon'ka tries to sidestep his aunt's schemes to marry him off, the narrative itself avoids any meaningful action or plot. With "Shpon'ka" Gogol finds a new way to engage his readers. Using a technique that evolves further in the Petersburg tales and in *Mertvye dushi,* Gogol focuses his attention on seemingly irrelevant detail and the development of comic moments. Readers strain to discern the significance of the story to no avail. Indeed the world around the text, rather than within the text, takes on importance, beginning with the opening line: "S ètoi istoriei sluchilas' istoriia" (There is a story about this story). The description of events that follow is almost entirely devoid of narrative direction and breaks off suddenly because Rudyi Panko's wife uses its final pages for the more practical task of baking fish (one reader playfully suggests that the text becomes food for thought). Gogol shifts the literary spotlight from the text onto the readers' extratextual experience of frustrated discovery. The evasive narrative technique in "Shpon'ka" illuminates Gogol's desire to direct readers' reactions to his work and hints at the increasing primacy of the narrative personality.

Although lacking a progressive plot, "Shpon'ka" offers rich and comic treatments of themes that later become central to Gogol's work. Much of what is humorous in the tale derives from sexual ambiguity; Gogol inverts gender stereotypes in the characterization of Shpon'ka and his aunt. Shpon'ka is given to typically feminine pursuits: fretting over his wardrobe and telling fortunes. A woman "rosta ispolinskogo" (of gigantic stature), his auntie hunts, fishes, and oversees Shpon'ka's small estate with a sharp eye and iron fist. Her life more closely resembles that of a nineteenth-century country bachelor than that of a middle-aged unmarried woman. Her strength necessarily implies her nephew's weakness; at thirty-eight he is reduced to a child as she addresses him by the diminutive Vaniusha and lifts him off the ground with her embraces. Related to this theme of sexual ambiguity is the question of Shpon'ka's paternity. His aunt tells him that he has been deeded a tract of land by a neighbor who used to visit his mother when her husband was away from home. The deed has been usurped by Shpon'ka's blustering neighbor Storchenko; the urgency of retrieving the deed fades, however, when Shpon'ka's aunt hatches a plan to marry her nephew to Storchenko's sister. Shpon'ka is panicked at the prospect of having a wife because, as he reasons, he has never had one before. The absurdity of Shpon'ka's logic extends into his nightmare, which provides rich material for Freudians. In the dream, wives with gooselike faces pop up everywhere Shpon'ka looks; he himself turns into a bell. In Gogol's folk-inspired tales, dreams often access magical and surreal parallel worlds; here, however, Gogol uses the dream symbolically to represent the anxiety of Shpon'ka's psyche.

"Zakoldovannoe mesto" (A Bewitched Spot) concludes the *Vechera* collection, acting as a final commentary on man's dubious ability to wield any power over the supernatural forces of evil. The sexton's grandfather is again the hero. He stumbles onto treasure in the illusory world of a "bewitched spot." Although this place abuts the grandfather's melon patch, he cannot relocate the site in daylight. The sudden transitions between the rational world and the fantastic are beyond his control and defy ordinary laws of time and space. He finally succeeds in carrying his pot of gold back home with him, only to discover that it has turned into slop. Despite its humor, "Zakoldovannoe mesto" suggests that man cannot regulate the evil that constantly encroaches upon the rational world. Enchanted patches are close by, perhaps just beyond one's own field, and they resist man's cultivation. The grandfather's melon patch was rented out, the sexton says at the end of his tale. But "zaseiut kak sleduet, a vzoidet takoe, chto i razobrat' nel'zia: arbuz–ne arbuz, tykva–ne tykva, ogurets–ne ogurets . . . chert znaet, chto takoe!" (they may sow it properly, but there's no saying what it is that comes up: not a melon–not a pumpkin–not a cucumber, the devil only knows what it is!).

Although the Patriotic Institute lay beyond his family's means and social standing, Gogol managed to

Sculpture in St. Petersburg of Major Kovalev's nose, inspired by Gogol's story "Nos," published in Sovremennik *(The Contemporary) in 1836 (photograph by Edward Alan Cole, 1997)*

enroll his two younger sisters, Anna and Elizaveta, in 1832. Gogol was inattentive to the girls' care and also to his teaching position. Yet he did harbor plans for a multivolume history of the world and in 1833 filed with the minister of education Sergei Semenovich Uvarov a report, "O prepodavanii vseobshchei istorii" (On the Teaching of World History), which was later included in *Arabeski* (Arabesques, 1835). Determined to become a great historian, Gogol managed to secure for himself an assistant professorship of history at the University of St. Petersburg in 1834 despite his lack of training or degree. His inaugural lecture that September was unforgettable. Gogol memorized the sweeping overview of the Middle Ages he created from brilliant images of crusades, chivalry, and the Inquisition and, without a single reference to historical names or dates, performed, rather than delivered, the lecture. However, Gogol could not repeat such a performance, nor did he seem willing or able to support his poetic rendition of history with facts. By the spring of 1835 it was clear that Gogol's teaching career, both at the Patriotic Institute and the university, was over.

Gogol's failure in scholarship was offset by a period of productivity in literature. In January 1835 Gogol published the two-volume *Arabeski,* a collection of stories and articles on subjects ranging from art and architecture to geography and history (much of the latter culled from his university lectures). By March the *Mirgorod* collection, also in two parts, appeared in publication. Although *Arabeski* and *Mirgorod* proved financial disappointments, they received high praise from the young critic Vissarion Grigor'evich Belinsky, who wrote that Gogol was taking the place of Pushkin in Russian literature.

Arabeski seems to be an eclectic grouping of Gogol's lecture notes, essays, and fiction. The remains of his short-lived assistant professorship are evident in "O srednikh vekakh" (On the Middle Ages), "Vzgliad na sostavlenie Malorossii" (A Glance at the Composition of Little Russia), "Al-Mamun" (Al-Mamun), "Zhizn'" (Life), "Schletser, Miller i Gerder" (Schlözer, Müller and Herder), "Mysli o geografii," and "O dvizhenii narodov v kontse V veka" (On the Movements of Peoples at the End of the Fifth Century). Gogol gathered his thoughts on music, architecture, literature, sculpture, and painting in "Skul'ptura, zhivopis' i muzyka" (Sculpture, Painting and Music), "Neskol'ko slov o Pushkine" (A Few Words about Pushkin), "Ob arkhitekture nyneshnego vremeni" (On Present-day Architecture), "O Malorossiiskikh pesniakh" (The Songs of the Ukraine), and "Poslednii den' Pompei" (The Last Day of Pompeii). Despite its appearance as a miscellany, *Arabeski* derives an inner unity when it is understood as an expression of Gogol's increasingly mature conception of art and the artist.

For Gogol the sphere of the artist is not limited to the arts. Rather the artist must be engaged in every area of culture and society. Although it is not necessary that the artist himself be a genius, it is essential that he detect genius and bring it to light. Thus, as Fanger shows, in Gogol's "Skul'ptura, zhivopis' i muzyka" the poet detects the greatness of the Greek world that has been lost to the centuries; in "O srednikh vekakh" the artist must construct a meaningful order out of the swirl of historical chaos; and in "Ob arkhitekture nyneshnego vremeni" only the architect who is both genius and poet will render his creations genuine. By perceiving and describing the universal truth and global wholeness that genius represents, Gogol's artist effectively counters the modern conditions of fragmentation and isolation that burden the individual with the loneliness of selfhood.

In the essays "Poslednii den' Pompei" and "Neskol'ko slov o Pushkine" Gogol suggests that art can stir a deadened soul. And for Gogol the soul is the instrument by which man transcends the constrictive bounds of his individual or social self. Thus in *Arabeski* the beginnings of Gogol's treatment of art as a religion advocating universal unity becomes evident. The truly aesthetic becomes for Gogol a spiritual force, lifting the viewers or readers out of the mundane, the banal, and the superficial. In the same way, bad art and the waste or abuse of genuine art becomes the realm of the devil. Gogol's artist is obliged to find the unusual in the ordinary without finding himself mired down by the subject of his representation. It is a difficult role to play. Like a ladder between heaven and earth, the artist joins the everyday with the sublime. Yet by representing the ordinary the artist risks losing a public that expects only grand, sweeping portraits of heroic subjects. Tempted by devilish greed and human weakness, the artist may also acquiesce to the demands of public approval.

By the time Gogol wrote the first volume of *Mertvye dushi,* his ideas and concerns about the role of the artist in society were explicit. In *Arabeski* they are clouded by unfocused rhetoric and lack of development. Yet Gogol expresses himself best in his creative prose. Gogol included three short works of fiction in *Arabeski:* "Zapiski sumasshedshego" (The Diary of a Madman), "Nevskii Prospekt" (Nevsky Prospect, revised for the 1842 edition of Gogol's *Sochineniia* [Works]), and "Portret" (The Portrait, also revised for the 1842 *Sochineniia*). In these stories Gogol develops the relationship among women, evil, and art that appears in its nascent stage in the *Vechera* collection. Gogol first envisioned "Zapiski sumasshedshego" as a story about a mad musician but later reworked it. In the resulting tale Poprishchin, a middle-aged clerk of little promise, records in his diary how he has fallen in love with the daughter of his departmental director. The clerk's obsession becomes the point of entry into a delusional world of madness. Although Poprishchin is not an artist, the insight he derives from his madness echoes with a hint of self-parody the notion of the perceptive aesthetic eye that Gogol explores in the *Arabeski* essays. Poprishchin's disregard for temporal chronology suggests comically that he perceives a mad order beneath the worldly calendar; Poprishchin dates his diary entries with "Martober 86," "2000 A.D., April 43" and "February thirtieth" as his sanity slips away. In addition his ears discern the language of dogs, allowing him to use their intercepted letters to spy on his chief's daughter. Finally he makes the most important discovery of all—woman is the consort of the devil: "O, èto kovarnoe sushchestvo—zhenshchina! Ia teper' tol'ko postignul, chto takoe zhenshchina. Do sikh por nikto eshche ne uznal, v kogo ona vliublena: ia pervyi otkryl èto. Zhenshchina vliublena v cherta" (Oh, woman is a treacherous creature! I have discovered now what women are. So far no one has found out with whom she is in love: I have been the first to discover it. Woman is in love with the devil).

The urban setting of the stories in *Arabeski* provides a field of play for devilry. The deceptive city becomes as much of a character in the later collection as the enchanted spots and magical forest do in *Vechera*. As women often do in Gogol's work, the streets and houses of St. Petersburg join forces with the devil to confound the artist. In "Nevskii Prospekt" the deceptions of woman, city, and devil result in the suicide of the young artist Piskarev. The artist succumbs to the fragmentation and superficiality of the modern urban environment, taking along with him the "genius" that may have restored in Russia the sacred unity for which Gogol longed: "Tak pogib, zhertva bezumnoi strasti, bednyi Piskarev, tikhii, robkii, skromnyi, detski prostodushnyi, nosivshii v sebe iskru talanta, byt' mozhet, so vremenem by vspykhnuvshego shiroko i iarko" (So perished the victim of a frantic passion, poor Piskarev, the gentle, timid, modest, childishly simplehearted artist whose spark of talent might with time have glowed into the full bright flame of genius).

Nevsky Prospect, the main thoroughfare of St. Petersburg, is the title character of the tale. Gogol's depiction of a typical day in the "life" of the street opens the narrative and personifies the street. Perceived by an almost cinemographic eye, Nevsky Prospect is lively and colorful, yet it lacks whole forms. The various pieces of clothing and parts of the body that Gogol describes are so dissociated from the people who own them that they seem to stroll along the avenue of their own volition. The fragmentation of life on Nevsky is augmented by superficiality. In one account the stylish clothes that parade up and down the street hold their owners' fancy for only a short time: "Tysiachi sortov shliapok, plat'ev, platkov-pestrykh, legkikh, k kotorym inogda v techenie tselykh dvukh dnei sokhraniaetsia priviazannost' ikh vladetel'nits, oslepiat khot' kogo na Nevskom prospekte" (Thousands of varieties of hats, dresses, and kerchiefs, bright colored and sheer, for which their owners feel sometimes an adoration that lasts two whole days, dazzle everyone on Nevsky Prospect).

Nighttime on Nevsky Prospect is a "tainstvennoe vremia, kogda lampy daiut vsemu kakoi-to zamanchivyi, chudesnyi svet" (mysterious time when the street lamps throw a marvelous enchanting light upon everything). Like the fairgrounds in "Sorochinskaia iarmarka," the vibrant colors and diverse

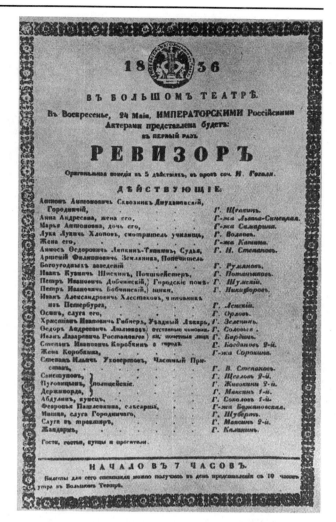

Poster for the first Moscow performance of Gogol's play Revizor *(The Inspector General), 24 May 1836*

human activity at play on Nevsky Prospect delight the senses. But the narrator warns that the "enchantment" of Nevsky is not to be trusted; the street is the devil's path:

On lzhet vo vsiakoe vremia, ètot Nevskii prospekt, no bolee vsego togda, kogda noch' sgushchennoiu massoiu naliazhet na nego i otdelit belye i palevye steny domov, kogda ves' gorod prevratitsia v grom i blesk, miriady karet valiatsia s mostov, foreitory krichat i prygaiut na loshadiakh, i kogda sam demon zazhigaet lampy dlia togo tol'ko, chtoby pokazat' vse ne v nastoiashchem vide.

(It deceives at all hours, Nevsky Prospect does, but most of all when night falls in masses of shadow on it, throwing into relief the white and dun-colored walls of the houses, when all the town is transformed into noise and brilliance, when the myriad carriages roll over the bridges, postilions shout and jolt up and down on their horses, and when the devil himself lights the street lamps only to show everything in false colors.)

In the story two young men, the artist Piskarev and a Lieutenant Pirogov, venture out one evening into the beguiling world of Nevsky Prospect. The men part ways to pursue the attractive young women each has spotted on the street. Neither of the women lives up to the men's expectations, but the friends react differently to their disappointment. Pirogov's romantic interest turns out to be the simple and satisfied wife of a rather uncouth German tinsmith. Undaunted, Pirogov orders spurs and then a dagger sheath from the German and returns to the home repeatedly on the pretense of inquiring about his orders. When the tinsmith finally realizes the true nature of Pirogov's visits, he unceremoniously throws the young lieutenant out of the house. On his way to report the tinsmith's insulting conduct to the authorities, Pirogov stops in at a cafe, and his indignation subsides over a dish of cream puffs. By nightfall he has forgotten about the tinsmith's pretty wife. The mediocre and superficial life of Pirogov's regiment society effectively saves him from real heartbreak.

Piskarev does not fare so well. He is unable to reconcile the innocent appearance of the young woman he follows with her life of prostitution. In "Nevskii Prospekt" good and evil, beauty and corruption become as indistinguishable to Piskarev as dream and reality and ultimately result in his destruction. Initially, Piskarev interprets the pale beauty and youth of the mysterious belle as innocence and purity of spirit. As does Gogol's essay "Zhenshchina," "Nevskii Prospekt" equates beauty with purity and innocence. For Piskarev the fresh loveliness of the young woman also imbues her with a holiness bordering on divinity. The language of his thoughts reveals his understanding of his romantic pursuit as something of a holy pilgrimage: "Kak uteriat' èto bozhestvo i ne uznat' dazhe toi sviatyni, gde ono opustilos' gostit'?" (How could he lose this divine being without even discovering the sacred place in which she condescended to stay?). Piskarev is not motivated by base physical attraction. As he follows the young woman into her house and up the stairs, he is consumed only by innocent desire for her, the proper state when approaching a sacred shrine.

When Piskarev steps across the threshold of the apartment into which the young woman leads him, he is shocked to discover that he is standing in a brothel, "gde chelovek sviatotatstvenno podavil i posmeialsia nad vsem chistym i sviatym, ukrashaiushchim zhizn'" (where man sacrilegiously tramples and ridicules all that is pure and holy, all that makes life beautiful). In such a place, woman—the manifestation of beauty in the world—becomes "strannoe, dvusmyslennoe sushchestvo" (a strange, equivocal creature) surrendering the purity of her heart and all that is "womanly" about her. When the beauty finally speaks to Piskarev, her words are vulgar and her gaze suggestive. The artist is unable to tolerate such a wrenching dislocation of beauty from purity and holiness, and he flees in horror.

At home Piskarev convinces himself that the young woman is far too lovely to have willingly succumbed to such a life of vice; her presence in the brothel must be the work of the devil. The artist's delusional belief manifests itself in a dream. In fitful sleep he sees an enormous ballroom crowded with gowns and uniforms. Like the descriptions of Nevsky Prospect, the shattered kaleidoscope of colors and movement in this room suggest the work of the devil: "Neobyknovennaia pestrota lits privela ego v sovershennoe zameshatel'stvo; emu kazalos', chto kakoi-to demon iskroshil ves' mir na mnozhestvo raznykh kuskov i vse èti kuski bez smysla, bez tolku smeshal vmeste" (The extraordinary brightness and variety of the scene completely staggered [Piskarev]; it seemed to him as though some demon had crumbled the whole world into bits and mixed all these bits indiscriminately together). For Gogol unity of form expresses goodness in both life and art. Piskarev's mysterious beauty moves elegantly through this scene. She seems ready to entrust him with the terrible secret of her coercion into a sinful life, a secret that would restore innocence to her beauty. However, before she can speak, he wakes up.

From that point forward Piskarev devotes his life to the resurrection of his ideal of beauty. Afraid to approach "tainstvennyi obraz, original mechtatel'nykh kartin" (the mysterious divinity, the original of his dream pictures), he begins to regard his oneiric visions as reality, losing the distinction between waking and dream. Opium-induced dreaming becomes his obsession; only in dreams can the artist reunite the sacred and the beautiful that reality so insistently pulls apart. The aim of all art, the identification of beauty and good, is at odds with forces that threaten to conceal evil within beauty. Piskarev expresses his frustration with this struggle in terms of his dreaming and waking hours: "Bozhe, chto za zhizn' nasha! vechnyi razdor mechty s sushchestvennost'iu!" (My God, what is our life! An eternal battle of dream with reality!).

When Piskarev finally musters the courage to approach the young prostitute again, he proposes to her the simple life of an artist's wife. But she prefers her life of relative ease and scornfully rejects his idea of a life of redemptive drudgery that would serve his art. With no hope of reconciling beauty and truth through art, the disconsolate Piskarev commits suicide. The deceit of demonic beauty destroys a potentially genuine artist. In the end the tale serves as a warning: "O, ne ver'te ètomu Nevskomu prospektu! . . . Vse obman, vse mechta, vse ne to, chem kazhetsia!" (Oh, do not trust that Nevsky Prospect! . . . Everything is a cheat, everything is a dream, everything is other than it seems!).

Gogol continues to explore the fate of the artist in the city in "Portret," the third piece of fiction included in *Arabeski*. This Hoffmanesque tale develops further Gogol's concern with morality and aesthetics. In it the poor artist Chertkov (Chartkov in the expanded 1842 version) buys the portrait of an old moneylender, whose horribly lifelike eyes seem to animate the face on the canvas. As the young prostitute in "Nevskii Prospekt" embodies the disjunction of truth and beauty, the painting represents truth without beauty. The moneylender's portrait reflects "uzhasnaia deistvitel'nost'" (a horrible reality) where human existence and experience is without meaning and grace. Looking at the portrait, Chertkov senses a dark presence in the very absence of art:

Èto bylo uzhe ne iskusstvo: èto razrushalo dazhe garmoniiu samogo portreta. Èto byli zhivye, èto byli chelovecheskie glaza! Kazalos', kak budto oni byli vyrezany iz zhivogo cheloveka i vstavleny siuda. Zdes' ne bylo uzhe togo vysokogo naslazhden'ia, kotoroe ob"emlet dushu pri vzgliade na proizvedenie khudozhnika, kak ni uzhasen vziatyi im predmet; zdes' bylo kakoe-to boleznennoe, tomitel'noe chuvstvo.

(This is no longer art. [The eyes] actually destroyed the harmony of the portrait. They were alive, human! It was as if they had been cut from a living man and inserted in the canvas. Here was none of that sublime feeling of enjoyment which imbued the spirit at the sight of an artist's endeavors, regardless of how terrible the subject he may have put on canvas. Instead, there was a painful, joyless sense of anxiety.)

The strange vitality of the portrait extends even into the world of Chertkov's dreams. In his sleep he sees the moneylender come to life, step out of the painting's frame, and move around the room. The next morning the frame does indeed break, and Chertkov discovers a roll of gold coins inside the eerie portrait. However, Chertkov's apparent boon turns out to be the source of his demise. Instead of living on the money while he painstakingly and humbly develops his artistic talent, he indulges his desire for material comforts and the empty praise of high society. He places an advertisement full of self-praise in the newspaper and is then inundated with requests for portraits. At first Chertkov tries to ren-

Gogol in 1841

der a true likeness of his subjects but soon realizes that his paying customers only want him to paint them in a more flattering, idealized light than reality reflects. Pandering to the tastes of society and his own vanity, Chertkov no longer attempts to capture the true nature of his subjects in his portraits. Doing so, he divorces art from nature and thus renders his work trivial and banal.

In "Portret" Gogol shows how evil—in the form of the devil or human philistinism—can destroy both art and the artist. In the moneylender's portrait and those Chertkov paints, nature and art fail to combine with the kind of balance that evokes a "sublime feeling of enjoyment" from the viewer. The portrait of the moneylender is too much infused with the real spirit of its subject while Chertkov's work becomes a series of tired and meaningless forms. Years later when Chertkov finally understands that he has squandered his talent, he himself becomes the agent of art's destruction. With a fortune at hand, he buys all the genuine paintings he can find and destroys them: "Nikogda ni odno chudovishche nevezhestva ne istrebilo stol'ko prekrasnykh proizvedenii, skol'ko istrebil ètot svirepyi mstitel'" (No ignorant monster ever destroyed so many marvelous works of art as this raving avenger). The first part of "Portret" ends with Chertkov's tortured death.

As with "Strashnaia mest'," the second part of "Portret" explains the first. At an auction an artist's son describes the strange circumstances under which his father painted the portrait of the moneylender. Before his death the moneylender entreated the artist to paint his portrait so that his spirit might remain in the world. The portrait passes from hand to hand, inspiring ill will and causing failure; thereafter the artist's work is pervaded by a vague sense of the demonic. For Gogol the artist resides in a lofty yet precarious realm. Although the salvation of the world depends on his aesthetic vision and his talent, the artist is often coerced by a terrible or petty force of evil to render human experience meaningless and devoid of value. To purge himself of the evil that has invaded his art and his life, the artist enters a monastery and for years lives the life of an ascetic. Only when his soul is pure can he paint guided by "sviataia vysshaia sila" (a holy and higher power). Turning to the painting after hearing the fantastic story about the artist, the auctiongoers are shocked to see that the terrible portrait has turned into an innocuous landscape (in the revised version it disappears).

The *Mirgorod* collection appeared in March 1835. Although the title page indicated the book would continue in the vein of the Ukrainian folktales of *Vechera,* the Little Russian setting receded into the background. With "Starosvetskie pomeshchiki" (Old-World Landowners) Gogol shifts the position of the narrator. Gone is the insider's perspective that Rudyi Panko offers in *Vechera.* The narrator of "Starosvetskie pomeshchiki" immediately establishes a distance between himself and his subject, the provincial world of Afanasii Ivanovich and Pul'kheriia Ivanovna Tovstogub, into which he sometimes likes "soiti na minutu" (to enter for a moment). Assuming this remote point of view, the narrator invites readers to share his experience of the Tovstogub home and also his ambivalent attitude toward the friendly, old couple. "Starosvetskie pomeshchiki" is not a story but a meditation on a disappearing way of life and the response of the narrator's modern consciousness to this loss. The theme is not new, but as Fanger points out, the role of the narrator as main character was a novelty in Russian literature: "By eschewing plot . . . Gogol alters the code of Russian fiction, producing something midway between a story and a performance—a verbal artifact whose charm lies entirely in the modulations of its unfolding."

The narrator's characterization of his tale as a portrait reflects the lack of movement in the narrative itself; life on the Tovstogub homestead is literally a "still life." Referring to the loving couple in

Greek myth who graciously provide Zeus and Hermes food when all others turn them away, the narrator says, "Esli by ia byl zhivopisets i khotel izobrazit' na polotne Filemona i Bavkidu, ia by nikogda ne izbral drugogo originala, krome ikh" (If I were a painter and wanted to portray Philemon and Baucis on canvas, I could choose no other models [than the Tovstogubs]). Yet these "models" of kindness turn out to be nothing more than human husks as grotesquely empty of true feeling as Piskarev's work in "Portret." The young social critic Belinsky plumbed the hollow depths of the Tovstogubs when he described them as "two parodies of humanity who, in the course of several decades, drink and eat, eat and drink, and then, as custom has it, die." And despite the narrator's apparent affection for the peace and plenty of the Tovstogub home, Renato Poggioli points out that "Starosvetskie pomeshchiki" represents an inversion of the eclogue, which traditionally celebrates the fullness of the idyll.

In "Starosvetskie pomeshchiki" the narrator's perspective alternates between that of the distant "outsider" and the more intimate viewpoint of a frequent houseguest. Moving between the "here" of St. Petersburg society and the "there" of the Ukrainian provinces, the narrative structure of the tale parallels the narrator's vacillating attitude toward the ironic Tovstogub idyll. The spatiality of "Starosvetskie pomeshchiki" describes the intangible pangs of feeling that are unclear to the narrator. Craving the cloying comforts of Tovstogub's traditional homestead at a distance, the narrator is vaguely repelled by their overfed and overheated lifestyle when he shares it with them. Ultimately it is through literary space that the narrator must reluctantly admit the moral depravity of the "old-fashioned" world he vainly attempts to sentimentalize. The Tovstogubs and their home succumb to the overwhelming force of habit, and the spiritual void that had all the while lurked behind the idyllic facade shows through when it becomes a vacant lot. The narrator says, "Chuvstva moi stranno szhimaiutsia, kogda voobrazhu sebe, chto priedu so vremenem opiat' na ikh prezhnee, nyne opusteloe zhilishche i uvizhu kuchu razvalivshikhsia khat, zaglokhshii prud, zarosshii rov na tom meste, gde stoil nizen'kii domik—i nichego bolee. Grustno!" (I feel a strange pang in my heart when I imagine myself going sometime again to their old, now deserted dwelling, and seeing the heap of ruined huts, the pond choked with weeds, an overgrown ditch on the spot where the little house stood—and nothing more. How depressing!). As in Gogol's earlier *Vechera* tales, the new evil—no longer petty devilry but the "immortal banality" of man that Dmitrii Sergeevich Merezhkovsky

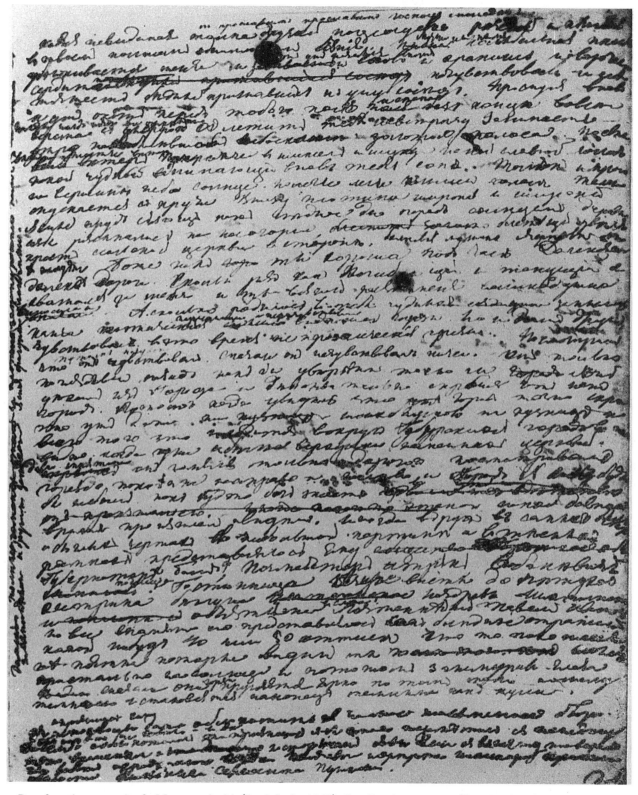

Page from the manuscript for Mertvye dushi *(Dead Souls, 1842), Gogol's epic prose poem (from David Magarshack,* Gogol:
A Life)

detects in Gogol—dwells in wild and overgrown natural chaos where humanity is no longer evident.

Like "Starosvetskie pomeshchiki," "Taras Bul'ba" depicts a vanished way of life. This literary legend about a fifteenth-century Dnieper Cossack *sech,* or community, grew out of the historical work included in *Arabeski* and was supposedly part of Gogol's efforts to preserve the ancient traditions of his native Ukraine. Despite his best intentions, Gogol's accuracy in detail and chronology suffered from his tendency toward intuitive history. Nevertheless, in "Taras Bul'ba" Gogol brings to life the merrily uncouth ways, vivid traditions, and warrior pride of the Cossack encampment. Gogol's revisions in 1839–1840 (for the 1842 edition of *Sochineniia*), which expanded the tale and emphasized Homeric similes, reoriented "Taras Bul'ba" toward a more generally Russian, rather than specifically Ukrainian, patriotism. Yet the later edition retains the pervasiveness of wild abandon and heroism even in the face of tragedy.

There is little tension between revelry and tragedy in "Taras Bul'ba." The ineffectiveness of Gogol's pathos often stems from a formulaic approach to the genre of historical novel. The gruesome and triumphant deaths of the Cossack heroes are of the boyhood adventure-novel variety. Each man, whether beheaded or impaled on a lance, remembers to praise his comrades and their mission before dying. At other times Gogol denigrates the object of narrative pity. The grieving Cossack mother, for example, who runs after her two young sons as they set off for war, pursues them "so vseiu legkost'iu dikoi kozy, nesoobraznoi ee letam" (with the nimbleness of a wild goat, hardly believable at her years). She is never mentioned again in the story.

The young Polish woman with whom Taras's younger son Andrei falls in love plays a role familiar in Gogol's work; she initiates the ruin of the Bul'ba family. Before he leaves the seminary in Kiev to return to his father's house, Andrei encounters her, "krasavitsu, kakoi eshche ne vidyval otrodu: chernoglazuiu i beluiu, kak sneg, ozarennyi utrennim rumiantsem solntsa" (the loveliest creature he had seen in his life, with black eyes and skin white as snow when it is lighted up by the flush of the dawning sun). Andrei's love overcomes the fact that she is the daughter of his enemy, and on the night before the Cossacks battle the Poles, he forsakes his country by defecting to her father's side. Andrei's treachery sets off a chain of events that end in the death of every male member of the Bul'ba household. Gogol's weak representation of Andrei's love hardly justifies such a heavy loss. As with the descriptions

of nature and battle, the narrative heights from which Gogol portrays the love story prove too heady. His language breaks down into cliché that is overly emotive and ultimately unconvincing. Omniscient narration does not suit Gogol. In order to ground his writing, his narrative persona needs to have some kind of involvement with the action he describes.

Gogol is self-involved in "Vii" to the extent that the tale gives shape to his personal anxiety about women as agents of evil. Many critics examine the roots of Gogol's fears in a Freudian context while Simon Karlinsky, in *The Sexual Labyrinth of Nikolai Gogol* (1976), conjectures that the author's latent homosexuality generates the misogynist dread in stories such as "Vii." But these fears may be given a broader, cultural text. Both oral and written literary traditions in Russia express the terror of powerlessness before the erotic and the supernatural, which are represented in fiction as the beauty and power of woman and her perceived alliance with the uncontrollable forces of nature. In one Russian folktale, which closely resembles "Vii," a young man must read prayers over the body of a young witch. She is resurrected and is married to the man but refuses to live the pious and obedient life of a wife. Her body is burned, dismembered, and restored to a whole before she will conform. Although Gogol's claim that "Vii" is pure folklore is inaccurate, the folk patterns and motifs he invokes express a cultural fear of the supernatural and of female eroticism.

In "Vii" an old woman gives a night's lodging in her forest homestead to the young philosophy student Khoma Brut. In a scene that recalls the flight scene in "Noch' pered Rozhdestvom" of *Vechera,* the woman compels Khoma to ride through the night sky as she sits astride him with her broom in hand. Although he is repelled by the witch's suggestive advances, Khoma experiences orgasmic sensations during the ride: "Pot katilsia s nego gradom. On chuvstvoval besovski-sladkoe chuvstvo, on chuvstvoval kakoe-to pronzaiushchee, kakoe-to tomitel'no-strashnoe naslazhdenie" (The sweat was pouring out of him. He was aware of a fiendishly voluptuous feeling; he felt a stabbing, exhaustingly terrible delight). For the philosophy student such feelings are further proof that he is in the clutches of a frightening and evil force. Despite the circumstances, Khoma is able to compose himself enough to pronounce the prayers that counteract the witch's power. Back on the ground, Khoma beats the old woman until he notices that she has undergone a startling change. He flees in horror when he sees that "pered nim lezhala krasavitsa s rastrepannoiu

Front wrapper for the first edition of Mertvye dushi, *designed by Gogol to illustrate the work*

roskoshnoiu kosoiu, s dlinnymi, kak strely, resnitsami" (before him lay a beautiful girl with luxuriant, tangled tresses and eyelashes as long as arrows).

Several days later Khoma is asked to read prayers and psalms for three nights over the body of a young Cossack girl who returned from the forest beaten and dying. When he looks at the body, he realizes with horror that the girl is the witch he killed days before. For three nights he is locked in a church with the body. As he reads prayers, the corpse sits up in its coffin and with eyes shut and teeth gnashing, proceeds to walk around the church in search of Khoma. Remembering the words of a monk, Khoma draws a circle in chalk around himself and repeats exorcisms. While inside the circle Khoma is invisible to the dead witch, and the multitude of evil spirits she summons on the second night

cannot harm him. Finally on the third night the witch calls on Vii, the forest gnome with eyelids that reach the ground. Although Khoma's inner voice beseeches him not to look at this horrible creature, he cannot restrain himself. When his eyes fall on Vii, Khoma is visible, and the evil spirits descend upon him, causing him to die of fright. Ultimately the evil of feminine power and eroticism destroys Khoma. As in Gogol's earlier work the physical or emotional enjoyment of a woman results in the spiritual or actual death of the hero.

As Gogol's writing matures, spiritual death—the loss of value and significance in human life—begins to replace physical death as the most chilling phenomenon. In "Povest' o tom, kak possorilsia Ivan Ivanovich s Ivanom Nikiforovichem" (The Tale of How Ivan Ivanovich Quarreled with Ivan Nikiforovich), the two title characters end their long-standing friendship with a petty quarrel that continues for a decade. Of all the *Mirgorod* tales, "Povest' o dvukh Ivanakh" (The Tale of the Two Ivans), as the story is popularly known, is the only one attributed to Rudyi Panko, the folksy narrator of the earlier Dikanka cycle. The tale opens humorously with the ironic naiveté of the insider's point of view. Praising Ivan Ivanovich's and Ivan Nikiforovich's fine qualities, the narrator actually exposes the pettiness and absurdity of their existence. Ivan Ivanovich collects the seeds of any melon he eats in a piece of paper and dates it; he is a pious man who never fails to question the beggars who throng the church but refuses them money. The narrator vehemently denies that Ivan Nikiforovich was born with a tail like a witch (insisting that a tail is solely a woman's affliction) or that this respectable Mirgorod citizen ever considered marriage. Yet Ivan Nikiforovich endures long visits from Agafiia Fedoseevna, an unrelated and meddling woman who rubs his entire body with vinegar and turpentine. The narrator's exuberance extends to the town of Mirgorod, which he breathlessly describes as a cluster of ramshackle houses and laundry-strewn fences surrounding an enormous puddle.

By the end of the tale the narrator's perspective is decidedly more distant—he is passing through Mirgorod after a five-year absence—and his attitude toward the quarrel of the two Ivans is one of morose exhaustion. "Skuchno na ètom svete, gospoda!" (It is a dreary world, gentlemen!), he says in conclusion. Recalling the closing tone of "Starosvetskie pomeshchiki," this final line indicates that time and distance have altered the narrator's relationship to his subjects. Throughout the story the narrator's role as primary character grows increasingly evident. The mastery and the artistic value of his narrative skills eventually displace the content of the story and its plot in importance, a narrative style known as *skaz*. Here, Gogol wants to demonstrate the primacy of the word. In fact, what little plot there is in "Povest' o dvukh Ivanakh" turns on a single word—*gusak* (gander)—with which Ivan Nikiforovich initiates the quarrel and then, with a second slip of the tongue, ensures it long life. The richness of the verbal display throughout this tale and the others in the collection turns *Mirgorod* into a landmark in the development of the role and position of the narrator in Gogol's work, as well as the timbre of the narrative voice.

In 1833, languishing under the burdens of his teaching positions, Gogol produced several short stories. Among these was "Nos" (The Nose), which he did not include in *Mirgorod* but submitted instead

in 1834 to the journal *Moskovskii nabliudatel'* (Moscow Observer), where the editorial board rejected it as vulgar and trivial. "Nos" was finally published in Pushkin's *Sovremennik* (The Contemporary) in 1836. As Viktor Vladimirovich Vinogradov shows, "Nos" follows a trend in early-nineteenth-century Europe that turned the nose into a thematic and phallic centerpiece. Gogol repeatedly declared himself incapable of inventing plots; it was Pushkin who supplied him with the subject for both *Revizor* (The Inspector General, 1836) and *Mertvye dushi*. However, Gogol's approach to well-known stories, themes, and motifs was so radically innovative that it seems unique. Gogol first conceived "Nos" as a dream, calling it "Son" (The Dream). With this idea in mind it is easy to view the contents of "Nos" as a Freudian example of castration anxiety, but a purely psychoanalytical reading of the story ultimately limits a fuller understanding.

In "Nos" the barber Ivan Iakovlevich wakes up on 25 March to the smell of hot bread. When he cuts into the loaf, he finds buried in it a nose that he recognizes as that of Major Kovalev, a pretentious civil servant preoccupied with social rank, whom Ivan Iakovlevich shaves regularly. Terrified, the barber flings the nose into the Neva, the central river in St. Petersburg, and for no apparent reason he is arrested.

Meanwhile, Major Kovalev wakes to find that indeed his nose is missing. On his way to report the loss, Kovalev is shocked to see his nose, dressed in a gentleman's uniform, stepping jauntily out of a carriage. Kovalev approaches his nose to express his surprise that it is not in its proper place on his face. The nose replies haughtily that it is an independent individual of more advanced rank and therefore entirely unconcerned with Kovalev's problems. Kovalev then tries to place an ad in the newspaper; he also consults a doctor; finally he registers a complaint with the police inspector. All who listen to his dilemma fail to consider it seriously and even question Kovalev's respectability. Although a policeman returns Kovalev's nose a few days later, it will not stick back in its place. Finally on 7 April, without warning or reason, Kovalev wakes up to find his nose has been restored to his face. Overjoyed, Kovalev dances a jig around the room and then resumes the superficial and self-centered social life he found impossible to conduct without a nose.

Despite its ribald tone, "Nos" represents an important step in Gogol's development as a writer. The independence of Kovalev's nose echoes Gogol's growing awareness of the autonomy of the word. While Kovalev grapples with his predicament, fantastic rumors about the strange event

Gogol in the study at his estate, Vasil'evka

spread throughout St. Petersburg, filling the newspapers. Fanciful additions to the story allow it to take on a life of its own, as Kovalev's nose becomes an "independent individual." Reading "Nos" as a literary manifesto, Fanger suggests that Gogol is attempting to define his own tradition and readership by creating new forms that challenge the validity of their antecedents. In "Nos" plot does not generate narrative form; language does not clearly indicate intentionality; and the reader's hope that the story holds some deeper meaning remains unrealized. For Gogol the pleasurable act of reading the story is itself significant.

Embedded within the story "Nos," however, is a task that Gogol considered more serious than advocating art for art's sake. In search of what Ivan Ermakov calls a "unique, Gogolian self," Gogol examines himself in the mirror he creates through narrative self-focus and skaz. At the end of "Nos" Gogol turns the reader's attention to both the indecent subject matter and the narrative self: "Vot kakaia istoriia sluchilas' v servernoi stolitse nashego obshirnogo gosudarstva! . . . No chto strannee, chto neponiatnee vsego, èto to, kak avtory mogut brat' podobnye siuzhety. Priznaius' èto uzh sovsem nepostizhimo" (So this is the strange event that oc-

curred in the northern capital of our spacious empire! . . . But what is stranger, what is more difficult to understand than anything is that authors can choose such subjects. I confess that is quite incomprehensible).

Praising the work and ascetic lifestyle of the painter Aleksandr Andreevich Ivanov, Gogol contended that a writer cannot create positive characters until his own heart is pure. In a prelude to the more formal "Avtorskaia ispoved'" (An Author's Confession, published in the 1855 edition of *Mertvye dushi*), "Nos" allowed Gogol to examine within himself the impurity and vulgarity that prevented his art from truly reflecting the spiritual in life. The desire for purity and perfection, which begins on a light note in "Nos," would gradually reach unrealistic proportions in Gogol's life and work and in the end prove fatal to the artist.

Readers consistently choose "Shinel'" (The Greatcoat) as Gogol's best piece of short fiction. Gogol worked on the story from 1839 through 1841. During Gogol's lifetime it appeared only once, in the third volume of the four-volume *Sochineniia* of 1842. There it was grouped with "Nevskii Prospekt," "Portret," and "Zapiski sumasshedshego" from *Arabeski* and "Nos" as part of the so-called Petersburg tales.

Like "Nos," "Shinel'" is more of a verbal performance than a plot-driven tale. As Boris Eikhenbaum shows in his essay "How Gogol's 'Overcoat' Is Made," the source of dynamism and the organizing force in the story is tension created by one layer of language play overlaid by another.

The first layer of what Eikhenbaum calls "purely comic *skaz*" includes etymological and sound puns. The best example of both types is found in the name of Gogol's hero, Akakii Akakievich, a name, Daniel Rancour-Laferriere shows, whose fecal overtones provide the basis of the anal-erotic theme running throughout the story. The hero's last name demonstrates the absurdity of Gogol's puns:

> Familiia chinovnika byla Bashmachkin. Uzhe po samomu imeni vidno, chto ona kogda-to proizoshla ot bashmaka; no kogda, v kakoe vremia i kakim obrazom proizoshla ona ot bashmaka, nichego ètogo neizvestno. I otets, i ded, i dazhe shurin i vse sovershenno Bashmachkiny khodili v sopogakh.

> (The clerk's surname was Bashmachkin. From the very name, it is clear that it must have been derived from shoe; but when, and in what way it was derived from a shoe, is not known. Both his father and his grandfather and even the brother-in-law, and all the Bashmachkins without exception wore boots.)

With the frequent repetition of the words *bashmaka* and *Bashmachkin,* readers associate the clerk with a shoe rather than a human face. Further breaching the limits of logic, the narrator emphasizes that "even" a Bashmachkin brother-in-law wore boots although, by definition, the brother-in-law is not a Bashmachkin at all.

The second layer of narration in "Shinel'" consists of an emotive, declamatory style into which the narrator slips when, for instance, he describes how Akakii Akakievich's beleaguered plea ("Ostav'te menia, zachem vy menia obizhaete?" [Leave me alone, why do you insult me?]) resounds within one of his colleagues: "I v ètikh pronikaiushchikh slovakh zveneli drugie slova: 'Ia brat tvoi.'. . . I mnogo raz sodrogalsia on potom na veku svoem, vidia, kak mnogo v cheloveke beschelovech'ia . . . Bozhe! dazhe v tom cheloveke, kotorogo svet priznaet blagorodnym i chestnym" (Within those moving words he heard others: 'I am your brother.'. . . And many times afterward in his life he shuddered, seeing how much inhumanity there is in man . . . my God! even in a man whom the world considers a gentlemen and a man of honor). Such evocative passages inspired Dostoyevsky to advocate compassion for the weak members of society in his novels *Bednye liudi*

(Poor Folk, 1846) and *Unizhennye i oskorblennye* (The Insulted and Injured, 1861).

In "Shinel'" the alternation between comedy and pathos creates a tension that Eikhenbaum calls grotesque. These narrative dynamics isolate Akakii Akakievich's experiences from the world at large, allowing Gogol to distort reality. Gogol uses the text to challenge the normal proportions of literary conventions as well and to innovate with unlikely combinations of comic and pathetic. As in "Nos," in "Shinel'" Gogol steps forward as a comic writer who vaguely senses his role as ethicist, moralist, and shaper of society. At a dinner party in 1832 an anecdote about the compassion a group of civil servants showed for an unfortunate colleague provided Gogol the basic plot for his tale. But in "Shinel'" the nature of the hero and the mixed reactions of the reader to him, along with narrative structure, endless qualifications, and relativism, serve to complicate the matter of simple decency. In the end Gogol's tale raises more questions than it answers.

In "Shinel'" the poor, reclusive Akakii Akakievich must replace his worn-out greatcoat as a matter of survival. Living on a clerk's salary, he endures great privation to save enough money for the new greatcoat. On the first day Akakii Akakievich wears his coat to the office, his frivolous colleagues decide to throw a party in honor of his new acquisition. Crossing a vast and poorly lit city square—the urban equivalent of Dikanka's enchanted forests—on the way home from the gathering, Akakii Akakievich is set upon and robbed of his treasured coat. Akakii Akakievich meekly appeals for an investigation into the robbery to a "znachitel'noe litso" (important person), who is unduly severe with the clerk. Numb from fright and without a proper coat, Akakii Akakievich catches cold and soon dies as anonymously as he lived. Gogol's tale moves from the real into the realm of the fantastic as the ghost of Akakii Akakievich appears to the horrified "important person" and angrily yanks the fur coat from his shoulders. Sadly, Akakii Akakievich seems a more substantial character in death than in life.

Those characters with whom Akakii Akakievich has contact hardly note his passing until his ghost appears in the city. It is into this lacuna of compassion that Gogol invites the readers. Yet while obliged to have sympathy for Akakii Akakievich, readers cannot fail to sense the pettiness and banality of his character. Akakii Akakievich's preference for form over content thwarts his career advancement; he wants only to copy documents letter by letter, unconcerned with words or their meaning. On the other hand Akakii Akakievich assigns excessive meaning to his new greatcoat, which plays the role

An 1844 letter from Gogol to Viktor Balabin (Kilgour Collection, Harvard University Library)

of a new wife in the clerk's dreary existence. The ability of this inanimate object to animate Akakii Akakievich is unsettling; it is not that his life is so pathetic but rather that his moral sense is corrupt. In the end Akakii Akakievich's very soul is preoccupied with the lost greatcoat, a fate more haunting than the ghost itself.

Gogol's "Koliaska" (The Carriage, 1836) is a small story that falls outside the bounds of his Ukrainian and Petersburg collections. Set in the sleepy Russian provinces, "Koliaska" briefly examines the shallowness and absurdity of human existence from a new angle—boredom. In the story the presence of a cavalry regiment brings a drowsy, provincial town to life. A local landowner, Pifagor Pifagorovich Chertokutsky, spends an evening at cards with the local gentry and the ranking mem-

bers of the regiment. Boasting at dinner about his extraordinary carriage, Chertokutsky invites the regimental general and officers to view it the next day while they dine at his house. Quite drunk when he leaves the gathering, Chertokutsky fails to inform his household about the impending visit. He wakes the next afternoon only as the general and his entourage are approaching the house. The unprepared Chertokutsky is too ashamed to greet his guests and hides in the carriage house to avoid them. But when the officers decide to inspect the carriage anyway, they find their host huddled inside. "A, vy zdes'!" (Ah, here you are!) the general says in surprise before he slams the carriage door and rides off with his men.

"Koliaska" is Gogol's first foray into the empty and mind-numbing absurdity of provincial life. By the time he finished *Mertvye dushi*—begun in late 1835—the boredom and emptiness of the Russian provinces would take on greater meaning. Here he starts to explore the setting of a backwater town and the effect of unrelenting ennui on its inhabitants. With such a scanty plot, however, the richness of Gogol's narrative comes to the forefront, making language once again the only real event in the story.

The verbal presence of Gogol's narrators grew with his awareness of an artist's role as social commentator. In the 1830s Gogol saw the stage as an opportunity to further shorten the distance between author and audience. In 1833 he described in a letter to Mikhail Petrovich Pogodin how the audience materialized before him when he considered drama: "Peredo mnoiu dvizhetsia stsena, shumit aplodisment, rozhi vysovyvaiutsia iz lozh, iz raika, iz kresel" (The stage moves before me, applause thunders, mugs thrust out of the loges, the balcony, the stalls). Gogol's theatrical works—one unfinished and three complete plays plus the fragment "Al'fred" (King Alfred), an historical play—are satirical critiques of society at all levels. Subjects range from official corruption and confidence games to marriage contracting, and the theme of deception lies at the heart of each play.

For Gogol the audience members are characters as much as the actors onstage and as susceptible to petty shortcomings and flaws. To implicate spectators in his dramas, Gogol transgressed the limits of the stage, thus violating the integrity of its "frame." In *Revizor* characters directly address the audience; in *Igroki* (The Gamblers, probably written in 1836) a group of cardsharpers dupe the audience as well as the hero; in *Zhenit'ba* (The Marriage, begun in 1833) the hero jumps through the window frame to escape both his fiancée and the stage. Thus blurring the boundary between spectator and actor, Gogol inverts the relationship. Gogol's epigram for *Revizor* encapsulates his wish to confront his audience by suggesting they reserve their own judgment for themselves: "Na zerkalo necha peniat', koli rozha kriva" (It is no use blaming the mirror if your mug is crooked).

In 1833 Gogol began his first theatrical endeavor, "Vladimir tret'ei stepeni" (Vladimir of the Third Class). The three surviving scenes show how a bureaucrat's preoccupation with the Vladimir service award ends in madness and failure. In the spirit of "Zapiski sumasshedshego," the bureaucrat believes in the end that he himself is the Vladimir of the Third Class. However, the bizarre psychological twist of the play could not sustain the otherwise

common themes and stock characters that forced Gogol to abandon the project.

Gogol was desperate to find a subject for a "purely Russian" comedy. In October 1835 Pushkin suggested the plot for *Revizor,* a story of mistaken identity that exhibits the vanity and corruption of small-town officials. A provincial mayor learns that an inspector general plans to visit the town incognito. In their apprehension the town officials believe that Khlestakov, a low-ranking St. Petersburg clerk stranded at the local inn with no money, is the inspector general. Khlestakov quickly catches on and takes full advantage of the townspeople. He collects money from them, enjoys their obsequious hospitality, and betroths himself to the mayor's daughter. By the time the town officials realize their mistake, Khlestakov is gone. The play ends with the arrival of the real inspector general.

In many ways Khlestakov is a precursor to Chichikov, the hero of *Mertvye dushi,* which Gogol set aside for the three months it took to write *Revizor.* Neither hero enjoys the rank and prestige he wants, but both manufacture the semblance of success out of wit and guile. Khlestakov's elaborations on his simple life in the capital are memorable. He claims to have written *The Marriage of Figaro* (1784) and popular Russian works. When he hosts a dinner party, he alleges that the soup is brought in a saucepan on a steamship directly from Paris. As does Chichikov, Khlestakov meets a procession of town officials, merchants, and citizens. However, in *Revizor* the townspeople present themselves to the hero, whereas in *Mertvye dushi* Chichikov ventures out himself. Nevertheless, in both works the visits allow Gogol to showcase the ignorance and petty concerns of provincial dwellers. In the play Khlestakov's letter to a friend in St. Petersburg performs the same function.

Khlestakov's letter depicts the townspeople in a less-than-flattering light. It is also the fulcrum on which Gogol's dramatic inversion turns. Angered at the letter and the spectators' laughter, the mayor turns the "mirror" on the audience. He asks them directly: "Chemu smeetes'? Nad soboiu smeetes'! . . . Ekh vy!" (What are you laughing at? You are laughing at yourselves! . . . You are a fine lot!). In the final, unsettling moments of *Revizor*, Gogol again challenges the audience. A gendarme arrives at the mayor's house to announce the arrival of the real inspector general. The assembled officials are literally petrified in a one-and-one-half-minute mute scene that Fanger calls a parody of Judgment Day. Gogol's audiences in the spring of 1836 did not appreciate the opportunity for self-reflection. Actors and directors of *Revizor* shared critics' discomfort. Although

Gogol insisted on direction for understated acting, *Revizor* was presented as vaudeville; the mute scene was shortened or cut altogether. The sense that his work had been misunderstood stunned Gogol as much as the poor reviews. Gogol left for Europe in June.

Before his departure Gogol met with Pushkin for the last time. He read the beginning of *Mertvye dushi* to the poet, who detected sadness rather than humor in Gogol's caricatures. At the time, both men were troubled—Gogol by debts and the response to *Revizor,* Pushkin by the rumors about his wife and the French baron Georges Charles d'Anthès-Heeckeren. Gogol's travels took him to Germany, Switzerland, and Paris, where in February 1837 he learned that d'Anthès-Heeckeren had killed Pushkin in a duel. In March, Gogol left Paris for Italy, where the warm climate and work on *Mertvye dushi* helped dull the painful loss of his mentor and friend. In Rome, Gogol associated with other Russian artists, notably the painter Aleksandr Ivanov, whose work, Gogol believed, truly reflected the purifying torments of his soul. Gogol's time in Italy was rather productive. In addition to working on *Mertvye dushi,* he revised "Taras Bul'ba," "Portret," "Nos," "Vii," and *Revizor.* He also rewrote the comedy *Zhenit'ba* but could not find an appropriate ending.

Work on these smaller pieces interfered with *Mertvye dushi.* In September 1839 a trip to Russia also delayed Gogol's progress on the novel. Gogol's widowed sister Maria was in danger of choosing an undesirable suitor, and the two youngest, Anna and Elizaveta, were about to complete their studies at the Patriotic Institute. Arriving first in Moscow, Gogol made a disagreeable impression on his friends. He was moody and reclusive, alternately eating enormous quantities of food, which he often prepared himself, and complaining about an assortment of stomach ailments. Gogol then traveled to St. Petersburg under considerable financial constraint, returning to Moscow in December with his two youngest sisters. Elizaveta stayed on in Moscow while the painfully shy Anna returned to Vasil'evka with Gogol's mother, who had traveled to Moscow to visit her son. Gogol remained in Moscow until his family and financial affairs were tentatively settled. In May 1840 he returned to Rome, where he completed the first volume of *Mertvye dushi*—for which Pushkin had provided the plot—and in August 1841 he returned to Moscow to oversee its publication.

As in many of Gogol's earlier works, *Mertvye dushi* turns on deception. Chichikov arrives in the town of N. and in the first five chapters visits a succession of landowners. He proposes to each that they transfer to him ownership of those serfs, or

Gogol's grave in Moscow .

"souls," whose deaths have yet to be registered by the census and are therefore still taxable property. Chichikov plans to mortgage his nonexistent "souls" to buy an estate. The plan falls through, and Chichikov must quickly leave town.

The image of the road dominates *Mertvye dushi,* but the movement of the novel is not clearly linear. Narrative digressions into distant realms and long-winded description threaten to divert Chichikov's tale from its course. Meanwhile a swirling mass of irrelevant details destroys any hierarchy of meaning but creates the dizzying impression that the world of *Mertvye dushi* is spinning on its narrative axis. In a circular relationship the landowners project the dominant aspect of their character onto the faceless Chichikov. Manilov is vacuous and sentimental; Korobochka, frugal and suspicious; Sobakevich, a misanthropic bear; Nozdrev, an inveterate liar; and Pliushkin, a passionately acquisitive miser. Like the landowners' homes, Chichikov in turn becomes a collective reflection of their *zadory* (passions).

Gogol's interest in the theater is evident in *Mertvye dushi*. Chichikov's meetings with the five landowners are strongly reminiscent of similar scenes in *Revizor* and *Zhenit'ba*. The suggestion of staged drama in the novel allows the narrator to engage the readers as the townspeople in *Revizor* turn to the audience and address them directly. Again in *Mertvye dushi* Gogol challenges his readers to divert to themselves the judgment they so harshly train on his narrator and characters, asking themselves: "A net li i vo mne kakoi-nibud' chasti Chichikov?" (And isn't there some part of Chichikov in me too?).

In *Mertvyi dushi* Gogol further defines the position and role of the artist in Russian society. The narrator is a "bessemeinyi putnik" (homeless wayfarer). But only from his isolated perspective can the writer discern beauty in the everyday—the definition of the artist that harkens back to *Arabeski*—and also glean meaning from the empty expanse of Russian plains. In keeping with the picaresque genre Gogol creates a strong authorial presence in the novel that mediates the readers' response to Chichikov's experience. Using the hero's exploits to showcase his own opinions and linguistic talents, Gogol's narrator positions himself at the center of the novel. Indeed he presents his own biography in the sixth chapter—the middle point in the novel—while Chichikov's life story comes much later. Hero and narrator vie for the role of main character in *Mertvye dushi* until their consciousnesses seem to merge in a vanishing point at the end.

Coupled with the task of authorship was Gogol's epic intent to portray in his work a truly "Russian Russia." To do so Gogol strove to inscribe meaning on the vast expanses of Russia and the *blankovyi list* (blank page) of its history. *Mertvye dushi* grew out of the absence of a Russian novelist tradition. In Gogol's work the emptiness of the Russian landscape and the moral hollowness of its inhabitants reflect this aesthetic void. By producing a *perl sozdan'ia* (pearl of creation) out of nothingness, Gogol hoped to revive the Russian "soul" as the seat of its realized self. Gogol envisioned three volumes of *Mertvye dushi* that would trace the transformation of his hero, Chichikov, from a wayfaring swindler into what Vasilii Vasil'evich Gippius calls "ideal khoziaev-domostrioitel'" (the ideal family man) and at the same time would kindle a cohesive Russian national consciousness. However, drafts of the second volume were a source of frustration and disappointment for him. In despair he burned them; the fragments that remain escaped the fire by chance and do not represent what Gogol meant to publish. The first volume of *Mertvye dushi* shows Gogol at the height of his verbal talents as he weaves the story of

an emerging artist—whose words bespeak Russia itself—into the anticlimactic tale of his trickster hero.

In *Mertvye dushi* negation, imprecision, and what Andrei Belyi describes as the law of "ne to" (not quite) become important leitmotivs that convey the pervasive emptiness of Russia. Gogol's famous nondescription of Chichikov's physiognomy reflects the blank slate of the hero's own "dead soul." As Chichikov enters the town N., the narrator portrays him in a series of negatives: "ne krasavets, no i ne durnoi naruzhnosti, ni slishkom tolst, ni slishkom tonok; nel'zia skazat', chtoby star, odnako zh i ne tak, chtoby slishkom molod" ([he was] not handsome, nor was he ugly, neither too fat nor too thin; one wouldn't say he was old, although neither would one say that he was too young).

As the townspeople of N. devise identities for the faceless Chichikov, Gogol's narrator insists that the emptiness of Russia holds great meaning. As Grigorii A. Gukovsky and Leon Stilman note, the narrator's estrangement from Russia—like his homelessness—allows him expansive vision as well as superior insight. "Iz chudesnogo, prekrasnogo daleka" (From a miraculous, wondrous afar), the narrator lists what Russia lacks:

> Rus! Rus! I see you: you are poor, far-flung and uncomfortable; cities with tall, many-windowed palaces growing on cliffs, picturesque trees and ivy-covered houses will not gladden the eye. . . . You are open, empty and flat; your low slung towns imperceptibly dot the plains like points, like marks; nothing beguiles and nothing charms the eye.

However, in this elegy to nothingness Gogol's narrator implies that there is some larger meaning in the open space of the plains:

> What does this unbounded expanse prophesy?. . . And the powerful expanse envelops me menacingly, reflecting with a terrible force in the depths of me; my eyes are lighted with a supernatural power: oh! what glittering, wondrous, unfathomable infinity of space! Rus!

The narrator suggests that in him the reflection of Russia's emptiness will give rise to some "bespredel'naia mysl'" (boundless thought) to express its significance. However, at this point the double-voiced narrative structure of the picaresque genre allows Chichikov to interrupt. The hero's ambiguously placed intrusion seems directed at both his reckless coachman, Selifan, and the narrator, with the implication that the latter should "get hold" of himself ("Derzhi! Derzhi, durak!"). Placed near the end of *Mertvye dushi*, Chichikov's command emphasizes the culmination of struggle between hero and narrator for prominence. Frederick T. Griffiths and Stanley J. Rabinowitz describe Chichikov and Gogol's narrator as two sides of the same personality. But when the narrative relationship between the two unites them in the final pages of *Mertvye dushi,* there is little resolution of conflict, but only the doubting hope that the striking barrenness of Russia holds any meaning at all.

The originality of *Mertvye dushi* delighted and shocked Gogol's readers. Critics such as Belinsky praised the novel for its artistry, humor, and social commentary. However, the slow movement of the novel through the censorship process forecast the critical reviews to come. Dissenting censors balked at the paradoxical notion of a "dead" soul and at Gogol's celebration of Chichikov's criminality. Later reviewers questioned the literariness of the work. Ironically the objections of Gogol's detractors—Polevoi, Nikolai Ivanovich Grech, Osip Ivanovich Senkovsky, and Konstantin Petrovich Masalsky—marked points of innovation in *Mertvye dushi* and illustrated its parody of selected sectors of Russian society. Reviewers' protestations about the indecency, banality, and base humor in the novel constitute an early reaction against the Natural School, of which Gogol is considered a founder. Similarly, as Belyi notes, the odd similes and metaphors for which Gogol's contemporaries chided him lie at the heart of Russian Symbolism. Negative reviews also failed to discern the parody of Gogol's circular speech and heavily stylized passages. Finally critics further inflamed the question of the writer's place in society by taking issue with Gogol's combination of the comic and the philosophic.

In May 1842 Gogol returned to Rome, imploring friends in Russia to describe in detail the reception of the novel. Gogol was also absent for the debut of his plays *Zhenit'ba* and *Igroki* in 1842 and 1843 after almost a decade of writing and revisions. Both plays focus on the theme of deception. In *Igroki* a cardsharper allies himself with a band of confidence men to cheat a landowner but falls prey to the elaborate hoax himself. Like *Revizor, Igroki* uses a provincial setting to satirize bureaucratic corruption. A treasury clerk suggests that the excesses of small-town officials depicted in works such as *Igroki* reflects widespread abuses: "Ved' vot uzhe i gospoda sochiniteli vse podsmeivaiutsia nad temi, kotorye berut vziatki; a kak rassmotrish' khoroshen'ko, tak vziatki berut i te, kotorye povyshe nas" (The gentlemen who write stories are always making jokes about people taking bribes, but when you look closely, our superiors take bribes too).

In *Zhenit'ba* the setting moves back to St. Petersburg, where Podkolesin, a government clerk, finds himself one of four suitors a matchmaker has arranged for a merchant's daughter. As in *Mertvye dushi,* the characters in *Zhenit'ba* are sketches of various physical types and humors. Determined to marry off the hero, Podkolesin's friend Kochkarev tricks the other suitors and arranges for a wedding that same day. In a moment of panic before the ceremony, Podkolesin jumps through an open window and rides away in a carriage, like Khlestakov in *Revizor* and Chichikov in *Mertvye dushi.*

Gogol believed that Russia expected *Mertvye dushi* to define for the country a collective cultural identity. He was frustrated by the public's misunderstanding of the work and his inability to produce the next volume. In 1843 and 1845 he burned two versions of the sequel. In 1847 Gogol published *Vybrannye mesta iz perepiska s druz'iami* (Selected Passages from Correspondence with Friends), a collection of real and fictitious letters. In part the work presents Gogol's interpretation of the intent and the failure of *Mertvye dushi.* With a mixture of humility and pride typical of *Vybrannye mesta,* Gogol's four letters on *Mertvye dushi* at once acknowledge the shortcomings of his work while berating his readership for not helping him accurately portray Russian life.

In general *Vybrannye mesta* sought to point Russia toward redemption by modeling proper social, political, and spiritual behavior. Thus directed, Russia would undergo a spiritual rebirth as it realized its true cultural identity. Literature is central to Gogol's project. The insight of the prophet-writer is necessary to the creation of Russia as a religious civilization; only the writer can discern from his "miraculous, wondrous afar" the proper order of Russia's institutions and the daily life of its citizens. Again, Gogol saw his position outside of society and outside of Russia as an advantageous perspective. Now inspired by God rather than muse, he could more clearly discern, diagnose, and advise on the problems that confronted Russia.

As part of Gogol's lifetime meditation on good and evil, *Vybrannye mesta* outlines Russia's salvation through good social practices. In it Gogol outlines proper conduct for a governor's wife, the clergy, and a person in "high office"; he offers practical advice on running a household, an estate, a government office, and a courtroom. In the same work Gogol discusses eternal redemption and an intricate system of keeping household accounts. This odd mixture of concerns prompted Abram Terts to call the book a cross between the Christian gospels and the *Domostroi* (House Law), the medieval book of Russian mores and manners. Like the *Domostroi, Vybrannye mesta* instructed Russians of all classes and occupations to live according to the station into which they were born. Thus, according to the work, universal education is harmful to peasants, but a master is morally obligated to beat and humiliate his serfs. In some places Gogol defends Russia's conservative political, religious, and social institutions so zealously that suspicious church and government censors cut large parts of the collection. Liberal critics were outraged; the work was attacked by both friend and foe as servile, moralistic, and permeated with an insane pride thinly disguised as religious humility. After reading *Vybrannye mesta* Belinsky—usually a champion of Gogol's work—sent an invective letter to the author on 15 July 1847 that called him a "preacher of the knout, apostle of ignorance, champion of obscurantism, panegyrist of barbarism."

What is useful in *Vybrannye mesta* are Gogol's analyses of Russian literature and its role in Russian society. In Gogol's mind the resurrection of the Russian soul depended on the literary word. Gogol likened the need to produce a work that would unify the Russian cultural consciousness to the need to feel "doma" (at home) in the country's "pustye, bespriiutnye prostranstva" (empty, shelterless expanses). The writer needed to lead Russia from what Ruth Sobel calls the "post-house condition"—rootless, misdirected wandering symptomatic of alienation and fragmentation of self—to the warmth and integration of a cultural "homecoming."

The fate and duty of the writer, Gogol states, is to lead Russia toward a heartfelt, "brotherly" welcome at "home." Gogol believed that Russian *poèziia* (literature) must fulfill a spiritual mission—to assemble and unite Russia under one roof as a nation of brothers. The notion of achieving spirituality through unity lies at the heart of the Russian idea of spiritual *sobornost'* (communality). In addition to the connotations of oneness inherent in *sobornost'*, the term conveys the meaning of unanimity or "consent" in the sense of a single (singing) voice comprised of many. In *Vybrannye mesta* Gogol wrote that Russian literature would produce a truly "Russian Russia." The clarity of this image would unite the country "v odin golos" (in one voice) to proclaim its long-awaited homecoming:

> Our literature will call forth for us our Russia—our Russian Russia . . . that, which it will draw out of us and show us in such a way so that every last one of us, regardless of differing thought, upbringing and opinion, will say in one voice: "This is our Russia; in it we are warm and comfortable, and now we are indeed at home, under our own native roof, and not in a foreign land."

In contrast, for Gogol the post-house condition represents the persistent absence of a warm welcome at one's own home and life on the road. However, Sobel says, the post-house metaphor suggests movement in the present from alienation and the cold reception at the post-house to a brotherly welcome and the joy of homecoming in the future. Ironically, while the road represents Russia's alienation from itself, it is also the means by which it will ultimately realize its "homecoming." In keeping with Gogol's image of Russia as a homeward-bound pilgrim, the image of the post-house suggests both the potential transformation of the Russian soul and the promise of eternal wandering.

In 1847 Gogol also began his association with Father Matvei Konstantinovsky, the spiritual advisor to Count Aleksandr Petrovich Tolstoi, the one-time governor of Tver'. Ignorant and narrowly faithful, Father Matvei regarded art that did not celebrate Orthodoxy as potentially heretical. Gogol was taken with the certainty of such convictions and corresponded with Father Matvei for months before he actually met him in November 1848. Gogol had long been seeking a spiritual locus for his writing. In January 1848 he traveled to Jerusalem but was disappointed by the mundane reality of what he imagined the Holy Land to be. Over the next four years Gogol attempted to reconcile his increasingly intense sense of spirituality with his authorship; this effort was the purpose of "Avtorskaia izpoved'," which he had drafted in 1847. Early in February 1852 Gogol gave several chapters of the second volume of *Mertvye dushi* to Father Matvei to read. The priest condemned the work and advised Gogol to purify his body instead of writing such nonsense. When Gogol countered that spirituality and prose could serve each other, Father Matvei erupted into a horrifying description of what awaited Gogol at the Last Judgment.

Believing that he was purifying his soul, Gogol soon stopped writing altogether and began the fast that would end his life. In mid February, living at the house of Count Tolstoi, he burned the latest version of the second volume of *Mertvye dushi*. Friends, doctors, and other clergy vainly implored Gogol to eat. Throughout the night of 20 February, doctors tried to save the author's life. About 11 P.M. he cried out his last words: "Dai lestnitsu!" (Give me a ladder!). At 8 A.M. in the morning on 21 February 1852 Gogol died at the age of forty-two.

Gogol's final words reveal the author's life-long attempt to bridge the earthly and the sublime in his art. Gogol offered his early work to a Russia that was unprepared for his challenges to preexisting art forms and the designated place of the author. Partisanship and lack of vision split nineteenth-century critics in their appreciation of Gogol. It was Dostoyevsky who summed up Gogol's role as the progenitor of Russian literature. Referring to the mastery of "Shinel'," he was reported to have said that he and his fellow authors "all came out from under Gogol's 'Overcoat.'"

Letters:

Vladimir Ivanovich Shenrok, *Ukazatel' k pis'mam Gogolia* (Moscow: Ris', 1886);

Shenrok, ed., *Pis'ma,* 4 volumes (St. Petersburg: A. F. Marks, 1901);

Vladimir V. Kallash, *N. V. Gogol' v vospominaiiakh sovremennikov i perepiske* (Moscow: Sytin, 1909);

Vasilii V. Gippius, ed., *N. V. Gogol' v pismakh i vospominaniiakh* (Moscow: Federatsiia, 1931);

Carl R. Proffer, ed., *Letters of Nikolai Gogol,* translated by Proffer and Vera Krivoshein (Ann Arbor: University of Michigan Press, 1967);

S. I. Mashinsky and M. B. Khrapchenko, eds., *Pis'ma* (Moscow: Khudozhestvennaia literatura, 1979);

A. A. Karpov and M. N. Virolainen, eds., *Perepiska N. V. Gogolia: v dvukh tomakh,* 2 volumes (Moscow: Khudozhestvennaia literatura, 1988).

Bibliographies:

Ia. Gorozhansky, *Bibliograficheskii ukazatel' literatury o Nikolae Vasilieviche Gogole 1829–1882* (Moscow: I. N. Kushnerev, 1883);

Gosudarstvennaia biblioteka SSSR imeni V. I. Lenina. Otdel rukopisei, *Rukopisi N. V. Gogolia: katalog* (Moscow: Sotsekgiz, 1940);

Ivan Z. Boiko, *Hohol i Ukraina: bibliohrafichnyi pokazhchyk do 100-richchia z dnia smerti M.V. Hoholia* (Kiev: Akademiia nauk URSR, 1952);

L. P. Arkhipova, *Pis'ma k N. V. Gogoliu: bibliografiia* (Leningrad: Biblioteka Akademii nauk, 1965);

Philip E. Frantz, *Gogol: A Bibliography* (Ann Arbor, Mich.: Ardis, 1989).

Biographies:

Panteleimon Oleksandrovych Kulish, *Opyt biografii N. V. Gogolia: so vkliucheniem do soroka ego pisem* (St. Petersburg: E. Prats, 1854);

A. Tarasenkov, *Poslednie dni zhizni N. V. Gogolia* (St. Petersburg: Korolev, 1857);

A. N. Annenskaia, *N. V. Gogol': ego zhizn' i literaturnaia deiatel'nost'. Biograficheskii ocherk* (St. Petersburg: Novost', 1891);

Vladimir Ivanovich Shenrok, *Materialy dlia biografii Gogolia,* 4 volumes (Moscow: Mamontova, 1892–1897);

Vasilii P. Avenarius, *Uchenicheskie gody Gogolia* (St. Petersburg: Lukovnikov, 1900);

Aleksandr I. Kirpichnikov, *Somneniia i protivorechiia v biografii Gogolia: Kommentarii k biograficheskoi kanve* (St. Petersburg: Akademiia nauk, 1900);

Nikolai Ivanovich Nadezhdin, *Gimnazicheskie gody Gogolia: biograficheskii rasskaz* (St. Petersburg-Moscow, 1909);

Vasilii V. Gippius, *Gogol* (Leningrad: Mysl', 1924);

Janko Lavrin, *Gogol* (London: Routledge, 1925);

Vladimir V. Nabokov, *Nikolai Gogol* (Norfolk, Conn.: New Directions, 1944);

Oleksii Poltoratsky, *Detstva Gogolia* (Leningrad: Sovetskii pisatel', 1956);

David Magarshack, *Gogol: A Life* (London: Faber & Faber, 1957);

Vasilii Vasil'evich Zenkovsky, *N. V. Gogol* (Paris: YMCA Press, 1961);

Vsevolod Setchkarev, *Gogol: His Life and Works* (London: Owen, 1966);

Victor Erlich, *Gogol* (New Haven: Yale University Press, 1969);

Vasilii V. Rozanov, *O Gogole* (Letchworth: Prideaux Press, 1970);

Henri Troyat, *Gogol* (Paris: Flammarion, 1971);

Leon Stilman, *Gogol* (Tenafly, N.J.: Hermitage Publishers, 1990);

Iurii Mann, *Skvoz' vidnyi miru smekh . . . : zhizn' N. V. Gogolia: 1809–1852* (Moscow: MIROC, 1994).

References:

Sergei Timofeevich Aksakov, *Istoriia moego znakomstva s Gogolem* (Moscow: Akademiia nauk SSSR, 1960);

Vissarion Grigor'evich Belinsky, *Pis'mo k Gogoliu* (St. Petersburg: Svetoch, 1905);

Andrei Belyi, *Masterstvo Gogolia: issledovanie* (Moscow: Khudozhestvennaia literatura, 1934);

Lina Bernstein, *Gogol's Last Book: The Architectonics of "Selected Passages from Correspondence with Friends"* (Birmingham, U.K.: Department of Russian Language and Literature, University of Birmingham, 1994);

Valerii Ia. Briusov, *Ispepelennyi: k kharakteristike Gogolia. Doklad, prochitannyi na torzhestvennom zasedanii Obshchestva liubitelei rossiiskoi slovestnosti, 27 aprelia 1909 g.* (Moscow: Skorpion, 1910);

Sergei Sergeevich Danilov, *Gogol' i teatr* (Leningrad: Khudozhestvennaia literatura, 1936);

Paul Debreczeny, *Nikolay Gogol and His Contemporary Critics* (Philadelphia: American Philosophical Society, 1966);

Boris Eikhenbaum, "How Gogol's 'Overcoat' Is Made," in *Gogol from the Twentieth Century: Eleven Essays,* edited by Robert A. Maguire (Princeton, N.J.: Princeton University Press, 1974), pp. 269–291;

Anna A. Elistratova, *Gogol i problemy zapadnoevropeiskogo romana* (Moscow: Nauka, 1972);

Ivan Ermakov, "The Nose," translated by Robert A. Maguire in *Gogol from the Twentieth Century,* edited by Maguire (Princeton, N.J.: Princeton University Press, 1974), pp. 156–198;

Donald Fanger, *The Creation of Nikolai Gogol* (Cambridge, Mass.: Belknap Press of Harvard University Press, 1979);

Susanne Fusso, *Designing "Dead Souls": An Anatomy of Disorder in Gogol* (Stanford, Cal.: Stanford University Press, 1993);

Fusso and Priscilla Meyer, eds., *Essays on Gogol: Logos and the Russian Word* (Evanston, Ill.: Northwestern University Press, 1992);

Frederick T. Griffiths and Stanley J. Rabinowitz, *Novel Epics: Gogol, Dostoevsky, and National Narrative* (Evanston, Ill.: Northwestern University Press, 1990);

Grigorii A. Gukovsky, *Realizm Gogolia* (Leningrad: Khudozhestvennaia literatura, 1959);

Simon Karlinsky, *The Sexual Labyrinth of Nikolai Gogol* (Cambridge, Mass.: Harvard University Press, 1976);

Antonina N. Lazareva, *Dukhovnyi opyt Gogolia* (Moscow: In-t filosofii RAN, 1993);

Robert A. Maguire, *Exploring Gogol* (Stanford, Cal.: Stanford University Press, 1994);

Semen Mashinsky, *"Mertvye dushi" N. V. Gogolia* (Moscow: Khudozhestvennaia literatura, 1978);

Mashinsky, *N. V. Gogol' i V. G. Belinsky* (Moscow: Znanie, 1952);

Dmitrii S. Merezhkovsky, *Gogol i chert: izledovanie* (Moscow: Skorpion, 1906);

Merezhkovsky, *Gogol': tvorchestvo, zhizn' i religiia* (St. Petersburg: Panteon, 1909);

Konstantin Mochulsky, *Dukhovnyi put' Gogolia* (Paris: YMCA Press, 1934);

Dmitrii N. Ovsianko-Kulikovsky, *Gogol' v ego proizvedeniiakh* (St. Petersburg: I. L. Ovsianiko-Kulikovskaia, 1911);

Richard A. Peace, *The Enigma of Gogol: An Examination of the Writings of N. V. Gogol and Their Place in the Russian Literary Tradition* (Cambridge, U.K. & New York: Cambridge University Press, 1981);

Valerian F. Pereverzev, *Tvorchestvo Gogolia* (Ivanovo-Voznesensk: Osnova, 1928);

Renato Poggioli, "Gogol's 'Old Fashioned Landowners': An Inverted Eclogue," *Indiana Slavic Studies,* 3 (1963): 54–72;

Cathy Popkin, *The Pragmatics of Insignificance: Chekhov, Zoshchenko, Gogol* (Stanford, Cal.: Stanford University Press, 1993);

Carl R. Proffer, *The Simile and Gogol's "Dead Souls"* (The Hague: Mouton, 1968);

Daniel Rancour-Laferriere, *Out from under Gogol's Overcoat* (Ann Arbor, Mich.: Ardis, 1982);

Sergei Konstantinovich Shambinago, *Trilogiia romantizma: N. V. Gogol* (Moscow: Pol'za, 1911);

Gavriel Shapiro, *Nikolai Gogol and the Baroque Cultural Heritage* (University Park: Pennsylvania State University Press, 1993);

Aleksandr Leonidovich Slonimsky, *Tekhnika komicheskogo u Gogolia* (Petrograd: Akademiia, 1923);

Ruth Sobel, *Gogol's Forgotten Book: "Selected Passages" and Its Contemporary Readers* (Washington, D. C.: University Press of America, 1981);

Leon Stilman, *Gogol* (Tenafly, N.J.: Hermitage, 1990);

Abram Terts, *V teni Gogolia* (Paris: Sintaksis, 1981);

William Mills Todd III, *Fiction and Society in the Age of Pushkin: Ideology, Institutions, and Narrative* (Cambridge, Mass.: Harvard University Press, 1986);

Iurii N. Tynianov, *Dostoevsky i Gogol': k teorii parodii* (Petrograd: Opoiaz, 1921);

V. V. Veresaev, *Gogol' v zhizni* (Moscow: Moskovskii rabochii, 1990);

Viktor Vladimirovich Vinogradov, *Etiudy o stile Gogolia* (Leningrad: Akademiia, 1926);

Vinogradov, *Evoliutsiia russkogo naturalizma: Gogol' i Dostoevsky* (Leningrad: Akademiia, 1929);

Vinogradov, *Gogol i natural'naia shkola* (Leningrad: Obrazovanie, 1925);

Vinogradov, "Siuzhet i kompozitsiia povesti Gogolia: 'Nos,'" *Nachala,* 1 (1921): 82–105;

James B. Woodward, *Gogol's "Dead Souls"* (Princeton, N.J.: Princeton University Press, 1978);

Woodward, *The Symbolic Art of Gogol: Essays on His Short Fiction* (Columbus, Ohio: Slavica, 1982);

Jesse Zeldin, *Nikolai Gogol's Quest for Beauty: An Exploration into His Works* (Lawrence: Regents Press of Kansas, 1978).

Papers:

The main portion of Gogol's archive is located in the Russian State Library (formerly the Lenin Library) in Moscow and the Institute of Russian Literature (Pushkin House) in St. Petersburg.

Timofei Nikolaevich Granovsky
(9 March 1813 – 4 October 1855)

Edward Alan Cole
Grand Valley State University

BOOKS: *Ioumsberg i Vineta. Istoricheskoe issledovanie* (Moscow: Universitetskaia tipografiia, 1845);

Abbat Sugerii: istoricheskoe issledovanie (Moscow: Universitetskaia tipografiia, 1849);

Pesni Eddy o Nifungakh (Moscow: Universitetskaia tipografiia, 1851);

O sovremennom sostoianii i znachenii vseobshchei istorii (Moscow: Universitetskaia tipografiia, 1852);

Istoriia voiny Rossii c Frantsiei v tsarstvovanie imperatora Pavla I v 1799 godu. Spb. 1853. Retsenziia (Moscow: Izdatel'stvo Imperatorskogo Moskovskogo Universiteta, 1853).

Editions and Collections: *Sochineniia T. N. Granovskogo* (Moscow: V. Got'e, 1856);

Sochineniia T. N. Granoskogo. S portretom avtora (Moscow: Grachevi, 1866);

Sochineniia (Moscow: A. I. Mamontov, 1892);

Izbrannye sochineniia (Moscow, 1905);

Polnoe sobranie sochineniia, 2 volumes, edited by N. F. Mertts (St. Petersburg: Izdatel'stuo Mertsa, 1905);

Granovskogo po istorii srednevekov'ia, compiled by T. N. Lektsy, edited by S. A. Asinkovskaia (Moscow, 1961);

Timofei Nikolaevich Granovsky, Sbornik statei (Moscow, 1970);

Lektsii po istorii srednevekov'ia, edited by S. A. Asinovskaia (Moscow: Nauka, 1986).

OTHER: "Ispanskaia inkvizitsiia," in *Zhivopisnaia entsiklopediia,* volume 1 (Moscow, 1847), pp. 278–281;

"Kvakery," in *Zhivopisnaia entsiklopediia,* volume 1 (Moscow, 1847), pp. 177–180;

"Petr Ramus," in *Zhivopisnaia entsiklopediia,* volume 1 (Moscow, 1847), pp. 57–70;

"Pesni Eddy o Nifungakh," in *Kometa: ucheno-literaturnyi almanakh* (Moscow, 1851), pp. 181–204;

"O sovremennom sostoianii i znachenii vseobshchei istorii. Rech', proiznessenaia v torzhestvennom sobranii imp. Moskovskogo universiteta 12 ianvaria 1852 goda," in *Rechi i otchet, pro-*

Timofei Nikolaevich Granovsky

iznessenye v torzhestvennom sobranii imperatorskogo Moskovskogo universiteta 12 ianvaria 1852 goda (Moscow: Izdatel'stuo Moskovskogo Universiteta, 1852), pp. 1–26;

"O fiziologicheskikh priznakakh chelovecheskikh porod i ikh otnoshenii k istorii. Pis'mo V. F. Edvardsa k Amadeiu Tyrri, avtoru istorii gallov, perevedennoe i dopolnennoe T. N. Granovskim," in *Magazin zemlevedenikh i puteshestvii. Geograficheskii sbornik, izdavaemyi N. Frolovym,* volume 1 (Moscow, 1852), pp. 308–379 (notes, pp. 367–379);

"Chteniia Nibura o drevnei istorii. Retsenziia," in *Propilei, sbornik izdav aemyi P. Leont'evym,* book 3, section 2 (Moscow, 1853), pp. 155–190; book 5, section 2 (Moscow, 1856), pp. 41–62;

"Granovskii Timofei Nikolaevich 'Avtobiografiia,'" in *Biograficheskii slovar' professorov i prepodavatelei imperatorskogo Moskovskogo universiteta, 1755–1855* (Moscow: Universitetskaia tipografiia, 1855), part 1, pp. 263–265; "Vigant Iogann 'Biografiia,'" pp. 165–166; "Cherpanov Nikifor Evtropievich 'Biografiia,'" part 2, pp. 553–554;

"O rodovoi byte u drevnikh germantsev," in *Arkhiv istoriko-iuridicheskikh svedenii, otnosiashchikhsia do Rossii, izdavaemyi N. Kalachovym,* book 2, part 1 (Moscow, 1855), pp. 143–170;

"O krestovykh pokhodakh," in *Pomoshch' golodaiushim: nauchno-lituraturnyi sbornik* (Moscow, 1892), pp. 261–264;

P. G. Vinogradov, "Zadachi vseobshchei istorii. Otryvok iz universitetskogo kursa Granovskogo," in *Sbornik v pol'zu nedostatochnykh studentov universiteta sv. Vladimira* (St. Petersburg, 1895), pp. 308–322.

SELECTED PERIODICAL PUBLICATIONS:
"Stradalets," *Damskii zhurnal,* no. 8 (April 1828): 87–89;

"Lektsii Pogodina po Gerenu. Retsenziia," *Biblioteka dlia chteniia,* 13, section 5 (1835): 1–24;

"O nyneshnem sostoianii povarennoi promyshlennosti i gastronomii v Evrope," *Biblioteka dlia chteniia,* 12, section 4 (1835): 25–76;

"Svidrigailo kniaz' Litovskii. Sochinenie Avgust Kotsebu. Retsenziia," *Biblioteka dlia chteniia,* 13, section 5 (1835): 25–50;

"Sud'by evreiskogo naroda. Ot padeniia Makaveev po nyneshnee vremia," *Biblioteka dlia chteniia,* 13, section 3 (1835): 57–92;

"Ocherki Konstantinoplia Bazili. Retsenziia," *Biblioteka dlia chteniia,* 15, section 5 (1836): 1–22;

"Rukovodstvo k poznaniiu srednei istorii dlia srednikh uchebnikh zavedenii, sochinennoe S. Smaragodym. Spb. 1841, c. 357. Retsenziia," *Moskvitianin,* section 6, book 12 (1841): 428–432;

"Geschichte des Preussischen Staats, von C. A. Stenzel. T. 1–3. Hamburg 1830–1841. 2. Geschichte Deutschlands von 1806–1830, von Fr. Buklau. Hamburg, 1842. Retsenziia," *Moskvitianin,* no. 4, section 2 (1843): 441–463;

"Nemetskie narodnye predaniia 1. Predaniia o Karle Velikom," *Biblioteka dlia vospitaniia,* section 1, part 3 (1845): 191–205;

"Rytsar Baiard," *Biblioteka dlia vospitaniia,* section 1, part 2 (1845): 249–286;

"Pis'mo iz Moskvy. 25 marta 1847 g," *Otechestvennye zapiski,* no. 4, section 8 (1847): 200–203;

"Otvet gospodinu Khomiakovu," *Moskovskie vedomosti* (26 April 1847): 386–387;

"Istoricheskaia literatura vo Frantsii i Germanii v 1847 godu," *Sovremennik,* no. 9, section 3 (1847): 1–26; no. 1, section 3 (1848): 1–24;

"Histoire de Henri VIII et du Schisme d'Angleterre, par M. Audin. Paris, 1847. 2 vols. Retsenziia," *Sovremennik,* no. 11, section 4 (1848): 29–40;

"Latinskie imperatory v Konstantinople i ikh otnosheniia k nezavisimym vladiteliam grecheskim i tuzemnomu narodnonaseleniiu voobshche. Istoricheskoe issledovanie P. Mel'gunova. Moskva, 1850. Retsenziia," *Sovremennik,* no. 5, section 3 (1850): 1–13;

"Bartold' Georg Nibur," *Sovremennik,* 19, no. 1, section 2 (1850): 49–64; no. 2, section 2 (1850): 113–130;

"Gosudarstvennye muzei Drevnei Gretsii v epokhu ee vozrozhdeniia. Istoricheskoe rassuzhdenie Ivana Babsta. Moskva 1851. Retsenziia," *Moskovskie vedomosti* (15 May 1851): 512–514;

"Rech' v chest' I. K. Aivazovskogo (proiznesennaia Granovskim 19 marta 1851)," *Moskvitianin,* no. 8, book 2 (April 1851): 201;

"Sud'by Italii ot padeniia Zapadnoi Rimskoi imperii do vostanovleniia ee Karlom Velikim. Obozrenie Ostgotlangobardskogo perioda italianskoi istorii. Sochineniia Petra Kudriavtseva. Moskva, 1850. Retsenziia," *Otechestvennye zapiski,* no. 4, section 5 (1851): 33–46; no. 6, section 5 (1851): 29–51;

"*Chetyre istoricheskie kharakteristiki. Publichnye lektsii, chitannye v 1851 godu.* Timur. Aleksandr Velikii. Liudovik IX. Bekon" (Moscow, 1852);

"Istoriia voiny Rossii c Frantsiei v tsarstvovanie imperatora Pavla I v 1799 godu. Spb. 1853. Retsenziia," *Moskovskie vedomosti* (21 May 1853): 623–624;

"Rech' na 'Proshchal'noi obedne M. S. Shchepkinu,'" *Moskvitianin,* no. 10, book 2 (May 1853): 49;

"Dozy. Recherches sur l'histoire politique et littéraire de l'Espagne pendant le moyen age. Retsenziia," *Otechestvennye zapiski,* no. 6, section 5 (1854): 37–54;

"Ob Okeanii i ee zhiteliakh. Chtenie T. N. Granovskogo. Lektsiia chitalas' v 1852 g. v krugu druzei," *Russkii vestnik,* 1, book 2 (1856): 173–184;

"Moskva," "Vopros i otvet," and "Tsena iz zhizni Kalliostro," in "Granovskii do ego professorstva v Moskve," by V. V. Grigor'ev, *Russkaia beseda*, book 3 (1856): 27–31.

Timofei Granovsky, professor of history at Moscow University, 1840–1855, had the great misfortune of maturing as a writer during the most repressive years of the reign of Tsar Nicholas I, and as a consequence Granovsky's published works are few. Nevertheless, Granovsky influenced many of the writers and critics of his age—including Aleksandr Ivanovich Herzen, Ivan Turgenev, Fyodor Dostoyevsky, and Vissarion Grigor'evich Belinsky—and through his teaching as well as his writing earned a reputation as "the Pushkin of history." Moreover, Granovsky's moral influence was surpassed only by that of the friend of his youth, Nikolai Vladimirovich Stankevich. With respect to literature and literary criticism, Granovsky taught the "historicist" view that literature was a part of its age; as a stylist he emphasized a liveliness, elegance, and simplicity that reflected his early love of Nikolai Mikhailovich Karamzin. With respect to his political ideas Granovsky is usually classified as a moderate Westernizer, opposed to the radicals of his own persuasion as well as to the Official Nationalists and the Slavophiles.

Timofei Nikolaevich Granovsky was born on 9 March 1813 at Orel on the River Oka to a family of the middle gentry with interests in law and commerce. His father was Nikolai Timofeevich Granovsky. His paternal grandfather had arrived in the province penniless and unknown but had built up a substantial fortune through shrewdness and hard work. Granovsky's mother, Anna Vasil'eva Charnysha Granovskaia, came from a wealthy Ukrainian family, and she shared much of her regional culture with her son. Granovsky received the usual domestic education of his class and time and was taught French and English at an early age. Possibly influenced by his mother, he developed a precocious interest in the novels of Sir Walter Scott; the family library also included works of travel literature, history, and geography. Another important influence was religion in the form of Russian Orthodox Christianity, which made a permanent impression on the future writer and historian. At age thirteen Granovsky was sent to Moscow and enrolled in Kuester's boarding school, where he fell under the spell of Karamzin's twelve-volume *Istoriia gosudarstva rossiiskogo* (History of the Russia State, 1818–1829). The education he received at the boarding school was primarily literary, and Granovsky was inspired to write poems, one of which, "Stradalets" (The Sufferer), won a school prize and was published in the April 1828 issue of *Damskii zhurnal* (The Ladies Journal). For many years Granovsky read and attempted to write sentimental and romantic poetry about suffer-

Granovsky's home in Orel

ing, self-searching, mysticism, Russia, religion, and other current themes. These efforts, duly preserved in his collected works, are of little poetic interest, but they testify to Granovsky's knowledge of European Romanticism. He also translated several novels, including those of George Sand, for the family circle in Orel, where he returned after only two years of study in Moscow.

In 1831 Granovsky departed for St. Petersburg to seek state employment. There he obtained a modest position in the Ministry of Foreign Affairs. However, he proved temperamentally unsuited for bureaucratic service, and within a year he had resigned his post and entered St. Petersburg University. Because he was unprepared in classical languages, the young Granovsky had to select the faculty of law rather than his first love, the faculty of philology, within which literary studies were then taught; however, the university curriculum was liberal enough to allow him considerable opportunity to indulge his true interests in history, literature, and philosophy.

Granovsky's years at St. Petersburg University, 1832–1835, were devoted mainly to study, in part because of the financial troubles continually besetting his father; nevertheless, he refused a state scholarship, which would have obligated him to become a teacher or professor, perhaps because he aspired to a career as a writer. Apart from his studies, the poetry of Aleksandr Sergeevich Pushkin seems to have been his main diversion, and he attempted several translations of Pushkin into French and English. These were skillful enough to attract the attention of Petr Aleksandrovich Pletnev, the literary critic, who was then a professor of literature. In 1835 Pletnev presented Granovsky to Pushkin, and others began to take note of the young man's talents and abilities. Count Sergei Grigor'evich Stroganov, chief of the St. Petersburg educational region, offered him a scholarship for study in Germany, but again Granovsky refused. He also participated in several student circles, including one centered on Vasilii Vasil'evich Grigor'ev, who has left some interesting accounts of those times. Apparently the circles were more important to the students than the classrooms were.

Upon completion of his university studies Granovsky again entered state service, this time as a secretary in the hydrographic department of the Ministry of the Marine. Fortunately he was able to publish a brilliant article, "Sud'by evreiskogo naroda. Ot padeniia Makaveev po nyneshnee vremia" (The Destinies of the Jewish People) in 1835 in the journal *Biblioteka dlia chteniia* (The Library for Reading), edited by Osip Ivanovich Senkovsky (Baron Brambeus). Impressed by this piece, Senkovsky and Vladimir Konstantinovich Rzhevsky, secretary to Count Stroganov, exerted their influence to obtain for Granovsky a scholarship for study in Germany and the promise of the chair of history at Moscow University. This time Granovsky accepted the offer, probably because he recognized that his talents lay in the direction of history rather than poetry.

Prior to his departure for Europe, Granovsky visited Moscow and, apparently recommended by his St. Petersburg friend Ianuarii Mikhailovich Neverov, entered the famous circle of Stankevich, which already included many of the principal figures of the next decade, among them Sergei Mikhailovich Stroev, Ivan Nikolaevich Obolensky, Belinsky, Konstantin Sergeevich Aksakov, Mikhail Aleksandrovich Bakunin, and Mikhail Nikiforovich Katkov. The circle was in its last years, but this proved to be a fateful association. Granovsky became a close friend and confidant of Stankevich when the two found themselves together in Berlin in 1838, studying under the same professors and meeting the same literary celebrities at the Frolov salon.

Most of Granovsky's years abroad (1836–1839) were spent at the University of Berlin, which was then at the height of its prestige. In addition to his studies, the young Russian also visited Prague, Vienna, and Dresden, but his funds were so limited and the intellectual attractions of Berlin so strong that he felt little desire to wander further afield. Four great professors left their marks on the future historian. Karl Ritter, professor of history, was actually more famous for his lectures on geography, in which he taught an "organic" approach to the subject; from Ritter, Granovsky derived a lasting respect for geography as a strong deterministic force shaping the destinies of nations. Friedrich Karl von Savigny, professor of Roman law, belonged to the historical school of jurists; Savigny, like the future Moscow professor sitting in his lecture hall, stressed both continuity and progress as historical themes. It was also from Savigny that Granovsky acquired the love of medieval history that would one day result in his own most important scholarship.

Hegel was gone, but Hegelianism remained strong at Berlin, and one of its most articulate champions was Karl Werder, professor of philosophy and specialist on William Shakespeare. Werder influenced many young Russians, including Stankevich and Turgenev. Granovsky's interest in Hegelian thought gradually matured into the belief that history always falls under the influence of philosophy, that it develops in an "organic" and dialectic fashion, that great individuals are essential to it, and that the proper subject of historical study is the development of the human spirit. In Granovsky's view of history and historical literature, elements of idealism, historicism, and determinism were always strong. But they were offset by his respect for free will and the authority of primary sources, both of which were inculcated by the fourth of his great professors, Leopold von Ranke, professor of history. Ranke was then engaged in publishing his famous history of the papacy. In his seminars he sought to counter the prevalent theoretical approaches to history and, in particular, Hegelianism. His most famous dictum was that history ought to be written "as it really happened," that is, inductively, from primary sources and documents. The young Russian historian emerged from Ranke's tutelage with his idealism tempered by devotion to the modern historical method. Ranke's faith in a providential God and his belief that history was an art akin to poetry also deeply impressed Granovsky, who found his own convictions reinforced by those of the great professor.

At the university Granovsky read widely and deeply, bringing himself into contact with many books and authors previously unknown to him, including Thomas Babington Macauley, whose politics and narrative strategies were important influences on Granovsky's intellectual life. As before at St. Petersburg his studies seem to have been his main occupation.

Moscow University as it appeared when Granovsky taught there from 1840 to 1855

But this time he also maintained an interesting social life.

In 1838 Stankevich came to Berlin for a time, and Granovsky immediately gravitated toward this attractive figure and spent much time with Stankevich and his light-hearted mistress, Berta. It was Granovsky who introduced Turgenev to Stankevich, and it was Granovsky who became the latter's chief correspondent of his last years. On the basis of their letters Stankevich emerges as the dominant figure, characterized by open-heartedness, intelligence, and levity; in comparison Granovsky seems somewhat staid and unimaginative. It is difficult to establish Stankevich's exact influence on his companion and confidant. They were already alike in many ways; for example, both were fascinated by idealist and historicist philosophy but remained true believers in a providential God. The real heart of their relationship was probably simple friendship and delight in one another's company. At any rate, when Granovsky learned of his friend's death in Italy of tuberculosis in 1840, the news stunned him. And although their association had been relatively brief, the Stankevich circle came to look upon Granovsky as the heir to the master. Stankevich left Berlin first, traveling toward Italy; soon after, in the autumn of 1839, Granovsky returned to Russia.

The next, and last, phase of Granovsky's life and career belonged to Moscow University, where he gave his first lecture on 12 September 1839. There he became famous for his survey courses. The university was then administered by his patron, Count Stroganov, and by Sergei Semenovich Uvarov, the classicist and propounder of the reigning state ideology, "Official Nationality" (orthodoxy, autocracy, and nationality). The leading history professors were Mikhail Petrovich Pogodin and Stefan Petrovich Shevyrev, both Official Nationalists. Tactlessness, bluntness, and intolerance for anything that questioned the greatness of Russia's past characterized historical studies at the university, all contrasting vividly with Granovsky's recent experiences in Berlin. He was a disruptive force in this little world, the more so when students began to flock to hear his lectures. Despite his St. Petersburg lisp and his quiet tone, Granovsky proved to be a spell-binding lecturer, captivating students with his thoughtful and artful presentations. To many he became the voice of the new age and the voice of Europe at the university. It was not long before Granovsky was embroiled in controversies with the university establishment; in these disputes he came to be grateful not only for the loyalty of the students but also for the occasional but timely support of Stroganov and Uvarov, who respected his learning.

Building on his previous contacts, Granovsky moved vigorously to establish a reputation as one of the most prominent intellectual figures in Moscow outside the university. He frequented the salon of Avdot'ia Elagina, who put him in touch with the Slavophiles. Although the Stankevich circle had really broken up when Belinsky went to St. Petersburg in 1839 and Bakunin went to Berlin in the following year, the remaining membership rallied around the returned Granovsky and shared with him their grief at the terrible news from Italy of Stankevich's death. Granovsky also sought friends among the rival circle led by Herzen and Nikolai Platonovich Ogarev. In his memoirs Herzen remembers Granovsky as the first man to unite all the various factions and camps of the intellectual world of Moscow. Herzen may have been romanticizing about those days, but in the same passages he pays tribute to Granovsky's affectionate and pacific nature, which succeeded in removing all vestiges of misunderstanding among the young intellectuals of Moscow. And as his friendships became many and close, Granovsky also fell in love. In 1841 he married Elizaveta Bogdanova Muhlhausen, an uneducated Moscow German from an undistinguished family; although the couple remained childless, mutual respect and affection characterized their life together until they were separated by Granovsky's untimely death.

Increasingly prominent in university and intellectual circles, Granovsky became a well-known figure in 1843 and 1844 when he delivered several public lectures on the Middle Ages in Europe. This series was the outstanding cultural event of its time, and all of educated Moscow celebrated it. Nevertheless, the lecturer's strong views generated criticisms that reflected the divisions between Slavophiles and Westernizers. Slavophiles admired Granovsky's "organic" view of history so much like their own and so obviously derived from the writings of Gottlieb von Herder, one of their favorite authors; they could not but sense Granovsky's admiration for the universal values of the progressive West. The sharpest criticisms came from the Official Nationalists of the university, who disliked Granovsky's Hegelianism and his neglect of Russia in the lectures. Something of a controversy developed when Granovsky's senior colleague Shevyrev criticized him in the journal *Moskvitianin* (The Muscovite) and Herzen defended him from the *Moskovskie Vedomosti* (Moscow News).

Passions began to mount within the university as well and came to a head on the occasion of the historian's public defense of his master's thesis (21 February 1845). This work, "Volin, Iumsberg, i Vineta," utilized historical methods learned at Berlin to demolish myths dear to both Official Nationalists and Slavophiles. Granovsky's senior colleague Pogodin was particularly offended, and feelings ran high. Alarmed for their favorite professor, the students staged the only demonstration at the university in the reign of Nicholas I. Once again a public presentation of Granovsky's ideas served to polarize opinion and to identify him as a *zapadnik* (Westernizer). The thesis, though interesting, understandably remained unpublished. By 1845 and 1846, when the historian delivered a second series of public lectures, this time comparing the political histories of France and England, the various camps were so well established that there was little stir.

In the mid 1840s Granovsky became one of the principal spokesmen for the Westernizer point of view. Soon that camp began to break up as well, and he began to be marginalized as a "moderate Westernizer," one of that brave but forlorn little band of conservative-liberal reformers whom Nikolai Aleksandrovich Berdiaev would later identify as so removed from "the Russian idea" that they were without effect on the history of Russia. Having alienated the Slavophiles, Granovsky found that he could not follow the radical Westernizers in their drift toward what would one day emerge as Socialism. The progress of this new division can be traced in the cooling relations between Granovsky and his friend Herzen, who in any case departed Russia permanently in 1847. Belinsky's death in the following year severed another personal link with the radicals. Granovsky found that his gradualism and his complex personal beliefs were incompatible with the moral absolutism, materialism, and atheistic tendencies that characterized the extremists.

As Granovsky became increasingly isolated within the Westernizer camp, the Official Nationalist establishment offered him an unusual opportunity. Count Uvarov, who appreciated Granovsky's worth in a country suffering from a scarcity of responsible intellectuals, invited the popular Moscow historian to deliver a series of lectures to a select audience at Porech', the Uvarov estate. This event is all the more remarkable when viewed against the general and severe crackdown that the intellectual life of Russia suffered at the time of the 1848 revolutions in Europe. Delivered in August of that year, Granovsky's lectures were about "transitional epochs" in history, a subject dear to his heart; his favorite periods were the European Middle Ages through the ninth century and the thirteenth through the sixteenth centuries. The thesis of the lectures was that superficial events do not always reveal the deeper forces of progress at work in history; this thesis was susceptible to "aesopian" interpretation and was taken by some as a commentary on current events, although it is not clear that this was the lecturer's intent. In the repressive period that followed, the historian found his activities confined to the academic world.

Granovsky's major work, *Abbat Sugerii: istoricheskoe issledovanie* (Abbot Suger: An Historical Investigation), his doctoral dissertation of 1849, was defended in public and printed at the university press. In the stifled atmosphere of the times, the kind of disturbances that had characterized his master's defense were unthinkable; in any case, his dissertation had no clear ideological implications. Nevertheless, it marks a certain point in the integration

Granovsky's library and study

of Russian civilization into general European culture.

A study based on original documents from the reign of Louis VI of France, the dissertation *Abbat Sugerii* generated controversy, but of a purely academic nature. The dissertation was an extended criticism of a work by the French historian Louis Joseph Carne. Granovsky portrayed the great abbot as the architect of royal centralization, a policy that led French monarchs to overcome the local and universal powers obstructing the formation of modern national government. Pogodin led the critics from his journal *Moskvitianin* in 1850; he praised the style of Granovsky's critique but deplored the failure of his junior colleague to appreciate the civilizing effect of the Church and the Christian religion. Konstantin Dmitrievich Kavelin refuted Pogodin in *Sovremennik* (The Contemporary), and younger historians, in particular Mikhail Matveevich Stasiulevich and Ivan Kondrat'evich Babst, seized upon the occasion to debate among themselves about the proper use of sources. It fell to an anonymous reviewer in *Otechestvennye zapiski* (Notes of the Fatherland) to point out in February 1851 the real importance of Granovsky's study: it was the first original Russian monograph on western European history. As scholarship Granovsky's interpretation stood the test of time, and as literature *Abbat Sugerii* was a fine example of what Granovsky meant in his frequent assertions that scholarship had to be made accessible to the educated public. In this he showed his debt to the tradition of Karamzin.

Granovsky's last years were increasingly melancholy because he found his ambitions frustrated by the rigidity of the regime, the iron censorship, and his own isolation as a moderate in a radicalized intellectual milieu. His last major public contribution was a series of four lectures given in 1851 to challenge the idea that the people are an agent of history; the Hegelian thesis was that history was a rational process and therefore only rational individuals could be its agents. Granovsky supported his arguments by reference to Tamerlane, Alexander the Great, Louis IX, and Sir Francis Bacon. But in a university address the next year Granovsky advanced the idea, alarming to some, that history might be more of a science than an art. He also published some articles on Spanish and German literature, on Friedrich Wilhelm Nietzsche, and on the historians Barthold Georg Niebuhr and Jules Michelet, all of which are marked by a historicist approach. He received a commission to write a textbook on world history. In 1855 he published an article on the clan organization of the ancient German tribes, which led to a last flurry of controversy, with Slavophiles upset because it tended to undermine their historical theories of the peasant land commune. Granovsky was defended by Nikolai Gavrilovich Chernyshevsky, writing in *Sovremennik*. In general the impression left by his last years is one of a powerful but restless mind confined and constrained by circumstances. On the very eve of a new order, Granovsky suddenly died in Moscow of a stroke on 4 October 1855, aged forty-two years. On Friday 7 October 1855 he was interred in the Piatnitsky Cemetery.

Granovsky's funeral was a solemn and wonderful event, with relays of students carrying his remains from the university to their resting place in the city. This was the last of many tributes paid to him during his career as a university professor, and from the strictly worldly point of view these solem-

Granovsky lecturing; drawing by his student, N. I. Tikhomirov (from Priscilla Reynolds Roosevelt,
Apostle of Russian Liberalism: Timofei Granovsky, *1986)*

nities celebrated his primary claim to fame: that he was the greatest teacher of his day. His list of published works is short, but the good that he did at the university lived on in the hearts and minds of his students, and he became one of those "secular saints" revered in the Russian tradition. He kept alive the humanistic approach to history and transmitted this to many of the leading writers of history in Russia, among whom were Kavelin, Sergei Mikhailovich Solov'ev, Boris Nikolaevich Chicherin, Petr Nikolaevich Kudriavtsev, Vladimir Ivanovich Ger'e, Stepan Vasil'evich Eshevsky, and Konstantin Nikolaevich Bestuzhev-Riumin. Many more students never wrote history but were profoundly affected by his ideas and his example.

Like Karamzin's, Granovsky's history at the deepest level rested on a belief in a providential God; to this he added Hegelian idealism, concern for the life of the spirit, belief in progress, respect for historical individuals, and an eye for geography, romantic detail, and local color. His was a rich and paradoxical view of history, filled with an awareness of historical irony arising from the fact that the living seldom appreciate the deeper forces underlying superficial events. In his teaching, determinism, voluntarism, the universal, the organic, the inductive, and the deductive all were held together in a synthesis that kept his auditors spellbound. He

taught that history was rational, that scholarship was not an end in itself, and that historical literature should be written for the educated public. He opposed philosophical skepticism, and his politics were the politics of gradualism and reform. A victim of the chilling effect of official repression, Granovsky nevertheless believed that a strong, yet progressive, monarchy was the best hope for the future of Russia. If he was the true heir of Stankevich, his own mantle passed on to Chicherin.

The obituaries for Granovsky written by his fellow Westernizers were understandably marked by uncritical admiration for a figure whom most had abandoned in the war of ideas. Over time Granovsky became a legendary figure, and his name entered the geneology of the intelligentsia alongside Aleksandr Nikolaevich Radishchev, Pushkin, Herzen, and others. Granovsky's contemporaries and his biographers agree that he stood at the center of the literary life of his age and exerted an important influence on many writers. Today his importance probably lies in his typicality. As much as any other figure of his time Granovsky exemplifies the Russian intellectual of the 1840s. This was appreciated by one of the greatest Russian novelists, Dostoyevsky, who immortalized him as the pathetic character Stefan Trofimovich Verkhovensky in *Besy* (Devils, also known as The Possessed,

1872). The portrayal of the liberal who unwittingly inspired a generation of nihilists is unfair to Granovsky but is nevertheless another tribute to his importance as an inspiring teacher and a man of his age.

Letters:

"Iz pisem' Timofeia Nikolaevicha Granovskogo," *Severnyi Vestnik,* no. 1 (1869): 62–69;

"Iz pisem' T. N. Granovskogo k E. F. K. v Peterburge," in *Pomoshch' golodaiushchim: nauchno-literaturnyi sbornik* (Moscow, 1892), pp. 528–530;

A. V. Stankevich, ed., *T. N. Granovsky i ego perepiska,* 2 volumes (Moscow: A. I. Mamontov, 1897);

N. V. Stankevich, *Perepiska Nikolaia Vladimiorovicha Stankevicha, 1830–1840,* edited by A. V. Stankevich (Moscow: A. I. Mamontov, 1914);

V. G. Belinsky, "Iz neizdannoi perepiski V. G. Belinskogo," in *Literaturnoe nasledstvo,* volume 55 (Moscow, 1948), pp. 415–428;

Belinsky, "Belinsky v neizdannoi perepiske sovremennikov (1834–1848)," in *Literaturnoe nasledstvo,* volume 56 (Moscow, 1950), pp. 87–200;

R. G. Eimontov, "Iz perepiski T. N. Granovskogo s P. V. Pavlovym (1850 g.)," in *Arkheologicheskii ezhegodnik za 1988 god* (Moscow, 1989), pp. 288–292.

Bibliographies:

"Arkhiv T. N. Granovskogo," in *Zapiski otdela rukopisei, Gosudarstvennoi Biblioteki SSSR imeni V. I. Lenina* (Moscow: Gosudavstvennoe sotsial'no-eknomicheshop Izdatel'stvo, 1959), pp. 3–32;

S. S. Dmitriev, ed., *Granovsky, Timofei Nikolaevich: Bibliografiia, 1828–1967* (Moscow: Izdatel'stvo Moskovskogo Universiteta, 1969).

Biographies:

V. V. Grigor'ev, *T. N. Granovsky do ego professorstva v Moskve* (Moscow: Beseda, 1856);

V. E. Cheshikin (Ch. Vetrinskii), *T. N. Granovsky i ego vremia* (St. Petersburg: Popovaia, 1905);

A. V. Stankevich, *Timofei Nikolaevich Granovsky. Biograficheskii ocherk* (Moscow: A. I. Mamontov, 1914);

N. V. Minaeva, *Granovskii v Moskve* (Moscow: Moskovskie rabochi, 1963);

Priscilla Reynolds Roosevelt, *Apostle of Russian Liberalism: Timofei Granovsky* (Newtonville, Mass: Oriental Research Partners, 1986);

Z. A. Kamensky, *Timofei Nikolaevich Granovsky* (Moscow: Mysl', 1988);

A. A. Levandovsky, *T. N. Granovsky v russkom obshchestvennom dvizhenii* (Moscow: Izdatel'stvo Moskovskogo Univesiteta, 1989).

References:

M. A. Alpatov, "Retsenziia na knige: Granovsky, Timofei Nikolaevich. Bibliografiia (1828–1967), Moscow, 1969, 237cc," *Voprosy istorii,* no. 11 (1969): 171–173;

B. V. Alpers, *Teatr Mochalova i Shchepkina* (Moscow: Iskusstvo, 1979), pp. 267–269, 271–273;

S. A. Asinovskaia, *Iz istorii peredovykh idei v russkoi medivistike [T. N. Granovsky]* (Moscow: Akademia Nauk, 1955);

I. Babst, "Neskol'ko zamechanii po povodu kritiki gospodina Stasiulevicha na knigu 'Abbat Sugerii,' istoricheskoe rassuzhdenie T. Granovskogo," *Otechesvennye zapiski,* 70, no. 7, part 8 (1850): 54–67;

P. Bartenev, "Sochineniia T. N. Granovskogo, t. 2, Moskva 1856, retsenziia," *Otechestvennye zapiski,* no. 2 (1857): 61–65;

P. P. Cherkasov, "175-letie so dnia rozhdeniia T. N. Granovskogo," *Voprosy istorii,* no. 7 (1988): 183–184;

Nikolai G. Chernyshevsky, "Sochineniia T. N. Granovskogo," in his *Polnoe sobranie sochineniia,* volume 3 (Moscow: Khudozhestvennaia literature, 1947);

A. L. Danilov, "Granovsky i nekotorye voprosy sotsial'noi istorii rannego srednovekov'ia," *Uchenye zapiski Tomskogo universiteta,* 16 (1951): 75–90;

A. G. Dement'ev, "Granovsky i Shevyrev," in *Chtenye zapiski Leningradskogo G. U.: seriia filogicheskikh nauk,* volume 3 (1939);

N. Gabidulina, "Liberalizm v Rossii (istoriko-filosofskii analiz)," *Vestnik vyshykh shkol,* nos. 7–9 (1992): 71–76;

V. N. Ger'e, *Professor Timofei Nikolaevich Granovsky v pamiat' stoletnogo iubileia ego rozhdeniia* (Moscow, 1914);

M. O. Gershenzon, *Istoriia molodoi Rossii* (Moscow: Gosudarstvennoe Izdatel'stvo, 1923);

Gershenzon, *A History of Young Russia* (Irvine, Cal.: Schlacks, 1986);

M. M. Grigor'ian, "Filosofskie i sotsiologicheskie vzgliady T. N. Granovskogo," in *Russkaia progressivnaia i sotsiologicheskaia mysl' XIX veka* (Moscow, 1959), pp. 33–120;

I. V. Gurrier, *Timofei Nikolaevich Granovsky* (Moscow, 1914);

E. V. Gutnova and S. A. Asinovskaia, "Granovsky kak istorik," in Granovsky's *Lektsii po istorii srednovekov'ia,* edited by Asinovskaia (Moscow: Nauka, 1986), pp. 336–362;

Gutnova, "T. N. Granovsky ob istoricheskoi nauke," *Novaia i noveishaia istoriia,* no. 4 (1989): 184–192;

D. Hecht, *Russian Radicals Look to America* (Cambridge, Mass.: Harvard University Press, 1947);

Aleksandr Ivanovich Herzen, *Byloe i dumy,* in his *Sobranie sochineniia,* volume 9 (Moscow, 1956);

Herzen, "Neopublichnaia stat'ia," *Novyi Mir,* no. 3 (1962);

Herzen, "Publichnye chteniia g. Granovskogo (Pis'mo v Peterburg); O publichnykh chteniiakh g-a. Granovskogo (Pis'mo vtoroe)," in his *Sobranie sochineniia,* volume 2 (Moscow: Akademiia Nauk, 1954);

Z. A. Kamensky, "O vozzreniiakh T. N. Granovskogo na istoricheskii protsess," *Izvestiia A. N. SSSR: seriia istorii i filosofii,* 3, no. 6 (1946): 489–496;

N. M. Kareev, *Istoricheskoe mirosozertsanie T. N. Granovskogo* (St. Petersburg: Stasiulevich, 1896);

K. D. Kavelin, "Abbat Sugerii. Istoricheskoe issledovanie T. Granovskogo. Moskva, 1849 (Retsenziia)," *Sobranie Sochinenii,* volume 3 (St. Petersburg: Stasiulevich, 1899), columns 1248–1255;

Kavelin, "K. D. Kavelin o smerti Nikolaia Pervogo. Pis'ma k T. N. Granovskomu," *Literaturnoe nasledstvo,* 67 (1959): 591–614;

L. E. Kerman, "Evolutsiia istoricheskikh vzgliadov T. N. Granovskogo," *Nauchnye zapiski Kievskogo universiteta,* volume 6, issue 1 (1947): 91–196;

M. N. Kovalensky, "Neizdannye universitetskie kursy Granovskogo," *Golos minuvshego,* no. 9 (1913): 210–233;

E. A. Kozminsky, "Zhizn' i deiatel'nost' T. N. Granovskogo," *Vestnik MGU,* no. 4 (1956);

V. Leontowitsch, *Geschichte des Liberalismus in Russland* (Frankfurt-am-Main: Klostermann, 1957);

A. A. Levandovsky, *Vremia Granovskogo: u istokov formirovaniia russkoi intelligentsii* (Moscow, 1990);

D. M. Levshin, *T. N. Granovsky: opyt istoricheskogo sinteza* (St. Petersburg: Tip. khudozhestvennoi pechaty, 1901);

A. S. Lichtenstein, *Granovsky and the Roots of the Politics of Enlightenment, 1813–1844,* dissertation, Indiana University, 1973;

P. Miliukov, "Universitetskii kurs Granovskogo," in P. Miliukov, *Iz istorii russkoi intelligentsii. Sbornik statei i etiudov* (St. Petersburg: Znanie, 1903), pp. 212–265;

N. V. Minaeva, "Amerikanskii istorik o T. N. Granovskom," *Voprosy istorii,* no. 11 (1988): 162–165;

Ia. M. Neverov, *Russkoe obshchestvo 30-kh godov XIXv.: Liudi i idei: memuary sovremennikov* (Moscow: Izdatel'stvo Moskoskogo Universiteta, 1989), p. 352ff;

A. S. Nifontov, *Rossiia v 1848 godu* (Moscow: Gosudarstvennoe uchebno-pedagogicheskoe izdatel'stvo, 1949);

Derek Offord, *Portraits of Early Russian Liberals* (Cambridge, U.K. & New York: Cambridge University Press, 1985);

I. S. Pichgina, "T. N. Granovsky, lektsii po istorii srednovekov'ia (retsenziia)," *Srednie veka,* issue 53 (1990): 242–243;

M. P. Pogodin, "Abbat Sugerii (chit. Siuger). Istoricheskoe issledovanie T. Granovskogo v univ. tip. 1849 (Retsenziia)," *Moskvitianin,* no. 2, book 2, part 4 (1850): 8;

V. I. Prilenskii, *Opyt issledovaniia mirovozreniia rannikh russkikh liberalov* (Moscow: Rossiiskoia Akademiia Nauk, 1995);

N. S. Racheotes, "T. N. Granovsky: On the Meaning of History," *Studies in Soviet Thought,* 18 (1978): 197–221;

Priscilla Reynolds Roosevelt, "Granovsky at the Lectern: A Conservative-Liberal's View of History," *Forschungen zur osteuropaeischen Geschichte,* 29 (1981): 61–192;

"Russkaia literatura v 1850 godu," *Otechestvennye zapiski,* 74, section 5 (February 1851): 67–150;

V. V. Selivanov, "Timofei Nikolaevich Granovsky: vospominanie V. V. Selivanova," *Russkaia Starina,* no. 20 (1877): 205–221;

S. P. Shevyrev, "Publichnyia lektsii ob istorii srednykh vekov g. Granovskogo," *Moskvitianin,* no. 3, part 4 (1843): 525–526;

A. Shklarevskii, *T. N. Granovsky: Po povodu stoletiia so dnia ego rozhdeniia* (Moscow, 1913);

I. S. Simonov, *Granovsky-uchitel'. Ko 50-letiu so dnia smerti: 4-ogo oktiabria 1855g.—4-ogo oktiabria 1905g.* (St. Petersburg, 1906);

M. M. Stasiulevich, "Abbat Sugerii. Istoricheskoe issledovanie T. Granovskogo. Moskva, 1849 (Retsenziia)," *Moskvitianin,* no. 10, book 2, part 4 (1850): 67–96;

V. N. Storonezh, *Vospominanie o T. N. Granovskom* (Rostov, 1905);

Ivan Turgenev, "Dva slova o Granovskom," in his *Sobranie sochineniia v 12 tomakh,* volume 11 (Moscow: Gosudarstvennoe izdatel'stvo khudozhestvennoi literatury, 1956), pp. 225–228;

L. A. Ushakova, "K voporosu ob otnoshenii T. N. Granovskogo k revoliutsii," *Uchenye zapiski Tomskogo universiteta,* 34 (1958): 71–85;

"Volin, Iomsburg i Vineta. Istoricheskoe issledovanie. Masterskaia dissertattsiia," *Sbornik istoricheskikh i statisticheskikh svedenii o Rossii i narodakh ei edinovernykh edinoplemennykh,* volume 1 (Moscow: Izdatel'stvo Moskovskogo Universiteta, 1845), pp. 143–184.

Nikolai Ivanovich Grech

(3 August 1787 – 12 January 1867)

Ruth Sobel

Defence School of Languages

BOOKS: *Uchebnaia kniga rossiiskoi slovesnosti,* 4 volumes (St. Petersburg: N. Grech, 1819–1822) corrected and enlarged edition (St. Petersburg: Printed by K. Zhernakov, 1844);

Opyt kratkaia istorii russkoi literatury (St. Petersburg: Izdatelia, 1822);

Prostrannaia russkaia grammatika (St. Petersburg: Izdatelia, 1827);

Nachal'nyia pravila russkoi grammatiki (St. Petersburg: Tip. Imp. Sanktpeterburgskogo vospitatel'nago doma, 1828);

Osnovnye pravila russkoi grammatiki (St. Petersburg, 1828; reprinted in 1843 as *Kratkaia russkaia grammatika*);

Poezdka v Germaniiu (St. Petersburg: N. Grech, 1831);

Sochineniia, 5 volumes (St. Petersburg, 1833–1838);

Chernaia zhenshchina (St. Petersburg: N. Grech, 1834);

Puteshestvie v Germaniiu (St. Petersburg, 1836);

28 dnei za granitsei ili deistvitel'naia poezdka v Germaniiu (St. Petersburg: N. Grech, 1837);

Literaturnye poiasneniia (St. Petersburg, 1838);

Putevye pis'ma iz Anglii, Germanii i Frantzii (St. Petersburg: N. Grech, 1839);

Chteniia o russkom iazyke (St. Petersburg, 1840);

Pis'ma s dorogi po Germanii, Shveitsarii i Italii (St. Petersburg: N. Grech, 1843);

Rukovodstvo k izucheniiu russkoi grammatiki (St. Petersburg: N. Grech, 1843);

Sochineniia, 3 volumes (St. Petersburg: Iakov Trei, 1855);

Zapiski o moei zhizni (St. Petersburg, 1880).

Editions and Collections: *Zapiski o moei zhizni* (St. Petersburg: A. S. Suvorin, 1886);

Zapiski o moei zhizni, edited by D. M. Ivanov-Razumnik and D. M. Pines (Moscow: Akademiia, 1930);

Sochineniia (Moscow: Kniga, 1990);

Chernaia zhenshchina, in *Tri starinnykk romana,* 2 volumes, edited by Vsevolod Iur'evich Troitsky (Moscow: Sovremennik, 1990);

Zapiski o moei zhizni (Moscow: Kniga, 1990).

Nikolai Ivanovich Grech

Grech's journalistic and literary career spanned more than five decades; yet despite his enormous output (articles, translations, reviews, novels, grammar books, memoirs, travelogues, and some genuinely valuable contributions to Russian language and literature, especially in the field of journalism) the memory he left is decidedly negative. His is one of the odious names of Russian letters, usually pronounced in one breath with those of Faddei Venediktovich Bulgarin and Osip Ivanovich Senkovsky, who became the symbols of corrupt and venal men of letters and did not flinch from writing denunciations of their enemies and rivals to the secret police. Although many contemporaries agree that Grech was not as morally base as his confederate Bulgarin and that their collaboration stemmed mainly from Grech's financial difficulties, in the final analysis his is not an unblemished reputation.

Probably because of the negative aura surrounding Grech, critics have virtually passed over his early liberal, and even radical, leanings in silence; they rarely mention his friendship with the Decembrists, whose works he continued to publish after the 1825 revolt. Today no one rates him highly as a grammarian, a writer, or a literary critic, though he wrote what actually were the first histories of Russian literature in 1822, *Uchebnaia kniga rossiiskoi slovesnosti* (A Textbook of Russian Literature, 1819–1822) and *Opyt kratkoi istorii russkoi literatury* (An Attempt at a Short History of Russian Literature). In addition his *Prostrannaia russkaia grammatika* (Detailed Russian Grammar, 1827), which ultimately saw eleven printings, gained him admittance as a corresponding member to the Academy of Sciences. Though this grammar, as well as his 1840 *Chteniia o russkom iazyke* (Readings on Russian Language) earned Grech no praise, they were a positive force in his day. His memoirs remain his best endeavor, most highly praised for a wealth of valuable and entertaining information on the reign of Alexander I and on the Decembrists in particular.

On the whole Grech belongs to the ranks of second- or even third-rate nineteenth-century men of letters whose names probably would have sunk into deeper oblivion were it not for their notoriety. Yet an attempt to embrace the whole panorama of literary life in a given period warrants a discussion of such a person as Grech.

Nikolai Ivanovich Grech came from a Russianized Bohemian-German family. His great-grandfather, a Protestant and a native of Bohemia, moved to Germany in the middle of the seventeenth century in order to escape Catholic persecution. His grandfather, Johann Ernst Gretsch, a graduate of Leipzig University, came to Russia during the reign of the Empress Anna Ivanovna together with Biron, the Duke of Courland and her all-powerful favorite. Gretsch first taught at the *gimnaziia* (Grammar school) in Mittau, the capital of Courland and later moved to St. Petersburg to take up a post at the Gentry Cadet Corps (for the Land Forces). When the future empress Catherine arrived in Russia, he was appointed as one of her tutors and taught her history and politics. Grech's father, Ivan Ivanovich (Johann-Ernst) on the other hand, became a civil servant; toward the end of his career he reached a fairly high position in the Senate, although he never became wealthy. On 23 August 1786 he married Ekaterina Iakovlevna Freigol'd (Freyhold).

Nikolai Ivanovich Grech was born in St. Petersburg on 3 August 1787 and first was educated at home. He wanted to study at Moscow University, as he had literary ambitions, but his father, whose financial affairs were in disarray, wanted him to pursue a career in the civil service. Consequently he enrolled Nikolai in the Junkers' School, where future civil servants destined for the Senate received their education. Grech studied there between 1801 and 1813, yet he did not abandon his wish to follow a different career. Thus he enrolled as a "free auditor" in the newly-opened Pedagogical Institute, where he attended lectures from 1803 through 1805.

In 1804 Grech embarked on his first career—teaching. He was invited to teach Russian language and literature initially in private schools and later in state-run educational establishments of the capital, among them the St. Petersburg *gimnaziia.* Between 1805 and 1815 Grech combined his teaching career with one in civil service, working for the St. Petersburg Censorship Committee, first as a clerk and later as the committee secretary. At that time his teaching career also progressed rapidly, and in 1809 he was appointed senior teacher in Russian language and literature in the main German school of the capital, where he taught until 1814. In 1811 he became a parish school inspector and held that post until 1814. That same year he was promoted to senior teacher at the St. Petersburg *gimnazium,* where he taught until 1817.

On a personal level at this time Grech was embarking on a new family life. He married Varvara Danilovna Miussar (Mussard) in 1808. They had five children.

One of Grech's great interests was Russian grammar, and in this field he made one of his most important contributions. His works on Russian grammar were closely connected with his teaching. While studying in Paris from 1817 to 1818, Grech took on the task of setting up a central school for the lower ranks of the guards regiments. During his stay in the French capital Grech studied the Lancasterian system of teaching, which employs more able and more advanced students to teach the less able ones under the supervision of a tutor. Later Grech introduced this system to Russia. In 1820 he was appointed head of the regimental school of the Guards Corps, where he served until 1821. His work merited steady promotion—in 1823 to the rank of collegiate assessor, in 1829 to state counselor, and in 1839 to veritable state counselor. As one of his duties in service Grech participated in the compilation of the 1828 censorship code, one of the most liberal in the history of Russian legislation. As a civil servant from 1829 until 1836 Grech was employed in the Ministry of Internal Affairs, and

Watercolor caricature by N. Stepanov of Osip Ivanovich Senkovsky, Grech, and Faddei Venediktovich Bulgarin at Smirdin's bookshop in St. Petersburg (National Pushkin Museum, St. Petersburg)

during the period 1836 through 1843 he was employed in the Ministry of Finance. Later he served as a council member in the Ministry of Education. After his dismissal from the Ministry of Education, Grech was transferred back to the Ministry of Internal Affairs and promoted to the rank of privy counselor.

Like many other men of letters of that period Grech combined a literary career with other activities. He was a teacher, a civil servant, a journalist, a man of letters, a publisher, a grammarian, and a novelist—to name but the chief of his occupations. He began his literary career as a translator of anti-Napoleonic tracts, such as "Germany in Her Deepest Humiliation," published in 1806 and 1807. A year later he embarked on his journalistic career when together with Fedor Andreevich Schroeder, he began to edit an historical-political journal of liberal tendency, *Genii vremen* (The Genius of the Times, 1807–1809), which was soon

closed by the censor. However, Grech continued his editorial work with Schroeder, publishing *Zhurnal noveishikh puteshestvii* (Journal of Newest Travels) and *Evropeiskie muzhi* (European Men, 1810). In addition Grech translated many literary works, among them August Friedrich Ferdinand von Kotzebue's novel, *Leontine,* which he translated in 1808. Grech also became a member of the liberal Obshchestvo Liubitelei rossiliskoi slavesnosti (Society of Lovers of Russian Literature), in which he sided with the anti-Shishkovite camp.

During the period of Napoleonic Wars Grech was a liberal and associated with liberal-minded journalists and guards officers. The year 1812 became a turning point in his career as journalist. He obtained a loan of one thousand rubles from the government for the purpose of setting up his own publication, which he called *Syn otechestva* (Son of the Fatherland). The inspiration for the title of his journal came from a letter written by his brother, an artillery officer wounded at the battle of Borodino: "I will die," Grech's brother wrote, "but as a true son of the fatherland." Grech intended the journal to focus on the progress of the war against Napoleon (it was launched in October 1812) but continued its publication after the end of the campaign. *Syn otechestva* became one of the best Russian publications of its time and maintained its leading position for more than a decade. Some of the contributors whom Grech, thanks to his editorial skills, succeeded in attracting were Ivan Andreevich Krylov, Gavrila Romanovich Derzhavin, Nikolai Mikhailovich Karamzin, Aleksandr Sergeevich Griboedov, Konstantin Nikolaevich Batiushkov, Vasilii Andreevich Zhukovsky, Petr Andreevich Viazemsky, Nikolai Ivanovich Gnedich, the young Aleksandr Sergeevich Pushkin, future Decembrists, the Bestuzhev brothers, Kondratii Fedorovich Ryleev, Fedor Nikolaevich Glinka, Vil'gel'm Karlovich Kiukhel'beker, and others. Publishing their works in his journal contributed to its long-deserved reputation as one of the best of the age; *Syn otechestva* and its editor both enjoyed a reputation as promoters of liberal, sometimes radical, views.

The time Grech spent working as the editor of *Syn otechestva* in its heyday constitutes his most important contribution to Russian letters. Yet in later years his views underwent a radical change; he became an arch-conservative who, together with Bulgarin and Senkovsky, symbolized reaction and obscurantism. This process was gradual. Some consider the 1820 mutiny in one of the elite guard regiments, the Semenovsky, a catalyst in the emergence of Grech's new conservative outlook. It seems that the Lancasterian system of teaching, which Grech introduced to the guards, was seen as one of the contributing factors to the mutiny, thus making Grech partly responsible for the occurrence.

By 1825, the year of the Decembrist uprising, Grech had already moved to the conservative camp, or as he said in his memoirs: "willy-nilly I 'sobered up' from liberal ideas." It is highly plausible that the secret surveillance over his journal and his person ordered by Tsar Nicholas I was another important factor in Grech's "defection" to the conservative faction.

Grech's 1820 meeting with Bulgarin and their subsequent partnership played a significant role in his professional literary career. The two men struck up a friendship and later embarked on a close collaboration in journalistic ventures. In 1829 *Syn otechestva* merged with Bulgarin's *Severnyi arkhiv* (The Northern Archive); and in 1831 Grech was appointed coeditor of Bulgarin's notorious *Severnaia pchela* (The Northern Bee), though in actual fact he had been editing it since 1825. Nevertheless, despite his increasingly conserva-

tive outlook, Grech still maintained literary links with the Decembrists in Siberia and elsewhere, as well as with Pushkin, who had been returned from exile by the tsar. Grech also published Bestuzhev's works in *Syn otechestva*. Additional editorial enterprises which Grech undertook in the course of his long career include editorship of the official *Zhurnal Ministerstva vnutrennikh del* (Journal of the Ministry of Internal Affairs) from 1829 to 1831, the important *Éntsiklopedicheskii leksikon* (Encyclopedic Lexicon) for Pluchard, and the *Voenno-entsiklopedicheskii leksikon* (Military-Encyclopedic Lexicon). He simultaneously edited the latter two publications from 1835 until 1840.

Among all of Grech's professional activities, the area which gave him the most pleasure was his involvement in Russian literature. Judged harshly because of his designation as one of the "Unholy Triumvirate of the Reptile Press," along with Senkovsky and Bulgarin, Grech nevertheless did add some works of merit to Russian letters, although his views were not altogether consistent.

At *Syn otechestva* Grech not only acted as the editor but also engaged in writing literary criticism. His main contribution to that nascent genre, often ignored, was the annual survey of new works (1814, 1815, 1816, . . .), later continued by other critics, among them Belinsky. In his early days as a critic he published reviews of Griboedov's play *Gore ot uma* (Woe from Wit, 1833) and Pushkin's *Tsygany* (The Gypsies, 1824). Even in his reactionary period he wrote a positive critique of Mikhail Iur'evich Lermontov's *Geroi nashego vremeni* (A Hero of Our Time, 1840); and yet from 1830 to 1831 Grech supported Bulgarin in his famous polemic with Pushkin. In 1842 Grech wrote a blatantly negative review of Nikolai Vasil'evich Gogol's masterpiece *Mertvye dushi* (Dead Souls, 1842); the critic deplored Gogol's lack of taste as well as his vulgar tone. Grech also condemned the Marquis de Custine's famous indictment of imperial Russia *La Russie en 1839,* which had angered the tsar. Grech's brochure, which aimed at discrediting the Frenchman's criticism, was published with the approval of the all-powerful chief of the secret police, Count Aleksandr Benckendorf, in 1844.

Grech's forays into novel writing were far from successful. In 1834 he published his initial attempt, *Chernaia zhenshchina* (The Black Woman), followed in 1836 by *Puteshestvie v Germaniiu* (A Trip to Germany), the first detailed study of the German community in St. Petersburg to appear in Russia (his own description of the book). He also wrote travelogues, five in all, between 1817 and 1847.

Grech's travel notes from an 1817 trip abroad, *Pis'ma o Shveitsarii* (Letters About Switzerland), appeared in *Poliarnaia zvezda* (The Polar Star) in 1823 and set a new tone for the genre. Eschewing the highly emotional, subjective style popular in the early part of the nineteenth century, Grech instead presents informal, objective notes, almost journalistic in manner, about his travels to Rousseau's birthplace, various cantons, the Alps, the Danube, the Rhine, and Lake Geneva. A description of his visit to Ferney is almost terse and matter-of-fact. Other travel notes of Grech's trips abroad include *28 dnei za granitsei ili deistvitel'naia poezdka v Germaniiu,* (28 Days Abroad or An Actual Trip to Germany, 1837)—as opposed to his fictional trip to Germany; *Putevye pis'ma iz Anglii, Germanii i Frantzii* (Travel Letters from England, Germany and France, 1839); and *Pis'ma s dorogi* (Letters from the Road, 1843).

The critical appraisal of Grech's first novel, *Chernaia zhenshchina,* was anything but praise. John Mersereau, who in *Russian Romantic Fiction* likens the work to a modern soap opera, calls it a "tale of endless tribulation, machination, devastation, and resignation" that combines "picaresque adventure, the supernatural, and social satire." This mix of elements probably contributed to the tremendous success the novel enjoyed: it had "something for everyone." A massive work, it encompasses almost a century in its narration, going back to Peter the Great. The events of the tale are fragmented and develop through flashbacks. Grech also provides interminable biographies of minor characters along with the adventures of the main hero. The action alternates among such disparate sites as "Moscow . . . , the Caucasus, Lombardy, Nice, Paris, Holland, Revel, and Petersburg."

Greed and avarice lie at the base of the action and provide the motivation for the evil, negative characters of the book. The characters in general are flat, stock types who fight on the side either of good or of evil. The story centers on the morally upright Prince Kemsky and his half sister, Alevtina, who plots to steal all of his money and estates. Supposedly sacrificed in the process are Kemsky's wife, Natasha, and their daughter, Nadezhda, who nevertheless somehow survive. Rather than develop his characters and reveal their psychological complexity, Grech relies on an overly convoluted, melodramatic plot based on implausible coincidences involving orphans, missing parents, and cases of mistaken identity to move the story along.

As if to add to the confusion, the narrator engages in bombastic soliloquies on good, evil, and almost any other abstraction under the sun. According to Mersereau, the novel suffers from lack of humor and ultimately is dull, lifeless, and cliché ridden. The narrator, according to Mersereau, even makes the 1755 Lisbon earthquake sound dreary.

Grech in his study; drawing by V. Timm, 1853 (frontispiece from Zapiski omoeizhizni, *1930)*

One question remains, though: who is the woman in black? It seems that she is a woman Kemsky first saw when he was a five-year-old child in Moscow during the plague. Even though she fell to her death from a balcony as she threw herself on the body of her dead child, the woman in black appears to Kemsky as an apparition at times of trial in his life. Kemsky ultimately confuses her—to his great joy—with his long-lost wife, Natasha, who really does appear, dressed in black, on the same balcony as the original lady in black. Natasha is thus clad because she has spent many years in a convent while Kemsky presumed she was dead.

Even a brief analysis of *Chernaia zhenshchina* gives a bleak picture of the prose scene in Russia during the 1830s, especially in light of its tremendous success. According to Mersereau, Grech's next effort, *Poezdka v Germaniiu* is hardly any better; on the contrary, this work "mercifully signalled the end of his efforts at major fiction."

Grech's contribution in the sphere of education was probably the most valuable and the most durable of all his efforts. His interest in Russian grammar evolved from teaching. His first textbook *Uchebnaia kniga rossiiskoi slovesnosti* in *Izbrannye mesta iz russkikh sochinenii i perevodov v stikhakh i proze s prisovokupleniem kratkikh pravil ritoriki i piitiki i istorii russkoi slovesnosti* (Selected Passages from Russian Compositions and Translations in Poetry and Prose with an Appendix of Short Rules of Rhetoric, Poetics, and History of Russian Literature) appeared in 1822 in four volumes. *Opyt kratkaia istorii russkoi literatury* is the first Russian study of this type. As an historian of literature Grech assimilated many ideas popular in his day; for example, he viewed literature as a social phenomenon and recognized the link between literature and national history, a key Romantic concept. Because of this latter idea, Grech acknowledged the special importance the War of 1812 against Napoleon held in the development of Russian literature.

Grech continued his studies in Russian grammar from the 1820s through the 1840s in his *Prostrannaia russkaia grammatika* (second edition, 1834) and *Nachal'nyia pravila russkoi grammatiki* (The Basic Rules of Russian Grammar, 1828). This last book went into ten editions and was renamed in 1843 as *Kratkaia russkaia grammatika* (A Short Russian Grammar); it became an official textbook in Russian schools until the 1860s. *Prostrannaia russkaia grammatika* (Expanded Russian Grammar, 1827) brought him important recognition: Grech was elected as a corresponding member of the Imperial Academy of Sciences. In 1840 Grech published his *Chteniia o russkom iazyke* (Lectures on Russian Language). In addition, toward the end of his life he helped Vladimir Ivanovich Dal' in his lexicographic work.

Grech also tried his hand in writing memoirs, which, unfortunately, he did not finish. He devoted the final years of his life to the writing of *Zapiski o moei zhizni* (Notes on My Life, 1880). Grech's memoirs—though extremely diffuse, verbose, and digressive—possess a wealth of interesting detail. Though biased in the spirit of official nationality, Grech nevertheless provides some unflattering descriptions of both Paul I and Alexander I. Before he enters the world of society, literature, and publishing, Grech furnishes his readers with a detailed history of his forebears. He also occasionally describes with some deep feeling personal events in his life, such as the death of one young daughter and the birth of another on the same day. The real value of the memoirs, though, lies in its portraits of his friends and acquaintances, among whom one finds such conflicting characters as the Decembrists and his close colleague Bulgarin. Grech's memoirs remain an important source for information about Russia in the first half of the nineteenth century.

In 1854 Grech celebrated fifty years of his literary and journalistic work. Most well-known and respected men of letters of the day did not attend the banquet in his honor, and the tsar neither awarded an order nor sent a present, as was the custom. Such was the measure of Grech's bad reputation. By that time Grech's notoriety as a "partisan of falsehood and darkness" (in the words of Nikolai Aleksandrovich Dobroliubov) had been firmly established for years; this ill-attended celebration only highlighted Grech's low standing in the world of Russian letters. In the final fifteen years of his life he continued to work on his memoirs. Grech died in St. Petersburg on 12 January 1867.

Letters:
"Pis'ma" ("Letters") in *Shchukinskii sbornik,* vypusk 8 (St. Petersburg, 1909), pp. 437–457.

Biographies:
Iubilei piatidesiatiletnei literaturnoi deiatel'nosti, N. I. Grech (St. Petersburg, 1855);
D. V. Solov'ev, *N. I. Grech, ego zhizn' i literaturno-zhurnal'naia deiatel'nost'. Filologicheskie zapiski,* nos. 1–6 (1916); no. 1 (1917).

References:
V. G. Belinsky, "Sochineniia N. Grecha" in *Polnoe sobranie sochinenii,* volume 2 (Moscow: Academy of Sciences of the USSR, 1953), pp. 530–549;
I. G. Dobrodomov, "N. I. Grech—grammatist," *Russkaia rech',* 6 (November/December 1987): 58–62;
N. F. Dubrovin, "K istorii russkoi literatury. F. V. Bulgarin i N. I. Grech kak izdateli zhurnalov," *Russkaia starina,* no. 9 (1900): 559–591;
Thomes Louis Koepnick, "The Journalistic Careers of F. V. Bulgarin and N. I. Grech: Publicism and Poetics in Tsarist Russia," dissertation, Ohio State University, 1976;
Ronald D. LeBlanc, "Notes on My Life, N. I. Grech," *Slavic and East European Journal,* 38 (1994): 493–499;
John Mersereau Jr., *Russian Romantic Fiction* (Ann Arbor, Mich.: Ardis, 1983);
V. N. Peretts, "K stoletiiu 'istorii' russkoi literatury (po povodu opyta kratkoi istorii russkoi literatury N. I. Grecha)," *Izvestiia iazyka i slovesnosti,* 28 (1924): 200–213;
A. P. Piatkovskii, "Zhurnal'nyi triumvirat" in *Iz istorii nashego literaturnogo i obshchestvennogo razvitiia,* second edition (St. Petersburg: Khromolit. A. Transhel', 1888), pp. 206–235;
N. Polevoi, "Dnevnik," *Istoricheskii vestnik,* no. 3 (1888): 654–674; no. 4: 163–183.

Ivan Vasil'evich Kireevsky
(22 March 1806 - 12 June 1856)

Rosina Neginsky
University of Illinois at Urbana-Champaign

BOOKS: *Polnoe sobranie sochinenii Ivan Vasilevicha Kireevskogo,* 2 volumes, edited by Aleksandr I. Koshelev (Moscow: P. Bakhmeter, 1861);
Polnoe sobranie sochinenii I. V. Kireevskogo, 2 volumes, edited by Mikhail O. Gershenzon (Moscow: Put', 1911);
I. V. Kireevsky, kritika i estetika (Moscow, 1979).

SELECTED PERIODICAL PUBLICATIONS:
"Nechto o kharaktere poezii Pushkina," *Moskovskii vestnik,* part 8, no. 6 (1828): 171–196;
"Obozrenie russkoi slovesnosti za 1829 god," *Dennitsa, almanakh* (1830): ix–lxxiv;
"Khor iz tragedii Andromakh," *Dennitsa, almanakh* (1830);
"Deviatnadtsati vek," *Evropeets,* part 1, no. 1 (1832): 3–23; no. 3 (1832): 371–379 (not published);
"Neskol'ko slov o sloge Vil'mena," *Evropeets,* part 1, no. 1 (1832): 48–51;
"Obozrenie russkoi literaturi za 1831 god," *Evropeets,* part 1, no. 1 (1832): 102–115; no. 2 (1832): 259–269;
" 'Gore ot uma'–na moskovskoi stsene," *Evropeets,* part 1, no. 1 (1832): 135–141;
"Russkie al'manakhi na 1832 god," *Evropeets,* part 1, no. 2 (1832): 285–289;
"O russkikh pisatel'nitsakh," *Podarok bednym, almanakh* (1834): 120–151;
"O stikhotvoreniiakh g. Iazykova," *Teleskop,* part 19, no. 3 (1834): 163–177; no. 4 (1834): 232–242;
"Tsaritsynskaia noch'" *Annals,* no. 5 (1845);
"E. A. Baratynsky," *Biblioteka dlia vospitaniia,* part 3 (1845): 1–6;
"Bibliographicheskie stat'i," *Moskvitianin,* parts 1, 2, 3 (1845): 1–5;
"Obozrenie sovremennoi russkoi literatury," *Moskvitianin,* part 1, no. 1 (1845): 1–28; part 2, no. 2 (1845): 56–78; part 3, no. 3 (1845): 18–30;
"Publichnye lektsii professora Shevyreva," *Moskvitianin,* part 1, no. 1, (1845): 1–6;
"Sel'skoe khoziaistvo," *Moskvitianin,* part 1 (1845);

Ivan Vasil'evich Kireevsky

"Sochineniia Paskalia," *Moskvitianin,* part 3, no. 3 (1845): 73–78;
"Zhizn' Steffensa," *Moskvitianin,* part 1, no. 1 (1845): 1–2; part 3 (1845): 45–46;
"O kharaktere prosveshcheniia Evropy i ego otnoshenie k prosveshcheniiu Rossii," *Moskovskii sbornik,* 1 (21 April 1852): 1–68;
"O neobkhodimosti i vosmoshnosti novykh nachal dlia filosophii," *Russkaia beseda,* 2 (1856): 1–48;
"Mitskevichu," *Russkii arkhive,* 2 (1874): 223;

"Das Tagebuch Ivan Vasil'evic Kireevskijs, 1852–1854," *Jahrbucher fur Geschichte Osteuropas,* 14 (June 1966): 167–194;

"Zapiska o napravlenii i metodakh pervonachal'nogo obrazovaniia naroda v Rossii," published as an appendix to Eberhard Muller's *Russischer Intellekt in Europaischer Krise* (Cologne: Bohlau, 1966), pp. 485–496.

Kireevsky was one of Russia's first literary critics and journal publishers. He was also known as one of the main theoreticians of Russian Slavophilism, a movement that attempted to define the essence of Russia's historical development and identity. He was the first to complete critical studies of Aleksandr Pushkin's poetry, with his "Nechto o kharaktere poezii Pushkina" (Something About Pushkin's Poetry, 1828); he did an early survey of current Russian literature; and he was the first to dedicate an article to Russian women writers: "O russikh pisatel'nitsakh" (On Russian Women Writers, 1834). He was also one of the first to import Western ideas to Russia and apply them in the construction of his own Slavophile philosophical system. His journalistic activity mirrors his development as a literary critic and thinker. Two issues of *Evropeets* (The European) published in 1832, particularly his article "Deviatnadtsati vek" (The Nineteenth Century), are typical of his early development, especially his interest in and understanding of European culture at that time. This understanding of another culture later fostered an appreciation of the identity, authenticity, and historical development of his own. His later development is best seen in three issues of *Moskvitianin* (The Moscovite) that Kireevsky published in 1845 and in his articles "O kharaktere prosveshcheniia Evropy i ego otnoshenie k prosveshcheniiu Rossii" (On The Enlightenment in Europe and its Relationship to Enlightenment in Russia, 1852) and "O neobkhodimosti i vosmoshnosti novykh nachal dlia filosofii" (On the Necessity and Possibility of New Principles of Philosophy, 1856), which became the foundation for the unfolding of the Slavophile movement in Russian historical evolution.

Ivan Vasil'evich Kireevsky was born on 22 March 1806 in Moscow. Kireevsky's family belonged to the oldest nobility of the Belev-Kozel'sk area, where they owned properties acquired since 1600. Their main estate, the village of Dolbino, which had been in the Kireevsky family since the early seventeenth century, was located close to Belev. On 13 January 1805, thirty-two-year-old Vasilii Ivanovich Kireevsky, the owner of Dolbino and of one thousand souls, married sixteen-year-old

Avdot'ia Petrovna Iushkova, who was a granddaughter of a former governor of the Tula province, Afanasii Ivanovich Bunin. The latter's wife was a well-educated woman who provided an excellent education for her own daughters and granddaughters and also for Vasilii Andreevich Zhukovsky, one of the greatest Russian poets and her husband's illegitimate son by a Turkish girl he brought back from the wars.

The marriage of Vasilii Ivanovich Kireevsky and Iushkova brought together not only two noble Russian families but also two educated families endowed with literary talents and scientific interests. Kireevsky knew five languages and had a wonderful library including books in Russian, German, French, English, and Italian. In his youth he dedicated considerable time to translations and literary writings; as an adult his interest lay mainly in natural sciences. At Dolbino he built a chemistry laboratory, studied medicine, and had an informal medical practice. In 1812, during the Napoleonic Wars, the Kireevskys moved to Orel, where Vasilii Ivanovich transformed both his city and his country houses into hospitals. On 1 November 1812 he died of typhoid contracted at one of the hospitals during his service there.

Avdot'ia Petrovna Iushkova was a daughter of Varvara Afanaseevna Bunina-Iushkova, known for her poetic nature and musical talents. She was also a good actress and performed occasionally at the theater in Tula, where the Iushkov family spent its winters. Avdot'ia Petrovna inherited her mother's love for music and poetry. After Varvara's death in 1794 her daughters went to live with their grandmother Mme. Bunina at her estate, Mishenskoe, three versts from Belev. There Avdot'ia Petrovna became interested in the literature that she studied with her tutor, Filat Gavrilovich Pokrovsky; under the guidance of her governess, Mme. Dore, she improved her skills in French. The brilliant poet Vasilii Andreevich Zhukovsky, Avdot'ia Petrovna's close relative, played an important role in the evolution of her personality. They shared literary interests, and during her Moscow visits she met Zhukovsky's friends the Turgenevs and the Sokovinins. Following her marriage to Kireevsky, Avdot'ia Petrovna and her husband spent time reading and discussing serious historical novels. Five years after Kireevsky's death in 1812, she was to marry Aleksei Andreevich Elagin, a well-educated man and a scholar of German philosophy with some reputation as a translator of works by Friedrich Wilhelm Joseph von Schelling. Through him she deepened her interest in literature and became acquainted with philosophy. Avdot'ia Petrovna herself was an excellent translator of French and German and, according to Zhukovsky, had a beautiful writing style. In 1830 she founded a Russian literary and philosophical salon in her house in Moscow near *Krasnye Vorota* (Red Gates). Her salon was open to a broad range of writers, and she actively participated in the literary life of the period. She was close to and corresponded with Zhukovsky, Nikolai Ivanovich Gogol, Nikolai Mikhailovich Iazykov, Mikhail Petrovich Pogodin, and many others. This correspondence reflects the epoch with its major literary events and describes Avdot'ia Petrovna's life and the lives of her friends and writers.

After the death of Vasily Ivanovich Kireevsky, Avdot'ia Petrovna, together with her children—Ivan, Petr, and Maria—moved to Muratovo near Orel, the estate belonging to her grandparents. In the early summer of 1813 she decided to go back to Dolbino but, influenced by Zhukovsky, postponed her return and stayed in Muratovo until the spring of 1814. Tormented by his love for a niece who refused to marry him, Zhukovsky hastened after Avdot'ia Petrovna and joined her and her children at Dolbino, where he stayed until late in 1815.

Zhukovsky's presence was a strong influence on the development of Ivan's personality. Zhukovsky conveyed the feeling that literature plays a significant part in the life of an individual and that the creation of a high literary culture in Russia was a necessity to which Kireevsky could and should make a contribution. Later, after Zhukovsky left Dolbino, he remained spiritually close to Avdot'ia Petrovna and her sons, especially to Ivan. Zhukovsky was interested in Ivan's education and supportive of his later literary activities; Zhukovsky also protected Ivan from the vagaries of social life. By age ten, he was already well acquainted with the best of Russian literature and with classic French literature; at the age of twelve he was literate in German.

In 1817, when Ivan Kireevsky was eleven years old, his mother married her third cousin, Aleksei Andreevich Elagin. Because it was difficult to find suitable tutors, he received his education under the guidance of his stepfather and his mother. He learned mathematics, read historical and literary texts, and studied philosophy, an interest that was awakened by his stepfather. The latter had read Immanuel Kant's *Critique of Pure Reason* (1781) and the philosophy of Schelling, originally provided by his friend Professor Daniil Mikhailovich Vellansky of the University of St. Petersburg. Kireevsky's interest in philosophy went further, and while still in Dolbino he read the works of John Locke and Claude Adrien Helvétius that he found in his step-

Kireevsky's mother, Avdot'ia Petrovna Kireevskaia, in 1812

father's library. Kireevsky's studies were also enriched by Zhukovsky's reading recommendations: William Shakespeare, Sir Walter Scott, Adam Smith, David Hume, and the Scottish philosophers Dugald Stewart and Thomas Reid.

In 1822 Ivan Kireevsky's family moved to Moscow to continue the children's education. He did not attend the university there because that was not a place where the gentry sent their children; rather, he studied privately with Moscow University professors Ivan Mikhailovich Snegirev, who taught him Latin; Aleksei Fedorovich Merzliakov, who tutored him in literature; and Lev Alekseevich Tsvetaev, who guided his study of law and political economy. Kireevsky also studied Greek and attended public lectures given by Professor Mikhail Grigor'evich Pavlov, another follower of Schelling. In November 1824 Kireevsky took the "committee examination" necessary for entry into the state service and was accepted by the Archives Department of the Foreign Ministry in Moscow.

The "Young Men of the Archives"—Dmitrii Vladimirovich Venevitinov, Aleksandr Ivanovich Koshelev, Stepan Petrovich Shevyrev, Vladimir Pavlovich Titov, Prince Vladimir Fedorovich Odoevsky, and Nikolai Matveevich Rozhalin—were closely involved with two intellectual groups: the *kruzhok Raicha* (Raich circle) and the *Obshchestvo liubomudriia* (Society of the Lovers of Wisdom). Kireevsky belonged to both. The *kruzhok Raicha* circle gathered around Semen Egorovich Raich, a famous classical scholar and translator of Virgil; *Obshchestvo liubomudriia* evolved from literary afternoons at Professor Merzliakov's apartment. The former circle was public and mainly centered on literary discussions and the techniques of translation. *Obshchestvo liubomudriia* was private and its access limited. Discussions centered on German philosophy, and particularly the work of the Dutch philosopher Benedict de Spinoza. This group prudently terminated its activities shortly after the Decembrist revolt of 14 December 1825.

Around 1827 Kireevsky chose his future path. He wrote in a letter to Koshelev: "It seems to me that I can be more useful outside the civil service. . . . I can be a force in literature. Isn't the best deed to contribute to the education of the people? . . . I can and I will give literature its direction." In 1828 he resigned from the archives of the Foreign Ministry and began his literary and philosophical career. Kireevsky's first famous work, "Tsaritsynkaia noch" (Tsaritsyn Night, 1845), was written in 1827 at Petr Andreevich Viazemsky's behest for a literary evening at the home of Princess Zinaida Aleksandrovna Volkonskaia, herself a writer, singer, and composer. "Tsaritsynkaia noch" was published posthumously in Kireevsky's collected works (1861), edited by Koshelev.

"Tsaritsynkaia noch" is a short literary étude. It is an attempt to re-create an atmosphere that existed among Kireevsky's close friends, several of whom may have been a part of *Obshchestvo liubomudriia*. The style of the essay is somewhat ponderous and artificial, but it conveys the feeling of the unity and warmth that existed among members of the society. The essay finishes with a kind of poetic coda glorifying six stars—Faith, Love, Poetry, Freedom, Glory, and Friendship—and an unnamed but most important seventh star symbolizing the dedication of these young men united in their love of Mother Russia. The poem contains little of literary interest, but it illustrates the cultural and aesthetic attitudes of the period, especially those of the *Obshchestvo liubomudriia*.

Kireevsky's other literary and poetic writings were limited but promising. In 1830 he wrote a beautiful fairy tale, "Opal," also not published until 1861; while it has little significance for Kireevsky's later bibliography, which consists mainly of literary criticism and essays, it was a seminal creative work for later Russian writers. In a way the beginning of

Gogol's "Nevskii prospekt" (Nevsky Prospect), first published in *Arabeski* (1835), owes a debt to Kireevsky's "Opal," even though "Nevskii prospekt" is much more complex and its overall conclusion is entirely different from that of Kireevsky's work. In 1831 Kireevsky wrote "Otryvok iz romana: *Dve zhizni*" (An Extract from the Novel: Two Lives) and published it in 1834 in *Teleskop* (Telescope). It is a short but interesting piece in which Kireevsky examines the essence of beauty. For him real beauty was inseparable from the beauty of the soul. He believed that beauty must involve a harmony between inward and outward attributes. In 1838 Kireevsky began to write the unfinished novella *Ostrov* (An Island). It was not published until 1858, when it appeared in *Russkoe bogatstvo* (Russian Wealth). The novella, which has a certain ease and elegance, carries the seeds of future Slavophile thinking and emphasizes the importance of the Orthodox Church.

Kireevsky's verse is mainly limited to two poems: "Mitskevichu" (To Mickiewicz) and "Khor iz tragedii Andromakh" (Chorus from the Tragedy *Andromache,* 1831), published in 1830 in *Dennitsa, Almanakh* (Dawn, Almanac). "Mickiewicz" was written in 1828 on the occasion of Adam Mickiewicz's departure from Moscow to St. Petersburg and was read to him at a farewell soiree. Like Kireevsky's other creative writings, this poem reflects his interest and faith in the mystical aspects of existence and his belief in the eternity of friendship.

Kireevsky's principal literary fame came through his critical writings. His first critical article, "Nechto o kharaktere poezii Pushkina," appeared in 1828 in the *Moskovskii vestnik* (Moscow Herald), the journal formed by what was left of the *Obshchestvo liubomudriia*. This first critical study of Pushkin's poetical writing is perceptive, subtle, and profound. Kireevsky perceives Pushkin's works in all of their diversity. He divides Pushkin's poetry into three periods. In Pushkin's first period, his Italian-French stage, he is a pure *tvorets-poet* (poet-creator). In the second period he becomes the *poet-filosof* (poet-philosopher) and outlines his worldview. In the third period, which Kireevsky calls *Russko-Pushkinskoi poezii* (The Russian Poetry of Pushkin), Pushkin reveals his interest in Russian popular culture, although Kireevsly studies the foreign influences on Pushkin's poetry as well.

In the same year Kireevsky wrote another successful article, "Obozrenie russkoi slovesnosti za 1829 god" (A Survey of Russian Literature in 1829) and published it in the almanac *Dennitsa,* edited by his friend and former colleague in the archives, Mikhail Aleksandrovich Maksimovich. This article reveals Kireevsky's encyclopedic knowledge of contemporary Russian and Western European literature, history, and theater, as well as his astute literary intuition. He broadly reviews contemporary literary journals; includes a critical study of Pushkin's "Poltava" (1829); analyzes Zhukovsky's and Baron Anton Antonovich Del'vig's literary translations; describes French and German influences on Russian poetry; and assesses the condition of the Russian contemporary theater, which he believes must improve in quality and establish its own unique identity. This article was well received by Kireevsky's readers and praised by everyone except Zhukovsky, who disliked Kireevsky's systematic critical approach to literature. However, these two articles established Kireevsky's future path—the comparative study of Russian and Western cultures and their interaction.

In January 1830 Kireevsky left Moscow and went to Germany. His departure interrupted his literary work but was necessary because of his emotional condition. He had hoped to marry his second cousin, Natal'ia Petrovna Arbeneva, but her rejection of his proposal of marriage made him so unhappy that he felt he must leave the country. It was fortunate that at this time his younger brother, Petr, was studying in Munich, and Ivan could join him. On the way Kireevsky visited St. Petersburg for the first time and stayed with his friends Titov, Koshelev, and Odoevsky. He then went to Germany and Austria, where he lived in Dresden, Berlin, Munich, and Vienna. He attended lectures of Georg Wilhelm Friedrich Hegel in Berlin and of Schelling and Lorenz Oken in Munich. He also became a friend of Fedor Ivanovich Tiutchev, who at that time worked at the Russian Embassy in Bavaria. After having spent ten months in Germany, Kireevsky returned to Russia on 16 November. He had planned to go to Italy late in 1830 but returned to Russia out of concern that his family might have been victims of an outbreak of cholera in Moscow. Kireevsky was generally impressed by Europe and found its intellectual environment stimulating to his personal development; while in the West, however, he suffered from homesickness.

The year after his return to Russia, in the fall of 1831, Kireevsky began preparation for publication of the journal *Evropeets* (The European). The desire to publish a journal was born out of his wish to enrich Russian culture and "to give direction to the evolution of Russian literature." The journal's name reveals Kireevsky's intention to inform the most educated part of the Russian population concerning pertinent intellectual events that had taken place in Europe in the late eighteenth and early nine-

Kireevsky's uncle, Vasilii Andreev Zhukovsky, a poet who was a great influence on his nephew

teenth centuries. In September 1831 he asked permission from the Moscow Censorship Committee to edit a journal, and on 13 October the Main Administration of the Censorship granted his request. The first two issues of *Evorpeets* appeared in 1832. The main contributors were Zhukovsky, Evgenii Abramovich Baratynsky, Iazykov, and Kireevsky himself; Aleksei Stepanovich Khomiakov and Aleksandr Ivanovich Turgenev also participated in the publication. The centerpiece of the journal was Kireevsky's article "Deviatnadtsati vek" (The Nineteenth Century), accompanied by another Kireevsky essay, "Obozrenie russkoi literatury za 1831 god" (A Survey of Russian Literature in 1831).

The article "Deviatnadtsati vek" examines the place of Russia within a Western European cultural context, its period of Enlightenment, and its history—which Kireevsky calls *obshchechelovecheskoe prosveshchenie* (enlightenment common to all mankind). Kireevsky expresses the belief that Russian culture should blend with Western European culture. In describing the history and evolution of Western European culture Kireevsky attempts to explain and justify the lateness of Russian Enlightenment and express his faith in Russia's cultural future.

Kireevsky's views in this article are still remote from his later ideas regarding Russia's special and independent destiny. At this point in his life he still promoted a Russian future linked to that of Western Europe. Kireevsky's deep understanding of European culture, the questions that he raised, and the format of *Evropeets* represented a new way to approach the art of journalism. Regrettably, the end of the article was never published because the government suppressed the journal after the publication of the second issue. The reason given was unclear. The government used Kireevsky's article to accuse him of revolutionary activity, although this was never his intention. Count Aleksandr Khristoforovich Benckendorff, the chief of the third section, wrote to Karl Andreevich Lieven, the minister of public education:

> the entire article is . . . a discussion of high politics, in spite of the fact that the author himself asserts at the beginning that he is speaking not about politics, but about literature. One has only to read this article casually to see that the author . . . by the word "enlightenment" means freedom (*svoboda*), . . . the activity of the mind means revolution for him, and the skillfully contrived middle ground is nothing else but a constitution.

Kireevsky's other article, "*Gore ot uma*–na moskovskoi stsene" (Woe from Wit on the Moscow Stage, 1832), also caused problems with the authorities. His criticism of Russian admiration for everything foreign was taken as a criticism of foreigners in Russia. Several non-Russians in the government were offended by the article, particularly Count Benckendorff, who had difficulties in speaking correct Russian himself. It was only because Zhukovsky, who at that time was a tutor to children in the royal family, made an appeal to Dmitrii Vladimirovich Golitsyn, the Governor-General of Moscow, that Kireevsky was not arrested and possibly executed. The demise of *Evropeets* pained Kireevsky greatly; the depression that followed caused him to avoid involvement in literary activity for many years. Over the course of the next six years he spent most of his time in the country and published only two articles, "O stikhotvoreniiakh g. Iazykova" (On Iazykov's Poetry) in *Teleskop* (The Telescope) and "O russkikh pisatel'nitsakh" (On Russian Women Writers) in the almanac *Podarok bednym, Almanakh* (A Gift for the Poor). Both articles appeared in 1834, though the first article was signed "V-z" with no mention of Kireevsky's name. Shocked by the closing of his journal and the persecution of him as a writer and editor, Kireevsky was very secretive about the appearance of his new articles, especially the one on Iazykov's poetry. He hoped to publish it in one of the leading metropolitan journals such as *Telegraf* (Tele-

graph) and did not want the article to be rejected because of his unjustly ruined reputation.

Iazykov was one of Kireevsky's favorite poets. Kireevsky's readings of Iazykov not only elucidate the poetry to the reader but also bring out the critic's own profound understanding of and sensitivity to poetry in general and Iazykov's poetry in particular. The article gradually peels away layers of meaning to disclose the core of Iazykov's poetry as multidimensional and boundless. Kireevsky saw in Iazykov's poetry an aspiration to *dushevnii prostor* (the wide expanse of the soul). Iazykov's poetry had, in Kreevsky's opinion, "the effect of a divine wine that doubles life: one life is narrow, shallow and banal; the other is festive, poetic and spacious. The first oppresses the soul; the second frees it, elevates it and fills it with ecstasy." Kireevsky pictures Iazykov's poetry as a bridge between the two lives. Certain elements of life "make the soul go from one life to another: . . . love, glory, friendship, wine, thoughts about the Motherland, thoughts about poetry and . . . joy." The notion of two worlds and their union through creativity was later developed in Vladimir Sergeevich Solov'ev's works and became fundamental to understanding the Russian Symbolists. Kireevsky perceives Iazykov's poetry as one of the most beautiful expressions of the Russian language.

The article "O russkikh pisatel'nitsakh" appeared in 1834 under Kireevsky's name, but not in Moscow; it appeared in an almanac published in the provincial city of Odessa. Though the article praises and describes the poetic, prosaic, critical, and translating skills of particular women–such as Evdokiia Petrovna (Sushkova) Rostopchina, Zinaida Aleksandrovna Volkonskaia, Karolina Karlovna Pavlova, Ekaterina Aleksandrovna Timasheva, and Anna Davydovna (Abamelek-Lazareva) Baratynskaia–and discusses their contributions to Russian literature, it does not mention their names.

On 29 April 1834 Kireevsky married Natal'ia Petrovna Arbeneva, by whom he had six children: three daughters–Ekaterina, Aleksandra, and Maria–and three sons–Nikolai, Vasilii, and Sergei. Kireevsky found emotional and psychological stability and spiritual growth in his marriage. His psychological and spiritual conversion to the Russian Orthodox Church and his later Slavophile evolution can be traced to it. Natal'ia Petrovna was very pious; through her influence her confessor, Father Filaret (Vasilii Mikhailovich Drozdov, Metropolitan of Moscow), also became her husband's. Filaret introduced Kireevsky to the writings of the fathers of the Eastern Church. Kireevsky's readings in theology later led to his closeness with the monks of

Optina Monastery. An intriguing document, "The Story of the Conversion of Ivan Kireevsky," written in the hand of Koshelev, was found in Kireevsky's papers after his death. It describes the path of Kireevsky's "conversion." Mikhail Osipovich Gershenzon published this story in his edition of Kireevsky's collected works in 1911:

I. V. Kireevsky was married in 1834 to a girl, Natal'ia Petrovna Arbeneva, who had been brought up according to the dictates of strict Christian piety. In the period immediately following their marriage, her performance of the rites and customs of our church struck him unpleasantly; but with a customary patience and delicacy, he in no way hindered her in this observance. She, on her part, was even more sorrowful to observe his absence of belief and complete neglect of all the customs of the Russian Orthodox Church. There were conversations between them which ended in an agreement that he would not hinder her in her fulfillment of her obligations. He was to be free in his own actions, but promised her not to scoff at sacred things and even to put a complete stop to those conversations of his friends which were so unpleasant for her. In the second year of their marriage, he asked his wife to read *Cousin*. She did this eagerly, but when he began to ask her opinion about this book, she said that there was much in it that was good, but she found nothing new, for all of it was set forth in a much deeper and more satisfying way in the writings of the Church Fathers. He smiled and was silent. He began to ask his wife to read Voltaire with him. She declared to him that she was ready to read any serious book which he recommended to her, but raillery or any kind of scoffing at the sacred was alien to her, and she could neither listen to nor read such things. Sometime after that they began to read Schelling together, and when his great, luminous thoughts appeared at the end, I. V. Kireevsky turned to his wife, expecting her to be surprised. She answered him forthwith that these thoughts were known to her from the writings of Church Fathers. More than once she pointed out in the works of the Church Fathers that which sometimes compelled I. V. to read whole pages. It was unpleasant for him to have to admit that really a great deal of what had so enraptured him in Schelling was in the Church Fathers. He would surreptitiously take his wife's books and read them with enthusiasm, although he did not like to admit to having done so.

Acquaintance with the Novospassky monk, Filaret, conversations with the holy *starets* (elder), and the reading of various works of the Church Fathers delighted him and drew him to the side of piety. He would go to Fr. Filaret, but always as if under duress. It was evident that he wanted to go to him, but always felt some kind of constraint. Finally the death of the elder Filaret in 1842 confirmed him once and for all in the path of piety.

Ivan Kireevsky had never worn a cross. His wife had asked him about this more than once, but I. V. would fall silent. At length, however, he said to her that he

Kireevsky's brother, Petr Vasil'evich

would wear a cross if it were sent to him by Fr. Filaret, whose intelligence and piety he already prized highly. Na. Petr. went to Fr. Filaret and communicated this to him. The elder, crossing himself, took off his own cross and gave it to Nat. Petr. saying "May it work to his salvation." When Natal'ia Petrovna came home, I. V. met her and asked: "Well, what did Father Filaret say?" She took out the cross and gave it to I. V., who asked her: "What sort of cross is this?" Nat. Petr. said that Fr. Filaret had taken it from his own person and said "Let it work to his salvation." I. V. fell on his knees and said: "Well now I hope for the salvation of my soul, for it must be that if Fr. Filaret has taken off his cross and sent it to me, God has clearly called me to salvation." From this moment, a decisive change in I. V.'s thoughts and feelings was perceptible.

At this period of his life Kireevsky also became sensitive and open to the views of his brother, Petr, and to the views of his friend Khomiakov, who valued Russia's unique historical and cultural destiny more than anything else. In 1839 at the Elagin Salon, in his talk "V otvet A. S. Khomiakovu" (An Answer to Khomiakov), Kireevsky set forth theses for the future evolution of Slavophile thinking. He emphasized the impossibility and senselessness of Russia's attempt to free itself from its European past, given the European influence on its development. He also stressed the role the Russian Orthodox

Church played in the Enlightenment of Russia and contrasted it to the role Catholicism played in the Enlightenment in Western Europe. He expressed a belief that religion must establish a harmonious balance between reason and faith yet did not see this harmony in the Roman faith. He saw it flourishing only in Russian Orthodoxy. He perceived Catholicism as a religion of reason, which he considered the equivalent of godlessness, the source of many undesirable developments in European history. In contrast, he saw that the Eastern Church in its reliance on faith had accepted God without recourse to reason and had avoided similar destructive effects on Russian cultural history and the Russian people. He believed that Russia had its own path, which should combine the aspects of European culture that had already passed through the consciousness of Russian people and the richness of Russian religious identity existing in the mystical body of the Russian Orthodox Church. This talk was published in the first edition of his *Polnoe sobranie sochinenii* (Collected Works) in 1861.

During 1839, when Kireevsky occupied the position of honorary supervisor of the chief school of the Belev district, he wrote to Count Sergei Grigor'evich Stroganov, the trustee of the Moscow Educational District, "Zapiska o napravlenii i metodakh pervonachal'nogo obrazovaniia narodov v Rossii" (A Note about Methods of Primary Education of People in Russia). In 1840 Kireevsky attempted to obtain a position at the department of philosophy at Moscow University, without success. According to Gershenzon, Kireevsky was not retained because of problems that he had encountered with the authorities over *Evropeets*. According to Abbott Gleason, Kireevsky was denied the position because he lacked the systematized preparation necessary to be a professor at the university. Perhaps both reasons worked against Kireevsky's appointment.

In 1845 he returned to his journalistic career; on the invitation of Pogodin, Kireevsky joined the editorial staff of the Pogodin's journal, *Moskvitianin*. Though Kireevsky became an editor, he never received an official authorization from the government to occupy this position; nevertheless, he published three issues in 1845; wrote a significant article in three parts, "Obozrenie sovremennogo russkoi literatury" (A Survey of the State of Modern Literature); and composed book reviews.

"Obozrenie" spanned three issues of the *Moskvitianin* and is a model of scholarship. In it Kireevsky demonstrates his deep and intuitive understanding of Russian literature, language, and culture, analyzed from his well-conceived philosophical position. The article is divided into three parts. In the first part Kireevsky gives an overview of Western European literature and philosophy and concludes that this culture has exhausted itself; it lacks ideas and is full of empty rhetoric. Western European culture, he says, needs the revitalization that can come only through fresh, external influences. Kireevsky proposes Russia as the obvious source for the rebirth of European culture, which needs the essence of Russia's Christianity to survive. In the second part of the article Kireevsky argues that while this Russian essence is inseparable from certain aspects of Western European culture, it does not follow that Russia should be led blindly by Western Europe. Russia has incorporated European influences but has also developed a unique Russian cultural identity heavily invested in the Eastern Church. If Russia is to take her place as a cultural, and especially spiritual, leader in the world, it must direct its future development by carefully incorporating Western influences into its own unique cultural and religious heritage without losing its own special character. In the third part of the article Kireevsky surveys the contemporary journals and endeavors to show that none of them has established a determined philosophical direction. Though some of them appear to have succeeded in defining their philosophical stance, this success is an illusion; their philosophical bearings change with the winds of fashion and suffer from a lack of real erudition. Kireevsky ends his article by identifying a new and determined trend in Russian literature: Christian Slavs, he thinks, will liberate Russia from its dependency and worship of Western European culture and will guide it in expanding its own inner richness. Kireevsky's first written comprehensive expression of his fully articulated position on Russia and the West, this article communicates the fundamental ideas of Russian Slavophiles. At the end of 1845, because of health reasons and a disagreement with Pogodin, Kireevsky resigned from his position at the *Moskvitianin*. Thus began a literary hiatus of more than seven years.

1846 was a sad year for the Kireevsky-Elagin family. Both Kireevsky's daughter Ekaterina and his dear friend Iazykov died that year, and A. A. Elagin suffered a fatal stroke. As a result Kireevsky felt a necessity for solitude and turned to spiritual life for his salvation. He became close to the monks of Optina Monastery, located forty versts (approximately 26 miles) from Dolbino. The major intellectual influence on him at this time was a monk of the

The prominent Slavophile Aleksei Stepanovich Khomiakov (fifth from left) and his friends; Kireevsky is fourth from left (from Peter K. Christoff, An Introduction to 19th Century Russian Slavophilism, *1961)*

Optina Monastery, *starets* (elder) Makarii; Filaret, his predecessor as Kireevsky's spiritual advisor, had died in 1842. Kireevsky's new field of activity became the study, translation, and publication of the writings of the Eastern Church under the guidance of and in collaboration with Father Makarii. The first fruit of this effort appeared in 1847: *Zhizn' i trudy Moldavskogo Startsa Paisiia Velichkovskogo* (The Life and Works of the Moldavian Elder Paisy Velichkovsky). Paisy Velichkovsky was a Russian mystic who greatly renewed Russian spiritual life in the eighteenth century. His biography and the translations of his works by the fathers, edited by Kireevsky and Father Makarii, were published in 1849.

Kireevsky published his next article, "O kharaktere prosveshcheniia Evropy i ego otnoshenii k prosveshcheniiu Rossii" (On the Character of the Enlightenment of Europe and Its Relationship to the Enlightenment of Russia), in 1852. While preparing to write this article, Kireevsky read widely in the areas of patriotic literature, Russian spirituality (works by Nil Sorsky, Velichkovsky, and Tikhon of Voronezh), and mystical writings of the Orthodox canon, including works of Isaac the Syrian, Simeon the New Theologian, Maximus the Confessor, and Gregory Palamas. The article appeared in the Slavophile journal *Moskovskii sbornik* (Moscow Miscellany) published by Ivan Sergeevich Aksakov in the form of a letter to his friend Egor Evgafovich Koma-

rovsky. Like his previous articles, this "epistle" demonstrates Kireevsky's impressive erudition. However, the most striking aspect of the article lies in Kireevsky's complete change of philosophical understanding of Russia's place within world culture. Rather than acknowledge Western influence in Russia's cultural development as he had previously, Kireevsky minimizes the importance of Western European culture on Russian society and claims for Russia a rich and unique cultural heritage. The essence of this culture is based in the religious teaching of the Fathers of the Eastern Church, which had retained the purity of Christ's teachings after the separation of the Roman and Eastern churches. Kireevsky sees the role of Russian culture as evangelical; Russia's mystical spirituality, he believed, would save Europe.

In the article "I.V. Kireevsky i tsenzura *Moskovskogo sbornika* 1852 god" (I.V. Kireevsky and the censorship of the *Moscow Miscellany,* 1852), published in *Russkii Arkhiv* (Russian Archive) in 1897, Mikhail Alekseevich Venevitinov notes that censors drastically cut the first version of Kireevsky's article, which did not appear in complete form until the publication of his collected works in 1911. The article evoked several antagonistic reactions among Kireevsky's fellow Slavophiles. While Khomiakov agreed with Kireevsky's general idea about the difference between the cultural inheritance of the West and the East, he could not accept Kireevsky's idealization of the Russian historical past. He prepared a response to Kireevsky's article, "Po povodu stat'i I.V. Kireevskogo" (On the Occasion of I. V. Kireevsky's Article) that was scheduled to appear in the second issue of *Moskovskii sbornik* but appeared in 1878 in Khomiakov's complete collected works. The second issue of *Moskovskii sbornik* was never published because the government found the journal dangerous.

Kireevsky's last years were not satisfying. Not happy with his own accomplishments, he felt that everything in his life—his family, his financial situation, the upbringing of his children—was in disorder. He attributed such personal chaos to "the disorder" of his "inner force." Emotionally paralyzed by self-discontent, he gave way to melancholy and passivity. Though he spent the years between 1851 and 1855 in Moscow, his social and intellectual life remained empty, though the Kireevskys occasionally hosted literary readings at their home. However, Kireevsky maintained his interest in education, and in 1854 in a note to Count Stroganov, Minister of Education, he stressed the need to teach Church Slavonic in the district schools.

Kireevsky's last important work, his article "O neobkhodimosti i vosmoshnosti novykh nachal dlia filosofii" (On the Necessity and Possibility of New Sources for Philosophy), appeared posthumously in 1856 in the Slavophile periodical *Russkaia beseda* (Russian Colloquy), edited by Koshelev and Aksakov. This article in many ways continues Kireevsky's "O kharaktere proisveshcheniia Evropy." By examining the history of Europe, Kireevsky endeavors to prove that contemporary European ideas lead nowhere because they are nothing but a rhetorical mind game. He is convinced that Europe needs greater spirituality; he sees proof of this need in Shelling's attempt to create his own religion in his philosophy. Kireevsky emphasizes the obvious differences between philosophy and religion, and as he had stated previously, he believes salvation comes only when humanity returns to God, to the essence of real mystical religion—that is, the Eastern Church. He reasserts his earlier claim that European rationality is destructive: "If that rationality could realize its limits and be able to conceive itself only as a tool necessary to discover the truth, and not as the *ne plus ultra* of human existence, then that rationality would see itself in the appropriate conditional and limited way, beneficial to humanity." For the Eastern Church to be accepted by Western culture, however, Kireevsky believes Western culture must relinquish the Roman Church. According to Khomiakov, "O neobkhodimosti" was not fin-

ished because it was interrupted by Kireevsky's death. Khomiakov believes a final version would have been not only "a critique of the historical development of philosophy" but also "a systematic working out of new principles."

On 10 June 1856 Kireevsky contracted cholera while he was visiting his son Vasilii in St. Petersburg during Vasilii's final examination at the Lyceum. Kireevsky died two days after. At the moment of his death he was surrounded by his St. Petersburg friends, Venevitinov and Count Komarovsky, and his son. He was buried at the Optina Monastery. The following words were written on his grave: "I loved wisdom and sought her out from my youth. . . Nevertheless, when I perceived that I could not otherwise obtain her, except God should give her me, I prayed unto the Lord and sought him with my whole heart."

Russia's repressive political atmosphere acted negatively on Kireevsky. Political circumstances prevented his realizing all his immense literary and philosophical potential and completing all that he sought to accomplish. One of his plans was to write "Istoriia drevnego khristianstva do V ili VI vekov" (A History of Ancient Christianity up to the Fifth or Sixth Century), but this volume never materialized. While Kireevsky did not leave a large literary legacy in volume, his work remains an essential part of Russian cultural development and has had a major impact on the later development of Russian philosophy and literature. The resurgence of interest in Orthodox theology at the end of the nineteenth century evolved from Kireevsky's writings. Kireevsky's concept of anti-rationalism became a central theme in the works of Fyodor Dostoyevsky and a basic principle of the writings of Vladimir Sergeevich Solov'ev, Sergei Nikolaevich Bulgakov, Nikolai Aleksandrovich Berdiaev, Lev Shestov, and other Russian philosophers. His perception of genuine beauty and understanding of genuine literature inspired the trend in Russian literature that opposed civic literature and literary criticism and reached its apogee in the works of the Russian Symbolists.

Unfortunately, Kireevsky's universality—his aspiration to ennoble not only Russia but also the entire world—was not accepted by either his contemporaries or the next generation of Russian Slavophiles. Just as National Socialism expropriated the symbols of nineteenth-century German nationalism without its ideals, those involved in late-nineteenth- and early-twentieth-century Russian social movements became Slavophiles in name, but without Kireevsky's nobility and idealism. Perhaps Russia's gradual return to its rich cultural heritage and its renewed interest in pre-Soviet historical, theological, and philosophical writings will restore Kireevsky to his rightful place as one of Russia's leading thinkers of the nineteenth century.

Letters:

To A. M. Iazykov, *Russkaia starina,* 39 (September 1883): 633–634; *Russkii arkhiv,* no. 10 (1897): 208–210;

To A. A. Elagin, "Pis'ma brat'ev Kireevskikh," *Russkii archiv,* no. 10, (1894): 208–210;

To Zhukovsky, "Pis'ma k V. A. Zhukovskomu raznikh lits," *Russkaia starina,* 115 (August 1903): 452–454; *Russkii arkhiv,* no. 4, (1909): 600; *Blagonamerennyi,* no. 1 (1926): 143–146;

To Prince Vladimir Odoevsky, "Iz perepiski kniazia V. F. Odoevskogo," *Russkaia starina,* 118 (April 1904): 215–217;

Russkii Arkhiv, no. 12 (1906): 571–595; no. 5 (1909): 95–114;

To Koshelev, "Pis'ma I.V. Kireevskogo k A. I. Koshelevu," *Russkii arkhiv,* no. 5 (1909): 99, 104;

To S. P. Shevyrev, *Golos minuvshego,* no. 7 (July 1914): 220–224;

"Kireevsky's letters to Father Makary," edited by S. I. Chetverikov, *Optina Pustyn'* (Paris: YMCA Press, 1926);

To Aleksandr Sergeevich Pushkin in his *Polnoe sobranie sochineny,* 14 (Moscow: Akademiia nauk SSSR, 1941), p. 328; 15 (Moscow: Akademiia nauk SSSR, 1948), pp.19–20.

Biographies:

Valerii Liaskovsky, *Brat'ia Kireevskie, zhizn' i trudy ikh* (St. Petersburg, 1899);

Aleksandr G. Lushnikov, *Ivan Vasil'evich Kireevsky* (Kazan', 1918);

Eberhard Muller, *Russischer Intellect in europaischer Krise: Ivan V. Kireevskii* (Cologne: Bohlau, 1966);

Abbott Gleason, *European and Moscovite: Ivan Kireevsky and the Origins of Slavophilism* (Cambridge, Mass.: Harvard University Press, 1972).

References:

Peter K. Christoff, "I. V. Kireevsky," in *An Introduction to Nineteenth-Century Russian Slavophilism: A Study in Ideas,* volume 2 (The Hague: Mouton, 1972);

Mikhail Osipovich Gershenzon, "Uchenie o lichnosti: I. V. Kireevsky," in *Istoricheskie zapiski* (Berlin: Gelikon, 1923);

Albert Gratieux, *A. S. Khomiakov et le mouvement Slavophile* (Paris: Editions du Cerf, 1939);

Vasil'evich Ivanov-Razumnik, *Istoriia russkoi obshchestvennoi mysli* (St. Petersburg: M. M. Stasiulevich, 1908);

"Kireevsky, Ivan Vasilevich," *Russkie pisateli 1800–1917, biographicheskii slovar',* volume 2 (Moscow: Nauchnoe izdatel'stvo "Bol'shafa rossiiskaia èntsiklopediia" fianit, 1992): 534–538;

Georgii Alekseevich Kniazev, *Brat'ia Kireevskie* (St. Petersburg, 1898);

Nil Petrovich Koliupanov, *Biografiia Kosheleva* (Moscow: O. F. Kosheleva, 1889–1892);

Veiiacheslav Anatolevich Koshelev, *Esteticheskoe I literaturnoe vozzrenie russkogo slavianofil'stva, 1840–1850* (Leningrad: Nauka, 1984);

M. Kovalevsky, "Rannie revniteli filosofii Shellinga v Rossii, Chaadaev i Ivan Kireevsky," *Russkaia mysl'* (December 1916): 115–135;

Alexandre Koyré, *Etudes sur l'histoire de la pensee philosophique en Russie* (Paris: J. Vrin, 1950);

Henry Lanz, "The Philosophy of Ivan Kireevsky," *Slavonic Review,* 4 (1926): 594–604;

Iurii Mann, "Esteticheskaia èvoliutsiia I. Kireevskogo," in *Kritika i èstetika* by I. V. Kireevsky (Moscow: Iskusstvo, 1979);

Nicholas Riasanovsky, *Russia and the West in the Teaching of the Slavophiles* (Gloucester, Mass.: Peter Smith, 1965);

N. I. Tsymbaev, *Slavianofil'stvo. Iz istorii russkoi obshchestvenno-politicheskoi mysli XIX veka* (Moscow: Moskovskii universitet, 1986);

Andrzej Walicki, *The Slavophile Controversy: History of a Conservative Utopia in Nineteenth-Century Russian Thought,* translated by Hilda Andrews-Rusiecka (South Bend, Ind. & London: University of Notre Dame Press, 1989).

Ivan Ivanovich Lazhechnikov
(14 September 1790 or 1792 – 26 June 1869)

Veronica Shapovalov
San Diego State University

BOOKS: *Pervye opyty v proze i stikhakh* (Moscow: Moskovskii Universitet, 1817);

Pokhodnye zapiski russkago ofitsera (St. Petersburg, 1820);

Poslednii Novik, ili Zavoevanie Lifliadii v tsarstvovanie Petra Velikago. Istoricheskii roman, 4 parts (Moscow, 1831–1833);

Ledianoi dom (Moscow, 1835);

Basurman (Moscow, 1838);

Sobranie sochinenii, 8 volumes (St. Petersburg: P. I. Krashennikov, 1857–1858);

Gorbun (St. Petersburg, 1858);

Nemnogo let nazad (Moscow, 1862);

Oprichnik (Moscow, 1867);

Vnuchka pantsyrnogo boiarina (St. Petersburg, 1868).

Editions and Collections: *Sochineniia. Posmertnoe polnoe izdanie,* 12 volumes (St. Petersburg & Moscow: M. O. Vol'f, 1883–1884);

Sochineniia v dvukh tomakh (Moscow: Khudozhestvennaia literatura, 1963).

Editions in English: *The Heretic,* translated by Thomas B. Shaw (3 volumes, Edinburgh & London: Blackwood, 1844; 1 volume, New York: Harper, 1844);

The Palace of Ice, translated from the French of Alexandre Dumas by H. L. Williams (New York: E. D. Long, 1860);

The Russian Gipsy; or, the Palace of Ice (London: Henry Lea, 1861).

PLAY PRODUCTIONS: *Gorbun,* Moscow, Malyi Teatr, 1853;

Okopirovalsia, St. Petersburg, Aleksandrinskii Teatr, November 1854; Moscow, Malyi Teatr, November 1854;

Oprichnik, St. Petersburg, Aleksandrinskii Teatr, 1867; and Moscow, Malyi Teatr, 1867;

Materi-sopernitsy, St. Petersburg, Aleksandrinskii Teatr, 1868; Moscow, Malyi Teatr, 1868.

One of the most popular historical novelists of his time, Ivan Ivanovich Lazhechnikov was, according to D. S. Mirsky's *History of Russian Literature* (1949),

Ivan Ivanovich Lazhechnikov, circa 1835 (portrait by A. Tiranov; from William Edward Brown, A History of Russian Literature of the Romantic Period, *1986)*

"the best of Russian Scottists." His mix of patriotism, sensationalism, complex characters, moral sense, and wealth of historical detail appealed to the Romantic reader in Russia. In spite of his language, which some call "colorless," and his prolix, ponderous prose, he could tell a good story with ease. Though he did not advance Russian prose beyond its sentimental-Romantic boundaries, most critics agree that Lazhechnikov was the best of the historical writers of the period, with the exception of Aleksandr Pushkin.

Ivan Ivanovich Lazhechnikov was born on 14 September 1790 or 1792 into a wealthy merchant family in Kolomna, near Moscow. His father was one of the richest bread-and-salt merchants in the area, and the Lazhechnikovs were one of the oldest merchant families in town. Lazhechnikov's family must have seemed unusual against the background of the uneducated "dark kingdom" of the merchant class at the end of the eighteenth century. Not only did the family have a large, beautiful house in Kolomna, but they also owned an estate, Krasnoe Sel'tso, not far from there. Local nobility, as well as government officials from Moscow, often came to the Lazhechnikov home to enjoy lavish receptions and an amateur orchestra. Lazhechnikov's father zealously believed in education, a belief intensified by his acquaintance with Nikolai Ivanovich Novikov, a pioneering journalist, philosopher, critic, and publisher. The friendship with Novikov refined the senior Lazhechnikov's taste in reading and inspired him to give his son the best possible education. Unfortunately this friendship also played an important role in the downfall of the family. In the summer of 1799 Lazhechnikov's father was arrested for "free thought" and incarcerated first in Moscow and later in the Peter and Paul Fortress in St. Petersburg. The priest who taught Russian to the Lazhechnikov children had denounced their father in the hope of a reward.

Lazhechnikov's mother, a beautiful woman pampered by both her parents and her husband, was brave and strong willed. Although she could barely read and write, she used the family's connections to find influential protectors in St. Petersburg—the Princes Kurakin and Lobanovo-Rostovsky, who pleaded her husband's case before Tsar Paul I. Their efforts, in addition to great sums of money, set the prisoner free within a short time; the priest who had denounced Lazhechnikov's father was demoted and transferred to a parish far from Kolomna. Lazhechnikov's father was freed in September on St. Michael's Day, and from then on the family celebrated this event annually. For Lazhechnikov his father's temporary imprisonment had mysterious and exotic overtones and intensified his interest in Romantic adventures. The tragic aspect of this event was not obvious to him until many years later. The imprisonment of Lazhechnikov's father had cost the family a great deal because the business had been left unattended for almost a year. This neglect, coupled with the poor weather conditions of 1811, contributed to the ruin of the Lazhechnikov family, who found themselves in 1812 in a state of almost total bankruptcy.

In spite of these difficulties, Lazhechnikov received a good education at home and developed early a love for reading, familiarizing himself first with Russian, then with French and German literature. At the recommendation of Novikov, Lazhechnikov's father

hired a French tutor for his son. Monsieur Beaulieu, a graduate of Strasbourg University, taught Lazhechnikov and his older brother French, German, the sciences, and drawing. At that time Lazhechnikov's favorite authors were Jean-Jacques Rousseau, Voltaire, Jean Racine, Tacitus, Titus Livius, and Friedrich Schiller. He read both French and German writers in the original languages. When he was fourteen he began his first literary experiments in French, at that time a rather common occurrence. He wrote a description of Miachnov Hill, located on the road from Kolomna to Moscow and famous for the historical legends connected with it. In the following year, 1807, Lazhechnikov's essay titled "Moi mysli" (My Thoughts) was published by the critic and translator Mikhail Trofimovich Kachenovsky in the journal *Vestnik Evropy* (The Herald of Europe). "Moi mysli" imitated the seventeenth-century classical French author Jean de La Bruyère and was written in the spirit of the French Enlightenment.

Even before his literary debut Lazhechnikov began to work in the Moscow Archives of the Ministry of Foreign Affairs. This work helped fire his passion for history. While working there Lazhechnikov continued his education and took private lessons with two professors of Moscow University, Aleksei Fedorovich Merzliakov and Petr Vasil'evich Pobedonostsev. In 1810 Lazhechnikov left the archives and began to work at the office of the general-governor of Moscow. This change, however, did not prevent him from continuing both his education and his literary work.

Soon Lazhechnikov's compositions began to appear in *Vestnik Evropy, Russkii vestnik* (Russian Herald) and *Aglaia. Russkii vestnik* was published from 1808 to 1824 by Sergei Nikolaevich Glinka, a poet, translator, and dramatist opposed to the Francomania that flourished in the circles of the nobility; instead he endeavored to awaken Russian patriotic sentiments. *Aglaia* was published by Petr Ivanovich Shalikov, a poet and a journalist who followed the traditions of sentimental literature.

Lazhechnikov's early works belong to the sentimentalist tradition. Although still unoriginal and undeveloped, these works nevertheless include the antidespotic and patriotic themes that would later play such a dominant role in Lazhechnikov's novels. One of his earliest experiments was a patriotic poem, "Voennaia pesn'" (The War Song), which had the subtitle "The Slavo-Russian Woman Sends Her Only Son Off to War." Published in 1808 in *Russkii vestnik,* the poem deserves mention because it seems to foretell the actual situation in which Lazhechnikov was to find himself only four years later when he ran away from his parents' home to join the army. The publication of this poem, which for the first time bore Lazhechnik-

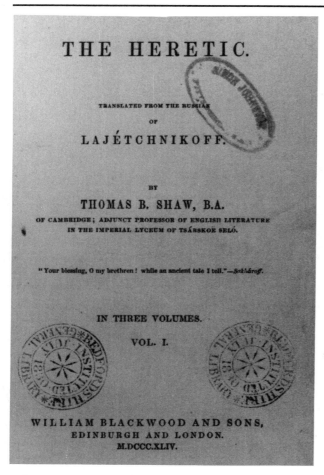

THE HERETIC.

TRANSLATED FROM THE RUSSIAN

OF

LAJÉTCHNIKOFF.

BY

THOMAS B. SHAW, B.A.

OF CAMBRIDGE; ADJUNCT PROFESSOR OF ENGLISH LITERATURE
IN THE IMPERIAL LYCEUM OF TSÁRSKOE SELÓ.

"Your blessing, O my brethren! while an ancient tale I tell."—*Sakhároff.*

IN THREE VOLUMES.

VOL. I.

WILLIAM BLACKWOOD AND SONS,
EDINBURGH AND LONDON.
M.DCCC.XLIV.

Title page for an English translation of Lazhechnikov's 1838 historical novel, Basurman

ceived a medal for his participation in the capture of Paris.

During his participation in the final stage of the Patriotic War and the military activities in Europe in 1813–1814 and 1815, Lazhechnikov observed the life and culture of Poland, Germany, France, and the Baltic areas, comparing the latter to scenes from Russian life. He spent the winter of 1814–1815 in Derpt, where he met the poet Vasilii Ivanovich Zhukovsky as well as Aleksandr Fedorovich Voeikov, a poet, critic, journalist, and the publisher of *Syn otechestva* (Son of the Fatherland), *Russkii invalid* (Russian Invalid), and other periodicals. Lazhechnikov read to them excerpts from his new work, *Pokhodnye zapiski russkago ofitsera* (Travel Notes of a Russian Officer, serialized 1817–1820). Both Zhukovsky and Voeikov encouraged Lazhechnikov to continue his literary work. At their suggestion he wrote a chapter on the history of the city of Derpt. In *Pokhodnye zapiski* he developed his interest in history and his desire to compare and contrast the past with the present. Many notes and observations in the book illustrate Lazhechnikov's ideological closeness to the cultural and political movements that culminated in the Decembrists. Lazhechnikov dedicated his work to Empress Elizaveta Alekseevna, who accepted it and presented him with a gold watch. *Pokhodnye zapiski* enjoyed a significant success at the time and upon demand was republished in 1836.

In 1817 Lazhechnikov published his first collection of works that had previously appeared separately in journals. The collection was titled *Pervye opyty v proze i stikhakh* (First Experiments in Prose and Poetry). The collection was divided into three parts: *Povesti* (Stories), *Rassuzhdeniia* (Thoughts), and *Stikhi* (Poems). The first part included such stories as the sentimental "Spasskaia Luzhaika" (The Spassky Glade) and the historical short story "Malinovka." In his autobiographical essay Lazhechnikov admitted that these stories were imitations of Nikolai Mikhailovich Karamzin's "Bednaia Liza" (Poor Liza) and "Natalia, boiarskaia doch" (Natalia, the Boyar's Daughter), which had both appeared in *Moskovskii zhurnal* (Moscow Journal) in 1792. "Spasskaia Luzhaika," a sentimental story of tragic love, must be viewed within the context of late Russian sentimentalism. Since the story was published after the Patriotic War, when sentimentalism gave way to Romanticism and the tastes of the reading public changed rapidly and dramatically, the story has never been appreciated. "Malinovka," a love story set in the times of Boris Godunov, was Lazhechnikov's first experiment in the genre of an historical story. Because he had no predecessors in this genre, he used the clichés of sentimental prose. Although artistically "Malinovka" is far from perfect, it should be viewed as a first step in the development of Russian

ov's full name, made the author "happy for a few days," and inspired him to further literary experiments. He published several poems and stories in *Aglaia.*

Overtaken by patriotic sentiments in 1812, Lazhechnikov ran away to join the Russian army. His patriotic feelings, brought on by Napoleon Bonaparte's capture of Moscow, were expressed with great force and sincerity in his essay "Novobranets 1812" (The Recruit of 1812). In this autobiographical essay he wrote that he applied to enter the army and was waiting for parental permission. He was eager to fight the enemy of his motherland, but instead of the expected permission, he received an order from his father to come home immediately. Regardless of the consequences, he decided to disobey his father and join the army. After many setbacks Lazhechnikov was first accepted as an officer in the Moscow defense, then subsequently transferred to the Moscow grenadier troops. He experienced the campaign of 1813–1814 in the capacity of a deputy commander to the Second Grenadier division. Lazhechnikov re-

historical narration. *Pervye opyty* was not successful and received no notice from either critics or the reading public. Lazhechnikov bought and destroyed almost all copies of the book, thus making *Pervye opyty* a bibliographical rarity.

In 1818 Lazhechnikov was appointed aide-de-camp to Count Aleksander Ivanovich Osterman-Tolstoi, the head of the Grenadiers corps, and was sent to Warsaw. During the winter of 1819–1820 Lazhechnikov lived in St. Petersburg in the house of the count, where he catalogued books and manuscripts on military history in the count's famous library, which had been collected under the guidance of military theorist Gen. Antoine Henri Jomini. It was the work in this library that prompted Lazhechnikov to start his novel about the times of Peter the Great. In December 1819 Lazhechnikov resigned from the army and soon thereafter married Count Osterman-Tolstoi's distant relative, Avdotia Alekseevna Shurupova, who had been brought up in the count's family.

Also in 1819 Lazhechnikov met Pushkin, of whom he was a devoted fan, and even prevented the poet's duel with Major Denisevich. Lazhechnikov later wrote about this event in his autobiographical sketch "Znakomstvo moe s Pushkinym" (My Acquaintance with Pushkin), published in February 1856 in Mikhail Nikiforovich Katkov's *Russkii vestnik,* a new journal with the same name as Glinka's publication. Although Lazhechnikov and Pushkin never met again after December 1819, they occasionally corresponded. Lazhechnikov sent Pushkin first editions of his novels as well as an historical manuscript about the Pugachev uprising. Pushkin admired Lazhechnikov's novels, although he reproached the author for distorting historical truth.

After his discharge from the military, Lazhechnikov began to work at the Ministry of Education, where he continued with few interruptions until 1837. In 1820 he was appointed director of public schools in Penza. He found the schools in neglect and disarray and worked hard to raise the level of education in the gymnasium. He not only hired new teachers but also opened a library as well as science and natural-history laboratories, and in 1821 he helped to open two more schools in the Penza district. During the course of his work he had occasion to meet the future literary critic Vissarion Grigor'evich Belinsky, who at that time was a second-form student in one of the schools Lazhechnikov helped to open. Lazhechnikov was favorably impressed with Belinsky's independence and intelligence, and in time this acquaintance turned into friendship. In the 1830s, when the aspiring young critic had financial problems, Lazhechnikov took care of him and found him a position as literary secretary for Aleksandr Markovich Poltoratsky, who published

humorous stories under the pen name Dormedon Vasil'evich Prutikov. Belinsky in turn sought to promote Lazhechnikov's career as a novelist. Many years later, after Belinsky's death, Lazhechnikov helped the critic's family. The history of this friendship is told in Lazhechnikov's sketch "Zametki dlia biografii Belinskogo" (Notes for the Biography of Belinsky, 1859), which first appeared in *Moskovskii vestnik* (Moscow Herald).

In December 1823 Lazhechnikov was appointed director of public schools for the Kazan' *guberniia* (district) and director of the Imperial Kazan' Gymnasium. Both in Penza and Kazan', Lazhechnikov worked under the supervision of the administrator of the local educational district, Mikhail Leont'evich Magnitsky, who was famous for his conservatism and obscurantism. Lazhechnikov's dedication to his work, as well as his warm and friendly personality, helped him to win the respect of Magnitsky. Of course Lazhechnikov's close relations to the powerful Osterman-Tolstoi, as well as the recognition of the Empress Elizaveta Alekseevna, played an important role in Magnitsky's attitude toward Lazhechnikov.

Lazhechnikov tried to use his positive relationship with Magnitsky to promote education and high culture as much as he could, not only in the educational establishments but also in the city of Kazan'. He played a key role in the erection of a monument to the Russian poet Gavrila Romanovich Derzhavin, who had been a student in the Kazan' Gymnasium. In January 1826 Lazhechnikov was appointed inspector of students at Kazan' University. By that time he was tired and frustrated from working with Magnitsky and requested a leave of absence. He then left for Moscow and began to make arrangements for his retirement. He did not want to return to Kazan', and for almost a year and a half he petitioned the ministry to renew his leave. While he did not like even to recall his service in Kazan', he maintained close relationships with his former colleagues from Penza. Lazhechnikov often helped students from Penza, Belinsky among them, to settle in Moscow and enter Moscow University. Lazhechnikov's pension was granted in the fall of 1827, and he was then able to devote himself completely to his work on the historical novel *Poslednii Novik, ili Zavoevanie Lifliandii v tsarstvovanie Petra Velikago* (The Last Novik, or The Conquest of Livonia During the Time of Peter the Great, 1831–1833).

The genre of the historical novel, which was first promoted by Sir Walter Scott in the 1810s, did not achieve worldwide acclaim by accident. The French Revolution, the Napoleonic dictatorship, wars for independence, and the Patriotic War in Russia increased the tempo of social life. People became involved in the earth-shattering historical events surrounding them and thus became fascinated with history and the interrelationship of the "large scale" historical events with "smaller" personal events. This wave of historical awareness initiated by a stormy epoch led to the birth of the historical novel and its growing popularity. The national past became a subject of collections and loving study as well as a source of poetic inspiration.

Lazhechnikov's historical novels portray those moments of history when passionate individuals sacrifice themselves in the name of people who are suffering. Hence Lazhechnikov's favorite protagonist, whether historical or fictional, possesses a complicated inner world and a particularly tragic fate. Lazhechnikov's protagonist usually moves about in a rarified atmosphere high above the occurrences of ordinary daily life. Thus he functions almost on a symbolic scale in an aura of poetic expressiveness. A certain "poetics of contrast" in the novels, as well as an emphasis on the hero's special character, put Lazhechnikov's historical narratives more in the tradition of Victor Hugo than of Scott.

Lazhechnikov's first novel, *Poslednii Novik* (a sixteenth- and seventeenth-century term for a young nobleman who has registered for military service but has not yet served), has a characteristically Romantic plot. It takes place in the years of the Northern War when Peter I fought against the Swedes for access to the Baltic Sea. Like the Decembrist authors Aleksandr Aleksandrovich Bestuzhev (Marlinsky) and Vil'gel'm Karlovich Kiukhel'beker, Lazhechnikov turned to the Baltics in his search for a topic. It should be remembered that serfdom had been abolished in the Baltics in 1813–1814 while in Russia it existed until 1861. Whereas the Decembrists were attracted to the Middle Ages and the idea of personal freedom, Lazhechnikov chose another era and another idea. The subject and conflict in the novel do not typify the era of Peter the Great. They were suggested to Lazhechnikov by contemporary history and his own participation in the Napoleonic wars. The conflict of a patriot with authority, along with his bitter awareness of the dichotomy between love for the motherland and the possibility that his actions might somehow work toward her detriment, reflect the realities of the Decembrist era rather than that of seventeenth-century Russia. The very image of a lonely, unrecognized hero who is forced to hide while somehow influencing the flow of events follows the pattern of the Romantic image prevalent in Western European literature at the beginning of the nineteenth century.

The fate of Vladimir, the protagonist, signals the victory of Peter the Great's cause. Tsarevna Sofia and Andrei Denisov raised Vladimir to be a sworn enemy of Peter the Great. After making an unsuccessful attempt on the tsar's life, he flees far from his beloved motherland, but with time realizes the significance of Peter the Great's reforms and makes it his life's goal to vindicate himself to the tsar and Russia. After the beginning of the war between Russia and Sweden, he secretly helps the Russian army that had invaded Livonia. He becomes a confidant of Shlippenbach, the leader of the Swedish troops, and feeds information on Swedish plans to the commander of the Russian Army in Livonia, thereby promoting Russian victory over Sweden. The situation of the main character is a typically Romantic one: he is simultaneously hero and criminal. He is a secret friend of Peter the Great but knows that Peter considers him an enemy. The conflict is resolved when Vladimir clandestinely returns to his motherland and is forgiven. However, he is too tired to participate in Peter the Great's reforms and therefore joins a monastery, where he dies.

The hero's dramatic fate, contradictory roles, and mysterious adventures were meant to reflect the two main historical conflicts of the epoch of Peter the Great: the struggle of Peter with Tsarevna Sofia and old boyar Russia and the war between Russia and Sweden. Although Lazhechnikov was impressed by the dramatic personality and strong character of Sofia, he portrays both Sofia and the boyars as the dark forces of pre-Petrine Russia. The old conservative Russia is symbolized by the sinister character of Andrei Denisov (whose secular name was Prince Myshetsky), one of Sofia's followers and the leader of the Old Believers. In Lazhechnikov's novel Denisov is ready to commit any crime for the good of the cause. It is significant, then, that Vladimir becomes the instrument of his death. In creating the negative image of Denisov, Lazhechnikov upheld the position of the official Russian Orthodox Church. Since Denisov was an Old Believer, the author deprives him of all positive characteristics and portrays him as the ultimate villain. The victory of Peter the Great over Denisov and his cause was, to Lazhechnikov, an unambiguously important moment in the historical development of Russia.

Vladimir's psychology remains flat and uninteresting. His pining for the motherland is portrayed realistically, yet his courageous attitude at the beginning of the novel inexplicably declines into dullness and passivity by the end. Although Lazhechnikov states that Vladimir is ambitious and passionate, he never displays these traits except in his zealous love for his country. However, Vladimir plays an important role in the composition of the novel. As Belinsky noted, the influence of Scott can clearly be seen in the portrayal of the main character, for the last *novik* fulfills the same function as analogous characters in such Scott novels as *Old Mortality* (1816) and *Quentin Dur-*

Two rulers about whom Lazhechnikov wrote historical novels: Peter the Great and Anna Ivannovna

ward (1823). Because of his position as a character whose adventures place him inside the scenes of both warring factions, on a structural level the last *novik* serves not only as a link between the two sides but also as a natural reflector of the tensions that simultaneously unite and separate them.

Historical figures occasionally appear in the text but usually occupy secondary places. Lazhechnikov closely adheres to historical facts in his rendering of Johann Reingold Patkul, the true patriot of Livonia, who becomes aware that the salvation of his suffering country lies in joining forces with the Russian empire of Peter the Great. Lazhechnikov depicts Peter the Great both as a politician and as a family man. His character combines simplicity and greatness, not unlike Pushkin's portrayal of him in two scenes of *Arap Petra Velikogo* (The Moor of Peter the Great, 1827). However, while Pushkin shows Peter the Great to be a contradictory and complex character, Lazhechnikov merely idealizes Peter and his followers. In Lazhechnikov's version of the tsar, Peter sits lost in thought, unaware of his surroundings as he contemplates the future of St. Petersburg. True to the Romantic model of the solitary genius, Lazhechnikov's Peter emerges as the lone visionary, the creator of a new nation.

The theme of the interrelationship between Russian and Western European cultures, which begins in *Poslednii Novik,* runs through all of the author's works. In this first novel the barons Zevelgodov and Fuerenhof resemble Lazhechnikov's contemporaries, those Baltic and German nobles at the tsar's court who despised all things Russian. But at the same time Lazhechnikov highly regards those quiet and talented representatives of foreign cultures who were impressed by the activities of Russia's reformer. Lazhechnikov used his novel to campaign for further progressive changes in the country, for the development of education, for the spread of humanitarian ideas, and for bringing Russia closer to Western Europe, where he did not foresee any danger to Russian national self-determination. Lazhechnikov claimed that love for the motherland was the predominant feeling in his novel.

As an artist Lazhechnikov strove for a painstaking and truthful representation of the historical past. During the Napoleonic Wars he traveled extensively in Livonia; while working on the novel he returned for a two-month stay in the area. During this trip he crossed Livonia many times, mostly by rural roads. The descriptions of costumes, location, traditions, and customs are true to life. Lazhechnikov studied the era and people of that time extensively, especially the historical figures whom he depicted. He not only read historical books but also studied rare sources such as manuscripts and documents.

Poslednii Novik brought Lazhechnikov acclaim. The novel was published in parts, from 1831 to 1833, and the reading public impatiently awaited each new installment. In 1834, a year after publication of the last installment, a separate edition of the complete novel appeared in print. Despite the high price, the book sold out almost immediately, and a second edition came out a few years later. The young Belinsky praised Lazhechnikov as the first Russian novelist whose work reflected talent, experience, education, and vivid imagination.

In 1831 Lazhechnikov returned to his job at the Ministry of Education. He was appointed director of the gymnasium and public schools in Tver'. There he became friends with Tat'iana Petrovna and Vadim Vasil'evich Passek. He gave advice to both Tat'iana Petrovna, who translated French novels, and Vadim Vasil'evich, who wrote *Putevye zapiski* (Travel Notes, 1834). In her memoirs, *Iz dal'nikh let* (From Faraway Years, first published in 1878), Tat'iana Petrovna recounted how Lazhechnikov read excerpts from his new novel *Ledianoi dom* (The Ice Palace, 1835) to the Passeks and their friends.

Ledianoi dom is Lazhechnikov's finest achievement as a novelist. The novel was a great success and strengthened the literary reputation of the author. In *Ledianoi dom* Lazhechnikov turned to the era of national regression and reaction that followed the glorious reign of Peter the Great. He re-created the events of the winter of 1739–1740, the last year of Anna Ivannovna's rule. The empress's sickness and lack of an heir exacerbated the tension at court and in the government. After the death of Peter I, Russia appeared demeaned and overtaken by the Baltic German nobility. Lazhechnikov focuses his novel on the struggle between the Russian patriots, led by the cabinet minister Artemii Petrovich Volynsky, and the foreigners, personified by the empress's favorite, Ernst-Johann Biron (with whose name the people titled the reign *bironovshchina*). The concept of *Ledianoi dom* is based on an actual palace of ice, ordered by the empress for court entertainment in the severe winter of 1739–1740. Lazhechnikov makes the ice palace the symbol of the empress's reign and her despotic power. The ice palace cast a shadow on the twisted political intrigues and on the Romantic story of the passionate love between Volynsky and Marioritsa, supposedly the Moldavian princess Lelemiko (though Volynsky was real, Marioritsa and the love story were Lazhechnikov's inventions). Volynsky, a fiery Romantic in both love and

politics, is Lazhechnikov's favorite hero. Lazhechnikov characterized Volynsky as purely and originally Russian. To Lazhechnikov's contemporaries, Volynsky's death in an unfair fight appeared martyrlike and invoked the history of the Decembrists.

The choice of subject and the contrast of the epoch of Peter the Great with the one immediately following it are not accidental phenomena. *Ledianoi dom* instantly reminded the contemporary reader of the contrast between the gloomy era of Nicholas I and the heroic time of 1812 to 1825. The *bironovshchina* epoch also brought to mind the large number of Germans active in Russian government circles in the 1830s. The novel came out shortly before the centennial of Volynsky's struggle with Biron. Thus not only the originality and artistic qualities of *Ledianoi dom* but also its allusions to contemporary issues ensured its success.

In this second novel Lazhechnikov again strove to re-create a true version of the past. He later revealed that the main objective in his writing of historical fiction had always been to paint an accurate picture of whatever epochs served as their settings. However, he felt that the historical novelist's principal task lies not in strict adherence to known facts but rather in fidelity to the poetic truth of the era, to its faces and its events.

Ledianoi dom presents the historical past in a much more concrete manner than did *Poslednii Novik*. The events take place precisely when the tensions between Volynsky and Biron were at their height, during that winter of 1739–1740. The image of the cruel and power-hungry Biron is historically accurate, although somewhat flat and one-sided, as noted by Pushkin in a letter to Lazhechnikov dated 3 November 1835. Biron owned serfs, accepted bribes, sold the national interests of Russia to England, and headed the feared Secret Chancellery. It is not surprising, then, that Biron became an object of hatred for the Russian people. In answer to Pushkin's comment that Biron had exhibited some positive traits, Lazhechnikov characterized Anna Ivannovna's favorite as a "bloodthirsty, evil man"; Pushkin ultimately agreed with this unequivocable assessment. Lazhechnikov defends his position in his 22 November 1835 letter to Pushkin by appealing to national opinion about the era; after all, the people gave the name to that period of Russia's history. He then posits that the people always name epochs in a just manner. He also tries to put forth a more balanced view of the era of *bironovshchina* by claiming it got its name not because Biron was a German but because of his abuse of power. Lazhechnikov notes that many foreigners served Russia honestly and left behind a good memory of themselves.

Lazhechnikov portrays the positive Romantic hero, Volynsky, in all of his glory as a direct descendant and guardian of Peter the Great's traditions and deeds, so specifically hailed in *Poslednii Novik*. The novelist uses the Decembrist poet Kondratii Fedorovich Ryleev's patriotic poem "Volynsky" (1822) as the source for his own depiction of his hero. He also notes that the "noble aura" that surrounded Volynsky's grave in the 1830s had an effect on his own characterization of the man. Pushkin took exception to the aspects of the novel that diverged from historical truth; he criticized Lazhechnikov for idealizing Volynsky while caricaturing the eighteenth-century poet Vasilii Kirillovich Trediakovsky. True to his Romantic outlook, Lazhechnikov did not take the poet's criticism to heart; instead he maintained that in a historical novel truth must always give way to poetry should the former impede the latter.

As a Romantic author Lazhechnikov was more interested in Volynsky from a psychological viewpoint, namely as a person of fiery passion and not as an historical figure. In this regard Volynsky's image was an artistic achievement in Russian prose. Belinsky saw in the characterization of Volynsky a truthful combination of contradictory qualities. Lazhechnikov's Volynsky emerges as a person who is deep and mighty in spirit, a zealous patriot with a clean and noble soul but light and flighty, a clever politician yet a boy unable to control himself, a government statesman, and a rowdy reveler. Such a successfully drawn combination of contradictions in one person remains a remarkable accomplishment for the novelist.

Similarly Romantic is the portrayal of the love between Volynsky and Marioritsa. Belinsky was fascinated by the bright and wholesome image of the young princess, who was devoted to Volynsky with all the passion of youth. In depicting Volynsky's patriotism and Marioritsa's passion, Lazhechnikov turns to the Romantic literature of his time. The letters of Volynsky to his beloved are written in the Romantic style, while the story of Marioritsa and her love includes all the elements of a Romantic "oriental" poem. One of them is the image of Marioritsa's mother, the dark and gloomy gypsy Mariula, devoted to her daughter to the point of self-sacrifice. The image of a mysterious gypsy enhances the Romantic tenor of Marioritsa's love story. Esmeralda and her mother in Victor Hugo's *Notre-Dame de Paris* (1831) may serve as a possible source for Lazhechnikov's characters Marioritsa and Mariula, especially their mother-daughter relationship. In addition Marioritsa and Esmeralda both endure an equally tragic fate.

Ledianoi dom also relies on enough realistic elements to provide readers with an historically accurate background for the action. Lazhechnikov truthfully depicts how in the time of Anna Ivannovna government business was intertwined with the private life of the empress and her court. The scene that shows the fear of the crowd upon the appearance of the disguised informant known as *iazyk* (the tongue) and the mention of the frightening phrase *slovo i delo* (word and deed), which was followed by torture in the Secret Chancellery, is historically accurate. The belief in magicians and clairvoyants, the image of the gypsy, the court jesters, the game with the ice palace that was to be arranged by the cabinet minister himself—all of these were colorful and true characteristics of that time. Belinsky noted that the details in the depiction of Volynsky in the scene where he disguises himself as a driver in order to meet the princess were also realistic.

The nature of Lazhechnikov's descriptions somewhat resembles the style of Scott, though his second novel relies less on the English novelist. In contrast to *Poslednii Novik* the story of *Ledianoi dom* centers not around a fictional character but rather around a true historical figure. As in Scott's novels history does not follow the lives of the characters; rather their fate depends on the flow of historical events.

Lazhechnikov published three chapters of the novel in 1834 in the almanac *Dennitsa* (Dawn) and the journal *Teleskop* (Telescope). After the first complete publication of the novel in 1835, a second edition of *Ledianoi dom* was in demand as soon as 1838. Belinsky called *Ledianoi dom* a present to the Russian public, a "shining star in the desert sky of Russian literature." However, in 1850 *Ledianoi dom* was banned by the censorship committee, which noted that the main point of Lazhechnikov's novel was the unjust decision of the empress to execute Volynsky regardless of how right his mission had been. Thus a third edition of the novel did not appear until 1858, as part of his *Sobranie sochinenii* (Collected Works). Of all of Lazhechnikov's works *Ledianoi dom* became the most popular.

Inspired by the success of *Ledianoi dom*, Lazhechnikov created his last completed historical novel over the next three years—*Basurman* (The Heretic, 1838). In it Lazhechnikov retreats to the fifteenth century and the harsh epoch of Ivan III, who, by destroying the feudal princedoms in old Muscovy, built up his capital city and created a new empire. This new empire grew out of a struggle between emerging forces in Russia: one based on the humanism of the Western Renaissance, the other based on fanaticism, cruelty, and deceit. Lazhechnikov's success lies undoubtedly in the complex character of Ivan III, whom he depicts as a careful and farsighted politician, a smart monarch, a tireless conqueror of land for Russia, and a despot attaining his goals through perfidy and might.

In this novel the architect Aristotele Fioravanti and the doctor Anton Erenshtein, like their real-life counterparts, arrive from Europe in the distant Moscow principality with the honorable goal of aiding the happiness of a country struggling for a new existence. Ivan III bestows his benevolence upon the two but also subverts their humanitarian plans to his own needs. Lazhechnikov's characters, the Romantics and the creators, suffer profoundly because of Ivan's manipulations.

Lazhechnikov was faced with many contradictions when he turned to the historical image of Ivan III, whose role had been evaluated in a variety of ways. For Nikolai Karamzin, Ivan III was a great historical figure who had strengthened the country's independence and laid the foundation for the greatness of Russia as a nation. The Decembrist writers, although they understood the leading role Ivan III played in overcoming Tatar domination, nevertheless considered him a despot who had destroyed the ancient Russian democracy-free Novgorod. They contrasted Ivan III with the heroic image of Marfa Posadnitsa, the celebrated patriot who tried to rally the city against the attack of the Muscovites under the command of Ivan. In his view of Ivan III, Lazhechnikov disagrees with Karamzin. Although the novel reflects a certain echo of the Decembrist preoccupation with Marfa Posadnitsa, this is not due to the author's conception of history but rather to his humanitarian feelings toward the famous prisoner of the ruler of all Russia.

Basurman depicts an important aspect of Ivan III's rule—his struggle with Tver'. Lazhechnikov portrays the fall of Tver' as an historically inescapable, long overdue event. He is fascinated by the clever and refined politics of Ivan III, who preferred to conduct his government not with force but with intrigue and diplomacy. In Lazhechnikov's portrayal Ivan III is a great historical figure, but unlike Karamzin the author is not inclined to idealize his personality. The novel includes scenes illustrating the despotism and avarice of Ivan, for example his deceitful capture of his brother, Prince Uglitsky (Andrei Vasil'evich).

Lazhechnikov highlights the political relationships in Russia at the end of the fifteenth century, but his main emphasis falls on the penetration of humanistic ideas and the culture of the Western European Renaissance into semibarbaric Moscow. Lazhechnikov shows Moscow in the time of Ivan III in the same light as Russia in Pushkin's *Arap Petra Velikogo,* namely as a place that is changing and growing.

To render a dramatic confrontation of humanism and education with the backwardness and barbarism of Russia at the time of Ivan III was a significant undertaking not only because of its historical meaning but also because of a possible social resonance in the Russia of Nicholas I. In the novel Western ideas are personified by the figure of the genius architect Aristotele Fioravanti, who dreams of creating in Moscow a grandiose temple, even greater than St. Peter's Basilica in Rome. The great prince of Moscow, in all his striving for greatness, needs more practical buildings; thus he rejects Fioravanti's plan. Although Fioravanti does succeed in building Uspenskii Cathedral under the tsar's approval, he nevertheless feels himself deprived and suffers the tragedy of a genius whose plans remain unrealized.

In depicting Fioravanti and the drama of his life, Lazhechnikov turned to many examples from Russian history: the fate of Vasilii Ivanovich Bazhenov's abortive plans in the 1760s to build a classical Moscow and the contemporary story of the talented architect A. L. Vitberg building the shrine of Christ the Savior in Moscow. Underhanded dealings of many people involved in its construction led to the completely innocent architect's prosecution under direct order of Nicholas I and eventual exile to Viatka in 1835. At the time Lazhechnikov was writing *Basurman,* Vitberg's case was on the front pages of Russian papers. The daring project of Lazhechnikov's contemporary was reflected in *Basurman* in Fioravanti's unrealized plans.

Also tragic was the story of the young scientist Anton Erenshtein. While working on the novel Lazhechnikov carefully studied chronicles for material on fifteenth-century life in Russia. The fate of Anton was suggested to him by a few lines of a chronicle entry of 1485 concerning a German doctor, Anton, who came to Karakacha, a Tatar Prince in Russia. Karakacha entertained him royally. However, the doctor poisoned Karakacha's son, Prince Daniarov. Karakacha gave the doctor to the Tatars, who took him to a bridge on the Moscow River and killed him as they would a sheep, with a knife. In re-creating the historical atmosphere Lazhechnikov turned not only to quotations from the chronicles but also to folklore. As a result he described most vividly details of everyday life. There are few sources to which Lazhechnikov did not resort in establishing historical accuracy.

The theme of *Basurman* brought it within the group of historical novels written in the 1830s in which the heroes were cultural leaders or intelligentsia (for example, Nikolai Alekseevich Polevoi's *Abbadonna,* 1833). It is a testament to Lazhechnikov's humanism that the hero of his novel is an unknown doctor whose positive qualities derive not from his descent but rather from his knowledge and culture. Such a hero was quite new in the Russian literature of the 1830s.

Basurman was praised by both the literary critics and the reading public. A reviewer for *Biblioteka dlia chteniia* (Library for Reading) considered *Basurman* an excellent historical novel, one of the best in contemporary literature. Another critic, for *Otechestvennye zapiski* (Notes of the Fatherland), placed *Basurman* on the same level as Pushkin's play *Boris Godunov* (1831). During the author's lifetime *Basurman* was published only three times: in 1838, in 1849–1850, and finally in 1858 in an eight-volume collection of the author's works. In the last edition, the archaic spelling that had caused much confusion and derision among Lazhechnikov's contemporary critics is missing, and Lazhechnikov replaced many archaic words and expressions with contemporary ones. In an effort to improve his style, Lazhechnikov sought simplicity of expression and mercilessly edited the verbose passages.

Basurman was the last great achievement of Lazhechnikov. The role of the historical novel diminished with the advent of authors of the Natural School. In 1837, before the publication of *Basurman,* Lazhechnikov began to work on a novel about the times of Peter II. The introduction was published in 1840 in *Otechestvennye zapiski* under the title "Koldun na Sukharevoi bashne" (The Sorcerer in Sukharev Tower). The action of the novel takes place in 1727–1728. Lazhechnikov planned to make Iakov Villimovich Brius and Prince Vasilii Luki'ch Dolgorukov the main characters of the novel; however, he never finished it. Neither his letters nor his autobiographical works give any reasons Lazhechnikov could not finish this work. He made several attempts to continue "Koldun na Sukharevoi bashne" but failed. It is quite possible that while collecting archival material in Tver' for *Basurman,* he became more interested in the times of Ivan III instead.

In May 1837 Lazhechnikov retired again and bought the estate Konoplino, where he settled. In Konoplino he finished *Basurman* and suddenly became interested in a genre that was completely new to him—historical drama in verse. In 1841 he published the first three acts of the drama *Khristiern II i Gustav Vaza* (Christiern II and Gustav Vasa) in *Otechestvennye zapiski.* He worked quickly, and in 1842 the complete text of the drama was published in the collection *Dagerotip* (Daguerrotype), edited by Nestor Vasil'evich Kukol'nik. Although Belinsky wrote a favorable review, the drama was not a success among the reading public. Always objective in the evaluation of his works, Lazhechnikov apparently was not satisfied with *Khristiern II i Gustav Vaza* and therefore did not include it in the complete collection of his works.

In 1842 Lazhechnikov wrote *Oprichnik,* a play in which he clearly condemns the tyranny of Ivan the Terrible. Belinsky read the drama in manuscript form and wrote favorably about it. Osip Ivanovich Senkovsky, the publisher of *Biblioteka dlia chteniia,* accepted *Oprichnik* for publication in his journal. The drama, however, was suppressed by censorship and did not appear until 1859 in *Russkoe Slovo.* In 1867 *Oprichnik* was published as a book and was successfully

Lazhechnikov's grave at Novodevich'e cemetery in Moscow

staged in St. Petersburg and Moscow theaters. Lazhechnikov dedicated the 1867 edition to the memory of Belinsky. After Lazhechnikov's death, in 1870–1872 Petr Ilich Tchaikovsky wrote an opera titled *Oprichnik,* based on Lazhechnikov's drama. It was staged in 1874 at the Mariinskii Theater in St. Petersburg and in 1875 in the Malyi Theater in Moscow.

In 1842 Lazhechnikov returned to government service. He was appointed honorable guardian of Tver' Gymnasium and later, in the spring of 1843, he became the vice governor of the city. In November 1852 Lazhechnikov's wife died; it was emotionally hard for him to stay in Tver', and he decided to go to St. Petersburg to petition for his transfer. His petition was granted, and he was appointed vice governor of Vitebsk. In October 1853 Lazhechnikov arrived in the town, where he planned to live for a long time. Vitebsk, however, disappointed Lazhechnikov. Despite the fact that as a vice governor he spent long hours toiling in his office, the results of his work did not satisfy him. Besides, he could not get used to the poverty of Belorussian peasants, the remoteness from Moscow and St. Petersburg, and the lack of intellectual life. He missed

Russia, and there were times when he was ready to petition for retirement. Vitebsk turned out to be a place of exile for Lazhechnikov. In his letters he wrote that he stayed in such a remote corner as Vitebsk only because he wanted to serve his country.

In Vitebsk, Lazhechnikov married Mariia Ivanovna Ozerova, who at that time was twenty-two. In spite of the age difference their marriage was happy. They had two daughters and a son, Ivan, who later became a journalist and poet. Lazhechnikov did not want to stay in Vitebsk any longer, and in June 1854 he returned to Moscow. In spite of his preoccupation with his work as a vice governor, Lazhechnikov did not abandon his literary career. During his years in Tver' and Vitebsk, Lazhechnikov worked on new editions of *Poslednii Novik* and *Ledianoi dom*. However, the censorship committee refused to allow republication of the novels. He also wrote two dramas—*Doch' evreiia* (Daughter of a Jew, 1847) and *Gorbun* (The Hunchback, 1858)—and a vaudeville, *Okopirovalsia* (The Miscopying, 1855). In Moscow Lazhechnikov became actively involved in the production of his plays. While *Okopirovalsia* and *Gorbun* were moderately successful (*Okopirovalsia* was staged in November 1854 in both the Aleksandrinskii Theater in St. Petersburg and the Malyi Theater in Moscow; *Gorbun* was staged in the Malyi Theater in 1853), *Doch' evreiia* was a failure.

Lazhechnikov's financial problems forced him to return to government service again. This time he had to move to St. Petersburg, where he became a member of the censorship committee. Although he started working there during the liberal years after the death of Nicholas I, he constantly experienced the conflict between his work and his moral convictions. He was assigned to censor the journal *Sovremennik* (The Contemporary), which had been founded by Pushkin in 1836. Ivan Ivanovich Panaev, who copublished the journal with Nekrasov beginning in 1846, wrote in his memoirs that Lazhechnikov suffered profoundly at this job and retired as soon as he received his pension in 1858.

In 1856 he published a story of the memoir genre, "Belen'kie, chernen'kie i seren'kie" (Whether White, Black or Gray), in Katkov's *Russkii vestnik*. In "Belen'kie, chernen'kie, seren'kie" Lazhechnikov describes his family and his childhood. Later followed his memoir essays "Znakomstvo moe s Pushkinym," "Novobranets 1812," and "Zametki dlia biografii Belinskogo." In 1856–1857 Lazhechnikov worked on the complete edition of his works that was published in 1857–1858. With the help of Ivan Andreevich Goncharov, a novelist who also worked as a censor, Lazhechnikov was allowed to republish his three historical novels, minus censored portions.

After his retirement Lazhechnikov settled down in the village of Khoroshevo, not far from Moscow. His house was built according to his own plans. In Khoroshevo he wrote further autobiographical essays for *Russkii khudozhestvennyi listok* (Russian Art Sheet), published by Vasilii Fedorovich Timm; an essay, "Kak ia znal Magnitskogo" (How I Knew Magnitsky), published in Katkov's *Russkii vestnik* in 1866; and his last two novels, *Nemnogo let nazad* (A Few Years Ago, 1862) and *Vnuchka pantsyrnogo boiarina* (The Granddaughter of a Polish Boyar, 1868), in which he turned from historical themes to contemporary ones. Neither novel was successful, which led Lazhechnikov to conclude that his best works were his historical novels. He wrote a stage version of his novel *Basurman* that he titled *Materi-sopernitsy* (Rival Mothers). It was produced in 1868 in the Aleksandrinskii Theater in St. Petersburg and in the Malyi Theater in Moscow. Although the leading roles were played by well-known actors of the time, the drama failed. Lazhechnikov did not attend the performance since he was already rather old and no longer left his house.

In May 1869 *Obshchestvo liubitelei rossiiskoi slovesnosti* (The Society of Lovers of Russian Literature) celebrated the fiftieth anniversary of Lazhechnikov's literary career. At this celebration Lazhechnikov's last work—his autobiographical notes—was read to the public. The writer was too old and ill to attend the celebration. Lazhechnikov's letter of gratitude to the society was the last one he wrote. He died on 26 June 1869 in Moscow and was buried in Novodevich'e cemetery near the east wall of the Smolensk Cathedral. He had written in his last will and testament, "To my wife and children I do not leave any fortune except my good name, which I bequeath to them in order that they guard and protect it in all of its purity."

Lazhechnikov's historical novels *Ledianoi dom* and *Basurman* were translated into English and German in the nineteenth century. In Russia the complete collection of his works was published in 1883 and went through several editions before 1917. In the history of Russian literature Lazhechnikov is known as a historical novelist. His autobiographical and memoir works (which are in no way inferior to his historical novels) never received attention or recognition; they remain among the unexplored pages of nineteenth-century Russian literature.

Letters:

To I. A. Krylov, *Sbornik statei Otdeleniia russkogo iazyka i slovesnosti,* 6 (1869): 311;

To A. N. Ostrovky, in *Prazdnovanie iubileia literatunoi deiatel'nosti I. I. Lazhechnikova* (Moscow, 1869);

To V. V. Passek, *Russkaia starina,* no. 7 (1876): 543–544; no. 7 (1877): 435–436;

To P. V. Pobedonostsev, *Russkaia starina*, no. 10 (1891): 230–231;

To A. V. Starchevsky, *Istoricheskii vestnik*, no. 11 (1892): 326–328;

To B. A. Almazov, *Russkoe obozrenie*, no. 9 (1894): 371–375;

To S. P. Pobedonostsev and K. P. Pobedonostsev, *Russkoe obozrenie*, no. 4 (1895): 881–887;

To A. V. Nikitenko, *Russkaia starina*, no. 12 (1896): 595–596;

To P. V. Pobedonostsev, *Russkii arkhiv*, no. 1 (1897): 306–307;

To A. F. Pisemsky, *Izvestiia knizhnogo magazina M. O. Vol'f*, no. 9–10 (1899): 181;

To A. K. Zhiznevsky, *Shchukinsky sbornik*, vypusk 1 (Moscow, 1902), pp. 89–90;

To Ia. A. Boiarkin, *Istoricheskii vestnik*, no. 3 (1910): 1066;

To E. S. Tilichev, *Trudy Vitebskoi arkhivnoi komissii*, no. 1 (1910): 25;

To A. F. Koni, *Russkii arkhiv*, no. 9 (1912): 141–151;

To S. A. Gedeonov, *Russkii arkhiv*, no. 1 (1915): 26–27;

To M. N. Longinov, in *Anatolii Fedorovich Koni. Iubileinyi sbornik* (Leningrad, 1925), pp. 126–132;

To A. A. Kraevsky, *Zven'ia*, volume 5 (Moscow-Leningrad, 1935), pp. 749–750;

To A. S. Pushkin, in Pushkin's *Polnoe sobranie sochinenii*, volume 14 (Moscow-Leningrad, 1941), pp. 249–250; volume 15 (Moscow-Leningrad, 1948), p. 122; volume 16 (Moscow-Leningrad, 1949), pp. 63–67;

To V. G. Belinsky, in *V. G. Belinsky i ego korrespondenty* (Moscow, 1948), pp. 174–190;

To A. M. Marin, in S. N. Marin, *Polnoe sobranie sochinenii* (Moscow, 1948), pp. 521–522;

To N. A. Nekrasov, *Literaturnoe nasledstvo*, 51–52 (1949): 354–356.

Biographies:

Prazdnovanie iubileia literatunoi deiatel'nosti I. I. Lazhechnikova (Moscow, 1869);

V. I. Nechaeva, *I. I. Lazhechnikov* (Penza: Gostlitizdat, 1945);

A. I. Opul'sky, *I zhizn' i pero na blago otechestva* (Moscow: Moskovskii rabochii, 1968).

References:

Vissarion Grigor'evich Belinsky, *Polnoe sobranie sochinenii*, 13 volumes (Moscow-Leningrad: AN SSSR, 1953–1959);

Sergei Nikolaevich Durylin, "I. I. Lazhechnikov," in his *Russkie pisateli v Otechestvennoi voine 1812 goda* (Moscow: Sovetskii pisatel', 1943), pp. 100–106;

E. I. Garshin, *I. I. Lazhechnikov kak istoricheskii romanist. Kritiko-biograficheskii etiud* (St. Petersburg, 1895);

N. G. Il'inskaia, "Roman Lazhechnikova *Ledianoi dom* (Obshchestvenno politicheskaia problematika)," *Uchenye zapiski Leningradskogo pedagogicheskogo instituta imeni A. I. Gertsena*, 184, no. 6 (Leningrad, 1958): 43–78;

G. S. Litvinova, "Roman I. I. Lazhechnikova *Basurman*," *Uchenye zapiski moskovskogo pedagogicheskogo instituta imeni V. P. Potemkina*, 98 (Moscow, 1959): 143–172;

Boris L'vovich Modzalevsky, "Pushkin i Lazhechnikov," in his *Pushkin* (Leningrad: Priboi, 1929), pp. 7–122;

Ivan Ivanovich Panaev, *Literaturnye vospominaniia* (Moscow: Pravda, 1988);

Tatiana Petrovna Passek, *Iz dal'nikh let,* 2 volumes (Moscow-Leningrad: Academiia, 1931);

S. M. Petrov, *Istoricheskii roman v russkoi literature* (Moscow: Gosudarstvennoe uchebno-pedagogicheskoe izdatel'stvo, 1961);

Petrov, *Istoriia russkogo romana* (Moscow-Leningrad: AN SSSR, 1962);

Leon I. Twarog, "The Soviet Revival of a Nineteenth-Century Historical Novelist: I. I. Lažečnikov," *Harvard Slavic Studies*, 4 (1957): 107–126;

S. A. Vengerov, "I. I. Lazhechnikov. (Kritiko-biograficheskii ocherk)," in *Sochineniia. Posmertnoe polnoe izdanie*, by Lazhechnikov, volume 1 (St. Petersburg & Moscow: M. O. Vol'f, 1883), pp. i–clxxxviii;

Vitaly Vowk, "'Antediluvian' Fiction in Russian Literature: I. I. Lazhechnikov's First Historical Novel *The Last Page* (1831) in Russian Criticism," *Proceedings of the Kentucky Foreign Language Conference: Slavic Section*, 3, no. 1 (1985): 17–27;

Vowk, "The Historical Novels of I. I. Lažečnikov," dissertation, Ohio State University, 1972;

Vowk, "I. I. Lažečnikov: His Role in the Evolution of Russian Historical Fiction," *Proceedings of the Kentucky Foreign Language Conference: Slavic Section*, 2, no. 1 (1984): 43–52;

A. K. Zhiznevsky, *Pamiati I. I. Lazhechnikova* (Tver', 1895).

Nikolai Ivanovich Nadezhdin

(5 October 1804 – 11 January 1856)

Leonard A. Polakiewicz
University of Minnesota

BOOKS: *De poseos romantica. De origine, natura et fatis poseos, juae romantica audit* (Moscow: Mosquae, typis universitatis caesareae, 1830); first complete Russian translation in *Literaturnaia kritika. Estetika* (Moscow: Khudozhestvennaia literatura, 1972), pp. 124–253;

Rod Kniazhevichei (Odessa, 1842);

Issledovanie o skopcheskoi eresi (St. Petersburg: Ministry of Internal Affairs, 1845);

O zagranichnykh raskol'nikakh (St. Petersburg: Ministry of Internal Affairs, 1846).

Collection: *Literaturnaia kritika. Èstetika* (Moscow: Khudozhestvennaia literatura, 1972).

OTHER: *Teleskop* (edited by Nadezhdin, 1831–1836);

Adol'f Aleksandrovich Pliushar, *Entsyklopedicheskii Leksikon,* volumes 8, 9, 10, 11, and 12 (1835–1841)—includes more than 100 essays by Nadezhdin;

Sorok odna povest' Luchshikh inostrannykh pisatelei: Bal'zaka i dr., edited by Nadezhdin (Moscow: N. Stepanov, 1836);

"Sila voli" in *Sto russkikh literatorov,* volume 2 (St. Petersburg: Tip. Smirdina, 1841): 399–558;

Zhurnal Ministerstva vnutrennikh del, edited by Nadezhdin, 1843;

"Ob etnograficheskom izuchenii russkogo naroda," *Zapiski Russkogo geograficheskogo obshchestva,* book 2 (St. Petersburg, 1847): 61–115;

Geograficheskie Izvestiia, edited by Nadezhdin, 1848;

Ètnograficheskii Sbornik, edited by Nadezhdin, 1853;

"Dva otveta Nadezhdina Chaadaevu" in M. Lemke's *Nikolaevskie zhandarmy i literatura. 1826–1855* (St. Petersburg: S. Bunin, 1909).

SELECTED PERIODICAL PUBLICATIONS: "O vysokom," *Vestnik Evropy,* nos. 3–6 (1828);

"O proiskhozhdenii, sushchestvovanii i padenii ital'ianskikh torgovykh poselenii v Tavride," *Vestnik Evropy,* nos. 15–19 (1828);

"Literaturnye opaseniia za budushchii god," *Vestnik Evropy,* nos. 21–22 (1828);

Nikolai Ivanovich Nadezhdin

"Sonmishche nigilistov," *Vestnik Evropy,* nos. 1–2 (1829);

"O nastoiashchem zloupotreblenii i iskazhenii romanticheskoi poezii" [excerpt from Nadezhdin's dissertation], *Vestnik Evropy,* nos. 1–2 (1830);

"Razlichie mezhdu klassicheskoiu i romanticheskoiu poeziei, ob'iasniaemoe iz ikh proiskhozhdeniia" [excerpt from Nadezhdin's dissertation], *Atenei,* no. 1 (1830);

"Sovremennoe napravlenie prosveshcheniia," *Teleskop,* no. 1 (1831);

"*Istoriia russkogo naroda.* Sochinenie Nikolaia Polevogo. Tom pervyi," *Vestnik Evropy,* no. 1 (1831);

"Chto takoe khoroshii ton? Severoamerikanskii roman . . . St. Peterburg, 1831," *Teleskop,* no. 5 (1831);

"Sochineniia D. V. Venevitinova. Chap. 2. Proza," *Teleskop,* no. 7 (1831);

"Neobkhodimost', znachenie i sila èsteticheskogo obrazovaniia," *Teleskop,* no. 10 (1831);

"Zamechaniia na vykhodki *Severnoi pchely,*" *Teleskop,* no. 16 (1831);

"Primechanie k stat'e M [M. A. Maksimovicha] 'Ob istorii filosofii Asta. Kriticheskie otmetki,'" *Teleskop,* no. 17 (1831);

"Logika, vybrannaia iz Kleina A. Galichem, 1831. Sistema logiki. Sochineniia F. Bakhmana, 1831," *Teleskop,* no. 20 (1831);

"Lehrbuch der naturphilosophie von Oken. Jena, 1831," *Teleskop,* no. 8 (1832);

"Primechanie k stat'e 'Sovremennyi dukh,'" *Teleskop,* no. 19 (1832);

"Tysiacha vosem'sot tridtsat' vtoroi god," *Teleskop,* no. 1 (1833);

"O sovremennom napravlenii iziashchnykh iskusstv," *Uchenye zapiski Moskovskogo universiteta,* part 1, nos. 1–3 (1833);

"Parizhskie kofeinye doma," *Molva,* no. 14 (1833);

"Vseobshchee nachertanie teorii iziashchnykh iskusstv Bakhmana," *Molva,* part 2, no. 67 (1833);

"Evropeizm i narodnost' v otnoshenii k russkoi slovesnosti," *Teleskop,* nos. 1–2 (1836);

"Bartelemi i Barb'e," *Teleskop,* no. 6 (1836);

"Dlia g. Shevyreva. Poiasneniia kriticheskikh zamechanii na ego *Istoriiu poezii,*" *Teleskop,* part 32, no. 8 (1836);

"Rechi, proiznesennye v torzhestvennom sobranii Imperatorskogo Moskovskogo universiteta 9 iiunia 1836 goda," *Teleskop,* no. 9 (1836);

"Priznaki myslitel'nosti i zhizni v *Moskovskom nabliudatele,*" *Teleskop,* no. 10 (1836);

"Ne dlya g. Shevyreva, a dlia chitatelei. Poslednee slovo ob *Istorii poezii,*" *Teleskop,* part 33, no. 11 (1836);

"Osnovaniia fiziki Mikhaila Pavlova, 1836, ch. 1 (izd. 2-e), ch. 2 (izd. 1-e)," *Teleskop,* no. 12 (1836);

"Primechanie k stat'e 'Filosoficheskie pis'ma'," *Teleskop,* no. 15 (1836);

"Novyi kurs filosofii. Sochineniia E. Zheriuze," Literaturnoe pribavlenie k *Russkomu invalidu,* no. 1 (1837);

"Ob istoricheskoi istine i dostovernosti," *Biblioteka dlia chteniia,* 20, section 2 (1837): 137–174;

"Ob istoricheskikh trudakh v Rossii," *Biblioteka dlia chteniia,* 20, section 3 (1837): 93–136;

"Opyt istoricheskoi geografii russkogo mira. Stat'ia pervaia," *Biblioteka dlia chteniia,* 22 (1837): 27–79;

"Svetleishii Knyaz' Potemkin-Tavricheskii, obrazovatel' Novorossiiskogo kraia," *Odesskii Al'manakh* (1839): 1–96;

"Novorossiiskie stepi," *Zhurnal Ministerstva vnutrennikh del,* part 1 (1843): 5–73;

"Plemia russkoe v obshchem semeistve slavian," *Zhurnal Ministerstva vnutrennikh del,* part 1 (1843): 163–170;

"Issledovaniia o gorodakh russkikh," *Zhurnal Ministerstva vnutrennikh del,* part 6 (1844?): 3–52; part 7 (1844?): 207–256, 323–364;

"Ob'em i poriadok obozreniia narodnogo bogatstva," *Zhurnal Ministerstva Vnutrennikh Del,* part 9 (1845?): 5–39, 269–290;

"O filologicheskikh nabliudeniiakh protoiereia Pavskogo nad sostavom russkogo iazyka," *Otechestvennye zapiski,* no. 6 (1851);

"Avtobiografia," *Russkii vestnik,* no. 3, book 2 (1856): 49–78 (includes a complete list of essays published in Adol'f Aleksandrovich Pliushar's *Èntsyklopedicheskii Leksikon,* volumes 8, 9, 10, 11, and 12);

"O russkikh mifakh i sagakh v primenenii ikh k geografii i osobenno ètnografii russkoi," *Russkaia beseda,* books 3–4 (1857);

"Lektsii po arkheologii i teorii iziashchnykh iskusstv," *Zhurnal Ministerstva narodnogo prosveshcheniia* (May, June, July 1907).

With the appearance of his second article "O proiskhozhdenii, sushchestvovanii i padenii ital'ianskikh torgovykh poselenii v Tavride" (On the Origin, Existence and the Decline of Italian Trade Settlements on the Northern Black Sea Coast, 1828) followed by controversial articles on "Literaturnye opaseniia za budushchii god" (Literary Apprehensions Over the Past Year, 1828) and "Sonmishche nigilistov" (The Crowd of Nihilists, 1829) in Mikhail Trofimovich Kachenovsky's *Vestnik Evropy* (The Messenger of Europe) under the pseudonym "Ex-student Nikodin Nadoumko," Nadezhdin began his literary career and attracted immediate attention as a literary critic. In these articles he attacked the works of romantic poets. Although he responded favorably to Aleksandr Pushkin's *Boris Godunov* (1831) and the historical works of Mikhail Petrovich Pogodin and Mikhail Nikolaevich Zagoskin, for their manifest interest in Russian history, and works by Nikolai Vasil'evich Gogol, such as *Vechera na khutore bliz Dikan'ki* (Evenings on a Farm Near Dikanka, 1831–1832) and *Revizor* (The Inspector General, 1836) as well as the novellas of Honoré de Balzac, he attacked George Gordon, Lord Byron and Victor Hugo, and found certain works by Pushkin—including *Evgeny Onegin* (1833), particularly Canto VII; "Graf Nulin" (Count Nulin, 1827); and "Domik v Kolomne" (Little House in Kolomna, 1833)—lacking in lofty aesthetic ideas or philosophical depth. He dismissed most of the Russian literary works of his time, finding them dull, incoherent, strained, and lacking in artistic unity, ideas, action, and clearly delineated characters (even the authors themselves seemed not to understand them).

In his philosophical views, Nadezhdin was an objective realist. His aesthetic approach was shaped by his knowledge of German philosophy, which, however, he criticized in "Sovremennoe napravlenie prosveshcheniia" (Contemporary Direction of Enlightenment, 1831) for its subjectivity and for its "passion for systems, ending quite often in transcendental violation of reality. . . ." It was Friedrich Wilhelm Joseph von Schelling's *Naturphilosophie* (Philosophy of Nature), however, which exerted perhaps the strongest influence on Nadezhdin's intellectual makeup and helped formulate the argument in his attacks on Russian Romanticism. Under Schelling's influence Nadezhdin developed and applied dialectic ideas to literature. He viewed art as one of the stages in the development of *Weltgeist* (world-spirit). Extending the idea of conformity with natural laws to the process of artistic creativity, Nadezhdin found in it unity of poetic necessity and freedom, "the union of taste and genius," as he wrote in "Neobkhodimost', znachenie i sila èsteticheskogo obrazovaniia" for *Teleskop* (1831). He traced the course of poetry from its objective, classical form in antiquity, depicting "outer life," through its subjective, romantic form in the Middle Ages, embodying the world of purely spiritual sensations, to the synthetic poetry of contemporary times. Nadezhdin considered Western-European Classicism and, particularly, the newest Romanticism in Western and Russian literatures anachronistic and, on this basis, sharply criticized the Romantic works of Byron, Hugo, and the early Pushkin. He is credited with using the term "pseudo-Classicism" in reference to French art of the seventeenth century and "pseudo-Romanticism" when speaking about certain works of contemporary art. For his own period, Nadezhdin proposed a kind of synthesis of Classicism and Romanticism. He regarded the principal features of synthetic poetry as natural feeling, simplicity, and the expression of "essence."

Nadezhdin's dialectic views led him to advocate the principle of unity in the laws of being and thinking, as he said in "Dlia g. Shevyreva. Poiasneniia kriticheskikh zamechanii na ego *Istoriiu poezii*" (For G. Shevyrev. An Explanation of Critical Observations of his *History of Poetry,* 1836) for *Teleskop,* to perceive the struggle of opposing forces both in the process of cognition and in the development of nature.

As a literary critic, specifically for his role in developing the aesthetics of Realism, Nadezhdin is regarded as a forerunner of Vissarion Grigor'evich Belinsky. Nadezhdin played a discernible role in shaping Belinsky's aesthetics, but from the beginning there were principal differences in their positions. Polemicizing with Nadezhdin, Belinsky demanded from contemporary literature "merciless frankness" and strongly criticized Nadezhdin for having seriously underestimated the merits of Pushkin's art. Yet Belinsky was quick to note in volume 17 of the 1841 *Otechestrennye zapiski* that Nadezhdin, "the opponent of Romanticism had a better understanding of it than its proponents." In his works of literary criticism, Nadezhdin attempted to develop a unified aesthetic theory. He considered that his most important task was to affirm the national originality of Russian literature, of its right to deal with actual Russian reality and to struggle against Romanticism. However, by criticizing the subjectivism and "dissolute willfulness" of the Romantics of the end of the 1820s and the beginning of the 1830s and thereby objectively promoting the development of Realism, Nadezhdin also rejected the "progressive Romanticism" of Byron and Pushkin, for example, which played into the hands of reactionary forces.

Nikolai Ivanovich Nadezhdin was born in the village of Nizhnyi-Beloomut, Riazan' province. His father, Ioann Ioannovich Nadezhdin was a deacon who only knew how to read and sing but instilled a love for reading in his son, especially books on history. Nadezhdin studied at the Riazan' Seminary (1815–1820) and then at the Moscow Theological Academy, from which he graduated in 1824. At the academy he studied the Hebrew, Greek, Latin, German, French, and English languages. Under the guidance of Fedor Aleksandrovich Golubinsky, Nadezhdin became acquainted with German philosophy, which helped him formulate his view of the history of mankind as a process in the development of ideas under the influence of time and place, and he began studying general and church history. After graduation he taught literature, rhetoric, logic, and Latin and German languages; he also served as a librarian at the Riazan' Seminary (1824–1826). He left the Riazan' Seminary post to take a job as house tutor with the Fedor Vasil'evich Samarin family in

Moscow. Samarin, a wealthy Moscow landowner, was the father of the future well-known Slavophile, Iurii Fedorovich Samarin, whom Nadezhdin helped educate. Taking advantage of the family's rich collection of books in Russian, French, German, and classical languages, Nadezhdin read Edward Gibbon (complete works), François Guizot, Jean-Charles-Léonard Simonde de Sismondi's twelve-volume *Histoire des républiques italiennes du moyen age* (History of the Italian Republics of the Middle Ages, 1809–1818) and Johann Paul Friedrich Richter. Exposure to these writers enabled him to see in a new light the philosophical theories of Plato, Franz von Baader, Immanuel Kant, and Schelling that he had studied at the Theological Academy. He was well acquainted with both classical and contemporary authors and translated Orpheus's hymns, Horace's odes, and Alphonse de Lamartine's *Méditations poétiques* (1820). Encouraged by Kachenovsky, Nadezhdin matriculated at Moscow University and wrote his dissertation in Latin titled *De Poseos, quae Romantica audit, origine, indole et fatis* (On the Origin, Nature, and Fate of Romantic Poetry), which he defended in 1830 as part of the requirements for the degree of doctor of philology.

The main thesis of his dissertation was that the forces of art are determined by the spirit of the age. Another important thesis developed by Nadezhdin was that "where there is life, there is poetry." He maintained that creative force is actually "life regenerating itself." He spoke of an idea as being the spirit of a work of art and of art as a union of form and idea. He viewed literature as an example of individual reflections of a common national life. He demanded that literature be conscious of its mission: it should not be idle play of the poet's personal fantasy, but rather, an expression of national consciousness.

Nadezhdin attributed the poverty of Russian poetry to the lack of serious and vigorous social life in Russia. He saw no possibility of Russian antiquity's offering any material for renewal of the national spirit in literature. He considered Russian medieval history as a period of purely physical expansion lacking any real life. The latter, he maintained, required "a powerful beginning of life" that did not take place during that period. During the Muscovite period the shape of the Russian national character had still not been formed. This period was only a preparatory stage toward a true national history initiated by Peter the Great. In regard to a national literature, it did not exist during the ancient period of Russian history because the spoken language was unsuitable for literary expression. Turning to the contemporary period, Nadezhdin asked how there

could be a Russian literature when a Russian literary language was still lacking. He maintained that a fuller and more active literary life as well as criticism could contribute to the improvement of the Russian language. He noted that related Slavic languages could help enrich the Russian language lexically while folk songs, proverbs, and sayings could contribute to its syntactical enrichment. Nadezhdin saw in Ivan Andreevich Krylov's fables and Zagoskin's novels the first serious attempts at elevating the language of the common people to the level of literary respectability. During the first three years of his own literary activity Nadezhdin published quite a large number of poems (he had begun writing poetry as a child) in the spirit of Friedrich Schiller, which were artistically rather weak. Later, in 1841 he published a short story titled "Sila voli" (Willpower), which appeared in a collection called *Sto russkikh literaturov* (A Hundred Writers).

From 1831 to 1835 Nadezhdin was an ordinary professor in the subdepartment of fine arts and archeology at Moscow University. His first assignment included the teaching of a course on the theory of fine arts and a course on the history of art (which he called archeology). In addition to his position at Moscow University, he began teaching in 1831 courses on logic, mythology, and Russian literature at the Moscow Theatrical School. In the second half of 1832 Nadezhdin made a trip to Germany, France, and Italy where he met important writers and gained new impressions. At Moscow University he lectured on the theory of fine arts, archeology, and logic. He did not read from his lecture notes, as was customary in those days; rather, his lectures were brilliant improvisations that made a lasting impression on his listeners, among them Nikolai Platonovich Ogarev, Nikolai Vladimirovich Stankevich, Konstantin Sergeevich Aksakov, and Ivan Aleksandrovich Goncharov. Some of them, including Aksakov, later found these lectures lacking significant content. In his lectures on the early 1830s Nadezhdin compared Russians (in endearing terms) to a horde of life-invigorating barbarians sweeping over degenerate Europe. Due to poor health, he resigned from his university position in 1835.

As a man of diverse interests Nadezhdin began his career as a publicist in two ways: first by contributing to Kachenovsky's *Vestnik Evropy* and in 1830 to Pogodin's *Moskovskii Vestnik* (Moscow Herald), then by founding the monthly *Teleskop* (Telescope) in 1831, a journal of "contemporary enlightenment," with its supplement *Molva* (Rumor), a newspaper of "fashions and news." As of 1833 Belinsky, who eventually became Russia's most influential literary critic during the nineteenth century, contributed to both publications. In fact, from June through December 1835 Belinsky was the acting editor of *Teleskop*. In 1836 new collaborators joined the journal, including Aleksandr Ivanovich Herzen, Mikhail Aleksandrovich Bakunin, Vasilii Petrovich Botkin, Aleksei Vasil'evich Kol'tsov, and Petr Iakovlevich Chaadaev.

Having begun to publish in Kachenovsky's journal, which was identified with defending all that was outdated and vapid in literature and regarded as an enemy of all that was modern and talented, Nadezhdin acquired the reputation of a detractor and pedant. He became the target of Nikolai Alekseevich Polevoi's harsh criticism and Pushkin's caustic epigrams of 1829 "Sapozhnik (Pritcha)" (The Shoemaker [A Parable]), "Mal'chishka Febu gimn podnes" (The Lad Who Composed a Hymn to Phoebus), "Nadeias' na moe prezrenie . . . " (Expecting My Scorn . . .), and "Sedoi Svistov! Ty tsarstvoral so slavoi" (Grey-haired Svistov! You Reigned with Fame). Eventually, Pushkin realized that Nadezhdin harbored no personal animosity toward him and placed in *Teleskop* two well-known polemical articles under the pseudonym "Feofilakt Kosichkin." Nadezhdin's heated polemics with Pushkin's enemy Faddei Venediktovich Bulgarin contributed to further understanding between Nadezhdin and Pushkin. The *Teleskop* also published Romantic writers such as Alexandre Dumas and Eugène Sue. Nadezhdin was particularly proud for having published Balzac, whose works he regarded as excellent examples of transition toward synthetic art. The *Teleskop* continued to develop ideas expressed by Nadezhdin in his early essays but with only limited success. His criticism did not gain favor with the public.

A key development of the 1830s that helped pave the way for the emergence of the "thick journals" at the end of the decade was the literary critics' assuming the role of social critics, shaped initially by Belinsky in his writings for Nadezhdin's journals. In 1834 Belinsky published *Literary Musings,* which may be regarded as the beginning of Russian journalism of the intelligentsia. Owing to Belinsky and other journalists of this period, a public opinion began to take shape. As the post-Decembrist government became uneasy with the growing sociopolitical tone of Russian journalism, it began closing many journals, including *Moskovskii Telegraf* (Moscow Telegraph) in 1834 and *Teleskop* (including the newspaper supplement *Molva*) in 1836. Nadezhdin's journal was closed down by the government for publishing Chaadaev's "Philosophical Letter," while Chaadaev was officially declared a lunatic and placed under medical supervision. Nadezhdin was

exiled to Siberia—first to Ust' Sysol'sk, then to Vologda (1836–1838). This sad event also brought an end to his long attraction to Elizaveta Vasil'evna Sukhovo-Kobylina (pseudonym Evgeniia Tur), who married a French count named Sailhas de Tournemire. As Nadezhdin later confessed in his unpublished letters to Pogodin, his exile plunged him into such despair that he never again engaged in independent journalistic activity. With the closing of the *Teleskop,* Belinsky was temporarily left without a regular job.

During his exile Nadezhdin developed a keen interest in historical ethnography. He wrote nearly one hundred essays for Adol'f Aleksandrovich Pliushar's *Èntsyklopedicheskii Leksikon* (Encyclopedic Lexicon, 1835–1841) on Russian and Slavic ethnography, ancient and modern, church and general Russian history, geography, philosophy, and aesthetics. His diverse scholarly activity also had a significant impact upon Russian historical geography. In addition to his reputation as a literary critic and publicist, for his scientific contributions, such as "Opyt istoricheskoi geografii russkogo mira. Stat'ia pervaia" (On Historical Geography of the Russian World), "Ob istoricheskikh trudakh v Rossii" (On Historical Research in Russia), and "Ob istoricheskoi istine i dostovernosti" (On Historical Truth and Authenticity), published in *Biblioteka dlia chteniia* (Library for Reading, 1837), he became recognized as a pioneer in historical geography. Following his return from exile to St. Petersburg in 1838, Nadezhdin spent the next several years living in Odessa, where he worked on the history of southern Russia for the Odessa Society of Lovers of History and Antiquity. From 1840 to 1841, on the instructions of Dimitrii Maksimovich Kniazhevich, Nadezhdin made an extensive trip to various Slavic countries and published in Varfolomei Ernei Kopitar's *Jahrbucher der Literatur* (part 95, 1841) an article on the dialects of the Russian language. In 1842 Nadezhdin settled in St. Petersburg.

After returning from exile Nadezhdin adopted reactionary political views. In 1843 he became editor of *Zhurnal Ministerstva vnutrennikh del* (Journal of the Ministry of Internal Affairs) and served in this capacity until 1856. He published in it a series of valuable works related to the geographic, ethnographic and statistical study of Russia: "Novorossiiskie stepi" (The Novorossiisk Steppes), "Plemia russkoe v obshchem semeistve slavian" (The Russian People as Part of the Slavic Family), "Issledovaniia o gorodakh russkikh" (Essays on Russian Cities), and "Ob'em i poriadok obozreniia narodnogo bogatstva" (Scope and System of Surveys of the National Wealth). During the administration of Minister Lev Alekseevich Perovsky, Nadezhdin became an expert resource person regarding historical, religious, and moral matters. He made two trips abroad—one from 1845 to 1846, the other from 1847 to 1848—for the purpose of gathering information for two articles commissioned by the ministry titled *Issledovanie o skopcheskoi eresi* (Investigations of the Skoptsy [Castrati] Heresy, 1845) and *O zagranichnykh raskol'nikakh* (Essay on Emigré Schismatics, 1846). The two articles were reprinted in London in a collection titled *Official Information Regarding Schismatics* (1860–1862). The essay on émigré schismatics, which offers much valuable information regarding this topic, reflects the views that were popular in the government circles at the time. The essay includes hints as to when and how Nadezhdin lived among the schismatics and how he obtained his information while carefully concealing the purpose of his research. Nadezhdin was an energetic worker in the Ethnographic Society, becoming its chairman and editor of *Geograficheskie Izvestiia* (Geographic News) in 1848 and editor of *Ètnograficheskii Sbornik* (Ethnographic Collection) in 1853. In the article "Ob ètnograficheskom izuchenii russkogo naroda" (About the Ethnographic Study of the Russian People), published in *Zapiski russkogo geograficheskogo obshchestva* (1847), Nadezhdin offers a broad outline of the scope of ethnographic research and its branching out into various areas of Russian life, including the study of nationality from the historical-geographic perspective and the perspectives of national psychology, archeology, and other matters. He produced several model works on historical geography and created an ethnographic survey, the distribution of which provided the Geographic Society with a mass of valuable data.

In 1851 Nadezhdin published an article called "O filologicheskikh nabliudeniiakh protoiereia Pavskogo nad sostavom russkogo iazyka" (About the Philosophical Observations of Archpriest Pavsky Regarding the Structure of the Russian Language) in *Otechestvennye zapiski* (Notes of the Fatherland) and in 1857 "O russkikh mifakh i sagakh v primenenii ikh k geografii i osobenno ètnografii russkoi" (Russian Myths and Sagas Applied to Russian Geography and Particularly Ethnography) in *Russkaia beseda* (Russian Debate). Aleksandr Nikolaevich Pypin in volume one of his *Istoriia russkoi ètnografii* (History of Russian Ethnography, 1890) characterized Nadezhdin's approach to the study of ethnography as "ethnographic pragmatism" that proceeded from direct and precise facts, and credited him with improving the methods of investigating and collecting ethnographic materials, that made

an impact on the work of ethnographers that followed.

Nadezhdin embodied his historical views, which strongly reflected the official viewpoint on nationality, in his articles "Evropeizm i narodnost' v otnoshenii k russkoi slovesnosti" (Europeanism and National Character in Russian Literature) in *Teleskop* (nos. 1 and 2, 1836) and "Ob istoricheskoi istine i dostovernosti" (On Historical Research in Russia) in *Biblioteka dlia chteniia* (no. 1, 1837). Nadezhdin's weltanschauung was contradictory. He tried to reconcile his liberal tendencies with his strong conservative views in his *Avtobiografia* (Autobiography, 1856). Although he supported autocratic rule and gradual progress and was critical of revolutionary upheaval, including the French Revolution, he nevertheless sharply exposed "the deep, motionless sleep . . . " (*Teleskop,* part 25, 1835, pp. 156–157) of Russian social life and supported democratization and enlightenment. Nadezhdin valued highly Peter the Great's reforms, regarding them as the beginning of Russia's historical development. Nadezhdin assigned primary significance to two genres: the novel and the novella. He believed that, with the exception of great historical events such as the War for the Fatherland of 1812 (hence his high esteem for Zagoskin's novels), the lack of development in Russian social life fails to offer the Russian novelist material needed for creative transformation. In a series of critical articles (for example, "Evropeizm i narodnost' v otnoshenii k russkoi slovesnosti") Nadezhdin established the relationship between the history of literature and the development of the literary language. After the suppression of *Teleskop,* Nadezhdin concentrated mainly on archeological, historical-ethnographic, and linguistic studies. Following a stroke in 1854, Nadezhdin's intellectual capacity declined perceptibly, and until his death 11 January 1856 in St. Petersburg he produced only a single work that is of any interest, his autobiography.

In the year Nadezhdin died Nikolai Gavrilovich Chernyshevsky pointed out Nadezhdin's significance for the history of Russian literature. According to Chernyshevsky—in volume three of his *Polnoe sobranie sochinenii* (1947)—Nadezhdin's greatest contribution was his introduction of genuine philosophical perception into Russian thinking. In his "Ocherki gogolevskogo perioda russkoi literatury" (Sketches of the Gogolian Period of Russian Literature), published in *Sovremennik* (1855–1856), Chernyshevsky went so far as to credit Nadezhdin with introducing German aesthetic theory into Russian literary thought and praised him for calling for a literature of greater ideological significance.

Chernyshevsky also attributed to Nadezhdin the role of Belinsky's mentor. Some have denied a direct tie between Nadezhdin and Belinsky. Perhaps a more accurate assessment is offered by Pavel Nikolaevich Miliukov in "Glavnye techeniia russkoi istoricheskoi mysli,"(Mainstream of Russian Historical Thought) published in *Russkaya Mysl'* (Russian Thought, no. 4, 1895), who observed that although Nadezhdin sided with the intellectual movement which embraced Schelling's philosophy, he was late in taking an active part in developing the basic ideas of the new ideology—whose representatives were Danil Mikhailovich Vellansky, Aleksandr Ivanovich Galich, Dmitrii Vladimirovich Venevitinov, and Prince Vladimir Fedorovich Odoevsky—as early as the 1820s. Most literary historians, however, admit that owing to Nadezhdin's influence, Russian literary criticism ceased to consist of brief passing remarks generated by personal impressions and instead became based on a theoretical foundation.

Nadezhdin was one of the most talented Russians of his time. He was a man of broad historical, theological, and literary knowledge and possessed considerable wit and a good theoretical mind. He was also known for his excessive patriotism, which led him to poeticize the Russian kulak, or wealthy peasant farmer, and employ the standard pronouncements on official nationality that were at variance with his basic views. These contradictions led some to conclude that Nadezhdin lacked firm convictions.

Most credit Ivan Vasil'evich Kireevsky, Venevitinov, Odoevsky, and Nadezhdin for having founded Russian philosophical aesthetics. At the beginning of the 1830s they represented its strongest wing, and they strove to create an integral system of poetics based on the principle of the unity of being and thinking. As a critic Nadezhdin helped to promote a realistic artistic consciousness, thereby laying the groundwork for the work of Russian literary critics that followed.

Letters:

To the Editor of *Vestnik Evropy* (22 December 1828), in *Vestnik Evropy*, no. 24 (1828): 300–304;

To The Publication Box of *Syn otechestva* and *Severnyi arkhiv* (26 March 1829); undated in *Vestnik Evropy*, no. 6 (1829): 152–162; and no. 7 (1829): 233–243;

To Iu. N. Bartenev (undated) in *Russkii arkhiv*, no. 1 (1864): 41–48;

To M. A. Maksimovich (1835–1849), in *Poliarnaia zvezda*, no. 4 (1881): 3–31; also excerpts (1837–1840), in *Russkii filologicheskii vestnik*, no. 2 (1911): 340–342, 353, 555;

To E. V. K-oi [E. V. Sukhovo-Kobylina] (1834–1835), in supplement to *Zhurnaly zasedanii Ryazanskoi uchenoi arkhivnoi komissii za 1883–1885 gg.* (Riazan', 1885), pp. 11–16; also in *Russkii arkhiv*, no. 8 (1885): 573–583;

Selected excerpts of letters addressed to M. A. Maksimovich, M. P. Pogodin (1840–1842), and S. P. Shevyrev [undated], in N. Barsukov, *Zhizn' i trudy M. P. Pogodina,* volume 3 (St. Petersburg, 1890), pp. 266, 323, 335; volume 5 (1892), pp. 51–56, 325–326, 435, 436; volume 6 (1892), pp. 330, 331; volume 9 (1895), p. 423; volume 10 (1896), pp. 44–48, 456, 457;

To Andrei Aleksandrovich Kraevsky in *Russkaia starina*, no. 5 (1904): 393–399; also in *Izvestiia otdeleniia russkogo iazyka i slovesnosti*, 10, no. 4 (1905): 303–311;

To V. V. Ganke (9 May 1843), in *Pis'ma k Ganke iz slavianskikh zemel'* (Warsaw, 1905), pp. 808–809;

To D. N. Bolgovsky (10 February–31 August 1837), in M. Lemke, *Nikolaevskie zhandarmy i literatura 1826–1855* (St. Petersburg, 1908), pp. 459–461.

Bibliographies:

G. N. Gennadi, "Spisok sochinenii i izdanii N. I. Nadezhdina," *Vestnik imperatorskogo russkogo geograficheskogo obshchestva,* 16, book 1, section 5 (1856): 16–19;

Gennadi, *Zhurnal Ministerstva narodnogo prosveshcheniya* (a list of fifty of Nadezhdin's works written 1829–1853), part 90, section 7 (1856): 92–96.

Biography:

N. K. Kozmin, *N. I. Nadezhdin. Zhizn' i nauchno-literaturnaia deiatel'nost'. 1804–1836* (St. Petersburg: M. A. Aleksandrova, 1912).

References:

I. O. Andronikov, "O dissertatsii S. M. Osovtseva 'Nadezhdin–teatral'nyi kritik'," *Teatr,* no. 5 (1967);

Anonymous, "Obozrenie sovremennykh russkikh zhurnalov," *Moskovskii telegraf,* no. 5 (1832): 98–104; no. 6: 123–152; no. 8: 170–181;

Aleksandra Andreevna Bazhenova, "N. I. Nadezhdin" in *Istoriia filosofii v SSSR,* edited by V. E. Evgrafov and others, volume 2, chapter 14 (Moscow: Nauka, 1968);

Vassarion Grigor'evich Belinsky, "Literaturnye mechtaniia," in *Polnoe sobranie sochinenii,* volume 1 (Moscow: Akademiia Nauk, 1953–1954), p. 86; "Nichto o nichem, ili otvet g. izdateliu *Teleskopa* za poslednee polugodie (1835) russkoi literatury," volume 2, pp. 7–50; "*Utrenniaia zarya. Al'manakh* na 1839 god," volume 3, pp. 66, 106–108; "*Odesskii al'manakh* na 1839 god," volume 5, pp. 213–214; "Sto russkich literatorov," volume 17, no. 7;

Nikolai Gavrilovich Chernyshevsky, "Ocherki gogolevskogo perioda russkoi literatury," *Sovremennik,* 54, no. 12 (1855); 55–60, nos. 1, 2, 4, 7, 9–12 (1856);

Chernyshevsky, *Polnoe sobranie sochinenii,* volume 3 (Moscow: Goslitizdat, 1947), pp. 140–143, 146–165, 169, 170, 177–196, 763, 764;

I. Z. Derkachev, "Ocherk èstetiki N. I. Nadezhdina," in *Uchenye zapiski Ul'ianovskogo gosudarstvennogo pedagogicheskogo instituta imeni I. N. Ul'ianova,* issue 8 (1956): 431–447;

Mikhail Mikhailovich Filippov, "Sud'by russkoi filosofii" (N. I. Nadezhdin i ego otnoshenie k Belinskomu), *Russkoe bogatstvo,* no. 9, section 1 (1894): 149–176;

Arusiak Georgievna Gukasova, "Iz istorii literaturno-zhurnal'noi bor'by vtoroi poloviny 20-kh godov XIX veka," *Uchenye zapiski Moskovskogo pedagogicheskogo instituta imeni V. I. Lenina,* 115, no. 7 (1957): 23–30;

Ivan Ivanovich Ivanov, *Istoria russkoi kritiki,* chapter 2 (St. Petersburg: Izdanie zhurnala "MirBozhii," 1898);

Vladimir Vladimirovich Kallash, "Pobornik narodnosti," *Russkaya mysl',* no. 12, section 2 (1904): 89–93;

I. Kamashev, "Neskol'ko zamechanii na rassuzhdenie g. Nadezhdina o proiskhozhdenii, svoistvakh i sud'be poezii, tak nazyvaemoi romanticheskoi," *Moskovskii vestnik,* part 3, no. 9 (1830): 44–57;

Zakhar Abramovich Kamensky, "Kommentarii," in *Russkie esteticheskie traktaty pervoi treti XIX veka,* volumes 1–2 (Moscow, 1974);

Kamensky, "Kurs logiki N. I. Nadezhdina v Moskovskom universitete," *Filosofskie nauki,* no. 2 (1981);

Kamensky, *N. I. Nadezhdin–Ocherk filosofskikh i èsteticheskikh vzglyadov 1828–1836* (Moscow, 1984);

E. N. Kiiko, "Nadezhdin" in *Istoriia russkoi kritiki,* volume 1, chapter 6 (Moscow-Leningrad: Akademiia Nauk SSSR, 1958), pp. 262–278;

P. Kogan, "N. I. Nadezhdin," in *Ocherki po istorii russkoi kritiki,* volume 1, edited by Anatoly Vasil'evich Lunacharsky and Pavel Ivanovich Lebedev-Poliansky (Moscow/Leningrad: GIZ, 1929), pp. 172–187;

Nikolai Kirovich Kozmin, "Nadezhdin i ego otnoshenie k Belinskomu," *Izvestiia otdeleniia russkogo iazyka i slovesnosti,* 10, no. 4 (1905): 303–311;

A. Lavretsky, "Istoriko-literaturnaia kontseptsiia Belinskogo, ee predshestvenniki, posledovateli i kritiki," *Belinsky—istorik i teoretik literatury* (Moscow/Leningrad: Akademiia Nauk SSSR, 1949), pp. 49–51;

Mikhail Konstantinovich Lemke, *Nikolaevskie zhandarmy i literatura 1826–1855 gg.* (includes Nadezhdin's testimony from the inquiry regarding the closing of the *Teleskop*) (St. Petersburg: S. Bunin, 1908), pp. 361–464;

L. Lobov, "N. I. Nadezhdin v russkoi kritike," *Zhurnal Ministerstva narodnogo prosveshcheniia,* no. 9, section 2 (1903): 29–44;

Iu. V. Mann, "Fakul'tety Nadezhdina," in N. I. Nadezhdin's *Literaturnaia kritika. Èstetika* (Moscow: Khudozhestvennaia literatura, 1972), pp. 3–44;

Mann, "Kommentarii," in *Nadezhdin N. I. Literaturnaia kritika. Estetika* (Moscow: Khudozhestvennaia literatura, 1972);

Mann, "N. I. Nadezhdin–predshestvennik Belinskogo," *Voprosy literatury,* no. 6 (1962): 143–166;

Petr Andreevich Mezentsev, "N. I. Nadezhdin i V. G. Belinsky," *Uchenye zapiski Kishinevskogo universiteta,* 22 (1956): 15–34;

P. N. Miliukov, "Glavnye techeniia russkoi istoricheskoi mysli," *Russkaya Mysl',* no. 43 (1895): 85–86;

Miliukov, "Nadezhdin i pervye kriticheskie stat'i Belinskogo," *Na slavnom postu. 1860–1900. Literaturnyi sbornik, posvyashchennyi N. K. Mikhailovskomu,* part 2 (St. Petersburg: N. N. Klobukova, 1900), pp. 409–430;

Nikolai Ivanovich Mordovchenko, "N. I. Nadezhdin. *Teleskop i Molva,*" in *Ocherki po istorii russkoi zhurnalistiki i kritiki,* volume 1 (Leningrad: Izdatel'stvo Leningradskogo gosuderstvennogo universiteta, 1950), pp. 342–370;

Moskovskii zhitel' [Makarov, M. N.], "O rechi Nadezhdina, proiznesennoi v Moskovskom universitete 6 iiulia 1831 g, 'Slovo o sovremennom napravlenii iziashchnykh iskusstv,'" *Severnaia pchela,* no. 208 (1833): 829–831; no. 209: 833–835;

Vera Stepanovna Nechaeva, "Stankevich i Nadezhdin" in Nechaeva, *V. G. Belinsky,* volume 2 (Moscow: Akademiia Nauk SSSR, 1954), pp. 177–202;

S. M. Osovtsev, *N. I. Nadezhdin—teatral'nyi kritik* (Leningrad, 1966);

Osovtsev, "Predshestvennik V. G. Belinskogo," *Uchenye zapiski Leningradskogo pedagogicheskogo instituta imeni A. I. Gertsena*, 144 (1957): 113–127;

M. G. Pavlov, "Pis'mo prof. Pavlova k izdateliu *Teleskopa* po povodu retsenzii na ego fiziku," *Teleskop*, no. 20 (1834);

Nikolai Alekseevich Polevoi, "O nachale, sushchnosti i uchasti poezii, romanticheskoi nazyvaemoi. Rassuzhdenie istoriko-kritiko-sostiazatel'noe. Sochinenie N. Nadezhdina," *Ocherki russkoi literatury*, part 2 (St. Petersburg, 1839), pp. 284–298;

Nil Aleksandrovich Popov, "N. I. Nadezhdin," *Zhurnal Ministerstva narodnogo prosveshcheniia*, no. 1, section 2 (1880): 1–43;

Aleksandr Sergeevich Pushkin, "Nadeyas' na moe prezrenie . . . ," *Polnoe sobranie sochinenii v desyati tomakh*, volume 3 (Moscow: Akademiia Nauk SSSR, 1959–1962), p. 279; "Epigramma" ("Sedoi Svistov! Ty tsarstvoval so slavoi . . . "), p. 280; "Epigramma" ("Mal'chishka Febu gimn podnes . . . "), p. 282; "Vozrazheniya kritikam 'Poltavy,'" volume 6, pp. 74–76;

A. N. Pypin, "N. I. Nadezhdin," *Vestnik Evropy*, no. 6 (1882): 624–662;

S. Shevyrev, "Vozmozhno kratkii i poslednii otvet avtora *Istorii poezii* g. izdateliu *Teleskopa*," *Moskovskii nabliudatel'*, part 7 (1836);

Gustav Gustavovich Shpet, *Ocherk razvitiia russkoi filosofii*, part 1 (Petrograd: Izdatel'stvo "Kolos," 1922), pp. 284–286, 299, 300, 339, 340;

Aleksandr Mikhailovich Skabichevsky, "Sorok let russkoi kritiki," *Sochineniia A. Skabichevskogo* (St. Petersburg: Tip. Tovarishchestva "Obshchestvennaia pol'za," 1895), pp. 285–291;

Sergei S. Trubachev, "Predshestvennik i uchitel' Belinskogo," *Istoricheskii vestnik*, no. 8 (1889): 307–330; no. 9: 449–527;

Mstislav Aleksandrovich Tsiavlovsky, "Epigramma 'Sedoi Svistov . . . ,'" *Zven'ia*, volume 9 (Moscow: Goskul'tprosvetizdat, 1951), pp. 163–167;

V. V. "Pis'mo k Nikodimu Aristarkhovichu Nedoumke," *Argus*, no. 4. Pribavlenie k zhurnalu *Galateia*, part 15 (1830);

Ivan Ivanovich Zamotin, "Literaturnye techeniia i literaturnaia kritika 30–kh godov." *Istoriia russkoi literatury XIX v*, volume 1, edited by D. N. Ovsyaniko-Kulikovsky (Moscow: Mir, 1908), pp. 316–329;

E. I. Zhegalkina, "Nadezhdin—kritik Pushkina," *Uchenye zapiski Moskovskogo oblastnogo pedagogicheskogo instituta imeni N. K. Krupskoi*, 66, no. 4 (1958): 29–101.

Papers:

Collections of Nadezhdin's papers are held at the Institut russkoi literatury (IRLI) and the Gosudarstvennaia publichnaia biblioteka (GPB); they include "Vtoroi kurs lektsii N. I. Nadezhdina po teorii izyashchnykh iskusstv 1832/33 akademicheskogo goda," RO IRLI, f. 199, op. 2, no. 84, l. 409–578 ob.; "Zhurnal lektsii iz klasa estetiki, chitannoi 1833, noiabria 25," edited by Ivan Kurasovsky, *Istoriia chuvstvitel'nogo*, RO IRLI, f. 199, op. 2, no. 87; "Zapiski lektsii professorov Moskovskogo universiteta . . . Lektsii logiki professora N. I. Nadezhdina v Imperatorskom Moskovskom universitete v 1834 godu. Logika N. Nadezhdina. s.s.s. O.N. M.U. P.Iu. Betskogo. OR and RK GPB, f. 71 (I. E. Betskii), no. 1, l. 249–283; "Lektsii po istorii iziashchnykh iskusstv," RO IRLI, f. 199, op. 2, no. 68, l. 1–77, ob. Published as fragments edited by N. K. Kozmin in *Russkie esteticheskie traktaty pervoi treti XIX veka*, volume 2; "Lektsii po logike, chitannye v Moskovskom universitete i zapisannye studentami," RO IRLI, f. 199, op. 2, no. 69, l. 1–28; "Pis'mo k E.V. Sukhovo-Kobylinoi," RO IRLI, f. 199, op. 2, ed. khr. 49; "Rassuzhdenie ob opasnosti izlishnego doveriia razumu pri iz" iasnenii Sviashchennogo pisaniia," RO IRLI, f. 199, op. 2, no. 4, l. 1–6, ob.; "Lektsii po teorii iziashchnykh iskusstv, chitannye v Moskovskom universitete," RO IRLI, f. 199, op. 2, no. 67; published as fragments edited by N. K. Kozmin in *Russkie esteticheskie traktaty pervoi treti XIX veka*, volume 2.

Vasilii Trofimovich Narezhny

(1780 – 21 June 1825)

Ronald D. LeBlanc
University of New Hampshire

BOOKS: *Dimitrii samozvanets* (Moscow, 1804);

Slavenskie vechera (St. Petersburg, 1809; expanded, St. Petersburg, 1826);

Rossiiskii Zhilblaz, ili Pokhozhdeniia kniazia Gavrily Simonovicha Chistiakova, parts 1–3 (St. Petersburg: Voennoe ministerstvo, 1814); complete, edited by Nikolai L. Stepanov (Moscow: Khudozhestvennaia literatura, 1938);

Aristion, ili Perevospitanie (St. Petersburg: V. Plavil'shikov, 1822);

Bursak, malorossiiskaia povest' (Moscow, 1824);

Novye povesti Vasiliia Narezhnogo (St. Petersburg, 1824);

Dva Ivana, ili Strast' k tiazhbam (Moscow, 1825);

Chernyi god, ili Gorskie kniazia (Moscow, 1829).

Editions and Collections: *Romany i povesti. Sochineniia Vasiliia Narezhnogo,* izdanie vtoroe, 10 volumes (St. Petersburg: A. Smirdin, 1835–1836);

Izbrannye romany, edited by Valerian Fedorovich Pereverzev (Moscow-Leningrad: Academia, 1933);

Izbrannye sochineniia, 2 volumes, edited by A. M. Zhigulev (Moscow: Goslitizdat, 1956).

Vasilii Trofimovich Narezhny

Although no less an authority than Vissarion Grigor'evich Belinsky acknowledged him to be Russia's "first" novelist, Narezhny has been given remarkably little credit for the important pioneering role he played in the development of the novel as a literary genre in early-nineteenth-century Russia. Instead he has been made to dwell in relative obscurity within the annals of Russian literary history, overlooked in the long shadows cast by contemporary giants such as Aleksandr Pushkin, Mikhail Iur'evich Lermontov, and Nikolai Gogol. Peculiarities of fate, as much as critical biases in favor of major writers, help to account for this lack of recognition for Narezhny's artistic achievement. For one thing, Narezhny was born in the Ukraine rather than Russia proper, and thus he wrote a coarse, humorous brand of prose fiction that might have been quite typical for writers who were "Little" Russians but was largely unusual, unfamiliar, and thus unsettling for readers who were "Great" Russians. Moreover, he was a novelist who wrote lengthy prose works—long, rambling narratives filled with extensive travels, many adventures, and complicated intrigues—during what was essentially a "golden age" of poetry in Russia (1810–1825), a period when the lyrical, elegiac, and epigrammatic were preferred over the comic, satiric, and ironic. Dismissed by many contemporary readers and critics alike as a literary anachronism, as an old-fashioned writer whose poetics were perhaps better suited to the eighteenth-century Enlightenment than to nineteenth-century Romanticism, Narezhny was also hounded by tsarist censors who withheld or delayed the publication of two of his best works until long after his death. Misunderstood by his audience, unappreciated by his critics, and oppressed by his censors, Narezhny was a writer who in many ways was simply out of step with his time.

Little is known about the details of Narezhny's personal life. He has left no memoirs or correspondence that might help to fill in the many blank spaces that exist in his biography; and because he avoided the fashionable salons and literary societies where the cultural elite of his day gathered, he is not mentioned often in the reminiscences left by some of his more famous contemporaries. The known facts are that Vasilii Trofimovich Narezhny was born in 1780 in Ustivitsa, a town located in the Mirgorod district of what was then the Poltava province of Ukraine. His father, Trofim Ivanovich Narezhny, served as a sergeant-major in a Cossack cavalry unit, the Chernigov carabineer regiment, until his retirement in 1786 when he was promoted to the rank of cornet and granted nobility status. Although Narezhny's father officially became a member of the gentry class, he remained in actuality a poor small landowner—a typical Ukrainian petty *shliakhtich* (squire)—who owned no serfs and who lived in a manner little different from that of a simple Cossack. For Soviet critics, these humble social origins are often invoked as a way to help explain the democratic sympathies and progressive views that the author purportedly displays in his literary works. As a child Narezhny was taught at home by an uncle, although the keen familiarity with seminary life that the author reveals in some of his novels has led some scholars to speculate that he might have attended a *bursa* (seminary school) in Chernigov. In 1792, when he had reached the age of twelve, Narezhny was sent away to attend the preparatory academy for *dvorianskaia gimnaziia* (gentry children) that was affiliated with Moscow University. Upon graduation from this school in 1799 Narezhny proceeded to enroll as a student at Moscow University, where he studied philosophy for two years before suddenly dropping out of school in 1801, apparently for reasons of financial and material hardships.

It was during his brief stay at Moscow University that Narezhny began his literary activity. He became acquainted with several classmates who would later become relatively influential men of letters in Russia (Aleksei Fedorovich Merzliakov, Aleksandr Fedorovich Voeikov, V. R. Vronchenko) as well as with Pavel Afanas'evich Sokhatsky, a teacher of classics who lectured on Greek and Latin literature and who served as editor for two university publications, *Priiatnoe i poleznoe preprovozhdenie vremeni* (Pleasant and Useful Passing of Time) and *Ippokrena, ili Utekhi liubosloviia* (Hippocrene, or the Pleasures of Philology). In these two journals Narezhny published his earliest literary efforts: two heroic poems on Russian historical themes, "Brega Alty" (The Banks of the Alta, 1798) and "Osvobozhdennaia Moskva" (Moscow Liberated, 1798), and two tragic dramas on classical themes, "Den' zlodeistva i uzhasa" (A Day of Villainy and Terror, 1799) and "Krovavaia noch', ili Konechnoe padenie domu Kadmova" (A Bloody Night, or The Final Collapse of the House of Cadmus, 1800). It was during these years as a student at Moscow University that Narezhny likewise wrote *Dimitrii samozvanets* (Dimitrii the Pretender), a pre-Romantic tragedy patterned largely after Friedrich Schiller's *Die Räuber* (1781), which was published in 1804 and performed on stage for the first time in 1809. The two years at Moscow University were largely a period of literary apprenticeship for Narezhny, who was required to study works of both classical antiquity and modern European literature. One detects an imitative and derivative quality to Narezhny's earliest works, especially the heroic poems on historical themes, which owe an obvious debt to Ossian, who was extremely popular at this time.

Upon leaving the university, Narezhny accepted an offer to work in the chancellery office of Petr Ivanovich Kovalensky, the newly appointed civilian ruler of Georgia. In 1802, therefore, Narezhny departed for the Caucasus where he assumed the duties of secretary in the headquarters office for the militia and spent a year in Tbilisi witnessing much of the administrative corruption that characterized Russian rule in this new imperial possession. These experiences in the Caucasus would later provide the material for Narezhny's novel, *Chernyi god, ili Gorskie kniazia* (The Black Year, or Mountain Princes, 1829), which satirizes the vices of Russian colonial rule as well as local Georgian political and ecclesiastical officialdom. Narezhny returned to St. Petersburg in 1803 and took up service in the Ministry of Internal Affairs, working for the next several years at the dispatch office for the department of state management. In 1809 Narezhny published the first part of *Slavenskie vechera* (Slavonic Evenings), a cycle of tales written in rhythmic prose that depicted certain well-known figures and legendary events from the Kievan period of Russian history heroically and poetically. Written under the influence of Ossianic poetry as well as the recently discovered national folk epic, *Slovo o polku Igoreve* (The Lay of Igor's Campaign, composed in the 1180s), these highly patriotic "poems in prose" were well received by the critics and brought Narezhny his first true literary recognition. Indeed, the huge success of *Slavenskie vechera* encouraged Narezhny in 1813 to get married and leave his civil service job in order to devote himself exclusively to his current work on a lengthy satiric novel of mores and manners that depicted life in contemporary Russia.

The novel that resulted from this temporary hiatus in his career of government service, *Rossiiskii Zhilblaz, ili Pokhozhdeniia kniazia Gavrily Simonovicha Chistiakova* (A Russian Gil Blas, or The Adventures of Prince Gavrily Simonovich Chistiakov, 1814), a scathing satire that attacks the vices of bureaucratic and gentry Russia alike, is artistically one of Narezhny's most significant and most successful works. The satire in *Rossiiskii Zhilblaz* is so strong and bitter, however, that only the first three parts of the novel were allowed to be published in 1814, and copies of them were quickly ordered to be confiscated from the shelves of bookstalls; the last three parts, meanwhile, were held up by the tsarist censors and did not appear in print until the Soviet period (in 1938).

In terms of genre and narrative structure, the very title of Narezhny's novel seems openly to acknowledge the Russian author's debt to Alain Réné Lesage's French classic, *Histoire de Gil Blas de Santillane* (1715–1735), the adventure plot that, based on the hero's series of picaresque escapades, allowed him to paint a broad panoramic canvas of various aspects of contemporary life. In *Rossiiskii Zhilblaz,* Chistiakov's travels take him from gentry estates located in the Russian countryside to the homes of high-ranking government officials living in the capital. Along the way he encounters a wide variety of social and professional types: despotic landowners, corrupt civil servants, greedy merchants, immoral actors, hypocritical clergy, hedonistic aristocrats, imitative writers. Soviet critics, following the lead of Nikolai L. Stepanov, have characterized *Rossiiskii Zhilblaz* as a work of "Enlightenment Realism," linking it with European novels such as Tobias Smollett's *The Adventures of Roderick Random* (1748) and Henry Fielding's *Tom Jones* (1749), because of the strong faith the Russian author displays in man's essential rationality and innate moral goodness. The label "Enlightenment Realism" also has been applied to Narezhny's poetics as a way to account for the elements of didacticism, rationalism, and utopianism present in his works. Narezhny's Enlightenment values and beliefs, Soviet Marxist critics have maintained, help to explain this "democratic" writer's inability to appreciate the objective laws of historical determinism and class struggle at work in the world he depicts. Narezhny's poetics, however, are rather more complex and complicated

than such critics have been able or willing to recognize; his relationship to Lesage's picaresque model, moreover, can be seen as playful and parodic rather than merely imitative.

The practical (nonaesthetic) failure of *Rossiiskii Zhilblaz,* due to the censorship problems that prevented its complete publication, seems to have affected the author deeply; according to his son's testimony in A. D. Galakhov's *Istoricheskaia khrestomatiia novogo perioda russkoi slovestnosti* (1864), Narezhny seriously considered giving up a literary career altogether. In any event he was forced to return to government service in order to maintain a livelihood. In 1815, therefore, Narezhny joined the Inspector's Department at the headquarters of the Ministry of War as a desk chief, and three years later he was promoted to the rank of court counselor. It was around this time, in 1818, that he attempted to get *Chernyi god* published by the *Vol'noe obshchestvo liubitelei rossiiskoi slovesnosti* (Free Society of Lovers of Russian Literature), a literary organization to which he did not belong but of which many of his friends and acquaintances were members. The Free Society, however, refused to publish *Chernyi god,* mainly because it feared that the bitter satiric tone of Narezhny's Caucasian novel, aimed directly at autocratic rulers and representatives of organized religion, would prevent the work from ever passing the censors. *Chernyi god* was not published until 1829, by which time it was already perceived as a literary anachronism by a contemporary audience that had been nurtured for more than a decade on Romantic tales and poems about the exotic Caucasian landscape. Instead of being hailed as the "Columbus of the Caucasus," Narezhny was chastised for reverting back to the eighteenth century and the now-archaic literary models provided by Voltaire, Jonathan Swift and Montesquieu. One contemporary reviewer complained that *Chernyi god* "carries upon itself the imprint of *Candide, Gulliver's Travels,* and a host of other works that some time ago inundated all of European literature." Although *Chernyi god* tends to be dismissed even today as merely another philosophical journey or adventure narrative that uses the clichéd devices of the old-fashioned Eastern tale (particularly the Oriental "mask") to satirize political vices, some modern critics, such as Pavel Mikhed, have underscored the presence of Rabelaisian elements in this satiric novel. The carnivalesque scenes, robust humor, and prandial imagery in *Chernyi god* are all part of the "grotesque realism" with which Narezhny's works, according to Mikhail Bakhtin's "Rable i Gogol (Iskusstvo slova i narodnaia smekhovaia kul'tyra)" (1975), are saturated.

Title page for Narezhny's novel Aristion, ili Perevospitanie
(Aristion, or Reeducation)

The late part of the 1810s and early part of the 1820s proved to be the most active period of Narezhny's brief literary career; during this time he produced a series of novels on Ukrainian themes. He retired from government service in 1821 and devoted the last four years of his life exclusively to literary activity. In 1822 he published *Aristion, ili Perevospitanie* (Aristion, or Reeducation), an *Erziehungsroman* (novel of education) written in the tradition of François de Salignac de La Mothe-Fénelon's *Les Aventures de Télémaque* (1699) and Jean-Jacques Rousseau's *Émile: ou, de l'éducation* (1762), in which the eponymous hero, a young wastrel who leads a life of gambling, wenching, and squandering money in decadent St. Petersburg, is remade into a model gentleman through a rigorous program of moral and intellectual reeducation based on the pedagogic principles of Rousseau. The elaborate hoax that is devised by his father in order to trick Aristion into agreeing to undergo this reeducation program defies credulity, and the moralizing lectures delivered by the hero's mentor are didactically dull. The protagonist's tour of neighboring estates, however, during which time the reader is introduced to colorful char-

acter types such as the miserly Tarakh, the hedonistic Paramon, and the ardent hunter Silvester, is informed by the kind of robust realism and coarse humor that led his contemporaries to call Narezhny the "Russian Teniers" (after Flemish genre painter David Teniers the Younger). Indeed, many critics point to Narezhny's characterizations in *Aristion* as prototypes for some of the grotesque landowners, such as Pliushkin, Nozdrev, and Petukh, that Chichikov later encounters during his "grand tour" of the Russian countryside in Nikolai Gogol's *Mertvye dushi* (Dead Souls, 1842).

Two years later, in 1824, Narezhny published *Novye povesti* (New Stories), a collection of six primarily humorous tales that included "Mariia" (Marie), "Nevesta pod zamkom" (The Fiancée Under Lock and Key), "Zaporozhets" (The Zaporozhian Cossack), "Zamorskii prints" (The Foreign Prince), "Turetskii sud" (Turkish Justice), and "Bogatyi bedniak" (The Wealthy Beggar). During that same year Narezhny published *Bursak, malorossiiskaia povest'* (The Seminary Student, a Little Russian Tale, 1824), a combination of picaresque novel and historical romance that many consider the most accomplished of the works he succeeded in having published during his lifetime. Written just prior to the time when Sir Walter Scott's novels became popular in Russia, *Bursak* freely fictionalizes events from seventeenth-century Ukrainian history, depicting scenes and figures that seem to come straight out of a fairy tale rather than the historical Russian past. The most interesting section of the novel occurs at the very beginning, before the hero's travels and adventures even commence, when the narrator describes the student years of Neon Khlopotinsky while he is attending a seminary school in Pereiaslavl. In a series of lively and colorful scenes where the author depicts these schoolboys drinking, brawling, and wenching, Narezhny draws upon the rich sources of Ukrainian folk culture, thus preparing the ground for Gogol's memorable portrayal of seminary life in his tales "Vii" and "Taras Bul'ba" (in *Mirogorod*, 1835) a decade later.

Narezhny's talent for describing the Ukrainian physiognomy in a humorous, satirical manner is likewise evident in *Dva Ivana, ili Strast' k tiazhbam* (The Two Ivans, or A Passion for Litigations, 1825), a comic novel of mores and manners that appeared in print just two weeks after the author's sudden, unexplained death on 21 June 1825. Like Gogol's pair of protagonists in the later "Povest' o tom, kak possorilis' Ivan Ivanovich s Ivanom Nikiforovichem" (The Tale of How Ivan Ivanovich Quarreled with Ivan Nikiforovich, in *Mirgorod,* 1835), Narezhny's "two Ivans" become involved in a long, protracted litigation—not against each other, however, but against a common neighbor, Pan Khariton. The lawsuit serves as the narrative device that allows the author to describe at some length, and in comic hues, these three Ukrainian petty squires and their provincial way of life. The "Flemish" artistic traits of this "Russian Teniers" are particularly evident in Narezhny's earthy depictions of scenes of eating, drinking, and carousing that appear regularly throughout this tale. The rather utopian "happy ending" to this mock epic in prose mars its realism, however, and reveals the lingering influence that the eighteenth-century Enlightenment, especially its rationalism and didacticism, continued to exert upon the author's poetics.

Narezhny's final literary work, an unfinished "robber novel" titled *Garkusha, malorossiiskii razboinik* (Garkusha, the Little Russian Bandit), provides a fictional account of the life and adventures of the legendary Ukrainian Robin Hood. In Narezhny's version of the biography of this famous eighteenth-century outlaw, the hero evolves from a simple peasant lad who peacefully tends a flock of sheep to a powerful robber who preys upon the wealth of neighboring Polish landowners—all as a result of a social wrong he had been made to suffer as a young man. Posthumous attempts by family and friends to have Narezhny's uncompleted manuscript published in Russia repeatedly failed, largely because tsarist censors observed in the text a tendency on the author's part to justify Garkusha's crimes on the grounds that he was a victim of social injustice. Like the full text of *Rossiiskii Zhilblaz,* Narezhny's final novel was not published until the Soviet period (in Boris S. Meilakh, ed., *Russkie povesti XIX veka 20-x-30-x godov,* 1950).

Although largely forgotten or ignored over the years, Narezhny is a writer who played an important role in the development of prose fiction—and especially the novel—in Russia during the early part of the nineteenth century. As an immediate precursor of Gogol and the writers of the Natural School, he was instrumental in preparing the way for the rise of Realism in Russian literature. Indeed, the novelist Ivan Aleksandrovich Goncharov wrote to M. I. Semevsky on 11 December 1874 that, had Narezhny been fortunate enough to have been born a few generations later, he would have been an "impressive figure" on the contemporary literary scene. Since Narezhny has in essence been "discovered" only during the Soviet period, his works have been analyzed mainly by critics who have shown a tendency to overstate the writer's Enlightenment values and thus to link him closely with the eighteenth-century Russian satirical tradition of Ivan Andreevich Krylov, Denis Ivanovich Fonvizin, and Mikhail Dmitrievich Chulkov. In recent years, however, several scholars have instead highlighted the Baroque features of Narezhny's works, especially their connection with the grotesque realism that derives from Ukrainian folk culture. There is general agreement among most critics, however, that despite the occasional heaviness of his style (with its archaisms and Slavonicisms), Narezhny helped to enrich the Russian literary language by introducing regionalisms, colloquialisms, and other popular forms of oral speech. Through his colorful depictions of native life in provincial Little Russia, Narezhny also helped to democratize Russian letters by portraying characters from various social levels that had previously been excluded from artistic treatment.

It would be well to keep in mind, when assessing this largely forgotten writer's contribution to Russian literary history, that Narezhny was a literary pioneer who could count upon few indigenous models to guide him as he went about the task of "Russianizing" the genre of the novel on native soil. His works nonetheless reveal a surprisingly high degree of artistic sophistication and a keen discriminating sense of what was (and, more importantly, what was not) appropriate to the Russian cultural context: to his country's social and political institutions as well as its literary traditions, spiritual values, and historical conditions.

References:

Nadezhda Aleksandrovna Belozerskaia, *Vasilii Trofimovich Narezhnyi. Istoriko-literaturnyi ocherk,* 2 volumes (St. Petersburg: L. F. Panteleev, 1896);

William E. Brown, "The Picaresque and Adventure Novel: Vasily Narezhny," in his *A History of Russian Literature of the Romantic Period,* volume 2 (Ann Arbor: Ardis, 1986), pp. 175–202;

V. A. Budrin, "Poslednii roman V. T. Narezhnogo *Garkusha, malorossiiskii razboinik,*" *Uchenye zapiski Permskogo gosudarstvennogo pedagogicheskogo instituta,* no. 10 (1946): 41–79;

Jean Chopin, "Oeuvres de Basile Narejny," *Revue Encyclopédique,* 44 (1829): 111–122;

Vladimir V. Danilov, "Zemliak i predtecha Gogolia," *Kievskaia starina,* 92, nos. 3–4 (1906): 285–298;

A. D. Galakhov, *Istorichiskaia khrestomatiia novogo perioda russkoi slovestnosti* (St. Petersbury, 1864);

S. A. Goncharov, "Zhanrovaia struktura romana V. T. Narezhnogo *Rossiiskii Zhilblaz,*" in *Literaturnoe proizvedenie i literaturnyi protsess v aspekte istoricheskoi poetiki,* edited by M. N. Darvin (Kemerevo: Kemerovskii gos. univ., 1988), pp. 75–86;

R. F. Iusufov, "Roman V. T. Narezhnogo *Chernyi god ili gorskie kniaz'ia,*" *Uchenye zapiski instituta istorii, iazyka i literatury im. G. Tsadasy* (seriia filologicheskaia), 18 (1968): 147–166;

Ronald D. LeBlanc, "The Monarch as Glutton: Vasily Narezhny's *The Black Year,*" in *Diet and Discourse: Eating, Drinking and Literature,* edited by Evelyn Hinz (Winnipeg: Mosaic, 1991), pp. 53–67;

LeBlanc, "Narrative Strategy in Nareznyj's *Rossijskij Zilblaz,*" *Russian Language Journal,* no. 135 (1986): 55–62;

LeBlanc, "Vasily Narezhny's *Rossiiskii Zhilblaz,*" in his *The Russianization of Gil Blas: A Study in Literary Appropriation* (Columbus, Ohio: Slavica, 1986), pp. 85–144;

Iurii Mann, "U istokov russkogo romana," *Voprosy literatury,* 5 (1983): 151–170;

Halina Mazurek-Wita, *Powieści Wasyla Narieznego na tle prozy satyryczno-obyczajowej XVIII i początku XIX wieku* (Wrocław: Akademia Nauk, 1978);

Pavel Mikhed, "O prirode i kharaktere smekha v romanakh V. T. Narezhnogo," *Voprosy russkoi literatury,* 42, no. 2 (1983): 87–92;

Mikhed, "Romany V. T. Narezhnogo i Ukraina," in V. T. Narezhnyi, *Bursak, malorossiiskaia povest'. Dva Ivana, ili Strast' k tiazhbam. Garkusha, malorossiiskii razboinik* (Kiev: Dnipro, 1988), pp. 5–18;

Mikhed, "V. T. Narizhnyi i barokko (Do pytannia pro styl' pys'mennyka)," *Radians'ke literaturoznavstvo,* no. 11 (1979): 74–83;

T. G. Orlova, "Parodirovanie v romane V. T. Narezhnogo *Rossiiskii Zhilblaz* kak otrazhenie literaturnoi i iazykovoi pozitsii avtora," *Funktsional'noe i sistemno-tipologicheskoe izuchenie iazyka i literatury* (Moscow: univ. im. Patrisa Lumumby, 1984), pp. 298–307;

N. K. Ostrovskaia, "Ukraina v tvorchestve V. T. Narezhnogo," *Trudy Odesskogo gosudarstvennogo universiteta,* 150, no. 4 (1960): 77–87;

Valerian Pereverzev, "Provozvestnik romana 'natural'noi shkoly' V. T. Narezhnyi," in his *U istokov russkogo real'nogo romana* (Moscow: Khudozhestvennaia literatura, 1937), pp. 7–43;

Vano Shaduri, *Pervyi russkii roman o Kavkaze* (Tbilisi: Zaria vostoka, 1947);

Iurii Sokolov, "V. T. Narezhnyi (Dva ocherka)," *Besedy. Sbornik Obshchestva istoril literatury v Moskve,* volume 1 (Moscow, 1915), pp. 77–109;

E. E. Sollertinskii, "Povest' V. T. Narezhnogo *Dva Ivana,*" *Uchenye zapiski Moskovskogo oblastnogo pedagogicheskogo instituta,* 40, no. 2 (1956): 3–32;

Sollertinskii, "Roman V. T. Narezhnogo *Rossiiskii Zhilblaz,*" *Uchenye zapiski Ural'skogo pedagogicheskogo instituta,* 2, no. 4 (1955): 101–134;

Nikolai L. Stepanov, "Pervyi russkii romanist—V. T. Narezhnyi," in his *Poety i prozaiki* (Moscow: Khudozhestvennaia literatura, 1966), pp. 23–65;

Jurij Striedter, "V. T. Nareznyjs *Russischer Gil Blas,*" in his *Der Schelmenroman in Russland: Ein Beitrag zur Geschichte des russischen Romans vor Gogol'* (Berlin: Erisch Blaschker, 1961), pp. 181–211;

Liane Teml, *Vasilij T. Nareznyjs satirische Romane: Ein Beitrag zur russischen Satire vor Gogol'* (Munich: Tuduv, 1979);

V. E. Zhukovskii, "V. T. Narezhnyi i tsenzura," *Trudy Azerbaidzhanskogo gosudarstvennogo universiteta im. S. M. Kirova (seriia filologicheskaia),* no. 2 (1947): 71–90.

Vladimir Fedorovich Odoevsky
(30 July 1804 or 1803 – 27 February 1869)

Neil Cornwell
University of Bristol

BOOKS: *Chetyre apologa* (Moscow, 1824);

Pestrye skazki s krasnym slovtsom, sobrannye Irineem Modestovichem Gomozeikoiu, magistrom filosofii i chlenom raznykh uchenykh obshchest, izdannye V. Bezglasnym (St. Petersburg: Ekspeditsiia zagotovleniia Gosudarstvennykh bumag, 1833);

Detskaia knizhka dlia voskresnykh dnei (St. Petersburg, 1833);

Gorodok v tabakerke. Detskaia skazka Dedushki Irineia (St. Petersburg, 1834);

Kniazhna Mimi: domashnye razgovory, as V. Bezglasnyi (St. Petersburg: Russkaia slovesnost', no date);

Skazki i povesti dlia detei Dedushki Irineia (St. Petersburg, 1841);

Sochineniia kniazia V. F. Odoevskogo, 3 volumes (St. Petersburg: A. I. Ivanov, 1844);

Sbornik detskikh pesen Dedushki Irineia (St. Petersburg, 1847);

Lettre et plaidoyer en faveur de l'abonné russe (Nice, 1857);

Nedovol'no (Moscow, 1867);

Publichnye lektsii professora Liubimova (Moscow, 1868);

4338-yi god: fantasticheskii roman (Moscow, 1926);

Izbrannye muzykal'no-kriticheskie stat'i (Moscow-Leningrad: Muzgiz, 1951);

Stat'i o M. I. Glinke, edited by G. B. Bernandt (Moscow: Muzgiz, 1953);

Izbrannye pedagogicheskie sochineniia, edited by V. I. Struminsky (Moscow: Uchpedgiz, 1955);

Muzykal'no-literaturnoe nasledie, edited by Bernandt (Moscow: Muzgiz, 1956);

O literature i iskusstve, edited by Vsevolod Ivanovich Sakharov (Moscow: Sovremennik, 1982).

Editions and Collections: *Dedushki Irineia skazki i sochinenia dlia detei* (Moscow, 1871);

Skazki i rasskazy Dedushki Irineia (St. Petersburg: A. S. Suvorin, 1889);

Povesti, 3 volumes (St. Petersburg: A. S. Suvorin, 1890);

Russkie nochi, edited by S. A. Tsvetkov (Moscow: Put', 1913); revised, edited by B. F. Egorov, E. A.

Vladimir Fedorovich Odoevsky

Maimin, and M. I. Medovoi (Leningrad: Nauka, 1975);

Romanticheskie povesti, edited by Orest Tsekhnovitser (Leningrad: Priboi, 1929);

Deviat' povestei (New York: Chekhov Publishers, 1954);

Povesti i rasskazy, edited by E. Iu. Khin (Moscow: Khudozhestvennaia literatura, 1959);

Povesti, edited by Vsevolod Ivanovich Sakharov (Moscow: Sovetskaia Rossiia, 1977);

Sochineniia v dvukh tomakh, edited by Sakharov (Moscow: Khudozhestvennaia literatura, 1981);

Poslednii kvartet Betkhovena: povesti, rasskazy, ocherki, Odoevsky v zhizni, edited by Vladimir Bronislavovich Murav'ev (Moscow: Moskovskii rabochii, 1982);

Pestrye skazki, edited by Neil Cornwell (Durham, U.K.: University of Durham, 1988);

Povesti i rasskazy, edited by A. Nemzer (Moscow: Khudozhestvennaia literatura, 1988);

Pestrye skazki, with *Skazki Irineia Modestovicha Gomozeiki,* edited by V. Grekov (Moscow Khudozhestvennaia literatura, 1993);

Pestrye skazki, edited by Marietta A. Tur'ian (St. Petersburg: Nauka, 1996).

Editions in English: *Russian Nights,* translated by Olga Koshansky-Olienikov and Ralph E. Matlaw (New York: Dutton, 1965);

Old Father Frost: A Russian Fairy Tale, translated by James Riordan (Moscow: Progress, 1981);

The Salamander and Other Gothic Tales, translated by Neil Cornwell (London: Bristol Classical Press, 1992; Evanston, Ill.: Northwestern University Press, 1992).

OTHER: *Mnemozina,* nos. 1–4, edited by Odoevsky and Vil'gel'm Karlovich Kiukhel'beker (Moscow, 1824–1825);

"Segeliel'. Don Kikhot XIX stoletiia. Skazka dlia starykh detei (otryvok iz 1-i chasti')," *Sbornik na 1838 A. F. Voeikova i V. A. Vladislavleva* (St. Petersburg, 1838), pp. 89–104;

"Sirota," *Al'manakh na 1838 god* (St. Petersburg, 1838), pp. 237–288;

"Zapiski grobovshchika," *Al'manakh na 1838 god* (St. Petersburg, 1838), pp. 221–236;

Sel'skoe chtenie, 4 books, edited by Odoevsky and A. P. Zablotsky (1844–1847);

"Sirotinka," *Vchera i segodnia* (St. Petersburg, 1845), pp. 3–16;

Rasskazy o boge, prirode i cheloveke: kniga dlia chteniia, edited by Odoevsky and Zablotsky (St. Petersburg, 1849);

"Iz bumag kniazia V. F. Odoevskogo," edited by Odoevsky, *Russkii arkhiv,* 7–8 (1864): 804–849;

Russkie èsteticheskie traktaty pervoi treti XIX veka v dvukh tomakh, edited by Zakhar Abramovich Kamensky, volume 2 (Moscow, 1974), pp. 156–192.

SELECTED PERIODICAL PUBLICATIONS: "Peterburgskie pis'ma," *Moskovskii nabliudatel',* 1 (1835): 55–69;

"Kto sumasshedshie?," *Biblioteka dlia chteniia,* 14 (1836): 50–64;

"Iz bumag kniazia V. F. Odoevskogo," *Russkii arkhiv,* 1 (1874): 278–360;

"Iz bumag kniazia V. F. Odoevskogo," *Russkii arkhiv,* 2 (1874): 11–54;

"Grazhdanskie zavety kniazia V. F. Odoevskogo," *Russkii arkhiv,* 2, no. 5 (1895): 36–54;

"'Tekushchaia khronika i osobye proisshestviia.' Dnevnik V. F. Odoevskogo 1859–1868gg.," *Literaturnoe nasledstvo,* 22, no. 4 (1935): 79–308.

In the 1830s Vladimir Odoevsky was one of the most popular authors in Russia, rated as a prose writer not far below Aleksandr Pushkin and Nikolai Gogol. His star rapidly waned as he went prematurely into a virtual literary retirement in the mid 1840s, some quarter of a century before his death, as the Romantic style of writing gave way to the new "Natural School" in prose and to the rise of Russian realism. Odoevsky was also well known as a thinker, a children's writer, a popular educator, a literary entrepreneur, an amateur scientist, and the first serious Russian musicologist, as well as a distinguished public servant and the host of a leading artistic salon through five decades. One contemporary recorded that "on Odoevsky's divan sits the whole of Russian literature." A central figure of his time, Odoevsky was close to the major historical events of the period and closely acquainted with its leading personalities, from Pushkin and Mikhail Ivanovich Glinka to Leo Tolstoy and Petr Il'ich Tchaikovsky. His reputation as an exponent of Russian Romantic prose, which had undergone occasional revivals (for instance at the turn of the century and again in the 1950s), in the 1990s stands at its highest point with the Russian reading public since his own heyday. A reputation for eccentricity, "encyclopedism," and dilettantism had caused him to be taken less seriously, both during his lifetime and for some time thereafter, than was his due. However, since 1975 more editions of his works have appeared than in the whole of the previous hundred years (although some editions carry the same title—to wit *Povesti i rasskazy,* Tales and Stories—the selections of material in fact differ).

Prince Vladimir Fedorovich Odoevsky was born in 1804 (or, according to some sources, in 1803—Odoevsky himself cited both years) into one of the oldest families in Russia, which traced its lineage back to the Varangian prince, Rurik. Indeed, as a *kniaz'* (prince), Odoevsky had in theory at least as much right to the throne as did the Romanov family, and was in later life recognized in the honorary position of Russia's "premier nobleman," the last of his line. Although several Odoevskys had played prominent roles over the centuries in Russian history, the family fortunes were largely dissipated in the eighteenth century, and as a result the later Odoevskys, while not exactly existing in abject poverty, were forced to work for a living. Vladimir's father, Fedor Sergeevich Odoevsky, was a state councillor and director of the Moscow Assignation Bank. Vladimir Odoevsky was financially dependent on his government salary; additional income from writing, journalism, and musical reviewing was always welcome. Aleksandr Ivanovich Odoevsky, his first cousin, who was to become a Decembrist poet, served as a Guards officer. Furthermore, his aristocratic lineage notwithstanding, Odoevsky was long thought to have been something of a *raznochinets* (person of mixed rank), because his mother, Ekaterina Alekseevna Fillipova, was widely supposed to have been a serf until her marriage. However, more recent research by biographer Marietta A. Tur'ian reveals this belief to have been an exaggeration; Odoevsky's mother in fact hailed from the lower reaches of the landowning classes.

Tur'ian's 1991 biography has provided much new information and a clearer picture of certain aspects of at least the first half of Odoevsky's life—what might be called the literary half. Nevertheless, much still remains hazy. Biographers gain little help from Odoevsky's consciously perfunctory attempts at autobiography: many of his recollections and comments on his life are far from being fully dependable in detail. His planned memoirs were never written; his diaries, though invaluable in certain respects, are devoid of detail (much from his diaries and his travel notes remains unpublished); his correspondence is scattered; and his autobiographical notes are teasingly fragmentary. In addition, Odoevsky scholars have never had the benefit of any of the usual run of study-aid volumes and collections normally supplied by the Soviet literary scholarly establishment on favored writers; such potential volumes as "Odoevsky in the Memoirs of his Contemporaries," "Odoevsky in Russian Criticism," "Odoevsky in St. Petersburg," or a day-by-day (insofar as the information might have been available) "Chronology of the Life and Work of V. F. Odoevsky," have never been produced. There was not even a volume on Vladimir Odoevsky (although his less significant Decembrist cousin, the poet Aleksandr, was accorded one in 1980) in the dubious series "Lives of Remarkable People." Consequently, researchers on Odoevsky have had to go back to the original nineteenth-century sources and explore a wide variety of scattered critical, memoir, and epistolary material, as well as attempt to deal with his colossal archival remains.

Following the early death of his father in 1808, the young Vladimir Odoevsky was brought up mainly by relatives in Moscow, with long visits in the country with his mother, who soon remarried. He received the best available education of the day at the "Noblemen's Pension" of Moscow University (Moscow's equivalent of the more famous *lycée* at Tsarskoe Selo near St. Petersburg), from which he graduated in 1822 with a gold medal. In particular, his literary and philosophical inclinations were excellently served: he had already begun writing, translating, and publishing by 1820.

The next four years, the only period in Odoevsky's adult life in which he did not serve the government of the day, were spent in a hectic whirl of intellectual activity. Odoevsky began the regular publication of translations, essays, stories, and music criticism in the Moscow journals. He attended the philosophical discussions of Semen Egorovich Raich's literary circle and presided over the *Obshchestvo liubomudriia* (Society of Wisdom Lovers), a philosophical circle influenced mainly by the nature-philosophy of Friedrich Wilhelm Joseph von Schelling; the society included among its adherents Dmitrii Vladimirovich Venevitinov and Ivan Vasil'evich Kireevsky and was a principal originator of both Westernist and Slavophile leanings. Together with the future Decembrist Vil'gel'm Karlovich Kiukhel'beker, Odoevsky founded, edited, and contributed much material to the four published numbers of the almanac *Mnemozina* (Mnemosyne, 1824–1825), which attracted contributions from the leading writers of the day, setting a new intellectual standard in Russian journalism and arousing considerable critical controversy.

Mnemozina foundered for lack of subscribers. In any case, this flourishing period of Russian intellectual life was soon brought to an abrupt end by the events in St. Petersburg on 14 December 1825, known thereafter in history as the Decembrist uprising. Aleksandr Odoevsky and Kiukhel'beker, who were active participants in the abortive revolt, suffered imprisonment and exile that led to early deaths. Though he was in Moscow, for a time Vladimir Odoevsky feared arrest by association. The *Obshchestvo liubomudriia* disbanded, burning their papers. A period of general intellectual paralysis followed. Odoevsky immersed himself ever deeper in idealist philosophy, mysticism, and European (especially German) Romanticism, channeling his thought into creative activity that reached fruition a decade later.

In 1826 Odoevsky obtained court permission to marry Ol'ga Stepanovna Lanskaia, sister of a future minister (the husband of one of Odoevsky's aunts) of Alexander II. In the same year he entered government service and moved to St. Petersburg, where he remained until 1862. During this period his literary career both flourished and declined. His marriage, which was childless, remained intact despite a lengthy extramarital affair (details of which Tur'ian has only recently established). He held several posts in various government ministries and committees, although because he was a writer and therefore a person with dubious contacts, he never enjoyed the full confidence of Nicholas I's government. He achieved lasting renown as a writer of children's stories (some of which remain widely in print to this day) and became strenuously involved in educational and subsequently philanthropic projects; time spent on the latter was a main factor in the cessation of his literary activities in the mid 1840s.

Odoevsky's salon, over which he presided while Princess Odoevskaia poured the tea, became a leading meeting place for literary and artistic celebrities from home and abroad: Franz Liszt, Hector Berlioz, and (much later in Moscow) Richard Wagner were among his famous visitors, not to mention all the important Russian writers from Pushkin to Tolstoy. He was indubitably a leading personality in the musical life of the period, both through his critical writings and by his association with, and promotion of, Glinka and other composers (both homegrown and European), and in the development of Russian journalism—as cofounder of Pushkin's *Sovremennik* (The Contemporary) and the main backer of Andrei Aleksandrovich Kraevsky's *Otechestvennye zapiski* (Notes of the Fatherland), the two most famous literary journals in nineteenth-century Russia. In 1842 he traveled to Western Europe and met his idol, Schelling.

A bureaucratic workaholic, as well as an encyclopedic reader and inveterate scribbler, Odoevsky served on various committees and commissions of the Ministries of Internal Affairs (including the censorship committee), State Domains, and the Tsar's Own Chancery, before being appointed deputy director of the Imperial Public Library and director of the Rumiantsev Museum. He thus held an extremely varied range of posts, often two or more simultaneously. His phenomenal capacity for work, study, and sociability—if not his domestic life—was greatly enhanced by an ability to do largely without sleep. His reputation as an eccentric came not merely from his multifarious artistic and official activities, but from what might be called his additional fringe interests: these included culinary experimentation, the invention of musical instruments, amateur science, and a long-standing pose as an unreconstructed alchemist.

Always among the more progressive elements of the nobility, though wary of radicalism and revolution, Odoevsky has misleadingly been labeled a "conservative" by some commentators; he later became an enthusiastic supporter of the reforms of Alexander II. At this stage he wearied of the social and financial strains of life in St. Petersburg, and in 1862 he took an appointment to the Moscow Senate. His salon continued to flourish during his last years in Moscow, and at the time of his death in 1869 he was busy with more projects than ever: musical, historical, scientific, and, once again, literary.

Throughout an intellectual career lasting half a century, Odoevsky never ceased to conceive grandiose literary, philosophical, encyclopedic, and educational projects. Few of these achieved more than a fragmentary existence, and many remained in little more than the planning stage, confined to his vast archive. This tendency is partly in character with the restless spirit of the man himself and in part corresponds to the Romantic preoccupation with both the fragmentary and the process for its own sake, rather than the end goal. The two literary projects that actually did reach completion, *Pestrye skazki* (Variegated Tales, 1833) and *Russkie nochi* (Russian Nights, published as a volume of *Sochineniia* [Works], 1844), were both conceived in the 1820s, yet mark the onset and the climax, respectively, of Odoevsky's "mature" period as a writer.

The compositional and publishing history of Odoevsky's rich and prolific writings is therefore more complicated than usual. Most of his literary output, for instance, appeared in journals or almanacs. Textual problems are frequently caused by revisions to republications. Much of his work was not collected into book form within his lifetime; indeed, a good proportion of it remains uncollected and no small amount unpublished (although considerable progress in publication and republication of Odoevsky's outpourings has been made since his day, much remains to be done). The nearest approach to a "collected works" (his own compilation—the three-volume *Sochineniia* of 1844) omitted much of the literary work, not to mention everything else. This situation has been only partly remedied (for instance by major collections in the 1950s of his musical and educational writings). There is still no satisfactory collection of Odoevsky's philosophical essays, while his letters lie scattered through a plethora of minor publications or else languish in the archives. Virtually the complete range of Odoevsky's literary writings and much more besides—published and unpublished, completed, fragmentary, or merely planned—has been summarized, with liberal quotation, in the compendious 1913 study by Pavel

Nikitich Sakulin, which remains an unparalleled source.

Summaries of Odoevsky's juvenilia can be found in Sakulin (and more briefly in Neil Cornwell's 1986 biography). The most interesting of these is the unpublished "Dnevnik studenta" (Diary of a Student, 1820–1821), written in confessional diary form and relating the (presumably autobiographical) protagonist's alienation from family and society and his strong feelings of friendship for "Aleksandr" (presumably A. I. Odoevsky); it includes several characteristics of Odoevsky's mature writing. Certainly the accusatory and didactic tone of the diary produces the type of discourse that largely determined the structure of Odoevsky's fiction, from the apologues of the first half of the 1820s—including the slim volume *Chetyre apologa* (Four Apologues, 1824)—to *Russkie nochi.* Of the former, the best known is "Stariki ili Ostrov Pankhai" (The Old Men, or the Island of Panchaea), published in *Mnemozina* in 1824. In this story, on the mystical island of Panchaea as supposedly described by Diodorus Siculus, time runs backwards for those who imbibe "the waters of the sun," so that they gradually become younger and can achieve the state of immortal youth or, for those who drink too much, deterioration into total infancy and eventual "one-day-old death." The latter category of "infant geriatrics" indulge in absurdly frivolous pastimes, enabling Odoevsky to satirize in allegorical (or apologue-parable) form various social and cultural norms, such as society small talk, the pursuit of honors, high-society upbringing, foreign fads and fetishes, and the time-honored practice of holding down the younger generation in the name of "experience."

Vissarion Grigor'evich Belinsky, reviewing Odoevsky's *Sochineniia* for *Otechestvennye zapiski* in 1844, praised the apologues as something completely new in Russian literature and went so far as to reprint the texts of two of them (including "Stariki") in his review. Another apologue of interest was one in *Mnemozina* titled "Novyi demon" (The New Demon, 1825), partly inspired by the demon within, mentioned in Pushkin's poem "Moi demon" (My Demon, later known as simply "Demon," which appeared in *Mnemozina* in 1824). Prominent among the twenty or so items that Odoevsky published in *Mnemozina* is the society tale "Elladii," which Belinsky lauded as the first real *povest'* (novella or tale) of Russian reality. As a story it compares unfavorably with, but points the way toward, Odoevsky's main society tales of the 1830s. The eponymous protagonist, Elladii, was a hapless victim of society intrigue.

Odoevsky in the 1820s

More typical of this early period of Odoevsky's prose, and possibly more consequential to the development of Russian literature, was the figure of Arist, the protagonist of several pieces from 1822–1823 and assumed to be something of an authorial alter ego. Arist in fact appears with increasing importance in all but the first of a series of works that bear the title or subtitle "Letters to the Luzhnitskii Elder," notably the stories "Strannyi chelovek" (The Strange Man, 1822) and "Dni dosad" (Days of Vexation, 1823), both published in *Vestnik Evropy* (The Herald of Europe). The publication of these "Letters" first drew Aleksandr Sergeevich Griboedov's attention to the young Odoevsky, giving rise to subsequent comparisons between Arist and Griboedov's Chatsky, while both the figure of Arist and the title "Strannyi chelovek" have prompted suggestions of the role played by Odoevsky in establishing an early prototype of the "superfluous man." Odoevsky's characterizations have frequently been regarded as on the weak side, particularly in his works of the 1820s; nevertheless Sakulin regards "Dni dosad" as the most significant of Odoevsky's works of the period and a kaleidoscopic picture of high-society Moscow. The instructional-didactic basis of these early works, grounded in the eighteenth-century Enlightenment tradition in fiction, foreshadows more successful mature works of the 1830s in this vein. However, it is unfortunate that Odoevsky, unlike Mikhail Iur'evich Lermontov, failed to develop this "strange man" prototype in his subsequent fiction.

Odoevsky's highest output of the decade was during 1824–1825. His contributions to *Mnemozina* were doubled by his pieces in Nikolai Alekseevich Polevoi's new journal, *Moskovskii telegraf* (Moscow Telegraph): short stories and apologues, articles, and musical criticism. The main influences on Odoevsky's fiction at this stage were Jean de La Bruyère and the Eastern tale, in particular the stories of the *Pañca-tantra,* a medieval Sanskrit collection of beast fables. However, the events of December 1825 and his new life in St. Petersburg meant that Odoevsky published only one item in 1826 (although his habit of publishing under a wide range of pseudonyms leaves open the possibility of further works of this and other periods coming to light). In 1827 he published ten pieces, all but one in *Moskovskii vestnik* (Moscow Herald), a new journal edited by Mikhail Petrovich Pogodin and regarded as the organ established for a revival of the German idealist-based program of the *Obshchestvo liubomudriia*. The last years of the 1820s brought a decline in Odoevsky's published output, which can probably be accounted for by two factors: Odoevsky's increasing involvement in tasks of government service, and his ruminations over vastly more ambitious literary projects that either remained unrealized (such as his unfinished novel of the Italian Renaissance, "Giordano Bruno and Pietro Aretino") or that only achieved fruition much later (including the long-standing project that underwent considerable metamorphosis before finally materializing as *Russkie nochi* in 1844). In addition, his archive reveals several other projects (for instance novels and plays) abandoned at an early stage—a propensity that Odoevsky had throughout his career and that he may well have cultivated as a Romantic fetish.

Perhaps Odoevsky's most striking experimental work of this period is the short story "Dva dni v zhizni zemnogo shara" (Two Days in the Life of the Terrestrial Globe), written in 1825 and published in *Moskovskii vestnik* in 1828, a story speculating upon the possible results of the impact of a comet on the earth (a theme to which Odoevsky later returned in *4338-i god* [The Year 4338], the fullest version of which was not published until 1926). What is remarkable about this work of just five pages is that it begins as a society tale, takes on an air of proto-science fiction, and concludes with a Schellingian aura of benign apocalypse in which there is a harmonious merging of the sun with the earth.

Virtually none of Odoevsky's works of the 1820s were included by him in his collected works of 1844, and few have been reprinted since. Many remained unfinished, while many more, notwithstanding a certain originality, appear immature, artless in construction, and paper-thin in characterization—even compared to many of his lesser works of the 1830s. Nevertheless, they did have a certain impact on the reader of the time (as Belinsky has testified) and they did play a definite part in the shaping of Russian prose in its most formative decade of the nineteenth century. Moreover, the basic lines and genres of Odoevsky's mature prose were apparent even in his writings of the *Mnemozina* period.

Odoevsky's fiction published in the years 1830–1844 represents by far the greatest quantity of his literary output (especially since he also wrote most of his children's stories during these years) and, by universal critical consent, is superior to that of the abundant earlier and sparse later periods in both quality and diversity. While it is not possible to maintain hard and fast chronological divisions over this fruitful decade and a half (*Russkie nochi,* for a start, having roots that stretch back to the 1820s), the period is approximately bounded by the publication of two "cycles": *Pestrye skazki* in 1833 and *Russkie nochi* in 1844. Other subdivisions can only be thematic: tales of artists, society tales, philosophical/romantic tales, and utopian/science-fiction tales. The picture is further complicated by the publication of more stories, later drawn into *Russkie nochi,* throughout the 1830s and by the partial construction of further grandiose projects that either metamorphosed into *Russkie nochi* (as with the proposed cycle "Dom sumasshedshikh," House of Madmen) or achieved only fragmentary publication (as with the unrealized novel "Segeliel'").

Odoevsky's fiction of the 1830s appears to be the product of a more mature artistic consciousness than might have been predicted from his writings of the 1820s. Whereas device, artifice, and motivation are used to somewhat clumsy and obvious effect in the earlier period, much of the work of the 1830s, which is certainly no less adventurous or experimental in form, takes on a dimension of subtlety and ambivalence. His study and application of Romantic aesthetics (its Germanic theory and its Germanic, but also French and Russian, practice) adds a question mark to any Odoevsky text from this period on (indeed, in the case of *Pestrye skazki,* with its quirky punctuation and use of the Spanish reverse interrogative sign, two question marks). This ambiguity is occasioned by the use of a variety of narrational devices (multiple narrators and spokesmen—even the "publisher" of *Pestrye skazki;* embedded narratives; and other framing contrivances), plus an irony that frequently undercuts the narrative at several levels, self-conscious play on the author-reader relationship (in the manner of what in the twentieth century is called metafiction), and other forms of Romantic irony, as well as various forms of parody and allegory. Initial naive readings of the works of this period tend to pale in the light of subsequent readings. The recent revival of interest in Romantic poetics has brought a greater understanding of its dependence on intertextuality; just as Pushkin and his contemporaries read and reflected Lord Byron, Laurence Sterne, and André-Marie de Chénier, so Odoevsky, particularly as a member of the *Obshchestvo liubomudriia,* read and used Schelling, E. T. A. Hoffmann, and Novalis.

The full title of Odoevsky's first cycle of stories must be one of the longest in Russian literature: *Pestrye skazki s krasnym slovtsom, sobrannye Irineem Modestovichem Gomozeikoiu, magistrom filosofii i chlenom raznykh uchenykh obshchestv, izdannye V. Bezglasnym* (Variegated Tales with a Witty Turn of Phrase, Collected by Irinei Modestovich Gomozeiko, Master of Philosophy and Member of Various Learned Societies, Published by V. Bezglasnyi). It was printed in a small deluxe format, appropriately adorned with variegated designs and illustrations, in St. Petersburg in 1833. The collection, as an entity, was republished for the first time only in 1988 (in the new orthography in the West; and in a facsimile edition in Moscow in 1991).

Odoevsky published many works over several decades under a variety of pseudonyms, and Bezglasnyi (the "publisher" of *Pestrye skazki*) was one of his favorite sobriquets of that period. Gomozeiko, however, was more than just another pen name; he was a persona over whom Odoevsky took considerable trouble. "Master of Philosophy and member of various learned societies," an aficionado of occult sciences who knows all possible languages "living, dead and half-dead," and just about everything else, Gomozeiko is a poverty-stricken encyclopedist; as such he assumes the role of a whimsical alter ego, a middle-aged eccentric and thus an older and exaggerated self-projection. The fact that Odoevsky had elaborate further plans for the figure of Gomozeiko adds a dimension beyond Pushkin's conception of Ivan Belkin, or Gogol's of Rudyi Panko.

Gomozeiko was conceived as the first resident of the unrealized "House of Madmen"; his "autobiography" and "historical researches" are alluded to in Bezglasnyi's introduction to *Pestrye skazki*. Of the historical researches there is no trace, but the autobiography was started, covering Gomozeiko's provincial upbringing, education, and government service (in which he struggled for the public good,

only to be accused of practicing "Carbonari-type" ideas). Connected with this project, or extracted from it, is "Istoriia o petukhe, koshke i liagushke" (The Story of a Cock, a Cat and a Frog), first published in *Biblioteka dlia chteniia* (Library for Reading) in 1834 under the title "An Extract from the Notes of Irinei Modestovich Gomozeiko," subtitled "a provincial story" and set in Rezhensk (the scene in *Pestrye skazki* of Ivan Sevast'ianych's traumatic experience with a body that belonged to no one knew whom). Odoevsky's knowledge of provincial life and officialdom, rarely displayed outside these two stories and often seen as Gogolian, probably derives from rural visits to his mother and his stepfather. There was to have been much more of Gomozeiko, including a whole cycle of adventures in the provinces and in the capital. However, the only complete tale in which Gomozeiko makes a return appearance is "Prividenie" (The Apparition, 1838), published in *Literaturnye pribavleniia k Russkomu invalidu* (Literary Supplement to the Russian Invalid).

Pestrye skazki can be seen in many ways as a transitional work between Odoevsky's fictional output of the 1820s and that of the 1830s. It is also a text that has never produced any real critical consensus. Such doubts seem equally to have applied to the author himself; when appropriating "Fragments from *Pestrye skazki* (1833)" as a section for part three of his 1844 *Sochineniia,* Odoevsky omitted much of the original cycle and rearranged the rest: only four stories were included here and a fifth ("Igosha") was revised and placed in a different section. As early as 1829, following his latest withdrawal from literature, Odoevsky referred to *Pestrye skazki* in a letter to Pogodin, claiming not to wish to remind the public of himself "by the commission of old sins." The "old sins" remained, however—at least as far as some readers were concerned: writing for *Moskovskii telegraf* in 1833, Polevoi saw in these stories cold imitations of Hoffmann and evidence of Odoevsky's aristocratic aloofness. Originality and the presence therein of Romantic philosophy were noted by others, but the reception was in general mixed and the readers slightly puzzled. This confusion can perhaps be attributed to the mixing of "old sins" (didactic and allegorical satirical apologues) along with more innovative works. However, even brief examination of *Pestrye skazki* reveals diversity and complexity, so that the original critical doubts and differences persist.

Between the two prefaces at the beginning (from the "publisher" and the "author," or rather collector) and the epilogue (itself merely a restating of the epigraph to the last story) the stories are numbered I to VIII; arguably, the real total of stories is seven, as VIII is a sequel, or rather a reverse of VII. There is an elaborate design, in terms of layout, punctuation, and illustrations, as well as cover, in which Odoevsky's close friend of that period, Gogol, is thought to have had a hand.

The first story, "Retorta" (The Retort), opens its four short chapters with an "Introduction" that reads like a veritable credo of Romanticism on the part of the narrator, or supposed author. Chapter two of the story finds the somewhat eccentric narrator at the usual venue for the opening of an early Odoevsky tale—a society ball. Annoyed when the conspiratorial ritual of the card table asserts its supremacy over the hot air of narrative digression, the storyteller retreats to cool himself by a ventilating window, only to find the air there just as hot despite the twenty degrees of frost outside. The entire house and its occupants prove to be enclosed in a glass retort that is (in chapter four) cast by a *satanenok* (young devil) into a Latin dictionary; on his travels from page to page through the dictionary, the narrator meets a spider, a dead body, a nightcap, the folk imp Igosha, and "other amiable young people whom the accursed young devil had gathered from all sides of the world and forced to share my fate." Some of these denizens of the dictionary are so steeped in words that they are turning into fairy tales, and the narrator himself begins to undergo such a transformation. Then the ball ends and the exodus from it breaks the retort; the young devil makes off in alarm, dropping a few pages from his dictionary in his haste, along with some of its fictional captives—the narrator ("Your humble servant") included. The narrator grabs his erstwhile comrades from among the dropped pages, stuffing them into his pocket in order to present them subsequently to the "esteemed reader" as the remaining *pestrye* (variegated or motley) stories that comprise the cycle.

Such is the intricate motivation behind the ensuing unlikely arrangement of stories. By this whimsical interplay of society tale and fairy tale, and its play on the relationship between narrator and reader, integral text and its component parts (characters and devices, words and punctuation), Odoevsky orchestrates his discourse to present what amounts to "fairy tales for old children" (a concept widely utilized elsewhere by Odoevsky in this period, including in the works he wrote specifically for children).

Discourse, both in writing and in incongruous dialogue, is also a strong sub-theme of "Skazka o mertvom tele neizvestno komu prinadlezhashchem" (The Tale of a Dead Body, Belonging to No One Knows Whom); indeed the stress on written articulation in this story almost matches Gogol's emphasis in his later "Shinel'" (The Greatcoat, 1842) on incoherence in speech. "Zhizn'i pokhozhdeniia odnogo iz zdeshnikh obyvatelei v stekliannoi banke, ili Novyi Zhoko" (The Life and Adventures of One of Our Local Inhabitants in a Glass Jar, or The New Zhoko), a spider's view of the universe, ironically subtitled "a classical tale," is primarily a burlesque of French freneticist Romantic forms; its polemical parodic thrust has long since been lost, but an unusual quality of the bizarre still lingers. "Skazka o tom, po kakomu sluchaiu kollezhskomu sovetniku Ivanu Bogdanovichu Otnosheniiu ne udalos' v svetloe voskresen'e pozdravit' svoikh nachal'nikov s prazdnikom" (The Tale of How it Happened that Collegiate Councillor Ivan Bogdanovich Otnoshenie Failed to Offer Holiday Greetings to his Superiors on Easter Sunday—such were the unwieldy titles that Odoevsky frequently cultivated) offers again a pre-Gogolian look inside a St. Petersburg chancellery and culminates in a demonic card game (cards, along with society balls, were a pet hate of Odoevsky's). "Igosha" builds a study in child psychology onto a Russian folkloric base, while "Prosto skazka" (Just a Fairy Tale) is more or less just what its title suggests.

"Skazka, o tom, kak opasno devushkam khodit' tolpoiu po Nevskomu prospektu'" (The Tale of How it is Dangerous for Girls to Walk in a Crowd along Nevsky Prospect) is an allegorical cautionary tale of the rape of Russian beauty. Together with "Ta zhe skazka, tol'ko na izvorot" (The Same Tale, Only in Reverse)—a narrational digression and Gomozeiko's parting shot, which balances his introduction at the beginning—this story leads into "Derevyanni gost', ili Skazka ob ochnuvsheisia kukle i gospodine Kivakele," (The Wooden Guest, or the Tale of the Awakened Doll and Mr. Kivakel), and represents a censure of the absurdities of female upbringing in St. Petersburg society, motivated perhaps more by concerns of artistic taste than with crude preoccupations of proto-Slavophilism. The repetition of the epigraph from Johann Wolfgang von Goethe's *Die Leiden des jungen Werthers* (The Sorrows of Young Werther, 1774) as an epilogue reinforces the theme of puppetry (who is manipulating whom?).

The tales of *Pestrye skazki* may be slight individually, but they are diverse in their use of inventive whimsy, satire, and the grotesque; not for the only time in Odoevsky's work the suspicion arises that the whole may exceed the sum of the parts. Soviet Russian criticism of this generally neglected cycle has tended to emphasize the angle of social satire; *Pestrye skazki* is said to anticipate Gogol's Petersburg stories and to prefigure some of Odoevsky's own slightly later stories that continue a similar grotesque-satirical line. However, this cycle is not to be pinned down as easily as that. Shrewder critics also point to the constantly undercutting effects of the use of Romantic irony. The importance of Gomozeiko and some of the quirks of narration have been noted; the work is clearly best read in the light of both the theory and the practice of the poetics of Romanticism.

The tales have more recently been seen as allegories, "complicated by such Hoffmannian romantic motifs as puppetry, automatonism and the spectrality of bureaucratic life," directed primarily still towards social satire, according to Vsevolod Ivanovich Sakharov in a 1982 essay. The cycle also represents a conjunction of pre-Romantic Russian prose with a poetics newly acquired from Romanticism and, like much of Odoevsky's work, is connected at another level with the literary polemics of the day. In any case, Odoevsky's experimentation with a whimsical brand of Germanic philosophical Romanticism, tinged both with fairy tale and the fantastic, ran contrary to the more robust variety established by Victor Hugo in France and favored in Russia by such writers as Polevoi and Aleksandr Aleksandrovich Bestuzhev (Marlinsky).

Nevertheless, despite their transitional place in Odoevsky's development and in Russian Romantic prose, the tales in *Pestrye skazki* are not quite as ephemeral in their significance as their author modestly indicated a decade later when, introducing the selection deemed worthy of inclusion in his 1844 *Sochineniia,* Odoevsky referred to the cycle as "a joke, the main aim of which was to demonstrate the possibilities for luxury editions in Russia and to launch woodcuts and other forms of illustration." Earlier he had remarked in a letter to Aleksandr Ivanovich Koshelev that *Pestrye skazki,* his "harlequinesque fairy tales," had been written in the "most bitter" moments of his life. Tur'ian takes this statement as a reference to his extramarital preoccupation that had developed during this period. While *Pestrye skazki* can be seen both as a series of tongue-in-cheek exercises parodying various forms of Romantic excess (in tune with Odoevsky's own critical articles of the 1830s) and as a preliminary workout for many of the themes and ideas that inform *Russkie nochi,* the cycle still retains its own idiosyncratic and enigmatic qualities.

Odoevsky's early rebellious protagonist, Arist, had withdrawn from society to the seclusion of his books on his country estate. When he, or rather his counterpart in Odoevsky's fiction of the 1830s, reemerged, it was as a mellow and learned

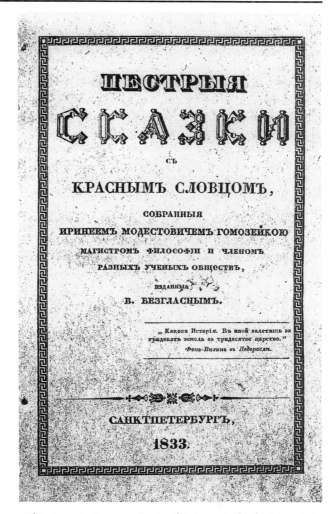

Title page for Pestrye skazki *(Variegated Tales), Odoevsky's first collection of stories*

middle-aged eccentric, considerably older than Odoevsky himself but with many of his qualities and in effect an exaggerated self-portrait: Gomozeiko (and later Faust of *Russkie nochi*). Odoevsky's other readily identifiable character type of this period is another kind of "strange man," the creative artist. The tormented genius, the deluded creator, and the intellectual crank: all were candidates for residence in the uncompleted "House of Madmen."

Odoevsky published separately four artistic tales in the first half of the 1830s; originally intended for the "House of Madmen," they were eventually incorporated into *Russkie nochi.* Why and when the former project evolved into the latter is, like a good deal else in Odoevsky's rather complicated literary career, less than clear. Of the four artists depicted, two are great composers; one is a deluded but harmless madman who imagines himself to be the architect and antiquarian Giovanni Battista Piranesi; the fourth is an ungifted poet whose talent, when boosted by occult means, gives him no satisfaction.

The two biographical stories are unconcerned with history; they are intuitive, sensitive pictures of the predicament of the great artist: in adversity (the deaf, unappreciated, and frustrated Beethoven at the end of his tether and of his life) and over the whole span of his artistic development (the comparatively extended tale of the life of Bach). The depiction of the composer in "Poslednii kvartet Betkhovena" (Beethoven's Last Quartet), published in the 1831 *Severnye tsvety* (Northern Flowers), is fittingly Romantic; the misunderstood genius descends into delirium, starving in his Viennese garret in the company of his one remaining student, the girl Louisa. The core of this story of only six pages is a three-page monologue—a kind of stream-of-consciousness *profession de foi*—by the composer, which, in its moving and frenzied catalogue of the tragedies of creative non-fulfillment, dominates the passages dealing with the misconceptions and conflicts between the artist and society by which it is framed. Beethoven, in true Odoevsky fashion, bemoans the abyss that divides thought from expression. This realization is compounded in the case of the musician, however, since even what he does write is not played as intended, if it is played at all. Rather like Piranesi's grandiose architectural plans, Beethoven's music seems to remain chained to the paper on which it is scored.

It is not coincidental that Odoevsky was foremost in Russia in promoting the music of Beethoven and Bach. His story "Sebastian Bach" was published in *Moskovskii nabliudatel'* (The Moscow Oberver) in 1835. The biography of the composer is related by a "researcher" whose particular task in life is the revelation of that "mysterious language . . . common to all artists" that lies hidden beneath the creative minutiae of "all the works of artists without exception," just as, allegedly, the poetry of all ages and peoples is one and the same "harmonious work." The introduction to the story provides, in the words of the eccentric researcher, a clear statement of Odoevsky's own idealized and idealist Romantic position. The researcher's other Romantic innovation as a biographer is to see an artist's works as the only source for his life: just as the universe is man's sole clue to the Almighty, so do an artist's works reveal a life in which there are no unpoetic moments. There then follows an intuitive artistic chronicle that begins with the Bach family and ends with the composer's death when his inspiration and imagination fail.

Odoevsky's conception of artistic biography appears to be particularly close to that of Wilhelm Heinrich Wackenroder, with whom he shares several other Romantic ideas such as the inadequacy of language, the work of art as a hieroglyph, and the religiously symbolic significance of art (Wackenroder's *Phantasien über die Kunst,* Fantasies on Art, 1799, had been translated into Russian by three of the former members of *Obshchestvo liubomudriia* in 1826). Particularly striking is the mystical vision of religion and art that the young Sebastian undergoes in his nocturnal visit to the church in Eisenach. The other, much later major episode is the infatuation of Bach's half-Italian wife, Magdalena, with the "impure seductive melody" of a visiting Venetian vocalist, Francesco. Impossible love for an unworthy object is Magdalena's undoing. Bach, who pursues to the exclusion of all else his own brand of artistic dedication, ends up as a dry professor within his own family: "half of his soul was a corpse."

Despite, or perhaps even because of, their greatness as artists, Beethoven and Bach were nevertheless flawed as human beings, *bezumtsy* (madmen of a special talent), passionately obsessed by their *idée fixe* and zealously devoted to the idea of creativity. These stories were an unusual innovation in Russian literature; held in high esteem by such discerning contemporaries as Pushkin, Gogol, Aleksandr Ivanovich Herzen, Polevoi, Nikolai Ivanovich Nadezhdin, and Belinsky, they elevated Odoevsky to the pinnacle of his literary reputation in the first half of the 1830s. Almost equally well received, and also still counted in the twentieth century as among the best of his stories, were his tales of the two pseudo-artists, the self-proclaimed Piranesi and Kipriano "the Improviser."

"Opere del Cavaliere Giambattista Piranesi" (The Works of the Chevalier Giambattista Piranesi; Odoevsky left his title in Italian), published in the 1832 *Severnye tsvety,* invites comparison with Hoffmann's "Ritter Gluck" (1809) in its presentation of a character purporting to be, or believing himself to be, an artistic figure who has been dead for years. In Odoevsky's case, however, there is no doubt as to the false identity of the protagonist: this Piranesi claims to have been taught by Michelangelo. This particular eccentric (dubbed, even before he claims to be Piranesi, a *chudak* or crank) empathizes to such a degree, presumably in a vast exaggeration of his own artistic frustrations, with the stupendous architectural fantasies and imaginary views of Piranesi that he projects himself into what he imagines might have been Piranesi's state of mind, had Piranesi seriously intended his designs to be realized. However, worse is in store within the psyche of the supposed

Piranesi: "each work which comes out of an artist's head engenders an avenging spirit" (*dukh efiroid*), he avers; these spirits of his frustrated creations persecute him through his existence, which (like that of the Wandering Jew) they themselves prolong. The real Piranesi was an important inspirational figure in the history of European Romanticism, and Odoevsky's symbolic portrayal has attracted less attention than might be its due.

Kipriano (or Cyprian), the Improviser (of "Improvizator," published in *Al'tsiona* [Alcyone], 1833), composed his verses with immense difficulty as a young poet and therefore relapsed into the poverty in which he had originated. He turns to Doctor Segeliel' (a name, like several others, used by Odoevsky in more than one work), a man of diabolical reputation, who accords him the ability to produce verse without effort and "to see, know and understand everything." Kipriano's perception and comprehension are immediately transformed: books on the shelves and the letters on their pages assume a state of mobility, and everything is reduced to "an arithmetical progression"—the whole of nature lies before Kipriano "like the skeleton of a beautiful woman, whom the dissector had boiled down so skillfully that there did not remain on her a single living vein." His beloved Charlotte is reduced in his eyes to an anatomical specimen; his microscopic vision reduces the world to a mechanistic model, dividing him permanently from the rest of its inhabitants, artifice replacing art and music yielding to a mere mechanical vibration. He composes poetry instantly and effortlessly, but with no personal satisfaction; he ends as a wandering jester jabbering nonstop verses in a mixture of all languages.

In this story, which also has affinities with Hoffmann, Odoevsky's imaginative writing can be seen at its best: within the framework of a fantastic variation on the theme of artistic inspiration, he attacks the mechanistic philosophy introduced through the European Enlightenment; presents the contrasting coupling of sinister mage and ineffectual Romantic poet; and, in the Romantic manner, employs occult motivation to introduce the kind of enhanced vision more usually found in science fiction of the twentieth century. "Improvizator" is a story that also attracted wider attention. Like the Beethoven and Piranesi tales, it was translated into French (1855); it was also plagiarized (presumably via the French version) by the Irish-American writer Fitz-James O'Brien and appeared under his name in *Harper's New Monthly Magazine* in 1857 under the title "Seeing the World."

As Odoevsky himself realized, whether immediately or only subsequently, links among these four stories inevitably suggest themselves. These tales explore the nature of artistic feeling and the relationship of the artist to those around him. The mechanical, sterile vision of Kipriano, a Salieri (or Petro Aretomp) figure who has acquired knowledge and creative ability illicitly from without, rather than from within, may be compared to the exhausted imagination of the dying Bach which, instead of sounds, "presented to him only the keys, the pipes, the valves of the organ." Something of the grandiose unrealized literary edifices of Odoevsky may be reflected in the anguish of his Piranesi; he also indicated to Koshelev that something of his own grief was incorporated into "Sebastian Bach." The theme of artistic inspiration and its many frustrations was undoubtedly a personal one.

One further artistic tale, belonging to an entirely different and uncompleted cycle, is "Zhivopisets" (The Painter), published in *Otechestvennye zapiski* in 1839. The artist in question here subsides into purist delirium and dire poverty, brought about by his principled refusal to execute commercial commissions. When, to placate his wife and ward off total starvation, he finally paints a shop sign, he promptly expires. This story cannot be regarded on the same philosophical or artistic plane as its predecessors; however, it demonstrates the direction of movement toward realism and the Natural School of the 1840s in at least a certain strand of Odoevsky's writing in the second half of the 1830s. It also presents a somewhat unusual structural twist; the story of the unfortunate painter is told by a woman of the merchant classes, who relates her tale in an affectionate *skaz* manner, devoid of any understanding of the artistic feeling at the root of her narrative.

Odoevsky's *svetskie povesti* (society tales) largely continue the main trend in his fiction of the 1820s: the tone is frequently didactic; the setting is predominantly the salon and the ballroom; the subject matter is society intrigue; the mores of aristocratic society and such associated factors as *zhenskii vopros* (the women's question) are under scrutiny. Sometimes in Odoevsky's fiction there can be a considerable overlap between a predominant society element and other features, such as a touch of the fantastic; the converse can also be the case, since the dividing lines among these elements are by no means hard and fast.

The category of society tale may also include one of the shorter stories later incorporated into *Russkie nochi*: "Brigadir" (The Brigadier), published in *Novosel'e* (Housewarming) in 1833. In this story, a phantom of the dead brigadier forms before the eyes of the narrator from his own confused thoughts and feelings; however, this seemingly fantastic event is of minor importance in comparison to the dead man's monologue, the confession of a wasted life through the normal immoral upbringing of his class followed by years of craven conformity to the social norms (strongly anticipatory here of Tolstoy). In "Bal" (The Ball), also in *Novosel'e* in 1833, a story of merely two pages but written with the intensity of a prose poem, the narrator moves from the horrific scene of a manic ball being engaged "with voluptuous madness" to a religious vision of love and harmony in a nearby church; again, the main thrust is the questioning of values of the highest society. The fantastic and grotesque events of "Nasmeshka mertvetsa" (The Mockery of a Corpse), first published in *Dennitsa* (Dawn) as "Nasmeshka mertvogo" (The Mockery of a Dead Man) in 1834—dramatic coincidence, an apocalyptic flood, and a corpse revived for vengeance—rather overshadow the prosaic explanation of a fainting fit. However, the main purpose of the story still comes through: to decry the abandonment by "prudent Liza" (a reversal here of Nikolai Mikhailovich Karamzin's more famous "poor Liza") of her beloved for the sake of a beneficial arranged marriage and to condemn the further self-perversion of her true spirit, even after her horrific, albeit illusory, experience.

Another society tale with a difference is the short story "Novyi god" (New Year), dated 1831 but published in *Literaturnye pribavlennia k Russkomu invalidu* in 1837; this story deals with the idealistic intelligentsia of the 1820s and in reality reflects on the members of *Obshchestvo liubomudriia*. Based no doubt on the deterioration of the idealism of the surviving members of the group during their "second breath" in St. Petersburg during the years 1827–1831, the story (which relates three New Year gatherings some years apart) looks back nostalgically on the high ideals, the literary and philosophical activities, and the bruising literary polemics of the early 1820s. The mark of time (and perhaps too of political events) diverts the lofty aspirations of the regular host of the gatherings, Viacheslav, first to family preoccupations and then to careerism and the accordant cynical exploitation of the *beau monde*. This poignant story of lost ideals, wasted talent, and erosion of all-male camaraderie is one of Odoevsky's best-executed short works.

What might be considered Odoevsky's society tales proper can be said to begin with the publication in 1834 of "Katia, ili istoriia vospitannitsy" (Katia, or the Story of a Young Ward), which appeared in *Novosel'e,* and *Kniazhna Mimi* (Princess Mimi). "Katia" deals with what Odoevsky calls "the life of our middle class," the *vospitannitsy* (wards) from the lower orders, brought up "charitably" by the more "benevolent" sections of the aristocracy and normally destined for eternal spinsterhood or a somewhat lowly marriage. In this story, which includes considerable social detail, an interesting situation is developing between Katia and a male ward of artistic sensibilities (Vladimir); at this point, though, the narrative of this intended novel breaks off. There is, however, archival evidence that Odoevsky intended to turn his heroine eventually into a ruthless exploiter.

Kniazhna Mimi has claims to be considered Odoevsky's society tale par excellence. It is his most outspoken attack on the destructive, hypocritical, and sterile aspects of high society; it includes authorial comments on the literary situation of the day and on the anomalous state of the Russian literary language—particularly with respect to the fictional presentation of society dialogue, given the real-life preponderance of French in salon conversation. Furthermore it constitutes, in the persona of its eponymous protagonist, Odoevsky's most serious attempt at psychological characterization. Odoevsky's ire (for such is the tone of the story) falls upon the usual social frivolities: balls; whist; that perpetual social barbarity, the duel; and, in this instance, the virtuous guardians of social morality. He further condemns "the moral estate," epitomized by the embittered Mimi herself (the self-appointed "soul of society") and the underlying situation in which the only purpose in life for girls in society is to get married. In the name of the preservation of "moral standards" Princess Mimi causes two needless deaths and blights the lives of many others. The development of Mimi into a venomous persecutor of those who incur her displeasure, through her conscious adoption of a policy of calculated perfidy, is sketched and explained by means of potted biography (by narration, or telling); her orchestration of a vicious whispering campaign against a blameless baroness is revealed in action (by demonstration, or showing).

For all the relative realism and social detail included in this story, it is not so far removed from Odoevsky's more overtly Romantic tales as might be imagined. The expression "the soul of this society," applied to Mimi, is the only remaining suggestion of a discarded prologue in which Mimi is afflicted by devils residing in her cellar. In terms of structure and narrative technique, it is, like so many of Odoevsky's works, executed in a mixture of styles, experimental and self-conscious. The "preface," coming two-thirds of the way through the story, is given over to authorial digression; various narrative quirks of the "shall I tell you?" and "by right of the indiscretion permitted to storytellers" variety appear throughout. Perhaps the main weakness of *Kniazhna Mimi* to the modern reader is its somewhat abrupt and melodramatic denouement, which seems to be heavily predetermined by its didactic motivation.

"Kniazhna Zizi" (Princess Zizi), published in *Otechestvennye zapiski* in 1839 but written in 1836, in time to gain the approbation of Pushkin, is one of Odoevsky's longest stories, amounting to some forty-five pages. Less schematic than *Kniazhna Mimi,* without formal sectioning, it is unexpectedly successful "in combining Byronism with the stock-exchange," in the narrator's words. As usual, the narrative structure is complicated and contrived. Following the framing device of a wager over love stories, a second narrator takes over, but the ensuing narrative method is mainly epistolary for the first half of the story (this narrator just happens to have the relevant bundle of letters at hand) and subsequently revolves around that narrator's own reminiscences, filled out by the assumed reports of a further, unseen narrator, Mar'ia Ivanovna (the original recipient of the letters and a vital background figure in the plot). From what seems to be an epistolary novel of romantic intrigue, the plot turns into a society thriller hinging upon emotional and sexual deception and a property swindle. Notwithstanding the predominantly masculine narration, cohesion stems from the dominant theme throughout the tale: the social and legal position of women. Once again the apparent realism of the story (the detail of provincial social life, the legal system, social responses) and the consequent impact of the positive heroine Zizi's familial, societal, and legal victory are undercut by the deliberate literariness that permeates both character and text, to the extent of furnishing the work with a strong veneer of Romantic pastiche.

Odoevsky's handling of the women's question in his society tales requires further comment. While it is true that the portrayal of Princess Mimi is unambiguously negative, her motivation is tackled from the standpoint of the unfortunate social position of women at the time; and in any case her depiction is arguably balanced by the positive treatment of Princess Zizi. As always, Odoevsky submerges his real attitudes beneath literary artifice and gentle irony. These two stories, in which women characters gain an unusual prominence, nevertheless represent just about the most progressive contribution from a male Russian writer of the period to the discussion of the plight of women and, at the very least, deserve the epithet of "quasi-feminist" rather critically bestowed by Joe Andrew.

Portrait of Odoevsky by A. Pokrovsky, 1844 (from Pushkin v 1833 godu: Khronika *[Pushkin in 1833: A Chronicle], 1994)*

Literariness, irony, and didacticism also come to the forefront in "Dusha zhenshchiny" (A Woman's Soul), which was published in *Russkaia beseda* (Russian Talk) in 1841 and has an unusual metaphysical setting, and in "Chernaia perchatka" (The Black Glove), which was published in *Literaturnye pribavlennia k Russkomu invalidu* in 1838 and is directed against excessive Anglophilia. Also a society tale of sorts is Odoevsky's only completed play, *Khoroshee zhalovan'e* (A Good Salary), which appeared in *Literaturnye pribavlennia k Russkomu invalidu* in 1837; it depicts the rise and fall of a Tartuffe-type figure. Of more interest than these examples is the story "Svidetel'" (The Witness), published in *Syn otechestva* (Son of the Fatherland) in 1839, a short work on the theme of the duel (carried over from *Kniazhna Mimi* and no doubt reelevated to prominence by the fate of Pushkin). Fyodor Dostoyevsky may later have elaborated on its plot in his biography of Zosima (*Brat'ia Karamazovy,* The Brothers Karamazov, 1880). Indeed, visible in Odoevsky's society tales (as in many works by Pushkin) are the basic plotlines, dramatic situations, character types, and configurations, albeit often in a relatively primitive form, that shaped the staple diet of Russian prose for the rest of the century, from the young Dostoyevsky through Tolstoy to Anton Chekhov.

Because of their fantastic or Romantic tone, many of Odoevsky's stories from this prolific period are best mentioned under the category of philosophical/romantic tales, although their interest or artistic success may be somewhat restricted in comparison with the main works of this category. "Prividenie," which brought the return of Gomozeiko, is an embedded narrative that deals with antics of mystification at a Gothic castle and subsequently leaves the reader guessing. "Neoboidennyi dom" (The Uninhabited House), published in *Al'manakh v pamiat' dvukhsotletnego iubileia imp. Aleksandrovskogo universiteta* in 1842, imitates the form of a folk legend in which an old woman is somehow caught in a time warp. "Imbroglio," first published in Odoevsky's 1844 *Sochineniia,* is a readable potboiler tale, Romantic in both manner and Italian setting, in which a Russian traveler to Naples is plunged into a complex series of adventures.

"Orlakhskaia krest'ianka" (The Peasant Girl from Orlach) published in *Otechestvennye zapiski* in 1842, is rather more philosophical/romantic than the other stories in this category. Opening in a society-tale setting with an exposition of the views of Louis Claude de Saint-Martin and John Pordage (two mystics whose ideas Odoevsky had investigated in his post-Schellingian phase), the story then relates the experiences of Anchen, the Orlach peasant girl, within whom is enacted a spectral struggle in which the dead speak through the living to resolve a four-hundred-year-old multiple-murder case. This anecdote is based on a supposed actual occurrence in Germany in the 1830s.

However, three stories were quite justifiably nominated in 1913 by Sakulin as the most significant and elaborate of what he termed "the works of mystical content": these were "Sil'fida" (The Sylph), published in *Sovremennik* (The Contemporary) in 1837; "Kosmorama" (The Cosmorama) published in *Otechestvennye zapiski* in 1840; and *Salamandra* (The Salamander), a two-part novella, the first part of which appeared in *Utrenniaia zaria* in 1841 and the second part of which appeared in *Otechestvennye zapiski* that same year. As Odoevsky's most overtly Romantic tales, these three were long neglected, especially for much of the Soviet period; indeed, "Kosmorama" had to wait until the 1988 edition of *Povesti i rasskazy* to achieve its second appearance in print.

"Sil'fida," subtitled "From the Notes of a Reasonable Man," begins with seven letters from Mikhail Platonovich (a kind of older Arist or younger Gomozeiko figure who has retired to his country es-

tate) to his friend and eventual publisher, the "reasonable man," who has little grasp of the artistic spirit. Bored with provincial life, Mikhail Platonovich discovers the cabalistic books and folios of his deceased uncle's secret library and immerses himself in the pursuit of sylphs until he avows himself ready to break off all social relations. There follows a letter of complaint to the publisher from Mikhail Platonovich's neighboring landlord and prospective father-in-law. The reasonable man's account of the "saving" of his friend (by means largely of "bouillon baths") for marriage and a conventional provincial lifestyle frames the extracts from Mikhail Platonovich's journal, in which the jottings about his relationship with the sylph (involving the discarding of clothing and the "cold membrane" that covers everything living, and the separation of time and space leading to "the soul of the soul" where "poetry is truth") gradually descend into incoherence. The tale concludes with an "authorial" confession of having understood "nothing in this story."

In "Sil'fida" (as in *Salamandra*) Odoevsky makes overt use of alchemical and cabalistic authorities such as Paracelsus and "the Count of Gabalis" (Monfaucon de Villars), who were sources common also to Hoffmann. The fantastic nature of the story as well as Odoevsky's ironic treatment of Mikhail Platonovich and the latter's complaints about his "cure" (which seem to resurface in Chekhov's Gothic tale "The Black Monk," 1894), have led to varying critical views of the story from Pushkin and Belinsky up to the Soviet era. However, the return to critical favor of the Romantic style of writing in the second half of the twentieth century has established the story as among the best and most poetic of Odoevsky's tales. Although, unlike "Improvizator," it was not subjected to outright plagiarism, it appears certain that "Sil'fida" must have been a strong influence on Fitz-James O'Brien's best-known story, "The Diamond Lens" (1858), again via the French translation.

Odoevsky's most overt and uncompromising depiction of the Romantic concept of dualism (or *dvoemirie,* parallel worlds) resides in "Kosmorama." This time the story, narrated in the first person by the protagonist, Vladimir Andreevich, is comprised of a manuscript bought at an auction, provenance unknown. In a preface, the "publisher" claims the story as printed to be a "separate work," yet he purports to be preparing a book-length commentary in which all will be explained. He also declares that he is laboring over the continuation of the manuscript, which "is written highly illegibly" and which is supposed to be a sequel or an account of the narrator's later life. Much of this elaboration is probably pure

Romantic mystification, although Sakulin did unearth notes for a proposed continuation.

As a child Vladimir Andreevich is given (by a mysterious Doctor Bin) a *kosmorama*—a toy "box" of moving pictures, in which he is somehow able to see scenes of family life not meant for his eyes. His life is said to be connected with another, or rather "extraneous" life (*postoronnaia zhizn'*), to which a mysterious network links him from boyhood. This extraneous life would seem, from the epigraph (and Sakulin's claims of Pordage's influence upon the story) to be an "inner" life; however, it may equally be a "parallel" life, since other characters apart from Vladimir (at least, in his conception of events) appear to have some awareness of it. Vladimir rediscovers the *kosmorama* in adult life, when he finds that the scope of its vision has increased. However, this mysterious toy is only of initial importance, as Vladimir's clairvoyant powers, once fully awakened, need no instrument to sustain them. The scope of Vladimir's perception in time and space (somewhat parallel to Kipriano the Improviser's, though Vladimir's is not merely mechanistic), the grotesque phantasmagoria of visions, and the ensuing Gothic chain of events, interwoven with some skill between "vision" and "reality" (involving amorous intrigue, the walking dead, crime and torture in "that" life as well as in this, supernatural arson, and spontaneous human combustion), would tax the abilities of the most experienced plot summarizer. As the preface implies, many puzzles remain—in particular the enigmatic roles of Doctor Bin and the unfortunate Sof'ia (who may owe something to Pordage's conception of the figure of Sophia, eternal maid of divine wisdom). The tale remains within the realms of the fantastic, where ultimately nothing can be decided because irony reinforces the ambiguities. Nevertheless, degeneration into madness (the inspirational nature of which was always a strong theme in Odoevsky's work) remains an underlying, though not necessarily wholly satisfying, explanation of the course of events.

Odoevsky's most ambitious tale, in terms of both length and setting, involving somewhat similar themes, is the "dilogy" (a two-part story, eventually combined as one), *Salamandra*. Restored to favor in Soviet criticism only in the 1970s, this work has since been accorded stimulating readings, both as an anthropological/psychological tale (by Tur'ian in 1978) and as an historical novel (by Sakharov in 1979). Western criticism, given present fashions, is perhaps more likely to treat it, along with "Kosmorama" and "Sil'fida," as Gothic extravaganza, though of a highly readable order, that compares favorably with many of its Western counterparts.

Originally envisaged in a West European setting, the work in fact opens on "The southern shore of Finland at the beginning of the eighteenth century" (the title of part one). From the rugged Finnish setting and the atmosphere of Finnish legend (mythic depiction of the Great Northern War from a Finnish standpoint and quotations from the *Kalevala,* the Finnish national epic first compiled by Elias Lönnrot in 1835) the action moves to St. Petersburg. Yakko, the adopted son of a poor Finnish fishing family caught up in the Russo-Swedish conflict, witnesses the clairvoyant powers of his foster-sister, Elsa, who is made by her grandfather to "see" the fate of her father at the hands of the Swedes. Brought to St. Petersburg by Zverev, a young Russian officer, Yakko is educated in Holland (having caught the attention of Peter the Great) and subsequently returns to Russia to find favored service with Peter the Great as an instrument of Russian enlightenment. Ivan Ivanovich Yakko, as he is now called, returns to Finland to seek out the semi-wild Elsa and to take her back to St. Petersburg. A conflict of cultures ensues between Elsa and her Russian hosts, the Zverevs—primitivism versus *embourgeoisement,* with "sorcery" held to be responsible on both sides. However, Yakko alone is bewitched, equally by the homely charms of the dark-haired Mar'ia Zvereva and by the untrammeled abandon of the blonde Elsa. The latter, who already had earned the reputation of a sorceress in Finland, and was apparently capable of undertaking an out-of-body visit to her homeland, picks up the threads of sorcery again because of jealousy. Her "sister in the fire" tells her that she and Yakko are to be one, united in "a single fiery thread," although her time has yet to come. Yakko's dilemma seems resolved when Elsa is rescued by a Finn during the great 1722 St. Petersburg flood and taken home to Finland. Yakko salves his conscience by delivering a purse of money for Elsa's wedding; "the last thread," he thinks, is broken.

In this first part of *Salamandra,* historical setting and detail and the values of European technology take precedence over the element of the fantastic, which is based on folklore. In part two the reverse is the case; the sorcery of old Finnish tales blends into the hoary tradition of European alchemy, the legend of Finnish treasure (*Sampo*), and the quest for the philosopher's stone, to overshadow the enlightenment introduced into Peter's Russia. Part one has an impersonal, more or less omniscient narration; part two opens a hundred years later in Moscow with a conversation between a common-sense authorial narrator and his Gomozeiko-like uncle, an adept in occult matters. Following a haunted-house visitation, the uncle takes over the narration (via the author's "memory"). Yakko's fortunes have deteriorated since the death of Peter the Great; dismissed from his posts and saddled with a nagging alcoholic wife (Mar'ia) in Moscow, he misses his "sister" Elsa and is reduced to an alchemical search for gold at the behest of a miserly count. In the course of the search he encounters in the fire a salamander in the likeness of Elsa. The real Elsa then returns, apparently oblivious to her other self. There is once again a hectic Gothic denouement that seems to involve a merging of Finnish magic with Western alchemy amid a fantastic ending, the apparent fulfillment of the salamander's prophecy. The haunted house of the opening of part two had been built on the ruins of Yakko's incinerated dwelling; at the conclusion, the uncle offers alternative versions of Yakko's fate.

A variation on this brand of Romantic historicism, closer to the process of threads and links observed in "Kosmorama," is the tale "Zhivoi mertvets" (The Live Corpse), dated 1838 but first published in *Otechestvennye zapiski* in 1844, which for all its own phantasmagoria is ultimately based more in reality, depending heavily on the chain of cause and effect. This latter preoccupation, heralded by Odoevsky's invented epigraph stressing the consequences of every thought and action, is shared with and may derive from the Romantic thought of Wackenroder. Having strong affinities with such stories as "Brigadir" and "Dusha zhenshchiny," "Zhivoi mertvets" features the wasted and corrupt life of the middle-aged clerk, Aristidov, who, in what turns out to be a dream, reviews the whole of his past life and the disastrous future of his dependents in an out-of-body, out-of-time experience that he thinks is death. This story manages to blend, or synthesize, almost all the strands of Odoevsky's work so far encountered: the fantastic element of the Romantic tale (life after death, the distortion of time and space, and an inner search of protopsychological depth), although this element is ultimately resolved by the revelation of the dream; the satirical/didactic approach of the society tale; and the short story as a vehicle for philosophical ideas (an attack on the worship of reason, the examination of a behavior pattern over a whole life, and an underlying existential pessimism). It is the philosophical side that eventually predominates, however, due to the close weaving of the central idea (expressed in the epigraph) into the text of the story, which emerges as a chronicle of the consequences of the deeds, the example, or even the thoughts, of a seemingly inconsequential man. At the same time, like many of Odoevsky's works, it has a strongly experi-

mental quality and can therefore appear somewhat disjointed in structure. An amalgam of styles and devices, written with varying intentions on several levels, it includes elements of pastiche and irony, dramatic dialogue, and a conversation in thieves' slang. "Zhivoi mertvets," perhaps best of any single work, indicates the direction of Odoevsky's fiction in the late 1830s.

A story that must be considered one of Odoevsky's most ambitious failures is "Segeliel'. Donkikhot Nineteenth stoletiia. Skazka dlia starykh detei" (Segeliel'. A Don Quixote of the Nineteenth Century: A Fairy-tale for Old Children), of which one fragment was published in 1838. Besides that piece, only drafts of certain sections and plans survive, despite the considerable time and effort Odoevsky devoted to the project from 1832 until at least the late 1830s. Even the proposed genre of the work is not clear; the published fragment is in the form of dramatic dialogue, and Sakulin reports that the language elsewhere "approaches the diction of poetry." Given that Dante, John Milton, Friedrich Gottlieb Klopstock, and Goethe seem to have been the main compositional influences, something in the nature of poetic drama was apparently planned, but almost any mixture of styles was possible with Odoevsky.

Sakulin has characterized this project as an attempt to "render the whole mystical conception of human history" and to "join heaven and earth." It was to begin with a heavenly prologue at the time of the fall of angels. Segeliel' is characterized as an all-loving figure similar to Klopstock's Abbadona; Odoevsky later refers to him as a spirit created by the Neoplatonists and the cabalists. Expelled from Paradise along with Lucifer, as one of his followers, Segeliel' displeases Lucifer by taking too sympathetic an interest in the fate of people on earth. In the cosmic struggle between good and evil, between Lucifer and the Creator, a secret strength in man (presently in the thrall of evil spirits) could tip the balance. Accordingly Segeliel' is dispatched to earth, but there, undergoing various metamorphoses, he ends up fighting on behalf of the forces of good and for mankind, despite Lucifer's frequent interventions. The existence here of *dvoemirie* may, as in the case of "Kosmorama," owe something to Swedenborgian ideas, as well as to Saint-Martin, Pordage, and the alchemists. In the published portion, Segeliel's immersion into bureaucratic philanthropy on earth introduced a strong autobiographical element into the work and was seen also as an updating of Quixotry (philanthropy as "the chivalry of our time"). However, Odoevsky's attempt to insinuate a "fallen spirit" into Russian society and institutions and to transform him into an ideal bureaucrat did not look too likely, on the evidence of the published fragment, to be accomplished with any great artistic felicity. The scale of the setting and the subject matter, and the form chosen for the endeavor, seemed to lie beyond his powers. As a grandiose failure that was never completed, it bears comparison with Gogol's *Mertvye dushi* (Dead Souls, 1842) in the totality of its conception and with Dostoyevsky's projected "Life of a Great Sinner."

Apart from the early "Dva dni v zhizni zemnogo shara," Odoevsky wrote three works that come under the category of utopian/science-fiction tales: "Gorod bez imeni" (City Without a Name), first published in *Sovremennik* in 1839, and "Poslednee samoubiistvo" (The Last Suicide), both of which form part of *Russkie nochi;* and the unfinished utopian work, *4338-i god.* "Gorod bez imeni" and "Poslednee samoubiistvo," stories directed polemically at the ideas of Jeremy Bentham and Thomas Malthus respectively, may be considered antiutopian (or dystopian). The story of the Benthamite colony, "Gorod bez imeni," is narrated in a characteristically spirited manner, recounting the triumphant mercantile expansion and ensuing self-destruction through strife between sectional interests (virtually class warfare). "Poslednee samoubiistvo" is a horrific depiction of overpopulation extending over the whole planet until finally the inhabitants turn against life itself. Escape from life into love, poetry, and philosophy is inadequate, according to the "prophets of despair"; by universal agreement (itself "the dream of the ancient philosophers"), preparations are made to destroy the planet with a gigantic explosion. These stories are an early example of the kind of potted histories of a planet, or the rise and fall of a civilization, with which readers are familiar in works such as Dostoyevsky's "Son smeshnogo cheloveka" (The Dream of a Ridiculous Man, 1877) and in the twentieth-century science fiction of writers such as Olaf Stapledon and Stanisław Lem.

In *4338-i god,* however, Odoevsky envisages the world lasting for at least two and a half millennia beyond his own time, until threatened in 4338 by a comet—the same one that had inspired Odoevsky's 1826 story. This work was originally conceived as the third part of a trilogy that was to have featured depictions of Russia in the era of Peter the Great and in the contemporary period (the 1830s); the first part was never written, and the second and futuristic third parts remained unfinished. Fragments were published in *Moskovskii nabliudatel'* in 1835 (as "Petersburg Letters") and in *Utrenniaia zaria* in 1840 (as "4338-i god"), and the fullest version of just the utopian part appeared as a book in 1926.

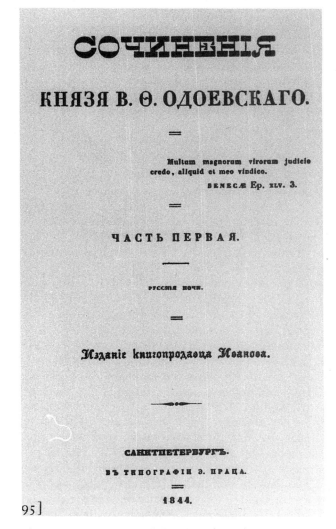

Title page for Odoevsky's Sochineniia *(Works), a three-volume collection that includes* Russkie nochi *(Russian Nights), his second cycle of stories*

Knowledge of this distant epoch is obtained by the supposed ability of the anonymous donor of the letters that comprise the work to travel through time at will via an advanced form of Mesmerism (an early-nineteenth-century equivalent to modern theories of science fiction). The world described is in some ways similar to the twentieth century (or perhaps the twenty-first); in other ways it is quite different. Many now-familiar technological advances are present: air travel (though it can take eight days by balloon from Peking to St. Petersburg), space travel (to the moon, but it is not clear how), the telephone, and photocopying. Hallucinogenic and truth drugs (in the form of gaseous drinks and "magnetic baths") remove all hypocrisy from social life. However, Russia and China are now the centers of world power (Russia covers half the globe and Moscow is a part of St. Petersburg); China is definitely the junior, backward partner (something like Russia in relation to Europe in the nineteenth century). Europe seems to be of no account (the English appear to be privatizing the British Isles, with Russia the purchaser). There is a marked absence of strife, suffering, and misery; various grandiose feats of engineering and climatic control have been accomplished. "Elastic glass" seems to be a basic, multipurpose material. The question of the imminent comet seems to be of minor import.

Interest inevitably centers on the social features of Odoevsky's utopia, though once again the ironic presentation should signal the advisability of exercising a certain caution. Due mainly to the lack of durability of books and texts, emphasized several times, knowledge of such distant epochs as the nineteenth century is extremely hazy. It is perhaps not surprising, therefore, that institutions such as the monarchy and the Church seem to have disappeared without a trace somewhere along the way. Technology and art are the dominant values and a republic (albeit of an aristocratic nature) seems to constitute the highly stable status quo. Education is highly elitist; poets, historians, and philosophers occupy high ministerial positions. An important (and quite Odoevskian, not to say Schellingian) feature of this system, which smacks more of enlightened technocracy than of democracy, is the presence of a "minister of conciliations," one whose main duty is the settling of scientific and literary disputes. The lower orders remain essentially outside the civilized scholarly establishment. The literary life appears to have reached that level of factions and squabbles with which Odoevsky was familiar in his own day; the work has topical allusions too, and was intended in part as a riposte to Faddei Venediktovich Bulgarin. Despite its fragmentary nature, there is no denying the achievement of imagination present in "4338-i god"; the leading authority on the history of science fiction, Darko Suvin, has written that "Odoevsky remains one of the more interesting SF writers of the pre-Wellsian age of Europe."

When considered as an entity, *Russkie nochi,* first published as an integral work as part of the 1844 *Sochineniia,* represents Odoevsky's major literary achievement and also provides a significant contribution to Russian thought of the period, standing somewhere between the positions of the Westernizers and the Slavophiles and including within itself elements of both. From the viewpoint of Romantic poetics, it also contrives to combine the forms of drama and novel within a framing device of a different order from, for example, Pushkin's *Povesti pokoinogo Ivana Petrovicha Belkina* (Tales of the Late Ivan Petrovich Belkin, 1830), Gogol's *Vechera na khutore bliz Dikan'ki* (Evenings on a Farm near Dikanka, 1831–1832), or, for that matter, Odoevsky's own *Pestrye skazki.* The most applicable generic description that can be given to this idiosyncratic work is probably that of "philosophical frame-tale."

Formal comparisons have been made between *Russkie nochi* and several supposed predecessors: Hoffmann's *Die Serapions-Brüder* (The Serapion Brothers, 1819–1821); Giovanni Boccaccio's *Decameron* (1348–1353); the Platonic dialogues; works from the German Romantic period by Goethe, Christoph Martin Wieland, Ludwig Tieck, and Heinrich Heine; and Joseph de Maistre's *Les soirées de Saint-Pétersbourg* (1821). None of these models in isolation is apt; however, while a case can be argued that *Russkie nochi* developed predominantly out of the Russian literary and philosophical movements of the 1820s and 1830s, the work demands assessment in the more general context of the poetics of European, and especially German, Romanticism. In this light it can be seen as something of a synthesis of the novella tradition of the frame-tale, stemming from the Eastern tale, notably *The Thousand and One Nights,* and the philosophical tradition that comes down from Plato. The synthesis, as a concept in itself, embodies one of the fundamental notions of Romantic philosophy and provides in this instance a unique Russian illustration of the Romantic aesthetic of the mixing of genres. Schelling and various of his antecedents are acknowledged sources for *Russkie nochi* and known influences on Odoevsky, while Novalis, who was also preoccupied with the concepts of reconciliation, through a process involving symbols, and of quest leading to revelation by stages, may function as an obvious ideational parallel.

In the most general terms, *Russkie nochi* consists of some eighteen sections or units, including an authorial introduction (lying outside the framework device, yet written in the spirit of the book as a whole, an integral part of the text since it includes and foreshadows several motifs and themes of the work that follows) and an epilogue (if not exactly a conclusion to the frame, at least a part of it). Eleven of the eighteen sections are stories, interpolated or embedded in the overall frame. Between the authorial introduction and the frame epilogue, the work is divided unequally into nine "nights" on which the frame-device gatherings purport to take place. Totaling (in the 1975 edition) some 177 pages, the stories taken together comprise a little more than half of the whole. In such works the frame represents a substantial proportion of the total text, obviously therefore taking on an importance greater than that

*Inscribed title page of a notebook presented by Odoevsky to Mikhail
Iur'evich Lermontov (from V. V. Afanas'ev, ed.,* I Love My
Native Land: In Lermontov's Footsteps, *1989)*

of a mere device of convenience; the epilogue in itself is more than half the length of the total frame
and the longest section in the book. There is also a
considerable introductory frame portion totaling
some twenty pages. The interstory frame discussions are either short or absent altogether and the
overall structure is irregular: the first story does not
occur until the Third Night, while the Fourth Night
includes six stories (some of which are quite short).

No work illustrates more clearly the apparent
contradiction in Odoevsky's approach to the composition of his fiction, and at the same time, the underlying element of inner unity. The writing of the
work occurred intermittently over a period of at
least fifteen years; the connections between each of
the parts were only revealed to the author with

hindsight. The framing device is motivated around
the nocturnal visits of a group of friends, representing various philosophical positions, to Faust, a kind
of serious, philosophical Gomozeiko or a learned
and older alter ego of Odoevsky himself. He argues
for a kind of synthesis between idealist aesthetics of
a largely Schellingian hue and nineteenth-century
ideas of progress, with a strong role of moral leadership projected for Russia, faced with a collapsing
Europe. Many thinkers are discussed and attacked,
including Adam Smith, Bentham, and Malthus, and
subtle connections are woven between these discussions and the interpolated stories, which include artistic tales, society tales, and antiutopias. *Russkie nochi* is Odoevsky's one completed large-scale project
to have achieved eventual critical success (particu-

larly from the 1969 assessment by Iu. V. Mann onward). It has a place as one of the most original works of Russian, and indeed European, Romanticism; it also marks the zenith and the swan song of Odoevsky's literary career.

There is no evidence of any psychological or spiritual crisis that may have caused Odoevsky to abandon his literary career at the height of his powers. The explanation seems to lie in the expansion of his bureaucratic and educational activities and was confirmed with the onset of his philanthropic enterprises (the management from 1846 of the Society for Visiting the Poor of St. Petersburg), although the somewhat disappointing reception of *Russkie nochi* may also have been a factor. In any case, while the publication of his fiction virtually ceased in 1844, the writing of it, aside from the finishing touches to the frame sections of *Russkie nochi,* had probably all but ceased four or five years before that. Almost all of Odoevsky's stories published from 1840 to 1844 are dated, or known to have been worked on, during the late 1830s. Even the two stories that he published in 1845 and 1846, "Sirotinka" (The Little Orphan) in *Vchera i segodnia* and "Martingal'" (The Martingale) in *Peterburgskii sbornik* seem to be scrapings from an earlier period, produced reluctantly to placate the demands of editors. Both stories, in any case, are far from being among Odoevsky's better works (although "The Martingale" provides a variant treatment of the theme of cards).

There may have been no grand gesture involved, therefore, in Odoevsky's premature literary retirement. Rather it seems to have been circumstantial, gradual, and haphazard. He had intended to prepare a second edition of his collected works as early as 1845 but became bogged down with other matters. Editors continued to request stories from Odoevsky for some years, and as late as 1858 Stepan Petrovich Shevyrev wrote to him: "I don't know why you have left literature completely and have indeed become *Voiceless*" (*Bezglasny*—the name of Odoevsky's fictitious publisher). After his release from his philanthropic toils (in 1855), Odoevsky did not find it easy to resume the literary career he had abandoned a decade and a half earlier; other priorities had come to the fore, although he did produce a variety of musical, scientific, and other articles in the late 1850s. He kept a diary (only partially published in *Literaturnoe nasledstvo* in 1935), which, although disappointing in its failure to resolve the mysteries of his inner life, nevertheless comprises valuable source material for the period. He also produced sketches of Moscow life and the polemical pieces "Nedovol'no" (Not Good Enough), published in *Besedy v obshchestve liubitelei rossiiskoi*

slovestnosti in 1867 as a spirited reply to Ivan Sergeevich Turgenev's purportedly valedictory "Dovol'no" (Enough, 1865), and "Perekhvachennye pis'ma" (Intercepted Letters), published in *Sovremennye izvestiia* in 1868, an unfinished satire in which Griboedov's Famusov returns to Moscow.

On the belletristic front, Odoevsky finally began to prepare a new edition of his works in the early 1860s. Full-scale revision was rejected as impossible seventeen years after the previous publication, and in any case a writer's word at a given time was considered "historical fact." However, minor corrections and alterations were made and some extra items were intended for inclusion (some of these amendments have been incorporated into subsequent editions of *Russkie nochi,* from 1913). It is not known why this edition never came to be printed. Odoevsky also attempted new literary works in his last years. A diary entry for 1867 mentions a plan for a comedy. More interestingly, from 1863 he engaged himself on a realistic novel to be called "Samarianin" (The Samaritan). Archival drafts and plans suggest that this work would have covered a wide Russian canvas over the period 1842–1861, bringing in historical detail on the Crimean War and the reforms.

The de facto abandonment by Odoevsky of his literary career after 1844 was a considerable misfortune for Russian literature, which had already lost many of its greatest writers through early and violent deaths. His work throughout the 1830s had shown a surprising degree of development; by the end of that decade he was demonstrating a psychological depth (in the fantastic stories), a presentation of realistic detail (in the society tales), and an interest in character depiction that earlier would have seemed beyond his range.

It is ironic that Odoevsky's most substantial achievement, *Russkie nochi,* proved to be, in effect, his literary farewell. A retrospective work by the time of its publication, it was outmoded by at least a decade and too complex in its design to satisfy the tastes of those years. Psychological (or Romantic) realism, together with a somewhat less overtly mystical element of the fantastic, soon resurfaced in Russian literature and was strongly in vogue elsewhere: Dostoyevsky and Edgar Allan Poe are but two names that spring to mind. It is regrettable that Odoevsky played no further role in this movement. A part of Odoevsky's close relations with the leading writers of his age entailed a considerable literary impact of his works and ideas on them: Griboedov, Pushkin, and Gogol all took something from Odoevsky as well as giving something back; his younger contemporaries (Lermontov, Turgenev, Dostoyevsky

The graves of Odoevsky (right) and his wife, Ol'ga Stepanovna Odoevskaia (née Lanskaia) in the Donskoi Monastery cemetery, Moscow

and Tolstoy) all exploited features, devices, or ideas from Odoevsky's fiction. His repercussions on later periods of Russian literature remain largely still to be traced.

Apart from the multigenre *Russkie nochi,* which has a significance in Russian cultural history that goes beyond its own ample belletristic qualities, Odoevsky's most lasting literary achievement rests in his fantastic and philosophical tales. The society tales, even at their best, are arguably of a more transitory stature, lacking the sparkle or the qualities of portraiture of the best examples of that genre. Greater imagination and originality (even if "originality" is understood as a relatively unusual treatment of preexisting sources) is found in the more Romantic stories. Some of these are predominantly fictional illustrations of Romantic philosophical or aesthetic positions, executed well or less well, as the case may be; others have an additional imaginative spark.

The main underlying compositional feature of many of these works is their posing of the question: "what if?" This question is normally posed early in the story, the remainder of which depicts the ensuing consequences. What if someone could get out of his body if he thought he was going to freeze to death? What if a mediocre poet could suddenly versify with ease and see and know everything? What if a man woke up to find he was dead and could go anywhere in time or space to consider the meaning of his life? This imaginative approach links Odoevsky with the tradition of incredible storytelling and inspired lying in Russian literature—from Gogol (what if a man suddenly lost his nose and it took on an independent existence?) to Mikhail Afanas'evich Bulgakov (what if Satan and his retinue suddenly visited Stalin's Moscow to cause havoc?). However, the approach is also quite European, as an examination of Odoevsky's ideas and sources readily indicates, where it stretches as if in parallel from Hoffmann (what if a cat wrote an autobiography that got mixed up with his master's memoirs?) to Franz Kafka (what if a man woke up one morning to find he had turned into a beetle?). It is amid this general Russian and European tradition of striking tales of the imagination that Odoevsky's fiction will be remembered.

Odoevsky's Romantic style of writing went out of fashion midway through his own lifetime. His reputation suffered a little-deserved eclipse for half a century thereafter at the hands of a largely utilitarian brand of criticism. It revived around the turn of the century, with the advent of a reborn interest in the Romantic movement occasioned by the growth of its natural successor, symbolism, which formed a part—in Russia as in Europe—of modernism (which of course had its own roots in Romanticism). The main fruits of this revival were a new edition of *Russkie nochi* in 1913 (only its second ever at that point) and the publication in the same year of Sakulin's monumental study (which, like many of the works of its subject, was also destined to remain uncompleted). Modernism in the Soviet Union, together with philosophical or idealist Romanticism, suffered for decades under the heavy shadow of socialist realist criticism; however, the outgrowing of that disastrously imposed perspective in Russia and the consequent rediscovery of interest there in Romanticism and modernism, together with a renewed Western fascination with Gothic fiction, looks set to ensure an established place for Odoevsky among the most esteemed storytellers of Europe.

Bibliography:

Katalogi biblioteki V. F. Odoevskogo (Chastnye sobraniia v fondakh Gosudarstvennoi Biblioteki SSSR imeni V. I. Lenina: Katalogi) (Moscow, 1988).

Biographies:

Neil Cornwell, *V. F. Odoyevsky: His Life, Times and Milieu* (London: Athlone, 1986);

Marietta A. Tur'ian, *"Strannaia moia sud'ba . . .": O zhizni Vladimira Fedorovicha Odoevskogo* (Moscow: Kniga, 1991).

References:

Joe Andrew, *Narrative and Desire in Russian Literature, 1822–49: The Feminine and the Masculine* (London: Macmillan, 1993), pp. 50–84;

Claud Backvis, "Trois notes sur l'oeuvre littéraire du prince Vladimir Odoevski," *AIPS* (Brussels), 19 (1968): 517–597;

Lewis Bagby, "V. F. Odoevskij's 'Kniažna Zizi'," *Russian Literature,* 17–18 (April 1985): 221–242;

Winfried Baumann, *Die Zukunftsperspektiven des Fürsten V. F. Odoevskii: Literatur, Futurologie und Utopie* (Frankfurt & Bern: Peter Lang, 1980);

Vissarion Grigor'evich Belinsky, "Sochineniia kniazia V. F. Odoevskogo," in his *Polnoe sobranie sochinenii,* volume 8 (Moscow: Akademia Nauk SSSR, 1955), pp. 297–323;

William Edward Brown, *A History of Russian Literature of the Romantic Period,* volume 2 (Ann Arbor, Mich.: Ardis, 1986), pp. 219–240;

J. S. Campbell, *V. F. Odoyevsky and the Formation of Russian Musical Taste in the Nineteenth Century* (New York: Garland, 1989);

Neil Cornwell, *Vladimir Odoevsky and Romantic Poetics: Collected Essays* (Providence, R.I. & Oxford, U.K.: Berghahn Books, 1998);

Cornwell, ed., *The Society Tale in Russian Literature: From Odoevskii to Tolstoi* (Amsterdam & Atlanta, Ga.: Rodopi, 1998);

Vasilii Gippius, "'Uzkii put': Kn. V. F. Odoevsky i romantizm," *Russkaia mysl',* 12 (1914): 1–26;

Norman W. Ingham, *E. T. A. Hoffmann's Reception in Russia* (Würzburg: Jal Verlag, 1974), pp. 177–193;

Zakhav Abramovich Kamensky, *Moskovskii kruzhok liubomudrov* (Moscow: Nauka, 1980);

Simon Karlinsky, "A Hollow Shape: The Philosophical Tales of Prince Vladimir Odoevsky," *Studies in Romanticism,* 5 (Spring 1966): 169–182;

L. A. Levina, "Avtorskii zamysel i khudozhestvennaia real'nost' (Filosofskii roman V. F. Odoevskogo 'Russkie nochi')," *Izvestiia Akademii nauk SSSR Seriia literatury i iazyka,* 49 (January–February 1990): 31–40;

Boris Andreevich Lezin, *Ocherki iz zhizni i literaturnoi deiatel'nosti kn. V. F. Odoevskogo* (Khar'kov: Tip. M. Zil'berberg, 1907);

Iu. V. Mann, "V. F. Odoevsky i ego 'Russkie nochi,'" in his *Russkaia filosofskaia èstetika (1820-30ye gody)* (Moscow: Iskusstvo, 1969), pp. 104–148;

Ralph E. Matlaw, introduction to *Russian Nights,* by Odoevsky (New York: Dutton, 1965), pp. 7–20;

E. A. Maimin, "Vladimir Odoevsky i ego 'Russkie Nochi,'" in *Russkie nochi,* by Odoevsky (Leningrad: Nauka, 1975), pp. 247–276;

M. I. Medovoi, "Neosushchestvlennyi zamysel V. F. Odoevskogo," in *Uchenye zapiski LGPA: russkaia literatura i obshchestvenno-politicheskaia bor'ba XVII-XIX vekov,* 414 (Leningrad, 1971), pp. 156–167;

Medovoi, "Izobrazitel'noe iskusstvo i tvorchestvo V. F. Odoevskogo," in *Russkaia literatura i izobratitel'noe iskusstvo XVIII-nachalo XX veka: sbornik nauchnykh trudov* (Leningrad: Nauka, 1988), pp. 84–95;

B. S. Meilakh, ed., *Russkaia povest' XIX veka: istoriia i problematika zhanra* (Leningrad: Nauka, 1973);

John Mersereau Jr., *Russian Romantic Fiction* (Ann Arbor, Mich.: Ardis, 1983), pp. 175–181, 229–230;

Fitz-James O'Brien, *The Fantastic Tales of Fitz-James O'Brien* (London: John Calder, 1977);

Charles E. Passage, *The Russian Hoffmannists* (The Hague: Mouton, 1963), pp. 89–114;

Robert Reid, ed., *Problems of Russian Romanticism* (Aldershot: Gower, 1986);

Vsevolod Ivanovich Sakharov, "Eshche o Pushkine i V. F. Odoevskom," in *Pushkin: issledovaniia i materialy,* edited by Vadim Erazmovich Vatsuro, volume 9 (Leningrad, 1979), pp. 224–230;

Sakharov, "E. T. A. Gofman i V. F. Odoevsky," in *Khudozhestvennyi mir E. T. A. Gofmana* (Moscow: Nauka, 1982), pp. 173–184;

Sakharov, "Seiatel' myslei (V. F. Odoevsky)," in his *Pod sen'iu druzhnykh muz: o russkikh pisateliakh-romantikakh,* edited by Igor' F. Belza and others (Moscow: 1984), pp. 203–255;

Pavel Nikitich Sakulin, *Iz istorii russkogo idealizma kniaz' V. F. Odoevsky Myslitel'-pisatel',* volume 1, parts 1 and 2 (Moscow: M. & S. Sabashnikovy, 1913);

S. E. Shatalov, ed., *Istoriia romantizma v russkoi literature. Romantizm v russkoi literature 20-30-kh godov XIX v. (1825–1840)* (Moscow: Nauka, 1979), pp. 108–172;

Heinrich Stammler, "Nachwort," in *Russische Nächte,* by Odoevsky, translated by Stammler and Johannes von Guenther (Munich: Wilhelm Fink, 1970), pp. 367–410;

Darko Suvin, *Metamorphoses of Science Fiction: On the Poetics and History of a Literary Genre* (New Haven & London: Yale University Press, 1979);

Orest Tsekhnovitser, "Predislovie" and "Siluet, vstupitel'naia stat'ia," in *Romanticheskie povesti,* by Odoevsky (Leningrad: Priboi, 1929), pp. 5–20, 25–99;

Marietta A. Tur'ian, "Evoliutsiia romanticheskikh motivov v povesti V. F. Odoevskogo 'Salamandra,'" in *Russkii romantizm,* edited by K. N. Grigor'ian (Leningrad: Nauka, 1978), pp. 187–206;

V pamiat' o kniaze Vladimire Fedoroviche Odoevskom (Moscow, 1869);

Andrzej Walicki, *The Slavophile Controversy: History of a Conservative Utopia in Nineteenth-Century Russian Thought,* translated by Hilda Andrews-Rusiecka (Oxford, U.K.: Clarendon Press, 1975), pp. 64–82;

I. I. Zamotin, *Romantizm dvadtsatykh godov XIX stol. v russkoi literature,* volume 2: *Romanticheskii idealizm v russkom obshchestve i literature 20-30-kh godov XIX stoletiia* (St. Petersburg: M. O. Vol'f, 1907), pp. 361–418;

V. V. Zenkovsky, *A History of Russian Philosophy,* translated by George L. Kline, volume 1 (London & New York, 1953), pp. 134–148.

Papers:

The bulk of Odoevsky's abundant manuscripts is held in St. Petersburg at the Saltykov-Schedrin State Public Library, *fond* 539, *opis* 1 and 2. A not-fully-reliable catalogue of *opis* 1 is to be found in: I. Bychkov, "Bumagi kn. V. F. Odoevskogo," *Otchet Imperatoskoi publichnoi biblioteki za 1884 g.* (St. Petersburg, 1887), prilozhenie 2-oe, pp. 1–65. *Opis* 2 is listed on a card index. Further papers are kept at the Institute of Russian Literature (Pushkin House) in St. Petersburg, and at the Russian State Library (formerly the Lenin Library) and the Central State Archive of Literature in Moscow.

Ivan Ivanovich Panaev
(15 March 1812 – 18 February 1862)

Carolyn Jursa Ayers
University of Groningen, The Netherlands

BOOKS: *Sobranie stikhotvorenii Novogo poeta* (St. Petersburg: Glavnyi shtab ego Imp. Velichestva po voenno-uch. Zavedeniiam, 1855);

Ocherki iz peterburgskoi zhizni Novogo poeta, parts 1–2 (St. Petersburg: K. Vul'f, 1860);

Sochineniia, 4 volumes (St. Petersburg: Kushulev-Bezborodko, 1860);

Literaturnye vospominaniia i Vospominaniia o Belinskom (St. Petersburg: V. Kovalevskii, 1876);

Sobranie sochinenii, 6 volumes (Moscow: V. M. Sablin, 1912);

Literaturnye vospominaniia (Leningrad: Academia, 1928).

Editions and Collections: *Pervoe polnoe sobranie sochinenii,* 6 volumes (St. Petersburg: N. G. Martynov, 1888–1889);

Literaturnye vospominaniia (Moscow: Goslitizdat, 1950);

Izbrannye proizvedeniia (Moscow: Goslitizdat, 1962);

Povesti. Ocherki (Moscow: Sovetskaia Rossiia, 1986);

Sochineniia (Leningrad: Khudozhestvennaia literatura, 1987);

Literaturnye vospominaniia (Moscow: Pravda, 1988).

OTHER: *Sovremennik*–copublished and coedited by Panaev and Nikolai Alekseevich Nekrasov, 1847–1862;

Illiustrirovannyi al'manakh, edited by Panaev and Nikolai Alekseevich Nekrasov (St. Petersburg: E. Prats, 1848).

Ivan Ivanovich Panaev

Ivan Panaev's literary legacy consists mainly of his memoirs, in which he comments on literary Russia of the 1830s and 1840s from his association with the Natural School and from his work as copublisher and coeditor, with Nikolai Alekseevich Nekrasov, of the journal *Sovremennik* (The Contemporary) from 1847 until his death in 1862. His tales and sketches (he was one of the main practitioners of the "physiological sketch" promoted by Vissarion Grigor'evich Belinsky) rate as quite respectable and still provide enjoyable reading. Nevertheless, Pan-

aev has traditionally been appreciated more for his polemical comments and commentaries, as a memoirist, journalist, and friend and colleague of the progressive literary figures Belinsky, Nekrasov, and Nikolai Gavrilovich Chernyshevsky. Perhaps because his own memoirs are sufficiently detailed, little independent scholarly writing exists on Panaev's life and work. Most introductory articles to the various editions of his works apologize, as it were, for his status as a second-rate writer of fiction, but all laud his persistent championing of progressive social and literary trends. For better and worse, he appears not only to have published but also to have assumed a personal identity under the label *Sovremennik* throughout his life.

Ivan Ivanovich Panaev was born on 15 March 1812 into a reasonably wealthy noble family with notable cultural and service connections. On his father's side Panaev was a grandnephew of the poet Gavril Romanovich Derzhavin; his uncle Viktor Alekseevich Panaev was a poet (a composer of idylls) and a high government official; and his father had collaborated on various journals, including Aleksandr Efimovich Izmailov's *Blagonamerennyi* (The Loyalist). Panaev's father, however, died when Ivan was still a child, and his mother brought him up in what he later described as a conservative household.

Panaev studied for five years, from 1825 to 1830, at the *Blagorodnyi Pansion* (Boarding School for the Nobility) attached to St. Petersburg University, which in 1830 became the First Petersburg Gimnaziia. He graduated with rank directly into a promising career in the civil service, serving first in the Department of the Treasury and then from 1834 to 1844 in the Department of Public Enlightenment, where he edited the journal of that ministry. He felt early on, however, that literature was his calling; according to some sources he tended to neglect his civil service career in favor of cultivating literary friendships and involving himself in literary activities. Even during his years in the Pansion, Panaev edited a weekly literary journal for his fellow students and teachers.

With what would be his characteristic urge to identify himself with the dominant literary movement of the moment, Panaev began his literary life as an enthusiastic devotee of Romanticism. In his memoirs he identifies Victor Hugo, Nikolai Alekseevich Polevoi, Aleksandr Aleksandrovich Bestuzhev (Marlinsky), and Nestor Vasil'evich Kukol'nik as particular idols. In the early 1830s Panaev wrote some verse in the Romantic style; several of his original verses as well as some translations from Hugo appeared in various journals and almanacs. Panaev soon turned exclusively to prose, however, with much more success. He wrote several society tales of short-story to novella length: "Spal'nia svetskoi zhenshchiny (Epizod iz zhizni poeta v obshchestve)" (The Boudoir of a Society Woman [An Episode from the Life of a Poet in Society], 1835), "Ona budet schastliva" (She Will Be Happy, 1836), "Segodnia i zavtra" (Today and Tomorrow, 1837), "Sumerki u kamina" (Evenings by the Fireside, 1838), and "Kak dobry ludi" (How Good People Are, 1838). These works earned the writer stead-

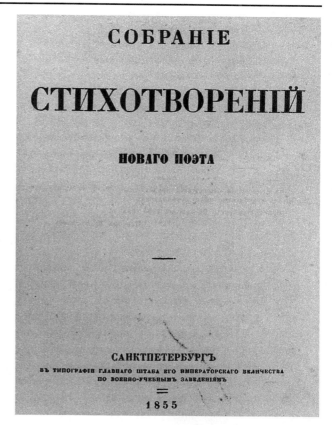

Title page for Panaev's Sobranie stikhotvorenii *(Collection of Poems)*

ily increasing critical acclaim and popularity; in hindsight, however, they seem to be rather literal, unsubtle renderings of the traditional Romantic conflict between the poet, or the sensitive soul, and society. They are especially lacking in convincing psychological motivation. Panaev himself was later embarrassed to recall his first attempts at prose, which he described as a "slavish imitation of Marlinsky."

Despite an obviously derivative style, even in his earliest works Panaev's eye for social detail is evident. He describes the milieu of the aristocratic elite with a discerning and critical exactness that portends his future career as a critical journalist. Also, in the latter tales of this early group he begins to draw characters from the lower classes of urban society, again with an unerring eye for external characterization.

Panaev remained in his Romantic mode long enough to embark on his own romantic adventure, his marriage to the then eighteen-year-old Avdotia Iakovlevna Brianskaia. According to the memoirs of Panaev's cousin, the writer's mother would not approve the match because Avdotia Iakovlevna was the daughter of an actor and therefore of low social standing. After trying for more than two years to

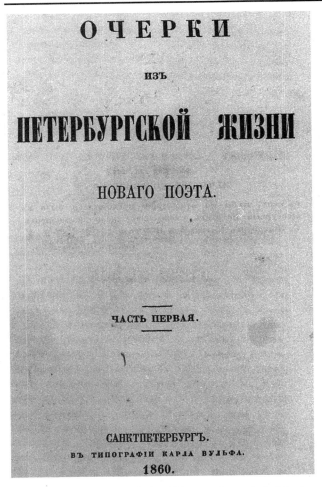

Title page for Panaev's Ocherki iz peterburgskoi zhizni Novogo poeta *(Essays of Petersburg Life)*

win her approval, the pair finally eloped and fled immediately to Kazan, followed the same day by a letter from her in which she cursed the couple. Although Panaev's mother soon reconciled with her son, the curse on the marriage seemed to remain. The couple had no children who survived infancy, and apparently it was Panaev's own thoughtless and frivolous behavior that soon rendered their marriage a mere formality (according to various accounts, Panaev "understood his spousal duty quite arbitrarily" and "could not manage to rearrange his life according to the family manner, not having renounced the habits of a free bachelor"). After some years of this unpleasantness Panaev's wife eventually turned to a liaison with his close associate Nekrasov that lasted fifteen years.

The Panaev home, despite the personal traumas of its occupants, became a thriving literary salon where the brightest lights of literary society were entertained and several young careers were nurtured.

The pair met Belinsky for the first time on their honeymoon in the spring of 1839 (Panaev had been an admirer of the critic since he had encountered Belinsky's "Literaturnye mechtaniia" in 1834), and an intimate friendship soon developed that proved influential over Panaev's subsequent career. The Panaevs also counted among their circle figures such as Aleksandr Ivanovich Herzen, Mikhail Aleksandrovich Bakunin, Vladimir Fedorovich Odoevsky, Ivan Sergeevich Turgenev, Ivan Aleksandrovich Goncharov, Timofei Nikolaevich Granovsky, Vladimir Aleksandrovich Sollogub, and the young Fyodor Dostoyevsky, who reportedly fell briefly in love with Avdotia Panaeva when he visited her salon in 1845. Avdotia Iakovlevna Panaeva herself became a respected prose writer under the pseudonym N. Stanitsky.

Panaev's relationship with Belinsky became the overriding influence in the former's literary and social outlook from 1839 on. The favor Belinsky had extended in 1838 through the poet Aleksei Vasil'evich Kol'tsov, inviting Panaev to contribute to the journal *Moskovskii nabliudatel'* (The Moscow Observer), Panaev returned in 1839 by helping to convince Andrei Aleksandrovich Kraevsky to hire Belinsky as the chief critic for the new journal *Otechestvennye zapiski* (Notes of the Fatherland). As his collaborator Panaev remained a champion of Belinsky's aesthetic views and of the critic personally, even after Belinsky's death in 1848; a desire to speak out in favor of Belinsky's name and literary legacy was certainly one of the motivating forces that led Panaev a decade later to begin writing his memoirs, which were dedicated to the memory of Belinsky.

Otechestvennye zapiski soon became the leading voice in print of the most progressive Russian men of letters. Its pages provided the forum in which Belinsky, Herzen, and others worked out a new "realistic" aesthetic for literature, one that reflected their leftward-leaning social agenda. The writers and critics of the "new generation" championed their views in ongoing polemics with more conservative journals, such as Mikhail Petrovich Pogodin and Stepan Petrovich Shevyrev's *Moskvitianin* (The Muscovite), Faddei Venediktovich Bulgarin's *Severnaia pchela* (The Northern Bee), and Osip Ivanovich Senkovsky's *Biblioteka dlia chteniia* (Library for Reading).

From 1839 through 1846 Panaev published, mainly in *Otechestvennye zapiski,* several successful tales and sketches, which followed the artistic prescriptives of the Natural School and helped to forward its goals. In tales such as "Doch' chinovnogo cheloveka" (Daughter of a Man of Rank, 1839),

*Panaev (center) beside Vissarion Grigor'evich Belinsky on his deathbed, 1884
(painting by A. Naumov; N.A. Nekrasov Flat-Museum, Moscow)*

"Prekrasnyi chelovek" (A Wonderful Man, 1840), "Onagr" (The Onager, 1841), and "Akteon" (Acteon, 1842) Panaev joined writers such as Nekrasov, Dmitrii Vasil'evich Grigorovich, and Vladimir Ivanovich Dal' in taking up Honoré de Balzac's avowed task of studying and accurately portraying the "physiology" of contemporary Russian society in all its different genres. Panaev described some of these types so vividly that they became stock figures in the Russian literary gallery; for instance, he introduced the "monsher" (from the French *mon cher*), the drawing room habitué who affects French expressions without quite reaching a credible level of sophistication.

One of Panaev's favorite themes, and one he returned to again and again in his journalistic writings and eventually in his memoirs, was the nature of literary life. With a wide circle of literary acquaintances, he was in a good position to know the habits, idiosyncracies, and personal politics of literary society. These he described, often in rather harsh and sarcastic terms, in tales such as "Peterburgskii fel'etonist" (Petersburg Feuilletonist, 1841), "Literaturnaia tlia" (Literary Louse, 1843), and "Literaturnyi zaiats" (Literary Hare, 1844).

Included in "Literaturnaia tlia" were some parodies of the kind of verse Panaev considered to be affected, amateurish, and all too often served up by the aspiring poets swarming around the contemporary literary scene. These "pseudoverses" were the first of many as Panaev soon adopted parody as one of his principal modes of writing. Under the pseudonym "Novyi poet" (a New Poet) Panaev created a semifictional persona who observed and copied the latest and most banal literary trends. The Novyi poet was in

some ways a rather primitive predecessor of the more polished parodic persona Koz'ma Prutkov (joint pseudonym of Aleksei Konstantinovich Tolstoi and Aleksandr Mikhailovich Zhemchuzhnikov), but the persona of the Novyi poet tended to blur into Panaev's own personality and to reflect his tastes and priorities with little artistic detachment. In addition to parodies, the Novyi poet moved on to sketches and feuilletons over his almost twenty-year literary "life," a life which was devoted exclusively to exposing the folly of outdated literary and social views.

By the mid 1840s Panaev, along with Belinsky and Nekrasov, had begun to chafe under the mainly commercially oriented editorial policies of Kraevsky at *Otechestvennye zapiski*. The friends dreamed of publishing their own journal, which would take a more idealistic course in the ongoing literary polemics of the day. Avdotia Panaeva was apparently instrumental in convincing her husband to sell some of his property to put up money for the purchase of such a journal. In 1846 Panaev purchased from Petr Aleksandrovich Pletnev the journal "with the illustrious name of 'Sovremennik'" (The Contemporary—this had been the name of Pushkin's short-lived literary journal). The first issue with Panaev listed as publisher appeared in January 1847 with a contribution from the Novyi poet, as well as a tale under Panaev's own name. This work, "Rodstvenniki" (The Relatives), articulated what would be a ubiquitous literary theme in the nineteenth century, that of the predicament of the "superfluous man," and it has been mentioned as a source for Turgenev's more famous first novel, *Rudin* (1856).

From this date on all Panaev's literary activity was devoted to *Sovremennik*. After the first year he nominally assumed editorship in addition to his responsibilities as publisher, but Nekrasov remained the de facto editor. Belinsky was the inspirational force of the journal from the beginning, and together this formidable trio became the core of what soon proved itself the leading journal in Russia. Panaev published the works of writers such as Herzen, Nekrasov, Turgenev, Goncharov, Grigorovich, and others. He also worked hard to keep the flame of liberal journalism alive during several difficult years when *Sovremennik* had to endure Herzen's emigration in 1847, the death of Belinsky in 1848, and a crackdown in censorship as the regime of Nicholas I grew ever more repressive.

Panaev harbored few illusions about the extent of his literary talents. (Surprisingly modest, he did not spare himself from his own fault-finding.) Nevertheless, he continued to labor as one of the "literary fleas" and produced credible work in diverse genres. He attempted two novels, *Mamen'kin synok* (Mama's Boy, 1845) and *L'vy v provintsii* (Lions of the Province, 1852), but these were not well received. More successful were his monthly installments, *Zametki* (later *Zametki i razmyshleniia) Novogo poeta po povodu russkoi zhurhalistiki* (Notes [later Notes and Reflections] by a New Poet on Russian Journalism), from 1851 through 1855. In these Panaev wrote as a critic, sustaining often harsh polemics with his old journal, Kraevsky's *Otechestvennye zapiski,* and with the conservative journal *Moskvitianin.*

Despite his harsh journalistic postures Panaev was well liked by his colleagues, and he continued to maintain good personal relations with most of the leading liberal writers, but the split between liberals and radicals was widening, and Panaev could not remain neutral in matters that he passionately believed to be critical for Russia's literary future. In 1855 Chernyshevsky joined the staff at *Sovremennik,* followed by Nikolai Aleksandrovich Dobroliubov in 1856. These standard-bearers of the new generation quickly assumed leadership roles at the journal; Nekrasov's endorsement of their views eventually drove away the more moderate writers such as Turgenev, Grigorovich, Aleksandr Vasil'evich Druzhinin, and Vasilii Petrovich Botkin. Consciously choosing to stake his claim with the radical critics, Panaev left his friends of many years, remained with the journal, and continued to press for what he believed was progress.

In 1855 he began a new monthly feuilleton titled "Peterburgskaia zhizn'. Zametki Novogo poeta" (Petersburg Life. Notes by the New Poet). Besides purely polemical observations on Russian life and letters, he included in this column sketches (some of his separately published tales feature characters from these pages), reviews, and notes on concerts, exhibitions, and performances. A particularly noteworthy effort

from this period is his collection of sketches *Opyt o khlyshchakh* (Investigation on Dandies, 1854–1857; the word "khlyshch" is Panaev's own untranslatable characterization of a certain type of social creature). In 1860 he published a four-volume collection of his literary works. Finally, as part of the ongoing debate over the future path of Russian literature, Panaev began to write and publish his literary memoirs. In them he clearly found his true voice, which he uses to bring to life the literary atmosphere of the 1840s, the decade of his and Belinsky's youth.

Panaev left his memoirs unfinished. He died unexpectedly of a heart attack at his home in Petersburg on 18 February 1862 at the age of forty-nine. He was still working actively on *Sovremennik* at the time. Despite the awkwardness of her relationship with Panaev's close associate Nekrasov, Avdotia Panaeva had continued to hold her husband in some esteem, and she was at his bedside when he died.

Chernyshevsky had planned to give a speech at Panaev's funeral but changed his mind when it appeared that the authorities might be there waiting for him, but his affectionate obituary for his older colleague testifies to the personal respect Panaev had earned among his acquaintances. As Chernyshevsky stated, Panaev remained "to the end of his life a champion of the new generation."

References:

Nikolai Gavrilovich Chernyshevsky, "Nekrolog Ivana Ivanovicha Panaeva," *Polnoe sobranie sochinenii v 15 tomay;* tom XVI (dopolnitel'nyi) (Moscow: Khudozhestvennai a literatura, 1953), pp. 662–666;

Isaak Grigor'evich Iampol'sky, "Literaturnaia deiatel'nost' I. I. Panaeva," introduction to Panaev's *Literaturnye vospominaniia* (Moscow: Pravda, 1988);

F. M. Ioffe, "Ivan Ivanovich Panaev," introduction to Panaev's *Izbrannye proizvedeniia* (Moscow: Goslitizdat, 1962);

J. L. Keynes, "Ivan Ivanovich Panaev: A Literary Figure from the Background of Nineteenth-Century Russian Literature," dissertation, University of Pennsylvania, 1954;

M. V. Otradin, "Tvorchestvo Ivana Panaeva," introduction to Panaev's *Sochineniia* (Leningrad: Khudozhestvennaia literatura, 1987);

Viktor Alekseevich Panaev, "Vospominaniia," *Russkaia starina,* 8 (1893): 343–346; 9 (1893): 469–483; 9 (1901): 481–491, 501–506;

Vladimir Artemovich Tunimanov, "Povesti i ocherki Ivana Panaeva," introduction to Panaev's *Povesti. Ocherki* (Moscow: Sovetskaia Rossiia, 1986), pp. 3–20.

Nikolai Filippovich Pavlov

(? September 1803 – 29 March 1864)

Carolyn Jursa Ayers

University of Groningen, The Netherlands

BOOKS: *Tri povesti* (Moscow: N. Stepanov, 1835)—comprises "Imeniny," "Auktsion," "Iatagan";

Novye povesti (St. Petersburg: Gutenberg, 1839)—includes "Maskarad," "Demon," "Million";

Razbor komedii grafa Solloguba 'Chinovnik' (Moscow, 1857);

Statskii—armeitsu (Nauburg, Germany, 1860).

Editions and Collections: *Imeniny. Auktsion. Iatagan. Povesti* (Leningrad: Izdatel'stvo pisatelei v Leningrade, 1931);

N. F. Pavlov. Povesti i stikhi (Moscow: Khudozhestvennaia literatura, 1957);

Tri povesti (Moscow: Khudozhestvennaia literatura, 1958);

N. F. Pavlov. Sochineniia (Moscow: Sovetskaia Rossiia, 1985);

N. F. Pavlov. Izbrannoe i povesti, stikhotvoreniia stat'i (Moscow: Khudozhestvennaia literatura, 1988).

TRANSLATIONS: Friedrich von Schiller, *Maria Stuart* (Moscow, 1825);

Honoré de Balzac, "Mshchenie" (Epizod iz letopisei sovremennoi zhizni), *Teleskop,* nos. 5–8 (1831);

Balzac, "Nevestka-aristokratka," *Teleskop,* part 5, nos. 17–19 (1831);

William Shakespeare, *Venetsianskii kupets. Otechestvennye zapiski,* part 5, no. 9 (1839).

OTHER: *Nashe vremia,* edited and published by Pavlov (17 January 1860 – June 1863).

SELECTED PERIODICAL PUBLICATION– UNCOLLECTED: "Moskovskii Otryvok iz romana," *Teleskop,* part 7 (1832): 27–43.

Nikolai Pavlov is now considered a minor figure in the Russian literary tradition, remembered as much for his unhappy marriage to the poet Karolina Pavlova as for his own small body of tales, translations, poetry, and criticism. At one time, however, he was one of the most influential personalities in Moscow literary society, active in virtually every literary institution. He was a contradictory individual, described by an acquaintance as talented and full of promise but one of those men for whom things continually fall apart rather than come together. Although his career unfolded roughly parallel to the evolution of Russian letters from the 1820s to the 1860s, he often found himself out of step with the social and literary mood of the day. Born a serf, Pavlov was always attracted to society life; he was one of the first *raznochintsy* (non-nobles) to succeed in a literary world that had been dominated by aristocrats. In his best-known tales, "Imeniny" (The Name Day) and "Iatagan" (The Scimitar), he created a sensation by broaching the normally forbidden topics of serfdom and the military. Here and elsewhere Pavlov directly addressed the abuses of these hierarchies and the inhumanity rampant among the social elite. In this practice he followed the example of Honoré de Balzac, whose tales Pavlov is credited with introducing to Russian readers; he was sometimes called "the Russian Balzac." Yet Pavlov indulged in many of the vices he criticized, to the extent that he eventually brought about his own downfall. Throughout his career he tried to work within the system, beginning as an enthusiastic civil servant who tried to use the law to effect social justice, then in the 1840s as host for a salon that sought to bring together members of opposing philosophical camps. He ended, however, by sharing with his journal *Nashe vremia* (Our Time) a reputation as an ineffective dupe of the government.

Nikolai Filippovich Pavlov was probably born in September of 1803 in the Tambov province on the estate of the landowner Vladimir Mikhailovich Grushetsky. (Some accounts date his birth in 1804 or 1805 and place it in Moscow, but most data suggests the first alternative). His mother was a house serf of Georgian origin and Grushetsky's concubine, so it is likely that Pavlov was really the landowner's illegitimate son. That Pavlov and his sister

Nikolai Filippovich Pavlov

received a thorough early education of the sort usually reserved for noble children supports this conjecture. This supposition also would explain why he and his sister were granted their freedom in 1811 by Grushetsky's son after the death of the old landowner. Upon their release both children were enrolled in a theatrical institute under the direction of the Imperial Theaters of Moscow. This institute, which prepared actors to join government-sponsored troupes, accepted mainly children of the merchant class, craftsmen's children, and freed serfs. Pavlov was able to pay his own way (probably financed by his former landlord) until 1816, but from then until he finished the institute in 1821 he was subsidized by the government, a fact which meant that he enjoyed even fewer privileges than others in this already austere environment.

Despite this less-than-ideal situation, Pavlov was a talented and energetic student, and he attracted the attention and patronage of Fedor Fedorovich Kokoshkin, the new, relatively enlightened director of the institute. Kokoshkin broadened Pavlov's horizons by inviting him to his home for literary gatherings and performances. It was here that Pavlov made his first connections among the

Moscow literati. Kokoshkin counted among his regular visitors Mikhail Nikolaevich Zagoskin, Aleksandr Aleksandrovich Shakhovskoi, and Sergei Timofeevich Aksakov. The young acting student was hardly treated as an equal in this company, however. One guest remembered later that Pavlov attended those evenings in the capacity of a servant, standing behind the guests at the table with a napkin over his arm. This early experience was certainly more crucial for the development of Pavlov's sensibilities than his formal education, since in this society he was able to feed his hunger for knowledge, hone his powers of observation, perfect his French, polish his manners, and at the same time nurture a sensitivity to the callousness of the upper class.

Upon finishing the institute, Pavlov was assigned to a theatrical troupe. Though Pavlov reportedly had excellent elocution (in later years he found himself quite in demand for speeches and often called upon to declaim other writers' works), he had no love of performing. In fact, he already had a literary career in mind. Through his connection with Kokoshkin he was able to obtain a medical discharge from the theater, which released him after only seven months of the five- to ten-year stint that was required as payment for his education. Pavlov had already attended lectures at Moscow University while he was at the institute, and in 1822 he enrolled in the division of philological sciences, finishing in 1825. During his student years, according to his biographer Nikolai Alekseevich Trifonov, Pavlov mixed in literary circles and became especially close with the future critic and scholar Stepan Petrovich Shevyrev and the writer Prince Vladimir Fedorovich Odoevsky. In spite of his low social standing, Pavlov was able to gain entry into the best circles and "gain his footing on the parquet."

According to all accounts, Pavlov owed his success to his remarkable talent, his sociability, and his brilliant and interesting conversation. Yet because of his low birth and his lack of means, he was still not entirely accepted in high society, a fact of which he was acutely conscious and which is reflected in his creative work all the way through the 1830s. Also around this time Pavlov married for the first time, apparently rashly and unhappily. Little is known about the woman or about the circumstances of their disillusionment with each other, but it is possible that the misogynous streak often remarked in Pavlov's tales dates to his own unfortunate experience. The two lived apart, and his wife died when they had been married a little more than a year.

Pavlov's earliest literary activity was, logically enough, connected with the theater. He had begun translating drama from French and English while he was still at the theatrical institute, and some of his translations were staged as early as 1820. There was at this time a great demand for both translations and vaudevilles to be performed on the Russian stage, and Pavlov followed the fashion, working in both popular forms. His first real success came with the staging and publication in 1825 of his translation of Friedrich von Schiller's tragedy *Maria Stuart* (1800). Throughout the 1820s, Pavlov published a series of poems, mainly elegies (again, the fashionable form). Pavlov began to participate in the literary society clustered around the various journals of the day; in addition to his poems and translations, he contributed critical articles. Literary alliances and affiliations with the different journals were still quite fluid, and it was not unusual for personal friendships and animosities to override literary philosophy in bringing writers together or driving them to competing journals. The literary-social divisions that would mark the 1830s and 1840s were just beginning. It was characteristic of Pavlov that he valued personal ties over literary polemics, contributed to journals with different agendas, and held the rather old-fashioned view that all literary criticism should be conducted in a manner of friendly conver-

sation. Pavlov was now making his way into the highest circles in Moscow, and he was anxious to please.

At the same time he was much less accommodating in his civil career. After finishing the university, Pavlov had taken a post as an assessor in the first department of the Moscow court system. His conscientiousness and zeal in seeking just redress in every case, even when he clashed with well-connected nobles, did not win him friends within the system. When in 1831 he denounced a powerful nobleman who had offered him a bribe, Pavlov was relieved of his post.

Fortunately, his literary career was beginning to blossom. At this time he was affiliated with the leading journal of the day—*Teleskop* (Telescope). In 1831 *Teleskop* published Pavlov's translations of Balzac's "Vendetta" ("Mshchenie") and "The Ball at Sceaux" ("Nevestka-aristokratka"). These were the first translations of Balzac into Russian, and they helped initiate the craze for the French writer that continued in Russia throughout the 1830s.

In his early exercises in the well-worn literary tracks of vaudevilles, elegies, and translations Pavlov had demonstrated enough talent to gain the attention of the literary establishment, but the works included little that was original. The prose fragment "Moskovskii bal" (Moscow Ball), published in 1832 in *Teleskop,* brought him more into what would be his own element: detailed and insightful renderings of the life of high society. And with the publication in 1835 of *Tri povesti* (Three Tales), Pavlov joined the ranks of Russia's best writers. This small volume—having the subtitle *domestica facta* and consisting of the tales "Imeniny," "Auktsion" (The Auction), and "Iatagan"—caused a sensation and immediately sold out its first printing. In depicting various trials of the heart, the tales exhibit subtle psychological characterization, detailed descriptions of contemporary reality, and expressive use of language. But their notoriety springs from their treatment of social relations and conflicts.

In "Imeniny" Pavlov broke with convention by choosing as his hero a sensitive, musically talented, and educated serf in whose voice most of the story is told. The tale's "message" is in the narrator's daring (for that time) statement: "Any man anywhere is equally worthy of attention . . . no matter who he is." "Auktsion" is a more compact, more cynical tale about winners and losers in the games of love, vanity, and revenge in high society. "Iatagan," probably Pavlov's best work, details the unfortunate downfall of a promising young cornet who provokes his superior's jealousy, is punished by him, and, unable to endure the insult, kills him in

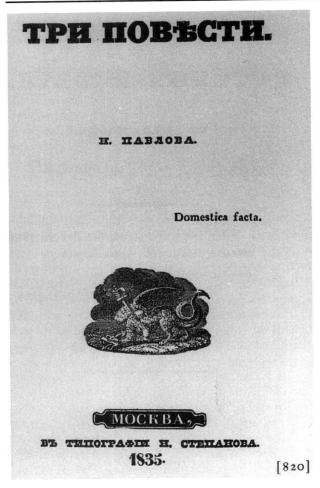

ТРИ ПОВѢСТИ.

Н. ПАВЛОВА.

Domestica facta.

МОСКВА,

ВЪ ТИПОГРАФІИ Н. СТЕПАНОВА.

1835.

[820]

Title page for Pavlov's Tri povesti *(Three Tales), which established his reputation as a leading Russian author*

retaliation. Four lives, including those of the heroine and the young officer's mother, are senselessly destroyed, not just because of the romantic entanglement but also because of the personal vanity that rules the characters' behavior. Most noteworthy in the tale, however, is the blatant way the author depicts the absolute and arbitrary power wielded by a military officer over his subordinates and the suffering caused by this state of affairs.

The army was considered an almost untouchable subject in literature except in works that celebrated heroic military feats, so Pavlov's tale represented a venture into new and controversial waters, despite its conventional and decorous rendering. The attention paid to Pavlov's social themes did not escape the notice of the censors. Although they had originally approved the work, the censors now, with Tsar Nicholas's personal agreement, forbade any future editions of the tales to be published (and indeed they were not reprinted in Russia until the twentieth century).

In 1837 Pavlov's personal fortunes took a dramatic turn when he married the poet and heiress Karolina Karlovna Jaenisch. The two had met some years earlier at the famous salon of Zinaida Volkonskaia. Though they appear to have had genuine regard for each other's literary talent, this was clearly a marriage of convenience, not of love. For her part Karolina Pavlova nurtured a lifelong, romantic passion for the Polish poet Adam Mickiewicz, who had courted her but whom her family had not allowed her to marry. And Pavlov later admitted to a friend that "in his life he had committed one vile act—he had married for money."

With his newly acquired wealth Pavlov could finally live the life he had enviously observed for so long. He threw himself into managing his wife's estates (with her approval, since she was of a decidedly impractical bent), and freely indulged his passion for gambling. He was known for giving spectacular dinners. In addition, the Pavlovs hosted one of the largest and most heterogeneous literary salons in Moscow in the 1840s. They counted many illustrious names among their guests, including Aleksandr Ivanovich Turgenev, Petr Andreevich Viazemsky, the Aksakovs, the Kireevskys, and many others. Reportedly Mikhail Iur'evich Lermontov spent his last night in Moscow there before he left on his final journey into exile in the Caucasus. The salon was successful, but in many ways it was also an anachronism in its decorousness, an imitation of the vibrant salons that the Pavlovs remembered from the 1820s. While the life of literary Russia during the 1840s lay in the raging polemics between (in simplistic terms) the Westernizers, Pavlov resisted recognizing a split between the two camps, and, in a way, retreated from the storm. But because he maintained close ties with many of the leading Slavophiles, he began to be mistrusted by the more progressive camp.

While Pavlov's social life was thriving, his literary output declined drastically. In 1839 he published three more tales in the collection *Novye povesti* (New Tales), but he had written them by 1835. His successful translation of Shakespeare's *The Merchant of Venice* also appeared in 1839. The stories in *Novye povesti* continue the social themes of Pavlov's *Tri povesti,* but they have less literary merit than the earlier tales and display considerably more of Pavlov's cynical worldview. Moreover, his criticism of the hypocrisy of high society seems to be more than balanced by his evident fascination with the social elite. In the first tale, "Maskarad" (Masquerade), a young socialite discovers the disillusioning secret of a hero similar in external characteristics to Lermontov's Pechorin the protagonist of *Geroi nashego vremeni*

14 Rozhdestvensky Boulevard, where Pavlov and his wife, Karolina Pavlova, hosted a literary salon in the 1840s

(Hero of Our Time, 1841). The hero had seemingly enjoyed that rare circumstance in high society, a happy marriage, only to discover upon his wife's untimely death that she had always loved someone else. Thus Pavlov continues to write around the motif of a woman who gives a vow of love that she cannot honor.

For the second story, "Demon" (The Demon), the author turns once again to a hero from the lower classes, this time one of the "poor clerks" who were later to receive more sympathetic treatment from the likes of Nikolai Vasil'evich Gogol and Fedor Mikhailovich Dostoevsky. Pavlov's story, however, is as much an indictment of human nature as of the social conditions that stifle it. The hero, initially downtrodden and unable to advance in the Petersburg bureaucracy, conceives a plan to exploit the system and make a pleasant life for himself. Through various persistent efforts, he manages to bring his young and beautiful wife to the attention of a powerful general. This "fortunate" circumstance brings the hero the material success and leisure that his own

labor never could, and the tale ends happily, if cynically.

The final tale in the collection, "Million" (A Million), concerns a favorite theme of the society-tale genre—the encroachment through marriage of the lower classes into the "territory" of the elite. In Pavlov's version, a marriage is being tastefully arranged between a well-bred but impoverished princess, in whom the family is placing its hopes, and a rich but uninteresting businessman. The man, grimly determined to expose the situation for what it is (even at the expense of his own happiness), offers the princess a million paper rubles if she will admit that she does not love him. The bargain is really less a test of her feelings than an indictment of the whole social structure that does not allow her even to know her own heart, much less heed it. The girl refuses the money, but her answer reveals a disillusionment at least as strong as that of the man: "If I did love you, then I stopped loving you at this moment." Pavlov's new tales, however diverting, suffer from a cynical tone that is distinctly at odds with an emerging age of idealism in Russian letters.

Based on his personal experience, Pavlov had reason to be cynical. Around 1840 he made another stab at a civil service career. Upon the recommendations of friends, he was appointed to a position as an intercessor on behalf of arrestees who wished to present petitions to the authorities. Once again Pavlov undertook his duties energetically, and once again he clashed with his superiors. He was forced to resign his position after he insisted on pursuing a complaint from a merchant against a well-connected count.

Pavlov's only literary work from the 1840s worth remarking is his series of three (some accounts say four) letters printed in *Moskovskie vedomosti* (Moscow Gazette) in response to Gogol's *Selected Passages from Correspondence with Friends* (1847). Pavlov's criticism of Gogol's notoriously unpopular literary endeavor was not only harsh but also insightful and witty. Vissarion Grigor'evich Belinsky praised Pavlov's letters, which preceded his own famous "Letter to N. V. Gogol," and saw that they were reprinted in the journal *Sovremennik* (The Contemporary).

Meanwhile, Pavlov's personal life was unraveling. Relations between the practical-minded Pavlov and his wife, who was frequently described as having an "exalted" temperament, grew less and less amicable. When Karolina invited a relative to come and live in their home as a companion, Pavlov fell in love with her. Eventually he installed her in a separate residence and began to support two families. An acquaintance reports that this second family (which grew to include two sons and a daughter) received much more of his attention than did his legal wife and son. Karolina and her father decided to take action. Wishing to humiliate Pavlov, in 1853 they took the drastic public step of appealing to the governor-general of Moscow, Arsenii Andreevich Zakrevsky, on the grounds that Pavlov was squandering the family fortune through his gambling. Zakrevsky already held a grudge against Pavlov over some unflattering verses Pavlov had written and circulated about him and was only too willing to order a search of Pavlov's home, on the premise of looking for marked cards. The inspectors found no marked cards, but Pavlov did have in his personal library forbidden works by Aleksandr Ivanovich Herzen, Prince Petr Vladimirovich Dolgorukov, and others. Pavlov was charged immediately and exiled to Perm; Karolina soon left Russia permanently. Although Pavlov was treated well in exile by the local governor-general, who welcomed him into his home, the writer was miserable. Once again through the intervention of friends, he was granted permission to return to Moscow after less than a

year of his ten-year sentence. Sobered by the whole experience, Pavlov gave up gambling and devoted all his energies to journalism.

The late 1850s were years of reform in Russia, and Pavlov was active in organizing many dinners and benefits supporting the government's efforts and advocating moderate reform. He labored as a critic and publicist for *Russkii vestnik* (The Russian Herald), which was at that time a liberal journal. During this period he published several important articles—a scathing review of Count Vladimir Aleksandrovich Sollogub's "Chinovnik" (The Clerk) in 1856, "Biograf-orientalist" (Biographer-Orientalist) in 1857 in response to an article by the conservative critic Apollon Aleksandrovich Grigor'ev; and in 1859 "Statskii-armeitsu" (Civilian to Military Man), a call for more tolerance for criticism of the military in the press. By this time, however, his liberal views were out of sync with both the radical democrats and the conservative Slavophiles. Nor did he return to writing fiction. Just as the radical critics Nikolai Gavrilovich Chernyshevsky and Nikolai Aleksandrovich Dobroliubov were dominating the literary scene with their utilitarian theories, Pavlov grew even more cynical about the social value of literature, deciding that "in its provisional demands and declarations, literature has invented nothing and created nothing."

From 1859 until his death from heart disease in 1864 Pavlov concentrated his efforts on launching a new journal. After extensive negotiations with the authorities Pavlov accepted several restrictions in order to begin publishing *Nashe vremia* (Our Time) as a weekly in January 1860. This was an ill-fated enterprise. The radical democrats declared war on this "organ of the government" from the pages of *Sovremennik*; at the same time the government for whom Pavlov had, in Herzen's words, "dropped his dagger," would not allow him to include political commentary, a restriction which was guaranteed to limit the journal's readership. Pavlov's sarcastic articles aimed against the radical democrats also put off many of the editor's former friends. *Nashe vremia* folded in June 1863. Pavlov immediately began to work toward the creation of a newspaper that he envisioned as having broader appeal, but he did not live to witness the success of *Russkie vedomosti* (Russian News). His reputation destroyed by his involvement with *Nashe vremia*, Pavlov had already outlived his moment in the limelight of Russian culture.

Partly because his interests did not keep up with the development of Russian prose in the mid nineteenth century, Pavlov is remembered less than he deserves to be. His important role in the literary society of his day is largely preserved in the memoirs of his contemporaries (memoir is the one genre in which Pavlov did not make a significant contribution; he left only a few fragments which have never been published), but his few original tales still provide rewarding reading.

Bibliography:

Vsevolod Panteleimonovich Vil'chinsky, in *Nikolai Filippovich Pavlov, Zhizn' i tvorchestvo* (Leningrad: Nauka, 1970), pp. 167–176.

References:

Vissarion Grigor'evich Belinsky, "O russkoi povesti i povestiakh g. Gogolia," *Polnoe sobranie sochinenii,* volume 1 (Moscow: Akademiia Nauk SSSR, 1953–1956), pp. 280–283;

N. V. Berg, "Posmertnye zapiski," *Russkaia starino,* no. 2 (1891): 262–270;

Boris Nikolaevich Chicherin, *Vospominaniia. Moskovskii universitet, Moskva sorokovykh godov* (Moscow: Izdatel'stvo M. i. S. Sabashnikovykhi, 1929);

Iurii Granin, "N. F. Pavlov," in *Ocherki po istorii russkoi literatury pervoi poloviny,* volume 19, part I (Baku: Izdanie Narkomprosa, 1941);

Sergei Ivanovich Ponomarev, *Materialy dlia istorii russkoi literatury (N. F. Pavlov),* in *Sbornik, Otde-lenie russkogo iazyka i slovesnosti Akademiia Nauk,* 46, no. 3 (1889): 1–19;

Elizabeth Colvin Shepard, "Pavlov's 'Demon' and Gogol's 'Overcoat,'" *Slavic Review,* 33 (1974): 288–301;

Stepan Petrovich Shevyrev, "*Tri povesti* N. Pavlova," *Moskovskii nabliudatel',* 1, nos. 1–2 (March 1835): 120–130;

Nikolai Stepanov, introduction to *Imeniny. Auktsion. Iatagan. Povesti* (Leningrad: Izdatel'stvo pisatelei v Leningrade, 1931), pp. 7–29;

Nikolai Alekseevich Trifonov, introduction to N. F. Pavlov's *Izbrannoe* (Moscow: Khudozhestvennaia literatura, 1988);

Trifonov, "Pervyi perevodchik Bal'zaka v Rossii," in *Nauchnye doklady vysshei shkoly: Filologicheskie nauki,* 2 (1960): 99–112;

Trifonov, "Povesti N. F. Pavlova," in *Uchennye zapiski, Kafedry russkoi literatury moskovskogo gosudarstvennogo pedagogicheskogo instituta im. N. K. Krupskoi, vypusk II* (Moscow, 1939), pp. 69–135;

Vsevolod Panteleimonovich Vil'chinsky, "Kriticheskie stat'i N. F. Pavlova (Iz istorii kritiki i zhurnalistiki 50-kh godov)," in *Iz istorii russkikh literaturnykh otnoshenii XVII–XIX vekov* (Moscow/Leningrad: Akademiia Nauk SSSR, 1959): 166–176;

Vil'chinsky, *Nikolai Filippovich Pavlov. Zhizn' i tvorchestvo* (Leningrad: Nauka, 1970).

Aleksei Alekseevich Perovsky
(Antonii Pogorel'sky)
(1787 – 9 July 1836)

Thomas Berry
Johns Hopkins University

BOOKS: *Wie sind Thiere und Gëwachse von einander unterschieden und welches ist ihr Verhältniss zu den Mineralien; Sur le but et l'utilité du système des plantes de Linné; O rasteniikh, kotoriia by polezno bylo razmnozhit' v Rossii* (Moscow, 1808);

Dvoinik, ili Moi vechera v Malorossii, as Pogorel'sky (St. Petersburg: pri Imperatorskoi akademii nauk, 1828);

Chernaia kuritsa, ili zhiteli podzemnogo tsarstva. Volshebnaia povest' dlia detei (St. Petersburg, 1829);

Monastyrka, as Pogorel'sky, part 1 (St. Petersburg, 1830); *Monastyrka,* parts 1 and 2 (St. Petersburg: N. Grech, 1833).

Editions and Collections: *Sochineniia Antoniia Pogorel'skogo,* 2 volumes (St. Petersburg: Aleksandr Smirdin pri Imperatorskoi akademii nauk, 1853);

Dvoinik, ili Moi vechera v Malorossii—Monastyrka, edited by N. L. Stepanov (Moscow: Khudozhestvennaia literatura, 1960);

Izbrannoe, edited by Marietta A. Tur'ian (Moscow: Sovetskaia Rossiia, 1985);

Dvoinik: Izbrannye proizvedeniia, edited by Zinaida Vasil'evna Kiriliuk (Kiev: Dnipro, 1990).

Editions in English: *The Convent Girl* (excerpts), translated by Christine Rydel, in *The Ardis Anthology of Russian Romanticism,* edited by Rydel (Ann Arbor: Ardis, 1984), pp. 267–280;

The Double, or My Evenings in Little Russia, translated by Ruth Sobel (Ann Arbor: Ardis, 1988).

SELECTED PERIODICAL PUBLICATIONS:
"Zamechaniia na pis'mo k sochiniteliu kritiki na poemu 'Ruslan i Liudmila,'" as K. Grigorii B–V, *Syn otechestva,* volume 9, part 10, no. 41 (1820): 39–44;

"Zamechaniia na razbor poemy 'Ruslan i Liudmila,' napechatannyi v 34, 35, 36, 37 Knizhkakh *Syna otechestva,*" as P. K.–V., *Syn otechestva,* volume 16, part 10, no. 42 (1820): 72–86;

Aleksei Alekseevich Perovsky in the 1820s

"Posetitel' magika," *Babochka,* volume 27, part 2, no. 17 (27 February 1829); volume 27, part 3, no. 18 (2 March 1829);

"Magnatizer," *Literaturnaia gazeta,* volume 1, part 1, no. 1 (1830): 1–2; volume 6, part 1, no. 2 (1830): 9–10;

"O narodnom prosveshchenii v Rossii," *Russkaia starina,* 5 (1901): 363–367;

"The Black Hen, or The Inhabitants of the Underground Kingdom," translated by Ruth Sobel, *Russian Literature Triquarterly,* no. 23 (1990): 115–134.

Though little known outside of his native country, Aleksei Alekseevich Perovsky (Antonii Pogorel'sky) at one time played a significant role in the development of Russian prose. A brilliantly educated man, he was adept in science as well as the arts. He was also able to combine a career in service to the state with an active participation in the literary life of his times. His major contribution to Russian letters lies in the fact that his works provided models for writers who followed. Known as Russian Hoffmannist, he wrote one of the first Russian fantasy tales, which elicited delight from his peers as well as from the reading public. He also wrote one of the first novels of manners in Russia. Seen from the twentieth century, his works may seem dated; however, his imagination and humor, as well as narrative skill, save them from oblivion. In fact, his tales inspired some of the best writers of the day; one can find echoes of Perovsky in Aleksandr Pushkin, Nikolai Gogol, and Vladimir Fedorovich Odoevsky. Such appeal to Perovsky's discerning contemporaries hints at something more in his seemingly simple narratives. Indeed Perovsky's works carry within them an element of parody and satire that suggest he was no stranger to Romantic irony, though in embryonic form. Destined to be known as one of the best of the "lesser lights" of his era, Perovsky nevertheless needs to be recognized as one of the most important forerunners of the prose tradition that flourished in Russia in the second half of the nineteenth century.

Aleksei Alekseevich Perovsky was born in 1787 into one of the most accidentally aristocratic families in Russian history. He was the illegitimate son of Count Aleksei Kirillovich Razumovsky and Maria Mikhailovna Sobolevskaia, whose illicit liaison produced seven children awarded legitimacy and nobility under the name Perovsky, after an estate, Perov, that belonged to Razumovsky. Aleksei Kirillovich was the nephew of Aleksei Grigor'evich Razumovsky, the peasant singer who became the Empress Elizabeth's secret husband. Aleksei Grigor'evich attained one of the highest positions of influence during her reign; he and his brother, Kiril Grigor'evich, were raised into the aristocracy with the title of count.

During the reign of the Emperor Paul, the wealthy Aleksei Kirillovich Razumovsky moved his family to another of his estates, Pochepa, where Aleksei Alekseevich Perovsky was raised. Though his father was a noted mason and Voltairean who avoided his children, he provided Aleksei Alekseevich with an excellent education. When Perovsky entered Moscow University at the age of eighteen, he was fluent in three languages. In 1807 he translated Nikolai Mikhailovich Karamzin's "Bednaia Liza" (Poor Liza, 1792) into German; it was published in Moscow with a dedication to Perovsky's father. In 1808 Perovsky received the degree of doctor of philosophy and letters

in botany. He conducted his thesis defense in three separate speeches in three languages: German, French, and Russian. He published his defense as a book in three parts: (1) *Wie sind Thiere und Gewächse von einander unterschieden und welches ist ihr Verhältniss zu den Mineralien;* (2) *Sur le but et l'utilité du système des plantes de Linné;* (3) *O rasteniiakh, kotoriia by polezno bylo razmnozhit' v Rossii* ([1] How Animals and Plants Differ from Each Other and Their Relationship to Minerals; [2] On the Aim and Usefulness of Linnaeus's Classification of Plants; [3] On Plants Which Would Be Useful to Propagate in Russia).

Because of his erudition and family influence, in 1808 Perovsky received the position of collegiate councilor in a department of the Senate. In 1809 he accompanied Senator Petr Alekseevich Obreskov on a tour of several provinces, among them Perm, Kazan', Nizhegorod and Vladimir; provinical life made a great impression on him and influenced his future prose works.

In 1810, drawn by the literary circle that surrounded Karamzin, Prince Petr Andreevich Viazemsky, and Vasilii Andreevich Zhukovsky, Perovsky accepted a position with the Senate in Moscow. When Napoleon invaded in 1812, Perovsky disregarded his father's threats of disinheritance and became an officer in a Cossack regiment, serving until 1816 and participating in battles in Germany. His fluency in German earned him a position with Prince Nikolai Grigor'evich Repnin-Volkonsky, the governor-general of the kingdom of Saxony. While serving in Dresden, Perovsky became imbued with German Romantic literature, especially the works of E. T. A. Hoffmann.

Perovsky left military service in 1816 and settled in St. Petersburg, where he participated in meetings of the Arzamas Society, a well-known literary group that included many brilliant Russian authors. Meanwhile, family affairs changed his life forever. His sister Anna Alekseevna Perovskaia married Count Konstantin Petrovich Tolstoi. After the birth of her son, the future writer Aleksei Konstantinovich Tolstoi, she left her husband and moved with Perovsky to another Razumovsky family estate, Pogorel'tsy, located in the Ukraine. For several years he divided his time between activities in St. Petersburg and the upbringing of his nephew in the country.

In 1820, after critics had attacked Aleksandr Pushkin for not upholding the classical style in "Ruslan i Liudmila" (published that year), Perovsky wrote an article, "Zamechaniia na pis'mo k sochiniteliu kritiki na poemu 'Ruslan i Liudmila'" (Observations on a Letter to the Author of Criticism of the Poem 'Ruslan and Liudmila'), which Viazemsky sent to the journal *Syn otechestva* (Son of the Fatherland). Pushkin greatly appreciated Perovsky's comments that the work showed genius and gave Russian literature a much-needed new direction. Later in 1820 Perovsky was elected a member of *Obshchestvo liubitelei rossiiskoi slovestnosti* (the Society of Lovers of Russian Literature), another famous group that included the major writers of the period.

Perovsky's father died in 1822, and Perovsky inherited two estates: Pogorel'tsy and Krasnyi Rog, a magnificent hunting lodge created by the famous architect Bartolomeo Rastrelli, who designed the Winter Palace for the Empress Elizabeth. The eighteenth-century lodge was a three-story octagonal structure built on a hill overlooking the Rog River. Unfortunately the building with its great library was destroyed during World War II. At different periods Perovsky lived at one estate or the other while helping with the education of his nephew. Perovsky's pseudonym, Antonii Pogorel'sky, was created at the estate Pogorel'tsy when he wrote stories for his young charge, and all of his fiction appeared under this name. Not everyone knew that Pogorel'sky was Perovsky, though those in literary circles suspected that he was.

In 1824 Perovsky was made trustee of the Khar'kov School District, which included the University of Khar'kov and the Nizhinsky Gymnasium, where Gogol studied at the time. After an investigation into the impoverished condition of the University of Khar'kov, Perovsky appealed to the Minister of Education, Aleksandr Semenovich Shiskhov, in 1825. Perovsky's zeal and erudition caused him to be named to the Committee for the Renovation of Educational Institutions; and in 1826, by an order of Nicholas I, Perovsky wrote a tract, "O narodnom prosveshchenii v Rossii" (On Public Education in Russia), which was a critical review of the directives of Mikhail Leont'evich Magnitsky, the director of the University of Khar'kov. At this time Pushkin, also at the command of Nicholas I, wrote his famous article on public education. Perovsky's report was published in *Russkaia starina* (Russian Antiquities) in 1901.

Countess Sobolevskaia, Perovsky's mother, married Major General Denis'ev in 1826 in Moscow. Perovsky's sister and nephew moved to the city, while he returned to St. Petersburg, dividing his time between the two capitals. In the spring of 1827 he accompanied his sister and nephew to Germany, where they visited Johann Wolfgang von Goethe in Weimar.

In 1828 Perovsky published a collection of stories, *Dvoinik, ili Moi vechera v Malorossii* (The Double, or My Evenings in Little Russia). One of the tales, "Lafertovskaia makovnitsa" (The Lafertovsky Poppy-seed-Cake Seller, first published in *Novosti literatury* in 1825), is considered the first fantastic tale in Russian literature; Pushkin thought this piece of sheer fantasy to be thoroughly enjoyable. In *Dvoinik* one finds no ef-

fort to explain the unusual and miraculous. However, Perovsky did make an effort to combine the stories through a realistic guise borrowed from Hoffmann: over several evenings, the narrator, Antonii, talks and trades stories with his own double, an apparition that serves to connect the tales. Victor Terras, in his *A History of Russian Literature* (1991), states that Hoffmann's stories inspired Russian writers "to write *Künstlernovellen* about an artist's conflict with society or with himself, as well as fantastic tales dealing with themes of romantic philosophy or the nocturnal aspect of human nature."

The first tale of *Dvoinik* is "Isidor i Aniuta," a sentimental story in the style of Karamzin. It is told by Antonii and takes place during the retreat of the populace from Moscow during the Napoleonic onslaught in 1812. Isidor, a young Russian officer, returns to the capital after the Battle of Borodino and finds his mother too sick for travel and his orphaned fiancée, Aniuta, destined to stay as her protectress. Isidor is torn between betraying his family honor or his military obligations, a human conflict in the true nature of the *Künstlernovelle*. His mother demands that he abandon her, which he does, only to return and find that she and Aniuta have perished. The visitation of his love's ghost leads to his own demise.

"Isidor i Aniuta" is followed by several tales about ghosts, which Antonii and his Double analyze. After the Double tells a story of an old countess who is visited by the ghost of a murdered woman seeking revenge, Antonii remarks that the tale reminds him of a mystery by Cicero in which a murdered man visits his friend to ask for help in exposing his murderer. Antonii and the Double then discuss Johann Heinrich Jung-Stilling's *Theorie der Geister-Kunde* (Theory of Pneumatology, 1808) and refer in their talk to "a white woman," who appeared among several German families after the death of a family member. This element recalls Pushkin's grandmother Osipova, who was also haunted three times by a "white woman" ghost; the poet never doubted the truth of his relative's account.

The third evening in *Dvoinik* is devoted to "Pagubnye posledstviia neobuzhdannogo voobrazheniia" (The Pernicious Effects of an Unbridled Imagination). Here Hoffmann's story "Der Sandmann" (The Sandman, 1817) serves as a model. The mechanical doll of Hoffmann's tale not only influenced Perovsky but also gave the world of opera the famous first act of Jacques Offenbach's *Les Contes d'Hoffmann* (The Tales of Hoffmann, 1881). In Perovsky's story a young Russian, the rich and handsome Alcest, is accompanied to Leipzig by Count F., an older companion. Alcest falls in love with a girl he espies sitting in a window. The young beauty, Adelina, turns out to be the daughter of

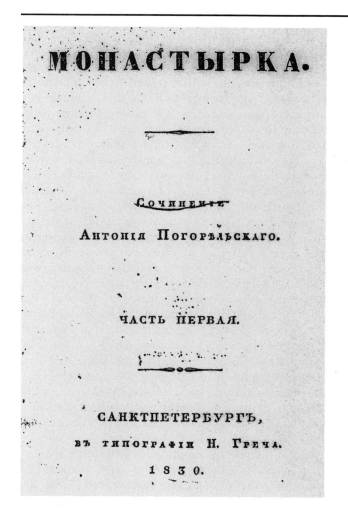
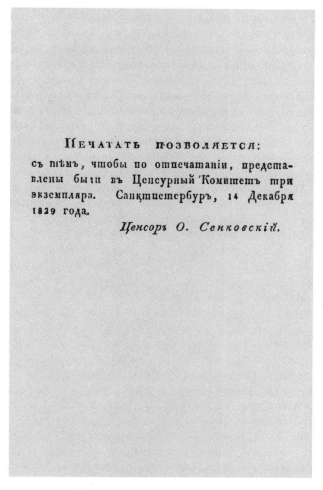

Title page and censor's approval (provided by Osip Ivanovich Senkovsky) for Monastyrka *(The Convent Girl), Perovsky's novel of manners about a spirited heroine*

a Neapolitan scientist, Androni. Count F. arranges a meeting with him and thus with the daughter, who is never allowed to be alone with Alcest.

While Count F. is away on business he hears that Alcest and Adelina plan to marry. He returns to Leipzig as quickly as he can in order to protect his young charge, but arrives only to learn that the newly-wed couple has retired for the night. Later Alcest rushes into the count's rooms in fright; his wife has burst open during a passionate embrace, and cotton stuffing spilled out. When the two return to Androni's, they see the old man sewing up his "daughter." It turns out that Alcest is the victim of a plot Androni has devised as revenge against the young man's father, who had earlier committed some offense against the scientist. Alcest disappears; he presumably commits suicide by throwing himself into a river. Upon his return home Count F. learns that Alcest's father has joined his son in death.

Antonii asks his Double how anyone could fall in love with a doll. He answers with an explanation that anticipates Vladimir Fedorovich Odoevsky's 1833 story, "Skazka, o tom, kak opasno devushkam khodit' tolpoiu po Nevskomu prospektu" (The Tale of How it is Dangerous for Young Girls to Walk in a Crowd along Nevsky Prospect): the young girls in St. Petersburg society resemble mechanical dolls to such a degree that it is nearly impossible to see a difference between them and the beautiful toys. Though Perovsky's story most resembles Hoffmann's tale, it also owes a debt to the French movement *l'école frénétique* (the frenetic school), which influenced several Russian writers in the 1830s.

On the fourth evening the Double offers an essay rather than a story and explains why people who are considered clever often commit follies. Dividing intellect into several types such as common sense, perspicacity, and foresight, the Double works out a scale by which one can judge a person's abilities. Antonii doubts the usefulness of such figures, stating that judgment is a given trait that cannot be learned.

The fifth evening is comprised of "Lafertovskaia makovnitsa." Pushkin was delighted with the cat in the story and wrote to his brother on 27 March 1825: "my dear, what a charming cat Granny has! I read that tale twice in one sitting and now I can only rave about Ar. Fal. Murlykin." Onufrich, the retired postman of the tale, later influenced Pushkin when he wrote his "Grobovshchik" (The Undertaker) in *Povesti pokoinogo Ivana Petrovicha Belkina* (Tales of the Late Ivan Petrovich Belkin, 1830). In Perovsky's story Onufrich has an aunt who sells poppyseed cakes in the Lafertov district of Moscow, where she is known as a witch. When the aunt arranges a marriage for Onufrich's daughter, Masha, the young girl realizes that the bridegroom is her aunt's cat; she breaks the spell by refusing her aunt's riches, and a new bridegroom brings her happiness. In a comic episode Masha sees dogs chasing her former fiancé down the street. At the funeral of the aunt, when Masha's greedy mother leans over the coffin for a farewell kiss, the dead woman's mouth opens in an effort to bite her. This incident may be a source for Pushkin's countess, who winks at her "murderer," Hermann, from her coffin, in the story "Pikovaia dama" (Queen of Spades, 1834).

During the sixth evening the Double relates "Puteshestvie v dilizhanse" (A Journey in a Diligence), a tale based on a story published in Paris in 1824 and in Russian translation in 1825: "Jocko, anecdote détachée des lettres inédites sur l'instinct des animaux" (Jocko, An Anecdote from Unedited Letters about Animal Instinct), by Marie-Charles- Joseph Pougens. In Perovsky's adaptation, long before Edgar Rice Burroughs created Tarzan, a Colonel Van der K. tells how he had been lost as a child on the island of Borneo and brought up by an ape named Tutu. When the colonel returns to his family as a grown man he becomes engaged to a girl named Amalia; however, Tutu visits and his fiancée resents the ape's presence. The poor hero is forced to kill the animal, only later to be killed himself by cannibals in North Holland.

This tale remains the most controversial of the collection in many ways. In her introduction to the 1988 English translation of *Dvoinik,* Ruth Sobel notes that the "motif of a tender attachment between an animal and a human being was not new in Romantic fiction but Pogorel'sky seems to take it to extremes, thereby undermining its psychological effect." Even Antonii doubts the depths of emotion the colonel feels for the ape, but the Double assures him that such suffering over the loss of an animal is not an unnatural phenomenon in humans. Sobel offers the possibility

that Perovsky intended this tale "as a parody of Romantic emotions carried to excess."

John Mersereau also discusses Perovsky's intentions and role in the story. He describes the complex narrative construction of the story as a "Chinese-box structure, with Antoni as the exterior surface, [the] Double inside the frame, then the Muscovite [who told the Double the tale], and finally Van der K., [which] provides sufficient distance between Perovsky and the events of the innermost box to relieve him of responsibility for them." Mersereau also disagrees with those who see "Puteshestvie v dilizhanse" as a sentimental tale; he, too, sees it as a parody, but of the already passé theme of the "noble savage." He posits that the story also parodies the love triangle (here with the other woman "not even a rival, but a one-pawed ape") as well as the already tritely common "scenes of forgiveness and remorse" at the death of a loved one (here the ape Tutu). Mersereau concludes that Perovsky does not take himself too seriously, but seems to value common sense above all else.

Dvoinik did not enjoy great success among readers and critics. Stepan Petrovich Shevyrev, who knew German literature, wrote in *Moskovskii vestnik* (The Moscow Herald) in 1828 that Perovsky's work was the "limit of capricious and unbridled fantasy, having passed the borders of any plausibility."

In 1829 Perovsky published two works comprising the fantastic: the beginning of a novel called "Posetitel' magika" (A Magician's Visitor), and a children's story, *Chernaia kuritsa, ili zhiteli podzemnogo tsarstva. Volshebnaia povest' dlia detei* (The Little Black Hen, or The Inhabitants of the Underground Kingdom). The first work was never completed; the first five chapters were published in the journal *Babochka* (The Butterfly). At the end of the text appeared the phrase, "From the English: Anton Pogorelsky"; however, the source has never been found in English literature. The story does relate to the French novel *The Magic Mirror. An Episode from the Life of Cornelius Agripina,* by Amédée Pichot, which was published in Russian translation in the paper *Molva* (Rumor) in 1833. In Perovsky's tale a stranger in thirteenth-century Florence visits the astrologer, magician, and philosopher Kornelii Agrippa, who owns a mirror that can show the reflection of any deceased person. After seeing his dead daughter Miriam in the mirror, the stranger admits that he is the Eternal Jew of historical legend.

Chernaia kuritsa, which Perovsky wrote for his nephew, achieved lasting success in children's literature. In 1828 Zhukovsky wrote to Anton Antonovich Del'vig, the editor of *Severnye tsvety* (Northern Flowers), that he had a children's story by Perovsky that was "very humorous and beautiful." The tale involves the secret life of a small, lonely boy at boarding school. He makes friends with a black hen, whose life he saves by bribing the school cook. The hen becomes a human figure when they enter a supernatural, underground land, where the boy is rewarded for his kindness. Unfortunately the boy betrays the trust of the underground people. The denouement reveals the sadness that human error and weakness can unwillingly bring on other mortals. Totally whimsical, this charming, didactic tale has become a classic.

Perovsky was elected a member of the Russian Academy in 1829. At this time a close relationship with Pushkin developed, and Perovsky spoke with the poet using the familiar form of address in Russian. In his memoirs Viazemsky recounts how Pushkin used to read his poetry at Perovsky's salon. In January 1830 the paper *Literaturnaia gazeta* (Literary Gazette) began to print excerpts from Perovsky's new novel, "Magnatizer" (The Mesmerist), about a young girl who falls under the spell of a hypnotist, to the alarm of her parents. The work was never finished, and no additional fragments have been found.

Perovsky's next work, *Monastyrka* (The Convent Girl, 1830), a novel of manners, created a polemic among critics of the period. In 1829 Faddei Venediktovich Bulgarin's own novel of manners, *Ivan Vyzhigin,* was published and had great success among the public but brought about a sharp reaction from progressive writers. When Perovsky's book appeared, Viazemsky heralded it in *Literaturnaia gazeta* as the first Russian "novel of manners because it opens the inner logic of its characters and gives a realistic picture of the environment and manners of the period." In the heroes of the book Viazemsky found the exact psychological characteristics and daily actions of the provincial gentry. Perovsky's book was considered superior to Bulgarin's because the latter did not directly correspond or relate to the Russian environment of the period.

Bulgarin answered Viazemsky's criticism in an article in *Severnaia pchela* (The Northern Bee). He praised Perovsky's novel as a work of "humorous and satirical nature which belongs to a number of those sweet creations in which one need not bother to look for great truths, or strong characters or sharp scenes, but rather for typical incidences of life, and characters who are well-known and heard from daily." The Pushkin group attacked Bulgarin for not admitting that *Monastyrka* was the first true Russian novel of manners of the period. Orest Mikhailovich Somov stated in *Severnye tsvety* in 1831 that Bulgarin wrote like "a foreigner who has achieved only the mechanisms of the Russian language, whereas Pogorel'sky presented a series of characters taken from life itself."

Monastyrka was praised in general for its depiction of the daily mode of life, its freedom from acci-

dental and implausible incidents, and its departure from concentration on the low and crude. Perovsky skillfully portrays the provincial attitude of the "Little Russians" with their native customs by having the heroine, Aniuta, a more sophisticated student from the Smolny Institute, return after graduation. Her astonishment at what she finds skillfully contrasts two cultures. The work is not a realistic novel since it has traditionally Romantic situations and heroes, yet it was a step forward because of its literary style and character development. Evgenii Abramovich Baratynsky, having read Gogol's *Vechera na khutore bliz Dikan'ki* (Evenings on a Farm near Dikanka, 1831–1832), wrote to Ivan Vasil'evich Kireevsky on 12 April 1832 that he would have ascribed that work to Perovsky because of its similarities to *Monastyrka.*

Though not a major literary work, *Monastyrka* nevertheless played an important role as a transitional novel in the development of that genre. While Perovsky may have used stock character types and situations already commonplace in Russia in the 1830s, he gave them a certain freshness by adding new dimensions to characters and story. For example, he places the narrative in a frame, a device that was a cliché by that time; however, the narrator knows the characters both in and out of the frame and even marries one of them. Thus Perovsky's narrator goes to great lengths to establish the authenticity of his story.

The novel does retain remnants of an earlier time: stale character types such as an odious villain in battle with a virtuous hero, badly educated provincial girls, and a gypsy based solely on literary models; and situations involving kidnapping, a mysterious hut deep in a dark forest, misunderstandings and mixups in the game of courtship, mockery of provincial French, and a poor orphan at the mercy of a cruel guardian. However, this poor orphan evolves into a crafty young woman who cleverly outwits her enemy.

The novel becomes more innovative in the area of narration. By reordering events, relying on switches in time and using flashbacks to great effect, Perovsky manages to endow his story with a plot and provide some suspense. For example, the main narrator describes Aniuta's life in St. Petersburg only after the reader experiences, through her letters, her dismay at the life she sees in Little Russia upon her return. Aniuta's descriptions are charming and perform a dual function: they provide scenes of local color required in Romantic prose and provide insights to the young girl's character. In addition, having Aniuta describe the rural scenes makes the inclusion of local color and local customs more real and natural. However, outdated artificial devices survive in *Monastyrka* as the intrusive narrator offers his opinions on the characters and strews broad

Perovsky in 1836

hints to the reader about the eventual outcome of the story. Perhaps the narrator's most endearing trait is his ability to lighten the tone of what could easily fall into melodrama by including some farcical scenes in the narrative. In Perovsky's narrator one may also find rudimentary traces of Romantic irony and the Romantic grotesque.

The interplay between the primary narrator and Aniuta also adds interest to the telling of the story. The two share a tendency to be charitable and fair in their dealings with others. They are also both "traveling" narrators, though readers ultimately hear their tale after they have settled down. The main contrast between the two, quite naturally, lies in their language. The narrator's prose is full of self-conscious literary usage, such as parallel constructions and a heavy reliance on participles. Aniuta's letters, on the other hand, retain the fresh, natural idiom of a young girl, who has been educated in St. Petersburg, writing to a close school friend.

In his depiction of Aniuta, Perovsky has advanced the cause of women in Russian literature, albeit in a tiny increment. She has little in common with her sentimental predecessors; rather, Aniuta emerges as a spirited, capable girl. Readers see her character develop, especially in the first half of the novel; the combination of the letters and her actions reveals her to be an adventurous, intelligent, naive, generous young woman who can admit her faults and experience true and lasting emotions.

Though the other characters may not be as developed, and actually do at times appear to be flat, they act as foils to each other and, as a whole, perform a structural function in the novel. *Monastyrka* is built upon contrasts: Aniuta's true guardian versus her two guardians, especially in their reactions to her appearance in their tightly maintained world. The narrator's skill at storytelling and plot manipulation saves the schematic formula from total triteness. Unfortunately Perovsky could not sustain the quality of the novel in part 2, published in 1833, a disappointing conclusion to the first half.

In 1830 Perovsky retired to Pogorel'tsy and concentrated on the education of his nephew, the future poet Aleksei Konstantinovich Tolstoi. Perovsky's last work was a humorous philosophical tract to Baron Alexander von Humboldt, "Novaia tiazhba o bukve " " (New Tensions about the Russian Letter 'hard sign'), which was published in *Literaturnaia gazeta* in 1830. In 1831 Perovsky traveled through Italy with his sister and nephew. Returning to St. Petersburg, the uncle, through his friendship with Zhukovsky, arranged for his nephew to become a playmate of the future Tsar Alexander II. At this time Perovsky developed problems with his lungs, probably tuberculosis. In 1836 he sought a cure abroad and set out again on a trip with his sister and nephew. His condition worsened, and he died on 9 July in Warsaw, where he was buried.

Though not a major author, Perovsky can rightfully claim a solid place in the second ranks of Russian writers of early-nineteenth-century Russia. His works, more than others, reflect the broad spectrum of Romantic prose. The emotional pitch of some works identifies him with Karamzinian sentimentalism, and the fantastic elements of *Dvoinik* clearly make him a Ludwig Tieck/Hoffmann Romantic. He resorts to typical Romantic elements such as the use of local color and dialect; he also introduced elements of Romantic irony and the Romantic grotesque as well as advanced narrative techniques. Perovsky's moral tone and opinions link him to Odoevsky, while some of his works look forward to Pushkin and Gogol. Perhaps Perovsky is fated to be, in Apollon Grigorev's terminology, a *dopotopnyi pisatel'* (an antediluvian writer), that is, one who embodies the major elements of his age but does not possess sufficient talent to step beyond it. His works pave the way for the great writers who follow his lead and then surpass him.

Letters:

To Nikolai Ivanovich Grech, in *Admiral Shishkov i kantsler graf Rumiantsov,* by Aleksandr Aleksandrovich Kochubinsky (Odessa: Tip. Odesskago vestnika, 1887–1888), pp. c–civ;

To Alexei Koustantinovich Tolstoi, in *Polnoe sobranie stikhotvorenii,* by Tolstoi, volume 1 (Leningrad: Sovetskii pisatel', 1937), p. 8;

To A. A. Pushkin, in *Polnoe sobranie sochinenii,* by Aleksandr Sergeevich Pushkin, volume 15 (Moscow: Akademiia Nauk, 1948), p. 48.

References:

Antonina Petrovna Babushkina, "'Chernaia ptitsa' Antoniia Pogorel'skogo," in her *Istoriia russkoi detskoi literatury* (Moscow: Uchpedgiz, 1948), pp. 196–203;

Faddei Venediktovich Bulgarin, "Monastyrka, part I," *Severnaia pchela,* no. 32 (15 March 1830): 1–4;

N. G. Chernyshevsky, "Polnoe sobranie sochinenii russkikh avtorov," in his *Polnoe sobranie sochinenii,* volume 2 (Moscow: Goslitizdat, 1949), pp. 1128–1136;

Philip Edward Frantz, "A. A. Perovskij (Pogorel'skij): Gentleman and Literateur," dissertation, University of Michigan, 1981;

V. Gorlenko, "A. A. Perovsky," *Kievskaia starina,* no. 4, section 1 (1888): 109–124;

S. S. Ignatov, "A. Pogorel'skii i E. Goffman," *Russkii filologicheskii vestnik,* volume 72, nos. 3–4, section 1 (1914): 249–278;

Zinaida Vasil'evna Kiriliuk, "Anton Pogorel'sky: Dvoinik," in *Dvoinik: Izbrannye proizvedeniia* (Kiev: Dnipro, 1990), pp. 5–19;

Aleksandr Ivanovich Kirpichnikov, "Bylye znamenitosti russkoi literatury. Antonii Pogorel'sky, (A. A. Perovsky)" in his *Ocherki po istorii novoi russkoi literatury* (St. Petersburg: L. F. Panteleev, 1896), pp. 76–120;

Kirpichnikov, "Nemetskii istochnik odnogo russkogo romana," *Russkaia starina,* no. 12 (1900): 617–619;

John Mersereau Jr., *Russian Romantic Fiction* (Ann Arbor: Ardis, 1983), pp. 75–77, 94–100, 153–158;

Charles E. Passage, "Pogorel'skij, the First Russian Hoffmannist," *American Slavic and East European Review,* 15 (1956): 247–264;

Nikolai Alekseevich Polevoi, "Dvoinik, ili Moi vechera v Malorossii," *Moskovskii telegraf,* 20, no. 7 (1828): 358–362;

Stepan Petrovich Shevyrev, "Dvoinik, ili Moi vechera v Malorossii. Sochinenie Antoniia Pogorel'skogo. 2 chasti. St. P., 1828," *Moskovskii vestnik,* 10, no. 14 (1828): 160–164;

Orest Mikhailovich Somov, "Obzor rossiiskoi slovesnosti za 1828," *Severnye tsvety* (1828): 85–93;

N. N. Tatarinova, "A. A. Perovsky," in *Materialy po istorii russkoi detskoi literatury (1750–1855)* (Moscow: Institut metodov vneshk. raboty, 1928), pp. 151–156;

Victor Terras, *A History of Russian Literature* (New Haven & London: Yale University Press, 1991), p. 235;

Marietta A. Tur'ian, "Anton Pogorel'sky," in *Izbrannoe,* by Perovsky (Moscow: Sovetskaia Rossiia, 1985), pp. 3–22.

Mikhail Petrovich Pogodin

(11 November 1800 – 8 December 1875)

Dan I. Ungurianu
University of Missouri–Columbia

BOOKS: *O proiskhozhdenii Rusi, rassuzhdenie, sochinennoe Imperatorskogo Moskovskogo Universiteta kandi-
datom Slovesnykh nauk Mikhailom Pogodinym, dlia
polucheniia stepeni magistra* (Moscow: Univer-
siteskaia tip., 1825);
Chernaia nemoch (Moscow, 1829);
*Marfa, posadnitsa novgorodskaia, tragediia v piati deistvi-
iakh v stikhakh* (Moscow: Universitetskaia tip.,
1830);
Istoriia v litsakh o Dimitrie Samozvantse (Moscow: Universitetskaia tip., 1835);
Nachertanie russkoi istorii dlia uchilishch (Moscow,
1835);
Istoricheskie aforizmy (Moscow: Universitetskaia tip.,
1836);
Nevesta na iarmarke. Povest' v dvukh chastiakh (Moscow: Tip. N. Stepanova, 1837);
Nachertanie russkoi istorii dlia gimnazii (Moscow: Universitetskaia tip., 1837; revised and enlarged,
1838);
*Kratkoe nachertanie russkoi istorii: sokrashchenie gimnazi-
cheskogo kursa* (Moscow: Tip. N. Stepanova,
1838);
*Nestor, istoriko-kriticheskoe rassuzhdenie o nachale russkikh
letopisei* (Moscow: Universitetskaia tip., 1839);
God v chuzhikh kraiakh (Moscow: Universitetskaia
tip., 1839);
Sud nad tsarevichem Alekseem Petrovichem (Moscow:
Tip. A. Semena, 1860);
*Pis'ma i stat'i o politike Rossii v otnoshenii slavianskikh
narodov i Zapadnoi Evropy* (Berlin: A. Ascher,
1860);
A. P. Ermolov, materialy dlia ego biografii (Moscow:
Universitetskaia tip., 1863);
*N. M. Karamzin, po ego sochineniiam, pis'mam i otzyvam
sovremennikov,* 2 volumes (Moscow: Tip. A. I.
Mamontova, 1866);
*Pol'skii vopros, sobranie rassuzhdenii i zamechanii, pisan-
nykh v 1830–1866 g.* (Moscow: Tip. gazety
Russkii, 1867);
Istoriia v litsakh o Tsare Borise Feodoroviche Godunove
(Moscow: Tip. gazety Russkii, 1868);

Mikhail Petrovich Pogodin

Drevniaia russkaia istoriia do mongol'skogo iga, 3 vol-
umes (Moscow: Sinodal'naia tip., 1871);
Petr I, tragediia v piati deistviiakh, v stikhakh (Moscow:
V. M. Frish i S. P. Annenkov, 1873);
Prostaia rech' o mudrenykh veshchakh (Moscow: V. M.
Frish, 1873; Moscow, 1874; Moscow: E. A.
Vil'de, 1875);

Istoriko-politicheskie pis'ma i zapiski v prodolzhenie Krymskoi voiny, 1853–1856 (Moscow: V. M. Frish, 1874);

Bor'ba ne na zhivot, a na smert' s novymi istoricheskimi eresiami (Moscow: Tip. F. B. Millera, 1874);

Semnadtsat' pervykh let v zhizni imperatora Petra Velikogo (Moscow: V. M. Frish, 1875).

Editions and Collections: *Povesti Mikhaila Pogodina,* Parts I–III, 2 volumes (Moscow, 1832);

Istoriko-kriticheskie otryvki, 2 volumes (Moscow: Tip. A. Semena [volume 1]; Tip. Sinodal'naia [volume 2], 1846–1867);

Issledovaniia, zamechaniia i lektsii M. Pogodina o russkoi istorii, 7 volumes (Moscow: Universitetskaia tip. [volumes 1–6]; Tip. L. Stepanova [volume 7], 1846–1854);

Povesti. Drama, edited by Mariia Naumovna Virolainen (Moscow: Sovetskaia Rossiia, 1984).

OTHER: *Uraniia, karmannaia knizhka na 1826 god dlia liubitel'nits i liubitelei russkoi slovesnosti,* edited by Pogodin (Moscow: S. Selivanovskii, 1825);

Moskovskii vestnik (editor, 1827–1830);

Vedomosti o sostoianii goroda Moskvy (editor, 1830–1831);

Moskvitianin (editor, 1841–1856);

Utro (editor, 1859, 1866, 1868);

Russkii (editor, 1867–1868).

SELECTED PERIODICAL PUBLICATION: "Pis'mo o russkikh romanakh," in *Severnaia lira na 1827 god* (1826): 133–140.

A versatile and energetic person, Pogodin was a prominent historian and paleologist, journalist, translator, and writer. In historiography he is best remembered for studies in the early Russian period, publication of primary sources, and an impressive collection of Russian antiquities. His journalistic ventures include editing *Moskovskii vestnik* (Moscow Herald) from 1827–1830 and *Moskvitianin* (The Muscovite) from 1841–1856, the former representing a link between *Obshchestvo liubomudriia* (The Society of the Lovers of Wisdom) and the nascent Slavophilism, the latter being the leading publication directed against Westernizers. A proponent of Russian exceptionalism, Pogodin was among main contributors to the doctrine of Official Nationality. He was also one of the founding fathers of Pan-Slavism. His literary fiction (a dozen prose tales and several historical tragedies) is less notable, although it is of significance within the context of Russian literature of the 1820s and 1830s. A friend of many luminaries—including Aleksandr Sergeevich Pushkin, Nikolai Vasil'evich Gogol and Leo Tolstoy—and himself a major cultural figure over the course of five de-

cades, Pogodin lived a life that vividly reflects the peculiarities and contradictions of nineteenth-century Russia.

Mikhail Petrovich Pogodin was born on 11 November 1800 in Moscow, the city where he would spend most of his life. His father, Petr Moiseevich, an enserfed steward of the Saltykov family, was manumitted in 1806 for exemplary service. Mikhail's education began with lessons from a household scribe and advanced to a new level when he moved in with publisher Andrei Gordevich Reshetnikov, where he was tutored in foreign languages and had access to a large library. In 1812 the Pogodins fled Moscow, suffering substantial property losses.

In 1814 Mikhail enrolled at Moscow Guberniya Gymnasium (later known as First Moscow Gymnasium), which offered special fees to victims of Napoleon's invasion. Aside from attending classes there, he frequented the theater and also developed a passion for Russian history, avidly reading Nikolai Mikhailovich Karamzin. In 1818 Pogodin entered Moscow University, where among his professors were the famous *littérateur* Aleksei Fedorovich Merzliakov and the historian Mikhail Trofimovich Kachenovsky, Pogodin's future adversary. In the summer of 1819 Pogodin was invited to serve as a tutor to the princely Trubetskoi family. He stayed in their country estate for nine consecutive summers. Pogodin's contact with the Trubetskois broadened his intellectual vistas, as he was exposed to various European authors and also introduced into Russian high society. (Despite his warm relations with the Trubetskois, Pogodin could never overcome a "plebeian complex," although later, himself attaining nobility, he visited the Noble Assembly and joined the prestigious English Club.)

Upon graduating in 1821 with a gold medal, Pogodin accepted the position of geography instructor at the Noble Pension of Moscow University and pursued many academic and literary projects. He published several translations (including Johann Wolfgang von Goethe's *Götz von Berlichingen,* 1773) and made his debut as a journalist in Kachenovsky's *Vestnik Evropy* (Herald of Europe). In 1825 Pogodin defended his master's thesis *O proiskhozhdenii Rusi* (On the Origins of Rus), which laid the foundation for his scholarly reputation and gained recognition for him from Karamzin. In 1826 Pogodin was appointed Professor of General History at Moscow University.

Through his research interests and tutoring Pogodin met Aleksei Fedorovich Malinovsky, the head of the Moscow Archives of the Ministry of Foreign Affairs, and as well as the famous *arkhivny iu-*

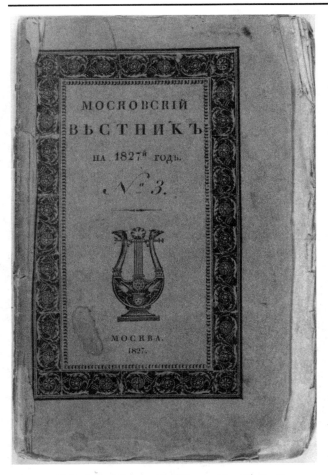

A copy of Moskovskii vestnik *(Moscow Herald) for the year Pogodin became its editor*

noshi (Archival Youths), who constituted the core of the *Obshchestvo liubomudriia* (The Society of Wisdom Lovers): the Venevitinov brothers (Dmitrii and Aleksei Vladimirovich), the Kireevsky brothers (Ivan and Petr Vasil'evich), Stepan Petrovich Shevyrev, and others. Pogodin participated in the gatherings of the society, although he felt himself somewhat handicapped due to his insufficient knowledge of German philosophy, in particular Friedrich von Schelling, the idol of the Wisdom Lovers. Using his connections among the Moscow intellectual elite, Pogodin edited the almanac *Urania* (1825), which boasted many outstanding contributors from older and younger literati: Merzliakov, Pushkin, Shevyrev, Prince Petr Andreevich Viazemsky, Evgenii Abramovich Baratynsky, Dmitrii Venevitinov, and Fedor Ivanovich Tiutchev (Pogodin's fellow student at Moscow University).

In 1827 Pogodin became the editor of *Moskovskii vestnik,* founded by the former Wisdom Lovers with the purpose of promoting German philosophy and the aesthetics of German Romanticism. The inspira-

tion for the journal came from Dmitrii Venevitinov, and its active participants included Shevyrev (coeditor, 1827–1829), Prince Vladimir Fedorovich Odoevsky, Aleksei Stepanovich Khomiakov, and the Kireevskys. The belles-lettres section also printed contributions from such prominent authors as Pushkin (who at one time was rather close to the young Muscovites), Baratynsky, Denis Vasil'evich Davydov, and Nikolai Mikhailovich Iazykov. However, deemed too highbrow by general audiences, *Moskovskii vestnik* could not compete against Nikolai Alekseevich Polevoi's well-rounded *Moskovskii telegraf* (Moscow Telegraph) and had to be terminated in 1830. Although short-lived, *Moskovskii vestnik* left a visible trace in Russian intellectual history and can be viewed as a protoSlavophile publication. During the 1830–1831 cholera epidemic, Pogodin stayed in Moscow and courageously launched another periodical: *Vedomosti o sostoianii goroda Moskvy* (Bulletin on the State of the City of Moscow), a chronicle of events in the afflicted city.

Significant out of Pogodin's own articles and essays written during these years is "Pis'mo o russkikh romanakh" (A Letter on Russian Novels) in the almanac *Severnaia lira na 1827 god* (Northern Lyre for the Year 1827). Passionately arguing against the opinion that Russian history is too bleak for literary adaptations à la Sir Walter Scott, Pogodin points to dramatic collisions in the Russian past and to the astounding variety of nature, climates, ethnic groups, and religions found within the borders of the country. Pogodin's article presages the boom in the Russian historical novel that began in 1829 with the release of Mikhail Nikolaevich Zagoskin's *Iurii Miloslavsky*.

The 1820s and early 1830s were the peak years of Pogodin's activity as a fiction writer. He created more than a dozen prose tales, which in 1832 were gathered in a three-part collection. Pogodin's works reflect a wide spectrum of themes explored in contemporary Russian literature and can be divided loosely into the following categories: Romantic love tales, society tales, brigand and criminal tales, folktales, and tales describing everyday life of the middle and lower classes with an element of social criticism.

The most memorable of his love tales is "Adel'" (1830), a tragic story of two kindred souls unable to unite in this world. Following the Romantic convention of "documentary" narrative, the tale purports to be based on a genuine diary of the narrator's friend, Dmitrii. The prototype for Dmitrii was Dmitrii Venevitinov, who had met an untimely death. This lofty and pure young man falls in love with the equally gentle and high-minded Adel', who dies of a sudden illness. Dmitrii does not survive her by long, collapsing beside her coffin at the funeral service. An unconsummated love is also at the center of "Petrus'" (1831), which is set in eighteenth-century Little Russia and pays tribute to the fashionable Ukrainian theme. The plot is based on the comic opera *Natalka-Poltavka* (1819) by Ivan Petrovich Kotliarevsky, whom Pogodin met in 1829 during his trip to the Ukraine. However, departing from its comic origins, "Petrus'" has a somber ending.

A bright key prevails in "Rusaia kosa" (A Light-Brown Braid, 1825) and "Sokol'nitskii sad" (Sokolniki Park, 1829). "Rusaia kosa" is a playful story about the aspiring scholar Minsky, whose erotic sensibility is awakened by the splendid hair of the young Countess O. Minsky's premonitions of a blissful union are realized later when he marries another possessor of an adorable braid, the beautiful and enlightened Mariia. These characters have autobiographic prototypes: Minsky is the author's double, while the girls are based on subjects of Pogodin's romantic infatuation (his student, Princess Aleksandra Trubetskaia, and Elizaveta Vagner, a visitor at the Trubetskois', whom Pogodin indeed married eight years later, in 1833). "Sokol'nitskii sad" is written in an epistolary form, an eighteenth-century genre which experienced its last revival in the 1820s and 1830s. The tale ends in the happy marriage of the protagonist, who meets the love of his life in a suburban park.

A less idyllic matrimony is achieved in "Kak auknetsia, tak i otkliknetsia" (What You Sow That Shall You Reap, 1825), which describes a duel between a clever and calculating coquette and her similarly strong-spirited suitor, who poses as a meek simpleton in order to be taken for an obedient husband-to-be. In its subject matter this piece resembles a society tale; however, it also has ties to the eighteenth-century satire, since the plot is based on a collision of character types and not on their conflict with the high society.

In many of his tales Pogodin concentrates on conspicuously Russian settings, choosing characters from un-Westernized lower and middle classes: peasants, clergymen, townspeople, merchants, and provincial noblemen. The hero of "D'iachok-koldun" (The Sexton-Sorcerer, 1832) is a village sexton who supplements his income by practicing fake sorcery. False magic (a frequent motive in Romantic fiction) is also present in "Suzhenyi" (The Intended Bridegroom, 1828), which belongs to the genre of *sviatochnyi rasskaz* (Christmas tale) with its savoring of folk beliefs and superstitions. The hero of "Suzhenyi" is a young shop assistant who over-

comes the social gap between himself and his beloved, the daughter of a rich merchant, by resorting to a ruse during the traditional Christmas fortune-telling. The Christmas-tale genre is combined with a brigand story in "Vasil'ev vecher" (St. Basil's Night, 1831), which has certain similarities to Vasilii Andreevich Zhukovsky's famous ballad "Svetlana" (composed, 1808–1812; published, 1813) in which a girl is kidnapped by a dead man. In "Vasil'ev vecher" the kidnapper is the robbers' chieftain, who avenges the humiliation of his gang at the hands of a brave maiden.

The crime theme is treated in more serious fashion in "Prestupnitsa" (The Criminal, 1830) and especially in "Psikhologicheskie iavleniia" (Psychological Phenomena, 1827–1832). "Prestupnitsa" is a story of an "innocent murderer," the virtuous daughter of a merchant who is drawn into a dark affair by corrupted servants. While "Prestupnitsa" is based on a common plot known since the Middle Ages, "Psikhologicheskie iavleniia" includes real-life anecdotes, describing bizarre crimes and suicides that reflect paradoxes of the human psyche.

Pogodin's most successful stories include elements of social criticism and *bytopisanie* (portrayal of everyday life). Social concerns are already evident in his early piece "Nishchii" (The Beggar, 1825), which tells of the sad life of an old Moscow beggar, Egor. The rustic idyll of Egor's youth was destroyed when his master took away his bride. The infuriated serf made an attempt on the landlord's life, then was drafted into the army, where he bravely fought under General Aleksandr Vasil'evich Suvorov. Retiring after twenty-five years of service, he has to support himself by begging. Although written largely according to sentimental conventions, the tale touches upon two topical issues: serfdom and the plight of Russian soldiers. After the Decembrist revolt, Pogodin was afraid that "Nishchii" might be used against him as incriminating evidence by government authorities.

While "Nishchii" is largely devoid of everyday realities, they come to prominence in Pogodin's most acclaimed tale, "Chernaia nemoch'" (Black Sickness, 1829). It is replete with details of *byt*, from food (including the notorious sauerkraut) to fashion. These "realistic" props serve to accentuate a Romantic conflict, as the "chosen" lofty hero perishes in his stifling environment. The protagonist is an "anointed" young man, an unrealized Johann Gottfried von Herder or Mikhailo Vasil'evich Lomonosov, who is horrified by the traditional, materialistic world of his abusive and heavy-handed merchant father. The young man passionately desires an education, but his parents treat his wish as a

ГЕЦЪ

ФОНЪ-БЕРЛИХИНГЕНЪ,

ЖЕЛѢЗНАЯ РУКА.

ТРАГЕДІЯ

ВЪ ПЯТИ ДѢЙСТВІЯХЪ.

СОЧИНЕНІЕ ГЕТЕ.

ПЕРЕВОДЪ СЪ НѢМЕЦКАГО.

МОСКВА.
ВЪ УНИВЕРСИТЕТСКОЙ ТИПОГРАФІИ.
1828.

[843]

Title page for Pogodin's Russian translation of Johann Wolfgang von Goethe's tragedy Goetz von Berlichingen, with the Iron-Hand

strange malady (hence the title) that should be cured by their son's marriage to a daughter of a fellow merchant: a short, fat girl of thirteen, with puffy cheeks and heavily painted face, clad in gold, silver, and many precious stones. Seeing no other alternative, the frustrated young man commits suicide.

Nevesta na iarmarke (A Bride at a Fair) originally consisted of two separate tales: "Nevesta na iarmarke" (1827–1828), and "Schastie v neschastii" (Happiness in Misfortune, 1832), which were published as a diptych in the 1837 edition. "Nevesta" begins with the satirical depiction of a provincial household. A greedy and hypocritical widow wants to restore her dwindling fortune by marrying off her daughters to wealthy suitors, whom she hopes to find at the bustling fair in Nizhny Novgorod. Whereas the two elder girls are much like their mother, the younger one, having been fostered in an aristocratic family, is lofty, sensitive, and pure. At

the fair they meet a hussar lieutenant, a petty nobleman posing as a well-connected aristocrat. He has gambled away regimental money and is anxious to find a rich bride. The two parties dupe each other successfully, until the truth is revealed on the very eve of the marriage. While the elder sisters reject the impostor, the meek younger one agrees to marry him, her dowry being sufficient only to repay his debt. Abandoning the comical overtones of Part One, Part Two turns into melodrama. The hussar abuses his spouse, sinking into gambling and drinking, typical of the military life, which Pogodin portrays in a rather unflattering light. Forced to resign, the young man goes to Moscow, where he becomes involved in criminal activities. His wife is subjected to new hardships and humiliations, as she and their baby dwell in a thieves' den. She dies from tuberculosis, remaining a devout Christian and still loving her dissolute husband. In the epilogue the former hussar, transformed by her love and a feeling of guilt, takes monastic vows.

Contemporary responses to Pogodin's prose were mixed. He was severely criticized by his literary foes, the Polevoi brothers (Ksenofont and Nikolai Alekseevich) and Osip Ivanovich Senkovsky. The Polevois found Pogodin's use of lowly details offensive, and Senkovsky ridiculed Pogodin's "anecdotes." In contrast, the bellwether critic Vissarion Grigor'evich Belinsky, the emerging icon of Russian civic criticism, highly praised "Nishchii," "Chernaia nemoch'," and "Nevesta na iarmarke," hailing Pogodin as a precursor of Gogol and a creator of genuine Russian prose dealing with the life of *prostonarodnaia povest'* (the lower classes). Modern scholars, although admitting the limited artistic merits of Pogodin's tales, emphasize his importance in the evolution of Russian literature, especially in the area of *bytopisanie,* which presages preoccupations of the Natural School. Pogodin also approaches psychological prose, although he stops at an external psychologism (not unlike his great contemporary Pushkin), merely stating psychological phenomena without an attempt to dissect the human soul. Recent commentators additionally point out that Pogodin foreshadows important themes in subsequent Russian literature: a gloomy depiction of the merchants' milieu, later found in Aleksandr Nikolaevich Ostrovsky, and the lot of the "humiliated and insulted" as well as the problem of the criminal mind, which were haunting concerns for Fedor Mikhailovich Dostoevsky.

In the early 1830s Pogodin wrote four historical dramas. The most significant of them is *Marfa, posadnitsa novgorodskaia* (Marfa, the Mayoress of Novgorod, 1830), which treats—with considerable poetic license—the fall of the republican Novgorod in its confrontation against the autocratic Moscow (a prominent topic since Karamzin's tale "Marfa-Posadnitsa," 1803). Echoing Karamzin, Pogodin shows sympathy for the ancient liberties of Novgorod, yet emphasizes that the city was in decline and that its inevitable demise ultimately contributed to the formation of a unified Russian state. An incarnation of this idea in the play is Marfa's fictional son, who betrays his homeland for the benefit of all Russia. Written under the strong influence of Pushkin's *Boris Godunov* (written in 1825, though not published until 1831) in its form and style, *Marfa* likewise includes many "popular scenes" reflecting discord among the Novgorodians. Pushkin highly commended *Marfa* (both in private communications with Pogodin and in the unfinished yet important article, "O narodnoi drame i drame *Marfa Posadnitsa*" [On the National Drama and the Drama Marfa the Mayoress, 1830]), greeting it as one of the first successful Russian historical plays and praising, in particular, the "popular scenes." The latter, however, provoked a negative response from the reviewer of *Syn otechestva* (Son of the Fatherland), edited by Nikolai Ivanovich Grech and Faddei Venediktovich Bulgarin, who deemed the play excessively "vulgar." *Marfa* was followed by another tragedy in verse, *Petr I* (written in 1825, though not published until 1831), which, after being banned by Nicholas I for its "risky" subject matter, appeared in print in 1873. After *Petr I,* Pogodin turned to the Time of Troubles, writing two "dramatic chronicles" in prose: *Istoriia v litsakh o Tsare Borise Feodoroviche Godunove* (Enacted History of Tsar Boris Feodorovich Godunov, written in 1833, published in 1868), and *Istoriia v litsakh o Dimitrie Samozvantse* (Enacted History of Dmitrii the Impostor, 1835), which was criticized by Senkovsky, who pointed out that Pogodin's boyars use the coarse diction of modern plebeians. Although Pogodin's dramas did not reach the stage and never enjoyed much acclaim, they are of interest within the context of debates about *narodnost'* (nationality) in Russian literature.

After the mid 1830s Pogodin abandoned literary fiction and concentrated on historical research, which covered a wide range of topics: the origins of Rus', the rise of Muscovy, the roots of serfdom, the Time of Troubles (in his 1827 article, Pogodin argues for Godunov's innocence in the death of Tsarevich Dmitrii), the Petrine epoch, and recent history, including biographies of Karamzin and General Aleksei Petrovich Ermolov. Pogodin's method, reflected most vividly in *Istorichekie aforizmy* (Historical Aphorisms, 1836), includes a combination of Romantic organicism, belief in Divine Providence, and a thorough analysis of sources dovetailed in what he

called a "mathematical" system of proof. According to Boris Mikhailovich Eikhenbaum, who accents "archaist" features in Tolstoy, Pogodin made a strong impact on the philosophy of history in Tolstoy's *Voina i mir* (War and Peace, 1865–1869).

Pogodin's foremost contribution remains in the area of early Russian history and study of chronicles. In his best scholarly work, *Nestor* (published in 1839, based on his doctoral dissertation defended in 1834) Pogodin refuted the reasoning of Kachenovsky's "Critical School," which dismissed *Povest' vremennykh let* (Tale of Bygone Years, sometimes called the Primary Chronicle, circa 1113) as a fable. Beginning with his master's thesis, Pogodin staunchly advocated the Norman origin of the first Russian rulers, accepting neither the "southern" Khazar version (supported by Gustav Evers and Kachenovsky) nor the nativist theory, which stressed the local Slavic element (supported by Pogodin's friend Mikhail Aleksandrovich Maksimovich, and later Dmitrii Ivanovich Ilovaisky). Pogodin remained a convinced Normanist throughout his life, challenging Nikolai Ivanovich Kostomarov, the champion of Rurik's Lithuanian lineage, in a much-publicized dispute in 1860 at St. Petersburg University. The "invitation of the Varangians" had, in Pogodin's view, profound implications for Russian history. Whereas Western feudalism was rooted in conquest, the Russian state had as its foundation an act of voluntary submission, which—combined with geographical factors and Slavic character—precluded social antagonisms and revolutions typical of the West. Speaking of a harmonious, family-like relationship between the Russian people and their authorities, Pogodin emphasized the creative role of the state and, in particular, of Peter the Great. Pogodin's historical views made him a sincere proponent of Count Sergei Semenovich Uvarov's triad "Orthodoxy, Autocracy, Nationality"—to the degree that he was perceived by younger radicals as an "official" historiographer; thus, the "Publisher" in Mikhail Evgrafovich Saltykov-Shchedrin's satire *Istoriia odnogo goroda* (History of a Town, 1869), confessed to fearing admonition from the stern Pogodin.

The decade starting in 1835 was the apex of Pogodin's academic career. In 1835 he received the chair of Russian History at Moscow University, and in 1841 he was honored with the title of Academician by the St. Petersburg Academy of Sciences. However, in 1844, amid faculty intrigues, Pogodin resigned his position at the university, citing reasons of health. His attempt to return a year later failed, as the chair was already occupied by the young star Sergei Mikhailovich Solov'ev; this fact

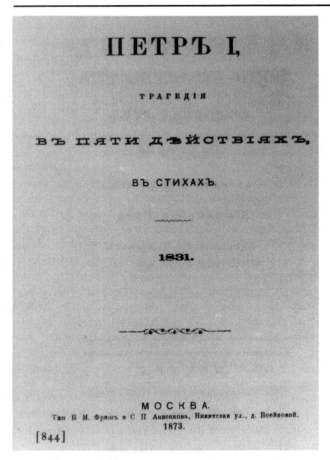

ПЕТРЪ I,

ТРАГЕДІЯ

ВЪ ПЯТИ ДѢЙСТВІЯХЪ,

ВЪ СТИХАХЪ.

1831.

МОСКВА.
Тип. В. М. Фриш. в С. П. Анненкова, Никитская ул., д. Воейковой.
1873.

[844]

Title page for Pogodin's five-act tragedy Peter I

added a touch of personal animosity to the subsequent polemics between the two historians. Nonetheless, Pogodin did not abandon his scholarly pursuits and made a substantial contribution to Russian paleography, publishing many important primary sources and assembling his famous *drevlekhranilishche,* a rare collection of old Russian manuscripts, books, and artifacts. This collection was later purchased by the Imperial Public Library at St. Petersburg.

Pogodin continued his journalistic activities as well. From 1835 to 1837 he contributed to *Moskovskii nabliudatel'* (Moscow Observer), which was aimed against the "commercial journalism" of Bulgarin, Grech, and Senkovsky. In 1841 Pogodin embarked on his most lasting journalistic enterprise, launching *Moskvitianin* (The Muscovite), which was supported by many dignitaries, including Zhukovsky and the Minister of Education, Count Uvarov. Conceived as a mouthpiece of conservative Muscovites, the journal advocated the principles of Official Nationality, directing its main polemical thrust against Westernizers (Belinsky, Herzen, and others) and their periodi-

cals, especially *Otechestvennye zapiski* (Notes of the Fatherland) and, from 1846, Nekrasov's *Sovremennik* (The Contemporary). Among the authors of *Moskvitianin* were some prominent Slavophiles (the Kireevskys, Khomiakov, and Samarin), although they disapproved of the overzealous loyalism of the journal and diverged from Pogodin in their appraisal of Peter I. (The inaugural issue of *Moskvitianin* included Pogodin's eulogy to Peter I.) Literary criticism in the journal was overseen by Pogodin's old collaborator Shevyrev, who attacked the emerging Natural School and was among the few reviewers who greeted the notorious *Vybrannye mesta* (Selected Passages, 1847) by Gogol. Pogodin edited the historical section, which held interesting materials on Russian history and philology, and also "Slavic News" from outside of Russia; Pogodin established extensive contacts with Slavic scholars in the Austrian Empire—Pavel Josef Šafařik, Vaćlav Hanka, Frantisek Palacký—during his first trip abroad in 1835. Pogodin was a vocal proponent of pan-Slavism, dreaming of a federation of all Slavic nations headed by Russia—an idea which ran counter to Nicholas's "legitimism" and emphasis on preserving the established international order. The weakest section of *Moskvitianin* was the belles-lettres. Successful at the beginning, the journal plunged into a continuous crisis in the mid 1840s and was revived only in 1850 with the advent of the "Young Editorial Board," which included some highly promising writers of the new generation: Aleksandr Nikolaevich Ostrovsky, Aleksei Feofilaktovich Pisemsky, Pavel Ivanovich Mel'nikov-Pechersky, and the brilliant, albeit erratic, thinker Apollon Aleksandrovich Grigor'ev. However, by 1853 to 1854 the "Young Board" was alienated by conflicts with the "Old Board" and Pogodin's stinginess; the journal ceased to exist in 1856. The subsequent journalistic ventures of Pogodin—the almanac *Utro* (Morning, 1859, 1866, 1868), and the newspaper *Russkii* (The Russian, 1867–1868), were of relatively little importance.

Pogodin's most interesting work as a publicist dates back to the period of the Crimean War, when he wrote a series of open letters, subjecting to sweeping criticism both the foreign and domestic policies of Nicholas I. In his opinion, the Russian strategy of containing revolution in Europe was a waste of resources desperately needed for domestic improvements. Reiterating his idea about Russia's uniqueness, Pogodin asserted that the country was immune to Western revolutions; however, it was threatened by peasant rebellions similar to those led by the Emel'ian Ivanovich Pugachev in 1773. Pogodin warned that a social upheaval was imminent unless the government implemented drastic reforms, beginning with the introduction of *glasnost* (openness) in public administration. These bold letters of the usually cautious Pogodin could not appear in print but were widely circulated throughout Russia, with some of them being presented to the tsar.

Pogodin spent the last four decades of his life at his estate in Moscow near Novodevichy Convent (in which he was buried after his death in 1875.) To this estate he added in 1856 the famous Pogodinskaia izba (Pogodin's Hut), one of the first buildings in the pseudo-Russian style (architect N. V. Nikitin). Pogodin's residence was the site of many gatherings and was visited by Zagoskin, Gogol, Viazemsky, Tiutchev, Ostrovsky, Petr Iakolevich Chaadaev, Mikhail Iur'evich Lermontov, Timofei Nikolaevich Granovsky, Ivan Sergeevich Turgenev, and many others. Throughout his long life Pogodin came in contact with virtually all figures of prominence in Russian culture from the 1820s to the 1870s. Contemporaries and subsequent biographers portray Pogodin as a person full of contradictions. He combined sober calculation with daydreaming and sentimentality, avarice with selflessness, rudeness and tactlessness with readiness to help people, and pettiness with the proverbial Russian breadth. The extensive body of Pogodin's work displays a certain roughness and lack of finishing touches. He did not create a single "Masterpiece" that would firmly enter the cultural canon. But overall, one should pay tribute to his indefatigable energy and many contributions to Russian culture. In a way, Pogodin was the living embodiment of the Russian nineteenth century. The complexity of his life in a broad contemporary context is well reflected in the monumental twenty-two volume biography by Nikolai Platonovich Barsukov. Although the commentary is somewhat naive, this work includes extensive excerpts from archival materials and represents an extremely valuable resource for the student of Russian culture of the period, in which Pogodin occupies such a distinguished place.

Bibliographies:

"Sochineniia i perevody M. P. Pogodina," in *Piatidesiatiletie grazhdanskoi i uchenoi sluzhby M. P. Pogodina* (Moscow, 1872), pp. 129–131;

I. V. Koz'menko, "Arkhiv M. P. Pogodina," in *Zapiski Otdela rukopisei Biblioteki SSSR im. V. I. Lenina,* 11 (1950): pp. 39–54.

Biographies:

Nikolai Platonovich Barsukov, *Zhizn' i trudy M. P. Pogodina,* 22 volumes (St. Petersburg: Tip. M. M. Stasiulevicha, 1888–1910);

Konstantin Nikolaevich Bestuzhev-Riumin, "M. P. Pogodin," in K. Bestuzhev-Riumin, *Biografii i kharakteristiki* (St. Petersburg: Tip. V. S. Balasheva, 1882), pp. 231–254;

Dmitrii Dmitrievich Iazykov, *M. P. Pogodin* (Moscow: Universitetskaia tip., 1901).

References:

Vissarion Grigor'evich Belinsky, "O russkoi povesti i povestiakh g. Gogolia," in *Polnoe sobranie sochinenii,* volume 1 (Moscow: A. N. SSSR, 1953), pp. 259–307;

Aleksandr Grigor'evich Dement'ev, *Ocherki po istorii russkoi zhurnalistiki 1840–1850 gg.* (Leningrad: GIKhL, 1951), pp. 183–240;

Boris Mikhailovich Eikhenbaum, *Lev Tolstoi. Kniga vtoraia. 60-e gody.* (Leningrad/Moscow: GIKhL, 1931), pp. 325–340;

Istoriia russkoi dramaturgii. XVII–pervaia polovina XIX veka., edited by Lidiia Mikhailovna Lotman and others (Leningrad: Nauka, 1982), pp. 332–338; 341–343;

Vladimir Dmitrievich Morozov, *"Moskovskii vestnik" i ego rol' v razvitii russkoi kritiki* (Novosibirsk: Izd-vo Novosibirskogo universiteta, 1990);

Aleksandr Sergeevich Pushkin, "O narodnoi drame i drame *Marfa Posadnitsa,*" in *Polnoe sobranie sochinenii,* volume 7 (Moscow: AN SSSR, 1964), pp. 211–220;

Nicholas Valentine Riasanovsky, *Nicholas I and Official Nationality in Russia, 1825–1855* (Berkeley & Los Angeles: University of California Press, 1959);

S. Rozanova, "'Liubeznye razgovory' (Pushkin, Leo Tolstoy i Pogodin)," *Voprosy literatury,* 5 (1993): 81–129;

Nikolai Leonidovich Rubinshtein, *Russkaia istoriografiia* (Moscow: Goslitizdat, 1941), pp. 254–271;

Russkaia povest' XIX veka. Istoriia i problematika zhanra, edited by Boris Solomonovich Meilakh, ed., (Leningrad: Nauka, 1973), pp. 208–214;

Iasif Markovich Toibin, *Pushkin i filosofsko-istoricheskaia mysl' v Rossii na rubezhe 1820 i 1830 godov* (Voronezh: Izdatel'stvo Voronezhskogo universiteta, 1980);

Mariia Naumovna Virolainen, "Molodoi Pogodin," in M. P. Pogodin's *Povesti. Drama,* edited by M. N. Virolainen (Moscow: Sovetskaia Rossiia, 1984), pp. 3–18.

Nikolai Alekseevich Polevoi

(22 June 1796 – 22 February 1846)

Mary Jo White
University of Washington

BOOKS: *Povesti i literaturnye otryvki,* 6 parts (Moscow, 1829–1830);

Istoriia russkogo naroda, 6 volumes (Moscow: A. Semen, 1829–1833);

Kliatva pri grobe Gospodnem. Russkaia byl' XV-go veka., 4 parts (Moscow, 1832);

Novyi zhivopisets obshchestva i literatury, 6 parts (Moscow: N. Stepanov pri Imperatorskom teatre, 1832);

Abbaddonna, 4 parts (Moscow: A. S. Shiriaev, 1833);

Russkaia Vivliofika, ili sobranie materiialov dlia otechestvennoi istorii, geografii, statistiki i drevnei russkoi literatury (Moscow: A. Semen, 1833);

Mechty i zhizn'. Byli i povesti, 4 parts (Moscow, 1833–1834);

Russkaia istoriia dlia pervonachal'nogo chteniia, 4 parts (Moscow: A. Semen, 1835–1841);

Ugolino; dramaticheskoe predstavlenie (St. Petersburg, 1838);

Igolkin, kupets novogorodskii; istoricheskaia byl' v 1 deistvii s epilogom (St. Petersburg, 1839);

Ocherki russkoi literatury, 2 parts (St. Petersburg: Sakharov, 1839);

Istoriia Petra Velikogo, 4 volumes (St. Petersburg: K. Zhernakov, 1842);

Dramaticheskie sochineniia i perevody N. A. Polevago, 4 parts (St. Petersburg, 1842–1843);

Istoriia kniazia Italiiskogo, grafa Suvorova-Rymnikskogo, generalissimusa rossiiskikh voisk (St. Petersburg, 1843);

Povesti Ivana Gudoshnika, sobrannye Nikolaem Polevym (St. Petersburg: A. Borodin, 1843);

Povest' o velikoi Bitve Borodinskoi byvshei 26-go Avgusta 1812 goda (St. Petersburg, 1844);

Starinnaia skazka ob Ivanushke Durachke, rasskazannaia moskovskim kupchinoiu Nikolaem Polevym (St. Petersburg: M. Ol'khin, 1844);

Istoriia Napoleona. Sochinenie N. Polevago, 5 volumes (St. Petersburg: M. Ol'khin and F. Nagel, 1844–1848);

Ermak Timofeich, ili, Volga i Sibir'; dramaticheskoe predstavlenie v piati deistviiakh (St. Petersburg: K. Krai, 1845);

Nikolai Alekseevich Polevoi, 1833

Russkie polkovodtsy ili zhizn' i podvigi Rossiiskikh polkovodtsev ot vremen Imperatora Petra Velikago do tsarstvovaniia Imperatora Nikolaia I (St. Petersburg, 1845);

Stoletie Rossii s 1745 po 1845 ili istoricheskaia kartina dostopamiatnykh sobytii v Rossii za 100 let, 3 parts (St. Petersburg: P. I. Martynov, 1845–1846);

Obozrenie russkoi istorii do edinoderzhaviia Petra Velikago / Sochinenie Nikolaia Polevogo (St. Petersburg: K. Zhernakov, 1846).

Editions and Collections: *Tsarstvovanie Ioanna Grozhago: obryvok iz istorii gosudarstva rossisskago,* second edition (Berlina: B. Behr, 1870);

Povest' o Suzdal'skom kniaze Simeone; istoricheskaia povest' N. A. Polevogo (St. Petersburg: A. Suvorin, 1885);

Dramaticheskie sochineniia iz russkoi istorii (St. Petersburg, 1899);

Sochineniia, 3 parts (Moscow: A. A. Petrovich, 1903);

Materialy po istorii russkoi literatury i zhurnalistiki tridtsatykh godov, edited by Vladimir Nikolaevich Orlov (Leningrad, 1934);

Mechty i zhizn', edited by B. S. Kondrat'ev (Moscow: Sovetskaia Rossiia, 1988);

Izbrannaia istoricheskaia proza, edited by A. Kurilov (Moscow: Pravda, 1990);

Literaturnaia kritika, stat'i i retsenzii 1825-1842: N. A. Polevoi, Ks. A. Polevoi, edited by V. Berezina and I. Sukhikh (Leningrad: Khudozhestvennaia literatura, 1990);

Meshok s zolotom; povesti, rasskazy, ocherki, edited by Mark D. Sergeev (Irkutsk: Vostochno-Sibirskoe knizhnoe izd-vo, 1991).

OTHER: *Moskovskii telegraf,* edited by Polevoi, 1825–1834;

Ekaterina Alekseevna Avdeeva, *Zapiski o starom i novom russkom byte,* edited by Polevoi (St. Petersburg, 1842).

Critical interest in Nikolai Polevoi in both the nineteenth and twentieth centuries has focused on the same aspects of his career. In the nineteenth century, though he was regularly accounted a publicist, a critic, a novelist and short-story writer, a versifier, an historian, and a man of letters in general, Polevoi was chiefly known as a journalist—the outstanding journalist of his day, in the opinion of the most important Russian critic of the period, Vissarion Grigor'evich Belinsky. In the twentieth century as well Polevoi has been most highly valued for his journalistic accomplishments, particularly for the critical essays and reviews he published in almost every issue of the celebrated journal he founded, *Moskovskii telegraf* (The Moscow Telegraph), and for the role these articles played in the development of Russian Romanticism and prose. Today he is also esteemed for his early contribution to the genre of critical biography and for his tireless pursuit of the editorial aim of *Moskovskii telegraf:* to cultivate a wider reading public, a broad middle-class audience, and so to democratize literature and learning.

Any estimate of Polevoi, in its scope and to some degree in its detail, will be indebted to the first critical overview of his life's work, which was written on the occasion of his death by Belinsky. As he did for so many other leading personalities of the age, Belinsky set the tone and established the standard for all subsequent evaluations of Polevoi. Rehabilitating what many have thought an undeservedly tarnished reputation, Belinsky paid enormous

tribute in death to the writer whose most unrelenting critic he had been in life, a man whose legacy Belinsky himself had obviously inherited.

Belinsky called Polevoi "romanticism's warrior," and the ideas for which Polevoi fought, the themes that are foremost in his journalistic essays and reviews, will be readily familiar to readers already acquainted with the world of European Romanticism, with Romantic poetics and historiography in particular. These themes, motives, and concerns, which recur throughout Polevoi's criticism and are met with again in Belinsky's, include the notions of originality, imagination, enthusiasm or rapture, and free creativity; the organic relation of form and content; the mixing of genres and levels of diction; the development of national literatures; and the role of history in literary works. In relation to the development of a distinctly Russian literature and the role of Russian history in it, the notions of *narodnost'* (a sense of national originality) and *mestnost'* (a sense of place or locality) figure prominently as well. All of these themes and concerns also play a leading role in the fiction, history, and drama that Polevoi wrote in the years following the government-ordered suspension of *Moskovskii telegraf,* when he joined forces with his former opponents and published in the journals then supporting the autocracy.

Nikolai Alekseevich Polevoi was born on 22 June 1796 in Irkutsk. His father, Aleksei Evsev'evich Polevoi, who came from a wealthy and well-established merchant family, was fond of books and kept a sizable library. Polevoi later recalled that among his earliest memories was a scene he saw often while growing up: an image of his father musing, book in hand. But despite his fondness for reading and literature, the elder Polevoi was skeptical about the world of letters and learning; and this feeling, combined with his ambitions for his son in the world of commerce, meant that Nikolai did not receive a systematic education. Still, Nikolai had learned to read and write by the time he was six, taught by his sister Ekaterina Alekseevna; he read voraciously throughout his youth, using whatever spare time his apprenticeship to his father left him, often stinting himself on sleep.

By his own account Polevoi had a prodigious memory, and much of what he read as a boy he soon learned by heart. He first found most of these books in his father's library, including works by Aleksandr Petrovich Sumarokov, Mikhailo Vasil'evich Lomonosov, and Nikolai Mikhailovich Karamzin; Mikhail Matveevich Kheraskov's *Rossiada* (1778); and a wide variety of travel tales, geographies, histories, and plays. His early acquaintance with these authors and subjects set him on the path toward his future career, and at the age of ten—or so he was later to record—he began writing verse and stories, composing plays, compiling histories, and "publishing" journals modeled on those he read aloud to his father. These youthful exercises were soon followed by more serious efforts in the same vein. But to his father's way of thinking all of this juvenilia pointlessly diverted energy and money needed for the family business. And so, to Polevoi's dismay, all of his earliest work met with a single fate: as soon as his father found it, he consigned it to the fire.

In 1811, when Polevoi was fifteen, his father decided to leave Irkutsk and move to Kursk, returning to the family's ancestral home. At the same time he decided to send Polevoi to Moscow on business, where the young merchant was to stay for the year. Here, on his own for the first time, Polevoi studiously attended university lectures, enjoyed the theater, and haunted bookshops. This and subsequent business trips to Moscow and St. Petersburg impressed upon him the inadequacy of his patchwork learning, and he soon undertook to correct it with serious and systematic study. In the course of this study he concentrated particularly on Russian grammar and on foreign languages—the Greek, Latin, French, and German from which he later translated many essays, articles, and excerpts on a wide variety of topics for inclusion in *Moskovskii telegraf*. This study, which was to occupy all of his free time for years, was not only systematic but also, of necessity, surreptitious. Since his own hopes of becoming a writer disrupted his father's ambitions for him, he literally had to work in the dark to realize them. For at least three years, at the end of each business day, he retreated to his books and dreams, careful to keep hidden from his father's eyes the stolen light by which he studied.

In 1820 his father sent him to Moscow once again, this time with the specific commission of establishing the family in the business of distilling vodka. This circumstance and the facts of his self-styled education were later held against him by the gentleman writers—including Aleksandr Pushkin—in whose company he traveled as the editor of *Moskovskii telegraf*. Although he had their cooperation and some contributions from them in the beginning of his enterprise, he soon earned their enmity with his reconsideration of Karamzin's *Istoriia gosudarstva Rossiiskogo* (History of the Russian State, 1816–1818; revised, 1818–1829) and with the publication of his own *Istoriia russkogo naroda* (History of the Russian People, 1829–1833), a work that Pushkin is believed to have parodied in his "Istoriia sela Goriukhina" (History of the Village of Goriukhino), written in 1830 but not published until 1837. No matter the hardships in his upbringing, the roadblocks to his learning, or the improbability of his achieving as much as he did, all Polevoi had succeeded in becoming in the end (or so the gentlemen said) was a puffed-up autodidact, a charlatan, a know-nothing who thought he knew it all.

Polevoi reports that despite Aleksei Evsev'evich's strong resistance to the idea that his son's future might be made in the world of letters, he was proud of his son's achievement from the moment the family name first appeared in print. This event occurred in 1817 when *Russkii vestnik* (The Russian Herald) carried a piece of reportage Polevoi had submitted, an account of the Emperor Alexander I's passage through Kursk. From that time forward his byline appeared with increasing frequency in several publications. He appeared most often in the journals of Nikolai Ivanovich Grech and Faddei Venediktovich Bulgarin, and this circumstance quickly led to the suggestion that he join them as a regular contributor. With other aims in mind he declined the offer and instead sought permission from Adm. Aleksandr Semenovich Shishkov, the Minister for Public Education, to bring out a new journal of his own, one that would be unlike anything currently being published by the monopoly Grech and Bulgarin controlled. This request was soon granted, and in 1824 Polevoi announced that *Moskovskii telegraf* would begin publication in the new year.

When it was first announced, the new journal was intended to have an encyclopedic program of coverage, with plans to publish widely on literature, criticism, science, and the arts. From its earliest issues to its last, *Moskovskii telegraf* included articles on aesthetics, archaeology, economics, ethnology, geography, history, mathematics, philology, philosophy, natural science, statistics, and technology. It broadcast the latest works of well-known Russian, European, and American authors, and it featured poetry from the most exalted—Pushkin, Vasilii Andreevich Zhukovsky, and Evgenii Abramovich Baratynsky among others, thanks to Prince Petr Andreevich Viazemsky's editorial involvement—alongside many more modest efforts as well. It included anecdotes, artwork, news from home and abroad about books and politics, and biographical sketches of famous men: George Washington, Benjamin Franklin, Simón Bolívar, and Jeremy Bentham all received treatment of this kind. In its foreign outlook the journal paid closest attention to the literature and history of France and England, and much coverage was devoted to the French revolution and Napoleon Bonaparte.

Both as a writer and as a translator Polevoi was responsible for almost half of what appeared in

Moskovskii telegraf over the course of its ten-year life, and what he translated to publish for its pages further illustrated its wide range: from Plato's *Philebus* to the tales of Washington Irving; from the German historian Barthold Georg Niebuhr's investigations of Roman history to Charles Maturin's *The Albigenses* (1824) and Napoleon's diary, *Le Memorial de Saint Hélène* (1823). He also translated William Shakespeare's *Hamlet* (1604) and discussed *A Midsummer Night's Dream* (1600); and along with publishing Viazemsky's translation of Benjamin Constant's 1816 novel, *Adolphe,* he translated the same novel himself. Polevoi published translations of the major European writers of the period and writers of interest to them—a list that begins with Lord Byron, Sir Walter Scott, and Shakespeare, and includes the best known among the French and German figures who have come to mean "Romanticism" to modern audiences: Madame de Staël, François-René de Chateaubriand, Alphonse-Marie-Louis de Prat de Lamartine, Prosper Mérimée, Alfred de Vigny, Charles-Augustin Sainte-Beuve, Jean-Jacques Rousseau, E. T. A. Hoffmann, August Wilhelm Schlegel, Friedrich Schiller, Friedrich Wilhelm Joseph von Schelling, Johann Wolfgang von Goethe, and Ludwig Tieck. Polevoi also published articles in which these authors' countrymen discussed them, as for example with William Hazlitt's review of Byron's *Manfred* (1817) and Sir Edward Bulwer-Lytton's remarks on the death of Scott. Not least among its unusual features, *Moskovskii telegraf* reproduced artworks and so contributed to popularizing the images of such artists as Jacques-Louis David, Henry Fuseli, Jean-Honoré Fragonard, Théodore Gericault, Nicolas Poussin, Raphael, and Rembrandt.

In his capacity as critic Polevoi regularly participated in discussions of the most pressing literary questions of the day, an activity that he plunged into almost immediately upon founding *Moskovskii telegraf* when he reviewed the first chapter of Pushkin's *Evgeny Onegin* (1823–1831, published in full in 1833) in 1825. In this, his first significant review, he proclaims and celebrates Pushkin's achievement rather than analyzing it in terms of poetics or versification, an approach to evaluating works of verbal art that in retrospect can be seen as characteristic of him. The review is brief, but in these few pages he touches on many issues that provide a key to understanding his own work and his age, including questions of genre, genius, rules, originality, feeling, the nature of the hero, and *narodnost'*. Beginning with the genre question, he observes that nothing like Pushkin's new work will have been described in Aristotle's *Poetics* or in any of the rule books of Aristotle's neoclassical imitators, whether French or Russian. What kind of

thing is it that seems to be a poem but has chapters like a book, he asks, and answers: the novel in verse, a genre to which the long poems of Goethe and Byron also belong.

Evgeny Onegin is a wholly new kind of literature, Polevoi says, and it is evidence that the real rules guiding poetic creation lie in the poet's imagination, not in the rule books. Pushkin himself is an original talent, and by virtue of his novel in verse he now takes his rightful place alongside Byron. Both Pushkin and Byron are national geniuses whose excellence does honor not only to their countries and countrymen but also to all men of their age. Their creations stem from inspiration and induce raptures of aesthetic pleasure in those who read them, he asserts, each expressing in its own mysterious way the secrets of the human heart. Both poets touch their readers as they do, he concludes, because they sing what is sung to them, never allowing rules to substitute for song. Polevoi then likens poetry to music and compares the first chapter of *Evgeny Onegin* to Byron's *Beppo* (1818) and *Don Juan* (1819–1824); all three, he says, are like a capriccio.

Asserting that the hero is the only thing threading the events of the first chapter together, Polevoi recounts the apparent plot of *Evgeny Onegin* and outlines what he calls its charming and lively series of pictures, the sketches whose only common element is Onegin himself. As Pushkin draws him, Onegin is not only light-hearted but illuminating as well: his character throws light on the relationship of the individual and his society. There is nothing coarse in Pushkin's depiction of Onegin and his world, and the tale is no mere jest, he says. Instead *Evgeny Onegin* lays bare the human heart with its mixture of melancholy and mirth. Pushkin's narration takes his readers through the full gamut of feeling, and the novel in verse is replete with *narodnost'*, Polevoi contends. It speaks directly to Russian minds and feelings and to the Russian character; it speaks of Russian mores; and it speaks in Russian words and sayings.

Polevoi made his next major contribution to literary controversy in 1829, when, engaged in writing a multivolume history of the Russian *narod* (people), he turned his attention as a critic to Karamzin's *Istoriia gosudarstva Rossiiskogo*. Belinsky remarked about Polevoi's entire career that no one had ever brought down so many established reputations as had Polevoi, and few among the figures of authority whose reconsideration he prompted were so well established and revered as Karamzin. A generation later, when Belinsky wrote his appraisal of Polevoi's life as a writer, he could agree with several of Polevoi's points about Karamzin as an historian, particularly with his remarks about Karamzin's ahistori-

Nikolai Polevoi

cal perspective and his creation of costume dramas. By then Belinsky could also commend the tone and taste of what some still viewed as Polevoi's assault. But when Polevoi's article first appeared, many of its more influential readers were outraged by Polevoi's presumption and suspicious of his motives. One result of the battles that ensued, the most important from Polevoi's point of view as publisher of *Moskovskii telegraf,* was that the gentlemen authors who had been associated with his journal from the start, notably Viazemsky, Karamzin's brother-in-law, angrily took their leave of him and it.

Polevoi begins this essay (which bears the same title as Karamzin's work) by praising Karamzin while reiterating the mission of *Moskovskii telegraf.* If his journal mirrors contemporary thinking and serves its educational purpose, it must broadcast the voices of the country's most learned and cultivated men, making plain their views on matters of significance. In Russia, he says, Karamzin's is such a voice; he was the first Russian man of letters, the most cultivated of his contemporaries. Those who knew him when he lived were singularly honored, but those who follow

can only judge him on the basis of his work. And that, Polevoi says, is what he proposes to do: to judge not the man but the work, the whole of which he believes can be found in Karamzin's *Istoriia gosudarstva Rossiiskogo.* Polevoi contends that Karamzin wrote his twelve-volume monument at the height of his powers but in an age already so far distant intellectually and artistically that, despite the literary merits of the work, it is outdated as history. This point, Polevoi stresses, is one of utmost importance in assessing the contemporary value of the work.

Comparing Karamzin to Lomonosov, Polevoi asserts that their accomplishments were equally great and equally important for the development of the Russian language and Russian literature. But, he continues, Karamzin was a fully mature talent when he turned to writing history after scaling the heights of literature; as he burrowed into the one, he gradually lost track of the other. As a consequence he did not keep pace with the new poetry that was emerging in Russia or with the study of philosophy and politics in relation to the new ideas coming to Russia from Germany, France, and England. However ardently he worked on his *Istoriia* for the twenty-three years he gave it (and he gave it the best years of his life from 1802–1826), he was not a man of modern times, so neither could his *Istoriia* be.

Polevoi next defines history as a philosophical understanding of the world and man's place in it, as a true recovery of the past, an explanation of the present, a prophecy of the future, and—most importantly for his criticism of Karamzin—as an intellectual enterprise that always highlights this notion: that each people has a leading idea. Karamzin tries to write, he says, as Herodotus, Tacitus, and even Napoleon did, by narrating the inner life of the events and people whose stories give history its shape. Had Karamzin succeeded, Polevoi says, he would have produced the historical equivalent of the Homeric poems. But Karamzin falls short of success in many ways and for several reasons, not least because he cannot leave his own time imaginatively and enter another with sympathy. Polevoi also sees no general principles evident in Karamzin's work and so no link between Russian and universal history. Nor is the genuine spirit of the people (*narodnost'*) represented, Polevoi emphasizes. Because he treats Russia as a modern state from its earliest tribal beginnings, Karamzin patriotically ennobles the barbarians, making them wellborn, wise, and refined simply because they are Russian. Karamzin fails to bring across to his readers the character of his personages or the spirit of their times, and he works in such a way that his feelings and ideas become the feelings and ideas of people who lived eight hundred years earlier and knew nothing of "Russia." His work is full of artistry, Polevoi contends, but it is a chronicle and not a history.

The first volume of Polevoi's *Istoriia russkogo naroda* came out in the same year as did his review of Karamzin, and he continued to work on it throughout the latter half of the life of *Moskovskii telegraf*, completing the sixth and final volume of the history in 1833. Following Viazemsky's departure from the journal, a move made inevitable by the Karamzin review, Polevoi increasingly turned its pages over to young men of the middle class like himself—he said he was proud to be a plebeian—and grew to rely most heavily on his brother, Ksenofont Alekseevich Polevoi. At the same time, *Moskovskii telegraf* began to commit substantial space to translations of European historians, idealist philosophers, and Romantic and historical novelists. Between his break with the aristocrats in 1829 and the government banning of his journal in 1834 Polevoi continued to publish prose of the highest quality—Pushkin's *Povesti pokoinogo Ivana Petrovicha Belkina* (Tales of the Late Ivan Petrovich Belkin) first appeared in the pages of his journal in 1831. He published the most popular prose writers of the day as well: the one aristocrat to remain with the plebeians of *Moskovskii telegraf* was Aleksandr Aleksandrovich Bestuzhev (Marlinsky). And it was during these same years that Polevoi produced the essay that has won him the highest praise for its intellectual content: a discussion in 1832 of Romanticism and prose, titled "O romanakh V. Giugo i voobshche o noveishikh romanakh" (On the Novels of Victor Hugo and on Modern Novels in General).

In the essay on Hugo and the modern novel Polevoi continues to take part in the long-fought battle between the proponents of Romanticism and the defenders of neoclassicism. Here he is careful to distinguish the genuinely classical from the neoclassical and to claim the former for the Romantic camp: genuine classicism is also new. This new study of Greece is exemplified by Nikolai Ivanovich Gnedich's translation of Homer's *Iliad,* from which *Moskovskii telegraf* had already published a major episode—"The Shield of Achilles"—in 1829. In the course of the essay Polevoi makes the point that the novel is both the product and the instrument of freedom, and that free creation unbounded by rules produces genuine art reflective of *narodnost'*. Such an art is the embodied voice of the people, just as the *Iliad* is, and it speaks of popular aspirations coinciding with the movement of history in its advance toward perfect civil liberty and community. The novel has no ties to the old political order, he says, but is the free and original creation of a new order; it is not an act of anarchy, as its neoclassical critics would have it, but a state of freedom.

Polevoi makes it his business in this essay to lay out the argument against Romanticism made by "the literary Old-Believers," the defenders of neoclassical rules and strictures, who are here represented in French dress rather than Russian and in approach and target of attack by Victor Chauvet, a minor critic long since forgotten, and Hugo, a writer whose works and reputation live on. Chauvet had undertaken to judge Hugo's novels in terms of the canons of taste and morals; and working with the assumption that there is nothing new under the sun, he had decided that there was nothing new in Hugo. Chauvet had also found that in what was then his most recent novel, *Notre-Dame de Paris* (1831), Hugo had failed to represent the character of the age accurately. But, Polevoi contends, Chauvet was wrong about the possibility of the new and about what was new in Hugo. He was also wrong from the perspective of taste and morals when these terms were properly understood—that is, as a Romantic would understand them. To satisfy the canons of taste the Romantic novelist heeds the vox populi, Polevoi says, the voice of the *narod* whose spirit guides the intellectual and cultural life of a nation by virtue of its connection with the laws of history and its intimate ties to the local landscape.

This taste that *narodnost'* inspires, the taste that drives public demand for Hugo's new approach and new work, cannot be wrong, Polevoi insists. This taste is moral; it reflects the good, the true, and the beautiful, and it springs from the same source as poetry: the free contemplation of nature and the original development of the spirit of the people. Unlike neoclassicism, Romanticism does not bind taste and morals to genres, Polevoi continues. Romantic taste, inspired by the popular spirit, finds the *Iliad*—an epic poem of anger, war, and madness—morally instructive. It finds similar instruction in the Greek tales of Phaedra, Andromache, and Iphigenia and in the characters of Don Quixote, Faust, King Lear, Macbeth, and Othello. The genuine moral heights, Polevoi contends, have been reached by Miguel de Cervantes, Shakespeare, Schiller, Goethe, and now by Hugo, and all have worked identically: by way of rapture and inspiration, surrendering to these rather than to genres. Rapture has led them to view the world with both mind and heart, to see it as a riddle, and the solution is the work they have created. For the freely creating poet whose work is original, Polevoi maintains, the form his work takes—its genre—will come from his inspiration; form and content will be one.

On the question of the novel itself Polevoi observes that this genre has only just come into its own, thanks to the genius of Scott. But what exactly is a novel, generically speaking, he asks—is it fantasy, history, satire, or fairy tale? And he answers that it is every one of these things and none of them; its form is not dictated by rules, he says, but invented anew by everyone who writes it. Scott was the first to recognize the ties of the novel to history, but Hugo now surpasses Scott with his *Notre-Dame de Paris,* the essential historical novel. If critics such as Chauvet fail to understand the morality of Hugo's work, Polevoi suggests, it is because this morality is not tricked out in moral phrases. Instead it is represented in characters and events truthfully portrayed in panoramic sweep on an enormous canvas. Hugo's Romanticism as readers know it from his prose is Romanticism in general, Polevoi argues; in it one sees the creating originality of the human spirit at work. Also evident is how Romanticism develops not only in every people but also in every great writer and how Romanticism mixes genres to make whatever it pleases. The first condition that Romanticism must satisfy is one that Hugo satisfies superlatively: the demand for the truthful depiction of humankind and human nature in both its everyday and ideal aspect. To meet this demand successfully Romanticism and the novel will always honor and depend on *narodnost'.* And this, Polevoi concludes, is exactly what Hugo has done.

The review of Hugo's work was published in 1832 at the height of Polevoi's success and influence; two years later *Moskovskii telegraf* fell victim to government censure. The immediate cause of the government-ordered closure was Polevoi's negative review of a patriotic play, one of the tsar's favorites—*Ruka Vsevyshnego otechestvo spasla* (The Hand of the Almighty Saved the Fatherland) by Nestor Vasil'evich Kukol'nik—but his liberal politics and democratic instincts had been earning him well-placed and powerful enemies for years. By the time the journal was banned Polevoi had already written everything on which his modern reputation rests; but his writing career was not over. He produced several historical studies, including multivolume histories of Peter the Great and of Napoleon. In addition he went on writing journalistic essays and reviews that were published in *Biblioteka dlia chteniia* (Library for Reading), *Literaturnaia gazeta* (The Literary Gazette), *Zhivopisnoe obozrenie* (Picturesque Review), and *Syn otechestva* (Son of the Fatherland).

Between 1834 and his death in 1846 Polevoi wrote forty plays on historical themes, all of them staged and none of them well received by the critics. Increasingly patriotic in tone, these works resulted in charges of jingoism. Though D. S. Mirsky labels these dramatic efforts as the "romantic and patriotic plays of the unfortunate Polevoi" and groups him

with other "untalented" writers such as Kukol'nik and Baron Egor Fedorovich Rozen, Polevoi enjoyed success among the theatergoing public, if not among the critics. He culled his subjects from both European and Russian history and used the latter to glorify the doctrine of Official Nationality created by Minister of Education Sergei Semenovich Uvarov, a typical ploy of most playwrights of the Nicolaevan period. Polevoi especially wanted to depict in his plays the loyalty and patriotism of the merchant class to Russia and the tsar; he did so in several plays, such as *Kupets Igolkin* (The Merchant Igolkin, 1839). Other works in his dramatic repertoire include *Lomonosov, Elena Glinskaia, Kostromskie lesa* (Kostroma Forests), and his personal favorite, *Parasha-Sibiriachka* (Parasha the Siberian Girl), based on a novel by Count Joseph de Maistre. Tsar Nicholas I loved *Dedushka russkogo flota* (Grandfather of the Russian Fleet, 1838), which he attended often with his children. A piece of "nonsense" according to the critic Boris Vasil'evich Varneke, it nevertheless paid obeisance to Official Nationalism.

Of the plays based on European sources, *Ugolino* (1838) became a favorite of tragic actors. Dramatizing a portion of Dante's *Inferno,* it is set in medieval Italy with an entire gallery of flat, schematically drawn characters, which Varneke called either "incredible villains or meek angels" who act without any motivation at all. Nevertheless, actors loved it as a source for tragic declamation. However, Polevoi's greatest contribution to Russian theater of the nineteenth century remains his verse translation of Shakespeare's *Hamlet,* which introduced the play to the Russian public. The great actors Pavel Stepanovich Mochalov in Moscow and Vasilii Karatygin in St. Petersburg popularized the play with their own interpretations in the starring role. Although Polevoi's original dramas added little to Russian dramatic arts, he must be credited with providing a worthy vehicle for two of her greatest actors.

Apart from his *Istoriia Petra Velikogo* (History of Peter the Great, 1842), the second edition of which appeared at the end of the nineteenth century when writers and artists of the Silver Age were taking a new look at modern Russia's epic founder, only Polevoi's prose fictions were considered successful enough to be reprinted after his death. Chief among these were the novels *Abbaddonna* (1833), republished in 1898, and *Kliatva pri grobe Gospodnem* (The Oath at the Lord's Sepulchre, 1832), republished in 1900, and the short stories and novellas collected under the title *Mechty i zhizn'* (Dreams and Life, 1834), republished in 1988, all of which had enjoyed a measure of success and acclaim while he lived. As with his republished history, the reappearance of Polevoi's prose was due to the appeal these works held for the period of their revival. While a renewed interest in Romantic and religious-historical themes drew attention to the novels at the turn of the century, Polevoi's tales of peasant life were not republished until the early 1950s and again in the late 1980s. These tales, first published as the collection *Mechty i deistvitel'nost'* (Dreams and Reality, 1834) included *Rasskazy russkogo soldata* (Stories of a Russian Soldier), which Belinsky once judged the best thing of its kind and which subsequent commentators have remarked as noteworthy in the development of the literature of Russian village life. Less florid than his historical novels and in a style characterized by William Edward Brown as "awkward and artless," *Rasskazy russkogo soldata* depicts the ill-fated love of two peasants, Duniasha and Sidor, as the latter tells his tale to a traveling narrator. In the first part Sidor describes the bleak life of the peasants in the village while in the second he relates his life in the military. The underplayed realism of this tale looks forward to the physiological sketches of the Natural School.

Most of Polevoi's major prose works were written during his later years at *Moskovskii telegraf* when he was also writing his *Istoriia russkogo naroda,* and they reflect the same concerns that he brought to his ongoing critical, editorial, and authorial tasks. *Kliatva pri grobe Gospodnem,* an historical novel after the manner of Scott, is set in the midst of fifteenth-century political events in the duchies of Suzdal and Moscow. In it Polevoi attempts an imaginative reconstruction of a past age that the reader views through a few dramatic personages; these characters function as types and represent the spirit of the nation and will of the people. They take their place in a story of foreign domination and the struggle for freedom, a story moved along by a humble character who had once taken an oath at the Holy Sepulchre in Jerusalem to see his land set free. Nevertheless, the novel is not without its faults: Polevoi completely misrepresents Dmitrii Shemiakin—Tsar Vasilii II's cousin and enemy, a cruel, unjust, untrustworthy intriguer—as a hero, and he creates an absurd, improbable character, the Gudok-Player, who somehow manages to become a positive force in Polevoi's fractured version of Russian history.

Abbaddonna, on the on other hand, is set in Polevoi's own time and is about things he knew firsthand. Like his earlier tales "Zhivopisets" (The Painter, 1833) and "Emma" (1834), *Abbaddonna* pictures the middle-class artist's simultaneous attraction to ideal and worldly love and beauty, his doubts about them both and about himself in relation to them, and his battle with the wearying distractions of daily life and human pettiness. "Zhivopisets" set the

model for all other *Künstlernovellen* (novellas about artists), which became popular in Russia during the 1830s and 1840s. In this tale Polevoi describes the fate of an artist, Arkady, the son of a petty official who has trouble being accepted by the educated, aristocratic class of high society. As Dmitrij Čiževskij notes, Arkady's problems are not social, political, or legal. Instead Polevoi portrays the artist's psychological conflict with society. Flying in the face of crass materialism, Arkady defends Romantic ideals. He ultimately dies of consumption, but not before he has painted the pictures that bring to life those very ideals.

Set in Germany, *Abbaddonna* chronicles the trials of a poet torn between a pure love for the mayor's daughter and passion for a society lady (Abbaddonna). Ultimately idyllic love wins as the poet, Reichenbach, rejects the vanity of high society. In his discussion of the novel John Mersereau Jr. notes the elements of satirical humor that relieve the "drudgery" of reading the novel, with its interminable digressions, overblown style, and "quite unattractive" characters. He concedes, though, that Polevoi is an amusing satirist who shows no mercy to any level of society. No one is safe from his humor. Especially successful are Polevoi's satirical barbs at editors, journalists, and publishers.

On another level Polevoi wrote clever parodies of literary figures, including Pushkin and Gogol. Along with humorous poems, these parodies appeared in his 1832 collection, *Novyi zhivopisets* (The New Painter). With his *Rasskazy russkogo soldata* Polevoi came full circle as a writer, returning to his own earliest beginnings by having his soldier unfold his tales—about the misfortunes of love and war and the mean circumstances of village life—to a young merchant narrator who meets him while traveling around Kursk in 1817.

Refurbishing Polevoi's reputation, Belinsky afforded him a position of highest honor in the history of Russian letters, placing him on a par with Lomonosov and Karamzin. Each marked the literature of his time in his own way, Belinsky said, impressing it with his own image and with the image of its historical period. What Polevoi is best remembered for today is indeed an indication of his era. Against the aristocratic and neoclassical interest in the proprieties of style and the dictates of genres, Polevoi emphasized the subject matter of prose works, calling attention to the successful painting of scenes and capturing of spirit rather than to the sculpting of phrases and adherence to rules. Although his discussions of prose often employ a vocabulary developed for, and better suited to, the description of lyrics and song, he still concentrated on issues that mark the descent of the novel from drama, especially in his concern with plot and character. Not unexpectedly for a political liberal from the merchant class whose rise to prominence is tied to the fortunes of Decembrists and their revolt, Polevoi firmly believed that works of art have a social dimension and their authors and critics a social responsibility. In the layout of his argument this sense of civic responsibility is often connected to his interest in how the work under consideration advances the Romantic program—as much a matter of politics as artistry for him—how it heeds historical imperative, how it satisfies public demand and so allows itself to be guided by the spirit of *narodnost'*.

Belinsky also hailed Polevoi's passion. It was, he said, a gentleman's passion, though Polevoi was himself not a gentleman; it was a passion for the enlightenment of his native land. This emotion was what had made *Moskovskii telegraf* great. Polevoi was a born journalist, one by calling and not by accident, Belinsky insisted, and by virtue of his gentleman's passion his journal towered over the competition and triumphed on behalf of the new direction in Russian literature, mingling the vital questions of life with art and taking them all up together in the arena of journalism.

Letters:

Izbrannye proizvedeniia i pis'ma, edited by A. A. Karpov (Leningrad: Khudozhestvennaia literatura, 1986).

Bibliographies:

Nikolai Kirovich Kozmin, "Bibliograficheskii ukazatel' proizvedenii N. A. Polevogo i literatury o nem (1817–1903)," in *Ocherki iz istorii russkogo romantizma N. A. Polevoi, Kak vyrazitel' literaturnykh napravlenii sovremennoi emu èpokhi* (St. Petersburg: I. N. Skorokhodov, 1903);

N. A. Popkova, *Moskovskii Telegraf, izdavaemyi Nikolaem Polevym: ukazatel' soderzhaniia,* 3 volumes (Saratov: Zonal'naia nauchnaia biblioteka Saratovskogo universiteta, 1990).

Biography:

Ksenofont Alekseevich Polevoi, *Zapiski o zhizni i sochinenniiakh N. A. Polevogo* (St. Petersburg: I. Fishon, 1860).

References:

Vissarion Grigor'evich Belinsky, *Sobranie sochinenii v deviati tomakh,* edited by Nikolai Konstantino-

vich Gei, volume 8 (Moscow: Khudozhestvennaia literatura, 1982), pp. 157–182;

William Edward Brown, *A History of Russian Literature of the Romantic Period,* volume 2 (Ann Arbor, Mich.: Ardis, 1986), pp. 271–273, 287–289;

Dmitrij Čiževskij, *History of Nineteenth-Century Russian Literature,* translated by Richard Noel Porter, volume 1 (Nashville: Vanderbilt University Press, 1974), pp. 107–109;

V. E. Evgen'ev-Maksimov and V. G. Berezina, *N. A. Polevoi: Ocherk zhizni i deiatel'nosti* (Irkutsk, 1947);

B. S. Kondrat'ev, "Tri zhizni Nikolaia Polevogo," in *Mechty i zhizn',* by Polevoi (Moscow, 1988);

Lauren G. Leighton, commentary on "Eugene Onegin, Chapter 1," by Polevoi, in *Russian Romantic Criticism, an Anthology,* edited and translated by Leighton (New York: Greenwood Press, 1987), pp. 101–110;

Leighton, *Russian Romanticism: Two Essays* (The Hague: Mouton, 1975);

John Mersereau Jr., *Russian Romantic Fiction* (Ann Arbor, Mich.: Ardis, 1983), pp. 84–86, 206–210;

D. S. Mirsky, *A History of Russian Literature,* edited and abridged by Francis J. Whitfield (New York: Knopf, 1966), pp. 121, 140;

Vladimir Dmitrievich Morozov, *Ocherki po istorii russkoi kritiki vtoroi poloviny 20-30-kh godov XIX veka* (Tomsk: Tomskii universitet, 1979);

Vladimir Nikolaevich Orlov, *Nikolai Polevoi: materialy po istorii russkoi literatury i zhurnalistiki tridtsatykh godov* (Leningrad: Izdatel'stvo pisatelei v Leningrade, 1934);

Ksenofont Alekseevich Polevoi, *Zapiski Ksenofonta Alekseevicha Polevogo* (St. Petersburg: A. S. Suvorin, 1888);

Nicholas V. Riasanovsky, *The Image of Peter the Great in Russian History and Thought* (New York: Oxford University Press, 1985), pp. 116–119;

Alla Ervandovna Shiklo, *Istoricheskie vzgliady N. A. Polevogo* (Moscow: Moskovskii universitet, 1981);

I. N. Sukhikh, "Poslednii romantik," in *Literaturnaia kritika,* by Polevoi (Leningrad: Khudozhestvennaia literatura, 1990);

Boris Vasil'evich Varneke, *History of the Russian Theatre, Seventeenth through Nineteenth Centuries,* translated by Boris Brasol, revised and edited by Belle Martin (New York: Macmillan, 1951), pp. 222–223, 243–245, 248–249.

Osip Ivanovich Senkovsky
(Józef-Julian Sekowski, Baron Brambeus)
(19 March 1800 – 4 March 1858)

Louis Pedrotti
University of California–Riverside

BOOKS: *Supplément à l'histoire générale des Huns, des Turcs et de Mongols* (St. Petersburg: University of St. Petersburg Press, 1824);

Fantasticheskie puteshestviia Barona Brambeusa (St. Petersburg: Vdova Pliushar s synom, 1833);

Listki barona Brambeusa (St. Petersburg: I. I. Glazunov, 1858).

Collections: *Sobranie sochinenii Senkovskogo (Barona Brambeusa)*, 9 volumes, edited by P. Savel'ev (St. Petersburg: Imperatorskaia Akademiia Nauk, 1858–1859);

Sochineniia Barona Brambeusa, edited by V. A. Koshelev and A. E. Novikov (Moscow: Sovetskaia Rossiia, 1989).

Editions in English: *The Fantastic Journeys of Baron Brambeus*, translated by Louis Pedrotti (New York: Peter Lang, 1993).

TRANSLATIONS: Lokman, *Amtsal Lokman el-Hakim* (Wilno: Towarzystwo Szubrawców, 1818), pp. i–xx, 1–32;

"Beduin," *Poliarnaia zvezda* (May 1823): 378–385;

"Vitiaz' bulanogo konia," *Poliarnaia zvezda* (January 1824): 297–307;

"Dereviannaia krasavitsa. Tatarskaia povest'," *Poliarnaia zvezda* (June 1825): 174–182;

"Istinnoe velikodushie. Arabskaia povest'," *Poliarnaia zvezda* (July 1825): 239–248;

"Urok neblagodarnym," *Poliarnaia zvezda* (July 1825): 258–262;

"Smert' Shanfariia," *Al'bom Severnykh Muz* (February 1828): 279–321;

"Beduinka," *Severnye Tsvety* (August 1828): 166–185;

James Morier, *Pokhozhdeniia mirzy Khadzhi-Baby Isfagani v Londone* (St. Petersburg, 1830);

"Vor," *Severnye Tsvety* (March 1830): 242–276;

Morier, *Pokhozhdeniia Khadzhi-Baby Isfagani v Persii i Turtsii, ili persidskii Gilblaz* (St. Petersburg, 1831).

Osip Ivanovich Senkovsky (Józef-Julian Sekowski, Baron Brambeus)

OTHER: *Bałamut Peterburski*, edited by Senkovsky (1831–1833);

Novosel'e (edited by Senkovsky, 1833–1834);

Biblioteka dlia chteniia (edited by Senkovsky, 1834–1856);

Èntsyklopedicheskii leksikon (edited by Senkovsky, 1838–1839);

Voennaia biblioteka (edited by Senkovsky, 1838–1840);

Prevrashchenie golov v knigi i knig v golovy and *Mikeriia, nil'skaia liliia*, in *Sto russkikh literatorov*, volume 1

(St. Petersburg, 1839), pp. 1–47; volume 3 (St. Petersburg, 1845), pp. 596–692;

Syn otechestva (edited by Senkovsky, 1841);

Uchenoe puteshestvie na Medvezhii ostrov, in *Vzgliad skvoz' stoletiia. Russkaia fantastika XVIII i pervoi poloviny XIX veka*, edited by Viktor Guminsky (Moscow: Molodaia Gvardiia, 1977), pp. 130–214;

"Antar," in *Russian 19th-Century Gothic Tales*, edited by Valentin Korovin (Moscow: Raduga, 1984), pp. 229–250.

SELECTED PERIODICAL PUBLICATIONS–
UNCOLLECTED:"Egipetskie drevnosti v S. Peterburge," *Severnaia pchela*, no. 9 (1825);

Pis'mo Tiutiundzhiu-Oglu-Mustafy-Agi, *Severnaia pchela*, nos. 129–133 (1827);

"Lettre à M. Silvestre de Sacy," *Journal Asiatique*, 2 (1828): 237ff;

Antar. Vostochnaia povest', *Novosel'e* (1833): 69–108;

Arifmetika, *Severnaia pchela*, nos. 209–210 (1833);

Bol'shoi vykhod u Satany, *Novosel'e* (1833): 129–186;

Chelovechik, *Severnaia pchela*, no. 137 (1833);

Chto takoe liudi! Basnia v proze, *Kometa Bely* (1833): 179–204;

Lichnosti, *Severnaia pchela*, no. 17 (1833);

"Moia zhena," *Severnaia pchela*, no. 152 (1833);

Neznakomka, *Severnaia pchela* (1833): 1–36;

Peterburgskaia baryshnia, *Severnaia pchela*, no. 4 (1833);

Zakoldovanni klad, *Severnaia pchela*, no. 220 (1833);

Auktsion. Ob'iavlenie: prodaetsia za ot"ezdom, *Severnaia pchela*, nos. 6–7 (1834);

Chin-chun, ili Avtorskaya slava, *Novosel'e* (1834): 9–44;

Pokhozhdeniia odnoi revizhskoi dushi, *Novosel'e* (1834): 130–236;

Shchastlivets. Vostochnaia povest', *Novosel'e* (1834): 81–106;

Liubov' i smert'. Nochnoe mechtanie, *Biblioteka dlia chteniia*, 2 (1834): 141–191;

"Brambeus i iunaia slovesnost'," *Biblioteka dlia chteniia*, 3 (1834): 33–60;

"Fizika Vellanskogo," *Biblioteka dlia chteniia*, 4 (1834): 7–12;

Visiashchiy gost', *Biblioteka dlia chteniia*, 6 (1834): 68–87;

Povesti. Povest', *Biblioteka dlia chteniia*, 7 (1834): 27–29;

Predubezhdenie. Stat'ia odnogo cheloveka, *Biblioteka dlia chteniia*, 7 (1834): 79–159;

Èbsambul. Nubiiskie stseny, *Biblioteka dlia chteniia*, 8 (1835): 219–244; 9 (1835): 69–110;

Poteriannaia dlia sveta povest', *Biblioteka dlia chteniia*, 10 (1835): 134–150;

Turetskaia tsyganka, *Biblioteka dlia chteniia*, 12 (1835): 134–174;

Teoriia obrazovannoi besedy, *Biblioteka dlia chteniia*, 12 (1835): 75–88;

Zapiski domovogo, *Biblioteka dlia chteniia*, 13 (1835): 71–120;

Dzhulio, *Biblioteka dlia chteniia*, 18 (1836): 20–122;

Liubov' muzykal'nogo uchitelia, *Biblioteka dlia chteniia*, 19 (1836): 70–86;

Pervoe pis'mo trëkh tverskikh pomeshchikov k baronu Brambeusu, *Biblioteka dlia chteniia*, 22 (1837): 65–96;

"Zoologiia i botanika," *Biblioteka dlia chteniia*, 25 (1837): 75–78;

"Biographie de M-lle. Taglioni," *Biblioteka dlia chteniia*, 26 (1838): 15;

Mamzel' Katish', ili Lovlia zhenikhov, *Biblioteka dlia chteniia*, 27 (1838): 17–62;

"Sochineniia N. Grecha," *Biblioteka dlia chteniia*, 27 (1838): 25–30; 33 (1839): 29–31;

Chasy mamzell' Katish', *Biblioteka dlia chteniia*, 31 (1838): 157–164;

Fan'su, ili Plutovka-gornichnaia. Kitaiskaia komediia, *Biblioteka dlia chteniia*, 35 (1839): 52–140;

Ivan i Roza. Povest' iz letopisei Vasil'evskogo ostrova, *Biblioteka dlia chteniia*, 39 (1840): 101–126; 40 (1840): 89–112;

"Sokrashchenie russkoi grammatiki," *Biblioteka dlia chteniia*, 41 (1840): 3–6;

Uzhasnaia taina, *Biblioteka dlia chteniia*, 43 (1840): 53–68;

"Po povodu Odissei," *Biblioteka dlia chteniia*, 44 (1841): 15–42; 46 (1841): 1–66;

Ideal'naia krasavitsa, *Biblioteka dlia chteniia*, 49 (1841): 141–254; 50 (1842): 17–130, 139–230; 61 (1843): 77–121; 63 (1844): 77–156;

"O posmertnykh sochineniiakh Pushkina," *Biblioteka dlia chteniia*, 49 (1841): 1–4;

Padenie Shirvanskogo tsarstva, *Biblioteka dlia chteniia*, 52 (1842): 9–74, 79–164;

"Pokhozhdeniia Chichikova Gogolia," *Biblioteka dlia chteniia*, 53 (1842): 24–54;

Lukii, ili Pervaia povest', *Biblioteka dlia chteniia*, 55 (1842): 75–132;

Umnitsy. Predmet vziat iz romana mistris Trollop, "The blue belles of England," i obdelan baronom Brambeusom, *Biblioteka dlia chteniia*, 58 (1843): 119–254;

"Gamlet. O perevodakh voobshche," *Biblioteka dlia chteniia*, 61 (1844): 33–35;

"Mify slavianskogo iazychestva," *Biblioteka dlia chteniia*, 99 (1850): 13–16;

"Neliudimka, drama gr. Rostopchinoi," *Biblioteka dlia chteniia*, 102 (1850): 13–36;

"Sochineniia Kukol'nika," *Biblioteka dlia chteniia*, 117 (1853): 1–16;

"O srodstve iazyka slavianskogo s sanskritskim," *Biblioteka dlia chteniia*, 123 (1854): 1–42; 124 (1854): 1–42;

"Listki Barona Brambeusa," *Syn otechestva,* nos. 14–21, 23–24, 26–27, 29–36, 38 (1856); nos. 1–2, 10, 12–13, 15, 17–18, 22–24, 27–29, 31–32, 35–36, 38–41, 43–45, 48, 50 (1857); nos. 5, 7, 8 (1858).

Perhaps the single most popular writer of the 1830s and 1840s in Russia, Osip Senkovsky fell into such disfavor under the onslaught of the utilitarian critics of the nineteenth and twentieth centuries that his name has scarcely survived to the present day. Beginning with Vissarion Grigor'evich Belinsky, the traditional critical attitude toward him was firmly set on a negative course. To Belinsky and the socially oriented critics who followed, Senkovsky was a reactionary, a man who turned his formidable irony and beguiling wit against almost every aspect of contemporary life—delving, probing, exposing, and ridiculing. His skepticism of all accepted values, whether scientific or aesthetic, was seen as a form of cynicism by the Socialist Realist critics of the Soviet era. Few Poles or Russians were willing to accept him as their own, even those who acknowledged his erudition, intellectual capacities, wit, and genius for scientific research. Despite the brilliance of his early studies at the University of Wilno and his extraordinary successes in examining the literary heritage of the Near East, Senkovsky chose to make an official break with his Polish past. In his adopted society of St. Petersburg, as the newly baptized "Baron Brambeus," he quickly rose to literary prominence, captivated the reading public with his witty stories, and enjoyed for many years an immense following in the world of journalism as the autocratic editor of the *Biblioteka dlia chteniia* (Library for Reading), the most widely read magazine of the day.

Osip Ivanovich Senkovsky was born on St. Joseph's Day, 19 March 1800, on his mother's estate in the village of Antagotony, about thirty miles from Wilno (today known as Vilnius, the capital of the Republic of Lithuania). Christened Józef-Julian Sekowski, he began his formal schooling at the Minsk Collegium (Rhetorum Collegium Minscensis) and matriculated at the University of Wilno. By the beginning of the nineteenth century the University of Wilno had risen to the level of the best universities of Western Europe, and it was there that Senkovsky came under the influence of several outstanding professors. Gottfried Groddeck, the German professor of Greek and Latin who was married to Senkovsky's mother's maternal aunt, instilled in the young scholar a lasting love for the classical world and provided him with a firm basis for his later philological pursuits. To another professor, the histo-

Senkovsky as a young man

rian and philologist Joachim Lelewel, Senkovsky owed his inspiration in the area of Orientalism, especially the worlds of the Near East and Northern Africa. To no lesser degree was Senkovsky indebted to another Wilno professor, Jedrzej Śniadecki, a noted physician, naturalist, and professor of chemistry who directed the young student toward the study of the natural sciences and philosophy. Senkovsky's love for scientific investigation and experimentation, controlled by an empirical skepticism, remained with him throughout his later professional career. In Śniadecki, Senkovsky also found a role model for his later satirical approach to all accepted principles and proclaimed infallibilities. While he was studying at the University of Wilno, Senkovsky joined the *Towarzystwo Szubrawców* (Society of Scamps), an intellectual club that published its own satirical magazine, *Wiadomości Brukowe* (Pavement News). While a member of the *Szubrawcy,* Senkovsky honed his satirical ability and gained valuable experience in the management of a periodical, assets that he would put into practice in his later journalistic enterprises in St. Petersburg.

In 1819 Senkovsky completed his studies at the University of Wilno, married Marja Rodziewiczówna, and left almost immediately thereafter to begin an extensive journey through the Near East and Northern Africa. The trip, sponsored by his friends at the University of Wilno, took him first to Constantinople, where he was appointed to the post of interpreter to Baron Sergei Grigor'evich Stroganov at the Russian Embassy. From there he traveled to Syria, Egypt, Nubia, and the upper reaches of the Nile, dressed in Arabic garb and speaking the local dialects that he encountered along the way. During this time he sent back many articles recounting his adventures to several Polish periodicals, including the *Dziennik Wilekńi* (Wilno Daily), *Tygodnik Wilekńi* (Wilno Weekly) and *Pamitnik Warszawski* (Warsaw Journal). He returned to Europe in 1821 and was appointed translator at the Ministry of Foreign Affairs in St. Petersburg. There he also received his appointment as member of the *Vol'noe Obshchestvo Liubitelei Slovesnosti* (Free Society of Lovers of Literature). The next year he was named professor of Oriental languages and literatures at the University of Wilno, but he declined this offer in favor of a more attractive one made to him by the University of St. Petersburg.

During his early years at the University of St. Petersburg, Senkovsky published many articles on his Near Eastern travels, as well as translations of Arabic and Persian stories. In 1823 he was named a corresponding member of the *Towarzystwo Przyjaciół Naukowe* (Scientific Society of Friends) in Warsaw, and in 1826 he was awarded the degree of doctor of philosophy by the Cracow Academy at the same time that he was named a member of the *Towarzystwo Naukowe* (Society of Science) in that city. In 1827 he became a member of the Asiatic Society in London, and in 1828 he received an appointment as censor from the Russian government and was named a corresponding member of the Akademiia Nauk (Academy of Sciences) in the Russian capital.

In 1829, a year after the annulment of his first marriage, Senkovsky married Adelaida Aleksandrovna Rall, daughter of the court banker Baron Aleksandr Rall. In 1830 he became editor of the humorous Polish journal *Batamut Peterburski* (St. Petersburg Trifler), a position he held until 1833. The year 1833 proved to be a turning point in Senkovsky's career. It was in this year that Aleksandr Smirdin, owner of the largest and most popular bookstore in the country, invited the young professor to help in putting together an anthology of works by the leading Russian literary figures, to be known as *Novosel'e* (The Housewarming). Senkovsky had first attracted Smirdin's attention by his translations of Arabic literature. Smirdin urged Senkovsky to try his hand at original fictional writing. Smirdin had also been impressed by Senkovsky's translation of James Morier's *The Adventures of the Mirza Hadji-Baba of Isfahan in London,* which had appeared in 1830. Senkovsky contributed to *Novosel'e* his first original works in Russian, a satirical attack on the Romantic school as well as on German speculative philosophy called *Bol'shoi vykhod u Satany* (Satan's Great Audience), along with an inspiration from his translations of Arabic folklore, a short story that he called "Antar." The latter story was the basis for Nikolai Andreevich Rimsky-Korsakov's *Symphony No. 2,* composed in 1868 and reorchestrated as a "symphonic suite" in 1878 and 1897. Rimsky-Korsakov makes much use of Senkovsky's Near Eastern scene to produce a series of movements in a pseudo-Oriental style. The melodies are languorously Oriental in mood and filled with ornate Eastern arabesques. Perhaps as significant as the stories themselves was Senkovsky's use of what became his most popular pseudonym, "Baron Brambeus."

It turned out that 1833 was to be a banner year for Senkovsky as a prose writer. In this year he produced a series of stories, that he later gathered under the title *Peterburgskie nravy* (St. Petersburg Manners) for *Severnaia pchela* (no. 4, 1833), in which he launched a scorching attack on the contemporary scene in Russia. The superficialities of French fashions, the rearing of children, the passion for card playing, senseless social climbing—these are a sampling of the vices Senkovsky laid bare in these seven satirical tales. The opening story is called "Peterburgskaia baryshnia" (A Young Lady of St. Petersburg). In it Senkovsky assails the typical education of young ladies with its ultimate aim of getting them married: modest behavior; Romantic sensitivity; a passion for the latest Parisian fashions; a cultivated shyness; skill in dancing, singing, painting, and playing the harp and piano; and most important of all, the accumulation of a sizable dowry. Personal tragedy strikes Nadezhda, however, when she is forced to give up her romantic love for a young (but impoverished) lieutenant to marry an elderly (but wealthy) German baron. "Poor Nadenka!" Senkovsky concludes. "The unhappy child of an ambitious mother and stupid father! And there are among us a prodigious number of such parents. I have had my fill of this. Next time I shall refuse to attend the wedding of a Young Lady of St. Petersburg."

The second story in the series, "Lichnosti" (Getting Personal), is a short piece that makes fun of modern litigation and the problem of trying to avoid offending the sensibilities of other people, people who are ready to believe that it is just about them that Baron Brambeus is writing. The third entry in the series, "Chelovechik" (The Little Man), laments the readiness of people to spread and believe slander in the refined society of St. Petersburg. The fourth story in the series is called "Moia zhena" (My Wife). Its subject is the Romantic concern with women's liberation. It tells of a husband who tries to speak to his wife "once and for all about a certain matter." However, she is seldom at home. She is always out on various ventures, shopping and haggling in stores or helping some friend in need. It turns out that the husband never does get a chance to speak to his wife "once and for all." "And now, beloved reader," Senkovsky concludes, " get back to your business, and I shall return home. If, after reading this piece, you find that your wife is out, don't get upset. She's probably gone to the bazaar with my Daria Kondratievna. When it's convenient, drop by my place after dinner. We'll go together to the silk shops to look for our spouses."

The fifth story in the series, "Arifmetika" (Arithmetic), brings the Szubrawcy satire against the passion for card playing to Russian literature. The story is a poorly disguised attack on compulsive card playing and the ruinous effects of this time-consuming pastime on intellectual activity. As a mathematical exercise Senkovsky suggests that all the playing cards in Russia have been buried deep in the ground near St. Petersburg. Suddenly the ground begins to shake and the entire atmosphere is filled with a volcanic shower of cards from Mount Pulkov, now a card-breathing mountain, and the capital is covered over, as Pompeii had been, but with playing cards. Playing on the topical sensations of recent discoveries around Mount Vesuvius, Senkovsky suggests that someday St. Petersburg may also be rediscovered from beneath its card-ashes:

> But what if they begin to rummage around everywhere and search all corners? Oh, let us beseech the powerful fate that sends down trumps to us mortals that Mount Pulkov may never turn into a card-Vesuvius! What would the pedants and antiquaries of the thirty-first or fiftieth centuries say about the purity of the morals of our time? However, ladies and gentlemen, have no fear. Continue to amuse yourselves as before. I know by arithmetic that this will never happen.

The sixth story, "Zakoldovannyi klad" (Enchanted Treasure), laments the rise of crass com-

Senkovsky dressed in Near-Eastern garb as "Baron Brambeus"

mercialism in Russian society, with all its unpoetic concerns about interest rates, balance of trade, budgets, bank accounts, and debts. The final story in the series, titled "Auktsion" (The Auction), originally appeared in 1834. It reflects Senkovsky's own skepticism, his bitterness and disillusionment with life. A man who is leaving the world forever wants to auction off all his belongings. Justice is bought for two million and two rubles, but it is paid for in bribes. A profiteer buys intelligence for seven kopecks. Literature goes for fifty rubles. A society of Germans buys the sciences for thirty-six pounds of tobacco. Fame is bought by a charlatan for ten rubles cash and for eighteen rubles and twenty-five kopecks on credit. An author's reputation is sold to a bad writer. As the most bitter blow of all, the auctioneer discovers that someone has stolen happiness.

However, Senkovsky's greatest achievement in prose during 1833 (and, indeed, during his entire career) was the four-part work called *Fantasticheskie puteshestviia Barona Brambeusa* (The Fantastic Journeys of Baron Brambeus). It is really with this work that Senkovsky made his pseudonym, Baron Brambeus, a household item in Russia. The first entry in this collection is not a journey at all. Rather, it serves as the preface to the other three stories, which are supposedly accounts of journeys undertaken by Baron Brambeus. This preface, titled "Osenniaia skuka" (The Boredom of Autumn), serves as a vehicle for Senkovsky's crusade for a more harmonious literary language and an attack on the bookish style in use at the time, with its heavy reliance on stiff and outdated official, or chancery, forms. Words such as *sey, ony, toliko,* and *kokliko,* he insisted, had no place in contemporary fiction. So strongly did Senkovsky resent the misuse of these antiquated official forms that he made the stern prediction that "Russian literature would be invigorated and would penetrate the higher classes of society only when it began to speak the Russian of its own time, free from such words and expressions, namely, the language spoken by proper people."

The second selection, the first true travel narrative, is called "Poèticheskoe puteshestvie po belu-svetu" (The Poetic Journey over the Great, Wide World). The theme of this story is literary, and Baron Brambeus aims his satire at the Romantic movement and the search for "strong feelings." Unable to find any excitement in St. Petersburg or Moscow, the baron heads for the warm lands of the south, where he finally experiences some rather strong sensations. In Ukraine (in a none-too-subtle lampoon on the "dirty realities" of Gogol's stories) he is bitten by fleas, drenched in garbage, beset by a pack of wild dogs, and quarantined for the plague. He is so entranced by the sight of Constantinople as seen from the bridge of his ship that he resolves to write a bombastic sea novel, "in the style of Eugène Sue." When he revives from the effects of having had the house burn down around him while he was making love to his Turkish sweetheart, he is informed by the doctor that he is now out of danger. Brambeus is warned, however, that under no circumstances should he experience any more strong feelings.

Senkovsky's fictional works often served as vehicles for a favorite literary device: the fusion of science and satire. The third entry in *Fantasticheskie puteshestviya Barona Brambeusa* is titled "Uchenoe puteshestvie na Medvezhii ostrov" (The Scientific Journey to Bear Island). Here Senkovsky turns his satire toward various aspects of the sciences, including archaeology, Egyptology, astronomy, and paleontology. Specifically, he calls to question tenets of two recently deceased French scientists, Jean François Champollion, who worked out a system for deciphering Egyptian hieroglyphs through the medium of the Rosetta Stone, and Baron Georges Cuvier, the noted naturalist. Senkovsky was also capitalizing on a topical scientific sensation: the eagerly anticipated arrival of Halley's Comet, predicted to oc-

cur in 1835. Accompanied by a learned German naturalist named Doctor Spurtzmann, Baron Brambeus sets out to explore a mysterious cave of Egyptian hieroglyphs located at the summit of an island in the Arctic Ocean off the mouth of the Lena River. In the cave they find not only hieroglyphs but also fossil remains of various prehistoric animals. The bulk of the story concerns the contents of the hieroglyphs, written on the walls of the cave by the last man remaining from a terrible flood caused in Tunguska by the impact of an immense comet. The comet's assault on the planet has not only destroyed the local civilization but has also turned what was a lush, tropical land of bananas and mastodons into the icy wastes of present-day Siberia. The two scholars are overjoyed at their great discoveries and dream of the great fame they will receive in Europe when they return with the news. Unfortunately, the bubble of their heady elation is pricked when the leader of the expedition, a level-headed mineralogist, coolly informs them that these symbols are not hieroglyphs, Egyptian or otherwise, but merely the crystallization of a stalagmite, the work of water and weather. As the group returns morosely to Europe, the baron vows never again to undertake any scientific journeys. It is curious that in this story Senkovsky anticipated the actual destructive impact of a gigantic explosion that occurred in the same region of Tunguska in 1908. Current thought is that this greatest of fireballs was caused by the penetration of Earth's atmosphere by either a comet or an asteroid.

The final entry in *Fantasticheskie puteshestviya Barona Brambeusa* is called "Sentimental'noe puteshestvie na goru Ètnu" (The Sentimental Journey to Mount Etna). Here the thrust of Senkovsky's satire is philosophical, seen on the background of recent sensational discoveries made at Pompeii and Herculaneum. Baron Brambeus goes on a sentimental journey (mostly after pretty Italian girls) to Mount Etna in the company of a Swedish companion and a local Sicilian girl. Unfortunately his jealous Swedish rival pushes him into the crater of Mount Etna, and the poor baron falls headlong into the funnel of the volcano, finally breaking through to a land where everything is upside down. Here he finds the local inhabitants walking in a topsy-turvy manner. They, of course, think it is the baron who is walking on the ceiling, and they beg him to come down and join them in the dance that he has interrupted by his intrusion. Brambeus soon learns that the locals also think upside down and backwards, and this phenomenon provides him with the opportunity to ridicule German idealist philosophy, including the ideas of Immanuel Kant, Johann Gottlieb Fichte, Wilhelm Joseph von Schelling, and the latter's Rus-

Editorial cartoon titled "The Fall of the First Man in Literature," in which Senkovsky is tempted by Faddei Bulgarin as "Eve" and Nikolai Grech as "the Serpent" in Veniamin A. Karavin's Baron Brambeus *(1929)*

sian disciple Daniil Mikhailovich Vellansky. After several years of adventures in the underground land Baron Brambeus is eventually ejected through the funnel of Mount Vesuvius and reunited with his disgruntled Russian wife. In Rome, however, officers of the Holy Inquisition throw him into prison for his heresy of insisting on walking on the ceiling. He is released from imprisonment on the conditions that he grant his wife a divorce and promise not to walk upside down again until he arrives in France.

So efficient and tireless did Senkovsky prove himself in his participation in Aleksandr Smirdin's *Novosel'e* project that he was the publisher's logical choice for the editorship of his new adventure in journalism, the magazine called *Biblioteka dlia chteniia*. So it was that in 1834 Senkovsky became editor of the new journal that on its title page proclaimed its dedication to the service of "literature, the sciences, the arts, industry, news, and fashion." Many critics immediately took issue with Senkovsky for his autocratic handling of the journal, especially his persistence in editing all articles submitted to him. There is no doubt that Senkovsky ran a tight ship in his editorial office. And there is no doubt, either, that he did much to improve the status of journalism during his tenure on the magazine. During the 1830s and 1840s *Biblioteka dlia chteniia* became the most widely circulated magazine in Russia, with a subscription list of more than five thousand. Publishers of other periodicals were happy to have a thousand, or even five hundred, subscribers. Already in its first year of production Senkovsky's magazine achieved a near monopoly in the field of journalism. Indeed, Senkovsky to no small degree revolutionized the Russian periodical. With his immense talent for organization he created in his own enterprise a model of journalistic practice that was emulated by other magazines not only in their exterior appearance but also in the internal format by sections. *Biblioteka dlia chteniia* became the first "fat magazine" in Russia.

The punctuality of the appearance of *Biblioteka dlia chteniia*, on the first day of each month, was another characteristic of Senkovsky's editorial policy. Another innovation attributed to the magazine was the final break with the "Maecenas" tradition in Russian letters, wherein the writer played the role of protégé to some wealthy or noble personage. Smirdin authorized Senkovsky to pay as much as 250 to 300 rubles for a sheet of prose and up to 5 rubles for a verse of poetry. This generous policy not only made good business sense but also produced a reform in the whole psychology of writing. There were purists, however, who feared the besmirching of the muse by such a turn to rank commercialism. Nevertheless, *Biblioteka dlia chteniia*, with its handsome payment policy, continued to attract outstanding contributors to its fold. Even from the list of names in its first issue the Russian reader could sense the large number and quality of contributors from which Senkovsky could draw: Evgenii Abramovich Baratynsky, Baron Brambeus (Senkovsky), Faddei Venediktovich Bulgarin, Prince Petr Andreevich Viazemsky, Fedor Nikolaevich Glinka, Nikolai Ivanovich Grech, Denis Vasil'evich Davydov, Vasilii Andreevich Zhukovsky, Mikhail Nikolaevich Zagoskin, Aleksandr Bestuzhev-Marlinsky, Prince Vladimir Fedorovich Odoevsky, Petr Aleksandrovich Pletnev, Mikhail Petrovich Pogodin, Antonii Pogorel'sky (Aleksei Alekseevich Perovsky), Nikolai Alekseevich Polevoi, Aleksandr Pushkin, Semen Egorovich Raich, Nikolai Gogol, Count Dmitrii Ivanovich Khvostov, Aleksei Stepanovich Khomiakov, Prince Aleksandr Aleksandrovich Shakhovskoi, Stepan Petrovich Shevyrev, Aleksandr Semenovich Shishkov, and Nikolai Mikhailovich Iazykov.

Senkovsky lent his great experience, including his apprenticeship with the *Towarzystwo Szubrawców* back in Wilno, to making his magazine a mirror of his own immense knowledge. He set for journalism a valuable example of punctuality, organization, accuracy, and perseverance at the same time that he provided his Russian readers with the greatest quantity of useful and thought-provoking information in a simple and attractive form. There can be little doubt that as editor and guiding spirit of *Biblioteka dlia chteniia* he remained faithful to the concept of the periodical as outlined in the Szubrawcy code. His despotic behavior in "correcting" manuscripts submitted to him, his conscientious observance of his own code of journalistic ethics, and his indefatigability as a critic and author gave his magazine an ap-

pearance of directional uniformity and operational discipline. There is no doubt that Senkovsky regarded the task of educating the Russian reading public as a sacred duty.

All this time Senkovsky was intimately involved with his original professional career, that of Professor of Oriental Languages at the University of St. Petersburg, where he gave his inaugural lecture on 18 August 1822. During his tenure at the University, from 1822 to 1847, he taught an enlightened approach to the study of Near Eastern languages and literatures, urging his students (among whom was included the later major novelist Ivan Turgenev) to shed all prejudices in their approach to Arabic studies and to make their European way of thinking conform to the psychology of the peoples under study. Senkovsky's twenty-five years as professor were crowded with various activities. He was appointed dean of the faculty at one time, and he occupied positions as member of the Educational Committee and as an inspector of public schools. In 1828 he was appointed to the government board of censorship. His first academic love, however, remained the world of the Near East. His lectures were not confined to bare linguistics and language courses but embraced the whole spectrum of the Orient—its geography, history, literature, and culture. In maintaining his high standards and scholarly methods Senkovsky did much to ensure the emergence of future generations of Russian Orientalists. At the conclusion of the war between Russia and Persia in 1828 Senkovsky urged Nicholas I to demand from the Persians, as terms for the treaty of peace, certain manuscripts and documents from their libraries. The result was that whole archives in Persian libraries were sent by the victorious Russian armies to St. Petersburg. To this day the Academy of Sciences in St. Petersburg remains one of the world's richest repositories of Persian literature, thanks in great measure to Senkovsky's enterprising activity. Indeed, Senkovsky's important contributions as an Oriental scholar still await the specialist's treatment.

Senkovsky's scholarly Oriental works embraced nearly the entire span of his life in St. Petersburg. Even before he returned from his Near Eastern travels, he had sent articles on his impressions to Polish periodicals. And upon his arrival in St. Petersburg he continued submitting his travel notes to Russian journals. But Senkovsky's serious literary activity began with direct translations of Oriental stories. These translations were rare in the foreign literatures available to the Russian reading public. Indeed, Senkovsky was the first to introduce the Oriental short story into Russia directly from the

East. Such stories had previously appeared through the medium of Western European translations. Prompted by Smirdin, Senkovsky soon began to experiment with his own original parodies of the Oriental short story. The Eastern motif became one of the favorite devices of his literary activity and served him as a means of introducing local color into his stories. This technique may be seen in many of his later works: he used Egypt in *Povesti. Povest'* (Stories. A Story, 1834) and *Mikeriia, nil'skaia liliia* (Mikeria, Lily of the Nile, 1845); India in *Chto takoe liudi! Basnia v proze* (What People Are Like! A Fable in Prose, 1833); Turkey in "Poèticheskoe puteshestvie po belu-svetu" (The Poetic Journey Over the Great, Wide World) and *Turetskaia tsyganka* (The Turkish Gypsy Girl, 1835); Baghdad in *Shchastlivets. Vostochnaia povest'* (A Happy Man, 1834); China in *Chin-chun, ili Avtorskaia slava* (Chin-Chun, or the Fame of an Author, 1834) and *Sovershenneishaia iz vsekh zhenshchin. Kitaiskie dela* (The Most Perfect of All Women. Chinese Affairs, 1845); Mongolia in *Pokhozhdeniia odnoi revizhskoi dushi* (The Adventures of a Registered Soul, 1834); Transcaucasia in *Predubezhdenie. Stat'ia odnogo cheloveka* (Prejudice. An Article by a Certain Man, 1834) and *Padenie Shirvanskogo tsarstva* (The Fall of the Kingdom of Shirvan, 1842); and Africa in *Prevrashchenie golov v knigi i knig v golovy* (The Transformation of Heads into Books and of Books into Heads, 1839).

Although his activities at the university had by necessity to yield to his exhausting duties as a writer and as editor of *Biblioteka dlia chteniia,* the classical training and inspiration that Senkovsky had received from Joachim Lelewel in Wilno remained close to his heart. The Orient was Senkovsky's first love, and it remained the guiding passion of his entire career. The Muslim world was not merely a source of rich material advantage for him. It was a way of life. At home he loved to re-create the atmosphere of the Near East as he had experienced it in his travels. Visitors to his home would often be announced by a lackey clapping his hands in the Oriental manner. From behind the portieres would come a similar sound in reply, and the guest would then be admitted to Senkovsky's presence. His study was furnished in Oriental style, and in its depths, among a multitude of multicolored Turkish cushions, reclined "Baron Brambeus." He was usually dressed in a blue Albanian jacket and red Turkish trousers, wearing a red fez on his head. On the Oriental carpets stood a crystal hookah, through which Senkovsky would emit a stream of aromatic smoke.

Ideal'naia krasavitsa (An Ideal Beauty), one of Senkovsky's most entertaining novels, appeared serially in *Biblioteka dlia chteniia* from 1841 to 1844. It

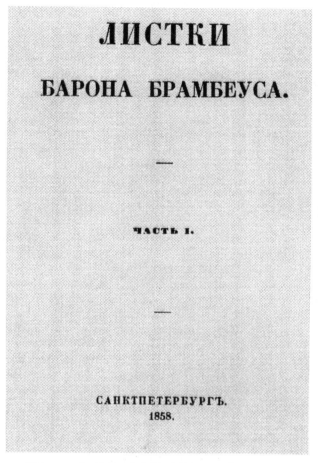

ЛИСТКИ

БАРОНА БРАМБЕУСА.

—

ЧАСТЬ I.

—

САНКТПЕТЕРБУРГЪ.
1858.

Title page for Senkovsky's Listki Barona Brambeusa
(The Notes of Baron Brambeus)

includes some of his most critical appraisals of the social concepts and institutions of the Romantic school. In this five-part work Senkovsky tells the story of Anna, a girl of great beauty, who defies her parents and falls in love with Valerian, a young poet, because of his "great soul and inner beauty." Senkovsky creates a deliberate twist in the usual Romantic plot by having Anna fall out of love with Valerian when the poet forsakes his poetry in order to ensure her a conventional future happiness. By the time the former poet returns to St. Petersburg, he finds Anna the unhappy wife of Count Edward, an empty-headed dandy. Valerian, now a celebrated general, once again pursues Anna, but she tells him, in an obvious parody of Pushkin's *Evgenii Onegin* (1833), that she is married to another. When, after many travels, she learns that he has killed her husband in a duel in Geneva, she parts from Valerian forever since she cannot even think of marrying the murderer of the father of her two children. Rejected by her children, she dies brokenhearted and penniless. Here, as throughout his other novels, Senkovsky turns to his women readers and begs them not to succumb to the wiles of the contemporary Romantic novel. He warns them to be on their guard against the wiles of those novelists who would like nothing more than

> . . . to turn you, the queens of nature, you, the sovereigns over the bearded sex, into their drudges, into housewives and nurses, into accurate and industrious German *fraus,* into commonplace mamas, lacking poetry and luster. Take care! I am giving you fair warning, I, your constant well-wisher, your faithful and humble servant, Baron Brambeus.

In a long, sustained passage of satirical metaphor Senkovsky takes aim at one of the most persistent social realities of nineteenth-century Russia, the "winter campaign" of mothers to procure husbands for their unmarried daughters. This is the battlefield of winter balls, on which takes place the "frightful slaughter of bachelors in which so many amiable young men perish every winter," victims of "petticoat generals," the mamas, among whom there are, indeed, "some amazing strategists." Senkovsky concludes his ironic description of the "winter campaign" with a parody of Famusov's famous lament at the end of act 1 of Aleksandr Sergeevich Griboedov's comedy *Gore ot uma* (Woe from Wit, 1861):

> . . . It's a great enterprise to be the mother of grown-up girls of marriageable age! And, on the other hand, how indifferent the world is to real talent. To this day there is not a single biography of a great mother who has won several brilliant campaigns one after the other, without losing a single kopeck of dowry.

In 1846 Senkovsky went abroad for four months on the advice of his physicians. In August of the next year he retired from the University of St. Petersburg. Stricken with cholera, he gave up his editorship of *Biblioteka dlia chteniia* in 1848. Broken in health and wearied by the incessant attacks made on him by the civic-minded critics, Senkovsky felt that his ten years of association with *Biblioteka dlia chteniia* had accomplished nothing permanent. This despondency over his literary career remained with him to his last days. And yet, almost on the eve of his death, Senkovsky began writing feuilletons for *Syn otechestva* (The Son of the Fatherland) under the title "Listki Barona Brambeusa" (Leaflets of Baron Brambeus). In these final articles he gave his advice to the would-be journalist. A person preparing to found a magazine, he insisted, should try to discover one thing above all: the tastes of the majority of the reading public. "Only a fool," he concluded bitterly, would "imagine that he is in a position to remake mankind or to instruct people according to his own intelligence." Disappointed and disillusioned with what he saw transpiring in the literary world and troubled by grave doubts of his own role in that sphere, Senkovsky felt increasingly a sense of frustration and hopelessness. In the last years of his life he lamented that "the Russia that used to read me in bygone days knew me and loved me, but the present generation neither knows me nor loves me." Senkovsky died on 4 March 1858.

Although he was arguably the most popular writer of the 1830s and 1840s in Russia, Senkovsky remained under a cloud for more than a century after his death. Times had changed drastically. His bantering wit, one of the enduring hallmarks of his talent, seemed out of place in the serious world of literary criticism and art fostered by Belinsky, Nikolai Gavrilovich Chernyshevsky, and Nikolai Aleksandrovich Dobroliubov, with its emphasis upon the utilitarian and the socially progressive. Endowed by nature with a cool, almost classical, detachment, he made few close friends and many bitter enemies. His provokingly skeptical attitudes toward contemporary social and literary phenomena; his light, mocking treatment of the most sacred subjects; his "fool's wit," as Ivan Andreevich Krylov called it, placed him in the role of a perverse dealer in cynicism in the opinion of the serious-minded and dedicated men of the time. Only in the twentieth century has there appeared an attempt to reassess Senkovsky's contributions to Russian literature, including his pioneering work in the realm of Russian science fiction and fantasy. This second look at the Polish-Russian enigma was made by Veniamin Kaverin (in *Baron Brambeus,* in 1929 and *Literator. Dnevniki i pis'ma,* in 1988). Kaverin's seminal work has prompted renewed interest in Senkovsky, leading to a reprinting of the fiction of Senkovsky in the final years of the Soviet Union.

Biographies:

Veniamin A. Kaverin, *Baron Brambeus* (Leningrad: Izdatel'stvo Pisatelei v Leningrade, 1929);

Louis Pedrotti, *Józef-Julian Sekowski. The Genesis of a Literary Alien* (Berkeley & Los Angeles: University of California Press, 1965).

References:

Elizaveta N. Akhmatova, "Osip Ivanovich Senkovskii (Baron Brambeus)," *Russkaia Starina* (May 1889): 273–312; (August 1889): 317–360;

Larisa Gulianovna Alieva, *O. I. Senkovskii-puteshestvennik i vostokoved* (Moscow: Aftoreferat, 1977);

Vsevolod Igorevich Avdiev and Nina Pavolvna Shastina, eds., *Ocherki po istorii russkogo vostok-ovedeniia,* (Moscow: Izdatel'stvo Akademii nauk SSSR, 1953);

Nikolai Gavrilovich Chernyshevsky, *Ocherki gogo-levskogo perioda russkoi literatury* (Moscow: Gosu-darstevennoe izdatel'stvo khudozhestvennoi literatury, 1953);

Aleksandr Vasil'evich Druzhinin, "O. I. Senkovskii," *Sobranie sochinenii,* volume 7 (St. Petersburg: Imperatorskaia Akademiia Nauk, 1865);

Nikolai Gogol, "O dvizhenii zhurnal'noi literatury v 1834 i 1835 godu," *Sobranie sochinenii v shesti to-makh,* volume 6 (Moscow: Gosudarstvennoe izdatel'stvo khudozhestvennoi literatury, 1959);

Viktor M. Guminsky, ed., "O russkoi fantastike," *Vzgliad skvoz' stoletiia. Russkaia fantastika XVIII i pervoi poloviny XIX veka* (Moscow: Molodaia Gvardiia, 1977), pp. 320–334;

Guminsky, *Otkrytie mira, ili Puteshestviia i stranniki* (Moscow: *Sovremennik,* 1987);

Veniamin A. Kaverin [Zil'ber], *Literator. Dnevniki i pis'ma* (Moscow: Sovetskii Pisatel', 1988);

Kaverin, "Senkovskij (Baron Brambeus)," in *Russian Prose,* edited by B. M. Èikhenbaum and Yury Tynyanov, translated by Ray Parrott (Ann Arbor: Ardis, 1985), pp. 127–149.

Fedor L'vov, "Zamechaniia na slog Barona Bram-beusa," *Moskovskii Telegraf,* 1, part 55 (1834): 666–676;

Aleksandr Miliukov, "Znakomstvo s O. I. Senkovskim," in *Literaturnye vstrechi i znakomstva* (St. Petersburg: Izdanie A. S. Suvorin, 1890), pp. 82–104;

Vladimir Dmitrievich Morozov, "O. I. Senkovskiy i ego «Biblioteka dlia chteniia»," in *Ocherki po isstorii russkoi kritiki vtoroi poloviny 20-30-kh godov XIX veka* (Tomsk: Izdatel'stvo Tomskogo universiteta, 1979), pp. 271–305;

Nikolai Ivanovich Pavlishchev, "Zdravyi smysl i baron Brambeus," *Teleskop,* 221 (1834): 249–259;

Louis Pedrotti, "Senkowski's Defense of Pushkin's Prose," *The Slavic and East European Journal,* 7, no. 1 (1964): 18–25;

Pedrotti, "Senkovsky's Baron Brambeus and the Rosetta Stone," in *Language. Literature. Linguistics,* edited by Michael S. Flier and Simon Karlinsky (Berkeley: Berkeley Slavic Specialties, 1987), pp. 178–191;

Pedrotti, "Warfare Celestial and Terrestrial: Osip Senkovsky's 1833 Russian Science Fantasy," in *Fights of Fancy. Armed Conflict in Science Fiction and Fantasy,* edited by George Slusser and Eric S. Rabkin (Athens: University of Georgia Press, 1993), pp. 49–58;

T. Roboli, "Literatura «puteshestvii»," in *Russkaia proza,* edited by B. M. Èikhenbaum and Yurii Tynianov (Leningrad: Academia, 1926); reprinted and edited by C. H. Van Schoneveld (The Hague: Mouton, 1963);

Roboli, "The Literature of Travel," in *Russian Prose,* edited by B. M. Èikhenbaum and Yurii Tynyanov, translated by Ray Parrott (Ann Arbor: Ardis, 1985), pp. 45–66;

Pavel Stepanovich Savel'ev, "O zhizni i trudakh O. I. Senkovskogo," in *Sobranie sochinenii Senkovskogo (Barona Brambeusa),* volume 1, by O. I. Senkovsky (St. Petersburg: Imperatorskaia Akademiia Nauk, 1858), pp. xi–cxii;

Teodor Adamovich Shumovskiy, "Put' arabista Senkovskogo," *Vostochnyi Al'manakh,* Vypusk 7-oi, edited by S. Khokhlova (Moscow: Izdatel'stvo "Khudozhestvennaia literatura," 1979), pp. 603–625;

S. Stavrin, "O. I. Senkovskiy," in *Delo,* volume 6 (St. Petersburg, 1874), p. 33.

Papers:

Some of Senkovsky's papers are located in the Library of the Jagiellonian University in Cracow, Poland, as well as in the Paskinskii Dom in St. Petersburg, Russia.

Vladimir Aleksandrovich Sollogub

(20 August 1813 – 17 June 1882)

Maxim D. Shrayer
Boston College

BOOKS: *Na son griadushchii. Otryvki iz povsednevnoi zhizni,* 2 volumes (St. Petersburg: A. Ivanov, 1841–1843);

Bukety, ili peterburgskoe tsvetobesie. Shutka v odnom deistvii (St. Petersburg: Imperatorskaia Akademiia Nauk, 1845);

Tarantas. Putevye vpechatleniia (St. Petersburg: A. Ivanov, 1845);

Biografiia generala Kotliarevskogo (Tiflis: Kantseliariia namestnika kavkazskogo, 1854);

Tridtsat' chetyre al'bomnykh stikhotvoreniia (Tiflis, 1855);

Chinovnik. Komediia vodnom deistvii (St. Petersburg: E. Veimar, 1856);

Une Preuve d'amitié (Paris, 1859);

Vospominania grafa Solloguba. Gogol', Pushkin i Lermontov Novyia svedeniia o predsmertnom poedinke Pushkina. Chitano v Obshchestve liubitelei rossiiskoi slovesnosti (Moscow: Grachev, 1866);

Razocharovannye. Komediia v 1-m deistvii (Moscow: T. Ris, 1867);

Novyi Egipet (Publichnyi otchet i putevye vpechatleniia) (St. Petersburg: Skariatin, 1871).

Editions and Collections: *Sochineniia,* 5 volumes (St. Petersburg: A. Smirdin, 1855–1856);

Povesti i rasskazy, 3 volumes (St. Petersburg, 1886);

Vospominaniia grafa Vladimira Aleksandrovicha Solloguba (St. Petersburg: A. S. Suvorin, 1887);

Dnevnik Vysochaishego prebyvaniia imperatora Aleksandra II za Dunaem v 1877 godu (St. Petersburg, 1888);

Povesti i rasskazy, third edition, 3 volumes (St. Petersburg: A. S. Suvorin, 1902–1903);

Tarantas. Putevye vpechatleniia (Moscow-Petrograd: GIZ, 1923);

Vospominaniia, edited by S. P. Shesterikov (Moscow-Leningrad: Akademiia, 1931);

Vodevili (Beda ot nezhnogo serdtsa. Sotrudniki, ili chuzhim dobrom ne nazhivësh'sia. Gorbun, ili vybor nevesty) (Moscow: Goslitizdat, 1937);

Povesti i rasskazy, edited by E. I. Kiiko (Moscow: Gosudarstvennoe izdatel'stvo khudozhestvennoi literatury, 1962);

Tri povesti, edited by A. Ospovat (Moscow: Sovetskaia Rossiia, 1978);

Vladimir Aleksandrovich Sollogub

Izbrannaia proza, edited by V. A. Mil'china (Moscow: Pravda, 1983);

Povesti i rasskazy, edited by N. I. Iakushin (Moscow: Sovetskaia Rossiia, 1988);

Povesti i vospominaniia, edited by I. S. Chistova (Leningrad: Khudozhestvennaia literatura, 1988);

Tarantas. Izbrannie proizvedeniia (Kiev, 1989);

Peterburgskie stranitsy vospominanii grafa Solloguba, edited by E. D. Zavalishina (St. Petersburg: Afina, 1993).

Editions in English: *The Tarantas. Travelling Impressions of Young Russia by Count Sollogub* (London: Chapman & Hall, 1850);

His Hat and Cane. A Comedy in One Act, translated from the French by members of the Bellevue dramatic club of Newport (Boston: W. H. Baker, 1902);

"The Snowstorm," translated by William Edward Brown, in *Russian Romantic Prose: An Anthology,* edited by Carl R. Proffer (Ann Arbor: Translation Press, 1979), pp. 263–277;

The Tarantas. Impressions of a Journey (Russia in the 1840s), translated and edited by William Edward Brown (Ann Arbor, Mich.: Ardis, 1989).

OTHER: *Vchera i segodnia,* 1–2, edited by Sollogub (St. Petersburg: Kantseliariia namestnika kavkazskogo, 1845–1846);

"Sa canne et son chapeau," in *Théatre de campagne,* second series (Paris: P. Ollendorff, 1877–1884), pp. 165–187;

"L'embarras du choix," in *Théatre de campagne,* sixth series (Paris: P. Ollendorff, 1881), pp. 165–175.

TRANSLATION: Ivan Turgenev, *Une nichée de gentilhommes; moeurs de la vie de province en Russie,* translated by Sollogub and A. de Calonne (Paris, J. Hetzel, n.d.).

SELECTED PERIODICAL PUBLICATION–UNCOLLECTED: "O kak prokhladno i veselo nam. . . , " by Sollogub and M. Iu. Lermontov, *Literaturnoe nasledstvo,* 58 (1952): 369–372.

Literary history has not been kind to Vladimir Sollogub: his fame lasted but a decade while memories of his faded popularity amused the reading public throughout the late 1860s. Sollogub was viewed by many of his contemporaries in the 1840s as Russia's most popular belletrist–hailed by Vissarion Grigor-'evich Belinsky after Lermontov's death as second only to Gogol. Both his short novels dealing with society, such as *Bol'shoi svet* (Great High Society, 1840), and his tales of the provinces, such as *Aptekarsha* (The Druggist's Wife, 1841), caused sensations in the Russia of Nicholas I; they were read by St. Petersburg society ladies and provincial petty landowners alike. Sollogub's 1845 *Tarantas* (Tarantas)–a novel-length work of mixed genres and narrative modes–became one of the earliest Russian best-sellers. The success of *Tarantas,* partly because of its appearance at the height of the Slavophile-Westernizer ideological controversy, compelled Belinsky to say the following in a letter to Aleksandr Ivanovich Gertsen: "Only three books were consumed in Russia with such ferocity: *Dead Souls, Tarantas,* and *The Petersburg Collection.*" The importance of Sollogub as a cultural phenomenon becomes evident if one peruses the correspondence and memoirs of nineteenth-century Russian writers and critics. His name figures in the correspondence of Aleksandr Sergeevich Pushkin, Nikolai Vasil'evich Gogol, Ivan Turgenev, and Leo Tolstoy. Ivan Ivanovich Panaev and Petr Dmitrievich Boborykin devoted lengthy, albeit critical, passages to Sollogub in their memoirs. A

gifted playwright, Sollogub created several vaudevilles and comedies that became part of the solid repertoire of the mid-nineteenth-century Russian theater; at least one of the vaudevilles, *Beda ot nezhnogo serdtsa* (Trouble from a Tender Heart, 1850), enjoys occasional productions even today.

Sollogub entered the literary scene in the 1830s and remained associated with it, if more and more remotely, until the 1870s. His remarkable memoirs present a self-portrait of a litterateur who was familiar with several pleiads of nineteenth-century Russian writers, from the writers of the Pushkin circle to Tolstoy and Fyodor Pavlovich Dostoyevsky. Sollogub witnessed many major developments in Russian letters, from the Romantic-ironic tales of late Pushkin and the adventurous narratives of Aleksandr Aleksandrovich Bestuzhev (pseudonym, Marlinsky) to the physiological sketch of the Natural School to the novels of high realism. He knew half a century of Russian literature firsthand but never associated intimately with any of its actors or trends, maintaining a remarkable stability of a liberal aristocratic world vision. Certainly one of the most gifted writers of his time, a possessor of a pen much finer than that of either Nikolai Alekseevich Polevoi, Faddei Venediktovich Bulgarin, or Marlinsky, to name a few popular contemporaries, Sollogub has not earned the place he deserves in Russian literary history. Passionate for literature but often aloof from fellow writers, a literary dilettante par excellence, Sollogub remained, in the estimation of a contemporary, a litterateur in high society and an aristocrat in literary circles.

Count Vladimir Aleksandrovich Sollogub was born on 20 August 1813 in St. Petersburg to an aristocratic family of Polish-Lithuanian stock (*magnaty*) dating back to the second half of the fifteenth century. The writer's paternal grandfather, Ivan Antonovich Sollogub, came to the court of Catherine II in 1790 after the first partition of Poland in 1773. While excelling in service at the court, he married Natal'ia L'vovna Naryshkina, a union that made him a relation of the royal dynasty of the Romanovs. (Peter the Great's mother was a Naryshkin.) Sollogub's father, Count Aleksandr Ivanovich, achieved prominence in the high society of St. Petersburg, gained the rank of Privy Counselor and Master of Court Ceremonies, and drifted away from his ancestors' Catholicism toward Orthodoxy. Sollogub's father married Sofia Ivanovna Arkharova, the daughter of Moscow's legendary military governor, Ivan Petrovich Arkharov, whose name gave way to a new coinage in Russian, *arkharovtsy* (bullies, cutthroats), originally referring to his ever-vigilant and fast police force; the Arkharov Moscow house is mentioned in Tolstoy's *War and Peace* (1863–1869).

Both by birth and social standing, the Sollogubs belonged to the cream of Russian society and played a visible role in the affairs of the court. Alexander I thought highly of Sollogub's mother, Sofia Ivanovna, and enjoyed lengthy conversations with her. In his memoirs Sollogub recalls the tsar's visits to their house, where his mother would receive the tsar in the company of her children but without her husband. A telling incident was etched forever in the would-be writer's memory. A large portrait of the emperor hung in the sitting room; the sign in French read: "Alexander I, Autocrat of All the Russias." In the midst of his mother's conversation with the tsar, Sollogub asked what *autocrat* meant. The tsar supposedly smiled and said: "It is apparent that he is recently from Paris. They did not teach him this word there." The Sollogubs were fairly rich: Sollogub's paternal grandfather is said to have owned up to 80,000 serfs. Through other familial ties the Sollogubs were related to Russia's most aristocratic families: the Rimsky-Korsakovs, the Kochubeis, the Shakhovskois, and others. Sollogub's father was well-known as a theater-lover and patron of the arts; Pushkin mentions him in the drafts of chapter one of *Evgeny Onegin*: "The ubiquitous Sollogub carouses." Thanks to his familial and social origins, Sollogub could hope for a brilliant career as civil servant and courtier. Fate made different arrangements, however.

Sollogub received a first-rate French-style early education at home, which, along with visits to France during his childhood, yielded good results: he wrote several comedies in French and even translated Ivan Turgenev's *Dvorianskoe gnezdo* (A Nest of the Gentry, 1859) into French in the 1860s. Sollogub's Russian teacher was Petr Aleksandrovich Pletnev, an elegiac poet and fine critic. As an adolescent Sollogub frequented the house of his relative, Aleksei Nikolaevich Olenin, president of the Academy of Arts and director of the Imperial Library. There he was first exposed to Russia's best writers and painters: Pushkin, Vasilii Andreevich Zhukovsky, Nikolai Ivanovich Gnedich, and Karl Pavlovich Briullov. Sollogub spent his summers in Pavlovsk, where his grandmother from Moscow had a summer house. The Arkharov household put Sollogub in touch with the patriarchal Moscow tradition, the tradition of pre-Petrine Russia.

Sollogub's first experiments at versification date back to the 1820s: he translated George Gordon, Lord Byron, and composed a Romantic long poem, *Stan* (The Army Camp). In 1830 Sollogub entered Derpt University (present-day Tartu [Estonian], or Iur'ev [Russian]) in Estonia. An old German university with medieval traditions of student brotherhood and active participation in the affairs of the university, Derpt differed from other universities of the Russian Empire.

Additionally, the intellectual climate of post-Kantian idealism, with the ideas of Friedrich Wilhelm Joseph von Schelling and Friedrich von Schlegel and his school influencing Sollogub's generation of students, must have had an impact on Sollogub's worldview. The acute sense of fine form and the authorial distance from his subjects that mark Sollogub's best prose go back to his Derpt, schooling. At Derpt, Sollogub befriended the sons of the great historian Nikolai Mikhailovich Karamzin, Andrei and Aleksandr, as well as the future pioneer of Russian surgery, Nikolai Ivanovich Pirogov. Along with the other Russian students of the predominantly German university, Sollogub experienced the legendary presence of Nikolai Mikhailovich Iazykov, a fine poet who had studied earlier at Derpt. Sollogub later collected his own imitative poems in an 1855 edition, *Tridtsat' chetyre al'bomnykh stikhotvoreniia* (Thirty-Four Album Poems). Several of Sollogub's lyrics, such as his "Serenada" (A Serenade), were made into popular *romansy* (love songs) and still remain part of the Russian classical repertoire. The Romantic spirit of Sollogub's student years was reflected in his 1843 *Neokonchennye povesti* (Unfinished Tales).

Another high point of Sollogub's student years was his meeting with Gogol in the summer of 1831. Sollogub was vacationing in Pavlosk when he was advised to meet the tutor of the Vasil'chikovs, to whom the Sollogubs were related. Sollogub first treated with condescension the "skinny young man" who "was dressed poorly and seemed timid"; then Sollogub heard Gogol read: "I shall never forget his facial expression! What an acute mind showed in his slightly squinting eyes, what a caustic smile slanted his thin lips but for a moment. . . . When he was finished, I threw myself at his neck and wept. What he read to us, I could not say even now, but, despite my youth, I felt, with my instinct if you will, how much high artistry was present in what he read. The name of the young man was Nikolai Vasil'evich Gogol." Sollogub's friendly relationship with Gogol continued until Gogol's death in 1852; Gogol and Sollogub were especially friendly when they both lived in Nice (1843–1844). During the 1831 vacation Sollogub also met Pushkin.

In his memoirs Sollogub dwells at length on his two-year acquaintance with Pushkin, Russia's greatest writer. In 1865, when Sollogub was elected member of the Society of Lovers of Russian Literature, he gave a public lecture that centered on his never-consummated duel with Pushkin in 1836 and on Pushkin's 1837 fatal duel with Baron Georges Charles d'Anthès-Heeckeren. Upon graduation from the university in 1834 Sollogub joined the civil service and began to appear in St. Petersburg high society. At a social gathering Sollogub—then a twenty-three-year-old dandy—addressed Pushkin's wife, Natal'ia Nikolaevna, with some semi-innocent jokes concerning her marriage and her dancing partners. Pushkin found this out from his wife and, protective of her honor, challenged the young count to a duel. Sollogub was eager to end the quarrel peacefully; after several rounds of negotiations and Sollogub's ornate apologetic note to Mme Pushkin, the duel was called off. After the incident Pushkin began to take an interest in Sollogub, especially since they both belonged to the same literary circles (Sofia Karamzin's salon and Olenin's salon, for example). According to Sollogub's memoirs Pushkin on one occasion "told me a few words so flattering [about my early writings] that I would not dare repeat them; however, these words remain the most delightful memory of my literary life." Sollogub played an important part in Pushkin's first duel with d'Anthès by serving as Pushkin's second. His account of the circumstances of the first duel with d'Anthès (it was called off) and the second, fatal one add an interesting perspective to the vast literature about Pushkin's last years.

Sollogub joined the civil service in 1835 as a special envoy at the Ministry of Internal Affairs. His first rank was only of the twelfth class in Russia's fourteen-class Table of Ranks. Had he done better on the exit examinations at Derpt he would have earned the degree of Candidate and a higher rank. Unfortunately Sollogub graduated only as a *deistvitel'nyi student* (certified student). His first assignment involved investigation of the old-believers' rituals in the Tver' region. Serving predominantly in the provinces (Smolensk, Vitebsk, Tver') and making frequent appearances in both capitals, Sollogub advanced his career and in 1837 received a promotion to *kollezhskii sekretar'* (captain's rank in civil service). In 1838 he was granted the court rank of *kamer-iunker,* prestigious for a man of his age. Further promotions followed.

In 1840 Sollogub married Sofia Mikhailovna Viel'gorskaia, the daughter of Count Mikhail Iur'evich Viel'gorsky, an important figure at the court and a famous patron of the arts. The wedding took place in the small chapel of the Winter Palace; Nicholas I was the bride's proxy. The Sollogubs had several children, although from the 1860s until Sofia Mikhailovna's death in 1878, the couple lived separately. Despite many opportunities and major connections, Sollogub did not distinguish himself in service; he lacked bureaucratic zeal, eschewed servility, and carried himself with an air of enormous self-importance. Throughout his career he would also take long leaves to travel and live on his estates; he even took a two-year trip to Europe from 1843 through 1844.

In 1842, already a *kollezhskii assessor* (major's equivalent), Sollogub switched to the State Chancellery, where he served until 1848 and earned two more promotions. In 1849 Sollogub left the service and lived for a year on his estate Nikol'skoe in the Simbirsk region. There is speculation that Sollogub was asked to retire because his superiors were not happy with his work. However, in 1850 Sollogub reentered the service, now in Tiflis (Tbilisi), Georgia, as special assistant to the governor-general of the Caucasus, Mikhail Semenovich Vorontsov. This time Sollogub was apparently seeking an opportunity to earn recognition for his service, but in part because of his dandyish mannerisms and his artistic inclinations, his superior did not take him seriously. Sollogub did receive a general's rank (*statskii sovetnik*) in 1852; but a chance for a "brilliant" career had been lost.

While in the Caucasus, Sollogub was active in promoting Russian theater in the region, wrote for the Tiflis newspaper *Kavkaz,* and also collected materials for a biography of Gen. Petr Stepanovich Kotiarevsky, one of the heroes of Russia's wars in the Caucasus. General Vorontsov asked Sollogub to write Kotliarevsky's biography, which came out in Tiflis in 1854 and subsequently underwent two more editions, the last one in 1901 in St. Petersburg. In 1856 Sollogub returned to the capital, where, with the ascension of Alexander II to the throne, changes were sweeping the imperial court. Sollogub was asked to compile a description of the new tsar's coronation. The court of the new ruler favored Sollogub more than had the court of the previous tsar, Nicholas I. Sollogub received a highly prestigious court rank of *kamerger* (equivalent to lieutenant general) and was popular among the royal princesses as a skillful storyteller.

From 1857 through 1859 Sollogub was in France on an assignment from the Minister of the Court, Count Vladimir Fedorovich Adlerberg, to study Paris theaters in order to adopt their practices in Russia. Upon his return from abroad, Sollogub took on a post in Derpt, where he served in the office of the Governor-General of the Baltic Province. Sollogub's next major assignment was—ironically, considering his society tales and vaudevilles—in the field of correctional facilities. In the 1860s he dedicated a great deal of his time to research in the field of correctional institutions and even wrote special studies on the subject: a monograph, *Ob organizatsii v Rossii tiuremnogo truda* (On the Organization of Prison Labor in Russia, 1866), and a long essay with the provocative title "Tiur'my i teatry" (Prisons and Theaters, 1867). These seemingly unconnected spheres—prisons and theaters—were to be brought together through philanthropy. After a research trip to France in 1870 Sollogub headed the

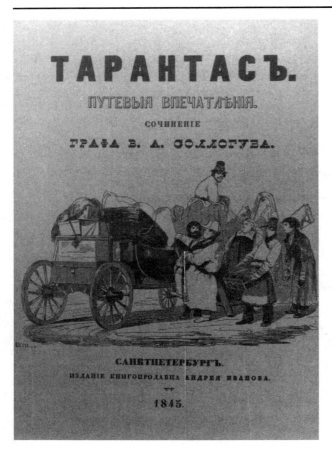

Cover and frontispiece for Sollogub's novel Tarantas, *inspired by his 1839 trip with painter*
Grigorii Grigor'evich Gagarin to the Kazan' region

Moscow Prison Council, and in 1875 he was appointed chairman of the Committee on Prison Improvement.

Sollogub was appointed to his last major position—a triumph of sorts for a rather vain official in his sixties—in 1877 during the Russo-Turkish War. He was made official historian and traveled with Alexander II across the Danube to the imperial headquarters. The trip resulted in a homiletic narrative, published in St. Petersburg in 1878 and titled *Dnevnik vysochaishego prebyvaniia imperatora Aleksandra II za Dunaem v 1877 godu* (Journal of the Royal Sojourn of the Emperor Alexander II Beyond the Danube in 1877). In 1878 after his wife's death Sollogub married a much younger woman with whom he had been living for some time. Vera Ivanovna Arkudinskaia did not come from an aristocratic family; her station and her age evoked disapproval in high society. Sollogub spent the last five years of his life abroad; he died on 17 June 1882 in Hamburg, Germany.

While Sollogub's career in the civil service may not have been spectacular, it progressed steadily and brought him high ranks and at least some public recognition in his later years. His career in letters, on the other hand, was completely different: short and turbulent. Sollogub the writer enjoyed his heyday throughout the 1840s, when the Russian reading public favored him. However, he experienced oblivion and contempt during the radical, brooding 1860s and 1870s, when critics viewed him as a literary anachronism, a barren extension of the Pushkinian Golden Age.

Sollogub's career as a prose writer falls under the triple shadow of Lermontov, Gogol, and Pushkin, with whom he shares some literary kinship. Several works of the 1830s, Sollogub's early period, reveal thematic and structural affinities with Lermontov's prose, especially the tale "Serezha" (1838) and the short novel *Bol'shoi svet* (Great High Society, 1840). Both are society stories that dissect the complex codes of Russia's aristocracy. Both portray young officers, in part Byronic passionate loners, in part small-time heirs of provincial gentry seeking careers in society; Sollogub's protagonists share traits of both Pechorin and Grushnitsky from Lermontov's *Geroi nashego vremeni* (Hero of Our Time, 1840). In terms of narrative design, Sollogub's early fiction resembles that of Lermontov's in many ways, especially in the "architecture" of the denouement and ending. However, Sollogub's prose does not include the romantic adventures and fatal intrigues of Lermontov's fiction. Thus, a duel between the protagonist, Leonin, and his rival, Shchetinin, is called off, and the protagonist leaves the capital and his dreams of high society, unlike the protagonist in *Geroi nashego vremeni,* who kills his rival.

The literary relationship between Sollogub and Lermontov, both the authors and their texts, was never of a simple, unilateral nature. Sollogub and Lermontov were almost the same age; they entered the literary scene roughly at the same time; they were personally well acquainted through Sofia Karamzin's salon; and together they composed an album poem, "O kak prokhladno i veselo nam . . . " (O, how cool and happy we feel). In his memoirs Sollogub gives a vivid account of his meetings with Lermontov, including a scene in Mme Karamzin's salon, where Lermontov read the first part of his long poem *Demon* (1829–1839): "When he finished, tears began to roll down his cheeks, and all of us, fascinated by the great poeticity of his piece and the unique musicality of his sounds, began to praise it." Lermontov was then compared to Pushkin; he responded, addressing Sollogub: "No, . . . I still have a long way to go toward Pushkin's level . . . and I have very little time left to work; I will be killed, Vladimir." Lermontov perished in a duel in 1841. Throughout his long career Sollogub carried memories of the "young genius," as he calls Lermontov in his memoir.

Sollogub never merely borrowed from Lermontov. For half a decade both men wrote and lived in the same milieu. Some of their works were even published around the same time in the same journals. For instance, the "Taman'" chapter of *Geroi nashego vremeni* was printed in *Otechestvennye zapiski* (Notes of the Fatherland) in February 1840; *Bol'shoi svet* appeared in the same journal in March 1840. Sollogub was certainly aware of several Lermontovian features in his own works, such as the masquerade motif in *Bol'shoi svet,* which is similar to that in Lermontov's verse drama *Maskarad* (Masquerade, written in 1834–1835, published in 1842), but Sollogub lacked Lermontov's deeply philosophical sense of the tragedy of a Romantic subject. Where Lermontov is skeptical and fatalistic, Sollogub is melodramatic. Where Lermontov is dark and demonic, Sollogub is light and airy. The great age of Russian Romanticism nevertheless needed both a Lermontov and a Sollogub.

Sollogub's prose debut, the short story "Tri zhenikha" (Three Marriage Suitors), appeared in 1837 in *Sovremennik* (The Contemporary). This publication, along with the short story "Dva studenta" (Two Students) and the tale "Serezha," which followed several

months later, were noted in literary circles but did not bring Sollogub fame. However, 1839 was a pivotal year in Sollogub's literary career–he became famous overnight when *Otechestvennye zapiski* (Notes of the Fatherland) printed his tale "Istoriia dvukh kalosh" (A Story of Two Galoshes). Ivan Ivanovich Panaev, a prominent literary figure of the 1840s and 1850s, testifies to the great popularity of the work in his memoirs: "Istoriia dvukh kalosh" created such an uproar that it was read even by those who never ever read anything . . . at least in Russian; for a week society spoke of nothing but those 'Galoshes.'. . . Sollogub was in great demand." Several memoirs of the 1830s, including a chapter in Panaev's memoirs, mention an anecdotal incident caused by the publication of Sollogub's tale. While waiting for his carriage after a ball, Sollogub decided to make fun of a certain A. With ironic solemnity, Sollogub announced "A.'s carriage over here!" To Sollogub's dismay, A. responded with "Sollogub's galoshes over here!"

"Istoriia dvukh kalosh" is a skillfully constructed narrative about a talented German musician, Karl Schultz, who seeks both professional recognition and love in St. Petersburg. Like many of his German compatriots, he is drawn by the many opportunities for success in the Russia of the first third of the nineteenth century. Karl is also fatally in love with Henrietta, a poor young woman of Baltic-German extraction and a *demoiselle de compagnie* to a rich Russian princess. Although Henrietta promised Karl she would wed him in the future, she is married off to Fedorenko, an older man and an opportunistic bureaucrat of middle rank. Karl's musical talent has no room for expression in St. Petersburg, where even the musicians are concerned with appearance and social intrigues. Karl ultimately dies of a brain infection. What holds the narrative together are the two pairs of galoshes, ordered from the same shoemaker, also a German, by Fedorenko and Schultz. During Schulz's visits to Henrietta, the galoshes–her husband's good pair and the musician's poor one–get mixed up; this allows the semi-omniscient narrator to furnish his story with a flavor of light irony. This is not to say that Sollogub's prose lacks moments of penetrating pathos–for instance, Schultz's words to his beloved at the end of the tale: "–I am telling you that I am a beggar. . . . I teach children to read, I entertain apprentices, I lie and bow; I bow when they push me and beat me. . . . I am telling you that I am a beggar. . . . " Written in elegant, modern Russian, "Istoriia dvukh kalosh" holds interest even today.

The "German theme" appears in several of Sollogub's early works and deserves closer examination. Several tales of the 1840s take place in Germany or depict German characters in a Russian setting, especially

One of Gagarin's 1839 travel illustrations, which were used by Sollogub as the basis for Tarantas

the so-called *ostzeiskie nemtsy,* the Baltic Germans. Sollogub's interest in and knowledge of the German culture goes back to his schooling at Derpt. He can be credited with introducing the milieu of German universities into Russian fiction. A case in point is the short novel *Aptekarsha* (The Druggist's Wife, 1841), which centers on Baron Firnheim, one of the many Baltic Germans (the Baltic lands belonged to the Russian crown) in the Russian imperial service. *Aptekarsha* was pronounced the best tale of the year by Belinsky, a leading critic of the time. Firnheim, the hero, is only a remote literary cousin of Hermann in Pushkin's "The Queen of Spades" (1833); Firnheim is rich and lacks fatal passions.

A St. Petersburg dandy bent on his career, Firnheim is sent to a remote provincial Russian town on an assignment. There he encounters a German druggist, his former classmate at the university, who is married to Firnheim's former college sweetheart, the daughter of an old German professor. A meeting with Charlotte, Firnheim's first love, brings a wave of memories that the narrator offers the reader in a flashback of free indirect discourse.

Sollogub's descriptions of life in a German university town, reminiscent of Derpt, have no equivalents in Russian literature. Both thematically and artistically, they possess a distinct flavor of German Romantic prose, namely that of Johann Wolfgang von Goethe and Heinrich Wilhelm von Kleist; yet they present a Russocentric perspective of a young Baltic German making a career in Russia. *Neokonchennye povesti* (Unfinished Tales, 1843) deals with three Russian friends during their schooling in Germany at the University of Heidelberg.

The short novel *Bol'shoi svet,* published in 1840 in *Otechestvennye zapiski,* typifies Sollogub's early Romantic period. The novel carries a subtitle, "Povest' v dvukh tantsakh" (Tale in Two Dances), which signals a mazurka-like narrative pace and a focus on ballroom intrigues. In his memoirs Sollogub provides the background for his short novel: "I became well acquainted with Lermontov at the Karamzins and was a contributor to *Otechestvennye zapiski* at the same time that he was. I portrayed his status in high society [*svetskoe znachenie*] under the name Leonin in my short novel *Bol'shoi svet,* written upon a request [*po zakazu*] from the Grand Princess Mariia Nikolaevna." Sollogub uses the phrase "status in high society" in order to make a distinction between, on the one hand, the status of Lermontov the great writer, and on the other, that of Lermontov the young junior officer in the society of St. Petersburg in the 1830s. Speculation has it that the Grand Princess Mariia Nikolaevna, daughter of Nicholas I (whose court ill-tolerated the young, daring poet), wanted Lermontov mocked and requested that Sollogub do so in a society tale.

Bol'shoi svet created quite a sensation and became a subject of heated discussions in both capitals. As Petr Andreevich Viazemsky put it, "much of Petersburg was sought and found in it through both hints and actualities." However, one would have to stretch the evidence in order to see *Bol'shoi svet* as an assault on Lermontov. Lermontov himself thought highly of the work as did both Andrei Aleksandrovich Kraevsky and Belinsky. Shadows of several other of Sollogub's contemporaries flit through the text, although there is never a full correspondence. Thus, for example, Saf'ev's prototype might have been Sergei Aleksandrovich Sobolevsky, a good friend of Pushkin and a bibliophile; Countess Vorotynskaia somewhat resembles Countess Aleksandra Kirillovna Vorontsova-Dashkova, one of the most celebrated beauties of her time; Naden'ka has something of Sollogub's first wife Viel'gorskaia; and Prince Shchetinin carries some traits of the author himself. Still, in real life Sollogub's first wife was never a bride without a dowry; Sollogub never served in the Guards; and Sobolevsky and Dashkova never had a love affair. In addition, Sollogub makes a point of separating both Lermontov and himself from the characters they supposedly inform; at one point Shchetinin says to Vorotynskaia: "Would you like me to play whist with your deaf auntie, and then go to a recital of L's verses and S-b's tales?" In the context of the late 1830s, the encoded names refer to Lermontov the poet and Sollogub the prose writer. Another Lermontov connection may be found in the masquerade motif, prominent in Sollogub's short novel. The possible connections between Lermontov's drama in verse *Masquerade* and Sollogub's *Bol'shoi svet* still await investigation.

Sollogub's piece opens with a masquerade scene. Leonin—a young officer from a good, albeit provincial, family—has just been transferred to the Guards from the Army. Accompanied by Saf'ev, an older, unmarried skeptic and prominent society figure, Leonin makes his first appearance in high society. The naive Leonin desires acceptance into society, which appears masquerade-like due both to its glamour and to its practice of covering spiritual emptiness with a mystifying facade. Despite Saf'ev's many warnings, Leonin falls in love with Countess Vorotynskaia, a married woman and a careful intriguer, and becomes her hopeless admirer. What he does not know, however, is that the Countess allows him to admire her only to keep him at bay and manipulate him. Vorotynskaia's younger sister, Nadina, newly adolescent at the beginning of the play and a seventeen-year-old at the end, was betrothed to Leonin in her mother's will, a fact Vorotynskaia takes quite seriously. What makes the intrigue more tangled is that Prince Shchetinin, a brilliant officer and a sophisticated society lion, has been in love with Nadina since he first saw her as a thirteen-year-old.

The description of Shchetinin's first encounter with Nadina foregrounds what a modern reader might call "the Lolita motif," an adult's fatal infatuation with a teenage girl. What is surprising is that portraits of Nadina are even given semantic overtones similar to Vladimir Nabokov's descriptions of Lolita in the eponymous novel. Namely, what attracts Shchetinin to Nadina is some sort of otherworldly aura, some angelic beauty, some hope of paradise regained: "At this moment a girl of about thirteen fluttered (*porkhnula*) past him chasing a butterfly. . . . Never had Shchetinin seen anything better, fresher than this semiterrestrial being (*poluzemnoe sushchestvo*). It was as though she had stepped down from one of Raphael's paintings, from a crowd of his angels, and mixed with the colors of Spring, with the rays of the morning sun for a celebration of Nature. Shchetinin's soul grew brighter and seemed to have expanded. . . . He felt, not knowing why, that upon beholding her, his soul rested [*dusha otdykhala*] from heavy labor." At the denouement, Leonin challenges Shchetinin to a duel, thinking him his main rival in his pursuit of Vorotynskaia. At the last moment, the duel is called off as Leonin's old grandmother (possibly based on Lermontov's grandmother, E. A. Arsen'eva) arrives from the provinces and rescues her grandson. Leonin has no claims for Nadina and leaves her to Shchetinin. His career in Petersburg comes to an end.

Sollogub's "Gogolian" period has received more attention in criticism, both from his contemporaries and from twentieth-century critics, than all of his other works combined. The reasons have more to do with the epistemological situation of the mid 1840s, when Sollogub published *Tarantas,* than with the literary value of this travelogue. The first seven chapters of *Tarantas* were printed in *Otechestvennye zapiski* in 1840; the complete book edition did not appear until 1845. The years 1843 to 1844 marked the height of Sollogub's friendship with Gogol; they were both living in Nice at the time. Sollogub's memoirs present an insight into Gogol's artistic temperament in the mid 1840s. Gogol thought highly of Sollogub's work and tried to encourage him to write on a regular basis, as a professional, and not to write upon fits of inspiration: "How many times did Gogol' scold me for my laziness!—Somehow I cannot get myself to write today, I would say.—But still you must write. . . . Take a fine little feather, sharpen it well, place a sheet of paper in front of yourself, and begin as follows: 'Today I cannot get myself to write' [*Mne segodnia chto-to ne pishetsia*]. Write this several times, and suddenly a good idea will visit you, then another one, a third one, because no one writes otherwise, while those who are constantly burdened by their imagination are quite rare, Vladimir Aleksandrovich!" In several letters to Sollogub's mother-in-law, his first wife, and in at least one surviving letter to Sollogub, Gogol inquires about his

Sollogub in 1830

friend's literary news and asks that all Sollogub's new publications be sent to him abroad.

Several critics, from the early Petr Aleksandrovich Pletnev and Iurii Fedorovich Samarin to the recent William Edward Brown and Andrei Semenovich Nemzer, have commented on the discrepancy of style between the earlier chapters of *Tarantas* and the later chapters, added in the book edition. Sollogub conceived *Tarantas* in the autumn of 1839 during a trip to his Simbirsk estate from Moscow via Kazan', which Sollogub undertook with his friend the painter Ggrigorii Grigor'evich Gagarin. As they were riding across provincial Russia, Gagarin made sketches of the landscape and local life. They decided that Sollogub would write an account of their trip and thereby "illustrate" Gagarin's drawings with descriptions of their journey. Etchings from several of Gagarin's sketches were printed in the 1845 edition, a testament to the highly sophisticated book techniques of the time. (Several copies still survive in major research libraries.)

Tarantas is a colorful account of a trip from Moscow to the Kazan' region. Two protagonists inhabit its

textual space. Vasilii Ivanovich, a landowner from the Kazan' region, is wrapping up his business in Moscow when he encounters his neighbor's son, a young man by the name of Ivan Vasil'evich who has just returned from abroad where he has spent several years traveling and studying the "current ideas." Since both are heading home, Vasilii Ivanovich offers to give his neighbor's son a ride in his tarantas, an old-fashioned four-wheeled Russian traveling carriage without springs. Ivan Vasil'evich accepts his neighbor's invitation, for it would give him a chance to reacquaint himself with his "ancient homeland." The young man has brought with him from Europe a contempt for Western civilization and a yearning to embrace the native Russian traditions unspoiled by rationalism and progress. Whether and to what extent Ivan Vasil'evich's ideas represent and parody those of the Slavophiles is still open to discussion. Suffice it to say that the young patriot fails in his plan to write an account of his trip that would restore the pride of the Russian people.

Ivan Vasil'evich suffers from what Brown calls myopia; what Ivan Vasil'evich perceives as *realia* of Russian life are in fact distorted fictions of his exalted imagination. Ivan Vasil'evich's myopia is especially ironic since he aspires to produce a panoramic, comprehensive picture of Great Russia. As Samarin puts it, Ivan Vasil'evich is consciousness devoid of life. This certainly makes his character counterbalance that of Vasilii Ivanovich, who lacks consciousness and is all life, Rabelesian and unbridled. Toward the end of their journey, Ivan Vasil'evich has a vatic dream in which Russia's future appears to him endowed with the law and grace of the pre-Petrine era. In the dream, the tarantas turns into a giant bird with folklore overtones (a fire-bird, for example), which flies Ivan Vasil'evich over his idealized Russia, which is now like the folktale Kitezh-grad embraced by the Slavophiles. To the young philosopher's dismay he wakes up as the tarantas is making its way into a classic Russian roadside ditch some two feet deep.

Although not the best of Sollogub's fiction, *Tarantas* received an enormous share of public attention in the mid 1840s and was considered a major literary event of the decade. In fact Sollogub is generally mentioned in literary histories as the author of *Tarantas,* his other fiction rarely given as much attention. A quick glance at the history of the reception of the novel might explain the reasons for such a judgment. In an 1845 review published in *Otechestvennye zapiski* Belinsky set the tone for considering *Tarantas* as Sollogub's response to the Slavophile-Westernizer ideological debate. Calling Ivan Vasil'evich one of the secondary "heroes of his time," a petty Don Quixote and a little worm (*cherviachok*), Belinsky insisted that the Slavophiles received a terrible blow in the person of

Ivan Vasil'evich. Nothing, says Belinsky, is scarier than the ridiculous (and he clearly implies that the Slavophiles are ridiculous) because the ridiculous is the execution of "ugly nonsense." Vasilii Ivanovich represents, in Belinsky's reading, the complete opposite of his young companion. A member of an earlier generation, he possesses a great deal of common sense and is "smart like nature herself is smart." The fellow-travelers do not communicate well: Ivan Vasil'evich's abstract and lofty phrases say nothing to the well-grounded Vasilii Ivanovich. That Ivan Vasil'evich's name happens to coincide with Ivan Vasil'evich Kireevsky, one of the leading Slavophiles, permitted Belinsky to speculate about Sollogub's satirical intentions. Many important literary figures wrote about *Tarantas,* including Nikolai Alekseevich Nekrasov in *Literaturnaia gazeta* (The Literary Gazette).

Tarantas overshadowed most of Sollogub's literary production, including the conspicuous tales of the middle period such as "Sobachka" (A Lap Dog, 1845) and "Vospitannitsa" (The Countess's Ward, 1846), published in the first and second volumes of the remarkable collection *Vchera i segodnia* (Yesterday and Today, 1845–1846), which Sollogub put together and edited. "Sobachka" and "Vospitannitsa" are the two parts of a compositional whole titled *Temenevskaia iarmarka* (The Temenev Fair). The Gogolian traits of *Tarantas* have been observed by several critics: the transformation of the tarantas into a giant bird at the end of the travelogue recalls Gogol's archetypal image of Russia as *ptitsa-troika* (bird-troika) at the end of volume one of Gogol's *Mertvye dushi* (Dead Souls, 1842). However, no one has yet noticed the strong Gogolian overtones in *Temenevskaia iarmarka,* the title of which recalls Gogol's tale "Sorochinskaia iarmarka" (The Soroka Fair, 1831). Features of Gogol's celebrated Nozdrev from *Mertvye dushi* surface in the description of landowners trading horses at the Temenev fair. Both the character of the mayor and the dramatic irony of "Sobachka" must have been informed by Gogol's 1836 comedy *Revizor* (The Inspector-General).

"Vospitannitsa," a story of a poor ward making a career in provincial theater, reveals remarkable parallels with Aleksandr Ivanovich Gertsen's fine tale "Soroka-Vorovka" (A Magpie-Thief), also published in 1846; it, too, dwells on the subject of actresses' dubious status in early Russian theater. In her memoir *Iz dal'nikh let* (From Distant Years, 1878–1889) Tat'iana Petrovna testifies that Sollogub knew Gertsen in the 1840s in Moscow and even visited him with Petr Iakovlevich Chaadaev. Passek also claims that Sollogub belonged to the wing of the Westernizers along with Chaadaev, Boborykin, and others. These connections illustrate the complexity of the cultural climate of the 1840s when Sollogub reached literary fame. In 1846, when "Vospitannitsa" came out, Sollogub was destined for only four more years of active prose writing. He used them well.

Soviet critics of Sollogub insist that his prose underwent the necessary evolution from the aristocratic Romanticism of his early tales to the realistic presentation of Russian life in *Tarantas.* Even the most sensitive of them, Nemzer, while speaking of a surprising stability of Sollogub's artistic sensibility and therefore seemingly defying the Marxist evolutionary arguments, still considers Sollogub a transitional link between tales of the Romantic era and those of the Natural School. The attributing of Sollogub to the Natural School may be considered hasty and forced, given the evidence about his aesthetics and ethics. The Natural School itself is a highly problematic term—referring both to a circle of litterateurs from the 1840s to the early 1850s who grouped around Nekrasov, Panaev, and Belinsky and participated in the 1844–1845 collection *Fiziologiia Peterburga* (The Physiology of Petersburg) and to a wide range of writers on the mid-nineteenth-century literary scene with some interest in representation of the mores of the population. While many fine writers, including Vladimir Ivanovich Dal' and Dmitrii Vasil'evich Grigorovich, made a contribution to the physiological sketch, the emblematic genre of the Natural School, Sollogub's leanings of the late 1840s were of an entirely different kind.

Disproving the evolutionary schemas of his would-be critics, Sollogub's later tales such as the 1849 "Metel'" (The Snowstorm) and the 1850 "Starushka" (The Little Old Lady) display a movement toward the absolute perfection of Pushkin's prose tales. Thus Sollogub's literary development moves—backward in terms of chronology—from the Lermontovian via the Gogolian towards the Pushkinian. Pushkinian elements had begun to manifest themselves in Sollogub's earlier fictions. For instance, "Sud'ba" (Fate), the last chapter of "Istoriia dvukh kalosh," subtextualizes the sequence of "The Queen of Spades," in which the old Countess winks at Hermann from her coffin. This passage suggests Sollogub already had Romantic/ironic leanings.

The problem of Romantic irony as underlying the poetics and philosophy of Sollogub's later works calls for a separate scholarly inquiry. Sollogub's ties to German Romantic idealism quite likely go back to his years at Derpt. However, it took Sollogub fifteen years, most of his short career in prose fiction, to arrive at an understanding of Romantic irony that comes close to that of Pushkin. The beginning of "Metel'" acknowledges its indebtedness to Pushkin's tale of the same title from *The Tales of I. P. Belkin* (1831).

In Sollogub's tale, written in eloquent, first-rate Russian with a fine economy of artistic means and devices, an officer of the Guards gets stuck at a transit station in the midst of an awful snowstorm. He meets a remarkable young woman, the wife of a provincial landowner. A communication develops: "Pri ètikh slovakh ofitser nevol'no vzglianul na svoiu sosedku: legkaia ulybka edva zametnym mertsaniem probezhala po ee chertam. Oni poniali drug druga." (At these words the officer could not help but look at the lady sitting next to him: a shadowy smile flickered across her features. They understood each other). The statement "they understood each other," so simple and yet so powerful, pointing as do several of Pushkin's prose tales to the covert modernist perfection of Ivan Alekseevich Bunin's prose, explains the nighttime revelatory conversation between the officer and the provincial lady. They both know that they will never see each other again and that their communication is possible only as long as the snowstorm continues. "The Snowstorm" is an open text par excellence that leaves etched in the reader's memory an ephemeral sadness and a sense of unreconciled and yet harmonizing ambiguities: "Oloviannoe solntse vyrezyvalos' piatnom na serom tumannom nebosklone. Metel' konchilas'." (The tin-like sun carved itself across the gray foggy horizon. The snowstorm ended).

"Starushka" carries perhaps a stronger dose of Romantic irony than "Metel'." Its ties to Pushkin's text, this time directly to "The Queen of Spades," become apparent from an early scene in the story. The tale describes a lesson in aristocratic sensibility that an old countess gives her young grandson. Like the Countess in Pushkin's tale, Sollogub's *starushka* is old and rich. She lives in a huge house with a plethora of servants and companions who are slowly robbing her as best they can. The old countess decides to take in a new companion, Nasten'ka, a young daughter of a poor civil servant, who in turn agrees to investigate the situation of the countess's provincial estates, which do not yield enough income. Like poor Lizan'ka of "The Queen of Spades," Nasten'ka develops an infatuation with a young aristocrat whom she sees only from the window of her father's apartment. After she moves to the countess's house, Nasten'ka finds out that the young man is the countess's grandson, Prince Andrei (in Pushkin's tale, the countess's grandson Tomsky is also a prince).

The affection between the two young people grows and thus compels the old countess to offer her grandson a lecture about his responsibilities as an aristocrat. In her view a love affair only befits a young aristocrat, while a marriage to a poor companion goes against both the code of high society and the laws of their family's heredity. The tale ends on an indeterminate note. Prince Andrei does not dispute his grandmother's words but only kisses her hand. The final short paragraph describes the old countess in a mystical state as she catches a glimpse of eternity: "The countess . . . sat for a while in her deep armchair, playing with a golden snuffbox. Her lips whispered some soundless indistinct words while all her features reflected her sad mocking smile." Thus ends Sollogub's short but brilliant career in prose fiction.

Sollogub gave Russian Romantic motifs and designs a plasticity of presentation; he popularized them and adjusted them for mass consumption. Sollogub was one of the first proper Russian belletrists—that is, a writer with a perfect sense of how literary devices (Gogolian and Pushkinian in this case) and composition ought to be balanced with theme to ensure that the reader is engaged. Although understanding such a balance may sound obvious today, one should keep in mind that Russia did not have a native belle lettres until the 1830s; prior to that time Russian readers consumed primarily French novels and translations. The old Countess in Pushkin's "The Queen of Spades" cannot hide her great astonishment when her grandson offers her a Russian novel: "Do Russian novels really exist?"

Sollogub never stopped writing. Wherever he went—to the Caucasus, to Europe, or back to his alma mater in Derpt—he would contribute to the local publications, write one-time comedies for various occasions, or give public lectures. However, nothing he wrote after 1850, save his remarkable—albeit unfinished—memoirs, would eclipse either *Bol'shoi svet* or "Metel'." In 1857 the radical critic Nikolai Aleksandrovich Dobroliubov contributed a long review article on Sollogub to *Sovremennik* (The Contemporary) on the occasion of the publication of a five-volume edition of Sollogub's works, produced by a major publisher, Aleksandr Filippovich Smirdin. Dobroliubov gave Sollogub credit for his "brilliant eloquence in treating descriptions and conversations" and for his "remarkable wit." He described Sollogub's later career as many attempts to attract the public's attention. In Dobroliubov's relentless judgment, by the mid 1850s the public had come to identify Sollogubian types (cold dandies indifferent to societal problems) with their author and had turned away. However true this assertion may be, although Sollogub's collected works underwent at least three editions in the pre-1917 era, by the 1850s the aesthetics of Sollogub's prose had become passé and was being superceded by the approaching wave of high realism.

Sollogub almost made a serious comeback in 1856 when his play *Chinovnik* (A Civil Servant) premiered in St. Petersburg. Sollogub had been known in the 1850s for his masterful vaudevilles and comedies. The most notable of these, *Beda ot nezhnogo serdtsa* (Trouble from a Tender Heart, 1850) and *Sotrudniki, ili chuzhim dobrom ne nazhivesh'sia* (Collaborators, or You Cannot Benefit from Other Peoples' Good, 1851), have been discussed (and anthologized) in conjunction with crucial transformations in the Russian theater by the great playwright Aleksandr Nikolaevich Ostrovsky. *Chinovnik* deals with the plight of an honest government worker surrounded by the universal corruption of Russia, a country on the verge of the major reforms of the 1860s. A rather predictable play with a banal ideological spring, *Chinovnik* was at first hailed by the court (where it was originally presented) but earned deserved disapproval from the leading writers and critics of the time. The most excruciating blow was struck by Nikolai Filippovich Pavlov in a long analysis printed in *Russkii vestnik* (Russian Messenger). In a letter written in 1856, Ivan Turgenev, well-acquainted with Sollogub but always irritated by his aristocratism, called the play artificial and perfectly fit for the Parisian Théatre du Gymnase. Turgenev predicted the future: during Sollogub's assignment in Paris from 1857 to 1859, his French comedy, *Une preuve d'amitié* (A Proof of Friendship) premiered at Théatre du Gymnase on 21 May 1859. Sollogub wrote several other comedies in French.

Sollogub lived a remarkably long life. He was a year older than Lermontov and four years Gogol's junior; he died a year after Dostoevsky and less than a year before Turgenev, both his juniors by several years. The correspondence of Turgenev includes thirteen letters to Sollogub and at least a dozen mentions, including a sarcastic quotation from Sollogub's popular song "Blagodariu—ne ozhidal" (Thank you—I didn't expect that). In the 1840s Sollogub held a literary salon, which was frequented by the writers Vladimir Fedorovich Odoevsky, Ivan Aleksandrovich Goncharov, Turgenev, Nekrasov, Grigorovich, the composer M A. Glinka, and the actor Mikhail Semenovich Shchepkin. Despite his aristocratic aloofness (which disturbed his fellow litterateurs, especially the ones of lower birth) Sollogub is described as having had a passion for new works and a welcoming heart for new writers.

In the 1860s Sollogub and a few living witnesses of the Russian Golden Age (Odoevsky, Sobolevsky, and Mikhail Petrovich Pogodin) formed a circle that maintained the traditions of the 1830s. A need to preserve his precious memories compelled Sollogub to reminisce, first in shorter essays, such as "Iubilei kniazia P. A. Viazemskogo" (The Anniversary of Prince P. A. Viazemsky, 1861), and then in longer memoir articles. Written in fragments throughout the 1860s, Sollogub's unfinished *Vospo-minaniia* (Memoirs) present the students of the Age of Pushkin and Gogol with a rare perspective of an ideal memoirist, both as an insider and active litterateur, and as an outsider, an estranged witness with sharp powers of observation. Sollogub's memoirs, in which chronology and thematic organization are unified by their author's persona, now capable of high society *causerie,* now of profound insights, include a wealth of information about the interaction among literary circles and aristocratic society in the 1830s and have few equivalents in Russian letters.

The main subjects of Sollogub's memoirs are Pushkin, Gogol, and Lermontov—his literary beacons; however, many other participants in the social and literary life of the 1830s also appear—including members of the imperial family and major courtiers. The following description of Pushkin a few months before his fatal duel is especially memorable: "Then he read to me the well-known letter to the Dutch ambassador [Heeckeren, stepfather of Baron d'Anthes-Heeckeren]. His lips began to tremble, his eyes filled with blood. He was so shaken with anger that it was only then that I understood that he was indeed of African descent. What could I object to in view of such excruciating passion?" Sollogub never completed his memoirs. An old, ill man, not happy with his young wife, he described his experiences in the unfinished novel *Cherez krai* (Over the Edge), published posthumously in *Nov'* (Virgin Soil) in 1885. Sollogub spent the last five years of his life away from Russia, in the Crimea and in Europe. He died in Hamburg on 17 June 1882 and was buried in Moscow at the Donskoi Monastery in the family sepulchre.

In 1846 Sollogub contributed a peculiar poem to Nekrasov's famous collection *Peterburgskii sbornik* (The Petersburg Collection), an anthology which introduced the young Dostoevsky to Russian readers. Sollogub's poem, titled "Moi autographe" (My Autograph), begins as follows: "K chemu vam autographe? / Skazhite mne po sovesti! / Chto byl kakoi-to graph, / Pechataiushchii povesti. . . ." (Why would you need my autograph? / Tell me in all honesty! / So there was once some Count, / Who published tales . . .). This poem, hardly a coquettish album piece, especially when printed next to Turgenev's translation of one of Goethe's *Roman Elegies,* can be read as Sollogub's prophetic and sad pronouncement on his literary destiny.

Letters:

To Vasilii Andreevich Zhukovsky, two letters from 1840–1844, *Russkii arkhiv,* No. 7 (1902): 454–456;

To Leo Tolstoy, two letters from 1863–1873, in Tolstoy's *Pis'ma Tolstogo i k Tolstomu. Iubileinyi sbornik* (Moscow-Leningrad, 1928), pp. 259–263;

To Aleksandr Sergeevich Pushkin, four letters from 1936, in Pushkin's *Polnoe sobranie sochinenii,* volume 16 (Moscow-Leningrad: Akademiia, 1949), pp. 78, 84, 89, 110.

References:

Vissarion Grigor'evich Belinsky, *Polnoe sobranie sochinenii,* volumes 5, 9 (Moscow: Akademia Nauka SSR, 1954–1955)–"Review of *Na son griadushchii,*" volume 5, pp. 153–158; "Review of *Vchera i segodnia,*" volume 9, pp. 28–37; "Review of *Tarantas,*" volume 9, pp. 75–117; "Russkaia literatura v 1845 godu," volume 9, pp. 388–390;

M. Belkina, "Vodevil' Solloguba," in Sollogub's *Vodevili* (Moscow, 1937), pp. 3–46;

Petr Dmitrievich Boborykin, *Vospominaniia,* volumes 1–2 (Moscow, 1965), volume 1, pp. 165–167 and passim; volume 2, p. 437 and passim;

Aleksandr Kornil'evich Borozdin, "V. A. Sollogub" in *Russkii biograficheskii slovar'* (St. Petersburg, 1909), pp. 96–98;

William Edward Brown, "Translator's Afterword: Literary and Ideological Aspects of Sollogub's Tarantas," in Sollogub's *The Tarantas. Impressions of a Journey (Russia in the 1840s),* translated and edited by William Edward Brown. (Ann Arbor, Mich.: Ardis, 1989);

Nikolai Gavrilovich Chernyshevsky, "Review of Sollogub's *Aptekarsha,*" in *Polnoe sobranie sochinenii,* volume 2 (Moscow: Goslitizdat, 1949), p. 755;

I. S. Chistova, "Belletristika i memuary Vladimira Solloguba," in Sollogub's *Povesti i vospominaniia* (Leningrad, 1988);

Nikolai Aleksandrovich Dobroliubov, "Review of *Sochineniia grafa Solloguba, 1855–1856,*" in *Sobranie sochinenii,* volume 1 (Moscow-Leningrad: Gosudarstvennoe izdatel'stvo khudozhestvennoi literatury, 1961), pp. 520–543;

Nikolai Ivanovich Iakushin, "Pisatel' s zamechatel'nym darovaniem," in V. A. Sollogub's *Povesti i rasskazy* (Moscow, 1988), pp. 3–20;

Ivan Vasil'evich Kireevsky, "Review of Na son griadushchii'," *Moskvitianin,* no. 1, part 2 (1845): 22–23;

Nikolai Alekseevich Nekrasov, "Review of *Tarantas,*" in *Polnoe sobranie sochinenii i pisem,* volume 9 (Moscow: Gosudarstvennoe izdatel'stvo khudozhestvennoi literatury, 1950), pp. 151–162;

Andrei Semenovich Nemzer, "Povesti Solloguba na fone romanticheskoi traditsii," *Vestnik moskovskogo universiteta. Seria 9, Filologiia,* no. 6 (1982): 45–50;

Nemzer, "Proza Vladimira Solloguba," in Sollogub's *Izbrannaia proza* (Moscow, 1983), pp. 3–20;

Ivan Ivanovich Panaev, *Literaturnye vospominaniia* (Moscow: Gos. izd-vo khudozh. Lit-ry, 1950), pp. 128–130, 269–274, 303–304, and passim;

Nikolai Filippovich Pavlov, "Razbor komedii grafa Solloguba *Chinovnik,*" *Russkii vestnik* (June 1856): 454–511; (July 1856): 385–418;

Iuri Fedorovich Samarin, "Review of *Tarantas,*" in *Sochineniia,* volume 1: *Stat'i raznorodnogo soderzhaniia i po pol'skomu voprosu* (Moscow, 1900), pp. 1–27;

John Schillinger, "V. A. Sollogub," in *Handbook of Russian Literature,* edited by Victor Terras (New Haven, Conn.: Yale University Press, 1985), p. 433;

Maxim D. Shrayer, "Rethinking Romantic Irony: Pushkin, Byron, Schlegel and *The Queen of Spades,*" *Slavic and East European Journal,* 36 (Winter 1992): 397–414;

Semyon Afanas'evich Vengerov, "Sollogub," in *Èntsiklopedicheskii slovar'* (Brokgauz i Éfron), 30a (St. Petersburg, 1900), pp. 756–758;

Anna Ivanovna Zhuravleva, "V. A. Sollogub," in *Russkaia drama èpokhi Ostrovskogo,* edited by A. I. Zhuravleva (Moscow, 1984), pp. 439–445.

Papers:

The papers of Sollogub are deposited in the Rossiiskii Gosudarstvennyi Arkhiv Literatury i Iskusstva (Russian State Archive of Literature and Art; formerly the Central State Archive of Literature and Art), Moscow, fond (Archive) No. 453; and at RGB (Russian State Library, formerly the Lenin Library, Moscow), fond No. 622.

Orest Mikhailovich Somov

(10 December 1793 – 27 May 1833)

John Mersereau Jr.
University of Michigan

BOOK: *O romanticheskoi poezii. Opyt v 3-kh stat'iakh* (St. Petersburg, 1823).

Editions and Collections: *Orest Somov: Selected Prose in Russian,* edited by John Mersereau Jr. and George Harjan, Michigan Slavic Materials no. 11 (Ann Arbor: Department of Slavic Languages and Literatures, University of Michigan, 1974);

Byli i nebylitsy, edited by Nina Nikolaevna Petrunina (Moscow: Sovetskaia Rossiia, 1984).

SELECTED PERIODICAL PUBLICATIONS–
UNCOLLECTED: "O parizhkikh teatrakh. Pis'ma k kniaziu Tsertelevu," *Blagonamerennyi,* no. 10 (1820) 348–355;

"Pis'mo k Fedoru Nikolaevichu Glinke. Dresden," *Sorevnovatel',* 11 (1820): 370–375;

"Prazdnik v Sadu Tivoli. Pis'mo k izdateliu 'Blagonamerennogo'," *Blagonamerennyi,* no. 19 (1820): 33–43;

"Gaidamak. Malorossiiskaia byl'," *Nevskii al'manakh* (1827);

"Obzor rossiiskoi slovesnosti za 1827 god," *Severnye tsvety* (1828): 3–82;

"Gaidamak," *Severnye tsvety* (1828): 227–300;

"Obzor rossiiskoi slovesnosti za 1828 god," *Severnye tsvety* (1829): 3–110;

"Otryvok iz malorossiiskoi povesti 'Gaidamak'," *Syn otechestva,* no. 23 (1829): 133–150; no. 24 (1829): 197–213; no. 25 (1829): 261–273;

"Obozrenie rossiiskoi slovesnosti za pervuiu polovinu 1829 goda," *Severnye tsvety* (1830): 3–114;

"Ispolin-rak. Anekdot (iz rasskazov puteshestvennika)," *Podsnezhnik* (1830): 1–19;

"Ispolinskie gory (iz rasskazov puteshestvennika)," *Literaturnaia gazeta,* no. 69 (1830): 263–267; no. 70 (1830): 271–274; no. 71 (1830): 279–282; no. 72 (1830): 287–290;

"Nochleg gaidamakov (Iz malorossiiskoi povesti 'Gaidamak')," *Dennitsa* (1830): 67–88;

"Obozrenie rossiiskoi slovesnosti za vtoruiu polovinu 1829 i za pervuiu 1830 goda," *Severnye tsvety* (1831): 3–100;

"Videnie na iavu (Improvizatsiia odnogo vesel'chaka v svetskom krugu)," *Girlianda,* no. 4 (1831): 93–103;

"Ispolinskie gory," *Sanktpeterburgskii vestnik,* 1 (1831);

"Boroda Bogdana Bel'skogo. Otryvok iz byli vremen Godunova," and "Brodiashchii ogon' (Iz malorossiiskikh bylei i nebylits)," *Al'tsiona* (1832): 121–130; 153–159.

Orest Somov was one of the major figures in the Russian Romantic movement, but he was virtually forgotten almost immediately after his early death in 1833 at the age of thirty-nine. Only in the second half of the twentieth century has interest in him revived enough that efforts have been made to evaluate his contributions to the theory of Romanticism, to the development of the prose literary language, and to fiction itself. This earlier neglect doubtless was caused by the complex literary and political conditions that prevailed during the century after his death: first, his talent as an author was eclipsed by better-known contemporaries, especially Aleksandr Pushkin and Nikolai Gogol; then, with the advent of realism in the 1840s, interest in Romantic fiction quickly waned. In the Soviet period critical attention was paid to authors who might best be exploited for their political views and activities, such as Aleksandr Aleksandrovich Bestuzhev (Marlinsky), Kondratii Fedorovich Ryleev, Aleksandr Ivanovich Polezhaev, and others. But Somov, despite his close association with several of the Decembrists, particularly Bestuzhev and Ryleev, and notwithstanding his having been arrested immediately after the abortive revolution of 14 December 1825, was in fact not one of the conspirators and apparently was not even aware of the plot to overthrow Tsar Nicholas I. Moreover, his fictional works, unlike those of Bestuzhev, for example, did not provide grist for the propaganda mills of Soviet literary scholarship, so Somov was exiled to the limbo of footnotes. The deliberate or casual indifference to his contribution was not only unfair to his reputation but it also became a factor in the distortion of

Russian literary history. There was no individual collection of his works published in the Soviet Union until 1984, the 150th anniversary of his death, when Nina Nikolaevna Petrunina published some twenty Somov stories in a volume titled *Byli i nebylitsy* (True Tales and Legends). The collection includes Petrunina's comprehensive introduction and notes, and, as if to compensate for many years of neglect, 400,000 copies were printed.

In addition to Somov's important contribution to belles lettres and criticism, he was also one of the first professional journalists in Russia. There had of course been many people before him who worked more or less full-time in the service of writing and publishing, but they typically enjoyed some supplementary support, such as a sinecure in a government office, a wealthy patron, or inherited funds. For the last seven years of his life, however, Somov depended entirely for his livelihood upon his efforts as author, journalist, editor, and publisher.

Details about Somov's biography are scarce, and much of what is known has been gleaned from casual remarks in his personal or business correspondence, from scant information provided by his contemporaries, or from "Kartiny detstva" (Pictures of Childhood), a brief autobiographical sketch that appeared in *Syn otechestva* (Son of the Fatherland) in 1834, the year following his death.

Somov was born into a modest Ukrainian gentry family in the town of Volchansk. Tutored at home, he subsequently attended school at Nezhin. In 1809 he matriculated at the University of Khar'kov, and while he was still a student there his poetry began appearing in local periodicals. In 1817 he moved to St. Petersburg, where he resided for the rest of his life. In 1818 the nomination of his countryman, Prince Nikolai Andreevich Tsertelev, gained him membership in *Vol'noe obshchestvo liubitelei rossiiskoi slovesnosti* (The Free Society of Lovers of Russian Literature, and soon he began contributing to its periodical, *Sorevnovatel'* (The Emulator). The following year he also joined the older and more conservative *Vol'noe obshchestvo liubitelei slovesnosti, nauk i khudozhestv* (Free Society of Lovers of Russian Literature, Science and Arts) and in 1820 contributions by Somov began to appear in its publication, *Blagonamerennyi* (Well-Intended).

Both *Sorevnovatel'* and *Blagonamerennyi* printed "letters" that Somov wrote while on an extended tour of Europe from the summer of 1819 through the spring of 1820 during which he visited Kraków, Vienna, Dresden, and Paris, where he spent several months. These letters, of which eight have been published, were really essays or sketches of various places of interest, such as the Tivoli amusement park

in Paris and the hospital at Bicêtre. In these pieces Somov's style is informal and often humorous, as in "Progulka po bul'varam" (A Stroll along the Boulevards), published in *Blagonamerennyi* in 1820, where the author adopts the pose of a cicerone whose rambling descriptions and comments about street names, beggars, street performers, and the crowds convey the lively atmosphere of the Parisian boulevards. Somov did not return to this genre until some ten years later, with six letters jointly titled "Chetyre dnia v Finlandii" (Four Days in Finland), the first three published in *Severnaia pchela* (The Northern Bee) in 1829 and the last three in *Literaturnaia gazeta* (The Literary Gazette) the following year. These letters were a tour de force of natural description combined with delightful anecdotes from a brief excursion to the Imatra Falls in the company of Baron Anton Antonovich Del'vig and several others.

At meetings of the two literary societies Somov became acquainted with many of the leading figures of St. Petersburg cultural life, and in the winter of 1820–1821 he was welcomed at the salon of Sofia Dmitrievna Ponomareva, which was frequented by Aleksandr Efimovich Izmailov, Nikolai Ivanovich Gnedich, Petr Aleksandrovich Pletnev, Evgenii Abramovich Baratynsky, Del'vig, and other famous or soon-to-be-famous writers and poets. Doubtless it was at meetings of *Vol'noe obshchestvo liubitelei rossiiskoi slovesnosti* that he met Ryleev and Bestuzhev, whose literary annual, *Poliarnaia zvezda* (Polar Star), enjoyed the collaboration of Russia's foremost men of letters. Somov contributed a short essay, "Frantsuskie chudaki" (French Eccentrics), to the first volume of *Poliarnaia zvezda* (1823). He also served on a committee with Ryleev, Aleksandr and Nikolai Bestuzhev, and Fedor Nikolaevich Glinka, the permanent president of *Vol'noe obschestvo liubitelei rossiiskoi slovesnosti,* that sought to revitalize the society and reorganize its *Sorevnovatel'*. Somov was given six hundred rubles to publish the first six issues for 1823, but having no money advanced for the issues from July to December, he undertook to publish these at his own expense in exchange for some sets of works by the poet Ivan Ivanovich Dmitriev previously published by the society.

Early in 1824 Somov became employed as a head clerk by the Russian-American Company, of which Ryleev was an executive, and shared an apartment in a company building on Galley Port with Aleksandr Bestuzhev, who was then an officer in the dragoons. The Ryleev family also had their apartment in the same building. As Bestuzhev was often away from the capital on military business and Ryleev was heavily involved in his political activities, Somov's role in the preparation and publication of

Cover for the final volume of Severnye tsvety *(Northern Flowers), which was compiled by Somov and included his tale* Svatovstvo *(Matchmaking)*

the 1825 volume of *Poliarnaia zvezda* became increasingly important.

Literary almanacs were profitable for their editors because they were popular with the public and the contributors were not paid. The success of *Poliarnaia zvezda* was noticed by Del'vig, and since he was well acquainted with the literary mandarins of St. Petersburg, among them Pushkin, Prince Petr Andreevich Viazemsky, and Vasilii Andreevich Zhukovsky, he determined to initiate an almanac of his own, to be called *Severnye tsvety* (Northern Flowers). The project attracted the collaboration of many well-known literati, including several of the best contributors from *Poliarnaia zvezda*. In November 1824 there was a disastrous flood in St. Petersburg, and Somov barely escaped drowning. In a letter to Ryleev, he wrote that Galley Port had been inundated, and that only a few of his books had survived by floating on a table in his apartment. On 25 November he jocularly reported that some printed portions of the 1825 *Severnye tsvety* had been "soaked in the bulb" and might therefore "bloom tardily," that is, later than the anticipated release in late December. However, both rival almanacs appeared before the end of the year.

Severnye tsvety was so successful that Bestuzhev and Ryleev decided to phase out *Poliarnaia zvezda*

with a smaller edition to be called *Zvezdochka* (Little Star). The attempted assassination of the tsar on 14 December 1825 intervened, and the editors, including Somov, were arrested. Those sections of *Zvezdochka* already printed were seized and kept sequestered in a government warehouse for almost four decades.

Somov was soon exonerated of any collaboration in the Decembrist plot and released. Bestuzhev had testified that the conspirators considered Somov "useless for the society, both because of his poor health and because of his faint heart and lack of dedication." In the immediate post-Decembrist period Somov continued working for the Russian-American Company, and he also began working as a journalist and critic for the publications of Nikolai Ivanovich Grech and Faddei Venediktovich Bulgarin: *Severnaia pchela* and *Syn otechestva,* and *Severnyi arkhiv* (Northern Archive). Somov was ruthlessly exploited by these two; in a letter of June 1826 to Vladimir Vasil'evich Izmailov, Somov referred to his employment as "manual labor, that is journalistic labor, but it doesn't deserve the title, and moreover it appears so often in three of the local periodicals that it is truly shameful to sign my name." He then went on to express his pleasure in planning stories about his homeland and some fairy tales, which, however, he lacked the time to write. He also announced his forthcoming resignation from the Russian-American Company.

In 1827 he began assisting Del'vig in publishing *Severnye tsvety*. Del'vig had previously handled the editorial end of production of the almanac, with the bookseller Ivan Vasil'evich Slenin in charge of the printing and distribution. Now, however, Del'vig decided to reap all the profits for himself, and to this end he hired Somov as assistant editor, paying him four thousand rubles. Del'vig, who was notoriously lazy, went off to Revel for the summer, leaving Somov unassisted and declaring himself unable even to read the galley proofs owing to a sprained wrist. Somov was almost in despair, since Del'vig had contracted to pay Pushkin six thousand rubles for "Graf Nulin" (Count Nulin), and an engraving of Pushkin by Orest Adamovich Kiprensky cost an additional thousand.

The collaboration of Somov and Del'vig proved quite successful, however, and contributions were so plentiful that they were able to publish an additional almanac for 1829 called *Podsnezhnik* (Snowdrop). Meanwhile, *Severnye tsvety* was increasingly popular, and with the volume for 1830 it became the almanac with the record for the longest consecutive publication. The four volumes from 1828 through 1831 opened with long critical articles by Somov surveying works published in Russia the previous year. While engaged with his critical and editorial duties, he was also increasingly active as a writer of fiction and stylized fairy tales. Some of his stories with Ukrainian settings were signed with his pseudonym, Porfiry Baisky. In an amusing letter of 1829 to the natural scientist Mikhail Aleksandrovich Maksimovich, who had written to congratulate him on his stories appearing under this pseudonym, Somov wrote that Porfiry Baisky was a gentleman living in Volchansk with a wife and ten children.

In the summer of 1830 Somov married a Ukrainian woman named Aleksandra Bestuzheva. Little is known about this woman or their marriage, other than that in the summer of 1831 she bore him a son, Nikolai, whom he amusingly described in a letter to Maksimovich that year as "a fine lad, only noisy beyond measure, since his measure is quite short: the finger-sized boy (*mal'chik s pal'chik*) about whom the Russian fairy tales speak."

Del'vig and his literary circle, in particular Pushkin and Viazemsky, were increasingly vexed by the attitudes and expressions of the Grech-Bulgarin camp, which was not averse to slanderous personal accusations and deliberately prejudicial critical commentaries. Accordingly, it was decided to counterattack with a literary newspaper, *Literaturnaia gazeta,* with Del'vig as editor and Somov as his assistant. It would appear every five days and consist of eight pages of poetry, prose, critical essays, reviews, and a literary miscellany section. According to Grech's memoir, *Zapiski o moei zhizni* (Notes on My Life, 1886), when word of this enterprise reached Grech and Bulgarin, for whom Somov had continued to work, the irate Bulgarin rudely fired him, shouting, "Von Somych, von ego!" (Out with that Son-of-a-Catfish, out with him!). Bulgarin also attempted to discredit Somov by spreading the rumor that on the night of the Decembrist Revolt, Somov had come to his apartment and demanded money and clothes to facilitate his escape, later threatening to expose Bulgarin as an accessory if he insisted on the return of the money. This story was obviously a malicious prevarication, since Somov had been arrested on the night of the revolt and imprisoned for two weeks thereafter.

Many of those who knew Del'vig and Somov prophesied that *Literaturnaia gazeta* would have a brief life, but it was still being published in the fall of 1830 despite a dearth of contributions, for which Somov valiantly sought to compensate with his own reviews, short stories (serialized), translations, and other copy. In October, Del'vig was severely rebuked by the tsar's watchdog, Count Aleksandr Khristoforovich Benckendorff, for the appearance in the 28 October issue of *Literaturnaia gazeta* of a four-line poem by Casimir Delavigne alluding to the July Revolution in France. Benckendorff suspended the paper and threatened Del'vig, along with Pushkin and Viazemsky, with exile to Siberia. This unjustified bullying so disheartened Del'vig that he lost all interest in literary affairs. Somov requested that he be allowed to continue publication of the paper, which was permitted presumably as a favor to the prepaid subscribers.

With Del'vig's withdrawal from literary activity, Somov had to bear the full burden of the paper and the forthcoming volume of *Severnye tsvety* for 1831. His situation was made even more difficult by the sudden death of Del'vig, whom he idolized, in early January 1831. Despite his personal loss, Somov's activities did not diminish. He continued to publish *Literaturnaia gazeta,* and even made up for the issues missed following the proscription of Del'vig as editor. However, by early summer the issues began to falter, and with number thirty-seven for 1831 the paper ceased publication. This break in fact freed Somov for his other literary endeavors, the most important of which was preparation of a final volume of *Severnye tsvety*. This volume was to be in honor of its late editor and presumably would provide a modest fund for his widow and two younger brothers, all of whom were in straitened circumstances. Somov was partially assisted by Pletnev and Pushkin in soliciting contributions, but only thanks to his own persistence and personal commitment did the 1832 *Severnye tsvety* appear before Christmas. This final edition did not include, as had the previous four volumes, Somov's survey of contemporary literature, because Pushkin felt that the polemical nature of his reviews would be out of place in a memorial volume. However, it did include his *Svatovstvo (Iz vospominanii starika o ego molodosti)* (Matchmaking [From an Old Man's Memories About His Youth]), a work of more than 9,000 words. Once the almanac was published, Somov had to seek employment elsewhere; and, doubtless to his personal distaste, he signed on with the notorious literary pirate Aleksandr Fedorovich Voeikov, editor of *Russkii invalid* (The Russian Invalid). Somov's efforts as a critic were somewhat conditioned by the prejudices of his employer, who was at odds with many authors whom Somov respected, and perhaps that is why he signed his contributions with the pseudonym Nikita Lugovoi.

Somov was well represented by his fiction in the almanacs for 1833. There was some indication then that he might be hired as an editor by Pushkin, who was awaiting official approval for a new journal, *Dnevnik* (The Diary). But the position did not materialize, and meanwhile Pushkin had developed a mistrust of Somov owing to the fact that the money expected from publication of the final volume of *Severnye tsvety* had simply disappeared. Somov, who had unsuccessfully requested that he not be involved in the financial details of publishing the edition for 1832, had been obliged to handle the costs and sales, but inexplicably the anticipated profit of three thousand rubles was not realized. He wrote a plaintive letter to Pushkin in January 1833, acknowledging the shortfall and offering to cover it from his own future earnings. But at that time he was out of work and had no resources. This letter particularly notes his ill health, which in fact led to his death in late May. The only person among the St. Petersburg literary figures to come to his funeral was the poet Baron Egor Fedorovich Rozen, Pushkin having ignored an invitation to attend. Somov was buried in a corner of the Smolensk Cemetery on Vasil'ev Island with a modest tombstone inscribed: "Orest Mikhailovich Somov. Died May 27, 1833, at the age of 40." The site has since been obscured by German shells or bombs.

The discussion of Somov's contribution to Russian fiction is best preceded by some remarks about his efforts and attitudes as a critic, not only because of his extensive involvement in the critical polemics of his time but also because certain statements may help illuminate what he sought to achieve with his artistic works. After his return from abroad, Somov eagerly entered into the noisy and often pointless polemics that characterized the criticism of the times. Authors were faulted for what were perceived as violations of the "spirit" of the Russian language, inept translations, and slavish imitation of Western literary models. Somov's contributions to some of these skirmishes, which he signed "Zhitel' Galernoj gavani" (A Resident of Galley Port), were typical of the period with respect to caustic comments and self-assured statements.

His first significant effort as a critic was a three-part essay titled *O romanticheskoi poezii* (On Romantic Poetry), which initially appeared in *Sorevnovatel'* in 1823. The first two parts are derived largely (with credit) from Madame de Stael's *De l'Allemagne* (Germany, 1810), while the third makes a strong case for an independent Russian Romantic Movement embodying *narodnost'*, national identity or national character, and *mestnost'*, national locale. (*Narod* means "people" and *mesto* means "place," while the *nost'* suffix is for abstract nouns.) Somov lauded Zhukovsky and Pushkin as exemplars of Romanticism in Russia, and he urged others to create with them an independent Russian Romanticism by drawing inspiration from the nation's impressive history, as preserved in its chronicles, and by exploiting its many ethnic groups and cultures, embodied in Russians, Poles, Cossacks, Tatars, Finns, and others. He concluded with a call to Russian bards to use their rich and magnificent language to reflect the spirit of their people.

Some common denominators uniting the broad scope of Somov's criticisms are insistence upon originality, that is, rejection of foreign clichés, and the importance of verisimilitude. Study of the chronicles and travel notes is the means for authors to familiarize themselves with the real lives of the people who inhabit the Russian land. In "O sushchestvennosti v literature" (On Substantiality in Literature), published in *Syn otechestva* in 1826, Somov defines "substantiality" as "the most true imitation of the things we wish to represent." The term *realism* did not at that time exist in the Russian critical vocabulary, but Somov's call for substantiality seems to prompt something akin to literary realism. In fact, in subsequent critical works he faulted those who failed to represent people, events, and places in accordance with reality. Bulgarin was chided for his false picture of St. Petersburg and Moscow society in the popular satirical novel *Ivan Vyzhigin* (1829), and even Pushkin was criticized for his lack of historical and psychological accuracy in the execution scene in *Poltava* (1829). Somov did not always satisfy his own admonitions about *narodnost'* or *mestnost'*, and his stories with foreign settings—such as "Mariia, ili sluzhanka traktira" (Mary, or the Tavern Servant), which appeared in *Literaturnaia gazeta* in 1830, a vapid and cliché-ridden Gothic tale with a supposed English setting—suffer from this oversight. The same may be said of "Strannyi poedinok (Rasskaz puteshestvennika)" (The Strange Duel [A Traveler's Tale]), published in *Podsnezhnik* in 1830, a work set in French society with a ridiculously improbable plot and characters whose psychology is unbelievable.

Another of Somov's principal concerns was the development of an adequate prose literary language. Writing in the 1829 *Severnye tsvety* he particularly lamented the absence of a narrative style for novels and short tales, the lack of a conversational style for dramatic works in prose, and even the absence of an epistolary style. Young authors, he goes on to say, become lost in the plowland of Slavano-Russian, or fall over Gallicisms and Teutonisms, or sink into the marsh of crude vernacular. With his own compositions, Somov's contribution to the development of the prose literary language was especially notable when his fiction dealt with characters whose language was conditioned by class affiliation, such as the idiom of the peasant driver in "Kikimora (Rasskaz russkogo krest'ianina na bol'shoi doroge)" (Monster [The Story of a Russian Peasant on the Highway]), published in *Severnye tsvety* in 1830, or the rambling discourse of the pathetic petty clerk in *Svatovstvo*.

Somov's artistic body of work is represented by poetry (which is not significant), "letters," *rasskazy* (short stories), and *povesti* (short novels or tales). He did not write *romany* (novels), as far as scholars know, although one of his longer tales, published in *Al'tsiona* (Alcyone) in 1832, is called *Roman v dvukh pis'makh* (A Novel in Two Letters). There is a problem in dealing with Somov's fiction, which arises from the scanty details of his creative biography: in most cases scholars do not know when his works were composed, only when they were published. There are also no manuscripts or galley proofs, which might provide some information as to the extent and nature of his rewriting, changes in emphasis, and so forth. Under such circumstances, it is difficult to generalize as to his artistic development.

Somov has been characterized as a Ukrainian author since many of his works deal with the customs and peoples of his native land; one of his professed aims was to use his art to provide a repository for the customs, traditions, folklore, and legends of Little Russia, which he felt were rapidly being forgotten as education spread into rural areas. However, to describe Somov simply as a Ukrainian author would be to disregard the fact that the majority of his works have no Ukrainian connection; and in any case his fiction was written in Russian, not Ukrainian.

Inasmuch as the publication of Somov's fiction embraced only the six-year period from 1827 to 1833, and since there is no information on dates of composition, a discussion of his legends, fairy tales, and stories based on order of publication cannot legitimately focus upon artistic development or the evolution of his weltanschauung. Instead, his fiction can be rather arbitrarily grouped into several separate categories, although that too is hardly satisfactory, since some stories might qualify for representation under more than one heading. For example, "Prikaz s togo sveta" (A Command from the Other World), published in *Literaturnyi muzeum* in 1827, may qualify as a story of the supernatural and/or a story from abroad, since it is set in Germany. "Iurodivyi. Malorossiiskaia byl'" (The Holy Fool: A Little Russian Tale), published in *Severnye tsvety* in 1827, may be a supernatural tale and/or a society tale.

First, those legends that Somov adapted from popular lore anticipated the later efforts of the better-known Vladimir Ivanovich Dal' (whose pseudonym was Cossack Lugansky). Essentially, they are stylizations or imitations in the spirit of folktales, and perhaps may have simply sprung from their author's fertile imagination. Three are quite short: "Oboroten'" (The Werewolf), published in *Podsnezhnik* in 1829; "Rusalka. Malorossiiskoe predanie" (The Water Sprite: A Little Russian Legend), also in *Podsnezhnik* in 1829 and signed Porfiry Baisky; and a work of 1831, "Kupalov vecher (Iz malorossiiskikh bylei i nebylits)" (Kupala Eve [From Little Russian Tales and Tall Stories]), published in *Literaturnaia gazeta* and also signed with his pseudonym. This latter work concerns a pagan celebration that later merged with St. John's Eve, and the tale is presented in a language heavily seasoned with locutions typical of folk narratives. The story relates how Konchislav, a pagan knight, returning to Kiev on Kupala Eve, encounters a group of beautiful maidens dancing in a meadow. Unbeknownst to him, they are *rusalki* (water sprites), who drown unwary males or tickle them to death. At their invitation, he joins them in dancing before the idol of Kupala and then falls prey to their leader, the ravishing Uslada, who lures him to a watery grave.

Several of Somov's folktales briefly (in fewer than one thousand words) and humorously depict how a modest but brave hero triumphs over an evil enemy. "Skazanie o khrabrom vitiaze Ukrometabunshchike (Kartina iz russkikh narodnykh skazok)" (Legend of the Brave Knight Ukrom-Tabunshchik [A Scene from Russian Popular Folktales]), published in *Nevskii al'manakh* (The Neva Almanac) in 1830, relates how the clever knight defeats the Pecheneg giant Baklan-Bogatyr by so ridiculing his sword and helmet that the unsuspecting warrior discards them—and is then easily defeated. "Skazka o Medvede kostolome i Ivane—kupetskom syne" (The Tale of Bone-Breaker Bear and Ivan the Merchant's Son), published in *Tsarskoe selo* (Tsar's Village) in 1830, amusingly recounts how an intrepid young man rids the Murom Forest of an evil bear that had been devouring livestock and even people. On his way to a fair, Ivan learns of this menace and volunteers to destroy it. The villagers anticipate the worst when he has not returned from the forest by nightfall, but suddenly there is a frightful roar and Ivan appears riding the fearsome beast and kicking its flanks with his iron-bound shoes. The bear stampedes into the village and drops dead. In return for his heroic deed, Ivan asks only for the villagers' good wishes, and he departs, leaving them to feast for three days and three nights.

The last of this cycle of humorous tales is "V pole s'ezzhaiutsia, rodom ne schitaiutsia" (In the Field, Origin Doesn't Count), published in the 1832–1833 *Russkii al'manakh*. The story is related in a rhythmical language with heavy emphasis on the phraseology peculiar to the oral tradition. Motifs typical of the fairy tale dominate the action: Elisia the half-wit is sent by his cruel master to find some stray horses. On a jade borrowed from the priest, he starts his search, and soon the road divides in three. Taking the middle road, he encounters the Tatar knight Kalga who by virtue of his rank demands that Elisia move aside. Elisia responds that in the field origin does not count; they fight, and he kills the Tatar. Disguised in Kalga's armor, he goes to the Tatar camp, demands that three dozen horses be provided him, and returns to his own village. His master is given three horses; the priest is given two; and Elisia makes his fortune by selling the rest.

Three considerably longer folk tales have a more somber atmosphere, and in these the protagonists are ultimately destroyed by demonic powers. "Skazka o Nikite Vdovinyche" (The Tale of Nikita the Widow's Son), also published in the 1832–1833 *Russkii al'manakh,* is related in a racy and quite unliterary language filled with vulgarisms, colloquial expressions, sayings and idioms common to substandard speech, and provincialisms. The work seems to have been created as a vehicle for Somov to preserve a description of the game of *babki,* a kind of knucklebones, in which the *babka,* usually a vertebra from a sheep, is thrown to win the opponents' bones by knocking them out of a circle. The protagonist, Nikita, whose wastrel father had died of drink, is a master at the game. While burying on his father's grave some *babki* he had won, he hears the deceased tell him to come three nights in a row and play *babki*

but that he must win or suffer the consequences. For two nights Nikita is victorious over ghostly adversaries, whose awesome forces are insufficient to confuse the lad; on the third night he wins the black *babka,* which grants its possessor any wish. For seven years Nikita enjoys the fruits of his victory, then marries a demanding woman whose expensive tastes are barely satisfied by the talisman. A son is born, and when he is twelve he finds the black *babka* which the now-alcoholic Nikita has carelessly dropped. The son is challenged by a mysterious black boy sent by satanic forces, and he loses the miraculous bone. The family possessions vanish; Nikita dies of drink; the widow withers away; and the foolish son becomes a beggar.

Despite the grim conclusion of the story, it is filled with humorous circumstances and images, not the least of which concern the unsportsmanlike behavior of the ghosts who seek to distract Nikita when it is his turn to play. The theme of the story and its unusual narrative style reveal Somov as an inventive raconteur with a talent for exploiting both an unusual subject and a little-known linguistic source.

The same may be said of "Kievskie ved'my" (Kiev Witches), published in *Novosel'e* (Housewarming) in 1833, although here the colorful language is confined to the speech of the characters. Simply told, a Cossack, Fedor, marries Katrusia, who is rumored to be the daughter of a witch. Suspicious of his wife's strange behavior, he spies on her and ultimately follows her up the chimney and off to Bald Mountain. There he secretly observes a witches' Sabbath, which is described through the eyes of the horrified youth. An enormous bear with a double ape snout, goat horns, a snake's tail, hedgehog bristles, and cat's claws presides over the wild dances of witches, sorcerers, nixies, werewolves, vampires, and other unholy types. Fedor's presence is discovered, and he is saved only when Katrusia sends him flying home on a shovel. When she returns, she tells him he must die, since he has been witness to their orgy. She kills him and disappears, and a rumor develops that she has been burned at the stake on Bald Mountain for seeking to enter a nunnery.

Although the exposition itself is not colloquial, Somov does season his work with several dozen lexical items peculiar to the Kiev dialect, and he comments on these in explanatory footnotes. Here again his concern for preserving ethnographic material is evident. The story has also been seen as a source for Pushkin's ballad *Gusar* (The Hussar, written in 1833).

The last of the somber folktales, "Nedobryi glaz. Malorossiiskoe predanie"(The Evil Eye: A Little Russian Legend), appeared in the Khar'kov journal *Utrenniaia zvezda* (Morning Star) in 1833 and was signed Porfiry Baisky. It is the most artistic of Somov's folk stories, a dramatic tale in fourteen parts in which suspense and a mood of impending disaster are masterfully augmented. The exposition is stylized to resemble a folktale, with the same descriptive epithet repeated whenever a character is mentioned; homey or unliterary comparisons; repetition; and parallelism. The first two parts introduce the well-to-do Kozak Nikita and his three beautiful daughters: Galia the black browed, Dokiika the rosy one, and Natalka the pale one. An ominous, mysterious stranger on a fiery steed arrives at their homestead; his beetling brows become a metonymic symbol for his repulsiveness, and readers share the daughters' increasing unease in his presence. At dinner he "peered avidly through his beetling brows at the comely daughters of Kozak Nikita, like a pike peers avidly through the reeds at tiny, sportive little fishes." The stranger evades all of Nikita's questions, but finally gives his name as Lavro Khorobit. In part nine he asks for each girl's hand in turn (the three-fold repetition is typical of the fairy tale), and as he is refused his reddish brows rear up like spines on a hedgehog and his pale-gray eyes transfix each of the girls with two burning threads of fatal light. Lavro departs with thinly veiled threats, and the tale ends with the scene of three fresh graves.

Between 1826 and 1830 Somov published a series of episodes united by the figure of Garkusha, a Ukrainian Robin Hood, who with his jolly band protects his countrymen from usurpation by the Poles, unites lovers, and rewards the virtuous. These stories bear a variety of titles which share the word *Gaidamak* (The Rebel), and in three of the four separate publications there is additional indication that the piece is an excerpt from a Little Russian tale or short novel: "Otryvok iz malorossiiskoi byl'" or "Otryvok iz malorossiiskoi povesti." Although the pieces are provided with chapter numbers, nothing about this cycle suggests excerpts from an historical novel, for it has no organic plot, no force of history, no continuity of characters, and no historical personages. These pieces are merely episodes that resemble scenes from the Ukrainian puppet theater with its conventionalized characters: the proud but foolish Pole, the timorous servant, the dull-witted soldier, the avaricious Jew, and the clever and daring hero. Owing to their heavy ethnographic content, these "chapters" have been seen as an effort at an historical novel in the manner of Sir Walter Scott, but such an argument is implausible. Somov, incidentally, was well acquainted with Scott, and his essay "O romanakh" (About Novels), which appeared in *Severnaia pchela* in 1825, shows his familiarity with almost a dozen of Scott's works. Somov admired Scott's art, and he

credited him with having brought the past to life, remarking that it was as if an old magician had awakened after a lengthy sleep and began to talk about the past.

Somov has been overlooked as a precursor of Dal' in the fairy tale and of Gogol as author of Ukrainian folktales. It has also been his misfortune to have lacked recognition for the many innovations he introduced into prose fiction in general. Not least of these was his authorship not later than 1827 of an early version of what was to become the *svetskaia povest'* (society tale), thus anticipating Aleksandr Bestuzhev's "Ispytanie" (The Test), published in 1830, by three years. In Somov's "Iurodivyi. Malorossiiskiia byl'," the protagonist is a young officer named Melsky whose adventure provides the plot of the story. The "holy fool" of the title, Vasil the Half-Wit, plays only a secondary role, and in fact those parts of the story that detail his peculiar appearance, nature, and actions may be taken separately as a kind of physiological sketch, a genre in which various occupational types were characterized or generalized, such as the cook, the porter, the water carrier, or the postman. Dal' later provided many such sketches, which are usually associated with his name. Here Somov describes the typical fool-in-Christ, a mendicant beggar who attracts sympathy and awe by his religious fanaticism, scorn for creature comforts, enigmatic speech, and presumed ability to predict the future.

Melsky's carriage almost runs over Vasil one night while he is sleeping on the highway. Curious as to the nature of this enigmatic being, Melsky befriends him and provides him a place to sleep. The next evening, as Melsky sets off to a soiree, the fool cautions him, "Nash iazyk, nash vrag" (Our tongue is our enemy). At the gathering Melsky and a superficial young lady amuse themselves with remarks about the other guests, thus arousing the anger of an artillery officer, who confronts Melsky and challenges him to a duel. At the duel Vasil suddenly rushes out between the antagonists and is wounded. The duelists, horrified at the consequences of their petty quarrel, are reconciled, and Vasil is taken to a peasant's hut for treatment. Several days later he disappears and is found dead on the grave of Melsky's aunt, thus fulfilling his prediction that he would lead Melsky to his aunt's grave.

The motifs and plot elements of the canonical society tale are found here: characters from the gentry class, young and heedless *jeunesse doree;* a soiree (or dance or ball); jealousy; the challenge; preparations for the duel; the duel itself; the fatal consequences; and the contrition of the guilty. Somov also recounts at length the kaleidoscope of images and thoughts that torment Melsky as he suffers from insomnia on the night he first encounters Vasil. This rather circumstantial depiction of the mental state of the protagonist is unusual for a story written at that period.

Also appearing in 1827 was a humorous story with a supernatural theme, "Prikaz s togo sveta." The Russian narrator, who is traveling through Bavaria, stops in Helnhausen at the local hostelry, The Golden Sun. The pompous innkeeper, Johann Gottlieb Cornelius Stauf, relates how his ghostly ancestor, the illustrious Georg von Hohenstaufen, appointed a rendezvous and admonished Stauf to cease opposing the marriage of his daughter, Minna, to the honest but poor teacher, Ernst German. As the story progresses, it becomes increasingly obvious that the visitation by the innkeeper's ancestor was actually a hoax perpetrated by the local worthies in order to overcome Stauf's prejudice against Ernst, whose lineage was presumably less illustrious than that of the Staufs.

The traveler's comments about his journey from Hamburg to Helnhausen, which precede Stauf's account, are quite amusing. He describes his fellow passenger, a know-it-all French officer, and discourses on the obstinacy of German postilions who refuse to drive faster than at a walk, regardless of the smooth road or the passengers' verbalized irritation and promises of a *Trinkgeld* (tip). In Stauf's account, as related by the traveler, the humor derives from the language of the garrulous and conceited innkeeper, whose manner of expression is peculiar and entertaining, and from the reader's gradual realization that Stauf had been deceived by the very people who confirm the reality of his "command from the other world."

Somov utilized a similar structure—a first-person account framed by the remarks of a traveler—in "Vyveska. Rasskaz puteshestvennika" (The Signboard: A Traveler's Story), which was published in *Nevskii al'manakh* for 1829. Here the traveler stops at the Hotel de la Poste in Verdun and while making some purchases nearby is attracted by the sign outside a barber shop, *Le soleil luit pour tout le monde* (The Sun Shines for Everyone). Curious as to the person responsible for such a sign, he enters the shop and meets the barber, Achilles, a garrulous Frenchman whose business prospers but who has been unable to gain the permission of the hotel owner to marry his daughter. This obstacle is overcome through the intercession of the traveler, who recounts in the epilogue how two years later he returned to Verdun and found everyone reconciled.

The center of this story is Achilles's lengthy autobiography, which includes his participation in Napoleon's invasion of Russia, the occupation of Moscow, and the terrible hardships of the retreat. It is one of the first accounts in Russian literature of the role of Russian partisans in the War of 1812, and the barber provides many graphic details about the horrors he experienced: skirmishes, wounds, corpses, and his ultimate capture. What is unique about this tale, however, is the language of the interior narrator, the talkative barber, whose pithy and unliterary manner of expression reflects his insouciant personality and unneurotic egocentricity.

Somov's interest in capturing the idiom of commoners, as distinct from that of the gentry, is evident in several other tales, but most notably in "Kikimora." Here readers find a fully realized *skaz,* that is, a tale related in an individualized "oral" style that reflects the narrator's class affiliation, education, personality, and intellect. This story begins with the words of a peasant driver, Faddei, who provides his passenger (whose presence as exterior narrator becomes evident only halfway through the story) with a rambling and colorful account of a family in his village that was bedeviled by *kikimora* (a monster). This invisible spirit chose to play its games in the house of Faddei's neighbors, Marfa and Pankrat, at first just washing and combing little Varia, their granddaughter, while everyone was asleep. Still, the presence of *kikimora* was enough to cause them to ask the priest to exorcize the interloper. He rebuked them for their superstitions, so they turned to the German bailiff, who was known as *Vot-on* Ivanovich. His exorcism was performed while dead drunk and seemed only to irritate the pest. An ancient woman then volunteered her services, but before anything could be done, Varia climbed to the top of the house and threw herself to the ground. Apparently dead, she was prepared for burial, but the old crone reappeared and mysteriously returned the child to life, finally ridding the family of the incubus.

Faddei not only reports what he knew of the "possession," but comments in a sly way as to its credibility. He clearly does not share the villagers' conviction about the existence of *kikimora,* nor was he impressed by the bailiff's powers: "The peasants believed that *Vot-on* Ivanovich had *plenty in his nose.* I never noticed nothin' but snuff." And when the passenger asks him if he saw the pest when, following the directions of the crone, the peasants put it on a sled covered with a sheepskin coat and hauled it out of the village, he responds that he saw the coat and the sled, nothing more. Faddei remains pointedly reticent when his passenger suggests the whole episode was a plot of jealous neighbors. So the reader is left to consider three alternatives: to believe in *kikimora* along with the villagers, to share Faddei's noncommital attitude, or to be completely skeptical along with the passenger.

In "Kikimora" Somov weaves the ethnographic material into the fabric of the story so that it is not conspicuous. Such is not the case with "Skazki o kladakh" (Tales of Buried Treasure), published in *Nevskii al'manakh* in 1830. In a footnote, the author states that his purpose is to bring together as many popular legends and beliefs as possible from among the people of Little Russia in order to preserve them for future archaeologists and poets. Therefore, he states, rather than presenting them in a dictionary, he has distributed them among various tales. The plot thus serves as a framework on which Somov arranges his material, often in the form of stories related by various narrators who are friends of the central figure, Major Maksim Kirilovich Neshpeta. The story concerns the efforts of the major to locate buried treasure, which he urgently needs to cover debts incurred by his mania for hunting and also to provide a dowry for his daughter, Gannusia. Meanwhile, the girl is saved from drowning by Lieutenant Levchinsky, who risks his life to save her when the village dam breaks. Ultimately, after many futile efforts to find treasure, the major discovers that a fortune is hidden in an old chest under his bed, and all ends happily.

The value of this work depends upon the digressive material connected with Ukrainian ethnology and sociology, since the daughter and her lieutenant are flat characters and the other narrators–the Serbian corporal, Fedor Pokutin, and the Jew, Itska–are stylized and two-dimensional. There is some situational humor of a slapstick nature deriving from the major's efforts to find his treasure, but what is really engaging are the tales about witches, magicians, spells, and treasures, as well as all the material about daily life and habitual activities of the Little Russian villagers. The story is equipped with many footnotes explaining various terms and expanding upon the information presented in the text.

The least successful of Somov's stories were those with foreign settings, and "Pochtovyi dom v Shato-T'erri (Iz rasskazov puteshestvennika)" (The Post Station in Chateau Thierry [From Tales of a Traveler]), published in *Literaturnaia gazeta* in 1830, may serve as an example. The exterior narrator's frame recounts his meeting the station master and hearing from him the story behind his happy marriage to a deaf-mute German woman whom he saved from dishonor by a band of marauding soldiers. Prolix and heavily sentimentalized, the tale falls well below Somov's standard.

An interesting feature of most Russian authors' Romantic tales of the supernatural is that the super-

natural is "unmasked," that is, in the end it turns out that what was perceived as not-of-this-world was the product of a dream, a trick, or some natural phenomenon. This trait is evident in those stories of Somov such as "Prikaz s togo sveta" and "Kikimora"; and even in "Iurodivyi" it is uncertain whether Vasil the holy fool possessed supernatural powers or not. Somov's "Strashnyi gost'. Anekdot (Iz rasskazov puteshestvennika)" (The Frightening Guest: An Anecdote [From Tales of a Traveler]), which appeared in *Literaturnaia gazeta* in 1830, also has a presumed supernatural content, but as it turns out the otherworldly manifestation is only a dream. The story is interesting primarily because of its frame, which describes a gathering at which a foreign poet, obviously Polish, improvises a tale to amuse the other guests. The description of the improvisator, as well as his remarks about fancy and imagination, strongly suggest that Somov was describing Adam Mickiewicz, well known in Russian literary circles for his improvisations.

Oddly enough, "Samoubiitsa. Povest' (Iz rasskazov puteshestvennika)" (The Suicide: A Story [From Tales of a Traveler]) has a "real" supernatural element, although in this particular story the supernatural could easily be attributed to the gnawing anxiety of guilt that drives a murderer to kill himself. The story appeared in *Literaturnaia gazeta* (1830) in five installments, the first consisting of a frame in which a traveler tells of spending the night at the house of a village *zemsky* or constable, from whom he hears the fearsome tale (the next four parts) of his old master's apparent suicide and the subsequent self-inflicted death of his spendthrift nephew, who was haunted by a ghost later identified as that of his uncle. The constable's story is narrated in a simple style consistent with what readers have learned about him in the introductory frame: that he is literate, familiar with some domestic and foreign classics, and that he is an orderly and disciplined person. His "voice" does include many nonliterary idioms and some bookish expressions, but these accord well with his peasant background and what he has learned from his reading. The only inconsistency occurs when he describes the members of the official inquest sent to investigate the death of the old master. Here the satire is well beyond what readers could expect from the narrator; however, Somov can be forgiven, because the descriptions of the clerks and the doctor are extremely amusing.

Svatovstvo is another of Somov's stories that features the individualized "oral" style of the first-person narrator, in this case a retired clerk, Demid Kalistratovich. His account is filled with Russianized Latin words (a result of his education in a seminary), and his later career as a court clerk is evidenced by stilted and bookish expressions. At the same time, his speech is filled with regionalisms and homey locutions, while in general the presentation is digressive, even rambling. Although these features give the story a humorous quality that is further enhanced by several amusing incidents, the tale is at best bittersweet, for it concerns Demid's unsuccessful courtship of Nastasia, which is thwarted by her widowed mother, and his sincere but fruitless efforts to protect the abused girl after she is forced to marry a brutal officer.

Considerable detail is devoted to mundane features of daily life in provincial Little Russia, with particular attention being paid to the custom of matchmaking, a traditional ritual involving formalities presided over by a professional marriage broker. The matchmaker here is the sly and devious Savelii Dement'evich Peresypchenko, a retired functionary from the chancery court, a weaver of words whose rigamarole employs pompous locutions and extraneous filler words as he tries to spellbind the widow into accepting his proposal on Demid's behalf. Even his persuasive presentation fails to overcome the snobbish mother's reluctance, however. Finally, the tragicomic content of this poor clerk's misfortunes, his pathetic efforts to secure happiness for Nastasia and himself, and his modesty create a strong empathy in the reader, who comes to sympathize with this humble but attractive raconteur, incidentally the first of his profession to achieve protagonist status in Russian fiction.

The 1832 volume of Rozen's almanac *Al'tsiona* included one of Somov's longest works, *Roman v dvukh pis'makh,* some 7,000 words comprising two letters of a supercilious young man to a St. Petersburg acquaintance recounting his adventures on returning to his native Ukraine after four years abroad and in the capital. Leon, the blasé protagonist, identifies with Pushkin's Eugene Onegin, whom he mentions on occasion; he also shares with Onegin, at least initially, a somewhat contemptuous attitude toward the rustic neighbors he encounters. To his dismay, Leon's aunt intends to marry him off to a local girl, Nadezhda, a proposition he rejects out of hand, finding her on initial acquaintance pretty but shy and, apparently, hopelessly provincial. However, by the end of the long postscript to the second letter (the title could logically have been "A Novel in Three Letters"), he has overcome his reluctance and eloped.

There are several amusing characters in this story, particularly Leon's earthy aunt and Avdei Kochevalkin, the crude hunter whom Leon saves from quicksand and dubs *bolotnyj muzhichok* (the bog boor), a simple soul who secretly hopes to marry Nadezhda.

Leon's own unrealized pretentiousness also provides much humor, as in his description of the village ball where he invents all kinds of new dance steps and provides whimsical names, such as *pas de chamois, pas de gazelle* (the chamois step, the gazelle step). He also displays his superficiality by his constant use of French, which an "editor's" afterword explains is typical of worldly young Russians of the time, who write as they speak, half in French and half in Russian. Somov's attitude toward provincial Ukraine and its rustic but unaffected gentry is reminiscent of Aleksei Alekseevich Perovsky's (Antonii Pogorel'sky) *Monastyrka* (The Convent Girl, 1830), a novel that also depicts the sunny Ukraine and its provincials with gentle irony.

"Matushka i synok" (Mommy and Sonny-Boy), perhaps Somov's most amusing satirical treatment of the follies of the provincial gentry, was published in *Al'tsiona* for 1833. Readers first become acquainted with the nouveau riche proprietors of the hamlet of Zakurikhino (Beyond the Henhouse): a bribe-taking, pathologically stingy judge and his nitwitted wife, who bears him a son, Valerii. Subsequently, she overcomes her husband's reluctance to spend money on tutors and hires a German, a recently retired clown from a troupe of bareback riders, whose wagon-load of degrees from all German universities has been left behind in Moscow, and a Frenchman, a valet's valet whose diplomas bear signatures of members of the French Academy dead long before he was born. A third tutor, a seminarian, claims expertise in all subjects from the spurious disciplines of *Infima* and *Synatacima* to theology. Valerii learns little, although his mother is convinced that he is the eighth wonder of the world.

The father dies unmourned, but for the sake of appearances the mother and son remain closeted at home, where he reads sentimental novels and she Gothic ones. Valerii becomes imbued with the tender passions and refined sentiments depicted in his reading, while the mother identifies with the protagonists of her literary favorites and becomes increasingly domineering. After a proper period of mourning, Valerii is dispatched, under the watchful eye of a servant, on a four-year tour to round out his education.

Shortly after departing Zakurikhino he writes his mother a letter, a wonderful parody of the Sentimental epistolary style with its turgid phraseology, emotional exclamations, and periphrastic euphemisms. At the first village Valerii, a great admirer of nature and the natural man, falls head over heels in love with Malasha, the quite ordinary daughter of his landlady. His pledge of eternal love to Malasha, now addressed as "Melania," the angel of beauty and innocence, is overheard by her mother, who informs him that a church and priest can properly handle the matter. The servant also witnesses this scene, and he writes to Valerii's mother that her son has been bewitched. She hastens to the village and finds Valerii uncharacteristically intransigent, so she drags him home and incarcerates him in a Gothic tower to pine, presumably forever, over his lost love.

This work incorporates several features later utilized by Gogol, such as ridiculous lists interrupted by unexpected absurdities (the seminarian's areas of expertise), the banal conversation of the would-be lover and his beloved, and the unanticipated and ironic denouement, not to mention the absence of any positive characters. Here again, as with the stylized Ukrainian folktales and legends, Gogol's indebtedness to Somov has been overlooked or ignored.

Published in the almanac *Kometa Bialy* (Bialy's Comet) in 1833, *Epigraf vmesto zaglavia* (An Epigraph Instead of a Title) may have been Somov's last work. It is a society tale, and with the exception of certain innovations with regard to characterization, it is disappointing. It is too long (12,000 words); the plot is improbable; and there are several overly sentimental episodes.

The central figure is Count Krinsky, a wealthy and promising young officer who has eschewed appointment to a fashionable guards regiment in order to serve in an obscure hussar regiment far from the capital. The story opens with an amusing depiction of a provincial ball, where a discussion among some of those who know Krinsky leads to the conclusion that there are only two possible candidates for the count's future wife: the beautiful young widow Felitsiata Nelskaia and seventeen-year-old Liubov' Vishaeva, the daughter of wealthy gentry. Count Krinsky is first taken with Felitsiata, but he loses interest when her innate arrogance is revealed. Then he becomes enamored of Liubov', and just as he is about to propose, she exposes her mean nature. Disillusioned, the count goes to a nearby village and meets the Reiev family, whose eighteen-year-old daughter, Olga, lacks the brilliance of his two previous attachments but proves to have a truly virtuous spirit; and they are wed.

What is interesting here, in addition to the satire on provincial society with its concern for rank and wealth, is Somov's effort to depict an emotional confrontation without resorting to the clichés prevalent at the time. The scene in which Krinsky quarrels with Felitsiata is marked by a dialogue that reveals their suppressed emotions and increasing irritation not only through their words but also by gestures. The overall effect is highly graphic and produces a strong illusion of reality.

It is not incorrect to rank Somov below Pushkin and Gogol with respect to the quality of his fiction, but he can legitimately stand in the company of Perovsky, Aleksandr Bestuzhev, Vladimir Fedorovich Odoevsky, and Aleksander Fomich Vel'tman, and his place on the Russian Parnassus is arguably above Bulgarin, Nikolai Alekseevich Polevoi, and Mikhail Petrovich Pogodin. Somov was not only a master raconteur of folktales and legends, but he was also an innovator whose stories and style in many respects anticipated the advent of realism. In utilizing new devices and in broadening the range of fictional content, however, he sometimes produced a work in which the Romantic features were not compatible with the elements of realism, most notably in his stories with foreign settings. But such deficiencies must not obscure Somov's originality and success in employing various styles of "oral" narration, his achievements in the development of the society tale, and his significant contribution to Russian criticism and belles lettres.

Letters:

"Iz pisem O. M. Somova k M. A. Maksimovicha," *Russkii arkhiv*, 3 (1908).

Biographies:

Z. V. Kiriliuk, *O. Somov—Kritik ta beletrist pushkins'koi epokhi* (Kiev: Vidavnitstvo kiivs'kogo universitetu, 1965);

John Mersereau Jr., *Orest Somov: Russian Fiction between Romanticism and Realism* (Ann Arbor: Ardis, 1989).

References:

John Mersereau Jr., "Orest Somov: An Introduction," *The Slavonic and East European Review,* 43 (June 1965): 354–370;

Mersereau, "Orest Somov and the Illusion of Reality," in *American Contributions to the Sixth International Congress of Slavists, Prague, 1968, August 7–13,* volume 2, edited by W. E. Harkins (The Hague: Mouton, 1968), pp. 307–331;

Mersereau, "Orest Somov: Life and Literary Activities," in *Papers in Slavic Philology 1: In Honor of James Farrell,* edited by Benjamin A. Stoltz (Ann Arbor: Michigan Slavic Publications, 1978), pp. 198–224;

Mersereau, "Orest Somov's Ukrainian and Russian Legends," in *Festschrift for Deming Brown* edited by Kenneth N. Brostrom (Ann Arbor: Michigan Slavic Publications, 1984), pp. 368–380.

Nikolai Vladimirovich Stankevich

(27 September 1813 – 25 June 1840)

Edward Alan Cole
Grand Valley State University

BOOK: *Vasilii Shuiskii* (Moscow, 1830).

Editions and Collections: *Stikhotvoreniia. Tragediia: Vasilii Shuiskii. Proza,* edited by A. V. Stankevich, (Moscow: O. O. Gerbek, 1890);

Poety kruzhka N. V. Stankevicha, edited by Semen Iosifovich Mashinsky (Moscow-Leningrad: Sovetskii pisatel', 1964);

Izbrannoe, edited by G. G. Elizavetina (Moscow: Sovetskaia Rossiia, 1982);

Poeziia. Proza. Stat'i. Pis'ma, edited by B. T. Udovov (Voronezh: Tsentral'no-Chernozemnoe Knizhnoe izdatel'stvo, 1988).

TRANSLATIONS: Johann Wolfgang von Goethe, "Gesang der Geisteruber den Wassern," translated as "Pesn' dukhov nad vodami," *Severnye tsvety* (1832): 147–148;

Goethe, "An den Mond," translated as "K mesiatsu," *Teleskop,* 9 (1832): 28–30.

SELECTED PERIODICAL PUBLICATIONS:
"Luna," *Babochka* (10 July 1829): 218–219;

"Nadpis' k pamiatniku Pozharskogo i Minina" and "Eksprompt," *Babochka* (3 August 1829): 247;

"Na igru gospozhi Ostriakovoi," *Babochka* (25 December 1829): 411;

"Stansy," *Babochka* (4 January 1830): 6–7;

"Prosti!" *Babochka* (25 January 1830): 31;

"Otryvki iz stikhotvornoi povestii," *Babochka* (22 February 1830): 63–64;

"Uteshenie," *Babochka* (29 March 1830): 103;

"Vesna," *Babochka* (19 April 1830): 127–128;

"Elegiia," *Babochka* (4 June 1830): 179–180;

"Izbrannyi" and "Zhelanie slavy," *Atenei,* no. 8 (1830): 118–130, 198;

"Ne sozhalei," *Molva* (30 August 1830): 277;

"Filin," *Severnye tsvety* (1831): 30–31;

"Nochnye dukhi," *Teleskop,* no. 8 (1831): 470–473;

"Kreml'," *Literaturnaia gazeta* (31 January 1831): 54;

"Grust'," *Literaturnaia gazeta* (27 March 1831): 146;

Nikolai Vladimirovich Stankevich

"Kalmytskii plennik," *Molva* (16 September 1832): 297–298;

"Mgnovenie," *Teleskop,* no. 6 (1832): 173;

"Boi chasov na Spasskoi bashne," *Severnye tsvety* (1832): 173;

"Na mogilu sel'skoi devitsy," *Syn otechestva i Severnyi arkhiv,* no. 16 (1834): 560;

"Fantaziia" and "Na mogile Emilii," *Dennitsa* (1834): 21, 127–128;

"Ianuariiu Mikhailovichu i Timofeiu Nikolaevichu, otpravliaiushchimsia naslazhdat'sia zhizn'iu" and "Poslanie k Ia. M. Neverovu po sluchaiu pechal'nykh zvukhov, kotorye on izvlekal iz muzikiiskogo strumenta," *Voronezhskaia literaturnaia beseda* (1925): 25, 31–32.

In the Russian literary tradition Nikolai Vladimirovich Stankevich is regarded as an important figure; despite the fact that he wrote little, and nothing of significance, Stankevich was the central personality of the 1830s. As the leader of the famous Moscow University student circle that bore his name, he inspired and fascinated an entire generation of Russian poets, writers, and intellectuals. On Friday afternoons and evenings in Stankevich's rooms at the home of Professor Mikhail Grigor'evich Pavlov, many of the leading minds of the rising generation found an intellectual refuge from the ignorance and oppressiveness of Russian life under Tsar Nicholas I, and there they became acquainted with the literature and philosophy of Europe. Stankevich managed to hold future Westernizers, Slavophiles, patriots, radicals, conservatives, moderates, and apolitical aesthetes together in a community of interest that did not break up into factions until his untimely death.

Nikolai Vladimirovich Stankevich was born on 27 September 1813 to a rich gentry family whose seat was at the village of Uderevko (today called Mukho-Uderevko) in the Ostragozhskii district of south-central Voronezh Province, which borders on the Ukraine. The estate was large, probably within the top fifteenth percentile of gentry establishments in terms of wealth and number of serfs. The family home was warm and busy, with a balcony from which the steppe could be viewed; Stankevich always spoke of home and the Russian countryside with affection. Remoteness ensured that the family was not insulated from the life of villagers and peasants, and Stankevich spent much of his infancy and youth among the children of the lower classes. He learned Ukrainian songs and stories from the servants; grew up in the Orthodox Church, which he never abandoned; and got his earliest tutoring from his parents and relatives. At age nine he was sent to the district public school to be instructed along with pupils of all social classes. At age twelve he entered the school for the nobility at the provincial capital of Voronezh, where he was trained in French and German; but even there his most important friendship was with Aleksei Vasil'evich Kol'tsov, the son of a cattle merchant. Stankevich admired Kol'tsov, who eventually emerged as a pioneer in the translation of folk culture into artistic poetry.

In 1830 Stankevich was sent to the nation's capital to enter Moscow University as a student of literature. Offsetting somewhat the oppressive nature of the tsar's regime was the fact that the age of amateurs and dilettantes was passing; a university education was established as the prerequisite for both career advancement and serious intellectual life, and therefore a lively society gathered around the institution. Unfortunately the university was closed much of that year because of the cholera. In these circumstances the Pavlov home, where Stankevich took rooms, became one of the centers of cultural life. The house, which no longer exists, was on Bol'shaia Dmitrovka (now Pushkinskaia) Street near the old site of the university. From the *Liubomudry* (members of *Obshchestvo liubomudriia,* the Society of Wisdom Lovers), Pavlov had acquired an interest in German idealist philosophy, which he even introduced into his courses on the natural sciences. Through Pavlov, Stankevich and his new friends also met Nikolai Ivanovich Nadezhdin, whose journal *Teleskop* (The Telescope) criticized the poverty of Russian literature and later became famous for publishing Petr Iakovlevich Chaadaev's "First Philosophical Letter" in 1836. Stankevich developed a close connection with *Teleskop,* in which he published most of his writing, and for which he and members of his circle served as an editorial staff; they also adopted Nadezhdin's gazette, *Molva* (Rumor). Another important influence was Nikolai Aleksandrovich Mel'gunov, who was well-read in German philosophy and another living link to the heritage of the *Liubomudry.*

Perhaps it was the example of this older group, which had prudently disbanded at the time of the Decembrist rebellion in 1825, that inspired Stankevich and his friends to begin a *kruzhok* (circle) of their own. At any rate, students began to gather, and the Stankevich Circle was born. Early members were Ivan Petrovich Kliushnikov and Vasilii Ivanovich Krasov, both aspiring poets. Ianuarii Mikhailovich Neverov was close to Stankevich and left some interesting accounts of those times; other early members were Ivan Afanas'evich Obolensky, Iakov I. Pocheka, and the future historian Sergei Mikhailovich Stroev. In 1833 the membership changed somewhat—Neverov departed for St. Petersburg, where he founded a kind of filial circle, one member of which was future historian Timofei Nikolaevich Granovsky. In Moscow, Stankevich's circle was enhanced by the presence of Konstantin Sergeevich Aksakov, the poet and future Slavophile, and Vissarion Grigor'evich Belinsky, the future critic. Other new members included Aleksandr Pavlovich Efremov and Aleksandr Keller.

Stankevich departed for a career in his native province in 1834, but he spent considerable time in Moscow, and the life of the circle continued, attracting Mikhail Nikiforovich Katkov, the future publi-

Lines from the manuscript for "Professor budushchii!" (Future Professor!), an 1838 poem by Stankevich (from Poety kruzhka N. V. Stankevicha, *edited by Semen Iosifovich Mashinsky, 1964)*

cist; Vasilii Petrovich Botkin, another future historian; and Mikhail Aleksandrovich Bakunin, the future anarchist ideologue. Granovsky joined the circle briefly on his way to Berlin. The poet Kol'tsov was an associate of the circle, along with Aleksei Beyer, his sisters Natal'ia and Aleksandra, and the Bakunin sisters Varvara, Tatiana, and Liubov'. There were also links to the Kireevskys, of future Slavophile fame.

The Stankevich Circle was the best known of several such groups that, along with the literary salons of educated society, served as the heart of intellectual life in the early reign of Nicholas I. Its chief rival, at least in the memory of contemporaries, was the circle of Aleksandr Ivanovich Herzen; but as the latter recalled, there was a kind of specialization at work, with those interested in politics gravitating to Herzen's group, and those captivated by aesthetics and philosophy to Stankevich's. For those interested in any of these subjects, the 1830s were difficult years, dominated by the activities of the Third Section and the censorship.

The period that began in 1825 has been called, with some justification, the age of silence, because with rare exceptions the intellectual ferment characteristic of the times usually did not achieve public expression. There were few literary journals worthy of the name, and those that published had limited readerships and existed at the pleasure of the authorities. Nevertheless, the importation and adaptation of European ideas continued, and the circle and the salon provided a kind of critical public. Literary Russians were particularly concerned with the poverty of their national literature in an age that, in Europe, was dominated by the concerns of nationalistic literary Romanticism, and the circle was one of the few forums within which this problem could be openly discussed.

The life of Stankevich's circle, not unlike that of the more fashionable salons of the time, had a strong social dimension, and was not always devoted to serious discussion. Stankevich studied music under Friedrich Karl Gebel, and his piano figures prominently in memoirs of participants. The circle did not demand alienation, and all the evidence suggests that most members retained important ties to friends and family, as well as to the general context of Russian life. Nevertheless, they also formed bonds of lifetime friendship and a sense of cohesion that at times bordered on the ascetic; references to "brotherhood" are frequent, and the agonies of alienation were not unknown.

Alienation is one of the themes of Stankevich's only work of prose fiction, the fragmentary short story "Neskol'ko mgnovenii iz zhizni grafa Z . . . " (A Few Moments in the Life of Count Z . . .), published in *Teleskop* in 1834. It tells the story of a sensitive youth educated by his father in the depths of the Russian countryside. Impassioned by a thirst for truth, the young count travels to Moscow to find teachers and comrades who would go hand-in-hand with him in the search. Unfortunately, he finds instead a world that he can only scorn and tolerate, and from which he is rescued only by an unexpected friendship with one Manuel, who has obviously been in touch with the truths the count has sought so ardently. The count discovers worlds he had never suspected, reading in metaphysics, history, religion, and art. Eventually he sails for Europe; in Vienna his soul is awakened by exposure to great music, and he falls in love, discovers truth, and dies, mourned by his love and his best friend, who arrive from Russia too late. As literature, this story has little to recommend it, but it may reflect with some accuracy the attitudes of the time.

Like most of the putative intellects of the 1830s, Stankevich attempted the art of poetry, beginning at age fifteen, before he came to Moscow. No critic has ever stepped forward to claim anything more than an honorific secondary importance either for the forty-two verses that comprise Stankevich's complete body of poetic work, or for the long verse tragedy *Vasilii Shuiskii,* which the seventeen-year-old author himself abhorred to such a degree that he bought up and destroyed every available copy of it. Stankevich's first original published verse appeared in 1829 on the pages of *Babochka* (The Butterfly), a journal of "novelties." It was titled "Nadpis' k pamiatniku Pozharskogo i Minina" (An Inscription for a Statue of Pozharsky and Minin), and packed into its four short lines was a feeling of strong, albeit conventional, patriotic gratitude to the "sons of the fatherland" who had "saved the Russian throne." In some ways it was his best verse.

The chief value of Stankevich's mostly lyric poetry is biographical, and what it reveals is that he understood and appreciated the Romantic style with all its themes and images—except for those of rebellion, which never appear. The poems are thoughtful

and reflect the circle's concern with the aesthetic concepts of Friedrich Schiller and Friedrich Wilhelm Joseph von Schelling. In general, the universe is presented as an organic unity of which man is a part, and pantheistic phrases abound. No particular poem emerges as most important, and it is difficult to trace any development until 1834, when for all intents and purposes Stankevich wisely abandoned serious poetry.

"Luna," an 1829 imitation of a lost French original, addresses the moon and compares her to Ossian. "Prosti!" (Farewell!, 1830) bids adieu to a cold beauty whom the poet had loved only to be mocked in return. "Izbrannyi" (The Chosen, 1830) features a celestial debate between the spirits of war and peace, with the latter prevailing. "Nochnye dukhi" (Night Spirits, 1831) is set on a cliff. "Kreml'" (The Kremlin, 1831) and "Boi chasov na Spasskoi bashne" (The Chimes of the Savior Tower, 1832) combine local color with historical reverie and perhaps evoke the environs of the university. The elegiac content of several poems, such as "Na mogilu sel'skoi devitsy" (On the Grave of a Village Damsel, 1834), is easily inferred. "Dva puti" (Two Paths), which first appeared in Pavel Vasil'evich Annenkov's 1857 biography of Stankevich, poses a dilemma for the wanderer: should he choose the path of gloom or of gaiety? The former is surprisingly the better, for sorrow leads to life.

"Podvig zhizni" (The Exploit of Life), written in the middle of Stankevich's university career and published in Annenkov's biography, clearly expresses the ideal asceticism of the literary circle, and pushes the familiar theme of religious, or at least spiritual, renunciation: it urges those who thirst for knowledge to flee from vanity and "sorrowing people" into the realm of *povsiudnaia zhizn'* (universal life), where the terrestrial will be annihilated but the soul will be saved. "Dve zhizni" (Two Lives), which concludes Stankevich's period of serious poetry, returns to the dilemma, this time in the form of a maiden who is the object of terrestrial passion, and another who is the object of prayer. Stankevich sent this poem to *Molva* in 1834 under the pseudonym V. Girchenko, but it was not published until 1857, in Annenkov's biography. Throughout these poems, misty images, the moon, and dreamy, obscure landscapes prevail, along with all sorts of tensions and sometimes surprising contradictions.

In addition to Stankevich, at least three other members of the circle eventually laid claim to the status of poet: Krasov, Kliushnikov, and Aksakov. Those of their works written in Stankevich's lifetime reveal many of the same philosophical and aesthetic ideas, but all three went separate ways as poets. To their number should be added Kol'tsov, whose poetry clearly developed outside the circle, but who was championed by Stankevich.

From 1831 to 1834, during his university years, Stankevich's circle was primarily occupied with the aesthetics of Schiller and Schelling, but any account of its activities would have to list the music of Wolfgang Amadeus Mozart, Ludwig van Beethoven, Franz Schubert, and Ferdinand Hérold, especially the latter's opera *Zampa* (1831). Favorite foreign authors included Adam Mickiewicz, E. T. A. Hoffmann, and Honoré de Balzac, and favorite Russians were Petr Vasil'evich Kireevsky, Kol'tsov, Nestor Vasil'evich Kukol'nik, and Ivan Ivanovich Lazhechnikov. In general, Stankevich's correspondence, particularly with Neverov, reveals a serious attempt to understand the value of art as revealed in the theories and concepts not only of Schelling, but also of August Wilhelm von Schlegel, Friedrich Bouterwek, and Karl Friedrich Bachman. Certain critical ideas, such as that of art as "thought in images," later expounded more fully by Belinsky, appear in Stankevich's letters. By the time of his departure from Moscow University, his true literary phase was coming to a close and philosophy was exerting the pull that eventually drew him to Berlin.

In 1834 Stankevich graduated with high honors and returned to Voronezh Province to become a school inspector at Ostrogozhsk. Despite this move he managed to remain the central figure of his circle at Moscow, where he visited as often as circumstances permitted. These visits, in addition to the onset of tuberculosis, prevented him from carrying out various reform projects at Ostrogozhsk, and in any case Stankevich was more interested in philosophy than in provincial education. It was also in these years that he deeply involved himself in the affairs of Bakunin's three sisters, with consequences that pursued him to Italy and his end. His romance was a tale that exemplifies the sad relationship of Romantic individualism to actual life. Along with many other figures of his generation, Stankevich was invited to the Bakunin home estate at Premukhino. There he participated in a campaign by the younger generation to "liberate" the Bakunin daughters from the "tyranny" of the traditional family. In the course of this adventure, Stankevich became engaged to one sister, Liubov', but developed a true bond of love with the married sister, Varvara. A need to escape this entanglement encouraged him in his decision in 1837 to travel to Europe. Another reason was his tuberculosis, for which Stankevich obtained a physician's prescription for travel abroad; but the foremost motive was his desire to study philosophy at the University of Berlin.

Relief portrait of Stankevich

Stankevich's interest in philosophy derived from the *Liubomudry*, who had rejected the rationalism of the Enlightenment and who bequeathed posterity with a vague system of notions chiefly gathered from Schelling. The vagueness of their philosophy derived in large part from the fact that such subjects were not permitted at Russian universities, and few students found any original German sources. A kind of synthesis, or wisdom, had been contrived, in which the universe was viewed as an organic whole united by a higher consciousness realizing itself in that of mankind. Human consciousness, it was believed, was thus able to discover the essential truths of the universe by means of artistic creation and sensibility. There was a strong sense of world history as a process that manifested itself in different ways through the histories of individual nations. Most of these elements appear in Stankevich's 1833 essay "Moia metafizika" (My Metaphysics), written as a letter to Neverov, which announced his growing interest in philosophy. He began to read systematically the works of Immanuel Kant, Johann Gottlieb Fichte, and eventually, Georg Wilhelm Friedrich Hegel, whose names began to pepper his letters to friends such as Neverov and Belinsky. The former remained true to literature, but Belinsky began his own investigations leading to the notorious "reconciliation with reality" that nearly vitiated his critical abilities in the late 1830s.

Stankevich himself experienced no such crisis, in part because he did not confront Hegelian realism until his Berlin days, and in part because for Stankevich, religion took precedence over philosophy. For him, the desire to know God was the inspiration for the philosophic search for intellectual understanding. In a sense, Stankevich already was reconciled to the world through faith, and his philosophic researches constituted a kind of nineteenth-century scholasticism. Also, Stankevich was much more systematic and thorough in his reading, and much less inclined to jump to conclusions than his friends Belinsky and Bakunin, who also entered a philosophic phase. Stankevich, for his part, brought rigor and a sense of purpose unusual in the previous history of philosophic studies in Russia, and like many students of his time he was drawn toward Berlin, the recognized capital of philosophic learning.

Stankevich entered the Berlin lecture halls chiefly to study under the renowned Karl Werder, who was famous for propagating the ideas of Hegel. The young Russian found himself in good company at the salon maintained by Nikolai Grigor'evich Frolov and his wife, Elizaveta Pavlovna, who regularly entertained the leading lights of the university and the city. There Stankevich met his new friend Granovsky, who introduced him to the writer Ivan Turgenev. Stankevich acquired a fun-loving mistress, Berta, who figures prominently in the memoirs of the visiting Russians. He also learned of the untimely death of his erstwhile fiancée, Liubov' Bakunina. Studies with Werder went well, and the two became close friends. Stankevich not only grasped the concept of Hegelian realism but—perhaps influenced by Granovsky, who was studying under Leopold von Ranke—he also undertook a systematic study of history. Indeed, there is something Faustian about Stankevich's Berlin sojourn, and his letters also mention studies in practical subjects such as agriculture and manufacturing.

Although Herzen's observation that Stankevich and his circle took little interest in politics is largely true, there is some evidence, chiefly in letters to his parents, that Stankevich was influenced by the idea of the *Rechtsstaat* (constitutional state) that dominated German theorizing. Indeed, the slim evidence of his early years indicates that Stankevich had political views, and that he had always been a loyal, patriotic monarchist. His first verse was patriotic, and one of his more elaborate poems, "Izbrannyi," depicts an ideal ruler who is strong, firm, and loved for his glory, justice, mercy, and law. In 1834 Stankevich lavished praise on the Official Nationalist dramas of

Kukol'nik. In 1835, in a letter to Bakunin, Stankevich depicted the state as an organic body that progressed according to internal necessity; progress, he held, is hampered by an egoism that can only be overcome by wise direction on the part of state functionaries. In an oblique remark presumably about revolutionaries (this was not an era in which it was prudent to discuss them even in private correspondence), he noted that "they must break a machine in order to fix it . . . we see examples of this in the West."

Residence in Berlin seemed to stimulate political thoughts that departed somewhat from Stankevich's earlier positions, such as they were. A diary entry for September 1837 repudiated incipient Slavophilism, noting that those who would define the Russian character by its old customs were those who would keep the people in a childlike state of development. By 1838 he was expressing a more practical political view, pointing out that order was the first requirement of liberty and crediting German education for producing an environment of respect for lawful power and an atmosphere of intellectual freedom. As for Russia, Stankevich disapproved of serfdom, but he believed that time and education would efface even the shortcomings of his own homeland. This expression of conservative liberalism is as close as Stankevich ever got to proposing a solution to the social problems of his day. To the end he remained a patriot, observing that the fatherland is the soil in which one's being is planted; a man without a country is like a seed blowing in the wind.

Stankevich left Berlin in the summer of 1839, traveling to Rome by way of Salzbrunn and other famous European cities. His health worsened, and at news of this his beloved Varvara, obtaining her husband's permission and taking her child with her, departed Russia to find him. She caught up with him in Italy, but on his way to the Lake Como district, on 25 June 1840, Stankevich died in her presence. He was buried at Novi Ligure, north of Genoa. Years later his remains were returned to his native village.

News of Stankevich's death shocked and saddened his friends and marked a turning point in the intellectual life of Russia. Belinsky raged against the Absolute, which had thus rendered life meaningless. Bakunin almost returned to the traditional religion he had abandoned. Granovsky, whose radiant personality and similar views caused many to regard him as Stankevich's spiritual heir, simply refused for a long time to believe that his friend was gone.

Over time the image of Stankevich underwent refinement in the memories of those who had known him, and he became one of the secular saints of the intelligentsia: chaste, pure, brilliant, and, above all, influential. Until 1857 and the publication of Annenkov's biography, Stankevich was remembered only by those who had known him. Thereafter a voluminous literature built up. Edward J. Brown, who studied the Stankevich "narrative" or "legend" in detail, concludes in *Stankevich and the Moscow Circle, 1830–1840* (1966) that, in the Aristotelian sense, Stankevich's image was more poetic than historical, and that it changed with the character of each stage in the history of the intelligentsia. Critics skeptical of the legendary Stankevich have been few and have been promptly and effectively refuted, and to the present his image as a great luminary has survived.

Obviously the real Stankevich was, as are most figures who have been idealized, both more and less than his legendary image. He was a young man of great talent, considerable wit, and magnetic personality; but just as obviously, he was a fallible human being who made some regrettable mistakes in his life. There are indications that, as his knowledge of philosophy deepened, Stankevich was moving away from the views of his circle in his last years. His conservative side has received little attention. But this figure, itself the product of the poetic imagination, exemplifies the ideals of a formative period in Russian literature—ideals which have been so attractive that even Leo Tolstoy, who knew him only through the biographical literature, declared that he had never loved anyone as he loved Stankevich.

Letters:

"I. S. Turgenevu, 11 iunia 1840," *Vestnik Evropy,* 11 (1899);

Perepiska Nikolaia Vladimirovicha Stankevicha, 1830–1840, edited by Aleksei Stankevich (Moscow: Mamontov, 1914);

Nikolai Leont'evich Brodsky, ed., *Belinsky i ego korrespondenty. Sbornik Otdela rukopisei Gosudarstvennoi Publichnoi Biblioteki SSSR imeni V. I. Lenina* (Moscow: Gosudarstvennaia biblioteka SSSR imeni V. I. Lenina, otdel rukopisei, 1948);

"V. G. Belinskomu, seredina aprelia 1837," *Literaturnoe nasledstvo,* 55 (1948);

"V. G. Belinskomu, 20 oktiabria 1838," *Literaturnoe nasledstvo,* 57 (1948);

"M. A. Bakuninu, 7 Iulia 1835" and "T. N. Granovskomu, 25 iunia 1839," *Literaturnoe nasledstvo,* 56 (1950).

Biographies:

Pavel Vasil'evich Annenkov, "Nikolai Vladimirovich Stankevich, biograficheskii ocherk," *Russkii vestnik,* 7 (1857): 441–449, 695–738;

published with additional material as *Nikolai Vladimirovich Stankevich. Perepiska ego i biografiia* (Moscow: Katkov, 1857);

Mikhail Osipovich Gershenzon, *N. V. Stankevich* (Moscow, 1904);

Fedor Fedorovich Nelidov, ed., *Zapadniki 40-kh godov: N. V. Stankevich, V. G. Bielinskii, A. I. Gertsen, T. N. Granovskii i dr.* (Moscow: I. D. Sytin, 1910);

Nikolai Aleksandrovich Dobroliubov, *N. V. Stankevich* (St. Petersburg: Probuzhdeniie, 1911);

N. Kashin, "Romany N. Stankevicha," *Sovremennyi mir,* nos. 7–8 (1915): 1–41;

Edward J. Brown, *Stankevich and Belinsky* (The Hague: S. Gravenhage, 1958);

Brown, *Stankevich and His Moscow Circle, 1830–1840* (Stanford: Stanford University Press, 1966);

A. Bourmeister, *Stankevic et L'idealisme humanitaire des anees 1830,* 2 volumes (Lille, 1974).

References:

Konstantin Sergeevich Aksakov, *Vospominaniia studentchestva, 1832–1835 godov* (St. Petersburg: Ogni, 1911);

Vladimir Astrov, *Ne nashi puti iz istorii religioznago Krizisa: Stankevich, Belinsky, Gertsen, Kireevsky, Dostoevsky* (St. Petersburg: M. M. Stasiulevich, 1914);

Nikolai Leont'evich Brodsky, *Literaturnye salony i kruzhki, pervaia polovina XIX veka* (Moscow: Akademia, 1930);

Brodsky, ed., "Ia. M. Neverov i ego avtbiografiia," *Vestnik vospitaniia,* 6 (1915): 73–136;

Nikolai Gavrilovich Chernyshevsky, *Ocherki gogolevskogo perioda russkoi literatury* (Moscow: Khudozhestvennaia literatura, 1953);

Dmitrij I. Čiževskij, *Gegel' v Rossii* (Paris: Dom knigi, 1939);

B. V. Emel'ianov and B. G. Tomilov, "N. V. Stankevich kak istorik i kritik nemetskoi filosofii kontsa XVIII-nachalo XIX veka," *Kantovskii sbornik,* no. 12 (1987): 11–26;

Aleksandr Ivanovich Gaivoronsky, *Zolotye arkhivnye rossypi* (Voronezh: Chernozem, 1971);

Aleksandr Ivanovich Herzen, *Byloe i dumy,* 2 volumes (Minsk: Gosudarstvennoe uchebnopedagogicheskoe izdatel'stvo, 1959);

V. K. Iarmershtedt, "Mirosozertsanie kruzhka Stankevicha i poeziia Kol'tsova," *Voprosy filosofii i psikhologii,* 20 (1893): 94–124;

Ivan Ivanovich Ivanov, *Istoriia russkoi kritiki,* 2 volumes (St. Petersburg: Mir Bozhii, 1900);

Zakhar Abramovich Kamensky, *Moskovskii kruzhok liubomudrov* (Moscow: Nauka, 1980);

Aleksandr Aleksandrovich Kornilov, *Molodye gody Mikhaila Bakunina; iz istorii russkago romantizma* (Moscow: Saboshnikovy, 1915);

Edmund Kostka,"At the Roots of Russian Westernism: N. V. Stankevich and His Circle," *Slavic and East European Studies,* 6: 158–176;

A. Kriazhnikov, comp., *Byl dushoi studentcheskogo bratstva: k 175-letiiu so dnia rozhdeniia N. V. Stankevicha (1813–1840)* (Belgorod, 1989);

I. L'khovsky, "Po povodu biografii Stankevicha," *Biblioteka dlia chteniia,* no. 3 (1858);

Iurii Vladimirovich Mann, *Russkaia filosofskaia èstetika (1820–1830)* (Moscow: Iskusstvo, 1969);

Mann, *Russkaia literatura i ee zarubezhnye kritiki* (Moscow: Khudozhestvennaia literatura, 1974);

Mann, *V kruzhke Stankevicha: istoricheskii literaturnyi ocherk* (Moscow, 1983);

Semen Iosifovich Mashinsky, *Nasledie i nasledniki* (Moscow: Sovetskii pisatel, 1967);

Mashinsky, "Stankevich i ego kruzhok," *Voprosy literatury,* no. 5 (1964);

Pavel Nikolaevich Miliukov, *Iz istorii russkoi intellegentsia* (St. Petersburg: Znanie, 1902);

Lidiia Il'inichna Nasonkina, *Moskovskii universitet posle vosstaniia dekabristov* (Moscow: Moskovskii universitet, 1972);

Vera Stepanovna Nechaeva, *V. G. Belinsky; nachalo zhiznnego puti i literaturnoi deiatel'nosti* (Moscow: Akademiia nauk SSSR, 1949);

Mark Iakovl'evich Poliakov, *Vissarion Belinsky. Lichnost'-idei-epokha* (Moscow: Khudozhestvennaia literatura, 1960);

Poliakov, *Belinsky v Moskve, 1829–1839* (Moscow: Moskovskii rabochii, 1948);

Aleksandr Nikolaevich Pypin, ed., *Belinsky, ego zhizn i perepiska* (St. Petersburg: Kolos, 1908);

Pavel Nikitich Sakulin, "Idealizm N. V. Stankevicha," *Vestnik Evropy* (1915): 246–264;

John L. Scherer, "The Myth of the 'Alienated' Russian Intellectual: Michael Bakunin, Vissarion Belinsky, Nikolai Stankevich, Alexander Herzen," dissertation, Indiana University, 1968;

Aleksandr Mikhailovich Skabichevsky, *Sochineniia,* 2 volumes (St. Petersburg: Pavlenkov, 1903);

Evgenii Sorokin, *Priamukhinskie romany: povestvovanie osnovannoe na podlinnykh pis'makh* (Moscow: Sovetskaia Rossiia, 1988);

N. I. Zhuraleva, "O poetakh kruzhke Stankevicha," *Vestnik Moskovskogo Universiteta,* no. 4 (1967).

Aleksandr Ivanovich Turgenev

(23 March 1784 – 3 December 1845)

Vladimir Shatskov
St. Petersburg University of Civil Engineering and Architecture

BOOKS: *Historica Russiae Monumenta ex antiquis exterarum gentium archivis deprompta ab A. I. Turgenevio*, 3 volumes (Petropoli: E. Prats, 1841–1848);

Akty istoricheskie otnosiashchiesia k Rossii, izvlechennye iz innostrannykh Arkhivov i Bibliotek A. I. Turgenevym (St. Petersburg: E. Prats, 1841–1848);

Ukazatel' k Aktam istoricheskim (St. Petersburg: E. Prats, 1843);

Supplementum ad Historia Russiae monumenta, ex archivis ac bibliothecis extráneis deprompta, ita Collegio archaegraphico edita (Petropoli: E. Prats, 1848);

La cour de Russie il y a cent ans, 1724–1783 (Paris: E. Dentu; Berlin: F. Schneider, 1858–1860);

Arkhiv brat'ev Turgenevykh, by A. I., S. I., and N. I. Turgenev, edited by Nikolai Karlovich Kul'man (St. Petersburg: Izdatel'stvo otdela russkago iazyka i slovesnosti Imperatorskot akademii Nauk, 1911–1921);

Khronika russkogo. Dnevniki, 1825–1826, compiled by M. I. Gillel'son (Moscow: Nauka, 1964).

Collection: *Politicheskaia proza,* edited by Aleksandr L. Ospovat (Moscow: Sovetskaia Rossiia, 1989).

Aleksandr Ivanovich Turgenev

In Aleksandr Pushkin's circle of writers, where every individual played a specific historical role, Aleksandr Ivanovich Turgenev occupied a special place. His extraordinary journalistic ability enabled him to convey many profound opinions about Russian history and European reality, about distinguishing characteristics of literature at home and abroad, and about the great contemporaries he met in the course of his life. The name Aleksandr Turgenev holds a prominent position in the history and literature of the first half of the nineteenth century. A friend of the great writers Pushkin, Vasilii Andreevich Zhukovsky, Petr Andreevich Viazemsky, and Nikolai Mikhailovich Karamzin and a brother of the Decembrist Nikolai Turgenev, Aleksandr Turgenev was an active public administrator who passionately promoted all of the most liberal ideas of his time. An avid collector of Russian historical antiquities, he was a man of letters who corresponded with illustrious contemporaries such as Johann Wolfgang von Goethe and Pushkin, leaving in his letters an account of nearly half a century of European life. Turgenev was visible in the social scene of his time, yet he stayed in the background in an accompanying, supportive role. His name is always brought up when Pushkin or Nikolai Turgenev are the subjects of discussion or when anyone speaks of Goethe's relationship with Russian writers, yet his own persona, his own life and deeds are considerably less well known.

An enlightened man, Aleksandr Turgenev had no inclination for writing, nor did he become an historical scholar. He could have become a great governmental official had it not been for his younger brother Nikolai's involvement in the Decembrist movement, which led to his own resignation from state service and many years of residence abroad. According to Viazemsky, Turgenev had an eclectic, multifaceted, cosmopolitan character. He was not at home in any of the fields of human knowledge, but he was never left out. For his contemporaries he was a kind friend, intercessor, and protector of the literary figures who had fallen out of grace with the Crown, a support and help to aspiring poets and writers. For later generations his epistolary legacy holds great interest. Through his voluminous correspondence can be traced events in the literary and social life of the enlightened Russian circles of the beginning of the nineteenth century. His letters are a mine of diverse information, opinions, facts, and projects.

Aleksandr Ivanovich Turgenev was born on 23 March 1784. His father, Ivan Petrovich, was a rich landowner, an enlightened man, and a close friend of Nikolai Ivanovich Novikov, the celebrated author and publisher of progressive literature during the reign of Catherine the Great. For this friendship, Ivan Petrovich, a Freemason, was exiled to live on his family's lands in the Turgenevo-Simbirsk region. Aleksandr's mother was Ekaterina Semenova Kachalova. The emperor Paul I repatriated Ivan Petrovich, brought him back to Moscow, and made him the president of Moscow University. Ivan Petrovich was a highly educated man and a Christian who taught his children high morality and respect for their fellow man. He spent a great deal of time with his children and was to a large degree responsible for their liberal views as well as their interest in history and Russian literature.

In the Turgenev family there were four sons. The oldest, Andrei (1781–1803), a poet and close friend of Zhukovsky, died when he was only twenty-two. He was a highly talented individual who left his mark on Russian literature. Writing his first poems at the age of thirteen, he soon became the nucleus of a junior literary circle, *Druzheskoe literaturnoe obshchestvo* (The Literary Friendship Society), which was formed because of the interest in German Romantic poetry exhibited by such poets as Zhukovsky, Viazemsky, and Konstantin Nikolaevich Batiushkov. Had it not been for his early death, Andrei might well have become a leading Russian literary figure.

Aleksandr was the second son in the family. After his eldest brother's death he felt a great deal of responsibility for his younger brothers. To help them he chose an administrative career. Like the rest of his brothers, Aleksandr received a brilliant education: at first he studied in the Moscow University Gentry Pension from 1797 to 1800, then at Göttingen University in Germany.

The third son, Nikolai, was one of the organizers of the Decembrist movement and consequently spent a great part of his life abroad. He is the best known of the brothers, particularly because of his progressive views. (His main political goal was freedom for the serfs.) He wrote two books, *Opyt teorii nalogov* (An Empirical Theory of Taxation, 1818) and *La Russie et les Russes* (Russia and the Russians, 1847), which are considered major contributions to Russian political thought in the first half of the nineteenth century. Although a member of *Soiuz Blagodentstviia* (The Union of Welfare), the secret society that sought the destruction of the monarchy, Nikolai could not take part in the uprising of 14 December 1825 because he had been forced to leave Russia six months earlier. He spent the rest of his life abroad without a chance of returning to his homeland. Out of the entire Turgenev family he was the only one who had a son, Petr Nikolaevich, to whom Russian researchers are greatly indebted for keeping, in accordance with Aleksandr Turgenev's will, the vast archives of the Turgenev family. Like his brother Nikolai, the fourth son, Sergei, was a bitter enemy of despotism and serfdom, but he was rather unhealthy and died at an early age.

United by their literary interests, Aleksandr Turgenev's small literary society became a noticeable force on the Russian cultural scene. Zhukovsky became a famous poet; Aleksei Fedorovich Merzliakov became a known literary figure and a professor at Moscow University; and Andrei Sergeevich Kaisarov became a professor at Dorpat University. The members of *Druzheskoe literaturnoe obshchestvo* loved German Romantic poetry, subscribed to all the major German literary publications, translated the works of August Friedrich Ferdinand von Kotzebue, and even attempted translations of German poets such as Christoph Martin Wieland, Friedrich von Schiller, and Goethe. Their favorite works were Goethe's *Die Leiden des jungen Werthers* (The Sorrows of Young Werther, 1774) and the dramas of Schiller. The main goal of the Turgenev brothers and their friends was the incorporation of German Romanticism into Russian literature.

When considering the literary society of the young Turgenevs, it is important to mention a group to which the senior Turgenev belonged: *Druzheskoe uchenoe obshchestvo* (The Friendly Learned Society). Among its members were the brothers Ivan and Petr Lopukhin (Turgenev's neighbors in the Simbirsk region), the well-known poet and historian Karamzin, the historian and philosopher Ivan Ivanovich Dmitriev, and other landowner-neighbors who made their way to the top of the Russian literary circles of pre-Pushkin times with the help of the senior Turgenev. The two societies interacted closely, although their interests and goals were different. The younger generation focused primarily on literature, while the older generation was more interested in history. Also, *Druzheskoe uchenoe obshchestvo* had strong masonic leanings, while *Druzheskoe literaturnoe obshchestvo* had nothing to do with freemasonry.

Aleksandr Turgenev's social circle was interesting. Friendships formed during his youth continued for the rest of his life. It is safe to say that particularly during this time (1800–1802) his moral as well as his social base was formed. Also during this time he experienced his first romance, the subject of which was Anna Sokovnikova. His feelings for her were rather shallow, and after two years of correspondence, their relationship was over.

Turgenev's excitement at the prospect of studying at Göttingen University is understandable, considering his love for German Romantic literature, for he would have a chance to study in the land of his literary gods. But two years of study in Göttingen changed his focus from literature to history. His university mentor was one of the most important historians of the time: August Ludwig Schlötzer. Under his guidance Turgenev became increasingly interested in historical science. He assisted with Schlötzer's work on the chronicler Nestor and in 1804 published an essay on ancient Russian history in the newspaper *Severnaia pchela* (Northern Bee). His professor held a high opinion of him and at his graduation gave him a written recommendation for further work in the field of history. Turgenev's stay abroad culminated in a trip through Central and Eastern Europe, made with his friend Kaisarov. (They had studied together in Moscow as well as Göttingen.) The friends visited Leipzig, Dresden, Prague, Vienna, Budapest, and Venice. After the journey was over, Kaisarov returned to Göttingen and Turgenev returned to Russia. Full of patriotic zeal, Turgenev was ready to devote his life to the study of Russian history and to the collection of antiquities.

Unfortunately, his homecoming did not bring him much joy. After already having lost his older brother, he was now faced with a dying parent. Following the death of his father, Turgenev became the head of the family, which meant that he had to care for his two younger brothers. In order to let his brothers have a chance at a good education, he had to abandon his career as an historian and to embark on an administrative one. He entered civil service in 1806 in the department of the assistant to the minister of justice, Nikolai Nikolaevich Novosil'tsev;

soon he was offered a second job as an assistant in the Committee of Law Compilation. Schlötzer's recommendation, which Turgenev could not use as intended, had at least assured him a favorable disposition within St. Petersburg's bureaucracy as well as stable employment. Turgenev's administrative career was successful; by 1816 he had attained the post of assistant to the Chairman of the Department of Law. He considered his main job in the Committee of Law Compilation to be the creation of laws that would limit the landlords' rights of serf ownership.

In fact, the Turgenev brothers, Aleksandr and Nikolai, were among the most consistent fighters against serfdom in early-nineteenth-century Russia. They were responsible for proposing, in the Committee of Law Compilation, a law that would forbid the sale of serfs without land. In their own villages in the Simbirsk region, they enforced the changes that they stood for. In a letter to Viazemsky, Aleksandr Turgenev wrote: "My brother returned from the village. . . . There he enforced his liberalism, abolished the *barshchina* [corvee], and put our peasants on *obrok* [quitrent], thus lessening our income. But his actions were correct." Later, however, the revolutionary views of the brothers diverged.

Aleksandr opposed any forced changes in the governing order, especially any curtailment of power or attempt on the tsar's life; he always upheld a moderately liberal position. Nikolai, at the time, held radical opinions as a member of the *Soiuz Blagodentstviia,* which favored the overthrow of the autocracy by any means. He was fired from his civil service position for having such free-thinking opinions. Soon, in 1824, Aleksandr was also fired.

The brothers left Russia in the spring of 1825. In a few months they heard the news of the failed Decembrist attempt to establish radical reforms through an armed rebellion. A little later they discovered that in Russia, Nikolai was now considered a class I criminal. Thus, he could no longer return, for any such attempt would automatically result in a life sentence at hard labor. The youngest brother, Sergei, was also implicated in Nikolai's case. He survived the legal ordeal but died in 1827 after a long illness. Even though they were abroad, the Turgenev brothers tried to realize their political ideas back in their hereditary lands. In 1827 they instructed their bailiff to free their serfs. This attempt failed because their agent refused to follow their orders. Two years later Aleksandr tried to exempt his serfs from the mandatory draft. These isolated feats of liberalism accomplished almost nothing. Sometimes even Aleksandr considered his own ideas "amusing," yet this hopeless but persistent doctrine later had much to do with the formation of a new democratic ideology in the mid nineteenth century.

Turgenev was not a writer or a poet; he did not leave behind any great literary work, but from an early age he was well acquainted with the highest literary circles of his time. He was actively involved in the cultural life of his contemporaries, and he knew and corresponded with many literary figures of his time; because of these associations, his name is mentioned in discussions of Zhukovsky, Viazemsky, Pushkin, and Evgenii Abramovich Baratynsky. His main creative output was his correspondence and diaries. A true man of letters, Turgenev was a chronicler of contemporary life. In his letters and diaries are allusions to nearly all of the literary and social events of his day. In the nineteenth century a letter was not only a means of personal communication but also a description of cultural events (an alternative to the regular press). Considering that Turgenev maintained up regular correspondence with Baratynsky, Karamzin, Viazemsky, Dmitriev, Zhukovsky, Nikolai Ivanovich Grech, and Aleksandr Fedorovich Voeikov, his role as a kind of journalist becomes apparent; in a way he helped to form the collective tastes of his contemporaries.

The literary niche that Turgenev strove to occupy would be considered journalistic today. In fact, that is precisely what Pushkin called it in his review of Turgenev's serial publication in *Sovremennik* (The Contemporary) under the title of "Khronika russkogo v Parizhe" (Chronicles of a Russian in Paris). "We had a chance . . . to take a peek at his daily and even hourly comments, and as is the custom in this age of exposing all secrets to rush to share the latest news with readers of *Sovremennik;* in other words, to give a shorthand view of . . . the fevered pace of Paris life." Viazemsky, too, was interested in Turgenev's journalistic talents and hired him as one of the Paris correspondents for the *Moskovskii telegraf* (Moscow Telegraph). He was particularly interested in Turgenev's private letters, which he considered masterful, and saw them as a remedy for the dearth of European news in Russia at that time.

Turgenev possessed an encyclopedic knowledge of many fields. This knowledge helped him to be a brilliant chronicler of a wide spectrum of political, literary, and artistic events. Combined with his rare energy, this learning helped him to receive and disseminate news and opinions. His thoughts were often original and inventive but primarily consisted of answers to the questions before him. These made him a brilliant conversationist whom everyone valued.

In order to understand better the importance of Turgenev's correspondence, one has to consider that after confiscation of Aleksandr Nikolaevich Radishchev's *Puteshestvie iz Peterburga v Moskvu* (A Journey from Petersburg to Moscow, 1790), good examples of Russian journalism were scarcely available to readers. Karamzin's *Zapiski drevnei i novoi Rossii* (Memoir on the Old and the New Russia, written December 1810–January 1811, published 1861) was addressed only to the Grand Duchess Ekaterina Pavlovna, the sister of Alexander I. And "Remarks Concerning a Mutiny," the preface to Pushkin's *Istoria Pugacheva* (History of Pugachev, 1834), was written only for the personal use of Nicholas I. Turgenev, on the other hand, opened his writings to the public, trying to develop in his readers free opinions, tolerance, and respect for the new and extraordinary.

One of Turgenev's closest friends was the poet Petr Viazemsky. Their friendship mainly manifested itself through letters: they never lived in the same city and because of this met only a few times in their lives. Viazemsky's description of Turgenev is vivid:

> The whole day he was in constant movement, mental and physical. In the morning he took care of his civil service job and spent the rest of the day running around town trying to help his friends. . . . He was an active literary correspondent, who brought to society the literary works of Zhukovsky, Pushkin, and others. His letter writing was phenomenal. I ask you: when did he find time to write and mail all of these letters on so many topics all over the world? He corresponded with his petitioners, with his brothers, with friends and acquaintances, with students, with spiritual leaders of all possible persuasions, with ladies of all ages, divers years and generations; he corresponded with all of Russia, France, Germany, Austria. . . .

In the period from 1806 to 1824—that is, in the period of his settled life in St. Petersburg and of incessant, endless administrative activity—friendship with the Viazemskys was the principal, most lively factor for Turgenev.

His relationship with Pushkin also held a special place in his life. He had become acquainted with the Pushkins in Moscow. Together with the poet's uncle, Vasilii L'vovich Pushkin, Turgenev had been inducted into the St. Petersburg literary society *Arzamas,* where he received the nickname Aeolian Harp. Later the two went to great pains to assure Pushkin a place at the Tsarskoe Selo Lyceum. In 1820 Turgenev stood up in Pushkin's defense when the young poet was threatened with exile to the Solovetskii monastery. He helped Pushkin to get a post in the department of Prince Mikhail Semenovich Vorontsov and worked tirelessly to end the poet's exile in Kishinev. From the few letters of their correspondence that have survived, it is apparent that Pushkin considered Turgenev to be his faithful defender and sponsor. Before 1825 a certain theme runs through these letters: that Turgenev, as a civil servant with an impeccable record, constantly interceded on Pushkin's behalf whenever the latter had his frequent clashes with government censors. After Turgenev left Russia, Pushkin hired him as a literary correspondent for the journal *Sovremennik*.

One of Turgenev's last visits to Russia coincided with Pushkin's duel and death. In December 1836 and January 1837 the two men frequently met and discussed different literary topics. Pushkin's death came as a complete surprise to Turgenev. Left in a state of bewilderment, he nevertheless managed to leave one of the most impressive accounts of the duel, death, and funeral of the poet: his diary includes a detailed description of the events from January 27 to February 7. Turgenev alone was permitted to follow the coffin to its place of burial in the Sviatogorsky monastery near Pskov, close to the family estate Mikhailovskoe so he alone knew the facts of Pushkin's burial.

During the twenty years that Turgenev spent abroad, traveling throughout Europe, he met and corresponded with some of the most notable figures of West European culture. In 1826 he met Goethe in Weimar, subsequently visiting him on several occasions. In 1828 he became acquainted with Sir Walter Scott and Robert Peel. Around 1829 he became well known in European literary circles. His list of correspondents includes Scott; François-René, vicomte de Chateaubriand; Wilhelm Freiherr von Humboldt; Johann Martin Miller; and even Kaiser Friedrich Wilhelm IV. During this era of extreme censorship in Nicolaevan Russia, Aleksandr Turgenev was truly a "window to Europe" for his Russian readers.

Turgenev made another contribution to Russian culture that has drawn considerably less attention than his correspondence. Though he never became a professional historian and scholar, he was one of the founders of Russian archival studies. Collection of rare documentation interested him even during his studies at Göttingen with Schlötzer. Upon his return to Russia, though, he did little archival work due to his involvement in civil service, yet he did find time to help Karamzin in his historical research. Abroad, free from service responsibilities, he dedicated his time to obtaining archival documents of Russian culture. Working in the archives of London, Paris, Rome, and the Hague, he collected a great many documents of Russia's past. Starting in 1841 he began to publish these materials under the title *Akty istoricheskie otnosiashchiesia k Rossii izvlechennye iz innostrannykh Arkhivov i Bibliotek A. I. Turgenevym* (Historical Documents Pertaining to Ancient Rus', Obtained by A. I. Turgenev in Foreign Archives and Libraries). In 1844 Turgenev published a volume of documents dedicated to eighteenth-century Russia. Between 1858 and 1860 Turgenev's book based on reports of British and French ambassadors, *La cour de Russie il y a cent ans, 1724–1783* (The Russian Court a Hundred Years Ago, 1724–1783), was published in Berlin and reprinted three times. Turgenev's impact on Russian archival studies was immense.

After spending two years more in France and Germany, Turgenev went back to Russia, on the way visiting Zhukovsky in Frankfurt-am-Main, where he also saw Gogol several times. Having "taken the waters" in Germany, he returned to Moscow at the end of August 1845. He spent his last months visiting friends, going through his archives, and planning to write his memoirs, but he caught cold while distributing money to convicts on Sparrow Hills and died on 3 December 1845. His papers were sealed soon after by the Moscow authorities, but Nicholas I ordered that a part of them, dealing mainly with sensitive issues such as the schism in the Russian Orthodox Church and Aleksandr I's correspondence with King George III, be transferred to the Archives of the Third Section in St. Petersburg.

Aleksandr Ivanovich Turgenev's name will forever be associated with Russia's Golden Age. Not only did he advance the cause of Russian history and historiography with his archival work and preservation of documents, but also he played an active role in the development of literature, principally through his association with the major writers of the day and in his dissemination of news of European and Russian culture. Turgenev's able administrative skills and his philanthropic activities also added to his reputation as one of the leading personages of the day. His fame mainly rests, however, on his voluminous correspondence and diaries, in which he chronicled contemporary literary, political, and social history. Turgenev deserves a prominent place as one of the most distinguished figures of his age.

Letters:

"Pis'ma A. I. Turgeneva I. I. Dmitrievu," *Russki arkhiv* (1867): 639–670;

Pis'ma A. I. Turgeneva N. I. Turgenevu (Leipzig: F. A. Brokganz, 1872);

"Pis'ma K. S. Serbinovichu," *Russkaia starina* (1881–1882);

Correspondence with Prince Petr Andreevich Viazemsky, in Viazemsky's *Ostaf'evskii arkhiv kniazei Viazemskikh,* 5 volumes in 8, edited by Vladimir Ivanovich Saitov, volume 8 edited by P. N. Shefter (St. Petersburg: S. B. Sheremetev, 1899–1913);

Pis'ma A. I. Turgeneva Bulgakovym, edited by A. A. Saburov and Iakov Kapitonovich Luppol (Moscow: Gosuderstvennae sotsial'noè-konomicheskoe izdatel'stvo, 1939).

References:

Nikolai Ivanovich Grech, *Zapiski o moei zhizni* (Moscow-Leningrad: Akademia, 1930), pp. 492–501, 649–654, and passim;

Barry Hollingsworth, "Aleksandr Turgenev and the Composition of *Khronika russkogo:* A Note and a Query," *Slavonic and East European Review,* 45: 531–536;

Hollingsworth, "The Friendly Literary Society," *New Zealand Slavonic Journal,* 1 (1976): 23–41;

Vasilii Mikhailovich Istrin, "Mladshii Turgenevskii Kruzhok i Aleksandr Ivanovich Turgenev," in *Arkhiv brat'ev Turgenevykh,* volume 2 (St. Petersburg, 1911);

Ekaterina O. Larionova, "A. I. Turgenev v 'Arzamase,'" *Graduate Essays on Slavic Language and Literature* (Pittsburg: University of Pittsburg, 1991);

Larionova, "Frantsuzskaia monografiia ob A. I. Turgeneve," *Russkaia literatura,* no. 4 (1992): 233–241;

Larionova, "K istorii stikhotvoreniia V. A. Zhukovskogo 'Imperatoru Aleksandru': Pis'ma A. I. Turgeneva V. A. Zhukovskomu," *Russkaia literatura,* 9, no. 3 (May/June 1989): 60–65;

Boris Livovich Modzalevsky, "Zhukovsky i brat'ia Turgenevy," in *Dekabristy: neizdannye materialy i stat'i,* edited by Modzalevsky and Iulian Grigor'evich Oksman (Moscow: Vsesoiuznoe obshehestvo politicheskikh katorzhani ssyl'noposelen'tsev, 1925), pp. 149–154;

Andrei Nikolaevich Shebunin, "Brat'ia Turgenevy i dvorianskoe obshchestvo Aleksandrovskoi epokhi," in *Dekabrist N. I. Turgenev,* edited by N. G. Svirin (Moscow: AN SSSR, 1936), pp. 26–79;

Gleb Struve, "Alexander Turgenev, Ambassador of Russian Culture in Partibus Infidelium," *Slavic Review,* 29 (1970): 444–459;

M. Thierry, "Russkii kosmopolitizm v pervoi polovine XIX veka," 5 volumes, dissertation, University of Paris, Sorbonne, 1982;

William Mills Todd III, *The Familiar Letter as a Literary Genre in the Age of Pushkin* (Princeton, N.J.: Princeton University Press, 1976);

Aleksandr Nikolaevich Veselovsky, *V. A. Zhukovsky. Poeziia chuvstva i "serdechnogo voobrazheniia"* (St. Petersburg: Imperatorskoi akademii nauk, 1904), pp. 137–219;

Veselovsky, "V. A. Zhukovsky i A. I. Turgenev v literaturnykh kruzhkakh Drezdena. 1826–1827 godu," *Zhurnal Ministerstva narodnogo prosveshcheniia,* no. 5 (1905): 159–183;

Viktor Vladimirovich Vinogradov, "Al'bom I. I. Dmitrieva," *Don,* no. 6 (1957): 149–155;

Vremennik Pushkinskoi komissii, volume 1 (Moscow-Leningrad: AN SSSR, 1936), pp. 191–220;

Patrick H. Waddington, "Document: Some Letters from A. I., S. I. and N. I. Turgenev to Richard Monckton Milnes (Lord Haughton)," *New Zealand Slavonic Studies,* 2: 61–83.

Papers:
There are archives on Turgenev in the Institute of Russian Literature, Pushkin House, fond 309.3.

Aleksandr Fomich Vel'tman

(8 July 1800 – 11 January 1870)

Brian J. Horowitz
University of Nebraska, Lincoln

BOOKS: *Nachalnye osnovaniia arifmetiki* (Moscow, 1817);

Nachertanie drevnei istorii Bessarabii: s prisovokupleniem istoricheskikh vypisok i karty (Moscow, 1828);

Beglets: povest' v stikhakh (Moscow, 1831);

Muromskie lesa: povest' v stikhakh (Moscow, 1831);

Strannik, 3 parts (Moscow, 1831–1832);

Koshchei bessmertnyi: bylina starogo vremeni (Moscow: A. Semen, 1833);

MMMCDXLVIII god: rukopis' Martyna Zadeki, 3 volumes (Moscow: A. Semen, 1833);

Lunatik: sluchai, 2 volumes (Moscow: N. Stepanov, 1834);

O Gospodine Novgorode Velikom: pis'mo, s prilozheniem vida Novgoroda v XII stoletii i plana okrestnostei (Moscow: S. Selivanovsky, 1834);

Sviatoslavich vrazhii pitomets: diva vremen krasnogo solntsa Vladimira (Moscow, 1835);

Predki Kalimerosa: Aleksandr Filippovich Makedonskii (Moscow, 1836);

Povesti (Moscow, 1837);

Virginiia; ili, Poezdka v Rossiiu (Moscow, 1837);

Serdtse i dumka: prikliuchenie (Moscow, 1838);

General Kalimeros: roman (Moscow, 1840);

Ratibor Kholmogradskii (Moscow, 1841);

Dostopamiatnosti moskovskago Kremlia (Moscow: N. Stepanov, 1843);

Povesti (St. Petersburg: M. D. Ol'khin, 1843);

Moskovskaia oruzheinaia palata (Moscow, 1844);

Novyi Emelia; ili, Prevrashcheniia: roman, 4 volumes (Moscow: N. Stepanov, 1845);

Troian i Angelitsa: povest' rasskazannaia svetloi Dennistsei iasnomu Mesiatsu (Moscow: N. Stepanov, 1846);

Prikliucheniia pocherpnutye iz moria zhiteiskago: Salomeia (Moscow, 1848);

Prikliucheniia pocherpnutye iz moria zhiteiskago: Chudodei (Moscow, 1849);

Opisanie novogo Imperatorskogo dvortsa v Kremle moskovskom (Moscow: A. Semen, 1851);

Indo-germany, ili saivane: opyt svoda i poverki skazanii o pervobytnykh naselentsakh Germanii (Moscow, 1856);

O Svevakh, Gunnakh i Mongolakh (Moscow, 1856);

Aleksandr Fomich Vel'tman, 1839 (portrait by K-F. P. Bodri; from Strannik *[The Wanderer], edited by Iurii M. Akutin, 1977)*

Attila i Rus' IV i V veka: svod istoricheskikh i narodnykh predanii (Moscow, 1858);

Magi i Midiiskie Kagany XIII stoletiia (Moscow: Universitetskaia tipografiia, 1860);

Prikliucheniia pocherpnutye iz moria zhiteiskago: Vospitannitsa Sara (Moscow: Katkov, 1862);

Prikliucheniia pocherpnutye iz moria zhiteiskago: Schast'e-neschast'e, 2 volumes (Moscow: A. Semen, 1863);

Pervobytnoe verovanie i Buddizm. (Moscow: Universitetskaia tipografiia, 1864);

Don: Mesto ssylki Ovidiia Nazona. Metropoliia Velikoi i Maloi Rusi na Donu s IV do IX veka (Moscow, 1866);

Dneprovskie porogi po Konstantinu Badrianovodnomu, (Moscow, n.d.).

Editions and Collections: *Prikliucheniia pocherpnutye iz moria zhiteiskago: Salomeia,* edited by Valerian

Fedorovich Pereverzev (Moscow: Khudozhestvennaia literatura, 1957);

Strannik, edited by Iurii M. Akutin (Moscow: Nauka, 1957);

Povesti i rasskazy, edited by Iurii M. Akutin (Moscow: Sovetskaia Rossiia, 1979);

Romany, edited by V. I. Kalugin (Moscow: Sovremennik, 1985);

Serdtse i dumka: prikliuchenie: roman v 4-kh chastiakh, edited by Viacheslav Anatol'evich Koshelev and A. V. Chernov (Moscow: Sovetskaia Rossiia, 1986).

TRANSLATIONS: *Mahabharata,* excerpts translated as "Nalo: povest' Urikhadazvy rasskazannaya Bgaratu," *Otechestvennye zapiski,* 3 (1839): 253–274;

William Shakespeare, *A Midsummer Night's Dream,* translated as "Volshebnaia noch': dramaticheskaia fantaziia," *Literaturnyi vecher* (1844): 35–143.

OTHER: *Moskvitianin,* edited by Vel'tman, 1849–1850;

Drevnosti rossiiskogo gosudarstva, edited, with contributions, by Vel'tman (Moscow, 1849–1853);

Amalat-bek, liberetto opery v 4 deistviiakh v 5 kartinakh (St. Petersburg, 1870);

"Travel Impressions," in *Russian Romantic Prose: An Anthology,* edited by Carl R. Proffer (Ann Arbor: Ardis, 1979);

SELECTED PERIODICAL PUBLICATIONS: "O vospitanii: Otryvok iz *Opyta o voennoi nravstvennosti,* sochineniia Al. Vel'tmana," *Syn otechestva,* 109, nos. 18–19 (1826): 200–211;

"Iunaia greshnitsa," "Ozhidanie," *Syn otechestva,* 17, no. 1 (1828): 86–87;

"Megamed," *Moskovskii telegraf,* 26, no. 5 (1829): 45;

"Drevniaia zmeia" and "Aleksandr Velikii," *Moskovskii telegraf,* 29, no. 17 (1829): 37–38;

"Zoroastr," *Moskovskii telegraf,* 31, no. 2 (1830): 177–178;

"Eskander," *Moskovskii telegraf,* 31, no. 2 (1831): 195–202;

"Provintsial'nie aktery," *Biblioteka dlia chteniia,* 10, no. 1 (1835): 208–243;

"Erotida: povest'," *Moskovskii nabliudatel',* 1 (1835): 330–381;

"Vospominaniia o Bessarabii," part 1, *Sovremennik,* 7 (1837): 226–49;

"Iolanda: povest'," *Moskovskii nabliudatel',* 12 (1837): 397–448;

"Radoi: povest'," *Syn otechestva,* 7, no. 1 (1839): 107–176;

"Kosteshtskie skaly: rasskaz," *Odesskii al'manakh na 1840 god* (1839);

"Putevye vpechatleniia i mezhdu prochim, gorshok erani: komicheskii rasskaz v rode povesti," *Syn otechestva,* 1 (1840): 35–84;

"Portfel' sluzhebnoi deiatel'nosti M. V. Lomonosova iz sobstvennoruchnikh bumag," *Ocherki Rossii,* 2 (1841);

"Likhomanka: soldatskaia skazka," *Literaturnaia gazeta,* 5 (1841);

"Priezzhii iz uezda; ili, sumatokha v stolitse," *Moskvitianin,* 1, no. 1 (1841): 131–218;

"Zakharushka dobraia dusha," *Russkaia beseda,* 2 (1841): 1–32;

"Otvet gospodinu Shevyrevu," *Moskvitianin,* 11 (1841): 194–213;

"Karriera," *Biblioteka dlia chteniia,* 55, no. 1 (1842): 13–66;

"Kolumb: dramaticheskie kartiny," *Russkii vestnik,* nos. 5–6 (1842): 85–132;

"Ob obretenii i vozobnovlenii drevneishei tserkvi Voskreseniia Lazaria," *Literaturnaia gazeta,* 28 (1842): 584–585;

"Raina, koroleva bolgarskaia," *Biblioteka dlia chteniia,* 59 (1843): 13–126;

"Volgin," *Biblioteka dlia chteniia,* 60 (1843): 17–88;

"Lechenie tsarevicha Alekseia Mikhailovicha," *Moskvitianin,* 1, no. 2 (1844): 265;

"Ilia Larin: rasskaz," *Moskovskii gorodskoi listok,* 10 January 1847, pp. 29–32;

"Dva maera: povest'," *Moskvitianin,* 1, no. 1 (1848): 33–90;

"Naem dachi: povest'," *Biblioteka dlia chteniia,* 91, no. 2 (1848): 1–64;

"Doch' Ippokrata: 'ellinkoe predanie ostrova Kosa,'" *Moskvitianin,* 3, no. 10 (1849): 61–76;

"Vengerskie trofei v Moskve," *Moskvitianin,* 5, no. 18 (1849): 31–32;

"Vengriia: istoricheskii obzor," *Moskvitianin,* 1, no. 1 (1849): 1–8;

"Vengriia i Kroatsiia: istoricheskii obzor," *Moskvitianin,* 1, no. 2 (1849): 37–44;

"Moskovskie gorodskie riady i gostinyi dvor," *Moskvitianin,* 4, no. 16 (1849): 48–64;

"O znachenii slova 'posadnik'," *Moskvitianin,* 2, no. 5 (1849): 13–14;

"Osveshchenie novogo moskovskogo dvortsa v Kremle," *Moskvitianin,* 2, no. 8 (1849): 149–154;

"Torzhestvennye prazdnestva v novom imperatarskom kremlevskom dvortse," *Moskvitianin,* 3, no. 9 (1849): 16–25;

"Imperatorskii kremlevskii dvorets," *Moskvitianin,* 1, no. 3 (1849): 92–95;

"Meteorologiia v prilozhenii ee k botanike, zemlede-liiu, lesovodstvu, geologii, publichnim rabo-tam, gigiene, i meditsine," *Moskvitianin,* 1, no. 3 (1849): 19–26;

"Russkoe tsarstvo v litsakh," *Moskvitianin,* 1, no. 3 (1849): 112–113;

"Zlatoi i Bela: cheshskaia skazka," *Al'manakh v poda-rok chitateliam' 'Moskvitianina'* (1850): 3–52;

"Doch' matrosa," by Vel'tman, E. I. Vel'tman, and Mikhail Petrovich Pogodin, *Al'manakh v poda-rok chitateliam 'Moskvitianina'* (1850): 189–251;

"Otryvok Illiady, pisannyi na papiruse i naidennyi v rukakh Egipetskoi mumii," *Moskvitianin,* 1, no. 2 (1850);

"Eksprompt," *Pushkiniana,* 45 (1902);

"Roland the Furious," translated by James J. Geb-hard, *Russian Literature Triquarterly,* 22 (1988): 27–54.

During his life Aleksandr Vel'tman experi-enced both tremendous popularity and public indif-ference. His fall from the position of one of Russia's leading writers in the 1830s to that of a forlorn fig-ure by the 1840s is a major feature of his literary ca-reer. He was a productive writer, a stylistic innova-tor who created an inimitable verbal world, and an imaginative craftsman who expanded the linguistic scope and literary forms of Russian literature. Be-sides writing more than fifteen novels, Vel'tman was a noted historian and ethnographer and briefly the editor of the important journal *Moskvitianin* (The Muscovite); he also served for more than a decade as the director of the Museum of the Kremlin's Ar-maments.

One reason why Vel'tman fell in popularity is that he did not change in response to changing times. As literary and social norms shifted, and as readers and critics began demanding realistic treat-ment and social themes, Vel'tman remained behind. Having discovered a manner of writing suitable for expressing his idiosyncratic, anarchic voice, Vel't-man held unwaveringly to that idiom.

Vel'tman, however, played an important role in Russian literary history. Writing at the period in which poetry was yielding to prose, Vel'tman pro-duced novels that serve as a bridge from the adven-ture novels of the eighteenth century to the realistic fiction of the nineteenth century. He was a master of a variety of genres—the historical novel, the senti-mental journey, and the fantastic tale—although he molded these genres to fit his particular appetite for narrative digression and verbal and conceptual dis-ruption. Since the politically progressive ideology that so strongly governed Russian literary criticism of the nineteenth century prevented an objective

evaluation of Vel'tman's role, the task of reassessing Vel'tman has fallen to twentieth-century literary his-torians. The Formalists were particularly interested in his fiction; and since the 1950s, Russian scholar Iurii M. Akutin and three Americans—James J. Geb-hard, Charles Alexander Ward, and David La-peza—have greatly contributed to readers' knowl-edge with full-length works on Vel'tman.

Many contemporary descriptions of Vel'tman show him as an urbane gentleman, the host of a Moscow social salon. His "Thursday evenings," to which all of literary Moscow was invited, were an institution for nearly forty years. Vissarion Gri-gor'evich Belinsky, Mikhail Iur'evich Lermontov, Nikolai Gogol, Vladimir Fedorovich Odoevsky, Vladimir Ivanovich Dal', the historian Mikhail Petrovich Pogodin, and the publisher Semen Ioannik'evich Selivanovsky, as well as many others, were among those who attended. Vel'tman was also a workaholic whose schedule reflected his feverish creative temperament. In 1871 Pogodin described Vel'tman this way:

> He belonged to that group of typical Moscow toilers who work from morning till night in their studies, who go nowhere and almost never leave their houses except for occasional necessities, who know no pleasure in the world and are completely devoted to their work. It is useless to wish them imitators, for can such people be found who will eagerly sweat over a desk for fifteen hours a day?

Another image, this one offered by the essayist and memoirist Anatolii Fedorovich Koni, depicts Vel'tman as a superstitious mystic. According to Koni, Vel'tman "was quite taken with spiritualism and seriously believed the messages he received through the medium of the rotating table," a form of spiritualism that was quite widespread in Russian society during the nineteenth century. Still another portrait shows Vel'tman as a generous and benevo-lent individual who took pains to aid others and en-courage young talent.

Aleksandr Fomich Vel'tman was born in St. Petersburg on 8 July 1800. His father, Foma Fedoro-vich Vel'tman, was descended from Swedish nobil-ity (though Gebhard believes that Vel'tman's Ger-man background was more important than the Swedish, since Foma Vel'tman was a native speaker of German). Foma Vel'tman served in the cavalry of the Russian Life Guards and was a veteran of the campaigns against Sweden (1789–1790). In 1799 he married Maria Petrovna Kolpanicheva, the daugh-ter of a court official in St. Petersburg. Once Alek-sandr, the first of four children, was born, Foma Vel'tman retired from the army, seeking a civilian

Page from the manuscript (with a drawing by Vel'tman) for Strannik *(1830), his best-known novel (from* Strannik, *edited by Iurii M. Akutin, 1977)*

occupation. Because he was not successful in the civilian service (he never rose higher than titular councillor, ninth rank), the Vel'tmans were poor, and therefore Aleksandr did not have the financial security that writers from the nobility enjoyed.

Vel'tman was taught Russian by his mother, who invented her own educational system of rewarding her son for good school work in order to combat his laziness. The other influence of Vel'tman's early years was his father's batman, Diad'ka Boris, who acted as Aleksandr's babysitter. A shoemaker by profession, Boris was a storyteller by vocation. In his informative and unpublished autobiographical essay, "Povest' o sebe" (Story of Myself), Vel'tman portrays this literary mentor as a resourceful old man who kept his ward from running away by spinning endless fantastic tales.

In 1808, at age eight, Aleksander was admitted to a private boarding school in Plesko. In 1814 he transferred to the private pension run by Ivan and Aleksei Terlikov for the preparation of candidates entering Moscow University. In 1816 Vel'tman enrolled in the *Korpus Kolonnovozhatykh* (Moscow Educational Institution for Staff Officers), a newly established military school in Moscow that provided an unusual nurturing atmosphere in which the teachers inculcated a genuine desire for learning and high moral aims. In addition to the powerful positive influence the school had on Vel'tman's emotional and intellectual development, its graduates were offered commissions as junior officers on the emperor's military staff. It appears that Vel'tman received these privileges exclusively by virtue of his hard work and scholastic achievements. He excelled in languages, mathematics, and geography; was proficient in music; and read extensively the works of Russia's eighteenth-century writers: Mikhailo Vasil'evich Lomonosov, Vasilii Kirillovich Trediakovsky, Ivan Ivanovich Dmitriev, Gavrila Romanovich Derzhavin, and Nikolai Mikhailovich Karamzin. Imitating his literary heroes, Vel'tman began to write plays and poetry. He also earned money by giving violin lessons, and he wrote a textbook, *Nachalnye osnovaniia arifmetiki* (The Basics of Arithmetic, 1817), at age seventeen.

The Napoleonic invasion in 1812 made a profound and lasting impact on Vel'tman. Although his family evacuated Moscow for Kostroma and he was far from the dangers of the front, Vel'tman made lavish use of his limited war experience in his writing. The image of burned-out Moscow appears as the locale for the novel *Lunatik: sluchai* (Lunatic: An Occurrence, 1834), while the presence of Napoleon Bonaparte in Moscow is the subject of an entire novel, *General Kalimeros* (1840). The events of 1812 also play an important role in the novels *Virginiia; ili, Poezdka v Rossiiu* (Virginia; or, A Trip to Russia, 1837) and *Novyi Emelia; ili, Prevrashcheniia* (The New Emelia; or, Metamorphoses, 1845).

Having graduated from the academy in 1817, Vel'tman was enlisted directly into the armed forces and spent more than a decade on the southwestern border of the empire, serving as a cartographer and military officer. His exploits included service as a member of a team making a topological survey of the newly acquired province of Bessarabia and as the aide-de-camp of the army headquarters before he retired with the rank of lieutenant in 1831. In his travels throughout the southeastern parts of the Russian empire Vel'tman accumulated ethnographical information and personal impressions. This experience became a major source for his literary work.

Another inspiration was his short-lived but deeply influential relationship with the poet Aleksandr Pushkin. While stationed in Kishinev in 1821, Vel'tman met Pushkin, and although they never became close since Vel'tman avoided cards and the social world of the Kishinev elite, Pushkin esteemed Vel'tman. They read poems to each other and debated questions of literature. Vel'tman dared to present his opinions of Pushkin's work, although according to Vel'tman's own testimony Pushkin did not like to be criticized. Ivan Petrovich Liprandi, a friend of the two, wrote in his memoirs that "Vel'tman was one of a few who could provide nourishment to Pushkin's mind and curiosity." Soon called away for duty, however, Vel'tman did not see Pushkin again until 1831.

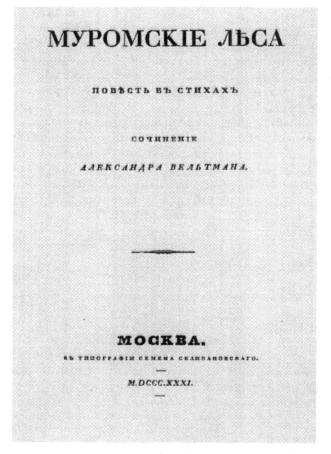

Title page for Muromskie lesa: povest' v stikhakh *(The Murom Forests: A Tale in Verse), one of Vel'tman's romantic poems*

During his time spent in the army Vel'tman continued to develop as a writer, setting himself ambitious plans for his future. He wrote two romantic poems, or "tales in verse," *Muromskie lesa* (The Forests of Murom, 1831) and *Beglets* (The Fugitive, 1831), which were influenced by Pushkin's "Ruslan i Liudmila" (1820) and "Kavkazskii plennik" (The Prisoner of the Caucasus, 1820–1821). Showing his ability to transform his own experience into art, in these early satirical poems Vel'tman deflated the Kishinev elite by portraying their pettiness, greed, and bourgeois self-contentment. It should be noted that, although far from the capitals, Vel'tman kept in touch with the latest intellectual trends, befriending many of the men who were members of the southern group of Decembrists (though Vel'tman was cleared of all charges connected with their 1825 conspiracy).

In the late 1820s Vel'tman was confronted with personal difficulties. His brother Nikolai and his father died, and his younger siblings were taken into a foster family. Furthermore, while stationed in

Shumla during the Russo-Turkish War in 1828, he fell in love with Elizaveta Isupova, the wife of a fellow officer. The relationship became so serious that the two planned Elizaveta's divorce so that they could marry. Elizaveta's husband, however, did not want to let her go, and by the time of Vel'tman's retirement from the army in 1831, their passions had cooled. In 1832 Velt'man married his distant cousin Anna Pavlovna Veidel' and settled in Moscow. In 1835 a son was born, but he died three days later. A daughter, Nadezhda, was born in 1837. Since the income for a retired lieutenant did not suffice for a growing family, Vel'tman went to work in the civil service as a clerk. Later, with the help of novelist Mikhail Nikolaevich Zagoskin, Vel'tman got the position of assistant director of the Museum of the Kremlin's Armaments.

In 1828 Vel'tman published his first work about Bessarabia, *Nachertanie drevnei istorii Bessarabii: s prisovokupleniem istoricheskikh vypisok i karty* (An Outline of the Ancient History of Bessarabia: With an Appendix of Historical Materials and a Map, 1828). Gebhard astutely notes the significance of the fact that this first major work consisted of historical scholarship, since Vel'tman was always pulled by two vocations—writer and historian-archaeologist.

Vel'tman's career as a fiction writer really began when he published his novel *Strannik* (The Wanderer) in the journal *Moskovskii telegraf* (The Moscow Telegraph) in 1830 and 1831, with subsequent book publication. *Strannik* was touted as the best novel of the year, and Vel'tman was considered a rising star. Among others, Belinsky, the leading critic of the day, hailed the work in his essay "Literaturnye mechtaniia" (Literary Reveries) in *Molva* (The Rumor) in 1834: "Vel'tman possesses such a vivacious, light, original talent that he is able to give so much fascination to each trifle, each joke. Oh, he is a true magician, a real poet." The survey article in *Moskovskii telegraf* for the year 1831 stated: "From two-hundred books, listed in the bibliography of *The Telegraph* of this year 1831, with which can one be content? Pushkin's *Boris Godunov* and Vel'tman's *Strannik*."

Although Vel'tman wrote many other novels, *Strannik* became the best known and had the greatest influence on later writers; it also set a pattern for his later novels in terms of language, form, and style. Vel'tman's novel has its sources in the two realms of life and literature. While much of the raw material of the novel is garnered from real life—the life of a Russian soldier in Bessarabia—the construction of the novel recalls the influence of the leading genres of the time: the sentimental travelogue, the military memoir, and the society tale. Out of these different genres, however, Vel'tman created something new and unusual. Ostensibly weaving a colorful, vibrant narrative about his travels in Bessarabia during the years he served there, Vel'tman undercuts the pretense that he is describing a genuine journey by asserting that the hero is actually sitting immobile in his Moscow study examining a map. In addition, while recalling several events pertinent to his own biography and presenting many facts concerning the history of Bessarabia, Vel'tman tells his story in an original way, using a first-person *skaz* narrator who is compulsively digressive. Instead of telling a straight and direct tale, the narrator stops and starts, introducing various themes from other literary discourses not connected with the story of the narrator's Bessarabian travels. Furthermore, Vel'tman invents an idiosyncratic and colorful language, splicing in Bessarabian dialects and diverse and unusual words from literary and conversational Russian. The rich linguistic and formal texture of *Strannik* plays as large a role in the novel as do the events described.

The fictionalized journey through Bessarabia is forty-five days long, composed of three parts covering fifteen days each. During that time, however, the narrator is able to take the reader through far more material than could occur in so many days. The extension of time is created not by the narrator providing more information about himself and his life but through digressions about literature, poetry, philosophy, and the history of Bessarabia. The narrator's musings on love, art, genius, immorality, and immortality are encyclopedic, although basically unmotivated by the travel story. Lapeza has described the various ways in which Vel'tman motivates digression: Vel'tman presents the fantasies of an educated traveler; the narrator's imagination operates independently of the maps in the Moscow apartment; and he uses structural conceits that are characteristic of Laurence Sterne's prose—free association and digressive rhetorical figures such as the catalogue, the scholarly citation, the extended comparison, the pun, and the realized commonplace. The open form in which the narrator can insert a digression on any subject at any time allows for involved and imaginative discussions on philosophical, historical, and personal themes.

The device of digression plays such a large role in Vel'tman's novel because for the author, the creative act is a linguistic act. Vel'tman plays with language, using his inventiveness to transmit, seemingly without selection or artistic rendering, the explosive chaos of the world he sees. The reader's feeling of encountering complete spontaneity is heightened by constant disjunctions, digressions, and non sequiturs. Although the result leads to the impression of haphazard chaos, the effect is intentional. Vel'tman carefully chooses what to include and how to present his material. He describes his method:

> I treat those things nobody ever noticed or noticed very rarely. But is there a similar thing in the world?—this is only a joke!—In the hands of the writer all the words, all the ideas, all the philosophizing is like the colorful little stones of a kaleidoscope. In the same way everyone will turn it in his own fashion, will see a different figure; he is happy if it seems to his mind that he has invented it.

Vel'tman, half realist, half Romantic, claims that the material of his fiction is the real world, while the artist merely shows it in a unique way. From the above passage many scholars have adopted the simile of a child's toy, the kaleidoscope, to grasp Vel'tman's colorful, dynamic descriptive method.

Vel'tman's wide use of digression has led scholars to investigate the connection of *Strannik* to the conventional Sternean narrator. While *Strannik* is related to Sterne's *Tristram Shandy* (1759–1767) since both have digressive narrators, the form of *Strannik* has a closer model in the genre of the sentimental journey and its examples in Russian literature. The development of the genre in Russia began primarily with *Pis'ma russkogo puteshestvennika* (Letters of a Russian Traveler, 1797–1801), Karamzin's factual travelogue written according to the model of Charles Dupaty's *Lettres sur l'Italie* (Letters on Italy, 1788). Alongside Karamzin, the translations of Count Xavier de Maistre's *Voyage autour de ma chambre* (Voyage around My Room, 1802) and *Expedition nocturne autour de ma chambre* (Night Expedition around My Room, 1803) were highly influential. De Maistre's work was Sternean in style, playfully engaging the reader in a fanciful parody of the informative travelogue. Based on these two models—Karamzin representing the factual treatment and de Maistre the parodic—two distinct groups of literary "journeys" emerged.

The stylistic devices linking *Strannik* with the factual travelogue are the descriptions of exotic places, the pretense of an epistolary form, the direct address to the reader, the inclusion of verses, and the motivation of the plot through travel from one place to another. The narrator describes his experiences as a soldier in Moldavia during the Russo-Turkish war of 1828. *Strannik,* however, belongs also to the category of parodic journeys, since the narrator is actually traveling in his mind on a fictional map. This latter aspect serves as a source of humor. For example, Vel'tman describes a flood in Spain and France, writing, "So this is what it means to place a glass of water on the map! . . . Would I

Vel'tman's second wife, writer Elena Ivanovna Krupenikova, in the 1840s

ever think that I would knock it off the Pyrennes with my elbow."

Z. S. Efimova, a critic of the 1920s, has also discovered the genre of the roman à clef submerged in the novel, since the narrator hints at an unrequited love that he cannot speak about directly or forget entirely. The narrator describes seeking the love of an unidentified married woman, but the romance story is left unresolved: the identity of the woman is never revealed, and the narrator's desire is never consummated. Actually, the love plot is purposely submerged because it is subservient to the other goals of the novel: the evocation of military life, digressions on history and the universal questions of mankind, and the spectacle of Vel't-man's play with language. In fact Vel'tman, posing to himself the question of why he writes the book, mockingly answers that he has no reason at all, but "at least we have been kept amused."

With the deliberately open form of *Strannik* one would expect to find a problem with closure, but there are elements that hold the work together. Most of all, the single personality of the omnipresent narrator plays this unifying role and gives sense to the various unconnected episodes. In addition, the most centrifugal aspect of the novel, the device of digression, paradoxically acts as a kind of cement, gradually linking the disparate elements. Digression constantly creates new relationships between what is already known by the reader and new information. The reader, while not understanding the meaning of these juxtapositions, is called upon to seek meaning in the chaos. The search for order by the reader, admittedly strenuous, actually grounds and orders this highly "messy" text.

Strannik has had a noticeable influence on subsequent writers. Scholars have discovered its links to Aleksandr Aleksandrovich Bestuzhev's (Marlinsky) military tales of the 1830s in the latter's portrayal of noble, candid, and sentimental heroes. Lermontov's *Geroi nashego vremeni* (A Hero of Our Time, 1840) also shares common elements with *Strannik*. For example, in "Taman'" Lermontov shuns psychology, describing an exotic and secretive Caucasus in which, no matter how much he tries, the narrator can never join. Moreover, both Vel'tman's and Lermontov's heroes are soldiers who are equally at home on the front line with the indigenous peoples and at the health spa, relaxing in the company of local high society. Vel'tman's historically informed, philosophically acute, and emotionally sensitive hero may even have influenced Pushkin in his *Puteshestvie v Arzrum* (Journey to Arzrum, 1836) and Leo Tolstoy in his creation of *Sevastopol'skie rasskazy* (The Sevastopol' Sketches, written in 1855–1856) and *Kazaki* (The Cossacks, 1863).

Following *Strannik,* in 1833 Vel'tman tried to build on his success by publishing a novel in three volumes, *MMMCDXLVIII god: rukopis' Martyna Zadeki* (The Year 3448: The Manuscripts of Martyn Zadeka). The action is situated in the thirty-fifth century in Bosforania, a Christian Slavic empire located in what was formerly Constantinople. In the novel Vel'tman depicts a future state in which the leader of Bosforania, a just and benevolent ruler, is overthrown by his tyrannical twin brother, Eol. Once in power, Eol creates chaos because his cruel, egoistic, and tyrannical form of governing is ineffective. Through his uncurbed ambition and his desire to place himself above all other people, Eol creates his own downfall and dies.

Critics of Vel'tman's time did not like the novel. Belinsky was especially caustic, addressing the author directly with a warning that Vel'tman was gambling with his talent and there was reason to fear he might lose. Many critics considered *MMMCDXLVIII god* a political satire of Russia under Tsar Nicholas I's reign, since Vel'tman depicted the evil rule of a tyrant. That interpretation seems stretched, however, since Vel'tman did not speak out against the idea of monarchy, only tyranny. It is interesting, however, to note that in Vel'tman's fictional world the dream of the nineteenth-century Slavophiles of recapturing Constantinople is realized. Bosforania–Constantinople–is presented as Orthodox Christian and Slavic.

Although this novel is one of the first examples of utopian fiction in Russia (the Decembrist Aleksandr Dmitrievich Ulybyshev's *Son* [Dream] is another), the work resembles the adventure stories popular in Russia during the eighteenth century. As Gebhard has pointed out, *MMMCDXLVIII god* includes shipwrecks, abductions, exchanges of identity, and the sudden reversals of fortune that are typical of the genre.

In the same year, 1833, Vel'tman improved his fortunes with the novel *Koshchei bessmertnyi: bylina starogo vremeni* (Koshchei the Deathless: A Tale of Old Times), which he called a *bylina* or historical epic. Set in the fourteenth century, *Koshchei bessmertnyi* consists of a series of loosely connected scenes in which Vel'tman parodies the chivalric quest. The hero, Iva, is a "half-wit, unaware of the reality around him," but as Ward explains, "Vel'tman used this hero because of the latitude it gave him to introduce the number of humorous episodes."

Koshchei bessmertnyi was well received because it was perceived as an historical novel. In truth, however, Vel'tman merely decorated his novel with extensive folklore while actually eliminating historical realism. The popularity of the work reflected the Romantic appreciation for historical novels that treat the quotidian life of the past more than well-known political and military events. Vel'tman appeared to depict the way people lived, the culture, the customs, and the daily life of the past. Furthermore, he lent authenticity to his narrative by using an idiosyncratic old-Russian dialect with which he intended to give the illusion of ancient spoken Russian. Given the state of the literary language at the time, this innovation should be seen as an attempt to infuse the language with fresh material. Gebhard has noticed that Vel'tman was not alone in using such unconventional Russian: "At approximately the same time as he there appeared other authors who introduced into their works unusual, nonliterary language material, material which in a given work is perceived as one of the means of *couleur locale,* but in the general course of literary evolution serves the cause of the creation of a new literary language. Such was the Ukranian language of Gogol' and the Russian dialects of Dal'." It should be noted, as Leonid Arsen'evich Bulakhovskii points out, that Vel'tman's dialect does not correspond to any real language ever spoken by Russians.

After *Koshchei bessmertnyi* Vel'tman wrote a novel a year until 1840. In 1834 Vel'tman published *Lunatik: sluchai,* a novel that takes the War of 1812 as its theme and concerns a young man who is deranged due to the education he received from his father. The hero, Avrelii, sleepwalks at night and has a variety of adventures in this double life. Besides using delirium as a motivation for adventure, the novel is characterized by descriptions of life in the countryside, which act as a counterbalance to Avrelii's urban world. Ward, viewing the work as unsuccessful due to an eclectic mixing of Romanticism and realism, claims that although the plot of the story features "mistaken identities, odd coincidences, and unlikely events" and thus is "heir to the devices of eighteenth-century adventure novels and comic opera," the novel has a realistic aspect "from Vel'tman's use of real peasant dialogue in minor characters." This mixture of contradictory influences characterizes Vel'tman's career.

In *Sviatoslavich vrazhii pitomets: diva vremen krasnogo solntsa Vladimira* (Sviatoslavich, The Devil's Nursling: Diva in the Time of the Red Sun Vladimir, 1835), Vel'tman returned to Russian folklore, setting his story in Kievan Russia in the last decades of the tenth century, when Vladimir became the ruler after his father, Sviatoslav, and converted Russia to Christianity. The novel uses the theme of the double or substitution, in which the soul of a miscarried son of Sviatoslav is taken by evil spirits and used in their fight against Christianity. Since this son, Sviatoslavich, resembles Vladimir, confusion arises, and in Vel'tman's version many of Vladimir's misdeeds are attributed to the double. Although Vladimir is responsible for the death of his brother Iaropolk, for example, Sviatoslavich receives the blame. In this way the plot is motivated by mistaken identity while the guilt of Vladimir, the Christianizer of Russia, is whitewashed.

In 1836 Vel'tman published *Predki Kalimerosa: Aleksandr Filippovich Makedonskii* (The Forefather of Kalimeros: Aleksandr Filippovich of Macedon), in which the author employs the device of imaginary travel through time in order to show history as a repetition of general moral and intellectual concepts and human types. The hero travels to Greece at the time of Alexander the Great, although Vel'tman emphasizes that the traveler is a nineteenth-century Russian. As in *Strannik,* Vel'tman uses imaginary travel as merely an excuse for digression. Interestingly, Vel'tman includes the creation of a time machine in the novel and therefore can be credited with the first literary flight through time, a concept later made famous by H. G. Wells and other science-fiction writers of the twentieth century.

Elena and Aleksandr Vel'tman with their children in the early 1860s

In 1837 Vel'tman completed the novel *Virginiia; ili, Poezdka v Rossiiu,* which concerns the impressions of a Frenchman, Hector, who comes to understand and appreciate the tragic history and deep personality of Russia. As Ward points out, although the characters are "stock types from the eighteenth century—an innocent girl, cad lover, understanding father," Vel'tman used his text "to express his Francophobia" and also "to praise Russia's eternal nature."

In 1838 Vel'tman wrote one of his best works of the period, *Serdtse i dumka: prikliuchenie* (Heart and Mind: An Adventure). In his usual fairy-tale, fantastic manner Vel'tman treats a provincial love story in which a witch is able to keep two predestined lovers apart until the end of the novel. The tale is infused with folklore as the witch and a spirit fight over control of Zoia, the heroine; and while Zoia sits at home entertaining possible suitors, her heart and mind travel to St. Petersburg and Moscow, where she experiences ten other love intrigues. This farfetched plot serves as a vehicle for Vel'tman to describe life in the capitals, with its high-society balls, and life in the country, with its minor civil and military officials.

In *General Kalimeros* Vel'tman addresses the difference between the life of the public statesman and that of the private man through the figure of Napoleon in Russia. In Vel'tman's treatment Napoleon falls in love with a Russian girl and secretly marries her, but amid the confusion of the retreat he loses her. The point of the novel is, as Ward puts it, that "those in power can not do good in society unless their hearts are satisfied."

Another important aspect of Vel'tman's career are his stories, written mainly in the last half of the 1830s and early part of the 1840s. Among the most well known are "Provintsial'nie aktery" (Provincial Actors; originally titled "Neistovyi Roland" [Roland the Furious], 1835), "Iolanda" (1837), "Radoi" (1839), and "Priezzhii iz uezda; ili, sumatokha v stolitse" (A Visitor from the Country; or, Disorder in the Capital, 1841). "Provintsial'nie aktery" deserves mention since its plot, concerning a provincial actor who impersonates an important official, anticipates Gogol's 1836 drama *Revizor* (The Inspector General).

During the second half of the 1830s, the critical response to Vel'tman's fiction was decidedly negative. Critics reproached Vel'tman for not revealing a clear idea or purpose. They accused the writer of failing to answer the needs and questions of society and ignoring the critical social role of the writer. In 1840 Vel'tman stopped writing, although the respite was probably not caused by his critics but by something much more serious. Ward explains:

> At this point in his career Vel'tman was at an impasse. His first two novels had had the greatest effect with their sparkling wit and endless intriguing digressions. In terms of plot, character and language, Vel'tman's works were most successful when he concentrated on language. His more recent works were less successful as his concentration shifted from language to the construction of elaborate adventure plots, with some hint of thematic motivation for his heroes' actions.

Vel'tman had two choices: either to return to the style of *Strannik,* which had propelled him to great popularity, or to learn to create full characters and probable, motivated plots. Perhaps for this reason, from 1840 to 1845 Vel'tman refrained from writing, considering a solution to this narrative problem before returning to print.

In 1845 Vel'tman published *Novyi Emelia; ili, Prevrashcheniia,* which has the form of a picaresque novel. The hero, Emelia, goes through many adventures before he marries the girl destined for him. It is not by coincidence that the title of the novel resembles two books by Jean-Jacques Rousseau, *Julie, ou la Nouvelle Héloïse* (Julie; or, The New Eloise, 1761) and *Émile, ou de l'éducation* (Émile; or, On Education, 1762), since there are parallels in terms of both the plot and the meaning of the novel. For example, like Émile, Emelia is an orphan; he is adopted by a Russian family. As Rousseau recommended not trying to reason with Émile until he had reached age twelve, so Emelia's foster mother does not try to teach him anything until he is twelve. Moreover, both Emelia and Émile leave their homes at the same age, twenty-two, and at the end of their travels both return to wed the girls who were too young for marriage when the heroes began their journeys. The parallels, however, go no further, since Emelia does not change and develop as does Émile. Furthermore, Rousseau's theme—that bad education ruins the character of the individual—is ignored by Vel'tman, who uses the theme of education as mere background to set the adventure in motion.

Vel'tman devoted the last twenty-five years of his life to his epic *Prikliucheniia pocherpnutye iz moria zhiteiskago* (Adventures Drawn from the Sea of Life), composed of five novels: *Salomeia* (1848), which first appeared in *Biblioteka dlia chteniia* (Library for Reading) in 1846–1847; *Chudodei* (The Eccentric, 1849); *Vospitannitsa Sara* (The Ward Sarah, 1862); *Schast'e-neschast'e* (Fortune-Misfortune, 1863); and "Poslednii v rode i bezrodnyi" (Last in Line and Disinherited; completed before Vel'tman's death in 1870 but not published). Set in contemporary Russia, the works combine elements of both the novel of manners and the picaresque novel, and they treat the rapid changes in social life such as the demise of the aristocracy, the democratization of the intelligentsia, the moral disintegration of the merchants, and the evident failure of serfdom as an institution. Vel'tman's attempts to fictionalize realistic trends, however, are undermined by his unrealistic, digressive literary style.

The first novel, *Salomeia,* resembles a picaresque novel: the protagonists, Dmitritsky and Salomeia, meet and then separately go through an enormous variety of adventures before they return to each other. The novel differs from Vel'tman's earlier works since he is able to create complex characters and a realistic social milieu. The economic changes of Russia in the 1840s create a concrete situation in which the characters encounter risk and opportunities to attain wealth or lose it, gaining knowledge of their distinct personalities in the process.

Salomeia is the beautiful and talented daughter of a state councillor. After making an unfortunate marriage just to hurt her younger sister, she runs away with the rogue Dmitritsky, who abandons her after taking her money. Left penniless, Salomeia pretends to be French and takes a position as a governess in a local estate, where the advances of the landowner irritate her. Soon after she is kidnapped by peasants loyal to the landowner's wife, Salomeia is again left to fend for herself. She meets an old millionaire who is willing to marry her, but Dmitritsky reappears and ruins her plans. After almost marrying a man named Tsarov, Salomeia is abandoned in a hospital, and at the end Dmitritsky discovers her and takes her to Siberia, where she is supposedly reformed through faith, although the transformation is hardly consistent with her personality.

Salomeia's inability to understand her fate is contrasted with Dmitritsky, who experiences similar ups and downs. Dmitritsky, however, displays mental strength and a realistic attitude. Furthermore, in the course of the novel Dmitritsky "emerges more and more as an ideological counterpoise," becoming increasingly contemplative and philosophic. Dmitritsky loses his regiment's money, works as a servant, becomes rich, and loses his money—only to become rich again and poor again. The interest in Dmitritsky, however, lies in his ability to ruminate about his situation and the vanity of his actions. His self-consciousness, quite unusual for a picaro, lends a psychological and realistic dimension to the novel.

Salomeia is successful not only because it depicts a wide variety of urban and provincial types but also because Vel'tman is able to create adventures that have meaning for the individual hero who goes through them. Dmitritsky's gambling losses show the volatile nature of wealth, but they also characterize the frivolity and instability of the hero, who is forced to reflect on his fate and choices. In *Salomeia* Vel'tman had finally shown his ability to create full characters who develop and change in response to experience.

The second novel in the series, *Chudodei,* returns to the old manner of writing. Although the book is composed of four storylines that include Dmitritsky and Salomeia as well as the protagonist of this work, Sergei Daianov, these lines hardly intersect. The action primarily concerns Daianov, whose eccentricities lead to adventures, mistaken identities, gossip, and love intrigues. The motivation for the plot is an exterior obstacle to happiness. Daianov wants to marry Sofi, who has recently been widowed, but he fears that she will marry someone

Vel'tman in the late 1860s

else. This dilemma propels him into a multitude of improbable situations until he gets married. The novel also includes an unmotivated digression about a restaurant offering French cuisine and engaging in competition with other restaurants. Lacking a proper focus, the novel soon loses its energy, and the interest generated at the beginning dissipates.

In the third novel, *Vospitannitsa Sara,* Vel'tman uses the device of substituted babies to motivate the plot. The mystery of the proper identity of the heroines is kept from the reader for most of the novel, but at the end the mix-ups are resolved to the satisfaction of all the characters. The plot concerns Sara, who had been abandoned by her mother and given to a woman named Viktorina, who agrees to bring her up with another child, Vera. As opposed to Vera, who has a rich benefactor, Sara has no support and is envious as a result. When the children reach the age of five, Vera is supposed to join her benefactor, but Viktorina switches them, and Sara grows up in Vera's place in the aristocratic Ligovskoi household. Only after two-thirds of the novel have passed do readers learn about Vera's father, Lutskii, who has been separated from his daughter for fifteen years. Once things are settled, however, Sara marries a prince and goes abroad, while Vera joins her father and Viktorina, and the plot ends happily. Although the mistaken identities and mystery of the unknown parents keep up the suspense of the novel, the main purpose of the work is to entertain. This aim, however, competes with another theme, that of the poverty and isolation that Sara experiences in her struggle to fend for herself in a difficult and unfriendly world.

In 1863 Vel'tman published *Schast'e-neschast'e,* which has an ingenious plot. Using the style, characters, and themes from *Strannik,* Vel'tman creates a situation in which the desire for ambition is reversed and a hero, who wants nothing but to live with his beloved in peace, is given endless promotions. The promotions that occur in Makhailo Ivanovich Gorazdovoi's life provide the motivation for many adventures as he is forced to go to Bessarabia and the Russian provinces to fulfill his duty in the civil service. The adventures could go on forever, but the novel ends with a deus ex machina when the wife who has been forced on Gorazdovoi abruptly dies at a masked ball, leaving the hero free to marry his childhood sweetheart, Lenochka.

Although *Prikliucheniia pocherpnutye iz moria zhiteiskogo* shows some development in Vel'tman's fiction, in fact the series shows greater similarities with his earlier works. For the most part the works feature adventure stories motivated by love intrigues, mistaken identities, and chance meetings. As in his earlier fiction, Vel'tman clings to the picaresque form, which gives him the opportunity to reduce character and plot development, while portraying strange random events that feature his forte: his imaginative use of language and creation of wild, intricate adventure plots. It is not surprising, then, that the heroes tend to be passive characters or bizarre figures who offer Vel'tman the chance to describe the world from an unusual and estranged point of view.

Not surprisingly, several critics have noted Vel'tman's influence on Russian realism in general and on the fiction of Fyodor Dostoyevsky in particular. The claim is that Vel'tman played a large role in the changeover from the genres of historical prose fiction to realism, since he portrayed various layers of Russian society and captured their own authentic language. Valerian Fedorovich Pereverzev, for example, claims that Dostoyevsky learned from Vel'tman how to present characters of the lower classes engaged in a conflict with their society and to create narratives of moral action. Although these claims are plausible, they must be balanced against the influence of Gogol and of the early realists of Western Europe: Honoré de Balzac, Stendhal, and George Sand.

Besides fiction, Vel'tman left behind a large body of historical and ethnographic works. In the 1830s Vel'tman began systematically to study world history, archaeology, folklore, religion, geography, and ethnography. In 1833 he translated the famous medieval Russian epic *Slovo o polku Igoreve* (The Tale of Igor's Campaign) into contemporary Russian. He also translated the thirteenth-century Middle High German epic poem *Nibelungenlied* (Song of the Nibelungs) in 1836 and parts of the Sanskrit epic *Mahabharata* in 1839. Also interested in pedagogy, Vel'tman published a reader composed of literary texts for use in schools in 1837. Besides using medieval and ancient Russian culture as the setting for his historical fiction, Vel'tman also wrote historical monographs, such as *O Gospodine Novgorode Velikom: pis'mo, s prilozheniem vida Novgoroda v XII stoletii i plana okrestnostei* (The State of Great Novgorod: A Letter with an Appended View of Novgorod in the Twelfth Century and a Plan of the Environs, 1834) and *Magi i Midiiskie Kagany XIII stoletiia* (Wizards and Midean Kings of the Thirteenth Century, 1860). In addition, Vel'tman studied ancient Scandinavia, writing a book about it: *Indo-germany, ili saivane: opyt svoda i poverki skazanii o pervobytnykh naselentsakh Germanii* (The Indo-Germans, or Saivan: An Attempt at Classifying and Verifying Written Sources on the Original Inhabitants of Germany, 1856).

Vel'tman's interests, however, were not exhausted even by these diverse subjects. He also wrote a book about Eastern religion, *Pervobytnoe verovanie i Buddizm* (The First Beliefs and Buddhism, 1864). Among his other nonfiction works are those associated with his position as head of the Museum of the Kremlin's Armaments: *Dostopamiatnosti moskovskago Kremlia* (The Landmarks of the Moscow Kremlin, 1843) and *Moskovskaia oruzheinaia palata* (The Moscow Museum of Armaments, 1844). In appreciation of his historical scholarship, Vel'tman was elected as a member of the Russian National Archaeological Society and the Russian Academy of Sciences.

During his lifetime, Vel'tman's historical work came under intense scrutiny. Many critics found factual errors and interpretive lapses. It was pointed out that in his study, *Attila i Rus' IV i V veka: svod istoricheskikh i narodnykh predanii* (Attila and Rus in the Fourth and Fifth Centuries: A Classification of Historical and Folk Legends, 1858), Vel'tman mistakenly asserted that the Huns were Slavs and Attila a Great Prince of Kiev. A contemporary, Nikolai Vasil'evich Berg, denigrated Vel'tman's historical endeavors, calling them "utter nonsense." Claiming that as an historian Vel'tman let his imagination roam at will with complete pleasure, Pogodin blamed Vel'tman's failures on the author's creative temperament, which could not be subordinated to the historian's objectivity. In the twentieth century, Akutin has contradicted this negative view, maintaining that Vel'tman tried to hold to the level of the objective historical scholarship of his day.

Among his many occupations, Vel'tman also served between 1849 and 1850 as the editor of *Moskvitianin*. While his contribution was extolled and did help the popularity of the journal, he often fought with executive editor Pogodin over which articles to print. During this time, since there was no money to pay contributors, Vel'tman wrote many of the articles in the journal himself. His book reviews were especially renowned as being creative works in themselves, since Vel'tman refrained from treating the books under investigation and instead offered personal observations on the literary scene.

The last two decades of Vel'tman's life were uneventful. After the death of his first wife, Vel'tman married a close acquaintance, Elena Ivanovna Krupenikova, a successful fiction writer. An efficient housewife and easygoing companion, Elena gave order to his life. It was during this time that the Vel'tmans' salon grew in public esteem. Freed from duties at home, he worked eagerly on his historical scholarship and his five-novel series. The couple also had two children, a boy and a girl. Elena died in 1868, and Vel'tman died two years later, on 11 January 1870.

Letters:

Iurii M. Akutin, ed., "Perepiska V. I. Dalia s A. F. Vel'tmanom," *Izvestiia literatury i iazyka,* 35, no. 6 (1976): 527–532.

Biography:

Iurii M. Akutin, "Aleksandr Vel'tman i ego roman *Strannik,*" in Vel'tman's *Strannik* (Moscow: Nauka, 1977), pp. 247–300.

References:

Iurii M. Akutin, "Aleksander Vel'tman v russkoy kritike XIX veka: neizvestnye stranitsy poezii A. Vel'tmana," *Problemy khudozhestvennogo metoda v russkoi literature* (1973): 56–89;

Akutin, "Izdrevle sladostnyi soiuz: Poetov mezh soboi sviazuet," *Nauka i zhizn',* 11, (1975): 138.

Boris Iakovlevich Bukhshtab, "Pervye romany Vel'tmana," in *Russkaia proza,* edited by Boris M. Eikhenbaum and Iu. N. Tynianov (The Hague: Mouton, 1963), pp. 192–231;

Leonid Arsen'evich Bulakhovskii, *Istoricheskii komentarii k literaturnomu russkomu iazyku* (Kharkov: Radian'ka shkola, 1937);

E. M. Dvoichenko-Markova, "Moldo-valashskie temy v proizvedeniiakh A. F. Vel'tmana," in her *Russko-rumynskie literaturnye sviazy v pervoi polovine XIX veka* (Moscow: Nauka, 1966);

Z. S. Efimova, "Nachal'nyi period literaturnoi deiatel'nosti A. F. Vel'tmana," in *Russkii romantizm,* edited by A. I. Beletsky (Leningrad: Akademiia, 1927), pp. 51–87;

James J. Gebhard, "A. F. Vel'tman's Unpublished Reply to Chaadaev's Philosophical Letter," *Canadian-American Slavic Studies,* 4, no. 2 (1970);

Gebhard, "The Early Novels of A. F. Vel'tman," dissertation, Indiana University, 1968;

Nin Golub-Lagatskaya, "A. F. Vel'tman as a Romanticist: An Analysis of the Compositional and Stylistic Characteristics of Two Novels (1830s)," dissertation, New York University, 1981;

Iu. A. Granin, "A. F. Vel'tman," *Ocherki po istorii literatury pervoi poloviny XIX veka,* part 1 (Baku: Azerbaidzhanskii Gosudarstvennyi Pedagogicheskii Institut, 1941);

A. Kidel', "V. G. Belinsky o bessarabskikh proizvedeniiakh A. F. Vel'tmana," *Dnestr,* 6 (1961): 135–137;

David Lapeza, "Kaleidoscope: The Poetics of Alexander Vel'tman's Early Novels," dissertation, University of Michigan, 1986;

Iurii D. Levin, "Volshebnaia noch' A. F. Vel'tmana: iz istorii vospriiatiia Shekspira v Rossii," in *Russko-evropeiskie literaturnye sviazi* (Moscow, 1966), pp. 83–92;

Valerian Fedorovich Pereverzev, "Predtecha Dostoevskogo," in his *U istokov russkogo realisticheskogo romana* (Moscow: Khudozhestvennaia literatura, 1965);

Mikhail Petrovich Pogodin, "Vospominaniia ob A. F. Vel'tmana," *Russkaia starina,* 4 (1871): 405–410;

T. A. Roboli, "Literatura puteshestvii," in *Russkaia proza,* edited by Eikhenbaum and Tynianov (The Hague: Mouton, 1963), pp. 42–71;

Semen Afanas'evich Vengerov, *Kritiko-biograficheskii slovar' russkikh pisatelei i uchenykh* (St. Petersburg, 1897), pp. 222–227;

Charles Alexander Ward, "The Later Novels of A. F. Vel'tman," dissertation, University of Chicago, 1974.

Papers:

Vel'tman's personal archive, including correspondence and the manuscript of "Povest' o sebe," is located in the Russian National Library, St. Petersburg.

Mikhail Nikolaevich Zagoskin

(14 July 1789 - 23 June 1852)

Dan I. Ungurianu
University of Missouri–Columbia

BOOKS: *Komediia protiv komedii, ili Urok volokitam* (St. Petersburg: Tipografiia Imperatorskogo teatra, 1816);

G. Bogatonov, ili Provintsial v stolitse (St. Petersburg, 1817);

Roman na bol'shoi doroge (St. Petersburg, 1819);

Vecherinka uchenykh (St. Petersburg: Tip. Imp. teatrov, 1820);

Dobryi maloi (St. Petersburg, 1820);

Urok kholostym (Moscow: A. Semen, 1822);

Derevenskii filosof (Moscow: Universitetskaia tip., 1823);

Bogatonov v derevne, ili, Siurpriz samomu sebe (Moscow: Imp. Moskovskii teatr, 1826);

Blagorodnyi teatr (Moscow: N. Stepanov, 1828);

Iurii Miloslavskii, ili Russkie v 1612 godu (Moscow: N. Stepanov, 1829);

Roslavlev, ili Russkie v 1812 godu (Moscow: N. Stepanov, 1831);

Askol'dova mogila (Moscow: N. Stepanov, 1833);

Askol'dova mogila [opera libretto] (Moscow, 1836);

Povesti, 2 volumes (Moscow: N. Stepanov, 1837)—includes *Koz'ma Roshchin, Vecher na Khopre* and *Tri zhenikha*;

Iskusitel' (Moscow: N. Stepanov, 1838);

Toska po rodine (Moscow: N. Stepanov, 1839);

Kuz'ma Petrovich Miroshev. Russkaia byl' vremen Ekateriny II (Moscow: N. Stepanov, 1842);

Moskva i moskvichi, Parts 1–4 (Moscow: A. Semen, 1842–1850);

Repetitsiia na stantsii (Moscow, 1845);

Brynskii les; epizod iz pervykh godov tsarstvovaniia Petra Velikago, 2 volumes (Moscow: N. Stepanov, 1846);

Russkie v nachale os'mnadtsatogo stoletiia; razskaz iz vremen edinoderzhavia Petra Pervogo (Moscow: N. Stepanov, 1848);

Poezdka za granitsu (Moscow, 1850);

Zhenatyi zhenikh (St. Petersburg, 1851).

Editions and Collections: *Sochineniia,* 7 volumes (St. Petersburg: V. I. Shtein, 1889);

Polnoe sobranie sochinenii, 10 volumes (St. Petersburg & Moscow: M. O. Vol'f, 1898);

Mikhail Nikolaevich Zagoskin

Sobranie sochinenii (Moscow: T-vo Kushnerev, 1902);

Polnoe sobranie sochinenii, 2 volumes (St. Petersburg: Izdanie V. I. Gubinskogo, 1902);

Sobranie sochinenii, 3 volumes (Moscow: Izd. M. V. Kliukina, 1902);

Polnoe sobranie sochinenii, 3 volumes (Petrograd: Aktsionernoe ob-vo Kopeika, n. d.);

Sobranie sochinenii, 4 volumes (Moscow, 1918);

Sochineniia, 2 volumes (Moscow: Khudozhestvennaia literatura, 1987);

Izbrannoe (Moscow: Sovetskaia Rossiia, 1988);

Askol'dova mogila: Romany, povesti (Moscow: Sovremennik, 1989);

Askol'dova mogila. Kuz'ma Roshchin, Vecher na Khopre: povesti (Kiev: Dnipro, 1990);

Istoricheskie romany (Moscow: Planeta, 1993).

Editions in English: *The Young Muscovite, or the Poles in Russia,* edited by Frederic Chamier (London: Cochrane & M'Crone, 1833);

Tales of Three Centuries, translated by Jeremiah Curtin (Boston: Little, Brown, 1891)—includes "An Evening on the Hopior," "The Three Suitors," and "Kuzma Roschin";

Askold's Grave [opera libretto], in *Askold's Grave,* by A. N. Verstovskii (New York: Consonance, 1996).

PLAY PRODUCTIONS: *Komediia protiv komedii, ili Urok volokitam,* St. Petersburg, Malyi Teatr, 3 November 1815;

Prokaznik, St. Petersburg, Malyi Teatr, 5 December 1815;

G. Bogatonov, ili Provintsial v stolitse, St. Petersburg, Malyi Teatr, 27 June 1817;

Vecherinka uchenykh, St. Petersburg, Malyi Teatr, 12 November 1817;

Roman na bol'shoi doroge, St. Petersburg, Bolshoi Teatr, 27 June 1817;

Dobryi maloi, St. Petersburg, Bolshoi Teatr, 23 June 1820;

Bogatonov v derevne, Moscow, 20 January 1821;

Urok kholostym, Moscow, 4 May 1822;

Derevenskii filosof, Moscow, 11 January 1823;

Repetitsiia na stantsii, Rozhdestveno estate of Prince D. V. Golitsyn, 29 October 1827;

Blagorodnyi teatr, 28 December 1827;

Nedovol'nye, Moscow, Bolshoi Petrovsky Teatr, 2 December 1835;

Poezdka za granitsu, Moscow, Malyi Teatr, 29 January 1850.

OPERA PRODUCTIONS: *Pan Tvardovsky* (music by Aleksei Nikolaevich Verstovsky), Moscow, 24 May 1828;

Askol'dova mogila (music by Verstovsky), Moscow, Bolshoi Petrovsky Teatr, 15 September 1835;

Toska po rodine (music by Verstovsky), Moscow, 31 August 1839.

One of the best-known writers of the 1820s and 1830s, Mikhail Nikolaevich Zagoskin started his literary career as a successful playwright and subsequently worked in several other prose genres, but he is remembered primarily as an historical novelist—the "Russian Walter Scott." His most acclaimed work is *Iurii Miloslavskii* (1829), the first full-fledged

Russian historical novel, which enjoyed enormous popularity and secured Zagoskin's place in literary history. His other prominent piece is *Roslavlev* (1831), one of the earliest Russian novels about the War of 1812. A later collection of sketches by Zagoskin, *Moskva i moskvichi* (Moscow and Muscovites, 1842–1850), has a certain extraliterary importance, as it deals with various aspects of Moscow life in the past and present and is of interest to the local historian. All of Zagoskin's works are permeated with the so-called Russian orientation: ardent patriotism, love of things Russian, and disdain for slavish admiration of the West. Zagoskin's outlook is rather simplistic and lacking in artistic or philosophical depth; however, his works are filled with good-hearted humor and genuine joviality. Zagoskin combined his artistic career with accomplishments in the civil service, attaining the rank of *deistvitel'nyi statskii sovetnik* (the equivalent of major general) and becoming director of the Moscow Imperial Theaters and director of the Kremlin Armory.

Mikhail Nikolaevich Zagoskin was born on 14 July 1789 on the Ramzai estate near the city of Penza into an old gentry family (whose founder, a Tatar nobleman from the Golden Horde, came to Muscovy in 1472). His father, Nikolai Mikhailovich, was a well-off provincial landlord, good-natured but known among the locals for his oddities, which were tempered by the influence of his wife, Natal'ia Mikhailovna (born Martynova). The eldest of nine siblings, Mikhail grew up on the family estate without receiving any systematic education but avidly reading books from his father's library and also writing some juvenilia. In the winter of 1802, when he had not yet turned thirteen, Zagoskin was sent to St. Petersburg to become a civil servant. He traveled to the capital in the company of Filipp Filippovich Vigel', a distant relative on his mother's side. The following decade Zagoskin spent in St. Petersburg, serving without particular success in various government departments. By 1811 he was still a *gubernskii sekretar',* third step from the bottom in the Table of Ranks, and often found himself in rather straitened financial circumstances. With Napoleon's invasion of Russia in 1812, Zagoskin joined the St. Petersburg Militia as a lieutenant. He fought with distinction at the capture of Polotsk (October 1812), where he sustained a wound and received a decoration for courage (the Order of St. Anna of the Fourth Degree on the Sword). Upon recovery he returned to the ranks and during the final period of the war participated in the siege of Danzig as an aide-de-camp to the commander of the Fourth Infantry Corps.

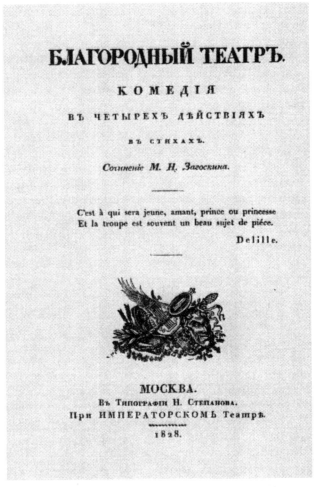

БЛАГОРОДНЫЙ ТЕАТРЪ.

КОМЕДІЯ

ВЪ ЧЕТЫРЕХЪ ДѢЙСТВІЯХЪ

ВЪ СТИХАХЪ.

Сочиненіе М. Н. Загоскина.

C'est à qui sera jeune, amant, prince ou princesse
Et la troupe est souvent un beau sujet de piéce.
Delille.

МОСКВА.
Въ Типографіи Н. Степанова.
При ИМПЕРАТОРСКОМЪ Театрѣ.
1828.

Title page for Zagoskin's verse comedy Blagorodnyi teatr
(The Amateurs' Theater)

After the dissolution of the militia in 1814, Zagoskin lived on the family estate, where he wrote his first comedy, *Prokaznik* (Prankster, performed in 1815). In 1815 he returned to St. Petersburg to resume his old position at the Department of Mineral and Salt Affairs and also to try his fortunes in literature. The beginning of Zagoskin's literary career is connected with favorable attention to his work from the theater mogul Prince Aleksandr Aleksandrovich Shakhovskoi. Zagoskin's rapprochement with Shakhovskoi occurred at the time of the controversy around Shakhovskoi's comedy *Urok koketkam, ili Lipetskie vody* (A Lesson for Coquettes, or the Lipetsk Spa), staged in September 1815. The comedy derided Vasilii Andreevich Zhukovsky and his ballads and provoked a literary battle that resulted in the creation of the Arzamas society. Zagoskin entered the conflict on the side of his patron Shakhovskoi, composing the comedy *Komediia protiv komedii, ili Urok volokitam* (A Comedy Against the Comedy, or

A Lesson for Womanizers), which lionized *Lipetskie vody*. Performed in St. Petersburg in November 1815, *Komediia protiv komedii* caused attacks from the opposing party but was well received by the public. The successful debut and the friendship with Shakhovskoi opened an access to the stage for Zagoskin. Five more of his comedies were staged from 1815 to 1820, the most acclaimed of them being *G. Bogatonov, ili Provintsial v stolitse* (Mr. Bogatonov, or A Provincial in the Capital), which premiered in 1817 and remained in the theater repertoire until 1829 in Moscow and 1831 in St. Petersburg. Zagoskin's comedies lack originality, as they follow the French clichés of the genre reproduced in many Russian adaptations. And yet his plays are marked by lively dialogue, merriment, and some keen observations in the portrayal of morals and manners.

Early in his literary career Zagoskin participated in journalistic undertakings as well. In the second half of 1817 he coedited (with Petr Aleksandrovich Korsakov) the journal *Severnyi nabliudatel'* (The Northern Observer), formerly *Russkii pustynnik* (The Russian Hermit), for which he wrote many articles and reviews, engaging at times in literary skirmishes. Thus his rather balanced critical opinion about Aleksandr Sergeevich Griboedov's play *Molodye suprugi* (Young Spouses, produced in 1815) provoked a vicious response by Griboedov, who ridiculed Zagoskin in the satiric poem "Lubochnyi teatr" (Cheap Theater, 1815). Another opponent of Zagoskin was Aleksandr Efimovich Izmailov, who edited (in the absence of Nikolai Ivanovich Grech) the journal *Syn otechestva* (Son of the Fatherland) and attacked Zagoskin's *Bogatonov*. Echoes of this polemic can be heard in Zagoskin's comedy *Vecherinka uchenykh* (A Soiree of the Learned People, produced in 1817). Zagoskin also published in *Severnyi nabliudatel'* his first serious attempt at prose fiction—the tale "Neravnyi brak" (Misalliance), subtitled "Otryvok iz russkogo romana" (A Fragment from a Russian Novel). The circle of Zagoskin's friends during these years included Nikolai Ivanovich Gnedich, Mikhail Evstaf'evich Lobanov, Ivan Andreevich Krylov, and Aleksei Nikolaevich Olenin. In 1819 he was accepted as a member of *Vol'noe obshchestvo liubitelei rossiiskoi slovesnosti* (Free Society of Lovers of Russian Literature).

Along with these literary activities, Zagoskin continued in the civil service but moved into areas more related to arts and humanities. From 1817 to 1818 he held a position in the Directorate of Imperial Theaters and from 1818 to 1820 was a librarian of the Imperial Public Library, where he participated in the cataloguing of the Russian collection (for which he received the Order of St. Anna of the

Third Degree). In 1816 Zagoskin married Anna Dmitrievna Vasil'tsovskaya, the natural daughter of Dmitrii Aleksandrovich Novosil'tsov, a despotic old grandee of the age of Catherine II, who openly disapproved of his son-in-law. This attitude caused Zagoskin much embarrassment, since for lack of money he had to live in Novosil'tsov's house for several years.

In 1820 Novosil'tsov and the Zagoskins with their two sons moved to Moscow. Zagoskin temporarily abandoned service and immersed himself in the social and theatrical life of Moscow, becoming close to Sergei Timofeevich Aksakov; Mikhail Aleksandrovich Dmitriev; Prince Ivan Mikhailovich Dolgorukov, an old family friend; and Fedor Fedorovich Kokoshkin. Zagoskin continued his theatrical pursuits, writing in 1820 a sequel to *G. Bogatonov—Bogatonov v derevne* (Bogatonov in the Country, 1826)—and also directing his own comedy *Dobryi maloi* (Good Fellow), which had previously been staged in St. Petersburg in 1820 and to which Pavel Aleksandrovich Katenin wrote a polemical response in his comedy *Spletni* (Gossip, 1821).

In 1821 Zagoskin, who had not composed poetry before, tried his hand at verse. He was incited to embark on this enterprise by friends who dismissed his opinion about a poem on the grounds that he understood nothing in verse. Zagoskin decided to prove that they were wrong by producing his own poetry. Not endowed with a poetic ear, he had to draw metrical schemes on paper in order to ensure the regularity of his verse. Despite such a laborious and uninspirational method of composition, Zagoskin's poems turned out to be rather lively and pleasant sounding. One of them, "Poslanie k Liudmilu" (An Epistle to Liudmil, 1823), even enjoyed critical acclaim. Zagoskin utilized his newly acquired skill to create several comedies in verse and vaudevilles: *Urok kholostym* (A Lesson for Bachelors, performed in 1822), *Derevenskii filosof* (Village Philosopher, performed in 1823), *Repetitsiia na stantsii* (Rehearsal at a Station, performed in 1827), and *Blagorodnyi teatr* (Amateurs' Theater, performed in 1827). The latter piece, which can be regarded as Zagoskin's best comedy, was especially popular. Produced originally by Shakhovskoi with stars such as Mikhail Semenovich Shchepkin and Pavel Stepanovich Mochalov in 1827, it was received with tremendous enthusiasm and remained on stage until 1841. In 1828 Zagoskin wrote the libretto for Aleksei Nikolaevich Verstovsky's opera *Pan Tvardovsky* (1828).

In 1822 Zagoskin was accepted into Obshchestvo liubitelei rossiiskoi slovesnosti (Society of Lovers of Russian Literature) at Moscow University

(becoming its secretary from 1827 to 1829 and president from 1833 to 1836). Zagoskin also used his first years in Moscow to bridge gaps in his education. In St. Petersburg he had learned French on his own by memorizing a dictionary and without paying much attention to the grammar and pronunciation. Consequently, he could make himself understood, but his mistakes gave ample food for jokes on the part of his aristocratic acquaintances. In Moscow, Zagoskin turned to the study of law, history, geometry, statistics, and other disciplines required for an exam qualifying him to be promoted to the rank of *kollezhskii assessor* (the civilian equivalent of major). Zagoskin had to take the exam since he did not possess any formal degree. Being industrious and endowed with a good memory, he easily passed the test in December 1821. In 1822 he received a position in the Theatrical Department, starting his long and successful career in Moscow theater administration. Extensive service responsibilities (he was in charge of theater logistics) account for his reduced literary productivity in the mid 1820s. In the period from 1823 to 1829 Zagoskin was promoted to the ranks of *kollezhskii assessor* and *nadvornyi sovetnik* (civilian lieutenant colonel). He was decorated with the Order of St. Anna of the Second Degree and St. Vladimir of the Fourth Degree.

In 1827 Zagoskin conceived the idea of a historical novel set in the Time of Troubles and grew completely absorbed with this project. The novel—*Iurii Miloslavskii, ili Russkie v 1612 godu* (Iurii Miloslavskii, or the Russians in 1612)—was to become Zagoskin's magnum opus and brought his popularity to an all-time high. Released in December 1829, the novel was met with almost universal admiration. Greeted by many prominent writers and cultural figures (Zhukovsky, Krylov, Gnedich, Aksakov, Olenin, Dmitriev, Prince Shakhovskoi, Aleksandr Pushkin, and others), it also reached to the base of the reader's pyramid, turning—as Aksakov attests in his biography of Zagoskin—into a kind of mass-culture phenomenon. (For example, scenes from *Miloslavskii* appeared on shawls and snuffboxes.) Zagoskin's triumph was crowned by warm commendations from Emperor Nicholas I, who granted the writer an audience and presented him with a ring. A reflection of the success of the novel can be seen in Nikolai Gogol's play *Revizor* (Inspector General, performed in 1836), in which the liar and braggart Khlestakov, claims to be, among other things, the author of *Miloslavskii*.

Alongside praise, reviewers outlined flaws in the novel. Thus, Pushkin spoke in *Literaturnaia gazeta* (The Literary Gazette) about the weakness of the actual historical episodes, and Aksakov pointed in *Moskovskii*

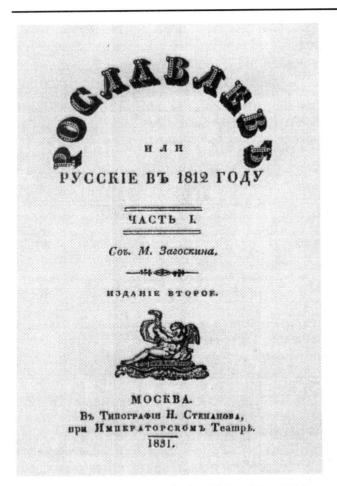

Title page for Zagoskin's Roslavlev, ili Russkie v 1812 godu *(Roslalev, or The Russsians in 1812), a novel about the Napoleonic Wars*

vestnik (The Moscow Herald) to the imcentury Muscovy. However, the general reaction improbability of the romantic love story in seventeenth-century Muscovy. However, the general reaction in the press was overwhelmingly positive. The only hostile review belonged to Faddei Venediktovich Bulgarin, who nearly lost his paper *Severnaia pchela* (The Northern Bee) for this critical demarche. Bulgarin's response was prompted by jealousy, since he was working on an historical novel from the Time of Troubles simultaneously with Zagoskin but had lost the "race," publishing his *Dimitrii Samozvanets* (Dimitrii the Impostor) at the beginning of 1830. The rivalry between Zagoskin and Bulgarin was a factor that contributed to the enthusiasm with which the anti-Bulgarin party accepted *Miloslavskii,* seeing it as a successful preemptive strike. This sentiment certainly seems to be the case with Pushkin, who suspected Bulgarin of plagiarizing in *Samozvanets* Pushkin's then-unpublished drama *Boris Godunov* (1831).

Overall, readers' acclaim of *Miloslavskii* surpassed anything the great Russian writers of the age could boast of: during Zagoskin's lifetime the novel went through eight publications and was translated into English, French, German, Italian, and even Dutch and Czech. The book received compliments from the "father of the historical novel," Sir Walter Scott, and gained praise from the French writer Prosper Mérimée. Aside from the merits of *Miloslavkii,* such an extraordinary success can be explained by the fact that the Russian reading public had been awaiting the appearance of a domestic historical novel. The historical genre came into vogue with the advent of Scott's novels, which fascinated Russian readers in the 1820s. Preceded by many historical tales and fragments, *Miloslavskii* was the first full-fledged Russian historical novel. Followed by an avalanche of other historical novels (which in the 1830s came to the forefront of Russian belles lettres in quantitative terms), *Miloslavskii* retained the advantage of primogeniture.

In *Miloslavskii,* Zagoskin largely follows Scott's novelistic model. The writer uses history at a dramatic point when two warring camps collide and the main hero, Iurii (a noble if somewhat bland young man), has access to both camps, going from one to the other and being torn by a conflict of loyalties. Thus, Iurii, a fervent Russian patriot, is in love with the daughter of a Polish sympathizer. Moreover, he is bound by an oath of loyalty to the Polish Prince Vladislav, which was a result of a bona fide delusion. The main focus is on the fictional romantic story (getting the bride) and on characters who are fictional but participate in some real events and come in touch with historical figures (Koz'ma Minin and Avraamy Palitsyn). Except for these brief moments of contact, the nonfictional characters exist in the background of the narration, since the novelist's goal is not to relate particular historical incidents but rather to convey the spirit of the epoch, often at the expense of chronological and factual exactitude. This general formula is accompanied by many motifs and episodes typical of Scott. The only formal Scottlike element absent from *Miloslavskii* is chapter epigraphs. Those, however, were duly supplied—selected from Scott, William Shakespeare, Lord Byron, Oliver Goldsmith, and other British writers—in the 1833 English translation by "a Russian lady and her daughters," edited by Frederic Chamier, who amended the plot and also modified names of several characters in order to make them more euphonious for the English reader (thus, Miloslavskii was transformed into Milolasky).

Having followed a proven literary recipe, Zagoskin competed successfully with his mentor Scott, creating a captivating and entangled story. Some well-read contemporaries (for example, Zhukovsky and Vigel') said that upon opening *Miloslavskii* they became so engrossed that they could not put the novel away before finishing all of its three volumes. Equally important for the success of *Miloslavskii* was that, having utilized a Western model, Zagoskin filled it with Russian content—portraying Russian types, reviving through fiction Russian history, and introducing colorful Russian folk or quasi-folk language. In the atmosphere of heated debates about *narodnost'* (nationality) in art, which reflected growing national self-awareness, this conspicuous Russianness of *Miloslavskii* was greeted by many reviewers as a long overdue phenomenon in domestic literature. Echoes from *Miloslavskii* are heard in Pushkin's *Kapitanskaia dochka* (The Captain's Daughter, 1836) in the opening scene of the snowstorm as well as in the themes of debt repayment and disproportionate gratitude.

Inspired by the success of *Miloslavskii,* Zagoskin began working in 1830 on a novel from contemporary history set during the War of 1812, *Roslavlev, ili Russkie v 1812 godu.* (Roslavlev, or The Russians in 1812), which was published in January 1831. In the wake of the Russian victory over Napoleon Bonaparte, the destruction of the Great Army was routinely likened to the expulsion of the Poles in 1612, since in both cases foreign invasions were crushed by strong popular resistance that unified all classes of Russian society. This parallel is implied in the subtitle of Zagoskin's second novel, which echoes the subtitle of *Miloslavskii*—that is, *Russkie v 1612 godu.* As in *Miloslavskii,* actual historical figures stay on the periphery of action and appear only briefly. On the French side they include Napoleon with his retinue and Marshal Murat. Among the Russians there are even fewer real-life characters, and they are not called by name since Zagoskin was wary of possible jealousies on the part of Russian veterans. However, some are easy to recognize—Count Mikhail Andreevich Miloradovich (the brave general in command of the Russian advance-guard); the poet-partisan Denis Vasil'evich Davydov (the "singer of wine, love and glory," who supplied Zagoskin with some information regarding the war); and another partisan commander known for his ruthlessness, Captain Aleksand Samoilovich Figner ("the silent officer"). Although Davydov and especially "the silent officer" play important roles in the plot, the action revolves around the love story of fictional characters.

The protagonist, Vladimir Roslavlev, is betrothed to Polina Lidina, but their relationship is clouded by a mystery in Polina's past: while in Paris, she had fallen in love with a married man, the French Count Senikur. The marriage between Roslavlev and Polina has to be postponed because of the war, and while Roslavlev spills his blood on the battlefield, his bride-to-be marries Count Senikur, now a widower who was captured by Russian troops. Polina follows her husband, sharing with him the changing fortunes of Napoleon's army. Eventually Senikur is killed in battle, and Polina dies too—from a Russian shell in the besieged Danzig. Roslavlev first grieves over Polina's betrayal but subsequently discovers his true love, Polina's sister Ol'ga, whom he marries. The love story in the novel is combined with many military adventures. In the final part Roslavlev serves as an aide-de-camp at the siege of Danzig, the description of which includes Zagoskin's own experiences. The peripeties of this convoluted plot are interlaced with lengthy nationalistic speeches and scenes displaying the patriotic élan of the Russian people.

As in *Miloslavskii,* Zagoskin was on the cutting edge of Russian literature in *Roslavlev,* since the creation of a novel about the Napoleonic Wars seemed to be in the air. *Roslavlev* appeared almost simultaneously with the novel of Zagoskin's rival Bulgarin—*Petr Ivanovich Vyzhigin* (1831), set in 1812—a sequel to *Ivan Vyzhigin* (1829). Other novels from the same epoch followed suit, including Rafail Mikhailovich Zotov's *Leonid, ili Nekotorye cherty iz zhizni Napoleona* (Leonid, or Some Features from the Life of Napoleon, 1832) and Nikolai Mikhailovich Konshin's *Graf Oboiansky, ili Smolensk v 1812 godu* (Count Oboiansky, or Smolensk in 1812, published in 1834). Pushkin reacted to Zagoskin's novel in a polemical fragment, also titled "Roslavlev" (1831), which offers a different perspective on patriotism. Zagoskin's *Roslavlev* was among Leo Tolstoy's sources for *Voina i mir* (War and Peace, 1865–1869). Despite a tremendous disparity between the two works and significant conceptual differences in the representation of the War of 1812 (for example, unlike Tolstoy, Zagoskin emphasizes the role of the Russian military and advocates the "patriotic" version of the fire of Moscow, according to which the city was set ablaze by Russians themselves), there are clear echoes from *Roslavlev* in *Voina i mir.* They include the juxtaposition of fictional and historical chapters and the use of polemical digressions, some of which are strikingly similar to those found in *Roslavlev.*

The reading public anxiously awaited Zagoskin's second novel. In anticipation of the high demand, the publisher Nikolai S. Stepanov paid Zagoskin 40,000 rubles in assignats for the exclusive right to print 4,800 copies of *Roslavlev* in the course of three years. These expectations, however, turned

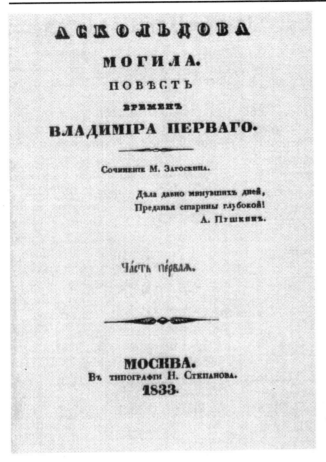

Title page for Zagoskin's historical novel Askol'dova mogila
*(Askol'd's Grave), set at the time of Prince Vladimir, the
dawn of Russian history*

out to be exaggerated: *Roslavlev* did not repeat the triumph of *Miloslavskii.* The plot of *Roslavlev* is less dynamic, and the entire novel is overburdened with patriotic discourse. In addition, as Zhukovsky had warned Zagoskin early during his work on *Roslavlev,* events of recent history witnessed by the writer's contemporaries were incomparably more resistant to novelistic conventions than subjects from bygone epochs. Reviewers of *Roslavlev* were also less unanimous in their enthusiasm, and Nikolai Alekseevich Polevoi in his journal *Moskovskii telegraf* (Moscow Telegraf) even launched an all-out attack against Zagoskin, accusing him of pandering to boastful patriotic instincts; of an inability to construct a genuine novelistic plot, which was replaced by a web of fairy-tale coincidences; and of lacking a broad historical picture, substituting instead petty stories of fictional characters. In his own historical novel *Kliatva pri grobe Gospodnem* (An Oath at the Holy Sepulchre, 1832) Polevoi concentrated on historical rather than fictional characters, thus following the example not of Scott but of the French writer Alfred

de Vigny with his novel *Cinq-Mars* (1826). Polevoi's criticism made him the archenemy of Zagoskin in the literary world. This hostility between the two writers was further exacerbated when *Moskovskii telegraf* denounced Zagoskin's handling of Moscow theaters, an action that led to an official complaint logged by Zagoskin against Polevoi in 1832. Although less successful than *Miloslavskii, Roslavlev* was by no means a failure: it went through three editions during Zagoskin's lifetime (actually equivalent to six editions, since the first printing of 4,800 copies consisted of four standard editions of 1,200 copies) and was translated into French and German.

Zagoskin's literary achievements, which were viewed favorably by the emperor himself, boosted the writer's career in the civil service. In 1830 he became the manager of the Bureau of Moscow Theater with the rank of *nadvornyi sovetnik,* and in 1831 he was appointed director of the Imperial Moscow Theaters, remaining in this capacity for more than a decade. His aide in theater administration was the composer Verstovsky, who handled many of the practical matters. In 1832 Zagoskin was promoted to the rank of *kollezhskii sovetnik,* in 1834 to *statskii sovetnik,* and in 1837 to *deistvitel'nyi statskii sovetnik.* In 1832 he received the court title of chamberlain and was also accepted as a member of the Russian Academy. In 1840 he was decorated with the Order of St. Vladimir of the Third Degree.

After *Roslavlev,* which was devoted to recent events, Zagoskin turned to another extreme of the historical genre, writing the novel *Askol'dova mogila* (Askol'd's Grave, 1833), the action of which takes place at the dawn of Russian history during the reign of Prince Vladimir at the end of the tenth century. Zagoskin's third historical novel differs in many aspects from the previous two. It is permeated with a somber Ossianic atmosphere and largely centers on a Byronic hero who overshadows the usual couple of bland lovers. This hero, the mysterious Unknown, is obsessed with the idea of overthrowing the Rurik dynasty in order to return the throne to descendants of the "legitimate" Kievan rulers Askol'd and Dir, who had been treacherously murdered by Oleg. Such a political monomaniac-cum-Romantic avenger is a typical figure in the historical fiction of the time—such as Gudoshnik in Polevoi's *Kliatva* (1832), Prince Myshetsky in Ivan Ivanovich Lazhechnikov's *Poslednii Novik* (The Last Page, 1831–1833), and the title character in Zotov's *Tainstvennyi monakh* (Mysterious Monk, 1834). The political intrigues of the Unknown unfold against the background of the penetration of Christianity into Russia. Contrary to the standard happy endings found in Zagoskin, *Askol'dova mogila* concludes with the deaths of all principal characters. However, the overall perspective remains optimistic, as Christianity triumphs in Kiev. Despite the well-known loyalty of its author, the novel had considerable problems with religious censorship, since Zagoskin speaks at length about the huge harems of Prince Vladimir, a canonized saint. Therefore, in the foreword the writer had to evoke the authority of Karamzin and to emphasize that Vladimir is shown *before* his baptism. During the preparation of the second edition of *Askol'dova mogila* in the early 1850s, the censor was also troubled by political aspects of the novel, expressing concerns over the inflammatory speeches of the Unknown against the ruling dynasty.

In 1835 Zagoskin remade *Askol'dova mogila* into an opera libretto (moving its action to the "safe" reign of Sviatoslav), the music for which was composed by Verstovsky. The operatic *Askol'dova mogila* enjoyed tremendous success and remained on stage for several decades. However, the novel itself was, compared to *Miloslavskii* and even *Roslavlev,* a failure, after which Zagoskin abandoned for a while the historical genre and moved to other areas of belles lettres. He returned to drama, writing in 1835 the play *Nedovol'nye* (The Discontented, performed the same year), which satirizes Russian noblemen who speak with contempt about their home country while taking for granted their wealth and privileges. This comedy in verse, which includes some parodic allusions to Griboedov's *Gore ot uma* (Woe from Wit, published in part in 1833), was directed against such Moscow dissidents as Petr Iakovlevich Chaadaev and Mikhail Fedorovich Orlov.

In 1837 Zagoskin published two volumes of tales, which include *Vecher na Khopre* (An Evening on the Khoper), *Tri zhenikha* (Three Suitors), and *Kuz'ma Roshchin.* All these tales, some of which had previously appeared in Senkovsky's *Biblioteka dlia chteniia* (Library for Reading), belong to different genres. *Tri zhenikha* is a comic sketch of provincial gentry (reworked in 1840 into the comedy *Urok matushkam* [A Lesson for Mothers]) written in a mixture of narrative and dramatic dialogue, a combination frequently found in Zagoskin's works. *Kuz'ma Roshchin* is a story of a repentant brigand with certain historical elements, as its second part concerns the Plague Mutiny in Moscow in 1771. And *Vecher na Khopre* is a series of horror stories recounted by several narrators. Such collections of "framed" evening or nighttime stories were a popular genre of Romantic prose similar to Aleksandr Aleksandrovich Bestuzhev's "Vecher na bivuake" (An Evening on Bivouac, 1823), Antonii Pogorel'sky's *Dvoinik, ili Moi vechera v Malorossii* (The Double, or My Evenings in Little

Russia, 1828), Gogol's *Vechera na khutore bliz Dikan'ki* (Evenings on a Farm Near Dikanka, 1831–1832), Mariia Semenovna Zhukova's *Vechera na Karpovke* (Evenings on the Karpovka, 1839), and Vladimir Fedorovich Odoevsky's *Russkie nochi* (Russian Nights, 1844). A similar collection of novellas is present in *Roslavlev,* where officers relate unusual occurrences in their lives, but whereas in *Roslavlev* each story receives a rational explanation, in *Vecher na Khopre* there is more room for supernatural interpretation. Zagoskin's attempts at fantastic fiction reflect a general trend in Russian literature that developed under the significant influence of E. T. A. Hoffmann—for example, Pogorelsky's *Dvoinik,* Pushkin's "Grobovshchik" (The Undertaker, 1831) and *Pikovaia dama* (Queen of Spades, 1834), Grech's *Chernaia zhenshchina* (The Black Woman, 1834), Gogol's tales, and Mikhail Iur'evich Lermontov's fragment "Shtoss" (1841).

Zagoskin continued experimentation with fantastic literature in his next big work, *Iskusitel'* (The Tempter, 1838), the first Russian novel about the devil's visiting Moscow. The opening part of *Iskusitel'* is completely of this world and describes the happy childhood of the hero in the Russian hinterland. It is largely autobiographical, since the village Tuzhilovka in the novel resembles Zagoskin's own Ramzai, while pictures of the nearby provincial city reflect the writer's memories of Penza. Supernatural elements come to the forefront in the second part (set in the late 1800s) with the appearance of the evil one, who poses under the guise of a sophisticated and wealthy foreign traveler, Baron Broken (the name refers to the Brocken Mountain, the site of Walpurgisnacht in Goethe's *Faust,* 1808 and 1832). On the personal level, the devil tries (unsuccessfully) to seduce the narrator-protagonist, matching him with a married woman and urging him to break up with his virtuous bride back home. On the social level, the devil corrupts the minds of the Moscow aristocracy with ideas of French philosophy and liberal rhetoric about humanity, enlightenment, Europeanism, and the demands of the time. Zagoskin tried to demonstrate that the contemporary socalled enlightenment was in part instigated by the devil himself. A counterbalance to this false enlightenment Zagoskin saw in the true one based on firm religious foundations. According to the judgment of critics and Zagoskin's own concessions, *Iskusitel'* was among his weakest works. However, it is certainly of interest as a precursor of the antinihilist novel and Fyodor Dostoyevsky's *Besy* (The Possessed, 1872). The chapter "Filosofskii razgovor v kharchevne" (A Philosophical Conversation in a Tavern) also presages many existential debates in

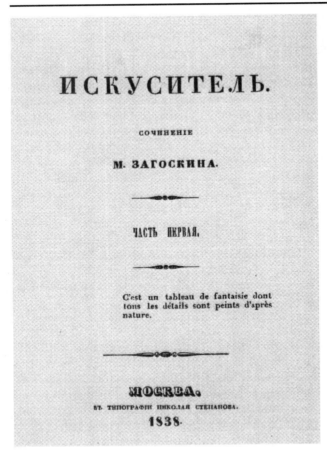

ИСКУСИТЕЛЬ.

СОЧИНЕНИЕ

М. ЗАГОСКИНА.

ЧАСТЬ ПЕРВАЯ.

C'est un tableau de fantaisie dont
tous les détails sont peints d'après
nature.

МОСКВА.
ВЪ ТИПОГРАФІИ НИКОЛАЯ СТЕПАНОВА.
1838.

Title page for Zagoskin's Iskusitel' *(The Tempter)*

pubs and taverns, which have become a trademark of Dostoyevsky. There are possible echoes from *Iskusitel'* in the demonology of Mikhail Afanas'evich Bulgakov's *Master i Margarita* (The Master and Margarita, completed in 1940, published in 1966–1967).

In 1839 Zagoskin published a long prose tale, *Toska po rodine* (Home Sickness), in which the protagonist, Vladimir Zavol'sky, flees abroad from an unhappy love affair. Languishing in nostalgia, he almost finds his death in Spain under the knives of hired killers, but at the last moment he is miraculously saved and returns to Russia, regaining both love and motherland. Many of the chapters with foreign settings are based on an early fragment by Zagoskin, "Puteshestvenik" (The Traveler), published in 1820 in *Sorevnovatel' prosveshcheniia i blagotvoreniia* (The Champion of Enlightenment and Beneficence). Emphasizing drawbacks of European life, both the fragment and the tale represent negativist travelogues, which were designed as an answer to contemporary Russian admirers of the West. Out of several countries described in the tale, Zagoskin visited only Germany, while his pictures of Britain, France, and Spain are at best secondhand. Recep-

tion of the tale was rather reserved. The operatic version of *Toska po rodine* (with Verstovsky's music) turned out to be even less successful than the original and disappeared from the stage soon after its premier in 1839.

Zagoskin's next major work was the novel *Kuz'ma Petrovich Miroshev* (1842), whose subtitle– *Russkaia byl' vremen Ekateriny II* (A True Russian Story from the Time of Catherine II)–suggests that it belongs to the historical genre. Several historical events and figures do appear in *Miroshev:* in the prologue the protagonist participates in the Seven Years' War, and in the main part he encounters the legendary criminal-turned-detective Van'ka Kain and the old grandee Count R*****, in whom it is easy to recognize Count Kiril Grigor'evich Razumovsky, the younger brother of Elizabeth's favorite. However, the significance of the actual historical elements in the novel is minimal. Another deviation from the model employed by Zagoskin in his previous works concerns the plot. Instead of being centered on a love affair set in a rather short span during a time of historical turmoil, *Miroshev* represents an extended biography of the title character. Events in the main part of the novel occur between 1780 and 1781, when the protagonist is already in his forties.

Kuz'ma Miroshev is a descendant of an ancient but impoverished family. Quiet, meek, and unassuming, he is ordinary and inconspicuous both in appearance and personality but is remarkable in his selflessness and ability to forgive. He also displays unwavering faith in God's grace and an acceptance of Divine Providence. These virtues are rewarded as Miroshev endures all adversities of fate and overcomes the evil intrigues of his enemies, gaining family happiness and material well-being. Throughout his life the protagonist is accompanied by the faithful attendant Prokhor Kondrat'evich, who resembles Savel'ich from *Kapitanskaia dochka* but is in fact modeled after Zagoskin's own *diad'ka* (bat man). On several occasions the writer laments the disappearance of this breed of servant who was a true member of the boyar household.

Miroshev enjoyed a moderate success among the reading public (the second edition of the novel appeared in 1847) but received little critical acclaim, except for Aksakov, who extolled the novel, deeming it on a par with *Miloslavskii*. According to Aksakov, Zagoskin portrays in Miroshev the type of the truly Russian Christian, who, without lofty rhetoric, displays miracles of heroism and self-sacrifice, being convinced that there is nothing unusual in such behavior.

The year 1842 marks the last change in the service career of Zagoskin, who was appointed director of the Kremlin Armory. He remained in this office throughout the final decade of his life. (Zagoskin's deputy and successor in the Armory was another writer and historical novelist, Aleksandr Fomich Vel'tman.) In 1845 Zagoskin was decorated with the Order of St. Stanislav of the First Degree and in 1851 with the Order of St. Anna of the First Degree.

In his literary pursuits Zagoskin returned to historical fiction, writing two novels: *Brynskii les* (Brynsky Forest, 1846) and *Russkie v nachale os'mnadtsatogo stoletiia* (The Russians at the Beginning of the Eighteenth Century, 1848), which are both set during the reign of Peter I. The action of *Brynskii les* dates back to the Strel'tsy (Musketeers) Mutiny of 1682, while *Russkie v nachale os'mnadtsatogo stoletiia* (the title of which is obviously intended to be reminiscent of the subtitles of *Miloslavskii* and *Roslavlev*) deals with the unfortunate Russian campaign against the Turks in Moldavia in 1711. Zagoskin's last novels are repetitive and strongly resemble his "firstling" *Miloslavskii* with its links to the Scott tradition. History is shown in connection with love affairs, which are complicated by the lovers' belonging to hostile camps. In *Brynskii les,* Dmitrii Levshin, the young officer of the Strel'tsy who abhors the riotous conduct of his comrades-in-arms and wholeheartedly supports the young Peter, falls for the adopted daughter of a Schismatic leader. In *Russkie v nachale os'mnadtsatogo stoletiia* Vasilii Simsky, a young ensign of the Preobrazhensky regiment and an ardent backer of Petrine reforms, is in love with the daughter of a conservative boyar. After many adventures, which unfold against the background of historic events and briefly involve nonfictional characters, the couples are happily united.

The last of Zagoskin's novels won little recognition, which is hardly surprising since the historical novel, having lived through its heyday in the 1830s, became obsolete in the following decade. Thus, the seventh edition of *Miloslavskii,* which appeared in 1846, was jeered at in *Otechestvennye zapiski* (Notes of the Fatherland) by Valerian Nikolaevich Maikov, who saw it as a blatant anachronism. Rather unsuccessful also were Zagoskin's last comedies: *Poezdka za granitsu* (Going Abroad, produced and published in 1850) and *Zhenatyi zhenikh* (The Married Bridegroom, 1851), which are based on earlier fragments.

The most interesting and acclaimed work written by Zagoskin during the final period of his life is the collection *Moskva i moskvichi,* which was released in four installments in 1842, 1843, 1848, and 1850. (The fifth installment remained unfinished.) *Moskva i moskvichi* represents a motley aggregation of prose and dramatic sketches and fragments devoted to recent history as well as contemporary life in the city. Though primarily valuable to historians of Moscow, *Moskva i moskvichi* is also noteworthy for its mixture of various literary traditions: elements of the nascent physiological sketch, the picture of morals in the spirit of the late eighteenth and early nineteenth centuries, and a Romantic play with narrative masks. Zagoskin purports to be a mere publisher of the sketches while their real author is allegedly a certain Bogdan Il'ich Bel'sky, whose biography is significantly different from that of Zagoskin. Moreover, Zagoskin occasionally appears in the collection as a character transparently disguised as a middle-aged chamberlain who figures as Belsky's interlocutor.

Despite its fragmented and eclectic nature, *Moskva i moskvichi* possesses a certain unity that reflects Zagoskin's concept of Moscow as a microcosm of the entire Russian world, or at least, the "heart" of this world, with its head residing in St. Petersburg. (An allegorical comparison of the two capitals is found in the sketch "Brat i sestra" [Brother and Sister].) The collection is permeated with a warm feeling for the ancient Russian capital, a drastic change of attitude from Zagoskin's first years in Moscow, when he deplored the boredom of local life and longed for St. Petersburg. But gradually he turned into a proud Muscovite and a great connoisseur of the city. In the capacity of armory director Zagoskin enthusiastically conducted tours of Moscow for Russian and foreign guests. (One such excursion and the innocent tricks of the guide, who strives to showcase his beloved city in the best possible light, are vividly described in the sketch "Vzgliad na Moskvu" [A Glance at Moscow].)

During his later years Zagoskin became a Moscow landmark of a kind. Among others, he hosted literary soirees frequented by the Aksakovs, Vel'tman, Nikolai Filippovich Pavlov, Mikhail Petrovich Pogodin, Nikolai Vasil'evich Sushkov, and sometimes by Gogol. Zagoskin fell ill in 1851 and died on 23 June 1852 after a long period of haphazard treatment. He is buried at the cemetery of the Novodevichy Convent.

Zagoskin was a prolific writer who experimented with a wide variety of genres, yet his body of works displays a significant unity in terms of recurrent characters, motifs, and themes. Zagoskin is also extremely consistent in his adherence to the "Russian orientation," a loyalty that bordered on xenophobia and prompted accusations (for example, from Polevoi and Vissarion Grigor'evich Belinsky) of the most lowbrow patriotism. His rather naive, patriotic ardor sometimes manifests itself in an absurd fashion, as in *Askol'dova mogila,* in which Russia turns out to be "holy" even prior to its Christian baptism. In his daily life Zagoskin was equally patriotic down to the smallest details. For example, he preferred to order clothes from Russian tailors and boycotted imported wines, trying to buy only the recently introduced Crimean ones. Despite his ardent patriotism, Zagoskin was not a Slavophile. The German philosophy that underlies Slavophilism was completely alien to him, and, unlike the Slavophiles, he did not idealize the pre-Petrine Russia; instead he eulogized Peter as a genius whose reforms elevated the country to the rank of a great power. Overall, Zagoskin's stance is rather close to Count Sergei Semenovich Uvarov's notorious triad of "Official Nationalism": orthodoxy, autocracy, and nationality. But regardless of its primitive overtones, Zagoskin's preoccupation with the national character is highly typical of the Romantic Age.

Zagoskin's patriotism was also sincere and "organic," an integral feature of his personality. In many ways he embodied the stereotype of the Russianness portrayed in his work. A person of robust constitution and considerable physical strength, he was sometimes likened to a bear—both in appearance and manners. Straightforward and open in his behavior, he was hot tempered and yet could not hold a grudge. All memoirists emphasize the absence of malice in his character and his disarming good-naturedness. Liveliness and joviality compensated for Zagoskin's lack of intellectual depth. Endowed with a comic disposition, he readily poked fun at others and himself, spicing his jokes with juicy Russian idioms. This brand of light, sprightly humor, remarked Aksakov, Zagoskin's old friend and first biographer, is devoid of serious dimensions and vastly differs from Gogol's "laughter through tears."

Zagoskin's personality left a strong imprint on his work, causing both criticism and recognition. For example, Pushkin praised Zagoskin (in connection with *Miloslavskii*) for his good-natured merriness and storyteller's talent. However, the caustic Prince Viazemsky retorted: "V Zagoskine tochno est' darovanie, no zato kak on i glup!" ("Zagoskin has a talent indeed, however, he is so stupid!"). Overall, one can apply to most of Zagoskin's body of works the opinion of Pushkin, which he formulated to amend the negative verdict of Viazemsky on *Roslavlev:*

Polozheniia, khotiia i natianutue, zanimatel'ny . . . Razgovory, khotia zhivy i . . . vse mozhno prochest' s udovol'stviem.

The situations are far-fetched, yet entertaining; the dialogue is unnatural, yet lively, and the whole can be read with enjoyment.

The literary reputation of Zagoskin reached its peak in the early 1830s with the release of *Miloslavskii* and *Roslavlev,* after which a gradual decline followed. Although Zagoskin was an active participant in the literary process of his time, his simplistic worldview and the unidimensionality of his characters prevented subsequent generations of readers from perceiving him as an equal of his great contemporaries: Pushkin, Lermontov, Gogol, and Griboedov. Nonetheless, Zagoskin remained a widely read author throughout the second half of the nineteenth and early twentieth centuries, retaining his audience among children and less-discriminating adults. As Aleksandr Mikhailovich Skabichevsky attested in the 1880s, virtually every literate Russian had read at least *Miloslavskii.* The lasting popularity of Zagoskin is proven by the continued printings of his books as well. Aside from individual pieces, five editions of his complete and collected works were published between the 1880s and the 1910s. From the 1870s to the 1910s there also appeared many remakes and adaptations of *Miloslavskii.* Zagoskin's return during the Soviet period began (not without debates) in the mid 1950s with the republication of *Miloslavskii* and *Roslavlev.* Starting with the early years of Perestroika, other works and collections by Zagoskin have been emerging in print. Some of them belong to the realm of cheap, mass-market publishing; others appear within the framework of the new ultrapatriotic and chauvinistic agenda; and still others (especially those edited by Aleksei Mikhailovich Peskov and Nikolai G. Okhotin) include thorough scholarly prefaces and commentaries and represent a valuable academic source for the author and his times.

Bibliographies:

Mikhail Nikolaevich Zagoskin, *Sochineniia,* volume 7 (St. Petersburg: V. I. Shtein, 1889);

"Opisanie rukopisei i perepiski M. N. Zagonskina," in *Otchet Imperatorskoi Publichnoi biblioteki za 1912 g.* (Petrograd, 1917), pp. 115–116.

Biographies:

Sergei Timofeevich Aksakov, *Biografiia M. N. Zagoskina* (Moscow, 1853); reprinted in Sergei T. Aksakov, *Sobranie sochinenii,* 3 volumes (Moscow: Khudozhestvennaia literatura, 1986), volume 3, pp. 383–430;

[Aleksandr Osipovich Kruglyi], *M. N. Zagoskin. Biograficheskii ocherk* (St. Petersburg, 1889);

D. M. Iazykov, *M. N. Zagoskin. Biograficheskii ocherk* (Moscow, 1902);

N. M. Vasin, *M. N. Zagoskin. Biograficheskii ocherk* (Moscow: Izd. M. V. Kliukin, 1902);

"Vospominaniia o Zagoskine" (S. T. Aksakov, F. F. Vigel', M. A. Dmitriev, K. A. Polevoi, I. I. Panaev, I. S. Turgenev, T. P. Passek, S. V. Engel'gardt, S. M. Zagoskin), in Zagoskin's *Moskva i moskvichi* (Moscow: Moskovskii rabochii, 1988), pp. 502–580.

References:

Sergei Timofeevich Aksakov, review of *Iurii Miloslavskii,* in his *Sobranie sochinenii,* volume 3 (Moscow: Khudozhestvennaia literatura, 1986), pp. 353–360;

Mark Grigor'evich Al'tshuller, *Epokha Val'tera Skotta v Rosii. Istoricheskii roman 1830–kh godov* (St. Petersburg: Akademi cheskii proekt, 1996), pp. 65–107;

N. G. Il'inskaia, "Stoit li 'voskreshat'' Zagoskina?" *Neva,* 1 (1957): 203–204;

Valerian Nikolaevich Maikov, review of *Iurii Miloslavskii,* in his *Kriticheskie opyty* (St. Petersburg, 1891), pp. 223–235;

Nikolai G. Okhotin, introduction to Zagoskin's *Moskva i moskvichi* (Moscow: Moskovskii rabochii, 1988), pp. 5–17;

Aleksandr Sergeevich Orlov, "Val'ter Skott I Zagoskin," in *Sergeiu Fedorovichu Ol'denburgu k 50-letiiu naucho-obshchestvennoi deiatel'nosti. 1882–1932, Sbornik statei* (Moscow-Leningrad: AN SSSR, 1934), pp. 413–20;

Aleksei Mikhailovich Peskov, introduction to Zagoskin's *Sochineniia v dvukh tomakh,* volume 1 (Moscow: Khudozhestvennaia literatura, 1987), pp. 5–34;

Nina Nikolaevna Petrunina, "Pushkin i Zagoskin," *Russkaia literatura,* 4 (1972): 110–120;

Vil'iam Vasil'evich Pokhlebkin, "M. N. Zagoskin," in his *Kushat' podano! Repertuar kushanii i napitkov v russkoi klassicheskoi dramaturgii s konsta XVIII do nachala XX stoletia* (Moscow: Artist. Rezhisser. Teatr, 1993), pp. 73–82;

Nikolai Alekseevich Polevoi, reviews of *Miloslavkii* and *Roslavlev,* in *Literaturnaia kritika. Stat'i i retsenzii,* by N. A. Polevoi and Ks. A. Polevoi (Leningrad: Khudozhestvennaia literatura, 1990), pp. 52–55; 89–95;

Ivan Pavolich Shcheblykin, "*Roslavlev* M. N. Zagoskina i *Voina i mir* L. N. Tolstogo," in *Tolstovskii sbornik,* edited by I. E. Grineva, volume 5 (Tula, 1973);

Aleksandr Mikhailovich Skabichevsky, "Nash istoricheskii roman v ego proshlom i nastoiashchem," in his *Sochineniia,* volume 2 (St. Petersburg, 1890), pp. 591–622;

Tat'iana Ivanovna Usakina, "Pamflet Zagoskina na P. Ia. Chaadaeva i M. F. Orlova," in *Dekabristy v Moskve* (Moscow: Muzei istorii I rekonstruktsii Moskvy, 1963), pp. 162–184;

Ivan Ivanovich Zamotin, *Romantizm 20-kh godov XIX stoletiia v russkoi literature,* volume 2 (St. Petersburg: Izdanie t-va M. O. Vol'f, 1913), pp. 283–379.

Papers:

Zagoskin's papers are housed at TsGALI (Tsentral'nyi gosudarstvennyi arkhiv literatury), fond 1768; IRLI (Institut russkoi literatury), fond 105; and Rossiiskaia natsianal'naia biblioteka (Russian National Library), St. Petersburg, fond 291. Family papers and materials for biography are located in the State Archive of the Penza region, fond 196, opis' 2, d. 79.

Checklist of Further Readings

Berry, Thomas Edwin. *Plots and Characters in Major Russian Fiction.* 2 volumes. Hamden, Conn.: Archon Books, 1977.

Billington, James H. *The Icon and the Axe: An Interpretive History of Russian Culture.* New York: Knopf, 1966.

Boyer, Arline. "A Description of Selected Periodicals in the First Half of the Nineteenth Century," *Russian Literature Triquarterly,* no. 3 (1972): 465–473.

Brooks, J. "Russian Nationalism and Russian Literature: Canonization of the Classics," in *Nations and Ideology: Essays in Honor of Wayne S. Vucinich,* edited by I. Banac and others. Boulder: *East European Quarterly,* 1981.

Brown, William Edward. *A History of Russian Literature of the Romantic Period.* 4 volumes. Ann Arbor, Mich.: Ardis, 1986.

Busch, Robert. "Russian Freneticism," *Canadian-American Slavic Studies,* 14 (1980): 269–283.

Bushmin, A. S., and others, eds., *Istoriia russkogo romana,* 2 volumes. Moscow: Akademiia Nauk SSSR, 1962–1964.

Canadian-American Slavic Studies, 29, nos. 3–4, special issues on Russian Romanticism (1995).

Čiževskij, Dmitrij. *History of Nineteenth-Century Russian Literature.* Translated by Richard Porter. Edited by Serge A. Zenkovsky. Volume 1: *The Romantic Period.* Volume 2: *The Realistic Period.* Nashville: Vanderbilt University Press, 1974.

Čiževskij. *On Romanticism in Slavic Literature.* The Hague: Mouton, 1957.

Čiževskij. *Russian Intellectual History.* Translated by J. Osborne. Ann Arbor, Mich.: Ardis, 1978.

Cornwell, Neil. *The Society Tale in Russian Literature: From Odoevskii to Tolstoi.* Amsterdam & Atlanta: Rodopi, 1998.

Debreczeny, Paul, and Jesse Zeldin, eds. and trans. *Literature and National Identity: Nineteenth-Century Russian Critical Essays.* Lincoln: University of Nebraska Press, 1970.

Eikhenbaum, Boris, and Iurii Tynianov, eds. *Russian Prose.* Translated by Ray Parrott. Ann Arbor, Mich.: Ardis, 1985.

Fehsenfeld, Nancy Kanach. "Prose in Nicolaevan Russia." Dissertation, Cornell University, 1980.

Fennell, John, ed. *Nineteenth-Century Russian Literature: Studies of Ten Russian Writers.* Berkeley: University of California Press, 1973.

Fuhrman, J. T., E. C. Bock, and L. I. Twarog. *Essays on Russian Intellectual History.* Austin: Texas University Press, 1971.

Gutsche, George J., and Lauren G. Leighton. *New Perspectives on Nineteenth-Century Russian Prose.* Columbus, Ohio: Slavica, 1982.

Harkins, William Edward. *Dictionary of Russian Literature.* New York: Philosophical Library, 1956.

Hingley, Ronald. *Russian Writers and Society, 1825–1904,* second revised edition. London: Weidenfeld & Nicolson, 1977.

Hollingsworth, Barry. *"Arzamas:* Portrait of a Literary Society." *Slavic and East European Review,* 44 (1967): 306–326.

Ingham, Norman. *E. T. A. Hoffmann in Russia, 1822–1845.* Wurzburg: Jal-Verlag, 1974.

Istoriia romantizma v russkoi literature. Volume 1: *Voznikhovenie i utverzhdenie romantizma v russkoi literature 1790–1825.* Volume 2: *Romantizm v russkoi literature 20–30kh godov XIX v., 1825–1840.* Moscow: Akademiia Nauk SSSR, 1979.

Jacobson, Helen Saltz, ed. and trans. *Diary of a Russian Censor: Alexander Nikitenko.* Amherst: University of Massachusetts Press, 1975.

Katz, Michael R. *Dreams and the Unconscious in Nineteenth-Century Russian Fiction.* Hanover, N.H.: New England University Press, 1984.

Kisselef, Natalia. "A Study of the Romantic Hero in the Nineteenth Century Novel." Dissertation, University of Toronto, 1976.

Kostka, Edmund. *Schiller in Russian Literature.* Philadelphia: University of Pennsylvania Press, 1965.

Layton, Susan. *Russian Literature and Empire: Conquest of the Caucasus from Pushkin to Tolstoy.* New York: Cambridge University Press, 1994.

Leatherbarrow, William J., and Derek C. Offord., eds. and trans. *A Documentary History of Russian Thought: From the Enlightenment to Marxism.* Ann Arbor, Mich.: Ardis, 1987.

LeBlanc, Ronald D. *The Russianization of Gil Blas: A Study in Literary Appropriation.* Columbus, Ohio: Slavica, 1986.

Leighton, Lauren G. *The Esoteric Tradition in Russian Romantic Literature: Decembrism and Freemasonry.* University Park: Pennsylvania State University Press, 1994.

Leighton. "A Romantic Idealist Nation in Russian Romantic Criticism." *Canadian-American Slavic Studies,* 7 (1973): 285-295.

Leighton. "Romanticism, Marxism-Leninism, Literary Movement." *Russian Literature,* 14, no. 2 (1983): 183–220.

Leighton. *Russian Romanticism: Two Essays.* The Hague: Mouton, 1975.

Leighton, ed. *Russian Romantic Criticism: An Anthology.* New York: Greenwood Press, 1987.

Likhachev, Dmitrii S., and others, eds. *Russkie pisateli. Bibliograficheskii slovar'. Spravochnik dlia uchitelia.* Moscow, 1971.

Mazour, Anatole *The First Russian Revolution.* Berkeley: University of California Press, 1937.

McLaughlin, Sigrid. "Russia/Romanicheskij–Romanticheskij–Romantizm," in *"Romantics" and Its Cognates: The European History of a Word,* edited by Hans Eichner. Toronto & Buffalo: University of Toronto Press, 1972, pp. 418–474.

Meliakh, B. S., ed. *Russkaia povest' XIX veka.* Leningrad: Akademia Nauk SSSR, 1973.

Mersereau, John Jr. "The Chorus and Spear Carriers of Russian Romantic Fiction," in *Russian and Slavic Literature,* edited by Richard Freeborn, R. R. Milner-Gulland, and Charles A. Ward. Cambridge, Mass.: Slavica, 1976, pp. 38–62.

Mersereau. "Normative Distinctions of Russian Romanticism and Realism," in *American Contributions to the Seventh International Congress of Slavists.* The Hague: Mouton, 1973.

Mersereau. *Russian Romantic Fiction.* Ann Arbor, Mich.: Ardis, 1983.

Mersereau. "Yes, Virginia, There Was a Russian Romantic Movement." *Russian Literature Triquarterly,* 3 (1972): 128–147.

Mirsky, D. S. *A History of Russian Literature,* edited and abridged by Francis J. Whitfield. New York: Knopf, 1949.

Moser, Charles A. *The Russian Short Story: A Critical History.* Boston: Twayne, 1986.

Neuhäuser, Rudolf. *Towards the Romantic Age: Essays on Sentimental and Preromantic Literature in Russia.* The Hague: Nijhoff, 1974.

Nilsson, Nils Åke. *Russian Romanticism: Studies in the Poetic Codes.* Stockholm, Sweden: Almqvist & Wiskell International, 1979.

Offord, Derek. *Portraits of Early Russian Liberals.* Cambridge, U.K. & New York: Cambridge University Press, 1985.

Passage, Charles E. *The Russian Hoffmannists.* The Hague: Mouton. 1963.

Phillips, Delbert Darwal. *Spook or Spoof? The Structure of the Supernatural in Russian Romantic Tales.* Lanham, Md.: University Press of America, 1982.

Proffer, Carl R., ed. *From Karamzin to Bunin.* Bloomington: Indiana University Press, 1969.

Proffer, ed. *Russian Romantic Prose: An Anthology.* Ann Arbor, Mich.: Ardis, 1977.

Reid, Robert, ed. *Problems of Russian Romanticism.* Brookfield, Vt.: Gower, 1986.

Riasanovsky, Nicholas V. *A History of Russia.* New York: Oxford University Press, 1963.

Riasanovsky. *The Image of Peter the Great in Russian History and Thought.* Oxford: Oxford University Press, 1985, pp. 88–152.

Riasanovsky. *Nicholas I and Official Nationality in Russia, 1825–1855.* Berkeley: University of California Press, 1959.

Riasanovsky. *A Parting of Ways: Government and the Educated Public in Russia, 1801–1855.* Oxford: Clarendon Press, 1976.

Riasanovsky. *Russia and the West in the Teaching of the Slavophiles.* Gloucester, Mass.: Peter Smith, 1965.

Riha, Thomas, ed. *Readings in Russian Civilization.* Volume 2: *Imperial Russia, 1700–1917.* Chicago: University of Chicago Press, 1965.

Russian Literature Triquarterly, no. 3, special issue on Romanticism (1972). See also *Russian Literature Triquarterly,* no. 10 (1974), *The Golden Age.*

Rydel, Christine A., ed. *The Ardis Anthology of Russian Romanticism.* Ann Arbor, Mich.: Ardis, 1984.

Shepard, E. C. "The Society Tale and the Innovative Argument in Russian Prose Fiction of the 1830s." *Russian Literature,* 10 (1981): 111–161.

Snow, Valentine. *Russian Writers: A Bio-Bibliographical Dictionary.* New York: International Book Service, 1946.

Stavrou, Theofanis G., ed. *Art and Culture in Nineteenth-Century Russia.* Bloomington: Indiana University Press, 1983.

Struve, Peter. "Walter Scott and Russia." *Slavic and East European Reviews,* 32 (1933): 397–441.

Terras, Victor, ed. *Handbook of Russian Literature.* New Haven: Yale University Press, 1985.

Terras. *A History of Russian Literature.* New Haven & London: Yale University Press, 1991.

Todd, William Mills. *The Familiar Letter as a Literary Genre in the Age of Pushkin.* Princeton, N.J.: Princeton University Press, 1976.

Todd. *Fiction and Society in the Age of Pushkin.* Cambridge, Mass.: Harvard University Press, 1986.

Todd. *Literature and Society in Imperial Russia.* Stanford, Cal.: Stanford University Press, 1978.

Tsvetkov, Olga S. "Aspects of the Russian Society Tale of the 1830's." Dissertation, University of Michigan, 1984.

Ungurianu, Dan I. "The Russian Historical Novel from Romanticism to Symbolism: Fact, Fiction, and the Poetics of Genre." Dissertation, University of Wisconsin, Madison, 1995.

Von Gronicka, André. *The Russian Image of Goethe: Goethe in Russian Literature in the First Half of the Nineteenth Century.* Philadelphia: University of Philadelphia Press, 1985.

Walicki, Andrzej. *The Slavophile Controversy.* Oxford: Oxford University Press, 1975.

West, James. "Walter Scott and the Style of Russian Historical Novels of the 1830s and 1840s" in *American Contributions to the Eighth International Congress of Slavists, Zagreb and Lyublijana, Sept. 3–9, 1978.* Volume 1: *Linguistics and Poetics.* Edited by Henrik Birnbaum. Columbus, Ohio: Slavica, pp. 757–772.

Wilson, Revel K. "The Literary Travelogue: A Critique with Special Revelance to Russian Literature from Fonvizin to Pushkin." Dissertation, University of Chicago, 1972.

Contributors

Amy Singleton Adams..*College of the Holy Cross*
Carolyn Jursa Ayers...*University of Groningen, The Netherlands*
Joachim T. Baer.....................................*University of North Carolina at Greensboro*
Lew Bagby ....*University of Wyoming*
Thomas Berry ....*Odyssey Program, Johns Hopkins University*
Edward Alan Cole ....*Grand Valley State University*
Neil Cornwell..*University of Bristol*
Jehanne M Gheith..*Duke University*
Brian J. Horowitz ....*University of Nebraska, Lincoln*
George L. Kline...*Bryn Mawr College*
Ronald D. LeBlanc ....*University of New Hampshire*
Irina Makarova ....*Russian State (Herzen) Pedagogical University*
John Mersereau Jr. ....*University of Michigan*
Rosina Neginsky ....*University of Illinois at Urbana–Champaign*
Derek Offord..*University of Bristol*
Louis Pedrotti..*University of California–Riverside*
Leonard A. Polakiewicz...*University of Minnesota*
Veronica Shapovalov ....*San Diego State University*
Vladimir Shatskov ....*St. Petersburg University of Civil Engineering and Architecture*
Maxim D. Shrayer ....*Boston College*
Ruth Sobel ....*Defence School of Languages*
Richard Tempest.............................*University of Illinois at Urbana–Champaign*
Dan I. Ungurianu ....*University of Missouri–Columbia*
Mary Jo White...*University of Washington*

Cumulative Index

Dictionary of Literary Biography, Volumes 1-198
Dictionary of Literary Biography Yearbook, 1980-1997
Dictionary of Literary Biography Documentary Series, Volumes 1-17

Cumulative Index

DLB before number: *Dictionary of Literary Biography,* Volumes 1-198
Y before number: *Dictionary of Literary Biography Yearbook,* 1980-1997
DS before number: *Dictionary of Literary Biography Documentary Series,* Volumes 1-17

A

Abbey, Edwin Austin 1852–1911. . . . DLB-188

Abbey Press DLB-49

The Abbey Theatre and Irish Drama,
1900-1945 . . . . DLB-10

Abbot, Willis J. 1863-1934 . . . . DLB-29

Abbott, Jacob 1803-1879 . . . . DLB-1

Abbott, Lee K. 1947- DLB-130

Abbott, Lyman 1835-1922 . . . . DLB-79

Abbott, Robert S. 1868-1940 . . . . DLB-29, 91

Abe, Kōbō 1924-1993 . . . . DLB-182

Abelard, Peter circa 1079-1142 . . . . . DLB-115

Abelard-Schuman DLB-46

Abell, Arunah S. 1806-1888 . . . . . . DLB-43

Abercrombie, Lascelles 1881-1938 . . . . DLB-19

Aberdeen University Press
Limited DLB-106

Abish, Walter 1931- DLB-130

Ablesimov, Aleksandr Onisimovich
1742-1783 . . . . DLB-150

Abraham à Sancta Clara
1644-1709 . . . . DLB-168

Abrahams, Peter 1919- DLB-117

Abrams, M. H. 1912- DLB-67

Abrogans circa 790-800 . . . . DLB-148

Abschatz, Hans Aßmann von
1646-1699 . . . . DLB-168

Abse, Dannie 1923- DLB-27

Academy Chicago Publishers DLB-46

Accrocca, Elio Filippo 1923- DLB-128

Ace Books DLB-46

Achebe, Chinua 1930- DLB-117

Achtenberg, Herbert 1938- DLB-124

Ackerman, Diane 1948- DLB-120

Ackroyd, Peter 1949- DLB-155

Acorn, Milton 1923-1986 . . . . DLB-53

Acosta, Oscar Zeta 1935?- DLB-82

Actors Theatre of Louisville DLB-7

Adair, Gilbert 1944- DLB-194

Adair, James 1709?-1783?. DLB-30

Adam, Graeme Mercer 1839-1912 . . . . DLB-99

Adam, Robert Borthwick II
1863-1940 . . . . DLB-187

Adame, Leonard 1947- DLB-82

Adamic, Louis 1898-1951 . . . . DLB-9

Adams, Alice 1926- Y-86

Adams, Brooks 1848-1927 . . . . DLB-47

Adams, Charles Francis, Jr.
1835-1915 . . . . DLB-47

Adams, Douglas 1952- Y-83

Adams, Franklin P. 1881-1960 . . . . . . DLB-29

Adams, Henry 1838-1918 . . . DLB-12, 47, 189

Adams, Herbert Baxter 1850-1901. . . . . DLB-47

Adams, J. S. and C.
[publishing house]. DLB-49

Adams, James Truslow
1878-1949 . . . . DLB-17; DS-17

Adams, John 1735-1826. . . . . . . DLB-31, 183

Adams, John 1735-1826 and
Adams, Abigail 1744-1818 . . . . . DLB-183

Adams, John Quincy 1767-1848 . . . . . DLB-37

Adams, Léonie 1899-1988 . . . . DLB-48

Adams, Levi 1802-1832. . . . . DLB-99

Adams, Samuel 1722-1803 . . . . . DLB-31, 43

Adams, Thomas
1582 or 1583-1652 . . . . DLB-151

Adams, William Taylor 1822-1897 . . . . DLB-42

Adamson, Sir John 1867-1950 . . . . . DLB-98

Adcock, Arthur St. John
1864-1930 . . . . DLB-135

Adcock, Betty 1938- DLB-105

Adcock, Fleur 1934- DLB-40

Addison, Joseph 1672-1719 . . . . . . DLB-101

Ade, George 1866-1944 . . . . . . DLB-11, 25

Adeler, Max (see Clark, Charles Heber)

Adonias Filho 1915-1990 . . . . DLB-145

Advance Publishing Company DLB-49

AE 1867-1935 . . . . DLB-19

Ælfric circa 955-circa 1010 . . . . . . DLB-146

Aeschines circa 390 B.C.-circa 320 B.C.
. . . . DLB-176

Aeschylus
525-524 B.C.-456-455 B.C. DLB-176

Aesthetic Poetry (1873), by
Walter Pater DLB-35

After Dinner Opera Company. Y-92

Afro-American Literary Critics:
An Introduction. DLB-33

Agassiz, Elizabeth Cary 1822-1907 . . . DLB-189

Agassiz, Jean Louis Rodolphe
1807-1873 . . . . DLB-1

Agee, James 1909-1955. . . . . DLB-2, 26, 152

The Agee Legacy: A Conference at
the University of Tennessee
at Knoxville Y-89

Aguilera Malta, Demetrio
1909-1981 . . . . DLB-145

Ai 1947- DLB-120

Aichinger, Ilse 1921- DLB-85

Aidoo, Ama Ata 1942- DLB-117

Aiken, Conrad
1889-1973 . . . . DLB-9, 45, 102

Aiken, Joan 1924- DLB-161

Aikin, Lucy 1781-1864. . . . . . DLB-144, 163

Ainsworth, William Harrison
1805-1882 . . . . DLB-21

Aitken, George A. 1860-1917 . . . . . . DLB-149

Aitken, Robert [publishing house]. DLB-49

Akenside, Mark 1721-1770 . . . . . . DLB-109

Akins, Zoë 1886-1958. . . . . DLB-26

Aksahov, Sergei Timofeevich
1791-1859 . . . . DLB-198

Akutagawa, Ryūnsuke
1892-1927 . . . . DLB-180

Alabaster, William 1568-1640 . . . . . DLB-132

Alain-Fournier 1886-1914 . . . . DLB-65

Alarcón, Francisco X. 1954- DLB-122

Alba, Nanina 1915-1968 . . . . DLB-41

Albee, Edward 1928- DLB-7

Albert the Great circa 1200-1280 . . . . DLB-115

Alberti, Rafael 1902- DLB-108

Albertinus, Aegidius
circa 1560-1620 . . . . DLB-164

Alcaeus born circa 620 B.C. DLB-176

Alcott, Amos Bronson 1799-1888 . . . . DLB-1

Alcott, Louisa May
1832-1888 . . . . . . DLB-1, 42, 79; DS-14

Alcott, William Andrus 1798-1859 . . . . DLB-1

Alcuin circa 732-804 . . . . DLB-148

Alden, Henry Mills 1836-1919 . . . . . DLB-79

Alden, Isabella 1841-1930 . . . . DLB-42

Alden, John B. [publishing house] DLB-49

Alden, Beardsley and Company DLB-49

Aldington, Richard
1892-1962 . . . . . . DLB-20, 36, 100, 149

Aldis, Dorothy 1896-1966 . . . . DLB-22

Aldis, H. G. 1863-1919 . . . . DLB-184

Aldiss, Brian W. 1925- DLB-14

Aldrich, Thomas Bailey
1836-1907 . . . . DLB-42, 71, 74, 79

Alegría, Ciro 1909-1967 . . . . DLB-113

Alegría, Claribel 1924- DLB-145

Aleixandre, Vicente 1898-1984 . . . . . DLB-108

Aleksandrov, Aleksandr Andreevich (see Durova,
Nadezhda Andreevna)

Aleramo, Sibilla 1876-1960 . . . . . . DLB-114

Alexander, Charles 1868-1923 . . . . . DLB-91

Alexander, Charles Wesley
[publishing house] DLB-49

Alexander, James 1691-1756 . . . . . DLB-24

Alexander, Lloyd 1924- DLB-52

Alexander, Sir William, Earl of Stirling
1577?-1640 . . . . DLB-121

Alexie, Sherman 1966- DLB-175

Alexis, Willibald 1798-1871 . . . . . . DLB-133

Alfred, King 849-899 . . . . DLB-146

Alger, Horatio, Jr. 1832-1899 . . . . . . DLB-42

Algonquin Books of Chapel Hill DLB-46

Algren, Nelson 1909-1981 . . . . DLB-9; Y-81, Y-82

Allan, Andrew 1907-1974 . . . . DLB-88

Allan, Ted 1916- DLB-68

Allbeury, Ted 1917- DLB-87

Alldritt, Keith 1935- DLB-14

Allen, Ethan 1738-1789 . . . . DLB-31

Allen, Frederick Lewis 1890-1954 . . . . DLB-137

Allen, Gay Wilson
1903-1995 . . . . DLB-103; Y-95

Allen, George 1808-1876 . . . . DLB-59

Allen, George [publishing house] DLB-106

Allen, George, and Unwin
Limited DLB-112

Allen, Grant 1848-1899 . . . . DLB-70, 92, 178

Allen, Henry W. 1912- Y-85

Allen, Hervey 1889-1949 . . . . DLB-9, 45

Allen, James 1739-1808 . . . . DLB-31

Allen, James Lane 1849-1925 . . . . . . DLB-71

Allen, Jay Presson 1922- DLB-26

Allen, John, and Company DLB-49

Allen, Paula Gunn 1939- DLB-175

Allen, Samuel W. 1917- DLB-41

Allen, Woody 1935- DLB-44

Allende, Isabel 1942- DLB-145

Alline, Henry 1748-1784 . . . . DLB-99

Allingham, Margery 1904-1966 . . . . . DLB-77

Allingham, William 1824-1889 . . . . . DLB-35

Allison, W. L.
[publishing house] DLB-49

The Alliterative Morte Arthure and
the Stanzaic Morte Arthur
circa 1350-1400 . . . . DLB-146

Allott, Kenneth 1912-1973 . . . . DLB-20

Allston, Washington 1779-1843 . . . . . DLB-1

Almon, John [publishing house] DLB-154

Alonzo, Dámaso 1898-1990 . . . . . . DLB-108

Alsop, George 1636-post 1673 . . . . . DLB-24

Alsop, Richard 1761-1815 . . . . DLB-37

Altemus, Henry, and Company DLB-49

Altenberg, Peter 1885-1919 . . . . . . DLB-81

Altolaguirre, Manuel 1905-1959 . . . . DLB-108

Aluko, T. M. 1918- DLB-117

Alurista 1947- DLB-82

Alvarez, A. 1929- DLB-14, 40

Amadi, Elechi 1934- DLB-117

Amado, Jorge 1912- DLB-113

Ambler, Eric 1909- DLB-77

America: or, a Poem on the Settlement of the
British Colonies (1780?), by Timothy
Dwight DLB-37

American Conservatory Theatre DLB-7

American Fiction and the 1930s DLB-9

American Humor: A Historical Survey
East and Northeast
South and Southwest
Midwest
West DLB-11

The American Library in Paris Y-93

American News Company DLB-49

The American Poets' Corner: The First
Three Years (1983-1986) Y-86

American Proletarian Culture:
The 1930s DS-11

American Publishing Company DLB-49

American Stationers' Company DLB-49

American Sunday-School Union DLB-49

American Temperance Union DLB-49

American Tract Society DLB-49

The American Trust for the
British Library Y-96

The American Writers Congress
(9-12 October 1981) Y-81

The American Writers Congress: A Report
on Continuing Business Y-81

Ames, Fisher 1758-1808 . . . . DLB-37

Ames, Mary Clemmer 1831-1884 . . . . DLB-23

Amini, Johari M. 1935- DLB-41

Amis, Kingsley
1922-1995 . . . . DLB-15, 27, 100, 139, Y-96

Amis, Martin 1949- DLB-194

Ammons, A. R. 1926- DLB-5, 165

Amory, Thomas 1691?-1788 . . . . . . DLB-39

Anania, Michael 1939- DLB-193

Anaya, Rudolfo A. 1937- DLB-82

Ancrene Riwle circa 1200-1225 . . . . . DLB-146

Andersch, Alfred 1914-1980 . . . . . . DLB-69

Anderson, Alexander 1775-1870 . . . . DLB-188

Anderson, Margaret 1886-1973 . . . . DLB-4, 91

Anderson, Maxwell 1888-1959 . . . . . DLB-7

Anderson, Patrick 1915-1979 . . . . . . DLB-68

Anderson, Paul Y. 1893-1938 . . . . . DLB-29

Anderson, Poul 1926- DLB-8

Anderson, Robert 1750-1830 . . . . . DLB-142

Anderson, Robert 1917- DLB-7

Anderson, Sherwood
1876-1941 . . . . . DLB-4, 9, 86; DS-1

Andreae, Johann Valentin
1586-1654 . . . . DLB-164

Andreas-Salomé, Lou 1861-1937 . . . . DLB-66

Andres, Stefan 1906-1970 . . . . DLB-69

Andreu, Blanca 1959- DLB-134

Andrewes, Lancelot
1555-1626 . . . . DLB-151, 172

Andrews, Charles M. 1863-1943 . . . . DLB-17

Andrews, Miles Peter ?-1814 . . . . . . DLB-89

Andrian, Leopold von 1875-1951 . . . . DLB-81

Andrić, Ivo 1892-1975 . . . . DLB-147

Andrieux, Louis (see Aragon, Louis)

Andrus, Silas, and Son DLB-49

Angell, James Burrill 1829-1916 . . . . DLB-64

Angell, Roger 1920- DLB-171, 185

Angelou, Maya 1928- DLB-38

Anger, Jane flourished 1589 . . . . . . DLB-136

Angers, Félicité (see Conan, Laure)

Anglo-Norman Literature in the
Development of Middle English
Literature DLB-146

The Anglo-Saxon Chronicle
circa 890-1154 . . . . DLB-146

The "Angry Young Men" DLB-15

Angus and Robertson (UK)
Limited DLB-112

Anhalt, Edward 1914- DLB-26

Anners, Henry F.
[publishing house] DLB-49

Annolied between 1077
and 1081 . . . . DLB-148

Anselm of Canterbury
1033-1109 . . . . DLB-115

Anstey, F. 1856-1934 . . . . . . DLB-141, 178

Anthony, Michael 1932- DLB-125

Anthony, Piers 1934- DLB-8

Anthony Burgess's *99 Novels:*
   An Opinion Poll Y-84

Antin, David 1932- DLB-169

Antin, Mary 1881-1949. . . . . Y-84

Anton Ulrich, Duke of Brunswick-Lüneburg
   1633-1714 . . . . DLB-168

Antschel, Paul (see Celan, Paul)

Anyidoho, Kofi 1947- DLB-157

Anzaldúa, Gloria 1942- DLB-122

Anzengruber, Ludwig
   1839-1889 . . . . DLB-129

Apess, William 1798-1839 . . . . DLB-175

Apodaca, Rudy S. 1939- DLB-82

Apollonius Rhodius third century B.C.
   . . . . DLB-176

Apple, Max 1941- DLB-130

Appleton, D., and Company DLB-49

Appleton-Century-Crofts. DLB-46

Applewhite, James 1935- DLB-105

Apple-wood Books DLB-46

Aquin, Hubert 1929-1977 . . . . DLB-53

Aquinas, Thomas 1224 or
   1225-1274 . . . . DLB-115

Aragon, Louis 1897-1982 . . . . DLB-72

Aralica, Ivan 1930- DLB-181

Aratus of Soli circa 315 B.C.-circa 239 B.C.
   . . . . DLB-176

Arbasino, Alberto 1930- DLB-196

Arbor House Publishing
   Company DLB-46

Arbuthnot, John 1667-1735 . . . . DLB-101

Arcadia House DLB-46

Arce, Julio G. (see Ulica, Jorge)

Archer, William 1856-1924 . . . . DLB-10

Archilochhus mid seventh century B.C.E.
   . . . . DLB-176

The Archpoet circa 1130?-? DLB-148

Archpriest Avvakum (Petrovich)
   1620?-1682 . . . . DLB-150

Arden, John 1930- DLB-13

Arden of Faversham DLB-62

Ardis Publishers Y-89

Ardizzone, Edward 1900-1979 . . . . . . DLB-160

Arellano, Juan Estevan 1947- DLB-122

The Arena Publishing Company DLB-49

Arena Stage DLB-7

Arenas, Reinaldo 1943-1990 . . . . DLB-145

Arensberg, Ann 1937- Y-82

Arguedas, José María 1911-1969 . . . . DLB-113

Argueta, Manilio 1936- DLB-145

Arias, Ron 1941- DLB-82

Arishima, Takeo 1878-1923 . . . . DLB-180

Aristophanes
   circa 446 B.C.-circa 386 B.C. . . . DLB-176

Aristotle 384 B.C.-322 B.C. DLB-176

Ariyoshi, Sawako 1931-1984 . . . . . . DLB-182

Arland, Marcel 1899-1986 . . . . DLB-72

Arlen, Michael
   1895-1956 . . . . DLB-36, 77, 162

Armah, Ayi Kwei 1939- DLB-117

Armantrout, Rae 1947- DLB-193

Der arme Hartmann
   ?-after 1150 . . . . DLB-148

Armed Services Editions DLB-46

Armstrong, Martin Donisthorpe 1882-1974
   . . . . DLB-197

Armstrong, Richard 1903- DLB-160

Arndt, Ernst Moritz 1769-1860 . . . . . DLB-90

Arnim, Achim von 1781-1831 . . . . . . DLB-90

Arnim, Bettina von 1785-1859 . . . . . DLB-90

Arnim, Elizabeth von (Countess Mary Annette
   Beauchamp Russell) 1866-1941 . . . DLB-197

Arno Press DLB-46

Arnold, Edwin 1832-1904 . . . . DLB-35

Arnold, Edwin L. 1857-1935 . . . . . . DLB-178

Arnold, Matthew 1822-1888 . . . . DLB-32, 57

Arnold, Thomas 1795-1842 . . . . DLB-55

Arnold, Edward
   [publishing house] DLB-112

Arnow, Harriette Simpson
   1908-1986 . . . . DLB-6

Arp, Bill (see Smith, Charles Henry)

Arpino, Giovanni 1927-1987 . . . . . . DLB-177

Arreola, Juan José 1918- DLB-113

Arrian circa 89-circa 155 . . . . DLB-176

Arrowsmith, J. W.
   [publishing house] DLB-106

The Art and Mystery of Publishing:
   Interviews Y-97

Arthur, Timothy Shay
   1809-1885 . . . . . . DLB-3, 42, 79; DS-13

The Arthurian Tradition and Its European
   Context DLB-138

Artmann, H. C. 1921- DLB-85

Arvin, Newton 1900-1963 . . . . DLB-103

As I See It, by
   Carolyn Cassady DLB-16

Asch, Nathan 1902-1964 . . . . DLB-4, 28

Ash, John 1948- DLB-40

Ashbery, John 1927- DLB-5, 165; Y-81

Ashburnham, Bertram Lord
   1797-1878 . . . . DLB-184

Ashendene Press DLB-112

Asher, Sandy 1942- Y-83

Ashton, Winifred (see Dane, Clemence)

Asimov, Isaac 1920-1992 . . . . . DLB-8; Y-92

Askew, Anne circa 1521-1546 . . . . . DLB-136

Asselin, Olivar 1874-1937 . . . . DLB-92

Asturias, Miguel Angel
   1899-1974 . . . . DLB-113

Atheneum Publishers DLB-46

Atherton, Gertrude 1857-1948 . . DLB-9, 78, 186

Athlone Press DLB-112

Atkins, Josiah circa 1755-1781 . . . . . DLB-31

Atkins, Russell 1926- DLB-41

The Atlantic Monthly Press DLB-46

Attaway, William 1911-1986 . . . . . . DLB-76

Atwood, Margaret 1939- DLB-53

Aubert, Alvin 1930- DLB-41

Aubert de Gaspé, Phillipe-Ignace-François
   1814-1841 . . . . DLB-99

Aubert de Gaspé, Phillipe-Joseph
   1786-1871 . . . . DLB-99

Aubin, Napoléon 1812-1890 . . . . . . DLB-99

Aubin, Penelope 1685-circa 1731 . . . . DLB-39

Aubrey-Fletcher, Henry Lancelot
   (see Wade, Henry)

Auchincloss, Louis 1917- DLB-2; Y-80

Auden, W. H. 1907-1973 . . . . . DLB-10, 20

Audio Art in America: A Personal
   Memoir Y-85

Audubon, John Woodhouse
   1812-1862 . . . . DLB-183

Auerbach, Berthold 1812-1882 . . . . . DLB-133

Auernheimer, Raoul 1876-1948 . . . . . DLB-81

Augier, Emile 1820-1889 . . . . DLB-192

Augustine 354-430 . . . . DLB-115

Austen, Jane 1775-1817 . . . . DLB-116

Austin, Alfred 1835-1913 . . . . DLB-35

Austin, Mary 1868-1934 . . . . DLB-9, 78

Austin, William 1778-1841 . . . . DLB-74

Author-Printers, 1476–1599 . . . . . . DLB-167

Author Websites Y-97

The Author's Apology for His Book
   (1684), by John Bunyan DLB-39

An Author's Response, by
   Ronald Sukenick Y-82

Authors and Newspapers
   Association DLB-46

Authors' Publishing Company DLB-49

Avalon Books DLB-46

Avancini, Nicolaus 1611-1686 . . . . . DLB-164

Avendaño, Fausto 1941- DLB-82

Averroëö 1126-1198 . . . . DLB-115

Avery, Gillian 1926- DLB-161

Avicenna 980-1037 . . . . DLB-115

Avison, Margaret 1918- DLB-53

Avon Books DLB-46

Awdry, Wilbert Vere 1911- DLB-160

Awoonor, Kofi 1935- DLB-117

Ayckbourn, Alan 1939- DLB-13

Aymé, Marcel 1902-1967 . . . . DLB-72

Aytoun, Sir Robert 1570-1638 . . . . . DLB-121

Aytoun, William Edmondstoune
1813-1865 . . . . DLB-32, 159

B

B. V. (see Thomson, James)

Babbitt, Irving 1865-1933 . . . . DLB-63

Babbitt, Natalie 1932- DLB-52

Babcock, John [publishing house] DLB-49

Babrius circa 150-200 . . . . DLB-176

Baca, Jimmy Santiago 1952- DLB-122

Bache, Benjamin Franklin
1769-1798 . . . . DLB-43

Bachmann, Ingeborg 1926-1973 . . . . . DLB-85

Bacon, Delia 1811-1859 . . . . DLB-1

Bacon, Francis 1561-1626 . . . . DLB-151

Bacon, Roger circa
1214/1220-1292 . . . . DLB-115

Bacon, Sir Nicholas
circa 1510-1579 . . . . DLB-132

Bacon, Thomas circa 1700-1768 . . . . . DLB-31

Badger, Richard G.,
and Company. DLB-49

Bage, Robert 1728-1801. . . . . DLB-39

Bagehot, Walter 1826-1877 . . . . DLB-55

Bagley, Desmond 1923-1983 . . . . . . DLB-87

Bagnold, Enid 1889-1981 . . . DLB-13, 160, 191

Bagryana, Elisaveta 1893-1991 . . . . . DLB-147

Bahr, Hermann 1863-1934 . . . . . DLB-81, 118

Bailey, Alfred Goldsworthy
1905- DLB-68

Bailey, Francis
[publishing house]. DLB-49

Bailey, H. C. 1878-1961 . . . . DLB-77

Bailey, Jacob 1731-1808. . . . . DLB-99

Bailey, Paul 1937- DLB-14

Bailey, Philip James 1816-1902 . . . . . DLB-32

Baillargeon, Pierre 1916-1967. . . . . . DLB-88

Baillie, Hugh 1890-1966 . . . . DLB-29

Baillie, Joanna 1762-1851 . . . . DLB-93

Bailyn, Bernard 1922- DLB-17

Bainbridge, Beryl 1933- DLB-14

Baird, Irene 1901-1981 . . . . DLB-68

Baker, Augustine 1575-1641. . . . . . . DLB-151

Baker, Carlos 1909-1987. . . . . DLB-103

Baker, David 1954- DLB-120

Baker, Herschel C. 1914-1990 . . . . . DLB-111

Baker, Houston A., Jr. 1943- DLB-67

Baker, Samuel White 1821-1893 . . . . DLB-166

Baker, Walter H., Company
("Baker's Plays") DLB-49

The Baker and Taylor
Company DLB-49

Balaban, John 1943- DLB-120

Bald, Wambly 1902- DLB-4

Balde, Jacob 1604-1668 . . . . DLB-164

Balderston, John 1889-1954. . . . . . . DLB-26

Baldwin, James
1924-1987 . . . . DLB-2, 7, 33; Y-87

Baldwin, Joseph Glover
1815-1864 . . . . DLB-3, 11

Baldwin, Richard and Anne
[publishing house] DLB-170

Baldwin, William
circa 1515-1563 . . . . DLB-132

Bale, John 1495-1563 . . . . DLB-132

Balestrini, Nanni 1935- DLB-128, 196

Balfour, Arthur James 1848-1930 . . . . DLB-190

Ballantine Books. DLB-46

Ballantyne, R. M. 1825-1894 . . . . . . DLB-163

Ballard, J. G. 1930- DLB-14

Ballerini, Luigi 1940- DLB-128

Ballou, Maturin Murray
1820-1895 . . . . DLB-79, 189

Ballou, Robert O.
[publishing house] DLB-46

Balzac, Honoré de 1799-1855 . . . . . DLB-119

Bambara, Toni Cade 1939- DLB-38

Bamford, Samuel 1788-1872. . . . . . . DLB-190

Bancroft, A. L., and
Company DLB-49

Bancroft, George
1800-1891 . . . . DLB-1, 30, 59

Bancroft, Hubert Howe
1832-1918 . . . . DLB-47, 140

Bandelier, Adolph F. 1840-1914 . . . . DLB-186

Bangs, John Kendrick
1862-1922 . . . . DLB-11, 79

Banim, John
1798-1842 . . . . DLB-116, 158, 159

Banim, Michael 1796-1874. . . . . DLB-158, 159

Banks, Iain 1954- DLB-194

Banks, John circa 1653-1706 . . . . . . DLB-80

Banks, Russell 1940- DLB-130

Bannerman, Helen 1862-1946. . . . . . DLB-141

Bantam Books. DLB-46

Banti, Anna 1895-1985 . . . . DLB-177

Banville, John 1945- DLB-14

Baraka, Amiri
1934- DLB-5, 7, 16, 38; DS-8

Barbauld, Anna Laetitia
1743-1825 . . . . . DLB-107, 109, 142, 158

Barbeau, Marius 1883-1969. . . . . . . DLB-92

Barber, John Warner 1798-1885 . . . . . DLB-30

Bàrberi Squarotti, Giorgio
1929- DLB-128

Barbey d'Aurevilly, Jules-Amédée
1808-1889 . . . . DLB-119

Barbour, John circa 1316-1395 . . . . DLB-146

Barbour, Ralph Henry
1870-1944 . . . . DLB-22

Barbusse, Henri 1873-1935 . . . . DLB-65

Barclay, Alexander
circa 1475-1552 . . . . DLB-132

Barclay, E. E., and Company DLB-49

Bardeen, C. W.
[publishing house]. DLB-49

Barham, Richard Harris
1788-1845 . . . . DLB-159

Barich, Bill 1943- DLB-185

Baring, Maurice 1874-1945 . . . . DLB-34

Baring-Gould, Sabine
1834-1924. . . . . DLB-156, 190

Barker, A. L. 1918- DLB-14, 139

Barker, George 1913-1991 . . . . DLB-20

Barker, Harley Granville
1877-1946 . . . . DLB-10

Barker, Howard 1946- DLB-13

Barker, James Nelson 1784-1858 . . . . DLB-37

Barker, Jane 1652-1727 . . . . . . DLB-39, 131

Barker, Lady Mary Anne
1831-1911 . . . . DLB-166

Barker, William
circa 1520-after 1576 . . . . DLB-132

Barker, Arthur, Limited DLB-112

Barkov, Ivan Semenovich
1732-1768 . . . . DLB-150

Barks, Coleman 1937- DLB-5

Barlach, Ernst 1870-1938 . . . . . . DLB-56, 118

Barlow, Joel 1754-1812 . . . . DLB-37

Barnard, John 1681-1770 . . . . DLB-24

Barne, Kitty (Mary Catherine Barne)
1883-1957 . . . . DLB-160

Barnes, Barnabe 1571-1609 . . . . . . DLB-132

Barnes, Djuna 1892-1982 . . . . . DLB-4, 9, 45

Barnes, Jim 1933- DLB-175

Barnes, Julian 1946- DLB-194; Y-93

Barnes, Margaret Ayer 1886-1967. . . . DLB-9

Barnes, Peter 1931- DLB-13

Barnes, William 1801-1886 . . . . DLB-32

Barnes, A. S., and Company. DLB-49

Barnes and Noble Books. DLB-46

Barnet, Miguel 1940- DLB-145

Barney, Natalie 1876-1972 . . . . DLB-4

Barnfield, Richard 1574-1627 . . . . . DLB-172

Baron, Richard W.,
Publishing Company DLB-46

Barr, Robert 1850-1912. . . . . . . DLB-70, 92

Barral, Carlos 1928-1989 . . . . DLB-134

Barrax, Gerald William
1933- DLB-41, 120

Barrès, Maurice 1862-1923 . . . . . . DLB-123

Barrett, Eaton Stannard
1786-1820 . . . . DLB-116

Barrie, J. M. 1860-1937 . . . . DLB-10, 141, 156

Barrie and Jenkins DLB-112

Barrio, Raymond 1921- DLB-82

Barrios, Gregg 1945- DLB-122

Barry, Philip 1896-1949 . . . . DLB-7

Barry, Robertine (see Françoise)

Barse and Hopkins DLB-46

Barstow, Stan 1928- DLB-14, 139

Barth, John 1930- DLB-2

Barthelme, Donald
1931-1989 . . . . DLB-2; Y-80, Y-89

Barthelme, Frederick 1943- Y-85

Bartholomew, Frank 1898-1985 . . . . . DLB-127

Bartlett, John 1820-1905 . . . . DLB-1

Bartol, Cyrus Augustus 1813-1900 . . . . DLB-1

Barton, Bernard 1784-1849 . . . . DLB-96

Barton, Thomas Pennant
1803-1869 . . . . DLB-140

Bartram, John 1699-1777 . . . . DLB-31

Bartram, William 1739-1823 . . . . . . DLB-37

Basic Books DLB-46

Basille, Theodore (see Becon, Thomas)

Bass, T. J. 1932- Y-81

Bassani, Giorgio 1916- DLB-128, 177

Basse, William circa 1583-1653 . . . . . DLB-121

Bassett, John Spencer 1867-1928 . . . . DLB-17

Bassler, Thomas Joseph (see Bass, T. J.)

Bate, Walter Jackson
1918- DLB-67, 103

Bateman, Christopher
[publishing house] DLB-170

Bateman, Stephen
circa 1510-1584 . . . . DLB-136

Bates, H. E. 1905-1974 . . . . . DLB-162, 191

Bates, Katharine Lee 1859-1929 . . . . DLB-71

Batsford, B. T.
[publishing house] DLB-106

Battiscombe, Georgina 1905- DLB-155

The Battle of Maldon circa 1000 . . . . DLB-146

Bauer, Bruno 1809-1882 . . . . DLB-133

Bauer, Wolfgang 1941- DLB-124

Baum, L. Frank 1856-1919 . . . . DLB-22

Baum, Vicki 1888-1960 . . . . DLB-85

Baumbach, Jonathan 1933- Y-80

Bausch, Richard 1945- DLB-130

Bawden, Nina 1925- DLB-14, 161

Bax, Clifford 1886-1962 . . . . . . DLB-10, 100

Baxter, Charles 1947- DLB-130

Bayer, Eleanor (see Perry, Eleanor)

Bayer, Konrad 1932-1964. . . . . DLB-85

Baynes, Pauline 1922- DLB-160

Bazin, Hervé 1911- DLB-83

Beach, Sylvia 1887-1962 . . . . . DLB-4; DS-15

Beacon Press. DLB-49

Beadle and Adams DLB-49

Beagle, Peter S. 1939- Y-80

Beal, M. F. 1937- Y-81

Beale, Howard K. 1899-1959. . . . . . DLB-17

Beard, Charles A. 1874-1948. . . . . . DLB-17

A Beat Chronology: The First Twenty-five
Years, 1944-1969 . . . . DLB-16

Beattie, Ann 1947- Y-82

Beattie, James 1735-1803 . . . . DLB-109

Beauchemin, Nérée 1850-1931 . . . . . DLB-92

Beauchemin, Yves 1941- DLB-60

Beaugrand, Honoré 1848-1906 . . . . . DLB-99

Beaulieu, Victor-Lévy 1945- DLB-53

Beaumont, Francis circa 1584-1616
and Fletcher, John 1579-1625 . . . . DLB-58

Beaumont, Sir John 1583?-1627 . . . . . DLB-121

Beaumont, Joseph 1616–1699 . . . . . DLB-126

Beauvoir, Simone de
1908-1986. . . . . DLB-72; Y-86

Becher, Ulrich 1910- DLB-69

Becker, Carl 1873-1945 . . . . DLB-17

Becker, Jurek 1937- DLB-75

Becker, Jurgen 1932- DLB-75

Beckett, Samuel
1906-1989 . . . . DLB-13, 15; Y-90

Beckford, William 1760-1844 . . . . . . DLB-39

Beckham, Barry 1944- DLB-33

Becon, Thomas circa 1512-1567 . . . . DLB-136

Becque, Henry 1837-1899 . . . . DLB-192

Bećković, Matija 1939- DLB-181

Beddoes, Thomas 1760-1808 . . . . . . DLB-158

Beddoes, Thomas Lovell
1803-1849 . . . . DLB-96

Bede circa 673-735. . . . . DLB-146

Beecher, Catharine Esther
1800-1878. . . . . DLB-1

Beecher, Henry Ward
1813-1887 . . . . DLB-3, 43

Beer, George L. 1872-1920. . . . . . . DLB-47

Beer, Johann 1655-1700 . . . . DLB-168

Beer, Patricia 1919- DLB-40

Beerbohm, Max 1872-1956 . . . . DLB-34, 100

Beer-Hofmann, Richard
1866-1945 . . . . DLB-81

Beers, Henry A. 1847-1926. . . . . . . DLB-71

Beeton, S. O.
[publishing house] DLB-106

Bégon, Elisabeth 1696-1755. . . . . . . DLB-99

Behan, Brendan 1923-1964 . . . . DLB-13

Behn, Aphra
1640?-1689 . . . . DLB-39, 80, 131

Behn, Harry 1898-1973. . . . . DLB-61

Behrman, S. N. 1893-1973 . . . . . DLB-7, 44

Belaney, Archibald Stansfeld (see Grey Owl)

Belasco, David 1853-1931 . . . . DLB-7

Belford, Clarke and Company. DLB-49

Belinksy, Vissarion Grigor'evich
1811-1848 . . . . DLB-198

Belitt, Ben 1911- DLB-5

Belknap, Jeremy 1744-1798. . . . . DLB-30, 37

Bell, Adrian 1901-1980 . . . . DLB-191

Bell, Clive 1881-1964. . . . . DS-10

Bell, Gertrude Margaret Lowthian
1868-1926 . . . . DLB-174

Bell, James Madison 1826-1902 . . . . DLB-50

Bell, Marvin 1937- DLB-5

Bell, Millicent 1919- DLB-111

Bell, Quentin 1910- DLB-155

Bell, Vanessa 1879-1961 . . . . DS-10

Bell, George, and Sons DLB-106

Bell, Robert [publishing house]. DLB-49

Bellamy, Edward 1850-1898 . . . . . . DLB-12

Bellamy, John [publishing house] DLB-170

Bellamy, Joseph 1719-1790 . . . . DLB-31

Bellezza, Dario 1944- DLB-128

La Belle Assemblée 1806-1837 . . . . . DLB-110

Belloc, Hilaire
1870-1953 . . . . . DLB-19, 100, 141, 174

Bellonci, Maria 1902-1986. . . . . . . DLB-196

Bellow, Saul
1915- DLB-2, 28; Y-82; DS-3

Belmont Productions DLB-46

Bemelmans, Ludwig 1898-1962. . . . . DLB-22

Bemis, Samuel Flagg 1891-1973 . . . . DLB-17

Bemrose, William
[publishing house] DLB-106

Benchley, Robert 1889-1945 . . . . . . DLB-11

Benedetti, Mario 1920- DLB-113

Benedictus, David 1938- DLB-14

Benedikt, Michael 1935- DLB-5

Benét, Stephen Vincent
1898-1943. . . . . DLB-4, 48, 102

Benét, William Rose 1886-1950 . . . . DLB-45

Benford, Gregory 1941- Y-82

Benjamin, Park 1809-1864 . . . . DLB-3, 59, 73

Benjamin, S. G. W. 1837-1914 . . . . . DLB-189

Benlowes, Edward 1602-1676 . . . . . DLB-126

Benn, Gottfried 1886-1956 . . . . DLB-56

Benn Brothers Limited DLB-106

Bennett, Arnold
1867-1931. . . . . . . DLB-10, 34, 98, 135

Bennett, Charles 1899- DLB-44

Bennett, Gwendolyn 1902- DLB-51

Bennett, Hal 1930- DLB-33

Bennett, James Gordon 1795-1872 . . . . DLB-43

Bennett, James Gordon, Jr.
1841-1918 . . . . DLB-23

Bennett, John 1865-1956 . . . . . . DLB-42

Bennett, Louise 1919- DLB-117

Benni, Stefano 1947- DLB-196

Benoit, Jacques 1941- DLB-60

Benson, A. C. 1862-1925 . . . . DLB-98

Benson, E. F. 1867-1940 . . . . . DLB-135, 153

Benson, Jackson J. 1930- DLB-111

Benson, Robert Hugh
1871-1914 . . . . DLB-153

Benson, Stella 1892-1933 . . . . . DLB-36, 162

Bent, James Theodore 1852-1897 . . . . DLB-174

Bent, Mabel Virginia Anna ?-? DLB-174

Bentham, Jeremy
1748-1832 . . . . DLB-107, 158

Bentley, E. C. 1875-1956 . . . . DLB-70

Bentley, Phyllis 1894-1977 . . . . DLB-191

Bentley, Richard
[publishing house] DLB-106

Benton, Robert 1932- and Newman,
David 1937- DLB-44

Benziger Brothers DLB-49

Beowulf circa 900-1000
or 790-825 . . . . DLB-146

Beresford, Anne 1929- DLB-40

Beresford, John Davys
1873-1947 . . . . DLB-162, 178, 197

Beresford-Howe, Constance
1922- DLB-88

Berford, R. G., Company DLB-49

Berg, Stephen 1934- DLB-5

Bergengruen, Werner 1892-1964 . . . . . DLB-56

Berger, John 1926- DLB-14

Berger, Meyer 1898-1959 . . . . DLB-29

Berger, Thomas 1924- DLB-2; Y-80

Berkeley, Anthony 1893-1971 . . . . . DLB-77

Berkeley, George 1685-1753 . . . . DLB-31, 101

The Berkley Publishing
Corporation DLB-46

Berlin, Lucia 1936- DLB-130

Bernal, Vicente J. 1888-1915 . . . . . . DLB-82

Bernanos, Georges 1888-1948 . . . . . DLB-72

Bernard, Harry 1898-1979 . . . . DLB-92

Bernard, John 1756-1828 . . . . DLB-37

Bernard of Chartres
circa 1060-1124? DLB-115

Bernari, Carlo 1909-1992 . . . . DLB-177

Bernhard, Thomas
1931-1989 . . . . DLB-85, 124

Bernstein, Charles 1950- DLB-169

Berriault, Gina 1926- DLB-130

Berrigan, Daniel 1921- DLB-5

Berrigan, Ted 1934-1983 . . . . . . DLB-5, 169

Berry, Wendell 1934- DLB-5, 6

Berryman, John 1914-1972 . . . . DLB-48

Bersianik, Louky 1930- DLB-60

Berthelet, Thomas
[publishing house] DLB-170

Berto, Giuseppe 1914-1978 . . . . . . DLB-177

Bertolucci, Attilio 1911- DLB-128

Berton, Pierre 1920- DLB-68

Besant, Sir Walter 1836-1901 . . . DLB-135, 190

Bessette, Gerard 1920- DLB-53

Bessie, Alvah 1904-1985 . . . . DLB-26

Bester, Alfred 1913-1987 . . . . DLB-8

The Bestseller Lists: An Assessment Y-84

Bestuzhev, Aleksandr Aleksandrovich (Marlinsky)
1797-1837 . . . . DLB-198

Bestuzhev, Nikolai Aleksandrovich
1791-1855 . . . . DLB-198

Betham-Edwards, Matilda Barbara (see Edwards,
Matilda Barbara Betham-)

Betjeman, John 1906-1984 . . . . DLB-20; Y-84

Betocchi, Carlo 1899-1986 . . . . DLB-128

Bettarini, Mariella 1942- DLB-128

Betts, Doris 1932- Y-82

Beveridge, Albert J. 1862-1927 . . . . . DLB-17

Beverley, Robert
circa 1673-1722 . . . . DLB-24, 30

Bevilacqua, Alberto 1934- DLB-196

Beyle, Marie-Henri (see Stendhal)

Bianco, Margery Williams
1881-1944 . . . . DLB-160

Bibaud, Adèle 1854-1941 . . . . DLB-92

Bibaud, Michel 1782-1857 . . . . DLB-99

Bibliographical and Textual Scholarship
Since World War II Y-89

The Bicentennial of James Fenimore
Cooper: An International
Celebration Y-89

Bichsel, Peter 1935- DLB-75

Bickerstaff, Isaac John
1733-circa 1808 . . . . DLB-89

Biddle, Drexel [publishing house] DLB-49

Bidermann, Jacob
1577 or 1578-1639 . . . . DLB-164

Bidwell, Walter Hilliard
1798-1881 . . . . DLB-79

Bienek, Horst 1930- DLB-75

Bierbaum, Otto Julius 1865-1910 . . . . DLB-66

Bierce, Ambrose
1842-1914? . . . DLB-11, 12, 23, 71, 74, 186

Bigelow, William F. 1879-1966 . . . . . DLB-91

Biggle, Lloyd, Jr. 1923- DLB-8

Bigiaretti, Libero 1905-1993 . . . . . . DLB-177

Bigland, Eileen 1898-1970 . . . . DLB-195

Biglow, Hosea (see Lowell, James Russell)

Bigongiari, Piero 1914- DLB-128

Billinger, Richard 1890-1965 . . . . . DLB-124

Billings, Hammatt 1818-1874 . . . . . DLB-188

Billings, John Shaw 1898-1975 . . . . DLB-137

Billings, Josh (see Shaw, Henry Wheeler)

Binding, Rudolf G. 1867-1938 . . . . . DLB-66

Bingham, Caleb 1757-1817 . . . . . . DLB-42

Bingham, George Barry
1906-1988 . . . . DLB-127

Bingley, William
[publishing house] DLB-154

Binyon, Laurence 1869-1943 . . . . . . DLB-19

Biographia Brittanica DLB-142

Biographical Documents I Y-84

Biographical Documents II Y-85

Bioren, John [publishing house] DLB-49

Bioy Casares, Adolfo 1914- DLB-113

Bird, Isabella Lucy 1831-1904 . . . . . DLB-166

Bird, William 1888-1963 . . . . . DLB-4; DS-15

Birken, Sigmund von 1626-1681 . . . . DLB-164

Birney, Earle 1904- DLB-88

Birrell, Augustine 1850-1933 . . . . . . DLB-98

Bisher, Furman 1918- DLB-171

Bishop, Elizabeth 1911-1979 . . . . . DLB-5, 169

Bishop, John Peale 1892-1944 . . . DLB-4, 9, 45

Bismarck, Otto von 1815-1898 . . . . . DLB-129

Bisset, Robert 1759-1805 . . . . DLB-142

Bissett, Bill 1939- DLB-53

Bitzius, Albert (see Gotthelf, Jeremias)

Black, David (D. M.) 1941- DLB-40

Black, Winifred 1863-1936 . . . . . . DLB-25

Black, Walter J.
[publishing house] DLB-46

The Black Aesthetic: Background DS-8

The Black Arts Movement, by
Larry Neal DLB-38

Black Theaters and Theater Organizations in
America, 1961-1982:
A Research List DLB-38

Black Theatre: A Forum
[excerpts] DLB-38

Blackamore, Arthur 1679-? DLB-24, 39

Blackburn, Alexander L. 1929- Y-85

Blackburn, Paul 1926-1971 . . . . DLB-16; Y-81

Blackburn, Thomas 1916-1977 . . . . . DLB-27

Blackmore, R. D. 1825-1900 . . . . . . DLB-18

Blackmore, Sir Richard
  1654-1729 . . . . DLB-131

Blackmur, R. P. 1904-1965 . . . . DLB-63

Blackwell, Basil, Publisher DLB-106

Blackwood, Algernon Henry
  1869-1951 . . . . DLB-153, 156, 178

Blackwood, Caroline 1931- DLB-14

Blackwood, William, and
  Sons, Ltd. DLB-154

Blackwood's Edinburgh Magazine
  1817-1980 . . . . DLB-110

Blades, William 1824-1890 . . . . . . DLB-184

Blair, Eric Arthur (see Orwell, George)

Blair, Francis Preston 1791-1876 . . . . . DLB-43

Blair, James circa 1655-1743 . . . . DLB-24

Blair, John Durburrow 1759-1823 . . . . DLB-37

Blais, Marie-Claire 1939- DLB-53

Blaise, Clark 1940- DLB-53

Blake, George 1893-1961 . . . . DLB-191

Blake, Nicholas 1904-1972 . . . . DLB-77
  (see Day Lewis, C.)

Blake, William
  1757-1827 . . . . DLB-93, 154, 163

The Blakiston Company DLB-49

Blanchot, Maurice 1907- DLB-72

Blanckenburg, Christian Friedrich von
  1744-1796 . . . . DLB-94

Blaser, Robin 1925- DLB-165

Bledsoe, Albert Taylor
  1809-1877 . . . . DLB-3, 79

Blelock and Company DLB-49

Blennerhassett, Margaret Agnew
  1773-1842 . . . . DLB-99

Bles, Geoffrey
  [publishing house] DLB-112

Blessington, Marguerite, Countess of
  1789-1849 . . . . DLB-166

The Blickling Homilies
  circa 971 . . . . DLB-146

Blish, James 1921-1975 . . . . DLB-8

Bliss, E., and E. White
  [publishing house] DLB-49

Bliven, Bruce 1889-1977 . . . . DLB-137

Bloch, Robert 1917-1994 . . . . DLB-44

Block, Rudolph (see Lessing, Bruno)

Blondal, Patricia 1926-1959 . . . . . . DLB-88

Bloom, Harold 1930- DLB-67

Bloomer, Amelia 1818-1894 . . . . . . DLB-79

Bloomfield, Robert 1766-1823 . . . . . DLB-93

Bloomsbury Group DS-10

Blotner, Joseph 1923- DLB-111

Bloy, Léon 1846-1917 . . . . DLB-123

Blume, Judy 1938- DLB-52

Blunck, Hans Friedrich 1888-1961 . . . . DLB-66

Blunden, Edmund
  1896-1974 . . . . DLB-20, 100, 155

Blunt, Lady Anne Isabella Noel
  1837-1917 . . . . DLB-174

Blunt, Wilfrid Scawen
  1840-1922 . . . . DLB-19, 174

Bly, Nellie (see Cochrane, Elizabeth)

Bly, Robert 1926- DLB-5

Blyton, Enid 1897-1968 . . . . DLB-160

Boaden, James 1762-1839 . . . . DLB-89

Boas, Frederick S. 1862-1957 . . . . . DLB-149

The Bobbs-Merrill Archive at the
  Lilly Library, Indiana University Y-90

The Bobbs-Merrill Company DLB-46

Bobrov, Semen Sergeevich
  1763?-1810 . . . . DLB-150

Bobrowski, Johannes 1917-1965 . . . . . DLB-75

Bodenheim, Maxwell 1892-1954 . . . DLB-9, 45

Bodenstedt, Friedrich von
  1819-1892 . . . . DLB-129

Bodini, Vittorio 1914-1970 . . . . . . DLB-128

Bodkin, M. McDonnell
  1850-1933 . . . . DLB-70

Bodley Head DLB-112

Bodmer, Johann Jakob 1698-1783 . . . . DLB-97

Bodmershof, Imma von 1895-1982 . . . DLB-85

Bodsworth, Fred 1918- DLB-68

Boehm, Sydney 1908- DLB-44

Boer, Charles 1939- DLB-5

Boethius circa 480-circa 524 . . . . . . DLB-115

Boethius of Dacia circa 1240-? DLB-115

Bogan, Louise 1897-1970 . . . . . DLB-45, 169

Bogarde, Dirk 1921- DLB-14

Bogdanovich, Ippolit Fedorovich
  circa 1743-1803 . . . . DLB-150

Bogue, David [publishing house] DLB-106

Böhme, Jakob 1575-1624 . . . . DLB-164

Bohn, H. G. [publishing house] DLB-106

Bohse, August 1661-1742 . . . . DLB-168

Boie, Heinrich Christian
  1744-1806 . . . . DLB-94

Bok, Edward W. 1863-1930 . . . DLB-91; DS-16

Boland, Eavan 1944- DLB-40

Bolingbroke, Henry St. John, Viscount
  1678-1751 . . . . DLB-101

Böll, Heinrich 1917-1985 . . . . . DLB-69; Y-85

Bolling, Robert 1738-1775 . . . . DLB-31

Bolotov, Andrei Timofeevich
  1738-1833 . . . . DLB-150

Bolt, Carol 1941- DLB-60

Bolt, Robert 1924- DLB-13

Bolton, Herbert E. 1870-1953 . . . . . DLB-17

Bonaventura DLB-90

Bonaventure circa 1217-1274 . . . . . DLB-115

Bonaviri, Giuseppe 1924- DLB-177

Bond, Edward 1934- DLB-13

Bond, Michael 1926- DLB-161

Boni, Albert and Charles
  [publishing house] DLB-46

Boni and Liveright DLB-46

Bonner, Paul Hyde 1893-1968 . . . . . DS-17

Robert Bonner's Sons DLB-49

Bonnin, Gertrude Simmons (see Zitkala-Ša)

Bonsanti, Alessandro 1904-1984 . . . . DLB-177

Bontemps, Arna 1902-1973 . . . . . DLB-48, 51

The Book Arts Press at the University
  of Virginia Y-96

The Book League of America DLB-46

Book Reviewing in America: I Y-87

Book Reviewing in America: II Y-88

Book Reviewing in America: III. Y-89

Book Reviewing in America: IV Y-90

Book Reviewing in America: V Y-91

Book Reviewing in America: VI Y-92

Book Reviewing in America: VII Y-93

Book Reviewing in America: VIII. Y-94

Book Reviewing in America and the
  Literary Scene Y-95

Book Reviewing and the
  Literary Scene Y-96, Y-97

Book Supply Company. DLB-49

The Book Trade History Group Y-93

The Booker Prize. Y-96

The Booker Prize
  Address by Anthony Thwaite,
  Chairman of the Booker Prize Judges
  Comments from Former Booker
  Prize Winners Y-86

Boorde, Andrew circa 1490-1549 . . . . DLB-136

Boorstin, Daniel J. 1914- DLB-17

Booth, Mary L. 1831-1889 . . . . DLB-79

Booth, Franklin 1874-1948 . . . . . . DLB-188

Booth, Philip 1925- Y-82

Booth, Wayne C. 1921- DLB-67

Booth, William 1829-1912 . . . . . . DLB-190

Borchardt, Rudolf 1877-1945 . . . . . . DLB-66

Borchert, Wolfgang
  1921-1947 . . . . DLB-69, 124

Borel, Pétrus 1809-1859 . . . . DLB-119

Borges, Jorge Luis
  1899-1986 . . . . DLB-113; Y-86

Börne, Ludwig 1786-1837 . . . . DLB-90

Borrow, George
  1803-1881 . . . . DLB-21, 55, 166

Bosch, Juan 1909- DLB-145

Bosco, Henri 1888-1976 . . . . DLB-72

Bosco, Monique 1927- DLB-53

Boston, Lucy M. 1892-1990 . . . . . . DLB-161

Boswell, James 1740-1795 . . . . . DLB-104, 142

Botev, Khristo 1847-1876 . . . . DLB-147

Bote, Hermann
circa 1460-circa 1520 . . . . DLB-179

Botta, Anne C. Lynch 1815-1891 . . . . . DLB-3

Bottome, Phyllis 1882-1963 . . . . . . DLB-197

Bottomley, Gordon 1874-1948 . . . . . DLB-10

Bottoms, David 1949- DLB-120; Y-83

Bottrall, Ronald 1906- DLB-20

Bouchardy, Joseph 1810-1870 . . . . . DLB-192

Boucher, Anthony 1911-1968 . . . . . . DLB-8

Boucher, Jonathan 1738-1804 . . . . . DLB-31

Boucher de Boucherville, George
1814-1894 . . . . DLB-99

Boudreau, Daniel (see Coste, Donat)

Bourassa, Napoléon 1827-1916 . . . . . DLB-99

Bourget, Paul 1852-1935 . . . . DLB-123

Bourinot, John George 1837-1902 . . . . DLB-99

Bourjaily, Vance 1922- DLB-2, 143

Bourne, Edward Gaylord
1860-1908 . . . . DLB-47

Bourne, Randolph 1886-1918 . . . . . . DLB-63

Bousoño, Carlos 1923- DLB-108

Bousquet, Joë 1897-1950 . . . . DLB-72

Bova, Ben 1932- Y-81

Bovard, Oliver K. 1872-1945 . . . . . . DLB-25

Bove, Emmanuel 1898-1945 . . . . . . DLB-72

Bowen, Elizabeth 1899-1973 . . . DLB-15, 162

Bowen, Francis 1811-1890 . . . . . . DLB-1, 59

Bowen, John 1924- DLB-13

Bowen, Marjorie 1886-1952 . . . . . . DLB-153

Bowen-Merrill Company DLB-49

Bowering, George 1935- DLB-53

Bowers, Claude G. 1878-1958 . . . . . DLB-17

Bowers, Edgar 1924- DLB-5

Bowers, Fredson Thayer
1905-1991 . . . . DLB-140; Y-91

Bowles, Paul 1910- DLB-5, 6

Bowles, Samuel III 1826-1878 . . . . . DLB-43

Bowles, William Lisles 1762-1850 . . . . DLB-93

Bowman, Louise Morey
1882-1944 . . . . DLB-68

Boyd, James 1888-1944 . . . . . DLB-9; DS-16

Boyd, John 1919- DLB-8

Boyd, Thomas 1898-1935 . . . . . DLB-9; DS-16

Boyesen, Hjalmar Hjorth
1848-1895 . . . . DLB-12, 71; DS-13

Boyle, Kay
1902-1992 . . . . . DLB-4, 9, 48, 86; Y-93

Boyle, Roger, Earl of Orrery
1621-1679 . . . . DLB-80

Boyle, T. Coraghessan 1948- Y-86

Božić, Mirko 1919- DLB-181

Brackenbury, Alison 1953- DLB-40

Brackenridge, Hugh Henry
1748-1816 . . . . DLB-11, 37

Brackett, Charles 1892-1969 . . . . . DLB-26

Brackett, Leigh 1915-1978 . . . . . . DLB-8, 26

Bradburn, John
[publishing house] DLB-49

Bradbury, Malcolm 1932- DLB-14

Bradbury, Ray 1920- DLB-2, 8

Bradbury and Evans DLB-106

Braddon, Mary Elizabeth
1835-1915 . . . . DLB-18, 70, 156

Bradford, Andrew 1686-1742 . . . . DLB-43, 73

Bradford, Gamaliel 1863-1932 . . . . . DLB-17

Bradford, John 1749-1830 . . . . DLB-43

Bradford, Roark 1896-1948 . . . . DLB-86

Bradford, William 1590-1657 . . . . DLB-24, 30

Bradford, William III
1719-1791 . . . . DLB-43, 73

Bradlaugh, Charles 1833-1891 . . . . . DLB-57

Bradley, David 1950- DLB-33

Bradley, Marion Zimmer 1930- DLB-8

Bradley, William Aspenwall
1878-1939 . . . . DLB-4

Bradley, Ira, and Company DLB-49

Bradley, J. W., and Company DLB-49

Bradshaw, Henry 1831-1886 . . . . . . DLB-184

Bradstreet, Anne
1612 or 1613-1672 . . . . DLB-24

Bradwardine, Thomas circa
1295-1349 . . . . DLB-115

Brady, Frank 1924-1986 . . . . DLB-111

Brady, Frederic A.
[publishing house] DLB-49

Bragg, Melvyn 1939- DLB-14

Brainard, Charles H.
[publishing house] DLB-49

Braine, John 1922-1986 . . . . . DLB-15; Y-86

Braithwait, Richard 1588-1673 . . . . . DLB-151

Braithwaite, William Stanley
1878-1962 . . . . DLB-50, 54

Braker, Ulrich 1735-1798 . . . . DLB-94

Bramah, Ernest 1868-1942 . . . . DLB-70

Branagan, Thomas 1774-1843 . . . . . DLB-37

Branch, William Blackwell
1927- DLB-76

Branden Press DLB-46

Brant, Sebastian 1457-1521 . . . . . . DLB-179

Brassey, Lady Annie (Allnutt)
1839-1887 . . . . DLB-166

Brathwaite, Edward Kamau
1930- DLB-125

Brault, Jacques 1933- DLB-53

Braun, Volker 1939- DLB-75

Brautigan, Richard
1935-1984 . . . . DLB-2, 5; Y-80, Y-84

Braxton, Joanne M. 1950- DLB-41

Bray, Anne Eliza 1790-1883 . . . . . . DLB-116

Bray, Thomas 1656-1730 . . . . DLB-24

Braziller, George
[publishing house] DLB-46

The Bread Loaf Writers'
Conference 1983 . . . . Y-84

The Break-Up of the Novel (1922),
by John Middleton Murry DLB-36

Breasted, James Henry 1865-1935 . . . . DLB-47

Brecht, Bertolt 1898-1956 . . . . . DLB-56, 124

Bredel, Willi 1901-1964 . . . . DLB-56

Breitinger, Johann Jakob
1701-1776 . . . . DLB-97

Bremser, Bonnie 1939- DLB-16

Bremser, Ray 1934- DLB-16

Brentano, Bernard von
1901-1964 . . . . DLB-56

Brentano, Clemens 1778-1842 . . . . . DLB-90

Brentano's DLB-49

Brenton, Howard 1942- DLB-13

Breslin, Jimmy 1929- DLB-185

Breton, André 1896-1966 . . . . DLB-65

Breton, Nicholas
circa 1555-circa 1626 . . . . DLB-136

The Breton Lays
1300-early fifteenth century DLB-146

Brewer, Luther A. 1858-1933 . . . . . DLB-187

Brewer, Warren and Putnam DLB-46

Brewster, Elizabeth 1922- DLB-60

Bridge, Ann (Lady Mary Dolling Sanders
O'Malley) 1889-1974 . . . . DLB-191

Bridge, Horatio 1806-1893 . . . . DLB-183

Bridgers, Sue Ellen 1942- DLB-52

Bridges, Robert 1844-1930 . . . . . DLB-19, 98

Bridie, James 1888-1951 . . . . DLB-10

Brieux, Eugene 1858-1932 . . . . DLB-192

Bright, Mary Chavelita Dunne
(see Egerton, George)

Brimmer, B. J., Company DLB-46

Brines, Francisco 1932- DLB-134

Brinley, George, Jr. 1817-1875 . . . . . DLB-140

Brinnin, John Malcolm 1916- DLB-48

Brisbane, Albert 1809-1890 . . . . DLB-3

Brisbane, Arthur 1864-1936 . . . . DLB-25

British Academy DLB-112

The British Library and the Regular
Readers' Group Y-91

The British Critic 1793-1843 . . . . DLB-110

The British Review and London
Critical Journal 1811-1825 . . . . . DLB-110

Brito, Aristeo 1942- DLB-122

Brittain, Vera 1893-1970 . . . . DLB-191

Broadway Publishing Company DLB-46

Broch, Hermann 1886-1951 . . . . DLB-85, 124

Brochu, André 1942- DLB-53

Brock, Edwin 1927- DLB-40

Brockes, Barthold Heinrich
1680-1747 . . . . DLB-168

Brod, Max 1884-1968 . . . . DLB-81

Brodber, Erna 1940- DLB-157

Brodhead, John R. 1814-1873 . . . . . DLB-30

Brodkey, Harold 1930- DLB-130

Brodsky, Joseph 1940-1996 . . . . Y-87

Broeg, Bob 1918- DLB-171

Brome, Richard circa 1590-1652 . . . . DLB-58

Brome, Vincent 1910- DLB-155

Bromfield, Louis 1896-1956 . . . . DLB-4, 9, 86

Bromige, David 1933- DLB-193

Broner, E. M. 1930- DLB-28

Bronk, William 1918- DLB-165

Bronnen, Arnolt 1895-1959 . . . . . . DLB-124

Brontë, Anne 1820-1849 . . . . DLB-21

Brontë, Charlotte 1816-1855 . . . . DLB-21, 159

Brontë, Emily 1818-1848 . . . . . . DLB-21, 32

Brooke, Frances 1724-1789 . . . . . DLB-39, 99

Brooke, Henry 1703?-1783 . . . . DLB-39

Brooke, L. Leslie 1862-1940 . . . . . DLB-141

Brooke, Margaret, Ranee of Sarawak
1849-1936 . . . . DLB-174

Brooke, Rupert 1887-1915 . . . . DLB-19

Brooker, Bertram 1888-1955 . . . . . . DLB-88

Brooke-Rose, Christine 1926- DLB-14

Brookner, Anita 1928- DLB-194; Y-87

Brooks, Charles Timothy
1813-1883 . . . . DLB-1

Brooks, Cleanth 1906-1994 . . . . DLB-63; Y-94

Brooks, Gwendolyn
1917- DLB-5, 76, 165

Brooks, Jeremy 1926- DLB-14

Brooks, Mel 1926- DLB-26

Brooks, Noah 1830-1903 . . . . . DLB-42; DS-13

Brooks, Richard 1912-1992 . . . . . . DLB-44

Brooks, Van Wyck
1886-1963 . . . . DLB-45, 63, 103

Brophy, Brigid 1929- DLB-14

Brophy, John 1899-1965 . . . . DLB-191

Brossard, Chandler 1922-1993 . . . . . DLB-16

Brossard, Nicole 1943- DLB-53

Broster, Dorothy Kathleen
1877-1950 . . . . DLB-160

Brother Antoninus (see Everson, William)

Brotherton, Lord 1856-1930 . . . . . . DLB-184

Brougham and Vaux, Henry Peter
Brougham, Baron
1778-1868 . . . . DLB-110, 158

Brougham, John 1810-1880 . . . . . . DLB-11

Broughton, James 1913- DLB-5

Broughton, Rhoda 1840-1920 . . . . . DLB-18

Broun, Heywood 1888-1939 . . . . DLB-29, 171

Brown, Alice 1856-1948 . . . . DLB-78

Brown, Bob 1886-1959 . . . . DLB-4, 45

Brown, Cecil 1943- DLB-33

Brown, Charles Brockden
1771-1810 . . . . DLB-37, 59, 73

Brown, Christy 1932-1981 . . . . DLB-14

Brown, Dee 1908- Y-80

Brown, Frank London 1927-1962 . . . . DLB-76

Brown, Fredric 1906-1972 . . . . DLB-8

Brown, George Mackay
1921- DLB-14, 27, 139

Brown, Harry 1917-1986 . . . . DLB-26

Brown, Marcia 1918- DLB-61

Brown, Margaret Wise
1910-1952 . . . . DLB-22

Brown, Morna Doris (see Ferrars, Elizabeth)

Brown, Oliver Madox
1855-1874 . . . . DLB-21

Brown, Sterling
1901-1989 . . . . DLB-48, 51, 63

Brown, T. E. 1830-1897 . . . . DLB-35

Brown, William Hill 1765-1793 . . . . . DLB-37

Brown, William Wells
1814-1884 . . . . DLB-3, 50, 183

Browne, Charles Farrar
1834-1867 . . . . DLB-11

Browne, Francis Fisher
1843-1913 . . . . DLB-79

Browne, Michael Dennis
1940- DLB-40

Browne, Sir Thomas 1605-1682 . . . . DLB-151

Browne, William, of Tavistock
1590-1645 . . . . DLB-121

Browne, Wynyard 1911-1964 . . . . . DLB-13

Browne and Nolan DLB-106

Brownell, W. C. 1851-1928 . . . . . . DLB-71

Browning, Elizabeth Barrett
1806-1861 . . . . DLB-32

Browning, Robert
1812-1889 . . . . DLB-32, 163

Brownjohn, Allan 1931- DLB-40

Brownson, Orestes Augustus
1803-1876 . . . . DLB-1, 59, 73

Bruccoli, Matthew J. 1931- DLB-103

Bruce, Charles 1906-1971 . . . . DLB-68

Bruce, Leo 1903-1979 . . . . DLB-77

Bruce, Philip Alexander
1856-1933 . . . . DLB-47

Bruce Humphries
[publishing house] DLB-46

Bruce-Novoa, Juan 1944- DLB-82

Bruckman, Clyde 1894-1955 . . . . . . DLB-26

Bruckner, Ferdinand 1891-1958 . . . . DLB-118

Brundage, John Herbert (see Herbert, John)

Brutus, Dennis 1924- DLB-117

Bryan, C. D. B. 1936- DLB-185

Bryant, Arthur 1899-1985 . . . . . . DLB-149

Bryant, William Cullen
1794-1878 . . . . DLB-3, 43, 59, 189

Bryce Echenique, Alfredo
1939- DLB-145

Bryce, James 1838-1922 . . . . . DLB-166, 190

Brydges, Sir Samuel Egerton
1762-1837 . . . . DLB-107

Bryskett, Lodowick 1546?-1612 . . . . . DLB-167

Buchan, John 1875-1940 . . . DLB-34, 70, 156

Buchanan, George 1506-1582 . . . . . DLB-132

Buchanan, Robert 1841-1901 . . . . . DLB-18, 35

Buchman, Sidney 1902-1975 . . . . . . DLB-26

Buchner, Augustus 1591-1661 . . . . . DLB-164

Büchner, Georg 1813-1837 . . . . . . DLB-133

Bucholtz, Andreas Heinrich
1607-1671 . . . . DLB-168

Buck, Pearl S. 1892-1973 . . . . . . DLB-9, 102

Bucke, Charles 1781-1846 . . . . DLB-110

Bucke, Richard Maurice
1837-1902 . . . . DLB-99

Buckingham, Joseph Tinker 1779-1861 and
Buckingham, Edwin
1810-1833 . . . . DLB-73

Buckler, Ernest 1908-1984 . . . . DLB-68

Buckley, William F., Jr.
1925- DLB-137; Y-80

Buckminster, Joseph Stevens
1784-1812 . . . . DLB-37

Buckner, Robert 1906- DLB-26

Budd, Thomas ?-1698 . . . . DLB-24

Budrys, A. J. 1931- DLB-8

Buechner, Frederick 1926- Y-80

Buell, John 1927- DLB-53

Bufalino, Gesualdo 1920-1996 . . . . . DLB-196

Buffum, Job [publishing house] DLB-49

Bugnet, Georges 1879-1981 . . . . . . DLB-92

Buies, Arthur 1840-1901 . . . . DLB-99

Building the New British Library
at St Pancras Y-94

Bukowski, Charles
1920-1994 . . . . DLB-5, 130, 169

Bulatović, Miodrag 1930-1991 . . . . . DLB-181

Bulgarin, Faddei Venediktovich
1789-1859 . . . . DLB-198

Bulger, Bozeman 1877-1932 . . . . . . DLB-171

Bullein, William
between 1520 and 1530-1576. . . . DLB-167

Bullins, Ed 1935- DLB-7, 38

Bulwer-Lytton, Edward (also Edward Bulwer)
1803-1873 . . . . DLB-21

Bumpus, Jerry 1937- Y-81

Bunce and Brother DLB-49

Bunner, H. C. 1855-1896 . . . . . DLB-78, 79

Bunting, Basil 1900-1985 . . . . DLB-20

Buntline, Ned (Edward Zane Carroll Judson)
1821-1886 . . . . DLB-186

Bunyan, John 1628-1688 . . . . DLB-39

Burch, Robert 1925- DLB-52

Burciaga, José Antonio 1940- DLB-82

Bürger, Gottfried August
1747-1794 . . . . DLB-94

Burgess, Anthony 1917-1993 . . . . DLB-14, 194

Burgess, Gelett 1866-1951 . . . . DLB-11

Burgess, John W. 1844-1931 . . . . . . DLB-47

Burgess, Thornton W.
1874-1965 . . . . DLB-22

Burgess, Stringer and Company DLB-49

Burick, Si 1909-1986. . . . . DLB-171

Burk, John Daly circa 1772-1808 . . . . DLB-37

Burke, Edmund 1729?-1797. . . . . . . DLB-104

Burke, Kenneth 1897-1993 . . . . . DLB-45, 63

Burke, Thomas 1886-1945 . . . . DLB-197

Burlingame, Edward Livermore
1848-1922 . . . . DLB-79

Burnet, Gilbert 1643-1715 . . . . DLB-101

Burnett, Frances Hodgson
1849-1924. . . . . DLB-42, 141; DS-13, 14

Burnett, W. R. 1899-1982 . . . . DLB-9

Burnett, Whit 1899-1973 and
Martha Foley 1897-1977 . . . . . DLB-137

Burney, Fanny 1752-1840 . . . . DLB-39

Burns, Alan 1929- DLB-14, 194

Burns, John Horne 1916-1953 . . . . . . Y-85

Burns, Robert 1759-1796 . . . . DLB-109

Burns and Oates. DLB-106

Burnshaw, Stanley 1906- DLB-48

Burr, C. Chauncey 1815?-1883 . . . . DLB-79

Burroughs, Edgar Rice 1875-1950. . . . DLB-8

Burroughs, John 1837-1921. . . . . . . DLB-64

Burroughs, Margaret T. G.
1917- DLB-41

Burroughs, William S., Jr.
1947-1981 . . . . DLB-16

Burroughs, William Seward
1914-. DLB-2, 8, 16, 152; Y-81, Y-97

Burroway, Janet 1936- DLB-6

Burt, Maxwell Struthers
1882-1954 . . . . DLB-86; DS-16

Burt, A. L., and Company. DLB-49

Burton, Hester 1913- DLB-161

Burton, Isabel Arundell
1831-1896 . . . . DLB-166

Burton, Miles (see Rhode, John)

Burton, Richard Francis
1821-1890 . . . . DLB-55, 166, 184

Burton, Robert 1577-1640. . . . . . DLB-151

Burton, Virginia Lee 1909-1968 . . . . DLB-22

Burton, William Evans
1804-1860 . . . . DLB-73

Burwell, Adam Hood 1790-1849. . . . DLB-99

Bury, Lady Charlotte
1775-1861 . . . . DLB-116

Busch, Frederick 1941- DLB-6

Busch, Niven 1903-1991 . . . . DLB-44

Bushnell, Horace 1802-1876 . . . . . . DS-13

Bussieres, Arthur de 1877-1913 . . . . DLB-92

Butler, Josephine Elizabeth
1828-1906 . . . . DLB-190

Butler, Juan 1942-1981 . . . . DLB-53

Butler, Octavia E. 1947- DLB-33

Butler, Pierce 1884-1953. . . . . . . DLB-187

Butler, Robert Olen 1945- DLB-173

Butler, Samuel 1613-1680 . . . . DLB-101, 126

Butler, Samuel 1835-1902. . . DLB-18, 57, 174

Butler, William Francis
1838-1910 . . . . DLB-166

Butler, E. H., and Company. DLB-49

Butor, Michel 1926- DLB-83

Butter, Nathaniel
[publishing house] DLB-170

Butterworth, Hezekiah 1839-1905 . . . DLB-42

Buttitta, Ignazio 1899- DLB-114

Buzzati, Dino 1906-1972. . . . . . . DLB-177

Byars, Betsy 1928- DLB-52

Byatt, A. S. 1936- DLB-14, 194

Byles, Mather 1707-1788 . . . . DLB-24

Bynneman, Henry
[publishing house] DLB-170

Bynner, Witter 1881-1968 . . . . . . DLB-54

Byrd, William circa 1543-1623 . . . . DLB-172

Byrd, William II 1674-1744 . . . . DLB-24, 140

Byrne, John Keyes (see Leonard, Hugh)

Byron, George Gordon, Lord
1788-1824 . . . . DLB-96, 110

Byron, Robert 1905-1941 . . . . . . DLB-195

C

Caballero Bonald, José Manuel
1926- DLB-108

Cabañero, Eladio 1930- DLB-134

Cabell, James Branch
1879-1958 . . . . DLB-9, 78

Cabeza de Baca, Manuel
1853-1915 . . . . DLB-122

Cabeza de Baca Gilbert, Fabiola
1898- DLB-122

Cable, George Washington
1844-1925. . . . . DLB-12, 74; DS-13

Cable, Mildred 1878-1952. . . . . . . DLB-195

Cabrera, Lydia 1900-1991. . . . . . . DLB-145

Cabrera Infante, Guillermo
1929- DLB-113

Cadell [publishing house] DLB-154

Cady, Edwin H. 1917- DLB-103

Caedmon flourished 658-680 . . . . . DLB-146

Caedmon School circa 660-899 . . . . DLB-146

Cafés, Brasseries, and Bistros. DS-15

Cage, John 1912-1992 . . . . DLB-193

Cahan, Abraham
1860-1951 . . . . DLB-9, 25, 28

Cain, George 1943- DLB-33

Caird, Mona 1854-1932 . . . . DLB-197

Caldecott, Randolph 1846-1886 . . . . DLB-163

Calder, John
(Publishers), Limited. DLB-112

Calderón de la Barca, Fanny
1804-1882 . . . . DLB-183

Caldwell, Ben 1937- DLB-38

Caldwell, Erskine 1903-1987 . . . . DLB-9, 86

Caldwell, H. M., Company DLB-49

Caldwell, Taylor 1900-1985 . . . . . . DS-17

Calhoun, John C. 1782-1850 . . . . . . DLB-3

Calisher, Hortense 1911- DLB-2

A Call to Letters and an Invitation
to the Electric Chair,
by Siegfried Mandel DLB-75

Callaghan, Morley 1903-1990 . . . . DLB-68

Callahan, S. Alice 1868-1894 . . . . . DLB-175

Callaloo Y-87

Callimachus circa 305 B.C.-240 B.C.
. . . . DLB-176

Calmer, Edgar 1907- DLB-4

Calverley, C. S. 1831-1884. . . . . . . DLB-35

Calvert, George Henry
1803-1889 . . . . DLB-1, 64

Calvino, Italo 1923-1985. . . . . . . DLB-196

Cambridge Press DLB-49

Cambridge Songs (Carmina Cantabrigensia)
circa 1050 . . . . DLB-148

Cambridge University Press. DLB-170

Camden, William 1551-1623 . . . . . DLB-172

Camden House: An Interview with
James Hardin. Y-92

Cameron, Eleanor 1912- DLB-52

Cameron, George Frederick
1854-1885 . . . . DLB-99

Cameron, Lucy Lyttelton
1781-1858 . . . . DLB-163

Cameron, William Bleasdell
1862-1951 . . . . DLB-99

Camm, John 1718-1778 . . . . DLB-31

Camon, Ferdinando 1935- DLB-196

Campana, Dino 1885-1932 . . . . . . DLB-114

Campbell, Gabrielle Margaret Vere
(see Shearing, Joseph, and Bowen, Marjorie)

Campbell, James Dykes
1838-1895 . . . . DLB-144

Campbell, James Edwin
1867-1896 . . . . DLB-50

Campbell, John 1653-1728 . . . . DLB-43

Campbell, John W., Jr.
1910-1971 . . . . DLB-8

Campbell, Roy 1901-1957 . . . . DLB-20

Campbell, Thomas
1777-1844 . . . . DLB-93, 144

Campbell, William Wilfred
1858-1918 . . . . DLB-92

Campion, Edmund 1539-1581 . . . . . DLB-167

Campion, Thomas
1567-1620 . . . . DLB-58, 172

Camus, Albert 1913-1960 . . . . DLB-72

The Canadian Publishers' Records
Database Y-96

Canby, Henry Seidel 1878-1961 . . . . DLB-91

Candelaria, Cordelia 1943- DLB-82

Candelaria, Nash 1928- DLB-82

Candour in English Fiction (1890),
by Thomas Hardy DLB-18

Canetti, Elias 1905-1994 . . . . . . DLB-85, 124

Canham, Erwin Dain
1904-1982 . . . . DLB-127

Canitz, Friedrich Rudolph Ludwig von
1654-1699 . . . . DLB-168

Cankar, Ivan 1876-1918 . . . . DLB-147

Cannan, Gilbert 1884-1955 . . . . DLB-10, 197

Cannan, Joanna 1896-1961 . . . . . . DLB-191

Cannell, Kathleen 1891-1974 . . . . . . DLB-4

Cannell, Skipwith 1887-1957 . . . . . . DLB-45

Canning, George 1770-1827 . . . . . . DLB-158

Cannon, Jimmy 1910-1973 . . . . . . DLB-171

Cantwell, Robert 1908-1978 . . . . . . DLB-9

Cape, Jonathan, and Harrison Smith
[publishing house] DLB-46

Cape, Jonathan, Limited DLB-112

Capen, Joseph 1658-1725 . . . . DLB-24

Capes, Bernard 1854-1918 . . . . . . DLB-156

Capote, Truman
1924-1984 . . . . . . DLB-2, 185; Y-80, Y-84

Caproni, Giorgio 1912-1990 . . . . . . DLB-128

Cardarelli, Vincenzo 1887-1959 . . . . DLB-114

Cárdenas, Reyes 1948- DLB-122

Cardinal, Marie 1929- DLB-83

Carew, Jan 1920- DLB-157

Carew, Thomas
1594 or 1595-1640 . . . . DLB-126

Carey, Henry
circa 1687-1689-1743 . . . . DLB-84

Carey, Mathew 1760-1839 . . . . . DLB-37, 73

Carey and Hart DLB-49

Carey, M., and Company DLB-49

Carlell, Lodowick 1602-1675 . . . . . DLB-58

Carleton, William 1794-1869 . . . . . DLB-159

Carleton, G. W.
[publishing house] DLB-49

Carlile, Richard 1790-1843 . . . . DLB-110, 158

Carlyle, Jane Welsh 1801-1866 . . . . . DLB-55

Carlyle, Thomas 1795-1881 . . . . DLB-55, 144

Carman, Bliss 1861-1929 . . . . DLB-92

Carmina Burana circa 1230 . . . . . . DLB-138

Carnero, Guillermo 1947- DLB-108

Carossa, Hans 1878-1956 . . . . DLB-66

Carpenter, Humphrey 1946- DLB-155

Carpenter, Stephen Cullen ?-1820? . . . DLB-73

Carpentier, Alejo 1904-1980 . . . . . . DLB-113

Carrier, Roch 1937- DLB-53

Carrillo, Adolfo 1855-1926 . . . . . . DLB-122

Carroll, Gladys Hasty 1904- DLB-9

Carroll, John 1735-1815 . . . . DLB-37

Carroll, John 1809-1884 . . . . DLB-99

Carroll, Lewis
1832-1898 . . . . DLB-18, 163, 178

Carroll, Paul 1927- DLB-16

Carroll, Paul Vincent 1900-1968 . . . . DLB-10

Carroll and Graf Publishers DLB-46

Carruth, Hayden 1921- DLB-5, 165

Carryl, Charles E. 1841-1920 . . . . . DLB-42

Carson, Anne 1950- DLB-193

Carswell, Catherine 1879-1946 . . . . . DLB-36

Carter, Angela 1940-1992 . . . . DLB-14

Carter, Elizabeth 1717-1806 . . . . . . DLB-109

Carter, Henry (see Leslie, Frank)

Carter, Hodding, Jr. 1907-1972 . . . . DLB-127

Carter, Landon 1710-1778 . . . . . . DLB-31

Carter, Lin 1930- Y-81

Carter, Martin 1927- DLB-117

Carter and Hendee DLB-49

Carter, Robert, and Brothers DLB-49

Cartwright, John 1740-1824 . . . . . . DLB-158

Cartwright, William circa
1611-1643 . . . . DLB-126

Caruthers, William Alexander
1802-1846 . . . . DLB-3

Carver, Jonathan 1710-1780 . . . . . . DLB-31

Carver, Raymond
1938-1988 . . . . DLB-130; Y-84, Y-88

Cary, Joyce 1888-1957 . . . . . . DLB-15, 100

Cary, Patrick 1623?-1657 . . . . DLB-131

Casey, Juanita 1925- DLB-14

Casey, Michael 1947- DLB-5

Cassady, Carolyn 1923- DLB-16

Cassady, Neal 1926-1968 . . . . DLB-16

Cassell and Company DLB-106

Cassell Publishing Company DLB-49

Cassill, R. V. 1919- DLB-6

Cassity, Turner 1929- DLB-105

Cassius Dio circa 155/164-post 229
. . . . DLB-176

Cassola, Carlo 1917-1987 . . . . DLB-177

The Castle of Perseverance
circa 1400-1425 . . . . DLB-146

Castellano, Olivia 1944- DLB-122

Castellanos, Rosario 1925-1974 . . . . DLB-113

Castillo, Ana 1953- DLB-122

Castlemon, Harry (see Fosdick, Charles Austin)

Čašule, Kole 1921- DLB-181

Caswall, Edward 1814-1878 . . . . . . DLB-32

Catacalos, Rosemary 1944- DLB-122

Cather, Willa
1873-1947 . . . . DLB-9, 54, 78; DS-1

Catherine II (Ekaterina Alekseevna), "The
Great," Empress of Russia
1729-1796 . . . . DLB-150

Catherwood, Mary Hartwell
1847-1902 . . . . DLB-78

Catledge, Turner 1901-1983 . . . . . . DLB-127

Catlin, George 1796-1872 . . . . . DLB-186, 189

Cattafi, Bartolo 1922-1979 . . . . . . DLB-128

Catton, Bruce 1899-1978 . . . . DLB-17

Causley, Charles 1917- DLB-27

Caute, David 1936- DLB-14

Cavendish, Duchess of Newcastle,
Margaret Lucas 1623-1673 . . . . DLB-131

Cawein, Madison 1865-1914 . . . . . . DLB-54

The Caxton Printers, Limited DLB-46

Caxton, William
[publishing house] DLB-170

Cayrol, Jean 1911- DLB-83

Cecil, Lord David 1902-1986 . . . . . DLB-155

Cela, Camilo José 1916- Y-89

Celan, Paul 1920-1970 . . . . DLB-69

Celati, Gianni 1937- DLB-196

Celaya, Gabriel 1911-1991 . . . . . . DLB-108

Céline, Louis-Ferdinand
1894-1961 . . . . DLB-72

The Celtic Background to Medieval English
    Literature. DLB-146

Celtis, Conrad 1459-1508 . . . . DLB-179

Center for Bibliographical Studies and
    Research at the University of
    California, Riverside Y-91

The Center for the Book in the Library
    of Congress. Y-93

Center for the Book Research. Y-84

Centlivre, Susanna 1669?-1723 . . . . . DLB-84

The Century Company. DLB-49

Cernuda, Luis 1902-1963 . . . . DLB-134

"Certain Gifts," by Betty Adcock. . . . DLB-105

Cervantes, Lorna Dee 1954- DLB-82

Chaadaev, Petr Iakovlevich
    1794-1856 . . . . DLB-198

Chacel, Rosa 1898- DLB-134

Chacón, Eusebio 1869-1948 . . . . . . DLB-82

Chacón, Felipe Maximiliano
    1873-? DLB-82

Chadwyck-Healey's Full-Text Literary Data-bases:
    Editing Commercial Databases of
    Primary Literary Texts Y-95

Challans, Eileen Mary (see Renault, Mary)

Chalmers, George 1742-1825 . . . . . . DLB-30

Chaloner, Sir Thomas
    1520-1565 . . . . DLB-167

Chamberlain, Samuel S.
    1851-1916 . . . . DLB-25

Chamberland, Paul 1939- DLB-60

Chamberlin, William Henry
    1897-1969 . . . . DLB-29

Chambers, Charles Haddon
    1860-1921 . . . . DLB-10

Chambers, W. and R.
    [publishing house]. DLB-106

Chamisso, Albert von
    1781-1838 . . . . DLB-90

Champfleury 1821-1889 . . . . DLB-119

Chandler, Harry 1864-1944 . . . . . . DLB-29

Chandler, Norman 1899-1973 . . . . . DLB-127

Chandler, Otis 1927- DLB-127

Chandler, Raymond 1888-1959 . . . . . . DS-6

Channing, Edward 1856-1931 . . . . . DLB-17

Channing, Edward Tyrrell
    1790-1856 . . . . DLB-1, 59

Channing, William Ellery
    1780-1842 . . . . DLB-1, 59

Channing, William Ellery, II
    1817-1901. . . . . DLB-1

Channing, William Henry
    1810-1884 . . . . DLB-1, 59

Chaplin, Charlie 1889-1977 . . . . . . DLB-44

Chapman, George
    1559 or 1560 - 1634 . . . . . DLB-62, 121

Chapman, John DLB-106

Chapman, Olive Murray
    1892-1977 . . . . DLB-195

Chapman, William 1850-1917 . . . . . DLB-99

Chapman and Hall DLB-106

Chappell, Fred 1936- DLB-6, 105

Charbonneau, Jean 1875-1960 . . . . . DLB-92

Charbonneau, Robert 1911-1967 . . . . DLB-68

Charles, Gerda 1914- DLB-14

Charles, William
    [publishing house]. DLB-49

The Charles Wood Affair:
    A Playwright Revived Y-83

Charlotte Forten: Pages from
    her Diary DLB-50

Charteris, Leslie 1907-1993 . . . . . . DLB-77

Charyn, Jerome 1937- Y-83

Chase, Borden 1900-1971. . . . . . . DLB-26

Chase, Edna Woolman
    1877-1957 . . . . DLB-91

Chase-Riboud, Barbara 1936- DLB-33

Chateaubriand, François-René de
    1768-1848 . . . . DLB-119

Chatterton, Thomas 1752-1770 . . . . DLB-109

Chatto and Windus DLB-106

Chatwin, Bruce 1940-1989 . . . . . . DLB-194

Chaucer, Geoffrey 1340?-1400 . . . . DLB-146

Chauncy, Charles 1705-1787 . . . . . DLB-24

Chauveau, Pierre-Joseph-Olivier
    1820-1890 . . . . DLB-99

Chávez, Denise 1948- DLB-122

Chávez, Fray Angélico 1910- DLB-82

Chayefsky, Paddy
    1923-1981 . . . . DLB-7, 44; Y-81

Cheesman, Evelyn 1881-1969 . . . . . DLB-195

Cheever, Ezekiel 1615-1708. . . . . . DLB-24

Cheever, George Barrell
    1807-1890 . . . . DLB-59

Cheever, John
    1912-1982 . . . . . DLB-2, 102; Y-80, Y-82

Cheever, Susan 1943- Y-82

Cheke, Sir John 1514-1557 . . . . . . DLB-132

Chelsea House DLB-46

Cheney, Ednah Dow (Littlehale)
    1824-1904. . . . . DLB-1

Cheney, Harriet Vaughn
    1796-1889 . . . . DLB-99

Chénier, Marie-Joseph 1764-1811 . . . DLB-192

Cherry, Kelly 1940. . . . . Y-83

Cherryh, C. J. 1942- Y-80

Chesnutt, Charles Waddell
    1858-1932. . . . . DLB-12, 50, 78

Chesney, Sir George Tomkyns
    1830-1895 . . . . DLB-190

Chester, Alfred 1928-1971. . . . . . . DLB-130

Chester, George Randolph
    1869-1924 . . . . DLB-78

The Chester Plays circa 1505-1532;
    revisions until 1575 . . . . DLB-146

Chesterfield, Philip Dormer Stanhope,
    Fourth Earl of 1694-1773 . . . . . DLB-104

Chesterton, G. K. 1874-1936
    . . . . . DLB-10, 19, 34, 70, 98, 149, 178

Chettle, Henry
    circa 1560-circa 1607 . . . . DLB-136

Chew, Ada Nield 1870-1945 . . . . . DLB-135

Cheyney, Edward P. 1861-1947 . . . . DLB-47

Chiara, Piero 1913-1986 . . . . DLB-177

Chicano History. DLB-82

Chicano Language DLB-82

Child, Francis James
    1825-1896 . . . . DLB-1, 64

Child, Lydia Maria
    1802-1880 . . . . DLB-1, 74

Child, Philip 1898-1978. . . . . DLB-68

Childers, Erskine 1870-1922 . . . . . . DLB-70

Children's Book Awards
    and Prizes DLB-61

Children's Illustrators,
    1800-1880 . . . . DLB-163

Childress, Alice 1920-1994. . . . . . DLB-7, 38

Childs, George W. 1829-1894 . . . . . DLB-23

Chilton Book Company DLB-46

Chinweizu 1943- DLB-157

Chitham, Edward 1932- DLB-155

Chittenden, Hiram Martin
    1858-1917 . . . . DLB-47

Chivers, Thomas Holley
    1809-1858. . . . . DLB-3

Cholmondeley, Mary 1859-1925 . . . DLB-197

Chopin, Kate 1850-1904 . . . . . . DLB-12, 78

Chopin, Rene 1885-1953 . . . . DLB-92

Choquette, Adrienne 1915-1973 . . . . DLB-68

Choquette, Robert 1905- DLB-68

The Christian Publishing
    Company DLB-49

Christie, Agatha 1890-1976 . . . . . DLB-13, 77

Christus und die Samariterin
    circa 950 . . . . DLB-148

Christy, Howard Chandler 1873-1952 . DLB-188

Chulkov, Mikhail Dmitrievich
    1743?-1792 . . . . DLB-150

Church, Benjamin 1734-1778 . . . . . . DLB-31

Church, Francis Pharcellus
    1839-1906 . . . . DLB-79

Church, Richard 1893-1972 . . . . . . DLB-191

Church, William Conant
    1836-1917 . . . . DLB-79

Churchill, Caryl 1938- DLB-13

Churchill, Charles
    1731-1764 . . . . DLB-109

Churchill, Sir Winston
1874-1965 . . . . DLB-100; DS-16

Churchyard, Thomas
1520?-1604 . . . . DLB-132

Churton, E., and Company. DLB-106

Chute, Marchette 1909-1994 . . . . . DLB-103

Ciardi, John 1916-1986 . . . . . . DLB-5; Y-86

Cibber, Colley 1671-1757. . . . . DLB-84

Cima, Annalisa 1941- DLB-128

Čingo, Živko 1935-1987 . . . . DLB-181

Cirese, Eugenio 1884-1955 . . . . . . DLB-114

Cisneros, Sandra 1954- DLB-122, 152

City Lights Books. DLB-46

Cixous, Hélène 1937- DLB-83

Clampitt, Amy 1920-1994 . . . . DLB-105

Clapper, Raymond 1892-1944 . . . . . DLB-29

Clare, John 1793-1864 . . . . . . DLB-55, 96

Clarendon, Edward Hyde, Earl of
1609-1674 . . . . DLB-101

Clark, Alfred Alexander Gordon
(see Hare, Cyril)

Clark, Ann Nolan 1896- DLB-52

Clark, C. E. Frazer Jr. 1925- DLB-187

Clark, C. M., Publishing
Company DLB-46

Clark, Catherine Anthony
1892-1977 . . . . DLB-68

Clark, Charles Heber
1841-1915 . . . . DLB-11

Clark, Davis Wasgatt 1812-1871. . . . . DLB-79

Clark, Eleanor 1913- DLB-6

Clark, J. P. 1935- DLB-117

Clark, Lewis Gaylord
1808-1873 . . . . DLB-3, 64, 73

Clark, Walter Van Tilburg
1909-1971. . . . . DLB-9

Clark, William (see Lewis, Meriwether)

Clark, William Andrews Jr.
1877-1934 . . . . DLB-187

Clarke, Austin 1896-1974 . . . . . DLB-10, 20

Clarke, Austin C. 1934- DLB-53, 125

Clarke, Gillian 1937- DLB-40

Clarke, James Freeman
1810-1888 . . . . DLB-1, 59

Clarke, Pauline 1921- DLB-161

Clarke, Rebecca Sophia
1833-1906 . . . . DLB-42

Clarke, Robert, and Company. DLB-49

Clarkson, Thomas 1760-1846 . . . . . DLB-158

Claudel, Paul 1868-1955. . . . . . . DLB-192

Claudius, Matthias 1740-1815 . . . . . DLB-97

Clausen, Andy 1943- DLB-16

Clawson, John L. 1865-1933 . . . . . DLB-187

Claxton, Remsen and
Haffelfinger DLB-49

Clay, Cassius Marcellus
1810-1903 . . . . DLB-43

Cleary, Beverly 1916- DLB-52

Cleaver, Vera 1919- and
Cleaver, Bill 1920-1981. . . . . . . DLB-52

Cleland, John 1710-1789 . . . . DLB-39

Clemens, Samuel Langhorne (Mark Twain) 1835-1910
. . . . . DLB-11, 12, 23, 64, 74, 186, 189

Clement, Hal 1922- DLB-8

Clemo, Jack 1916- DLB-27

Cleveland, John 1613-1658 . . . . . . DLB-126

Cliff, Michelle 1946- DLB-157

Clifford, Lady Anne 1590-1676. . . . . DLB-151

Clifford, James L. 1901-1978 . . . . . DLB-103

Clifford, Lucy 1853?-1929 . . . DLB-135, 141, 197

Clifton, Lucille 1936- DLB-5, 41

Clines, Francis X. 1938- DLB-185

Clode, Edward J.
[publishing house]. DLB-46

Clough, Arthur Hugh 1819-1861 . . . DLB-32

Cloutier, Cécile 1930- DLB-60

Clutton-Brock, Arthur
1868-1924 . . . . DLB-98

Coates, Robert M.
1897-1973 . . . . DLB-4, 9, 102

Coatsworth, Elizabeth 1893- DLB-22

Cobb, Charles E., Jr. 1943- DLB-41

Cobb, Frank I. 1869-1923 . . . . DLB-25

Cobb, Irvin S.
1876-1944. . . . . DLB-11, 25, 86

Cobbe, Frances Power 1822-1904 . . . DLB-190

Cobbett, William 1763-1835 . . . . DLB-43, 107

Cobbledick, Gordon 1898-1969 . . . . . DLB-171

Cochran, Thomas C. 1902- DLB-17

Cochrane, Elizabeth 1867-1922 . . . DLB-25, 189

Cockerill, John A. 1845-1896. . . . . . DLB-23

Cocteau, Jean 1889-1963 . . . . DLB-65

Coderre, Emile (see Jean Narrache)

Coffee, Lenore J. 1900?-1984 . . . . . DLB-44

Coffin, Robert P. Tristram
1892-1955 . . . . DLB-45

Cogswell, Fred 1917- DLB-60

Cogswell, Mason Fitch
1761-1830 . . . . DLB-37

Cohen, Arthur A. 1928-1986. . . . . . DLB-28

Cohen, Leonard 1934- DLB-53

Cohen, Matt 1942- DLB-53

Colden, Cadwallader
1688-1776. . . . . DLB-24, 30

Cole, Barry 1936- DLB-14

Cole, George Watson
1850-1939 . . . . DLB-140

Colegate, Isabel 1931- DLB-14

Coleman, Emily Holmes
1899-1974. . . . . DLB-4

Coleman, Wanda 1946- DLB-130

Coleridge, Hartley 1796-1849. . . . . . DLB-96

Coleridge, Mary 1861-1907 . . . . DLB-19, 98

Coleridge, Samuel Taylor
1772-1834 . . . . DLB-93, 107

Colet, John 1467-1519 . . . . DLB-132

Colette 1873-1954 . . . . DLB-65

Colette, Sidonie Gabrielle (see Colette)

Colinas, Antonio 1946- DLB-134

Coll, Joseph Clement 1881-1921 . . . . DLB-188

Collier, John 1901-1980. . . . . DLB-77

Collier, John Payne 1789-1883 . . . . . DLB-184

Collier, Mary 1690-1762 . . . . DLB-95

Collier, Robert J. 1876-1918 . . . . . . DLB-91

Collier, P. F. [publishing house]. DLB-49

Collin and Small DLB-49

Collingwood, W. G. 1854-1932. . . . . DLB-149

Collins, An floruit circa 1653. . . . . . DLB-131

Collins, Merle 1950- DLB-157

Collins, Mortimer 1827-1876. . . . . DLB-21, 35

Collins, Wilkie 1824-1889 . . . DLB-18, 70, 159

Collins, William 1721-1759 . . . . . . DLB-109

Collins, William, Sons and
Company DLB-154

Collins, Isaac [publishing house] DLB-49

Collis, Maurice 1889-1973. . . . . . . DLB-195

Collyer, Mary 1716?-1763?. DLB-39

Colman, Benjamin 1673-1747 . . . . . DLB-24

Colman, George, the Elder
1732-1794 . . . . DLB-89

Colman, George, the Younger
1762-1836 . . . . DLB-89

Colman, S. [publishing house] DLB-49

Colombo, John Robert 1936- DLB-53

Colquhoun, Patrick 1745-1820 . . . . . DLB-158

Colter, Cyrus 1910- DLB-33

Colum, Padraic 1881-1972 . . . . . . DLB-19

Colvin, Sir Sidney 1845-1927. . . . . DLB-149

Colwin, Laurie 1944-1992 . . . . Y-80

Comden, Betty 1919- and Green,
Adolph 1918- DLB-44

Comi, Girolamo 1890-1968 . . . . . . DLB-114

The Comic Tradition Continued
[in the British Novel]. DLB-15

Commager, Henry Steele
1902- DLB-17

The Commercialization of the Image of
Revolt, by Kenneth Rexroth. DLB-16

Community and Commentators: Black
Theatre and Its Critics. DLB-38

Compton-Burnett, Ivy
1884?-1969 . . . . DLB-36

Conan, Laure 1845-1924 . . . . DLB-99

Conde, Carmen 1901- DLB-108

Conference on Modern Biography Y-85

Congreve, William
1670-1729 . . . . DLB-39, 84

Conkey, W. B., Company DLB-49

Connell, Evan S., Jr. 1924- DLB-2; Y-81

Connelly, Marc 1890-1980 . . . . . DLB-7; Y-80

Connolly, Cyril 1903-1974 . . . . DLB-98

Connolly, James B. 1868-1957 . . . . . DLB-78

Connor, Ralph 1860-1937 . . . . DLB-92

Connor, Tony 1930- DLB-40

Conquest, Robert 1917- DLB-27

Conrad, Joseph
1857-1924 . . . . DLB-10, 34, 98, 156

Conrad, John, and Company DLB-49

Conroy, Jack 1899-1990 . . . . Y-81

Conroy, Pat 1945- DLB-6

The Consolidation ·of Opinion: Critical
Responses to the Modernists DLB-36

Consolo, Vincenzo 1933- DLB-196

Constable, Henry 1562-1613 . . . . . DLB-136

Constable and Company
Limited DLB-112

Constable, Archibald, and
Company DLB-154

Constant, Benjamin 1767-1830 . . . . DLB-119

Constant de Rebecque, Henri-Benjamin de
(see Constant, Benjamin)

Constantine, David 1944- DLB-40

Constantin-Weyer, Maurice
1881-1964 . . . . DLB-92

Contempo Caravan: Kites in
a Windstorm Y-85

A Contemporary Flourescence of Chicano
Literature Y-84

"Contemporary Verse Story-telling,"
by Jonathan Holden DLB-105

The Continental Publishing
Company DLB-49

A Conversation with Chaim Potok Y-84

Conversations with Editors. Y-95

Conversations with Publishers I: An Interview
with Patrick O'Connor Y-84

Conversations with Publishers II: An Interview
with Charles Scribner III Y-94

Conversations with Publishers III: An Interview
with Donald Lamm Y-95

Conversations with Publishers IV: An Interview
with James Laughlin Y-96

Conversations with Rare Book Dealers I: An
Interview with Glenn Horowitz Y-90

Conversations with Rare Book Dealers II: An
Interview with Ralph Sipper Y-94

Conversations with Rare Book Dealers
(Publishers) III: An Interview with
Otto Penzler Y-96

The Conversion of an Unpolitical Man,
by W. H. Bruford DLB-66

Conway, Moncure Daniel
1832-1907. . . . . DLB-1

Cook, Ebenezer
circa 1667-circa 1732 . . . . DLB-24

Cook, Edward Tyas 1857-1919. . . . . DLB-149

Cook, Michael 1933- DLB-53

Cook, David C., Publishing
Company DLB-49

Cooke, George Willis 1848-1923. . . . . DLB-71

Cooke, Increase, and Company DLB-49

Cooke, John Esten 1830-1886 . . . . . . DLB-3

Cooke, Philip Pendleton
1816-1850 . . . . DLB-3, 59

Cooke, Rose Terry
1827-1892 . . . . DLB-12, 74

Cook-Lynn, Elizabeth 1930- DLB-175

Coolbrith, Ina 1841-1928 . . . . . DLB-54, 186

Cooley, Peter 1940- DLB-105

Coolidge, Clark 1939- DLB-193

Coolidge, Susan (see Woolsey, Sarah Chauncy)

Coolidge, George
[publishing house] DLB-49

Cooper, Giles 1918-1966 . . . . DLB-13

Cooper, James Fenimore
1789-1851 . . . . DLB-3, 183

Cooper, Kent 1880-1965 . . . . DLB-29

Cooper, Susan 1935- DLB-161

Cooper, William
[publishing house] DLB-170

Coote, J. [publishing house] DLB-154

Coover, Robert 1932- DLB-2; Y-81

Copeland and Day DLB-49

Ćopić, Branko 1915-1984 . . . . DLB-181

Copland, Robert 1470?-1548 . . . . . DLB-136

Coppard, A. E. 1878-1957 . . . . . . DLB-162

Coppel, Alfred 1921- Y-83

Coppola, Francis Ford 1939- DLB-44

Copway, George (Kah-ge-ga-gah-bowh)
1818-1869. . . . . DLB-175, 183

Corazzini, Sergio 1886-1907 . . . . . DLB-114

Corbett, Richard 1582-1635 . . . . . DLB-121

Corcoran, Barbara 1911- DLB-52

Cordelli, Franco 1943- DLB-196

Corelli, Marie 1855-1924 . . . . . DLB-34, 156

Corle, Edwin 1906-1956 . . . . Y-85

Corman, Cid 1924- DLB-5, 193

Cormier, Robert 1925- DLB-52

Corn, Alfred 1943- DLB-120; Y-80

Cornish, Sam 1935- DLB-41

Cornish, William
circa 1465-circa 1524 . . . . DLB-132

Cornwall, Barry (see Procter, Bryan Waller)

Cornwallis, Sir William, the Younger
circa 1579-1614 . . . . DLB-151

Cornwell, David John Moore
(see le Carré, John)

Corpi, Lucha 1945- DLB-82

Corrington, John William 1932- DLB-6

Corrothers, James D. 1869-1917 . . . . . DLB-50

Corso, Gregory 1930- DLB-5, 16

Cortázar, Julio 1914-1984 . . . . . . DLB-113

Cortez, Jayne 1936- DLB-41

Corvinus, Gottlieb Siegmund
1677-1746 . . . . DLB-168

Corvo, Baron (see Rolfe, Frederick William)

Cory, Annie Sophie (see Cross, Victoria)

Cory, William Johnson
1823-1892 . . . . DLB-35

Coryate, Thomas
1577?-1617 . . . . DLB-151, 172

Ćosić, Dobrica 1921- DLB-181

Cosin, John 1595-1672. . . . . DLB-151

Cosmopolitan Book Corporation. DLB-46

Costain, Thomas B. 1885-1965 . . . . . . DLB-9

Coste, Donat 1912-1957 . . . . DLB-88

Costello, Louisa Stuart 1799-1870 . . . DLB-166

Cota-Cárdenas, Margarita
1941- DLB-122

Cotten, Bruce 1873-1954 . . . . DLB-187

Cotter, Joseph Seamon, Sr.
1861-1949 . . . . DLB-50

Cotter, Joseph Seamon, Jr.
1895-1919 . . . . DLB-50

Cottle, Joseph [publishing house] DLB-154

Cotton, Charles 1630-1687 . . . . . . DLB-131

Cotton, John 1584-1652. . . . . DLB-24

Coulter, John 1888-1980 . . . . DLB-68

Cournos, John 1881-1966. . . . . DLB-54

Courteline, Georges 1858-1929 . . . . DLB-192

Cousins, Margaret 1905- DLB-137

Cousins, Norman 1915-1990 . . . . . DLB-137

Coventry, Francis 1725-1754 . . . . . . DLB-39

Coverdale, Miles
1487 or 1488-1569 . . . . DLB-167

Coverly, N. [publishing house] DLB-49

Covici-Friede DLB-46

Coward, Noel 1899-1973 . . . . DLB-10

Coward, McCann and
Geoghegan DLB-46

Cowles, Gardner 1861-1946 . . . . . . DLB-29

Cowles, Gardner ("Mike"), Jr.
1903-1985. . . . . DLB-127, 137

Cowley, Abraham
    1618-1667. . . . . DLB-131, 151

Cowley, Hannah 1743-1809 . . . . DLB-89

Cowley, Malcolm
    1898-1989. . . . . . DLB-4, 48; Y-81, Y-89

Cowper, William
    1731-1800. . . . . DLB-104, 109

Cox, A. B. (see Berkeley, Anthony)

Cox, James McMahon
    1903-1974 . . . . DLB-127

Cox, James Middleton
    1870-1957 . . . . DLB-127

Cox, Palmer 1840-1924. . . . . DLB-42

Coxe, Louis 1918-1993. . . . . DLB-5

Coxe, Tench 1755-1824 . . . . DLB-37

Cozzens, James Gould
    1903-1978. . . . . . DLB-9; Y-84; DS-2

Cozzens's *Michael Scarlett* Y-97

Crabbe, George 1754-1832 . . . . . . DLB-93

Crackanthorpe, Hubert
    1870-1896 . . . . DLB-135

Craddock, Charles Egbert
    (see Murfree, Mary N.)

Cradock, Thomas 1718-1770. . . . . . DLB-31

Craig, Daniel H. 1811-1895 . . . . . . DLB-43

Craik, Dinah Maria
    1826-1887 . . . . DLB-35, 136

Cramer, Richard Ben 1950- DLB-185

Cranch, Christopher Pearse
    1813-1892 . . . . DLB-1, 42

Crane, Hart 1899-1932 . . . . DLB-4, 48

Crane, R. S. 1886-1967. . . . . DLB-63

Crane, Stephen 1871-1900. . . . DLB-12, 54, 78

Crane, Walter 1845-1915 . . . . DLB-163

Cranmer, Thomas 1489-1556 . . . . . DLB-132

Crapsey, Adelaide 1878-1914. . . . . . DLB-54

Crashaw, Richard
    1612 or 1613-1649 . . . . DLB-126

Craven, Avery 1885-1980 . . . . DLB-17

Crawford, Charles
    1752-circa 1815 . . . . DLB-31

Crawford, F. Marion 1854-1909 . . . . DLB-71

Crawford, Isabel Valancy
    1850-1887 . . . . DLB-92

Crawley, Alan 1887-1975. . . . . DLB-68

Crayon, Geoffrey (see Irving, Washington)

Creamer, Robert W. 1922- DLB-171

Creasey, John 1908-1973 . . . . DLB-77

Creative Age Press DLB-46

Creech, William
    [publishing house] DLB-154

Creede, Thomas
    [publishing house] DLB-170

Creel, George 1876-1953 . . . . DLB-25

Creeley, Robert
    1926- DLB-5, 16, 169; DS-17

Creelman, James 1859-1915 . . . . . . DLB-23

Cregan, David 1931- DLB-13

Creighton, Donald Grant
    1902-1979 . . . . DLB-88

Cremazie, Octave 1827-1879 . . . . . . DLB-99

Crémer, Victoriano 1909?- DLB-108

Crescas, Hasdai
    circa 1340-1412?. DLB-115

Crespo, Angel 1926- DLB-134

Cresset Press DLB-112

Cresswell, Helen 1934- DLB-161

Crèvecoeur, Michel Guillaume Jean de
    1735-1813 . . . . DLB-37

Crews, Harry 1935- DLB-6, 143, 185

Crichton, Michael 1942- Y-81

A Crisis of Culture: The Changing Role
    of Religion in the New Republic
    . . . . DLB-37

Crispin, Edmund 1921-1978 . . . . . DLB-87

Cristofer, Michael 1946- DLB-7

"The Critic as Artist" (1891), by
    Oscar Wilde DLB-57

"Criticism In Relation To Novels" (1863),
    by G. H. Lewes DLB-21

Crnjanski, Miloš 1893-1977 . . . . . . DLB-147

Crockett, David (Davy)
    1786-1836. . . . . DLB-3, 11, 183

Croft-Cooke, Rupert (see Bruce, Leo)

Crofts, Freeman Wills
    1879-1957 . . . . DLB-77

Croker, John Wilson
    1780-1857 . . . . DLB-110

Croly, George 1780-1860 . . . . DLB-159

Croly, Herbert 1869-1930 . . . . DLB-91

Croly, Jane Cunningham
    1829-1901 . . . . DLB-23

Crompton, Richmal 1890-1969 . . . . DLB-160

Cronin, A. J. 1896-1981. . . . . DLB-191

Crosby, Caresse 1892-1970. . . . . . . DLB-48

Crosby, Caresse 1892-1970 and Crosby,
    Harry 1898-1929. . . . . . . DLB-4; DS-15

Crosby, Harry 1898-1929. . . . . DLB-48

Cross, Gillian 1945- DLB-161

Cross, Victoria 1868-1952 . . . . DLB-135, 197

Crossley-Holland, Kevin
    1941- DLB-40, 161

Crothers, Rachel 1878-1958 . . . . . . DLB-7

Crowell, Thomas Y., Company DLB-49

Crowley, John 1942- Y-82

Crowley, Mart 1935- DLB-7

Crown Publishers DLB-46

Crowne, John 1641-1712 . . . . DLB-80

Crowninshield, Edward Augustus
    1817-1859 . . . . DLB-140

Crowninshield, Frank 1872-1947 . . . . . DLB-91

Croy, Homer 1883-1965. . . . . DLB-4

Crumley, James 1939- Y-84

Cruz, Victor Hernández 1949- DLB-41

Csokor, Franz Theodor
    1885-1969 . . . . DLB-81

Cuala Press. DLB-112

Cullen, Countee
    1903-1946 . . . . DLB-4, 48, 51

Culler, Jonathan D. 1944- DLB-67

The Cult of Biography
    Excerpts from the Second Folio Debate:
    "Biographies are generally a disease of
    English Literature" – Germaine Greer,
    Victoria Glendinning, Auberon Waugh,
    and Richard Holmes. Y-86

Cumberland, Richard 1732-1811 . . . . DLB-89

Cummings, Constance Gordon
    1837-1924 . . . . DLB-174

Cummings, E. E. 1894-1962 . . . . . DLB-4, 48

Cummings, Ray 1887-1957 . . . . DLB-8

Cummings and Hilliard. DLB-49

Cummins, Maria Susanna
    1827-1866 . . . . DLB-42

Cundall, Joseph
    [publishing house] DLB-106

Cuney, Waring 1906-1976 . . . . DLB-51

Cuney-Hare, Maude 1874-1936 . . . . . DLB-52

Cunningham, Allan 1784-1842 . . DLB-116, 144

Cunningham, J. V. 1911- DLB-5

Cunningham, Peter F.
    [publishing house]. DLB-49

Cunquiero, Alvaro 1911-1981. . . . . . DLB-134

Cuomo, George 1929- Y-80

Cupples and Leon DLB-46

Cupples, Upham and Company DLB-49

Cuppy, Will 1884-1949. . . . . DLB-11

Curll, Edmund
    [publishing house] DLB-154

Currie, James 1756-1805. . . . . DLB-142

Currie, Mary Montgomerie Lamb Singleton,
    Lady Currie (see Fane, Violet)

Cursor Mundi circa 1300 . . . . DLB-146

Curti, Merle E. 1897- DLB-17

Curtis, Anthony 1926- DLB-155

Curtis, Cyrus H. K. 1850-1933 . . . . DLB-91

Curtis, George William
    1824-1892 . . . . DLB-1, 43

Curzon, Robert 1810-1873 . . . . . . DLB-166

Curzon, Sarah Anne
    1833-1898 . . . . DLB-99

Cushing, Harvey 1869-1939. . . . . . . DLB-187

Cynewulf circa 770-840 . . . . DLB-146

Czepko, Daniel 1605-1660 . . . . DLB-164

D

D. M. Thomas: The Plagiarism
   Controversy. Y-82

Dabit, Eugène 1898-1936 . . . . DLB-65

Daborne, Robert circa 1580-1628 . . . . DLB-58

Dacey, Philip 1939- DLB-105

Dach, Simon 1605-1659 . . . . DLB-164

Daggett, Rollin M. 1831-1901 . . . . . . DLB-79

D'Aguiar, Fred 1960- DLB-157

Dahl, Roald 1916-1990 . . . . DLB-139

Dahlberg, Edward 1900-1977 . . . . DLB-48

Dahn, Felix 1834-1912 . . . . DLB-129

Dal', Vladimir Ivanovich (Kazak Vladimir
   Lugansky) 1801-1872 . . . . DLB-198

Dale, Peter 1938- DLB-40

Daley, Arthur 1904-1974 . . . . DLB-171

Dall, Caroline Wells (Healey)
   1822-1912 . . . . DLB-1

Dallas, E. S. 1828-1879 . . . . DLB-55

The Dallas Theater Center DLB-7

D'Alton, Louis 1900-1951 . . . . DLB-10

Daly, T. A. 1871-1948 . . . . DLB-11

Damon, S. Foster 1893-1971 . . . . . . DLB-45

Damrell, William S.
   [publishing house] DLB-49

Dana, Charles A. 1819-1897 . . . . . DLB-3, 23

Dana, Richard Henry, Jr.
   1815-1882 . . . . DLB-1, 183

Dandridge, Ray Garfield DLB-51

Dane, Clemence 1887-1965 . . . . . DLB-10, 197

Danforth, John 1660-1730 . . . . DLB-24

Danforth, Samuel, I 1626-1674 . . . . . DLB-24

Danforth, Samuel, II 1666-1727 . . . . . DLB-24

Dangerous Years: London Theater,
   1939-1945 . . . . DLB-10

Daniel, John M. 1825-1865 . . . . DLB-43

Daniel, Samuel
   1562 or 1563-1619 . . . . DLB-62

Daniel Press DLB-106

Daniells, Roy 1902-1979 . . . . DLB-68

Daniels, Jim 1956- DLB-120

Daniels, Jonathan 1902-1981 . . . . . DLB-127

Daniels, Josephus 1862-1948 . . . . . . DLB-29

Danis Rose and the Rendering
   of *Ulysses* Y-97

Dannay, Frederic 1905-1982 and
   Manfred B. Lee 1905-1971 . . . . . DLB-137

Danner, Margaret Esse 1915- DLB-41

Danter, John [publishing house] DLB-170

Dantin, Louis 1865-1945 . . . . DLB-92

Danzig, Allison 1898-1987 . . . . DLB-171

D'Arcy, Ella circa 1857-1937 . . . . . DLB-135

Darley, Felix Octavious Carr
   1822-1888 . . . . DLB-188

Darley, George 1795-1846 . . . . DLB-96

Darwin, Charles 1809-1882 . . . . DLB-57, 166

Darwin, Erasmus 1731-1802 . . . . . . DLB-93

Daryush, Elizabeth 1887-1977 . . . . . DLB-20

Dashkova, Ekaterina Romanovna
   (née Vorontsova) 1743-1810 . . . . DLB-150

Dashwood, Edmée Elizabeth Monica
   de la Pasture (see Delafield, E. M.)

Daudet, Alphonse 1840-1897 . . . . . DLB-123

d'Aulaire, Edgar Parin 1898- and
   d'Aulaire, Ingri 1904- DLB-22

Davenant, Sir William
   1606-1668 . . . . DLB-58, 126

Davenport, Guy 1927- DLB-130

Davenport, Marcia 1903-1996 . . . . . . DS-17

Davenport, Robert ?-? DLB-58

Daves, Delmer 1904-1977 . . . . DLB-26

Davey, Frank 1940- DLB-53

Davidson, Avram 1923-1993 . . . . . . DLB-8

Davidson, Donald 1893-1968 . . . . . . DLB-45

Davidson, John 1857-1909 . . . . DLB-19

Davidson, Lionel 1922- DLB-14

Davidson, Sara 1943- DLB-185

Davie, Donald 1922- DLB-27

Davie, Elspeth 1919- DLB-139

Davies, Sir John 1569-1626 . . . . . . DLB-172

Davies, John, of Hereford
   1565?-1618 . . . . DLB-121

Davies, Rhys 1901-1978 . . . . . DLB-139, 191

Davies, Robertson 1913- DLB-68

Davies, Samuel 1723-1761 . . . . DLB-31

Davies, Thomas 1712?-1785 . . . . DLB-142, 154

Davies, W. H. 1871-1940 . . . . . DLB-19, 174

Davies, Peter, Limited DLB-112

Daviot, Gordon 1896?-1952 . . . . . . DLB-10
   (see also Tey, Josephine)

Davis, Charles A. 1795-1867 . . . . . . DLB-11

Davis, Clyde Brion 1894-1962 . . . . . . DLB-9

Davis, Dick 1945- DLB-40

Davis, Frank Marshall 1905-? DLB-51

Davis, H. L. 1894-1960 . . . . DLB-9

Davis, John 1774-1854 . . . . DLB-37

Davis, Lydia 1947- DLB-130

Davis, Margaret Thomson 1926- . . . DLB-14

Davis, Ossie 1917- DLB-7, 38

Davis, Paxton 1925-1994 . . . . Y-94

Davis, Rebecca Harding
   1831-1910 . . . . DLB-74

Davis, Richard Harding 1864-1916
   . . . . . . DLB-12, 23, 78, 79, 189; DS-13

Davis, Samuel Cole 1764-1809 . . . . . DLB-37

Davison, Peter 1928- DLB-5

Davys, Mary 1674-1732 . . . . DLB-39

DAW Books DLB-46

Dawn Powell, Where Have You Been All
   Our lives? Y-97

Dawson, Ernest 1882-1947 . . . . . . DLB-140

Dawson, Fielding 1930- DLB-130

Dawson, William 1704-1752 . . . . . . DLB-31

Day, Angel flourished 1586 . . . . . . DLB-167

Day, Benjamin Henry 1810-1889 . . . DLB-43

Day, Clarence 1874-1935 . . . . DLB-11

Day, Dorothy 1897-1980 . . . . DLB-29

Day, Frank Parker 1881-1950 . . . . . DLB-92

Day, John circa 1574-circa 1640 . . . . DLB-62

Day, John [publishing house] DLB-170

Day Lewis, C. 1904-1972 . . . . . DLB-15, 20
   (see also Blake, Nicholas)

Day, Thomas 1748-1789 . . . . DLB-39

Day, The John, Company DLB-46

Day, Mahlon [publishing house] DLB-49

Dazai, Osamu 1909-1948 . . . . DLB-182

Deacon, William Arthur
   1890-1977 . . . . DLB-68

Deal, Borden 1922-1985 . . . . DLB-6

de Angeli, Marguerite 1889-1987 . . . . DLB-22

De Angelis, Milo 1951- DLB-128

De Bow, James Dunwoody Brownson
   1820-1867 . . . . DLB-3, 79

de Bruyn, Günter 1926- DLB-75

de Camp, L. Sprague 1907- DLB-8

De Carlo, Andrea 1952- DLB-196

The Decay of Lying (1889),
   by Oscar Wilde [excerpt] DLB-18

Dechert, Robert 1895-1975 . . . . . . DLB-187

Dedication, *Ferdinand Count Fathom* (1753),
   by Tobias Smollett DLB-39

Dedication, *The History of Pompey the Little*
   (1751), by Francis Coventry DLB-39

Dedication, *Lasselia* (1723), by Eliza
   Haywood [excerpt] DLB-39

Dedication, *The Wanderer* (1814),
   by Fanny Burney DLB-39

Dee, John 1527-1609 . . . . DLB-136

Deeping, George Warwick
   1877-1950 . . . . DLB 153

Defense of *Amelia* (1752), by
   Henry Fielding DLB-39

Defoe, Daniel 1660-1731 . . . . DLB-39, 95, 101

de Fontaine, Felix Gregory
   1834-1896 . . . . DLB-43

De Forest, John William
   1826-1906 . . . . DLB-12, 189

DeFrees, Madeline 1919- DLB-105

DeGolyer, Everette Lee 1886-1956 . . . DLB-187

de Graff, Robert 1895-1981 . . . . Y-81

de Graft, Joe 1924-1978 . . . . DLB-117

De Heinrico circa 980? DLB-148

Deighton, Len 1929- DLB-87

DeJong, Meindert 1906-1991 . . . . . . DLB-52

Dekker, Thomas
circa 1572-1632 . . . . DLB-62, 172

Delacorte, Jr., George T.
1894-1991 . . . . DLB-91

Delafield, E. M. 1890-1943 . . . . DLB-34

Delahaye, Guy 1888-1969 . . . . DLB-92

de la Mare, Walter
1873-1956 . . . . DLB-19, 153, 162

Deland, Margaret 1857-1945 . . . . . . DLB-78

Delaney, Shelagh 1939- DLB-13

Delano, Amasa 1763-1823 . . . . DLB-183

Delany, Martin Robinson
1812-1885 . . . . DLB-50

Delany, Samuel R. 1942- DLB-8, 33

de la Roche, Mazo 1879-1961 . . . . . DLB-68

Delavigne, Jean François Casimir 1793-1843
. . . . DLB-192

Delbanco, Nicholas 1942- DLB-6

De León, Nephtalí 1945- DLB-82

Delgado, Abelardo Barrientos
1931- DLB-82

Del Giudice, Daniele 1949- DLB-196

De Libero, Libero 1906-1981 . . . . . DLB-114

DeLillo, Don 1936- DLB-6, 173

de Lisser H. G. 1878-1944 . . . . DLB-117

Dell, Floyd 1887-1969 . . . . DLB-9

Dell Publishing Company DLB-46

delle Grazie, Marie Eugene
1864-1931 . . . . DLB-81

Deloney, Thomas died 1600 . . . . . . DLB-167

Deloria, Ella C. 1889-1971 . . . . . . DLB-175

Deloria, Vine, Jr. 1933- DLB-175

del Rey, Lester 1915-1993 . . . . DLB-8

Del Vecchio, John M. 1947- DS-9

de Man, Paul 1919-1983 . . . . DLB-67

Demby, William 1922- DLB-33

Deming, Philander 1829-1915 . . . . . DLB-74

Demorest, William Jennings
1822-1895 . . . . DLB-79

De Morgan, William 1839-1917 . . . . DLB-153

Demosthenes 384 B.C.-322 B.C. DLB-176

Denham, Henry
[publishing house] DLB-170

Denham, Sir John
1615-1669 . . . . DLB-58, 126

Denison, Merrill 1893-1975 . . . . DLB-92

Denison, T. S., and Company DLB-49

Dennery, Adolphe Philippe 1811-1899 . . . DLB-192

Dennie, Joseph
1768-1812 . . . . DLB-37, 43, 59, 73

Dennis, John 1658-1734 . . . . DLB-101

Dennis, Nigel 1912-1989 . . . . . . DLB-13, 15

Denslow, W. W. 1856-1915 . . . . . DLB-188

Dent, Tom 1932- DLB-38

Dent, J. M., and Sons DLB-112

Denton, Daniel circa 1626-1703 . . . . DLB-24

DePaola, Tomie 1934- DLB-61

Department of Library, Archives, and Institutional
Research, American Bible Society Y-97

De Quille, Dan 1829-1898 . . . . . . DLB-186

De Quincey, Thomas
1785-1859. . . . . DLB-110, 144

Derby, George Horatio
1823-1861 . . . . DLB-11

Derby, J. C., and Company DLB-49

Derby and Miller DLB-49

Derleth, August 1909-1971 . . . . DLB-9; DS-17

The Derrydale Press DLB-46

Derzhavin, Gavriil Romanovich
1743-1816 . . . . DLB-150

Desaulniers, Gonsalve
1863-1934 . . . . DLB-92

Desbiens, Jean-Paul 1927- DLB-53

des Forêts, Louis-Rene 1918- DLB-83

Desiato, Luca 1941- DLB-196

Desnica, Vladan 1905-1967 . . . . . . DLB-181

DesRochers, Alfred 1901-1978 . . . . . DLB-68

Desrosiers, Léo-Paul 1896-1967 . . . . . DLB-68

Dessì, Giuseppe 1909-1977 . . . . . . DLB-177

Destouches, Louis-Ferdinand
(see Céline, Louis-Ferdinand)

De Tabley, Lord 1835-1895 . . . . . . DLB-35

"A Detail in a Poem,"
by Fred Chappell DLB-105

Deutsch, Babette 1895-1982 . . . . . . DLB-45

Deutsch, Niklaus Manuel (see Manuel, Niklaus)

Deutsch, André, Limited DLB-112

Deveaux, Alexis 1948- DLB-38

The Development of the Author's Copyright
in Britain DLB-154

The Development of Lighting in the Staging
of Drama, 1900-1945 . . . . DLB-10

The Development of Meiji Japan DLB-180

De Vere, Aubrey 1814-1902 . . . . . . DLB-35

Devereux, second Earl of Essex, Robert
1565-1601 . . . . DLB-136

The Devin-Adair Company DLB-46

De Vinne, Theodore Low
1828-1914 . . . . DLB-187

De Voto, Bernard 1897-1955 . . . . . . DLB-9

De Vries, Peter 1910-1993 . . . . . DLB-6; Y-82

Dewdney, Christopher 1951- DLB-60

Dewdney, Selwyn 1909-1979 . . . . . . DLB-68

DeWitt, Robert M., Publisher DLB-49

DeWolfe, Fiske and Company DLB-49

Dexter, Colin 1930- DLB-87

de Young, M. H. 1849-1925 . . . . . . DLB-25

Dhlomo, H. I. E. 1903-1956 . . . . . DLB-157

Dhuoda circa 803-after 843 . . . . . . DLB-148

The Dial Press DLB-46

Diamond, I. A. L. 1920-1988 . . . . . DLB-26

Dibdin, Thomas Frognall
1776-1847 . . . . DLB-184

Di Cicco, Pier Giorgio 1949- DLB-60

Dick, Philip K. 1928-1982 . . . . DLB-8

Dick and Fitzgerald DLB-49

Dickens, Charles
1812-1870 . . . . . DLB-21, 55, 70, 159, 166

Dickinson, Peter 1927- DLB-161

Dickey, James 1923-1997
. . . . DLB-5, 193; Y-82, Y-93, Y-96; DS-7

Dickey, William 1928-1994 . . . . DLB-5

Dickinson, Emily 1830-1886 . . . . DLB-1

Dickinson, John 1732-1808 . . . . . . DLB-31

Dickinson, Jonathan 1688-1747 . . . . . DLB-24

Dickinson, Patric 1914- DLB-27

Dickinson, Peter 1927- DLB-87

Dicks, John [publishing house] DLB-106

Dickson, Gordon R. 1923- DLB-8

*Dictionary of Literary Biography
Yearbook* Awards Y-92, Y-93

The Dictionary of National Biography
. . . . DLB-144

Didion, Joan
1934- DLB-2, 173, 185; Y-81, Y-86

Di Donato, Pietro 1911- DLB-9

Die Fürstliche Bibliothek Corvey Y-96

Diego, Gerardo 1896-1987 . . . . DLB-134

Digges, Thomas circa 1546-1595 . . . . DLB-136

Dillard, Annie 1945- Y-80

Dillard, R. H. W. 1937- DLB-5

Dillingham, Charles T.,
Company DLB-49

The Dillingham, G. W.,
Company DLB-49

Dilly, Edward and Charles
[publishing house] DLB-154

Dilthey, Wilhelm 1833-1911 . . . . . . DLB-129

Dimitrova, Blaga 1922- DLB-181

Dimov, Dimitŭr 1909-1966 . . . . . . DLB-181

Dimsdale, Thomas J. 1831?-1866 . . . . DLB-186

Dingelstedt, Franz von
1814-1881 . . . . DLB-133

Dintenfass, Mark 1941- Y-84

Diogenes, Jr. (see Brougham, John)

Diogenes Laertius circa 200 . . . . . . DLB-176

DiPrima, Diane 1934- DLB-5, 16

Disch, Thomas M. 1940- DLB-8

Disney, Walt 1901-1966 . . . . DLB-22

Disraeli, Benjamin 1804-1881 . . . . DLB-21, 55

D'Israeli, Isaac 1766-1848 . . . . DLB-107

Ditzen, Rudolf (see Fallada, Hans)

Dix, Dorothea Lynde 1802-1887 . . . . . DLB-1

Dix, Dorothy (see Gilmer,
Elizabeth Meriwether)

Dix, Edwards and Company DLB-49

Dix, Gertrude circa 1874–? DLB-197

Dixie, Florence Douglas
1857-1905 . . . . DLB-174

Dixon, Ella Hepworth 1855 or
1857-1932 . . . . DLB-197

Dixon, Paige (see Corcoran, Barbara)

Dixon, Richard Watson
1833-1900 . . . . DLB-19

Dixon, Stephen 1936- DLB-130

Dmitriev, Ivan Ivanovich
1760-1837 . . . . DLB-150

Dobell, Bertram 1842-1914 . . . . . . DLB-184

Dobell, Sydney 1824-1874 . . . . DLB-32

Döblin, Alfred 1878-1957 . . . . DLB-66

Dobson, Austin
1840-1921 . . . . DLB-35, 144

Doctorow, E. L.
1931- DLB-2, 28, 173; Y-80

Documents on Sixteenth-Century
Literature DLB-167, 172

Dodd, William E. 1869-1940 . . . . . . DLB-17

Dodd, Anne [publishing house] DLB-154

Dodd, Mead and Company DLB-49

Doderer, Heimito von 1896-1968 . . . DLB-85

Dodge, Mary Mapes
1831?-1905 . . . . DLB-42, 79; DS-13

Dodge, B. W., and Company DLB-46

Dodge Publishing Company DLB-49

Dodgson, Charles Lutwidge
(see Carroll, Lewis)

Dodsley, Robert 1703-1764 . . . . DLB-95

Dodsley, R. [publishing house] DLB-154

Dodson, Owen 1914-1983 . . . . DLB-76

Doesticks, Q. K. Philander, P. B.
(see Thomson, Mortimer)

Doheny, Carrie Estelle
1875-1958 . . . . DLB-140

Doherty, John 1798?-1854 . . . . DLB-190

Domínguez, Sylvia Maida
1935- DLB-122

Donahoe, Patrick
[publishing house] DLB-49

Donald, David H. 1920- DLB-17

Donaldson, Scott 1928- DLB-111

Doni, Rodolfo 1919- DLB-177

Donleavy, J. P. 1926- DLB-6, 173

Donnadieu, Marguerite (see Duras,
Marguerite)

Donne, John 1572-1631 . . . . . DLB-121, 151

Donnelley, R. R., and Sons
Company DLB-49

Donnelly, Ignatius 1831-1901 . . . . . DLB-12

Donohue and Henneberry DLB-49

Donoso, José 1924- DLB-113

Doolady, M. [publishing house] DLB-49

Dooley, Ebon (see Ebon)

Doolittle, Hilda 1886-1961 . . . . . DLB-4, 45

Doplicher, Fabio 1938- DLB-128

Dor, Milo 1923- DLB-85

Doran, George H., Company DLB-46

Dorgelès, Roland 1886-1973 . . . . . . DLB-65

Dorn, Edward 1929- DLB-5

Dorr, Rheta Childe 1866-1948 . . . . . DLB-25

Dorris, Michael 1945-1997 . . . . . . DLB-175

Dorset and Middlesex, Charles Sackville,
Lord Buckhurst,
Earl of 1643-1706 . . . . DLB-131

Dorst, Tankred 1925- DLB-75, 124

Dos Passos, John
1896-1970 . . . . . DLB-4, 9; DS-1, DS-15

John Dos Passos: A Centennial
Commemoration Y-96

Doubleday and Company DLB-49

Dougall, Lily 1858-1923 . . . . DLB-92

Doughty, Charles M.
1843-1926 . . . . DLB-19, 57, 174

Douglas, Gavin 1476-1522 . . . . . . DLB-132

Douglas, Keith 1920-1944 . . . . DLB-27

Douglas, Norman 1868-1952 . . . . DLB-34, 195

Douglass, Frederick
1817?-1895 . . . . DLB-1, 43, 50, 79

Douglass, William circa
1691-1752 . . . . DLB-24

Dourado, Autran 1926- DLB-145

Dove, Arthur G. 1880-1946 . . . . . . DLB-188

Dove, Rita 1952- DLB-120

Dover Publications DLB-46

Doves Press DLB-112

Dowden, Edward 1843-1913 . . . . DLB-35, 149

Dowell, Coleman 1925-1985 . . . . . DLB-130

Dowland, John 1563-1626 . . . . DLB-172

Downes, Gwladys 1915- DLB-88

Downing, J., Major (see Davis, Charles A.)

Downing, Major Jack (see Smith, Seba)

Dowriche, Anne
before 1560-after 1613 . . . . DLB-172

Dowson, Ernest 1867-1900 . . . . . DLB-19, 135

Doxey, William
[publishing house] DLB-49

Doyle, Sir Arthur Conan
1859-1930 . . . . . . DLB-18, 70, 156, 178

Doyle, Kirby 1932- DLB-16

Doyle, Roddy 1958- DLB-194

Drabble, Margaret 1939- DLB-14, 155

Drach, Albert 1902- DLB-85

Dragojević, Danijel 1934- DLB-181

Drake, Samuel Gardner 1798-1875 . . . DLB-187

The Dramatic Publishing
Company DLB-49

Dramatists Play Service DLB-46

Drant, Thomas
early 1540s?-1578 . . . . DLB-167

Draper, John W. 1811-1882 . . . . . . DLB-30

Draper, Lyman C. 1815-1891 . . . . . . DLB-30

Drayton, Michael 1563-1631 . . . . . DLB-121

Dreiser, Theodore
1871-1945 . . . . DLB-9, 12, 102, 137; DS-1

Drewitz, Ingeborg 1923-1986 . . . . . . DLB-75

Drieu La Rochelle, Pierre
1893-1945 . . . . DLB-72

Drinkwater, John 1882-1937
. . . . DLB-10, 19, 149

Droste-Hülshoff, Annette von
1797-1848 . . . . DLB-133

The Drue Heinz Literature Prize
Excerpt from "Excerpts from a Report
of the Commission," in David
Bosworth's *The Death of Descartes*
An Interview with David
Bosworth Y-82

Drummond, William Henry
1854-1907 . . . . DLB-92

Drummond, William, of Hawthornden
1585-1649 . . . . DLB-121

Dryden, Charles 1860?-1931 . . . . . DLB-171

Dryden, John 1631-1700 . . . DLB-80, 101, 131

Držić, Marin circa 1508-1567 . . . . . DLB-147

Duane, William 1760-1835 . . . . DLB-43

Dubé, Marcel 1930- DLB-53

Dubé, Rodolphe (see Hertel, François)

Dubie, Norman 1945- DLB-120

Du Bois, W. E. B.
1868-1963 . . . . DLB-47, 50, 91

Du Bois, William Pène 1916- DLB-61

Dubus, Andre 1936- DLB-130

Ducange, Victor 1783-1833 . . . . . . DLB-192

Du Chaillu, Paul Belloni
1831?-1903 . . . . DLB-189

Ducharme, Réjean 1941- DLB-60

Dučić, Jovan 1871-1943 . . . . DLB-147

Duck, Stephen 1705?-1756 . . . . DLB-95

Duckworth, Gerald, and
    Company Limited DLB-112

Dudek, Louis 1918- DLB-88

Duell, Sloan and Pearce DLB-46

Duerer, Albrecht 1471-1528 . . . . . . DLB-179

Dufief, Nicholas Gouin 1776-1834 . . . DLB-187

Duff Gordon, Lucie 1821-1869 . . . . DLB-166

Duffield and Green DLB-46

Duffy, Maureen 1933- DLB-14

Dugan, Alan 1923- DLB-5

Dugard, William
    [publishing house] DLB-170

Dugas, Marcel 1883-1947 . . . . DLB-92

Dugdale, William
    [publishing house] DLB-106

Duhamel, Georges 1884-1966 . . . . . DLB-65

Dujardin, Edouard 1861-1949 . . . . . DLB-123

Dukes, Ashley 1885-1959 . . . . DLB-10

du Maurier, Daphne 1907-1989 . . . . DLB-191

Du Maurier, George
    1834-1896 . . . . DLB-153, 178

Dumas, Alexandre *fils* 1824–1895 . . . . DLB-192

Dumas, Alexandre *père*
    1802-1870 . . . . DLB-119, 192

Dumas, Henry 1934-1968 . . . . DLB-41

Dunbar, Paul Laurence
    1872-1906 . . . . DLB-50, 54, 78

Dunbar, William
    circa 1460-circa 1522 . . . . . DLB-132, 146

Duncan, Norman 1871-1916 . . . . . . DLB-92

Duncan, Quince 1940- DLB-145

Duncan, Robert 1919-1988 . . . DLB-5, 16, 193

Duncan, Ronald 1914-1982 . . . . DLB-13

Duncan, Sara Jeannette
    1861-1922 . . . . DLB-92

Dunigan, Edward, and Brother DLB-49

Dunlap, John 1747-1812 . . . . DLB-43

Dunlap, William
    1766-1839 . . . . DLB-30, 37, 59

Dunn, Douglas 1942- DLB-40

Dunn, Harvey Thomas 1884-1952 . . . DLB-188

Dunn, Stephen 1939- DLB-105

Dunne, Finley Peter
    1867-1936 . . . . DLB-11, 23

Dunne, John Gregory 1932- Y-80

Dunne, Philip 1908-1992 . . . . DLB-26

Dunning, Ralph Cheever
    1878-1930 . . . . DLB-4

Dunning, William A.
    1857-1922 . . . . DLB-17

Duns Scotus, John
    circa 1266-1308 . . . . DLB-115

Dunsany, Lord (Edward John Moreton
    Drax Plunkett, Baron Dunsany)
    1878-1957 . . . . . . DLB-10, 77, 153, 156

Dunton, John [publishing house] DLB-170

Dunton, W. Herbert 1878-1936 . . . . DLB-188

Dupin, Amantine-Aurore-Lucile (see Sand, George)

Durand, Lucile (see Bersianik, Louky)

Duranti, Francesca 1935- DLB-196

Duranty, Walter 1884-1957 . . . . DLB-29

Duras, Marguerite 1914- DLB-83

Durfey, Thomas 1653-1723 . . . . DLB-80

Durova, Nadezhda Andreevna (Aleksandr
    Andreevich Aleksandrov) 1783-1866
    . . . . DLB-198

Durrell, Lawrence
    1912-1990 . . . . DLB-15, 27; Y-90

Durrell, William
    [publishing house] DLB-49

Dürrenmatt, Friedrich
    1921-1990 . . . . DLB-69, 124

Dutton, E. P., and Company DLB-49

Duvoisin, Roger 1904-1980 . . . . DLB-61

Duyckinck, Evert Augustus
    1816-1878 . . . . DLB-3, 64

Duyckinck, George L. 1823-1863 . . . . DLB-3

Duyckinck and Company DLB-49

Dwight, John Sullivan 1813-1893 . . . . DLB-1

Dwight, Timothy 1752-1817 . . . . . . DLB-37

Dybek, Stuart 1942- DLB-130

Dyer, Charles 1928- DLB-13

Dyer, George 1755-1841 . . . . DLB-93

Dyer, John 1699-1757 . . . . DLB-95

Dyer, Sir Edward 1543-1607 . . . . . DLB-136

Dylan, Bob 1941- DLB-16

E

Eager, Edward 1911-1964 . . . . DLB-22

Eames, Wilberforce 1855-1937 . . . . DLB-140

Earle, James H., and Company DLB-49

Earle, John 1600 or 1601-1665 . . . . DLB-151

Early American Book Illustration,
    by Sinclair Hamilton DLB-49

Eastlake, William 1917- DLB-6

Eastman, Carol ?- DLB-44

Eastman, Charles A. (Ohiyesa)
    1858-1939 . . . . DLB-175

Eastman, Max 1883-1969 . . . . DLB-91

Eaton, Daniel Isaac 1753-1814 . . . . DLB-158

Eberhart, Richard 1904- DLB-48

Ebner, Jeannie 1918- DLB-85

Ebner-Eschenbach, Marie von
    1830-1916 . . . . DLB-81

Ebon 1942- DLB-41

Ecbasis Captivi circa 1045 . . . . DLB-148

Ecco Press DLB-46

Eckhart, Meister
    circa 1260-circa 1328 . . . . DLB-115

The Eclectic Review 1805-1868 . . . DLB-110

Eco, Umberto 1932- DLB-196

Edel, Leon 1907- DLB-103

Edes, Benjamin 1732-1803 . . . . DLB-43

Edgar, David 1948- DLB-13

Edgeworth, Maria
    1768-1849 . . . . DLB-116, 159, 163

The Edinburgh Review 1802-1929 . . . . . DLB-110

Edinburgh University Press DLB-112

The Editor Publishing Company DLB-49

Editorial Statements DLB-137

Edmonds, Randolph 1900- DLB-51

Edmonds, Walter D. 1903- DLB-9

Edschmid, Kasimir 1890-1966 . . . . . DLB-56

Edwards, Amelia Anne Blandford
    1831-1892 . . . . DLB-174

Edwards, Edward 1812-1886 . . . . . DLB-184

Edwards, Jonathan 1703-1758 . . . . . DLB-24

Edwards, Jonathan, Jr. 1745-1801 . . . . DLB-37

Edwards, Junius 1929- DLB-33

Edwards, Matilda Barbara Betham-
    1836-1919 . . . . DLB-174

Edwards, Richard 1524-1566 . . . . . . DLB-62

Edwards, James
    [publishing house] DLB-154

Effinger, George Alec 1947- DLB-8

Egerton, George 1859-1945 . . . . . . DLB-135

Eggleston, Edward 1837-1902 . . . . . DLB-12

Eggleston, Wilfred 1901-1986 . . . . . DLB-92

Ehrenstein, Albert 1886-1950 . . . . . DLB-81

Ehrhart, W. D. 1948- DS-9

Eich, Günter 1907-1972 . . . . . . DLB-69, 124

Eichendorff, Joseph Freiherr von
    1788-1857 . . . . DLB-90

1873 Publishers' Catalogues DLB-49

Eighteenth-Century Aesthetic
    Theories DLB-31

Eighteenth-Century Philosophical
    Background DLB-31

Eigner, Larry 1926-1996 . . . . . . DLB-5, 193

Eikon Basilike 1649 . . . . DLB-151

Eilhart von Oberge
    circa 1140-circa 1195 . . . . DLB-148

Einhard circa 770-840 . . . . DLB-148

Eiseley, Loren 1907-1977 . . . . DS-17

Eisenreich, Herbert 1925-1986 . . . . DLB-85

Eisner, Kurt 1867-1919 . . . . DLB-66

Eklund, Gordon 1945- Y-83

Ekwensi, Cyprian 1921- DLB-117

Eld, George
  [publishing house] DLB-170

Elder, Lonne III 1931- DLB-7, 38, 44

Elder, Paul, and Company DLB-49

Elements of Rhetoric (1828; revised, 1846),
  by Richard Whately [excerpt] DLB-57

Elie, Robert 1915-1973 . . . . DLB-88

Elin Pelin 1877-1949 . . . . DLB-147

Eliot, George 1819-1880 . . . . . DLB-21, 35, 55

Eliot, John 1604-1690 . . . . DLB-24

Eliot, T. S. 1888-1965 . . . . DLB-7, 10, 45, 63

Eliot's Court Press DLB-170

Elizabeth I 1533-1603 . . . . DLB-136

Elizabeth of Nassau-Saarbrücken
  after 1393-1456 . . . . DLB-179

Elizondo, Salvador 1932- DLB-145

Elizondo, Sergio 1930- DLB-82

Elkin, Stanley 1930- DLB-2, 28; Y-80

Elles, Dora Amy (see Wentworth, Patricia)

Ellet, Elizabeth F. 1818?-1877 . . . . . DLB-30

Elliot, Ebenezer 1781-1849 . . . . . DLB-96, 190

Elliot, Frances Minto (Dickinson)
  1820-1898 . . . . DLB-166

Elliott, George 1923- DLB-68

Elliott, Janice 1931- DLB-14

Elliott, William 1788-1863 . . . . DLB-3

Elliott, Thomes and Talbot DLB-49

Ellis, Alice Thomas (Anna Margaret Haycraft)
  1932- DLB-194

Ellis, Edward S. 1840-1916 . . . . . . DLB-42

Ellis, Frederick Staridge
  [publishing house] DLB-106

The George H. Ellis Company DLB-49

Ellis, Havelock 1859-1939 . . . . . . DLB-190

Ellison, Harlan 1934- DLB-8

Ellison, Ralph Waldo
  1914-1994 . . . . DLB-2, 76; Y-94

Ellmann, Richard
  1918-1987 . . . . DLB-103; Y-87

The Elmer Holmes Bobst Awards in Arts
  and Letters Y-87

Elyot, Thomas 1490?-1546 . . . . . . DLB-136

Emanuel, James Andrew 1921- DLB-41

Emecheta, Buchi 1944- DLB-117

The Emergence of Black Women
  Writers DS-8

Emerson, Ralph Waldo
  1803-1882 . . . . DLB-1, 59, 73, 183

Emerson, William 1769-1811 . . . . . . DLB-37

Emerson, William 1923-1997 . . . . . . Y-97

Emin, Fedor Aleksandrovich
  circa 1735-1770 . . . . DLB-150

Empedocles fifth century B.C. DLB-176

Empson, William 1906-1984 . . . . . . DLB-20

Enchi, Fumiko 1905-1986 . . . . . . DLB-182

Encounter with the West DLB-180

The End of English Stage Censorship,
  1945-1968 . . . . DLB-13

Ende, Michael 1929- DLB-75

Endō, Shūsaku 1923-1996 . . . . . . DLB-182

Engel, Marian 1933-1985 . . . . DLB-53

Engels, Friedrich 1820-1895 . . . . . . DLB-129

Engle, Paul 1908- DLB-48

English Composition and Rhetoric (1866),
  by Alexander Bain [excerpt] DLB-57

The English Language:
  410 to 1500 . . . . DLB-146

The English Renaissance of Art (1908),
  by Oscar Wilde DLB-35

Enright, D. J. 1920- DLB-27

Enright, Elizabeth 1909-1968 . . . . . . DLB-22

L'Envoi (1882), by Oscar Wilde DLB-35

Epictetus circa 55-circa 125-130 . . . . DLB-176

Epicurus 342/341 B.C.-271/270 B.C.
  . . . . DLB-176

Epps, Bernard 1936- DLB-53

Epstein, Julius 1909- and
  Epstein, Philip 1909-1952 . . . . . . DLB-26

Equiano, Olaudah
  circa 1745-1797 . . . . DLB-37, 50

Eragny Press DLB-112

Erasmus, Desiderius 1467-1536 . . . . . DLB-136

Erba, Luciano 1922- DLB-128

Erdrich, Louise 1954- DLB-152, 175

Erichsen-Brown, Gwethalyn Graham
  (see Graham, Gwethalyn)

Eriugena, John Scottus
  circa 810-877 . . . . DLB-115

Ernest Hemingway's Toronto Journalism
  Revisited: With Three Previously
  Unrecorded Stories Y-92

Ernst, Paul 1866-1933 . . . . . . DLB-66, 118

Erskine, Albert 1911-1993 . . . . Y-93

Erskine, John 1879-1951 . . . . . . DLB-9, 102

Erskine, Mrs. Steuart ?-1948 . . . . . DLB-195

Ervine, St. John Greer 1883-1971 . . . . DLB-10

Eschenburg, Johann Joachim 1743-1820 . . . DLB-97

Escoto, Julio 1944- DLB-145

Eshleman, Clayton 1935- DLB-5

Espriu, Salvador 1913-1985 . . . . . . DLB-134

Ess Ess Publishing Company DLB-49

Essay on Chatterton (1842), by
  Robert Browning DLB-32

Essex House Press DLB-112

Estes, Eleanor 1906-1988 . . . . DLB-22

Eszterhas, Joe 1944- DLB-185

Estes and Lauriat DLB-49

Etherege, George 1636-circa 1692 . . . . DLB-80

Ethridge, Mark, Sr. 1896-1981 . . . . . DLB-127

Ets, Marie Hall 1893- DLB-22

Etter, David 1928- DLB-105

Ettner, Johann Christoph
  1654-1724 . . . . DLB-168

Eudora Welty: Eye of the Storyteller Y-87

Eugene O'Neill Memorial Theater
  Center DLB-7

Eugene O'Neill's Letters: A Review Y-88

Eupolemius
  flourished circa 1095 . . . . DLB-148

Euripides circa 484 B.C.-407/406 B.C.
  . . . . DLB-176

Evans, Caradoc 1878-1945 . . . . . . DLB-162

Evans, Charles 1850-1935 . . . . DLB-187

Evans, Donald 1884-1921 . . . . DLB-54

Evans, George Henry 1805-1856 . . . . DLB-43

Evans, Hubert 1892-1986 . . . . DLB-92

Evans, Mari 1923- DLB-41

Evans, Mary Ann (see Eliot, George)

Evans, Nathaniel 1742-1767 . . . . . . DLB-31

Evans, Sebastian 1830-1909 . . . . . . DLB-35

Evans, M., and Company DLB-46

Everett, Alexander Hill 1790-1847 . . . . DLB-59

Everett, Edward 1794-1865 . . . . . DLB-1, 59

Everson, R. G. 1903- DLB-88

Everson, William 1912-1994 . . . . . DLB-5, 16

Every Man His Own Poet; or, The
  Inspired Singer's Recipe Book (1877),
  by W. H. Mallock DLB-35

Ewart, Gavin 1916- DLB-40

Ewing, Juliana Horatia
  1841-1885 . . . . DLB-21, 163

The Examiner 1808-1881 . . . . DLB-110

Exley, Frederick
  1929-1992 . . . . DLB-143; Y-81

Experiment in the Novel (1929),
  by John D. Beresford DLB-36

von Eyb, Albrecht 1420-1475 . . . . . DLB-179

"Eyes Across Centuries: Contemporary
  Poetry and 'That Vision Thing,'"
  by Philip Dacey DLB-105

Eyre and Spottiswoode DLB-106

Ezzo ?-after 1065 . . . . DLB-148

F

"F. Scott Fitzgerald: St. Paul's Native Son
  and Distinguished American Writer":
  University of Minnesota Conference,
  29-31 October 1982 . . . . Y-82

Faber, Frederick William
  1814-1863 . . . . DLB-32

Faber and Faber Limited DLB-112

Faccio, Rena (see Aleramo, Sibilla)

Fagundo, Ana María 1938- DLB-134

Fair, Ronald L. 1932- DLB-33

Fairfax, Beatrice (see Manning, Marie)

Fairlie, Gerard 1899-1983 . . . . DLB-77

Fallada, Hans 1893-1947 . . . . DLB-56

Falsifying Hemingway Y-96

Fancher, Betsy 1928- Y-83

Fane, Violet 1843-1905 . . . . DLB-35

Fanfrolico Press DLB-112

Fanning, Katherine 1927 . . . . DLB-127

Fanshawe, Sir Richard
1608-1666 . . . . DLB-126

Fantasy Press Publishers DLB-46

Fante, John 1909-1983 . . . . . DLB-130; Y-83

Al-Farabi circa 870-950 . . . . DLB-115

Farah, Nuruddin 1945- DLB-125

Farber, Norma 1909-1984 . . . . DLB-61

Farigoule, Louis (see Romains, Jules)

Farjeon, Eleanor 1881-1965 . . . . . . DLB-160

Farley, Walter 1920-1989 . . . . DLB-22

Farmer, Penelope 1939- DLB-161

Farmer, Philip José 1918- DLB-8

Farquhar, George circa 1677-1707 . . . DLB-84

Farquharson, Martha (see Finley, Martha)

Farrar, Frederic William
1831-1903 . . . . DLB-163

Farrar and Rinehart. DLB-46

Farrar, Straus and Giroux DLB-46

Farrell, James T.
1904-1979 . . . . . DLB-4, 9, 86; DS-2

Farrell, J. G. 1935-1979 . . . . DLB-14

Fast, Howard 1914- DLB-9

Faulkner and Yoknapatawpha Conference,
Oxford, Mississippi. Y-97

"Faulkner 100—Celebrating the Work," University
of South Carolina, Columbia Y-97

Faulkner, William 1897-1962
. . . . . . DLB-9, 11, 44, 102; DS-2; Y-86

Faulkner, George
[publishing house] DLB-154

Fauset, Jessie Redmon 1882-1961 . . . . DLB-51

Faust, Irvin 1924- DLB-2, 28; Y-80

Fawcett Books. DLB-46

Fawcett, Millicent Garrett 1847-1929 . . DLB-190

Fearing, Kenneth 1902-1961 . . . . DLB-9

Federal Writers' Project. DLB-46

Federman, Raymond 1928- Y-80

Feiffer, Jules 1929- DLB-7, 44

Feinberg, Charles E.
1899-1988 . . . . DLB-187; Y-88

Feind, Barthold 1678-1721. . . . . . . DLB-168

Feinstein, Elaine 1930- DLB-14, 40

Feiss, Paul Louis 1875-1952. . . . . . DLB-187

Feldman, Irving 1928- DLB-169

Felipe, Léon 1884-1968 . . . . DLB-108

Fell, Frederick, Publishers. DLB-46

Felltham, Owen 1602?-1668. . . . DLB-126, 151

Fels, Ludwig 1946- DLB-75

Felton, Cornelius Conway
1807-1862. . . . . DLB-1

Fenn, Harry 1837-1911 . . . . DLB-188

Fennario, David 1947- DLB-60

Fenno, John 1751-1798 . . . . DLB-43

Fenno, R. F., and Company DLB-49

Fenoglio, Beppe 1922-1963 . . . . . . DLB-177

Fenton, Geoffrey 1539?-1608 . . . . . DLB-136

Fenton, James 1949- DLB-40

Ferber, Edna 1885-1968. . . . . DLB-9, 28, 86

Ferdinand, Vallery III (see Salaam, Kalamu ya)

Ferguson, Sir Samuel 1810-1886 . . . . DLB-32

Ferguson, William Scott
1875-1954 . . . . DLB-47

Fergusson, Robert 1750-1774 . . . . . DLB-109

Ferland, Albert 1872-1943 . . . . DLB-92

Ferlinghetti, Lawrence 1919- DLB-5, 16

Fern, Fanny (see Parton, Sara Payson Willis)

Ferrars, Elizabeth 1907- DLB-87

Ferré, Rosario 1942- DLB-145

Ferret, E., and Company. DLB-49

Ferrier, Susan 1782-1854 . . . . DLB-116

Ferrini, Vincent 1913- DLB-48

Ferron, Jacques 1921-1985 . . . . . . DLB-60

Ferron, Madeleine 1922- DLB-53

Ferrucci, Franco 1936- DLB-196

Fetridge and Company DLB-49

Feuchtersleben, Ernst Freiherr von
1806-1849 . . . . DLB-133

Feuchtwanger, Lion 1884-1958 . . . . . DLB-66

Feuerbach, Ludwig 1804-1872. . . . . DLB-133

Feuillet, Octave 1821-1890. . . . . . . DLB-192

Feydeau, Georges 1862-1921 . . . . . DLB-192

Fichte, Johann Gottlieb
1762-1814 . . . . DLB-90

Ficke, Arthur Davison 1883-1945 . . . . DLB-54

Fiction Best-Sellers, 1910-1945 . . . . . DLB-9

Fiction into Film, 1928-1975: A List of Movies
Based on the Works of Authors in
British Novelists, 1930-1959 . . . . . DLB-15

Fiedler, Leslie A. 1917- DLB-28, 67

Field, Edward 1924- DLB-105

Field, Eugene
1850-1895. . . . . DLB-23, 42, 140; DS-13

Field, John 1545?-1588. . . . . DLB-167

Field, Marshall, III 1893-1956. . . . . DLB-127

Field, Marshall, IV 1916-1965 . . . . . DLB-127

Field, Marshall, V 1941- DLB-127

Field, Nathan 1587-1619 or 1620 . . . . DLB-58

Field, Rachel 1894-1942 . . . . DLB-9, 22

A Field Guide to Recent Schools of American
Poetry. Y-86

Fielding, Henry
1707-1754 . . . . DLB-39, 84, 101

Fielding, Sarah 1710-1768. . . . . . . DLB-39

Fields, James Thomas 1817-1881 . . . . DLB-1

Fields, Julia 1938- DLB-41

Fields, W. C. 1880-1946 . . . . DLB-44

Fields, Osgood and Company DLB-49

Fifty Penguin Years. Y-85

Figes, Eva 1932- DLB-14

Figuera, Angela 1902-1984 . . . . . . DLB-108

Filmer, Sir Robert 1586-1653 . . . . . DLB-151

Filson, John circa 1753-1788 . . . . . . DLB-37

Finch, Anne, Countess of Winchilsea
1661-1720 . . . . DLB-95

Finch, Robert 1900- DLB-88

"Finding, Losing, Reclaiming: A Note on My
Poems," by Robert Phillips. DLB-105

Findley, Timothy 1930- DLB-53

Finlay, Ian Hamilton 1925- DLB-40

Finley, Martha 1828-1909. . . . . . . DLB-42

Finn, Elizabeth Anne (McCaul)
1825-1921 . . . . DLB-166

Finney, Jack 1911- DLB-8

Finney, Walter Braden (see Finney, Jack)

Firbank, Ronald 1886-1926. . . . . . . DLB-36

Firmin, Giles 1615-1697. . . . . DLB-24

Fischart, Johann
1546 or 1547-1590 or 1591 . . . . DLB-179

First Edition Library/Collectors'
Reprints, Inc. Y-91

First International F. Scott Fitzgerald
Conference Y-92

First Strauss "Livings" Awarded to Cynthia
Ozick and Raymond Carver
An Interview with Cynthia Ozick
An Interview with Raymond
Carver Y-83

Fischer, Karoline Auguste Fernandine
1764-1842 . . . . DLB-94

Fish, Stanley 1938- DLB-67

Fishacre, Richard 1205-1248. . . . . . DLB-115

Fisher, Clay (see Allen, Henry W.)

Fisher, Dorothy Canfield
1879-1958. . . . . DLB-9, 102

Fisher, Leonard Everett 1924- DLB-61

Fisher, Roy 1930- DLB-40

Fisher, Rudolph 1897-1934 . . . . . DLB-51, 102

Fisher, Sydney George 1856-1927 . . . . DLB-47

Fisher, Vardis 1895-1968. . . . . DLB-9

Fiske, John 1608-1677. . . . . DLB-24

Fiske, John 1842-1901 . . . . DLB-47, 64

Fitch, Thomas circa 1700-1774. . . . . DLB-31

Fitch, William Clyde 1865-1909. . . . . DLB-7

FitzGerald, Edward 1809-1883 . . . . . DLB-32

Fitzgerald, F. Scott 1896-1940
. . . . . DLB-4, 9, 86; Y-81; DS-1, 15, 16

F. Scott Fitzgerald Centenary
Celebrations. Y-96

Fitzgerald, Penelope 1916- DLB-14, 194

Fitzgerald, Robert 1910-1985. . . . . Y-80

Fitzgerald, Thomas 1819-1891 . . . . . DLB-23

Fitzgerald, Zelda Sayre 1900-1948. . . . . Y-84

Fitzhugh, Louise 1928-1974. . . . . . . DLB-52

Fitzhugh, William
circa 1651-1701 . . . . DLB-24

Flagg, James Montgomery 1877-1960. . DLB-188

Flanagan, Thomas 1923- Y-80

Flanner, Hildegarde 1899-1987 . . . . . DLB-48

Flanner, Janet 1892-1978. . . . . DLB-4

Flaubert, Gustave 1821-1880 . . . . . DLB-119

Flavin, Martin 1883-1967 . . . . DLB-9

Fleck, Konrad (flourished circa 1220)
. . . . DLB-138

Flecker, James Elroy 1884-1915 . . . DLB-10, 19

Fleeson, Doris 1901-1970. . . . . DLB-29

Fleißer, Marieluise 1901-1974. . . . DLB-56, 124

Fleming, Ian 1908-1964. . . . . DLB-87

Fleming, Paul 1609-1640. . . . . DLB-164

Fleming, Peter 1907-1971 . . . . DLB-195

The Fleshly School of Poetry and Other
Phenomena of the Day (1872), by Robert
Buchanan DLB-35

The Fleshly School of Poetry: Mr. D. G.
Rossetti (1871), by Thomas Maitland
(Robert Buchanan) DLB-35

Fletcher, Giles, the Elder
1546-1611 . . . . DLB-136

Fletcher, Giles, the Younger
1585 or 1586-1623 . . . . DLB-121

Fletcher, J. S. 1863-1935 . . . . DLB-70

Fletcher, John (see Beaumont, Francis)

Fletcher, John Gould 1886-1950 . . . DLB-4, 45

Fletcher, Phineas 1582-1650 . . . . . DLB-121

Flieg, Helmut (see Heym, Stefan)

Flint, F. S. 1885-1960. . . . . DLB-19

Flint, Timothy 1780-1840. . . . . DLB-73, 186

Florio, John 1553?-1625 . . . . DLB-172

Fo, Dario 1926- Y-97

Foix, J. V. 1893-1987 . . . . DLB-134

Foley, Martha (see Burnett, Whit, and
Martha Foley)

Folger, Henry Clay 1857-1930 . . . . DLB-140

Folio Society DLB-112

Follen, Eliza Lee (Cabot) 1787-1860 . . . DLB-1

Follett, Ken 1949- DLB-87; Y-81

Follett Publishing Company DLB-46

Folsom, John West
[publishing house]. DLB-49

Folz, Hans
between 1435 and 1440-1513. . . . DLB-179

Fontane, Theodor 1819-1898 . . . . . DLB-129

Fonvisin, Denis Ivanovich
1744 or 1745-1792 . . . . DLB-150

Foote, Horton 1916- DLB-26

Foote, Mary Hallock 1847-1938. . DLB-186, 188

Foote, Samuel 1721-1777 . . . . DLB-89

Foote, Shelby 1916- DLB-2, 17

Forbes, Calvin 1945- DLB-41

Forbes, Ester 1891-1967. . . . . DLB-22

Forbes, Rosita 1893?-1967 . . . . . . DLB-195

Forbes and Company. DLB-49

Force, Peter 1790-1868 . . . . DLB-30

Forché, Carolyn 1950- DLB-5, 193

Ford, Charles Henri 1913- DLB-4, 48

Ford, Corey 1902-1969 . . . . DLB-11

Ford, Ford Madox
1873-1939 . . . . DLB-34, 98, 162

Ford, Jesse Hill 1928- DLB-6

Ford, John 1586-? DLB-58

Ford, R. A. D. 1915- DLB-88

Ford, Worthington C. 1858-1941 . . . . DLB-47

Ford, J. B., and Company DLB-49

Fords, Howard, and Hulbert. DLB-49

Foreman, Carl 1914-1984. . . . . DLB-26

Forester, C. S. 1899-1966 . . . . DLB-191

Forester, Frank (see Herbert, Henry William)

"Foreword to *Ludwig of Bavaria*," by
Robert Peters DLB-105

Forman, Harry Buxton 1842-1917 . . . DLB-184

Fornés, María Irene 1930- DLB-7

Forrest, Leon 1937- DLB-33

Forster, E. M. 1879-1970
. . . . DLB-34, 98, 162, 178, 195; DS-10

Forster, Georg 1754-1794 . . . . DLB-94

Forster, John 1812-1876 . . . . DLB-144

Forster, Margaret 1938- DLB-155

Forsyth, Frederick 1938- DLB-87

Forten, Charlotte L. 1837-1914. . . . . DLB-50

Fortini, Franco 1917- DLB-128

Fortune, T. Thomas 1856-1928 . . . . DLB-23

Fosdick, Charles Austin
1842-1915 . . . . DLB-42

Foster, Genevieve 1893-1979 . . . . . . DLB-61

Foster, Hannah Webster
1758-1840 . . . . DLB-37

Foster, John 1648-1681 . . . . DLB-24

Foster, Michael 1904-1956 . . . . DLB-9

Foster, Myles Birket 1825-1899 . . . . DLB-184

Foulis, Robert and Andrew / R. and A.
[publishing house] DLB-154

Fouqué, Caroline de la Motte
1774-1831 . . . . DLB-90

Fouqué, Friedrich de la Motte
1777-1843 . . . . DLB-90

Four Essays on the Beat Generation,
by John Clellon Holmes. DLB-16

Four Seas Company DLB-46

Four Winds Press. DLB-46

Fournier, Henri Alban (see Alain-Fournier)

Fowler and Wells Company DLB-49

Fowles, John 1926- DLB-14, 139

Fox, John, Jr. 1862 or 1863-1919. DLB-9; DS-13

Fox, Paula 1923- DLB-52

Fox, Richard Kyle 1846-1922 . . . . . DLB-79

Fox, William Price 1926- DLB-2; Y-81

Fox, Richard K.
[publishing house]. DLB-49

Foxe, John 1517-1587 . . . . DLB-132

Fraenkel, Michael 1896-1957. . . . . . DLB-4

France, Anatole 1844-1924 . . . . . DLB-123

France, Richard 1938- DLB-7

Francis, Convers 1795-1863 . . . . . . DLB-1

Francis, Dick 1920- DLB-87

Francis, Jeffrey, Lord 1773-1850 . . . . DLB-107

Francis, C. S. [publishing house]. DLB-49

François 1863-1910 . . . . DLB-92

François, Louise von 1817-1893 . . . . DLB-129

Franck, Sebastian 1499-1542. . . . . . DLB-179

Francke, Kuno 1855-1930. . . . . . . DLB-71

Frank, Bruno 1887-1945. . . . . DLB-118

Frank, Leonhard 1882-1961. . . . DLB-56, 118

Frank, Melvin (see Panama, Norman)

Frank, Waldo 1889-1967 . . . . . . DLB-9, 63

Franken, Rose 1895?-1988 . . . . Y-84

Franklin, Benjamin
1706-1790. . . . . . . DLB-24, 43, 73, 183

Franklin, James 1697-1735 . . . . . . DLB-43

Franklin Library. DLB-46

Frantz, Ralph Jules 1902-1979 . . . . . DLB-4

Franzos, Karl Emil 1848-1904. . . . . DLB-129

Fraser, G. S. 1915-1980. . . . . DLB-27

Fraser, Kathleen 1935- DLB-169

Frattini, Alberto 1922- DLB-128

Frau Ava ?-1127 . . . . DLB-148

Frayn, Michael 1933- DLB-13, 14, 194

Frederic, Harold
1856-1898. . . . . . . DLB-12, 23; DS-13

Freeling, Nicolas 1927- DLB-87

Freeman, Douglas Southall
1886-1953 . . . . DLB-17; DS-17

Freeman, Legh Richmond
1842-1915 . . . . DLB-23

Freeman, Mary E. Wilkins
1852-1930 . . . . DLB-12, 78

Freeman, R. Austin 1862-1943 . . . . . DLB-70

Freidank circa 117¿-circa 1233 . . . . . DLB-138

Freiligrath, Ferdinand 1810-1876 . . . . DLB-133

Frémont, John Charles 1813-1890 . . . DLB-186

Frémont, John Charles 1813-1890
and Frémont, Jessie Benton
1834-1902 . . . . DLB-183

French, Alice 1850-1934 . . . . . DLB-74; DS-13

French, David 1939- DLB-53

French, Evangeline 1869-1960 . . . . . DLB-195

French, Francesca 1871-1960 . . . . . . DLB-195

French, James [publishing house] DLB-49

French, Samuel [publishing house] DLB-49

Samuel French, Limited DLB-106

Freneau, Philip 1752-1832 . . . . . DLB-37, 43

Freni, Melo 1934- DLB-128

Freshfield, Douglas W.
1845-1934 . . . . DLB-174

Freytag, Gustav 1816-1895 . . . . . . DLB-129

Fried, Erich 1921-1988 . . . . DLB-85

Friedman, Bruce Jay 1930- DLB-2, 28

Friedrich von Hausen
circa 1171-1190 . . . . DLB-138

Friel, Brian 1929- DLB-13

Friend, Krebs 1895?-1967? DLB-4

Fries, Fritz Rudolf 1935- DLB-75

Fringe and Alternative Theater
in Great Britain DLB-13

Frisch, Max 1911-1991 . . . . . . DLB-69, 124

Frischlin, Nicodemus 1547-1590 . . . . DLB-179

Frischmuth, Barbara 1941- DLB-85

Fritz, Jean 1915- DLB-52

Fromentin, Eugene 1820-1876 . . . . . DLB-123

From *The Gay Science*, by
E. S. Dallas DLB-21

Frost, A. B. 1851-1928 . . . . . DLB-188; DS-13

Frost, Robert 1874-1963 . . . . . DLB-54; DS-7

Frothingham, Octavius Brooks
1822-1895 . . . . DLB-1

Froude, James Anthony
1818-1894 . . . . DLB-18, 57, 144

Fry, Christopher 1907- DLB-13

Fry, Roger 1866-1934 . . . . DS-10

Frye, Northrop 1912-1991 . . . . . DLB-67, 68

Fuchs, Daniel
1909-1993 . . . . DLB-9, 26, 28; Y-93

Fuentes, Carlos 1928- DLB-113

Fuertes, Gloria 1918- DLB-108

The Fugitives and the Agrarians:
The First Exhibition Y-85

Fulbecke, William 1560-1603? DLB-172

Fuller, Charles H., Jr. 1939- DLB-38

Fuller, Henry Blake 1857-1929 . . . . . DLB-12

Fuller, John 1937- DLB-40

Fuller, Margaret (see Fuller, Sarah Margaret,
Marchesa D'Ossoli)

Fuller, Roy 1912-1991 . . . . . . DLB-15, 20

Fuller, Samuel 1912- DLB-26

Fuller, Sarah Margaret, Marchesa
D'Ossoli 1810-1850 . . . DLB-1, 59, 73, 183

Fuller, Thomas 1608-1661 . . . . DLB-151

Fullerton, Hugh 1873-1945 . . . . . . DLB-171

Fulton, Alice 1952- DLB-193

Fulton, Len 1934- Y-86

Fulton, Robin 1937- DLB-40

Furbank, P. N. 1920- DLB-155

Furman, Laura 1945- Y-86

Furness, Horace Howard
1833-1912 . . . . DLB-64

Furness, William Henry 1802-1896 . . . . DLB-1

Furnivall, Frederick James
1825-1910 . . . . DLB-184

Furthman, Jules 1888-1966 . . . . DLB-26

Furui, Yoshikichi 1937- DLB-182

Futabatei, Shimei (Hasegawa Tatsunosuke)
1864-1909 . . . . DLB-180

The Future of the Novel (1899), by
Henry James DLB-18

Fyleman, Rose 1877-1957 . . . . DLB-160

G

The G. Ross Roy Scottish Poetry
Collection at the University of
South Carolina Y-89

Gadda, Carlo Emilio 1893-1973 . . . . DLB-177

Gaddis, William 1922- DLB-2

Gág, Wanda 1893-1946 . . . . DLB-22

Gagarin, Ivan Sergeevich 1814-1882 . . DLB-198

Gagnon, Madeleine 1938- DLB-60

Gaine, Hugh 1726-1807 . . . . DLB-43

Gaine, Hugh [publishing house] DLB-49

Gaines, Ernest J.
1933- DLB-2, 33, 152; Y-80

Gaiser, Gerd 1908-1976 . . . . DLB-69

Galarza, Ernesto 1905-1984 . . . . . . DLB-122

Galaxy Science Fiction Novels DLB-46

Gale, Zona 1874-1938 . . . . DLB-9, 78

Galen of Pergamon 129-after 210 . . . DLB-176

Gall, Louise von 1815-1855 . . . . . . DLB-133

Gallagher, Tess 1943- DLB-120

Gallagher, Wes 1911- DLB-127

Gallagher, William Davis
1808-1894 . . . . DLB-73

Gallant, Mavis 1922- DLB-53

Gallico, Paul 1897-1976 . . . . . . DLB-9, 171

Gallup, Donald 1913- DLB-187

Galsworthy, John
1867-1933 . . . DLB-10, 34, 98, 162; DS-16

Galt, John 1779-1839 . . . . DLB-99, 116

Galton, Sir Francis 1822-1911 . . . . . DLB-166

Galvin, Brendan 1938- DLB-5

Gambit DLB-46

Gamboa, Reymundo 1948- DLB-122

Gammer Gurton's Needle DLB-62

Gan, Elena Andreevna (Zeneida R-va)
1814-1842 . . . . DLB-198

Gannett, Frank E. 1876-1957 . . . . . . DLB-29

Gaos, Vicente 1919-1980 . . . . DLB-134

García, Lionel G. 1935- DLB-82

García Lorca, Federico
1898-1936 . . . . DLB-108

García Márquez, Gabriel
1928- DLB-113; Y-82

Gardam, Jane 1928- DLB-14, 161

Garden, Alexander
circa 1685-1756 . . . . DLB-31

Gardiner, Margaret Power Farmer (see
Blessington, Marguerite, Countess of)

Gardner, John 1933-1982 . . . . . . DLB-2; Y-82

Garfield, Leon 1921- DLB-161

Garis, Howard R. 1873-1962 . . . . . . DLB-22

Garland, Hamlin
1860-1940 . . . . . . DLB-12, 71, 78, 186

Garneau, Francis-Xavier
1809-1866 . . . . DLB-99

Garneau, Hector de Saint-Denys
1912-1943 . . . . DLB-88

Garneau, Michel 1939- DLB-53

Garner, Alan 1934- DLB-161

Garner, Hugh 1913-1979 . . . . DLB-68

Garnett, David 1892-1981 . . . . DLB-34

Garnett, Eve 1900-1991 . . . . DLB-160

Garnett, Richard 1835-1906 . . . . . . DLB-184

Garrard, Lewis H. 1829-1887 . . . . . DLB-186

Garraty, John A. 1920- DLB-17

Garrett, George
1929- DLB-2, 5, 130, 152; Y-83

Garrett, John Work 1872-1942 . . . . . DLB-187

Garrick, David 1717-1779 . . . . DLB-84

Garrison, William Lloyd
1805-1879 . . . . DLB-1, 43

Garro, Elena 1920- DLB-145

Garth, Samuel 1661-1719 . . . . DLB-95

Garve, Andrew 1908- DLB-87

Gary, Romain 1914-1980 . . . . DLB-83

Gascoigne, George 1539?-1577 . . . . . DLB-136

Gascoyne, David 1916- DLB-20

Gaskell, Elizabeth Cleghorn
1810-1865 . . . . DLB-21, 144, 159

Gaspey, Thomas 1788-1871 . . . . . . DLB-116

Gass, William Howard 1924- DLB-2

Gates, Doris 1901- DLB-22

Gates, Henry Louis, Jr. 1950- DLB-67

Gates, Lewis E. 1860-1924 . . . . DLB-71

Gatto, Alfonso 1909-1976 . . . . DLB-114

Gaunt, Mary 1861-1942 . . . . DLB-174

Gautier, Théophile 1811-1872 . . . . . DLB-119

Gauvreau, Claude 1925-1971 . . . . . . DLB-88

The Gawain-Poet
flourished circa 1350-1400 . . . . . DLB-146

Gay, Ebenezer 1696-1787 . . . . DLB-24

Gay, John 1685-1732 . . . . DLB-84, 95

The Gay Science (1866), by E. S. Dallas [excerpt]
. . . . DLB-21

Gayarré, Charles E. A. 1805-1895 . . . . DLB-30

Gaylord, Edward King
1873-1974 . . . . DLB-127

Gaylord, Edward Lewis 1919- DLB-127

Gaylord, Charles
[publishing house] DLB-49

Geddes, Gary 1940- DLB-60

Geddes, Virgil 1897- DLB-4

Gedeon (Georgii Andreevich Krinovsky)
circa 1730-1763 . . . . DLB-150

Geibel, Emanuel 1815-1884 . . . . . . DLB-129

Geiogamah, Hanay 1945- DLB-175

Geis, Bernard, Associates DLB-46

Geisel, Theodor Seuss
1904-1991 . . . . DLB-61; Y-91

Gelb, Arthur 1924- DLB-103

Gelb, Barbara 1926- DLB-103

Gelber, Jack 1932- DLB-7

Gelinas, Gratien 1909- DLB-88

Gellert, Christian Fürchtegott
1715-1769 . . . . DLB-97

Gellhorn, Martha 1908- Y-82

Gems, Pam 1925- DLB-13

A General Idea of the College of Mirania (1753),
by William Smith [excerpts] DLB-31

Genet, Jean 1910-1986 . . . . . . DLB-72; Y-86

Genevoix, Maurice 1890-1980 . . . . . DLB-65

Genovese, Eugene D. 1930- DLB-17

Gent, Peter 1942- Y-82

Geoffrey of Monmouth
circa 1100-1155 . . . . DLB-146

George, Henry 1839-1897 . . . . DLB-23

George, Jean Craighead 1919- DLB-52

George, W. L. 1882-1926 . . . . DLB-197

Georgslied 896? DLB-148

Gerhardie, William 1895-1977 . . . . . DLB-36

Gerhardt, Paul 1607-1676 . . . . DLB-164

Gérin, Winifred 1901-1981 . . . . DLB-155

Gérin-Lajoie, Antoine 1824-1882 . . . . DLB-99

German Drama 800-1280 . . . . DLB-138

German Drama from Naturalism
to Fascism: 1889-1933 . . . . DLB-118

German Literature and Culture from
Charlemagne to the Early Courtly
Period DLB-148

German Radio Play, The DLB-124

German Transformation from the Baroque
to the Enlightenment, The DLB-97

The Germanic Epic and Old English Heroic
Poetry: Widseth, Waldere, and The
Fight at Finnsburg DLB-146

Germanophilism, by Hans Kohn DLB-66

Gernsback, Hugo 1884-1967 . . . . DLB-8, 137

Gerould, Katharine Fullerton
1879-1944 . . . . DLB-78

Gerrish, Samuel [publishing house] . . . DLB-49

Gerrold, David 1944- DLB-8

The Ira Gershwin Centenary Y-96

Gersonides 1288-1344 . . . . DLB-115

Gerstäcker, Friedrich 1816-1872 . . . . DLB-129

Gerstenberg, Heinrich Wilhelm von
1737-1823 . . . . DLB-97

Gervinus, Georg Gottfried
1805-1871 . . . . DLB-133

Geßner, Salomon 1730-1788 . . . . . . DLB-97

Geston, Mark S. 1946- DLB-8

"Getting Started: Accepting the Regions You
Own—or Which Own You," by Walter
McDonald DLB-105

Al-Ghazali 1058-1111 . . . . DLB-115

Gibbings, Robert 1889-1958 . . . . . . DLB-195

Gibbon, Edward 1737-1794 . . . . . . DLB-104

Gibbon, John Murray 1875-1952 . . . . DLB-92

Gibbon, Lewis Grassic (see Mitchell,
James Leslie)

Gibbons, Floyd 1887-1939 . . . . DLB-25

Gibbons, Reginald 1947- DLB-120

Gibbons, William ?-? DLB-73

Gibson, Charles Dana 1867-1944 . . . . . DS-13

Gibson, Charles Dana
1867-1944 . . . . DLB-188; DS-13

Gibson, Graeme 1934- DLB-53

Gibson, Margaret 1944- DLB-120

Gibson, Margaret Dunlop
1843-1920 . . . . DLB-174

Gibson, Wilfrid 1878-1962 . . . . DLB-19

Gibson, William 1914- DLB-7

Gide, André 1869-1951 . . . . DLB-65

Giguère, Diane 1937- DLB-53

Giguère, Roland 1929- DLB-60

Gil de Biedma, Jaime 1929-1990 . . . . DLB-108

Gil-Albert, Juan 1906- DLB-134

Gilbert, Anthony 1899-1973 . . . . . . DLB-77

Gilbert, Michael 1912- DLB-87

Gilbert, Sandra M. 1936- DLB-120

Gilbert, Sir Humphrey
1537-1583 . . . . DLB-136

Gilchrist, Alexander
1828-1861 . . . . DLB-144

Gilchrist, Ellen 1935- DLB-130

Gilder, Jeannette L. 1849-1916 . . . . . DLB-79

Gilder, Richard Watson
1844-1909 . . . . DLB-64, 79

Gildersleeve, Basil 1831-1924 . . . . . . DLB-71

Giles, Henry 1809-1882 . . . . DLB-64

Giles of Rome circa 1243-1316 . . . . . DLB-115

Gilfillan, George 1813-1878 . . . . . . DLB-144

Gill, Eric 1882-1940 . . . . DLB-98

Gill, William F., Company DLB-49

Gillespie, A. Lincoln, Jr.
1895-1950 . . . . DLB-4

Gilliam, Florence ?-? DLB-4

Gilliatt, Penelope 1932-1993 . . . . . . DLB-14

Gillott, Jacky 1939-1980 . . . . DLB-14

Gilman, Caroline H. 1794-1888 . . . . DLB-3, 73

Gilman, W. and J.
[publishing house] DLB-49

Gilmer, Elizabeth Meriwether
1861-1951 . . . . DLB-29

Gilmer, Francis Walker
1790-1826 . . . . DLB-37

Gilroy, Frank D. 1925- DLB-7

Gimferrer, Pere (Pedro) 1945- DLB-134

Gingrich, Arnold 1903-1976 . . . . . . DLB-137

Ginsberg, Allen 1926- DLB-5, 16, 169

Ginzburg, Natalia 1916-1991 . . . . . . DLB-177

Ginzkey, Franz Karl 1871-1963 . . . . . DLB-81

Gioia, Dana 1950- DLB-120

Giono, Jean 1895-1970 . . . . DLB-72

Giotti, Virgilio 1885-1957 . . . . DLB-114

Giovanni, Nikki 1943- DLB-5, 41

Gipson, Lawrence Henry
1880-1971 . . . . DLB-17

Girard, Rodolphe 1879-1956 . . . . . . DLB-92

Giraudoux, Jean 1882-1944 . . . . . . DLB-65

Gissing, George 1857-1903 . . DLB-18, 135, 184

Giudici, Giovanni 1924- DLB-128

Giuliani, Alfredo 1924- DLB-128

Glackens, William J. 1870-1938 . . . . DLB-188

Gladstone, William Ewart
1809-1898 . . . . DLB-57, 184

Glaeser, Ernst 1902-1963 . . . . DLB-69

Glancy, Diane 1941- DLB-175

Glanville, Brian 1931- DLB-15, 139

Glapthorne, Henry 1610-1643? DLB-58

Glasgow, Ellen 1873-1945 . . . . . . DLB-9, 12

Glasier, Katharine Bruce 1867-1950 . . DLB-190

Glaspell, Susan 1876-1948 . . . . . DLB-7, 9, 78

Glass, Montague 1877-1934 . . . . DLB-11

The Glass Key and Other Dashiell Hammett
Mysteries Y-96

Glassco, John 1909-1981 . . . . DLB-68

Glauser, Friedrich 1896-1938 . . . . . . DLB-56

F. Gleason's Publishing Hall DLB-49

Gleim, Johann Wilhelm Ludwig
1719-1803 . . . . DLB-97

Glendinning, Victoria 1937- DLB-155

Glover, Richard 1712-1785 . . . . DLB-95

Glück, Louise 1943- DLB-5

Glyn, Elinor 1864-1943 . . . . DLB-153

Gobineau, Joseph-Arthur de
1816-1882 . . . . DLB-123

Godbout, Jacques 1933- DLB-53

Goddard, Morrill 1865-1937 . . . . . . DLB-25

Goddard, William 1740-1817 . . . . . . DLB-43

Godden, Rumer 1907- DLB-161

Godey, Louis A. 1804-1878 . . . . DLB-73

Godey and McMichael DLB-49

Godfrey, Dave 1938- DLB-60

Godfrey, Thomas 1736-1763 . . . . . . DLB-31

Godine, David R., Publisher DLB-46

Godkin, E. L. 1831-1902 . . . . DLB-79

Godolphin, Sidney 1610-1643 . . . . . DLB-126

Godwin, Gail 1937- DLB-6

Godwin, Mary Jane Clairmont
1766-1841 . . . . DLB-163

Godwin, Parke 1816-1904 . . . . . . DLB-3, 64

Godwin, William
1756-1836 . . . . DLB-39, 104, 142, 158, 163

Godwin, M. J., and Company DLB-154

Goering, Reinhard 1887-1936 . . . . . DLB-118

Goes, Albrecht 1908- DLB-69

Goethe, Johann Wolfgang von
1749-1832 . . . . DLB-94

Goetz, Curt 1888-1960 . . . . DLB-124

Goffe, Thomas circa 1592-1629 . . . . . DLB-58

Goffstein, M. B. 1940- DLB-61

Gogarty, Oliver St. John
1878-1957 . . . . DLB-15, 19

Gogol, Nikolai Vasil'evich
1809-1852 . . . . DLB-198

Goines, Donald 1937-1974 . . . . DLB-33

Gold, Herbert 1924- DLB-2; Y-81

Gold, Michael 1893-1967 . . . . . . DLB-9, 28

Goldbarth, Albert 1948- DLB-120

Goldberg, Dick 1947- DLB-7

Golden Cockerel Press DLB-112

Golding, Arthur 1536-1606 . . . . . . DLB-136

Golding, Louis 1895-1958 . . . . DLB-195

Golding, William 1911-1993 . DLB-15, 100; Y-83

Goldman, William 1931- DLB-44

Goldring, Douglas 1887-1960 . . . . . DLB-197

Goldsmith, Oliver
1730?-1774 . . . . DLB-39, 89, 104, 109, 142

Goldsmith, Oliver 1794-1861 . . . . . . DLB-99

Goldsmith Publishing Company DLB-46

Goldstein, Richard 1944- DLB-185

Gollancz, Victor, Limited DLB-112

Gómez-Quiñones, Juan 1942- DLB-122

Gomme, Laurence James
[publishing house] DLB-46

Goncourt, Edmond de 1822-1896 . . . DLB-123

Goncourt, Jules de 1830-1870 . . . . DLB-123

Gonzales, Rodolfo "Corky"
1928- DLB-122

González, Angel 1925- DLB-108

Gonzalez, Genaro 1949- DLB-122

Gonzalez, Ray 1952- DLB-122

González de Mireles, Jovita
1899-1983 . . . . DLB-122

González-T., César A. 1931- DLB-82

"The Good, The Not So Good," by
Stephen Dunn DLB-105

Goodbye, Gutenberg? A Lecture at
the New York Public Library,
18 April 1995 . . . . Y-95

Goodison, Lorna 1947- DLB-157

Goodman, Paul 1911-1972 . . . . . . DLB-130

The Goodman Theatre DLB-7

Goodrich, Frances 1891-1984 and
Hackett, Albert 1900- DLB-26

Goodrich, Samuel Griswold
1793-1860 . . . . DLB-1, 42, 73

Goodrich, S. G. [publishing house] . . DLB-49

Goodspeed, C. E., and Company DLB-49

Goodwin, Stephen 1943- Y-82

Googe, Barnabe 1540-1594 . . . . . . DLB-132

Gookin, Daniel 1612-1687 . . . . . . DLB-24

Gordimer, Nadine 1923- Y-91

Gordon, Caroline
1895-1981 . . . . DLB-4, 9, 102; DS-17; Y-81

Gordon, Giles 1940- DLB-14, 139

Gordon, Helen Cameron, Lady Russell
1867-1949 . . . . DLB-195

Gordon, Lyndall 1941- DLB-155

Gordon, Mary 1949- DLB-6; Y-81

Gordone, Charles 1925- DLB-7

Gore, Catherine 1800-1861 . . . . . . DLB-116

Gorey, Edward 1925- DLB-61

Gorgias of Leontini circa 485 B.C.-376 B.C.
. . . . DLB-176

Görres, Joseph 1776-1848 . . . . DLB-90

Gosse, Edmund 1849-1928 . . DLB-57, 144, 184

Gosson, Stephen 1554-1624 . . . . . . DLB-172

Gotlieb, Phyllis 1926- DLB-88

Gottfried von Straßburg
died before 1230 . . . . DLB-138

Gotthelf, Jeremias 1797-1854 . . . . . DLB-133

Gottschalk circa 804/808-869 . . . . . DLB-148

Gottsched, Johann Christoph
1700-1766 . . . . DLB-97

Götz, Johann Nikolaus
1721-1781 . . . . DLB-97

Goudge, Elizabeth 1900-1984 . . . . . DLB-191

Gould, Wallace 1882-1940 . . . . DLB-54

Govoni, Corrado 1884-1965 . . . . . . DLB-114

Gower, John circa 1330-1408 . . . . . DLB-146

Goyen, William 1915-1983 . . . . . DLB-2; Y-83

Goytisolo, José Augustín 1928- DLB-134

Gozzano, Guido 1883-1916 . . . . . . DLB-114

Grabbe, Christian Dietrich
1801-1836 . . . . DLB-133

Gracq, Julien 1910- DLB-83

Grady, Henry W. 1850-1889 . . . . . . DLB-23

Graf, Oskar Maria 1894-1967 . . . . . DLB-56

Graf Rudolf between circa 1170
and circa 1185 . . . . DLB-148

Grafton, Richard
[publishing house] DLB-170

Graham, George Rex
1813-1894 . . . . DLB-73

Graham, Gwethalyn 1913-1965 . . . . . DLB-88

Graham, Jorie 1951- DLB-120

Graham, Katharine 1917- DLB-127

Graham, Lorenz 1902-1989 . . . . . . DLB-76

Graham, Philip 1915-1963 . . . . . . DLB-127

Graham, R. B. Cunninghame
1852-1936 . . . . DLB-98, 135, 174

Graham, Shirley 1896-1977 . . . . . . DLB-76

Graham, Stephen 1884-1975 . . . . . . DLB-195

Graham, W. S. 1918- DLB-20

Graham, William H.
[publishing house] DLB-49

Graham, Winston 1910- DLB-77

Grahame, Kenneth
1859-1932 . . . . DLB-34, 141, 178

Grainger, Martin Allerdale
1874-1941 . . . . DLB-92

Gramatky, Hardie 1907-1979 . . . . . DLB-22

Grand, Sarah 1854-1943 . . . . . DLB-135, 197

Grandbois, Alain 1900-1975 . . . . . . DLB-92

Grange, John circa 1556-? DLB-136

Granich, Irwin (see Gold, Michael)

Granovsky, Timofei Nikolaevich
  1813-1855 . . . . DLB-198

Grant, Duncan 1885-1978 . . . . DS-10

Grant, George 1918-1988 . . . . DLB-88

Grant, George Monro 1835-1902 . . . . DLB-99

Grant, Harry J. 1881-1963 . . . . DLB-29

Grant, James Edward 1905-1966 . . . . . DLB-26

Grass, Günter 1927- DLB-75, 124

Grasty, Charles H. 1863-1924 . . . . . . DLB-25

Grau, Shirley Ann 1929- DLB-2

Graves, John 1920- Y-83

Graves, Richard 1715-1804 . . . . DLB-39

Graves, Robert
  1895-1985 . . . . . DLB-20, 100, 191; Y-85

Gray, Alasdair 1934- DLB-194

Gray, Asa 1810-1888 . . . . DLB-1

Gray, David 1838-1861 . . . . DLB-32

Gray, Simon 1936- DLB-13

Gray, Thomas 1716-1771 . . . . DLB-109

Grayson, William J. 1788-1863 . . . . DLB-3, 64

The Great Bibliographers Series Y-93

The Great War and the Theater, 1914-1918
  [Great Britain] DLB-10

The Great War Exhibition and Symposium at the
  University of South Carolina Y-97

Grech, Nikolai Ivanovich 1787-1867 . . DLB-198

Greeley, Horace 1811-1872 . . . DLB-3, 43, 189

Green, Adolph (see Comden, Betty)

Green, Duff 1791-1875 . . . . DLB-43

Green, Elizabeth Shippen 1871-1954 . . DLB-188

Green, Gerald 1922- DLB-28

Green, Henry 1905-1973 . . . . DLB-15

Green, Jonas 1712-1767 . . . . DLB-31

Green, Joseph 1706-1780 . . . . DLB-31

Green, Julien 1900- DLB-4, 72

Green, Paul 1894-1981 . . . . . DLB-7, 9; Y-81

Green, T. and S.
  [publishing house] DLB-49

Green, Thomas Hill 1836-1882 . . . . . DLB-190

Green, Timothy
  [publishing house] DLB-49

Greenaway, Kate 1846-1901 . . . . . . DLB-141

Greenberg: Publisher DLB-46

Green Tiger Press DLB-46

Greene, Asa 1789-1838 . . . . DLB-11

Greene, Belle da Costa 1883-1950 . . . DLB-187

Greene, Benjamin H.
  [publishing house] DLB-49

Greene, Graham 1904-1991
  . . . DLB-13, 15, 77, 100, 162; Y-85, Y-91

Greene, Robert 1558-1592 . . . . . DLB-62, 167

Greene Jr., Robert Bernard (Bob)
  1947- DLB-185

Greenhow, Robert 1800-1854 . . . . . . DLB-30

Greenlee, William B. 1872-1953 . . . . DLB-187

Greenough, Horatio 1805-1852 . . . . . . DLB-1

Greenwell, Dora 1821-1882 . . . . DLB-35

Greenwillow Books DLB-46

Greenwood, Grace (see Lippincott, Sara Jane
  Clarke)

Greenwood, Walter 1903-1974 . . . DLB-10, 191

Greer, Ben 1948- DLB-6

Greflinger, Georg 1620?-1677 . . . . . DLB-164

Greg, W. R. 1809-1881 . . . . DLB-55

Gregg, Josiah 1806-1850 . . . . . DLB-183, 186

Gregg Press DLB-46

Gregory, Isabella Augusta
  Persse, Lady 1852-1932 . . . . DLB-10

Gregory, Horace 1898-1982 . . . . DLB-48

Gregory of Rimini
  circa 1300-1358 . . . . DLB-115

Gregynog Press DLB-112

Greiffenberg, Catharina Regina von
  1633-1694 . . . . DLB-168

Grenfell, Wilfred Thomason
  1865-1940 . . . . DLB-92

Greve, Felix Paul (see Grove, Frederick Philip)

Greville, Fulke, First Lord Brooke
  1554-1628 . . . . DLB-62, 172

Grey, Sir George, K.C.B.
  1812-1898 . . . . DLB-184

Grey, Lady Jane 1537-1554 . . . . . . DLB-132

Grey Owl 1888-1938 . . . . . . DLB-92; DS-17

Grey, Zane 1872-1939 . . . . DLB-9

Grey Walls Press DLB-112

Grier, Eldon 1917- DLB-88

Grieve, C. M. (see MacDiarmid, Hugh)

Griffin, Bartholomew
  flourished 1596 . . . . DLB-172

Griffin, Gerald 1803-1840 . . . . DLB-159

Griffith, Elizabeth 1727?-1793 . . . DLB-39, 89

Griffith, George 1857-1906 . . . . . . DLB-178

Griffiths, Trevor 1935- DLB-13

Griffiths, Ralph
  [publishing house] DLB-154

Griggs, S. C., and Company DLB-49

Griggs, Sutton Elbert
  1872-1930 . . . . DLB-50

Grignon, Claude-Henri 1894-1976 . . . DLB-68

Grigson, Geoffrey 1905- DLB-27

Grillparzer, Franz 1791-1872 . . . . . DLB-133

Grimald, Nicholas
  circa 1519-circa 1562 . . . . DLB-136

Grimké, Angelina Weld
  1880-1958 . . . . DLB-50, 54

Grimm, Hans 1875-1959 . . . . DLB-66

Grimm, Jacob 1785-1863 . . . . DLB-90

Grimm, Wilhelm 1786-1859 . . . . DLB-90

Grimmelshausen, Johann Jacob Christoffel von
  1621 or 1622-1676 . . . . DLB-168

Grimshaw, Beatrice Ethel
  1871-1953 . . . . DLB-174

Grindal, Edmund
  1519 or 1520-1583 . . . . DLB-132

Griswold, Rufus Wilmot
  1815-1857 . . . . DLB-3, 59

Grosart, Alexander Balloch
  1827-1899 . . . . DLB-184

Gross, Milt 1895-1953 . . . . DLB-11

Grosset and Dunlap DLB-49

Grossman, Allen 1932- DLB-193

Grossman Publishers DLB-46

Grosseteste, Robert
  circa 1160-1253 . . . . DLB-115

Grosvenor, Gilbert H. 1875-1966 . . . DLB-91

Groth, Klaus 1819-1899 . . . . DLB-129

Groulx, Lionel 1878-1967 . . . . DLB-68

Grove, Frederick Philip 1879-1949 . . . DLB-92

Grove Press DLB-46

Grubb, Davis 1919-1980 . . . . DLB-6

Gruelle, Johnny 1880-1938 . . . . DLB-22

von Grumbach, Argula
  1492-after 1563? DLB-179

Grymeston, Elizabeth
  before 1563-before 1604 . . . . . . DLB-136

Gryphius, Andreas 1616-1664 . . . . . DLB-164

Gryphius, Christian 1649-1706 . . . . . DLB-168

Guare, John 1938- DLB-7

Guerra, Tonino 1920- DLB-128

Guest, Barbara 1920- DLB-5, 193

Guèvremont, Germaine
  1893-1968 . . . . DLB-68

Guidacci, Margherita 1921-1992 . . . . DLB-128

Guide to the Archives of Publishers, Journals, and
  Literary Agents in North American Libraries
  . . . . Y-93

Guillén, Jorge 1893-1984 . . . . DLB-108

Guilloux, Louis 1899-1980 . . . . DLB-72

Guilpin, Everard
  circa 1572-after 1608? DLB-136

Guiney, Louise Imogen 1861-1920 . . . DLB-54

Guiterman, Arthur 1871-1943 . . . . . . DLB-11

Günderrode, Caroline von
  1780-1806 . . . . DLB-90

Gundulić, Ivan 1589-1638 . . . . DLB-147

Gunn, Bill 1934-1989 . . . . DLB-38

Gunn, James E. 1923- DLB-8

Gunn, Neil M. 1891-1973 . . . . DLB-15

Gunn, Thom 1929- DLB-27

Gunnars, Kristjana 1948- DLB-60

Günther, Johann Christian
  1695-1723 . . . . DLB-168

Gurik, Robert 1932- DLB-60

Gustafson, Ralph 1909- DLB-88

Gütersloh, Albert Paris 1887-1973 . . . . DLB-81

Guthrie, A. B., Jr. 1901- DLB-6

Guthrie, Ramon 1896-1973 . . . . DLB-4

The Guthrie Theater DLB-7

Guthrie, Thomas Anstey (see Anstey, FC)

Gutzkow, Karl 1811-1878 . . . . DLB-133

Guy, Ray 1939- DLB-60

Guy, Rosa 1925- DLB-33

Guyot, Arnold 1807-1884 . . . . DS-13

Gwynne, Erskine 1898-1948 . . . . . . DLB-4

Gyles, John 1680-1755 . . . . DLB-99

Gysin, Brion 1916- DLB-16

H

H. D. (see Doolittle, Hilda)

Habington, William 1605-1654 . . . . . DLB-126

Hacker, Marilyn 1942- DLB-120

Hackett, Albert (see Goodrich, Frances)

Hacks, Peter 1928- DLB-124

Hadas, Rachel 1948- DLB-120

Hadden, Briton 1898-1929 . . . . DLB-91

Hagedorn, Friedrich von
1708-1754 . . . . DLB-168

Hagelstange, Rudolf 1912-1984 . . . . . DLB-69

Haggard, H. Rider
1856-1925 . . . . . . DLB-70, 156, 174, 178

Haggard, William 1907-1993 . . . . Y-93

Hahn-Hahn, Ida Gräfin von
1805-1880 . . . . DLB-133

Haig-Brown, Roderick 1908-1976 . . . . DLB-88

Haight, Gordon S. 1901-1985 . . . . . DLB-103

Hailey, Arthur 1920- DLB-88; Y-82

Haines, John 1924- DLB-5

Hake, Edward
flourished 1566-1604 . . . . DLB-136

Hake, Thomas Gordon 1809-1895 . . . . DLB-32

Hakluyt, Richard 1552?-1616 . . . . . DLB-136

Halbe, Max 1865-1944 . . . . DLB-118

Haldone, Charlotte 1894-1969 . . . . . DLB-191

Haldane, J. B. S. 1892-1964 . . . . . . DLB-160

Haldeman, Joe 1943- DLB-8

Haldeman-Julius Company DLB-46

Hale, E. J., and Son DLB-49

Hale, Edward Everett
1822-1909 . . . . DLB-1, 42, 74

Hale, Janet Campbell 1946- DLB-175

Hale, Kathleen 1898- DLB-160

Hale, Leo Thomas (see Ebon)

Hale, Lucretia Peabody
1820-1900 . . . . DLB-42

Hale, Nancy
1908-1988 . . . . DLB-86; DS-17; Y-80, Y-88

Hale, Sarah Josepha (Buell)
1788-1879 . . . . DLB-1, 42, 73

Hales, John 1584-1656 . . . . DLB-151

Halévy, Ludovic 1834-1908 . . . . . . DLB-192

Haley, Alex 1921-1992 . . . . DLB-38

Haliburton, Thomas Chandler
1796-1865 . . . . DLB-11, 99

Hall, Anna Maria 1800-1881 . . . . . DLB-159

Hall, Donald 1928- DLB-5

Hall, Edward 1497-1547 . . . . DLB-132

Hall, James 1793-1868 . . . . DLB-73, 74

Hall, Joseph 1574-1656 . . . . . DLB-121, 151

Hall, Radclyffe 1880-1943 . . . . DLB-191

Hall, Samuel [publishing house] DLB-49

Hallam, Arthur Henry 1811-1833 . . . . DLB-32

Halleck, Fitz-Greene 1790-1867 . . . . . DLB-3

Haller, Albrecht von 1708-1777 . . . . DLB-168

Halliwell-Phillipps, James Orchard
1820-1889 . . . . DLB-184

Hallmann, Johann Christian
1640-1704 or 1716? DLB-168

Hallmark Editions DLB-46

Halper, Albert 1904-1984 . . . . DLB-9

Halperin, John William 1941- DLB-111

Halstead, Murat 1829-1908 . . . . . . DLB-23

Hamann, Johann Georg 1730-1788 . . . DLB-97

Hamburger, Michael 1924- DLB-27

Hamilton, Alexander 1712-1756 . . . . DLB-31

Hamilton, Alexander 1755?-1804 . . . . DLB-37

Hamilton, Cicely 1872-1952 . . . DLB-10, 197

Hamilton, Edmond 1904-1977 . . . . . DLB-8

Hamilton, Elizabeth 1758-1816 . . . DLB-116, 158

Hamilton, Gail (see Corcoran, Barbara)

Hamilton, Ian 1938- DLB-40, 155

Hamilton, Mary Agnes 1884-1962 . . . DLB-197

Hamilton, Patrick 1904-1962 . . . . DLB-10, 191

Hamilton, Virginia 1936- DLB-33, 52

Hamilton, Hamish, Limited DLB-112

Hammett, Dashiell 1894-1961 . . . . . DS-6

Dashiell Hammett:
An Appeal in *TAC* Y-91

Hammon, Jupiter 1711-died between
1790 and 1806 . . . . DLB-31, 50

Hammond, John ?-1663 . . . . DLB-24

Hamner, Earl 1923- DLB-6

Hampson, John 1901-1955 . . . . . . DLB-191

Hampton, Christopher 1946- DLB-13

Handel-Mazzetti, Enrica von
1871-1955 . . . . DLB-81

Handke, Peter 1942- DLB-85, 124

Handlin, Oscar 1915- DLB-17

Hankin, St. John 1869-1909 . . . . . . DLB-10

Hanley, Clifford 1922- DLB-14

Hanley, James 1901-1985 . . . . DLB-191

Hannah, Barry 1942- DLB-6

Hannay, James 1827-1873 . . . . . . DLB-21

Hansberry, Lorraine 1930-1965 . . . . DLB-7, 38

Hapgood, Norman 1868-1937 . . . . . DLB-91

Happel, Eberhard Werner
1647-1690 . . . . DLB-168

Harcourt Brace Jovanovich DLB-46

Hardenberg, Friedrich von (see Novalis)

Harding, Walter 1917- DLB-111

Hardwick, Elizabeth 1916- DLB-6

Hardy, Thomas 1840-1928 . . . . DLB-18, 19, 135

Hare, Cyril 1900-1958 . . . . DLB-77

Hare, David 1947- DLB-13

Hargrove, Marion 1919- DLB-11

Häring, Georg Wilhelm Heinrich (see Alexis,
Willibald)

Harington, Donald 1935- DLB-152

Harington, Sir John 1560-1612 . . . . DLB-136

Harjo, Joy 1951- DLB-120, 175

Harkness, Margaret (John Law)
1854-1923 . . . . DLB-197

Harlow, Robert 1923- DLB-60

Harman, Thomas
flourished 1566-1573 . . . . DLB-136

Harness, Charles L. 1915- DLB-8

Harnett, Cynthia 1893-1981 . . . . . DLB-161

Harper, Fletcher 1806-1877 . . . . . . DLB-79

Harper, Frances Ellen Watkins
1825-1911 . . . . DLB-50

Harper, Michael S. 1938- DLB-41

Harper and Brothers DLB-49

Harraden, Beatrice 1864-1943 . . . . . DLB-153

Harrap, George G., and Company
Limited DLB-112

Harriot, Thomas 1560-1621 . . . . . . DLB-136

Harris, Benjamin ?-circa 1720 . . . . DLB-42, 43

Harris, Christie 1907- DLB-88

Harris, Frank 1856-1931 . . . . . DLB-156, 197

Harris, George Washington
1814-1869 . . . . DLB-3, 11

Harris, Joel Chandler
1848-1908 . . . . . DLB-11, 23, 42, 78, 91

Harris, Mark 1922- DLB-2; Y-80

Harris, Wilson 1921- DLB-117

Harrison, Charles Yale
1898-1954 . . . . DLB-68

Harrison, Frederic 1831-1923 . . . . DLB-57, 190

Harrison, Harry 1925- DLB-8

Harrison, Jim 1937- Y-82

Harrison, Mary St. Leger Kingsley
(see Malet, Lucas)

Harrison, Paul Carter 1936- DLB-38

Harrison, Susan Frances
1859-1935 . . . . DLB-99

Harrison, Tony 1937- DLB-40

Harrison, William 1535-1593 . . . . . DLB-136

Harrison, James P., Company DLB-49

Harrisse, Henry 1829-1910 . . . . . . DLB-47

Harryman, Carla 1952- DLB-193

Harsdörffer, Georg Philipp
1607-1658 . . . . DLB-164

Harsent, David 1942- DLB-40

Hart, Albert Bushnell 1854-1943 . . . . DLB-17

Hart, Julia Catherine 1796-1867 . . . . DLB-99

The Lorenz Hart Centenary Y-95

Hart, Moss 1904-1961 . . . . DLB-7

Hart, Oliver 1723-1795 . . . . DLB-31

Hart-Davis, Rupert, Limited DLB-112

Harte, Bret
1836-1902 . . . . . DLB-12, 64, 74, 79, 186

Harte, Edward Holmead 1922- DLB-127

Harte, Houston Harriman 1927- . . . DLB-127

Hartlaub, Felix 1913-1945 . . . . DLB-56

Hartleben, Otto Erich
1864-1905 . . . . DLB-118

Hartley, L. P. 1895-1972 . . . . . DLB-15, 139

Hartley, Marsden 1877-1943 . . . . . . DLB-54

Hartling, Peter 1933- DLB-75

Hartman, Geoffrey H. 1929- DLB-67

Hartmann, Sadakichi 1867-1944 . . . . DLB-54

Hartmann von Aue
circa 1160-circa 1205 . . . . DLB-138

Harvey, Gabriel 1550?-1631 . . . . . . DLB-167

Harvey, Jean-Charles 1891-1967 . . . . DLB-88

Harvill Press Limited DLB-112

Harwood, Lee 1939- DLB-40

Harwood, Ronald 1934- DLB-13

Haskins, Charles Homer
1870-1937 . . . . DLB-47

Hass, Robert 1941- DLB-105

The Hatch-Billops Collection DLB-76

Hathaway, William 1944- DLB-120

Hauff, Wilhelm 1802-1827 . . . . DLB-90

A Haughty and Proud Generation (1922),
by Ford Madox Hueffer DLB-36

Haugwitz, August Adolph von
1647-1706 . . . . DLB-168

Hauptmann, Carl
1858-1921 . . . . DLB-66, 118

Hauptmann, Gerhart
1862-1946 . . . . DLB-66, 118

Hauser, Marianne 1910- Y-83

Hawes, Stephen
1475?-before 1529 . . . . DLB-132

Hawker, Robert Stephen
1803-1875 . . . . DLB-32

Hawkes, John 1925- DLB-2, 7; Y-80

Hawkesworth, John 1720-1773 . . . . DLB-142

Hawkins, Sir Anthony Hope (see Hope, Anthony)

Hawkins, Sir John
1719-1789 . . . . DLB-104, 142

Hawkins, Walter Everette 1883-? DLB-50

Hawthorne, Nathaniel
1804-1864 . . . . DLB-1, 74, 183

Hawthorne, Nathaniel 1804-1864 and
Hawthorne, Sophia Peabody
1809-1871 . . . . DLB-183

Hay, John 1835-1905 . . . . . DLB-12, 47, 189

Hayashi, Fumiko 1903-1951 . . . . . . DLB-180

Haycraft, Anna Margaret (see Ellis, Alice Thomas)

Hayden, Robert 1913-1980 . . . . . DLB-5, 76

Haydon, Benjamin Robert
1786-1846 . . . . DLB-110

Hayes, John Michael 1919- DLB-26

Hayley, William 1745-1820 . . . . DLB-93, 142

Haym, Rudolf 1821-1901 . . . . DLB-129

Hayman, Robert 1575-1629 . . . . . . DLB-99

Hayman, Ronald 1932- DLB-155

Hayne, Paul Hamilton
1830-1886 . . . . DLB-3, 64, 79

Hays, Mary 1760-1843 . . . . . DLB-142, 158

Haywood, Eliza 1693?-1756 . . . . . . DLB-39

Hazard, Willis P. [publishing house] DLB-49

Hazlitt, William 1778-1830 . . . . DLB-110, 158

Hazzard, Shirley 1931- Y-82

Head, Bessie 1937-1986 . . . . DLB-117

Headley, Joel T.
1813-1897 . . . . DLB-30, 183; DS-13

Heaney, Seamus 1939- DLB-40; Y-95

Heard, Nathan C. 1936- DLB-33

Hearn, Lafcadio 1850-1904 . . . DLB-12, 78, 189

Hearne, John 1926- DLB-117

Hearne, Samuel 1745-1792 . . . . . . DLB-99

Hearst, William Randolph
1863-1951 . . . . DLB-25

Hearst, William Randolph, Jr
1908-1993 . . . . DLB-127

Heartman, Charles Frederick
1883-1953 . . . . DLB-187

Heath, Catherine 1924- DLB-14

Heath, Roy A. K. 1926- DLB-117

Heath-Stubbs, John 1918- DLB-27

Heavysege, Charles 1816-1876 . . . . . DLB-99

Hebbel, Friedrich 1813-1863 . . . . . . DLB-129

Hebel, Johann Peter 1760-1826 . . . . . DLB-90

Heber, Richard 1774-1833 . . . . . . DLB-184

Hébert, Anne 1916- DLB-68

Hébert, Jacques 1923- DLB-53

Hecht, Anthony 1923- DLB-5, 169

Hecht, Ben 1894-1964
. . . . DLB-7, 9, 25, 26, 28, 86

Hecker, Isaac Thomas 1819-1888 . . . . DLB-1

Hedge, Frederic Henry
1805-1890 . . . . DLB-1, 59

Hefner, Hugh M. 1926- DLB-137

Hegel, Georg Wilhelm Friedrich
1770-1831 . . . . DLB-90

Heidish, Marcy 1947- Y-82

Heißenbüttel 1921- DLB-75

Hein, Christoph 1944- DLB-124

Heine, Heinrich 1797-1856 . . . . . . DLB-90

Heinemann, Larry 1944- DS-9

Heinemann, William, Limited DLB-112

Heinlein, Robert A. 1907-1988 . . . . . DLB-8

Heinrich Julius of Brunswick
1564-1613 . . . . DLB-164

Heinrich von dem Türlin
flourished circa 1230 . . . . DLB-138

Heinrich von Melk
flourished after 1160 . . . . DLB-148

Heinrich von Veldeke
circa 1145-circa 1190 . . . . DLB-138

Heinrich, Willi 1920- DLB-75

Heiskell, John 1872-1972 . . . . DLB-127

Heinse, Wilhelm 1746-1803 . . . . . . DLB-94

Heinz, W. C. 1915- DLB-171

Hejinian, Lyn 1941- DLB-165

Heliand circa 850 . . . . DLB-148

Heller, Joseph 1923- DLB-2, 28; Y-80

Heller, Michael 1937- DLB-165

Hellman, Lillian 1906-1984 . . . . . DLB-7; Y-84

Hellwig, Johann 1609-1674 . . . . . . DLB-164

Helprin, Mark 1947- Y-85

Helwig, David 1938- DLB-60

Hemans, Felicia 1793-1835 . . . . DLB-96

Hemingway, Ernest 1899-1961 . . DLB-4, 9, 102;
Y-81, Y-87; DS-1, DS-15, DS-16

Hemingway: Twenty-Five Years
Later Y-85

Hémon, Louis 1880-1913 . . . . DLB-92

Hemphill, Paul 1936- Y-87

Hénault, Gilles 1920- DLB-88

Henchman, Daniel 1689-1761 . . . . . . DLB-24

Henderson, Alice Corbin
1881-1949 . . . . DLB-54

Henderson, Archibald
1877-1963 . . . . DLB-103

Henderson, David 1942- DLB-41

Henderson, George Wylie
1904- DLB-51

Henderson, Zenna 1917-1983 . . . . . . DLB-8

Henisch, Peter 1943- DLB-85

Henley, Beth 1952- Y-86

Henley, William Ernest
1849-1903 . . . . DLB-19

Henniker, Florence 1855-1923 . . . . . DLB-135

Henry, Alexander 1739-1824 . . . . DLB-99

Henry, Buck 1930- DLB-26

Henry VIII of England
1491-1547 . . . . DLB-132

Henry, Marguerite 1902- DLB-22

Henry, O. (see Porter, William Sydney)

Henry of Ghent
circa 1217-1229 - 1293 . . . . . . DLB-115

Henry, Robert Selph 1889-1970 . . . . DLB-17

Henry, Will (see Allen, Henry W.)

Henryson, Robert
1420s or 1430s-circa 1505 . . . . . DLB-146

Henschke, Alfred (see Klabund)

Hensley, Sophie Almon 1866-1946. . . . DLB-99

Henson, Lance 1944- DLB-175

Henty, G. A. 1832?-1902 . . . . . . DLB-18, 141

Hentz, Caroline Lee 1800-1856 . . . . . . DLB-3

Heraclitus flourished circa 500 B.C.
. . . . DLB-176

Herbert, Agnes circa 1880-1960. . . . . DLB-174

Herbert, Alan Patrick 1890-1971 . . DLB-10, 191

Herbert, Edward, Lord, of Cherbury
1582-1648. . . . . DLB-121, 151

Herbert, Frank 1920-1986 . . . . DLB-8

Herbert, George 1593-1633 . . . . . . DLB-126

Herbert, Henry William
1807-1858 . . . . DLB-3, 73

Herbert, John 1926- DLB-53

Herbert, Mary Sidney, Countess of Pembroke
(see Sidney, Mary)

Herbst, Josephine 1892-1969 . . . . DLB-9

Herburger, Gunter 1932- DLB-75, 124

Êercules, Frank E. M. 1917- DLB-33

Herder, Johann Gottfried
1744-1803 . . . . DLB-97

Herder, B., Book Company DLB-49

Herford, Charles Harold
1853-1931 . . . . DLB-149

Hergesheimer, Joseph
1880-1954. . . . . DLB-9, 102

Heritage Press DLB-46

Hermann the Lame 1013-1054 . . . . DLB-148

Hermes, Johann Timotheus
1738-1821 . . . . DLB-97

Hermlin, Stephan 1915- DLB-69

Hernández, Alfonso C. 1938- DLB-122

Hernández, Inés 1947- DLB-122

Hernández, Miguel 1910-1942 . . . . . DLB-134

Hernton, Calvin C. 1932- DLB-38

"The Hero as Man of Letters: Johnson,
Rousseau, Burns" (1841), by Thomas
Carlyle [excerpt] DLB-57

The Hero as Poet. Dante; Shakspeare (1841),
by Thomas Carlyle. DLB-32

Herodotus circa 484 B.C.-circa 420 B.C.
. . . . DLB-176

Heron, Robert 1764-1807 . . . . DLB-142

Herr, Michael 1940- DLB-185

Herrera, Juan Felipe 1948- DLB-122

Herrick, Robert 1591-1674 . . . . . . DLB-126

Herrick, Robert 1868-1938 . . . . DLB-9, 12, 78

Herrick, William 1915- Y-83

Herrick, E. R., and Company DLB-49

Herrmann, John 1900-1959 . . . . DLB-4

Hersey, John 1914-1993 . . . . . . DLB-6, 185

Hertel, François 1905-1985 . . . . . . DLB-68

Hervé-Bazin, Jean Pierre Marie (see Bazin, Hervé)

Hervey, John, Lord 1696-1743 . . . . . DLB-101

Herwig, Georg 1817-1875 . . . . DLB-133

Herzog, Emile Salomon Wilhelm (see Maurois, André)

Hesiod eighth century B.C. DLB-176

Hesse, Hermann 1877-1962 . . . . . . DLB-66

Hessus, Helius Eobanus
1488-1540 . . . . DLB-179

Hewat, Alexander
circa 1743-circa 1824 . . . . DLB-30

Hewitt, John 1907- DLB-27

Hewlett, Maurice 1861-1923 . . . . DLB-34, 156

Heyen, William 1940- DLB-5

Heyer, Georgette 1902-1974 . . . . DLB-77, 191

Heym, Stefan 1913- DLB-69

Heyse, Paul 1830-1914 . . . . DLB-129

Heytesbury, William
circa 1310-1372 or 1373 . . . . . . DLB-115

Heyward, Dorothy 1890-1961 . . . . . . DLB-7

Heyward, DuBose
1885-1940 . . . . DLB-7, 9, 45

Heywood, John 1497?-1580? DLB-136

Heywood, Thomas
1573 or 1574-1641 . . . . DLB-62

Hibbs, Ben 1901-1975 . . . . DLB-137

Hichens, Robert S. 1864-1950 . . . . . DLB-153

Hickman, William Albert
1877-1957 . . . . DLB-92

Hidalgo, José Luis 1919-1947 . . . . . DLB-108

Hiebert, Paul 1892-1987 . . . . DLB-68

Hieng, Andrej 1925- DLB-181

Hierro, José 1922- DLB-108

Higgins, Aidan 1927- DLB-14

Higgins, Colin 1941-1988 . . . . DLB-26

Higgins, George V. 1939- DLB-2; Y-81

Higginson, Thomas Wentworth
1823-1911 . . . . DLB-1, 64

Highwater, Jamake 1942?- DLB-52; Y-85

Hijuelos, Oscar 1951- DLB-145

Hildegard von Bingen
1098-1179 . . . . DLB-148

Das Hildesbrandslied circa 820 . . . . . DLB-148

Hildesheimer, Wolfgang
1916-1991 . . . . DLB-69, 124

Hildreth, Richard
1807-1865 . . . . DLB-1, 30, 59

Hill, Aaron 1685-1750 . . . . DLB-84

Hill, Geoffrey 1932- DLB-40

Hill, "Sir" John 1714?-1775 . . . . . . DLB-39

Hill, Leslie 1880-1960 . . . . DLB-51

Hill, Susan 1942- DLB-14, 139

Hill, Walter 1942- DLB-44

Hill and Wang DLB-46

Hill, George M., Company DLB-49

Hill, Lawrence, and Company,
Publishers DLB-46

Hillberry, Conrad 1928- DLB-120

Hilliard, Gray and Company DLB-49

Hills, Lee 1906- DLB-127

Hillyer, Robert 1895-1961 . . . . DLB-54

Hilton, James 1900-1954 . . . . . DLB-34, 77

Hilton, Walter died 1396 . . . . DLB-146

Hilton and Company DLB-49

Himes, Chester
1909-1984 . . . . DLB-2, 76, 143

Hindmarsh, Joseph
[publishing house] DLB-170

Hine, Daryl 1936- DLB-60

Hingley, Ronald 1920- DLB-155

Hinojosa-Smith, Rolando
1929- DLB-82

Hippel, Theodor Gottlieb von
1741-1796 . . . . DLB-97

Hippocrates of Cos flourished circa 425 B.C.
. . . . DLB-176

Hirabayashi, Taiko 1905-1972 . . . . . DLB-180

Hirsch, E. D., Jr. 1928- DLB-67

Hirsch, Edward 1950- DLB-120 The History of the
Adventures of Joseph Andrews
(1742), by Henry Fielding
[excerpt] DLB-39

Hoagland, Edward 1932- DLB-6

Hoagland, Everett H., III 1942- . . . DLB-41

Hoban, Russell 1925- DLB-52

Hobbes, Thomas 1588-1679 . . . . . . DLB-151

Hobby, Oveta 1905- DLB-127

Hobby, William 1878-1964 . . . . . . DLB-127

Hobsbaum, Philip 1932- DLB-40

Hobson, Laura Z. 1900- DLB-28

Hoby, Thomas 1530-1566 . . . . DLB-132

Hoccleve, Thomas
  circa 1368-circa 1437 . . . . DLB-146

Hochhuth, Rolf 1931- DLB-124

Hochman, Sandra 1936- DLB-5

Hocken, Thomas Morland
  1836-1910 . . . . DLB-184

Hodder and Stoughton, Limited DLB-106

Hodgins, Jack 1938- DLB-60

Hodgman, Helen 1945- DLB-14

Hodgskin, Thomas 1787-1869 . . . . . DLB-158

Hodgson, Ralph 1871-1962 . . . . DLB-19

Hodgson, William Hope
  1877-1918 . . . . . DLB-70, 153, 156, 178

Hoe, Robert III 1839-1909 . . . . DLB-187

Hoffenstein, Samuel 1890-1947 . . . . . DLB-11

Hoffman, Charles Fenno
  1806-1884 . . . . DLB-3

Hoffman, Daniel 1923- DLB-5

Hoffmann, E. T. A. 1776-1822 . . . . DLB-90

Hoffman, Frank B. 1888-1958 . . . . . DLB-188

Hoffmanswaldau, Christian Hoffman von
  1616-1679 . . . . DLB-168

Hofmann, Michael 1957- DLB-40

Hofmannsthal, Hugo von
  1874-1929 . . . . DLB-81, 118

Hofstadter, Richard 1916-1970 . . . . . DLB-17

Hogan, Desmond 1950- DLB-14

Hogan, Linda 1947- DLB-175

Hogan and Thompson DLB-49

Hogarth Press DLB-112

Hogg, James 1770-1835 . . . . DLB-93, 116, 159

Hohberg, Wolfgang Helmhard Freiherr von
  1612-1688 . . . . DLB-168

von Hohenheim, Philippus Aureolus
  Theophrastus Bombastus (see Paracelsus)

Hohl, Ludwig 1904-1980 . . . . DLB-56

Holbrook, David 1923- DLB-14, 40

Holcroft, Thomas
  1745-1809 . . . . DLB-39, 89, 158

Holden, Jonathan 1941- DLB-105

Holden, Molly 1927-1981 . . . . DLB-40

Hölderlin, Friedrich 1770-1843 . . . . . DLB-90

Holiday House DLB-46

Holinshed, Raphael died 1580 . . . . . DLB-167

Holland, J. G. 1819-1881 . . . . DS-13

Holland, Norman N. 1927- DLB-67

Hollander, John 1929- DLB-5

Holley, Marietta 1836-1926 . . . . DLB-11

Hollingsworth, Margaret 1940- DLB-60

Hollo, Anselm 1934- DLB-40

Holloway, Emory 1885-1977 . . . . . DLB-103

Holloway, John 1920- DLB-27

Holloway House Publishing
  Company DLB-46

Holme, Constance 1880-1955 . . . . . . DLB-34

Holmes, Abraham S. 1821?-1908 . . . . DLB-99

Holmes, John Clellon 1926-1988 . . . . DLB-16

Holmes, Oliver Wendell
  1809-1894 . . . . DLB-1, 189

Holmes, Richard 1945- DLB-155

Holmes, Thomas James 1874-1959 . . . DLB-187

Holroyd, Michael 1935- DLB-155

Holst, Hermann E. von
  1841-1904 . . . . DLB-47

Holt, John 1721-1784 . . . . DLB-43

Holt, Henry, and Company DLB-49

Holt, Rinehart and Winston DLB-46

Holtby, Winifred 1898-1935 . . . . . . DLB-191

Holthusen, Hans Egon 1913- DLB-69

Hölty, Ludwig Christoph Heinrich
  1748-1776 . . . . DLB-94

Holz, Arno 1863-1929 . . . . DLB-118

Home, Henry, Lord Kames (see Kames, Henry
  Home, Lord)

Home, John 1722-1808 . . . . DLB-84

Home, William Douglas 1912- DLB-13

Home Publishing Company DLB-49

Homer circa eighth-seventh centuries B.C.
  . . . . DLB-176

Homer, Winslow 1836-1910 . . . . . DLB-188

Homes, Geoffrey (see Mainwaring, Daniel)

Honan, Park 1928- DLB-111

Hone, William 1780-1842 . . . . . DLB-110, 158

Hongo, Garrett Kaoru 1951- DLB-120

Honig, Edwin 1919- DLB-5

Hood, Hugh 1928- DLB-53

Hood, Thomas 1799-1845 . . . . DLB-96

Hook, Theodore 1788-1841 . . . . . . DLB-116

Hooker, Jeremy 1941- DLB-40

Hooker, Richard 1554-1600 . . . . . . DLB-132

Hooker, Thomas 1586-1647 . . . . . . DLB-24

Hooper, Johnson Jones
  1815-1862 . . . . DLB-3, 11

Hope, Anthony 1863-1933 . . . . . DLB-153, 156

Hopkins, Ellice 1836-1904 . . . . DLB-190

Hopkins, Gerard Manley
  1844-1889 . . . . DLB-35, 57

Hopkins, John (see Sternhold, Thomas)

Hopkins, Lemuel 1750-1801 . . . . . . DLB-37

Hopkins, Pauline Elizabeth
  1859-1930 . . . . DLB-50

Hopkins, Samuel 1721-1803 . . . . . . DLB-31

Hopkins, John H., and Son DLB-46

Hopkinson, Francis 1737-1791 . . . . . DLB-31

Hoppin, Augustus 1828-1896 . . . . . DLB-188

Horgan, Paul 1903- DLB-102; Y-85

Horizon Press DLB-46

Horne, Frank 1899-1974 . . . . DLB-51

Horne, Richard Henry (Hengist)
  1802 or 1803-1884 . . . . DLB-32

Hornung, E. W. 1866-1921 . . . . . . DLB-70

Horovitz, Israel 1939- DLB-7

Horton, George Moses
  1797?-1883? DLB-50

Horváth, Ödön von
  1901-1938 . . . . DLB-85, 124

Horwood, Harold 1923- DLB-60

Hosford, E. and E.
  [publishing house] DLB-49

Hoskyns, John 1566-1638 . . . . DLB-121

Hotchkiss and Company DLB-49

Hough, Emerson 1857-1923 . . . . . . DLB-9

Houghton Mifflin Company DLB-49

Houghton, Stanley 1881-1913 . . . . . DLB-10

Household, Geoffrey 1900-1988 . . . . DLB-87

Housman, A. E. 1859-1936 . . . . . . DLB-19

Housman, Laurence 1865-1959 . . . . . DLB-10

Houwald, Ernst von 1778-1845 . . . . DLB-90

Hovey, Richard 1864-1900 . . . . . . DLB-54

Howard, Donald R. 1927-1987 . . . . DLB-111

Howard, Maureen 1930- Y-83

Howard, Richard 1929- DLB-5

Howard, Roy W. 1883-1964 . . . . . . DLB-29

Howard, Sidney 1891-1939 . . . . . DLB-7, 26

Howe, E. W. 1853-1937 . . . . . . DLB-12, 25

Howe, Henry 1816-1893 . . . . DLB-30

Howe, Irving 1920-1993 . . . . DLB-67

Howe, Joseph 1804-1873 . . . . DLB-99

Howe, Julia Ward 1819-1910 . . . . DLB-1, 189

Howe, Percival Presland
  1886-1944 . . . . DLB-149

Howe, Susan 1937- DLB-120

Howell, Clark, Sr. 1863-1936 . . . . . DLB-25

Howell, Evan P. 1839-1905 . . . . . . DLB-23

Howell, James 1594?-1666 . . . . DLB-151

Howell, Warren Richardson
  1912-1984 . . . . DLB-140

Howell, Soskin and Company DLB-46

Howells, William Dean
  1837-1920 . . . . . DLB-12, 64, 74, 79, 189

Howitt, William 1792-1879 and
  Howitt, Mary 1799-1888 . . . . . . DLB-110

Hoyem, Andrew 1935- DLB-5

Hoyers, Anna Ovena 1584-1655 . . . . DLB-164

Hoyos, Angela de 1940- DLB-82

Hoyt, Palmer 1897-1979 . . . . DLB-127

Hoyt, Henry [publishing house] DLB-49

Hrabanus Maurus 776?-856 . . . . . . DLB-148

Hrotsvit of Gandersheim
circa 935-circa 1000 . . . . DLB-148

Hubbard, Elbert 1856-1915. . . . . . . DLB-91

Hubbard, Kin 1868-1930 . . . . DLB-11

Hubbard, William circa 1621-1704. . . . DLB-24

Huber, Therese 1764-1829 . . . . DLB-90

Huch, Friedrich 1873-1913 . . . . DLB-66

Huch, Ricarda 1864-1947 . . . . DLB-66

Huck at 100: How Old Is
Huckleberry Finn? Y-85

Huddle, David 1942- DLB-130

Hudgins, Andrew 1951- DLB-120

Hudson, Henry Norman
1814-1886 . . . . DLB-64

Hudson, Stephen 1868?-1944 . . . . . . DLB-197

Hudson, W. H.
1841-1922 . . . . DLB-98, 153, 174

Hudson and Goodwin DLB-49

Huebsch, B. W.
[publishing house]. DLB-46

Hueffer, Oliver Madox 1876-1931 . . . DLB-197

Hughes, David 1930- DLB-14

Hughes, John 1677-1720 . . . . DLB-84

Hughes, Langston
1902-1967 . . . . . . DLB-4, 7, 48, 51, 86

Hughes, Richard 1900-1976. . . . DLB-15, 161

Hughes, Ted 1930- DLB-40, 161

Hughes, Thomas 1822-1896 . . . . DLB-18, 163

Hugo, Richard 1923-1982 . . . . DLB-5

Hugo, Victor 1802-1885 . . . . . DLB-119, 192

Hugo Awards and Nebula Awards DLB-8

Hull, Richard 1896-1973 . . . . DLB-77

Hulme, T. E. 1883-1917 . . . . DLB-19

Humboldt, Alexander von
1769-1859 . . . . DLB-90

Humboldt, Wilhelm von
1767-1835 . . . . DLB-90

Hume, David 1711-1776 . . . . DLB-104

Hume, Fergus 1859-1932 . . . . DLB-70

Hummer, T. R. 1950- DLB-120

Humorous Book Illustration DLB-11

Humphrey, William 1924- DLB-6

Humphreys, David 1752-1818 . . . . . DLB-37

Humphreys, Emyr 1919- DLB-15

Huncke, Herbert 1915- DLB-16

Huneker, James Gibbons
1857-1921 . . . . DLB-71

Hunold, Christian Friedrich
1681-1721 . . . . DLB-168

Hunt, Irene 1907- DLB-52

Hunt, Leigh 1784-1859 . . . . DLB-96, 110, 144

Hunt, Violet 1862-1942 . . . . . . DLB-162, 197

Hunt, William Gibbes 1791-1833 . . . . DLB-73

Hunter, Evan 1926- Y-82

Hunter, Jim 1939- DLB-14

Hunter, Kristin 1931- DLB-33

Hunter, Mollie 1922- DLB-161

Hunter, N. C. 1908-1971. . . . . DLB-10

Hunter-Duvar, John 1821-1899 . . . . . DLB-99

Huntington, Henry E.
1850-1927 . . . . DLB-140

Hurd and Houghton DLB-49

Hurst, Fannie 1889-1968 . . . . DLB-86

Hurst and Blackett. DLB-106

Hurst and Company DLB-49

Hurston, Zora Neale
1901?-1960 . . . . DLB-51, 86

Husson, Jules-François-Félix (see Champfleury)

Huston, John 1906-1987 . . . . DLB-26

Hutcheson, Francis 1694-1746 . . . . . DLB-31

Hutchinson, R. C. 1907-1975 . . . . . DLB-191

Hutchinson, Thomas
1711-1780 . . . . DLB-30, 31

Hutchinson and Company
(Publishers) Limited DLB-112

von Hutton, Ulrich 1488-1523 . . . . DLB-179

Hutton, Richard Holt 1826-1897 . . . . DLB-57

Huxley, Aldous
1894-1963 . . . . . DLB-36, 100, 162, 195

Huxley, Elspeth Josceline 1907- DLB-77

Huxley, T. H. 1825-1895. . . . . DLB-57

Huyghue, Douglas Smith
1816-1891 . . . . DLB-99

Huysmans, Joris-Karl 1848-1907 . . . . DLB-123

Hyde, Donald 1909-1966 and
Hyde, Mary 1912- DLB-187

Hyman, Trina Schart 1939- DLB-61

I

Iavorsky, Stefan 1658-1722 . . . . . . DLB-150

Ibn Bajja circa 1077-1138 . . . . DLB-115

Ibn Gabirol, Solomon
circa 1021-circa 1058 . . . . DLB-115

Ibuse, Masuji 1898-1993 . . . . DLB-180

The Iconography of Science-Fiction
Art DLB-8

Iffland, August Wilhelm
1759-1814 . . . . DLB-94

Ignatow, David 1914- DLB-5

Ike, Chukwuemeka 1931- DLB-157

Iles, Francis (see Berkeley, Anthony)

The Illustration of Early German
Literary Manuscripts,
circa 1150-circa 1300 . . . . DLB-148

"Images and 'Images,'" by
Charles Simic DLB-105

Imbs, Bravig 1904-1946 . . . . DLB-4

Imbuga, Francis D. 1947- DLB-157

Immermann, Karl 1796-1840 . . . . . DLB-133

Impressions of William Faulkner Y-97

Inchbald, Elizabeth 1753-1821 . . . . DLB-39, 89

Inge, William 1913-1973 . . . . DLB-7

Ingelow, Jean 1820-1897 . . . . . DLB-35, 163

Ingersoll, Ralph 1900-1985 . . . . . . DLB-127

The Ingersoll Prizes Y-84

Ingoldsby, Thomas (see Barham, Richard
Harris)

Ingraham, Joseph Holt 1809-1860 . . . . DLB-3

Inman, John 1805-1850 . . . . DLB-73

Innerhofer, Franz 1944- DLB-85

Innis, Harold Adams 1894-1952 . . . . DLB-88

Innis, Mary Quayle 1899-1972 . . . . . DLB-88

Inoue, Yasushi 1907-1991 . . . . DLB-181

International Publishers Company DLB-46

An Interview with David Rabe Y-91

An Interview with George Greenfield,
Literary Agent Y-91

An Interview with James Ellroy. Y-91

Interview with Norman Mailer Y-97

An Interview with Peter S. Prescott. . . . Y-86

An Interview with Russell Hoban. Y-90

Interview with Stanley Burnshaw Y-97

An Interview with Tom Jenks. Y-86

"Into the Mirror," by
Peter Cooley. DLB-105

Introduction to Paul Laurence Dunbar,
Lyrics of Lowly Life (1896),
by William Dean Howells DLB-50

Introductory Essay: Letters of Percy Bysshe
Shelley (1852), by Robert
Browning DLB-32

Introductory Letters from the Second Edition
of Pamela (1741), by Samuel
Richardson DLB-39

Irving, John 1942- DLB-6; Y-82

Irving, Washington 1783-1859
. . . . DLB-3, 11, 30, 59, 73, 74, 183, 186

Irwin, Grace 1907- DLB-68

Irwin, Will 1873-1948. . . . . DLB-25

Isherwood, Christopher
1904-1986 . . . . DLB-15, 195; Y-86

Ishiguro, Kazuo 1954- DLB-194

Ishikawa, Jun 1899-1987. . . . . DLB-182

The Island Trees Case: A Symposium on
School Library Censorship
An Interview with Judith Krug
An Interview with Phyllis Schlafly
An Interview with Edward B. Jenkinson
An Interview with Lamarr Mooneyham
An Interview with Harriet
Bernstein Y-82

Islas, Arturo 1938-1991 . . . . DLB-122

Ivanišević, Drago 1907-1981 . . . . . DLB-181

Ivers, M. J., and Company DLB-49

Iwano, Hōmei 1873-1920 . . . . DLB-180

Iyayi, Festus 1947- DLB-157

Izumi, Kyōka 1873-1939. . . . . DLB-180

J

Jackmon, Marvin E. (see Marvin X)

Jacks, L. P. 1860-1955. . . . . DLB-135

Jackson, Angela 1951- DLB-41

Jackson, Helen Hunt
1830-1885 . . . . DLB-42, 47, 186, 189

Jackson, Holbrook 1874-1948. . . . . . DLB-98

Jackson, Laura Riding 1901-1991 . . . . DLB-48

Jackson, Shirley 1919-1965. . . . . . . DLB-6

Jacob, Naomi 1884?-1964 . . . . DLB-191

Jacob, Piers Anthony Dillingham (see Anthony,
Piers)

Jacobi, Friedrich Heinrich
1743-1819 . . . . DLB-94

Jacobi, Johann Georg 1740-1841 . . . . . DLB-97

Jacobs, Joseph 1854-1916 . . . . DLB-141

Jacobs, W. W. 1863-1943. . . . . DLB-135

Jacobs, George W., and Company . . . DLB-49

Jacobson, Dan 1929- DLB-14

Jaggard, William
[publishing house] DLB-170

Jahier, Piero 1884-1966 . . . . DLB-114

Jahnn, Hans Henny
1894-1959 . . . . DLB-56, 124

Jakes, John 1932- Y-83

James, C. L. R. 1901-1989 . . . . . . DLB-125

James Dickey Tributes Y-97

James, George P. R. 1801-1860. . . . . DLB-116

James Gould Cozzens–A View from
Afar Y-97

James Gould Cozzens Case Re-opened . . . Y-97

James Gould Cozzens: How to Read
Him Y-97

James, Henry
1843-1916 . . . DLB-12, 71, 74, 189; DS-13

James, John circa 1633-1729 . . . . . . DLB-24

The James Jones Society. Y-92

James Laughlin Tributes Y-97

James, M. R. 1862-1936. . . . . . . DLB-156

James, P. D. 1920- DLB-87; DS-17

James, Will 1892-1942 . . . . DS-16

James Joyce Centenary: Dublin, 1982. . . . Y-82

James Joyce Conference Y-85

James VI of Scotland, I of England
1566-1625. . . . . DLB-151, 172

James, U. P. [publishing house] DLB-49

Jameson, Anna 1794-1860. . . . . . DLB-99, 166

Jameson, Fredric 1934- DLB-67

Jameson, J. Franklin 1859-1937. . . . . DLB-17

Jameson, Storm 1891-1986 . . . . DLB-36

Jančar, Drago 1948- DLB-181

Janés, Clara 1940- DLB-134

Janevski, Slavko 1920- DLB-181

Jaramillo, Cleofas M. 1878-1956 . . . . DLB-122

Jarman, Mark 1952- DLB-120

Jarrell, Randall 1914-1965 . . . . . . DLB-48, 52

Jarrold and Sons. DLB-106

Jarry, Alfred 1873-1907 . . . . DLB-192

Jarves, James Jackson 1818-1888 . . . . DLB-189

Jasmin, Claude 1930- DLB-60

Jay, John 1745-1829. . . . . DLB-31

Jefferies, Richard 1848-1887. . . . DLB-98, 141

Jeffers, Lance 1919-1985 . . . . DLB-41

Jeffers, Robinson 1887-1962 . . . . . . DLB-45

Jefferson, Thomas 1743-1826 . . . DLB-31, 183

Jelinek, Elfriede 1946- DLB-85

Jellicoe, Ann 1927- DLB-13

Jenkins, Elizabeth 1905- DLB-155

Jenkins, Robin 1912- DLB-14

Jenkins, William Fitzgerald (see Leinster,
Murray)

Jenkins, Herbert, Limited DLB-112

Jennings, Elizabeth 1926- DLB-27

Jens, Walter 1923- DLB-69

Jensen, Merrill 1905-1980 . . . . DLB-17

Jephson, Robert 1736-1803 . . . . DLB-89

Jerome, Jerome K.
1859-1927 . . . . DLB-10, 34, 135

Jerome, Judson 1927-1991 . . . . DLB-105

Jerrold, Douglas 1803-1857 . . . . DLB-158, 159

Jesse, F. Tennyson 1888-1958 . . . . . DLB-77

Jewett, Sarah Orne 1849-1909 . . . . DLB-12, 74

Jewett, John P., and Company. DLB-49

The Jewish Publication Society. DLB-49

Jewitt, John Rodgers 1783-1821 . . . . DLB-99

Jewsbury, Geraldine 1812-1880 . . . . DLB-21

Jhabvala, Ruth Prawer 1927- . . DLB-139, 194

Jiménez, Juan Ramón 1881-1958 . . . . DLB-134

Joans, Ted 1928- DLB-16, 41

John, Eugenie (see Marlitt, E.)

John of Dumbleton
circa 1310-circa 1349 . . . . DLB-115

John Edward Bruce: Three
Documents DLB-50

John O'Hara's Pottsville Journalism Y-88

John Steinbeck Research Center Y-85

John Updike on the Internet Y-97

John Webster: The Melbourne
Manuscript Y-86

Johns, Captain W. E. 1893-1968 . . . . DLB-160

Johnson, B. S. 1933-1973 . . . . . DLB-14, 40

Johnson, Charles 1679-1748 . . . . . DLB-84

Johnson, Charles R. 1948- DLB-33

Johnson, Charles S. 1893-1956. . . . DLB-51, 91

Johnson, Denis 1949- DLB-120

Johnson, Diane 1934- Y-80

Johnson, Edgar 1901- DLB-103

Johnson, Edward 1598-1672 . . . . . DLB-24

Johnson E. Pauline (Tekahionwake)
1861-1913 . . . . DLB-175

Johnson, Fenton 1888-1958 . . . . DLB-45, 50

Johnson, Georgia Douglas
1886-1966 . . . . DLB-51

Johnson, Gerald W. 1890-1980 . . . . DLB-29

Johnson, Helene 1907- DLB-51

Johnson, James Weldon
1871-1938 . . . . DLB-51

Johnson, John H. 1918- DLB-137

Johnson, Linton Kwesi 1952- DLB-157

Johnson, Lionel 1867-1902 . . . . DLB-19

Johnson, Nunnally 1897-1977 . . . . . DLB-26

Johnson, Owen 1878-1952 . . . . Y-87

Johnson, Pamela Hansford
1912- DLB-15

Johnson, Pauline 1861-1913 . . . . . . DLB-92

Johnson, Ronald 1935- DLB-169

Johnson, Samuel 1696-1772 . . . . . . DLB-24

Johnson, Samuel
1709-1784 . . . . . . DLB-39, 95, 104, 142

Johnson, Samuel 1822-1882 . . . . DLB-1

Johnson, Uwe 1934-1984 . . . . DLB-75

Johnson, Benjamin
[publishing house]. DLB-49

Johnson, Benjamin, Jacob, and
Robert [publishing house] DLB-49

Johnson, Jacob, and Company DLB-49

Johnson, Joseph [publishing house] . . . DLB-154

Johnston, Annie Fellows 1863-1931 . . . DLB-42

Johnston, David Claypole 1798?-1865 . DLB-188

Johnston, Basil H. 1929- DLB-60

Johnston, Denis 1901-1984 . . . . . . DLB-10

Johnston, George 1913- DLB-88

Johnston, Sir Harry 1858-1927 . . . . . DLB-174

Johnston, Jennifer 1930- DLB-14

Johnston, Mary 1870-1936 . . . . DLB-9

Johnston, Richard Malcolm
1822-1898 . . . . DLB-74

Johnstone, Charles 1719?-1800? DLB-39

Johst, Hanns 1890-1978 . . . . DLB-124

Jolas, Eugene 1894-1952 . . . . DLB-4, 45

Jones, Alice C. 1853-1933 . . . . DLB-92

Jones, Charles C., Jr. 1831-1893 . . . . . DLB-30

Jones, D. G. 1929- DLB-53

Jones, David 1895-1974 . . . . DLB-20, 100

Jones, Diana Wynne 1934- DLB-161

Jones, Ebenezer 1820-1860 . . . . DLB-32

Jones, Ernest 1819-1868 . . . . DLB-32

Jones, Gayl 1949- DLB-33

Jones, George 1800-1870 . . . . DLB-183

Jones, Glyn 1905- DLB-15

Jones, Gwyn 1907- DLB-15, 139

Jones, Henry Arthur 1851-1929 . . . . . DLB-10

Jones, Hugh circa 1692-1760 . . . . . . DLB-24

Jones, James 1921-1977 . . . DLB-2, 143; DS-17

Jones, Jenkin Lloyd 1911- DLB-127

Jones, LeRoi (see Baraka, Amiri)

Jones, Lewis 1897-1939 . . . . DLB-15

Jones, Madison 1925- DLB-152

Jones, Major Joseph (see Thompson, William
    Tappan)

Jones, Preston 1936-1979 . . . . DLB-7

Jones, Rodney 1950- DLB-120

Jones, Sir William 1746-1794 . . . . . DLB-109

Jones, William Alfred 1817-1900 . . . . DLB-59

Jones's Publishing House DLB-49

Jong, Erica 1942- DLB-2, 5, 28, 152

Jonke, Gert F. 1946- DLB-85

Jonson, Ben 1572?-1637 . . . . . . DLB-62, 121

Jordan, June 1936- DLB-38

Joseph, Jenny 1932- DLB-40

Joseph, Michael, Limited DLB-112

Josephson, Matthew 1899-1978 . . . . . DLB-4

Josephus, Flavius 37-100 . . . . DLB-176

Josiah Allen's Wife (see Holley, Marietta)

Josipovici, Gabriel 1940- DLB-14

Josselyn, John ?-1675 . . . . DLB-24

Joudry, Patricia 1921- DLB-88

Jovine, Giuseppe 1922- DLB-128

Joyaux, Philippe (see Sollers, Philippe)

Joyce, Adrien (see Eastman, Carol)

A Joyce (Con)Text: Danis Rose and the Remaking
    of *Ulysses* Y-97

Joyce, James
    1882-1941 . . . . . . DLB-10, 19, 36, 162

Judd, Sylvester 1813-1853 . . . . DLB-1

Judd, Orange, Publishing
    Company DLB-49

Judith circa 930 . . . . DLB-146

Julian of Norwich
    1342-circa 1420 . . . . DLB-1146

Julian Symons at Eighty Y-92

June, Jennie (see Croly, Jane Cunningham)

Jung, Franz 1888-1963 . . . . DLB-118

Jünger, Ernst 1895- DLB-56

Der jüngere Titurel circa 1275 . . . . . DLB-138

Jung-Stilling, Johann Heinrich
    1740-1817 . . . . DLB-94

Justice, Donald 1925- Y-83

The Juvenile Library (see Godwin, M. J., and
    Company)

K

Kacew, Romain (see Gary, Romain)

Kafka, Franz 1883-1924 . . . . DLB-81

Kahn, Roger 1927- DLB-171

Kaikō, Takeshi 1939-1989 . . . . DLB-182

Kaiser, Georg 1878-1945 . . . . DLB-124

Kaiserchronik circca 1147 . . . . DLB-148

Kaleb, Vjekoslav 1905- DLB-181

Kalechofsky, Roberta 1931- DLB-28

Kaler, James Otis 1848-1912 . . . . . . DLB-12

Kames, Henry Home, Lord
    1696-1782 . . . . DLB-31, 104

Kandel, Lenore 1932- DLB-16

Kanin, Garson 1912- DLB-7

Kant, Hermann 1926- DLB-75

Kant, Immanuel 1724-1804 . . . . DLB-94

Kantemir, Antiokh Dmitrievich
    1708-1744 . . . . DLB-150

Kantor, Mackinlay 1904-1977 . . . . DLB-9, 102

Kaplan, Fred 1937- DLB-111

Kaplan, Johanna 1942- DLB-28

Kaplan, Justin 1925- DLB-111

Kapnist, Vasilii Vasilevich
    1758?-1823 . . . . DLB-150

Karadžić,Vuk Stefanović
    1787-1864 . . . . DLB-147

Karamzin, Nikolai Mikhailovich
    1766-1826 . . . . DLB-150

Karsch, Anna Louisa 1722-1791 . . . . DLB-97

Kasack, Hermann 1896-1966 . . . . . . DLB-69

Kasai, Zenzō 1887-1927 . . . . DLB-180

Kaschnitz, Marie Luise 1901-1974 . . . . DLB-69

Kaštelan, Jure 1919-1990 . . . . DLB-147

Kästner, Erich 1899-1974 . . . . DLB-56

Kattan, Naim 1928- DLB-53

Katz, Steve 1935- Y-83

Kauffman, Janet 1945- Y-86

Kauffmann, Samuel 1898-1971 . . . . . DLB-127

Kaufman, Bob 1925- DLB-16, 41

Kaufman, George S. 1889-1961 . . . . . DLB-7

Kavanagh, P. J. 1931- DLB-40

Kavanagh, Patrick 1904-1967 . . . . DLB-15, 20

Kawabata, Yasunari 1899-1972 . . . . . DLB-180

Kaye-Smith, Sheila 1887-1956 . . . . . . DLB-36

Kazin, Alfred 1915- DLB-67

Keane, John B. 1928- DLB-13

Keary, Annie 1825-1879 . . . . DLB-163

Keating, H. R. F. 1926- DLB-87

Keats, Ezra Jack 1916-1983 . . . . DLB-61

Keats, John 1795-1821 . . . . . . DLB-96, 110

Keble, John 1792-1866 . . . . . . DLB-32, 55

Keeble, John 1944- Y-83

Keeffe, Barrie 1945- DLB-13

Keeley, James 1867-1934 . . . . DLB-25

W. B. Keen, Cooke
    and Company DLB-49

Keillor, Garrison 1942- Y-87

Keith, Marian 1874?-1961 . . . . DLB-92

Keller, Gary D. 1943- DLB-82

Keller, Gottfried 1819-1890 . . . . . . DLB-129

Kelley, Edith Summers 1884-1956 . . . . DLB-9

Kelley, William Melvin 1937- DLB-33

Kellogg, Ansel Nash 1832-1886 . . . . . DLB-23

Kellogg, Steven 1941- DLB-61

Kelly, George 1887-1974 . . . . DLB-7

Kelly, Hugh 1739-1777 . . . . DLB-89

Kelly, Robert 1935- DLB-5, 130, 165

Kelly, Piet and Company DLB-49

Kelman, James 1946- DLB-194

Kelmscott Press DLB-112

Kemble, E. W. 1861-1933 . . . . DLB-188

Kemble, Fanny 1809-1893 . . . . DLB-32

Kemelman, Harry 1908- DLB-28

Kempe, Margery circa 1373-1438 . . . . DLB-146

Kempner, Friederike 1836-1904 . . . . . DLB-129

Kempowski, Walter 1929- DLB-75

Kendall, Claude [publishing company] . . DLB-46

Kendell, George 1809-1867 . . . . DLB-43

Kenedy, P. J., and Sons DLB-49

Kennan, George 1845-1924 . . . . DLB-189

Kennedy, Adrienne 1931- DLB-38

Kennedy, John Pendleton 1795-1870 . . . . DLB-3

Kennedy, Leo 1907- DLB-88

Kennedy, Margaret 1896-1967 . . . . . . DLB-36

Kennedy, Patrick 1801-1873 . . . . . . DLB-159

Kennedy, Richard S. 1920- DLB-111

Kennedy, William 1928- DLB-143; Y-85

Kennedy, X. J. 1929- DLB-5

Kennelly, Brendan 1936- DLB-40

Kenner, Hugh 1923- DLB-67

Kennerley, Mitchell
    [publishing house] DLB-46

Kenneth Dale McCormick Tributes Y-97

Kenny, Maurice 1929- DLB-175

Kent, Frank R. 1877-1958 . . . . DLB-29

Kenyon, Jane 1947- DLB-120

Keough, Hugh Edmund 1864-1912. . . DLB-171

Keppler and Schwartzmann. DLB-49

Kerlan, Irvin 1912-1963 . . . . DLB-187

Kern, Jerome 1885-1945. . . . . DLB-187

Kerner, Justinus 1776-1862 . . . . DLB-90

Kerouac, Jack 1922-1969 . . . . DLB-2, 16; DS-3

The Jack Kerouac Revival. Y-95

Kerouac, Jan 1952- DLB-16

Kerr, Orpheus C. (see Newell, Robert Henry)

Kerr, Charles H., and Company DLB-49

Kesey, Ken 1935- DLB-2, 16

Kessel, Joseph 1898-1979 . . . . DLB-72

Kessel, Martin 1901- DLB-56

Kesten, Hermann 1900- DLB-56

Keun, Irmgard 1905-1982. . . . . DLB-69

Key and Biddle DLB-49

Keynes, John Maynard 1883-1946 . . . . DS-10

Keyserling, Eduard von 1855-1918 . . . DLB-66

Khan, Ismith 1925- DLB-125

Khaytov, Nikolay 1919- DLB-181

Khemnitser, Ivan Ivanovich
1745-1784 . . . . DLB-150

Kheraskov, Mikhail Matveevich
1733-1807 . . . . DLB-150

Khristov, Boris 1945- DLB-181

Khvostov, Dmitrii Ivanovich
1757-1835 . . . . DLB-150

Kidd, Adam 1802?-1831 . . . . DLB-99

Kidd, William
[publishing house] DLB-106

Kidder, Tracy 1945- DLB-185

Kiely, Benedict 1919- DLB-15

Kieran, John 1892-1981 . . . . DLB-171

Kiggins and Kellogg. DLB-49

Kiley, Jed 1889-1962 . . . . DLB-4

Kilgore, Bernard 1908-1967 . . . . DLB-127

Killens, John Oliver 1916- DLB-33

Killigrew, Anne 1660-1685 . . . . DLB-131

Killigrew, Thomas 1612-1683. . . . . . DLB-58

Kilmer, Joyce 1886-1918 . . . . DLB-45

Kilwardby, Robert
circa 1215-1279 . . . . DLB-115

Kincaid, Jamaica 1949- DLB-157

King, Charles 1844-1933 . . . . DLB-186

King, Clarence 1842-1901 . . . . DLB-12

King, Florence 1936 . . . . Y-85

King, Francis 1923- DLB-15, 139

King, Grace 1852-1932 . . . . DLB-12, 78

King, Henry 1592-1669 . . . . DLB-126

King, Stephen 1947- DLB-143; Y-80

King, Thomas 1943- DLB-175

King, Woodie, Jr. 1937- DLB-38

King, Solomon [publishing house] DLB-49

Kinglake, Alexander William
1809-1891 . . . . DLB-55, 166

Kingsley, Charles
1819-1875 . . . . DLB-21, 32, 163, 178, 190

Kingsley, Mary Henrietta
1862-1900 . . . . DLB-174

Kingsley, Henry 1830-1876. . . . . . . DLB-21

Kingsley, Sidney 1906- DLB-7

Kingsmill, Hugh 1889-1949 . . . . . . DLB-149

Kingston, Maxine Hong
1940- DLB-173; Y-80

Kingston, William Henry Giles
1814-1880 . . . . DLB-163

Kinnell, Galway 1927- DLB-5; Y-87

Kinsella, Thomas 1928- DLB-27

Kipling, Rudyard
1865-1936 . . . . . . DLB-19, 34, 141, 156

Kipphardt, Heinar 1922-1982 . . . . . . DLB-124

Kirby, William 1817-1906 . . . . DLB-99

Kircher, Athanasius 1602-1680 . . . . . DLB-164

Kireevsky, Ivan Vasil'evich
1806-1856 . . . . DLB-198

Kirk, John Foster 1824-1904 . . . . . . DLB-79

Kirkconnell, Watson 1895-1977 . . . . . DLB-68

Kirkland, Caroline M.
1801-1864 . . . . . . DLB-3, 73, 74; DS-13

Kirkland, Joseph 1830-1893. . . . . . . DLB-12

Kirkman, Francis
[publishing house] DLB-170

Kirkpatrick, Clayton 1915- DLB-127

Kirkup, James 1918- DLB-27

Kirouac, Conrad (see Marie-Victorin, Frère)

Kirsch, Sarah 1935- DLB-75

Kirst, Hans Hellmut 1914-1989 . . . . . DLB-69

Kiš, Danilo 1935-1989 . . . . DLB-181

Kita, Morio 1927- DLB-182

Kitcat, Mabel Greenhow
1859-1922 . . . . DLB-135

Kitchin, C. H. B. 1895-1967 . . . . . . DLB-77

Kizer, Carolyn 1925- DLB-5, 169

Klabund 1890-1928 . . . . DLB-66

Klaj, Johann 1616-1656 . . . . DLB-164

Klappert, Peter 1942- DLB-5

Klass, Philip (see Tenn, William)

Klein, A. M. 1909-1972. . . . . DLB-68

Kleist, Ewald von 1715-1759 . . . . . . DLB-97

Kleist, Heinrich von 1777-1811 . . . . . DLB-90

Klinger, Friedrich Maximilian
1752-1831 . . . . DLB-94

Klopstock, Friedrich Gottlieb
1724-1803 . . . . DLB-97

Klopstock, Meta 1728-1758. . . . . . . DLB-97

Kluge, Alexander 1932- DLB-75

Knapp, Joseph Palmer 1864-1951 . . . . DLB-91

Knapp, Samuel Lorenzo
1783-1838 . . . . DLB-59

Knapton, J. J. and P.
[publishing house] DLB-154

Kniazhnin, Iakov Borisovich
1740-1791 . . . . DLB-150

Knickerbocker, Diedrich (see Irving,
Washington)

Knigge, Adolph Franz Friedrich Ludwig,
Freiherr von 1752-1796 . . . . . . DLB-94

Knight, Damon 1922- DLB-8

Knight, Etheridge 1931-1992 . . . . . . DLB-41

Knight, John S. 1894-1981 . . . . DLB-29

Knight, Sarah Kemble 1666-1727 . . . . DLB-24

Knight, Charles, and Company. DLB-106

Knight-Bruce, G. W. H.
1852-1896 . . . . DLB-174

Knister, Raymond 1899-1932. . . . . . DLB-68

Knoblock, Edward 1874-1945 . . . . . DLB-10

Knopf, Alfred A. 1892-1984 . . . . Y-84

Knopf, Alfred A.
[publishing house]. DLB-46

Knorr von Rosenroth, Christian
1636-1689 . . . . DLB-168

"Knots into Webs: Some Autobiographical
Sources," by Dabney Stuart DLB-105

Knowles, John 1926- DLB-6

Knox, Frank 1874-1944. . . . . DLB-29

Knox, John circa 1514-1572. . . . . . . DLB-132

Knox, John Armoy 1850-1906 . . . . . DLB-23

Knox, Ronald Arbuthnott
1888-1957 . . . . DLB-77

Knox, Thomas Wallace 1835-1896. . . DLB-189

Kobayashi, Takiji 1903-1933 . . . . . . DLB-180

Kober, Arthur 1900-1975 . . . . DLB-11

Kocbek, Edvard 1904-1981 . . . . . . DLB-147

Koch, Howard 1902- DLB-26

Koch, Kenneth 1925- DLB-5

Kōda, Rohan 1867-1947. . . . . DLB-180

Koenigsberg, Moses 1879-1945. . . . . DLB-25

Koeppen, Wolfgang 1906- DLB-69

Koertge, Ronald 1940- DLB-105

Koestler, Arthur 1905-1983. . . . . Y-83

Kohn, John S. Van E. 1906-1976 and
Papantonio, Michael 1907-1978. . . DLB-187

Kokoschka, Oskar 1886-1980 . . . . . DLB-124

Kolb, Annette 1870-1967 . . . . DLB-66

Kolbenheyer, Erwin Guido
1878-1962 . . . . DLB-66, 124

Kolleritsch, Alfred 1931- DLB-85

Kolodny, Annette 1941- DLB-67

Komarov, Matvei
    circa 1730-1812 . . . . DLB-150

Komroff, Manuel 1890-1974 . . . . DLB-4

Komunyakaa, Yusef 1947- DLB-120

Koneski, Blaže 1921-1993 . . . . DLB-181

Konigsburg, E. L. 1930- DLB-52

Konrad von Würzburg
    circa 1230-1287 . . . . DLB-138

Konstantinov, Aleko 1863-1897 . . . . DLB-147

Kooser, Ted 1939- DLB-105

Kopit, Arthur 1937- DLB-7

Kops, Bernard 1926?- DLB-13

Kornbluth, C. M. 1923-1958 . . . . . . DLB-8

Körner, Theodor 1791-1813 . . . . . . DLB-90

Kornfeld, Paul 1889-1942 . . . . . . DLB-118

Kosinski, Jerzy 1933-1991 . . . . . DLB-2; Y-82

Kosmač, Ciril 1910-1980 . . . . DLB-181

Kosovel, Srečko 1904-1926 . . . . . . DLB-147

Kostrov, Ermil Ivanovich
    1755-1796 . . . . DLB-150

Kotzebue, August von 1761-1819 . . . . DLB-94

Kotzwinkle, William 1938- DLB-173

Kovačić, Ante 1854-1889 . . . . DLB-147

Kovič, Kajetan 1931- DLB-181

Kraf, Elaine 1946- Y-81

Kramer, Jane 1938- DLB-185

Kramer, Mark 1944- DLB-185

Kranjčević, Silvije Strahimir
    1865-1908 . . . . DLB-147

Krasna, Norman 1909-1984 . . . . . . DLB-26

Kraus, Hans Peter 1907-1988 . . . . . DLB-187

Kraus, Karl 1874-1936 . . . . DLB-118

Krauss, Ruth 1911-1993 . . . . DLB-52

Kreisel, Henry 1922- DLB-88

Kreuder, Ernst 1903-1972 . . . . . . DLB-69

Kreymborg, Alfred 1883-1966 . . . . DLB-4, 54

Krieger, Murray 1923- DLB-67

Krim, Seymour 1922-1989 . . . . . . DLB-16

Krleža, Miroslav 1893-1981 . . . . . DLB-147

Krock, Arthur 1886-1974 . . . . DLB-29

Kroetsch, Robert 1927- ‰DLB-53

Krutch, Joseph Wood 1893-1970 . . . . DLB-63

Krylov, Ivan Andreevich
    1769-1844 . . . . DLB-150

Kubin, Alfred 1877-1959 . . . . DLB-81

Kubrick, Stanley 1928- DLB-26

Kudrun circa 1230-1240 . . . . DLB-138

Kuffstein, Hans Ludwig von
    1582-1656 . . . . DLB-164

Kuhlmann, Quirinus 1651-1689 . . . . DLB-168

Kuhnau, Johann 1660-1722 . . . . . . DLB-168

Kumin, Maxine 1925- DLB-5

Kunene, Mazisi 1930- DLB-117

Kunikida, Doppo 1869-1908 . . . . . . DLB-180

Kunitz, Stanley 1905- DLB-48

Kunjufu, Johari M. (see Amini, Johari M.)

Kunnert, Gunter 1929- DLB-75

Kunze, Reiner 1933- DLB-75

Kupferberg, Tuli 1923- DLB-16

Kurahashi, Yumiko 1935- DLB-182

Kureishi, Hanif 1954- DLB-194

Kürnberger, Ferdinand
    1821-1879 . . . . DLB-129

Kurz, Isolde 1853-1944 . . . . DLB-66

Kusenberg, Kurt 1904-1983 . . . . . . DLB-69

Kuttner, Henry 1915-1958 . . . . . . DLB-8

Kyd, Thomas 1558-1594 . . . . DLB-62

Kyffin, Maurice
    circa 1560?-1598 . . . . DLB-136

Kyger, Joanne 1934- DLB-16

Kyne, Peter B. 1880-1957 . . . . . . DLB-78

L

L. E. L. (see Landon, Letitia Elizabeth)

Laberge, Albert 1871-1960 . . . . . . DLB-68

Laberge, Marie 1950- DLB-60

Labiche, Eugène 1815-1888 . . . . . . DLB-192

La Capria, Raffaele 1922- DLB-196

Lacombe, Patrice (see Trullier-Lacombe,
    Joseph Patrice)

Lacretelle, Jacques de 1888-1985 . . . . DLB-65

Lacy, Sam 1903- DLB-171

Ladd, Joseph Brown 1764-1786 . . . . DLB-37

La Farge, Oliver 1901-1963 . . . . . . DLB-9

Lafferty, R. A. 1914- DLB-8

La Flesche, Francis 1857-1932 . . . . DLB-175

Lagorio, Gina 1922- DLB-196

La Guma, Alex 1925-1985 . . . . . . DLB-117

Lahaise, Guillaume (see Delahaye, Guy)

Lahontan, Louis-Armand de Lom d'Arce,
    Baron de 1666-1715? DLB-99

Laing, Kojo 1946- DLB-157

Laird, Carobeth 1895- Y-82

Laird and Lee DLB-49

Lalić, Ivan V. 1931-1996 . . . . . . DLB-181

Lalić, Mihailo 1914-1992 . . . . . . DLB-181

Lalonde, Michèle 1937- DLB-60

Lamantia, Philip 1927- DLB-16

Lamb, Charles
    1775-1834 . . . . DLB-93, 107, 163

Lamb, Lady Caroline 1785-1828 . . . . DLB-116

Lamb, Mary 1764-1874 . . . . DLB-163

Lambert, Betty 1933-1983 . . . . . . DLB-60

Lamming, George 1927- DLB-125

L'Amour, Louis 1908?- Y-80

Lampman, Archibald 1861-1899 . . . . DLB-92

Lamson, Wolffe and Company DLB-49

Lancer Books DLB-46

Landesman, Jay 1919- and
    Landesman, Fran 1927- DLB-16

Landolfi, Tommaso 1908-1979 . . . . . DLB-177

Landon, Letitia Elizabeth 1802-1838 . . . DLB-96

Landor, Walter Savage
    1775-1864 . . . . DLB-93, 107

Landry, Napoléon-P. 1884-1956 . . . . DLB-92

Lane, Charles 1800-1870 . . . . DLB-1

Lane, Laurence W. 1890-1967 . . . . . DLB-91

Lane, M. Travis 1934- DLB-60

Lane, Patrick 1939- DLB-53

Lane, Pinkie Gordon 1923- DLB-41

Lane, John, Company DLB-49

Laney, Al 1896-1988 . . . . DLB-4, 171

Lang, Andrew 1844-1912 . . . DLB-98, 141, 184

Langevin, André 1927- DLB-60

Langgässer, Elisabeth 1899-1950 . . . . DLB-69

Langhorne, John 1735-1779 . . . . . . DLB-109

Langland, William
    circa 1330-circa 1400 . . . . DLB-146

Langton, Anna 1804-1893 . . . . . . DLB-99

Lanham, Edwin 1904-1979 . . . . . . DLB-4

Lanier, Sidney 1842-1881 . . . . DLB-64; DS-13

Lanyer, Aemilia 1569-1645 . . . . . . DLB-121

Lapointe, Gatien 1931-1983 . . . . . . DLB-88

Lapointe, Paul-Marie 1929- DLB-88

Lardner, John 1912-1960 . . . . DLB-171

Lardner, Ring
    1885-1933 . . . DLB-11, 25, 86, 171; DS-16

Lardner, Ring, Jr. 1915- DLB-26

Lardner 100: Ring Lardner
    Centennial Symposium Y-85

Larkin, Philip 1922-1985 . . . . DLB-27

La Roche, Sophie von 1730-1807 . . . . DLB-94

La Rocque, Gilbert 1943-1984 . . . . . DLB-60

Laroque de Roquebrune, Robert (see Roquebrune,
    Robert de)

Larrick, Nancy 1910- DLB-61

Larsen, Nella 1893-1964 . . . . DLB-51

Lasker-Schüler, Else
    1869-1945 . . . . DLB-66, 124

Lasnier, Rina 1915- DLB-88

Lassalle, Ferdinand 1825-1864 . . . . . DLB-129

Lathrop, Dorothy P. 1891-1980 . . . . DLB-22

Lathrop, George Parsons
    1851-1898 . . . . DLB-71

Lathrop, John, Jr. 1772-1820 . . . . . . DLB-37

Latimer, Hugh 1492?-1555 . . . . . . DLB-136

Latimore, Jewel Christine McLawler
  (see Amini, Johari M.)

Latymer, William 1498-1583 . . . . . DLB-132

Laube, Heinrich 1806-1884 . . . . . . DLB-133

Laughlin, James 1914- DLB-48

Laumer, Keith 1925- DLB-8

Lauremberg, Johann 1590-1658 . . . . . DLB-164

Laurence, Margaret 1926-1987 . . . . . DLB-53

Laurentius von Schnüffis
  1633-1702 . . . . DLB-168

Laurents, Arthur 1918- DLB-26

Laurie, Annie (see Black, Winifred)

Laut, Agnes Christiana 1871-1936 . . . . DLB-92

Lauterbach, Ann 1942- DLB-193

Lavater, Johann Kaspar 1741-1801 . . . . DLB-97

Lavin, Mary 1912- DLB-15

Law, John (see Harkness, Margaret)

Lawes, Henry 1596-1662 . . . . DLB-126

Lawless, Anthony (see MacDonald, Philip)

Lawrence, D. H.
  1885-1930 . . . DLB-10, 19, 36, 98, 162, 195

Lawrence, David 1888-1973 . . . . . . DLB-29

Lawrence, Seymour 1926-1994 . . . . Y-94

Lawrence, T. E. 1888-1935 . . . . . . DLB-195

Lawson, John ?-1711 . . . . DLB-24

Lawson, Robert 1892-1957 . . . . . . DLB-22

Lawson, Victor F. 1850-1925 . . . . . . DLB-25

Layard, Sir Austen Henry
  1817-1894 . . . . DLB-166

Layton, Irving 1912- DLB-88

LaZamon flourished circa 1200 . . . . . DLB-146

Lazarević, Laza K. 1851-1890 . . . . . . DLB-147

Lazhechnikov, Ivan Ivanovich
  1792-1869 . . . . DLB-198

Lea, Henry Charles 1825-1909 . . . . . . DLB-47

Lea, Sydney 1942- DLB-120

Lea, Tom 1907- DLB-6

Leacock, John 1729-1802 . . . . DLB-31

Leacock, Stephen 1869-1944 . . . . . . DLB-92

Lead, Jane Ward 1623-1704 . . . . . . DLB-131

Leadenhall Press DLB-106

Leapor, Mary 1722-1746 . . . . DLB-109

Lear, Edward 1812-1888 . . . DLB-32, 163, 166

Leary, Timothy 1920-1996 . . . . DLB-16

Leary, W. A., and Company DLB-49

Léautaud, Paul 1872-1956 . . . . DLB-65

Leavitt, David 1961- DLB-130

Leavitt and Allen DLB-49

Le Blond, Mrs. Aubrey
  1861-1934 . . . . DLB-174

le Carré, John 1931- DLB-87

Lécavelé, Roland (see Dorgeles, Roland)

Lechlitner, Ruth 1901- DLB-48

Leclerc, Félix 1914- DLB-60

Le Clézio, J. M. G. 1940- DLB-83

Lectures on Rhetoric and Belles Lettres (1783),
  by Hugh Blair [excerpts] DLB-31

Leder, Rudolf (see Hermlin, Stephan)

Lederer, Charles 1910-1976 . . . . . . DLB-26

Ledwidge, Francis 1887-1917 . . . . . . DLB-20

Lee, Dennis 1939- DLB-53

Lee, Don L. (see Madhubuti, Haki R.)

Lee, George W. 1894-1976 . . . . DLB-51

Lee, Harper 1926- DLB-6

Lee, Harriet (1757-1851) and
  Lee, Sophia (1750-1824) DLB-39

Lee, Laurie 1914- DLB-27

Lee, Li-Young 1957- DLB-165

Lee, Manfred B. (see Dannay, Frederic, and
  Manfred B. Lee)

Lee, Nathaniel circa 1645 - 1692 . . . . DLB-80

Lee, Sir Sidney 1859-1926 . . . . . DLB-149, 184

Lee, Sir Sidney, "Principles of Biography," in
  Elizabethan and Other Essays DLB-149

Lee, Vernon
  1856-1935 . . . . DLB-57, 153, 156, 174, 178

Lee and Shepard DLB-49

Le Fanu, Joseph Sheridan
  1814-1873 . . . . . . DLB-21, 70, 159, 178

Leffland, Ella 1931- Y-84

le Fort, Gertrud von 1876-1971 . . . . . DLB-66

Le Gallienne, Richard 1866-1947 . . . . . DLB-4

Legaré, Hugh Swinton
  1797-1843 . . . . DLB-3, 59, 73

Legaré, James M. 1823-1859 . . . . . . DLB-3

The Legends of the Saints and a Medieval
  Christian Worldview DLB-148

Léger, Antoine-J. 1880-1950 . . . . DLB-88

Le Guin, Ursula K. 1929- DLB-8, 52

Lehman, Ernest 1920- DLB-44

Lehmann, John 1907- DLB-27, 100

Lehmann, Rosamond 1901-1990 . . . . DLB-15

Lehmann, Wilhelm 1882-1968 . . . . . DLB-56

Lehmann, John, Limited DLB-112

Leiber, Fritz 1910-1992 . . . . DLB-8

Leibniz, Gottfried Wilhelm
  1646-1716 . . . . DLB-168

Leicester University Press DLB-112

Leigh, W. R. 1866-1955 . . . . DLB-188

Leinster, Murray 1896-1975 . . . . . . DLB-8

Leisewitz, Johann Anton
  1752-1806 . . . . DLB-94

Leitch, Maurice 1933- DLB-14

Leithauser, Brad 1943- DLB-120

Leland, Charles G. 1824-1903 . . . . . DLB-11

Leland, John 1503?-1552 . . . . DLB-136

Lemay, Pamphile 1837-1918 . . . . . . DLB-99

Lemelin, Roger 1919- DLB-88

Lemercier, Louis-Jean-Népomucène
  1771-1840 . . . . DLB-192

Lemon, Mark 1809-1870 . . . . DLB-163

Le Moine, James MacPherson
  1825-1912 . . . . DLB-99

Le Moyne, Jean 1913- DLB-88

Lemperly, Paul 1858-1939 . . . . DLB-187

L'Engle, Madeleine 1918- DLB-52

Lennart, Isobel 1915-1971 . . . . . . DLB-44

Lennox, Charlotte
  1729 or 1730-1804 . . . . DLB-39

Lenox, James 1800-1880 . . . . DLB-140

Lenski, Lois 1893-1974 . . . . DLB-22

Lenz, Hermann 1913- DLB-69

Lenz, J. M. R. 1751-1792 . . . . DLB-94

Lenz, Siegfried 1926- DLB-75

Leonard, Elmore 1925- DLB-173

Leonard, Hugh 1926- DLB-13

Leonard, William Ellery
  1876-1944 . . . . DLB-54

Leonowens, Anna 1834-1914 . . . . DLB-99, 166

LePan, Douglas 1914- DLB-88

Leprohon, Rosanna Eleanor
  1829-1879 . . . . DLB-99

Le Queux, William 1864-1927 . . . . . . DLB-70

Lerner, Max 1902-1992 . . . . DLB-29

Lernet-Holenia, Alexander
  1897-1976 . . . . DLB-85

Le Rossignol, James 1866-1969 . . . . . DLB-92

Lescarbot, Marc circa 1570-1642 . . . . . DLB-99

LeSeur, William Dawson
  1840-1917 . . . . DLB-92

LeSieg, Theo. (see Geisel, Theodor Seuss)

Leslie, Doris before 1902-1982 . . . . . DLB-191

Leslie, Frank 1821-1880 . . . . . . DLB-43, 79

Leslie, Frank, Publishing House DLB-49

Lesperance, John 1835?-1891 . . . . . . DLB-99

Lessing, Bruno 1870-1940 . . . . DLB-28

Lessing, Doris 1919- . . . DLB-15, 139; Y-85

Lessing, Gotthold Ephraim
  1729-1781 . . . . DLB-97

Lettau, Reinhard 1929- DLB-75

Letter from Japan Y-94

Letter from London Y-96

Letter to [Samuel] Richardson on Clarissa
  (1748), by Henry Fielding DLB-39

A Letter to the Editor of The Irish
  Times Y-97

Lever, Charles 1806-1872. . . . . DLB-21

Leverson, Ada 1862-1933 . . . . DLB-153

Levertov, Denise 1923- DLB-5, 165

Levi, Peter 1931- DLB-40

Levi, Primo 1919-1987 . . . . DLB-177

Levien, Sonya 1888-1960 . . . . DLB-44

Levin, Meyer 1905-1981 . . . . DLB-9, 28; Y-81

Levine, Norman 1923- DLB-88

Levine, Philip 1928- DLB-5

Levis, Larry 1946- DLB-120

Levy, Amy 1861-1889 . . . . DLB-156

Levy, Benn Wolfe
1900-1973. . . . . DLB-13; Y-81

Lewald, Fanny 1811-1889 . . . . DLB-129

Lewes, George Henry
1817-1878 . . . . DLB-55, 144

Lewis, Agnes Smith 1843-1926 . . . . DLB-174

Lewis, Alfred H. 1857-1914 . . . . DLB-25, 186

Lewis, Alun 1915-1944 . . . . . . DLB-20, 162

Lewis, C. Day (see Day Lewis, C.)

Lewis, C. S. 1898-1963 . . . . DLB-15, 100, 160

Lewis, Charles B. 1842-1924 . . . . . . DLB-11

Lewis, Henry Clay 1825-1850. . . . . . DLB-3

Lewis, Janet 1899- Y-87

Lewis, Matthew Gregory
1775-1818 . . . . DLB-39, 158, 178

Lewis, Meriwether 1774-1809 and
Clark, William 1770-1838. . . DLB-183, 186

Lewis, R. W. B. 1917- DLB-111

Lewis, Richard circa 1700-1734 . . . . . DLB-24

Lewis, Sinclair
1885-1951 . . . . DLB-9, 102; DS-1

Lewis, Wilmarth Sheldon
1895-1979 . . . . DLB-140

Lewis, Wyndham 1882-1957 . . . . . . DLB-15

Lewisohn, Ludwig
1882-1955 . . . . DLB-4, 9, 28, 102

Leyendecker, J. C. 1874-1951 . . . . . DLB-188

Lezama Lima, José 1910-1976. . . . . . DLB-113

The Library of America DLB-46

The Licensing Act of 1737. . . . . . . DLB-84

Lichfield, Leonard I
[publishing house] DLB-170

Lichtenberg, Georg Christoph
1742-1799 . . . . DLB-94

The Liddle Collection Y-97

Lieb, Fred 1888-1980 . . . . DLB-171

Liebling, A. J. 1904-1963. . . . . . . DLB-4, 171

Lieutenant Murray (see Ballou, Maturin
Murray)

Lighthall, William Douw
1857-1954 . . . . DLB-92

Lilar, Françoise (see Mallet-Joris, Françoise)

Lillo, George 1691-1739 . . . . DLB-84

Lilly, J. K., Jr. 1893-1966 . . . . DLB-140

Lilly, Wait and Company DLB-49

Lily, William circa 1468-1522. . . . . DLB-132

Limited Editions Club DLB-46

Lincoln and Edmands DLB-49

Lindesay, Ethel Forence (see Richardson, Henry
Handel)

Lindsay, Alexander William, Twenty-fifth Earl
of Crawford 1812-1880 . . . . . . DLB-184

Lindsay, Jack 1900- Y-84

Lindsay, Sir David
circa 1485-1555 . . . . DLB-132

Lindsay, Vachel 1879-1931 . . . . DLB-54

Linebarger, Paul Myron Anthony (see Smith,
Cordwainer)

Link, Arthur S. 1920- DLB-17

Linn, John Blair 1777-1804. . . . . . . DLB-37

Lins, Osman 1124-1978 . . . . DLB-145

Linton, Eliza Lynn 1822-1898 . . . . . DLB-18

Linton, William James 1812-1897 . . . . DLB-32

Lintot, Barnaby Bernard
[publishing house] DLB-170

Lion Books DLB-46

Lionni, Leo 1910- DLB-61

Lippincott, Sara Jane Clarke
1823-1904 . . . . DLB-43

Lippincott, J. B., Company. DLB-49

Lippmann, Walter 1889-1974. . . . . . DLB-29

Lipton, Lawrence 1898-1975 . . . . . . DLB-16

Liscow, Christian Ludwig
1701-1760 . . . . DLB-97

Lish, Gordon 1934- DLB-130

Lispector, Clarice 1925-1977 . . . . . . DLB-113

The Literary Chronicle and Weekly Review
1819-1828 . . . . DLB-110

Literary Documents: William Faulkner
and the People-to-People
Program. Y-86

Literary Documents II: Library Journal
Statements and Questionnaires from
First Novelists Y-87

Literary Effects of World War II
[British novel]. DLB-15

Literary Prizes [British] DLB-15

Literary Research Archives: The Humanities
Research Center, University of
Texas Y-82

Literary Research Archives II: Berg
Collection of English and American
Literature of the New York Public
Library Y-83

Literary Research Archives III:
The Lilly Library Y-84

Literary Research Archives IV:
The John Carter Brown Library Y-85

Literary Research Archives V:
Kent State Special Collections Y-86

Literary Research Archives VI: The Modern
Literary Manuscripts Collection in the
Special Collections of the Washington
University Libraries Y-87

Literary Research Archives VII:
The University of Virginia
Libraries. Y-91

Literary Research Archives VIII:
The Henry E. Huntington
Library Y-92

"Literary Style" (1857), by William
Forsyth [excerpt] DLB-57

Literatura Chicanesca: The View From Without
. . . . DLB-82

Literature at Nurse, or Circulating Morals (1885),
by George Moore DLB-18

Littell, Eliakim 1797-1870. . . . . . . DLB-79

Littell, Robert S. 1831-1896 . . . . . . DLB-79

Little, Brown and Company DLB-49

Little Magazines and Newspapers DS-15

The Little Review 1914-1929 . . . . . . DS-15

Littlewood, Joan 1914- DLB-13

Lively, Penelope 1933- DLB-14, 161

Liverpool University Press DLB-112

The Lives of the Poets DLB-142

Livesay, Dorothy 1909- DLB-68

Livesay, Florence Randal
1874-1953 . . . . DLB-92

"Living in Ruin," by Gerald Stern . . . DLB-105

Livings, Henry 1929- DLB-13

Livingston, Anne Howe
1763-1841 . . . . DLB-37

Livingston, Myra Cohn 1926- DLB-61

Livingston, William 1723-1790 . . . . . DLB-31

Livingstone, David 1813-1873. . . . . . DLB-166

Liyong, Taban lo (see Taban lo Liyong)

Lizárraga, Sylvia S. 1925- DLB-82

Llewellyn, Richard 1906-1983 . . . . . DLB-15

Lloyd, Edward
[publishing house] DLB-106

Lobel, Arnold 1933- DLB-61

Lochridge, Betsy Hopkins (see Fancher, Betsy)

Locke, David Ross 1833-1888 . . . . DLB-11, 23

Locke, John 1632-1704 . . . . . . DLB-31, 101

Locke, Richard Adams 1800-1871 . . . . DLB-43

Locker-Lampson, Frederick
1821-1895 . . . . DLB-35, 184

Lockhart, John Gibson
1794-1854 . . . . DLB-110, 116 144

Lockridge, Ross, Jr.
1914-1948 . . . . DLB-143; Y-80

Locrine and Selimus. DLB-62

Lodge, David 1935- DLB-14, 194

Lodge, George Cabot 1873-1909. . . . . DLB-54

Lodge, Henry Cabot 1850-1924 . . . . . DLB-47

Lodge, Thomas 1558-1625 . . . . DLB-172

Loeb, Harold 1891-1974 . . . . DLB-4

Loeb, William 1905-1981 . . . . DLB-127

Lofting, Hugh 1886-1947 . . . . DLB-160

Logan, James 1674-1751 . . . . . DLB-24, 140

Logan, John 1923- DLB-5

Logan, William 1950- DLB-120

Logau, Friedrich von 1605-1655 . . . . DLB-164

Logue, Christopher 1926- DLB-27

Lohenstein, Daniel Casper von
    1635-1683 . . . . DLB-168

Lomonosov, Mikhail Vasil'evich
    1711-1765 . . . . DLB-150

London, Jack 1876-1916 . . . . . DLB-8, 12, 78

The London Magazine 1820-1829 . . . . . DLB-110

Long, Haniel 1888-1956 . . . . DLB-45

Long, Ray 1878-1935 . . . . DLB-137

Long, H., and Brother DLB-49

Longfellow, Henry Wadsworth
    1807-1882 . . . . DLB-1, 59

Longfellow, Samuel 1819-1892 . . . . . . DLB-1

Longford, Elizabeth 1906- DLB-155

Longinus circa first century DLB-176

Longley, Michael 1939- DLB-40

Longman, T. [publishing house] DLB-154

Longmans, Green and Company DLB-49

Longmore, George 1793?-1867 . . . . . DLB-99

Longstreet, Augustus Baldwin
    1790-1870 . . . . DLB-3, 11, 74

Longworth, D. [publishing house] DLB-49

Lonsdale, Frederick 1881-1954 . . . . DLB-10

A Look at the Contemporary Black Theatre
    Movement DLB-38

Loos, Anita 1893-1981 . . . . DLB-11, 26; Y-81

Lopate, Phillip 1943- Y-80

López, Diana (see Isabella, Ríos)

Loranger, Jean-Aubert 1896-1942 . . . . DLB-92

Lorca, Federico García 1898-1936 . . . DLB-108

Lord, John Keast 1818-1872 . . . . . . DLB-99

The Lord Chamberlain's Office and Stage
    Censorship in England DLB-10

Lorde, Audre 1934-1992 . . . . DLB-41

Lorimer, George Horace
    1867-1939 . . . . DLB-91

Loring, A. K. [publishing house] DLB-49

Loring and Mussey DLB-46

Lossing, Benson J. 1813-1891 . . . . . DLB-30

Lothar, Ernst 1890-1974 . . . . DLB-81

Lothrop, Harriet M. 1844-1924 . . . . DLB-42

Lothrop, D., and Company DLB-49

Loti, Pierre 1850-1923 . . . . DLB-123

Lotichius Secundus, Petrus
    1528-1560 . . . . DLB-179

Lott, Emeline ?-? DLB-166

The Lounger, no. 20 (1785), by Henry
    Mackenzie DLB-39

Louisiana State University Press Y-97

Lounsbury, Thomas R. 1838-1915 . . . . DLB-71

Louÿs, Pierre 1870-1925 . . . . DLB-123

Lovelace, Earl 1935- DLB-125

Lovelace, Richard 1618-1657 . . . . . DLB-131

Lovell, Coryell and Company DLB-49

Lovell, John W., Company DLB-49

Lover, Samuel 1797-1868 . . . . DLB-159, 190

Lovesey, Peter 1936- DLB-87

Lovingood, Sut (see Harris,
    George Washington)

Low, Samuel 1765-? DLB-37

Lowell, Amy 1874-1925 . . . . . . DLB-54, 140

Lowell, James Russell
    1819-1891 . . . . . DLB-1, 11, 64, 79, 189

Lowell, Robert 1917-1977 . . . . . DLB-5, 169

Lowenfels, Walter 1897-1976 . . . . . . DLB-4

Lowndes, Marie Belloc 1868-1947 . . . . DLB-70

Lowndes, William Thomas
    1798-1843 . . . . DLB-184

Lownes, Humphrey
    [publishing house] DLB-170

Lowry, Lois 1937- DLB-52

Lowry, Malcolm 1909-1957 . . . . . . DLB-15

Lowther, Pat 1935-1975 . . . . DLB-53

Loy, Mina 1882-1966 . . . . DLB-4, 54

Lozeau, Albert 1878-1924 . . . . DLB-92

Lubbock, Percy 1879-1965 . . . . . . DLB-149

Lucas, E. V. 1868-1938 . . . DLB-98, 149, 153

Lucas, Fielding, Jr.
    [publishing house] DLB-49

Luce, Henry R. 1898-1967 . . . . . . DLB-91

Luce, John W., and Company DLB-46

Lucian circa 120-180 . . . . DLB-176

Lucie-Smith, Edward 1933- DLB-40

Lucini, Gian Pietro 1867-1914 . . . . DLB-114

Luder, Peter circa 1415-1472 . . . . . DLB-179

Ludlum, Robert 1927- Y-82

Ludus de Antichristo circa 1160 . . . . . DLB-148

Ludvigson, Susan 1942- DLB-120

Ludwig, Jack 1922- DLB-60

Ludwig, Otto 1813-1865 . . . . DLB-129

Ludwigslied 881 or 882 . . . . DLB-148

Luera, Yolanda 1953- DLB-122

Luft, Lya 1938- DLB-145

Lugansky, Kazak Vladimir (see Dal', Vladimir Iva-
    novich)

Luke, Peter 1919- DLB-13

Lummis, Charles F. 1859-1928 . . . . DLB-186

Lupton, F. M., Company DLB-49

Lupus of Ferrières
    circa 805-circa 862 . . . . DLB-148

Lurie, Alison 1926- DLB-2

Luther, Martin 1483-1546 . . . . . . DLB-179

Luzi, Mario 1914- DLB-128

L'vov, Nikolai Aleksandrovich
    1751-1803 . . . . DLB-150

Lyall, Gavin 1932- DLB-87

Lydgate, John circa 1370-1450 . . . . DLB-146

Lyly, John circa 1554-1606 . . . . . DLB-62, 167

Lynch, Patricia 1898-1972 . . . . . . DLB-160

Lynch, Richard
    flourished 1596-1601 . . . . DLB-172

Lynd, Robert 1879-1949 . . . . DLB-98

Lyon, Matthew 1749-1822 . . . . . . DLB-43

Lysias circa 459 B.C.-circa 380 B.C.
    . . . . DLB-176

Lytle, Andrew 1902-1995 . . . . . DLB-6; Y-95

Lytton, Edward (see Bulwer-Lytton, Edward)

Lytton, Edward Robert Bulwer
    1831-1891 . . . . DLB-32

M

Maass, Joachim 1901-1972 . . . . DLB-69

Mabie, Hamilton Wright
    1845-1916 . . . . DLB-71

Mac A'Ghobhainn, Iain (see Smith, Iain
    Crichton)

MacArthur, Charles
    1895-1956 . . . . DLB-7, 25, 44

Macaulay, Catherine 1731-1791 . . . . DLB-104

Macaulay, David 1945- DLB-61

Macaulay, Rose 1881-1958 . . . . . . DLB-36

Macaulay, Thomas Babington
    1800-1859 . . . . DLB-32, 55

Macaulay Company DLB-46

MacBeth, George 1932- DLB-40

Macbeth, Madge 1880-1965 . . . . . DLB-92

MacCaig, Norman 1910- DLB-27

MacDiarmid, Hugh 1892-1978 . . . . DLB-20

MacDonald, Cynthia 1928- DLB-105

MacDonald, George
    1824-1905 . . . . DLB-18, 163, 178

MacDonald, John D.
    1916-1986 . . . . DLB-8; Y-86

MacDonald, Philip 1899?-1980 . . . . . DLB-77

Macdonald, Ross (see Millar, Kenneth)

MacDonald, Wilson 1880-1967 . . . . DLB-92

Macdonald and Company
    (Publishers) DLB-112

MacEwen, Gwendolyn 1941- DLB-53

Macfadden, Bernarr
    1868-1955 . . . . DLB-25, 91

MacGregor, John 1825-1892 . . . . . . DLB-166

MacGregor, Mary Esther (see Keith, Marian)

Machado, Antonio 1875-1939 . . . . . DLB-108

Machado, Manuel 1874-1947 . . . . . . DLB-108

Machar, Agnes Maule 1837-1927 . . . . DLB-92

Machen, Arthur Llewelyn Jones
1863-1947 . . . . DLB-36, 156, 178

MacInnes, Colin 1914-1976 . . . . DLB-14

MacInnes, Helen 1907-1985 . . . . . . DLB-87

Mack, Maynard 1909- DLB-111

Mackall, Leonard L. 1879-1937 . . . . . DLB-140

MacKaye, Percy 1875-1956 . . . . DLB-54

Macken, Walter 1915-1967 . . . . DLB-13

Mackenzie, Alexander 1763-1820 . . . . DLB-99

Mackenzie, Alexander Slidell
1803-1848 . . . . DLB-183

Mackenzie, Compton
1883-1972 . . . . DLB-34, 100

Mackenzie, Henry 1745-1831 . . . . . DLB-39

Mackenzie, William 1758-1828 . . . . . DLB-187

Mackey, Nathaniel 1947- DLB-169

Mackey, William Wellington
1937- DLB-38

Mackintosh, Elizabeth (see Tey, Josephine)

Mackintosh, Sir James
1765-1832 . . . . DLB-158

Maclaren, Ian (see Watson, John)

Macklin, Charles 1699-1797 . . . . . . DLB-89

MacLean, Katherine Anne 1925- DLB-8

MacLeish, Archibald
1892-1982 . . . . DLB-4, 7, 45; Y-82

MacLennan, Hugh 1907-1990 . . . . . DLB-68

Macleod, Fiona (see Sharp, William)

MacLeod, Alistair 1936- DLB-60

Macleod, Norman 1906-1985 . . . . . . DLB-4

Mac Low, Jackson 1922- DLB-193

Macmillan and Company DLB-106

The Macmillan Company DLB-49

Macmillan's English Men of Letters,
First Series (1878-1892) DLB-144

MacNamara, Brinsley 1890-1963 . . . . DLB-10

MacNeice, Louis 1907-1963 . . . . DLB-10, 20

MacPhail, Andrew 1864-1938 . . . . . DLB-92

Macpherson, James 1736-1796 . . . . . DLB-109

Macpherson, Jay 1931- DLB-53

Macpherson, Jeanie 1884-1946 . . . . . DLB-44

Macrae Smith Company DLB-46

Macrone, John
[publishing house] DLB-106

MacShane, Frank 1927- DLB-111

Macy-Masius DLB-46

Madden, David 1933- DLB-6

Madden, Sir Frederic 1801-1873 . . . . DLB-184

Maddow, Ben 1909-1992 . . . . DLB-44

Maddux, Rachel 1912-1983 . . . . Y-93

Madgett, Naomi Long 1923- DLB-76

Madhubuti, Haki R.
1942- DLB-5, 41; DS-8

Madison, James 1751-1836 . . . . DLB-37

Maeterlinck, Maurice 1862-1949 . . . . DLB-192

Magee, David 1905-1977 . . . . DLB-187

Maginn, William 1794-1842 . . . . DLB-110, 159

Mahan, Alfred Thayer 1840-1914 . . . . DLB-47

Maheux-Forcier, Louise 1929- DLB-60

Mafûz, Najîb 1911- Y-88

Mahin, John Lee 1902-1984 . . . . . . DLB-44

Mahon, Derek 1941- DLB-40

Maikov, Vasilii Ivanovich
1728-1778 . . . . DLB-150

Mailer, Norman 1923-
DLB-2, 16, 28, 185; Y-80, Y-83; DS-3

Maillart, Ella 1903-1997 . . . . DLB-195

Maillet, Adrienne 1885-1963 . . . . . . DLB-68

Maimonides, Moses 1138-1204 . . . . . DLB-115

Maillet, Antonine 1929- DLB-60

Maillu, David G. 1939- DLB-157

Main Selections of the Book-of-the-Month
Club, 1926-1945 . . . . DLB-9

Main Trends in Twentieth-Century Book Clubs
. . . . DLB-46

Mainwaring, Daniel 1902-1977 . . . . . DLB-44

Mair, Charles 1838-1927 . . . . DLB-99

Mais, Roger 1905-1955 . . . . DLB-125

Major, Andre 1942- DLB-60

Major, Clarence 1936- DLB-33

Major, Kevin 1949- DLB-60

Major Books DLB-46

Makemie, Francis circa 1658-1708 . . . . DLB-24

The Making of a People, by
J. M. Ritchie DLB-66

Maksimović, Desanka 1898-1993 . . . . DLB-147

Malamud, Bernard
1914-1986 . . . DLB-2, 28, 152; Y-80, Y-86

Malerba, Luigi 1927- DLB-196

Malet, Lucas 1852-1931 . . . . DLB-153

Malleson, Lucy Beatrice (see Gilbert, Anthony)

Mallet-Joris, Françoise 1930- DLB-83

Mallock, W. H. 1849-1923 . . . . . DLB-18, 57

Malone, Dumas 1892-1986 . . . . DLB-17

Malone, Edmond 1741-1812 . . . . . . DLB-142

Malory, Sir Thomas
circa 1400-1410 - 1471 . . . . . . DLB-146

Malraux, André 1901-1976 . . . . DLB-72

Malthus, Thomas Robert
1766-1834 . . . . DLB-107, 158

Maltz, Albert 1908-1985 . . . . DLB-102

Malzberg, Barry N. 1939- DLB-8

Mamet, David 1947- DLB-7

Manaka, Matsemela 1956- DLB-157

Manchester University Press DLB-112

Mandel, Eli 1922- DLB-53

Mandeville, Bernard 1670-1733 . . . . DLB-101

Mandeville, Sir John
mid fourteenth century DLB-146

Mandiargues, André Pieyre de
1909- DLB-83

Manfred, Frederick 1912-1994 . . . . . . DLB-6

Manfredi, Gianfranco 1948- DLB-196

Mangan, Sherry 1904-1961 . . . . DLB-4

Manganelli, Giorgio 1922-1990 . . . . . DLB-196

Mankiewicz, Herman 1897-1953 . . . . . DLB-26

Mankiewicz, Joseph L. 1909-1993 . . . . DLB-44

Mankowitz, Wolf 1924- DLB-15

Manley, Delariviere
1672?-1724 . . . . DLB-39, 80

Mann, Abby 1927- DLB-44

Mann, Heinrich 1871-1950 . . . . DLB-66, 118

Mann, Horace 1796-1859 . . . . DLB-1

Mann, Klaus 1906-1949 . . . . DLB-56

Mann, Thomas 1875-1955 . . . . DLB-66

Mann, William D'Alton
1839-1920 . . . . DLB-137

Mannin, Ethel 1900-1984 . . . . DLB-191, 195

Manning, Marie 1873?-1945 . . . . . . DLB-29

Manning and Loring DLB-49

Mannyng, Robert
flourished 1303-1338 . . . . DLB-146

Mano, D. Keith 1942- DLB-6

Manor Books DLB-46

Mansfield, Katherine 1888-1923 . . . . DLB-162

Manuel, Niklaus circa 1484-1530 . . . . DLB-179

Manzini, Gianna 1896-1974 . . . . . . DLB-177

Mapanje, Jack 1944- DLB-157

Maraini, Dacia 1936- DLB-196

March, William 1893-1954 . . . . . DLB-9, 86

Marchand, Leslie A. 1900- DLB-103

Marchant, Bessie 1862-1941 . . . . . . DLB-160

Marchessault, Jovette 1938- DLB-60

Marcus, Frank 1928- DLB-13

Marden, Orison Swett
1850-1924 . . . . DLB-137

Marechera, Dambudzo
1952-1987 . . . . DLB-157

Marek, Richard, Books DLB-46

Mares, E. A. 1938- DLB-122

Mariani, Paul 1940- DLB-111

Marie-Victorin, Frère 1885-1944 . . . . DLB-92

Marin, Biagio 1891-1985 . . . . DLB-128

Marinković, Ranko 1913- DLB-147

Marinetti, Filippo Tommaso
1876-1944 . . . . DLB-114

Marion, Frances 1886-1973 . . . . DLB-44

Marius, Richard C. 1933- Y-85

The Mark Taper Forum DLB-7

Mark Twain on Perpetual Copyright Y-92

Markfield, Wallace 1926- DLB-2, 28

Markham, Edwin 1852-1940 . . . . DLB-54, 186

Markle, Fletcher 1921-1991 . . . . DLB-68; Y-91

Marlatt, Daphne 1942- DLB-60

Marlitt, E. 1825-1887 . . . . DLB-129

Marlowe, Christopher 1564-1593 . . . . DLB-62

Marlyn, John 1912- DLB-88

Marmion, Shakerley 1603-1639 . . . . . DLB-58

Der Marner
before 1230-circa 1287 . . . . . . DLB-138

The *Marprelate Tracts* 1588-1589 . . . . DLB-132

Marquand, John P. 1893-1960 . . . . DLB-9, 102

Marqués, René 1919-1979 . . . . DLB-113

Marquis, Don 1878-1937 . . . . . . DLB-11, 25

Marriott, Anne 1913- DLB-68

Marryat, Frederick 1792-1848 . . . . DLB-21, 163

Marsh, George Perkins
1801-1882 . . . . DLB-1, 64

Marsh, James 1794-1842 . . . . DLB-1, 59

Marsh, Capen, Lyon and Webb DLB-49

Marsh, Ngaio 1899-1982 . . . . DLB-77

Marshall, Edison 1894-1967 . . . . . . DLB-102

Marshall, Edward 1932- DLB-16

Marshall, Emma 1828-1899 . . . . . . DLB-163

Marshall, James 1942-1992 . . . . . . DLB-61

Marshall, Joyce 1913- DLB-88

Marshall, Paule 1929- DLB-33, 157

Marshall, Tom 1938- DLB-60

Marsilius of Padua
circa 1275-circa 1342 . . . . DLB-115

Marson, Una 1905-1965 . . . . DLB-157

Marston, John 1576-1634 . . . . . DLB-58, 172

Marston, Philip Bourke 1850-1887 . . . . DLB-35

Martens, Kurt 1870-1945 . . . . DLB-66

Martien, William S.
[publishing house] DLB-49

Martin, Abe (see Hubbard, Kin)

Martin, Charles 1942- DLB-120

Martin, Claire 1914- DLB-60

Martin, Jay 1935- DLB-111

Martin, Johann (see Laurentius von Schnüffis)

Martin, Violet Florence (see Ross, Martin)

Martin du Gard, Roger
1881-1958 . . . . DLB-65

Martineau, Harriet 1802-1876
. . . . DLB-21, 55, 159, 163, 166, 190

Martínez, Eliud 1935- DLB-122

Martínez, Max 1943- DLB-82

Martyn, Edward 1859-1923 . . . . DLB-10

Marvell, Andrew 1621-1678 . . . . . . DLB-131

Marvin X 1944- DLB-38

Marx, Karl 1818-1883 . . . . DLB-129

Marzials, Theo 1850-1920 . . . . DLB-35

Masefield, John
1878-1967 . . . . . . DLB-10, 19, 153, 160

Mason, A. E. W. 1865-1948 . . . . . . DLB-70

Mason, Bobbie Ann
1940- DLB-173; Y-87

Mason, William 1725-1797 . . . . DLB-142

Mason Brothers DLB-49

Massey, Gerald 1828-1907 . . . . DLB-32

Massey, Linton R. 1900-1974 . . . . . DLB-187

Massinger, Philip 1583-1640 . . . . . . DLB-58

Masson, David 1822-1907 . . . . DLB-144

Masters, Edgar Lee 1868-1950 . . . . . DLB-54

Mastronardi, Lucio 1930-1979 . . . . . . DLB-177

Matevski, Mateja 1929- DLB-181

Mather, Cotton
1663-1728 . . . . DLB-24, 30, 140

Mather, Increase 1639-1723 . . . . . . DLB-24

Mather, Richard 1596-1669 . . . . DLB-24

Matheson, Richard 1926- DLB-8, 44

Matheus, John F. 1887- DLB-51

Mathews, Cornelius
1817?-1889 . . . . DLB-3, 64

Mathews, John Joseph
1894-1979 . . . . DLB-175

Mathews, Elkin
[publishing house] DLB-112

Mathias, Roland 1915- DLB-27

Mathis, June 1892-1927 . . . . DLB-44

Mathis, Sharon Bell 1937- DLB-33

Matković, Marijan 1915-1985 . . . . . DLB-181

Matoš, Antun Gustav 1873-1914 . . . . DLB-147

Matsumoto, Seichō 1909-1992 . . . . . DLB-182

The Matter of England
1240-1400 . . . . DLB-146

The Matter of Rome
early twelfth to late fifteenth
century DLB-146

Matthews, Brander
1852-1929 . . . . DLB-71, 78; DS-13

Matthews, Jack 1925- DLB-6

Matthews, William 1942- DLB-5

Matthiessen, F. O. 1902-1950 . . . . . DLB-63

Maturin, Charles Robert
1780-1824 . . . . DLB-178

Matthiessen, Peter 1927- DLB-6, 173

Maugham, W. Somerset
1874-1965 . . DLB-10, 36, 77, 100, 162, 195

Maupassant, Guy de 1850-1893 . . . . DLB-123

Mauriac, Claude 1914- DLB-83

Mauriac, François 1885-1970 . . . . . . DLB-65

Maurice, Frederick Denison
1805-1872 . . . . DLB-55

Maurois, André 1885-1967 . . . . DLB-65

Maury, James 1718-1769 . . . . DLB-31

Mavor, Elizabeth 1927- DLB-14

Mavor, Osborne Henry (see Bridie, James)

Maxwell, William 1908- Y-80

Maxwell, H. [publishing house] DLB-49

Maxwell, John [publishing house] DLB-106

May, Elaine 1932- DLB-44

May, Karl 1842-1912 . . . . DLB-129

May, Thomas 1595 or 1596-1650 . . . . DLB-58

Mayer, Bernadette 1945- DLB-165

Mayer, Mercer 1943- DLB-61

Mayer, O. B. 1818-1891 . . . . DLB-3

Mayes, Herbert R. 1900-1987 . . . . . . DLB-137

Mayes, Wendell 1919-1992 . . . . DLB-26

Mayfield, Julian 1928-1984 . . . . DLB-33; Y-84

Mayhew, Henry 1812-1887 . . DLB-18, 55, 190

Mayhew, Jonathan 1720-1766 . . . . . . DLB-31

Mayne, Ethel Colburn 1865-1941 . . . DLB-197

Mayne, Jasper 1604-1672 . . . . DLB-126

Mayne, Seymour 1944- DLB-60

Mayor, Flora Macdonald
1872-1932 . . . . DLB-36

Mayrocker, Friederike 1924- DLB-85

Mazrui, Ali A. 1933- DLB-125

Mažuranić, Ivan 1814-1890 . . . . . . DLB-147

Mazursky, Paul 1930- DLB-44

McAlmon, Robert
1896-1956 . . . . DLB-4, 45; DS-15

McArthur, Peter 1866-1924 . . . . . . DLB-92

McBride, Robert M., and
Company DLB-46

McCabe, Patrick 1955- DLB-194

McCaffrey, Anne 1926- DLB-8

McCarthy, Cormac 1933- DLB-6, 143

McCarthy, Mary 1912-1989 . . . . DLB-2; Y-81

McCay, Winsor 1871-1934 . . . . DLB-22

McClane, Albert Jules 1922-1991 . . . . DLB-171

McClatchy, C. K. 1858-1936 . . . . . . DLB-25

McClellan, George Marion
1860-1934 . . . . DLB-50

McCloskey, Robert 1914- DLB-22

McClung, Nellie Letitia 1873-1951 . . . . DLB-92

McClure, Joanna 1930- DLB-16

McClure, Michael 1932- DLB-16

McClure, Phillips and Company DLB-46

McClure, S. S. 1857-1949 . . . . DLB-91

McClurg, A. C., and Company DLB-49

McCluskey, John A., Jr. 1944- DLB-33

McCollum, Michael A. 1946. . . . . Y-87

McConnell, William C. 1917- DLB-88

McCord, David 1897- DLB-61

McCorkle, Jill 1958- Y-87

McCorkle, Samuel Eusebius
1746-1811 . . . . DLB-37

McCormick, Anne O'Hare
1880-1954 . . . . DLB-29

McCormick, Robert R. 1880-1955. . . . DLB-29

McCourt, Edward 1907-1972. . . . . . DLB-88

McCoy, Horace 1897-1955 . . . . DLB-9

McCrae, John 1872-1918 . . . . DLB-92

McCullagh, Joseph B. 1842-1896. . . . DLB-23

McCullers, Carson
1917-1967 . . . . DLB-2, 7, 173

McCulloch, Thomas 1776-1843 . . . . DLB-99

McDonald, Forrest 1927- DLB-17

McDonald, Walter
1934- DLB-105, DS-9

McDougall, Colin 1917-1984 . . . . . . DLB-68

McDowell, Obolensky DLB-46

McEwan, Ian 1948- DLB-14, 194

McFadden, David 1940- DLB-60

McFall, Frances Elizabeth Clarke
(see Grand, Sarah)

McFarlane, Leslie 1902-1977 . . . . . . DLB-88

McFee, William 1881-1966 . . . . . . DLB-153

McGahern, John 1934- DLB-14

McGee, Thomas D'Arcy
1825-1868 . . . . DLB-99

McGeehan, W. O. 1879-1933 . . . DLB-25, 171

McGill, Ralph 1898-1969 . . . . DLB-29

McGinley, Phyllis 1905-1978 . . . . DLB-11, 48

McGinniss, Joe 1942- DLB-185

McGirt, James E. 1874-1930 . . . . . . DLB-50

McGlashan and Gill DLB-106

McGough, Roger 1937- DLB-40

McGraw-Hill DLB-46

McGuane, Thomas 1939- DLB-2; Y-80

McGuckian, Medbh 1950- DLB-40

McGuffey, William Holmes
1800-1873 . . . . DLB-42

McIlvanney, William 1936- DLB-14

McIlwraith, Jean Newton
1859-1938 . . . . DLB-92

McIntyre, James 1827-1906. . . . . . . DLB-99

McIntyre, O. O. 1884-1938 . . . . . . DLB-25

McKay, Claude
1889-1948 . . . . DLB-4, 45, 51, 117

The David McKay Company DLB-49

McKean, William V. 1820-1903 . . . . DLB-23

McKenna, Stephen 1888-1967 . . . . . DLB-197

The McKenzie Trust. Y-96

McKinley, Robin 1952- DLB-52

McLachlan, Alexander 1818-1896 . . . . DLB-99

McLaren, Floris Clark 1904-1978 . . . . DLB-68

McLaverty, Michael 1907- DLB-15

McLean, John R. 1848-1916 . . . . . . DLB-23

McLean, William L. 1852-1931 . . . . DLB-25

McLennan, William 1856-1904. . . . . DLB-92

McLoughlin Brothers DLB-49

McLuhan, Marshall 1911-1980 . . . . . DLB-88

McMaster, John Bach 1852-1932. . . . DLB-47

McMurtry, Larry
1936- DLB-2, 143; Y-80, Y-87

McNally, Terrence 1939- DLB-7

McNeil, Florence 1937- DLB-60

McNeile, Herman Cyril
1888-1937 . . . . DLB-77

McNickle, D'Arcy 1904-1977 . . . . . DLB-175

McPhee, John 1931- DLB-185

McPherson, James Alan 1943- DLB-38

McPherson, Sandra 1943- Y-86

McWhirter, George 1939- DLB-60

McWilliams, Carey 1905-1980 . . . . DLB-137

Mead, L. T. 1844-1914 . . . . DLB-141

Mead, Matthew 1924- DLB-40

Mead, Taylor ?- DLB-16

Meany, Tom 1903-1964. . . . . DLB-171

Mechthild von Magdeburg
circa 1207-circa 1282 . . . . DLB-138

Medill, Joseph 1823-1899 . . . . DLB-43

Medoff, Mark 1940- DLB-7

Meek, Alexander Beaufort
1814-1865. . . . . DLB-3

Meeke, Mary ?-1816? DLB-116

Meinke, Peter 1932- DLB-5

Mejia Vallejo, Manuel 1923- DLB-113

Melanchthon, Philipp 1497-1560 . . . DLB-179

Melançon, Robert 1947- DLB-60

Mell, Max 1882-1971 . . . . DLB-81, 124

Mellow, James R. 1926- DLB-111

Meltzer, David 1937- DLB-16

Meltzer, Milton 1915- DLB-61

Melville, Elizabeth, Lady Culross
circa 1585-1640 . . . . DLB-172

Melville, Herman 1819-1891 . . . . DLB-3, 74

Memoirs of Life and Literature (1920),
by W. H. Mallock [excerpt] DLB-57

Menander 342-341 B.C.-circa 292-291 B.C.
. . . . DLB-176

Menantes (see Hunold, Christian Friedrich)

Mencke, Johann Burckhard
1674-1732 . . . . DLB-168

Mencken, H. L.
1880-1956. . . . . . . DLB-11, 29, 63, 137

Mencken and Nietzsche: An Unpublished Excerpt
from H. L. Mencken's *My Life
as Author and Editor* Y-93

Mendelssohn, Moses 1729-1786 . . . . DLB-97

Méndez M., Miguel 1930- DLB-82

Mens Rea (or Something). Y-97

The Mercantile Library of
New York Y-96

Mercer, Cecil William (see Yates, Dornford)

Mercer, David 1928-1980. . . . . DLB-13

Mercer, John 1704-1768 . . . . DLB-31

Meredith, George
1828-1909 . . . . DLB-18, 35, 57, 159

Meredith, Louisa Anne
1812-1895 . . . . DLB-166

Meredith, Owen (see Lytton, Edward Robert Bulwer)

Meredith, William 1919- DLB-5

Mergerle, Johann Ulrich
(see Abraham ä Sancta Clara)

Mérimée, Prosper 1803-1870 . . . DLB-119, 192

Merivale, John Herman
1779-1844 . . . . DLB-96

Meriwether, Louise 1923- DLB-33

Merlin Press DLB-112

Merriam, Eve 1916-1992 . . . . DLB-61

The Merriam Company DLB-49

Merrill, James
1926-1995 . . . . DLB-5, 165; Y-85

Merrill and Baker. DLB-49

The Mershon Company DLB-49

Merton, Thomas 1915-1968 . . . . DLB-48; Y-81

Merwin, W. S. 1927- DLB-5, 169

Messner, Julian [publishing house] DLB-46

Metcalf, J. [publishing house] DLB-49

Metcalf, John 1938- DLB-60

The Methodist Book Concern DLB-49

Methuen and Company. DLB-112

Mew, Charlotte 1869-1928 . . . . . DLB-19, 135

Mewshaw, Michael 1943- Y-80

Meyer, Conrad Ferdinand 1825-1898 . . . DLB-129

Meyer, E. Y. 1946- DLB-75

Meyer, Eugene 1875-1959 . . . . DLB-29

Meyer, Michael 1921- DLB-155

Meyers, Jeffrey 1939- DLB-111

Meynell, Alice 1847-1922. . . . . . DLB-19, 98

Meynell, Viola 1885-1956 . . . . . . DLB-153

Meyrink, Gustav 1868-1932 . . . . . . DLB-81

Michael M. Rea and the Rea Award for the
Short Story Y-97

Michaels, Leonard 1933- DLB-130

Micheaux, Oscar 1884-1951 . . . . . . DLB-50

Michel of Northgate, Dan
circa 1265-circa 1340 . . . . DLB-146

Micheline, Jack 1929- DLB-16

Michener, James A. 1907?- DLB-6

Micklejohn, George
circa 1717-1818 . . . . DLB-31

Middle English Literature:
An Introduction DLB-146

The Middle English Lyric. DLB-146

Middle Hill Press DLB-106

Middleton, Christopher 1926- DLB-40

Middleton, Richard 1882-1911 . . . . . DLB-156

Middleton, Stanley 1919- DLB-14

Middleton, Thomas 1580-1627 . . . . . DLB-58

Miegel, Agnes 1879-1964 . . . . DLB-56

Mihailović, Dragoslav 1930- DLB-181

Mihalić, Slavko 1928- DLB-181

Miles, Josephine 1911-1985 . . . . . . DLB-48

Miliković, Branko 1934-1961 . . . . . . DLB-181

Milius, John 1944- DLB-44

Mill, James 1773-1836 . . . . . . DLB-107, 158

Mill, John Stuart 1806-1873 . . . . DLB-55, 190

Millar, Kenneth
1915-1983 . . . . DLB-2; Y-83; DS-6

Millar, Andrew
[publishing house] DLB-154

Millay, Edna St. Vincent
1892-1950 . . . . DLB-45

Miller, Arthur 1915- DLB-7

Miller, Caroline 1903-1992 . . . . DLB-9

Miller, Eugene Ethelbert 1950- DLB-41

Miller, Heather Ross 1939- DLB-120

Miller, Henry 1891-1980 . . . . DLB-4, 9; Y-80

Miller, Hugh 1802-1856 . . . . DLB-190

Miller, J. Hillis 1928- DLB-67

Miller, James [publishing house] DLB-49

Miller, Jason 1939- DLB-7

Miller, Joaquin 1839-1913 . . . . DLB-186

Miller, May 1899- DLB-41

Miller, Paul 1906-1991 . . . . DLB-127

Miller, Perry 1905-1963 . . . . . . DLB-17, 63

Miller, Sue 1943- DLB-143

Miller, Vassar 1924- DLB-105

Miller, Walter M., Jr. 1923- DLB-8

Miller, Webb 1892-1940 . . . . DLB-29

Millhauser, Steven 1943- DLB-2

Millican, Arthenia J. Bates
1920- DLB-38

Mills and Boon DLB-112

Milman, Henry Hart 1796-1868 . . . . DLB-96

Milne, A. A.
1882-1956 . . . . . . DLB-10, 77, 100, 160

Milner, Ron 1938- DLB-38

Milner, William
[publishing house] DLB-106

Milnes, Richard Monckton (Lord Houghton)
1809-1885 . . . . DLB-32, 184

Milton, John 1608-1674 . . . . . DLB-131, 151

Minakami, Tsutomu 1919- DLB-182

The Minerva Press DLB-154

Minnesang circa 1150-1280 . . . . . . DLB-138

Minns, Susan 1839-1938. . . . . DLB-140

Minor Illustrators, 1880-1914 . . . . . DLB-141

Minor Poets of the Earlier Seventeenth
Century DLB-121

Minton, Balch and Company DLB-46

Mirbeau, Octave 1848-1917 . . . . DLB-123, 192

Mirk, John died after 1414? DLB-146

Miron, Gaston 1928- DLB-60

A Mirror for Magistrates DLB-167

Mishima, Yukio 1925-1970 . . . . . . DLB-182

Mitchel, Jonathan 1624-1668 . . . . . . DLB-24

Mitchell, Adrian 1932- DLB-40

Mitchell, Donald Grant
1822-1908 . . . . DLB-1; DS-13

Mitchell, Gladys 1901-1983. . . . . . . DLB-77

Mitchell, James Leslie 1901-1935 . . . . . DLB-15

Mitchell, John (see Slater, Patrick)

Mitchell, John Ames 1845-1918 . . . . . DLB-79

Mitchell, Joseph 1908-1996 . . . . DLB-185; Y-96

Mitchell, Julian 1935- DLB-14

Mitchell, Ken 1940- DLB-60

Mitchell, Langdon 1862-1935 . . . . . . DLB-7

Mitchell, Loften 1919- DLB-38

Mitchell, Margaret 1900-1949 . . . . . . DLB-9

Mitchell, W. O. 1914- DLB-88

Mitchison, Naomi Margaret (Haldane)
1897- DLB-160, 191

Mitford, Mary Russell
1787-1855. . . . . DLB-110, 116

Mitford, Nancy 1904-1973. . . . . . . DLB-191

Mittelholzer, Edgar 1909-1965. . . . . . DLB-117

Mitterer, Erika 1906- DLB-85

Mitterer, Felix 1948- DLB-124

Mitternacht, Johann Sebastian
1613-1679 . . . . DLB-168

Miyamoto, Yuriko 1899-1951 . . . . . . DLB-180

Mizener, Arthur 1907-1988 . . . . . . DLB-103

Mo, Timothy 1950- DLB-194

Modern Age Books. DLB-46

"Modern English Prose" (1876),
by George Saintsbury DLB-57

The Modern Language Association of America
Celebrates Its Centennial Y-84

The Modern Library DLB-46

"Modern Novelists – Great and Small" (1855), by
Margaret Oliphant DLB-21

"Modern Style" (1857), by Cockburn
Thomson [excerpt] DLB-57

The Modernists (1932),
by Joseph Warren Beach DLB-36

Modiano, Patrick 1945- DLB-83

Moffat, Yard and Company DLB-46

Moffet, Thomas 1553-1604 . . . . . . DLB-136

Mohr, Nicholasa 1938- DLB-145

Moix, Ana María 1947- DLB-134

Molesworth, Louisa 1839-1921 . . . . . DLB-135

Möllhausen, Balduin 1825-1905. . . . . DLB-129

Momaday, N. Scott 1934- DLB-143, 175

Monkhouse, Allan 1858-1936. . . . . . DLB-10

Monro, Harold 1879-1932 . . . . DLB-19

Monroe, Harriet 1860-1936 . . . . DLB-54, 91

Monsarrat, Nicholas 1910-1979 . . . . . DLB-15

Montagu, Lady Mary Wortley
1689-1762 . . . . DLB-95, 101

Montague, C. E. 1867-1928. . . . . . DLB-197

Montague, John 1929- DLB-40

Montale, Eugenio 1896-1981 . . . . . . DLB-114

Monterroso, Augusto 1921- DLB-145

Montgomerie, Alexander
circa 1550?-1598 . . . . DLB-167

Montgomery, James
1771-1854 . . . . DLB-93, 158

Montgomery, John 1919- DLB-16

Montgomery, Lucy Maud
1874-1942 . . . . DLB-92; DS-14

Montgomery, Marion 1925- DLB-6

Montgomery, Robert Bruce (see Crispin, Edmund)

Montherlant, Henry de 1896-1972 . . . DLB-72

The Monthly Review 1749-1844 . . . . . DLB-110

Montigny, Louvigny de 1876-1955 . . . DLB-92

Montoya, José 1932- DLB-122

Moodie, John Wedderburn Dunbar
1797-1869 . . . . DLB-99

Moodie, Susanna 1803-1885 . . . . . . DLB-99

Moody, Joshua circa 1633-1697 . . . . . DLB-24

Moody, William Vaughn
1869-1910 . . . . DLB-7, 54

Moorcock, Michael 1939- DLB-14

Moore, Catherine L. 1911- DLB-8

Moore, Clement Clarke 1779-1863 . . . DLB-42

Moore, Dora Mavor 1888-1979 . . . . . DLB-92

Moore, George
1852-1933 . . . . DLB-10, 18, 57, 135

Moore, Marianne
1887-1972 . . . . DLB-45; DS-7

Moore, Mavor 1919- DLB-88

Moore, Richard 1927- DLB-105

Moore, T. Sturge 1870-1944 . . . . . . DLB-19

Moore, Thomas 1779-1852 . . . . . DLB-96, 144

Moore, Ward 1903-1978 . . . . DLB-8

Moore, Wilstach, Keys and
Company DLB-49

The Moorland-Spingarn Research
Center DLB-76

Moorman, Mary C. 1905-1994 . . . . . DLB-155

Moraga, Cherríe 1952- DLB-82

Morales, Alejandro 1944- DLB-82

Morales, Mario Roberto 1947- DLB-145

Morales, Rafael 1919- DLB-108

Morality Plays: *Mankind* circa 1450-1500 and
Everyman circa 1500 . . . . DLB-146

Morante, Elsa 1912-1985 . . . . DLB-177

Morata, Olympia Fulvia
1526-1555 . . . . DLB-179

Moravia, Alberto 1907-1990 . . . . . . DLB-177

Mordaunt, Elinor 1872-1942 . . . . . . DLB-174

More, Hannah
1745-1833 . . . . . DLB-107, 109, 116, 158

More, Henry 1614-1687 . . . . DLB-126

More, Sir Thomas
1477 or 1478-1535 . . . . DLB-136

Moreno, Dorinda 1939- DLB-122

Morency, Pierre 1942- DLB-60

Moretti, Marino 1885-1979 . . . . . . DLB-114

Morgan, Berry 1919- DLB-6

Morgan, Charles 1894-1958 . . . . DLB-34, 100

Morgan, Edmund S. 1916- DLB-17

Morgan, Edwin 1920- DLB-27

Morgan, John Pierpont
1837-1913 . . . . DLB-140

Morgan, John Pierpont, Jr.
1867-1943 . . . . DLB-140

Morgan, Robert 1944- DLB-120

Morgan, Sydney Owenson, Lady
1776?-1859 . . . . DLB-116, 158

Morgner, Irmtraud 1933- DLB-75

Morhof, Daniel Georg
1639-1691 . . . . DLB-164

Mori, Ōgai 1862-1922 . . . . DLB-180

Morier, James Justinian
1782 or 1783?-1849 . . . . DLB-116

Mörike, Eduard 1804-1875 . . . . . . DLB-133

Morin, Paul 1889-1963 . . . . DLB-92

Morison, Richard 1514?-1556 . . . . . DLB-136

Morison, Samuel Eliot 1887-1976 . . . . DLB-17

Moritz, Karl Philipp 1756-1793 . . . . . DLB-94

Moriz von Craûn
circa 1220-1230 . . . . DLB-138

Morley, Christopher 1890-1957 . . . . . DLB-9

Morley, John 1838-1923 . . . . DLB-57, 144, 190

Morris, George Pope 1802-1864 . . . . . DLB-73

Morris, Lewis 1833-1907 . . . . DLB-35

Morris, Richard B. 1904-1989 . . . . . DLB-17

Morris, William
1834-1896 . . DLB-18, 35, 57, 156, 178, 184

Morris, Willie 1934- Y-80

Morris, Wright 1910- DLB-2; Y-81

Morrison, Arthur
1863-1945 . . . . DLB-70, 135, 197

Morrison, Charles Clayton
1874-1966 . . . . DLB-91

Morrison, Toni
1931- DLB-6, 33, 143; Y-81, Y-93

Morrow, William, and Company DLB-46

Morse, James Herbert 1841-1923 . . . . DLB-71

Morse, Jedidiah 1761-1826 . . . . . . DLB-37

Morse, John T., Jr. 1840-1937 . . . . . DLB-47

Morselli, Guido 1912-1973 . . . . DLB-177

Mortimer, Favell Lee 1802-1878 . . . . DLB-163

Mortimer, John 1923- DLB-13

Morton, Carlos 1942- DLB-122

Morton, H. V. 1892-1979 . . . . DLB-195

Morton, John P., and Company DLB-49

Morton, Nathaniel 1613-1685 . . . . . DLB-24

Morton, Sarah Wentworth
1759-1846 . . . . DLB-37

Morton, Thomas
circa 1579-circa 1647 . . . . DLB-24

Moscherosch, Johann Michael
1601-1669 . . . . DLB-164

Moseley, Humphrey
[publishing house] DLB-170

Möser, Justus 1720-1794 . . . . DLB-97

Mosley, Nicholas 1923- DLB-14

Moss, Arthur 1889-1969 . . . . DLB-4

Moss, Howard 1922-1987 . . . . DLB-5

Moss, Thylias 1954- DLB-120

The Most Powerful Book Review in America
[*New York Times Book Review*] Y-82

Motion, Andrew 1952- DLB-40

Motley, John Lothrop
1814-1877 . . . . DLB-1, 30, 59

Motley, Willard 1909-1965 . . . DLB-76, 143

Motte, Benjamin Jr.
[publishing house] DLB-154

Motteux, Peter Anthony
1663-1718 . . . . DLB-80

Mottram, R. H. 1883-1971 . . . . DLB-36

Mouré, Erin 1955- DLB-60

Mourning Dove (Humishuma)
between 1882 and 1888?-1936 . . . . DLB-175

Movies from Books, 1920-1974 . . . . . DLB-9

Mowat, Farley 1921- DLB-68

Mowbray, A. R., and Company,
Limited DLB-106

Mowrer, Edgar Ansel 1892-1977 . . . . DLB-29

Mowrer, Paul Scott 1887-1971 . . . . . DLB-29

Moxon, Edward
[publishing house] DLB-106

Moxon, Joseph
[publishing house] DLB-170

Mphahlele, Es'kia (Ezekiel)
1919- DLB-125

Mtshali, Oswald Mbuyiseni
1940- DLB-125

Mucedorus DLB-62

Mudford, William 1782-1848 . . . . . DLB-159

Mueller, Lisel 1924- DLB-105

Muhajir, El (see Marvin X)

Muhajir, Nazzam Al Fitnah (see Marvin X)

Mühlbach, Luise 1814-1873 . . . . . DLB-133

Muir, Edwin 1887-1959 . . . . DLB-20, 100, 191

Muir, Helen 1937- DLB-14

Muir, John 1838-1914 . . . . DLB-186

Mukherjee, Bharati 1940- DLB-60

Mulcaster, Richard
1531 or 1532-1611 . . . . DLB-167

Muldoon, Paul 1951- DLB-40

Müller, Friedrich (see Müller, Maler)

Müller, Heiner 1929- DLB-124

Müller, Maler 1749-1825 . . . . DLB-94

Müller, Wilhelm 1794-1827 . . . . . . DLB-90

Mumford, Lewis 1895-1990 . . . . . . DLB-63

Munby, Arthur Joseph 1828-1910 . . . . DLB-35

Munday, Anthony 1560-1633 . . . . DLB-62, 172

Mundt, Clara (see Mühlbach, Luise)

Mundt, Theodore 1808-1861 . . . . . DLB-133

Munford, Robert circa 1737-1783 . . . . DLB-31

Mungoshi, Charles 1947- DLB-157

Munonye, John 1929- DLB-117

Munro, Alice 1931- DLB-53

Munro, H. H. 1870-1916 . . . . DLB-34, 162

Munro, Neil 1864-1930 . . . . DLB-156

Munro, George
[publishing house] DLB-49

Munro, Norman L.
[publishing house] DLB-49

Munroe, James, and Company DLB-49

Munroe, Kirk 1850-1930 . . . . DLB-42

Munroe and Francis DLB-49

Munsell, Joel [publishing house] DLB-49

Munsey, Frank A. 1854-1925 . . . . DLB-25, 91

Murakami, Haruki 1949- DLB-182

Munsey, Frank A., and
Company DLB-49

Murav'ev, Mikhail Nikitich
1757-1807 . . . . DLB-150

Murdoch, Iris 1919- DLB-14, 194

Murdoch, Rupert 1931- DLB-127

Murfree, Mary N. 1850-1922 . . . . DLB-12, 74

Murger, Henry 1822-1861 . . . . DLB-119

Murger, Louis-Henri (see Murger, Henry)

Murner, Thomas 1475-1537 . . . . . . DLB-179

Muro, Amado 1915-1971 . . . . DLB-82

Murphy, Arthur 1727-1805 . . . . . DLB-89, 142

Murphy, Beatrice M. 1908- DLB-76

Murphy, Emily 1868-1933 . . . . DLB-99

Murphy, John H., III 1916- DLB-127

Murphy, John, and Company DLB-49

Murphy, Richard 1927-1993 . . . . DLB-40

Murray, Albert L. 1916- DLB-38

Murray, Gilbert 1866-1957 . . . . DLB-10

Murray, Judith Sargent 1751-1820 . . . . DLB-37

Murray, Pauli 1910-1985 . . . . DLB-41

Murray, John [publishing house] DLB-154

Murry, John Middleton
1889-1957 . . . . DLB-149

Musäus, Johann Karl August
1735-1787 . . . . DLB-97

Muschg, Adolf 1934- DLB-75

The Music of *Minnesang* DLB-138

Musil, Robert 1880-1942 . . . . . . DLB-81, 124

Muspilli circa 790-circa 850 . . . . . . DLB-148

Musset, Alfred de 1810-1857 . . . . . DLB-192

Mussey, Benjamin B., and
Company DLB-49

Mutafchieva, Vera 1929- DLB-181

Mwangi, Meja 1948- DLB-125

Myers, Frederic W. H. 1843-1901 . . . DLB-190

Myers, Gustavus 1872-1942 . . . . . . DLB-47

Myers, L. H. 1881-1944 . . . . DLB-15

Myers, Walter Dean 1937- DLB-33

Myles, Eileen 1949- DLB-193

N

Nabl, Franz 1883-1974 . . . . DLB-81

Nabokov, Vladimir
1899-1977 . . . . . DLB-2; Y-80, Y-91; DS-3

Nabokov Festival at Cornell Y-83

The Vladimir Nabokov Archive
in the Berg Collection Y-91

Nadezhdin, Nikolai Ivanovich
1804-1856 . . . . DLB-198

Nafis and Cornish DLB-49

Nagai, Kafū 1879-1959 . . . . DLB-180

Naipaul, Shiva 1945-1985 . . . . DLB-157; Y-85

Naipaul, V. S. 1932- DLB-125; Y-85

Nakagami, Kenji 1946-1992 . . . . . . DLB-182

Nancrede, Joseph
[publishing house] DLB-49

Naranjo, Carmen 1930- DLB-145

Narezhny, Vasilii Trofimovich
1780-1825 . . . . DLB-198

Narrache, Jean 1893-1970 . . . . DLB-92

Nasby, Petroleum Vesuvius (see Locke, David
Ross)

Nash, Ogden 1902-1971 . . . . DLB-11

Nash, Eveleigh
[publishing house] DLB-112

Nashe, Thomas 1567-1601? DLB-167

Nast, Conde 1873-1942 . . . . DLB-91

Nast, Thomas 1840-1902 . . . . DLB-188

Nastasijević, Momčilo 1894-1938 . . . . DLB-147

Nathan, George Jean 1882-1958 . . . . DLB-137

Nathan, Robert 1894-1985 . . . . DLB-9

The National Jewish Book Awards Y-85

The National Theatre and the Royal
Shakespeare Company: The
National Companies DLB-13

Natsume, Sōseki 1867-1916 . . . . . . DLB-180

Naughton, Bill 1910- DLB-13

Naylor, Gloria 1950- DLB-173

Nazor, Vladimir 1876-1949 . . . . . . DLB-147

Ndebele, Njabulo 1948- DLB-157

Neagoe, Peter 1881-1960 . . . . DLB-4

Neal, John 1793-1876 . . . . DLB-1, 59

Neal, Joseph C. 1807-1847 . . . . . . DLB-11

Neal, Larry 1937-1981 . . . . DLB-38

The Neale Publishing Company DLB-49

Neely, F. Tennyson
[publishing house] DLB-49

Negri, Ada 1870-1945 . . . . DLB-114

"The Negro as a Writer," by
G. M. McClellan DLB-50

"Negro Poets and Their Poetry," by
Wallace Thurman DLB-50

Neidhart von Reuental
circa 1185-circa 1240 . . . . DLB-138

Neihardt, John G. 1881-1973 . . . . DLB-9, 54

Neledinsky-Meletsky, Iurii Aleksandrovich
1752-1828 . . . . DLB-150

Nelligan, Emile 1879-1941 . . . . DLB-92

Nelson, Alice Moore Dunbar
1875-1935 . . . . DLB-50

Nelson, Thomas, and Sons [U.S.] DLB-49

Nelson, Thomas, and Sons [U.K.] . . . DLB-106

Nelson, William 1908-1978 . . . . . . DLB-103

Nelson, William Rockhill
1841-1915 . . . . DLB-23

Nemerov, Howard 1920-1991 . . . DLB-5, 6; Y-83

Nesbit, E. 1858-1924 . . . . DLB-141, 153, 178

Ness, Evaline 1911-1986 . . . . DLB-61

Nestroy, Johann 1801-1862 . . . . . . DLB-133

Neukirch, Benjamin 1655-1729 . . . . DLB-168

Neugeboren, Jay 1938- DLB-28

Neumann, Alfred 1895-1952 . . . . . . DLB-56

Neumark, Georg 1621-1681 . . . . . . DLB-164

Neumeister, Erdmann 1671-1756 . . . . DLB-168

Nevins, Allan 1890-1971 . . . . . DLB-17; DS-17

Nevinson, Henry Woodd
1856-1941 . . . . DLB-135

The New American Library DLB-46

New Approaches to Biography: Challenges
from Critical Theory, USC Conference
on Literary Studies, 1990 . . . . Y-90

New Directions Publishing
Corporation DLB-46

A New Edition of *Huck Finn* Y-85

New Forces at Work in the American Theatre:
1915-1925 . . . . DLB-7

New Literary Periodicals:
A Report for 1987 . . . . Y-87

New Literary Periodicals:
A Report for 1988 . . . . Y-88

New Literary Periodicals:
A Report for 1989 . . . . Y-89

New Literary Periodicals:
A Report for 1990 . . . . Y-90

New Literary Periodicals:
A Report for 1991 . . . . Y-91

New Literary Periodicals:
A Report for 1992 . . . . Y-92

New Literary Periodicals:
A Report for 1993 . . . . Y-93

The New Monthly Magazine
1814-1884 . . . . DLB-110

The New *Ulysses* Y-84

The New Variorum Shakespeare Y-85

A New Voice: The Center for the Book's First
Five Years Y-83

The New Wave [Science Fiction] DLB-8

New York City Bookshops in the 1930s and
1940s: The Recollections of Walter
Goldwater Y-93

Newbery, John
[publishing house] DLB-154

Newbolt, Henry 1862-1938 . . . . DLB-19

Newbound, Bernard Slade (see Slade, Bernard)

Newby, P. H. 1918- DLB-15

Newby, Thomas Cautley
[publishing house] DLB-106

Newcomb, Charles King 1820-1894 . . . . DLB-1

Newell, Peter 1862-1924 . . . . DLB-42

Newell, Robert Henry 1836-1901 . . . . DLB-11

Newhouse, Samuel I. 1895-1979 . . . . DLB-127

Newman, Cecil Earl 1903-1976 . . . . . DLB-127

Newman, David (see Benton, Robert)

Newman, Frances 1883-1928 . . . . Y-80

Newman, Francis William
1805-1897 . . . . DLB-190

Newman, John Henry
1801-1890 . . . . DLB-18, 32, 55

Newman, Mark [publishing house]. . . . DLB-49

Newnes, George, Limited DLB-112

Newsome, Effie Lee 1885-1979. . . . . DLB-76

Newspaper Syndication of American
  Humor DLB-11

Newton, A. Edward 1864-1940. . . . DLB-140

Ngugi wa Thiong'o 1938- DLB-125

Niatum, Duane 1938- DLB-175

The *Nibelungenlied* and the *Klage*
  circa 1200 . . . . DLB-138

Nichol, B. P. 1944- DLB-53

Nicholas of Cusa 1401-1464 . . . . . DLB-115

Nichols, Beverly 1898-1983 . . . . . . DLB-191

Nichols, Dudley 1895-1960. . . . . . DLB-26

Nichols, Grace 1950- DLB-157

Nichols, John 1940- Y-82

Nichols, Mary Sargeant (Neal) Gove
  1810-1884. . . . . DLB-1

Nichols, Peter 1927- DLB-13

Nichols, Roy F. 1896-1973 . . . . . . DLB-17

Nichols, Ruth 1948- DLB-60

Nicholson, Edward Williams Byron
  1849-1912 . . . . DLB-184

Nicholson, Norman 1914- DLB-27

Nicholson, William 1872-1949 . . . . DLB-141

Ní Chuilleanáin, Eiléan 1942- DLB-40

Nicol, Eric 1919- DLB-68

Nicolai, Friedrich 1733-1811 . . . . . DLB-97

Nicolay, John G. 1832-1901 and
  Hay, John 1838-1905. . . . . . . DLB-47

Nicolson, Harold 1886-1968. . . . DLB-100, 149

Nicolson, Nigel 1917- DLB-155

Niebuhr, Reinhold 1892-1971 . . DLB-17; DS-17

Niedecker, Lorine 1903-1970 . . . . . DLB-48

Nieman, Lucius W. 1857-1935. . . . DLB-25

Nietzsche, Friedrich 1844-1900 . . . . DLB-129

Nievo, Stanislao 1928- DLB-196

Niggli, Josefina 1910- Y-80

Nightingale, Florence 1820-1910. . . . DLB-166

Nikolev, Nikolai Petrovich
  1758-1815 . . . . DLB-150

Niles, Hezekiah 1777-1839 . . . . . . DLB-43

Nims, John Frederick 1913- DLB-5

Nin, Anaïs 1903-1977 . . . . . . DLB-2, 4, 152

1985: The Year of the Mystery:
  A Symposium Y-85

The 1997 Booker Prize Y-97

Nissenson, Hugh 1933- DLB-28

Niven, Frederick John 1878-1944 . . . . DLB-92

Niven, Larry 1938- DLB-8

Nizan, Paul 1905-1940 . . . . DLB-72

Njegoš, Petar II Petrović
  1813-1851 . . . . DLB-147

Nkosi, Lewis 1936- DLB-157

"The No Self, the Little Self, and the Poets,"
  by Richard Moore DLB-105

Nobel Peace Prize

The 1986 Nobel Peace Prize:
  Elie Wiesel Y-86

The Nobel Prize and Literary Politics . . . Y-86

Nobel Prize in Literature

The 1982 Nobel Prize in Literature:
  Gabriel García Márquez. Y-82

The 1983 Nobel Prize in Literature:
  William Golding Y-83

The 1984 Nobel Prize in Literature:
  Jaroslav Seifert Y-84

The 1985 Nobel Prize in Literature:
  Claude Simon Y-85

The 1986 Nobel Prize in Literature:
  Wole Soyinka Y-86

The 1987 Nobel Prize in Literature:
  Joseph Brodsky. Y-87

The 1988 Nobel Prize in Literature:
  Najīb Mahfūz. Y-88

The 1989 Nobel Prize in Literature:
  Camilo José Cela. Y-89

The 1990 Nobel Prize in Literature:
  Octavio Paz. Y-90

The 1991 Nobel Prize in Literature:
  Nadine Gordimer Y-91

The 1992 Nobel Prize in Literature:
  Derek Walcott Y-92

The 1993 Nobel Prize in Literature:
  Toni Morrison Y-93

The 1994 Nobel Prize in Literature:
  Kenzaburō Ōe Y-94

The 1995 Nobel Prize in Literature:
  Seamus Heaney Y-95

The 1996 Nobel Prize in Literature:
  Wisława Szymborsha. Y-96

The 1997 Nobel Prize in Literature:
  Dario Fo Y-97

Nodier, Charles 1780-1844 . . . . . . DLB-119

Noel, Roden 1834-1894. . . . . DLB-35

Nogami, Yaeko 1885-1985. . . . . . . DLB-180

Nogo, Rajko Petrov 1945- DLB-181

Nolan, William F. 1928- DLB-8

Noland, C. F. M. 1810?-1858 . . . . . DLB-11

Noma, Hiroshi 1915-1991 . . . . DLB-182

Nonesuch Press DLB-112

Noonan, Robert Phillipe (see Tressell, Robert)

Noonday Press DLB-46

Noone, John 1936- DLB-14

Nora, Eugenio de 1923- DLB-134

Nordhoff, Charles 1887-1947 . . . . . DLB-9

Norman, Charles 1904- DLB-111

Norman, Marsha 1947- Y-84

Norris, Charles G. 1881-1945 . . . . . . DLB-9

Norris, Frank 1870-1902 . . . . DLB-12, 71, 186

Norris, Leslie 1921- DLB-27

Norse, Harold 1916- DLB-16

North, Marianne 1830-1890. . . . . . DLB-174

North Point Press. DLB-46

Nortje, Arthur 1942-1970 . . . . DLB-125

Norton, Alice Mary (see Norton, Andre)

Norton, Andre 1912- DLB-8, 52

Norton, Andrews 1786-1853. . . . . . DLB-1

Norton, Caroline 1808-1877 . . . . DLB-21, 159

Norton, Charles Eliot 1827-1908 . . . DLB-1, 64

Norton, John 1606-1663 . . . . DLB-24

Norton, Mary 1903-1992 . . . . DLB-160

Norton, Thomas (see Sackville, Thomas)

Norton, W. W., and Company DLB-46

Norwood, Robert 1874-1932 . . . . . DLB-92

Nosaka, Akiyuki 1930- DLB-182

Nossack, Hans Erich 1901-1977 . . . . DLB-69

A Note on Technique (1926), by
  Elizabeth A. Drew [excerpts]. DLB-36

Notker Balbulus circa 840-912 . . . . DLB-148

Notker III of Saint Gall
  circa 950-1022 . . . . DLB-148

Notker von Zweifalten ?-1095 . . . . . DLB-148

Nourse, Alan E. 1928- DLB-8

Novak, Slobodan 1924- DLB-181

Novak, Vjenceslav 1859-1905 . . . . . DLB-147

Novalis 1772-1801. . . . . DLB-90

Novaro, Mario 1868-1944. . . . . . . DLB-114

Novás Calvo, Lino 1903-1983 . . . . . DLB-145

"The Novel in [Robert Browning's] 'The Ring
  and the Book'" (1912), by
  Henry James DLB-32

The Novel of Impressionism,
  by Jethro Bithell DLB-66

Novel-Reading: *The Works of Charles Dickens,
  The Works of W. Makepeace Thackeray*
  (1879), by Anthony Trollope. . . . DLB-21

Novels for Grown-Ups Y-97

The Novels of Dorothy Richardson (1918),
  by May Sinclair DLB-36

Novels with a Purpose (1864), by
  Justin M'Carthy DLB-21

Noventa, Giacomo 1898-1960 . . . . . DLB-114

Novikov, Nikolai Ivanovich
  1744-1818 . . . . DLB-150

Nowlan, Alden 1933-1983 . . . . DLB-53

Noyes, Alfred 1880-1958 . . . . DLB-20

Noyes, Crosby S. 1825-1908 . . . . . . DLB-23

Noyes, Nicholas 1647-1717. . . . . . . DLB-24

Noyes, Theodore W. 1858-1946 . . . . . DLB-29

N-Town Plays circa 1468 to early
  sixteenth century DLB-146

Nugent, Frank 1908-1965 . . . . DLB-44

Nugent, Richard Bruce 1906- DLB-151

Nušić, Branislav 1864-1938 . . . . DLB-147

Nutt, David [publishing house] DLB-106

Nwapa, Flora 1931- DLB-125

Nye, Bill 1850-1896 . . . . DLB-186

Nye, Edgar Wilson (Bill)
  1850-1896. . . . . DLB-11, 23

Nye, Naomi Shihab 1952- DLB-120

Nye, Robert 1939- DLB-14

O

Oakes, Urian circa 1631-1681 . . . . . DLB-24

Oakley, Violet 1874-1961 . . . . DLB-188

Oates, Joyce Carol
  1938- DLB-2, 5, 130; Y-81

Ōba, Minako 1930- DLB-182

Ober, Frederick Albion 1849-1913 . . . DLB-189

Ober, William 1920-1993 . . . . Y-93

Oberholtzer, Ellis Paxson
  1868-1936 . . . . DLB-47

Obradović, Dositej 1740?-1811 . . . . . DLB-147

O'Brien, Edna 1932- DLB-14

O'Brien, Fitz-James 1828-1862 . . . . . DLB-74

O'Brien, Kate 1897-1974 . . . . DLB-15

O'Brien, Tim
  1946- DLB-152; Y-80; DS-9

O'Casey, Sean 1880-1964. . . . . DLB-10

Occom, Samson 1723-1792 . . . . . . DLB-175

Ochs, Adolph S. 1858-1935 . . . . . . DLB-25

Ochs-Oakes, George Washington
  1861-1931 . . . . DLB-137

O'Connor, Flannery
  1925-1964 . . . . . DLB-2, 152; Y-80; DS-12

O'Connor, Frank 1903-1966 . . . . . DLB-162

Octopus Publishing Group DLB-112

Oda, Sakunosuke 1913-1947 . . . . . DLB-182

Odell, Jonathan 1737-1818 . . . . . DLB-31, 99

O'Dell, Scott 1903-1989. . . . . DLB-52

Odets, Clifford 1906-1963 . . . . . . DLB-7, 26

Odhams Press Limited DLB-112

Odoevsky, Vladimir Fedorovich
  1804 or 1803-1869 . . . . DLB-198

O'Donnell, Peter 1920- DLB-87

O'Donovan, Michael (see O'Connor, Frank)

Ōe, Kenzaburō 1935- DLB-182; Y-94

O'Faolain, Julia 1932- DLB-14

O'Faolain, Sean 1900- DLB-15, 162

Off Broadway and Off-Off Broadway . DLB-7

Off-Loop Theatres DLB-7

Offord, Carl Ruthven 1910- DLB-76

O'Flaherty, Liam
  1896-1984 . . . . DLB-36, 162; Y-84

Ogilvie, J. S., and Company DLB-49

Ogot, Grace 1930- DLB-125

O'Grady, Desmond 1935- DLB-40

Ogunyemi, Wale 1939- DLB-157

O'Hagan, Howard 1902-1982 . . . . . DLB-68

O'Hara, Frank 1926-1966 . . . . DLB-5, 16, 193

O'Hara, John 1905-1970 . . . . DLB-9, 86; DS-2

Okara, Gabriel 1921- DLB-125

O'Keeffe, John 1747-1833. . . . . DLB-89

Okes, Nicholas
  [publishing house] DLB-170

Okigbo, Christopher 1930-1967. . . . . DLB-125

Okot p'Bitek 1931-1982 . . . . DLB-125

Okpewho, Isidore 1941- DLB-157

Okri, Ben 1959- DLB-157

Olaudah Equiano and Unfinished Journeys:
  The Slave-Narrative Tradition and
  Twentieth-Century Continuities, by
  Paul Edwards and Pauline T.
  Wangman DLB-117

Old English Literature:
  An Introduction DLB-146

Old English Riddles
  eighth to tenth centuries DLB-146

Old Franklin Publishing House DLB-49

Old German Genesis and *Old German Exodus*
  circa 1050-circa 1130 . . . . DLB-148

Old High German Charms and
  Blessings DLB-148

The *Old High German Isidor*
  circa 790-800. . . . . DLB-148

Older, Fremont 1856-1935 . . . . DLB-25

Oldham, John 1653-1683 . . . . DLB-131

Olds, Sharon 1942- DLB-120

Olearius, Adam 1599-1671 . . . . . . DLB-164

Oliphant, Laurence
  1829?-1888. . . . . DLB-18, 166

Oliphant, Margaret 1828-1897 . . . DLB-18, 190

Oliver, Chad 1928- DLB-8

Oliver, Mary 1935- DLB-5, 193

Ollier, Claude 1922- DLB-83

Olsen, Tillie 1913?- DLB-28; Y-80

Olson, Charles 1910-1970 . . . . DLB-5, 16, 193

Olson, Elder 1909- DLB-48, 63

Omotoso, Kole 1943- DLB-125

"On Art in Fiction "(1838),
  by Edward Bulwer. DLB-21

On Learning to Write Y-88

On Some of the Characteristics of Modern
  Poetry and On the Lyrical Poems of
  Alfred Tennyson (1831), by Arthur
  Henry Hallam DLB-32

"On Style in English Prose" (1898), by
  Frederic Harrison DLB-57

"On Style in Literature: Its Technical
  Elements" (1885), by Robert Louis
  Stevenson DLB-57

"On the Writing of Essays" (1862),
  by Alexander Smith DLB-57

Ondaatje, Michael 1943- DLB-60

O'Neill, Eugene 1888-1953. . . . . DLB-7

Onetti, Juan Carlos 1909-1994 . . . . . DLB-113

Onions, George Oliver
  1872-1961 . . . . DLB-153

Onofri, Arturo 1885-1928 . . . . DLB-114

Opie, Amelia 1769-1853 . . . . . . DLB-116, 159

Opitz, Martin 1597-1639. . . . . DLB-164

Oppen, George 1908-1984 . . . . . DLB-5, 165

Oppenheim, E. Phillips 1866-1946 . . . . DLB-70

Oppenheim, James 1882-1932 . . . . . DLB-28

Oppenheimer, Joel 1930-1988 . . . . DLB-5, 193

Optic, Oliver (see Adams, William Taylor)

Oral History Interview with Donald S.
  Klopfer Y-97

Orczy, Emma, Baroness
  1865-1947 . . . . DLB-70

Origo, Iris 1902-1988 . . . . DLB-155

Orlovitz, Gil 1918-1973. . . . . DLB-2, 5

Orlovsky, Peter 1933- DLB-16

Ormond, John 1923- DLB-27

Ornitz, Samuel 1890-1957 . . . . . DLB-28, 44

O'Rourke, P. J. 1947- DLB-185

Ortese, Anna Maria 1914- DLB-177

Ortiz, Simon J. 1941- DLB-120, 175

Ortnit and *Wolfdietrich*
  circa 1225-1250 . . . . DLB-138

Orton, Joe 1933-1967 . . . . DLB-13

Orwell, George 1903-1950 . . . DLB-15, 98, 195

The Orwell Year Y-84

Ory, Carlos Edmundo de 1923- . . . DLB-134

Osbey, Brenda Marie 1957- DLB-120

Osbon, B. S. 1827-1912 . . . . DLB-43

Osborne, John 1929-1994. . . . . DLB-13

Osgood, Herbert L. 1855-1918. . . . . . DLB-47

Osgood, James R., and
  Company DLB-49

Osgood, McIlvaine and
  Company DLB-112

O'Shaughnessy, Arthur
  1844-1881 . . . . DLB-35

O'Shea, Patrick
  [publishing house]. DLB-49

Osipov, Nikolai Petrovich
  1751-1799 . . . . DLB-150

Oskison, John Milton 1879-1947 . . . DLB-175

Osler, Sir William 1849-1919 . . . . . DLB-184

Osofisan, Femi 1946- DLB-125

Ostenso, Martha 1900-1963. . . . . . . DLB-92

Ostriker, Alicia 1937- DLB-120

Osundare, Niyi 1947- DLB-157

Oswald, Eleazer 1755-1795 . . . . DLB-43

Oswald von Wolkenstein
1376 or 1377-1445 . . . . DLB-179

Otero, Blas de 1916-1979 . . . . DLB-134

Otero, Miguel Antonio
1859-1944 . . . . DLB-82

Otero Silva, Miguel 1908-1985 . . . . . DLB-145

Otfried von Weißenburg
circa 800-circa 875? DLB-148

Otis, James (see Kaler, James Otis)

Otis, James, Jr. 1725-1783 . . . . DLB-31

Otis, Broaders and Company DLB-49

Ottaway, James 1911- DLB-127

Ottendorfer, Oswald 1826-1900 . . . . DLB-23

Ottieri, Ottiero 1924- DLB-177

Otto-Peters, Louise 1819-1895 . . . . . DLB-129

Otway, Thomas 1652-1685 . . . . DLB-80

Ouellette, Fernand 1930- DLB-60

Ouida 1839-1908 . . . . DLB-18, 156

Outing Publishing Company DLB-46

Outlaw Days, by Joyce Johnson DLB-16

Overbury, Sir Thomas
circa 1581-1613 . . . . DLB-151

The Overlook Press DLB-46

Overview of U.S. Book Publishing,
1910-1945 . . . . DLB-9

Owen, Guy 1925- DLB-5

Owen, John 1564-1622 . . . . DLB-121

Owen, John [publishing house] DLB-49

Owen, Robert 1771-1858 . . . . DLB-107, 158

Owen, Wilfred 1893-1918 . . . . DLB-20

Owen, Peter, Limited DLB-112

The Owl and the Nightingale
circa 1189-1199 . . . . DLB-146

Owsley, Frank L. 1890-1956 . . . . . . DLB-17

Oxford, Seventeenth Earl of, Edward de Vere
1550-1604 . . . . DLB-172

Ozerov, Vladislav Aleksandrovich
1769-1816 . . . . DLB-150

Ozick, Cynthia 1928- DLB-28, 152; Y-82

P

Pace, Richard 1482?-1536 . . . . DLB-167

Pacey, Desmond 1917-1975 . . . . . . DLB-88

Pack, Robert 1929- DLB-5

Packaging Papa: *The Garden of Eden* Y-86

Padell Publishing Company DLB-46

Padgett, Ron 1942- DLB-5

Padilla, Ernesto Chávez 1944- DLB-122

Page, L. C., and Company DLB-49

Page, P. K. 1916- DLB-68

Page, Thomas Nelson
1853-1922 . . . . DLB-12, 78; DS-13

Page, Walter Hines 1855-1918 . . . DLB-71, 91

Paget, Francis Edward
1806-1882 . . . . DLB-163

Paget, Violet (see Lee, Vernon)

Pagliarani, Elio 1927- DLB-128

Pain, Barry 1864-1928 . . . . . . DLB-135, 197

Pain, Philip ?-circa 1666 . . . . DLB-24

Paine, Robert Treat, Jr. 1773-1811 . . . DLB-37

Paine, Thomas
1737-1809 . . . . DLB-31, 43, 73, 158

Painter, George D. 1914- DLB-155

Painter, William 1540?-1594 . . . . . . DLB-136

Palazzeschi, Aldo 1885-1974 . . . . . . DLB-114

Paley, Grace 1922- DLB-28

Palfrey, John Gorham
1796-1881 . . . . DLB-1, 30

Palgrave, Francis Turner
1824-1897 . . . . DLB-35

Palmer, Joe H. 1904-1952 . . . . DLB-171

Palmer, Michael 1943- DLB-169

Paltock, Robert 1697-1767 . . . . DLB-39

Pan Books Limited DLB-112

Panama, Norman 1914- and
Frank, Melvin 1913-1988 . . . . . . DLB-26

Panaev, Ivan Ivanovich 1812-1862 . . . DLB-198

Pancake, Breece D'J 1952-1979 . . . . DLB-130

Panero, Leopoldo 1909-1962 . . . . . DLB-108

Pangborn, Edgar 1909-1976 . . . . . . DLB-8

"Panic Among the Philistines": A Postscript,
An Interview with Bryan Griffin Y-81

Panizzi, Sir Anthony 1797-1879 . . . . . DLB-184

Panneton, Philippe (see Ringuet)

Panshin, Alexei 1940- DLB-8

Pansy (see Alden, Isabella)

Pantheon Books DLB-46

Papantonio, Michael (see Kohn, John S. Van E.)

Paperback Library DLB-46

Paperback Science Fiction DLB-8

Paquet, Alfons 1881-1944 . . . . DLB-66

Paracelsus 1493-1541 . . . . DLB-179

Paradis, Suzanne 1936- DLB-53

Pareja Diezcanseco, Alfredo
1908-1993 . . . . DLB-145

Pardoe, Julia 1804-1862 . . . . DLB-166

Parents' Magazine Press DLB-46

Parise, Goffredo 1929-1986 . . . . . . DLB-177

Parisian Theater, Fall 1984: Toward
A New Baroque Y-85

Parizeau, Alice 1930- DLB-60

Parke, John 1754-1789 . . . . DLB-31

Parker, Dorothy
1893-1967 . . . . DLB-11, 45, 86

Parker, Gilbert 1860-1932 . . . . DLB-99

Parker, James 1714-1770 . . . . DLB-43

Parker, Theodore 1810-1860 . . . . . . DLB-1

Parker, William Riley 1906-1968 . . . . DLB-103

Parker, J. H. [publishing house] DLB-106

Parker, John [publishing house] DLB-106

Parkman, Francis, Jr.
1823-1893 . . . . DLB-1, 30, 183, 186

Parks, Gordon 1912- DLB-33

Parks, William 1698-1750 . . . . DLB-43

Parks, William [publishing house] . . . DLB-49

Parley, Peter (see Goodrich, Samuel Griswold)

Parmenides late sixth-fifth century B.C.
. . . . DLB-176

Parnell, Thomas 1679-1718 . . . . . . DLB-95

Parr, Catherine 1513?-1548 . . . . . . DLB-136

Parrington, Vernon L.
1871-1929 . . . . DLB-17, 63

Parrish, Maxfield 1870-1966 . . . . . . DLB-188

Parronchi, Alessandro 1914- DLB-128

Partridge, S. W., and Company DLB-106

Parton, James 1822-1891 . . . . DLB-30

Parton, Sara Payson Willis
1811-1872 . . . . DLB-43, 74

Parun, Vesna 1922- DLB-181

Pasinetti, Pier Maria 1913- DLB-177

Pasolini, Pier Paolo 1922- DLB-128, 177

Pastan, Linda 1932- DLB-5

Paston, George (Emily Morse Symonds)
1860-1936 . . . . DLB-149, 197

The *Paston Letters* 1422-1509 . . . . . DLB-146

Pastorius, Francis Daniel
1651-circa 1720 . . . . DLB-24

Patchen, Kenneth 1911-1972 . . . . DLB-16, 48

Pater, Walter 1839-1894 . . . . . DLB-57, 156

Paterson, Katherine 1932- DLB-52

Patmore, Coventry 1823-1896 . . . . DLB-35, 98

Paton, Alan 1903-1988 . . . . DS-17

Paton, Joseph Noel 1821-1901 . . . . . DLB-35

Paton Walsh, Jill 1937- DLB-161

Patrick, Edwin Hill ("Ted")
1901-1964 . . . . DLB-137

Patrick, John 1906- DLB-7

Pattee, Fred Lewis 1863-1950 . . . . . DLB-71

Pattern and Paradigm: History as
Design, by Judith Ryan DLB-75

Patterson, Alicia 1906-1963 . . . . . . DLB-127

Patterson, Eleanor Medill
1881-1948 . . . . DLB-29

Patterson, Eugene 1923- DLB-127

Patterson, Joseph Medill
1879-1946 . . . . DLB-29

Pattillo, Henry 1726-1801 . . . . DLB-37

Paul, Elliot 1891-1958 . . . . DLB-4

Paul, Jean (see Richter, Johann Paul Friedrich)

Paul, Kegan, Trench, Trubner and Company
Limited DLB-106

Paul, Peter, Book Company DLB-49

Paul, Stanley, and Company
Limited DLB-112

Paulding, James Kirke
1778-1860 . . . . DLB-3, 59, 74

Paulin, Tom 1949- DLB-40

Pauper, Peter, Press DLB-46

Pavese, Cesare 1908-1950 . . . . . DLB-128, 177

Pavić, Milorad 1929- DLB-181

Pavlov, Konstantin 1933- DLB-181

Pavlov, Nikolai Filippovich
1803-1864 . . . . DLB-198

Pavlović, Miodrag 1928- DLB-181

Paxton, John 1911-1985 . . . . DLB-44

Payn, James 1830-1898 . . . . DLB-18

Payne, John 1842-1916 . . . . DLB-35

Payne, John Howard 1791-1852 . . . . . DLB-37

Payson and Clarke DLB-46

Paz, Octavio 1914-1998 . . . . Y-90

Pazzi, Roberto 1946- DLB-196

Peabody, Elizabeth Palmer
1804-1894 . . . . DLB-1

Peabody, Elizabeth Palmer
[publishing house] DLB-49

Peabody, Oliver William Bourn
1799-1848 . . . . DLB-59

Peace, Roger 1899-1968 . . . . DLB-127

Peacham, Henry 1578-1644? DLB-151

Peacham, Henry, the Elder
1547-1634 . . . . DLB-172

Peachtree Publishers, Limited DLB-46

Peacock, Molly 1947- DLB-120

Peacock, Thomas Love
1785-1866 . . . . DLB-96, 116

Pead, Deuel ?-1727 . . . . DLB-24

Peake, Mervyn 1911-1968 . . . . . DLB-15, 160

Peale, Rembrandt 1778-1860 . . . . . . DLB-183

Pear Tree Press DLB-112

Pearce, Philippa 1920- DLB-161

Pearson, H. B. [publishing house] DLB-49

Pearson, Hesketh 1887-1964 . . . . . . DLB-149

Peck, George W. 1840-1916 . . . . . DLB-23, 42

Peck, H. C., and Theo. Bliss
[publishing house] DLB-49

Peck, Harry Thurston
1856-1914 . . . . DLB-71, 91

Peele, George 1556-1596 . . . . . . DLB-62, 167

Pegler, Westbrook 1894-1969 . . . . . . DLB-171

Pekić, Borislav 1930-1992 . . . . DLB-181

Pellegrini and Cudahy DLB-46

Pelletier, Aimé (see Vac, Bertrand)

Pemberton, Sir Max 1863-1950 . . . . DLB-70

Penfield, Edward 1866-1925 . . . . . . DLB-188

Penguin Books [U.S.] DLB-46

Penguin Books [U.K.] DLB-112

Penn Publishing Company DLB-49

Penn, William 1644-1718 . . . . DLB-24

Penna, Sandro 1906-1977 . . . . DLB-114

Pennell, Joseph 1857-1926 . . . . DLB-188

Penner, Jonathan 1940- Y-83

Pennington, Lee 1939- Y-82

Pepys, Samuel 1633-1703 . . . . DLB-101

Percy, Thomas 1729-1811 . . . . DLB-104

Percy, Walker 1916-1990 . . . DLB-2; Y-80, Y-90

Percy, William 1575-1648 . . . . DLB-172

Perec, Georges 1936-1982 . . . . DLB-83

Perelman, Bob 1947- DLB-193

Perelman, S. J. 1904-1979 . . . . . DLB-11, 44

Perez, Raymundo "Tigre"
1946- DLB-122

Peri Rossi, Cristina 1941- DLB-145

Periodicals of the Beat Generation DLB-16

Perkins, Eugene 1932- DLB-41

Perkoff, Stuart Z. 1930-1974 . . . . . . DLB-16

Perley, Moses Henry 1804-1862 . . . . DLB-99

Permabooks DLB-46

Perovsky, Aleksei Alekseevich (Antonii Pogorel'sky)
1787-1836 . . . . DLB-198

Perrin, Alice 1867-1934 . . . . DLB-156

Perry, Bliss 1860-1954 . . . . DLB-71

Perry, Eleanor 1915-1981 . . . . DLB-44

Perry, Matthew 1794-1858 . . . . DLB-183

Perry, Sampson 1747-1823 . . . . DLB-158

"Personal Style" (1890), by John Addington
Symonds DLB-57

Perutz, Leo 1882-1957 . . . . DLB-81

Pesetsky, Bette 1932- DLB-130

Pestalozzi, Johann Heinrich
1746-1827 . . . . DLB-94

Peter, Laurence J. 1919-1990 . . . . . . DLB-53

Peter of Spain circa 1205-1277 . . . . . DLB-115

Peterkin, Julia 1880-1961 . . . . DLB-9

Peters, Lenrie 1932- DLB-117

Peters, Robert 1924- DLB-105

Petersham, Maud 1889-1971 and
Petersham, Miska 1888-1960 . . . . DLB-22

Peterson, Charles Jacobs
1819-1887 . . . . DLB-79

Peterson, Len 1917- DLB-88

Peterson, Louis 1922- DLB-76

Peterson, T. B., and Brothers DLB-49

Petitclair, Pierre 1813-1860 . . . . . . DLB-99

Petrov, Aleksandar 1938- DLB-181

Petrov, Gavriil 1730-1801 . . . . . . DLB-150

Petrov, Vasilii Petrovich
1736-1799 . . . . DLB-150

Petrov, Valeri 1920- DLB-181

Petrović, Rastko 1898-1949 . . . . . . DLB-147

Petruslied circa 854? DLB-148

Petry, Ann 1908- DLB-76

Pettie, George circa 1548-1589 . . . . DLB-136

Peyton, K. M. 1929- DLB-161

Pfaffe Konrad
flourished circa 1172 . . . . DLB-148

Pfaffe Lamprecht
flourished circa 1150 . . . . DLB-148

Pforzheimer, Carl H. 1879-1957 . . . . DLB-140

Phaer, Thomas 1510?-1560 . . . . . . DLB-167

Phaidon Press Limited DLB-112

Pharr, Robert Deane 1916-1992 . . . . DLB-33

Phelps, Elizabeth Stuart
1844-1911 . . . . DLB-74

Philander von der Linde
(see Mencke, Johann Burckhard)

Philby, H. St. John B. 1885-1960 . . . . DLB-195

Philip, Marlene Nourbese
1947- DLB-157

Philippe, Charles-Louis
1874-1909 . . . . DLB-65

Phillipps, Sir Thomas 1792-1872 . . . . DLB-184

Philips, John 1676-1708 . . . . DLB-95

Philips, Katherine 1632-1664 . . . . . DLB-131

Phillips, Caryl 1958- DLB-157

Phillips, David Graham
1867-1911 . . . . DLB-9, 12

Phillips, Jayne Anne 1952- Y-80

Phillips, Robert 1938- DLB-105

Phillips, Stephen 1864-1915 . . . . . . DLB-10

Phillips, Ulrich B. 1877-1934 . . . . . DLB-17

Phillips, Willard 1784-1873 . . . . . . DLB-59

Phillips, William 1907- DLB-137

Phillips, Sampson and Company DLB-49

Phillpotts, Adelaide Eden (Adelaide Ross)
1896-1993 . . . . DLB-191

Phillpotts, Eden
1862-1960 . . . . . . DLB-10, 70, 135, 153

Philo circa 20-15 B.C.-circa A.D. 50
. . . . DLB-176

Philosophical Library DLB-46

"The Philosophy of Style" (1852), by
Herbert Spencer DLB-57

Phinney, Elihu [publishing house] DLB-49

Phoenix, John (see Derby, George Horatio)

PHYLON (Fourth Quarter, 1950),
The Negro in Literature:
The Current Scene DLB-76

Physiologus
circa 1070-circa 1150 . . . . DLB-148

Piccolo, Lucio 1903-1969 . . . . DLB-114

Pickard, Tom 1946- DLB-40

Pickering, William
[publishing house] DLB-106

Pickthall, Marjorie 1883-1922 . . . . . . DLB-92

Pictorial Printing Company DLB-49

Piercy, Marge 1936- DLB-120

Pierro, Albino 1916- DLB-128

Pignotti, Lamberto 1926- DLB-128

Pike, Albert 1809-1891 . . . . DLB-74

Pike, Zebulon Montgomery 1779-1813 . . DLB-183

Pilon, Jean-Guy 1930- DLB-60

Pinckney, Josephine 1895-1957 . . . . . DLB-6

Pindar circa 518 B.C.-circa 438 B.C.
. . . . DLB-176

Pindar, Peter (see Wolcot, John)

Pinero, Arthur Wing 1855-1934 . . . . . DLB-10

Pinget, Robert 1919- DLB-83

Pinnacle Books DLB-46

Piñon, Nélida 1935- DLB-145

Pinsky, Robert 1940- Y-82

Pinter, Harold 1930- DLB-13

Piontek, Heinz 1925- DLB-75

Piozzi, Hester Lynch [Thrale]
1741-1821 . . . . DLB-104, 142

Piper, H. Beam 1904-1964 . . . . DLB-8

Piper, Watty DLB-22

Pirckheimer, Caritas 1467-1532 . . . . . DLB-179

Pirckheimer, Willibald
1470-1530 . . . . DLB-179

Pisar, Samuel 1929- Y-83

Pitkin, Timothy 1766-1847 . . . . DLB-30

The Pitt Poetry Series: Poetry Publishing Today
. . . . Y-85

Pitter, Ruth 1897- DLB-20

Pix, Mary 1666-1709 . . . . DLB-80

Pixerécourt, René Charles Guilbert de
1773-1844 . . . . DLB-192

Plaatje, Sol T. 1876-1932 . . . . DLB-125

The Place of Realism in Fiction (1895), by
George Gissing DLB-18

Plante, David 1940- Y-83

Platen, August von 1796-1835 . . . . . . DLB-90

Plath, Sylvia 1932-1963 . . . . . DLB-5, 6, 152

Plato circa 428 B.C.-348-347 B.C.
. . . . DLB-176

Platon 1737-1812 . . . . DLB-150

Platt and Munk Company DLB-46

Playboy Press DLB-46

Playford, John
[publishing house] DLB-170

Plays, Playwrights, and Playgoers DLB-84

Playwrights and Professors, by
Tom Stoppard DLB-13

Playwrights on the Theater DLB-80

Der Pleier flourished circa 1250 . . . . DLB-138

Plenzdorf, Ulrich 1934- DLB-75

Plessen, Elizabeth 1944- DLB-75

Plievier, Theodor 1892-1955 . . . . DLB-69

Plimpton, George 1927- DLB-185

Plomer, William 1903-1973 . . DLB-20, 162, 191

Plotinus 204-270 . . . . DLB-176

Plumly, Stanley 1939- DLB-5, 193

Plumpp, Sterling D. 1940- DLB-41

Plunkett, James 1920- DLB-14

Plutarch circa 46-circa 120 . . . . DLB-176

Plymell, Charles 1935- DLB-16

Pocket Books DLB-46

Poe, Edgar Allan
1809-1849 . . . . DLB-3, 59, 73, 74

Poe, James 1921-1980 . . . . DLB-44

The Poet Laureate of the United States
Statements from Former Consultants
in Poetry Y-86

"The Poet's Kaleidoscope: The Element of Surprise
in the Making of the Poem," by Madeline De-
Frees DLB-105

"The Poetry File," by
Edward Field DLB-105

Pogodin, Mikhail Petrovich
1800-1875 . . . . DLB-198

Pogorel'sky, Antonii (see Perovsky, Aleksei Alekseevich)

Pohl, Frederik 1919- DLB-8

Poirier, Louis (see Gracq, Julien)

Polanyi, Michael 1891-1976 . . . . DLB-100

Pole, Reginald 1500-1558 . . . . DLB-132

Polevoi, Nikolai Alekseevich
1796-1846 . . . . DLB-198

Poliakoff, Stephen 1952- DLB-13

Polidori, John William
1795-1821 . . . . DLB-116

Polite, Carlene Hatcher 1932- DLB-33

Pollard, Edward A. 1832-1872 . . . . . DLB-30

Pollard, Percival 1869-1911 . . . . DLB-71

Pollard and Moss DLB-49

Pollock, Sharon 1936- DLB-60

Polonsky, Abraham 1910- DLB-26

Polotsky, Simeon 1629-1680 . . . . DLB-150

Polybius circa 200 B.C.-118 B.C. DLB-176

Pomilio, Mario 1921-1990 . . . . DLB-177

Ponce, Mary Helen 1938- DLB-122

Ponce-Montoya, Juanita 1949- DLB-122

Ponet, John 1516?-1556 . . . . DLB-132

Poniatowski, Elena 1933- DLB-113

Ponsard, François 1814-1867 . . . . . . DLB-192

Ponsonby, William
[publishing house] DLB-170

Pontiggia, Giuseppe 1934- DLB-196

Pony Stories DLB-160

Poole, Ernest 1880-1950 . . . . DLB-9

Poole, Sophia 1804-1891 . . . . DLB-166

Poore, Benjamin Perley
1820-1887 . . . . DLB-23

Popa, Vasko 1922-1991 . . . . DLB-181

Pope, Abbie Hanscom
1858-1894 . . . . DLB-140

Pope, Alexander 1688-1744 . . . . DLB-95, 101

Popov, Mikhail Ivanovich
1742-circa 1790 . . . . DLB-150

Popović, Aleksandar 1929-1996 . . . . . DLB-181

Popular Library DLB-46

Porlock, Martin (see MacDonald, Philip)

Porpoise Press DLB-112

Porta, Antonio 1935-1989 . . . . DLB-128

Porter, Anna Maria
1780-1832 . . . . DLB-116, 159

Porter, David 1780-1843 . . . . DLB-183

Porter, Eleanor H. 1868-1920 . . . . . . DLB-9

Porter, Gene Stratton (see Stratton-Porter, Gene)

Porter, Henry ?-? DLB-62

Porter, Jane 1776-1850 . . . . . . DLB-116, 159

Porter, Katherine Anne
1890-1980 . . . . DLB-4, 9, 102; Y-80; DS-12

Porter, Peter 1929- DLB-40

Porter, William Sydney
1862-1910 . . . . DLB-12, 78, 79

Porter, William T. 1809-1858 . . . . . DLB-3, 43

Porter and Coates DLB-49

Portis, Charles 1933- DLB-6

Posey, Alexander 1873-1908 . . . . . . DLB-175

Postans, Marianne
circa 1810-1865 . . . . DLB-166

Postl, Carl (see Sealsfield, Carl)

Poston, Ted 1906-1974 . . . . DLB-51

Postscript to [the Third Edition of] *Clarissa*
(1751), by Samuel Richardson DLB-39

Potok, Chaim 1929- DLB-28, 152; Y-84

Potter, Beatrix 1866-1943 . . . . DLB-141

Potter, David M. 1910-1971 . . . . . . DLB-17

Potter, John E., and Company DLB-49

Pottle, Frederick A.
1897-1987 . . . . DLB-103; Y-87

Poulin, Jacques 1937- DLB-60

Pound, Ezra 1885-1972 . . DLB-4, 45, 63; DS-15

Povich, Shirley 1905- DLB-171

Powell, Anthony 1905- DLB-15

Powell, John Wesley 1834-1902 . . . . DLB-186

Powers, J. F. 1917- DLB-130

Pownall, David 1938- DLB-14

Powys, John Cowper 1872-1963 . . . . DLB-15

Powys, Llewelyn 1884-1939 . . . . . . DLB-98

Powys, T. F. 1875-1953 . . . . . . DLB-36, 162

Poynter, Nelson 1903-1978 . . . . DLB-127

The Practice of Biography: An Interview
with Stanley Weintraub Y-82

The Practice of Biography II: An Interview
with B. L. Reid Y-83

The Practice of Biography III: An Interview
with Humphrey Carpenter Y-84

The Practice of Biography IV: An Interview with
William Manchester Y-85

The Practice of Biography V: An Interview
with Justin Kaplan Y-86

The Practice of Biography VI: An Interview with
David Herbert Donald. Y-87

The Practice of Biography VII: An Interview with
John Caldwell Guilds Y-92

The Practice of Biography VIII: An Interview
with Joan Mellen. Y-94

The Practice of Biography IX: An Interview
with Michael Reynolds Y-95

Prados, Emilio 1899-1962 . . . . DLB-134

Praed, Winthrop Mackworth
1802-1839 . . . . DLB-96

Praeger Publishers. DLB-46

Praetorius, Johannes 1630-1680 . . . . . DLB-168

Pratolini, Vasco 1913—1991. . . . . . . DLB-177

Pratt, E. J. 1882-1964. . . . . DLB-92

Pratt, Samuel Jackson 1749-1814. . . . . DLB-39

Preface to Alwyn (1780), by
Thomas Holcroft DLB-39

Preface to Colonel Jack (1722), by
Daniel Defoe DLB-39

Preface to Evelina (1778), by
Fanny Burney. DLB-39

Preface to Ferdinand Count Fathom (1753), by
Tobias Smollett DLB-39

Preface to Incognita (1692), by
William Congreve DLB-39

Preface to Joseph Andrews (1742), by
Henry Fielding DLB-39

Preface to Moll Flanders (1722), by
Daniel Defoe DLB-39

Preface to Poems (1853), by
Matthew Arnold DLB-32

Preface to Robinson Crusoe (1719), by
Daniel Defoe DLB-39

Preface to Roderick Random (1748), by
Tobias Smollett DLB-39

Preface to Roxana (1724), by
Daniel Defoe DLB-39

Preface to St. Leon (1799), by
William Godwin DLB-39

Preface to Sarah Fielding's Familiar Letters
(1747), by Henry Fielding
[excerpt] DLB-39

Preface to Sarah Fielding's The Adventures of
David Simple (1744), by
Henry Fielding DLB-39

Preface to The Cry (1754), by
Sarah Fielding. DLB-39

Preface to The Delicate Distress (1769), by
Elizabeth Griffin. DLB-39

Preface to The Disguis'd Prince (1733), by
Eliza Haywood [excerpt] DLB-39

Preface to The Farther Adventures of Robinson
Crusoe (1719), by Daniel Defoe . . . DLB-39

Preface to the First Edition of Pamela (1740), by
Samuel Richardson DLB-39

Preface to the First Edition of The Castle of
Otranto (1764), by
Horace Walpole DLB-39

Preface to The History of Romances (1715), by
Pierre Daniel Huet [excerpts] DLB-39

Preface to The Life of Charlotta du Pont (1723),
by Penelope Aubin DLB-39

Preface to The Old English Baron (1778), by
Clara Reeve DLB-39

Preface to the Second Edition of The Castle of
Otranto (1765), by Horace
Walpole DLB-39

Preface to The Secret History, of Queen Zarah,
and the Zarazians (1705), by Delariviere
Manley DLB-39

Preface to the Third Edition of Clarissa (1751),
by Samuel Richardson
[excerpt] DLB-39

Preface to The Works of Mrs. Davys (1725), by
Mary Davys DLB-39

Preface to Volume 1 of Clarissa (1747), by
Samuel Richardson DLB-39

Preface to Volume 3 of Clarissa (1748), by
Samuel Richardson DLB-39

Préfontaine, Yves 1937- DLB-53

Prelutsky, Jack 1940- DLB-61

Premisses, by Michael Hamburger. . . . DLB-66

Prentice, George D. 1802-1870. . . . . DLB-43

Prentice-Hall. DLB-46

Prescott, Orville 1906-1996. . . . . . . Y-96

Prescott, William Hickling
1796-1859 . . . . DLB-1, 30, 59

The Present State of the English Novel (1892),
by George Saintsbury DLB-18

Prešeren, Francè 1800-1849 . . . . . . DLB-147

Preston, May Wilson 1873-1949 . . . . DLB-188

Preston, Thomas 1537-1598 . . . . . . DLB-62

Price, Reynolds 1933- DLB-2

Price, Richard 1723-1791 . . . . DLB-158

Price, Richard 1949- Y-81

Priest, Christopher 1943- DLB-14

Priestley, J. B. 1894-1984
. . . . . . DLB-10, 34, 77, 100, 139; Y-84

Primary Bibliography: A
Retrospective Y-95

Prime, Benjamin Young 1733-1791 . . . DLB-31

Primrose, Diana
floruit circa 1630 . . . . DLB-126

Prince, F. T. 1912- DLB-20

Prince, Thomas 1687-1758 . . . . . DLB-24, 140

The Principles of Success in Literature (1865), by
George Henry Lewes [excerpt] . . . DLB-57

Printz, Wolfgang Casper
1641-1717 . . . . DLB-168

Prior, Matthew 1664-1721 . . . . DLB-95

Prisco, Michele 1920- DLB-177

Pritchard, William H. 1932- DLB-111

Pritchett, V. S. 1900- DLB-15, 139

Procter, Adelaide Anne 1825-1864 . . . DLB-32

Procter, Bryan Waller
1787-1874 . . . . DLB-96, 144

Proctor, Robert 1868-1903. . . . . . . DLB-184

Producing Dear Bunny, Dear Volodya: The Friendship
and the Feud. Y-97

The Profession of Authorship:
Scribblers for Bread Y-89

The Progress of Romance (1785), by Clara Reeve
[excerpt] DLB-39

Prokopovich, Feofan 1681?-1736 . . . . DLB-150

Prokosch, Frederic 1906-1989 . . . . . DLB-48

The Proletarian Novel DLB-9

Propper, Dan 1937- DLB-16

The Prospect of Peace (1778), by
Joel Barlow DLB-37

Protagoras circa 490 B.C.-420 B.C.
. . . . DLB-176

Proud, Robert 1728-1813. . . . . DLB-30

Proust, Marcel 1871-1922. . . . . DLB-65

Prynne, J. H. 1936- DLB-40

Przybyszewski, Stanislaw
1868-1927 . . . . DLB-66

Pseudo-Dionysius the Areopagite floruit
circa 500 . . . . DLB-115

Public Domain and the Violation of
Texts Y-97

The Public Lending Right in America
Statement by Sen. Charles McC.
Mathias, Jr. PLR and the Meaning
of Literary Property Statements on
PLR by American Writers Y-83

The Public Lending Right in the United Kingdom
Public Lending Right: The First Year in the
United Kingdom Y-83

The Publication of English
Renaissance Plays. DLB-62

Publications and Social Movements
[Transcendentalism] DLB-1

Publishers and Agents: The Columbia
　Connection Y-87

A Publisher's Archives: G. P. Putnam . . . Y-92

Publishing Fiction at LSU Press. Y-87

Pückler-Muskau, Hermann von
　1785-1871 . . . . DLB-133

Pufendorf, Samuel von
　1632-1694 . . . . DLB-168

Pugh, Edwin William 1874-1930 . . . . DLB-135

Pugin, A. Welby 1812-1852 . . . . . . DLB-55

Puig, Manuel 1932-1990 . . . . DLB-113

Pulitzer, Joseph 1847-1911 . . . . DLB-23

Pulitzer, Joseph, Jr. 1885-1955 . . . . . DLB-29

Pulitzer Prizes for the Novel,
　1917-1945 . . . . DLB-9

Pulliam, Eugene 1889-1975 . . . . . . DLB-127

Purchas, Samuel 1577?-1626 . . . . . . DLB-151

Purdy, Al 1918- DLB-88

Purdy, James 1923- DLB-2

Purdy, Ken W. 1913-1972 . . . . . DLB-137

Pusey, Edward Bouverie
　1800-1882 . . . . DLB-55

Putnam, George Palmer
　1814-1872 . . . . DLB-3, 79

Putnam, Samuel 1892-1950 . . . . DLB-4

G. P. Putnam's Sons [U.S.] DLB-49

G. P. Putnam's Sons [U.K.] DLB-106

Puzo, Mario 1920- DLB-6

Pyle, Ernie 1900-1945 . . . . DLB-29

Pyle, Howard
　1853-1911 . . . . DLB-42, 188; DS-13

Pym, Barbara 1913-1980 . . . . . DLB-14; Y-87

Pynchon, Thomas 1937- DLB-2, 173

Pyramid Books DLB-46

Pyrnelle, Louise-Clarke 1850-1907 . . . . DLB-42

Pythagoras circa 570 B.C.-? DLB-176

Q

Quad, M. (see Lewis, Charles B.)

Quaritch, Bernard 1819-1899 . . . . . . DLB-184

Quarles, Francis 1592-1644 . . . . DLB-126

The Quarterly Review
　1809-1967 . . . . DLB-110

Quasimodo, Salvatore 1901-1968 . . . . DLB-114

Queen, Ellery (see Dannay, Frederic, and
　Manfred B. Lee)

The Queen City Publishing House . . . DLB-49

Queneau, Raymond 1903-1976 . . . . . DLB-72

Quennell, Sir Peter 1905-1993 . . . DLB-155, 195

Quesnel, Joseph 1746-1809 . . . . . . DLB-99

The Question of American Copyright
　in the Nineteenth Century
　Headnote
　Preface, by George Haven Putnam
　The Evolution of Copyright, by Brander
　　Matthews
　Summary of Copyright Legislation in
　　the United States, by R. R. Bowker
　Analysis oæ the Provisions of the
　　Copyright Law of 1891, by
　　George Haven Putnam
　The Contest for International Copyright,
　　by George Haven Putnam
　Cheap Books and Good Books,
　　by Brander Matthews DLB-49

Quiller-Couch, Sir Arthur Thomas
　1863-1944 . . . . DLB-135, 153, 190

Quin, Ann 1936-1973 . . . . DLB-14

Quincy, Samuel, of Georgia ?-? DLB-31

Quincy, Samuel, of Massachusetts
　1734-1789 . . . . DLB-31

Quinn, Anthony 1915- DLB-122

Quinn, John 1870-1924 . . . . DLB-187

Quintana, Leroy V. 1944- DLB-82

Quintana, Miguel de 1671-1748
　A Forerunner of Chicano
　Literature DLB-122

Quist, Harlin, Books DLB-46

Quoirez, Françoise (see Sagan, Françoise)

R

R-va, Zeneida (see Gan, Elena Andreevna)

Raabe, Wilhelm 1831-1910 . . . . . . DLB-129

Rabe, David 1940- DLB-7

Raboni, Giovanni 1932- DLB-128

Rachilde 1860-1953 . . . . DLB-123, 192

Racin, Kočo 1908-1943 . . . . DLB-147

Rackham, Arthur 1867-1939 . . . . . . DLB-141

Radcliffe, Ann 1764-1823 . . . . . . DLB-39, 178

Raddall, Thomas 1903- DLB-68

Radichkov, Yordan 1929- DLB-181

Radiguet, Raymond 1903-1923 . . . . . DLB-65

Radishchev, Aleksandr Nikolaevich
　1749-1802 . . . . DLB-150

Radványi, Netty Reiling (see Seghers, Anna)

Rahv, Philip 1908-1973 . . . . DLB-137

Raičković, Stevan 1928- DLB-181

Raimund, Ferdinand Jakob
　1790-1836 . . . . DLB-90

Raine, Craig 1944- DLB-40

Raine, Kathleen 1908- DLB-20

Rainolde, Richard
　circa 1530-1606 . . . . DLB-136

Rakić, Milan 1876-1938 . . . . DLB-147

Rakosi, Carl 1903- DLB-193

Ralegh, Sir Walter 1554?-1618 . . . . . DLB-172

Ralin, Radoy 1923- DLB-181

Ralph, Julian 1853-1903 . . . . DLB-23

Ralph Waldo Emerson in 1982 . . . . . . Y-82

Ramat, Silvio 1939- DLB-128

Rambler, no. 4 (1750), by Samuel Johnson
　[excerpt] DLB-39

Ramée, Marie Louise de la (see Ouida)

Ramírez, Sergío 1942- DLB-145

Ramke, Bin 1947- DLB-120

Ramler, Karl Wilhelm 1725-1798 . . . . DLB-97

Ramon Ribeyro, Julio 1929- DLB-145

Ramous, Mario 1924- DLB-128

Rampersad, Arnold 1941- DLB-111

Ramsay, Allan 1684 or 1685-1758 . . . . DLB-95

Ramsay, David 1749-1815 . . . . DLB-30

Ranck, Katherine Quintana
　1942- DLB-122

Rand, Avery and Company DLB-49

Rand McNally and Company DLB-49

Randall, David Anton
　1905-1975 . . . . DLB-140

Randall, Dudley 1914- DLB-41

Randall, Henry S. 1811-1876 . . . . . . DLB-30

Randall, James G. 1881-1953 . . . . . . DLB-17

The Randall Jarrell Symposium: A Small
　Collection of Randall Jarrells
　Excerpts From Papers Delivered at
　the Randall Jarrel Symposium Y-86

Randolph, A. Philip 1889-1979 . . . . DLB-91

Randolph, Anson D. F.
　[publishing house] DLB-49

Randolph, Thomas 1605-1635 . . . DLB-58, 126

Random House DLB-46

Ranlet, Henry [publishing house] DLB-49

Ransom, Harry 1908-1976 . . . . DLB-187

Ransom, John Crowe
　1888-1974 . . . . DLB-45, 63

Ransome, Arthur 1884-1967 . . . . . . DLB-160

Raphael, Frederic 1931- DLB-14

Raphaelson, Samson 1896-1983 . . . . DLB-44

Raskin, Ellen 1928-1984 . . . . DLB-52

Rastell, John 1475?-1536 . . . . . DLB-136, 170

Rattigan, Terence 1911-1977 . . . . . . DLB-13

Rawlings, Marjorie Kinnan
　1896-1953 . . . . . DLB-9, 22, 102; DS-17

Raworth, Tom 1938- DLB-40

Ray, David 1932- DLB-5

Ray, Gordon Norton
　1915-1986 . . . . DLB-103, 140

Ray, Henrietta Cordelia
　1849-1916 . . . . DLB-50

Raymond, Ernest 1888-1974 . . . . . . DLB-191

Raymond, Henry J. 1820-1869 . . . DLB-43, 79

Raymond Chandler Centenary Tributes from Michael Avallone, James Elroy, Joe Gores, and William F. Nolan Y-88

Reach, Angus 1821-1856 . . . . DLB-70

Read, Herbert 1893-1968 . . . . . DLB-20, 149

Read, Herbert, "The Practice of Biography," in *The English Sense of Humour and Other Essays* DLB-149

Read, Opie 1852-1939 . . . . DLB-23

Read, Piers Paul 1941- DLB-14

Reade, Charles 1814-1884 . . . . DLB-21

Reader's Digest Condensed Books DLB-46

Readers Ulysses Symposium Y-97

Reading, Peter 1946- DLB-40

Reading Series in New York City Y-96

Reaney, James 1926- DLB-68

Rebhun, Paul 1500?-1546 . . . . DLB-179

Rèbora, Clemente 1885-1957 . . . . . DLB-114

Rechy, John 1934- DLB-122; Y-82

The Recovery of Literature: Criticism in the 1990s: A Symposium Y-91

Redding, J. Saunders 1906-1988 . . . . DLB-63, 76

Redfield, J. S. [publishing house] DLB-49

Redgrove, Peter 1932- DLB-40

Redmon, Anne 1943- Y-86

Redmond, Eugene B. 1937- DLB-41

Redpath, James [publishing house] DLB-49

Reed, Henry 1808-1854 . . . . DLB-59

Reed, Henry 1914- DLB-27

Reed, Ishmael 1938- DLB-2, 5, 33, 169; DS-8

Reed, Rex 1938- DLB-185

Reed, Sampson 1800-1880 . . . . DLB-1

Reed, Talbot Baines 1852-1893 . . . . DLB-141

Reedy, William Marion 1862-1920 . . . DLB-91

Reese, Lizette Woodworth 1856-1935 . . . . DLB-54

Reese, Thomas 1742-1796 . . . . DLB-37

Reeve, Clara 1729-1807 . . . . DLB-39

Reeves, James 1909-1978 . . . . DLB-161

Reeves, John 1926- DLB-88

"Reflections: After a Tornado," by Judson Jerome DLB-105

Regnery, Henry, Company DLB-46

Rehberg, Hans 1901-1963 . . . . DLB-124

Rehfisch, Hans José 1891-1960 . . . . DLB-124

Reid, Alastair 1926- DLB-27

Reid, B. L. 1918-1990 . . . . DLB-111

Reid, Christopher 1949- DLB-40

Reid, Forrest 1875-1947 . . . . DLB-153

Reid, Helen Rogers 1882-1970 . . . . . DLB-29

Reid, James ?-? DLB-31

Reid, Mayne 1818-1883 . . . . . . DLB-21, 163

Reid, Thomas 1710-1796 . . . . DLB-31

Reid, V. S. (Vic) 1913-1987 . . . . . DLB-125

Reid, Whitelaw 1837-1912 . . . . DLB-23

Reilly and Lee Publishing Company DLB-46

Reimann, Brigitte 1933-1973 . . . . . . DLB-75

Reinmar der Alte circa 1165-circa 1205 . . . . DLB-138

Reinmar von Zweter circa 1200-circa 1250 . . . . DLB-138

Reisch, Walter 1903-1983 . . . . DLB-44

Remarque, Erich Maria 1898-1970 . . . . DLB-56

"Re-meeting of Old Friends": The Jack Kerouac Conference Y-82

Reminiscences, by Charles Scribner Jr. . . DS-17

Remington, Frederic 1861-1909 . . . . DLB-12, 186, 188

Renaud, Jacques 1943- DLB-60

Renault, Mary 1905-1983 . . . . Y-83

Rendell, Ruth 1930- DLB-87

Representative Men and Women: A Historical Perspective on the British Novel, 1930-1960 . . . . DLB-15

(Re-)Publishing Orwell Y-86

Research in the American Antiquarian Book Trade Y-97

Responses to Ken Auletta Y-97

Rettenbacher, Simon 1634-1706 . . . . . DLB-168

Reuchlin, Johannes 1455-1522 . . . . . DLB-179

Reuter, Christian 1665-after 1712 . . . DLB-168

Reuter, Fritz 1810-1874 . . . . DLB-129

Reuter, Gabriele 1859-1941 . . . . DLB-66

Revell, Fleming H., Company DLB-49

Reventlow, Franziska Gräfin zu 1871-1918 . . . . DLB-66

Review of Reviews Office DLB-112

Review of [Samuel Richardson's] *Clarissa* (1748), by Henry Fielding DLB-39

The Revolt (1937), by Mary Colum [excerpts] DLB-36

Rexroth, Kenneth 1905-1982 . . . . . DLB-16, 48, 165; Y-82

Rey, H. A. 1898-1977 . . . . DLB-22

Reynal and Hitchcock DLB-46

Reynolds, G. W. M. 1814-1879 . . . . . DLB-21

Reynolds, John Hamilton 1794-1852 . . . . DLB-96

Reynolds, Mack 1917- DLB-8

Reynolds, Sir Joshua 1723-1792 . . . . DLB-104

Reznikoff, Charles 1894-1976 . . . . DLB-28, 45

"Rhetoric" (1828; revised, 1859), by Thomas de Quincey [excerpt] DLB-57

Rhett, Robert Barnwell 1800-1876 . . . . DLB-43

Rhode, John 1884-1964 . . . . DLB-77

Rhodes, James Ford 1848-1927 . . . . . DLB-47

Rhodes, Richard 1937- DLB-185

Rhys, Jean 1890-1979 . . . . . DLB-36, 117, 162

Ricardo, David 1772-1823 . . . . . DLB-107, 158

Ricardou, Jean 1932- DLB-83

Rice, Elmer 1892-1967 . . . . DLB-4, 7

Rice, Grantland 1880-1954 . . . . . DLB-29, 171

Rich, Adrienne 1929- DLB-5, 67

Richards, David Adams 1950- DLB-53

Richards, George circa 1760-1814 . . . . DLB-37

Richards, I. A. 1893-1979 . . . . DLB-27

Richards, Laura E. 1850-1943 . . . . . DLB-42

Richards, William Carey 1818-1892 . . . . DLB-73

Richards, Grant [publishing house] DLB-112

Richardson, Charles F. 1851-1913 . . . . DLB-71

Richardson, Dorothy M. 1873-1957 . . . . DLB-36

Richardson, Henry Handel (Ethel Florence Lindesay) 1870-1946 . . . . DLB-197

Richardson, Jack 1935- DLB-7

Richardson, John 1796-1852 . . . . . . DLB-99

Richardson, Samuel 1689-1761 . . . . DLB-39, 154

Richardson, Willis 1889-1977 . . . . . . DLB-51

Riche, Barnabe 1542-1617 . . . . DLB-136

Richepin, Jean 1849-1926 . . . . DLB-192

Richler, Mordecai 1931- DLB-53

Richter, Conrad 1890-1968 . . . . . . DLB-9

Richter, Hans Werner 1908- DLB-69

Richter, Johann Paul Friedrich 1763-1825 . . . . DLB-94

Rickerby, Joseph [publishing house] DLB-106

Rickword, Edgell 1898-1982 . . . . . . DLB-20

Riddell, Charlotte 1832-1906 . . . . . DLB-156

Riddell, John (see Ford, Corey)

Ridge, John Rollin 1827-1867 . . . . . . DLB-175

Ridge, Lola 1873-1941 . . . . DLB-54

Ridge, William Pett 1859-1930 . . . . . DLB-135

Riding, Laura (see Jackson, Laura Riding)

Ridler, Anne 1912- DLB-27

Ridruego, Dionisio 1912-1975 . . . . . DLB-108

Riel, Louis 1844-1885 . . . . DLB-99

Riemer, Johannes 1648-1714 . . . . . . DLB-168

Riffaterre, Michael 1924- DLB-67

Riggs, Lynn 1899-1954 . . . . DLB-175

Riis, Jacob 1849-1914 . . . . DLB-23

Riker, John C. [publishing house] DLB-49

Riley, James 1777-1840 . . . . DLB-183

Riley, John 1938-1978 . . . . DLB-40

Rilke, Rainer Maria 1875-1926. . . . . . DLB-81

Rimanelli, Giose 1926- DLB-177

Rinehart and Company. DLB-46

Ringuet 1895-1960. . . . . DLB-68

Ringwood, Gwen Pharis
1910-1984 . . . . DLB-88

Rinser, Luise 1911- DLB-69

Ríos, Alberto 1952- DLB-122

Ríos, Isabella 1948- DLB-82

Ripley, Arthur 1895-1961. . . . . DLB-44

Ripley, George 1802-1880. . . . . DLB-1, 64, 73

The Rising Glory of America:
Three Poems DLB-37

The Rising Glory of America: Written in 1771
(1786), by Hugh Henry Brackenridge and
Philip Freneau. DLB-37

Riskin, Robert 1897-1955. . . . . DLB-26

Risse, Heinz 1898- DLB-69

Rist, Johann 1607-1667 . . . . DLB-164

Ritchie, Anna Mowatt 1819-1870 . . . . DLB-3

Ritchie, Anne Thackeray
1837-1919 . . . . DLB-18

Ritchie, Thomas 1778-1854. . . . . . . DLB-43

Rites of Passage
[on William Saroyan] Y-83

The Ritz Paris Hemingway Award Y-85

Rivard, Adjutor 1868-1945 . . . . DLB-92

Rive, Richard 1931-1989 . . . . DLB-125

Rivera, Marina 1942- DLB-122

Rivera, Tomás 1935-1984 . . . . DLB-82

Rivers, Conrad Kent 1933-1968 . . . . DLB-41

Riverside Press DLB-49

Rivington, James circa 1724-1802 . . . . DLB-43

Rivington, Charles
[publishing house] DLB-154

Rivkin, Allen 1903-1990 . . . . DLB-26

Roa Bastos, Augusto 1917- DLB-113

Robbe-Grillet, Alain 1922- DLB-83

Robbins, Tom 1936- Y-80

Roberts, Charles G. D. 1860-1943. . . . DLB-92

Roberts, Dorothy 1906-1993 . . . . . . DLB-88

Roberts, Elizabeth Madox
1881-1941. . . . . DLB-9, 54, 102

Roberts, Kenneth 1885-1957. . . . . . . DLB-9

Roberts, William 1767-1849. . . . . . DLB-142

Roberts Brothers DLB-49

Roberts, James [publishing house] . . . DLB-154

Robertson, A. M., and Company DLB-49

Robertson, William 1721-1793 . . . . DLB-104

Robins, Elizabeth 1862-1952. . . . . . DLB-197

Robinson, Casey 1903-1979 . . . . . . DLB-44

Robinson, Edwin Arlington
1869-1935 . . . . DLB-54

Robinson, Henry Crabb
1775-1867 . . . . DLB-107

Robinson, James Harvey
1863-1936 . . . . DLB-47

Robinson, Lennox 1886-1958. . . . . . DLB-10

Robinson, Mabel Louise
1874-1962 . . . . DLB-22

Robinson, Mary 1758-1800 . . . . . . DLB-158

Robinson, Richard
circa 1545-1607 . . . . DLB-167

Robinson, Therese
1797-1870 . . . . DLB-59, 133

Robison, Mary 1949- DLB-130

Roblès, Emmanuel 1914- DLB-83

Roccatagliata Ceccardi, Ceccardo
1871-1919 . . . . DLB-114

Rochester, John Wilmot, Earl of
1647-1680 . . . . DLB-131

Rock, Howard 1911-1976 . . . . DLB-127

Rockwell, Norman Perceval
1894-1978 . . . . DLB-188

Rodgers, Carolyn M. 1945- DLB-41

Rodgers, W. R. 1909-1969 . . . . . . DLB-20

Rodríguez, Claudio 1934- DLB-134

Rodriguez, Richard 1944- DLB-82

Rodríguez Julia, Edgardo
1946- DLB-145

Roethke, Theodore 1908-1963. . . . . . DLB-5

Rogers, Jane 1952- DLB-194

Rogers, Pattiann 1940- DLB-105

Rogers, Samuel 1763-1855 . . . . . . DLB-93

Rogers, Will 1879-1935. . . . . DLB-11

Rohmer, Sax 1883-1959 . . . . DLB-70

Roiphe, Anne 1935- Y-80

Rojas, Arnold R. 1896-1988 . . . . . . DLB-82

Rolfe, Frederick William
1860-1913 . . . . DLB-34, 156

Rolland, Romain 1866-1944 . . . . . . DLB-65

Rolle, Richard
circa 1290-1300 - 1340 . . . . . . DLB-146

Rölvaag, O. E. 1876-1931 . . . . DLB-9

Romains, Jules 1885-1972. . . . . . . DLB-65

Roman, A., and Company DLB-49

Romano, Lalla 1906- DLB-177

Romano, Octavio 1923- DLB-122

Romero, Leo 1950- DLB-122

Romero, Lin 1947- DLB-122

Romero, Orlando 1945- DLB-82

Rook, Clarence 1863-1915 . . . . . . DLB-135

Roosevelt, Theodore 1858-1919 . . DLB-47, 186

Root, Waverley 1903-1982. . . . . . . DLB-4

Root, William Pitt 1941- DLB-120

Roquebrune, Robert de 1889-1978. . . . DLB-68

Rosa, João Guimarães
1908-1967 . . . . DLB-113

Rosales, Luis 1910-1992. . . . . DLB-134

Roscoe, William 1753-1831 . . . . . . DLB-163

Rose, Reginald 1920- DLB-26

Rose, Wendy 1948- DLB-175

Rosegger, Peter 1843-1918. . . . . . . DLB-129

Rosei, Peter 1946- DLB-85

Rosen, Norma 1925- DLB-28

Rosenbach, A. S. W. 1876-1952 . . . . DLB-140

Rosenbaum, Ron 1946- DLB-185

Rosenberg, Isaac 1890-1918. . . . . . . DLB-20

Rosenfeld, Isaac 1918-1956 . . . . . . DLB-28

Rosenthal, M. L. 1917- DLB-5

Rosenwald, Lessing J. 1891-1979 . . . . DLB-187

Ross, Alexander 1591-1654 . . . . . . DLB-151

Ross, Harold 1892-1951. . . . . DLB-137

Ross, Leonard Q. (see Rosten, Leo)

Ross, Lillian 1927- DLB-185

Ross, Martin 1862-1915 . . . . DLB-135

Ross, Sinclair 1908- DLB-88

Ross, W. W. E. 1894-1966 . . . . . . DLB-88

Rosselli, Amelia 1930- DLB-128

Rossen, Robert 1908-1966 . . . . . . DLB-26

Rossetti, Christina Georgina
1830-1894 . . . . DLB-35, 163

Rossetti, Dante Gabriel 1828-1882 . . . . DLB-35

Rossner, Judith 1935- DLB-6

Rostand, Edmond 1868-1918 . . . . . DLB-192

Rosten, Leo 1908- DLB-11

Rostenberg, Leona 1908- DLB-140

Rostovsky, Dimitrii 1651-1709 . . . . . DLB-150

Bertram Rota and His Bookshop Y-91

Roth, Gerhard 1942- DLB-85, 124

Roth, Henry 1906?- DLB-28

Roth, Joseph 1894-1939. . . . . DLB-85

Roth, Philip 1933- DLB-2, 28, 173; Y-82

Rothenberg, Jerome 1931- . . . . : DLB-5, 193

Rothschild Family DLB-184

Rotimi, Ola 1938- DLB-125

Routhier, Adolphe-Basile
1839-1920 . . . . DLB-99

Routier, Simone 1901-1987. . . . . . . DLB-88

Routledge, George, and Sons DLB-106

Roversi, Roberto 1923- DLB-128

Rowe, Elizabeth Singer
1674-1737. . . . . DLB-39, 95

Rowe, Nicholas 1674-1718 . . . . . . DLB-84

Rowlands, Samuel
circa 1570-1630 . . . . DLB-121

Rowlandson, Mary
circa 1635-circa 1678 . . . . DLB-24

Rowley, William circa 1585-1626 . . . . DLB-58

Rowse, A. L. 1903- DLB-155

Rowson, Susanna Haswell
circa 1762-1824 . . . . DLB-37

Roy, Camille 1870-1943 . . . . DLB-92

Roy, Gabrielle 1909-1983 . . . . DLB-68

Roy, Jules 1907- DLB-83

The Royal Court Theatre and the English
Stage Company DLB-13

The Royal Court Theatre and the New Drama
. . . . DLB-10

The Royal Shakespeare Company
at the Swan Y-88

Royall, Anne 1769-1854 . . . . DLB-43

The Roycroft Printing Shop DLB-49

Royde-Smith, Naomi 1875-1964 . . . . DLB-191

Royster, Vermont 1914- DLB-127

Royston, Richard
[publishing house] DLB-170

Ruark, Gibbons 1941- DLB-120

Ruban, Vasilii Grigorevich
1742-1795 . . . . DLB-150

Rubens, Bernice 1928- DLB-14

Rudd and Carleton DLB-49

Rudkin, David 1936- DLB-13

Rudolf von Ems
circa 1200-circa 1254 . . . . DLB-138

Ruffin, Josephine St. Pierre
1842-1924 . . . . DLB-79

Ruganda, John 1941- DLB-157

Ruggles, Henry Joseph 1813-1906 . . . . DLB-64

Rukeyser, Muriel 1913-1980 . . . . . . DLB-48

Rule, Jane 1931- DLB-60

Rulfo, Juan 1918-1986 . . . . DLB-113

Rumaker, Michael 1932- DLB-16

Rumens, Carol 1944- DLB-40

Runyon, Damon 1880-1946 . . DLB-11, 86, 171

Ruodlieb circa 1050-1075 . . . . DLB-148

Rush, Benjamin 1746-1813 . . . . DLB-37

Rushdie, Salman 1947- DLB-194

Rusk, Ralph L. 1888-1962 . . . . DLB-103

Ruskin, John 1819-1900 . . . . DLB-55, 163, 190

Russ, Joanna 1937- DLB-8

Russell, B. B., and Company DLB-49

Russell, Benjamin 1761-1845 . . . . . . DLB-43

Russell, Bertrand 1872-1970 . . . . . . DLB-100

Russell, Charles Edward
1860-1941 . . . . DLB-25

Russell, Charles M. 1864-1926 . . . . . DLB-188

Russell, Countess Mary Annette Beauchamp (see
Arnim, Elizabeth von)

Russell, George William (see AE)

Russell, R. H., and Son DLB-49

Rutherford, Mark 1831-1913 . . . . . . DLB-18

Ruxton, George Frederick
1821-1848 . . . . DLB-186

Ryan, Michael 1946- Y-82

Ryan, Oscar 1904- DLB-68

Ryga, George 1932- DLB-60

Rylands, Enriqueta Augustina Tennant
1843-1908 . . . . DLB-184

Rylands, John 1801-1888 . . . . DLB-184

Rymer, Thomas 1643?-1713 . . . . . DLB-101

Ryskind, Morrie 1895-1985 . . . . . . DLB-26

Rzhevsky, Aleksei Andreevich
1737-1804 . . . . DLB-150

S

The Saalfield Publishing
Company DLB-46

Saba, Umberto 1883-1957 . . . . DLB-114

Sábato, Ernesto 1911- DLB-145

Saberhagen, Fred 1930- DLB-8

Sabin, Joseph 1821-1881 . . . . DLB-187

Sacer, Gottfried Wilhelm
1635-1699 . . . . DLB-168

Sachs, Hans 1494-1576 . . . . DLB-179

Sack, John 1930- DLB-185

Sackler, Howard 1929-1982 . . . . . . DLB-7

Sackville, Thomas 1536-1608 . . . . . DLB-132

Sackville, Thomas 1536-1608
and Norton, Thomas
1532-1584 . . . . DLB-62

Sackville-West, Edward 1901-1965 . . . DLB-191

Sackville-West, V. 1892-1962 . . . . DLB-34, 195

Sadlier, D. and J., and Company DLB-49

Sadlier, Mary Anne 1820-1903 . . . . . DLB-99

Sadoff, Ira 1945- DLB-120

Saenz, Jaime 1921-1986 . . . . DLB-145

Saffin, John circa 1626-1710 . . . . . . DLB-24

Sagan, Françoise 1935- DLB-83

Sage, Robert 1899-1962 . . . . DLB-4

Sagel, Jim 1947- DLB-82

Sagendorph, Robb Hansell
1900-1970 . . . . DLB-137

Sahagún, Carlos 1938- DLB-108

Sahkomaapii, Piitai (see Highwater, Jamake)

Sahl, Hans 1902- DLB-69

Said, Edward W. 1935- DLB-67

Saiko, George 1892-1962 . . . . DLB-85

St. Dominic's Press DLB-112

Saint-Exupéry, Antoine de
1900-1944 . . . . DLB-72

St. John, J. Allen 1872-1957 . . . . . . DLB-188

St. Johns, Adela Rogers 1894-1988 . . . DLB-29

The St. John's College Robert
Graves Trust Y-96

St. Martin's Press DLB-46

St. Omer, Garth 1931- DLB-117

Saint Pierre, Michel de 1916-1987 . . . DLB-83

Saintsbury, George
1845-1933 . . . . DLB-57, 149

Saki (see Munro, H. H.)

Salaam, Kalamu ya 1947- DLB-38

Šalamun, Tomaž 1941- DLB-181

Salas, Floyd 1931- DLB-82

Sálaz-Marquez, Rubén 1935- DLB-122

Salemson, Harold J. 1910-1988 . . . . . DLB-4

Salinas, Luis Omar 1937- DLB-82

Salinas, Pedro 1891-1951 . . . . DLB-134

Salinger, J. D. 1919- DLB-2, 102, 173

Salkey, Andrew 1928- DLB-125

Salt, Waldo 1914- DLB-44

Salter, James 1925- DLB-130

Salter, Mary Jo 1954- DLB-120

Salustri, Carlo Alberto (see Trilussa)

Salverson, Laura Goodman
1890-1970 . . . . DLB-92

Sampson, Richard Henry (see Hull, Richard)

Samuels, Ernest 1903- DLB-111

Sanborn, Franklin Benjamin
1831-1917 . . . . DLB-1

Sánchez, Luis Rafael 1936- DLB-145

Sánchez, Philomeno "Phil"
1917- DLB-122

Sánchez, Ricardo 1941- DLB-82

Sanchez, Sonia 1934- DLB-41; DS-8

Sand, George 1804-1876 . . . . . . DLB-119, 192

Sandburg, Carl 1878-1967 . . . . . DLB-17, 54

Sanders, Ed 1939- DLB-16

Sandoz, Mari 1896-1966 . . . . DLB-9

Sandwell, B. K. 1876-1954 . . . . DLB-92

Sandy, Stephen 1934- DLB-165

Sandys, George 1578-1644 . . . . . DLB-24, 121

Sangster, Charles 1822-1893 . . . . . . DLB-99

Sanguineti, Edoardo 1930- DLB-128

Sansom, William 1912-1976 . . . . . . DLB-139

Santayana, George
1863-1952 . . . . DLB-54, 71; DS-13

Santiago, Danny 1911-1988 . . . . . . DLB-122

Santmyer, Helen Hooven 1895-1986 . . . Y-84

Sanvitale, Francesca 1928- DLB-196

Sapidus, Joannes 1490-1561 . . . . . . DLB-179

Sapir, Edward 1884-1939 . . . . DLB-92

Sapper (see McNeile, Herman Cyril)

Sappho circa 620 B.C.-circa 550 B.C.
. . . . DLB-176

Sardou, Victorien 1831-1908 . . . . . . DLB-192

Sarduy, Severo 1937- DLB-113

Sargent, Pamela 1948- DLB-8

Saro-Wiwa, Ken 1941- DLB-157

Saroyan, William
1908-1981 . . . . DLB-7, 9, 86; Y-81

Sarraute, Nathalie 1900- DLB-83

Sarrazin, Albertine 1937-1967. . . . . . DLB-83

Sarris, Greg 1952- DLB-175

Sarton, May 1912- DLB-48; Y-81

Sartre, Jean-Paul 1905-1980 . . . . DLB-72

Sassoon, Siegfried 1886-1967 . . . . DLB-20, 191

Sata, Ineko 1904- DLB-180

Saturday Review Press DLB-46

Saunders, James 1925- DLB-13

Saunders, John Monk 1897-1940. . . . . DLB-26

Saunders, Margaret Marshall
1861-1947 . . . . DLB-92

Saunders and Otley DLB-106

Savage, James 1784-1873 . . . . DLB-30

Savage, Marmion W. 1803?-1872 . . . . DLB-21

Savage, Richard 1697?-1743 . . . . . . DLB-95

Savard, Félix-Antoine 1896-1982 . . . . DLB-68

Saville, (Leonard) Malcolm
1901-1982 . . . . DLB-160

Sawyer, Ruth 1880-1970 . . . . DLB-22

Sayers, Dorothy L.
1893-1957 . . . . DLB-10, 36, 77, 100

Sayle, Charles Edward 1864-1924 . . . DLB-184

Sayles, John Thomas 1950- DLB-44

Sbarbaro, Camillo 1888-1967 . . . . . DLB-114

Scalapino, Leslie 1947- DLB-193

Scannell, Vernon 1922- DLB-27

Scarry, Richard 1919-1994 . . . . DLB-61

Schaeffer, Albrecht 1885-1950 . . . . . DLB-66

Schaeffer, Susan Fromberg 1941- DLB-28

Schaff, Philip 1819-1893 . . . . DS-13

Schaper, Edzard 1908-1984 . . . . DLB-69

Scharf, J. Thomas 1843-1898. . . . . . DLB-47

Schede, Paul Melissus 1539-1602 . . . . DLB-179

Scheffel, Joseph Viktor von
1826-1886 . . . . DLB-129

Scheffler, Johann 1624-1677 . . . . . . DLB-164

Schelling, Friedrich Wilhelm Joseph von
1775-1854 . . . . DLB-90

Scherer, Wilhelm 1841-1886. . . . . . . DLB-129

Schickele, René 1883-1940 . . . . DLB-66

Schiff, Dorothy 1903-1989 . . . . DLB-127

Schiller, Friedrich 1759-1805 . . . . . . DLB-94

Schirmer, David 1623-1687 . . . . . . DLB-164

Schlaf, Johannes 1862-1941 . . . . . . DLB-118

Schlegel, August Wilhelm
1767-1845 . . . . DLB-94

Schlegel, Dorothea 1763-1839. . . . . . DLB-90

Schlegel, Friedrich 1772-1829 . . . . . . DLB-90

Schleiermacher, Friedrich
1768-1834 . . . . DLB-90

Schlesinger, Arthur M., Jr. 1917- DLB-17

Schlumberger, Jean 1877-1968 . . . . . DLB-65

Schmid, Eduard Hermann Wilhelm (see
Edschmid, Kasimir)

Schmidt, Arno 1914-1979 . . . . DLB-69

Schmidt, Johann Kaspar (see Stirner, Max)

Schmidt, Michael 1947- DLB-40

Schmidtbonn, Wilhelm August
1876-1952 . . . . DLB-118

Schmitz, James H. 1911- DLB-8

Schnabel, Johann Gottfried
1692-1760 . . . . DLB-168

Schnackenberg, Gjertrud 1953- DLB-120

Schnitzler, Arthur 1862-1931 . . . . DLB-81, 118

Schnurre, Wolfdietrich 1920- DLB-69

Schocken Books. DLB-46

Scholartis Press. DLB-112

The Schomburg Center for Research
in Black Culture DLB-76

Schönbeck, Virgilio (see Giotti, Virgilio)

Schönherr, Karl 1867-1943 . . . . . . DLB-118

Schoolcraft, Jane Johnston
1800-1841 . . . . DLB-175

School Stories, 1914-1960 . . . . DLB-160

Schopenhauer, Arthur 1788-1860. . . . DLB-90

Schopenhauer, Johanna 1766-1838 . . . DLB-90

Schorer, Mark 1908-1977 . . . . DLB-103

Schottelius, Justus Georg
1612-1676 . . . . DLB-164

Schouler, James 1839-1920 . . . . DLB-47

Schrader, Paul 1946- DLB-44

Schreiner, Olive 1855-1920 . . DLB-18, 156, 190

Schroeder, Andreas 1946- DLB-53

Schubart, Christian Friedrich Daniel
1739-1791 . . . . DLB-97

Schubert, Gotthilf Heinrich
1780-1860 . . . . DLB-90

Schücking, Levin 1814-1883 . . . . . . DLB-133

Schulberg, Budd 1914- . . DLB-6, 26, 28; Y-81

Schulte, F. J., and Company DLB-49

Schulze, Hans (see Praetorius, Johannes)

Schupp, Johann Balthasar
1610-1661 . . . . DLB-164

Schurz, Carl 1829-1906 . . . . DLB-23

Schuyler, George S. 1895-1977 . . . DLB-29, 51

Schuyler, James 1923-1991 . . . . . DLB-5, 169

Schwartz, Delmore 1913-1966 . . . . DLB-28, 48

Schwartz, Jonathan 1938- Y-82

Schwarz, Sibylle 1621-1638 . . . . . . DLB-164

Schwerner, Armand 1927- DLB-165

Schwob, Marcel 1867-1905 . . . . . . DLB-123

Sciascia, Leonardo 1921-1989 . . . . . DLB-177

Science Fantasy. DLB-8

Science-Fiction Fandom and
Conventions DLB-8

Science-Fiction Fanzines: The Time
Binders DLB-8

Science-Fiction Films DLB-8

Science Fiction Writers of America and the
Nebula Awards. DLB-8

Scot, Reginald circa 1538-1599 . . . . . DLB-136

Scotellaro, Rocco 1923-1953. . . . . . . DLB-128

Scott, Dennis 1939-1991 . . . . DLB-125

Scott, Dixon 1881-1915 . . . . DLB-98

Scott, Duncan Campbell 1862-1947 . . . DLB-92

Scott, Evelyn 1893-1963 . . . . DLB-9, 48

Scott, F. R. 1899-1985 . . . . DLB-88

Scott, Frederick George 1861-1944. . . . DLB-92

Scott, Geoffrey 1884-1929 . . . . DLB-149

Scott, Harvey W. 1838-1910. . . . . . . DLB-23

Scott, Paul 1920-1978 . . . . DLB-14

Scott, Sarah 1723-1795 . . . . DLB-39

Scott, Tom 1918- DLB-27

Scott, Sir Walter
1771-1832. . . . DLB-93, 107, 116, 144, 159

Scott, William Bell 1811-1890 . . . . . DLB-32

Scott, Walter, Publishing
Company Limited. DLB-112

Scott, William R.
[publishing house]. DLB-46

Scott-Heron, Gil 1949- DLB-41

Scribe, Eugene 1791-1861 . . . . DLB-192

Scribner, Arthur Hawley
1859-1932. . . . . DS-13, 16

Scribner, Charles 1854-1930 . . . . . . DS-13, 16

Scribner, Charles, Jr. 1921-1995 . . . . . Y-95

Charles Scribner's
Sons DLB-49; DS-13, 16, 17

Scripps, E. W. 1854-1926. . . . . DLB-25

Scudder, Horace Elisha
1838-1902 . . . . DLB-42, 71

Scudder, Vida Dutton 1861-1954 . . . . DLB-71

Scupham, Peter 1933- DLB-40

Seabrook, William 1886-1945 . . . . . . DLB-4

Seabury, Samuel 1729-1796. . . . . . . DLB-31

Seacole, Mary Jane Grant
1805-1881 . . . . DLB-166

The Seafarer circa 970 . . . . DLB-146

Sealsfield, Charles (Carl Postl)
1793-1864. . . . . DLB-133, 186

Sears, Edward I. 1819?-1876 . . . . . . DLB-79

Sears Publishing Company DLB-46

Seaton, George 1911-1979 . . . . DLB-44

Cumulative Index

Seaton, William Winston
  1785-1866 . . . . DLB-43

Secker, Martin, and Warburg
  Limited DLB-112

Secker, Martin [publishing house] DLB-112

Second-Generation Minor Poets of the
  Seventeenth Century DLB-126

Sedgwick, Arthur George
  1844-1915 . . . . DLB-64

Sedgwick, Catharine Maria
  1789-1867 . . . . DLB-1, 74, 183

Sedgwick, Ellery 1872-1930 . . . . DLB-91

Sedley, Sir Charles 1639-1701 . . . . . DLB-131

Seeger, Alan 1888-1916 . . . . DLB-45

Seers, Eugene (see Dantin, Louis)

Segal, Erich 1937- Y-86

Šegedin, Petar 1909- DLB-181

Seghers, Anna 1900-1983 . . . . DLB-69

Seid, Ruth (see Sinclair, Jo)

Seidel, Frederick Lewis 1936- Y-84

Seidel, Ina 1885-1974 . . . . DLB-56

Seifert, Jaroslav 1901- Y-84

Seigenthaler, John 1927- DLB-127

Seizin Press DLB-112

Séjour, Victor 1817-1874 . . . . DLB-50

Séjour Marcou et Ferrand, Juan Victor (see Séjour,
  Victor)

Sekowski, Jósef-Julian, Baron Brambeus (see
  Senkovsky, Osip Ivanovich)

Selby, Hubert, Jr. 1928- DLB-2

Selden, George 1929-1989 . . . . DLB-52

Selected English-Language Little Magazines
  and Newspapers [France,
  1920-1939] DLB-4

Selected Humorous Magazines
  (1820-1950) DLB-11

Selected Science-Fiction Magazines and
  Anthologies DLB-8

Selenić, Slobodan 1933-1995 . . . . . . DLB-181

Self, Edwin F. 1920- DLB-137

Seligman, Edwin R. A. 1861-1939 . . . . DLB-47

Selimović, Meša 1910-1982 . . . . . . DLB-181

Selous, Frederick Courteney
  1851-1917 . . . . DLB-174

Seltzer, Chester E. (see Muro, Amado)

Seltzer, Thomas
  [publishing house] DLB-46

Selvon, Sam 1923-1994 . . . . DLB-125

Semmes, Raphael 1809-1877 . . . . . . DLB-189

Senancour, Etienne de 1770-1846 . . . . DLB-119

Sendak, Maurice 1928- DLB-61

Senécal, Eva 1905- DLB-92

Sengstacke, John 1912- DLB-127

Senior, Olive 1941- DLB-157

Senkovsky, Osip Ivanovich (Józef-Julian Sekowski,
  Baron Brambeus) 1800-1858 . . . . DLB-198

Šenoa, August 1838-1881 . . . . DLB-147

"Sensation Novels" (1863), by
  H. L. Manse DLB-21

Sepamla, Sipho 1932- DLB-157

Seredy, Kate 1899-1975 . . . . DLB-22

Sereni, Vittorio 1913-1983 . . . . DLB-128

Seres, William
  [publishing house] DLB-170

Serling, Rod 1924-1975 . . . . DLB-26

Serote, Mongane Wally 1944- DLB-125

Serraillier, Ian 1912-1994 . . . . DLB-161

Serrano, Nina 1934- DLB-122

Service, Robert 1874-1958 . . . . DLB-92

Sessler, Charles 1854-1935 . . . . DLB-187

Seth, Vikram 1952- DLB-120

Seton, Ernest Thompson
  1860-1942 . . . . DLB-92; DS-13

Setouchi, Harumi 1922- DLB-182

Settle, Mary Lee 1918- DLB-6

Seume, Johann Gottfried
  1763-1810 . . . . DLB-94

Seuse, Heinrich 1295?-1366 . . . . . . DLB-179

Seuss, Dr. (see Geisel, Theodor Seuss)

The Seventy-fifth Anniversary of the Armistice:
  The Wilfred Owen Centenary and the Great
  War Exhibit at the University of
  Virginia Y-93

Sewall, Joseph 1688-1769 . . . . DLB-24

Sewall, Richard B. 1908- DLB-111

Sewell, Anna 1820-1878 . . . . DLB-163

Sewell, Samuel 1652-1730 . . . . DLB-24

Sex, Class, Politics, and Religion [in the
  British Novel, 1930-1959] DLB-15

Sexton, Anne 1928-1974 . . . . . . DLB-5, 169

Seymour-Smith, Martin 1928- DLB-155

Sgorlon, Carlo 1930- DLB-196

Shaara, Michael 1929-1988 . . . . Y-83

Shadwell, Thomas 1641?-1692 . . . . . DLB-80

Shaffer, Anthony 1926- DLB-13

Shaffer, Peter 1926- DLB-13

Shaftesbury, Anthony Ashley Cooper,
  Third Earl of 1671-1713 . . . . . . DLB-101

Shairp, Mordaunt 1887-1939 . . . . . . DLB-10

Shakespeare, William
  1564-1616 . . . . DLB-62, 172

The Shakespeare Globe Trust Y-93

Shakespeare Head Press DLB-112

Shakhovskoi, Aleksandr Aleksandrovich
  1777-1846 . . . . DLB-150

Shange, Ntozake 1948- DLB-38

Shapiro, Karl 1913- DLB-48

Sharon Publications DLB-46

Sharp, Margery 1905-1991 . . . . . . DLB-161

Sharp, William 1855-1905 . . . . DLB-156

Sharpe, Tom 1928- DLB-14

Shaw, Albert 1857-1947 . . . . DLB-91

Shaw, George Bernard
  1856-1950 . . . . DLB-10, 57, 190

Shaw, Henry Wheeler 1818-1885 . . . . DLB-11

Shaw, Joseph T. 1874-1952 . . . . . . DLB-137

Shaw, Irwin 1913-1984 . . . . DLB-6, 102; Y-84

Shaw, Robert 1927-1978 . . . . DLB-13, 14

Shaw, Robert B. 1947- DLB-120

Shawn, William 1907-1992 . . . . . . DLB-137

Shay, Frank [publishing house] DLB-46

Shea, John Gilmary 1824-1892 . . . . . DLB-30

Sheaffer, Louis 1912-1993 . . . . DLB-103

Shearing, Joseph 1886-1952 . . . . . . DLB-70

Shebbeare, John 1709-1788 . . . . . . DLB-39

Sheckley, Robert 1928- DLB-8

Shedd, William G. T. 1820-1894 . . . . DLB-64

Sheed, Wilfred 1930- DLB-6

Sheed and Ward [U.S.] DLB-46

Sheed and Ward Limited [U.K.] DLB-112

Sheldon, Alice B. (see Tiptree, James, Jr.)

Sheldon, Edward 1886-1946 . . . . . . DLB-7

Sheldon and Company DLB-49

Shelley, Mary Wollstonecraft
  1797-1851 . . . . . . DLB-110, 116, 159, 178

Shelley, Percy Bysshe
  1792-1822 . . . . DLB-96, 110, 158

Shelnutt, Eve 1941- DLB-130

Shenstone, William 1714-1763 . . . . . DLB-95

Shepard, Ernest Howard
  1879-1976 . . . . DLB-160

Shepard, Sam 1943- DLB-7

Shepard, Thomas I,
  1604 or 1605-1649 . . . . DLB-24

Shepard, Thomas II, 1635-1677 . . . . DLB-24

Shepard, Clark and Brown DLB-49

Shepherd, Luke
  flourished 1547-1554 . . . . DLB-136

Sherburne, Edward 1616-1702 . . . . . DLB-131

Sheridan, Frances 1724-1766 . . . . DLB-39, 84

Sheridan, Richard Brinsley
  1751-1816 . . . . DLB-89

Sherman, Francis 1871-1926 . . . . . . DLB-92

Sherriff, R. C. 1896-1975 . . . . . . DLB-10, 191

Sherry, Norman 1935- DLB-155

Sherwood, Mary Martha
  1775-1851 . . . . DLB-163

Sherwood, Robert 1896-1955 . . . . DLB-7, 26

Shiel, M. P. 1865-1947 . . . . DLB-153

Shiels, George 1886-1949 . . . . DLB-10

Shiga, Naoya 1883-1971 . . . . DLB-180

Shiina, Rinzō 1911-1973 . . . . DLB-182

Shillaber, B.[enjamin] P.[enhallow]
1814-1890 . . . . DLB-1, 11

Shimao, Toshio 1917-1986 . . . . . . DLB-182

Shimazaki, Tōson 1872-1943 . . . . . DLB-180

Shine, Ted 1931- DLB-38

Ship, Reuben 1915-1975 . . . . DLB-88

Shirer, William L. 1904-1993 . . . . . DLB-4

Shirinsky-Shikhmatov, Sergii Aleksandrovich
1783-1837 . . . . DLB-150

Shirley, James 1596-1666 . . . . DLB-58

Shishkov, Aleksandr Semenovich
1753-1841 . . . . DLB-150

Shockley, Ann Allen 1927- DLB-33

Shōno, Junzō 1921- DLB-182

Short, Peter
[publishing house] DLB-170

Shorthouse, Joseph Henry
1834-1903 . . . . DLB-18

Showalter, Elaine 1941- DLB-67

Shulevitz, Uri 1935- DLB-61

Shulman, Max 1919-1988 . . . . DLB-11

Shute, Henry A. 1856-1943 . . . . . . DLB-9

Shuttle, Penelope 1947- DLB-14, 40

Sibbes, Richard 1577-1635 . . . . . . DLB-151

Sidgwick, Ethel 1877-1970 . . . . . . DLB-197

Sidgwick and Jackson Limited DLB-112

Sidney, Margaret (see Lothrop, Harriet M.)

Sidney, Mary 1561-1621 . . . . DLB-167

Sidney, Sir Philip 1554-1586 . . . . . DLB-167

Sidney's Press DLB-49

Siegfried Loraine Sassoon: A Centenary Essay
Tributes from Vivien F. Clarke and
Michael Thorpe Y-86

Sierra, Rubén 1946- DLB-122

Sierra Club Books DLB-49

Siger of Brabant
circa 1240-circa 1284 . . . . DLB-115

Sigourney, Lydia Howard (Huntley)
1791-1865 . . . . DLB-1, 42, 73, 183

Silkin, Jon 1930- DLB-27

Silko, Leslie Marmon
1948- DLB-143, 175

Silliman, Benjamin 1779-1864 . . . . . DLB-183

Silliman, Ron 1946- DLB-169

Silliphant, Stirling 1918- DLB-26

Sillitoe, Alan 1928- DLB-14, 139

Silman, Roberta 1934- DLB-28

Silva, Beverly 1930- DLB-122

Silverberg, Robert 1935- DLB-8

Silverman, Kenneth 1936- DLB-111

Simak, Clifford D. 1904-1988 . . . . . DLB-8

Simcoe, Elizabeth 1762-1850 . . . . . DLB-99

Simcox, Edith Jemima 1844-1901 . . . . DLB-190

Simcox, George Augustus
1841-1905 . . . . DLB-35

Sime, Jessie Georgina 1868-1958 . . . DLB-92

Simenon, Georges
1903-1989 . . . . DLB-72; Y-89

Simic, Charles 1938- DLB-105

Simmel, Johannes Mario 1924- DLB-69

Simmes, Valentine
[publishing house] DLB-170

Simmons, Ernest J. 1903-1972 . . . . DLB-103

Simmons, Herbert Alfred 1930- DLB-33

Simmons, James 1933- DLB-40

Simms, William Gilmore
1806-1870 . . . . DLB-3, 30, 59, 73

Simms and M'Intyre DLB-106

Simon, Claude 1913- DLB-83; Y-85

Simon, Neil 1927- DLB-7

Simon and Schuster DLB-46

Simons, Katherine Drayton Mayrant
1890-1969 . . . . Y-83

Simović, Ljubomir 1935- DLB-181

Simpkin and Marshall
[publishing house] DLB-154

Simpson, Helen 1897-1940 . . . . . . DLB-77

Simpson, Louis 1923- DLB-5

Simpson, N. F. 1919- DLB-13

Sims, George 1923- DLB-87

Sims, George Robert
1847-1922 . . . . DLB-35, 70, 135

Sinán, Rogelio 1904- DLB-145

Sinclair, Andrew 1935- DLB-14

Sinclair, Bertrand William
1881-1972 . . . . DLB-92

Sinclair, Catherine
1800-1864 . . . . DLB-163

Sinclair, Jo 1913- DLB-28

Sinclair Lewis Centennial
Conference Y-85

Sinclair, Lister 1921- DLB-88

Sinclair, May 1863-1946 . . . . . . DLB-36, 135

Sinclair, Upton 1878-1968 . . . . . . DLB-9

Sinclair, Upton [publishing house] . . . DLB-46

Singer, Isaac Bashevis
1904-1991 . . . . DLB-6, 28, 52; Y-91

Singer, Mark 1950- DLB-185

Singmaster, Elsie 1879-1958 . . . . . DLB-9

Sinisgalli, Leonardo 1908-1981 . . . . DLB-114

Siodmak, Curt 1902- DLB-44

Siringo, Charles A. 1855-1928 . . . . DLB-186

Sissman, L. E. 1928-1976 . . . . . . DLB-5

Sisson, C. H. 1914- DLB-27

Sitwell, Edith 1887-1964 . . . . . . DLB-20

Sitwell, Osbert 1892-1969 . . . . DLB-100, 195

Skármeta, Antonio 1940- DLB-145

Skeat, Walter W. 1835-1912 . . . . . DLB-184

Skeffington, William
[publishing house] DLB-106

Skelton, John 1463-1529 . . . . . . DLB-136

Skelton, Robin 1925- DLB-27, 53

Skinner, Constance Lindsay
1877-1939 . . . . DLB-92

Skinner, John Stuart 1788-1851 . . . . DLB-73

Skipsey, Joseph 1832-1903 . . . . . . DLB-35

Slade, Bernard 1930- DLB-53

Slamnig, Ivan 1930- DLB-181

Slater, Patrick 1880-1951 . . . . . . DLB-68

Slaveykov, Pencho 1866-1912 . . . . . DLB-147

Slaviček, Milivoj 1929- DLB-181

Slavitt, David 1935- DLB-5, 6

Sleigh, Burrows Willcocks Arthur
1821-1869 . . . . DLB-99

A Slender Thread of Hope: The Kennedy
Center Black Theatre Project DLB-38

Slesinger, Tess 1905-1945 . . . . . . DLB-102

Slick, Sam (see Haliburton, Thomas Chandler)

Sloan, John 1871-1951 . . . . DLB-188

Sloane, William, Associates DLB-46

Small, Maynard and Company DLB-49

Small Presses in Great Britain and Ireland,
1960-1985 . . . . DLB-40

Small Presses I: Jargon Society Y-84

Small Presses II: The Spirit That Moves
Us Press Y-85

Small Presses III: Pushcart Press Y-87

Smart, Christopher 1722-1771 . . . . . DLB-109

Smart, David A. 1892-1957 . . . . . . DLB-137

Smart, Elizabeth 1913-1986 . . . . . . DLB-88

Smellie, William
[publishing house] DLB-154

Smiles, Samuel 1812-1904 . . . . . . DLB-55

Smith, A. J. M. 1902-1980 . . . . . . DLB-88

Smith, Adam 1723-1790 . . . . DLB-104

Smith, Adam (George Jerome Waldo Goodman)
1930- DLB-185

Smith, Alexander 1829-1867 . . . . DLB-32, 55

Smith, Betty 1896-1972 . . . . Y-82

Smith, Carol Sturm 1938- Y-81

Smith, Charles Henry 1826-1903 . . . . DLB-11

Smith, Charlotte 1749-1806 . . . . DLB-39, 109

Smith, Chet 1899-1973 . . . . DLB-171

Smith, Cordwainer 1913-1966 . . . . . DLB-8

Smith, Dave 1942- DLB-5

Smith, Dodie 1896- DLB-10

Smith, Doris Buchanan 1934- DLB-52

Smith, E. E. 1890-1965 . . . . DLB-8

Smith, Elihu Hubbard 1771-1798 . . . DLB-37

Smith, Elizabeth Oakes (Prince)
1806-1893. . . . . DLB-1

Smith, F. Hopkinson 1838-1915 . . . . . DS-13

Smith, George D. 1870-1920 . . . . . DLB-140

Smith, George O. 1911-1981 . . . . DLB-8

Smith, Goldwin 1823-1910 . . . . DLB-99

Smith, H. Allen 1907-1976 . . . . . DLB-11, 29

Smith, Harry B. 1860-1936 . . . . . . DLB-187

Smith, Hazel Brannon 1914- DLB-127

Smith, Henry
circa 1560-circa 1591 . . . . DLB-136

Smith, Horatio (Horace)
1779-1849 . . . . DLB-116

Smith, Horatio (Horace) 1779-1849 and
James Smith 1775-1839. . . . . . . DLB-96

Smith, Iain Crichton
1928- DLB-40, 139

Smith, J. Allen 1860-1924. . . . . . . DLB-47

Smith, Jessie Willcox 1863-1935 . . . . DLB-188

Smith, John 1580-1631 . . . . . . DLB-24, 30

Smith, Josiah 1704-1781. . . . . DLB-24

Smith, Ken 1938- DLB-40

Smith, Lee 1944- DLB-143; Y-83

Smith, Logan Pearsall 1865-1946. . . . DLB-98

Smith, Mark 1935- Y-82

Smith, Michael 1698-circa 1771 . . . . DLB-31

Smith, Red 1905-1982. . . . . . . DLB-29, 171

Smith, Roswell 1829-1892 . . . . DLB-79

Smith, Samuel Harrison
1772-1845 . . . . DLB-43

Smith, Samuel Stanhope
1751-1819 . . . . DLB-37

Smith, Sarah (see Stretton, Hesba)

Smith, Seba 1792-1868. . . . . . . DLB-1, 11

Smith, Sir Thomas 1513-1577. . . . . DLB-132

Smith, Stevie 1902-1971. . . . . DLB-20

Smith, Sydney 1771-1845 . . . . DLB-107

Smith, Sydney Goodsir 1915-1975 . . . . DLB-27

Smith, Wendell 1914-1972. . . . . . . DLB-171

Smith, William
flourished 1595-1597 . . . . DLB-136

Smith, William 1727-1803 . . . . DLB-31

Smith, William 1728-1793 . . . . DLB-30

Smith, William Gardner
1927-1974 . . . . DLB-76

Smith, William Henry
1808-1872 . . . . DLB-159

Smith, William Jay 1918- DLB-5

Smith, Elder and Company. DLB-154

Smith, Harrison, and Robert Haas
[publishing house]. DLB-46

Smith, J. Stilman, and Company. . . . DLB-49

Smith, W. B., and Company DLB-49

Smith, W. H., and Son. DLB-106

Smithers, Leonard
[publishing house] DLB-112

Smollett, Tobias 1721-1771 . . . . . DLB-39, 104

Smythe, Francis Sydney
1900-1949 . . . . DLB-195

Snellings, Rolland (see Touré, Askia
Muhammad)

Snodgrass, W. D. 1926- DLB-5

Snow, C. P. 1905-1980 . . . DLB-15, 77; DS-17

Snyder, Gary 1930- DLB-5, 16, 165

Sobiloff, Hy 1912-1970 . . . . DLB-48

The Society for Textual Scholarship and
TEXT. Y-87

The Society for the History of Authorship, Reading and Publishing. Y-92

Soffici, Ardengo 1879-1964 . . . . . . DLB-114

Sofola, 'Zulu 1938- DLB-157

Solano, Solita 1888-1975 . . . . DLB-4

Soldati, Mario 1906- DLB-177

Šoljan, Antun 1932-1993 . . . . DLB-181

Sollers, Philippe 1936- DLB-83

Sollogub, Vladimir Aleksandrovich
1813-1882 . . . . DLB-198

Solmi, Sergio 1899-1981 . . . . DLB-114

Solomon, Carl 1928- DLB-16

Solway, David 1941- DLB-53

Solzhenitsyn and America Y-85

Somerville, Edith Œnone
1858-1949 . . . . DLB-135

Somov, Orest Mikhailovich
1793-1833 . . . . DLB-198

Song, Cathy 1955- DLB-169

Sono, Ayako 1931- DLB-182

Sontag, Susan 1933- DLB-2, 67

Sophocles 497/496 B.C.-406/405 B.C.
. . . . DLB-176

Šopov, Aco 1923-1982 . . . . DLB-181

Sorge, Reinhard Johannes
1892-1916 . . . . DLB-118

Sorrentino, Gilbert
1929- DLB-5, 173; Y-80

Sotheby, William 1757-1833 . . . . . . DLB-93

Soto, Gary 1952- DLB-82

Sources for the Study of Tudor and Stuart Drama
DLB-62

Souster, Raymond 1921- DLB-88

The South English Legendary
circa thirteenth-fifteenth
centuries DLB-146

Southerland, Ellease 1943- DLB-33

Southern Illinois University Press Y-95

Southern, Terry 1924- DLB-2

Southern Writers Between the
Wars DLB-9

Southerne, Thomas 1659-1746 . . . . . DLB-80

Southey, Caroline Anne Bowles
1786-1854 . . . . DLB-116

Southey, Robert
1774-1843 . . . . DLB-93, 107, 142

Southwell, Robert 1561?-1595. . . . . DLB-167

Sowande, Bode 1948- DLB-157

Sowle, Tace
[publishing house] DLB-170

Soyfer, Jura 1912-1939. . . . . DLB-124

Soyinka, Wole 1934- . . . DLB-125; Y-86, Y-87

Spacks, Barry 1931- DLB-105

Spalding, Frances 1950- DLB-155

Spark, Muriel 1918- DLB-15, 139

Sparke, Michael
[publishing house] DLB-170

Sparks, Jared 1789-1866 . . . . DLB-1, 30

Sparshott, Francis 1926- DLB-60

Späth, Gerold 1939- DLB-75

Spatola, Adriano 1941-1988 . . . . . . DLB-128

Spaziani, Maria Luisa 1924- DLB-128

The Spectator 1828- DLB-110

Spedding, James 1808-1881 . . . . . . DLB-144

Spee von Langenfeld, Friedrich
1591-1635 . . . . DLB-164

Speght, Rachel 1597-after 1630 . . . . DLB-126

Speke, John Hanning 1827-1864 . . . . DLB-166

Spellman, A. B. 1935- DLB-41

Spence, Thomas 1750-1814 . . . . . . DLB-158

Spencer, Anne 1882-1975. . . . . . DLB-51, 54

Spencer, Elizabeth 1921- DLB-6

Spencer, George John, Second Earl Spencer
1758-1834 . . . . DLB-184

Spencer, Herbert 1820-1903 . . . . . . DLB-57

Spencer, Scott 1945- Y-86

Spender, J. A. 1862-1942 . . . . DLB-98

Spender, Stephen 1909- DLB-20

Spener, Philipp Jakob 1635-1705 . . . . DLB-164

Spenser, Edmund circa 1552-1599 . . . DLB-167

Sperr, Martin 1944- DLB-124

Spicer, Jack 1925-1965 . . . . . DLB-5, 16, 193

Spielberg, Peter 1929- Y-81

Spielhagen, Friedrich 1829-1911. . . . DLB-129

"Spielmannsepen"
(circa 1152-circa 1500) DLB-148

Spier, Peter 1927- DLB-61

Spinrad, Norman 1940- DLB-8

Spires, Elizabeth 1952- DLB-120

Spitteler, Carl 1845-1924. . . . . . . DLB-129

Spivak, Lawrence E. 1900- DLB-137

Spofford, Harriet Prescott
1835-1921 . . . . DLB-74

Spring, Howard 1889-1965 . . . . . . DLB-191

Squier, E. G. 1821-1888 . . . . DLB-189

Squibob (see Derby, George Horatio)

Stacpoole, H. de Vere
1863-1951 . . . . DLB-153

Staël, Germaine de 1766-1817. . . DLB-119, 192

Staël-Holstein, Anne-Louise Germaine de
(see Staël, Germaine de)

Stafford, Jean 1915-1979 . . . . . . DLB-2, 173

Stafford, William 1914- DLB-5

Stage Censorship: "The Rejected Statement"
(1911), by Bernard Shaw
[excerpts] DLB-10

Stallings, Laurence 1894-1968 . . . . . DLB-7, 44

Stallworthy, Jon 1935- DLB-40

Stampp, Kenneth M. 1912- DLB-17

Stanev, Emiliyan 1907-1979 . . . . . . DLB-181

Stanford, Ann 1916- DLB-5

Stankevich, Nikolai Vladimirovich
1813-1840 . . . . DLB-198

Stanković, Borisav ("Bora")
1876-1927 . . . . DLB-147

Stanley, Henry M. 1841-1904 . DLB-189; DS-13

Stanley, Thomas 1625-1678 . . . . . . DLB-131

Stannard, Martin 1947- DLB-155

Stansby, William
[publishing house] DLB-170

Stanton, Elizabeth Cady 1815-1902 . . . DLB-79

Stanton, Frank L. 1857-1927 . . . . . . DLB-25

Stanton, Maura 1946- DLB-120

Stapledon, Olaf 1886-1950 . . . . DLB-15

Star Spangled Banner Office DLB-49

Stark, Freya 1893-1993 . . . . DLB-195

Starkey, Thomas circa 1499-1538. . . . DLB-132

Starkie, Walter 1894-1976 . . . . DLB-195

Starkweather, David 1935- DLB-7

Starrett, Vincent 1886-1974 . . . . . . DLB-187

Statements on the Art of Poetry DLB-54

The State of Publishing Y-97

Stationers' Company of
London, The DLB-170

Stead, Robert J. C. 1880-1959 . . . . . DLB-92

Steadman, Mark 1930- DLB-6

The Stealthy School of Criticism (1871), by
Dante Gabriel Rossetti DLB-35

Stearns, Harold E. 1891-1943 . . . . . . DLB-4

Stedman, Edmund Clarence
1833-1908 . . . . DLB-64

Steegmuller, Francis 1906-1994 . . . . DLB-111

Steel, Flora Annie 1847-1929 . . . DLB-153, 156

Steele, Max 1922- Y-80

Steele, Richard 1672-1729 . . . . . DLB-84, 101

Steele, Timothy 1948- DLB-120

Steele, Wilbur Daniel 1886-1970 . . . . DLB-86

Steere, Richard circa 1643-1721 . . . . . DLB-24

Stefanovski, Goran 1952- DLB-181

Stegner, Wallace 1909-1993 . . . . DLB-9; Y-93

Stehr, Hermann 1864-1940 . . . . . . DLB-66

Steig, William 1907- DLB-61

Stein, Gertrude
1874-1946 . . . . . . DLB-4, 54, 86; DS-15

Stein, Leo 1872-1947 . . . . DLB-4

Stein and Day Publishers DLB-46

Steinbeck, John 1902-1968 . . . . DLB-7, 9; DS-2

Steiner, George 1929- DLB-67

Steinhoewel, Heinrich
1411/1412-1479 . . . . DLB-179

Steloff, Ida Frances 1887-1989 . . . . DLB-187

Stendhal 1783-1842 . . . . DLB-119

Stephen Crane: A Revaluation Virginia
Tech Conference, 1989 . . . . Y-89

Stephen, Leslie 1832-1904 . . . DLB-57, 144, 190

Stephen Vincent Benét Centenary Y-97

Stephens, Alexander H. 1812-1883. . . . DLB-47

Stephens, Alice Barber 1858-1932. . . . DLB-188

Stephens, Ann 1810-1886 . . . . . . DLB-3, 73

Stephens, Charles Asbury
1844?-1931 . . . . DLB-42

Stephens, James
1882?-1950 . . . . DLB-19, 153, 162

Stephens, John Lloyd 1805-1852 . . . . DLB-183

Sterling, George 1869-1926 . . . . DLB-54

Sterling, James 1701-1763 . . . . DLB-24

Sterling, John 1806-1844 . . . . DLB-116

Stern, Gerald 1925- DLB-105

Stern, Gladys B. 1890-1973 . . . . . . DLB-197

Stern, Madeleine B. 1912- DLB-111, 140

Stern, Richard 1928- Y-87

Stern, Stewart 1922- DLB-26

Sterne, Laurence 1713-1768. . . . . . . DLB-39

Sternheim, Carl 1878-1942 . . . . . DLB-56, 118

Sternhold, Thomas ?-1549 and
John Hopkins ?-1570 . . . . DLB-132

Stevens, Henry 1819-1886 . . . . DLB-140

Stevens, Wallace 1879-1955 . . . . DLB-54

Stevenson, Anne 1933- DLB-40

Stevenson, D. E. 1892-1973 . . . . . . DLB-191

Stevenson, Lionel 1902-1973 . . . . . . DLB-155

Stevenson, Robert Louis 1850-1894
. . . . . DLB-18, 57, 141, 156, 174; DS-13

Stewart, Donald Ogden
1894-1980 . . . . DLB-4, 11, 26

Stewart, Dugald 1753-1828 . . . . DLB-31

Stewart, George, Jr. 1848-1906 . . . . . DLB-99

Stewart, George R. 1895-1980 . . . . . . DLB-8

Stewart and Kidd Company DLB-46

Stewart, Randall 1896-1964 . . . . . . DLB-103

Stickney, Trumbull 1874-1904 . . . . . . DLB-54

Stieler, Caspar 1632-1707 . . . . DLB-164

Stifter, Adalbert 1805-1868 . . . . . . DLB-133

Stiles, Ezra 1727-1795. . . . . DLB-31

Still, James 1906- DLB-9

Stirner, Max 1806-1856 . . . . DLB-129

Stith, William 1707-1755 . . . . DLB-31

Stock, Elliot [publishing house] DLB-106

Stockton, Frank R.
1834-1902. . . . . DLB-42, 74; DS-13

Stoddard, Ashbel
[publishing house] DLB-49

Stoddard, Charles Warren
1843-1909 . . . . DLB-186

Stoddard, Richard Henry
1825-1903 . . . . DLB-3, 64; DS-13

Stoddard, Solomon 1643-1729 . . . . . DLB-24

Stoker, Bram 1847-1912 . . . . DLB-36, 70, 178

Stokes, Frederick A., Company DLB-49

Stokes, Thomas L. 1898-1958 . . . . . . DLB-29

Stokesbury, Leon 1945- DLB-120

Stolberg, Christian Graf zu
1748-1821 . . . . DLB-94

Stolberg, Friedrich Leopold Graf zu
1750-1819 . . . . DLB-94

Stone, Herbert S., and Company DLB-49

Stone, Lucy 1818-1893 . . . . DLB-79

Stone, Melville 1848-1929. . . . . DLB-25

Stone, Robert 1937- DLB-152

Stone, Ruth 1915- DLB-105

Stone, Samuel 1602-1663 . . . . DLB-24

Stone and Kimball DLB-49

Stoppard, Tom 1937- DLB-13; Y-85

Storey, Anthony 1928- DLB-14

Storey, David 1933- DLB-13, 14

Storm, Theodor 1817-1888 . . . . . . DLB-129

Story, Thomas circa 1670-1742 . . . . . DLB-31

Story, William Wetmore 1819-1895. . . . DLB-1

Storytelling: A Contemporary
Renaissance Y-84

Stoughton, William 1631-1701 . . . . . DLB-24

Stow, John 1525-1605 . . . . DLB-132

Stowe, Harriet Beecher
1811-1896 . . . . . . DLB-1, 12, 42, 74, 189

Stowe, Leland 1899- DLB-29

Stoyanov, Dimitŭr Ivanov (see Elin Pelin)

Strabo 64 or 63 B.C.-circa A.D. 25
. . . . DLB-176

Strachey, Lytton
1880-1932 . . . . DLB-149; DS-10

Strachey, Lytton, Preface to *Eminent
Victorians* DLB-149

Strahan and Company DLB-106

Strahan, William
[publishing house] DLB-154

Strand, Mark 1934- DLB-5

The Strasbourg Oaths 842 . . . . . . DLB-148

Stratemeyer, Edward 1862-1930 . . . . DLB-42

Strati, Saverio 1924- DLB-177

Stratton and Barnard DLB-49

Stratton-Porter, Gene 1863-1924 . . . . . DS-14

Straub, Peter 1943- Y-84

Strauß, Botho 1944- DLB-124

Strauß, David Friedrich
1808-1874 . . . . DLB-133

The Strawberry Hill Press DLB-154

Streatfeild, Noel 1895-1986 . . . . . . DLB-160

Street, Cecil John Charles (see Rhode, John)

Street, G. S. 1867-1936 . . . . DLB-135

Street and Smith DLB-49

Streeter, Edward 1891-1976. . . . . . DLB-11

Streeter, Thomas Winthrop
1883-1965 . . . . DLB-140

Stretton, Hesba 1832-1911. . . . . DLB-163, 190

Stribling, T. S. 1881-1965 . . . . DLB-9

Der Stricker circa 1190-circa 1250 . . . DLB-138

Strickland, Samuel 1804-1867. . . . . . DLB-99

Stringer and Townsend. DLB-49

Stringer, Arthur 1874-1950 . . . . . . DLB-92

Strittmatter, Erwin 1912- DLB-69

Strniša, Gregor 1930-1987 . . . . DLB-181

Strode, William 1630-1645 . . . . . . DLB-126

Strong, L. A. G. 1896-1958 . . . . . . DLB-191

Strother, David Hunter 1816-1888 . . . . DLB-3

Strouse, Jean 1945- DLB-111

Stuart, Dabney 1937- DLB-105

Stuart, Jesse
1906-1984 . . . . . . DLB-9, 48, 102; Y-84

Stuart, Lyle [publishing house] DLB-46

Stubbs, Harry Clement (see Clement, Hal)

Stubenberg, Johann Wilhelm von
1619-1663 . . . . DLB-164

Studio. DLB-112

The Study of Poetry (1880), by
Matthew Arnold DLB-35

Sturgeon, Theodore
1918-1985 . . . . DLB-8; Y-85

Sturges, Preston 1898-1959 . . . . . . DLB-26

"Style" (1840; revised, 1859), by
Thomas de Quincey [excerpt] DLB-57

"Style" (1888), by Walter Pater DLB-57

Style (1897), by Walter Raleigh
[excerpt] DLB-57

"Style" (1877), by T. H. Wright
[excerpt] DLB-57

"Le Style c'est l'homme" (1892), by
W. H. Mallock. DLB-57

Styron, William 1925- DLB-2, 143; Y-80

Suárez, Mario 1925- DLB-82

Such, Peter 1939- DLB-60

Suckling, Sir John 1609-1641? . . . DLB-58, 126

Suckow, Ruth 1892-1960. . . . . . DLB-9, 102

Sudermann, Hermann 1857-1928 . . . . DLB-118

Sue, Eugène 1804-1857 . . . . DLB-119

Sue, Marie-Joseph (see Sue, Eugène)

Suggs, Simon (see Hooper, Johnson Jones)

Sukenick, Ronald 1932- DLB-173; Y-81

Suknaski, Andrew 1942- DLB-53

Sullivan, Alan 1868-1947 . . . . DLB-92

Sullivan, C. Gardner 1886-1965 . . . . DLB-26

Sullivan, Frank 1892-1976 . . . . DLB-11

Sulte, Benjamin 1841-1923 . . . . . . DLB-99

Sulzberger, Arthur Hays
1891-1968 . . . . DLB-127

Sulzberger, Arthur Ochs 1926- DLB-127

Sulzer, Johann Georg 1720-1779 . . . . DLB-97

Sumarokov, Aleksandr Petrovich
1717-1777 . . . . DLB-150

Summers, Hollis 1916- DLB-6

Sumner, Henry A.
[publishing house]. DLB-49

Surtees, Robert Smith 1803-1864. . . . DLB-21

Surveys: Japanese Literature,
1987-1995 . . . . DLB-182

A Survey of Poetry Anthologies,
1879-1960 . . . . DLB-54

Surveys of the Year's Biographies

A Transit of Poets and Others: American
Biography in 1982 . . . . Y-82

The Year in Literary Biography . . . Y-83–Y-96

Survey of the Year's Book Publishing

The Year in Book Publishing Y-86

Survey of the Year's Children's Books

The Year in Children's Books
. . . . Y-92–Y-96

Surveys of the Year's Drama

The Year in Drama
. . . . Y-82–Y-85, Y-87–Y-96

The Year in London Theatre Y-92

Surveys of the Year's Fiction

The Year's Work in Fiction:
A Survey Y-82

The Year in Fiction: A Biased View Y-83

The Year in
Fiction. Y-84–Y-86, Y-89, Y-94–Y-96

The Year in the
Novel Y-87, Y-88, Y-90–Y-93

The Year in Short Stories Y-87

The Year in the
Short Story Y-88, Y-90–Y-93

Survey of the Year's Literary Theory

The Year in Literary Theory Y-92–Y-93

Surveys of the Year's Poetry

The Year's Work in American
Poetry. Y-82

The Year in Poetry Y-83–Y-92, Y-94–Y-96

Sutherland, Efua Theodora
1924- DLB-117

Sutherland, John 1919-1956. . . . . . DLB-68

Sutro, Alfred 1863-1933. . . . . DLB-10

Swados, Harvey 1920-1972 . . . . DLB-2

Swain, Charles 1801-1874 . . . . DLB-32

Swallow Press. DLB-46

Swan Sonnenschein Limited. DLB-106

Swanberg, W. A. 1907- DLB-103

Swenson, May 1919-1989 . . . . DLB-5

Swerling, Jo 1897- DLB-44

Swift, Graham 1949- DLB-194

Swift, Jonathan 1667-1745 . . . DLB-39, 95, 101

Swinburne, A. C. 1837-1909 . . . . . DLB-35, 57

Swineshead, Richard floruit
circa 1350 . . . . DLB-115

Swinnerton, Frank 1884-1982. . . . . DLB-34

Swisshelm, Jane Grey 1815-1884. . . . DLB-43

Swope, Herbert Bayard 1882-1958. . . . DLB-25

Swords, T. and J., and Company. . . . DLB-49

Swords, Thomas 1763-1843 and
Swords, James ?-1844 . . . . DLB-73

Sykes, Ella C. ?-1939 . . . . DLB-174

Sylvester, Josuah
1562 or 1563 - 1618 . . . . DLB-121

Symonds, Emily Morse (see Paston, George)

Symonds, John Addington
1840-1893 . . . . DLB-57, 144

Symons, A. J. A. 1900-1941 . . . . . . DLB-149

Symons, Arthur 1865-1945 . . . DLB-19, 57, 149

Symons, Julian 1912-1994 . . DLB-87, 155; Y-92

Symons, Scott 1933- DLB-53

A Symposium on The Columbia History of
the Novel. Y-92

Synge, John Millington
1871-1909. . . . . DLB-10, 19

Synge Summer School: J. M. Synge and the Irish
Theater, Rathdrum, County Wiclow, Ireland
. . . . Y-93

Syrett, Netta 1865-1943 . . . . . . DLB-135, 197

Szymborska, Wisława 1923- Y-96

T

Taban lo Liyong 1939?- DLB-125

Tabucchi, Antonio 1943- DLB-196

Taché, Joseph-Charles 1820-1894. . . . DLB-99

Tachihara, Masaaki 1926-1980 . . . . . DLB-182

Tadijanović, Dragutin 1905- DLB-181

Tafolla, Carmen 1951- DLB-82

Taggard, Genevieve 1894-1948. . . . . DLB-45

Taggart, John 1942- DLB-193

Tagger, Theodor (see Bruckner, Ferdinand)

Tait, J. Selwin, and Sons DLB-49

Tait's Edinburgh Magazine
1832-1861 . . . . DLB-110

The Takarazaka Revue Company Y-91

Talander (see Bohse, August)

Talese, Gay 1932- DLB-185

Talev, Dimitŭr 1898-1966. . . . . . . DLB-181

Tallent, Elizabeth 1954- DLB-130

TallMountain, Mary 1918-1994. . . . . DLB-193

Talvj 1797-1870 . . . . DLB-59, 133

Tan, Amy 1952- DLB-173

Tanizaki, Jun'ichirō 1886-1965 . . . . . DLB-180

Tapahonso, Luci 1953- DLB-175

Taradash, Daniel 1913- DLB-44

Tarbell, Ida M. 1857-1944 . . . . DLB-47

Tardivel, Jules-Paul 1851-1905 . . . . . DLB-99

Targan, Barry 1932- DLB-130

Tarkington, Booth 1869-1946 . . . . DLB-9, 102

Tashlin, Frank 1913-1972. . . . . . . DLB-44

Tate, Allen 1899-1979 . . DLB-4, 45, 63; DS-17

Tate, James 1943- DLB-5, 169

Tate, Nahum circa 1652-1715 . . . . . DLB-80

Tatian circa 830 . . . . DLB-148

Taufer, Veno 1933- DLB-181

Tauler, Johannes circa 1300-1361. . . . DLB-179

Tavčar, Ivan 1851-1923 . . . . DLB-147

Taylor, Ann 1782-1866 . . . . DLB-163

Taylor, Bayard 1825-1878 . . . . . DLB-3, 189

Taylor, Bert Leston 1866-1921. . . . . DLB-25

Taylor, Charles H. 1846-1921 . . . . . DLB-25

Taylor, Edward circa 1642-1729 . . . . DLB-24

Taylor, Elizabeth 1912-1975. . . . . . DLB-139

Taylor, Henry 1942- DLB-5

Taylor, Sir Henry 1800-1886. . . . . . DLB-32

Taylor, Jane 1783-1824 . . . . DLB-163

Taylor, Jeremy circa 1613-1667 . . . . DLB-151

Taylor, John 1577 or 1578 - 1653. . . DLB-121

Taylor, Mildred D. ?- DLB-52

Taylor, Peter 1917-1994. . . . . . . Y-81, Y-94

Taylor, William, and Company DLB-49

Taylor-Made Shakespeare? Or Is
"Shall I Die?" the Long-Lost Text
of Bottom's Dream? Y-85

Teasdale, Sara 1884-1933 . . . . DLB-45

The Tea-Table (1725), by Eliza Haywood [excerpt]
DLB-39

Telles, Lygia Fagundes 1924- DLB-113

Temple, Sir William 1628-1699 . . . . DLB-101

Tenn, William 1919- DLB-8

Tennant, Emma 1937- DLB-14

Tenney, Tabitha Gilman 1762-1837 . . . DLB-37

Tennyson, Alfred 1809-1892 . . . . . . DLB-32

Tennyson, Frederick 1807-1898 . . . . DLB-32

Terhune, Albert Payson 1872-1942 . . . . DLB-9

Terhune, Mary Virginia
1830-1922 . . . . DS-13, DS-16

Terry, Megan 1932- DLB-7

Terson, Peter 1932- DLB-13

Tesich, Steve 1943- Y-83

Tessa, Delio 1886-1939 . . . . DLB-114

Testori, Giovanni 1923-1993 . . . . DLB-128, 177

Tey, Josephine 1896?-1952 . . . . . . DLB-77

Thacher, James 1754-1844 . . . . . . DLB-37

Thackeray, William Makepeace
1811-1863 . . . . . . DLB-21, 55, 159, 163

Thames and Hudson Limited. DLB-112

Thanet, Octave (see French, Alice)

Thatcher, John Boyd 1847-1909 . . . . DLB-187

The Theater in Shakespeare's Time. . . DLB-62

The Theatre Guild. DLB-7

Thegan and the Astronomer
flourished circa 850 . . . . DLB-148

Thelwall, John 1764-1834 . . . . . DLB-93, 158

Theocritus circa 300 B.C.-260 B.C.
. . . . DLB-176

Theodulf circa 760-circa 821 . . . . . DLB-148

Theophrastus circa 371 B.C.-287 B.C.
. . . . DLB-176

Theriault, Yves 1915-1983 . . . . DLB-88

Thério, Adrien 1925- DLB-53

Theroux, Paul 1941- DLB-2

They All Came to Paris DS-16

Thibaudeau, Colleen 1925- DLB-88

Thielen, Benedict 1903-1965. . . . . . DLB-102

Thiong'o Ngugi wa (see Ngugi wa Thiong'o)

Third-Generation Minor Poets of the
Seventeenth Century DLB-131

This Quarter 1925-1927, 1929-1932 . . . . . DS-15

Thoma, Ludwig 1867-1921. . . . . . . DLB-66

Thoma, Richard 1902- DLB-4

Thomas, Audrey 1935- DLB-60

Thomas, D. M. 1935- DLB-40

Thomas, Dylan
1914-1953 . . . . DLB-13, 20, 139

Thomas, Edward
1878-1917 . . . . DLB-19, 98, 156

Thomas, Gwyn 1913-1981 . . . . DLB-15

Thomas, Isaiah 1750-1831 . . . DLB-43, 73, 187

Thomas, Isaiah [publishing house] DLB-49

Thomas, Johann 1624-1679 . . . . . . DLB-168

Thomas, John 1900-1932 . . . . DLB-4

Thomas, Joyce Carol 1938- DLB-33

Thomas, Lorenzo 1944- DLB-41

Thomas, R. S. 1915- DLB-27

The Thomas Wolfe Collection at the University of
North Carolina at Chapel Hill Y-97

The Thomas Wolfe Society Y-97

Thomasîn von Zerclære
circa 1186-circa 1259 . . . . DLB-138

Thomasius, Christian 1655-1728 . . . . DLB-168

Thompson, David 1770-1857. . . . . . DLB-99

Thompson, Dorothy 1893-1961 . . . . DLB-29

Thompson, Francis 1859-1907 . . . . . DLB-19

Thompson, George Selden (see Selden, George)

Thompson, Henry Yates 1838-1928 . . DLB-184

Thompson, Hunter S. 1939- DLB-185

Thompson, John 1938-1976 . . . . . . DLB-60

Thompson, John R. 1823-1873 . . . DLB-3, 73

Thompson, Lawrance 1906-1973 . . . . DLB-103

Thompson, Maurice 1844-1901 . . . DLB-71, 74

Thompson, Ruth Plumly
1891-1976 . . . . DLB-22

Thompson, Thomas Phillips
1843-1933 . . . . DLB-99

Thompson, William 1775-1833 . . . . DLB-158

Thompson, William Tappan
1812-1882 . . . . DLB-3, 11

Thomson, Edward William
1849-1924 . . . . DLB-92

Thomson, James 1700-1748 . . . . . . DLB-95

Thomson, James 1834-1882 . . . . . . DLB-35

Thomson, Joseph 1858-1895 . . . . . DLB-174

Thomson, Mortimer 1831-1875 . . . . DLB-11

Thoreau, Henry David
1817-1862 . . . . DLB-1, 183

Thornton Wilder Centenary at Yale Y-97

Thorpe, Thomas Bangs
1815-1878 . . . . DLB-3, 11

Thoughts on Poetry and Its Varieties (1833),
by John Stuart Mill DLB-32

Thrale, Hester Lynch (see Piozzi, Hester
Lynch [Thrale])

Thucydides circa 455 B.C.-circa 395 B.C.
. . . . DLB-176

Thulstrup, Thure de 1848-1930 . . . . DLB-188

Thümmel, Moritz August von
1738-1817 . . . . DLB-97

Thurber, James
1894-1961 . . . . DLB-4, 11, 22, 102

Thurman, Wallace 1902-1934 . . . . . DLB-51

Thwaite, Anthony 1930- DLB-40

Thwaites, Reuben Gold
1853-1913 . . . . DLB-47

Ticknor, George
1791-1871. . . . . DLB-1, 59, 140

Ticknor and Fields DLB-49

Ticknor and Fields (revived) DLB-46

Tieck, Ludwig 1773-1853 . . . . DLB-90

Tietjens, Eunice 1884-1944 . . . . DLB-54

Tilney, Edmund circa 1536-1610 . . . . DLB-136

Tilt, Charles [publishing house] DLB-106

Tilton, J. E., and Company DLB-49

Time and Western Man (1927), by Wyndham
  Lewis [excerpts] DLB-36

Time-Life Books DLB-46

Times Books DLB-46

Timothy, Peter circa 1725-1782 . . . . . DLB-43

Timrod, Henry 1828-1867 . . . . DLB-3

Tinker, Chauncey Brewster
  1876-1963 . . . . DLB-140

Tinsley Brothers DLB-106

Tiptree, James, Jr. 1915-1987 . . . . . . DLB-8

Tišma, Aleksandar 1924- DLB-181

Titus, Edward William
  1870-1952 . . . . DLB-4; DS-15

Tlali, Miriam 1933- DLB-157

Todd, Barbara Euphan
  1890-1976 . . . . DLB-160

Tofte, Robert
  1561 or 1562-1619 or 1620 . . . . DLB-172

Toklas, Alice B. 1877-1967 . . . . DLB-4

Tokuda, Shūsei 1872-1943 . . . . DLB-180

Tolkien, J. R. R. 1892-1973 . . . . DLB-15, 160

Toller, Ernst 1893-1939 . . . . DLB-124

Tollet, Elizabeth 1694-1754 . . . . DLB-95

Tolson, Melvin B. 1898-1966 . . . . DLB-48, 76

Tom Jones (1749), by Henry Fielding
  [excerpt] DLB-39

Tomalin, Claire 1933- DLB-155

Tomasi di Lampedusa,
  Giuseppe 1896-1957 . . . . DLB-177

Tomlinson, Charles 1927- DLB-40

Tomlinson, H. M. 1873-1958
  . . . . DLB-36, 100, 195

Tompkins, Abel [publishing house] . . . DLB-49

Tompson, Benjamin 1642-1714 . . . . . DLB-24

Tondelli, Pier Vittorio 1955-1991 . . . . DLB-196

Tonks, Rosemary 1932- DLB-14

Tonna, Charlotte Elizabeth
  1790-1846 . . . . DLB-163

Tonson, Jacob the Elder
  [publishing house] DLB-170

Toole, John Kennedy 1937-1969 . . . . . . Y-81

Toomer, Jean 1894-1967 . . . . . . DLB-45, 51

Tor Books DLB-46

Torberg, Friedrich 1908-1979 . . . . . . DLB-85

Torrence, Ridgely 1874-1950 . . . . . . DLB-54

Torres-Metzger, Joseph V.
  1933- DLB-122

Toth, Susan Allen 1940- Y-86

Tottell, Richard
  [publishing house] DLB-170

Tough-Guy Literature DLB-9

Touré, Askia Muhammad 1938- DLB-41

Tourgée, Albion W. 1838-1905 . . . . . DLB-79

Tourneur, Cyril circa 1580-1626 . . . . . DLB-58

Tournier, Michel 1924- DLB-83

Tousey, Frank [publishing house] DLB-49

Tower Publications DLB-46

Towne, Benjamin circa 1740-1793 . . . . DLB-43

Towne, Robert 1936- DLB-44

The Townely Plays
  fifteenth and sixteenth
  centuries DLB-146

Townshend, Aurelian
  by 1583 - circa 1651 . . . . DLB-121

Tracy, Honor 1913- DLB-15

Traherne, Thomas 1637?-1674 . . . . . DLB-131

Traill, Catharine Parr 1802-1899 . . . . . DLB-99

Train, Arthur 1875-1945 . . . . . DLB-86; DS-16

The Transatlantic Publishing
  Company DLB-49

The Transatlantic Review 1924-1925 . . . . . DS-15

Transcendentalists, American DS-5

transition 1927-1938 . . . . DS-15

Translators of the Twelfth Century:
  Literary Issues Raised and Impact
  Created DLB-115

Travel Writing, 1837-1875 . . . . DLB-166

Travel Writing, 1876-1909 . . . . DLB-174

Traven, B.
  1882? or 1890?-1969? DLB-9, 56

Travers, Ben 1886-1980 . . . . DLB-10

Travers, P. L. (Pamela Lyndon)
  1899- DLB-160

Trediakovsky, Vasilii Kirillovich
  1703-1769 . . . . DLB-150

Treece, Henry 1911-1966 . . . . DLB-160

Trejo, Ernesto 1950- DLB-122

Trelawny, Edward John
  1792-1881 . . . . DLB-110, 116, 144

Tremain, Rose 1943- DLB-14

Tremblay, Michel 1942- DLB-60

Trends in Twentieth-Century
  Mass Market Publishing DLB-46

Trent, William P. 1862-1939 . . . . . . DLB-47

Trescot, William Henry
  1822-1898 . . . . DLB-30

Tressell, Robert (Robert Phillipe Noonan)
  1870-1911 . . . . DLB-197

Trevelyan, Sir George Otto
  1838-1928 . . . . DLB-144

Trevisa, John
  circa 1342-circa 1402 . . . . DLB-146

Trevor, William 1928- DLB-14, 139

Trierer Floyris circa 1170-1180 . . . . . DLB-138

Trillin, Calvin 1935- DLB-185

Trilling, Lionel 1905-1975 . . . . . DLB-28, 63

Trilussa 1871-1950 . . . . DLB-114

Trimmer, Sarah 1741-1810 . . . . . . DLB-158

Triolet, Elsa 1896-1970 . . . . DLB-72

Tripp, John 1927- DLB-40

Trocchi, Alexander 1925- DLB-15

Troisi, Dante 1920-1989 . . . . DLB-196

Trollope, Anthony
  1815-1882 . . . . DLB-21, 57, 159

Trollope, Frances 1779-1863 . . . . DLB-21, 166

Troop, Elizabeth 1931- DLB-14

Trotter, Catharine 1679-1749 . . . . . . DLB-84

Trotti, Lamar 1898-1952 . . . . DLB-44

Trottier, Pierre 1925- DLB-60

Troupe, Quincy Thomas, Jr. 1943- . . DLB-41

Trow, John F., and Company DLB-49

Truillier-Lacombe, Joseph-Patrice
  1807-1863 . . . . DLB-99

Trumbo, Dalton 1905-1976 . . . . . . DLB-26

Trumbull, Benjamin 1735-1820 . . . . . DLB-30

Trumbull, John 1750-1831 . . . . DLB-31

Trumbull, John 1756-1843 . . . . . . DLB-183

Tscherning, Andreas 1611-1659 . . . . DLB-164

T. S. Eliot Centennial Y-88

Tsubouchi, Shōyō 1859-1935 . . . . . DLB-180

Tucholsky, Kurt 1890-1935 . . . . . . DLB-56

Tucker, Charlotte Maria
  1821-1893 . . . . DLB-163, 190

Tucker, George 1775-1861 . . . . . DLB-3, 30

Tucker, Nathaniel Beverley
  1784-1851 . . . . DLB-3

Tucker, St. George 1752-1827 . . . . . DLB-37

Tuckerman, Henry Theodore
  1813-1871 . . . . DLB-64

Tunis, John R. 1889-1975 . . . . . DLB-22, 171

Tunstall, Cuthbert 1474-1559 . . . . . DLB-132

Tuohy, Frank 1925- DLB-14, 139

Tupper, Martin F. 1810-1889 . . . . . DLB-32

Turbyfill, Mark 1896- DLB-45

Turco, Lewis 1934- Y-84

Turgenev, Aleksandr Ivanovich
  1784-1845 . . . . DLB-198

Turnball, Alexander H. 1868-1918 . . . DLB-184

Turnbull, Andrew 1921-1970 . . . . . DLB-103

Turnbull, Gael 1928- DLB-40

Turner, Arlin 1909-1980 . . . . DLB-103

Turner, Charles (Tennyson)
  1808-1879 . . . . DLB-32

Turner, Frederick 1943- DLB-40

Turner, Frederick Jackson
  1861-1932 . . . . DLB-17, 186

Turner, Joseph Addison
1826-1868 . . . . DLB-79

Turpin, Waters Edward
1910-1968 . . . . DLB-51

Turrini, Peter 1944- DLB-124

Tutuola, Amos 1920- DLB-125

Twain, Mark (see Clemens, Samuel Langhorne)

Tweedie, Ethel Brilliana
circa 1860-1940 . . . . DLB-174

The 'Twenties and Berlin, by
Alex Natan DLB-66

Tyler, Anne 1941- DLB-6, 143; Y-82

Tyler, Moses Coit 1835-1900 . . . . DLB-47, 64

Tyler, Royall 1757-1826 . . . . DLB-37

Tylor, Edward Burnett 1832-1917 . . . . DLB-57

Tynan, Katharine 1861-1931 . . . . . DLB-153

Tyndale, William
circa 1494-1536 . . . . DLB-132

U

Udall, Nicholas 1504-1556 . . . . DLB-62

Ugrěšić, Dubravka 1949- DLB-181

Uhland, Ludwig 1787-1862. . . . . . . DLB-90

Uhse, Bodo 1904-1963 . . . . DLB-69

Ujević, Augustin ("Tin")
1891-1955 . . . . DLB-147

Ulenhart, Niclas
flourished circa 1600 . . . . DLB-164

Ulibarrí, Sabine R. 1919- DLB-82

Ulica, Jorge 1870-1926 . . . . DLB-82

Ulivi, Ferruccio 1912- DLB-196

Ulizio, B. George 1889-1969 . . . . . . DLB-140

Ulrich von Liechtenstein
circa 1200-circa 1275 . . . . DLB-138

Ulrich von Zatzikhoven
before 1194-after 1214 . . . . . . DLB-138

Ulysses, Reader's Edition Y-97

Unamuno, Miguel de 1864-1936 . . . . DLB-108

Under the Microscope (1872), by
A. C. Swinburne DLB-35

Unger, Friederike Helene
1741-1813 . . . . DLB-94

Ungaretti, Giuseppe 1888-1970 . . . . . DLB-114

United States Book Company DLB-49

Universal Publishing and Distributing
Corporation DLB-46

The University of Iowa Writers' Workshop
Golden Jubilee Y-86

The University of South Carolina
Press Y-94

University of Wales Press. DLB-112

"The Unknown Public" (1858), by
Wilkie Collins [excerpt] DLB-57

Uno, Chiyo 1897-1996 . . . . DLB-180

Unruh, Fritz von 1885-1970 . . . . DLB-56, 118

Unspeakable Practices II: The Festival of
Vanguard Narrative at Brown
University. Y-93

Unsworth, Barry 1930- DLB-194

Unwin, T. Fisher
[publishing house] DLB-106

Upchurch, Boyd B. (see Boyd, John)

Updike, John
1932- . . . DLB-2, 5, 143; Y-80, Y-82; DS-3

Upton, Bertha 1849-1912 . . . . DLB-141

Upton, Charles 1948- DLB-16

Upton, Florence K. 1873-1922 . . . . . DLB-141

Upward, Allen 1863-1926. . . . . . . DLB-36

Urista, Alberto Baltazar (see Alurista)

Urzidil, Johannes 1896-1976 . . . . . . DLB-85

Urquhart, Fred 1912- DLB-139

The Uses of Facsimile Y-90

Usk, Thomas died 1388 . . . . DLB-146

Uslar Pietri, Arturo 1906- DLB-113

Ustinov, Peter 1921- DLB-13

Uttley, Alison 1884-1976 . . . . DLB-160

Uz, Johann Peter 1720-1796 . . . . . . DLB-97

V

Vac, Bertrand 1914- DLB-88

Vail, Laurence 1891-1968 . . . . DLB-4

Vailland, Roger 1907-1965 . . . . DLB-83

Vajda, Ernest 1887-1954 . . . . DLB-44

Valdés, Gina 1943- DLB-122

Valdez, Luis Miguel 1940- DLB-122

Valduga, Patrizia 1953- DLB-128

Valente, José Angel 1929- DLB-108

Valenzuela, Luisa 1938- DLB-113

Valeri, Diego 1887-1976. . . . . DLB-128

Valesio, Paolo 1939- DLB-196

Valgardson, W. D. 1939- DLB-60

Valle, Víctor Manuel 1950- DLB-122

Valle-Inclán, Ramón del
1866-1936 . . . . DLB-134

Vallejo, Armando 1949- DLB-122

Vallès, Jules 1832-1885 . . . . DLB-123

Vallette, Marguerite Eymery (see Rachilde)

Valverde, José María 1926- DLB-108

Van Allsburg, Chris 1949- DLB-61

Van Anda, Carr 1864-1945 . . . . . . DLB-25

Van Dine, S. S. (see Wright, Williard Huntington)

Van Doren, Mark 1894-1972 . . . . . . DLB-45

van Druten, John 1901-1957 . . . . . . DLB-10

Van Duyn, Mona 1921- DLB-5

Van Dyke, Henry
1852-1933 . . . . DLB-71; DS-13

Van Dyke, John C. 1856-1932 . . . . . DLB-186

Van Dyke, Henry 1928- DLB-33

van Gulik, Robert Hans 1910-1967 . . . . DS-17

van Itallie, Jean-Claude 1936- DLB-7

Van Loan, Charles E. 1876-1919. . . . DLB-171

Van Rensselaer, Mariana Griswold
1851-1934 . . . . DLB-47

Van Rensselaer, Mrs. Schuyler (see Van
Rensselaer, Mariana Griswold)

Van Vechten, Carl 1880-1964 . . . . . DLB-4, 9

van Vogt, A. E. 1912- DLB-8

Vanbrugh, Sir John 1664-1726. . . . . . DLB-80

Vance, Jack 1916?- DLB-8

Vane, Sutton 1888-1963 . . . . DLB-10

Vanguard Press DLB-46

Vann, Robert L. 1879-1940 . . . . . . DLB-29

Vargas, Llosa, Mario 1936- DLB-145

Varley, John 1947- Y-81

Varnhagen von Ense, Karl August
1785-1858 . . . . DLB-90

Varnhagen von Ense, Rahel
1771-1833 . . . . DLB-90

Vásquez Montalbán, Manuel
1939- DLB-134

Vassa, Gustavus (see Equiano, Olaudah)

Vassalli, Sebastiano 1941- DLB-128, 196

Vaughan, Henry 1621-1695. . . . . . DLB-131

Vaughan, Thomas 1621-1666. . . . . . DLB-131

Vaux, Thomas, Lord 1509-1556 . . . . DLB-132

Vazov, Ivan 1850-1921 . . . . DLB-147

Vega, Janine Pommy 1942- DLB-16

Veiller, Anthony 1903-1965. . . . . . . DLB-44

Velásquez-Trevino, Gloria
1949- DLB-122

Veloz Maggiolo, Marcio 1936- DLB-145

Vel'tman Aleksandr Fomich
1800-1870 . . . . DLB-198

Venegas, Daniel ?-? DLB-82

Vergil, Polydore circa 1470-1555 . . . . DLB-132

Veríssimo, Erico 1905-1975 . . . . . . DLB-145

Verne, Jules 1828-1905 . . . . DLB-123

Verplanck, Gulian C. 1786-1870. . . . . DLB-59

Very, Jones 1813-1880 . . . . DLB-1

Vian, Boris 1920-1959 . . . . DLB-72

Vickers, Roy 1888?-1965 . . . . DLB-77

Victoria 1819-1901 . . . . DLB-55

Victoria Press DLB-106

Vidal, Gore 1925- DLB-6, 152

Viebig, Clara 1860-1952 . . . . DLB-66

Viereck, George Sylvester
1884-1962 . . . . DLB-54

Viereck, Peter 1916- DLB-5

Viets, Roger 1738-1811 . . . . DLB-99

Viewpoint: Politics and Performance, by
 David Edgar DLB-13

Vigil-Piñon, Evangelina 1949- DLB-122

Vigneault, Gilles 1928- DLB-60

Vigny, Alfred de 1797-1863 . . . . DLB-119, 192

Vigolo, Giorgio 1894-1983 . . . . DLB-114

The Viking Press DLB-46

Villanueva, Alma Luz 1944- DLB-122

Villanueva, Tino 1941- DLB-82

Villard, Henry 1835-1900 . . . . DLB-23

Villard, Oswald Garrison
 1872-1949 . . . . DLB-25, 91

Villarreal, José Antonio 1924- DLB-82

Villegas de Magnón, Leonor
 1876-1955 . . . . DLB-122

Villemaire, Yolande 1949- DLB-60

Villena, Luis Antonio de 1951- DLB-134

Villiers de l'Isle-Adam, Jean-Marie
 Mathias Philippe-Auguste, Comte de
 1838-1889 . . . . DLB-123, 192

Villiers, George, Second Duke
 of Buckingham 1628-1687 . . . . . DLB-80

Vine Press DLB-112

Viorst, Judith ?- DLB-52

Vipont, Elfrida (Elfrida Vipont Foulds,
 Charles Vipont) 1902-1992 . . . . . DLB-160

Viramontes, Helena María
 1954- DLB-122

Vischer, Friedrich Theodor
 1807-1887 . . . . DLB-133

Vivanco, Luis Felipe 1907-1975 . . . . DLB-108

Viviani, Cesare 1947- DLB-128

Vizenor, Gerald 1934- DLB-175

Vizetelly and Company DLB-106

Voaden, Herman 1903- DLB-88

Voigt, Ellen Bryant 1943- DLB-120

Vojnović, Ivo 1857-1929 . . . . DLB-147

Volkoff, Vladimir 1932- DLB-83

Volland, P. F., Company DLB-46

Vollbehr, Otto H. F. 1872?-
 1945 or 1946 . . . . DLB-187

Volponi, Paolo 1924- DLB-177

von der Grün, Max 1926- DLB-75

Vonnegut, Kurt
 1922- DLB-2, 8, 152; Y-80; DS-3

Voranc, Prežihov 1893-1950 . . . . . . DLB-147

Voß, Johann Heinrich 1751-1826 . . . . DLB-90

Voynich, E. L. 1864-1960 . . . . DLB-197

Vroman, Mary Elizabeth
 circa 1924-1967 . . . . DLB-33

Wace, Robert ("Maistre")
 circa 1100-circa 1175 . . . . DLB-146

Wackenroder, Wilhelm Heinrich
 1773-1798 . . . . DLB-90

Wackernagel, Wilhelm
 1806-1869 . . . . DLB-133

Waddington, Miriam 1917- DLB-68

Wade, Henry 1887-1969 . . . . DLB-77

Wagenknecht, Edward 1900- DLB-103

Wagner, Heinrich Leopold
 1747-1779 . . . . DLB-94

Wagner, Henry R. 1862-1957 . . . . . DLB-140

Wagner, Richard 1813-1883 . . . . . . DLB-129

Wagoner, David 1926- DLB-5

Wah, Fred 1939- DLB-60

Waiblinger, Wilhelm 1804-1830 . . . . DLB-90

Wain, John
 1925-1994 . . . . . . DLB-15, 27, 139, 155

Wainwright, Jeffrey 1944- DLB-40

Waite, Peirce and Company DLB-49

Wakeman, Stephen H. 1859-1924 . . . DLB-187

Wakoski, Diane 1937- DLB-5

Walahfrid Strabo circa 808-849 . . . . DLB-148

Walck, Henry Z. DLB-46

Walcott, Derek 1930- . . . DLB-117; Y-81, Y-92

Waldegrave, Robert
 [publishing house] DLB-170

Waldman, Anne 1945- DLB-16

Waldrop, Rosmarie 1935- DLB-169

Walker, Alice 1944- DLB-6, 33, 143

Walker, George F. 1947- DLB-60

Walker, Joseph A. 1935- DLB-38

Walker, Margaret 1915- DLB-76, 152

Walker, Ted 1934- DLB-40

Walker and Company DLB-49

Walker, Evans and Cogswell
 Company DLB-49

Walker, John Brisben 1847-1931 . . . . DLB-79

Wallace, Alfred Russel 1823-1913 . . . DLB-190

Wallace, Dewitt 1889-1981 and
 Lila Acheson Wallace
 1889-1984 . . . . DLB-137

Wallace, Edgar 1875-1932 . . . . DLB-70

Wallace, Lila Acheson (see Wallace, Dewitt,
 and Lila Acheson Wallace)

Wallant, Edward Lewis
 1926-1962 . . . . DLB-2, 28, 143

Waller, Edmund 1606-1687 . . . . . . DLB-126

Walpole, Horace 1717-1797 . . . . DLB-39, 104

Walpole, Hugh 1884-1941 . . . . DLB-34

Walrond, Eric 1898-1966 . . . . DLB-51

Walser, Martin 1927- DLB-75, 124

Walser, Robert 1878-1956 . . . . DLB-66

Walsh, Ernest 1895-1926 . . . . . . DLB-4, 45

Walsh, Robert 1784-1859 . . . . DLB-59

Waltharius circa 825 . . . . DLB-148

Walters, Henry 1848-1931 . . . . DLB-140

Walther von der Vogelweide
 circa 1170-circa 1230 . . . . DLB-138

Walton, Izaak 1593-1683 . . . . DLB-151

Wambaugh, Joseph 1937- DLB-6; Y-83

Waniek, Marilyn Nelson 1946- DLB-120

Warburton, William 1698-1779 . . . . DLB-104

Ward, Aileen 1919- DLB-111

Ward, Artemus (see Browne, Charles Farrar)

Ward, Arthur Henry Sarsfield
 (see Rohmer, Sax)

Ward, Douglas Turner 1930- DLB-7, 38

Ward, Lynd 1905-1985 . . . . DLB-22

Ward, Lock and Company DLB-106

Ward, Mrs. Humphry 1851-1920 . . . . DLB-18

Ward, Nathaniel circa 1578-1652 . . . . DLB-24

Ward, Theodore 1902-1983 . . . . . . DLB-76

Wardle, Ralph 1909-1988 . . . . DLB-103

Ware, William 1797-1852 . . . . DLB-1

Warne, Frederick, and
 Company [U.S.] DLB-49

Warne, Frederick, and
 Company [U.K.] DLB-106

Warner, Charles Dudley
 1829-1900 . . . . DLB-64

Warner, Marina 1946- DLB-194

Warner, Rex 1905- DLB-15

Warner, Susan Bogert
 1819-1885 . . . . DLB-3, 42

Warner, Sylvia Townsend
 1893-1978 . . . . DLB-34, 139

Warner, William 1558-1609 . . . . . . DLB-172

Warner Books DLB-46

Warr, Bertram 1917-1943 . . . . DLB-88

Warren, John Byrne Leicester
 (see De Tabley, Lord)

Warren, Lella 1899-1982 . . . . Y-83

Warren, Mercy Otis 1728-1814 . . . . DLB-31

Warren, Robert Penn
 1905-1989 . . . . DLB-2, 48, 152; Y-80, Y-89

Warren, Samuel 1807-1877 . . . . . . DLB-190

Die Wartburgkrieg
 circa 1230-circa 1280 . . . . DLB-138

Warton, Joseph 1722-1800 . . . . DLB-104, 109

Warton, Thomas 1728-1790 . . . DLB-104, 109

Washington, George 1732-1799 . . . . DLB-31

Wassermann, Jakob 1873-1934 . . . . DLB-66

Wasson, David Atwood 1823-1887 . . . DLB-1

Waterhouse, Keith 1929- DLB-13, 15

Waterman, Andrew 1940- DLB-40

Waters, Frank 1902- Y-86

Waters, Michael 1949- DLB-120

Watkins, Tobias 1780-1855. . . . . . . DLB-73

Watkins, Vernon 1906-1967 . . . . . . DLB-20

Watmough, David 1926- DLB-53

Watson, James Wreford (see Wreford, James)

Watson, John 1850-1907 . . . . DLB-156

Watson, Sheila 1909- DLB-60

Watson, Thomas 1545?-1592 . . . . . DLB-132

Watson, Wilfred 1911- DLB-60

Watt, W. J., and Company DLB-46

Watten, Barrett 1948- DLB-193

Watterson, Henry 1840-1921 . . . . . . DLB-25

Watts, Alan 1915-1973 . . . . DLB-16

Watts, Franklin [publishing house] DLB-46

Watts, Isaac 1674-1748 . . . . DLB-95

Wand, Alfred Rudolph 1828-1891 . . . DLB-188

Waugh, Alec 1898-1981. . . . . DLB-191

Waugh, Auberon 1939- DLB-14, 194

Waugh, Evelyn 1903-1966 . . DLB-15, 162, 195

Way and Williams DLB-49

Wayman, Tom 1945- DLB-53

Weatherly, Tom 1942- DLB-41

Weaver, Gordon 1937- DLB-130

Weaver, Robert 1921- DLB-88

Webb, Beatrice 1858-1943 and
    Webb, Sidney 1859-1947 . . . . . DLB-190

Webb, Frank J. ?-? DLB-50

Webb, James Watson 1802-1884. . . . DLB-43

Webb, Mary 1881-1927 . . . . DLB-34

Webb, Phyllis 1927- DLB-53

Webb, Walter Prescott 1888-1963 . . . . DLB-17

Webbe, William ?-1591 . . . . DLB-132

Webster, Augusta 1837-1894 . . . . . . DLB-35

Webster, Charles L.,
    and Company. DLB-49

Webster, John
    1579 or 1580-1634? DLB-58

Webster, Noah
    1758-1843 . . . . . . DLB-1, 37, 42, 43, 73

Weckherlin, Georg Rodolf
    1584-1653 . . . . DLB-164

Wedekind, Frank 1864-1918 . . . . . DLB-118

Weeks, Edward Augustus, Jr.
    1898-1989 . . . . DLB-137

Weeks, Stephen B. 1865-1918. . . . . . DLB-187

Weems, Mason Locke
    1759-1825. . . . . DLB-30, 37, 42

Weerth, Georg 1822-1856. . . . . . . DLB-129

Weidenfeld and Nicolson DLB-112

Weidman, Jerome 1913- DLB-28

Weigl, Bruce 1949- DLB-120

Weinbaum, Stanley Grauman
    1902-1935. . . . . DLB-8

Weintraub, Stanley 1929- DLB-111

Weise, Christian 1642-1708 . . . . . . DLB-168

Weisenborn, Gunther
    1902-1969 . . . . DLB-69, 124

Weiß, Ernst 1882-1940 . . . . DLB-81

Weiss, John 1818-1879. . . . . DLB-1

Weiss, Peter 1916-1982 . . . . . . DLB-69, 124

Weiss, Theodore 1916- DLB-5

Weisse, Christian Felix 1726-1804 . . . . DLB-97

Weitling, Wilhelm 1808-1871 . . . . . DLB-129

Welch, James 1940- DLB-175

Welch, Lew 1926-1971? DLB-16

Weldon, Fay 1931- DLB-14, 194

Wellek, René 1903- DLB-63

Wells, Carolyn 1862-1942 . . . . DLB-11

Wells, Charles Jeremiah
    circa 1800-1879 . . . . DLB-32

Wells, Gabriel 1862-1946 . . . . DLB-140

Wells, H. G.
    1866-1946 . . . . . . DLB-34, 70, 156, 178

Wells, Robert 1947- DLB-40

Wells-Barnett, Ida B. 1862-1931 . . . . . DLB-23

Welty, Eudora
    1909- DLB-2, 102, 143; Y-87; DS-12

Wendell, Barrett 1855-1921. . . . . . . DLB-71

Wentworth, Patricia 1878-1961 . . . . . DLB-77

Werder, Diederich von dem
    1584-1657 . . . . DLB-164

Werfel, Franz 1890-1945 . . . . . DLB-81, 124

The Werner Company DLB-49

Werner, Zacharias 1768-1823. . . . . . DLB-94

Wersba, Barbara 1932- DLB-52

Wescott, Glenway 1901- DLB-4, 9, 102

We See the Editor at Work. Y-97

Wesker, Arnold 1932- DLB-13

Wesley, Charles 1707-1788 . . . . . . DLB-95

Wesley, John 1703-1791. . . . . DLB-104

Wesley, Richard 1945- DLB-38

Wessels, A., and Company DLB-46

Wessobrunner Gebet
    circa 787-815. . . . . DLB-148

West, Anthony 1914-1988 . . . . DLB-15

West, Dorothy 1907- DLB-76

West, Jessamyn 1902-1984 . . . . . DLB-6; Y-84

West, Mae 1892-1980. . . . . DLB-44

West, Nathanael 1903-1940 . . . . DLB-4, 9, 28

West, Paul 1930- DLB-14

West, Rebecca 1892-1983 . . . . . DLB-36; Y-83

West, Richard 1941- DLB-185

West and Johnson DLB-49

Western Publishing Company DLB-46

The Westminster Review 1824-1914 . . . . DLB-110

Weston, Elizabeth Jane
    circa 1582-1612 . . . . DLB-172

Wetherald, Agnes Ethelwyn
    1857-1940 . . . . DLB-99

Wetherell, Elizabeth (see Warner, Susan Bogert)

Wetzel, Friedrich Gottlob
    1779-1819 . . . . DLB-90

Weyman, Stanley J. 1855-1928 . . DLB-141, 156

Wezel, Johann Karl 1747-1819. . . . . DLB-94

Whalen, Philip 1923- DLB-16

Whalley, George 1915-1983 . . . . . . DLB-88

Wharton, Edith
    1862-1937. . . DLB-4, 9, 12, 78, 189; DS-13

Wharton, William 1920s?- Y-80

Whately, Mary Louisa
    1824-1889 . . . . DLB-166

Whately, Richard 1787-1863 . . . . . . DLB-190

What's Really Wrong With Bestseller
    Lists Y-84

Wheatley, Dennis Yates
    1897-1977 . . . . DLB-77

Wheatley, Phillis
    circa 1754-1784 . . . . DLB-31, 50

Wheeler, Anna Doyle
    1785-1848? DLB-158

Wheeler, Charles Stearns
    1816-1843. . . . . DLB-1

Wheeler, Monroe 1900-1988. . . . . . DLB-4

Wheelock, John Hall 1886-1978 . . . . DLB-45

Wheelwright, John
    circa 1592-1679 . . . . DLB-24

Wheelwright, J. B. 1897-1940 . . . . . DLB-45

Whetstone, Colonel Pete (see Noland, C. F. M.)

Whetstone, George 1550-1587 . . . . . DLB-136

Whicher, Stephen E. 1915-1961 . . . . DLB-111

Whipple, Edwin Percy 1819-1886 . . DLB-1, 64

Whitaker, Alexander 1585-1617 . . . . . DLB-24

Whitaker, Daniel K. 1801-1881 . . . . . DLB-73

Whitcher, Frances Miriam
    1814-1852 . . . . DLB-11

White, Andrew 1579-1656 . . . . DLB-24

White, Andrew Dickson
    1832-1918 . . . . DLB-47

White, E. B. 1899-1985 . . . . DLB-11, 22

White, Edgar B. 1947- DLB-38

White, Ethel Lina 1887-1944 . . . . . . DLB-77

White, Henry Kirke 1785-1806 . . . . . DLB-96

White, Horace 1834-1916 . . . . DLB-23

White, Phyllis Dorothy James
    (see James, P. D.)

White, Richard Grant 1821-1885 . . . . DLB-64

White, T. H. 1906-1964. . . . . DLB-160

White, Walter 1893-1955 . . . . DLB-51

White, William, and Company DLB-49

White, William Allen 1868-1944 . . . DLB-9, 25

White, William Anthony Parker
(see Boucher, Anthony)

White, William Hale (see Rutherford, Mark)

Whitechurch, Victor L. 1868-1933. . . . DLB-70

Whitehead, Alfred North
1861-1947 . . . . DLB-100

Whitehead, James 1936- Y-81

Whitehead, William 1715-1785. . . DLB-84, 109

Whitfield, James Monroe 1822-1871. . . DLB-50

Whitgift, John circa 1533-1604 . . . . . DLB-132

Whiting, John 1917-1963 . . . . DLB-13

Whiting, Samuel 1597-1679. . . . . . . DLB-24

Whitlock, Brand 1869-1934. . . . . . . DLB-12

Whitman, Albert, and Company. . . . DLB-46

Whitman, Albery Allson
1851-1901 . . . . DLB-50

Whitman, Alden 1913-1990 . . . . Y-91

Whitman, Sarah Helen (Power)
1803-1878. . . . . DLB-1

Whitman, Walt 1819-1892 . . . . . DLB-3, 64

Whitman Publishing Company. DLB-46

Whitney, Geoffrey
1548 or 1552?-1601 . . . . DLB-136

Whitney, Isabella
flourished 1566-1573 . . . . DLB-136

Whitney, John Hay 1904-1982 . . . . . DLB-127

Whittemore, Reed 1919- DLB-5

Whittier, John Greenleaf 1807-1892. . . . DLB-1

Whittlesey House DLB-46

Who Runs American Literature? Y-94

Whose *Ulysses*? The Function of
Editing Y-97

Wideman, John Edgar 1941- DLB-33, 143

Widener, Harry Elkins 1885-1912 . . . . DLB-140

Wiebe, Rudy 1934- DLB-60

Wiechert, Ernst 1887-1950 . . . . DLB-56

Wied, Martina 1882-1957. . . . . DLB-85

Wiehe, Evelyn May Clowes (see Mordaunt,
Elinor)

Wieland, Christoph Martin
1733-1813 . . . . DLB-97

Wienbarg, Ludolf 1802-1872 . . . . . . DLB-133

Wieners, John 1934- DLB-16

Wier, Ester 1910- DLB-52

Wiesel, Elie 1928- DLB-83; Y-86, Y-87

Wiggin, Kate Douglas 1856-1923 . . . . DLB-42

Wigglesworth, Michael 1631-1705 . . . . DLB-24

Wilberforce, William 1759-1833. . . . . DLB-158

Wilbrandt, Adolf 1837-1911. . . . . . . DLB-129

Wilbur, Richard 1921- DLB-5, 169

Wild, Peter 1940- DLB-5

Wilde, Oscar 1854-1900
. . . . . DLB-10, 19, 34, 57, 141, 156, 190

Wilde, Richard Henry
1789-1847 . . . . DLB-3, 59

Wilde, W. A., Company. DLB-49

Wilder, Billy 1906- DLB-26

Wilder, Laura Ingalls 1867-1957 . . . . . DLB-22

Wilder, Thornton 1897-1975 . . . . DLB-4, 7, 9

Wildgans, Anton 1881-1932. . . . . . . DLB-118

Wiley, Bell Irvin 1906-1980 . . . . . . DLB-17

Wiley, John, and Sons DLB-49

Wilhelm, Kate 1928- DLB-8

Wilkes, Charles 1798-1877 . . . . DLB-183

Wilkes, George 1817-1885 . . . . DLB-79

Wilkinson, Anne 1910-1961 . . . . . . DLB-88

Wilkinson, Sylvia 1940- Y-86

Wilkinson, William Cleaver
1833-1920 . . . . DLB-71

Willard, Barbara 1909-1994 . . . . . . DLB-161

Willard, L. [publishing house] DLB-49

Willard, Nancy 1936- DLB-5, 52

Willard, Samuel 1640-1707 . . . . DLB-24

William of Auvergne 1190-1249 . . . . DLB-115

William of Conches
circa 1090-circa 1154 . . . . DLB-115

William of Ockham
circa 1285-1347 . . . . DLB-115

William of Sherwood
1200/1205 - 1266/1271 . . . . . . DLB-115

The William Chavrat American Fiction
Collection at the Ohio State University
Libraries. Y-92

William Faulkner Centenary. Y-97

Williams, A., and Company DLB-49

Williams, Ben Ames 1889-1953. . . . . DLB-102

Williams, C. K. 1936- DLB-5

Williams, Chancellor 1905- DLB-76

Williams, Charles
1886-1945. . . . . DLB-100, 153

Williams, Denis 1923- DLB-117

Williams, Emlyn 1905- DLB-10, 77

Williams, Garth 1912- DLB-22

Williams, George Washington
1849-1891 . . . . DLB-47

Williams, Heathcote 1941- DLB-13

Williams, Helen Maria
1761-1827 . . . . DLB-158

Williams, Hugo 1942- DLB-40

Williams, Isaac 1802-1865 . . . . DLB-32

Williams, Joan 1928- DLB-6

Williams, John A. 1925- DLB-2, 33

Williams, John E. 1922-1994 . . . . . . DLB-6

Williams, Jonathan 1929- DLB-5

Williams, Miller 1930- DLB-105

Williams, Raymond 1921- DLB-14

Williams, Roger circa 1603-1683. . . . . DLB-24

Williams, Rowland 1817-1870. . . . . . DLB-184

Williams, Samm-Art 1946- DLB-38

Williams, Sherley Anne 1944- DLB-41

Williams, T. Harry 1909-1979 . . . . . DLB-17

Williams, Tennessee
1911-1983 . . . . . . DLB-7; Y-83; DS-4

Williams, Ursula Moray 1911- DLB-160

Williams, Valentine 1883-1946 . . . . . DLB-77

Williams, William Appleman
1921- DLB-17

Williams, William Carlos
1883-1963 . . . . DLB-4, 16, 54, 86

Williams, Wirt 1921- DLB-6

Williams Brothers DLB-49

Williamson, Henry 1895-1977 . . . . . DLB-191

Williamson, Jack 1908- DLB-8

Willingham, Calder Baynard, Jr.
1922- DLB-2, 44

Williram of Ebersberg
circa 1020-1085 . . . . DLB-148

Willis, Nathaniel Parker
1806-1867 . . . DLB-3, 59, 73, 74, 183; DS-13

Willkomm, Ernst 1810-1886. . . . . . DLB-133

Wilmer, Clive 1945- DLB-40

Wilson, A. N. 1950- DLB-14, 155, 194

Wilson, Angus
1913-1991 . . . . DLB-15, 139, 155

Wilson, Arthur 1595-1652 . . . . DLB-58

Wilson, Augusta Jane Evans
1835-1909 . . . . DLB-42

Wilson, Colin 1931- DLB-14, 194

Wilson, Edmund 1895-1972 . . . . . . DLB-63

Wilson, Ethel 1888-1980 . . . . DLB-68

Wilson, Harriet E. Adams
1828?-1863? DLB-50

Wilson, Harry Leon 1867-1939 . . . . . DLB-9

Wilson, John 1588-1667 . . . . DLB-24

Wilson, John 1785-1854 . . . . DLB-110

Wilson, Lanford 1937- DLB-7

Wilson, Margaret 1882-1973 . . . . . . DLB-9

Wilson, Michael 1914-1978 . . . . . . DLB-44

Wilson, Mona 1872-1954 . . . . DLB-149

Wilson, Romer 1891-1930. . . . . . . DLB-191

Wilson, Thomas
1523 or 1524-1581 . . . . DLB-132

Wilson, Woodrow 1856-1924 . . . . . DLB-47

Wilson, Effingham
[publishing house] DLB-154

Wimsatt, William K., Jr.
1907-1975 . . . . DLB-63

Winchell, Walter 1897-1972 . . . . . . DLB-29

Winchester, J. [publishing house]. DLB-49

Winckelmann, Johann Joachim
　　1717-1768 . . . . DLB-97

Winckler, Paul 1630-1686 . . . . DLB-164

Wind, Herbert Warren 1916- DLB-171

Windet, John [publishing house] DLB-170

Windham, Donald 1920- DLB-6

Wing, Donald Goddard 1904-1972 . . . DLB-187

Wing, John M. 1844-1917 . . . . DLB-187

Wingate, Allan [publishing house] . . . DLB-112

Winnemucca, Sarah 1844-1921 . . . . . DLB-175

Winnifrith, Tom 1938- DLB-155

Winsloe, Christa 1888-1944 . . . . . . DLB-124

Winsor, Justin 1831-1897 . . . . DLB-47

John C. Winston Company DLB-49

Winters, Yvor 1900-1968 . . . . DLB-48

Winthrop, John 1588-1649 . . . . . DLB-24, 30

Winthrop, John, Jr. 1606-1676 . . . . . DLB-24

Wirt, William 1772-1834 . . . . DLB-37

Wise, John 1652-1725 . . . . DLB-24

Wise, Thomas James 1859-1937 . . . . DLB-184

Wiseman, Adele 1928- DLB-88

Wishart and Company DLB-112

Wisner, George 1812-1849 . . . . DLB-43

Wister, Owen 1860-1938 . . . . DLB-9, 78, 186

Wither, George 1588-1667 . . . . DLB-121

Witherspoon, John 1723-1794 . . . . . DLB-31

Withrow, William Henry 1839-1908 . . . . DLB-99

Wittig, Monique 1935- DLB-83

Wodehouse, P. G.
　　1881-1975 . . . . DLB-34, 162

Wohmann, Gabriele 1932- DLB-75

Woiwode, Larry 1941- DLB-6

Wolcot, John 1738-1819 . . . . DLB-109

Wolcott, Roger 1679-1767 . . . . DLB-24

Wolf, Christa 1929- DLB-75

Wolf, Friedrich 1888-1953 . . . . DLB-124

Wolfe, Gene 1931- DLB-8

Wolfe, John [publishing house] DLB-170

Wolfe, Reyner (Reginald)
　　[publishing house] DLB-170

Wolfe, Thomas
　　1900-1938 . . DLB-9, 102; Y-85; DS-2, DS-16

Wolfe, Tom 1931- DLB-152, 185

Wolff, Helen 1906-1994 . . . . Y-94

Wolff, Tobias 1945- DLB-130

Wolfram von Eschenbach
　　circa 1170-after 1220 . . . . DLB-138

Wolfram von Eschenbach's *Parzival*:
　　Prologue and Book 3 . . . . DLB-138

Wollstonecraft, Mary
　　1759-1797 . . . . DLB-39, 104, 158

Wondratschek, Wolf 1943- DLB-75

Wood, Benjamin 1820-1900 . . . . . . DLB-23

Wood, Charles 1932- DLB-13

Wood, Mrs. Henry 1814-1887 . . . . . DLB-18

Wood, Joanna E. 1867-1927 . . . . . . DLB-92

Wood, Samuel [publishing house] DLB-49

Wood, William ?-? DLB-24

Woodberry, George Edward
　　1855-1930 . . . . DLB-71, 103

Woodbridge, Benjamin 1622-1684 . . . . DLB-24

Woodcock, George 1912- DLB-88

Woodhull, Victoria C. 1838-1927 . . . . DLB-79

Woodmason, Charles circa 1720-? DLB-31

Woodress, Jr., James Leslie 1916- . . . DLB-111

Woodson, Carter G. 1875-1950 . . . . . DLB-17

Woodward, C. Vann 1908- DLB-17

Woodward, Stanley 1895-1965 . . . . . DLB-171

Wooler, Thomas
　　1785 or 1786-1853 . . . . DLB-158

Woolf, David (see Maddow, Ben)

Woolf, Leonard 1880-1969 . . . . DLB-100; DS-10

Woolf, Virginia
　　1882-1941 . . . . DLB-36, 100, 162; DS-10

Woolf, Virginia, "The New Biography," *New York Herald Tribune*, 30 October 1927
　　. . . . . DLB-149

Woollcott, Alexander 1887-1943 . . . . DLB-29

Woolman, John 1720-1772 . . . . DLB-31

Woolner, Thomas 1825-1892 . . . . . . DLB-35

Woolsey, Sarah Chauncy 1835-1905 . . . DLB-42

Woolson, Constance Fenimore
　　1840-1894 . . . . DLB-12, 74, 189

Worcester, Joseph Emerson
　　1784-1865 . . . . DLB-1

Worde, Wynkyn de
　　[publishing house] DLB-170

Wordsworth, Christopher 1807-1885 . . DLB-166

Wordsworth, Dorothy 1771-1855 . . . . DLB-107

Wordsworth, Elizabeth 1840-1932 . . . . DLB-98

Wordsworth, William 1770-1850 . . DLB-93, 107

Workman, Fanny Bullock 1859-1925 . . DLB-189

The Works of the Rev. John Witherspoon
　　(1800-1801) [excerpts] DLB-31

A World Chronology of Important Science
　　Fiction Works (1818-1979) DLB-8

World Publishing Company DLB-46

World War II Writers Symposium at the
　　University of South Carolina,
　　12–14 April 1995 . . . . Y-95

Worthington, R., and Company DLB-49

Wotton, Sir Henry 1568-1639 . . . . . DLB-121

Wouk, Herman 1915- Y-82

Wreford, James 1915- DLB-88

Wren, Percival Christopher 1885-1941 . . DLB-153

Wrenn, John Henry 1841-1911 . . . . . DLB-140

Wright, C. D. 1949- DLB-120

Wright, Charles 1935- DLB-165; Y-82

Wright, Charles Stevenson 1932- DLB-33

Wright, Frances 1795-1852 . . . . DLB-73

Wright, Harold Bell 1872-1944 . . . . . DLB-9

Wright, James 1927-1980 . . . . . . DLB-5, 169

Wright, Jay 1935- DLB-41

Wright, Louis B. 1899-1984 . . . . . . DLB-17

Wright, Richard 1908-1960 . . DLB-76, 102; DS-2

Wright, Richard B. 1937- DLB-53

Wright, Sarah Elizabeth 1928- DLB-33

Wright, Willard Huntington ("S. S. Van Dine")
　　1888-1939 . . . . DS-16

Writers and Politics: 1871-1918,
　　by Ronald Gray DLB-66

Writers and their Copyright Holders:
　　the WATCH Project Y-94

Writers' Forum Y-85

Writing for the Theatre, by
　　Harold Pinter DLB-13

Wroth, Lady Mary 1587-1653 . . . . . DLB-121

Wroth, Lawrence C. 1884-1970 . . . . DLB-187

Wurlitzer, Rudolph 1937- DLB-173

Wyatt, Sir Thomas
　　circa 1503-1542 . . . . DLB-132

Wycherley, William 1641-1715 . . . . . DLB-80

Wyclif, John
　　circa 1335-31 December 1384 . . . DLB-146

Wyeth, N. C.
　　1882-1945 . . . . DLB-188; DS-16

Wylie, Elinor 1885-1928 . . . . DLB-9, 45

Wylie, Philip 1902-1971 . . . . DLB-9

Wyllie, John Cook
　　1908-1968 . . . . DLB-140

Wynne-Tyson, Esmé 1898-1972 . . . . DLB-191

X

Xenophon circa 430 B.C.-circa 356 B.C.
　　. . . . . DLB-176

Y

Yasuoka, Shōtarō 1920- DLB-182

Yates, Dornford 1885-1960 . . . . . DLB-77, 153

Yates, J. Michael 1938- DLB-60

Yates, Richard 1926-1992 . . DLB-2; Y-81, Y-92

Yavorov, Peyo 1878-1914 . . . . DLB-147

Yearsley, Ann 1753-1806 . . . . DLB-109

Yeats, William Butler
　　1865-1939 . . . . . DLB-10, 19, 98, 156

Yep, Laurence 1948- DLB-52

Yerby, Frank 1916-1991 . . . . DLB-76

Yezierska, Anzia 1885-1970 . . . . DLB-28

Yolen, Jane 1939- DLB-52

Yonge, Charlotte Mary
  1823-1901 . . . . DLB-18, 163

The York Cycle
  circa 1376-circa 1569 . . . . DLB-146

A Yorkshire Tragedy DLB-58

Yoseloff, Thomas
  [publishing house]. DLB-46

Young, Al 1939- DLB-33

Young, Arthur 1741-1820 . . . . DLB-158

Young, Dick
  1917 or 1918 - 1987 . . . . DLB-171

Young, Edward 1683-1765 . . . . DLB-95

Young, Francis Brett 1884-1954. . . . . DLB-191

Young, Stark 1881-1963 . . . DLB-9, 102; DS-16

Young, Waldeman 1880-1938 . . . . . . DLB-26

Young, William [publishing house]. . . . DLB-49

Young Bear, Ray A. 1950- DLB-175

Yourcenar, Marguerite
  1903-1987. . . . . DLB-72; Y-88

"You've Never Had It So Good," Gusted by
  "Winds of Change": British Fiction in the
  1950s, 1960s, and After DLB-14

Yovkov, Yordan 1880-1937 . . . . . . DLB-147

Z

Zachariä, Friedrich Wilhelm
  1726-1777 . . . . DLB-97

Zagoskin, Mikhail Nikolaevich
  1789-1852 . . . . DLB-198

Zajc, Dane 1929- DLB-181

Zamora, Bernice 1938- DLB-82

Zand, Herbert 1923-1970. . . . . . . DLB-85

Zangwill, Israel 1864-1926. . . DLB-10, 135, 197

Zanzotto, Andrea 1921-. DLB-128

Zapata Olivella, Manuel 1920- DLB-113

Zebra Books. DLB-46

Zebrowski, George 1945- DLB-8

Zech, Paul 1881-1946. . . . . DLB-56

Zepheria DLB-172

Zeidner, Lisa 1955- DLB-120

Zelazny, Roger 1937-1995 . . . . DLB-8

Zenger, John Peter 1697-1746 . . . . DLB-24, 43

Zesen, Philipp von 1619-1689. . . . . DLB-164

Zieber, G. B., and Company DLB-49

Zieroth, Dale 1946- DLB-60

Zigler und Kliphausen, Heinrich Anshelm von
  1663-1697 . . . . DLB-168

Zimmer, Paul 1934- DLB-5

Zingref, Julius Wilhelm
  1591-1635 . . . . DLB-164

Zindel, Paul 1936- DLB-7, 52

Zinnes, Harriet 1919- DLB-193

Zinzendorf, Nikolaus Ludwig von
  1700-1760 . . . . DLB-168

Zitkala-Ša 1876-1938. . . . . DLB-175

Zola, Emile 1840-1902. . . . . DLB-123

Zolla, Elémire 1926- DLB-196

Zolotow, Charlotte 1915- DLB-52

Zschokke, Heinrich 1771-1848 . . . . . DLB-94

Zubly, John Joachim 1724-1781 . . . . DLB-31

Zu-Bolton II, Ahmos 1936- DLB-41

Zuckmayer, Carl 1896-1977 . . . . DLB-56, 124

Zukofsky, Louis 1904-1978 . . . . . DLB-5, 165

Zupan, Vitomil 1914-1987. . . . . . . DLB-181

Župančič, Oton 1878-1949 . . . . . . DLB-147

zur Mühlen, Hermynia 1883-1951 . . . . DLB-56

Zweig, Arnold 1887-1968. . . . . DLB-66

Zweig, Stefan 1881-1942 . . . . . DLB-81, 118